.744
1971

NEWS DICTIONARY 1971

NEWS DICTIONARY

an encyclopedic summary of contemporary history

Editor-in-Chief: LESTER A. SOBEL

Editor: SUSAN ANDERSON

Staff: Foreign Affairs—HAL KOSUT, JOANNE EDGAR, JOHN MINER, MYRNA LEBOV, ROBERT KRAMER

National Affairs—JOSEPH FICKES, MARY L. THOM, SETH ABRAHAM, SUSAN J. SCHOCH, DAVID SEISMAN

Associate Editors—DOROTHY KATTLEMAN, BARRY YOUNGERMAN, MARJORIE B. BANK

Facts on File, Inc.

119 West 57th Street, New York, N.Y. 10019

NEWS DICTIONARY

Library of Congress
Catalog Card Number: 65-17649

ISBN 0-87196-093-1 (cloth-bound)
ISBN 0-87196-094-X (paperback)

Using the News Dictionary

You will find the 1971 NEWS DICTIONARY as easy to use as the WEBSTER'S that stands beside it on the shelf. The editors of FACTS ON FILE—who themselves spend much of their time buried in reference books—designed the NEWS DICTIONARY to overcome the shortcomings of the typical yearbook: a complicated index, nine-month coverage, and an eclectic choice of material. Here you will find a self-index, complete coverage from January 1 through December 31, and the details of *every* significant news development of 1971.

The principle of the NEWS DICTIONARY is the alphabet. To find the story and facts of an event, the researcher simply looks up—as he would in a dictionary—the subject, the country concerned, or the name of a key person or organization involved in the event; if the story is not found in the first place he looks, an explicit cross-reference will direct him to the proper location without further effort or guesswork. Thus, the record of the kidnapings of foreign diplomats in Uruguay and the events surrounding them are found under URUGUAY; but the researcher would also be referred to the proper location from cross-references under ABDUCTIONS; KIDNAPINGS; and other headings.

A useful feature of the NEWS DICTIONARY is the system of numbered paragraphs to make the work of the researcher less time-consuming. Whenever there are more than a few paragraphs under any heading, numerals in the margin number the paragraphs consecutively. The cross-references refer the researcher—by number—to the specific paragraph(s) in which the desired information is recorded. For example, a researcher seeking material involving Sen. Mike Gravel will find after his name the reference "See PENTAGON PAPERS [10, 13]"; this refers him to paragraphs 10 and 13 of the PENTAGON PAPERS entry.

ABDUCTION—*See* ARGENTINA [11]; BRAZIL; CANADA [2-4]; COLOMBIA; CRIME [6]; LATIN AMERICA; MEXICO; PANAMA; SECURITY, U.S.; TURKEY [1, 6]; URUGUAY [9-12]; VENEZUELA

ABERNATHY, REV. RALPH D.—*See* AGNEW, SPIRO THEODORE; NEGROES

ABORTION—Nixon opposes unrestricted abortion. In what was believed to be his first statement on the issue, President Nixon said April 3 that he regarded abortion as "an unacceptable form of population control" and therefore had ordered the Defense Department to abandon its liberalized abortion policy and to conform with generally more restrictive state laws. The President's statement confirmed an April 2 report that he had directed the Pentagon to make its policy on abortions at military bases throughout the U.S. conform with the laws of the states in which the bases were situated.

The directive which the President struck down had been ordered into effect July 31, 1970, allegedly in an attempt to standardize abortion procedures throughout the armed services rather than to make it easier for servicemen's wives to obtain abortions. According to military sources, the wife of a serviceman could obtain an abortion on the recommendation of a military doctor and one consultant.

D.C. law upheld. In its first decision on the constitutionality of abortion laws, the Supreme Court, by a 5-2 vote April 21, upheld the constitutionality of the District of Columbia's 70-year abortion law that permitted abortions only to protect the life and health of the mother. The opinion, written by Justice Black (joined by Justices Blackmun, Harlan and White and Chief Justice Burger), reversed the November 1969 ruling of a U.S. judge who held that the D.C. statute was unconstitutionally vague. However, the decision defined health as including "psychological as well as physical well-being," a distinction not made in the D.C. law. It was expected that this qualifying language would limit enforcement of the D.C. law and others like it. Black's decision stated that in future abortion cases the government would have to prove not only that the abortion took place, but also that the woman's life or health was not in danger. Justices Brennan and Marshall did not participate in the decision because they felt the court lacked jurisdiction to hear the case upon direct appeal from a lower district court. Justices Stewart and Douglas dissented, Stewart on the grounds that the law should accept that a woman's health made an abortion necessary if a licensed physician performed the operation, and Douglas on grounds that the law was unconstitutionally vague.

New public position. The Commission on Population Growth and the American Future Oct. 27 made public a federal study showing that half the public was now in favor of liberalized abortion laws. In 1969, survey data indicated that 85% of the nation opposed liberalizing such laws. Of the 1700 adults questioned for the survey, 50% said the decision to abort should be made by the persons involved and their doctor, 41% said abortions should be allowed only in certain circumstances and 9% had no opinion. Nearly 80% of those interviewed said they favored voluntary sterilization and more than half thought people should limit the size of their family even if they could afford more children.

Canadian doctors approve liberalization. The Canadian Medical Association general council June 7 approved (by a 78-74 vote) a resolution recognizing justification for abortion on "non-medical, social grounds." June 8 the council voted that abortion should be decided on by a woman and her doctor and favored removal from the Criminal Code of a provision requiring the approval of a three-doctor hospital committee for an abortion.

Italian legislation introduced. According to a report June 19, three Italian Socialist senators introduced a bill legalizing abortion in cases where the mother's mental or physical health was endangered, the child was likely to be physically or mentally abnormal, the mother already had five children or was older than 45 and in cases of rape or incest.

Swedish committee recommends free abortion. A Swedish government committee Sept. 3 submitted a proposed law recommending free abortion and the right of a woman alone to decide to terminate a pregnancy.

See also CHURCHES [11, 14]; DRAFT & WAR PROTEST [19]; POPULATION; ROMAN CATHOLIC CHURCH [3]; YOUTH

ABU DHABI—*See* OIL
ACADEMY AWARDS—*See* MOTION PICTURES
ADVISORY COUNCIL ON EXECUTIVE REORGANIZATION—*See* GOVERNMENT REORGANIZATION

AFGHANISTAN—Noor Ahmad Etemadi, faced with a threat of censure by Parliament, resigned as premier of Afghanistan May 17. Critics contended that Etemadi's government had done little to improve what they charged was a stagnating economy. Abdul Zahir, ambassador to Italy, was appointed as Etemadi's successor by King Mohammed Zahir Shah June 9.

AFRICA—Rights team report. A six-man working group reported to the United Nations Human Rights Commission in Geneva Feb. 23 that "elements of genocide" in the treatment of black Africans existed in some parts of southern Africa. The report, which followed four years of investigation by the group, cited actions in South Africa, Rhodesia and the Portuguese African territories as examples of "genocide," listing 62 subjects which warranted closer examination. Among the subjects listed were the government removal of black Africans in South Africa and Rhodesia to barren lands in Namibia and Rhodesia, 340 inadequately investigated prisoner deaths in South African jails and 1968 and 1969 disturbances in the Caprivi Strip in eastern Namibia. The report also charged that in the Portuguese territories of Angola, Portuguese Guinea and Mozambique "Portugal had carried out mass executions of civilians and of persons suspected of opposing the regime and had carried out collective punishment against the civilian population."

River states meet. The foreign ministers of the Organization of Senegal River States (OERS) held an extraordinary session Feb. 19 in Nouakchott at the initiative of Mauritanian President Moktar Ould Daddah. A communique issued after the meeting said that the delegates had discussed the Portuguese invasion of Guinea in November 1970. (A meeting of OERS heads of state Jan. 18 in Bamako, Mali, had also been devoted to Guinea.)

"**Strategy for development.**" The U.N. Economic Commission for Africa adopted a "strategy for development" for the 1970s at the end of a six-day meeting in Tunis Feb. 13. The 29 delegates declared that aid programs now operating in Africa "reinforced the historical, geographical and political fragmentation of the region, thus aggravating the already difficult problems of cooperation and integration." A resolution sponsored by Algeria and Nigeria supported the principle of "permanent sovereignty" of African countries over their natural resources.

OAU postpones Uganda seating. The Ministerial Council of the Organization of African Unity ended its semi-annual meeting in Addis Ababa March 3 without deciding on claims to official recognition by two rival Ugandan delegations. The ministers Feb. 26 had excluded a delegation sent by Gen. Idi Amin until the delegation representing deposed President Milton Obote could be heard the following day. A Feb. 25 communique had described Britain's recent decision to sell helicopters to South Africa as "a new challenge to Africa and the Commonwealth." Ethiopian Emperor Haile Selassie told the delegates Feb. 26 that a dialogue with South Africa of the sort discussed by African leaders in 1970 would be "self-defeating and a waste of time."

Leaders meet in Abidjan. Four African presidents—Leopold Sedar Senghor (Senegal), Hamani Diori (Niger), Francois Tombalbaye (Chad) and Felix Houphouet-Boigny (Ivory Coast)—gathered for a joint meeting March 14-15 in Abidjan, Ivory Coast. Although no communique was issued after the session, the leaders were known to have discussed relations with South Africa, the January withdrawal of Cameroon from Air Afrique and the desire of the Congo (Kinshasa) government to make its currency unit, the zaire, completely convertible in the financial operations of the Common Organization of Africa, Malagasy and Mauritius (OCAM).

Amin for liberation army. In a message to the defense commission of the OAU, Ugandan President Amin Dec. 13 offered his country as a training area for the development of an all-African army and air force to be used in overthrowing white-controlled governments in the southern part of the continent.

See also CHURCHES [5]; GREAT BRITAIN [10]; HIJACKING [1]; MIDDLE EAST [37]; RACIAL & MINORITY UNREST [1]; SPACE [20]; TRACK & FIELD; UGANDA

AGENCY FOR INTERNATIONAL DEVELOPMENT (AID)—*See* FOREIGN AID

AGING—'Crisis' for aged reported. In preparation for the White House Conference on Aging in November, the Senate Special Committee on Aging, chaired by Sen. Harrison A. Williams Jr. (D, N.J.), issued reports Jan. 17 and April 4 on problems of the aging. The Jan. 17 report, titled "Economics of Aging," covered what Williams called "a retirement income crisis." The report said that poverty among Americans over 65 increased by 200,000 people between 1968 and 1969, while it decreased by 1.2 million for all other age groups. The increase in the aged poor was in both number and proportion. According to the study, poverty was most acute among the minority group elderly. It reported a 50.2% poverty rate among older blacks compared with 23.3% for elderly white Americans. Particularly troubling to the elderly, according to the report, were health care costs (six times that for young people and 2.5 times that for the 19-64 age group, with less than half the costs covered by Medicare) and unemployment, which often caused the elderly to lose not only their jobs but also their pensions. (Unemployment among workers over 45 had risen from 596,000 to 1,017,000 since January 1969.) Williams asked Congress to vote Social Security increases of 10% in 1971 and 20% in 1972. The committee advised that "serious consideration be given to the use of general revenues in the financing of the Social Security System."

The committee report issued April 4 centered on an evaluation of federal housing, health and retirement income programs for older Americans, which it stated continued to be "fragmented" and "haphazard." The report said that the Administration on Aging, established in 1965, failed to coordinate programs adequately for the 20 million Americans 65 years old or older. Citing housing problems, the committee said that six million persons of that group lived in substandard housing in 1970 and that many of the one million older persons now in nursing homes or mental institutions could be released if they had someplace to go. Among the recommendations of the report: that the government double its production of housing units for the elderly to 120,000 each year, that Medicare be entirely financed through payroll taxes and general revenues and that there be automatic cost-of-living raises in Social Security benefit levels.

Advisory council report. A 13-member federal advisory council headed by former Health, Education and Welfare Secretary Arthur S. Flemming issued a report on programs for the aging April 3. The council had been named in 1969 to review Social Security and Medicare as required by a provision of the Social Security Act. The council report recommended the alterations in Social Security and Medicare also recommended by the Special Committee in Aging and made the following additional recommendations: that the Social Security tax wage base be increased to $12,000 by 1974, that outside earnings permitted without reduction of Social Security benefits be raised from $1,650 to $2,000 a year, that Medicare be expanded to cover partial payment of prescription drugs for out-of-hospital use, that Medicare be extended to persons receiving disability benefits under Social Security and that extended Medicare coverage be given at a lower cost for persons with long illnesses.

Nixon urges improved care for elderly. In a June 25 speech before a joint meeting in Chicago of the National Retired Teachers Association and the American Association of Retired Persons, President Nixon called for a national effort to improve the inadequate status of many nursing homes for the elderly in America. The President cited nursing homes that were "unsanitary and ill-equipped, overcrowded and understaffed." While many nursing homes were "outstanding," he told the group, too many were considered "little more than warehouses for the unwanted, dumping grounds for the dying," serving "mainly to keep older people out of sight and out of mind, so that no one will notice their degradation and despair." Nixon pledged that the upgrading of nursing homes would get top priority at the White House Conference on Aging, and he indicated the possibility of withholding federal funds from substandard homes. He said that he was confident "that our federal, state and local governments, working together with the private sector, can do much to transform the nursing home." He said this was his Administration's goal. He also appealed for support of his revenue sharing plan, which, he said, would "ease the pressure on property taxes for older Americans and for all Americans."

Conference held. The White House Conference on Aging, chaired by Dr. Flemming, was held in Washington Nov. 28-Dec. 2. The gathering produced a series of committee reports on which President Nixon must, by law, comment within 90 days. A Cabinet-level committee on aging and a special post-conference board would review the recommendations, according to the President. Among the recommendations of the group was one passed by the income committee Dec. 1 for a minimum yearly income of $4,500 for elderly couples. A meeting of blacks, one of 17 "special concerns sessions," Dec. 1 backed a $9,000 figure. (A welfare reform bill, passed by the House of Representatives, would provide for a minimum income of $2,400 yearly for elderly couples and $1,800 yearly for single elderly persons.)

The conference had been authorized by Congress in 1968, called by Nixon in 1969 and preceded by about 6,000 local meetings.

Pension proposals. In a special message Dec. 8, President Nixon asked Congress to permit employees to have an income tax deduction of up to $1,500 a year or 20% of income, whichever was smaller, for investment in a private pension plan. Self-employed persons, under the proposed plan, could deduct up to $7,500 or 15% of income, whichever was smaller, for a contribution plan for themselves or for employees. (Currently, self-employed deductions were limited to $2,500 or 10%.) The President also proposed a minimum vesting standard, generally based on "a rule of 50," to protect workers who left their jobs before qualifying to receive pensions. Under the rule of 50, an employee would be half vested when his age plus his number of years in the pension plan equaled 50. Each year after that would bring an additional 10% in vesting until full vesting was reached in five years.

See also HEALTH CARE; POPULATION; SOCIAL SECURITY SYSTEM; WOMEN'S RIGHTS

AGNEW, SPIRO THEODORE—Diplomatic tour. Vice President Spiro Agnew returned to Washington July 28 from a 32-day diplomatic tour of 10 nations. Agnew was welcomed at the airport by Secretary of State William P. Rogers and proceeded to the White House where he and President Nixon discussed the trip.

The vice president held his most important talks in Kuwait and Saudi Arabia, where moderate leaders friendly to the U.S. were expected to be influential in attempts to settle the Middle East dispute. Agnew held what was described as an "animated, intense discussion" of the Arab-Israeli dispute July 7 with Kuwait's Sheikh Sabah as-Salim as Sabah. Agnew was reported to have held a "productive" meeting July 8 with Saudi Arabia's King Faisal and other Saudi leaders. During the discussions, Faisal was said to have repeated his suspicions about American military support for Israel, while stating the basic Arab position calling for total Israeli withdrawal from occupied Arab territory. Agnew emphasized that President Nixon favored neither side in the dispute and only wished to achieve a de facto settlement.

On the African part of his tour, Agnew visited Ethiopia July 10 for a conference with Emperor Haile Salassie, Kenya for a three-day visit which included a meeting with President Jomo Kenyatta and the Democratic Republic of the Congo for a two-day visit and a conference with President Joseph D. Mobutu. Agnew had visited South Korea June 29 and Singapore July 6. The original purpose of the tour was for Agnew to attend the inauguration of Korean President Chung Hee Park. The vice president represented the U.S. in a celebration in Spain July 18 marking the 35th anniversary of the uprising against the Spanish Republic in 1936. While in Spain, Agnew visited Generalissimo Francisco Franco July 17 and 19 and Prince Juan Carlos de Borbon, Franco's designated successor as Head of State July 19. After a four-day holiday with his family in the Spanish resort of Sotogrande, Agnew flew to Rabat, Morocco, where his official visit had been cut from two days to one for security reasons resulting from the recent abortive coup (*see* MOROCCO). In Morocco Agnew congratulated King Hassan II on behalf of President Nixon for his courage during the attempted coup and hailed Moroccan efforts at economic development, while pledging American assistance "within the limits of our resources." In his last stop, Agnew went to Lisbon, Portugal July 26 where he conferred with both Premier Marcello Caetano and President Americo Thomaz.

In a news conference aboard his plane traveling from the Congo to Madrid, Agnew delivered a broad indictment of unnamed black American leaders who he said could "learn much" from the three African leaders he met on his tour. He said that the quality of leadership evidenced by the three was "in distinct contrast" with those black leaders in the U.S. "who spend their time in querulous complaint and constant recrimination against the rest of society." According to the vice president, "many black people in the U.S. are tired of this constant complaining and ... would like to see some constructive action from these people." In the U.S., Rev. Ralph Abernathy, president of the Southern Christian Leadership Conference, said July 20 that Agnew was the "biggest complainer in America." Rep. William Clay (D, Mo.) said July 21 on the floor of the House that Agnew was "an intellectual sadist" who experienced "intellectual orgasms by attacking, humiliating and kicking the oppressed." In a press briefing July 11, Agnew said that all of the leaders he had talked to had been "appalled" by the publication of the Pentagon Papers (see PENTAGON PAPERS) and had expressed fear about a "retreat from responsibility" by the U.S., citing the Congressional defeat of the supersonic transport plane as an example (see AVIATION [1-3]).

Agnew visits Greece. A visit to Greece by Agnew Oct. 16-23 stirred controversy over the Nixon Administration's support for the military-backed regime of Greek Premier George Papadopoulos. His tour began with a three-day official visit and concluded with a private tour, the journey marking Agnew's first return to the land of his forefathers. Papadopoulos greeted Agnew upon his arrival in Athens Oct. 16, marked by elaborate ceremony. During the official visit, the two men conferred 6½ hours, including an unscheduled three-hour private meeting at the premier's suburban home Oct. 17. No official communique on the meetings was issued, both sides stating that the discussions related to Greece's NATO role. Some 170 former members of Parliament, representing the opposition leadership, had distributed a statement to the foreign press Oct. 15 denouncing U.S. support for the Papadopoulos regime, as symbolized by the Agnew visit. Demetrios Papaspyrou, Parliament's last president, issued an open letter to Agnew Oct. 14 calling upon the U.S. to "stop its intervention in favor of the dictatorial regime."

Visits to Turkey and Iran. Prior to his trip to Greece, Agnew visited Turkey Oct. 11-13 and Iran Oct. 15, where he attended the 2,500th anniversary celebration of the founding of the Persian Empire. At the fete, Agnew conferred with Greece's exiled monarch, King Constantine II. In Turkey, Agnew conferred Oct. 11 with Premier Nihat Erim and Oct. 12 with President Cevdet Sunay.

See also CONGRESS [10]; EARTHQUAKES; NEWSPAPERS; POLITICS [4]; TELEVISION & RADIO

AGRICULTURE—1970 farm subsidy payments. Federal farm subsidy payments in 1970 totaled $3.7 billion, the Agriculture Department reported April 8. Of the total, 45.5% went to 137,000 farmers in payments of $5,000 or more; the remainder went to about 2.3 million smaller operators for acreage reductions and price supports.

[2] Subsidy payments of $1 million or more were paid to nine large operators, the largest going to J. G. Boswell Co. of Corcoran, Calif., a cotton producer, which received $4.4 million, and to Giffen, Inc. of Huron, Calif., which received $4.1 million. Of the nine producers receiving $1 million, six were in California and received a total of $14.4 million. Six other California growers were among the 14 receiving payments of from $500,000 to $1 million. The other farms receiving the largest subsidy payments were in Hawaii (4), Arizona (3), Florida (2), Mississippi and Montana.

[3] Only six of the 23 growers receiving more than $500,000 would be eligible for such large subsidies in 1971 because of the 1970 farm legislation limiting individual growers to subsidies of $55,000 for each crop of wheat, feed grain or cotton. The six not affected were sugar producers, who were not covered by the new legislation.

[4] **Nixon pledges aid to farmers.** President Nixon addressed himself to the problems of farmers in a radio talk May 2. Deploring the "perennially troublesome cost-price squeeze" on farmers, the President announced a number of federal initiatives to help the farmer reap more income from the "surging vitality of our agriculture." Despite an anticipated higher total income for farmers in 1971 "than ever before in our history," he said, the farmer was

confronted with "the fact that increases in total income are not always reflected in more net income" because of "the high cost of farming." The President assured the farmers that definite progress was being made against inflation and asserted that "the brightest future for agriculture lies in actions that stimulate new energy in the market system."

[5] Nixon noted that farm exports were at their highest level and said, to aid that expansion, $1 million would be added to the $28.7 million funding for fiscal 1972 for the Foreign Agricultural Service. He also announced requests to Congress for: (a) a new system of federal guarantees for private farm operating loans, to replace a program of federal farm operating loans (the amount of insured ownership loans to farmers under the Farmers Home Administration was to be increased from $210 million to $350 million for fiscal 1972); (b) $7.6 million for research into crop and animal diseases; (c) an additional $12 million for the Soil Conservation Service and a rise to $105 million in federal grants for small watershed projects and to $300 million in fiscal 1972 for insured loans for rural water and sewer systems.

[6] (Nixon reiterated his concern about the problems of farmers in a $75,000 "salute to agriculture" on the White House grounds May 7. The cost of the "salute" was to be paid with Agriculture Department funds.)

[7] **Manpower program for migrants.** Labor Secretary James D. Hodgson June 19 announced a $20 million manpower program for migrant farm workers, to be administered by the Farm Labor Service. Hodgson said that the $20 million allocation, to run through June 30, 1972, would be in addition to the $23 million regular budget for the Service. He said the new money would provide health care, educational, food stamp and housing service. Training and job development would be provided for seasonal workers who wanted to leave the migrant work force. The program was immediately denounced by several migrant groups, who cited a Labor Department probe that had found the Service to be "a de facto institutional discriminator." Placement of the program under the Service was denounced by the Migrant Legal Action Program Inc. June 19 and by Mario Obledo, executive director of the Mexican-American Legal Defense and Educational Fund, who said "doubling the Farm Labor Service budget is a little like giving $20 million to the Ku Klux Klan to find jobs for blacks." Robert Gnaizda of California Rural Legal Assistance urged Hodgson to "express his faith in the farm worker by giving the farm worker an opportunity to run his own manpower program." (Sixteen organizations and 398 individual farm workers had petitioned Hodgson April 22 to replace the Service with a migrant-staffed Worker Service.) A bipartisan group of 38 representatives from Northeastern and Middle Atlantic states protested to the Labor Department June 30 that the new migrant manpower program excluded 30,000 migrants who came into their states to work each year.

[8] The problems of migrant workers had been a topic of concern throughout the first half of 1971. The National Committee on the Education of Migrant Children, in a 15-month study funded by the Ford Foundation, charged March 19 that $17 million of $97 million appropriated for educational aid for about 300,000 migrant children had been returned unused by states in fiscal years 1967-69. The study, written by Cassandra Stockburger, said that the Office of Education program, "as presently conceived and administered, ... cannot meet the needs of migrant children." The study also charged that many migrant children were found to be enrolled in segregated classes or schools and that, in the 42 states surveyed, only 22% or less of migrant children were enrolled beyond the sixth grade. The percentage was half that for the nation as a whole and only 1% higher than the number enrolled beyond the sixth grade in 1952. The American Friends Service Committee, in a report on a five-state investigation conducted in the summer of 1970, said that child labor abuse in American agriculture compared with "the sweatshop scene in 1938." Quaker investigating teams, aided by the National Committee on the Education of

Migrant Children, conducted studies in Ohio, Maine, California, Oregon and Washington. The report said that one-fourth of the farm wage workers in the U.S. were under 16 and some were as young as six. The study contended that as long as legislation against the employment of children, enforced since 1938 in industry, is not extended to farm labor, such employment would continue, with the increased labor supply resulting from such employment maintaining wages for all farm labor at a low level. The study found pay for children ranging from piecework wages such as 12¢ a crate for strawberries to an average hourly wage of $1.12 in California. The report also said that many migrant families lived in shacks without plumbing and worked in fields sprayed with DDT. A two-year study issued May 28 by the Migrant Research Project showed that less than 10% of the migrant families surveyed received welfare assistance of any kind, although the average income of the families in 1970 was only $2,021—less than half the federal poverty level for families of their size. Margaret Garrity, project director, said federal assistance programs were ineffective for migrants because of the mobility of the families, their ignorance of available benefits and bureaucratic conflicts.

[9]   **N.J. action.** New Jersey Gov. William T. Cahill (R) signed a series of bills June 7 to improve the working and living conditions of migrant laborers. One bill guaranteed wages equal to the state's $1.50 per hour minimum for seasonal farm workers who did piece-rate work. Another provided for registration of migrant crew leaders and prohibited hiring of crew leaders not certified by the state. Another bill required water and sanitary facilities for work sites. The legislation also provided $50,000 for interpreters to assist non-English speaking migrants. Many migrant laborers in the state were Puerto Ricans.

[10]   In another New Jersey development, the state Supreme Court ruled unanimously May 11 that farmers could not invoke trespass statutes to keep qualified visitors from migrant work camps. The ruling struck down trespass convictions of two federal antipoverty officials—Peter K. Shach, a legal services lawyer, and Frank Tejeras, a caseworker. The opinion by Chief Justice Joseph Weintraub said: "The employer may not deny the worker his privacy or interfere with his opportunity to live with dignity and to enjoy associations customary among our citizens. These rights are too fundamental to be denied on the basis of an interest in real property and too fragile to be left to the unequal bargaining strength of the parties." (Attorney General John Mitchell had announced March 11 that the government had filed suit seeking access to migrant worker camps for agents of federal assistance programs. The suit, the first of its kind, was filed in federal district court in Kalamazoo, Mich. against John Hassle, owner of the largest farm and orchard in Van Buren County, alleging that Hassle had tried to keep representatives of federal, state, local and private assistance programs from entering the camps, thus depriving the migrants of information about aid programs open to them. A U.S. district court judge in Michigan ruled Oct. 2 that migrant workers living on a grower's property "are clothed with their full bundle of rights," and ordered Hassle to pay $4,500 damages for interfering with visitors to a family residing in his migrant camp.)

[11]   **Subsidies increased.** Agriculture Secretary Clifford M. Hardin announced a program Oct. 18 designed to increase farm subsidies in 1972 to reduce surplus production of corn and other livestock feed grains. The program called for more acreage to be taken out of production and for higher subsidies to farmers idling the acreage. The new program was designed as a result of a record 1971 corn crop of 5.4 million bushels, almost one-third more than in 1970, when the corn blight cut output. The blight was not a factor in 1971. The new program was expected to cost $1.5 billion-$1.75 billion compared with costs of $1.2 billion in 1971. The goal was to reduce acreage by 38 million acres for feed grains, including corn, grain sorghums and barley. This would compare with an idling of 18.2 million acres in 1971 for farmers to qualify for federal price support loans.

[12] **Hardin replaced by Butz.** President Nixon announced Nov. 11 that he had accepted the resignation of Secretary Hardin, who was leaving his Cabinet position to accept a post with the Ralston Purina Company in St. Louis. At the same time, Nixon said that he had selected Earl L. Butz, dean of continuing education at Purdue University in Lafayette, Ind., and an assistant secretary of agriculture in the Eisenhower Administration, to replace Hardin. The Senate confirmed the controversial appointment of Butz by a 51-44 vote Dec. 2, and he was sworn in later the same day. Opposition to Butz centered around his alleged endorsement of corporate agriculture. Other critics said he was not sympathetic to programs to feed the poor and hungry. Still others were dissatisfied because of his past record in opposing price supports for farmers. During committee hearings on the nomination, spokesmen for organized labor, civil rights groups, the poor, consumer organizations and conservation associations called on senators to vote against Butz. On the final day of hearings, Nov. 19, the National Farmers Union made known its opposition to Butz, but the National Grange endorsed him the same day. Prior to the vote on the Senate floor, Butz conducted a personal lobbying campaign with promises to bolster the farm economy, preserve the family farm and support programs to alleviate hunger and poverty.

See also BUDGET; DISASTERS; EUROPEAN ECONOMIC COMMUNITY [3-4]

AIR FORCE, U.S.—*See* ESPIONAGE; MILITARY [7-8, 11]; PENTAGON PAPERS [11, 23, 27]; RACIAL & MINORITY UNREST [16]; WAR CRIMES [12]

AIR POLLUTION—*See* POLLUTION [1-3, 16-21]

ALBANIA—1970 economic results. The Albanian news agency Jan. 29 announced the results of the 1970 economic development plan. Measured against the figures for 1969, the following major increases were reported: national income rose 6%, the production of crude oil 14%, chromium ore 9%, blister copper 7%, copper ore 8%, phosphate fertilizer 12% and cement 9%. Agricultural field crops increased 5%, stock raising 4%, grain 4%, potatoes 4%, sugar 8%, sunflower 14%, rice 15%, cotton 3%, tobacco 15% and sugar beets 10%.

Party congress held. The 6th Congress of the Albanian Communist party, held Nov. 1-7 in Tirana, approved guidelines for the 1971-75 economic development plan and elected major party officials. Although the list of foreign delegations, released Nov. 1, did not include representatives of the People's Republic of China, observers attributed China's absence to its policy, adopted in 1969, of refusing to send delegates to international Communist events. The Chinese, whose country was mentioned favorably by a number of speakers during the congress, sent goodwill messages to the delegates Nov. 1 and 7. In discussing world issues in his opening address Nov. 1, party First Secretary Enver Hoxha echoed policies expressed by the Chinese: that the price of peace in the Middle East being offered to the Arabs by the U.S. and the U.S.S.R. was "very high" and an "insult"; that "true European security" could not exist as long as Nato and the Warsaw Pact continued; that the "problem of disarmament" had been "deliberately raised" by the U.S. and the Soviet Union in order to "lull the vigilance of the peoples and to intensify the plans for their schemes of aggression." Hoxha devoted a major part of the address to condemnation of the "imperialism and revisionism" of U.S. and Soviet foreign policy.

The principal objectives of the 1971-75 economic plan were outlined Nov. 4. Overall industrial production was expected to rise 61%-66%, with emphasis being given to production of producer goods. Other planned increases: agricultural output (65%-69%), investments (70%-75%), per capita income (14%-17%). The congress re-elected Hoxha as first secretary Nov. 7 and chose a new Central Committee of 111 members instead of the former 97. Hoxha told the delegates that a session of the new Central Committee had elected a Politburo of 13 full and four candidate members. The Politburo consisted of

Abdyl Kellezi, Kadri Hazbiu, Koco Theodhosi (new members) and Adil Carcani, Beqir Balluku, Enver Hoxha, Haki Toska, Hysni Kapo, Manush Myftiu, Mehmet Shehu, Ramiz Alia, Rita Marko and Spiro Koleka. Candidate members of the Politburo were Piro Dodbiba, Xhafer Spahiu (new members) and Petrit Dume and Pilo Peristeri.

See also GREECE [7]; UNION OF SOVIET SOCIALIST REPUBLICS [5]; UNITED NATIONS [7, 9]

AL FATAH—See JORDAN [1, 10, 12]; LEBANON; MIDDLE EAST [8, 26]

ALGERIA—Student union dissolved. The Interior Ministry dissolved the National Union of Algerian Students Jan. 15 following widespread unrest at the University of Algiers. The dissolution order claimed that the student union had become "a tool in the hands of a political movement organized in accordance with special methods similar to those of subversive organizations." The reference was reportedly to the clandestine Avant-Garde Socialist party (PAGS), a modern version of the Communist party which had been banned in 1962. The action came after many of the university's 13,000 students had struck to protest the arrest of six students earlier in January on charges of subversive activity. Authorities Jan. 19 established teams of special campus police, under the control of the university's rectors, to keep order. Students Feb. 14 were forbidden to use university buildings to hold protest meetings, organize demonstrations or distribute leaflets.

French oil firms seized. President Houari Boumedienne announced Feb. 24 in Algiers that his government was taking control of 51% of the shares of all French oil companies in Algeria as well as nationalizing the companies' assets in natural gas and gas pipelines. Boumedienne said Algeria would "make compensations" for the assets. (Algeria Feb. 26 rejected a Feb. 25 request by Elf-Erap, the French state-owned oil company in Algeria, for 100% nationalization of its interests, reportedly in order to insure compensation for the firm's entire investment.) The French government Feb. 25 declared that the nationalization, though coming at a time when oil negotiations between French and Algerian officials were in progress, had not been a surprise and that France's oil supply "poses no problems." The French statement requested Boumedienne to specify the "just and equitable" indemnity promised. Algerian and French representatives held discussions in March but made no apparent progress in determining compensation.

Oil prices rise. The government April 13 established the world's highest posted price per barrel of crude oil. The rise, from $2.85 to $3.60, was retroactive to March 20. The French Foreign Ministry noted April 15 that the action rendered "pointless" the talks being held with Algeria on nationalization. Herve Alphand, secretary general of the ministry, handed Algerian Foreign Minister Abdelaziz Bouteflika the French note April 15 declaring the negotiations over. The note halted the special government-to-government talks on "all aspects of cooperation between the two countries" and said that a solution would now be up to "the competent Algerian authorities and the companies operating in Algeria." Observers regarded the so-called "special relationship" between the two countries as being at an end. French oil companies suspended the purchase of Algerian crude oil April 22 "for the time being."

Oil pact signed. The government June 30 and Dec. 15 signed agreements providing for compensation to the two French oil companies nationalized in February. The first accord, resulting from talks begun May 25, was signed for Algeria by Sonatrach, the national oil trust. It gave $50 million to the Compagnie Francaise des Petroles Algerie, a group in which the French government owned 35% of the stock. The company agreed to settle back taxes estimated at $27 million and to invest most of its earnings in Algeria over the next 10 years. (The company had decided May 1 to repatriate its entire staff and their families. Although Sonatrach disclaimed any influence in the decision, the company said French technicians had received dismissal orders.) The second agreement, between Sonatrach and Elf-Erap, provided that Elf's demands for compensation of about $35 million would be canceled out by taxes owed the Algerian government. The government's claims on payment of $80 million in debts would be met by Elf's concession to some of its private holdings. Following the December pact, two new firms, Elf-Algerie and Total Algerie, were to have sole management of French oil interests. Disputes were to be settled by Algerian courts.

U.S. backs gas deal. The Nixon Administration was reported July 27 to have dropped its opposition to a contract by the El Paso Natural Gas Co. for the import of Algerian natural gas, pending since Jan. 12. The opposition had been requested by the French government because of the February nationalization. The El Paso contract required final approval from the U.S. Federal Power Commission.

See also AFRICA; FRANCE [6]; HIJACKING [1]; OIL; SUDAN

ALI, MUHAMMED (CASSIUS CLAY)—*See* BOXING; SELECTIVE SERVICE SYSTEM [14]

ALIOTO, JOSEPH L.—*See* CRIME [9]; DRAFT & WAR PROTEST [10]; ELECTIONS [8]

ALLIANCE FOR PROGRESS—*See* FOREIGN AID; LATIN AMERICA

ALL-STAR GAMES—*See* BASEBALL [4]; BASKETBALL; HOCKEY

AMCHITKA—*See* ATOMIC ENERGY [16-18]

AMERICAN ACADEMY OF MOTION PICTURE ARTS & SCIENCES—*See* MOTION PICTURES

AMERICAN BAR ASSOCIATION (ABA)—*See* JUDICIARY [6-7, 10]; POVERTY; SUPREME COURT

AMERICAN CIVIL LIBERTIES UNION (ACLU)—*See* DRAFT & WAR PROTEST [15, 17, 24]; ESPIONAGE; HOUSING; SECURITY, U.S.; SELECTIVE SERVICE SYSTEM [7, 11-12, 16]; VOTING RIGHTS

AMERICAN FEDERATION OF LABOR-CONGRESS OF INDUSTRIAL ORGANIZATIONS (AFL-CIO)—*See* ECONOMY, U.S. [27-28]; LABOR [2-3, 8-10, 12]; RAILROADS

AMERICAN FEDERATION OF TEACHERS (AFT)—*See* EDUCATION [14]

AMERICAN INDIAN MOVEMENT (AIM)—*See* INDIANS, AMERICAN

AMERICAN MEDICAL ASSOCIATION (AMA)—*See* MEDICINE

AMERICAN SELLING PRICE (ASP)—*See* TARIFFS & WORLD TRADE [2]

AMERICANS FOR DEMOCRATIC ACTION (ADA)—*See* SUPREME COURT

AMERICAN STOCK EXCHANGE (AMEX)—*See* STOCK MARKET

AMERICAN TELEPHONE & TELEGRAPH (AT&T)—*See* CIVIL RIGHTS [24]; CONSUMER AFFAIRS [17]; LABOR [11]

AMPHETAMINES—*See* DRUG USE & ADDICTION [15, 23]

AMTRAK—*See* RAILROADS

ANDEAN COMMON MARKET—*See* LATIN AMERICA

ANGLICAN CHURCH—*See* CHURCHES [17]; SOUTH AFRICA [4-5]

ANGOLA—*See* AFRICA; PORTUGAL; ZAMBIA

ANGUILLA—Great Britain named Arthur Watson as the new commissioner in Anguilla to replace Willoughby Thompson, it was reported Jan. 30. In accord with the Anguilla Act, which recommended that islanders be recruited and trained to replace the British police force, Britain announced Sept. 1 that it had ordered 60 military engineers and 30 policemen to return home to Great Britain. The military and police had been stationed in Anguilla since 1969 when the island declared its withdrawal from the St. Kitts-Nevis-Anguilla federation.

See also ST. KITTS-NEVIS-ANGUILLA

ANTIBALLISTIC MISSILE (ABM)—*See* ATOMIC ENERGY [17]; DISARMAMENT

ANTIGUA—In the first elections held in Antigua since it became an associated state of Britain in 1967, Premier Vere Cornwall Bird's Antigua Labor Party (ALP) was defeated Feb. 11 by labor leader George Walter's Progressive Labor Movement (PLM). The PLM won 14 parliamentary seats, the ALP three. Bird, also a union leader, had ruled Antigua for 25 years. Walter had split from Bird's union in 1967 and formed the Antigua Workers Union and subsequently the PLM.

See also VIRGIN ISLANDS

ANTITRUST ACTIONS—*See* BASEBALL [7]; BASKETBALL; BUSINESS [6-7, 9]; MINES; STOCK MARKET

APARTHEID—*See* AUSTRALIA [10]; AUTOMOBILES [8]; FOREIGN POLICY; SOUTH AFRICA [1-2, 6, 9, 11, 13]

APPOINTMENTS—*See* CONSUMER AFFAIRS [4]; NIXON, RICHARD MILHOUS [4, 7, 9]; POLITICS [2]; POSTAL SERVICE, U.S.; RAILROADS

APOLLO 14—*See* SPACE [1-2]

APOLLO 15—*See* SPACE [3]

ARAB LEAGUE—*See* MIDDLE EAST [19]

ARAB REPUBLIC OF EGYPT—*See* MIDDLE EAST [16]; UNITED ARAB REPUBLIC

ARAB WORLD—*See* FOREIGN POLICY; JORDAN; LEBANON; MIDDLE EAST; PERSIAN GULF STATES; UNITED ARAB REPUBLIC

ARAFAT, YASIR—*See* LEBANON; MIDDLE EAST [26]

ARCHEOLOGY & ANTHROPOLOGY—**Prehistoric drawings in Egypt.** Egyptian scientist-explorers discovered drawings dating back to 6,000 B.C. in caves on Uweinat Mountain in Egypt's Western Desert, according to a Jan. 3 report. The drawings of gazelles, giraffes, cows, deer and dogs—all of them resembling paleolithic drawings in caves in France and Spain—showed life when man and animals lived in the desert and had enough vegetation to support them.

Artifacts found inside mummies. Valuable artifacts imbedded in royal mummies in the Cairo Museum were discovered by a team of University of Michigan scientists headed by Dr. James E. Harris, it was announced Jan. 13. The artifacts—including gold armbands, sacred eye amulets, heart plates, statues and inscribed scarabs—were discovered through x-ray examination of 29 mummified pharoahs and their queens. The articles were hidden in body cavities and on the skin's surface under a thick resinous coating. The inscriptions were expected to produce positive identification and dating of the mummies. The x-rays also disclosed that Rameses II, the pharoah responsible for the construction of monumental pyramids, may have had smallpox and that, contrary to belief, the brains were still inside the skulls of some mummies.

Crucified skeleton unearthed. Israeli scholars, according to a Jan. 3 report, unearthed the first authenticated physical evidence of a crucifixion in the Holy Land, the skeleton of a man in his 20s. The man, whose heel bones were found pierced by a large iron nail, was believed to be one of thousands of Jews and Gentiles crucified about 2,000 years ago. The remains were discovered in a coffin bearing the common first name "Jehohanan" during excavations of cave tombs in an ancient cemetery in northeastern Jerusalem. The conclusions were published in the Israel Exploration Journal. Vasilius Tzaferis, an archaelogist associated with the Israeli government's Department of Antiquities and Museums, dated the crucifixion somewhere before the outbreak of a Jewish rebellion against Roman rule set off by the crucifixion of 3,600 Jews in 66 A.D.

Dr. Nicu Haas of the Hebrew University-Hadassah Medical Center, reporting on how the act of crucifixion was actually accomplished, indicated that the victim was nailed to the cross in a sitting position, with his feet pointing in the same direction, legs pressed tightly together, and both knees pointing away from the cross. This evidence negated the idealized image of a man draped down the cross as traditionally depicted by painters in their portraits of the crucifixion of Jesus. Dr. Haas attributed the preservation of the only material evidence of a crucifixion to an accident: the nail was bent as it hit a knot in the wood, making it impossible to remove the nail from the heel bones.

He noted that the calf bones of the victim disclosed a sharp, almost horizontal cut, "obviously created by a sharp tool, an ax or a hatchet."

Stone of second temple. Israeli archaelogists Jan. 4 reported unearthing in Old Jerusalem a cornerstone from the wall of the second Jewish temple destroyed by the Romans in 70 A.D. The six-foot-wide limestone fragment was the first remnant of the temple wall to be found with a Hebrew inscription. Benjamin Mazar, head of the Hebrew University Israel Antiquities Society, reported that the stone bore an inscription that matched a reference to the temple in the works of First Century historian Josephus Flavius. The inscription began "To the house of the blowing of the ram's horn..." Mazar said Josephus described the corner of the temple parapet where priests blew the ram's horn to herald the start and end of the Sabbath.

ARGENTINA—Severe problems within the economy, coupled with civil unrest, resulted during March in the ouster of the government of President Roberto Marcelo Levingston by a military junta. Levingston was replaced March 25 by Gen. Alejandro Agustin Lanusse, commander of the army. However, Lanusse too was threatened by abortive uprisings within the armed forces [8, 18-20], outbreaks of urban violence [13-14], economic problems [15, 23] and labor problems [17, 21].

[2]   **Levingston ousted, replaced by Lanusse.** President Levingston was ousted from his post March 23 by the commanders of Argentina's three armed services—Adm. Pedro Alberto Jose Gnavi of the navy, Gen. Lanusse of the army and Brig. Gen. Carlos Alberto Rey of the air force. The dismissal followed a week of severe riots in Cordoba and problems within the economy. The junta March 25 announced the appointment of Gen. Lanusse to the presidency. He was sworn in March 26. Lanusse announced April 15 that he would hand over power to a constitutional government within three years.

[3]   In an announcement broadcast over the government radio March 23, the three commanders said they would "resume political power until the Argentine revolution has been completed." (The three generals had installed Levingston in June 1970.) The junta urged all officials and governors to remain in their posts. Levingston left the presidential palace before dawn March 23. A military commission set up to study charges against his conduct announced April 1 that he should undergo trial before a special military "tribunal of honor."

[4]   *Cordoba riots.* General strikes and demonstrations in Cordoba March 12-19 resulted in at least three deaths, hundreds of injuries and arrests and an estimated $4 million in damages. Workers and students in Cordoba were protesting the government's wage policies and the economic situation, as well as the appointment of Jose Camilo Uriburu, a right-wing nationalist, as governor of Cordoba Province March 1, succeeding Bernardo Bas, who had resigned Feb. 25. Uriburu resigned March 16 and was temporarily succeeded by Helvio Gouzden, governor of La Pampa Province. Cordoba was declared an emergency zone March 18 and Gen. Lopez Aufranc of the Third Army Division took control of the city. In a move which aggravated the crisis, Levingston March 19 dismissed Brig. Gen. Ezequiel Martinez as chairman of the joint chiefs of staff for, in Levingston's words, "a disciplinary infraction of grave character." (Martinez, who allegedly had been plotting with Rey against Levingston, was restored to his post by the junta March 23.) In a last-ditch effort to save his government, Levingston March 22 fired Lanusse as commander in chief of the army for not having "acted with sufficient authority" to quell the Cordoba violence. Rey and Gnavi, however, announced support for Lanusse; and his replacement, Defense Minister Jorge Esteban Caceres Monie, announced he would hold the post only long enough to hand it back to Lanusse. Lanusse also received support from other key military leaders, particularly from Aufranc. The state of emergency in Cordoba was ended by the junta March 23.

[5] *Economic situation.* The economic situation had deteriorated sharply during late 1970 and the first two months of 1971. The rate of inflation, 6.6% in 1969 and 20% in 1970, had reached 9.5% for January and February. Economy Minister Aldo Ferrer had originally forecast a 10% inflation ceiling for 1970, but had been forced to raise the prediction to around 30%. In the face of union demands for 40%-200% wage increases, Levingston had announced March 7 that wage increases in 1971 would be held to a ceiling of 19%, of which 13% was to allow for inflation. (The ceiling was lifted by the junta March 23.) Price controls on items critical to the cost-of-living index went into effect March 8.

[6] An important element in the inflation was the increase in the price of meat by 130% during the previous 14 months. The shortage of beef had almost decimated Argentina's traditional beef exports and created a need for the importation of cattle. Levingston Feb. 26 had announced that the government, effective March 15, would fix a selling price of 14¢ a pound for live animals, above which special taxes would be instituted along with a possible cutoff of internal consumption for two weeks a month. In addition, credit facilities would be made available to meat packers and producers. (Deltec International Finance Corporation's Compania Swift de la Plata, the nation's largest private meat packer, had gone bankrupt in December 1970, as had the British-owned Anglo Meat Packing Co. in January and another British-owned house, Liebig's, in February. Swift was again declared bankrupt Nov. 8.) The junta March 25 announced a ban on the sale of meat. The ban would alternate every other week for an initial period of three months.

[7] *Cabinet named.* President Lanusse, who reportedly retained his control of the army, March 26 swore in two new cabinet ministers—Social Welfare Minister Francisco Guillermo Manrique and Interior Minister Arturo Mor Roig. The six other ministers in the Cabinet were retained from Levingston's administration—Foreign Affairs Minister Luis Maria de Pablo Pardo, Defense Minister Monie, Justice Minister Jaime Perriaux, Education Minister Jose Luis Cantini, Public Works Minister Óscar Colombo and Economy Minister Ferrer. In later changes in the cabinet: Colombo was replaced June 21 by Pedro Antonio Gordilla; Perriaux was replaced Oct. 11 by Ismael Bruno Quijano; Ferrer resigned May 29, reportedly under compulsion, after Lanusse announced May 26 that his post would be abolished in order to create four new posts—Finance (headed by Juan Quilici, who was replaced by Cayetano A. Licciardo Oct. 11), Commerce and Industry (headed by Gen. Oscar Chescotta, replaced Oct. 23 by Alfredo Jose Girelli as minister of commerce and Carlos Gerardo Casale as minister of industry and mining), Agriculture and Livestock (headed by Gabriel Perren, who was replaced by Antonio di Rocco July 20) and Labor (headed by Rubens San Sabastian). A fifth ministry, Transport, might be added later.

[8] **Abortive coup.** Lanusse retained control of the government after an attempted coup by what were described as "leftist-nationalist" elements failed May 11. The conspiracy centered in Tucuman, where Capt. Jose Meritello attempted to rally the garrison on May 10 to support a "nationalist revolution." He was arrested by his commanding officer. On May 14, Lanusse dismissed seven colonels implicated in the conspiracy. An arrest warrant was reported to have been issued for retired Gen. Eduardo Rafael LaBanca, an anti-Marxist and nationalist implicated as the central figure in the plot. Despite his anti-Communist stance, LaBanca had obtained the support of some left-wing groups, particularly within the Peronist labor movement.

[9] **Party organization permitted.** The government announced June 1 that the organization of political parties, first proposed April 1, would be permitted beginning July 1. The formation of parties had been officially banned since the 1966 military coup. Interior Minister Mor Roig said that, while the reinstatement of parties would first be declared by executive decree, plans were being made to codify electoral and political reforms in a constitutional

amendment. The government June 30 accepted the Organic Law of Political Parties.

[10] Agreement on Falklands. Secret talks which began June 21 between Argentina and Britain on the opening of air and sea links to the Falkland Islands (called the Malvinas by the Argentines) ended in agreement July 1. Both sides had agreed to put aside the difficult question of sovereignty over the islands in order to settle other key issues. They stated in a communique July 1 that nothing contained in the agreement could signify renunciation by either government of its position on the question of sovereignty. The agreement called for creation of a special consultative committee to resolve any problems in communications and movement of persons from the islands; grant of a document to the islands' residents permitting them free travel within Argentina; exemption from taxes on certain equipment for islanders who pass through Argentina; and exemption from military service for island residents. The agreement also provided for Argentina to establish a weekly air service for passengers, mail and cargo between the mainland and the islands and a similar maritime shipping service to be provided by Britain. Britain announced July 1 that it would construct an airport at Port Stanley, capital of the Falkland Islands, as a first step in improving relations between Britain and Argentina.

[11] 'Summit' on terrorist measures. President Lanusse and Uruguayan President Jorge Pacheco Areco met in Buenos Aires July 9 to discuss possible coordination of antiterrorist activities by the two countries. According to report, Lanusse was seeking support in implementing an "Argentine Doctrine," which called for no deals with political kidnapers, no aid to hijackers and a strong campaign against urban guerrillas. The two presidents also signed resolutions calling for collaboration on water resources and hydroelectric energy, proposed a joint commission on economic cooperation to seek to correct existing disadvantages in commercial relations and discussed measures to insure the application of the 200-mile territorial limit in the South Atlantic. (More than a dozen young men and women, members of a self-proclaimed Revolutionary People's Army (ERP) composed of both Argentines and Uruguayans, were arrested after police discovered a plot to assassinate both presidents while they reviewed a military parade on Argentine Independence Day, July 9.)

[12] Argentine-Chilean 'summit.' President Lanusse and Chilean President Salvador Allende held a "summit" meeting July 23-24 in the northern Argentine city of Salta. The meeting was regarded as historic, mainly because the two leaders represented different ideological political positions. Allende was a Marxist who favored socialism for Chile. The meeting was called to ratify a formula, negotiated by the foreign ministers of the two countries, for settlement of a dispute over the Beagle Channel in the extreme southern region of Tierra del Fuego. The agreement consisted of three parts: a list of 18 articles providing for the border to be established by Britain's Queen Elizabeth on the basis of a technical decision by a five-man arbitration court composed of judges from the World Court; a modus vivendi to be applied while the court was deliberating, and a joint declaration approving the eventual decision which would be binding on both sides. Both presidents signed the "Declaration of Salta," which ratified the arbitration agreement, called for maintenance of the 200-mile limit and urged joint efforts to expand trade, transport, tourism and the exchange of technology.

[13] Outbreak of urban violence. In what appeared to be a highly coordinated plan, bombing and terrorist attacks took place July 26 in Cordoba, Rosario, Tucuman and Buenos Aires. The events coincided with the 19th anniversary of the death of Eva Peron, late wife of the former Argentine dictator Juan Peron. Police in La Plata the same day announced that they had discovered a terrorist unit of the Armed Forces of Liberation (FAL) and detained 13 of its members, attributing various subversive acts to them during the past year. The police said the FAL had been part of a nationwide subversive network and received arms and precise instructions on their activities and national subversive developments. The group was allegedly in possession of 60 million pesos to finance its activities.

[14]   It was reported Aug. 9 that Argentine authorities estimated that armed subversive movements had reached an active membership of 6,000 persons. The report said that evidence indicated that, as in Brazil and Guatemala, "death squads" linked to security forces had been responsible for the killing of persons suspected of terrorist activities. Terrorism in Argentina also included Roman Catholic Priests, members of the Third World Priests Movement. Four members of the movement were arrested by the army Aug. 3 in Rosario along with 13 other persons in a roundup of "terrorist elements." Sixty priests gathered from all parts of the country during September to attend a movement conference in Rosario. A group of 47 of the priests was arrested Sept. 25 while carrying out a peaceful demonstration for the release of parish priest Santiago MacGuire and other political prisoners. The 47 were released Sept. 28. Besides demanding the release of political prisoners, the arrested priests made a public statement to the press criticizing the "growing participation of the army in investigation without proper legal controls."

[15]   **Wage increase, price freeze set.** The government invoked a "social accord" Sept. 2 which would consist of "a truce between those sectors that perform functions in both the economic and social fields." To solidify the accord, the following measures were announced: prices and taxes were frozen at their Aug. 24 level (until Jan. 31, 1972, according to a Sept. 9 report); tariffs from state enterprises would be maintained for the next 60 days; a family allowance for wives was increased by 6,000 pesos (national money); compensation to retired people and pensioners was readjusted beginning Oct. 1. Other measures announced by the government included an increase of 5,000 pesos (national money) in wages for workers in collective enterprises beginning Sept. 1. During the time of the "truce," the peso would not be devalued nor would taxes be increased. During the time the measures would take effect, the government would study the necessary means to place economic and social factors in equilibrium. Any abuses of the measures would lead to either a censure or a closing by the government of the companies involved. In another economic move, the government Sept. 13 imposed a 60-90-day ban on all imports.

[16]   **Eva Peron's body taken to Spain.** The government Sept. 3 returned the body of Eva Peron to former President Peron, in Spanish exile. The silver coffin containing the body of Eva Peron, who died in 1952, was turned over to Peron by Argentine embassy officials for reburial near his Madrid home. The government did not indicate where the body had been kept since its disappearance three months after Peron was ousted by the military in 1955. It was disclosed Sept. 7 that Eva Peron's body had been kept in a Milan, Italy, cemetery for 14 years before its transfer to Madrid. Italian press reports said Sept. 5 that the late Pope Pius XII had given permission for the secret burial on a request by President Pedro Aramburu, who headed the Argentine government after Peron was overthrown.

[17]   **Illegal CGT strike called success.** A 24-hour strike Sept. 29 called by the General Confederation of Workers (CGT), the country's largest labor union, was called a success by union leaders who claimed nearly 100% support by the union's 3.5 million members. The strike, seen as a protest against the military government, had been declared illegal by government authorities Sept. 27. The CGT, dominated by supporters of Peron, ostensibly called the strike to protest inflation and the decline of real wages and to demand increased salaries, pension benefits and family allowances. Police took no action against the illegal strikers.

[18] **Army revolt quelled.** Two army regiments garrisoned in the towns of Azul and Olavarria south of Buenos Aires Oct. 8 declared their rebellion against the government. The rebellion ended Oct. 9 with only a few shots fired and no casualties when the rebel commanders surrendered to 10,000 loyal government troops. Former President Levingston was placed under arrest Oct. 10 as the suspected organizer of the uprising. According to report Oct. 13, 65 persons had been arrested for complicity in the rebellion. Among those arrested were Brig. Gen. Ricardo Etchverry Boneo, commander of the 1st Armored Cavalry Brigade, and the Rev. Julio Meinvielle of Buenos Aires, who was reported to be an outspoken advocate of right-wing causes.

[19] Soldiers in the two garrisons seized control of the local radio stations Oct. 8 and called for Lanusse's immediate resignation. The rebels, under the command of Lt. Col. Florentino Diaz Loza in Olavarria and Col. Manuel Alejandro Garcia and Lt. Col. Fernando Amadeo Baldrich in Azul, said the Lanusse government was guilty of creating "political and economic chaos and moral disaster." They described the government plan (announced Sept. 17) to hold elections March 25, 1973 as "a farce" that would betray the army's nationalist goals. Lanusse announced that loyal units of the 1st Corps had been sent to quell the insurrection. While troops converged on the rebel zone, Lanusse received declarations of allegiance and support from commanders of several units of the army, the CGT, the Peronist movement and the Hour of the People, a coalition of leftist parties. (Because of his support of Lanusse, Jorge Paladino, Peron's personal representative and head of the Justicialist party, was replaced by Peron Nov. 5 with Hector Cumpira, a former Peronist deputy.)

[20] *Navy crisis resolved.* The revolt came one day after a crisis in the leadership of the navy was resolved Oct. 7 by the decision of the navy commander in chief, Gnavi, to retire in December. Lanusse announced Nov. 4 that Gnavi would be replaced by Vice Adm. Carlos G. N. Coda, effective Jan. 3, 1972. The crisis in the naval command was the result of Gnavi's attempt to dismiss several other high-ranking officers. Five senior naval officers were dismissed Oct. 3 by Gnavi. No reasons were given for the dismissals, although a reference was made to an "internal situation without any implication outside the navy." It was reported Oct. 7 that five admirals had applied for early retirement, a move believed to have been an attempt to force the resignation of Adm. Gnavi. Sources said the rebel naval officers wanted to oust Gnavi as a result of his cooperation in government overtures to supporters of former President Peron. The naval crisis was reportedly linked with the navy's traditional refusal to permit negotiations with Peronist supporters. The navy had had a prominent role in the overthrow of Peron's regime.

[21] **Cordoba strike brings police disorders.** A 14-hour general strike called by the CGT Oct. 22 in Cordoba virtually paralyzed the city, closing down radio and television stations, newspapers, transport and other essential services, it was reported Oct. 23. The federal government had imposed strict security measures in Cordoba's central district to impede disorders. The strike, however, provoked clashes between provincial and federal police, who had been mobilized in Cordoba to maintain order during the strike activities. The clash began when federal police, placing a roadblock on a principal city street, shot at and destroyed a car that ignored the barrier. The car's driver, Eduardo Romero, 25, was severely injured. The provincial police immediately issued statements condemning the assault, claiming that the federal police had abused their powers. The federal police responded Oct. 23 by attacking the Cordoba police headquarters, wounding several officers and damaging the building. Federal police also detained Cordoba Police Chief Alberto Villar and other police officials who were charged with obstruction of federal police activity.

[22] **Woman sentenced for guerrilla activity.** Luisa Velosa, a 27-year-old maid in a navy canteen, became the first Argentine to be sentenced by a special military tribunal to combat rising left-wing guerrilla activity. Miss Velosa, who told the tribunal that police had tortured her with electric shocks, was given a

seven-year sentence Nov. 3 after being found guilty of participating in an armed attempt by guerrillas to seize weapons from the Buenos Aires police July 20. Lawyers defending Miss Velosa attacked the tribunal as illegal on the ground that it contravened the constitution of 1853—theoretically still in force—which forbade setting up special tribunals for political offenses.

[23] **New economic plan.** President Lanusse July 7 proposed a new, moderately nationalistic plan that he said would strengthen his efforts to restore an elected government. The plan, invoked Dec. 3, consisted of 25 measures which were to remain in effect until May 1973. The new plan was to stimulate the flow of exports, provide periodic salary raises up to 25% while holding price increases to 20% and increase the cost of public services by 40%. (A 25% wage increase was decreed for all workers Dec. 30. Employees would receive a 15% wage increase Jan. 1, 1972 and another 10% increase July 1, 1972.) The plan would also lift the 15% import surcharge in steps, beginning with the removal of the entire surcharge on basic industrial and iron and steel imports, and would provide for an increase of 30% in family allowances and an adjustment in the wages of all workers to reassure maintenance of real salaries. In an effort to stem the rising rate of inflation, the plan provided that the Central Bank would not be able to issue more than two billion new pesos until May 1973.

See also EUROPEAN ECONOMIC COMMUNITY [8]; HIJACKING [2]; LATIN AMERICA; MIDDLE EAST [11]; PAKISTAN [42]; SPORTS; TARIFFS & WORLD TRADE [2]

ARMAMENTS, INTERNATIONAL—World arms outlay surveyed. The U.S. Arms Control and Disarmament Agency's fifth annual report on world military spending, published May 5, estimated that $204 billion had been spent on arms in 1970. The increase over the previous year's expenditures of $199 billion was described as "the smallest in recent years." The agency said that "in terms of constant dollars, i.e., had prices been unchanged, there would have been a slight decline—a hopeful sign that the sharp uptrend of the 1960s had been blunted." NATO arms spending was put at approximately $103 billion a year, while the outlay for Warsaw Pact countries continued on a "sharp upward slant" averaging $71 billion a year.

French nuclear missiles operational. France's first nine nuclear ballistic missiles had become operational with completion of their installation and testing Aug. 3 in the Vaucluse Mountains in southern France, Defense Minister Michel Debre announced to the Council of Ministers Aug. 4. The missiles, which were stocked underground, had a range of about 2,000 miles and had nuclear warheads reportedly in the 150 kiloton range. A second set of nine missiles was expected to become operational in 1972. Plans for a third stage of the missile program were canceled for economic reasons.

The nation's independent nuclear strike forces now included the ballistic missiles and 45 Mirage IV supersonic medium-range bombers. Also planned were five thermonuclear missile-launching nuclear submarines, two of which were on trial. By 1972, missiles stocked underground would amount to a force of 2,700 kilotons. By 1976, France was expected to have a nuclear deterrent force of about 40,000 kilotons.

Soviet missile cutback reported. The London-based Institute for Strategic Studies, an independent research group, said Sept. 2 in its annual report that the Soviet Union had curtailed its deployment of intercontinental ballistic missiles (ICBMs) since the beginning of 1970. Suggesting that the U.S.S.R. "may have reached or be approaching its planned level" of ICBMs, the institute estimated that the Soviet total of such missiles was 1,510, compared with 1,054 for the U.S. The report, which listed world military spending exclusive of Latin America to July 1971, said Israel had spent 26.5% of its gross national product on defense in 1970. The figure for Egypt was 19.6%. NATO reportedly had "little more than a third as many operational tanks as the Warsaw Pact and 2,500 fewer tactical aircraft." The institute reported that the U.S. had approximately 2.7 million men in its armed forces, while the Soviet Union had 3.4 million.

Israeli A-missile hinted. Israeli production of a missile capable of carrying atomic warheads was reported Oct. 4. The account was based on assessments made by American and other Western intelligence sources, according to the newspaper. The missile, called the Jericho, was being built to carry a warhead of 1,000-1,500 pounds 300 miles or more. It was believed the weapon was being manufactured at a rate of three to six a month. The report quoted one American specialist as saying: "It wouldn't make much sense to manufacture a costly weapon like Jericho merely to carry the equivalent of two or three 500-pound bombs. The decision to go into production suggests that Israel has, or believes it could have soon, nuclear warheads for the system." Israel was said to have started development of the Jericho in the early 1960s.

Soviet weapons lead seen. The Soviet Union "now has the initiative in weapons technology," according to *Jane's Weapons Systems 1971-72,* a British reference book which attributed the Soviet advantage to a duplication of effort by members of the North Atlantic Treaty Organization. The report said improvements in the Soviet early-warning radar system and "the modern Soviet navy and the nature of its armament and equipment and the existence of an operational antiballistic missile system around Moscow are evidence of the Soviet ability to take the initiative in weapons systems development and deployment.... Fragmentary evidence is emerging of a number of other Soviet developments and programs, one of which is directly comparable with but slightly ahead of a U.S. project. This is a new supersonic bomber, reported to carry the NATO designation 'Backfire,' and to be a swing-wing machine with low-altitude supersonic capability." The approximately equivalent U.S. B-1 bomber project was "as yet only at the mockup stage," the publication reported.

See also DISARMAMENT; FOREIGN POLICY; GERMANY, WEST [3]; JAPAN [4-5]; MIDDLE EAST [20-23]; PAKISTAN [37-38]; SOUTH AFRICA [7-12]; SPACE [22]; TERRITORIAL WATERS; VENEZUELA; ZAMBIA

ARMY, U.S.—*See* CHEMICAL & BIOLOGICAL WARFARE; MILITARY [2-7, 11-12]; PENTAGON PAPERS [27]; POLLUTION [16]; RACIAL & MINORITY UNREST; SELECTIVE SERVICE SYSTEM; WAR CRIMES

ASH, ROY L.—*See* GOVERNMENT REORGANIZATION

ASTRONOMY—Two nearby galaxies detected. Astronomers reported Jan. 10 that they had detected two "new" massive galaxies that had been previously overlooked because of a thick curtain of interstellar dust. The two galaxies, the scientists said, were "next door" to the Milky Way, earth's own galaxy. The discovery, made by astronomers from the University of California at Berkeley, the California Institute of Technology and the Carnegie Institution of Washington, was made public Jan. 11. The detection of the two galaxies brought to seven the number of what astronomers called the "local group" or "local cluster." The five original galaxies in the cluster were the Milky Way, the Andromeda galaxy and three small satellite galaxies. The two additions were the farthest distant of the local group. The astronomers named the two galaxies Maffei 1 and 2 to honor a young Italian astronomer who touched off the chain of events that led to their eventual detection. (In 1968, the Italian astronomer, Paolo Maffei, reported in a scientific journal that he had found two strange "objects" on an infrared photograph he had made of a region in the northern sky.)

ATOMIC ENERGY—U.S. radiation levels reported safe. A study released Jan. 25 by the National Council on Radiation Protection (NCRP) in Washington said current precautions against radiation exposure in the U.S. were safe and no tighter standards were required. The council was a nonprofit corporation chartered by Congress and provided information on radiation projects of government agencies, including the Atomic Energy Commission and the Public

Health Services. Its recommendations were to be submitted to the Environmental Protection Agency.

[2]   The council report, based on a 10-year study, said its "review of the current knowledge of biological effects of radiation exposure provides no basis for any drastic reductions in the recommended exposure levels despite the current urgings of a few critics." The NCRP took issue with recent assertions by Drs. John F. Gofman and Arthur R. Tamplin of the AEC's Radiation Laboratory in California. According to their own estimates of radiation dangers, the two scientists concluded that 32,000 excess cancer deaths would probably occur annually under the average permissible radiation exposure (170 millirems) of the American population. Gofman urged that the radiation exposure limits be reduced to one-tenth their present levels. The NCRP contended that exposure to the total permissible maximum would result in no more than 3,000 additional cancer deaths a year. It said that although average exposures were far lower than the recommended limit, no exposure could be regarded as safe.

[3]   The council recommended for the first time that a maximum permissible radiation dose of 0.5 rem (measurement of radiation dosage) be set specifically for pregnant women to protect the fetus.

[4]   **Hanford deactivation halted.** President Nixon Feb. 4 ordered a suspension of plans to deactivate one of two remaining nuclear reactors at the Atomic Energy Commission's reservation in Hanford, Wash. The reactor produced plutonium for nuclear weapons and electric power for the Washington Public Power Supply System. The suspension order came after hearings by the Joint Congressional Committee on Atomic Energy Feb. 4 at which Sen. Henry M. Jackson (D, Wash.) testified that the reactor's closure would severely affect power supplies and employment in the Hanford area. An unidentified Nixon Administration official, quoted Feb. 6, called the reactor "unreliable and a possible safety hazard."

[5]   **Soviet-French uranium pact.** France and the Soviet Union March 15 signed a pact worth approximately $7 million by which the Soviet Union agreed to enrich French uranium. The accord, breaking a monopoly held by the AEC in providing fissionable materials to Western countries, obliged the Soviet Union to enrich the uranium (increase its ratio of radioactive isotopes) for a French power plant to be constructed at Fessenheim in Alsace.

[6]   **U.S.S.R. builds atomic converter.** The Soviet Union announced March 25 that its scientists had succeeded in constructing a new engineering system that could convert nuclear energy directly into electricity. In a brief official statement, Tass, the Soviet Press Agency, said "comprehensive tests" had been completed on an advanced converter with an electrical capacity of "several kilowatts." Tass hailed the new converter as "a new major achievement of Soviet atomic science and technology." (AEC spokesmen called the Soviet accomplishment "an important technical step." They added, however, that not enough details were available to determine if it was a major breakthrough in the field of direct energy conversion.)

[7]   The Tass statement described the new device as a thermionic converter. Scientists in the U.S. and U.S.S.R. had been investigating the thermionic method for directly converting atomic energy into electric power rather than through the heating of steam to drive a turbine generator. The new development was seen as another step in the attempts by scientists in both the U.S. and the Soviet Union to develop compact generators for on-board power systems in space vehicles.

[8]   **Atom plant alterations.** The AEC June 7 proposed that nuclear power plants limit their radiation exposure to 1%, or less, of the amount of radiation permitted under current U.S. guidelines for power reactors. AEC spokesmen said only the Humboldt Bay reactor near Eureka, Calif., and the Dresden reactor no. 1 and possibly the Dresden reactor no. 2, both near Chicago, failed to meet the new guidelines. In another safety measure, the AEC June 19

ordered five atomic power plants to modernize their emergency cooling systems and three plants to lower their peak operating temperatures to 2,300 degrees Fahrenheit. The orders were described as part of an "interim core cooling policy" subject to future changes.

[9] AEC orders reactor permit reviews. Following a July 23 ruling of the U.S. Court of Appeals for the District of Columbia that AEC procedures made a "mockery" of the 1970 Environmental Policy Act by considering only radiation hazards, the AEC announced new rules Sept. 3 under which operating licenses or construction permits of more than 100 nuclear reactor power plants in 21 states would come under review. The affected utilities were required to show cause within 40 days why their permits or licenses should not be suspended pending completion of a review to produce a complete environmental impact statement. Ten plants that were granted provisional operating licenses before the 1970 act also would be reviewed for environmental effects, but their licenses would not be suspended. Seven other facilities, the oldest nuclear power plants in the country, faced no action because their full operating licenses were granted before 1970. It was estimated that adequate environmental safeguards could cost the nation's utilities as much as $25 million. The July 23 court ruling came in an environmental suit seeking to halt construction of the Calvert Cliffs plant of Chesapeake Bay in Maryland. The AEC Nov. 24 announced that it would not halt construction of the Calvert Cliffs plant while it conducted a review of its environmental impact. The announcement also gave tentative go-aheads to the Yankee station in Lincoln County, Me.; the Fitzpatrick plant, near Oswego, N.Y.; and the Oconie, S.C. power station. In a further development, a U.S. district court judge Dec. 13 enjoined the AEC from issuing a partial operating license for a Cordova, Ill. nuclear power plant until the agency issued a complete environmental impact statement called for by the 1969 National Environmental Policy Act. The injunction had been sought by the Illinois attorney general and the Izaak Walton League of America, a conservation group.

[10] Nuclear pact safeguards accords. Finland June 11 became the first nation to formally sign an agreement with the International Atomic Energy Agency (IAEA) in Vienna providing for application of IAEA safeguards to all Finnish nuclear material to insure their peaceful use. The agreement was in fulfillment of Article III of the Treaty on the Non-Proliferation of Nuclear Weapons. The safeguards accord still required adoption by the Finnish parliament. Austria signed a safeguards agreement with the IAEA Sept. 21. Uruguay Sept. 8 and Poland Sept. 16 initialed the text of safeguards agreements following the conclusion of negotiations with the IAEA. The agreements were based on guidelines established by the IAEA safeguards committee in March and approved by the board of governors April 20. The guidelines included provision for a national control system by each state, coupled with the IAEA's right to independently verify the national findings.

[11] France suspends Pacific nuclear tests. France Sept. 1 announced cancellation of two nuclear tests planned in 1971 in the Murora Atoll in the South Pacific. French Defense Minister Michel Debre said the first five tests (June 5 and 12, July 14, and Aug. 8 and 14) had "fully satisfied—without exception" the objectives of French scientists working on perfecting France's nuclear force. However, observers attributed the testing halt to protests from Peru, Japan, Australia, New Zealand and the South Pacific islands of Tonga, Nauru, Fiji, Western Samoa and Cook Island.

[12] Atoms for Peace conference. The Fourth International Conference on the Peaceful Uses of Atomic Energy was held under U.N. sponsorship in Geneva Sept. 6-16. It was attended by about 4,000 scientists from 79 nations and was presided over by Dr. Glenn Seaborg, former chairman of the U.S. AEC. The conference focused on the past and future expansion of nuclear power plants to supply electricity and the consequences of this development, including environmental problems.

[13]   **Euratom impasse ended.** The European Atomic Energy Community (Euratom) Council of Ministers broke an internal deadlock Sept. 20 between France and its five non-nuclear members—West Germany, Italy, Belgium, the Netherlands and Luxembourg—over Euratom inspection of civilian nuclear installations. The five nations bowed to French demands that only the civilian French nuclear plants using fuel obtained from nations outside France would continue to be subject to Euratom inspection. West Germany had demanded that France open its entire civilian nuclear industry to Euratom checks. With the internal dispute settled, the five non-nuclear members of the Council of Ministers also approved the terms of inspection for nuclear plants they would seek in negotiations with the IAEA under the nuclear nonproliferation treaty. The treaty was signed, but not yet ratified, by the five nations. They had opposed IAEA controls over their nuclear facilities. France, which had refused to sign the nonproliferation treaty, would not have been subject to IAEA inspection because it already possessed nuclear weapons.

[14]   **Pentagon aides back on-site checks.** The two leading Pentagon scientists, Dr. John S. Foster, Jr., director of defense research and engineering, and Dr. Stephen J. Lukasik, director of the Advanced Research Projects Agency, told the Congressional Joint Committee on Atomic Energy Oct. 27 that substantial advances by the U.S. in seismic technology in the last decade had not eliminated the need for on-site inspections to verify compliance with an underground nuclear testing ban. Their testimony was the Pentagon's first detailed report in 10 years on the U.S. program to develop more sophisticated methods of nuclear test detection. Among their disclosures: A $25 million network of U.S. "seismic array" stations, in operation in Alaska, Montana and Norway, could detect underground blasts as small as five kilotons (a kiloton explosion is equivalent to 1,000 tons of TNT) in Communist China or the Soviet Union and could pinpoint explosions within 60 miles of the actual sites. The U.S. had also deployed eight individual seismic listening stations in the U.S., Canada, Australia, Turkey and Thailand, with three others planned for Bolivia, Spain and Norway. The seismic arrays and the individual stations together would enable the U.S. to detect underground tests as small as two kilotons. Detonations, nevertheless, could be concealed or muffled by conducting tests during an earthquake, in a cavity or in soft material such as sand or gravel.

[15]   **U.S. underground test series.** The U.S. resumed underground nuclear tests at the AEC's Nevada test site with a low-yield (equivalent to the force of less than 20,000 tons of TNT) explosion June 19. The blast ended a six-month test suspension (the longest in nearly a decade) following an underground test Dec. 18, 1970 that had released radioactive material into the air. The AEC conducted nine more underground explosions, the 224th-230th and 232nd-233rd conducted by the AEC since the 1963 treaty banning all but underground tests, at the site. Low-yield tests took place July 1, Sept. 29, Oct. 8 and Nov. 24. Tests in the low-intermediate yield range (20,000 to 200,000 tons of TNT) took place June 23 and 24, July 8, Aug. 18 and Dec. 14.

[16]   *H-bomb exploded under Amchitka.* The most powerful underground nuclear test conducted by the U.S.—a five megaton blast equivalent to the explosive force of 5 million tons of TNT—was executed Nov. 6 on the remote Alaskan island of Amchitka in the Aleutians, five hours after the Supreme Court denied a last-minute appeal by environmental and antiwar groups for a temporary injunction. The 4-3 court vote (Chief Justice Warren E. Burger and Justices Harry A. Blackmun, Potter Stewart and Byron R. White voting with the majority and Justices William J. Brennan Jr., William O. Douglas and Thurgood Marshall dissenting) climaxed a four-month legal battle to block the test. President Nixon Oct. 27 had given special authorization for the test, code-named Cannikin, for national security reasons. Congress had barred the test until mid-1972 unless the President authorized it. The test, estimated to have cost about $200 million, was conducted in the face of strong opposition from Canada, Japan, some U.S. senators and thousands of U.S. citizens, all of whom

feared possible adverse ecological consequences. However, the earthquake and tidal wave feared by test opponents failed to materialize and the AEC reported the absence of any trace of radioactive leakage.

[17] The bomb was detonated at 5 p.m. (EST) in a 54-foot-wide chamber at the bottom of a 6,000-foot hole on Amchitka. It caused a ground side roll on Amchitka and on the Island of Adak, 190 miles from the test area. Seismographs in Alaska and Japan registered tremors five or six minutes after the explosion, which registered 7 on the Richter scale (equivalent to a major earthquake). AEC Chairman Schlesinger declared the blast to be "a successful test" and said "we will be able to certify, I think, this device for introduction into the stockpiles." Schlesinger reiterated his earlier claim that the test "minimized the likelihood of a defective warhead being used in the Spartan antiballistic missile." The underground cavern created by the blast collapsed Nov. 8, forming a large crater on the island's surface. The collapse registered 5 on the Richter scale. First reports released Nov. 8 on the test's environmental effects indicated that several rockfalls, "larger than expected," had destroyed four eagle nests and a peregrine falcon nest and killed 13 birds. No falcons or eagles, considered two of America's rarest birds, were killed. A report published Dec. 10 said that 900-1,000 sea otters had been killed by the blast. (The AEC had predicted 20-100 deaths.)

[18] In legal events preceding the Supreme Court decision: U.S. District Court Judge George L. Hart Aug. 26 dismissed a suit seeking release of secret government papers that had allegedly advised against the test; Hart ruled Aug. 30 that the test would comply "with all relevant laws and treaties" and refused to delay or cancel the blast; ordered by the Court of Appeals for the District of Columbia to reopen the case, Hart Oct. 26 directed the government to furnish him with the secret documents so he could determine if they should be released; the court of appeals Oct. 28 upheld Hart's request for the documents and also refused to block the test temporarily, contending that the action would "interject the court into national security matters that lie outside its province"; after examining the documents, Hart again refused to grant a preliminary injunction against the test Nov. 1; the AEC, in compliance with Hart's ruling, Nov. 3 released 187 pages of secret documents; the court of appeals Nov. 3 refused for a second time to halt the test but said the case did "present a substantial question as to the legality of the proposed test."

[19] **Soviet test series.** The AEC reported recording seismic signals indicating Soviet nuclear tests in the low-intermediate range March 21, Oct. 21, Oct. 22 and Dec. 30. The AEC Sept. 27 reported seismic signals presumed to be an underground nuclear test in the range of two to four megatons (equivalent to 2 million to 4 million tons of TNT) in the Novaya Zemlya region of the Soviet Arctic. It was the second biggest underground explosion recorded up to that time, exceeded only by a Soviet detonation in October 1970. The Uppsala University Seismological Institute in Sweden reported the detection of blast July 10, Oct. 5 and Oct. 9. The tests, not confirmed by the AEC, measured 5.1, 4.7 and 5.7, respectively, on the Richter scale. The AEC said the Russians were thought to have set off 10 tests in 1971.

[20] **Chinese test.** Communist China Nov. 18 conducted its first nuclear test since October 1970 and its 12th since China's first nuclear explosion in 1964. The test, estimated by the AEC to be in the 20 kiloton range, took place at China's Lop Nor test site in Sinkiang Province.

See also BUDGET; DEFENSE [5]; DISARMAMENT; ENERGY; GOVERNMENT REORGANIZATION; MEDICINE; PENTAGON PAPERS [22]; POLLUTION [11, 15]; SCIENCE

ATTICA CORRECTIONAL FACILITY—*See* PRISONS [6-8]

AUSTRALIA—McMahon sworn in. External Affairs Minister William McMahon, 63, was sworn in as prime minister March 10, replacing John Gorton after he had been ousted as leader of the Liberal party in a bitter political dispute triggered March 8 by the resignation of Defense Minister Malcolm Fraser over Gorton's failure to block publication of a newspaper article in which Fraser was accused of "extreme disloyalty" to the army. (Fraser's quarrel with the army stemmed from a clash over army plans to cut civic action programs in Vietnam and from allegations that Fraser had ordered an intelligence investigation of the army in Vietnam because he did not trust army reports.) At a closed session of the Liberal party, Gorton cast the deciding vote against himself to break a 33-33 tie on a vote of confidence. The party, which dominated the conservative coalition government, then elected Gorton as deputy leader, McMahon's former post. Party members had accused Gorton of dictatorial tendencies and a disregard of the states in important policy matters.

[2] McMahon's government March 15 survived a motion of no confidence introduced in the House of Representatives by Gough Whitlam, leader of the Labor party. The motion was defeated 62-58. Whitlam had called for an immediate general election so the electorate could vote on what he called the "extraordinary events" involving Fraser's resignation and Gorton's ouster.

[3] **Government reorganization.** McMahon announced a government reorganization March 12 designed "to support the operation of the cabinet system of government." (Gorton had been criticized for centralizing power in his own hands.) Under the reorganization, the Prime Minister's Department and the Department of the Cabinet Office were replaced by the Department of the Prime Minister and the Cabinet and the Department of the Vice President of the Executive Council. At the insistence of Governor-General Sir Paul Hasluck, the change would not involve the Executive Council itself.

[4] **Cabinet shakeup.** McMahon announced a cabinet shuffle March 21. (Gorton had been named defense minister March 10.) Leslie H. E. Bury, federal treasurer, was named minister of foreign affairs. Billy M. Snedden, previously minister of labor and national service, was named treasurer. Alexander Forbes was appointed immigration minister, succeeding Phillip Lynch who was named minister of labor. Two of Gorton's closest associates—Navy Minister James Killen and Attorney General Thomas Hughes—were replaced by Malcolm G. Mackay and Nigel Bowen, former minister of education and science. David Fairbairn, a cabinet member until 1969, was appointed minister for education and science. Ivor Greenwood was named minister for health, and Kevin Cairns became minister of housing.

[5] (Following the election Feb. 3 of Minister for Primary Industry John Douglas Anthony to replace Sir John McEwen as leader of the Country party, a partner in the coalition government, Country party cabinet posts were reshuffled Feb. 3. Anthony took over McEwen's posts as deputy prime minister and minister for trade and industry; Ralph Hunt, a rancher, was named minister for the interior to replace Peter Nixon, who became minister for shipping and transport; Ian Sinclair, who was replaced by Nixon, became minister for primary industry.)

[6] **Federal-state relations.** Federal-state relations, which had deteriorated under former Prime Minister Gorton, marked a sharp improvement April 5 with talks between the state premiers and Prime Minister McMahon and Treasurer Snedden. The federal government agreed to allocate $43 million in special assistance grants to the states to reduce cash deficits. Gorton had refused interim budget aid to the states on the ground that it would add to inflationary pressures. At a meeting in June, McMahon said he would grant the premiers the right to collect the payroll tax which, at the current rate of 2½%, would add an estimated $250 million to their revenues in 1971-72. McMahon said, however, that federal grants to the states would be reduced by the amount raised by the payroll tax receipts. The premiers decided to increase the rate of

the payroll tax to 3½% after McMahon said an increase in the payroll levy would not be deducted from the grants.

[7] Foreign minister ousted. Prime Minister McMahon announced Aug. 1 the resignation of Foreign Minister Bury and the appointment of Attorney General Bowen to the post. The dismissal was attributed to a dispute over Australia's policy toward the People's Republic of China in the wake of President Richard Nixon's announcement July 15 that he would visit Peking. *(See* COMMUNIST CHINA-U.S. DETENTE [6].) Earlier Aug. 1, Bury had told a Liberal party seminar that he had "profound misgivings about the process involved" in the planned summit meeting between Nixon and Premier Chou En-lai. In a minor Cabinet change also announced Aug. 1, McMahon named Health Minister Greenwood as attorney general to replace Bowen, Minister of Supply Sir Kenneth Anderson as minister of health and Ransley V. Garland as minister of supply. The ouster of Bury and the cabinet shuffle were seen as attempts to bolster the government in anticipation of parliamentary elections due no later than November 1972. The issue of Australia's policy toward China was emerging as a paramount question.

[8] Prior to Nixon's announcement of his visit, McMahon had harshly criticized Labor leader Whitlam for his comments during a trip to Communist China which ended July 14 as advocating a policy that would "isolate" Australia "from friends and allies." Whitlam had said during his trip that a Labor government would establish diplomatic relations with Peking and withdraw recognition from the government of Nationalist China. (Members of the delegation that accompanied Whitlam on his trip said that Chinese officials had expressed a willingness to resume suspended wheat purchases from Australia only after diplomatic relations were established.) After Nixon's announcement of his planned trip, McMahon returned to his proposal, first announced May 13, to open a "dialogue" with Peking and to end Australia's opposition to Communist Chinese membership in the United Nations. He disclosed for the first time that Australia had sought contact with China through diplomatic channels in Paris.

[9] Gorton ousted as defense chief. McMahon Aug. 12 dismissed Defense Minister Gorton amid a political controversy over comments by Gorton concerning other cabinet members. Minister of Education and Science Fairbairn was sworn in Aug. 13 as the new defense minister while retaining his former post. (He was replaced as minister of education and science Aug. 19 by former Defense Minister Fraser.) Gorton resigned as deputy leader of the Liberal party Aug. 16 and was replaced by Snedden Aug. 18. The controversy which sparked Gorton's ouster began with the publication Aug. 8 of the first of a series of newspaper articles containing Gorton's reply to a book that criticized his personal conduct during his tenure as prime minister. In his reply, Gorton said some of his Cabinet ministers had been "afflicted with a compulsion to try out ideas on their wives" and implied they had leaked government information. McMahon said in a statement Aug. 12 that Gorton's action "breached basic principles of Cabinet solidarity and unity and reflected on the integrity of some ministers." (Gough Whitlam Aug. 17 offered a no-confidence motion in McMahon's government because of his "methods and motives in removing his ministers and his subservience to outside influence." The motion was defeated 62-56.)

[10] S. Africa rugby tour sparks protests. The arrival of an all-white South African rugby team, known as the Springboks, in Perth June 26 provoked demonstrations for and against the planned tour. Protests disrupted rugby matches in Melbourne, Sydney and elsewhere during the tour that lasted until Aug. 8. The protesters, many of whom were students, viewed the visit as tacit acceptance by the Australian government of South Africa's apartheid policy. The visit led Robert J. Hawke, leftist head of the Australian Council of Trade Unions, to call on union workers to refuse to furnish transport or restaurant and hotel services to the team members, according to report June 27. The team used private charter planes and cars. According to report July 14, the

Queensland state government declared a state of emergency to help police control demonstrations expected with the arrival of the Springboks in Brisbane the following week. About 125,000 workers staged a 24-hour general strike in Queensland July 21 to protest the state of emergency. State police July 29 approved the declaration of a state of emergency but voted a no-confidence motion in their commissioner because of his alleged moderate tactics toward anti-apartheid demonstrators. The Australian Cricket Board of Control Sept. 8 canceled a forthcoming tour of Australia by an all-white South African cricket team on the grounds that matches would provoke anti-apartheid demonstrations.

[11] **Budget presented.** Treasurer Snedden presented to Parliament Aug. 17 a budget for 1971-72 designed to curb inflationary pressures. The budget increased personal and corporate income taxes, introduced higher rates for telephone and postal services, increased excise duties on cigarettes and gasoline, and doubled the charge for prescriptions under the National Health Scheme. The budget also introduced a one-year guaranteed price program for wool guaranteeing 36¢ a pound for a wool clip. Pensions and child endowment were increased and assistance to rural industries was announced. An overall deficit of $11 million was estimated in the budget, with expenditures totaling $8.833 billion and revenue amounting to $8.822 billion. However, after discounting overseas transactions, the domestic surplus was budgeted for $630 million.

[12] **Censure motion defeated.** The House of Representatives Nov. 3 defeated, by a 56-51 vote, an opposition Labor party motion of no confidence in Defense Minister Fairbairn for his failure to inform Prime Minister McMahon of a U.S. request for training of Cambodian troops in South Vietnam until nearly a month after the request had been received. The request was made by the U.S. Sept. 30 but did not reach McMahon before his departure for talks with President Nixon Oct. 27. McMahon called the Cabinet into special session in his absence Nov. 1 to approve the American request. During the parliamentary debate, Fairbairn admitted the failure of internal government communication in the matter. The central question raised by the opposition was why the request had been made by the U.S., not by Cambodia. It revived charges that the government had again yielded to U.S. pressure, echoing the circumstances under which Australia had committed troops to South Vietnam, reportedly in response to U.S. pressure. (Disclosure of those circumstances in publication of secret U.S. Pentagon documents had caused McMahon June 17 to assign the Defense Committee, composed of top-level government and military leaders, to investigate and report on Australia's commitment of troops to the war.)

See also ATOMIC ENERGY [11]; GREAT BRITAIN [9]; INDOCHINA WAR [61, 72]; INTERNATIONAL BANK FOR RECONSTRUCTION & DEVELOPMENT; MALAYSIA; PENTAGON PAPERS [18]; SOUTH AFRICA [6]; SOUTH PACIFIC FORUM; SPACE [19]

AUSTRIA—Jonas re-elected president. President Franz Jonas, 71, was re-elected April 25 to a new six-year term. He won 2,488,372 votes—52.7%— against 2,225,368—47.21%—for Dr. Kurt Waldheim, the conservative People's party candidate. Dr. Waldheim was a former foreign minister and the present Austrian representative to the United Nations. Jonas's re-election was generally seen as an endorsement of policies of the minority Socialist government of Dr. Bruno Kreisky.

Army reform. Austria's compulsory military service was reduced from nine months to six by Parliament July 15 as part of a reform of the military. The reduction had been proposed Feb. 5 by Liberals and accepted by the ruling Socialist party as a basis for further negotiations. The reform program had reportedly been opposed by former Defense Minister Johann Freihsler, who had resigned Feb. 4 for "health reasons." Freihsler was replaced Feb. 8 by Brig. Gen. Karl Luetgendorf, who reportedly supported the reform program.

Socialists win majority. The Socialist party, which had headed a minority government for 18 months, won 50.04% of the vote in national elections Oct. 10. It was the first time any party had won more than 50% of the vote in democratic elections since World War II. According to final figures published Oct. 13, the Socialists would hold 93 of the 183 seats in the new, enlarged Parliament. The People's party would hold 80 seats, and the right-wing Freedom party 10 seats. The Austrian Communist party again failed to win parliamentary representation. (A new election law increased the number of seats in the lower parliamentary house from 165 to 183 and based the geographical distribution of seats on population figures rather than on the number of voters in each area.) Percentage results (1970 vote in parentheses): Socialists 50.04% (48.4%); People's party 43.12% (44.7%); Freedom party 5.45% (5.4%); Communists 1.35% (.4%). A new Communist splinter group polled .04%.

Chancellor Kreisky was thought to have called for early elections to benefit from the confusion of the People's party in the aftermath of their election of Karl Schleinzer, a former minister of agriculture, as party president to replace Waldheim and of the party's reorganization. (If not for the early elections, the National Assembly's term would have expired in 1974.) Kreisky had announced July 6 that he would call for a dissolution of Parliament to obtain a clear election mandate to carry out his government's program. Parliament had voted July 14 to dissolve.

The new all-Socialist government was sworn in Nov. 4. Ingrid Leodolter and Elfriede Karl were named, respectively, to the newly created posts of health and environmental protection minister and secretary of state in the Chancellery charged with family affairs. The changes meant a reduced role for Rudolf Haeuser, vice chancellor and social welfare minister, who had opposed Kreisky's position on collectivization of the means of production. The only other government change was the appointment of Fred Sinowatz, a provincial government official, to replace Leopold Gratz as national education minister.

1972 budget presented. A deficit budget for 1972 was presented to Parliament Nov. 12 by Finance Minister Hannes Androsch. Expenditures were estimated at $4.9 billion, creating a $392 million deficit. Androsch said the government would introduce tax reform measures to replace the turnover tax, a form of sales tax, with a value-added tax by January 1973. The value-added tax was a levy imposed on each stage in the production of goods.

See also ATOMIC ENERGY;[10]; DRUG USE & ADDICTION[9]; EUROPEAN ECONOMIC COMMUNITY [10]; INTERNATIONAL MONETARY DEVELOPMENTS [2, 4, 10]; ITALY [15]

AUTOMOBILES—Chrysler, UAW agree on pact. Chrysler Corp. and the United Automobile Workers (UAW) reached agreement Jan. 19 on a new three-year contract following the pattern of pacts signed with General Motors Corp. (GM) and Ford Motor Co. The pact, covering some 110,000 Chrysler workers, called for a 51¢-an-hour average pay hike in the first year and 14¢ an hour more in each of the next two contract years plus a cost-of-living increase figured annually the first two years and quarterly in the third year. The wage increases were retroactive to Nov. 2, 1970. Prepact wages averaged $4.02 an hour. The pension provision would permit retirement on a $500-a-month pension after 30 years of service at age 58. Chrysler and the union also agreed to establish a joint committee to study establishment of a pilot program for a four-day week for assembly-line workers. Ratification of the pact by the rank and file membership was announced by the union Feb. 3. Some 10,000 salaried workers represented by the UAW went on strike against Chrysler for about three hours Feb. 2 before agreement was reached, and the pickets withdrawn, to include in their contract provisions for a 13% pay hike retroactive to Nov. 2, 1970.

[2] **Chrysler names consumer unit.** Chrysler Corp. created an Office of Public Responsibility in response to the growing consumer and environment movement and then named an ombudsman to handle customer complaints about products and company policy. It was reported Feb. 20 that Virgil Boyd, vice president of the Chrysler board of directors, would head the new consumer unit and would be assisted by Byron J. Nichols, vice president-consumer affairs, and Philip Buckminster, vice president-environmental and safety relations. Nichols was placed in charge of the company's ombudsman program March 3.

[3] **Safety systems for 1974 cars.** The Department of Transportation March 5 set Aug. 15, 1973 as its deadline for installation of automatic crash protection systems in front seats of automobiles. Installation of full protection passive restraint systems for both front and rear seat passengers was delayed until Aug. 15, 1975. The department order also called for an interim standard, effective Jan. 1, 1972, that provided for combination lap and shoulder belts with automatic retractors and warning devices for unbuckling, unless car makers chose to meet the 1973 or 1975 regulations at that time. Cars built after the 1973 deadline would be equipped with passive restraints (devices preventing passengers from being tossed about in crashes without the aid of safety belts or other preventive action) that would protect front-seat occupants in head-on crashes at 30 miles an hour. Unless the passive system also provided protection in lateral collisions and rollovers, lap belts and buzzers and lights warning passengers to buckle up would also be required.

[4] *Safety expert criticizes designs.* Dr. William Haddon Jr., former director of the National Highway Safety Bureau, testified before a Senate Commerce subcommittee March 10 that car manufacturers deliberately designed autos prone to costly damages because of the profitable market in replacement parts sales. Haddon, currently president of the Insurance Institute for Highway Safety, supported his remarks with the results of low-speed crash tests of 1971 models conducted by the institute. According to Haddon, the institute found that average estimated repair costs in four out of five test crashes were about 50% higher for 1971 models than for 1970 cars as a result of 5 mile-per-hour test crashes; in head-on crashes average damage for 1971 models cost $332, compared with $216 for 1970 cars; in rear-end crashes 1971 models averaged $329 compared with $219 for 1970 models. Haddon said the increases were caused chiefly by "designed-in delicateness" of the cars, rather than higher prices for labor or parts. Haddon contended that the auto industry had not taken advantage of body design changes and use of energy-absorbing bumpers to cut down damage potential.

[5] *Car bumper standard.* The Transportation Department April 14 issued a modified safety standard for protective bumpers on passenger cars. The new standard required front bumpers on 1973 models to be able to withstand crashes against fixed barriers at 5 mph without damage to specific safety-related parts. However, it cut the required rear-bumper strength level to 2½ mph. Slightly stiffer requirements for 1974 models called for additional absorption at various angles of 5 mph crashes by front bumpers and 2.81 mph blows by rear bumpers.

[6] **Nixon insurance plan.** Secretary of Transportation John A. Volpe, speaking for the White House, asked Congress March 18 to adopt an automobile insurance plan that would include passage of a resolution urging each state to pass no-fault insurance legislation. The plan apparently overruled recommendations of a $2 million study prepared by the Transportation Department and released by Volpe the day of his testimony before the Senate Commerce Committee. Volpe said the Administration was committed to abolition of the current liability system of insurance in favor of state-legislated no-fault insurance plans. Under the latter concept, accident victims would receive prompt compensation for medical costs and loss of income without regard to driver negligence. Sens. Philip A. Hart (D, Mich.) and Warren G. Magnuson (D, Wash.), sponsors of federal no-fault insurance legislation,

countered that leaving legislation to the states could delay implementation of no-fault insurance up to five years. Volpe defended the plan as a means to avoid "federal dictation."

[7] Features of the Administration program included full coverage of all medical benefits with small deductibles but high mandatory limits, providing income-loss benefits up to $1,000 for a maximum of three years; severe curtailment of rights to sue for damages resulting from negligence; and release of insurance carriers from obligation to pay benefits equal to costs covered by car insurance.

[8] **Car styling inquiry sought.** Ralph Nader and 39 members of the Yale Law Journal petitioned the Federal Trade Commission (FTC) April 18 to investigate annual new-car styling changes as possible antitrust violations. The petitioners argued that annual restyling by GM, Ford and Chrysler constituted an "unfair" trade practice because the prohibitive costs involved prevented new competitors from entering the industry. The petition asked the FTC to require the Big 3 auto makers either to divest themselves of all but one of their total 45 assembly plants in the U.S. or place a "moratorium" on all style changes unrelated to safety, pollution or improved performance.

[9] **GM defeats social critics.** Proposals from the Episcopal Church in the U.S. and from the Project on Corporate Responsibility were roundly defeated at the annual meeting of General Motors Corp. in Detroit May 21. Leaders of the Project, which led the second annual Campaign GM, conceded they would have to revise their strategy to force social responsibility on the giant corporation through its stockholders.

[10] The vote on the Episcopal Church's proposal that GM close its operations in South Africa received only 1.29% (3 million shares) of the nearly 230 million shares voted. The proposal was defeated despite impassioned pleas by the Rev. Leon Howard Sullivan, elected to the GM board of directors Jan. 4, assorted U.S. churchmen and two blacks from South Africa. Sullivan, who had informed his fellow directors in April he would vote against them in favor of the proposal, became the first GM director to speak against management at an annual meeting. Sullivan said American industry, which was "to a great measure" underwriting the system of apartheid in South Africa, could not "morally continue to do business in a country that so blatantly and ruthlessly and clearly maintains such dehumanizing practices against such large numbers of people." On the issue of aiding minorities, Sullivan said he had been encouraged by his fellow board members and that GM was heading in the right direction. GM Chairman James M. Roche countered that GM was better able to achieve racial equality by remaining in South Africa. He also argued that shutting down its highly specialized plants would be costly and would cause social hardship for its 6,100 employees there, 53% of whom were black.

[11] The Project, which owned 12 shares, had forecast that its three proposals would poll at least 3% but they ranged between only 1.11% and 2.36% of the shares voted. The proposal for more detailed reports of GM efforts concerning pollution, auto safety and minority hiring received votes of 5.4 million shares (2.36%). Voting in favor of the proposal were the First Pennsylvania Banking & Trust Co. of Philadelphia, the nation's 20th and oldest bank with an estimated one million shares, and New York City's pension fund with 350,000 shares. Two Project proposals would have weakened management's control over the selection of GM's board of directors. The vote on the proposal to allow GM employees, consumers and dealers to name three directors was 2.5 million shares (1.11% of the 229.7 million shares voted); the proposal for a new method of electing directors by providing for a list of 30 candidates proposed by stockholders, in addition to the management slate, was 3.1 million shares (1.36% of the 229.6 million shares voted).

[12] The annual meeting provided a forum for a full-scale debate on the corporate role in society. In his speech to stockholders, Roche said GM would increase 1971 corporate spending to curb car pollution by $26 million to a record $150 million. Another $64 million would be allocated for cleaning up GM plants. GM said it had spent $119 million in 1970 on pollution control.

[13] **Supreme Court cases.** The Supreme Court declared unconstitutional May 24 a Georgia law, similar to those in 36 other states, by which an uninsured driver's license could be revoked after an accident, regardless of who was at fault. The court held that the motorist must be given a hearing before his license could be taken away, at which the state must demonstrate "a reasonable possibility" that a court would hold the driver liable for damages incurred in the accident. The state "financial responsibility" law at issue provided that a driver involved in an accident could lose his license unless he held liability insurance or unless he could post a bond to cover any injuries. The court's ruling, written by Justice William J. Brennan Jr., said the law violated the driver's due process right since it denied him a "fault" hearing. The other members of the court either joined in Brennan's decision or concurred in the result of the ruling. The ruling did not affect compulsory insurance laws in New York, North Carolina and Massachusetts. Ten other states had laws requiring "fault" hearings before a driver's license could be revoked. (The court June 1 voided another provision of the financial responsibility laws by voting 5-4 that a state couldn't suspend the license of a driver pending payment of a traffic accident judgment against him if the driver had erased the debt by going bankrupt.)

[14] In a ruling May 17 on automobile accidents, the court held 5-4 that state "hit and run" laws were constitutional. The ruling overturned a decision by the California Supreme Court that such laws violated the Constitutional privilege against self-incrimination by requiring a driver involved in an accident to stop and give his name and address. Chief Justice Warren E. Burger, who wrote the opinion, held that a motorist's privilege against self-incrimination was outweighed by "the public need" for information. The majority argued that identification at the scene of an accident was essentially a neutral act that did not constitute admission of fault. Justices Brennan, William O. Douglas, Thurgood Marshall and Hugo L. Black dissented from the ruling. All 50 states had similar "hit and run" laws.

See also GREAT BRITAIN [5, 12]; POLLUTION [16, 18]; STATE & LOCAL GOVERNMENTS [6]; TARIFFS & WORLD TRADE [9]; TAXES

AVIATION—SST project at an end. Congressional opponents of the U.S. program to develop a supersonic transport plane scored a victory over the White House, aerospace industry officials and labor leaders March 24 as the Senate voted 51-46 to cut off funds March 30 for the development of two SST prototypes by 1973. Coupled with a House vote March 18 against further federal funding for the controversial aircraft, the project seemed dead. The margin by which the Senate cut off further funding was wider than expected. A decisive element seemed to be the President's inability to convert Republicans who opposed the project: 17 voted against the SST. The House roll-call vote against the SST was 215-204. The defeat was unexpected because the House had backed continued funds for the airplane three times before. Key elements in the House defeat were the votes of freshmen representatives (33 of the 51 freshmen voted against the SST) and a revised voting procedure—the "teller vote"—which forced members to take a public, recorded position at the amendment stage of a bill before a final roll-call vote on the full bill. The end of the government's project was expected to idle as many as 13,000 aerospace workers around the U.S. There was some consideration of financing the project with private funds, but William S. Magruder, chief of the SST office, was reportedly turned down March 24-25 by James R. Mitchell, vice president for aerospace at the Chase Manhattan Bank in New York; officials of the Boeing Co., General Electric Co. and Fairchild-Hiller Corp., the three major SST contractors; and George P. Shultz, director of the Office of Management and Budget. The three companies, the Transportation and Treasury Departments and representatives of the banking community would conduct a study, according to Fairchild-Hiller April 9, to see if the project could be continued with private financing.

[2] Opposition to the SST came from environmentalists concerned with anti-pollution and noise control, while much of the Administration's support of the program was based on the long-range economic benefits resulting from jobs on the project. Anti-SST forces, led by Sen. William Proxmire (D, Wis.) in the Senate, argued against the economic feasibility of the project, however, by citing an alleged British Overseas Airways Corp. (BOAC) statement that the running costs of operating and maintaining the French-British SST (the Concorde) would result in some financial losses. BOAC declined to confirm or deny the report. During Senate debate, Proxmire introduced three scientists who supported a theory that fleets of SSTs could significantly increase the incidence of skin cancer by thinning the layers of ozone in the atmosphere that shielded the earth from the sun's ultraviolet radiations. The White House scored the allegation as "a shocking attempt to create fear about something that is simply not the fact." In defending the project, Treasury Secretary John B. Connally Jr. said March 10 that he saw as "reasonable" the estimate that full-scale production of an SST fleet would produce a gain of up to $22 billion in the U.S. foreign trade account through 1990.

[3] *SST revived, rejected.* Congressional backers of the SST scored a stunning victory May 12 when the House voted 201-197 to continue development of the controversial aircraft. However, the success was short-lived, as the Senate voted 58-37 May 19 to kill the House appropriation. The House had voted $85.3 million for continued development of the airliner after Rep. Edward Boland (D, Mass.) sponsored an amendment that reworded the language of a bill that would have appropriated money to terminate the program. Boland's amendment turned the bill around to put the money into continued development rather than termination costs. The Senate, however, deleted (on an amendment by Proxmire) funds for the airliner from a $6.9 billion supplemental money bill. In a subsequent vote, the Senate sealed the aircraft's fate by voting 92-3 to make $155 million in termination payments to the airlines which had invested in the SST and to the plane's contractors for work already done. Following a House-Senate conference, a bill allowing $97.3 million to terminate the project, $85.3 million to the prime contractors and $12 million to the government was passed by the Congress May 24 and signed by the President May 25.

[4] **More Concordes authorized.** Britain and France April 22 authorized construction of four more Concordes, in addition to the six already being built, and the ordering of materials for six further production models. The agreement was reached during talks in London between two British ministers, Secretary of State for Trade and Industry John Davies and Minister for Aviation Supply Frederick Corfield, and the French minister for transport, Jean Chamant. The ministers did not irrevocably commit their governments to long-term continuation of the Concorde. A final decision would be based on commercial considerations. Sixteen airlines had taken options on 74 Concordes, but none had yet placed a definite order because of the plane's projected high cost. Davies said the question of price was discussed but no decision was reached. Davies said Britain and France had already spent nearly $1 billion on the plane's research and development. (The British and French Concorde manufacturers—British Aircraft Corp. and the National Industrial Aerospace Co. of France [formerly Sud Aviation]—had announced March 3 that costs of the Concorde program had risen from under $400 million, as originally estimated in 1962, to $2 billion. They attributed the rise to inflation—higher industrial prices and wages—and design modifications.) Doubts lingered in both France and Great Britain over the commercial feasibility of the project.

[5] **Soviet SST makes Western debut.** The Soviet Union's supersonic airliner, the TU-144, made its Western debut May 25 when it arrived in Paris for the city's 29th air show. The plane flew from Prague with its designer, Andrei N. Tupolev, and Soviet Aviation Minister Pyotr V. Dementyev aboard. It had made the flight to Le Bourget Airport at subsonic speed. Many SST experts said the TU-144 bore a strong resemblance to the Concorde. Soviet officials said the plane would be ready for commercial operation by the end of 1973.

[6] **Mohawk Airlines strike ends.** A five-month pilots' strike against Mohawk Airlines ended April 1 after agreement to submit the contract dispute to binding arbitration. The agreement had been reached March 19 and the strike, which had begun Nov. 12, 1970, ended April 1 when the arbitrator, David L. Cole, presented a back-to-work plan. The line employed 396 pilots and 1,900 stewardesses, mechanics and other employees, who were furloughed during the strike. The carrier, which served the Northeast, announced it would reduce its prestrike schedule by as much as 20% for economy reasons. The recall to work included only 355 pilots and 1,500 other employees. The issues to be resolved included wages and fringe benefits and job protection arising from subcontracting of routes. (Cole awarded pay increases averaging 21% over a three-year period May 14.) The airline resumed service April 14.

[7] **6% air fare hike.** The Civil Aeronautics Board (CAB) April 12 authorized a 6% increase in domestic air fares as the first step of a tentatively approved 9% boost. The increase could provide $115 million-$400 million annually to the financially depressed industry in which six of the 11 major domestic carriers reported losses in 1970. The authorization marked a two-fold break with past procedures by (1) requiring carriers to fill a certain percentage of their seating capacity and (2) setting the new fares as ceilings, permitting a new flexibility that could lead to price competition. The board warned the airlines to continue excess cost and seating capacity reductions. The industry had requested a 12%-24% increase. Industry leaders expressed doubts that fare increases alone could restore profits.

[8] **Mexico-Cuba air pact renewed.** Mexico and Cuba reached agreement on a new air pact, according to a report Aug. 3. The old pact had expired July 30. Agreement was reached after months of negotiations between the countries' foreign ministers. The old pact had been renounced by Mexico in 1970 over an extradition dispute involving hijackers. The new agreement called for the continuation of the twice-weekly flights between Mexico City and Havana by Cubana Airlines. A Mexican Foreign Ministry press release said the new pact would "update the conditions under which air communication between the two countries will develop."

[9] **IATA agreement nullified.** A rate schedule for North Atlantic fares for April 1, 1972 to March 31, 1973, agreed on after a stormy 44-day meeting of the International Air Transport Association, was nullified by the West German airline Lufthansa, which announced Aug. 12 that it would exercise its veto over the agreement. The meeting had been called to renew the 25-year agreement under which almost all scheduled North Atlantic airlines charged identical fares. Unanimous agreement was required to put any agreement into effect. The plan vetoed by Lufthansa would have continued most fares at their current levels until the summer of 1972 and would have called for several new discount plans. The discount rate was initially pushed by BOAC, Trans-World Airlines (TWA), Pan American World Airways and Air Canada, arguing that lower rates were necessary to fill seats in their new Boeing 747 jets and to compete with the growing fleet of nonscheduled charter airlines. The agreed plan included a controversial "advance purchase excursion" under which passengers would have to buy their tickets 90 days before a flight and would lose 25% of their payment if they canceled.

[10] In announcing Aug. 12 that it would not withdraw its veto by the Sept. 1 ratification deadline, Lufthansa specifically rejected the advance purchase plan, denouncing the "large number of limiting conditions." Lufthansa officially announced Sept. 15 that it would introduce Feb. 1, 1972 the lowest trans-Atlantic rates ever offered on scheduled jet flights. (The IATA agreement had an escape clause which allowed members to set any rates after Feb. 1.) The airline declared that its decision was irrevocable until Nov. 1, 1972. As a result of the decision to veto the agreement, each airline would be able to propose its own fare rates to its government, which would then take over tariff control from IATA.

[11] The IATA opened a special conference in Lausanne, Switzerland Oct. 26 to attempt to prevent the "open fare" competitive situation which would result from Lufthansa's actions, but the conference collapsed after four days when officials of the 25 members failed to agree on fares and the period of applicability of a proposed individual excursion fare which would have replaced the advance purchase plan. It was reported Sept. 29 that TWA and Pan American had appealed to the Nixon Administration to intervene with the West German government to roll back the fares proposed by Lufthansa. The State Department and the CAB had indicated Sept. 28 that they could not comply with the request.

[12] *Fare compromise.* Chief executives of the airlines belonging to IATA agreed Nov. 19 in Honolulu on a compromise package of reduced transatlantic fares for 1972. The pact was ratified at an IATA conference in Geneva, according to report Dec. 14. Lufthansa reportedly acceded to the package after the U.S. dollar, the chief currency in pricing flights, declined sharply in relation to other currencies. The package avoided the advance purchase excursion requirement. It reduced the present $271 New York-London winter 22-45 day round-trip excursion fare by $67. Summer rates would be $294. Youth fares would be the same as the 22-45 day excursion fare. A separate package would cover 14-21 day excursion fares. Normal economy class rates for a round trip between New York and London would be $404, $454, and $556, depending on the season. All round-trip fares would be raised $4 and one-way trips $2 to compensate for navigational charges imposed by governments. The package would also offer special round-trip fares for groups, with membership requirements still to be announced. New York-London prices would be $180, $200 and $270, depending on the season. One industry source was reported Dec. 14 as estimating that the scheduled lines would have to boost passenger volume 20%-30% on North Atlantic runs to offset revenue loss on lower fares.

[13] **Air disasters.** A Japanese Air Force plane flown by a student pilot collided with a commercial airliner July 30 over Honshu Island, killing 162 persons in the worst air disaster on record. The airliner, a Boeing 727 of All Nippon Airways with 155 passengers and a crew of seven, was on a domestic flight from Sapporo to Tokyo in an established commercial airlane when it struck an F-86 Sabrejet piloted by Sgt. Yoshimi Ichikawa about 275 miles north of Tokyo. Ichikawa parachuted to safety. Ichikawa, Capt. Tamotsu Kuma (his instructor) and Lt. Col. Masuo Tanaka of the air base at Matsushima, who had planned the flight, were arrested July 31 and charged with "professional negligence." All military training flights were temporarily suspended. Keikichi Masuhara, who had succeeded Yasuhiro Nakasone in July as director of the Defense Agency, resigned Aug. 1 as an acknowledgement of his organization's responsibility for the crash. He was succeeded by Naomi Nishimura.

[14] In other crashes: A Soviet Aeroflot Ilyushin-18 airliner crashed during takeoff from Leningrad's Smolny Airport Dec. 31, 1970. The 90 persons aboard were all reported killed. An Apache Airlines plane with 12 persons aboard crashed near Coolidge, Ariz. May 6. There were no survivors. It was the first crash of a scheduled airliner in the continental U.S. since November 1969. A Yugoslav airliner carrying 83 persons—72 of them British tourists on an

Adriatic holiday—crashed and burned May 23 at KRK, an island off Rijeka, Yugoslavia. Seventy-eight persons were reported dead. A Hughes Air West DC-9 airliner with 49 persons aboard collided with a Marine Phantom F-4 fighter jet June 6 over the San Gabriel Mountains in California. The pilot of the Phantom and all of the airline passengers died but another Marine crewman parachuted safely. A Japanese airliner attempting a landing in fog crashed on a mountainside near Hakodate, Japan July 3. All 68 persons aboard died. A Soviet Aeroflot airliner, with 97 aboard, crashed and exploded on takeoff from Siberia's Irkutsk Airport, officials reported Aug. 11. There were no survivors. Thirty-seven U.S. soldiers were killed Aug. 18 when their helicopter exploded and crashed in flames in a hayfield near Pegnitz, West Germany. It was the worst training accident involving U.S. troops in West Germany since the end of World War II. An Alaska Airlines 727 jet, flying through dense fog and rain Sept. 4, crashed into a mountain in the Tongass National Forest, about 20 miles west of Juneau. All 111 passengers were killed. It was the worst air accident involving a single plane in U.S. history. One of four turboprops on a British European Airways Vanguard airliner exploded Oct. 2, causing the plane to crash near Ghent, Belgium. All 63 passengers died. A Peruvian airliner, carrying 92 persons from Lima to Iquitos was presumed to have crashed in the jungle Dec. 24. Radio contact was lost shortly after takeoff.

See also AGNEW, SPIRO THEODORE; BUDGET; BUSINESS [3-5]; CHILE [8]; CHINA, COMMUNIST CONGRESS [1]; DEFENSE [1-2, 6, 9]; GREAT BRITAIN [5, 12]; HIJACKING; LABOR [1]; STATE & LOCAL GOVERNMENTS [6]

AWARDS—*See* MOTION PICTURES; NOBEL PRIZES; PULITZER PRIZES; RECORD INDUSTRY; SCIENCE; TELEVISION & RADIO; THEATER

BACON, LESLIE—*See* DRAFT & WAR PROTEST [5-6]
BAHAMAS—*See* HIJACKING [2]

BAHRAIN—The Persian Gulf sheikdom of Bahrain formally declared its independence from Great Britain Aug. 14. A new pact of friendship between the two countries was signed Aug. 15 by Sheik Issa Ben Salman al-Khalifa, Bahrain's ruler, and Sir Geoffrey Arthur, British representative. In decrees issued Aug. 16, the country was renamed the State of Bahrain and Khalifa's title was changed to emir.

    See also UNITED NATIONS [1]

BALANCE OF PAYMENTS—*See* ECONOMY,U.S. [8, 29]
BANGLA DESH—*See* PAKISTAN [1, 3, 5, 11-13, 18-19, 21-23, 30, 34, 36, 41]
BANK FOR INTERNATIONAL SETTLEMENTS (BIS)—*See* INTERNATIONAL MONETARY DEVELOPMENTS [6]

BANKS—Rules for one-bank holding companies. The Federal Reserve Board (FRB), in accordance with federal legislation passed in 1970, published Jan. 25 proposed regulations to restrict the acquisitions of one-bank holding companies to concerns engaged solely in 10 types of banking-related activities: (1) loan making operations, such as a mortgage, finance or factoring company; (2) operating as an industrial bank; (3) acting as fiduciary; (4) servicing loans; (5) acting as insurance agent or broker, chiefly in connection with credit extensions by the holding company or any of its subsidiaries; (6) acting as insurer for the holding company and its subsidiaries; (7) acting as investment or financial adviser; (8) leasing personal property where the initial lease provided for rental payments that would reimburse the lessor for the full purchase price of the property; (9) providing bookkeeping or data processing services for the holding company and subsidiaries or other financial institution under certain conditions; and (10) making equity investments in community rehabilitation and development corporations providing housing and employment for low and moderate income persons.

    Bank mutual funds barred. The Supreme Court ruled April 5 that operation by commercial banks of collective investment funds (mutual funds) would be illegal under the Glass-Steagall Banking Act of 1933 which separated commercial banking from investment banking. The decision upset the banking industry's efforts to win federal approval that would enable banks to capture a sizable share (estimated at about $2 billion) of the mutual fund industry's business. The 6-2 decision reversed a circuit court ruling in Washington validating the permission given by the Comptroller of the Currency in 1965 for a model investment plan set up by First National City Bank of New York City. The circuit ruling of the case, Investment Company Institute vs. William B. Camp (comptroller), had been written by Chief Justice Warren Burger, who did not participate in the Supreme Court decision.

The court's majority opinion, written by Justice Potter Stewart, said the Glass-Steagall Act specifically applied to the type of commingled managing agency account created by the banks to compete with mutual funds. It also stressed that the same potential dangers that precipitated the law in 1933 still existed; among those dangers, banks might (1) distort credit decisions or make unsound loans to companies in which the fund had invested; (2) exploit a confidential relationship with commercial and industrial creditors for the benefit of the fund; (3) make credit facilities available, directly or indirectly, to the fund; (4) make loans to facilitate the purchase of interests in the fund; and (5) risk losing public confidence in the bank itself because of imprudent or unsuccessful management of the fund, which in turn could pressure banks to rescue the fund through measures inconsistent with sound banking. The majority opinion said the comptroller's 1962 regulation allowing banks to pool managing agency accounts violated provisions of the banking law which stipulated that a bank's handling of securities and stock should be limited to buying and selling solely for the benefit of its clients without any gain for itself.

Interlocking directorates. A bill sponsored by Rep. Wright Patman (D, Tex.) to eliminate interlocking directorates and curb conflicts of interest in financial institutions (HR 5700) met opposition at hearings of the House Banking and Currency Committee April 26 and May 4. Arthur F. Burns, chairman of the FRB, and Richard W. McLaren, head of the Justice Department's antitrust unit, suggested that the bill was too strong. Both recommended that interlocks should be prohibited only among banks that were local competitors or among those with assets of $1 billion or more that were competing on a nationwide basis. Whereas the Patman bill would extend the ban against interlocks to insurance companies and brokerage firms, Burns would limit the ban to commercial banks, savings banks and savings and loan associations.

Chase takes over Parsons bank. Chase Manhattan Bank, the nation's third largest bank, took over effective operating control of the $1 billion-deposit Bank of the Commonwealth in Detroit Jan. 14. The Detroit bank had served as the flagship of a chain of 19 banks once controlled by investor Donald H. Parsons and his associates, known as the Parsons Group. In recent months, the group had been trying to dismantle its banking empire, worth $3 billion in 1969, in order to satisfy creditors. Chase, which had helped Parsons gain control of the Bank of the Commonwealth in 1964, took over on the basis of its 39% stock interest in the bank. Parsons had pledged the securities as collateral on two loans from Chase totaling $20 million. It was announced that John A. Hooper, one of Chase's senior lending officers, would become chairman and chief executive officer of the Detroit bank.

European bank groups. The Banco di Roma Jan. 11 joined the working partnership created in October 1970 by France's Credit Lyonnais and West Germany's Commerzbank. The enlarged group thus became the world's third largest banking group and the world's largest outside the U.S. Banco di Roma, with a capital of about $64 million, held deposits of $22.4 million. Louis Camu, president of the Banque de Bruxelles, announced creation of a new European banking group Feb. 24, bringing together two banks from West Germany, one from the Netherlands and one from Belgium. The four banks—the Banque de Bruxelles, the Dresdner Bank, the Bayerische Hypotheken und Wechselbank and the Algemen Bank Nederland—had assets totaling $17 billion at the end of 1969. The four banks were to be associated with an "outer" circle of banks with assets totaling $34 million—Barclays Bank, Banque Nationale de Paris and Banca Nazionale del Lavoro. It was reported Dec. 6 that a multinational European-Brazilian Bank, with issued capital of $10 million, would open in

London within 90 days, financing medium and long term industrial and commercial activities throughout the world, but principally in Latin America. Shares of the capital would be held by Banco do Brazil (35%), Bank of America Ltd. (17.5%), Ameribas (Luxembourg) (17.5%), and the Deutsche Bank (15%).

See also BUSINESS [1, 5]; COMMUNISM, INTERNATIONAL; ECONOMY, U.S. [2]; INTERNATIONAL MONETARY DEVELOPMENTS; KENYA

BARBADOS—Prime Minister Errol W. Barrow's Barbados Democratic Labor party retained power after the island's general elections Sept. 9. Barrow's party increased its majority from 15 to 18 seats in the 24-seat House of Assembly. Barrow also won a third five-year term. The opposition Barbados Labor party won six seats, one less than it had previously held.

See also CARIBBEAN; MIDDLE EAST [39]

BARBITURATES—*See* DRUG USE & ADDICTION [15]

BASEBALL—**Pirates win World Series.** The Pittsburgh Pirates overcame long odds and a two-game deficit to defeat the Baltimore Orioles, 2-1, Oct. 17 in the seventh and deciding game of baseball's 68th World Series in Baltimore. Down 2-0 in the best-of-seven series, Pittsburgh won three straight games in its home park, Three Rivers Stadium. The Orioles, defending world champions, evened the series at 3-all but failed to muster an offensive threat in the final game against Pirate hurler Steve Blass. Pittsburgh was managed by Danny Murtaugh. Earl Weaver piloted Baltimore. Roberto Clemente, the Pirate's 37-year-old hitting star, was named the series' outstanding player.

[2]   The game-by-game scores: Oct. 9 at Baltimore's Memorial Stadium—Baltimore 5, Pittsburgh 3; Oct. 11 in Baltimore—Baltimore 11, Pittsburgh 3; Oct. 12 at Pittsburgh—Pittsburgh 5, Baltimore 1; Oct. 13 at Pittsburgh—Pittsburgh 4, Baltimore 3; Oct. 14 in Pittsburgh—Pittsburgh 4, Baltimore 0; Oct. 16 in Baltimore—Baltimore 3, Pittsburgh 2; Oct. 17 in Baltimore—Pittsburgh 2, Baltimore 1. Pittsburgh, Eastern Division champion of the National League (NL), had dropped the opening game of pennant playoffs to the San Francisco Giants, 5-4, Oct. 2, but came back Oct. 3-6 to win three straight, 9-4, 2-1, 9-5. Baltimore, winner of the American League's (AL) Eastern race, disposed of the Oakland Athletics in three straight games, 5-3, 5-1, 5-3, Oct. 3-5 in the AL's pennant race.

[3]   Stories carried by the Associated Press Oct. 17 telling of rapes, assaults and serious crimes in downtown Pittsburgh in the wake of the Pirate's triumph were denied Oct. 18 by Pittsburgh Police Superintendent Robert E. Colville. The police said that 98 persons were arrested, 90 of whom were charged with intoxication. According to police, there were no rapes, no violent crimes against persons and no serious injuries. The AP's Pittsburgh bureau stood by its first dispatches about the rapes and assaults.

[4]   **AL snaps NL All-Star streak.** The AL's All-Stars rallied from three runs down to defeat the NL's All-Stars, 6-4, and break an eight-game losing streak in baseball's 42nd All-Star game in Detroit July 13. The AL's victory was its first since 1962 and it was only the second time the league had won in the last 14 All-Star games. The AL's triumph brought the overall record in the contests to 23 NL wins, 18 AL wins and one tie. Earl Weaver, manager of the Orioles, guided the AL club. The NL team was led by Sparky Anderson of the Cincinnati Reds.

[5]   **New York to buy Yankee Stadium.** New York City Mayor John V. Lindsay announced March 3 that the city planned to buy Yankee Stadium for $24 million, renovate it, and lease it to the New York Yankee baseball club. Lindsay said the city would take the 48-year-old ball park through condemnation proceedings if an agreement could not be reached. Yankee Stadium was owned by Rice University (Houston). The land on which it stood was owned by the Knights of Columbus. Lindsay said the city was buying Yankee Stadium to keep the Yankee baseball team and Giants football team in

New York. The plans called for the city to lease the stadium to the Yankees, who would sublet it to the Giants in the football season.

[6] Phillies dedicate new park. Philadelphia public officials, professional athletes and 35,000 fans turned out April 4 to dedicate the city's new $45-million Veterans Stadium. Mayor James H. J. Tate presided over ceremonies that included workouts by the baseball Phillies and football Eagles on the synthetic Astroturf field. With a capacity of 56,371 persons, the stadium was the largest NL baseball park.

[7] Flood loses appeal. Curt Flood, the star outfielder who was challenging professional baseball's reserve clause, lost the second inning April 7 when a federal appeals court in New York upheld a lower court ruling denying his multi-million dollar lawsuit. The Supreme Court Oct. 19 agreed to decide whether baseball's reserve clause, which bound a player to one team, violated the nation's antitrust laws. (Flood quit baseball April 27 because of "very serious personal problems.")

[8] Indians fined on contracts. Baseball Commissioner Bowie Kuhn fined the Cleveland Indian baseball club $5,000 June 15 after he learned of illegal bonus provisions between the club and four of its players. Kuhn said his investigation had shown that the Cleveland front office had worked out "performance bonus understandings" with Sam McDowell, Vada Pinson, Ken Harrelson and Craig Nettles.

[9] Senators move to Texas. Robert Short, owner of the Washington Senators, was granted permission by the other AL club owners Sept. 21 to move his team to Arlington, Tex., midway between Dallas and Fort Worth, for the 1972 season. AL President Joe Cronin announced in Boston that the club owners had voted 10-2 to allow the shift. The transfer was made conditional with terms relating to the seating capacity and a lease for Turnpike Stadium in Arlington. The transfer would mean that major league baseball would be without a representative in the nation's capital for the first time in 71 years. Short, who had made a fortune in trucking, conceded that he had "failed in Washington to field a team successfully." He said his team had lost $3 million over the last three seasons.

[10] Fans forced an end to the final game played by the Senators in the nation's capital Sept. 30. With the Senators leading the New York Yankees, 7-5, fans spilled out onto the playing field at Robert F. Kennedy Stadium, forcing the umpires to award the game to New York, 9-0, on a forfeit.

BASKETBALL—College: *UCLA wins NCAA title.* The University of California Los Angeles (UCLA) used clutch outside shooting in the first half and a slowdown in the second half to stop Villanova March 27, 68-62, in the finals of the National Collegiate Athletic Association (NCAA) tournament in the Houston Astrodome. For the Bruins, coached by John Wooden, it was an unprecedented fifth consecutive NCAA crown and the seventh in the last eight years. Villanova, coached by Jack Kraft, announced June 17 that it was forfeiting its second-place finish in the tournament after it was learned that Villanova star Howard Porter, All-American and outstanding performer of the tournament, had signed a professional contract in December 1970 with the American Basketball Association (ABA). (The contract, signed Dec. 15, was later assigned to the Pittsburgh Condors, who drafted Porter. Porter, who denied signing a contract with Pittsburgh, had signed April 24 with the Chicago Bulls of the National Basketball Association. His signing with Chicago prompted Pittsburgh to file a suit June 10 for an injunction to block him from playing for the NBA team.)

North Carolina wins NIT. North Carolina overpowered Georgia Tech, 84-66, to capture the 34th National Invitational Tournament (NIT) in New York's Madison Square Garden March 27. North Carolina was paced in the finals by Bill Chamberlain, who scored 34 points and was voted the tournament's outstanding player, Carolina was coached by Dean Smith and Georgia Tech by Whack Hyder.

East tops west. A team of college All-Stars representing the East topped a West All-Star college team, 106-104, in overtime April 3 in Dayton, Ohio in the Coaches' All-Star game. Jim Daniels, who played for Western Kentucky and had signed with the Carolina Cougars of the ABA, scored 29 points and took down ten rebounds. He was named the game's outstanding performer.

Professional: *All-Star games.* Lenny Wilkens, player-coach of the Seattle Supersonics, scored 21 points Jan. 12 to pace the West to a 108-107 triumph over the East in the NBA's 21st All-Star game in San Diego. He was named the game's outstanding player. Behind as much as 18 points in the third quarter, the East rallied to defeat the West, 126-122, in the ABA's fourth All-Star game in Greensboro, N.C. Jan. 23. The West was paced by Mel Daniels of the Indiana Pacers, most valuable player and high scorer of the game with 29 points. A team of NBA All-Stars defeated an All-Star squad of ABA players 125-120 in Houston May 28, in the first game between the two leagues. Milwaukee's Oscar Robertson and Walt Frazier of New York paced the NBA stars. (Lew Alcindor, named the NBA's most valuable player March 20, did not play.) Frazier, who scored 26 points, was named the game's outstanding performer.

Bucks win NBA crown. The Milwaukee Bucks, paced by Robertson and Alcindor, won the NBA title April 30 by completing a four-game sweep of the Baltimore Bullets. The Bucks, coached by Larry Costello, won the fourth and deciding game 118-106 in Baltimore. Baltimore was coached by Gene Shue. Alcindor, who averaged 27 points in the final playoff round, was named the outstanding player of the playoffs.

Utah wins ABA championship. The Utah Stars relied on a scoring spree by Zelmo Beaty and Willie Wise early in the fourth quarter of the seventh and deciding game May 18 to defeat the Kentucky Colonels, 131-121, and win the ABA championship in Salt Lake City. Utah was coached by Bill Sharman and Kentucky by Frank Ramsey.

Haywood case settled. The NBA announced March 26 that an out-of-court settlement had been reached in the Spencer Haywood case, clearing the way for Haywood to play for the Seattle Supersonics. Haywood was signed by Seattle in defiance of NBA bylaws after he left the Denver Rockets of the ABA. (Supreme Court Justice Douglas March 1 had ordered the NBA to reinstate Haywood in the interest of the league's playoffs, which began March 23.) NBA bylaws required that a player could not be hired until four years after he graduated from high school. (Walter Kennedy, NBA commissioner, announced June 24 that the league was revising the rule to allow a player who had not graduated from college to request permission to join an NBA team on the basis of hardship.) Under the terms of the settlement, the Supersonics would pay the NBA a $200,000 fine for violating regulations but would retain the rights to Haywood. The agreement held that all litigation involving Haywood, Seattle and the NBA would be dismissed "with prejudice," which meant the case could not be reopened. In another case, the Rockets March 30 settled their breach of contract suit against Haywood for his jump. A federal jury hearing the case in Los Angeles was dismissed.

NBA and ABA seek merger. The NBA and ABA agreed May 7 to seek Congressional approval for a merger of the two leagues. Merger talks, begun over a year before but broken off by the NBA after the ABA refused to drop an impending antitrust suit against the older league, were reopened by the NBA. Under the terms of the projected merger, the ABA would drop its suit and the two leagues would work out difficulties caused by those players who had signed with both leagues. It was also agreed that, if and when a merger took place, all 28 clubs—17 in the NBA and 11 in the ABA—would be included in the merger. Senate hearings on the merger began Sept. 21.

Rockets move to Houston. The NBA opened its 26th year of play with its first franchise in Texas—the Houston Rockets. The Rockets, based in San Diego, were sold to a group of Houston businessmen June 23. The Rockets were to play most of their home games on the University of Houston campus and round out their schedule with games in Houston's Astrodome, in Lubbock, San Antonio and El Paso.

See also SPORTS

BASQUES—*See* SPAIN [1, 4]
BAYH, BIRCH—*See* POLITICS [8-9]; SUPREME COURT

BELGIUM—Tax protest. Merchants staged a nationwide general strike Feb. 18 to protest the imposition of the European Economic Community's value-added tax Jan. 1. Shops, restaurants, banks, cinemas and other businesses were closed. Demonstrators totaling 60,000-150,000 held a protest march in Brussels. The strike was held despite the government's repeal Feb. 15 of an unpopular temporary measure that would have required shopkeepers to make provisional value-added tax payments before their full liability had been assessed. (About 40,000 shopkeepers in the province of Liege had staged a half-day strike Feb. 4 to protest the tax.)

Labor developments. Teachers staged a wildcat strike March 22-24 for higher pay, better working conditions and a voice in the reform of the educational system. About 75% of the schools in Brussels and about half the schools elsewhere were shut down. The teachers' unions, which had just reached agreement with the government on a new wage plan for civil servants, had opposed the strike. About 70,000 teachers struck again March 29. Municipal police staged wildcat strikes throughout Belgium March 22 and March 29.

Employers and trade unions agreed April 6 on a new collective agreement for 1971-72. The accord provided time for trade union activities during working hours in 1971 and a reduced work week of 42 hours in 1972. It increased pensions by 5% and added two days to the three-week vacation. The accord envisaged a 40-hour work week and four-week vacations by 1976. The trade unions failed to win their demand that employers pay all of the costs of the unemployment insurance program, but their request was to be reviewed as part of proposals for reform of the financing of social security.

Parliamentary crisis. A bitter conflict that threatened the existence of the coalition Cabinet of Social Christians and Socialists was resolved April 23 with agreement on a compromise economic program that would stiffen price controls but would provide recourse to the courts in controversial cases. The Socialists, demanding strict price controls, had clashed with the conservative wing of the Social Christians. (The government announced a 5% cut in administrative expenses as part of its anti-inflation program, according to an April 15 report.)

Language reform approved. The Chamber of Deputies July 16 approved (155-21, with 25 abstentions) with more than the necessary 2/3 majority two bills granting autonomy in cultural affairs to Belgium's three principal language groups and fixing the bilingual and administrative status of Brussels. The bills were part of a constitutional reform intended to solve the long-standing dispute between Belgium's French- and Flemish-speaking groups. The constitutional reform, which recognized three national communities—the northern Dutch-speaking Flemings, the French-speaking Walloon minority in the south, and the predominantly French-speaking population of bilingual Brussels—went into effect with ratification of the bills in the Senate July 19.

The reform decentralized the decision-making processes, with special powers delegated to local administrative bodies for the French and Flemish groups. In Brussels, the reform imposed a status quo on the city limits and regulated the bilingual rights of the two language groups. As a compromise to the French, the law authorized the father of a family in Brussels to choose the language of his children's education, repealing a law that restricted a child's education to the language of his native origin. The reform also made a disputed region near the German frontier into a bilingual area under the direct jurisdiction of the Interior Ministry.

Coalition retains majority. The coalition government partners retained their majority in the 212-seat Chamber of Deputies in general elections Nov. 7 despite sharp gains by Belgium's Dutch-speaking Flemish and French-speaking parties. Premier Gaston Eyskens, a Christian Social, handed in his Cabinet's resignation to King Baudouin Nov. 8 according to routine practice. He was to head a caretaker government until a new Cabinet was formed. However, Eyskens abandoned his effort to form a new coalition Dec. 22. His attempts had bogged down over differences between Socialists and Christian Socials and between the Flemish- and French-speaking factions of the Christian Social party. Edmond Leburton, co-president of the Socialist party, Dec. 23 accepted a request by the King to explore resolution of the crisis.

The sharpest gains in the elections were registered by the extremist anti-Flemish alliance of the Democratic Front of the French-speaking Bruxellois (FDF) and the Walloon Union which increased their vote percentage from 5.9% in the 1968 elections to 11.4%. The Flemish nationalists (Volksunie party) increased their percentage from 9.79% to 11%. The extremists' gains were made largely at the expense of the Party of Liberty and Progress (Liberals), whose vote percentage fell from 20.87% to 16.7% and whose actual parliamentary representation declined from 47 seats to 34. The election results (previous number of seats in parentheses): Social Christians—66 (68); Socialists—61 (59); Liberal—34 (47); Communist—5 (5); Volksunie—22 (20); FDF-RW—24 (13).

See also ATOMIC ENERGY [13]; DRUG USE & ADDICTION [9]; ESPIONAGE; EUROPEAN ECONOMIC COMMUNITY [1]; INTERNATIONAL BANK FOR RECONSTRUCTION & DEVELOPMENT; INTERNATIONAL MONETARY DEVELOPMENTS [2, 4, 8-10, 15]; JAPAN [10]; PAKISTAN [35, 39]; UNION OF SOVIET SOCIALIST REPUBLICS [13]

BERLIN—*See* EUROPEAN SECURITY; FOREIGN POLICY; GERMAN CONSULTATIONS; GERMANY, EAST; GERMANY, WEST [4]; NIXON, RICHARD MILHOUS [3]; NOBEL PRIZES
BERRIGAN, PHILIP—*See* SECURITY, U.S.
BHUTAN—*See* PAKISTAN [41]; UNITED NATIONS [1]
BHUTTO, ZULFIKAR ALI—*See* PAKISTAN [2, 4, 25, 29, 31, 42]
BIAFRA—*See* SUDAN
BIG FOUR—*See* GERMAN CONSULTATIONS; GERMANY, EAST; MIDDLE EAST [31, 33]
BIOLOGICAL WARFARE—*See* CHEMICAL & BIOLOGICAL WARFARE; DISARMAMENT

BIOLOGY—**Human growth hormone synthesized.** The University of California Medical Center in San Francisco announced Jan. 6 that two of its biochemists had succeeded in synthesizing the hormone responsible for growth in the human body. The synthesis was described as one of the most complex achievements in protein chemistry history. The synthesis was made by Dr. Choh Hao Li, 57, professor of biochemistry and director of the medical center's Hormone Research Laboratory. Li, a pioneer in hormone research, first isolated and purified the growth hormone in 1956. He was assisted by Donald H. Yamashiro, a research biochemist.

Li said the synthesized hormone amounted to only a few milligrams in his lab, but said he believed large-scale production could be accomplished by the large drug industries. The hormone served a variety of functions in the body. In early life, the hormone was chiefly responsible for the body's growth. The hormone was produced by the body in large quantities all through life, even though most growth ceased around adolescence. As a person aged, the hormone continued to promote development and enlargement of all bodily tissues and increase the size and number of the body's cells. Li noted that among the first applications of the hormone would be the treatment of nearly 7,000 children born in the U.S. each year afflicted with dwarfism as a result of deficient amounts of the growth hormone.

See also NOBEL PRIZES

BIRTH CONTROL—Canadian developments. The Canadian government Jan. 9 ordered all manufacturers of birth control pills to include in each packet a warning that the product is "potent and effective" medication that might cause health complications. The order was effective Feb. 1. In another development, Health Minister John Munro announced in the House of Commons May 6 a $100,000 grant to the Family Planning Federation of Canada for a program that would make birth control information available to low income groups.

Italy. The Italian Constitutional Court published a landmark decision March 17 that declared unconstitutional a 1926 law prohibiting dissemination of information on birth control. (The manufacture, sale or use of contraceptive devices was never banned in Italy.)

Ireland. The Irish Senate March 31 refused a first reading to a private bill introduced by Sen. Mary Bourke Robinson to end the 1935 ban on the import, sale and advertising of contraceptives. Majority Leader Thomas Mullin advised the Senate to await the government's decision on the issue. The government was known to favor an end to the ban but had to contend with strong opposition from the Roman Catholic hierarchy.

'Morning-after' pill tested. Dr. Lucille K. Kuchera, a senior physician at the University of Michigan Health Service, made public Oct. 25 findings that a "morning-after" birth control pill had safely prevented pregnancy of all 1,000 women of child-bearing age involved in a university study. Calculations indicated that at least 20-40 of the women would have become pregnant if they had not used the drug. The pill, a synthetic estrogenic substance called diethylstilbestrol (DES), was given twice a day for five days, beginning within 72 hours of intercourse. DES, a hormone substitute used to relieve several female ailments, had been linked to a number of cases in which young women whose mothers had taken it during pregnancy had been afflicted with vaginal cancer.

See also POPULATION

BIRTH RATE—*See* POPULATION
BLACK EXPO—*See* NEGROES
BLACK, HUGO L.—*See* OBITUARIES; SUPREME COURT

BLACK MILITANTS—Brown shot in New York. H. Rap Brown, the fugitive black militant leader who disappeared 17 months before, was shot and captured by police in New York City Oct. 16. He was arraigned on charges of robbery and attempted murder Oct. 20. Brown, 28, was shot twice in the stomach as he and three other men tried to make their getaway after they robbed a bar. Two policemen were wounded in the exchange of gunfire. One officer was hospitalized and the other treated for a hand wound. Brown, whose condition was listed by hospital authorities as fair Oct. 18, had been on the Federal Bureau of Investigation's (FBI) most wanted list of fugitives since May 6, 1970, shortly after he disappeared from his trial on arson and riot charges in Ellicott City, Md. Those charges stemmed from a speech he gave in Cambridge, Md. in July 1967 which state officials maintained touched off a wave of rioting there.

[2]   According to police, Brown was one of four or five men who robbed 25 customers of a Manhattan bar at gunpoint. When the suspects came out of the bar, police said, they saw a policeman and opened fire. A run-and-shoot gunbattle ensued during which 50 policemen joined the chase. Brown's three companions were arrested in a building a few blocks from the West Side bar they allegedly held up. Brown was shot and captured on the roof of the same building. New York Police Commissioner Patrick V. Murphy said the other three suspects had been tentatively identified as Sam Petty, 23; Arthur Young, 25; and Levi Valentine, 24. Police said they recovered two loaded carbines, three pistols and 300 rounds of ammunition carried by the robbers.

[3] **Angela Davis trial.** Angela Davis, a former UCLA professor and an avowed Communist, was arraigned Jan. 5 on charges of murder, kidnaping and criminal conspiracy in connection with the Aug. 1970 courtroom shootout in which four people, including presiding Judge Harold Haley, were slain. However, by the end of the year, her trial had still not begun. Although Miss Davis allegedly had only supplied guns used in the shootout and was not present at the gunbattle, under California law her alleged complicity made her equally guilty with the participants. Pretrial hearings into the case began March 16, but the courtroom had to be cleared twice that day because of bomb threats. Ruchel Magee (charged with firing the shots that killed Haley), who was being accused with Miss Davis, March 17 accused Superior Court Judge John P. McMurray of prejudice and McMurray withdrew without reasons. The California Judicial Council March 23 accepted Superior Court Justice Alan A. Lindsay to replace McMurray at the hearings, which resumed April 1. Miss Davis charged that Lindsay was prejudiced and asked that he be disqualified. Lindsay recessed for a week to consider the charge, but said April 8 that he saw no reason to remove himself. An appeal to the state supreme court by Miss Davis's attorneys failed, but Magee, against the advice of his attorneys, May 6 formally exercised his challenge to force Lindsay to step aside. (Under California law, the removal of the judge was necessary upon such a challenge.) Magee reportedly used the challenge after Lindsay declined to halt the hearings while Magee attempted to move the entire proceedings to federal court.

[4] Lindsay was replaced by Judge Richard Arnason, who reopened hearings May 24. Magee moved to have him disqualified when Arnason attempted to continue the hearings despite efforts for a change of jurisdiction. At the request of Miss Davis's attorneys, Arnason July 19 severed Magee from Miss Davis's trial. (Arnason refused to grant Miss Davis bail June 15.) Arnason set Nov. 1 as the starting date of the trial, allowing Miss Davis's attorneys a five-week delay to wind up arguments for a change of venue from San Rafael to San Francisco on the charge that she couldn't receive a fair trial in San Rafael. The change of venue was granted Nov. 2, but venue was changed to San Jose rather than San Francisco. Miss Davis's attorneys said they would appeal.

[5] **7 freed in Chicago slaying.** A Chicago jury Jan. 17 acquitted seven members of the Black P Stone Nation, a confederation of 60 black street gangs, of charges of murder and conspiracy to murder in the August 1970 sniper slaying of Chicago detective James A. Alfano Jr. Those freed were Charles Edward Bey, Lamar Bell, Tony M. Carter, Dennis Griffen, Ronald Florence, William Throop and Elton Wicks.

[6] **4 guilty in NYC police plot.** Four young black men were convicted May 13 in New York City of illegal possession of weapons and bombs that the prosecution charged were used to "kill a cop a week." The prosecution charged that the Harlem Five (Lloyd Butler was acquitted) had planned to raid an armory in New York to carry out their threat to murder policemen. The jury found Preston Lay Jr. and Hannibal Thomas guilty of possession of a weapon, in reference to a rifle and to a bomb. Wallace Marks was found guilty on two counts of possessing a loaded pistol and bombs. Ebb Glenn was convicted of a single charge of possessing a bomb. All were acquitted of a conspiracy charge. A sixth man, John Aykik Garrett, was charged in the case, but his charges were dismissed for lack of evidence.

[7] **11 charged in Mississippi slaying.** A Jackson, Miss. city judge Aug. 23 ordered the case of 11 black members of the Republic of New Africa charged with murdering Jackson policeman Lt. W. L. Skinner remanded to a grand jury. Skinner was fatally wounded in a gunfight which erupted Aug. 18 when police raided the headquarters of the black separatist group to serve three of its members with fugitive warrants. An agent of the FBI and another Jackson policeman were also wounded in the 20-minute exchange of gunfire. The 11 blacks were also charged Aug. 22 with treason under an old state law that

declared it illegal to participate in armed insurrection against the state. The charges carried the death penalty.

[8]   Panther-police conflicts. Police in Winston-Salem, N.C. investigating the theft of a truckload of meat opened fire Jan. 12 on Black Panther headquarters after two youths had pinned the officers down with gunfire from the building. The two surrendered after the 45-second police fusillade. Police said the meat, guns and 150 rounds of ammunition were found inside the building. Police in Memphis Jan. 17 arrested 13 Panthers following a dispute over the Panthers' moving families into a housing complex without permission from the city's housing authority. Eleven of the Panthers surrendered without resistance following negotiations with the police. The others were taken into custody after confronting policemen with a loaded shotgun and were booked on charges of assault to murder. A Detroit jury of 10 blacks and two whites June 30 cleared 12 Panthers of charges of murdering a policeman and conspiracy to murder in a gunfight with police at the party's headquarters in October 1970. Three of the Panthers were convicted of felonious assault and faced a maximum of four years imprisonment. David Hilliard, Panther chief of staff, was sentenced July 2 in Oakland, Calif. to a 1-10 year prison term for assault in connection with an April 1968 shootout with police. A jury of 10 blacks and two whites in New Orleans deliberated 31 minutes Aug. 6 before acquitting 12 Black Panthers of attempted murder of five New Orleans policemen in a gunfight in September 1970.

[9]   13 cleared on bombing charges. Thirteen Panthers were acquitted May 13 in New York City of 12 counts of plotting to bomb police stations, department stores and other public places throughout the city. Among those cleared were two Panthers who had fled to Algeria Feb. 6, forfeiting $100,000 bail, while the eight-month trial was still in progress. A total of 22 Panthers had been indicted in the alleged conspiracy. Some were never apprehended and others had their trials severed because of illness or their youth. The trial was one of the most costly in the state's history, with costs to city and state estimated at $750,000. Those acquitted were: Lumumba Shakur, his wife Afeni, Walter Johnson (Baba O Dinga), John J. Casson (Ali Bey Hassan), Robert Collier, Curtis Powell, Alex McKiever (Catarra), Clark Squire, Joan Bird, William E. King Jr. (Kinchasa), Lee Roper (Shaba Um), Michael Tabor (Ceyteyo) and Richard Moore (Analye Darhubi). Tabor and Moore had fled to Algeria.

[10]   Hilliard freed in Nixon case. A U.S. judge in San Francisco May 4 ordered David Hilliard released from federal custody after the government refused to divulge wiretap logs of conversations involving Hilliard. Hilliard had been charged with threatening the life of President Nixon in an antiwar speech he made in November 1969.

[11]   Charges dropped in Rackley case. A Connecticut state judge who had presided over the six-month trial of Panthers Bobby G. Seale and Mrs. Ericka Huggins on charges of kidnaping and murder in the death of Panther Alex Rackley dismissed all charges against the two May 25. Judge Harold H. Mulvey ordered the charges dropped and declared a mistrial one day after the jury in the case announced it was hopelessly deadlocked. Mulvey said "massive publicity" about the absence of a verdict in the case had made it too difficult to try them again. During the New Haven trial, which had begun Nov. 17, 1970, the state had attempted to prove that Seale, chairman of the Panthers, had ordered a group of Panthers to kill Rackley on suspicion of being a police informer. Mrs. Huggins, in addition to murder and kidnaping charges, was accused of participating in the alleged torture of Rackley before he died. Mulvey's decision allowed Mrs. Huggins, 23, to go free after spending two years in prison without bail. Seale was held by state authorities until May 28 when $25,000 bail was set in Chicago on his appeal of a contempt charge in connection with the 1969 Chicago conspiracy trial. State witness Warren Kimbro and the state's star witness George Sams Jr., both of whom had pleaded guilty to second-degree murder in the case, were sentenced to life imprisonment June 23.

[12]   7 indicted in party slaying. Seven Panthers were indicted in New York City July 7 on charges of murder and arson in connection with the gangland-style slaying of West Coast Panther official Samuel Lee Napier. The murder reportedly was tied to a power struggle between the Panther's East and West Coast factions. Among those indicted were Richard Moore (*see* [9]), Edward Josephs and Irving Mason, who were immediately arraigned following the announcement of the indictment. The other four were still being sought.

[13]   14 lawmen indicted in Hampton case. Illinois State's Attorney Edward V. Hanrahan, chief prosecutor of Chicago, was among 14 law enforcement officials named Aug. 24 in a long-suppressed indictment handed down in Chicago on charges of conspiring to obstruct justice in connection with a Dec. 4, 1969 police raid in which Fred Hampton, the Panther's Illinois chairman, and Mark Clark, another Panther official, were killed. The indictment was made public on orders issued Aug. 24 by the Illinois Supreme Court. Chief Criminal Court Judge Joseph A. Power, a former law partner of Chicago Mayor Richard J. Daley, had kept the indictment sealed since April, when it was prepared. Power had refused to accept the indictment because he contended that the grand jury had not heard all the pertinent witnesses and that it had been pressured into returning the true bills. It was on order of the Illinois Supreme Court that Power made the indictment public. The indictment accused Hanrahan and the 13 other defendants of knowingly conspiring to obstruct justice by attempting to thwart criminal prosecution of the eight policemen who participated in the predawn raid on Hampton's apartment. The indictment also accused the 14 defendants of planting false evidence and conspiring to obstruct the legal defense of the seven Panthers who survived the raid. Hanrahan was also accused by the grand jury of presenting evidence before another Cook County grand jury that "he knew or reasonably should have known to be false and inflammatory."

[14] Others named in the indictment were Assistant State Attorney Richard Jalovec, who headed the police section initiating the raid; eight policemen who took part in the raid and four police officials who later conducted departmental investigations into the raid. Chicago Police Superintendent James B. Conlisk Jr. was among five other Chicago law enforcement officials named as co-conspirators but not as defendants. No specific allegations were made against Conlisk other than his listing as a co-conspirator who had knowledge of the alleged conspiracy to obstruct justice.

[15]   Newton cleared of charges. The state of California Dec. 15 ended its four-year case against Huey P. Newton, 29, the Black Panther leader accused of killing an Oakland policeman, when Oakland District Attorney Lowell Jensen asked for dismissal of the charge. Judge William J. Hayes accepted the motion and dismissed the case against Newton. Jensen told Hayes, "I feel this is a frustration of justice and would prefer to retry the case, but I am compelled to ask at this time for a dismissal."

[16] Newton, co-founder of the Panthers, had been convicted in September 1968 of voluntary manslaughter in the 1967 death of Patrolman John Frey. He spent two years in prison before the California Court of Appeals overturned the conviction. Two subsequent retrials, the last June 29-Aug. 8, ended with deadlocked juries. In his motion to the court, Jensen said he had decided against a fourth trial because he believed that it, too, would fail to end with a verdict.

See also HIJACKING [1]; RACIAL & MINORITY UNREST [8]

BLACK PANTHERS—*See* BLACK MILITANTS [8, 16]; PRISONS [7]; RACIAL & MINORITY UNREST [8]

BLACK P STONE NATION—*See* BLACK MILITANTS [5]; POVERTY; PRISONS [11]

BLOUNT, WINTON M.—*See* POSTAL SERVICE, U.S.

BOLIVIA—Bolivia was torn during 1971 by revolts and threatened revolts against the leftist government of President Juan Jose Torres. The unrest culminated Aug. 22 in the overthrow of the Torres government and its replacement by a rightist government headed by Col. Hugo Banzer Suarez.

[2] **Torres blocks army revolt.** President Torres announced Jan. 11 that he had crushed an attempted military coup seeking to impose a "dictatorship of the right." The rebellion, reportedly led by Col. Banzer and Col. Edmundo Valencia Ibanez, had begun Jan. 10 when officers seized the army headquarters in La Paz, taking Army Commander Gen. Luis Reque Teran and other important military men as hostages. Torres had responded by calling out the presidential guard, which took control of strategic points in La Paz, and the air force, which sent fighter planes to strafe the occupied army headquarters with machinegun fire. Banzer and Valencia had both been sent to frontier posts in a reorganization of the armed forces Jan. 4 which had also included the forced retirement of two members (Gen. Efrain Guachalla and Rear Adm. Alberto Albarracin) of the junta set up following the military revolt against former President Alfredo Ovando Candia and the transfer of the third (Gen. Fernando Sattori) to be military attache to Bolivia's embassy in Washington, D.C. Following the attempted revolt, Torres dismissed 16 army officials, including Banzer and Valencia, according to report Jan. 16. Sixteen of the officers who allegedly participated in the coup attempt were among 23 persons expelled from Bolivia Jan. 17 to Arica, Chile.

[3] **Peasant revolt in Santa Cruz.** About 1,000 peasants invaded and assumed power in Santa Cruz March 2, then turned the city over to troops of the army's 8th Division, headed by Col. Remberto Torres, the president's cousin. The peasants described their revolt as an "action against communism." (The National Peasants Confederation had called a state of alert March 1, warning that 10,000 armed peasants were available to defend the national government.) They ousted the city's mayor, named Col. Torres as the new mayor and demanded the resignation of several cabinet members, whom they called "collaborators with the extreme left." In response to a threatened general strike by the Central Workers' Organization (COB), President Torres March 4 dismissed his cousin and reinstated the mayor of Santa Cruz. The government also agreed to workers' demands for an investigation of military complicity in the revolt, the removal of several local officials and the return of a local radio station from the peasants to leftists who had seized it in February.

[4] **Cabinet reorganization.** The Cabinet resigned en masse March 17 to make way for a reorganization of the government. The new Cabinet, named and sworn in the same day, was considered more leftist than the former Cabinet. The new Cabinet: foreign relations—Huascar Taborga; defense—Gen. Emilio Molina; interior—Jorge Gallardo; finance—Flavio Machicado; education—Hugo Poope; labor—Isaac Sandoval; public health—Javier Torres Goitia; mines—Gen. Eduardo Mendez Pereira; planning—Gustavo Luna; industry & commerce—Edmundo Roca Vaca Diez; transportation—Jaime Cadima Valdez; urban affairs—Jorge Prudencio; information—Ramiro Villaroel; gas & oil—Enrique Mariaca Bilbao; peasant affairs & agriculture— Col. Mario Candia Navarro.

[5] **Envoy to West Germany killed.** Former Bolivian Consul General to Hamburg Roberto Quintanilla was shot and killed in the Hamburg consulate April 1 by an unidentified woman. The Bolivian National Liberation Army (ELN) April 2 claimed responsibility for the murder and charged that Quintanilla was responsible for the death of guerrilla leader "Inti" Peredo in 1969. Quintanilla had retired as consul general but was remaining in Germany until his replacement arrived.

[6] **State of emergency declared.** President Torres June 22 declared a state of emergency in Bolivia after reports circulated of a right-wing military coup allegedly planned in response to the inauguration of the first session of the Popular Assembly June 22. (The Assembly was first established May 1 by the

Bolivian Confederation of Labor [CTB] and students. Torres had first assumed an equivocal position toward the Assembly, but finally gave tacit support to the body which would act only in an advisory capacity.) Indian peasants and workers had been converging on La Paz to form a militia in support of the leftist government. Troops loyal to the president had also been moving toward the capital to thwart any coup attempt. Gen. Reque Teran June 17 had vigorously denied accusations by labor groups that he was planning a right-wing coup. Reque Teran said the era of military insurrections in Bolivia had ended.

[7] **Popular Assembly demands.** The Popular Assembly ended its first session the first week of July after passing resolutions calling for the expulsion of U.S. military and FBI and CIA personnel, co-management of mines by workers' representatives and the eventual creation of popular tribunals and militias. The Assembly also voted June 24 to lead mass resistance to any attempted coup against the government and to seize all private businesses and call a general strike if necessary.

[8] **Torres overthrown; Banzer installed.** The 10-month regime of President Torres was deposed and replaced Aug. 22 by a rightist government headed by Col. Banzer. The coup, which began Aug. 19 in Santa Cruz with a right-wing demonstration headed by members of the Nationalist Revolutionary Movement (MNR) and the Bolivian Socialist Falange (FSB), touched off a virtual nationwide civil war and caused the death of over 120 persons. The Santa Cruz demonstration, which resulted in a state of national emergency being decreed Aug. 19, reportedly sprang from MNR and FSB anger over the arrest Aug. 18 of 30 persons (including Banzer) in Santa Cruz in what the government said was a move to block a coup attempt by a "fascist conspiracy." Leaders of the two opposition parties told demonstrators that the MNR and FSB, former enemies, were forming a National Popular Front "to keep the country from falling into the hands of communism." By Aug. 20, Santa Cruz and Cochabamba were in the hands of rebels who proclaimed Banzer president. The same day, the air force and Gen. Reque Teran declared their support for Torres. Peasants, students and miners fought in support of Torres, with over 35,000 peasants and miners marching against Santa Cruz, 50,000 peasants, students and miners gathered in La Paz around the presidential palace, and 10,000 peasants marching against the southern city of Oruro. (Oruro fell to the rebels by evening of Aug. 20.)

[9] By late Aug. 21, the rebels had taken possession of La Paz. Torres fled the palace and took shelter in the one military headquarters that remained loyal to him after the air force and the three largest army regiments in La Paz defected to the rebels. (Torres flew to exile in Peru Aug. 26. It was reported Oct. 12 that he had flown to Chile to join his family, which had been given asylum there.) With the help of the La Paz garrisons, the rebels were able to break through positions in the city held by armed workers, peasants and loyalist troops. The military junta, composed of Banzer, Gen. Jaime Florentino Mendieta and Col. Andres Selich (who led the revolt in Santa Cruz), declared itself in Santa Cruz the same day. The fighting ended in La Paz Aug. 22 and Banzer that day assumed the presidency by decision of the high command. The new Cabinet, announced Aug. 22: foreign affairs—Mario Gutierrez, FSB leader; interior—Col. Selich; finance—Raul Lema Pelaez, MNR leader; national defense—Gen. Antonio Arnez Camacho, ex-commander of the air force; education and culture—Agusto Mendizabal Moya (FSB); labor and union affairs—Ciro Humbolt Barrero (FSB); welfare and public health—Carlos Valverde (FSB); mines and petroleum—Carlos Serrate (MNR); information—Hugo Gonzalez (MNR); transportation and communication—Ambrosio Garcia (FSB); and urban planning—Enrique Leigue (an independent).

[10]   Banzer Aug. 22 issued a new state of emergency and curfew as troops held positions around La Paz and tanks patrolled the streets. The new government sought to consolidate its support Aug. 23 by crushing a resistance effort by leftist students at San Andres University. Army and air force units strafed a central university tower killing at least eight students and wounding 25 others. Following the attack on the university, 250 students were arrested, including 30 women. The women were later released. The government freed 52 more students Aug. 30.

[11]   **Government orders schools closed.** The government Sept. 4 ordered the country's universities closed until Feb. 28, 1972 in order to end "the acts of violence and terrorism" directed by "foreign mercenaries that altered the social peace." At the same time, the government ordered a reorganization of the nation's university system "to rediscover the moral and patriotic perfectability of the new generations." It was reported Sept. 9 that students and professors of the University of Potosi had decided to attend classes despite the new government law.

[12]   **Armed forces chief resigns.** President Banzer Oct. 18 forced the resignation of the armed forces chief, Gen. Remberto Iriarte. The two reportedly had "tactical disagreements." Iriarte was succeeded by Gen. Joaquin Zenteno Anaya, director of the antiguerrilla operations that led to the death of Ernesto "Che" Guevara in 1967. Iriarte's resignation was reportedly forced after a series of stories linking him with subversive plots against the government.

    See also HIJACKING [8]; LATIN AMERICA

BOMBING—*See* CIVIL RIGHTS [9]; CRIME [6]; DRAFT & WAR PROTEST [4-6]; GREAT BRITAIN [4]; NORTHERN IRELAND [6, 9, 18-19]; STUDENT UNREST [10]; UNION OF SOVIET SOCIALIST REPUBLICS [15]
BON VIVANT SOUPS, INC.—*See* CONSUMER AFFAIRS [8-9]
BOOKS—*See* COPYRIGHTS, INTERNATIONAL; PULITZER PRIZES
BOTULISM—*See* CONSUMER AFFAIRS [8-10]

BOXING—Frazier outpoints Ali. Joe Frazier established himself March 8 as the undisputed heavyweight champion of the world as he relentlessly slugged his way to a unanimous 15-round decision over Muhammed Ali, the deposed champion, before a sellout crowd of 19,500 at New York's Madison Square Garden. In the U.S., 360 theaters showed the fight on closed-circuit television. An estimated audience of 300 million in 35 foreign countries also watched the fight on television via cable or satellite. For Ali, 29, who had won the heavyweight title in 1964 as Cassius Clay, it was a first loss after 31 pro triumphs. Frazier registered his 27th pro victory without defeat. The fight's only knockdown was scored by Frazier, who floored Ali with a left hook in the 15th round. Judge Bill Recht awarded 11 rounds to Frazier and 4 to Ali, while the other judge, Artie Aidala, scored the fight 9-6 in Frazier's favor. The referee, Arthur Mercante, gave 8 rounds to Frazier, 6 to Ali and scored one even.

    Admissions at Madison Square Garden grossed $1.25 million, a record for an indoor fight. The bout's promoters, Jerry Perenchio and Jack Kent Cooke, estimated that the closed-circuit television hookup would bring in another $25 million in worldwide receipts. Frazier and Ali each received $2.5 million, record purses for a bout.

BRANDT, WILLY—*See* GERMAN CONSULTATIONS; GERMANY, WEST [1-2]; INTERNATIONAL MONETARY DEVELOPMENTS [5]; NOBEL PRIZES

BRAZIL—Swiss envoy freed. Giovanni Enrico Bucher, the Swiss Ambassador to Brazil kidnaped by terrorists Dec. 7, 1970, was released Jan. 16 in exchange for the government's release Jan. 14 of 70 political prisoners, who were sent to Chile. Bucher was in good health. Brazilian President Emilio Garrastazu Medici had signed a decree Jan. 13 banishing the 68 Brazilian and two foreign prisoners. The 70, plus the children of a couple among the prisoners, arrived in

Chile Jan. 14 and were given political asylum. Many of them were reported to bear scars and bruises from torture inflicted in prison. The prisoners accused police of killing Eduardo Leite, a prisoner whose body had been found just before Bucher's kidnaping. The police had reported Leite was shot during an escape attempt.

Death squad sentences. Two policemen were sentenced to 65 years in prison Jan. 29 on charges of murder in connection with the notorious death squads—groups reportedly composed of off-duty policemen who, on their own initiative, killed petty criminals. The sentences were reportedly the first given to alleged members of the death squads. It was reported Oct. 1 that Dimas Silvares Machado, a police detective, was sentenced by a Sao Paulo jury to 19 years in prison for death squad activity. Also convicted for participation in the squads were police detective Genesio Cunha, jailed in Victoria Nov. 19 for 33 years for taking part in the murders of 11 persons, and policeman Nelson Querido, sentenced in Sao Paulo Dec. 1 to 7.5 years in prison for the murder of a common criminal. In other developments concerning the squads: 15 Sao Paulo policemen were indicted March 9 on charges of murder in connection with the squads; the 13-member Brazilian Federal Court of Appeals in Brasilia unanimously decided June 24 that civil courts would try cases resulting from death squad executions in Sao Paulo; the Rio de Janeiro newspaper Ultima Hora said July 8 that military police had severely beaten one of its reporters July 7 in reprisal for a campaign waged by the paper against the squads; in response to criticism of the squads, the U.S. State Department July 15 announced it was ending a 12-year program of public safety assistance under which 600 Brazilian police had been trained in the U.S. and another 100,000 in Brazil; Helio P. Bicudo, the public prosecutor who had won indictments against more than 25 policemen in connection with the squads, was reportedly removed from his assignment in Sao Paulo state under government pressure Aug. 2; President Medici, according to report Sept. 25, issued a decree suspending the political rights of policemen accused of participating in Sao Paulo's squads.

Third political party launched. Former Vice President Pedro Aleixo formally announced the creation of the Democratic Republican party, Brazil's third political party, March 31, the seventh anniversary of the 1964 "revolution." (The two other legalized parties were the government-supported National Renovating Alliance, or ARENA, and the opposition Brazilian Democratic Movement.) The party was designed, according to Aleixo, not to oppose the current military government, but to support "the ideals of the revolution of March 31," 1964. Among the objectives of the party were the defense and perfection of representative democracy, the preservation of fundamental human rights, the prevention of violence and the maintenance of order, security and tranquility. By taking no official action preventing the new party's formation, the government apparently intended to tolerate it under the 1969 amendments to the constitution which had authorized the formation of new parties.

Agrarian reform law announced. President Medici July 6 unexpectedly announced a program of agrarian reform and rural modernization for the underdeveloped and densely populated northeast region. The program, which would cost an estimated 4 billion cruzeiros ($800 million), was to be financed by special taxes during the 1972-76 period. It would create a system for compensated expropriation of large under-utilized land holdings for redistribution as small farms for peasants and would finance the development of new markets, electrification of the region and the creation of transport facilities. It also called for stimulation of agricultural industry, granting financial aid and technical assistance to small farmers and credit to farmers colonizing the region.

New Indian policy ordered. President Medici July 12 ordered the formation of three new Indian reservations in the middle Amazon basin. The reservations were to be occupied by small primitive tribes living along the route of the Trans-Amazon highway, currently under construction. Medici also altered the area of the Xingu national park, which served as a reservation for 1,300 Indians who were being displaced by another highway. The actions were interpreted as a reaffirmation of the country's intention to forcibly relocate Amazon tribes that were said to impede the extensive Amazon region development program.

4 priests sentenced to prison. A military court in Sao Paulo Sept. 14 sentenced three Roman Catholic priests to four-year prison terms and another to a six-month sentence—all on charges of participation in the National Liberation Alliance (ALN), an urban guerrilla group. They were specifically charged with helping fugitives escape across the border to Uruguay and with disseminating subversive literature. (The priests said they had not known the men and had merely exercised the Christian right of asylum.) Fourteen others accused, including several priests, were absolved for lack of evidence. The four convicted priests, and three priests who were acquitted, had been in prison since being sentenced in November 1969 to indefinite terms on charges of aiding terrorist ALN leader Carlos Marighela, who had earlier been killed by police.

42 terrorists convicted. A military tribune in Juiz de Fora, according to report Dec. 1, convicted 42 persons and acquitted 26 others in the largest subversion trial ever held in Brazil. The sentences, given at the end of a seven-day trial, ranged from six months to four years imprisonment. The accused were linked to the "Corrente" terrorist organization. Thirty were awaiting sentencing on other charges of antigovernment activities.

Air force purge. In what was seen as a move to de-emphasize the role of the armed forces in the political structure, President Medici Dec. 3 dismissed two air force officials and the air force legal counsel one week after a policy dispute between Medici and Air Force Marshal Marcio de Souza e Melo resulted in Souza e Melo's resignation. Those dismissed were Air Force Zone Commander Brig. Joao Paulo Burnier, Director of Intelligence Carlos Alfonso Dellamora and legal counsel Caio Joaquim de Oliveira de Sa Freire. Other mass dismissals or resignations of senior officials whose appointments by Souza e Melo had caused resentment were reported to have followed. Souza e Melo, a member of the ruling junta that selected Medici as president in 1969, was considered a "hard-liner" and had disagreed with Medici over the use of torture, which the president reportedly was anxious to eliminate. Brig. Joelmir Campos de Araripe Macedo, a liberal, was chosen to replace Souza e Melo.

Medici visits U.S. President Medici Dec. 9 concluded a three-day visit to the U.S. which included talks with President Nixon. The visit represented a break with a U.S. policy tradition, at least a decade old, of keeping relations with Latin American military governments at the formal diplomatic level. A joint communique issued at the end of the visit said the two presidents had consulted, among other things, on the need for "intensified cooperation" among hemispheric nations on economic and social development "as well as their common security interest." The joint statement also declared that the future of the hemisphere "must be founded on . . . freedom and self-determination."

See also ARGENTINA [14]; BANKS; DISASTERS; DOMINICAN REPUBLIC; FLOODS; LATIN AMERICA; SPORTS; TERRITORIAL WATERS

BRITISH COMMONWEALTH—*See* EUROPEAN ECONOMIC COMMUNITY [14]; GREAT BRITAIN [9-10, 18]; NORTHERN IRELAND [17]; UGANDA; VIRGIN ISLANDS

BROWN, H. RAP—*See* BLACK MILITANTS [1-2]

BUDGET—**'Expansionary but not inflationary.'** President Nixon submitted to Congress Jan. 29 a $229.2 billion budget for fiscal 1972 (July 1, 1971 to June 30, 1972) with an estimated deficit of $11.6 billion. The budget, which Nixon called "expansionary but not inflationary," was the first U.S. budget formally committed to the "full employment" surplus concept—a theory evaluating spending in terms of the amount of money generated by the present taxing system at full efficiency under conditions of an acceptable 4% unemployment rate. Within this concept, the fiscal 1972 budget was approximately in balance and the fiscal 1971 budget, which was estimated as showing a deficit of $18.6 billion, was estimated to be in surplus. (The federal estimate of the 1971 deficit, revealed Jan. 29, was a drastic revision from the original estimate of a $1.3 billion surplus, revised in May 1970 to a $1.3 billion deficit.) Nixon stressed the idea of a full employment budget in his message, saying it was "in the nature of a self-fulfilling prophecy: By operating as if we were at full employment, we will help bring about that full employment."

The 1972 revenue estimate of $217.6 billion was based on an optimistic economic forecast of an $88 billion (12%) increase in the gross national product (GNP), or total private and government output, to a $1.065 trillion level in 1971. (The GNP rose $45 billion to $977 billion in 1970.) The government projection conflicted with the consensus of private forecasts that the GNP increase in 1971 would be in the 7% range from $1.045 trillion to $1.05 trillion.

The budget contained no new taxing proposals and incorporated the President's goal to forward "a peaceful revolution in which power will be turned back to the people." Basic to the goal were his plans for government reorganization—initiation of a revenue sharing program with states and localities (see STATE & LOCAL GOVERNMENTS [1-9]), a realignment of cabinet departments (see GOVERNMENT REORGANIZATION) and enactment of welfare reform (see WELFARE). As for spending priorities, defense spending would increase $1.5 billion but would decrease to 32% of total budget outlays and 6.8% of the GNP, the lowest proportions since 1950 and 1951, respectively. (The figures did not include defense-related programs of the Atomic Energy Commission and the Selective Service System, which would increase the proportion to 34% of the budget.) The projected increase in total spending for human resources increased from 41% of the budget to 42%. Increased spending also was projected for environment, parks and natural resources, poverty, welfare and Social Security, science, health, civil rights, education, law enforcement, housing, veterans and the supersonic transport (SST) project. Decreases in spending were projected for farm subsidy outlays, transportation, space and the Indochinese war.

Budget Outlays
(In millions of dollars for the fiscal year)

	1970 actual	1971 estimate	1972 estimate
National defense*	80,295	76,443	77,512
International affairs and finance	3,570	3,586	4,032
Space research and technology	3,749	3,368	3,151
Agriculture and rural development	6,201	*5,262	5,804
Natural resources	2,480	2,636	4,243
Commerce and transportation	9,310	11,442	10,937
Community development and housing	2,965	3,858	4,495
Education and manpower	7,289	8,300	8,808
Health	12,995	14,928	16,010
Income security	43,790	55,546	60,739
Veterans benefits and services	8,667	9,969	10,644
Interest	18,312	19,433	19,687
General government	3,336	4,381	4,970
Allowances for:			
Added amount for revenue sharing	-----	-----	4,019
Pay increase (excluding Department of Defense)	-----	500	1,000
Contingencies	-----	300	950
Undistributed intragovernmental transactions	-6,380	-7,197	-7,771
Total outlays	**196,588**	**212,755**	**229,232**
Budget deficit	**2,845**	**18,562**	**11,639**

*Includes allowance for all-volunteer force and civilian and military pay increases for Defense Department.

Budget Receipts
(In millions of dollars for the fiscal year)

	1970 actual	1971 estimate	1972 estimate
Individual Income taces................................	90,412	88,300	93,700
Corporation income taxes.............................	32,829	30,100	36,700
Social insurance taxes and contributions:			
Employment taxes and contributions................	39,133	42,297	50,225
Unemployment insurance.........................	3,464	3,604	4,183
Contributions for other insurance and retirement......	2,701	3,072	3,151
Excise taxes...	15,705	16,800	17,500
Estate and gift taxes.................................	3,644	3,730	5,300
Customs duties......................................	2,430	2,490	2,700
Miscellaneous receipts...............................	3,424	3,800	4,134
Total receipts..................................	**193,743**	**194,193**	**217,593**

The fiscal 1972 spending total, based on the assumption that unemployment—at 6% in January—would average 4.8% between mid-1971 and mid-1972, represented an increase of $16.4 billion, or 8%, over fiscal 1971. (The $16.2 billion spending increase for 1971 was originally estimated at $2.9 billion, but unemployment benefits alone nearly doubled from the estimate of $3.2 billion to $5.9 billion.) Of the $249 billion requested in new budget authority, or the right to make commitments to spend, more than $170 billion would require new Congressional action.

The President also requested reform of the budget process itself, particularly in federal credit programs that, he said, "escape regular review by either the executive or the legislative branch."

See also CONGRESS [11]; NIXON, RICHARD MILHOUS [1]; YOUTH

BULGARIA—1970 economic report. The Bulgarian news agency BTA announced the results of the 1970 economic development plan Jan. 28. Measured against the figures for 1969, the following major increases were reported: national income 7%, labor productivity 7.2%, foreign trade 7.9%, agricultural production 4%, housing construction 23.9%, retail trade 8% and average wages 4%.

Cabinet changes. The Presidium of the National Assembly Jan. 4 replaced Vladimir Kalaydzhiev as first deputy minister of health with Evgeni Apostolov, and Georgi Nastev as deputy minister with Ivan Kislarov. Kiril Ignatòv was replaced as minister of health March 15 by Angel Todorov. Ivan Golomeev, deputy foreign trade minister, was dismissed April 28. Peter T. Mladenov became foreign minister Dec. 16, replacing Ivan Bashev, who had died in a skiing accident Dec. 12.

Party congress held. The 10th Communist Party Congress was held April 20-25 in Sophia. The delegates approved a report by the Central Committee on its activities since the last congress, a new constitution and a draft of the 1971-75 economic development plan. Todor Zhivkov was elected for another term as party first secretary and an enlarged Central Committee was chosen.

Membership of the Central Committee was increased from 137 to 147. Those elected April 25 to the committee's Politburo as full members were Boris Velchev, Boyan Bulgaranov, Zhivko Zhivkov, Ivan Mikhailov, Ivan Popov, Pencho Kubadinski, Stanko Todorov, Tano Tsolov, Todor Zhivkov (also named Communist party first secretary), Todor Pavlov and Tsola Dragoycheva. The Politburo's alternate members were Angel Tsanev, Venelin Kotsev, Ivan Abadzhiev, Kostadin Gyaurov, Krustyu Trichkov and Peko Takov. (Gyaurov March 9 had been named chairman of the Central Trade Union Council, replacing Roza Koritarova, who became deputy chairman. Four of the council's six secretaries were transferred to other jobs.) Deputy

Premier Lachezar Avramov was dropped from the Politburo, apparently for his involvement as foreign trade minister in a 1969 controversy over a merchant shipping firm's trade with Western countries. (Avramov was relieved of his posts as minister of foreign trade and deputy premier April 28. He was replaced by Ivan Nedev, previously first deputy minister.) Mitko Grigorov, formerly considered a rival to First Secretary Zhivkov, regained the Central Committee membership he had lost at the previous congress.

Constitution approved. The new Bulgarian constitution, passed by the party congress April 25, was approved by national referendum May 16. The document established a State Council, replacing the Presidium of the National Assembly, which would conduct the general direction of foreign and domestic policy and would be headed by Zhivkov. (Zhivkov resigned as premier July 7 and was elected Bulgarian president. He was succeeded as premier by Stanko Todoro, a member of the CP Politburo considered the second-ranking figure in the party.)

See also DISARMAMENT; DRUG USE & ADDICTION [9]; SPACE [24]; SUDAN

BUNKER, ELLSWORTH—*See* VIETNAM, SOUTH
BUREAU OF INDIAN AFFAIRS—*See* INDIANS, AMERICAN
BUREAU OF MINES—*See* MINES
BURGER, WARREN E.—*See* CIVIL RIGHTS [2-3]; JUDICIARY [4, 6-7, 11]; PENTAGON PAPERS [7]; POSTAL SERVICE, U.S.

BURMA—Rebel developments. Thai officials reported Jan. 2 that former Burmese Premier U Nu, deposed in 1962 by Gen. Ne Win and leader of the rebel National Liberation Front since October 1970, had established headquarters in Thailand's Tak Province near the Burmese border. The rebels reportedly set up a powerful radio transmitting station in the Mae Sot district where thousands of rebels were stationed. In northern Kachin State a group of 200 Kachin Independence Army rebels ambushed a train Feb. 23, killing at least 16 passengers and injuring many others. Government troops later exchanged fire with the rebels, who fled taking property looted from passengers. The minority Karens of southern Burma, who had been fighting against the central government since being granted limited autonomy following a revolt in 1949, were reported Feb. 7 to be planning a new offensive aimed at toppling the Ne Win government. The announcement was made in Thailand by Mahn Ba Zan, president of the Karen National Union, the ruling Karen rebel authority, and recently named president of the United National Liberation Front, a coalition of rebel groups including the Karens and Mon, Chin and Shan minority groups. The Kachins cooperated with the Front but did not belong to it.

BURNS, ARTHUR—*See* BANKS; BUSINESS [3]

BURUNDI—Economics Minister Libere Ndabakwaje and Information Minister Maj. Jerome Ntungumburanye were arrested July 5 and charged with plotting to overthrow the government of Col. Michel Micombero.

BUSINESS—Overseas curbs extended. The government, in a joint announcement Jan. 7 by the Treasury, the Federal Reserve Board (FRB) and the Commerce Department, extended into 1971 existing curbs on U.S. private investment and bank lending abroad. Although the Administration had hoped to phase out the controls, the Treasury explained that the extension was necessary in view of a "serious continuing balance-of-payments problem." The announcement included minor changes in FRB banking rules and liberalization of the Commerce Department's regulations for direct corporate investment abroad. Although FRB ceilings on bank lending were essentially maintained, the changes exempted export credits from limits imposed on short-term lending in developed countries and permitted banks to buy bonds and notes of international institutions without counting them against the present ceilings. The Commerce Department (1) raised its limit on a company's worldwide investment from $1 million to $2 million annually, without requiring submission of a quarterly report to the department or observance of federal investment quotas; (2) increased the amount of "liquid foreign balances" that companies could have at the end of each month to a maximum $100,000, up from the previous ceiling of $25,000; and (3) relaxed limits on direct foreign investment, based on prior year earnings of foreign affiliates, by permitting companies to invest up to 40% rather than 30% of these earnings.

[2]   **IOS developments.** Investors Overseas Services said in Geneva Jan. 16 that Bernard Cornfeld, the mutual fund's founder and former chairman, had sold nearly all his seven million preferred shares in the company and resigned his posts as a director and member of the executive committee, ending all ties between them. Cornfeld's withdrawal climaxed a week of intensive negotiations centering on an effort by representatives of International Controls Corp. (ICC) of Fairfield, N.J., including ICC's chief executive officer, Robert I. Vesco, to remove Cornfeld. Cornfeld had opposed all dealings with Vesco since his acquisition of seats on the IOS board of directors through a $15-million loan to the company in 1970. Cornfeld said he could not disclose the terms of the sale nor identify the purchaser, whom he described as "affiliated with a major international financial institution." The unknown financial institution sold the 13% block of shares in May to American Interland Ltd., a Canadian ICC subsidiary. The stock transfer was one of the causes for a subpoena by the Securities and Exchange Commission (SEC) requiring Vesco to provide the SEC with information concerning ICC dealings with IOS. Vesco contended in a suit in U.S. district court that any information he divulged to the SEC would expose him to criminal prosecution under Swiss secrecy laws. However, the court May 24 dismissed the suit and May 26 ordered Vesco to supply the SEC with the information it required. Vesco and IOS President Milton F. Meissner were arrested and jailed in Geneva Nov. 30 on charges of influencing a misappropriation of shares, deposited as loan collateral, in a proxy fight by Vesco to retain control of IOS. IOS requested Vesco's and Meissner's resignations and they were given, according to report Dec. 3. In another development, IOS and Cornfeld were accused by the Justice Department, in a suit filed in the U.S. district court in New York Dec. 2, of illegally purchasing $38,193,000-worth of gold during the 1968 gold crisis. The suit, brought under the Gold Reserve Act of 1934 which barred ownership of gold by U.S. corporations except for specific uses, accused an IOS subsidiary of purchasing gold worth $31,917,000 and accused Cornfeld of personally causing another subsidiary to purchase gold worth $6,276,000. Citing a federal law imposing penalties equal to twice the value of gold involved in illegal transactions, the suit sought $62,394,000 from IOS and $12,552,000 from Cornfeld.

[3]   **Lockheed, Rolls accord.** Lockheed Aircraft Corp. signed a new contract in London May 11 with Rolls-Royce (1971) Ltd. (a nationalized company registered Feb. 23 after the original Rolls-Royce company declared bankruptcy) to proceed with the production of the Rolls-Royce RB-211 engine for Lockheed's L1011 Tri-star airbus. Britain's defense minister, Lord Carrington, and aerospace minister, Frederick Corfield, had announced in Parliament May 10 that Lockheed agreed to pay an additional $120 million above the previously agreed-upon price of $445 million for the first 555 Rolls engines. The contract was contingent upon Congressional approval of a Presidential request May 6 for loan guarantees to Lockheed to insure the necessary financial backing for the project. The legislation, providing a $250 million loan guarantee to prevent Lockheed from going bankrupt, was narrowly passed in the House July 30 by a 192-189 vote and in the Senate Aug. 2 by a 49-48 vote. It was signed into law by President Nixon Aug. 9. Nixon

appointed Treasury Secretary John B. Connally Jr., FRB Chairman Arthur Burns and SEC Chairman William J. Casey to a three-member Emergency Loan Guarantee Board to administer the loan guarantee.

[4] In the Congress, the legislation had been saved by a last-minute compromise before the Aug. 6 recess. It had been expected that the House would pass a broader bill, approved by the House Banking Committee July 21, that would have provided for a loan program of up to $2 billion, including other needy corporations. However, the House reverted to the Administration's Lockheed-only bill. After the close vote in the House, House leaders informed key senators July 31 that it was obvious that the House would settle only for the narrower bill. They pointed out that, in order to pass the legislation before the recess, the Senate would have to agree to the House measure to avoid a House-Senate conference on differences between the House bill and the broader version blocked by a filibuster in the Senate. At a strategy meeting the same day, the Administration, represented by Secretary Connally, and pro-Lockheed senators accepted a compromise proposal by Sen. William Proxmire (D, Wis.) and other Lockheed opponents under which the Senate bill would be scuttled and the Lockheed opposition would drop its filibuster in return for a vote on a Lockheed-only bill.

[5] *Loan pact signed.* A 24-bank consortium and the federal government Sept. 14 signed a $750 million financing package with Lockheed. The contract renewed an outstanding $400 million loan by the banks at an interest rate of 1% above the prevailing prime rate (6%) and provided for an immediate $50 million loan at an 8% interest rate under the $250 million federally guaranteed loan program that was unanimously approved by the Emergency Loan Guarantee Board Sept. 9. (Lockheed would pay the government a guarantee fee of 2.3% of the 8% total interest, in addition to a fee of less than 1% on the unused portion of the $250 million loan guarantee that would be divided equally between Lockheed and the banks. Lockheed would also receive from its three major airline customers—Trans World Airlines, Eastern Air Lines and Delta Air Lines—$100 million in prepayments on orders in addition to the $200 million already paid by the three toward development of the airbus. The Loan Guarantee Board Nov. 17 approved Lockheed's request to borrow another $25 million under the program.)

[6] **FTC challenges drug merger.** The Federal Trade Commission (FTC) April 20 announced a proposed complaint challenging the merger in 1970 of two giant drug companies—Warner-Lambert Pharmaceutical Co. and Parke, Davis & Co. The proposed complaint charged that the merger violated the Clayton Antitrust Act by substantially lessening competition in drug manufacturing, particularly in ethical drugs sold primarily on doctors' prescriptions and in 52 highly concentrated submarkets for specific drugs. Although the merger would not result in a significant increase of concentration in the ethical drug business, the FTC said the elimination of Parke, Davis as a competitor would encourage further acquisitions or mergers, thereby increasing concentration. In a separate proposed order, the FTC would require Warner-Lambert to divest itself of Parke, Davis within six months by distributing its stock to Warner-Lambert stockholders. In addition, Warner-Lambert would be prohibited for 20 years from acquiring any company in the drug or medical electronic-equipment industries without prior FTC approval. The settlement sought the restoration of Parke, Davis as a "separate, viable, independent, going concern," continuing in its former line of business.

[7] Action on the merger had been opposed by the Justice Department, against the advice of its antitrust division, and referred instead to the FTC. The merger was a politically sensitive one because of close personal ties between the Nixon Administration and Warner-Lambert. Attorney General John Mitchell had disqualified himself from the case because of his former partnership in the law

firm (in which President Nixon was also a partner) that represented Warner-Lambert—Mudge, Rose, Guthrie and Alexander. Warner-Lambert's honorary chairman, Elmer Bobst, was a personal friend of the President and had been one of the six biggest contributors to the Nixon-Agnew fund-raising committees in the 1968 presidential campaign.

[8] **DuPont grip on Delaware denounced.** A two-volume study, entitled "The Company State" and compiled by law students working under Ralph Nader, accused E. I. duPont de Nemours & Co. and the powerful duPont family of using their domination over "virtually every major aspect of Delaware life" for selfish interests. Among the allegations of the study released Nov. 26, the team of "Nader's Raiders" charged that the nation's 18th largest industrial corporation and members of the duPont family: did not pay their fair share of property and income taxes; used their control over community charities in Wilmington to sway decisions on projects irrespective of public sentiment; ignored problems of air and water pollution; condoned racism in Wilmington; prevented dissent by "a virtual monopoly" over the news through control of Delaware's two largest newspapers, the Morning News and the Evening Journal in Wilmington; nurtured a "business-coddling" judiciary; allowed a "disgraceful state of health and education for all but the well-to-do"; and curbed the social, political and professional freedom of action of its employees. The report recommended expansion of the chemical company's board of directors to include "representatives of consumers, the Delaware community, employees and minority stockholder interests," institution of a "formal mechanism by which workers can have substantial participation in running the company," selling the two newspapers to competing companies and efforts to make the state government and corporation "more accountable to the citizens of Delaware."

[9] **U.S. sues commodity board.** The Justice Department filed an antitrust suit against the Chicago Board of Trade Dec. 1 challenging its right to fix commission rates on commodity futures trade. It was the first such antitrust action against any commodity or securities exchange. The suit, filed in U.S. district court in Chicago, charged that the Board of Trade and its approximately 1,400 members (not defendants in the suit) violated Section 1 of the Sherman Antitrust Act by jointly fixing and maintaining minimum rates of commission, floor brokerage and other fees, thereby depriving the public of the right to trade at competitive rates and fees. The suit alleged that the sale of services among member brokers of the Board of Trade also eliminated price competition. Minimum commission rates were generally twice as large for non-members as for members. The suit asked the court to permanently enjoin the Board of Trade and its members from fixing rates and fees.

[10] In a separate action Dec. 1, the Justice Department Antitrust Division issued a memorandum to the SEC urging an end to similar fee-fixing by the New York (NYSE) and other stock exchanges. The reason identical practices of fee-fixing were the object of an antitrust suit against the Board of Trade but were merely the subject of recommendations to the SEC was apparently a matter of legal differences; the SEC was empowered to review brokerage rates set by the stock exchanges, while the Agriculture Department's Commodity Exchange Authority was essentially powerless. (*See* STOCK MARKET)

See also CONSUMER AFFAIRS [9]; ECONOMY, U.S.; GREAT BRITAIN [5]; TAXES

BUSING—*See* CIVIL RIGHTS [2-3, 7-12, 14-15, 19]; EDUCATION [12]
BUTZ, EARL L.—*See* AGRICULTURE [12]

CABLE TELEVISION—*See* TELEVISION & RADIO
CALLEY, WILLIAM A.—*See* DRAFT & WAR PROTEST [19]; WAR CRIMES [3-4, 6-8]

CAMBODIA—Government shakeup. Gen. Lon Nol resigned as premier of Cambodia April 20 because of ill health. Lon Nol had suffered a stroke Feb. 8 and returned to Cambodia April 12 only partially recovered after spending two months in Hawaii for medical treatment. Efforts to replace him following his resignation led to a government crisis that was finally resolved with an accord May 3 under which Lon Nol agreed to serve as titular premier while Lt. Gen. Sisowath Sirik Matak, deputy premier in the outgoing government, would hold the principal power as premier-delegate. The accord took effect May 6 when a new Cabinet was approved by the National Assembly by a 50-1 vote with nine abstentions. The new Cabinet had 16 members, as had the outgoing one, with only four holdovers, excluding Sirik Matak and Lon Nol. There were three vice premiers, each responsible for a group of ministries. Sirik Matak retained authority over defense and foreign affairs.

Despite Lon Nol's decision to step down, Chief of State Cheng Heng April 21 had given him a mandate to form a new government. Following several days of consultation, the premier had submitted his final resignation April 29. At the same time, he had been named chief of the Cambodian armed forces and Sirik Matak was appointed second in command. Cheng Heng had called on Sirik Matak to form a new government, but the deputy premier had declined the offer April 30. Chuop Hell, Counselor to Cheng Heng, had been mandated premier, but had announced May 1 that he could not "fulfill his delicate mission." In Tam, National Assembly president, had been called in to form a new government but had failed following consultations May 2.

Sihanouk sons acquitted. A Pnompenh military court July 17 acquitted the two sons of ousted Prince Norodom Sihanouk of charges of terrorism and collaboration with the enemy. Norodom Nararith and his half-brother, Norodom Naradipo, had been accused of terrorist attacks, including the bombing of the U.S. embassy in Pnompenh. Naradipo was already serving a five-year sentence for treason imposed by the same court April 6. Princess Norodom Botum Bopha, Sihanouk's daughter, had been acquitted of charges of antigovernment activities April 6.

U.S. envoy escapes bomb attack. Emory C. Swank, U.S. ambassador to Cambodia, escaped an assassination attempt in Pnompenh Sept. 7. Swank was being driven to the American embassy when two terrorists shoved a bomb-laden bicycle in front of his car. Cambodian police said the explosive failed to detonate. The two men escaped.

Emergency rule declared. Premier Lon Nol Oct. 22 declared a state of emergency in Cambodia and abolished constitutional rule. At the same time, the premier announced the formation of a new Cabinet, which he said would govern by "ordinance." He said his action was aimed at preventing anarchy in the country, which he contended was threatened by a "fifth column." The premier's moves followed the Cabinet's abolition of the National Assembly Oct. 16 by decreeing that the assembly's five-year mandate, due to expire Oct. 18, would not be renewed. The Cabinet instead ordered the legislative body replaced by a constituent assembly, charged with drawing up a new constitution. (The assembly met for the first time Nov. 8.) The U.S. declared Oct. 21 that it would continue to support Cambodia despite the constitutional curbs it had invoked. (The new Cabinet included all the former ministers and four new members. They were Tim Nguon, first vice president; Gen. Thappana Nginn, interior minister; Chhan Sokhum, industry minister; and May Lay Jhem, commerce minister.)

See also FOREIGN AID; INDOCHINA WAR [1-16, 35, 51, 55, 62, 64, 69, 72, 79]; PENTAGON PAPERS [23, 27]; VIETNAM, NORTH

CAMEROON—Three executed in plot; bishop spared. Three men found guilty of plotting to overthrow and assassinate President Ahmadou Ahidjo were executed near Yaounde Jan. 15. The death sentence of Albert Ndongmo, Roman Catholic archbishop of Nkongsamba arrested on the same charges in August 1970, was commuted to life imprisonment by Ahidjo Jan. 14. The dead men, shot publicly in Bafoussam, were Ernest Ouandie, leader of the clandestine Union of Cameroon Peoples (UPC); Raphael Fotsing, one of Ouandie's lieutenants; and Gabriel Tabeu, leader of a group called the Holy Cross for the Liberation of Cameroon.

The four, including Ndongmo, had been among 102 defendants in two trials beginning Dec. 26, 1970. They had been charged with "attempted revolution, the organizing of armed bands, murder, wilful destruction, rape, illegal detention, looting and complicity in the aforementioned crimes." Many of the defendants were members of the Bamileke tribe in the southern part of the country, who considered that Ahidjo's government was too closely associated with the Moslem Fulani in the north. Ndongmo, charged in both trials, was given life imprisonment as a result of the first verdict Jan. 5 and death at the second sentencing Jan. 6. Appeals for clemency on his behalf were lodged with Ahidjo by the Vatican Jan. 6 and by U.N. Secretary General U Thant the following day. The death sentences of Mathieu Niassep and Celestin Takala, both UPC members, were also commuted to life Jan. 14. Twenty-five persons were acquitted, with the remaining accused receiving sentences ranging from five years to life imprisonment.

Cabinent changes. President Ahidjo revised his Cabinet Jan. 25. Jean Keutcha was named minister of foreign affairs, replacing Raymond Nteppe, who was given responsibility for one of the missions at the presidency. Onana Awona remained minister of territorial planning but gave up territorial administration to Victor Ayissi Mvodo. Samuel Eboua was named assistant secretary to the presidency and Samuel Naoue was placed in charge of primary education in East Cameroon. It was reported March 12 that Francois-Xavier Ngoubeyou had been appointed minister of youth and sports, replacing Michel Njiensi.

See also AFRICA; MIDDLE EAST [37]

CAMPAIGN GM—*See* AUTOMOBILES [9-12]

CANADA—During 1971, Canada recovered from the state of emergency into which it had been thrown in 1970 by Quebec separatism and the kidnap-murder of Quebec Labor Minister Pierre Laporte. Of the four men accused of the kidnap and murder, three were brought to trial during 1971 and convicted. Canada also attempted during the year to ease federal-provincial relations with a proposed constitutional charter and attempts at bilingualism. In foreign trade and policy, the country's actions were influenced by a growing desire to escape from the influence of U.S. domination. At the end of 1971, Canada enacted a tax bill considered to be one of the most liberal and effective in the Western world.

[2] **Aftermath of Quebec terrorism.** Four members of the outlawed Front de Liberation du Quebec (FLQ)—Paul Rose, his brother Jacques Rose, Francis Simard and Bernard Lortie—Jan. 4 were held "criminally responsible" for the murder of kidnaped Labor Minister Laporte. The four were arraigned Jan. 5 on charges of noncapital murder. Paul Rose, reportedly head of the Chenier cell of the FLQ, was sentenced March 13 to one month in prison for contempt of court and to life imprisonment for his role in the murder of Laporte. The life sentence was mandatory for conviction on charges of noncapital murder. In trying Rose, the prosecution had presented as evidence a controversial 18-page confession statement which Rose allegedly made to two police officers Dec. 29, 1970. In the statement, Rose said that he, his brother, Simard and another unnamed person had murdered Laporte. Rose, however, refused to sign the statement, reportedly for "political reasons," and he denied March 9 that he had even made the statement. Rose was also sentenced Nov. 30 to serve a concurrent life sentence for kidnaping Laporte. He would be eligible for parole on both sentences in 10 years. Lawyer Robert Lemieux filed an appeal on Rose's murder conviction March 24 on the grounds that Rose had been tried in the news media and had been denied Lemieux's services during the trial. (Rose had requested that Lemieux be his lawyer, but Lemieux had been in jail under the War Measures Act invoked to deal with conditions following Laporte's kidnaping. Lemieux received bail Feb. 15 but was fired by Rose Feb. 17 on grounds that the trial was biased and Lemieux's presence would only serve to cover the court's actions.) Simard was sentenced May 20 to life imprisonment for noncapital murder. He also received a four-month sentence for contempt of court, in addition to his one-month sentence for contempt of court in Rose's trial. Lortie was sentenced Nov. 22 to 20 years for the kidnaping. Jacques Rose had not been tried for murder or kidnaping by the end of the year; Simard had not been tried for kidnaping, and Lortie had not been tried for murder.

[3] In other trial actions related to the Laporte kidnap-murder: Robert Langevon, a Quebec high school student, was acquitted Jan. 13 of publishing a seditious libel by drafting and circulating a plan to violently overthrow the Quebec government. The jury reached its decision after Justice Roger Quimet told them they had to decide whether the plan, which the defense admitted Langevon had written, was a "literary exercise" by an impressionable young man or a seditious libel as charged. Justice Quimet Feb. 12 quashed seditious conspiracy charges against five Quebec nationalists accused of being members of the FLQ—Pierre Vallieres, Charles Gagnon, Michel Chartrand, Lemieux and Jacques Larue-Langlois. The charges of advocating the overthrow of the Canadian and Quebec governments between Jan. 1, 1968 and Oct. 16, 1970 were dismissed on the grounds that they covered too long a period of time and lacked "sufficient details" to inform the accused of their alleged offense. However, Vallieres, Gagnon and Larue-Langlois were indicted March 10 on charges of seditious conspiracy through membership in the FLQ. The trial of Vallieres was postponed May 7 until September. Vallieres jumped bail in September and Dec. 20 announced his defection from the FLQ. Gagnon and Larue-Langlois were granted separate trials. Richard Therrien and his sister, Collette, were each sentenced to a year in jail April 15 after admitting that they had sheltered the Laporte kidnapers and communicated statements on behalf of

the FLQ; Francois Belisle and his sister, Francine, both of whom shared an apartment with the Therriens, were sentenced April 26 to jail terms of six months and nine months respectively after pleading guilty to charges of sheltering the kidnapers; Helene Quesnel was sentenced to six months imprisonment April 28 after pleading guilty to charges of sheltering the Rose brothers and Simard; Denise Quesnel and Yves Roy were sentenced April 30 to prison terms of one year and six months respectively on charges of sheltering the Rose brothers and Simard. Claude Lariviere and Louise Verreault were sentenced April 27 to jail terms of two years and one year respectively after pleading guilty to charges ranging from obstructing justice to aiding the FLQ.

[4] Justice Minister John Turner April 29 announced that the government would allow the emergency antiterrorist bill known as Public Order (Temporary Measures) Act 1970, which replaced the War Measures Act and gave police special powers during the Quebec separatist crisis surrounding Laporte's kidnap and murder, to expire on schedule April 30. (The government Jan. 5 had withdrawn the troops deployed in Quebec during the separatist disturbances.) Turner also announced that the government would establish a special joint parliamentary committee to draft a new permanent law against terrorism. Despite the expiration of the Public Order Act, the FLQ would remain an illegal organization under the seditious conspiracy section of the Criminal Code. All charges pending under the act remained valid after expiration.

[5] **External affairs reorganization.** The first major reorganization of the External Affairs Department in 25 years was announced Jan. 21. The reorganization plan, effective Feb. 1, provided for creation of four regional bureaus—European, African and Middle Eastern, Asian and Pacific, and Western Hemisphere affairs—whose directors-general would assume broad responsibility for day-to-day operations of the department areas. Two newly appointed assistant undersecretaries, J. G. H. Halstead and Michel Dupuy, and the department's two top officers, Undersecretary of State A. E. Ritchie and Associate Undersecretary Paul Tremblay, would concentrate on long-term formulation, coordination and supervision of policy. The reorganization plan established six functional bureaus to handle economic and scientific affairs, legal and consular affairs, defense and arms control, public affairs, United Nations affairs, and coordination of policy, including relations with Commonwealth and French-speaking states.

[6] **Labor developments.** Labor Minister Bryce Mackasey March 9 introduced into the Commons a bill amending the Canada Labor Code to provide new standards of protection for laidoff employees, to increase the federal minimum wage from $1.65 to $1.75 per hour (effective July 1) and to provide equal pay and benefits for women. The Labor Code applied to 550,000 employees in industries under federal jurisdiction as well as to about 250,000 federal public servants. Among the provisions of the proposed bill: the Cabinet was authorized to approve further increases in the minimum wage without legislative changes upon recommendation from the labor minister; employers would be required to give advance notice of 8-16 weeks in cases of mass layoffs; dismissed employees, except in cases of retirement or dismissal for just reasons, would be entitled to severance pay on the basis of two days of pay for each year of service for employees with at least five years of service; employers would be required to grant 17 weeks of maternity leave for pregnant female employees; employers would not be able to dismiss an employee solely on the basis of her pregnancy. The bill provided stricter provisions for federal inspection and enforcement procedures and stronger penalties for violations.

[7] Legislation revising the nation's unemployment insurance system was introduced into the Commons March 10. The plan would increase benefits to a maximum of $100 a week from the current $58 weekly, broaden the coverage to include an additional 1,200,000 persons and provide easier access to the plan. The bill would also provide up to 15 weeks of unemployment benefits for those

out of work because of illness or pregnancy. The new bill, which would phase out the existing Unemployment Insurance Act, would require employers and employees to finance most of the unemployment costs when unemployment was below the 4% level, but stipulated that Ottawa would meet almost the full cost of the extra benefits when national unemployment was above 4%. (Throughout 1971, unemployment was at 6% or above, reaching a high of 7.1% for a seasonally adjusted rate in September.)

[8] *Strike developments.* A last-minute contract settlement of a threatened national rail strike was reached April 5, hours before 7,000 members of the Brotherhood of Locomotive Engineers were scheduled to walk off the job. After nearly 90 hours of continuous bargaining, the union and the two major railroads—Canadian Pacific (CP) and Canadian National (CN)—agreed on a new three-year engineers contract providing wage increases of 8% in each of the first two years and 7% in the third year. The agreement was retroactive to March 16, 1970 for CP engineers and to May 1, 1970 for CN engineers. The contract also authorized a change in work rules that would reduce the number of hours to be worked before booking a rest period. Other contract changes included increased health, welfare and vacation benefits. Labor Minister Mackasey had intervened in the dispute March 1 after contract talks broke down and the date was set for the first railway strike in 63 years. The settlement followed a series of wildcat strikes by locomotive engineers in western Canada.

[9] The International Association of Machinists and Aerospace Workers, representing 6,000 ground service personnel of Air Canada, walked out for over 24 hours July 12 and voted overwhelmingly to initiate a series of rotating strikes. The union and airline had been negotiating a new contract since the expiration of their 26-month agreement Dec. 31, 1970. Issues in the dispute included the length of a new agreement, fringe benefits, shift agreements, overtime and job security. Another 24-hour strike took place July 17 at the Toronto International airport, forcing cancellation of over half the scheduled flights. Labor Minister Mackasey July 18 appointed mediators at the request of both parties.

[10] Quebec provincial police walked off the job Sept. 26 for 44 hours after Justice Minister Jerome Choquette refused to accede to an ultimatum which included a demand that they be paid time-and-a-half for 5,000 hours of overtime worked during the Quebec separatist crisis in 1970 (*see* [2-4]). The government had offered to pay half the time at that rate and the remainder in days off before the end of the year. Police returned to work Sept. 28 after agreeing to accept the mediation of Quebec Labor Minister Jean Cournoyer in the dispute.

[11] **Prison riot ends.** A riot broke out at Canada's largest prison, Kingston Penitentiary, April 4 when 500 inmates seized six guards as hostages and took over the main cell block to press demands for better conditions. The riot ended April 18 with one prisoner dead, the victim of his fellow inmates, and 11 others injured, one seriously. (The injured and dead prisoners were believed to be informers and sex deviates.) One guard had been released April 16 "as a sign of good faith," and the five others were released April 18. It was announced April 18 that prison officials had made no concessions to win the release of the hostages. According to a report Aug. 28, five convicts, who pleaded guilty to charges that they had seized the guards, were sentenced to three-year jail terms to run consecutively with their present terms. In response to complaints from prisoners, Solicitor-General Jean-Pierre Goyer announced July 20 that inmates in Canada's 32 federal penal institutions would be permitted to form committees to seek improved prison conditions. The committees, which would be elected by inmates at each institution, would have no administrative or decision-making powers, but would be encouraged to make recommendations on treatment, training, rehabilitation and parole procedures. Members of the committees would be elected twice a year by secret ballot from residential units, cell blocks and workshops to insure broad representation. Committee meetings would be held monthly with the recommendations forwarded to the warden at each institution.

[12]   **Home Oil to remain Canadian.** The purchase of controlling interest in Home Oil Ltd. of Calgary—the last major Canadian-controlled oil company—by Consumers' Gas Ltd. of Toronto was announced by Energy Minister J. J. Greene in the House of Commons April 22. The agreement achieved the federal government's aim to keep Home Oil in Canadian hands. It was reported April 23 that Consumers' Gas would pay $17.6 million for 50.3% of the voting shares of Cygnus Corp., an investment company which controlled Home Oil. R. A. Brown Jr., president of Cygnus and Home Oil, would continue as chief executive officer of the two companies. Pressure on the government to intervene in the sale of Home Oil built up in February after reports that Ashland Oil Inc. of Kentucky was negotiating for purchase of Brown's shares in Cygnus. Critics of foreign ownership of Canada's resources urged the Canadian government to acquire control of Cygnus, if necessary. After exploring that avenue, Greene had announced March 23 that private buyers had re-entered the negotiations. (Consumers' Gas was more than 97% owned by Canadian shareholders.)

[13]   **Cabinet changes.** Communications Minister Eric Kierans April 29 announced his retirement from the Cabinet because of his disagreement with the government's economic policies. He was temporarily replaced April 29 by Jean-Pierre Cote, minister without portfolio, responsible for the post office. Secretary of State Gerard Pelletier was named acting minister of communications May 12. In later changes, Fisheries Minister Jack Davis was sworn in June 11 as the new environment minister (*see* [17]) and Cote was sworn in as postmaster general. Prime Minister Trudeau Aug. 11 announced the elevation of Minister without Portfolio Robert Stanbury to full Cabinet rank as minister of communications. Trudeau also announced the appointment of Martin O'Connell as minister without portfolio and Alastair Gillespie as minister of state for science and technology (*see* [17]). Dr. N. Harvey Lithwick, who was responsible for laying the groundwork for the new Ministry of Urban Affairs (*see* [17]), resigned his top-level post in the ministry Aug. 12.

[14]   **Grain bill controversy.** Legislation was introduced in the Commons April 29 repealing the Temporary Wheat Reserves Act (TWRA) retroactive to July 31, 1970, and replacing its provisions with a plan by which the government would subsidize storage payments on commercially held wheat in excess of 178 million bushels. As a transitional step toward a grain farmers' income stabilization, the new legislation would provide for a payment of $100 million to farmers for the 1970-71 crop year ended July 31. The bill would create a fund to which farmers and the government would contribute on a 1-2 ratio. Grain farmers could draw from the fund in years when their gross income fell below the average of the five previous years. Anticipating passage of the legislation, the government Aug. 1, 1970 suspended payments under the act to the Canadian Wheat Board. Accusing the government of violating the TWRA by withholding grain payments, the opposition Conservatives Sept. 23 introduced a motion of no confidence in the Trudeau government. The motion was defeated 112-72, but opponents of the government decided Sept. 29 to halt all regular Commons business by filibuster and repeated motions to adjourn because the government had flouted the law. The government withdrew the law Oct. 13 after four Saskatchewan farmers refused to postpone legal action against Finance Minister Edgar Benson to force the government to make overdue payments to wheat farmers under the TWRA. In addition to their stalling methods in Commons, opponents of the legislation had encouraged the suit and had initiated impeachment proceedings against Benson, Justice Minister Turner and Otto Lang, minister in charge of the Wheat Board.

[15]   Report urges 37 bilingual districts. The Bilingual Districts Advisory Board, a 10-member body established by the Official Languages Act of 1969, May 4 recommended to the Commons the establishment of 37 bilingual districts in which federal services would be made available in both French and English. The report, which initiated a 90-day period within which the Cabinet must make a final decision on bilingual districts, urged that all of Quebec and New Brunswick be made bilingual districts, in addition to large areas of eastern and northern Ontario and portions of every other province. Among the issues not resolved by the board was bilingualism for minorities of less than 10% of a city's population. The Official Languages Act provided that the French or English minority must constitute at least 10% of the total population in a specific area in order to merit bilingual service in federal offices and agencies. In a later development, the federal government Aug. 17 announced that 29,000 public service employees would be told to conduct their business in French as part of a one-year experiment in bilingualism. The program started during September, October and November, with the emphasis on gradualism and a minimum disruption to services. (*See* [18].)

[16]   Canadian-Soviet pact signed. Prime Minister Trudeau and Soviet Premier Aleksei N. Kosygin signed a protocol agreement (not subject to parliamentary ratification) in Moscow May 19 on consultations designed to encourage greater cooperation between the two nations. The agreement did not interfere with commitments to either nation's allies, but called on both countries to "enlarge and deepen consultations by means of periodic meetings" in order to "strengthen relations of friendship, good-neighborliness and mutual confidence." It pledged the two nations' foreign ministers, or their representatives, to meet "whenever the need arises and, in principle, at least once a year" to discuss political, economic, cultural and environmental issues. It also declared the two governments would consult each other in the event of an international crisis endangering world peace. According to unidentified Canadian sources, the agreement was drafted at Soviet initiative. Explaining Canadian motives in signing, Trudeau said May 20 that Canada wanted "to diversify its channels of communications because of the overpowering presence of the United States."

[17]   Reorganization bill becomes law. The Government Organization Act was given final Senate approval June 10 after months of filibusters by the opposition and repeated compromises. It had been passed by the House of Commons May 25. The act established an Environment Department and permitted the prime minister to create new ministries of state with Commons approval. (The Commons June 21 approved the formation of a Ministry of State for Science and Technology and July 5 approved a Ministry of State for Urban Affairs.) An amendment was approved to allow the new environment minister to also carry the title of fisheries minister, with the Fisheries Department to be eliminated (*see* [13]). The act also would allow the prime minister to appoint as many Parliamentary secretaries as there were ministries. There were currently 16 secretaries and 26 Cabinet ministers.

[18]   Federal-provincial constitutional charter. Prime Minister Trudeau and 10 provincial premiers June 14-17 drafted a compromise constitutional charter after much acrimonious debate and discussion. The central controversy was between those provinces desiring a more centralized federal government and those, headed by Quebec Premier Robert Bourassa, wanting a more decentralized federation with extensive provincial rights. In order to become law, the charter had to be affirmed by all 11 provinces and then endorsed by the two houses of Parliament and the provincial legislatures. Premier Bourassa announced June 23 that Quebec would not accept the draft charter because of its "uncertainties" on points of social welfare. (Bourassa had been under heavy pressure within the province to reject the charter.) The constitutional conference had achieved a consensus which fell short of meeting Quebec's goal of primacy in the social security area, but gave the provinces the right to jurisdiction over family, youth and occupational training allowances. The federal government, however, would set national standards. The draft provided for regional parity, the nomination of Supreme Court justices by the federal justice minister after obtaining the support of the attorney general of the home province of the nominated judge, and a conference of the provincial premiers and the prime minister to be held at least once a year. A provision that would have placed a constitutional obligation on the provinces to provide schooling in the second official language, French, to French-speaking minority children was rejected by the four western premiers and Quebec. (Bourassa opposed any future commitment to provide English-language schools for English-speaking minorities. The Quebec government Jan. 18 had made it compulsory for English-language schools to teach French as a second language.) The charter recognized French as an official language in federal institutions, to be used with English in federal-provincial communications. The charter also permitted the provinces to "provide for more extensive use of English and French" within their "respective legislative jurisdiction."

[19] **New consumer law.** A new law on competition and fair pricing, introduced in the House of Commons June 29. The legislation was designed to crack down on deceptive selling, advertising and business practices that restrict competition, unless the benefits of the restriction would bring tangible benefits to the public. Service companies, including banks, insurance firms and all other previously unregulated activities, would be brought under the new law. New sanctions were proposed to insure that these and other companies—including transportation, manufacturing and retailing firms—would not act to restrict competition. The legislation also called for creation of a quasi-judicial competitive practices tribunal and commissioner to enforce provisions of the act. The tribunal would have broad jurisdiction over mergers, with the capacity to prohibit or dissolve them if they did not conform to broad criteria. Foreign takeovers of Canadian companies would have to insure that the Canadian people would benefit from the takeover.

[20] **White paper stresses new defense role.** The government Aug. 24 released a white paper, indicating policy, which emphasized a new defense role based on territorial sovereignty. The paper called for continued cooperation with the U.S. for continental defense and with North Atlantic allies for European defense, while Canada would direct more of its defense resources to the protection of its sovereignty (especially over the Arctic), its environment and backing up civil police in emergencies. Most of the paper dealt with civil use of defense personnel and resources. It also called for dismantling the Bomarc anti-aircraft missiles with American nuclear warheads. (The installation of the missiles in 1962 had caused a national political controversy, creating a split within the Conservative government and bringing the Liberals into power.) The government also announced that it would lift the freeze on defense spending in the 1972-73 fiscal year and that a revised military manpower ceiling of 83,000 men, an increase of 1,000 over the projected level, would be set for April 1973. While elimination of the Bomarc missiles would save $5 million a year, the Defense Department's budget would increase by about $18 million from the current figure of $1.8 billion. Canada planned no further cuts in military contributions to the North Atlantic Treaty Organization (NATO). The white paper gave qualified approval to Canadian participation in future peacekeeping operations and said the country would accept such an assignment only when governed by realistic terms of reference that reflected "a consensus by all parties on the purposes which the operation was intended to serve." The paper also announced a new government policy requiring that 28% of the total defense establishment be French-speaking to reflect the bilingual and bicultural nature of Canada.

[21] **Program for ethnic groups.** The Trudeau government Oct. 8 announced a program to help Canadians who were of neither British nor French background to preserve and develop their cultures. The program, reportedly designed to meet the complaints of the "New Canadians" of European and Oriental origin that make up nearly one-third of Canada's population, would include grants, commissioned studies and cultural incentives designed to meet the recommendations of the Royal Commission on Bilingualism and Biculturalism. Secretary of State Gerard Pelletier, head of the program, cited four policy objectives: financial assistance to ethnic groups; financing of histories and films stressing the contributions of ethnic groups to Canadian society; promotion of encounters between diverse ethnic groups; and government assistance to immigrants.

[22] **Kosygin visits Canada.** Soviet Premier Kosygin Oct. 17-26 toured Canada, reciprocating for Prime Minister Trudeau's visit to the Soviet Union (*see* [16]). He was the first Soviet leader to visit Canada. Kosygin and Trudeau Oct. 26 issued a joint communique reaffirming "the attachment of Canada and the Soviet Union to peace and security and the development of international peace." Both nations agreed to work together more closely in the economic, technical and scientific fields. The communique called for diversification and expansion of Soviet-Canadian trade and establishment of a joint commission for trade consultations. Kosygin and Trudeau also pledged to seek a ban on underground nuclear tests and proposed a conference on security and cooperation in Europe with the participation of all European states, Canada and the U.S. (*See* EUROPEAN SECURITY.) Rigid security was imposed throughout the trip. A young man Oct. 18 jumped on Kosygin's back and struggled briefly with the premier until Canadian security agents overpowered the assailant, reportedly a member of the Hungarian Freedom Fighters. During the first three days of the visit, Kosygin was also harassed by Jewish and Ukrainian demonstrators protesting the treatment of political prisoners and Jews in the Soviet Union. A crowd of 1,500 protesters demonstrated at the Soviet embassy Oct. 18, and nearly 8,000 Canadian Jews marched through downtown Ottawa Oct. 19 to demand freedom for Soviet Jewry. Kosygin Oct. 20 said that the Soviet Union had "no Jewish question" nor did it have a policy against permitting Jews to leave the country.

[23] **La Presse closes.** La Presse, Quebec's largest newspaper and the largest French-language daily in North America, Oct. 27 announced that publication would cease immediately. The daily had been faced with labor problems and with a public boycott. The labor dispute, centering on contract negotiations dealing with La Presse's plans to invest several million dollars in new equipment that would replace some existing jobs, had led to a lockout of 321 union members July 19. The paper continued publication despite the lockout and the boycott until journalists (not involved in the union dispute) issued a denunciation of the newspaper's management and staged a teach-in Oct. 28 to discuss unfair editorial practices. A union-led demonstration by 10,000 persons in Montreal Oct. 29, protesting the closing of the paper, erupted into a riot in which 200 persons were injured and one killed as demonstrators and police clashed around the La Presse building. An injunction had been issued against the demonstration on the grounds it would lead to violence. Fifty-six policemen were admitted to hospitals for emergency treatment. Sixty persons were arrested and 23 charged in court. Following the La Presse closing, union members Nov. 2 founded Le Quotidien Populaire, but the daily tabloid closed Nov. 15.

[24] **Military pay boost.** Defense Minister Donald Macdonald announced Nov. 5 that the government would increase the salary of most armed forces personnel by 11.5% at a cost to taxpayers of $39.5 million during the current fiscal year. Macdonald told Commons the increases, retroactive to Oct. 1, were designed to bring armed forces salaries in line with civil service employees. He said he hoped it would encourage recruitment.

[25] **Worsening U.S. relations.** Concern with U.S. economic moves that were damaging the Canadian economy (see ECONOMY [8] and TARIFFS & WORLD TRADE [8]) and with the Liberal government's foreign policy of pursuing closer relations with the Soviet Union (see [16, 22]), Communist China and other Communist nations, led Nov. 3 to the Conservative introduction of a motion of no-confidence in the government. The motion was rejected Nov. 4 by a vote of 134-60. In an indication of an apparent nationalist switch in energy policies (see [12]), the Canadian National Energy Board Nov. 19 rejected applications from six companies planning to export 2.66 trillion cubic feet of natural gas to the U.S. The gas was valued at approximately $1 billion. Although the applicants argued that untapped gas and oil resources in the Arctic and on the offshore continental shelf were assurance against any future shortage in Canada, their opponents felt that increasing sales of gas to the U.S. would force Canadian consumers to pay unnecessarily high prices for gas in Canada and would hamper efforts to clean up pollution caused by burning dirtier fuels.

[26] *U.S.-Canadian conference.* Prime Minister Trudeau conferred with President Nixon at the White House Dec. 6. According to Trudeau, the two leaders did not reach any firm trade or defense agreements in their talks, but they moved closer to settling the two countries' outstanding problems. The two leaders talked about the U.S. surcharge, the desirability of balanced trade between the two countries and Canada's movement toward a new foreign ownership policy (see [27]). Trudeau said that the U.S. wanted a "neutral" trade balance but was willing to allow Canada to maintain a trade surplus with the U.S. because it realized that Canada needed the surplus to pay dividends and interest to U.S. investors. Trudeau and Nixon also talked about the India-Pakistan situation (see PAKISTAN [15-21]), the Middle East and Nixon's forthcoming visit to China (see COMMUNIST CHINA-U.S. DETENTE [6]). A parallel meeting was held Dec. 6 between Finance Minister Benson, Industry, Trade and Commerce Minister Jean-Luc Pepin and U.S. Commerce Secretary Maurice Stans and Treasury Secretary John Connally. The four discussed currency exchange rates, defense production sharing (see [20]), problems associated with the 1965 Canadian-U.S. automotive pact and Canada's $25 duty exemption for Canadian visitors returning from the U.S. (The U.S. wanted it increased.) Also under review were Canadian demands that the U.S. end its embargo on Canadian uranium.

[27] **Major tax reform passed.** The Canadian Parliament Dec. 17 passed a sweeping 707-page tax reform bill after six months of debate. Finance Minister Benson, who had proposed the bill June 18, called it "the best system by far" in the Western world in the field of income and corporation taxes. The measure, which would go into effect Jan. 1, 1972, established Canada's first capital gains tax, exempted an estimated one million of Canada's lowest income earners from any income tax, raised income tax rates for an approximate 1.3 million in the upper-income brackets and contained measures to control foreign investment and slow down American takeovers of Canadian businesses. Under the reform in corporate taxation, Canadian businesses with a total yearly income of $400,000 would have to pay only 25% on their first $50,000 of income, while foreign-owned companies would have to pay the full tax rate of 50% on all earnings. Canadian corporations were enabled by the bill to deduct interest on money borrowed to buy shares in other companies. The new law required all pension plans and retirement-savings plans to invest no more than 10% of their funds outside Canada. Other provisions of the bill allowed higher dividend credits for resident shareholders in Canadian firms and an increase from 15% to 25% in the withholding tax on investment income paid to nonresidents.

[28] **Provincial affairs.** *Maritime premiers' council created.* New Brunswick Premier Richard Hatfield, Nova Scotia Premier Gerald Regan and Prince Edward Island Premier Alex Campbell May 25 signed an agreement establishing the Council of Maritime Premiers. The creation of the council had been recommended by a study group in November 1970 as a step toward full

political union in a decade. The three premiers agreed to: establish a Maritime Provinces Higher Education Commission and a Maritime Provinces Industrial Research Council; coordinate policy and programs on environmental matters; establish a central mapping and surveying program, and create a regional data bank and statistical service.

[29] *Ontario vetoes expressway.* Ontario Premier William G. Davis June 3 announced that construction on Toronto's controversial $137 million Spadina Expressway to connect northwest Toronto with the city's downtown core would be halted and a subway built instead. Davis said that in the future his government would emphasize public transit in towns and cities and would discourage systems that would proliferate the use of the passenger car. The expressway, less than a third completed, had been opposed by Toronto citizens, primarily because it would have required the destruction of about 700 homes in a close-knit neighborhood.

[30] *Restructuring of Ontario government.* Premier Davis announced Dec. 10 that he had accepted a massive reorganization plan, occurring "over a period of time," that would reduce the number of Ontario government ministries from 24 to 20, and group them in three policy areas overseen by coordinating ministers. The three areas would be social development, environment and resource development and justice. Two separate ministries that did not fit easily into the policy field concept would be incorporated into an expanded treasury and economic department and an expanded revenue department. These changes would replace the present vertical structure of the 21 departments. Davis said the aim of the recommended changes was to make it easier for ministers to reach day-to-day decisions. He also promised the province's 65,000 civil servants that no jobs would be lost as a result of the reorganization.

See also ABORTION; BIRTH CONTROL; COMMUNIST CHINA-U.S. DÉTENTE [3]; CONSERVATION; DISASTERS; GREAT BRITAIN [9]; GUYANA; HEALTH [10-11]; HIJACKING [8, 15-16]; INTERNATIONAL BANK FOR RECONSTRUCTION & DEVELOPMENT; INTERNATIONAL MONETARY DEVELOPMENTS [14-15]; LATIN AMERICA; NEWSPAPERS; NIXON, RICHARD MILHOUS [2]; OIL; PAKISTAN [35-39]; POLLUTION [11]; SPACE [20]; SPORTS; TARIFFS & WORLD TRADE [2-8]

CANCER—*See* ATOMIC ENERGY [2]; AVIATION [2]; BIRTH CONTROL; HEALTH [6, 8, 12]; MEDICINE; NIXON, RICHARD MILHOUS [1]; POLLUTION [8]
CANNIKIN—*See* ATOMIC ENERGY [16-18]
CAPE VERDE—*See* PORTUGAL
CAPITAL PUNISHMENT—*See* CHURCHES [5]; CRIME [3-4, 20]

CARIBBEAN—Communist influence. An unpublished report issued Oct. 7 by a Georgetown University research center warned that a confrontation between the U.S. and the Soviet Union in the Caribbean might be near. James D. Theberge, director of the research center, said the basic conclusion of the study was that "the Soviet Union ... is again pursuing a more active and adventurous diplomatic and military policy in the Caribbean which raises the risks of another hemispheric confrontation with the U.S."

West Indian unity plan. A blueprint for the formation of a new West Indian nation to incorporate the Republic of Guyana, Dominica, Grenada, St. Kitts-Nevis, St. Lucia and St. Vincent by April 22, 1973, was announced Nov. 1 in a document called the Declaration of Grenada. The declaration, which had been signed by the heads of government of the six states in Grenada July 25, also called for the end of British political presence in the West Indies by April 1973. (Guyana became independent from Britain in 1966; the other signatories were given semi-autonomous status in early 1967.) St. Lucia and Grenada withdrew from the accord Nov. 9, in disappointment that Trinidad & Tobago and Barbados had not agreed to join the union. The four remaining nations in the accord were reported Nov. 14 to be going ahead with the unity plan.

See also CUBA; TARIFFS & WORLD TRADE [10]; TERRITORIAL WATERS

CASTRO, FIDEL—See CHILE [19-20]; CUBA; SPORTS

CENSORSHIP—See OBSCENITY & PORNOGRAPHY; PENTAGON PAPERS

CENSUS, U.S.—See NEGROES; POPULATION; POVERTY; PRISONS [1]

CENTRAL AFRICAN REPUBLIC—President Jean-Bedel Bokassa relinquished the information portfolio in his government Feb. 5 to Joachim da Silva, but resumed it Aug. 3. Bokassa added responsibility for tourism to his other ministerial posts Feb. 5, replacing Claude Kissingou, but abandoned responsibility April 26 to allow tourism to be absorbed by the Ministry of Information. He took control of the newly created Ministry of Public Health and Social Welfare April 26, but gave up responsibility for the post Aug. 3 to Andre Dieu-Donne Magale, former police commandant. In other Cabinet changes Feb. 5: Clement Ngaya-Voueto replaced Maurice Gouandjia as foreign minister; Gouandjia became minister delegate in charge of the government secretariat; Auguste M'Bongo, minister for public works and housing, replaced Guillaume Mokemba-Kenguemba as minister of equipment. In changes April 26: Marie-Joseph Frank, former minister of public welfare, was dropped from the Cabinet, as was Louis Kpado, former interior minister, whose duties were taken over by Jean-Louis Phismis, named minister delegate to the presidency in charge of interior. In other Cabinet changes August 3: Ngaya-Voueto exchanged posts with Joseph Potolot, succeeding Potolot as minister of labor and civil service. In changes Sept. 13, Bokassa assumed Gouandjia's responsibility as keeper of the seals following Gouandjia's resignation as keeper and as minister of justice. Louis-Pierre Gamba was named the new justice minister.

CENTRAL INTELLIGENCE AGENCY (CIA)—See BOLIVIA [7]; COMMUNIST CHINA-U.S. DETENTE [11]; CUBA; ESPIONAGE; FEDERAL BUREAU OF INVESTIGATION [8]; GOVERNMENT REORGANIZATION; GUINEA; INDOCHINA WAR [29-32]; MILITARY [13]; PENTAGON PAPERS [16, 19, 23, 25-26]; TELEVISION & RADIO; WAR CRIMES [8]

CEYLON—Emergency declared. Prime Minister Mrs. Sirimavo R.D. Bandaranaike March 16 declared a state of emergency throughout Ceylon. Troops were called out to guard key centers in various parts of the country. In a further emergency move, Mrs. Bandaranaike March 21 ordered the death penalty for arson, looting, trespass and damage by explosives. The actions were in response to a series of incidents during the previous few weeks, including an alleged attempt to kill Social Services Minister Tikri Banda Tennekoon, the arrest of People's Liberation Front (PLF or "Che Guevarists") leader Rohan Wijeweera, an attack on the U.S. embassy in Colombo March 6 that prompted the mobilization of the armed forces March 7 to maintain order, and the discovery of a huge ammunition and explosives cache on the University of Ceylon campus in Colombo. Mrs. Bandaranaike told the House of Representatives March 23 that the incidents were part of a police-discovered plot by the PLF to mount violent attacks against the government.

Government battles rebels. Forces of the PLF launched an armed rebellion against the government April 5. Heavy fighting continued through April 12, losing in intensity April 13 as insurgents ran low on food and equipment. More than 3,978 rebels surrendered to the government during a May 1-4 amnesty period granted by the government in an effort to undercut the uprising, but battles continued through May. Mrs. Bandaranaike July 20 told the House of Representatives that about 1,200 persons, including 60 soldiers, had been killed in the two-month rebellion. According to the prime minister, damage caused by the guerrillas totaled millions of dollars and about 14,000 persons were under detention.

The uprising, which the PLF waged to overthrow the leftist coalition government on the ground that it had not carried out a program of socialist reform, was announced April 6. At that time, Mrs. Bandaranaike announced the imposition of a nationwide 3 p.m. to 6 a.m. curfew and formally banned the PLF. The curfew was extended for 24 hours April 9 as the fighting raged unabated. Mrs. Bandaranaike, in a radio appeal to the nation to help crush the uprising, said that many rebels had been killed and the situation was under control. She pledged to continue the struggle. Acknowledging the rebel demand for changes, she insisted that reforms must be achieved through peaceful democratic means. In a further crackdown against the rebellion, the government was reported April 10 to have decreed the death penalty for anyone aiding the insurgents or plotting to kill government officials, policemen or soldiers. The launching of a general offensive by Ceylonese forces was reported by official sources April 12. The curfew was relaxed April 15 as the fighting tapered off. The government April 18 formed a seven-member committee, headed by Irrigation, Power and Highways Minister Maithripala Senanayake, to "re-establish civil authority" in areas affected by the rebellion. Senanayake April 23 announced a rehabilitation program for rebels who surrendered to the government. Under the program, internees were sent to a rehabilitation center just outside Colombo where they were to "attend lectures ... that will lead them to think along democratic lines."

In response to Mrs. Bandaranaike's request for international assistance, arms and equipment were sent to the Ceylonese government by Britain, India, Pakistan and the Soviet Union. U.S.S.R. assistance included sending a military training mission to Ceylon May 7. The U.S. was also said to have been asked to supply arms, but had sent only spare aircraft parts.

Senate abolished. A bill abolishing Ceylon's senate was approved Oct. 3 by William Gopallawa, the royal governor. The measure had been passed by the House of Representatives, which became the country's sole legislative body.

See also PAKISTAN [7]

CHAD—Peace accord signed. President Francois Tombalbaye signed a peace agreement Jan. 18 at Fort Archambault with leaders of the six-year Chadian rebellion. Despite the accord, however, fighting continued in some parts of the country. The agreement, signed by Tombalbaye and six members of Frolinat (National Liberation Front of Chad), obliged the government to unify the country by practicing justice at the administrative level, especially in the north, releasing political detainees and meeting the other rebel leaders. (Frolinat headquarters in Algiers denounced the agreement Jan. 20, reaffirming its intention to oppose the Tombalbaye government.) A peace accord had been signed Jan. 6 at Fort-Lamy, the country's capital, with 12 leaders of the Moubi tribe, who were among the first to rebel against the government in 1965. A group of rebel leaders meeting at Mangalme Jan. 28 welcomed the Fort Archambault pact and expressed hope that the government would keep its promises. The group declared it had broken all contacts with Dr. Abba Sidick, one of the original leaders of Frolinat.

New government formed. A new Cabinet, including three former political prisoners, was announced May 23 as a result of President Tombalbaye's policy of "national reconciliation and development," adopted at a recent congress of the ruling Progressive party. The new ministers, who had been imprisoned in 1963 on charges of subversive activity, were Djibrine Kerallah (finance), Baba Hassane (foreign affairs) and Mohamed Abdel Kerim (stockbreeding). (Kerallah was appointed Dec. 26 to the post of minister of state to the presidency. He was replaced as finance minister by Elie Romba. In another change the same day, Tombalbaye assumed the defense portfolio.)

The congress, held March 30-April 5, had elected a new Political Bureau that included Kerallah. Tombalbaye declared April 18 that the congress "proved that our national reconciliation is a reality" and that it had given him "the mandate to free all our countrymen currently deprived of their freedom for political reasons." Tombalbaye announced that two other political prisoners, Silas Selingar, former permanent undersecretary in the president's office, and Jean Baptiste, former minister of social affairs, health and labor, were dead. The Chadian president explained that Selingar had been shot while trying to escape from prison after being arrested for ordering the killing of Jean Baptiste, who had been imprisoned for subversion in 1963. It was reported that 150 political prisoners were released May 11. Another 60 prisoners had been released May 6.

Libya accused in coup attempt. The Chadian government Aug. 27 broke diplomatic relations with Libya after what it described as a "foreign-directed" coup attempt launched that day had failed to oust President Tombalbaye. In a speech before the diplomatic corps at Fort-Lamy, Foreign Minister Hassane accused Libya of "openly trying to interfere in the internal affairs of our young republic with the help of a major imperialist power and through a third party intermediary." The government had long regarded Libya as a supporter of the armed rebellion against Tombalbaye's rule which had been in progress in the northern and eastern parts of the country since 1965. In the midst of a news blackout from Fort-Lamy, the events of the attempted coup were difficult to reconstruct. Hassane said in his speech that the move had been led by Ahmed Abdallah, reportedly a former deputy in the Chadian National Assembly, who had committed suicide after being captured with an undisclosed number of followers.

See also AFRICA, HEALTH [1]

CHAFEE JOHN H.—*See* PUERTO RICO

CHEMICAL & BIOLOGICAL WARFARE (CBW)—U.S. moves gas from Okinawa. The U.S. Army Jan. 13 began moving the first shipment of poisonous mustard gas from its Chibana ammunition dump in Okinawa to the port of Tengan for transfer to Johnston Island, 750 miles southwest of Hawaii. Removal of the gas was completed Sept. 10. The U.S. had pledged to remove the 13,000 tons of gas before returning Okinawa and other islands of the Ryukyu group to Japan in 1972. Okinawans protesting that not enough safety measures were being taken in moving the gas through civilian areas had staged violent demonstrations Jan. 10, 11 and 13.

U.S. use of tear gas backed. The wartime use of tear gas and herbicides was defended March 22 by a Pentagon official who urged that they not be dropped from the U.S. arsenal. G. Warren Nutter, assistant secretary of defense for international security affairs, made the assertion before the Senate Foreign Relations Committee. Nutter appeared before the panel to support Senate ratification of the 1925 Geneva Protocol banning chemical and biological weapons. (The Nixon Administration had said it supported the treaty with the understanding that it would not bar the use of tear gas and plant killers by the U.S.) Nutter described tear gas and plant killers as legitimate, humane weapons of war.

Stocks destroyed. In accordance with President Nixon's orders and his November 1969 announcement that the U.S. would destroy all its existing germ stocks, the Army began July 7 to destroy the nation's CBW stocks, most of which were stored at the Pine Bluff Arsenal in Arkansas. (Nixon had announced Jan. 27 that the Pine Bluff facilities would be dismantled and the installation's labs used for Food and Drug Administration research into the effects of chemical poisons on man.) At the same time, the Army began to dismantle the weapons that would have been used to deliver the lethal agents against an enemy. The Army estimated that it would take 48 weeks and cost about $10 million to destroy the stocks. According to the Army, only a small quantity of CBW agents was being kept at facilities around the U.S. to continue the development of serums and vaccines against them. There was no chance, the Army said, that the few remaining stocks would be used to rebuild an offensive arsenal. The stocks destroyed at the Arsenal, announced for the first time, included a shellfish poison, Botulinum Toxin A (a food poisoning),

Bacillus Anthacis (responsible for anthrax) and Coxiella Butnettii (responsible for Q fever).

Sen. Frank Church (D, Idaho) Jan. 22 had challenged the credibility of Nixon's renunciation of biological warfare in light of reports that the Army planned to expand its testing facilities at Deseret, Utah. According to Church, the installation would be the largest biological warfare center in the world, employing 190 military personnel and 250 civilians. Church alleged that the expansion was to be carried out under secret orders.

U.N. bans germ weapons. The United Nations General Assembly Dec. 16 approved a treaty outlawing biological methods of warfare. The document had been worked out jointly by the U.S. and the Soviet Union and had been submitted in September to the U.N. Conference of the Committee on Disarmament in Geneva.

See also DISARMAMENT; NIXON, RICHARD MILHOUS [3]; POLLUTION [15]

CHEMISTRY—*See* NOBEL PRIZES
CHIANG KAI-SHEK—*See* UNITED NATIONS [8]

CHILE—Enterprise visit canceled. The U.S. Department of Defense announced Feb. 27 that a courtesy call, planned for Feb. 28, by the U.S. aircraft carrier Enterprise to the Chilean port of Valparaiso had been called off. The department said "the operating schedule does not permit the ship to make this port of call and still make her scheduled commitments." President Salvador Allende had announced the planned visit in a national broadcast Feb. 25. He reportedly had extended the invitation for the ship's visit during a meeting with U.S. Chief of Naval Operations Adm. Elmo Zumwalt Feb. 19. Cancellation of the ship's visit reportedly came after bureaucratic in-fighting between the Defense and State Departments. According to report Feb. 28, the State Department had recommended cancellation of the visit and had been quickly supported by the White House.

[2] **Bethlehem Mines sales set.** President Allende confirmed March 27 that Chile had signed a contract with Bethlehem Iron Mines Co. of Pennsylvania to purchase its iron mines in Chile. The sale, the first major takeover in Chile's policy of nationalizing all mining resources, would reportedly bring Bethlehem $30 million, with payments to be made over 17 years with interest at 5.5%. The first instalment would be paid in July 1973. According to a report March 28, the Armco Steel Corp. had agreed on a sale to the Chilean government of 35.7% of its interest in Armco-Chile for $1 million. Armco would retain a 34.3% interest.

[3] **Ex-minister assassinated.** Edmundo Perez Zujovic, former interior minister and head of the rightist wing of the Christian Democrat party (DC), was assassinated June 8. He died of five bullet wounds in a car ambush outside his home by three men firing submachine guns. The government immediately placed the province of Santiago under a state of emergency, suspending some constitutional rights, and imposed a five-hour night curfew. Military units were placed on alert throughout the country. Police announced June 8 that they had implicated Roland Rivera Calderon, a member of the extremist Marxist group the Organized People's Vanguard (VOP), in connection with the slaying. Rivera Calderon was identified by Perez Zujovic's daughter, who was with her father at the time of the attack. Rivera Calderon, and his brother Arturo (also accused of Perez Zujovic's murder), were killed June 13 in a gunfire exchange with police as the police converged on a private garage that was apparently a munitions armory for the VOP. Three men and three women were arrested in the garage. A third VOP member suspected of the former interior minister's murder, Heriberto Salazar Bello, burst into police headquarters June 16, killed two detectives and pulled a grenade, killing himself. In a related development, the Communist and Socialist parties, the most powerful groups in the Allende Popular Unity coalition (UP), charged in official statements June 10 that the

U.S. Central Intelligence Agency (CIA) was behind the assassination of Perez Zujovic.

[4] **Copper nationalized.** The Chilean Congress July 11 unanimously approved a constitutional amendment authorizing the president to nationalize the copper properties of the American-owned Kennecott, Anaconda and Cerro corporations. The vote constituted final ratification of the constitutional amendment. In compensation proceedings, Chilean Comptroller General Hector Humeres announced Oct. 11 that Anaconda and Kennecott should receive no compensation for their nationalized properties. Cerro Corp., which owned 70% of a new mine, was held to have a claim of $14 million. Humeres set a book value of $242 million on Anaconda's Chuquicamata mine and a value of $319 million on Kennecott's El Teniente mine. (Under the nationalization law, the comptroller general was to determine indemnification based on the companies' book value as of Dec. 31, 1970.) President Allende, however, had announced Sept. 28 that $774 million in "excess profits" earned by the companies in the previous 10 years would be deducted from indemnification. After the deduction of $300 million in excess profits plus $18 million for other charges, Anaconda was left with a claim of $76 million against it. The Kennecott deduction of $410 million in excess profits plus other deductions left a claim of $310 million against the firm. Humeres said the nationalization law provided only for indemnification, not for the collection of a net deficit. U.S. Secretary of State William P. Rogers Oct. 13 told Chile that its decision not to compensate the firms was a "serious departure from expected standards of international law." Rogers warned that the action might jeopardize the flow of private investment funds to Chile and erode the base of support for foreign aid to Chile and other developing nations. Kennecott and Anaconda Dec. 3 appealed the compensation decision to a five-man copper tribunal created by the nationalization act. The court, which was to decide whether Allende's right to deduct excess profits was subject to review, was made up of three officials appointed by Allende, a member of the Supreme Court and a member of the Court of Appeals of Santiago.

[5] **Copper strike.** The first strike in the nationalized copper industry began Aug. 1 when 5,000 workers of the El Salvador mine refused a formula arrangement for a 38% pay increase offered by the company and asked for a raise of 45%. The position of the strikers was considered a direct challenge to the UP government. The strike ended Aug. 12 as workers reportedly accepted a 43% wage increase, including an automatic moving scale for cost-of-living adjustments. The labor conflict represented an estimated loss of $2,200,000 in production revenues.

[6] **Cabinet crisis.** President Allende faced his first Cabinet crisis when four ministers, members of the UP, submitted their resignations Aug. 7. The resignations were a result of divisions within both the Radical party and the Unified Popular Action Movement (MAPU). The four Cabinet members were Orlando Cantuarias (mines), Mario Astorga (education) and Alejandro Valdivia (defense) of the Radical party and Jacques Chonchol (agriculture) of MAPU. Radical party members told Allende that he must either "refuse or accept totally the resignations," leaving Allende in a position where he could not accept some resignations and reject others. The crisis was resolved Aug. 11 when Allende refused the four resignations and accepted the resignation of Oscar Jiminez Pinochet, health minister from the Socialist party. He resigned Aug. 10 to allow Allende to give the ministry to a MAPU representative.

[7] Offers to resign by ranking government officials were traditional when their party was undergoing an internal crisis. The Radical party had split Aug. 3 when Radical Senator Americo Acuna announced that he and 10 other senators and deputies had made an "irrevocable" decision to abandon the Radical party after a party congress declared the party to be "Socialist" and a "workers' party." Acuna said his faction would continue to work within the UP coalition, adding that they considered themselves "democratic socialists and not

Marxists." The defectors said they would form a new Independent Radical party, pledged to support the interests of the middle class. MAPU minister Chonchol and three MAPU representatives left MAPU, which had split from the DC in 1969, in order to affiliate themselves with the new Christian Left movement. (The Christian Left movement had been formed July 28 when leadership of the youth wing of the DC resigned to protest the party's alliance with the rightist National and Democratic Radical parties in a special congressional election in Valparaiso earlier in the month. The movement had gained strength July 31 as six parliamentary deputies resigned from the DC to join the movement.) Chonchol and his followers criticized MAPU for converting itself into a party "of strong Marxist content" and of adopting "as its fundamental basis a category of Marxist-Leninist thought."

[8]   U.S. refuses jet purchase loan. The U.S. Export-Import Bank (Eximbank) Aug. 11 rejected a Chilean request for $21 million in loans and loan guarantees for the purchase of three Boeing jetliners for the national airline LAN. The loan was refused because of the unresolved issue of compensation for the U.S. copper mining investments (*see* [4]). It was reported that Chile had been negotiating with the State Department, Eximbank and the Boeing Co. for six months, offering to pay $5 million toward the $26 million price, provided that Eximbank agreed to underwrite 40% of the cost in guarantees to five U.S. private banks plus another 40% as a direct loan to Boeing. Top officials of LAN left for the Soviet Union Sept. 13 to negotiate the purchase of eight Soviet commercial jets to replace their fleet of Boeing planes.

[9]   Land seizure developments. The government Sept. 12 acted to arrest the directors of an illegal campaign of seizing farms. The seizures, by peasants dissatisfied with the rate of agrarian reform instituted by the government, were allegedly led, in some instances, by leftist university students and members of the Movement of the Revolutionary Left (MIR), as well as by some local officials of Allende's government. Allende had asked Congress in February for the power to imprison leaders of the campaign. In two moves to redistribute land, Agriculture Minister Chonchol Nov. 24 gave deeds to houses and small parcels of land to 1,500 persons at Limache and Dec. 19 did the same to 1,330 farmers in Cochagua province.

[10]   Allende closes, reopens UPI office. President Allende Sept. 15 announced that his government had decided to close the United Press International (UPI) offices in Chile. Allende said the decision was based on a UPI report printed Sept. 14 which quoted the Colombian newspaper El Tiempo as saying that Colombia was investigating the possibility that a Chilean plane, carrying some of Allende's bodyguards from the president's trip to Colombia and reported lost en route to Ecuador, had landed in Colombia with arms and subversive literature for guerrillas. Allende also accused UPI of distributing false and partial news printed by foreign governments which presented a false image of his government. Interior Minister Jose Toha reportedly said Sept. 16 that the government's action was aimed at UPI, not at any of its correspondents, who would not be expelled. He said UPI would no longer be able to distribute international news in Chile nor send news from Chile outside the country. He said the action would not affect UPI's national service. The Interior Ministry announced Sept. 26 that Allende had reversed his decision and would permit UPI to continue operations, but that the conduct of the UPI bureau chief in Santiago, Martin P. Houseman, was "unacceptable" and he would have to be removed. It was reported that Allende reversed his decision following a series of talks with UPI's Latin American manager, William McCall, who allegedly had agreed that UPI "transmitted false news stories that affected Chile internationally."

[11]   Government takes over ITT operations. The government Sept. 24 decided to take over operation of the Chilean Telephone Co. in order to prevent interruption in service. Interior Minister Toha said the government was continuing to discuss nationalization plans with International Telephone and

Telegraph (ITT), which owned 70% of the operation. Toha said the intervention was due to "precariousness of service" which, unless remedied, "could harm national security."

[12] Christian Democrats drop support. The DC broke off its working compact with the UP government Sept. 24, reportedly as a result of a prolonged campaign against DC leaders in the leftist Santiago press. Included in the campaign was a series of personal attacks against former President Eduardo Frei Montalva, a Christian Democrat, in newspapers controlled by the Communist and Socialist parties that form the government. It was reported that detailed changes in DC party policy would soon be worked out, but the break from loyal opposition took effect immediately.

[13] Nationalization bill sent to Congress. President Allende Oct. 19 sent Congress a bill listing 150 Chilean firms, regarded by the government as playing a key role in the economy, to be nationalized. The bill, which left most of the nation's industries and businesses unaffected, divided the economy into three areas. The 150 firms, after compensation, would enter the "social area," becoming the property of the state. There would also be a mixed area of both state and private capital and a totally private sector. It was reported Oct. 21 that opposition to the legislation was already intense and that the DC had introduced a rival bill which would give nationalization power to the legislature rather than to the executive.

[14] Imports restricted. President Allende, according to report Nov. 3, ordered that imports be restricted to essentials in an attempt to avert a crisis in the country's foreign currency reserves, which had reportedly dropped from about $400 million to $175 million during the year in which the UP held power. The Chilean Central Bank imposed a 10,000% prior deposit charge on more than 75% of all capital and consumer goods imported from abroad. Under the restriction, a company that wanted to import $100 worth of goods would be required to deposit $10,000 in the central bank.

[15] Major reform bill rejected. President Allende Nov. 11 sent to Congress a sweeping constitutional reform bill to implement most of the government's revolutionary programs. The legislation was rejected, however, by the Constitutional Committee of the Chamber of Deputies Nov. 27 by a vote of 8-4 with one abstention. (The committee, dominated by opponents of the UP government, also moved to block any attempt by the president to dissolve Congress by introducing a bill that dissolution could be approved only by a national referendum.) Allende had said that he would call a national plebiscite if Congress rejected the bill. The DC opposition had decided to seek a plebiscite but was first inserting amendments in the bill to blur the simple issue requiring "yes" or "no" answers with which the government hoped to obtain a popular majority.

[16] The legislation would replace the existing two-house Congress with a unicameral legislature, broaden the president's powers and make basic changes in the Supreme Court. Under the reform, legislation would be permitted by petitioners who collected 5,000 signatures. The Communist-led Central Confederation of Labor would also be permitted to introduce legislation, and the president would be able to require Congress to act on certain bills within 30 days. The reform also suggested that Supreme Court judges be elected by Congress for unrenewable six-year terms.

[17] Renegotiation of foreign debt planned. President Allende announced Nov. 9 that the government would seek to negotiate its foreign debt, which totaled more than $3 billion. Allende said the government would fulfill its promise to assume all obligations contracted by previous Chilean governments, but that the debt repayment schedule was incompatible with sustaining a sufficient rate of development in the new Socialist structure of investment in Chile. (The current schedule called for payment of $300 million in 1971, with $400 million to be paid in both 1972 and 1973.) In his speech, Allende cited the closing of credit lines of $190 million by U.S. banks and the decline of international copper prices as causes for the debt renegotiation. Enrique Bernstein, head of the foreign affairs committee in the Chilean Foreign Ministry, arrived in London Dec. 7 to examine the possibility of renegotiating Chile's debts to Britain.

[18] University clashes. Clashes erupted Nov. 17, 22 and 26 in a conflict at the University of Chile between Marxist professors and students who wanted to restructure the university's 12 schools and anti-Marxists who claimed the restructuring was part of a plan to bring the autonomous institution under control of the government. The Marxists claimed a 57-47 majority on the university governing board. In fighting Nov. 17, anti-Marxists occupied two of the university's faculties and suspended 50% of classes. Students of the leftist Chilean Students Federation occupied the headquarters building of the university and detained university rector Edgardo Boeninger for several hours. Boeninger then led 200 students and professors to the presidential palace to protest the takeover of the headquarters, but they were prevented from entering the palace by police using tear gas. President Allende Nov. 19 ordered the criminal prosecution of Boeninger, opposition parliament members and students for "violent entry" and "assault" against the palace guard. The Nov. 22 clash involving more than 2,000 students erupted in the center of Santiago as anti-Marxist students from the private Catholic University staged a march to show solidarity with the University of Chile students who were demanding a plebiscite to determine whether a majority of students wanted restructuring of the university. The Nov. 26 clash erupted as 1,000 anti-Marxist students marched from the University of Chile law school, where students had occupied the building for a month, to Congress. The Marxist majority on the university governing board refused to approve the plebiscite and Nov. 26 challenged Boeninger and the university council to resign so that new elections of university officials could be held. The university crisis spread to Valparaiso Nov. 25 where more than a dozen students were injured.

[19] Castro visit. Cuban Premier Fidel Castro, a long-time friend of President Allende, visited Chile Nov. 10 to Dec. 4. The Cuban premier's trip, his first to Latin America since 1959, was to have lasted only 10 days but was extended to 25. The visit signified a breach in the united policy of diplomatic and economic boycott begun when the Organization of American States (OAS) expelled Cuba in 1962. (The Allende government had resumed relations with Cuba shortly after it took office in 1970.) Castro, who maintained a controlled, moderate position during his trip, received an enthusiastic welcome, mainly among organized students and workers.

[20] Riots bring on state of emergency. A state of emergency was declared in Santiago Dec. 2 after more than 150 persons were injured in violence set off by a Dec. 1 march by 5,000 women protesting food shortages and the Castro visit. The "March of the Empty Pots," organized by the DC and National parties, began peacefully as a march of women beating pots and pans, but turned into the largest and most violent demonstration since the Allende government took office. The violence began when bands of youths from the MIR and the Communist party's Ramona Parra Youth Brigade threw rocks at the women and 80 club-carrying youths escorting them. Riot police fired tear gas grenades among the demonstrators, but a group of 200 women regrouped and was intercepted by Communist youths. More than 100 rock-throwing youths were arrested by national police. Street clashes between Marxist and anti-Marxist youths continued through the night. Shortly after daybreak Dec. 2, Allende declared a state of emergency which banned street demonstrations, allowed arrests without warrants and imposed news censorship. Later in the day, anti-Marxist youths defied the state of emergency and demonstrated in a new outburst against the government. Gen. Augusto Pinochet, commander of the Santiago army garrison, Dec. 3 imposed a 1 a.m.-6 a.m. curfew. Interior Minister Toha Dec. 2 ordered the shutdown of two opposition radio stations which had broadcast repeated calls Dec. 1 for women to take part in the march.

(The DC voted Dec. 3 to begin impeachment proceedings against Toha on charges of tolerating armed extremist groups. Leftist Christian Democrats opposed the motion, which could lead to the resignation of a minister who was widely believed to be a moderating influence on the government.)

[21] *Allende imposes state food control.* President Allende Dec. 8 announced that the government would take over full control of food distribution as part of an "offensive against fascist sedition." He also called for the organization of "neighborhood vigilance committees" to fight food hoarders and black marketers. The government had assumed control of three major wholesale distributors and ordered 22 cattle auction markets under state management Dec. 7. Important sectors of wholesale food distribution were already under government control, particularly all marketing of beef, wheat, sugar and other basic products. The government had announced it also would extend state control and open state stores in populous low-income neighborhoods.

[22] **Broadcasters strike.** Broadcasting workers at all of Santiago's 23 radio stations struck Dec. 24 when union negotiations failed to meet their demands for 45% pay raises. Fourteen stations supporting the government accepted a government arbitrator's ruling Dec. 25 in favor of a 25% pay raise and went back to work. (Opposition politicians claimed that the stations had received promises that enough official advertising would be placed with them to pay for the salary increase.) The remaining nine stations, all aligned with the opposition, remained on strike until Dec. 30, when they agreed to concessions made by the government.

See also ARGENTINA [10]; COLOMBIA; CUBA; EARTHQUAKES; FOREIGN POLICY; HIJACKING [8]; LATIN AMERICA; PERU

CHINA, COMMUNIST (PEOPLE'S REPUBLIC OF CHINA)—Escapees to Hong Kong barred.

China was reported Jan. 11 to have ordered stricter border controls to prevent its citizens from escaping to Hong Kong. The order was contained in a directive issued in Kwangtung Province, adjacent to the British crown colony. The directive called for prison terms of "more than 10 years" for anyone caught attempting to flee and ordered border guards to "pursue and execute on the spot" persons resisting arrest. It included close surveillance of Chinese visitors from Hong Kong and the nearby Portuguese colony of Macao, the use of more political agents among the populated Chinese areas adjacent to Hong Kong and Macao and more stringent controls on goods entering and leaving Kwangtung. A dispatch from Hong Kong Sept. 11 said the number of Chinese fleeing to the colony was increasing and was expected to exceed 20,000 in 1971. Hong Kong authorities had reported Sept. 6 that about 2,500 Chinese had been arrested after swimming from the mainland to Hong Kong between January and August—almost three times the 1970 figure of 900, and only a small percentage of the refugees to reach the colony without arrest.

1970 economic report. According to statistical estimates released by the Japanese Foreign Office March 4, China's economy showed improvement in 1970. The report said: "In 1969 the Chinese economy recovered to the level before the (1965-69) Cultural Revolution. There was a further rise in 1970." Among the reported gains: industrial production increased by 15%-20%; agricultural output was up between 5%-10%; the gross national product grew by about 10% and reached $74 billion; 220-230 million metric tons of grain and vegetables were harvested; foreign trade increased slightly to about $4.3 billion. (According to a statistical report issued in Paris July 27, four-fifths of China's foreign trade was with capitalist countries in 1970, compared with only one-fifth in 1960. West Germany, followed by Great Britain and France, was China's largest trading partner in Western Europe. Peking's trade with other Asian countries had also increased sharply since 1966.)

Chi heads Foreign Ministry. Deputy Foreign Minister Chi Peng-fei was reported March 27 to have assumed the functions of foreign minister, although Foreign Minister Chen Yi retained his post. Chen had disappeared from public view April 1969.

Party rebuilding completed. The restructuring of the Communist party at the province level following the disruptions caused by the Cultural Revolution was completed Aug. 26 as the last three of China's 29 provincial party committees were formed.

Economics body formed. The formation of a new Ministry of Economic Affairs was reported Sept. 12. The new body was said to have been created from the former State Economic Commission, which apparently had ceased operations during the Cultural Revolution. The existence of the new ministry was first disclosed in a broadcast the previous week from Shihkhiachwang, capital of Hopeh Province, in a report on a conference on improved gasoline engines. Of the 40 government ministries that had existed in the central government before the Cultural Revolution, only 17 were known to be in operation.

National Day celebration. China celebrated National Day (marking the establishment of the country in 1949) in Peking Oct. 1 amid foreign speculation that the country was in the grip of a political crisis. The speculation had been touched off Sept. 21 by the announcement that the customary National Day parade was being canceled. China's Canton television station had announced Sept. 26 that "a special and important news program" concerning the "circumstances of the Oct. 1 National Day celebration" would be broadcast Sept. 28, but the program was delayed and then dropped. In addition to the cancellation of the parade, the Communist party newspaper Jenmin Jih Pao failed to carry its usual editorial marking the founding of the government and did not publish the customary large photographs of Chairman Mao Tsetung and Deputy Chairman and Defense Minister Lin Piao. Mao did not attend the National Day celebrations in Tienanmen Square; nor did the Politburo members of the armed services—Huang Yung-sheng (army), Wu Fa-hsien (air force) and Li Tso-peng (navy)—who had not been mentioned or seen in more than three weeks. Also adding to the speculation that China was faced with some kind of unrest was the absence of Premier Chou En-lai and other top-ranking officials from a National Day eve reception Sept. 30.

Lin Piao ouster hinted. A report Nov. 8 of the promotion of former army Marshal Yeh Chien-ying to fourth place in the Communist party's Politburo raised speculation that Defense Minister Lin, Mao's officially designated successor, had been ousted from his post in a major reshuffle of Peking's leadership. The report, listing six of the full members of the Politburo at a Peking rally Nov. 8 for the 30th anniversary of the Albanian Communist party, placed Yeh after Premier Chou and Chiang Ching, Mao's wife. Yeh's new duties were not specified, but it was believed he may have taken over Lin's defense post or his job as executive of the party's Military Commission. Lin, who along with other top military men had been absent from public view for several months, had been variously reported seriously ill or involved in an internal crisis. It was reported Nov. 9 that Lin and others had plotted to assassinate Mao on three separate occasions. The same report said that the Chinese plane reported to have crashed in Mongolia the night of Sept. 12-13 possibly carried Lin and eight others during an aborted attempt to flee China following an alleged hijacking of the aircraft. All nine persons aboard the plane were listed as dead, some from pistol shots. U.S. intelligence sources were reported as saying that the crisis in Peking had come to a head about Sept. 11 when Lin and his followers were forced out by Mao and Chou. According to the U.S. report, Lin and some military leaders were said to have advocated economic priorities favorable to the armed forces while the Mao-Chou faction preferred to have the country's economic resources allocated largely for non-military use. Lin was also said to have opposed Peking's new policy of detente with the West (*see* COMMUNIST CHINA-U.S. DETENTE).

Shifts forced. The apparent fall of Lin and other top military leaders from power was reported to have resulted in a major reshuffling of the government hierarchy. The upheaval was said to include Mao's takeover of the armed forces (reported in the U.S. Nov. 27 on the basis of Chinese radio broadcasts and newspapers) and the elevation of Chou to second position in the Politburo. A report Nov. 28 said that Chou, formerly listed third after Lin in the Politburo standing, was now directly behind Mao. The advancement of Chiang Ching from sixth to third place was said to have been brought about by the purging of Chen Po-ta and the disappearance from public life of Keng Sheng, both former top Politburo leaders. Other purges and illnesses were said to have reduced the Politburo membership from 21 to nine. Other Politburo members who had disappeared from view were: Yeh Chun, Lin's wife; Wu Fa-hsien (see above); Li Tso-peng (see above); Chieu Hui-tso, a deputy chief of staff; Hsu Shih-yu, a deputy defense minister; Hsieh Fuchih, head of the Peking Revolutionary Committee; and Chu Teh and Liu Po-cheng, military men. In continuation of the purge, U.S. specialists reported Nov. 29 that Li Hsueh-feng, an associate of Lin, had been dropped as an alternate Politburo member.

See also ATOMIC ENERGY [20]; AUSTRALIA [7-8]; BULGARIA; CANADA [25]; COMMUNISM, INTERNATIONAL; COMMUNIST CHINA-U.S. DETENTE; DISARMAMENT; ESPIONAGE; FOREIGN AID; FOREIGN POLICY; HIJACKING [7]; INDIA; INDOCHINA WAR [21, 72]; JAPAN [4, 9, 12-13]; KOREA, NORTH; KOREAN RELATIONS; MIDDLE EAST [26]; PAKISTAN [40, 42-43]; PENTAGON PAPERS [18-19, 22]; PERU; POLAND; RUMANIA; SINO-SOVIET DEVELOPMENTS; SOUTHERN YEMEN; SPACE [16]; SPORTS; STORMS; TURKEY [7]; UNION OF SOVIET SOCIALIST REPUBLICS [5]; UNITED NATIONS [7-10, 12-13]; VIETNAM, NORTH

CHINA, NATIONALIST (REPUBLIC OF CHINA)—U.S. missionary ousted. The
Nationalist Chinese government March 2 ordered the ouster from Taiwan of an American missionary, the Rev. M.L. Thornberry, and his wife. No explanation for the deportation was given, but the Thornberrys were known to have been friendly with a number of native Taiwanese opposed to the Taipei government. Thornberry was a missionary of the United Methodist Church and had served in Taipei since 1964. The expulsion order, along with other recent incidents, reportedly created an air of tension among government officials and dissident elements and within the foreign community in Taiwan. Some of the incidents were believed connected with a growing feeling of anti-Americanism reportedly linked to Washington's new stance toward Communist China. (*See* COMMUNIST CHINA-U.S. DETENTE) The Bank of America's Taipei branch was shaken by an explosion Feb. 4. Police attributed the blast to a gas leak, but bank officials denied there was any gas on the premises. Four windows of the U.S. embassy's consular office in Taipei were broken by stones Feb. 9.

U.S. aides linked to dissidents. The U.S. was reported May 31 to have transferred from Taiwan at least five aides following Nationalist Chinese government charges that they had assisted the outlawed Taiwanese independence movement. The Defense Ministry was said to have filed a protest in April with U.S. military and diplomatic authorities. The ousted men were said to have given the Taiwanese dissidents advice on the use of explosives and on means of promoting international support for their cause. The Americans also were accused of using their military postal privileges to assist the Taiwanese in contacting their countrymen abroad. These alleged activities were uncovered during interrogation of antigovernment Chinese and Taiwanese arrested in February and March, it was reported. Newsmen confirmed the transferred aides were two Army men, two Navy officers and a civilian employee of the U.S. Army Technical Group, the cover name for the Central Intelligence Agency.

Taiwan defense resolution repeal. The Senate Foreign Relations Committee unanimously approved July 21 repeal of a 1955 Congressional resolution providing the President with authority to employ forces to defend Taiwan and smaller islands off Mainland China held by the Chinese Nationalists. Committee Chairman J. W. Fulbright (D, Ark.) pointed out the action would not "technically" eliminate the U.S. defense commitment to the Chinese Nationalists since it was also provided in a 1955 defense treaty.

See also AUSTRALIA [8]; COMMUNIST CHINA-U.S. DETENTE [6, 8-9, 11]; EUROPEAN ECONOMIC COMMUNITY [5]; FOREIGN AID; FOREIGN POLICY; JAPAN [12-13]; PERU; TARIFFS & WORLD TRADE [3, 5]; TURKEY [7]; UNITED NATIONS [7-10]

CHOLERA—*See* HEALTH [1]; PAKISTAN [32]
CHOU EN-LAI—*See* CHINA, COMMUNIST; COMMUNIST CHINA-U.S. DETENTE [1, 3, 6, 9]; INDOCHINA WAR [72]; JAPAN [13]

CHURCHES—World Council of Churches. The Ethiopian Orthodox Church played host in Addis Ababa Jan. 10-21 to the Central Committee of the World Council of Churches, representing 235 Protestant and Eastern Orthodox member denominations. The agenda of the committee, the council's chief policy-making body, reflected the growing concern of the council with issues and problems confronting the Third World.
[2]   Much of the committee's business was devoted to debate over the executive committee's $200,000 grant in September 1970 to 19 antiracist organizations, including liberation groups. (The council repeated the $200,000 grant to 17 antiracist groups Sept. 9.) The grant had aroused opposition in Great Britain, West Germany, South Africa and Rhodesia because of objections to funding groups that allegedly endorsed the use of force. In his first report to the committee Jan. 10, Dr. M. M. Thomas, director of the Christian Institute for the Study of Religion and Society and the committee's chairman, defended the grant as an expression of protest against "the status quo ideology of violence and an attempt to break the moral and religious sanctions behind it." Thomas conceded that the council had not yet formed a consensus on the issue of war or violence as a last resort in situations where all nonviolent methods of change were either "illegal, unconstitutional or otherwise suppressed."
[3]   The Rev. Dr. Eugene Carson Blake, general secretary of the council, reported to the committee Jan. 11 that the grant had produced negative results, including added strain on ecumenical programs and persons not only in South Africa and Rhodesia, but in varying degrees in Portugal, Ireland, Greece, Great Britain and Germany. However, he said, the negative repercussions had been offset by the beginnings of "serious discussion of racism" in the council. The committee voted 84-0, with three abstentions, Jan. 16 that the grant was in accord with the general principles of the council's antiracism program. It also asked member churches to support further actions against racism.
[4]   By a unanimous vote Jan. 18, the committee sent an appeal to Great Britain's Prime Minister Edward Heath, who was attending the Commonwealth Conference in Singapore, to abandon plans to resume the sale of arms to South Africa. The resolution also mandated the general secretary to write French member churches, asking them to convey to President Georges Pompidou the committee's concern about the continued sale of arms by France to South Africa. Noting that the council had met twice with the International Jewish Committee on Interreligious Consultations (a new coalition of world Jewish groups, including the World Jewish Congress and the Synagogue Council of America), Dr. Blake Jan. 11 called for collaboration with major Jewish agencies on issues of racial justice and world peace.
[5]   Among resolutions adopted during its 12-day meeting, the committee called for an end to (1) capital punishment which it described as a violation of the "sanctity of life," (2) the use of the death penalty and "exorbitant" prison terms to punish political dissenters and minority groups, and (3) the

interference of rich and powerful nations in African affairs, which the committee said compounded the problems of tribalism and internal dissidence.

[6]   The final business session of the committee was boycotted Jan. 21 by Greek and other Eastern Orthodox leaders in a dispute over the council's recognition of the new Orthodox Church of America. The controversy grew out of a request by the new church, formerly the Russian Orthodox Greek Catholic Church of America (or the Metropolia), to be listed in the council's rolls by its new title. Representatives of the Ecumenical Patriarchate in Istanbul had objected to the request as a constitutional endorsement of the church's new status, which they did not recognize.

[7]   **NCC seeks wider base.** The general board of the National Council of Churches concluded a four-day meeting Jan. 26 in Louisville, Ky. The policy-making body of the council, a federation of 33 Protestant and Eastern Orthodox denominations, turned down proposals to dissolve the organization into independent agencies in favor of some kind of reorganization plan that would broaden the council's ecumenical base but still permit it to speak out collectively on controversial issues. A reorganization planning committee was authorized to draw up revised proposals for presentation in September. The NCC Sept. 10-11 adopted proposals opening the door to Roman Catholic membership and Jewish affiliation. The proposals also sought to widen the council's ecumenical scope with a periodic ecumenical congress and to strengthen its official pronouncements by replacing the general board with a 350-member governing board and decision-making body. The proposals required ratification by the next general assembly to be held in December 1972.

[8]   **Church of England Council meets.** The first Anglican Consultative Council, held in Limuru, Kenya, voted 24-22 during the first week of March for a resolution approving the ordination of women as priests under certain conditions. Opposition to the measure was based on concern that ordination of women would damage ecumenical ties with churches that do not permit women priests. The 50-member council, formed in 1969 to develop joint policies among the 47 million Anglicans in 90 countries, also adopted a resolution against racism and defeated an effort by the Most. Rev. Arthur Michael Ramsey, archbishop of Canterbury, to bar a statement of support for grants made by the World Council of Churches to militant antiracist groups in southern Africa (*see* [2-3]). The Church of England was a member of the World Council of Churches.

[9]   *Church weddings for divorced favored.* An eight-member commission, appointed by Ramsey three years before, proposed in London April 21 that divorced persons be allowed to remarry in the church. The commission's report was to be sent to the House of Bishops and then to the General Synod to be held later in the year.

[10]   **Southern Baptist Convention.** The Southern Baptist Convention reaffirmed its traditional conservatism at its three-day annual meeting in St. Louis June 1-3. The 11.6 million-member convention, the largest U.S. Protestant denomination, acted on several controversial resolutions and dismissed Dr. G. Henton Davis, the author revising its Bible commentary, because portions of his work did not adhere to a strict literal interpretation of the Scripture. The Rev. Carl E. Bates, a Charlotte, N.C. pastor, was reelected June 2 to a second term as president of the convention.

[11]   In resolutions passed at the meeting, the delegates: urged Baptists to work for legislation permitting abortions under specific conditions, including "rape, incest, clear evidence of severe fetal deformity, and carefully ascertained evidence of the damage to the emotional, mental and physical health of the mother"; asked President Nixon to recall Henry Cabot Lodge as his personal envoy at the Vatican because the post signified preferential recognition to the Roman Catholic Church and violated "our concept of separation of church and state"; refused to adopt a statement that the Vietnam war was morally ambiguous, but praised the troop reduction in Vietnam and changed a plea that

President Nixon "accelerate" troop withdrawal to "continue" withdrawal; and opposed public aid to parochial education.

[12] **Presbyterians study unity.** The general assemblies of the United Presbyterian Church and the Presbyterian Church in the U.S. (Southern) agreed separately to study a proposed plan of union that would reunite the two churches after their division from the Civil War period. The United Presbyterians held their general assembly May 17-26 in Rochester, N.Y.; the Southern Presbyterians met June 13-18 in Massanetta Springs, Va. The United Presbyterians defeated an attempt by a black caucus to shelve the draft plan until 1975 so that four largely black denominations—the African Methodist Episcopal Church, the African Methodist Episcopal Zion Church, the Christian Methodist Episcopal Church and the Second Cumberland—could be included in the plan. Jan. 15, 1973 was set as the date for receiving recommendations and revisions from both bodies.

[13] **Lutheran Church-Missouri Synod.** The 2.8 million-member Lutheran Church-Missouri Synod concluded a stormy eight-day convention in Milwaukee July 16 that was marked by dissension between conservatives, led by synod President Rev. Dr. Jacob A. O. Preus, and moderates. Amid heated debate, moderates scored key victories on two issues. The delegates rejected a resolution that would have made doctrinal statements voted at the biennial synod binding on pastors and teachers. The moderates had argued that only the Scriptures and Lutheran creeds could have a binding effect. In the other action, the convention elected four of five candidates supported by the moderates for posts on the board of control of Concordia Seminary in St. Louis, the church's main seminary. The faculty at Concordia had been the subject of an investigation begun by Preus in 1970 to discipline professors who taught that parts of the Bible were parables and did not have to be accepted literally. The elections apparently would diminish some of the investigation's impact.

[14] Underlying the two issues was the power of the 51-year-old president whom moderates accused of trying to purge the church of members who opposed his fundamentalist interpretation of the Bible or who held similar "unorthodox" views. The delegates gave Preus an indirect vote of confidence by rejecting a resolution July 13 that accused Preus of managing news, "suppression of free speech," having private aims for the Milwaukee convention" and "using his effort to assist American prisoners of war in Vietnam as a cynical political ploy." The issue of scriptural orthodoxy was linked with conservatives' reluctance to develop ecumenical ties with other Lutheran and non-Lutheran denominations. Acting cautiously on the advice of Preus, the delegates voted not to withdraw from the Lutheran Council in the U.S.A., but to study the agency. They also voted to continue, but not expand, a recent agreement to exchange pastors with the 2.5 million-member American Lutheran Church.

[15] In other actions, the synod: voted for a resolution asking the church to reconsider its approval in 1970 of the ordination of women and declaring that "the word of God does not permit women to hold pastoral office" or "exercise authority over men"; opposed abortions; acknowledged that racism still prevailed throughout the synod; appealed for efforts to alleviate hunger; and warned against "impetuous behavior" or "unrightful judgment of those who lead us" in the Vietnam war.

[16] **Coptic pope crowned.** Pope Shenuda III, 48, was crowned in Cairo Nov. 14 as the 117th patriarch of the Coptic Orthodox Church and Pope of Alexandria. The new pope, formerly a bishop in charge of theological education and a former Egyptian army officer, succeeded Pope Kyrollos VI who had died in March.

[17] **Accord on communion.** The Anglican-Roman Catholic International Commission, with the approval of Pope Paul VI and Archbishop Ramsey, announced agreement Dec. 30 on the "essential" meaning of the sacrament of holy communion (holy eucharist). The announcement, in the form of a

declaration "Agreed Statement on Eucharistic Doctrine," ended four centuries of theological dispute and removed one of the major obstacles to reunion between the Roman Catholic Church and the Church of England.

See also EDUCATION [18]; MOTION PICTURES; PRISONS [2]; ROMAN CATHOLIC CHURCH; SOUTH AFRICA [4-5, 13]

CHURCH OF ENGLAND—*See* CHURCHES [8-9, 17]

CIGARETTES—*See* HEALTH [4-12]

CITIZENSHIP, U.S.—The Supreme Court, in a 5-4 ruling April 5, overturned a district court ruling in favor of Aldo Mario Bellei (born in Italy of an Italian father and an American mother), holding that the government had the right to revoke citizenship through residency requirements in the case of persons born abroad of one American parent. The court upheld a 1952 law requiring that such individuals live in the U.S. for five consecutive years between the ages of 14 and 28 in order to retain citizenship. In a dissent, Justice Black contended that the ruling violated a 1967 decision that he had authored in which the court said a citizen could not be stripped of his citizenship unless he affirmatively renounced it. The majority, in an opinion by Justice Blackmun, held that the '67 ruling applied only to Americans who owed their citizenship to the 14th Amendment guarantee to "all persons born or naturalized in the United States." Blackmun said that in cases of a person naturalized abroad, Congress had granted citizenship and therefore Congress could legally impose the residency requirement. Also dissenting were Justices Douglas, Brennan and Marshall.

CIVIL AERONAUTICS BOARD (CAB)—*See* AVIATION [11]; GOVERNMENT REORGANIZATION

CIVIL RIGHTS—School desegregation in the South proceeded during 1971 with few major disturbances, but racial tension became stronger in the North and West as the courts and the federal government pressed for extension of desegregation there [4-12]. The primary concern was over the busing of schoolchildren out of their neighborhoods in order to aid desegregation. The Supreme Court ruled in April that busing was not unconstitutional [2], but the Nixon Administration continued its opposition to busing [14-16], and the House of Representatives passed a bill providing funds for desegregation efforts which prohibited spending the funds for busing [19]. In employment, the Administration's Philadelphia Plan survived two challenges and was extended to three additional cities [21]. In housing, the Department of Housing and Urban Renewal decided that it should have rejected subsidies for a previously approved housing project in Philadelphia [29].

School Desegregation

[2] **Supreme Court upholds busing.** The Supreme Court, in a series of unanimous decisions April 20, told school districts in the South that busing children as a means of dismantling dual school systems was constitutional. The rulings brought to a close final legal efforts by Southern school boards and by the Nixon Administration to stave off busing students to achieve racially balanced schools. Justice Department lawyers had contended that Southern school districts should be permitted to assign students to schools in their own neighborhoods even if it slowed down the pace of desegregation. In the opinions for the entire court, Chief Justice Warren E. Burger said that "desegregation plans cannot be limited to the walk-in school." The justices held that busing was proper "unless the time or the distance is so great as to risk either the health of the children or significantly impinge on the educational process." The court added that at times busing was an indispensable method of eliminating "the last vestiges" of racial segregation. The court, however, imposed some limitations on its decisions: it said that the rulings did not apply to de facto segregation, caused by neighborhood housing patterns and most often found in the North; it stopped short of ordering the elimination of all-black schools or of requiring

racial balance in the schools; and it said that young children may be improper subjects for busing if it is over long distances. The court's rulings: upheld a desegregation plan by U.S. Judge James B. McMillan for the Charlotte-Mecklenburg County, N.C. joint school system which required massive crosstown busing and which had been overturned by a U.S. appeals court on the grounds that it was unreasonable and burdensome; struck down as unconstitutional an antibusing statute enacted by the North Carolina legislature; overturned a desegregation plan that Mobile, Ala. city officials had devised and ordered further desegregation; and overturned a Georgia Supreme Court ruling that said certain desegregation efforts in Athens were unconstitutional because they took race into account.

[3] Chief Justice Burger Aug. 31 clarified the April decision in refusing to stay the enforcement of a court-ordered busing plan for the Winston-Salem, Forsyth County, N.C. school system. (The plea was rejected because of the lateness of the appeal and the lack of sufficient information to overturn the plan, which involved busing of 50,000 students.) In his opinion, Burger said the April ruling did not require "a fixed racial balance or quota" in order to constitutionally desegregate schools. He said a school district's racial balance should be used as "a starting point" to determine "whether in fact any violation existed," but he quoted language from the Charlotte-Mecklenburg decision saying "that every school in every community must always reflect the racial composition of the school system as a whole."

[4] **Integration results.** The federal government June 17 released the results of a nationwide survey showing that public school integration in the South had increased dramatically in the previous two years. Other figures, contained in a survey made public by the Department of Health, Education and Welfare (HEW), indicated that school integration in many of the North's large cities had shown a significant decline over the same two-year period. According to HEW: of the total Negro student population, the percentage attending white majority schools increased from 23% in the fall of 1968 to 33% in the fall of 1970. The increase was attributed by HEW almost wholly to the increase in integration in the South. The percentage of Negroes in Southern schools with a white majority rose from 18% in 1968 to 39% in 1970, while the Northern figure remained steady at 27%. Increased integration in some areas of the North and West (Los Angeles, Newark, San Diego and Denver) was offset by declines in the big cities (New York, Detroit, Philadelphia, St. Louis, Boston, San Francisco and Minneapolis). As schools opened for the 1972 school year in September, protests against desegregation centered in the North, while Southern and Border states school districts opened with a minimum of disruption. In major developments in school desegregation, by state:

[5] *Alabama.* Gov. George C. Wallace, ignoring federal Judge Sam C. Pointer's ruling that Wallace's executive orders to have two Alabama school boards defy school desegregation plans were "legally meaningless," ordered two more school boards Aug. 18 to disregard a court-approved integration plan. Pointer had called Wallace's executive orders to the Jefferson County-Birmingham school district Aug. 12 (to transfer a white student from a court-assigned predominantly black school to a predominantly white school nearer her home) and to the Limestone County school board Aug. 13 (to reopen a predominantly black school that had been closed by federal court order) merely an exercise of free speech. In his Aug. 18 action, Wallace directed the boards of education of Calhoun County and the city of Oxford to disregard orders from a federal district court to pair an all-black school in Hobson City with two predominantly white schools in Oxford. At a news conference in Hobson City, Wallace made it clear that he was purposely attempting to challenge the Administration and the Justice Department over busing. Wallace had said Aug. 17 that the federal government would have to take him to court to stop his antibusing orders to the school boards. He promised, however, to abide by any ultimate decision of the courts. In a later development, an Alabama judge Oct.

18 invoked for the first time a state law, passed at Wallace's urging, which required school boards to honor transfer requests if parents determined that their children's health or education was endangered by busing. The law was ruled unconstitutional Dec. 3 by Judge Pointer.

[6] Arkansas. Scores of white high school students walked out of classes Feb. 11 near Pine Bluff to protest a court-ordered desegregation plan. They were met by their parents and other supporters in a peaceful demonstration which was the only incident on the day the Watson Chapel School District No. 24 began operating under the desegregation order. The district implemented the plan "with great reluctance" after U.S. District Court Judge Oren Harris warned the school board's members Feb. 5 that they faced jail terms for the remainder of the school year and fines of $350 a day for each day they remained in contempt of court by ignoring the school order. The desegregation ruling had been ordered into effect by Harris Nov. 17, 1970. In his Feb. 5 warning, Harris said that the six board members had ignored his invitation for them to propose "reasonable alternative plans" to his plan.

[7] California. The San Francisco Board of Education June 4 adopted a plan to fully integrate its 102 elementary schools in September. The plan, involving 48,000 children, was adopted to comply with an April 28 order by U.S. District Judge Stanley A. Weigel. Weigel, ordering full integration in light of the Supreme Court's April 20 decision (*see* [2]), had given the school board until June 10 to submit a plan for his approval. He said that he had found that only 29% of the pupils in the city's elementary schools were black but that 80% of the blacks were concentrated in 27 schools. The board of education asked for a delay in implementation of the plan, but was refused by the U.S. Court of Appeals for the 9th Circuit Aug. 12 and by Associate Justice William O. Douglas of the Supreme Court Aug. 29. San Francisco schools reopened under the order Sept. 13.

[8] Massachusetts. HEW Dec. 1 formally notified Boston school officials that they were violating the 1964 Civil Rights Act by following policies that tended to create segregated school attendance patterns. Boston was the largest Northern school system to be so charged and could face court action and a cutoff of $10 million in annual aid if a remedial plan were not devised. (Massachusetts had withheld $14 million in operating funds from the Boston system after the School Committee Sept. 22 abandoned a scheduled integration plan for the downtown district. Efforts at integrating the district had begun Sept. 8 but withered when black and white parents refused to send their children to the new, integrated Lee School in a black neighborhood.) More than 78% of the city's nonwhite students were in majority nonwhite schools, although a 1965 state law required local officials to eliminate all such imbalance. HEW noted that a plan announced in 1965 for converting all junior high schools (grades 7-9) to middle schools (grades 6-8) had been implemented in only four schools, which had become predominantly nonwhite, as had the elementary and high schools with meshing grade structures. Other examples of discriminatory policies which had been uncovered by earlier investigations by the Massachusetts Department of Education included cases of busing nonwhites past predominantly white schools with empty seats, nearly adjacent elementary schools totally segregated by race and an all-white high school in a district that included large numbers of nonwhites. (The Massachusetts Commission Against Discrimination had directed the Boston School Committee June 23 to complete a sweeping integration of the city's public schools by the opening of the 1972 year.)

[9] Michigan. The U.S. Court of Appeals for the 6th Circuit May 28 let stand an order (handed down in February 1970) by District Court Judge Damon Keith which called for all elementary schoolchildren to attend neighborhood schools for two grades and be bused for four of the six elementary school years. Under the plan, each elementary school would have only two grades. In protest over the order, arsonists Aug. 30 set firebombs that destroyed 10 of the fleet of

90 school buses which were to be used to implement the order. Agents of the Federal Bureau of Investigation (FBI) Sept. 9 arrested six members of the Klu Klux Klan in connection with the bombing. Arrested were: Robert E. Miles, grand dragon of the Michigan Realm of the United Klans of America; Wallace E. Fruit; Alexander J. Distel Jr.; Dennis C. Ramsey; Raymond Quick Jr.; and Edmund Reimer. All except Reimer were indicted Oct. 20 by a federal grand jury in Detroit on charges of conspiring to intimidate black students in the exercise of their constitutional right to attend public schools. The five were accused of plotting at a statewide meeting of the Klan in July to blow up the buses. An affidavit filed in U.S. court in Detroit Sept. 10 charged that the Klansmen also planned to "knock out" a power station in the Pontiac area as a diversion for a full-scale mortar attack on the bus fleet. In other protests over the busing order, eight white students and one black youth were injured Sept. 8 in fights. Protesters carrying American flags marched in front of the school bus depot Sept. 8 daring bus drivers to run them down. A high percentage of white parents held a boycott at the opening of the schools. The Supreme Court Oct. 26 declined to hear an appeal by the school board of the order.

[10] Federal Judge Stephen J. Roth Oct. 4 directed the Michigan Board of Education to propose within four months a school integration plan that would encompass Detroit's inner city schools and schools in outlying suburban areas. Roth had ruled Sept. 27 that Detroit's school system had been deliberately segregated by the school board's actions in constructing small primary schools, redrawing attendance zones to circumvent integration and using busing to move some black students to other black schools instead of to white ones. Gov. William G. Milliken put himself at the head of antibusing forces in the state Nov. 3 when he announced that Michigan would appeal Roth's order for a desegregation plan.

[11] **Mississippi.** U.S. District Court Judge Dan Russell Oct. 20 issued a permanent injunction enjoining the State of Mississippi from inter-fering in a desegre-gation plan for public schools in Jackson or withholding funds from the Jackson district because of busing. Russell ordered the state tax commissioner, state auditor and attorney general not to interfere with implementation of a court-ordered desegregation plan. Jackson officials had sought relief from the federal court after Gov. John Bell Williams Sept. 11 issued an executive order directing the state auditor to withhold education funds until the system showed it was not using the money for busing purposes.

[12] **Texas.** U.S. District Court Judge Jack Roberts July 18 refused to accept a federal school desegregation proposal for schools in Austin which would have required extensive crosstown busing. Roberts instead accepted a school desegregation plan filed by the Austin school district. The federal plan, recommended May 14, had been rejected June 28 by Roberts, who had ordered the federal government and the Austin school district to try to draw up a plan that would keep busing to a minimum. Under the district's plan for elementary schools, new centers would be established for fine arts, avocations, social sciences and sciences. Pupils of all races would be bused to the new centers for a portion of the school day. The district's plan for junior high schools called for the reassignment of all black pupils to schools "that are not identifiable as Negro schools." The district and HEW had previously agreed to a plan for the desegregation of Austin's high schools which provided for the closing of a predominantly black high school with reassignment of all black students to schools not identifiable as black schools. (President Nixon Aug. 3 disassociated himself from his Administration's Austin plan and reasserted his strong opposition to busing as a means of racial balance.)

[13] **Administration policy. 23 academies lose tax privilege.** The Internal Revenue Service (IRS) said March 26 that it was ending the tax-exemption privileges of 23 private academies in Mississippi after the schools failed to adopt nondiscriminatory enrollment policies. (The action came nearly two months after the Southern Regional Council, a private organization

researching civil rights, Feb. 6 criticized the government for what it described as laxity in revoking tax exemptions of private schools that refused to admit blacks. The council had singled out for criticism the IRS policy of relying on written assurances of school officials that their academies did not discriminate.) The IRS revocations were tied to a lawsuit filed in 1970 by the parents of black schoolchildren who were denied admission to the private academies. In the original complaint, 41 private academies were named as defendants. Since the date of the suit, two of the 41 closed, nine submitted satisfactory evidence to the IRS that they were no longer discriminating against Negroes, one was being granted a tax exemption on a tentative basis and six were still under IRS scrutiny.

[14] *Nixon warns aides on busing.* The White House said Aug. 11 that President Nixon had warned HEW and Justice Department officials, orally and in writing, that they risked losing their jobs if they sought to impose extensive busing as a means of desegregating schools throughout the South. Nixon said in his warnings that he wanted the busing of schoolchildren kept to the minimum required by law (*see* [13]). According to White House Press Secretary Ronald L. Zeigler, the Administration did not object to busing plans drawn up by local school officials and would enforce any direct court orders requiring widespread busing. But he said the President had instructed government personnel to carry out school desegregation without using the busing of children as a "major technique." The U.S. Commission on Civil Rights said Aug. 12 that the Nixon directive would undermine efforts to desegregate schools.

[15] *Rights panel assails Administration.* The U.S. Commission on Civil Rights again used stern language Nov. 16 to accuse the Nixon Administration of failing to adequately enforce the nation's civil rights laws. The panel report criticized President Nixon, saying that he had not clearly defined his civil rights policy despite position statements on school busing (*see* [13]) and housing (*see* [27]). The report repeated its warning that Nixon's busing position might be interpreted as "a sign of a slowdown in the federal desegregation effort," and said that Nixon's housing statement was "restrictive" and limited the federal role in the housing area to an essentially passive one. The report included a performance rating in which the White House and 29 U.S. agencies were reviewed for their commitment to civil rights. In rating the civil rights performance of the 29 agencies, the panel based its conclusions on the progress made on recommendations by the commission in 1970. Four performance levels—poor, marginal, adequate and good—or a combination of those marks, were used in the rating system. The White House fared better than any of the agencies but received only a "less than adequate" mark. None of the agencies received a rating of adequate. The Office of Management and Budget, which was under the auspices of the White House, scored the best of any agency with a rating just below the adequate level. The commission noted, however, that some progress had been made by many of the U.S. agencies, mainly the establishment of an apparatus to begin enforcement.

[16] The individual agencies showing the best improvement were: the Department of Housing and Urban Development, Federal Home Loan Bank Board and the Department of Justice. Among those agencies which were given the lowest ratings were the Veterans Administration, Board of Governors of the Federal Reserve System, Comptroller of the Currency, Federal Deposit Insurance Corporation, higher education in the Department of Health, Education and Welfare, Internal Revenue Service, Interior Department, Law Enforcement Assistance Administration under the Justice Department, Transportation Department, Civil Aeronautics Board, Federal Power Commission, and the Interstate Commerce Commission.

[17] Congressional action. The Senate April 26 approved a compromise bill authorizing $1.4 billion in federal aid to help school districts integrate their schools. The vote was 74-8. The vote followed acrimonious debate that centered primarily on the distinctions between school integration in the North and in the South. The bill would give communities broad discretion over use of most of the funds allotted. In applying for grants, however, school districts would be required to have a broad plan for eliminating segregation and (except in the cases of districts under court-ordered desegregation plans) would have to use a portion of their grant to create at least one "stable, quality, integrated" model school. The model schools would have a "substantial portion of children from educationally advantaged backgrounds" but would be substantially representative of the racial makeup of the community. The bill was a compromise measure worked out by HEW Secretary Elliot L. Richardson and a group of civil rights advocates, among them Sens. Jacob K. Javits (R, N.Y.), Walter F. Mondale (D, Minn.) and Claiborne Pell (D, R.I.). The primary area of disagreement between the Administration and the civil rights proponents was over how the money should be allocated.

[18] The only amendment to get the Senate's backing was authored by Sen. John Stennis (D, Miss.) and approved April 22 by a 44-43 vote. The amendment put the Senate on record as declaring that it was "the policy of the United States" to enforce federal school desegration laws in communities where the segregation resulted from housing patterns as well as in areas where the segregation had been sanctioned by law. Stennis said his amendment would eliminate the "dual standard" of enforcement under which, he said, Southern schools were threatened with forfeiture of federal funds if they failed to desegregate while schools in Northern cities and suburban areas remained segregated. The Senate April 21 had voted down, by a 51-35 vote, an amendment by Sen. Abraham Ribicoff (D, Conn.) to force the nation's suburban communities to integrate their schools with neighboring inner-city public schools within 12 years. The Senate April 26 turned down a series of amendments by Sen. Sam J. Ervin Jr. (D, N.C.) designed to relax some of the U.S. desegregation guidelines.

[19] In the House, the bill, passed Nov. 5 by a 332-38 vote, was encumbered with three antibusing amendments. The key amendment would prohibit the use of any of the funds to pay for buses, drivers or any other cost of transporting children out of their neighborhoods for the purpose of racial integration. Dozens of liberal Democrats voted with nearly all Republicans and Southerners to pass that amendment by a 233-124 vote. Another amendment, passed by a 235-125 vote, would not allow federal court orders requiring busing to go into effect until all appeals had been exhausted or until the time for appeal had passed. The third amendment, adopted by a vote of 231-126, would forbid U.S. education officials from requiring, or even encouraging, communities to institute busing plans. Passage of the House bill set the stage for a protracted Congressional battle over busing, with the opening rounds to be fought in a House-Senate conference. (The Administration's original bill had been defeated Nov. 1 by a 222-135 vote after Democrats agreed to put it to a vote under a "suspension" procedure that forbade amendments and required two-thirds majority for passage. The suspension procedure had been a requirement of the Rules Committee, which had otherwise refused to pass the bill to the House floor.)

Equal Employment Actions

[20] Discriminatory job tests barred. The Supreme Court ruled 8-0 March 8 that employers could not use job tests that had the effect of screening out Negroes if the tests were not related to ability to do the work. The court held that the employment bias section of the 1964 Civil Rights Act involved the consequences of employment practices, not simply whether the practices were motivated by racial bias. The court limited the use of general educational and aptitude tests and said that "any tests used must measure the person for the job and not the person in the abstract." The case grew out of applications for promotion by 13 black laborers at the Duke Power Co. generating plant at Dan River in Draper, N.C.

[21]   Courts back Philadelphia Plan. The Nixon Administration's pilot job plan, known as the Philadelphia Plan, overcame two legal challenges in 1971 as the U.S. Court of Appeals for the 3rd Circuit April 23 upheld its legality and the Supreme Court Oct. 12 rejected a challenge to the plan without comment. Both challenges were by the Contractors Association of Eastern Pennsylvania, which claimed the plan violated the 1964 Civil Rights Act by setting up racial "quotas." The plan, devised by the Labor Department in 1969, required contractors bidding on federal or federally assisted projects to hire a fixed number of minority group workers by a certain date. The plan, which had also been imposed on Washington, was imposed on San Francisco June 3, on Seattle June 17 and on Atlanta, Ga. June 18.

[22]   House passes weakened rights bill. The House Sept. 16 passed an Administration-supported equal employment bill by a 285-106 vote. The measure empowered the Equal Employment Opportunity Commission (EEOC) to bring discrimination suits in a federal court and empowered the attorney general to institute appeals in cases of unfavorable lower court rulings. The legislation had been substituted for a stronger bill favored by civil rights and women's rights groups that would have given the EEOC power to issue cease-and-desist orders. (The EEOC could act against job discrimination only by means of conciliation efforts.) The bill including the cease-and-desist powers had been passed by the House Education and Labor Committee June 2 by a 21-12 vote. The Administration version, rejected in committee, was substituted for the committee-approved bill by a narrow 202-197 margin on the House floor Sept. 16. Opponents of the bill then lost a 270-129 vote to recommit the measure to committee after Democratic leaders decided that the Administration bill provided a "vehicle" that could be strengthened in the Senate. The Senate had passed a bill giving the EEOC cease-and-desist powers in the 91st Congress. Proponents of the increased powers for the EEOC argued that the cease-and-desist power would cut down on judicial backlogs.

[23]   Utility bias charged. After three days of hearings, the EEOC Nov. 17 charged the nation's gas and electric utilities with "rampant discrimination" in hiring and promoting minority group men and women. The commission reported that only 6% of the industry work force was black, the lowest percentage among the 23 largest industries, and that 1.6% had Spanish surnames compared with 3.6% of all major industry workers. Women, who constituted 34% of the major industry work force, held only 15% of the utility jobs and were traditionally relegated to clerical jobs with little management opportunity and relatively low pay. The commission contended that some utilities used "culturally biased" general hiring tests not directly related to job openings. Industry spokesmen claimed that efforts to upgrade blacks had uncovered few qualified for better positions. Low employee turnover and promotion from the ranks in the highly unionized industry were also cited by company executives and independent experts as major causes of continuing inequality.

[24]   AT&T job bias charged. The EEOC Dec. 1 charged the American Telephone & Telegraph Co. (AT&T) and its operating subsidiaries with systematic job discrimination against blacks and Spanish-Americans, and called AT&T, with nearly a million employees, "the largest oppressor of women workers in the United States." The charges were in a report to the Federal Communications Commission (FCC) in documentation of charges originally submitted to the FCC by the EEOC Dec. 10, 1970 in opposition to AT&T's requested rate increase (see CONSUMER AFFAIRS [17]). The FCC scheduled a public hearing beginning Jan. 31, 1972—the first job discrimination hearing by a federal regulatory agency.

Housing Developments
[25]   U.S. moves to end bias. The Department of Housing and Urban Renewal (HUD) May 25 issued federal guidelines to prevent the use of racial, religious and national origin designations in newspaper advertisements for housing. Under the policy, HUD would consider the placement in advertisements of certain words, signs and symbols as clear evidence of intent to discriminate. The evidence would be used in complaints filed under the Civil Rights Act of 1968. The guidelines, to be effective 30 days after issuance, would apply to designations that implied that sale or rental of dwelling units was for the benefit of any race, religion or national group.

[26]   Panel criticizes housing program. The U.S. Commission on Civil Rights charged June 10 that the Federal Housing Administration (FHA) "has abdicated its responsibility" in administering its home ownership program for low-income families and, "in effect, has delegated it to members of the private housing and home finance industry." According to the commission, the private groups had misused the program by largely ignoring the intent of civil law. The report, based on the commission's year-long study of the home ownership program in four cities (Denver, Little Rock, Philadelphia and St. Louis), said that, because of the FHA's ineffectiveness in running the program, housing under the plan was following the same pattern as most other housing—whites were getting new homes in the suburbs, and blacks were getting homes in the central cities. The program under fire was Section 235 of the Housing Act of 1968—the first large-scale effort to make available to low-income families the opportunity to own a home. A purchaser whose income was between $4,000 and $10,000 could purchase housing under the plan worth up to $21,000. The purchaser then would pay at least 20% of his income toward the monthly payments of principal, interest, insurance, taxes and FHA insurance premium, while the government would pay the remainder. The commission said that, in all four cities studied, "minority buyers received cheaper, inferior housing and smaller government subsidies than white buyers."

[27]   Nixon outlines housing policy. President Nixon, in a major position statement June 11, called racial discrimination in housing clearly unconstitutional and said it "will not be tolerated" by his Administration. The President, however, repeated his earlier view that racial and economic segregation in housing were not synonymous and therefore he would not use the government's legal apparatus to force communities to accept low- and moderate-income housing against their wishes. Nixon said that, based on his review of the legislative history of the 1968 Civil Rights Act, he did not believe that the act's "affirmative action" clause authorized "housing officials in federal agencies to dictate local land use policy." He said, however, that the federal government would move against zoning changes when it was determined that rezoning had been done by a community to exclude a federally assisted housing development. The policy statement was the result of nearly seven months of debate and discussion within the Administration over the limits to which federal leverage would be applied to induce local communities to integrate their housing.

[28]   *Romney announces proposed guidelines.* HUD Secretary George Romney Jan. 14 announced proposed guidelines (to take effect in 30 days) that would limit federal grants for community development to communities agreeing to plan for housing for low- and moderate-income families.

[29]   Subsidized slum housing challenged. HUD Sept. 22 informed the U.S. Court of Appeals for the 3rd Circuit that a subsidized housing project previously approved for a predominantly Negro renewal area in North Philadelphia should have been rejected. (The court had ruled Dec. 30, 1970 that HUD, in considering applications for rent supplements or mortgage insurance, had to determine whether the Philadelphia project would increase or maintain segregation. The court had said that HUD could not support housing projects that increased or maintained segregation unless it found that the need for renewal of a slum or additional housing in slums "clearly outweighs the disadvantage of increasing or perpetuating racial concentration.") In announcing its decision to the court, HUD said the project, Fairmount Manor, would add too much to racial concentration in the area and should not have been approved. The decision could have a national impact on location of subsidized housing complexes. If it were applied in other cities, it could lead to dispersal of poor families now in the central cities to outlying areas. The decision meant that the court would decide if federal rent subsidies to those living in the project should continue.

Public Services Developments

[30] **Court orders equality.** The U.S. 5th Circuit Court of Appeals Jan. 29 overturned a lower court's decision and ruled that Shaw, Miss., a small town in Mississippi's northwest farm belt, had to provide public services—such as street lights, drainage facilities, paved streets and traffic signals—equally to all its residents. Civil rights proponents said the court's decision (which governed Mississippi, Alabama, Florida, Georgia, Louisiana and Texas and could be cited as a precedent in other circuits) was a major breakthrough that could lead to court challenges all over the country against inadequate public services. The court also ordered the town to submit a plan to correct the "gross disparities." The ruling came in a case launched in September 1969 by the National Association for the Advancement of Colored People (NAACP) Legal Defense and Educational Fund, Inc., on behalf of black residents of Shaw.

[31] **Pool closings upheld.** The Supreme Court by a 5-4 vote June 14 ruled that a city could close its public pools to black and white citizens alike rather than comply with court orders to desegregate them. The decision was handed down in a case brought to the court by Jackson, Miss. Negroes who were challenging the closing of Jackson's five public pools in 1965 in response to a federal court order to desegregate them. The court held that, because the city closed the pools to both black and white citizens, it did not deny blacks equal protection of the laws.

See also AGRICULTURE [7-10]; BUDGET; EDUCATION [12]; HOUSING; NEGROES; PRISONS [8-9]; RACIAL & MINORITY UNREST [1, 11]; STATE & LOCAL GOVERNMENTS [9]; SUPREME COURT; VOTING RIGHTS; WOMEN'S RIGHTS

CLAY, CASSIUS (MUHAMMED ALI)—*See* BOXING; SELECTIVE SERVICE SYSTEM [14]
CLIFFORD, CLARK—*See* PENTAGON PAPERS [28]

COLOMBIA—**Pastrana calls state of siege.** President Misael Pastrana Borrero Feb. 26 declared a state of siege, or modified martial law, throughout Colombia following rioting that day in the industrial city of Cali. The state of siege authorized suspension of the right of assembly, use of curfews, closure of bars and use of courts-martial for breaches of the peace. At least seven persons were killed and more than 100 injured in the Cali violence, which erupted when police attempted to dislodge students, seeking the ouster of the president of the University del Valle, from the buildings they were occupying on the university campus. The riots followed several weeks of unrest which had included a teachers' strike for higher pay (settled the week following the riots), a national 24-hour general strike called by the Union of Colombian Workers for March 8 and the invasion and occupation of farms by peasant squatters.

Agreement with Chile. Colombia and Chile May 8 signed an agreement calling for "ideological pluralism" between states in the United Nations and within the inter-American system, and for the self-determination of nations. The declaration was significant as a step in bridging a widening gap of conflicting ideologies in Latin America. Observers said it would also impede efforts by the U.S. to continue the policy of ostracism of Cuba by the Organization of American States.

Cabinet resigns. Eleven Cabinet members resigned June 1 to enable President Pastrana to settle difficulties within the National Front coalition which arose following a split between progressive and moderate leaders of the Liberal party. Only defense minister Gen. Hernando Currea Cubides remained in the Cabinet. The new members of the Cabinet, announced June 9: foreign affairs—Alfredo Vesquez Carrizosa; interior—Abelardo Forero Benavides; justice—Miguel Escobar Mendez; agriculture—Hernan Jaramillo Ocampo; finance—Rodrigo Llorente Martinez; health—Jose Maria Salazar Buchelli; education—Luis Carlos Galan Sarmiento; communications—Juan B. Fernandez; public works—Argelino Duran Quintero; development—Jorge Valencia Jaramillo; mines—Rafael Caicedo Espinosa; labor—Crispin Villazon de Armas.

New party forms. The National Popular Alliance (ANAPO) became Colombia's third political party June 13 in what was described as the largest political gathering in recent years. ANAPO had been increasing its electoral strength in the past 10 years and won over 36% of the vote in the 1970 elections. Former Gen. Gustavo Rojas Pinilla, head of ANAPO, said the new party would fight for the establishment of a "Colombian socialism" that would favor women, workers and the people of Colombia. (Colombia's two other parties were the Liberals and the Conservatives.)

Petroleum strike. Petroleum workers, protesting the firing of several union directors who had participated in a work slowdown, occupied the installations of Colombia's principal petroleum complex (in Barrancabermeja) Aug. 6, leaving the industry totally paralyzed. The strikers had taken 17 engineers and technicians as hostages, and clashes were reported between the strikers and the armed forces.

Student unrest. The army occupied the National University in Bogota, the nation's largest school, and arrested more than 70 leftist students, according to reports Sept. 23. The army was called in after police failed to end rioting by leftist student groups who opposed government participation in the appointment of deans and presidents to the school. At least six policemen were reportedly injured in the clashes.

Emergency measures issued. President Pastrana Oct. 9 announced a series of emergency security measures to deal with guerrilla subversion: placing the armed forces in a state of alert and calling for prison sentences of 15 years for anyone found carrying firearms or any object capable of harming persons, for kidnaping or hijacking or for unjustly depriving another of life or liberty.

See also CHILE [10]; COMMUNIST CHINA-U.S. DETENTE [3]; ECUADOR; LATIN AMERICA; VENEZUELA

COMMISSION ON CIVIL RIGHTS, U.S.—See CIVIL RIGHTS [14-16, 26].
COMMON CAUSE—See TAXES
COMMON MARKET—See EUROPEAN ECONOMIC COMMUNITY
COMMON MARKET OF AFRICA, MALAGASY & MAURITIUS (OCAM)—See AFRICA
COMMONWEALTH OF NATIONS (BRITISH COMMONWEALTH)—See EUROPEAN ECONOMIC COMMUNITY [14]; GREAT BRITAIN [9-10, 18]; NORTHERN IRELAND [17]; UGANDA; VIRGIN ISLANDS

COMMUNISM, INTERNATIONAL—Comecon bank operational. The International Investment Bank, established in July 1970 by the Soviet bloc's common market organization, Comecon (Council for Mutual Economic Aid), began operations Jan. 1. The bank, which called up $192 million of its total authorized capital, was expected to serve in the Soviet bloc the function served in the West by the World Bank (see INTERNATIONAL BANK FOR RECONSTRUCTION & DEVELOPMENT). It would borrow and lend for profit in the Eurodollar area and engage in common ventures with capitalist banks. The bank unanimously admitted Rumania Jan. 12. The same day the board of the bank voted to increase the organization's initial capital, originally established at 1 billion rubles, about one-third of which was listed as freely convertible currency.

Comecon plans integration. Comecon ended a three-day session in Bucharest July 29 by approving plans for further integration of the economies of its member states and for a convertible ruble to be used in mutual business transactions. The program for coordinating economic policies, published Aug. 7, did not make clear how the new currency unit would differ from the transfer ruble already in use in Comecon states, although it said that by 1973 the organization would establish gold equivalent and exchange rates for the new ruble. A uniform exchange rate for the currencies of all member states was to be worked out during 1976-79. The program also covered other areas, including tourism, scientific research and the standardization of products and spare parts, and was to be implemented over a "15-20 year period."

Rumania absent from Crimea meeting. Rumania was not represented at a one-day meeting of East European premiers held Aug. 2 somewhere in the Crimea and attended by Soviet Communist party General Secretary Leonid I. Brezhnev and President Nikolai V. Podgorny. It was not known if Rumania had been invited to the gathering. The session was apparently called to discuss policy on President Nixon's planned visit to Communist China (*see* COMMUNIST CHINA-U.S. DETENTE) and on recent events in the Sudan (*see* SUDAN). A communique issued Aug. 2 implied criticism of Rumania, which had supported Nixon's projected trip. Regarding the Sudanese problem, the statement "expressed grave alarm in connection with the ruthless terror unleashed against the Communist party and other democratic organizations."

See also CARIBBEAN; CZECHOSLOVAKIA [8]; EUROPEAN SECURITY; GERMANY, EAST; POLAND

COMMUNIST CHINA-U.S. DETENTE—Relations between the United States and the People's Republic of China eased dramatically in 1971, culminating in the announcement July 15 that President Richard Nixon would visit China to confer with Communist party Chairman Mao Tsetung and Premier Chou Enlai. Although the United States government still did not officially recognize the government of the People's Republic of China, Nixon's visit and the admission of China to the United Nations (*see* UNITED NATIONS [7-10]) brought the U.S. and China into a closer relationship than at any time since the Communist takeover of the mainland in 1949.

[2] U.S. ends travel ban. The U.S. March 15 discontinued the requirement that its citizens obtain specially validated passports for travel to China. The measure did not affect the ban on travel to North Korea, North Vietnam and Cuba, which the State Department extended for an additional six-month period March 15.

[3] Table tennis. Nine U.S. table tennis players, four officials and two wives arrived in China April 10 in response to an invitation tendered by China April 6 at the world table tennis championships in Nagoya, Japan and accepted there the following day by Graham B. Steenhoven, president of the U.S. Table Tennis Association. Most sources reported that U.S. players had sought the invitation. The team left China April 17. Following several days of travel through China, the U.S. players were defeated in exhibition matches in Peking April 13. They were received April 14 by Premier Chou, who also received teams from Britain, Canada, Nigeria and Colombia. Chou informed all five visiting groups that Chinese teams would accept invitations to their countries. Steenhoven said April 20 that he had invited the Chinese team to the U.S. It was also announced April 20 by a U.S. official that China had accepted the invitation.

[4] *Western newsmen admitted.* Reversing a policy maintained since 1949, China April 10 granted visas to seven Western newsmen to cover the U.S. team's visit. The newsmen were representatives of the Associated Press, the National Broadcasting Company (NBC) and Life magazine. Tillman Durdin, chief of the New York Times Hong Kong Bureau, and Mark Gayn, a

Canadian correspondent, were authorized to enter China April 13. Durdin's stay was limited to one month.

[5] Trade embargo relaxed. President Nixon April 14 took another step aimed at easing U.S. relations with China by relaxing a 20-year embargo on trade with that country. Nixon's statement said that the U.S. was "prepared to expedite visas" for visitors or groups of visitors from China and that U.S. firms would be allowed to trade with China in dollars. (Treasury Secretary John B. Connally May 7 announced a general license for the use of dollars in transactions with China.) U.S. oil companies were to be allowed to supply fuel to ships or planes proceeding to or from mainland China with the exception of Chinese-owned or Chinese-chartered carriers going to or from North Vietnam, North Korea or Cuba. U.S. carriers were to be allowed to transport Chinese cargoes between non-Chinese ports, and U.S.-owned carriers under foreign flags could call at Chinese ports. After reviewing a list of proposed exports prepared by the National Security Council, Nixon June 10 released a list of 47 categories of items considered exportable to China and announced that Chinese exports to the U.S. would be treated in the same manner as items from other Communist countries. The President's list included such nonstrategic goods as farm products, household appliances, automobiles and basic metals. Omitted from the list, but described as exportable under special licenses following a review by the Commerce Department and other government agencies, were locomotives, trucks, high-grade computers, petroleum products and commercial aircraft. In a related development, Nixon June 10 lifted a requirement by which 50% of grain shipments to China, the U.S.S.R. and other East European countries were to be carried in U.S. ships.

[6] Nixon's China visit. President Nixon July 15, in a totally unanticipated announcement, said that he would visit Peking before May 1972 to confer with Chinese leaders "to seek the normalization of relations between the two countries and to exchange views on questions of concern to the two sides." A follow-up announcement by the Western White House at San Clemente, Calif. July 16 said the President would confer with both Mao Tsetung and Premier Chou. No American president had been received by a Chinese government. In his address to the American people, Nixon disclosed that arrangements for the projected meeting had been worked out in secret talks held in Peking July 9-11 by Henry Kissinger, Nixon's national security affairs adviser, and Premier Chou. Nixon said the plan was being announced simultaneously in the U.S. and Peking. Alluding to the Nationalist Chinese government, the President emphasized that "our action in seeking a new relationship with the People's Republic of China will not be at the expense of our old friends." Nixon said that Chou had extended the invitation to him to come to Peking in response to Nixon's expression of interest in a visit to China.

[7] *Kissinger mission.* The meeting between Kissinger and Chou mentioned by the President was held while Kissinger was on a fact-finding tour of Asia. While he was reportedly resting in the Pakistani mountain resort of Nattria Gali, temporarily incapacitated by a stomach ailment, Kissinger made a secret flight to Peking from Pakistan. The Kissinger mission, and preparations for it, were shrouded in such secrecy that only Nixon, Kissinger, Secretary of State William P. Rogers and "a very few White House staff members" knew what was happening. Arrangements for the trip were drawn up between April and June. Negotiations leading up to the trip were in two stages. The first required the establishment of a framework for negotiations and success in convincing the Chinese leaders that Americans were flexible and were not "prisoners of history." The second phase started in April as negotiations moved from the general framework to a more specific exploration of "where we might go from here."

[8] *Reaction to Nixon trip.* The announcement of Nixon's intention to visit China drew generally favorable comment, mainly within Congress, from U.S. political figures July 15-20. (Nixon briefed Congressional leaders July 19 on his plans.) However, some senators and congressmen expressed concern over the effect of the trip on foreign and domestic policy. The response of other nations to the visit ranged from positive acclaim to sharp criticism. Nationalist China expressed shock and dismay in a series of statements issued July 15-17 by government officials and envoys. The Viet Cong warned July 16 and 20 that the visit would not help to resolve the conflict in Indochina, but South Vietnam Vice President Nguyen Cao Ky predicted July 18 that the move would bring an early settlement of the Indochina war. Japan July 17 expressed hope that the visit would help improve relations between Japan and China. In Eastern Europe, comments varied; but all Western European governments, including those of France, Britain and West Germany, July 16 welcomed Nixon's decision to visit China. The Soviet Union July 21 endorsed criticism of Nixon's trip, but refrained from direct comment on it. In the first official Soviet reaction to the visit, the Communist party newspaper Pravda July 25 warned that "any designs to use the contacts between Peking and Washington for some pressure against the Soviet Union, or the states of the Socialist community, are nothing but the result of a loss of touch with reality." However, the Soviet position seemed to soften Aug. 10 when the Soviet news agency Tass distributed an article by Georgi A. Arbatov, a specialist in U.S. affairs, which expressed hope that the visit would not harm U.S.-Soviet relations or hinder the solution of major world problems.

[9] *Chou on visit.* In an interview published Dec. 5, Premier Chou implied that President Nixon would have to solve "the Taiwan [Nationalist China] question" during his visit. (Chou had declared July 19 that, in order to establish diplomatic relations with Peking, the U.S. would have to recognize Peking as the sole legitimate government of China and acknowledge Taiwan as an "internal affair" of China which "brooks no foreign intervention.") Chou said support of two Chinas amounted to "contradictions in U.S. foreign policy" and that it was "up to President Nixon to answer this question—otherwise, if he comes to China and yet the Taiwan question remains unsettled, how will he account for himself when he gets back?"

[10] **Nixon stresses dialogue.** President Nixon Aug. 4 cautioned against expectation that his visit would produce "instant detente." The President said: "We expect to make some progress, but to speculate about what progress will be made on any particular issue—to speculate, for example, as to what effect this might have on Vietnam—would not serve the interests of constructive talks." The President said that the meaning of his visit was that the U.S. was moving from "an era of confrontation without communication to an era of negotiations with discussion." While he would not speculate on the effect of his visit or the conversations to be held on Vietnam, Nixon said there would be "a wide-ranging discussion of issues concerning both governments" and the agenda would deal "with the hard problems as well as the easy ones."

[11] **Spy flights halted.** The U.S. government announced July 28 a suspension of American intelligence-gathering missions over China by manned SR-71 reconnaissance planes and unmanned drones. The decision was aimed at preventing any incident that might mar Nixon's trip. U.S. earth satellite missions were to continue over China, however, being considered less provocative because they were well above China's airspace. It was presumed that Nationalist China would continue to fly U-2 spy planes over the mainland. (It was reported Aug. 6 that incursion into Chinese territory of CIA (U.S. Central Intelligence Agency)-supported teams of Laotian tribesmen on reconnaissance patrols had been ordered halted.)

[12]   Telephone service restored. Direct telephone service between the U.S. and China, terminated by Peking without explanation in 1968, was restored Sept. 2. Direct telephone connection between Britain and China had been reopened April 15 after an interruption of 22 years.

[13]   2nd Kissinger visit. Henry Kissinger visited Peking Oct. 20-25 to arrange the agenda and itinerary for the Nixon visit. Kissinger originally had planned to stay only four days, but his stay was extended for two additional days without explanation. He reported to the President on his trip Oct. 27. He later told newsmen that Nixon and the Chinese leaders hoped to restrict their substantive talks to issues involving only the two countries. Other matters, such as Soviet-Chinese relations and the Indochina war, would not be discussed, he said.

   See also AUSTRALIA [8-9]; CANADA [26]; CHINA, COMMUNIST; CHINA, NATIONALIST; COMMUNISM, INTERNATIONAL; ESPIONAGE; FOREIGN POLICY; NIXON, RICHARD MILHOUS [3]; SINO-SOVIET DEVELOPMENTS

CONCERNED OFFICERS MOVEMENT—*See* WAR CRIMES [12]
CONDORS—*See* CONSERVATION

CONGO, DEMOCRATIC REPUBLIC OF THE (KINSHASA)—Aftermath of student unrest. The normalization of relations with the Congo (Brazzaville) suffered a setback Aug. 19 when Kinshasa expelled Brazzaville charge d' affaires Lt. Gaston Iyabo and charged him with complicity in a plot by a group of Louvanium University students to overthrow the government of Gen. Joseph Mobutu. (Mobutu had closed the university June 5 and ordered its Congolese students to report for induction into the army after police the previous day fired on a group of students commemorating 1969 disturbances on the campus. It was reported June 15 that 2,889 students had enrolled in the army and that 16 students failing to do so had been sentenced by a military court June 12 to 10 years in prison for desertion.) The students accused of the plot had been on trial since Aug. 14 for allegedly planning an urban guerrilla warfare campaign with the assistance of Nicolas Olenga, one of the leaders of the 1964-65 Congolese rebellion. Ten students were sentenced Aug. 26 to life imprisonment; three were given three years each in prison, and two were acquitted. Nineteen East European diplomats were expelled from the country July 27 for their reported involvement with the student demonstrations.

   Government changes. Four ministerial appointments were announced July 2 by Mobutu. Claude Mafema became minister of national affairs, replacing Jacques Risasi. Paul Mushiete was named minister of posts and telecommunications, replacing Nestor Watum. Leon Engulu was given control of public works and territorial planning, and Jean-Baptiste Alves became minister of commerce.

   Name changed. The government announced Oct. 27 that the country henceforth would be known as the Republic of Zaire because "our country is called after the majestic River Congo, but historically the name Congo was used for the ancient kingdom of Ekongo but not for the river Zaire." The Congo River was renamed the Zaire, Orientale Province became Upper Zaire Province and Central Congo Province became Lower Zaire Province. There would be a new flag and national anthem.

   See also AFRICA; AGNEW, SPIRO THEODORE; MIDDLE EAST [37]; SUDAN

CONGO, REPUBLIC OF (BRAZZAVILLE)— The Congolese Labor party Feb. 8 announced changes in the Council of State. The new Cabinet: Marien Ngouabi—president of the Council of State in charge of national defense and security; Alfred Raoul—vice president of the Council of State in charge of trade, industry and mines (replaced Dec. 16 as vice president by Aloyse Moudileno-Massengo and as minister of industry by Justin Lekounzou); Ange Djawara—development (ministry abolished Dec. 16), water and forestry resources; Moudileno-Massengo—information (ministry abolished Dec. 16), justice and keeper of the seals; Henri Lopes—national education, culture, arts, mass education and sports; Louis Sylvain Goma—public works and transport; Charles Ngouoto—social affairs, health (replaced Dec. 16 by Dieudonne Itoua) and labor; Itoua—territorial administration (ministry abolished Dec. 16); Auxence Ickonga—foreign affairs (replaced Dec. 16 by Lopes); Boniface Matingou—finance and budget (replaced June 12 by Edward Ange Poungui). The council continued to include three secretaries of state, but the secretariat headed by Elie Itsou became that of social affairs, health and labor. The functions of Pierre Ngounimba Tsari, secretary of state for development, were assumed by Djawara June 12. In further changes Dec. 16, Jean-Pierre Chicaya became minister of technical and professional education and Christophe Moukoueke was named minister of primary and secondary education.

See also CONGO, DEMOCRATIC REPUBLIC OF THE

CONGRESS—91st Congress adjourns. The 91st Congress adjourned Jan. 2. Its second session was the longest since 1950. The Senate decided to carry one controversial issue—funding of the supersonic transport plane (*See* AVIATION [1-3])—over to the new Congress, swore in new members William V. Roth Jr. (R, Del.) and John V. Tunney (D, Calif.) and adjourned at 2:29 p.m. Roth and Tunney were succeeding to seats held by Sens. John J. Williams (R, Del.), retiring after 24 years in the Senate, and George Murphy (R, Calif.), who lost to Tunney in November 1970. The House heard eulogies to its speaker, John W. McCormack (D, Mass.), 79, who was retiring after 42 years in the House and nine as speaker, then adjourned at 3:11 p.m. President Nixon said Jan. 5 that the 91st Congress would be remembered "not for what it did but for what it failed to do." Nixon directed much of his criticism against the Senate and said "the 91st Congress had the opportunity to write one of the most productive and memorable chapters in the history of the American government. The opportunity was lost. The nation was the loser." In rebuttal to Nixon's attack, Rep. Carl Albert (D, Okla.), the most likely successor to McCormack's vacated post, said later Jan. 5 that "not Congress but the Administration will surely be remembered for what it failed to do." A report Jan. 29 by Congressional Quarterly said that President Nixon had won 77% of Congressional roll call votes in 1970 which presented a clear test of support for his known position. The House support was 85%, the Senate's 71%.

[2]   Lobby spending reported. Congressional Quarterly Aug. 6 reported that $5.8 million was spent by organizations in 1970 to influence legislation, according to reports filed with the House File Clerk under the Federal Regulation of Lobbying Act. The total figure reported for 1969 was $5.4 million. Broken down by type of organization, the following total lobby spending was reported: business, $1,901,031; citizens, $1,064,600; employee and labor, $1,035,815; farm, $600,946; foreign, $32,404; individuals and firms, $42,821; military and veterans, $569,035; professional, $565,413; and miscellaneous, $29,469.

[3]   92nd Congress convenes. The 92nd Congress convened Jan. 21 with Democratic majorities in both houses. The political lineup in the Senate (after the Republican caucus accepted Sen. James L. Buckley, who was elected as a Conservative from New York, and the Democratic caucus accepted Sen. Harry F. Byrd, who had been re-elected as an independent from Georgia) was 54 Democrats, 45 Republicans and one vacancy created by the death of Georgia Democrat Richard B. Russell, who died Jan. 21. (Georgia Gov. Jimmy Carter Feb. 1 appointed David H. Gambrell, an Atlanta lawyer and Democratic state chairman, to fill Russell's unexpired term.) The political lineup in the House was 254 Democrats, 180 Republicans and one vacancy.

[4]   *Senate actions.* Sen. Mike Mansfield (Mont.) was re-elected majority leader by acclamation in the Senate Democratic caucus Jan. 21. The caucus ousted Sen. Edward M. Kennedy (Mass.) as assistant majority leader, replacing him with Sen. Robert C. Byrd (W. Va.) by a 31-24 vote. Kennedy's loss was largely attributed to complacency and to an uneven performance as assistant majority leader. In other Democratic organizational procedures Jan. 21, Frank E. Moss (Utah) was named by acclamation to succeed Byrd as secretary of the Democratic Conference, the third-ranking post in the Senate party leadership. After the caucus, Mansfield appointed Sens. William B. Spong (Va.), Quentin N. Burdick (N.D.) and Moss to the Democratic Steering Committee. In a further move to give the steering group, which controlled Senate committee assignments, a "more liberal orientation," Mansfield Jan. 23 named Kennedy and Sen. Lawton Chiles (Fla.), a freshman senator, to the committee. Sen. Allen J. Ellender (La.) was chosen by the Democrats Jan. 23 to be president pro tempore of the Senate, succeeding Russell.

[5]   In the Republican caucus Jan. 21, Sen. Hugh Scott (Pa.) retained his position as minority leader, despite a challenge by Sen. Howard H. Baker Jr. (Tenn.). Scott won by a 24-20 vote, a smaller margin than anticipated. Other GOP leaders re-elected were Sens. Robert P. Griffin (Mich.) as minority whip (assistant leader), Margaret Chase Smith (Me.) as chairman of the Senate Republican Conference, and Gordon Allott (Colo.) as chairman of the Republican Policy Committee. Sen. Norris Cotton (N.H.) was named to succeed Sen. Milton R. Young (N.D.), who chose not to run, as secretary of the GOP Conference. Republicans Jan. 23 chose Sen. Wallace F. Bennett (Utah) to head the GOP Committee on Committees, which made party committee assignments. Sen. Peter Dominick (Colo.) was named head of the Senate GOP Campaign Committee.

[6]   The Senate leadership agreed Jan. 19 to some procedural reforms to speed up the legislative process. Minor morning speeches were to be limited to three minutes. Members were expected to remain in Washington during sessions and the Senate was to take a five-day recess at the end of each month. The rule requiring a three-day interval between a committee report and floor action on appropriations bills was to be enforced to permit time to study hearings reports. The leadership also agreed to seek formation of a joint committee with the executive branch to study the feasibility of changing the fiscal year as a way to ease the problem of Congressional tardiness in processing appropriations bills. Senate Republicans Jan. 26 approved limiting members to no more than one ranking minority membership on standing committees and authorized a study of changes in the seniority system. Senate Democrats Jan. 26 approved in caucus, for the first time in recent history, the selection of committee chairmen. They also authorized a regular monthly meeting of the caucus, which would provide opportunity to subject committee chairmen and other leadership to the majority view. Both Republican and Democratic proposals were initiated by Sens. Fred Harris (D, Okla.) and Charles McC. Mathias Jr. (R, Md.), who had held, on their own initiative, informal hearings Jan. 18-19 on reform of the seniority system. They were seeking to gain acceptance of a Senate rule to require committee chairmen to be approved by party caucus and then by the Senate.

[7]   *House actions.* House Democrats Jan. 19 named Rep. Albert as their choice for speaker over Rep. John Conyers (Mich.), a Negro, who challenged Albert on the basis of his refusal to commit himself to strip members of the Mississippi delegation of seniority because they came from a state Democratic party that practiced racial segregation and had been refused recognition at the 1968 Democratic National Convention. The vote on the speakership was 220-20. The caucus later voted 111-55 to defeat a proposal to deny the Mississippians seniority, which would have ousted one committee chairman and two subcommittee chairmen. Other Democratic leadership selections at the caucus Jan. 19 were Rep. Hale Boggs (La.) as majority leader and Rep. Olin E. Teague (Tex.) as permanent chairman of the caucus. Teague gained the post by a surprise 155-91 victory over Rep. Dan Rostenkowski (Ill.), who was seeking a third two-year term as chairman. The major contest among the Democrats was for majority leader, which Boggs won on the second ballot. Boggs won after

Rep. Wayne L. Hays (Ohio) withdrew from the race, endorsing Boggs, and Rep. James G. O'Hara (Mich.) also withdrew. Boggs won with 140 votes to 88 votes for Rep. Morris K. Udall (Ariz.) and 17 votes for Rep. B. F. Sisk (Calif.). Boggs Jan. 22 selected Rep. Thomas P. O'Neill Jr. (Mass.) as majority whip and Reps. John Brademas (Ind.) and John J. McFall (Calif.) as assistant whips.

[8] In the House Republican caucus Jan. 20, conservative challenges were twice beaten back by moderates as Rep. John B. Anderson (Ill.) was re-elected to a second term as chairman of the House Republican Conference by an 89-81 vote over Rep. Samuel L. Devine (Ohio) and Rep. Robert T. Stafford (Vt.) defeated Rep. Jack Edwards (Ala.) by an 85-82 vote for the position of conference vice chairman. Minority Leader Gerald R. Ford (Mich.) and Minority Whip Leslie C. Arends (Ill.) were unopposed for re-election to those positions. Rep. Richard H. Poff (Va.) was renamed conference secretary and Rep. John Rhodes (Ariz.) chairman of the GOP Policy Committee. Rep. Barber B. Conable Jr. (N.Y.) was unopposed for chairmanship of the Research Committee.

[9] In separate caucuses Jan. 20, Democrats and Republicans authorized caucus approval of the selection of committee chairmen or ranking minority members of committees. Such a vote would be held by the Democrats whenever it was demanded by 10 members. The Republicans were to vote automatically by secret ballot on committee ranking. Both parties also agreed that seniority need not guide the drafting of committee assignments for caucus approval. House Democrats also approved a limitation of one subcommittee chairmanship to committee chairmen and other senior committee members. (The limit would open up to 30 subcommittee chairmanships.) Despite the slight easing of the seniority rule by the caucuses, a liberal drive in the Democratic caucus Feb. 3 failed to unseat Rep. John L. McMillan (S.C.), 72, as chairman of the Committee on the District of Columbia, a position he had held for 22 years. The 126-96 vote to uphold McMillan was still considered a surprising show of strength for the liberals. The House Democrats also rejected Feb. 3 reform proposals to limit the age of committee chairmen to 70 years and to limit a chairman's service to four two-year terms. Democratic liberals also failed Feb. 3 to unseat Rep. Joe D. Waggoner Jr. (La.), a leading spokesman for Southern conservatives, from the Ways and Means Committee and replace him with Rep. Donald M. Fraser (Minn.), chairman of the liberal Democratic Study Group.

[10] **Filibuster on filibuster change.** Sens. Frank Church (D, Idaho) and James B. Pearson (R, Kan.) Jan. 26 led a reform proposal by 51 senators to reduce the number of senators necessary to cut off a filibuster from two-thirds of those present and voting to three-fifths. Sens. James B. Allen (D, Ala.) and Sam J. Ervin Jr. (D, N.C.) launched a filibuster against the change the same day. (Proposals to change the filibuster rule were subject to a filibuster unless the presiding officer, in this case Vice President Spiro Agnew, ruled that the Senate, at the start of a new Congress, had a constitutional right to cut off debate by a simple majority. Agnew said he would put all constitutional questions during the debate to the Senate.) The effort to change the filibuster rule was abandoned March 9 after four attempts to invoke cloture (stop debate) had failed. The first cloture vote Feb. 18 failed by nine votes—48-37; the second vote Feb. 23 failed by eight votes—50-36; the third vote March 2 failed by eight votes—48-36, and the fourth vote March 9 failed by eight votes—55-39. Following the final vote, Sen. Jacob K. Javits (R, N.Y.) sought to force a ruling on the question whether a new Senate could amend its rules by a simple majority or was a "continuing body" bound by previous rules. However, a motion to table Javit's challenge was tabled 55-37, since some who were supporting reform did not want cloture by a simple majority vote.

[11] **Impounding conflict.** Conflict broke out between the Congress and the Administration during March over the Administration's withholding of what was first estimated as $8 billion in appropriated funds. The withholding was disclosed in testimony before the House Appropriations Committee during

hearings on the federal budget by Director of the Office of Management and Budget (OMB) George P. Shultz. Shultz's disclosure drew fire March 3 from Sen. John J. Sparkman (D, Ala.), who charged that "impounding" the funds was a "serious breach of faith" with Congress. Caspar W. Weinberger, deputy director of the OMB, and Secretary of Housing and Urban Development George Romney March 4 testified that the funds had been withheld mainly as a means of combating inflation. They said most of the impounded funds had been marked for construction, an area of central concern to the Administration because of spiraling wages and prices. Weinberger, in testimony before the Senate Subcommittee on Separation of Powers March 24, said that the President was not required to spend appropriated funds. He denied that the freeze was "a means by which the President attempts to thwart the will of Congress." The President, he said, could not be forced to spend automatically without regard to statutory debt and spending ceilings. Subcommittee member Sen. Mathias disagreed, calling the impounding "clearly in violation of the spirit and intent of our Constitution." Allowing the President to have a "line-item veto of appropriated money which cannot be overridden," he said, would "impound declared Congressional policy and threaten Congress's very existence." In criticism of the freeze March 25, Democratic leaders revealed that $12.8 billion in appropriated funds had been withheld—nearly $6 billion for highway construction, $757 million for farm programs, $200 million for water and sewer facilities, $191 million for Appalachian regional development and various sums for mass transit, anti-pollution, education, regional medical programs, air safety and other programs.

[12] Reserve status for congressmen illegal. U.S. District Court Judge Gerhard A. Gesell ruled April 2 in Washington that it was a violation of the Constitution's principle of "separation of powers" for members of Congress to hold commissions in military reserve units during their time in office. Gesell said, however, that he would not issue an order directing the 117 senators and representatives holding commissions to resign them or leave Congress. The ruling, which came in a suit against Secretary of Defense Melvin Laird filed by an organization called the Reservists Committee to Stop the War, was based on Article 1, Section 6, Clause 2 of the Constitution, which said: "No senator or representative shall, during the time for which he was elected, be appointed to any civil office under the authority of the United States, which shall have been created or the emoluments whereof shall have been increased during such time; and no person holding any office under the United States shall be a member of either house during his continuance in office."

[13] Prouty dies. Sen. Winston L. Prouty (R, Vt.), 65, died in Boston Sept. 10 of stomach cancer. Rep. Robert T. Stafford (R), Vermont's only member in the House, was appointed to the vacant Senate seat Sept. 16 by Vermont Gov. Deane C. Davis (R). A special election was scheduled for January 1972 to fill the seat for the five remaining years of the term won by Prouty in 1970.

[14] Congress adjourns. The first session of the 92nd Congress adjourned Dec. 17, the House at 12:59 p.m., the Senate at 1:32 p.m.

See also AGING; AGRICULTURE [12]; AUTOMOBILE [4, 6-7]; AVIATION [1-3]; BANKS; BUDGET; BUSINESS [3-4]; CHEMICAL & BIOLOGICAL WARFARE; CHINA, NATIONALIST; CIVIL RIGHTS [1, 17-19, 22]; COMMUNIST CHINA-U.S. DETENTE [8]; CONSERVATION; CONSTITUTION, U.S.; CONSUMER AFFAIRS [3-6, 12, 14]; CRIME [2-6, 22]; DEFENSE [9, 11, 14]; DISARMAMENT; DISTRICT OF COLUMBIA; DRAFT & WAR PROTEST [4-5, 7, 11-12, 14, 16]· DRUG USE & ADDICTION [1-2, 14, 16-17, 19]; ECONOMY, U.S. [4, 8-10, 13, 16]; EDUCATION [12-13, 18]; ELECTIONS [1]; ENERGY; ENVIRONMENT; EUROPEAN SECURITY; FEDERAL BUREAU OF INVESTIGATION [1, 3-5]; FOREIGN AID; FOREIGN POLICY; GOVERNMENT REORGANIZATION; GREECE [3]; HEALTH CARE; HOUSING; HUNGER; INDIANS, AMERICAN; INDOCHINA WAR [1, 18, 66-68]; INTERNATIONAL MONETARY DEVELOPMENTS [8, 14]; JAPAN [5];

JUDICIARY [2-3, 7]; LABOR [1]; LATIN AMERICA; MEDICINE; MEXICO; MIDDLE EAST [22]; MILITARY [3-6]; MINES; NIXON, RICHARD MILHOUS [1-2, 4, 7-8]; PAKISTAN [37]; PENTAGON PAPERS [3, 9-10, 13, 17]; POLITICS [1-2, 9]; POLLUTION [3, 14-15]; POPULATION; POSTAL SERVICE, U.S.; POVERTY; PRISONS [8]; PUBLIC LAND; PUERTO RICO; RACIAL & MINORITY UNREST [1, 3, 17]; RAILROADS; RHODESIA; SECURITY, U.S.; SELECTIVE SERVICE SYSTEM [2-3, 5-8]; SOCIAL SECURITY; STATE & LOCAL GOVERNMENTS [1-8]; SUPREME COURT; TARIFFS & WORLD TRADE [3, 7, 13]; TAXES; TELEVISION & RADIO; TERRITORIAL WATERS; UNEMPLOYMENT; UNITED NATIONS [8]; VOTING RIGHTS; WAR CRIMES [12]; WELFARE; WOMEN'S RIGHTS

CONGRESSIONAL BLACK CAUCUS—*See* RACIAL & MINORITY UNREST [1, 17]; TARIFFS & WORLD TRADE [13]

CONNALLY, JOHN B.—*See* AVIATION [2]; BUSINESS [3-4]; CANADA [26]; COMMUNIST CHINA-U.S. DETENTE [5]; DRUG USE & ADDICTION [7]; INTERNATIONAL BANK FOR RECONSTRUCTION & DEVELOPMENT; NIXON, RICHARD MILHOUS [4]

CONSCIENTIOUS OBJECTORS (COs)—*See* ROMAN CATHOLIC CHURCH [10]; SELECTIVE SERVICE SYSTEM [11-16]

CONSERVATION—U.S. bars whale hunting. Commerce Secretary Maurice H. Stans issued an order March 1 ending licensing of commercial whale hunters. The ban, which took effect in 30 days, was a followup to the Interior Department's action in December 1970 designating the kinds of whales most often hunted commercially as endangered species and banning the import of whale products from the species on the endangered list. The 1970 action did not affect domestic whaling. The Commerce Department order affected only the Del Monte Fishing Co., operated from San Francisco Bay, which hunted whales for animal foods and lubricating oils.

Seal hunt begins. The 1971 seal hunt in the northwest Atlantic and Arctic Oceans began March 12. Canadian Fisheries Minister Jack Davis announced March 29 the appointment of a six-man task force to study the annual hunt. He predicted that the kill-quota on seals would be drastically reduced in 1972 from the 1971 quota of 245,000. Canada and Norway signed an agreement July 15 to regulate seal hunting by the two nations. They agreed to establish a commission that would submit proposals regarding national catch-quotas, opening and closing days of the season and humane hunting methods. Norwegian rights to hunt seals were insured until the end of 1978. Following a visit to Alaska, Commerce Secretary Stans said July 14 that seals on the Pribilof Islands off Alaska were "being managed and harvested under scientific practices just as domestic animals are raised and harvested." He said that environmentalists' protests that harvesting depleted the herd or was conducted in an inefficient, inhumane or indiscriminate manner were "totally unfounded." A report released by the Commerce Department Sept. 8 defended the Pribilof harvest as "highly efficient and humane." The report was by a panel of veterinarians who had reviewed the hunt in July.

Hearings on ocean mammals. The House Fisheries and Wildlife Conservation Subcommittee was told Sept. 9 that several species of ocean mammals were threatened with extinction not only because of hunting but also because of pollution and destruction of their habitat. The hearings resulted from a public outcry, mostly in connection with the clubbing method used in the seal harvest in the Pribilofs. One bill, introduced by Rep. David Pryor (D, Md.) and cosponsored by 90 congressmen, would ban the killing of seals, whales, walruses, sea lions, polar bears, otters or porpoises in U.S. waters or by U.S. citizens in any waters. It would also ban importation of ocean mammal products and demand State Department negotiation with other countries to protect ocean mammals. Pryor said he was removing a provision to end the Pribilof harvest because it could endanger an international treaty against seal hunts on the high seas.

Shooting of eagles reported. A pilot, James O. Vogan, told the Senate Environmental Appropriations Subcommittee in testimony Aug. 2 and 3 that 770 rare bald and golden eagles had been illegally shot from helicopters over Wyoming and Colorado from September 1970 to March 1971. Vogan said sheep ranchers, ostensibly to protect livestock, paid $80 a day or from $10 to $25 per eagle for the hunt. Federal and state law prohibited the killing of the eagles, both on the Interior Department's list of endangered species. Bald eagles, the American national emblem, numbered about 2,000 in the U.S., and golden eagles numbered about 8,000-10,000. It was also illegal to hunt any wildlife from aircraft without a special permit from the Interior Department under a program to control predatory animals. Vogan, who was granted immunity from prosecution before testifying, said he had flown hunting parties seeking eagles and coyotes while working for the Buffalo (Wyo.) Flying Service. He said that antelope, elk, deer and Canadian geese had also been hunted from helicopters. An attorney for the Buffalo Flying Service said Aug. 3 that the firm had never had agreements to kill predators other than coyotes. Herman Werner, reportedly the largest sheep rancher in Wyoming, whom Vogan had accused of paying $15,000 to the flying service for the killing of eagles and coyotes, said Aug. 11 that he had nothing to do with the shooting of eagles. A search connected with the Senate hearings found an undetermined number of dead eagles on Werner's Bolton Ranch.

The appearance of Vogan before the subcommittee chaired by Sen. Gale W. McGee (D, Wyo.) followed an investigation earlier in the year of the thallium poisoning of eagles near Casper, Wyo. About 50 poisoned eagles had been discovered in May and June. As a result of that probe, criminal charges were filed against Van Irvine, former president of the Wyoming Stockgrowers Association, for killing an antelope out of season and using it for bait by lacing the carcass with poison. Irvine pleaded no contest to 29 state charges and was fined $679. Charges against four other men were dropped.

Hunting animals from planes barred. Legislation making it a federal crime to shoot or hunt birds, fish or other animals from an airplane was cleared by Congress Nov. 5 and signed by President Nixon Nov. 18. Penalties of up to $5,000 in fines and a year in prison were authorized. Such activity would be permitted to protect land, water, animals, people or crops, but participants would have to obtain state or federal permits. Final action Nov. 5 consisted of House approval of a Senate amendment to require permit holders to report quarterly on the number and type of animals killed in such activity.

Wild horses protected. A bill making it a federal offense to kill or harass the estimated 9,000-10,000 wild horses and 10,000 wild burros on public lands in the West was cleared by Congress Dec. 3 and signed Dec. 15. Refuges were to be set up if necessary.

Ban sought on poison shipments. Seven conservation organizations petitioned Environmental Protection Administrator William D. Ruckelshaus Aug. 18 to ban interstate shipment of poisons used to kill coyotes. The groups said the poisons threatened the ecology, were a "shotgun approach" to the coyote problem and also killed a variety of birds and pet dogs and cats. Signing the petition were the Natural Resources Defense Council, Defenders of Wildlife, Friends of the Earth, Humane Society of the United States, National Audubon Society Inc., New York Zoological Society and Sierra Club.

Save-condor effort begun. The Nature Conservancy and the U.S. Forest Service announced a joint project Aug. 19 to save the California condor. It was estimated that only 50-60 of the large birds were left. The groups bought 162 acres of condor nesting ground for a sanctuary.

See also ATOMIC ENERGY [17]; ENVIRONMENT; FEDERAL BUREAU OF INVESTIGATION [5]; INDIANS, AMERICAN; POLLUTION [4, 6-7]

CON SON ISLAND —*See* SECURITY, U.S.; VIETNAM, SOUTH

CONSTITUTION, U.S.—The Senate adopted by an 84-0 vote Oct. 19 a bill to establish additional procedure to amend the Constitution through a national convention. Amendment of the Constitution through the convention process, which could be called on petition of two-thirds of the states, had never been employed. Ratification by three-quarters of the states of any amendments issuing from a convention was the same procedure following adoption by two-thirds of both houses of Congress, the only method used so far to amend the charter.

The additional rules, sponsored by Sen. Sam J. Ervin Jr. (D, N.C.), stemmed from concern that a convention once called was under no current curb and could rewrite the entire Constitution. The concern was brought to a head from the near-miss of a movement led by the late Sen. Everett M. Dirksen (R, Ill.) to hold a convention on reapportionment and overturn the Supreme Court's one-man, one-vote decision. By July of 1969, 33 states, one short of the necessary two-thirds, had approved resolutions calling for a convention, although there were no set procedures for holding it. The Ervin bill would provide that: (a) a state calling for a convention must state the subject to be considered; (b) the same resolution must be adopted by two-thirds of the states within seven years; (c) Congress must call the convention and set the date, provide quarters and pay expenses; (d) delegates must be elected with each state entitled to the number of its Congressional delegation; (e) the convention must be limited to the subject of the call; (f) approval of any proposed Constitutional amendment must be by two-thirds of the convention; (g) the change would then be submitted to the states for ratification by at least three-quarters before becoming effective. The two-thirds vote of the convention needed for approval of the amendment was added to the Senate bill by a 45-39 vote on a proposal by Sen Birch Bayh (D, Ind.). The Ervin bill had sanctioned approval by a simple majority.

See also CONGRESS [11-12]; SUPREME COURT; VOTING RIGHTS; WOMEN'S RIGHTS

CONSUMER AFFAIRS—FTC acts on credit abuses. The Federal Trade Commission (FTC) Jan. 21 proposed a rule that sales agreements on installment credit plans must state that the holder of the contract was "subject to all defenses and claims" that a consumer could legally raise against the retailer. The customer's legal "defenses" included the right to refuse payment or bring suit in case of fraud or a defective product. The proposed regulation would define as unfair and deceptive the transfer of an installment payment contract without protection of the consumer's claims against the original retailer.

[2] New credit card rules. New rules went into effect Jan. 25 requiring all new credit cards to bear some type of cer-tain holder identification and providing that a card holder could not be held responsible for more than $50 of unauthorized purchases made on a lost or stolen card. Companies had to inform card holders of the liability and had to provide self-addressed, prestamped notices to be returned if a credit card was lost or stolen. The rules, part of a Truth-in-Lending Act amendment signed by President Nixon Oct. 26, 1970, were to be administered by the FTC. (A provision making it illegal to mail unsolicited credit cards had gone into effect upon signing of the amendment.)

[3] Combination drug rules set. The Food and Drug Administration (FDA) Feb. 17 proposed a new set of rules requiring that each active ingredient in a combination drug (one containing two or more active ingredients in a fixed dosage form) contribute to the medicine's effectiveness. The rules, which became effective 30 days following their proposition, affected up to 40% of the most widely sold prescription drugs and about 50% of over-the-counter (OTC) drugs—those sold without a prescription. In later drug developments, the FDA announced June 7, effective in October, that labels and advertisements for prescription drugs would have to include adverse findings on their effectiveness by the National Academy of Sciences-National Research Council. In a move announced Aug. 1, the FDA launched a study of the efficacy and safety of nonprescription tranquilizers and sleeping pills. The action gave drug manufacturers 180 days to submit "the best available evidence" of safety and effectiveness of numerous OTC products that contained an antihistamine called methapyrilene. (The substance was contained in such products as Compoz, Nytol, Sominex, Excedrin P.M. and Dormin.) FDA Commissioner Charles C. Edwards said July 21 that the study of mood drugs would be the first part of an assessment of all OTC medicines. The FDA Oct. 6 announced that it would begin an inventory of all prescription and OTC drugs, vitamins and antibiotics sold in the U.S. for human use. Manufacturers would be asked to comply voluntarily, though a bill passed by the House Sept. 16 would mandate industry cooperation. The inventory, to be completed and processed by April 1972, would list for each product the amount of production, formula, claimed effectiveness and individual coding on each pill or tablet.

[4] **Special consumer message.** President Nixon sent to Congress a consumer message Feb. 24 framing a legislative program designed as "a Buyer's Bill of Rights." He asked Congress to authorize mandatory federal safety standards for consumer products not already regulated by federal law. At the same time, the President created by executive order a White House Office of Consumer Affairs to coordinate federal consumer activities. Mrs. Virginia H. Knauer, special Presidential assistant for consumer affairs, was appointed by the President to assume the additional responsibility of director of the new office. The President proposed that the secretary of health, education and welfare be given authority to set minimum safety standards for products, following hearings by the FDA. The secretary would also be empowered to ban from the market products that failed to meet federal safety standards. Civil penalties of $10,000 would be levied for each violation of the standards. Violators would also be subject to unspecified criminal penalties.

[5]   The President's consumer package, which was similar to a program he had proposed Oct. 30, 1969, also would: (1) authorize the Justice Department to prosecute for 14 specific fraudulent advertising and selling practices, (2) empower the FTC to seek injunctions against unfair practices (but not to impose criminal penalties for known frauds or compel restitution to consumers), (3) call for a study of class-action suits that would permit consumers to seek damages in federal courts but only after successful prosecution by the Justice Department, (4) bar deceptive warranties, and (5) set up a National Business Council in the Commerce Department to assist business in meeting its obligations to consumers (see [13]). The President rejected an earlier proposal for legislation to set up an independent consumer protection agency to represent the consumer before federal courts and regulatory agencies as merely adding to "the proliferation of agencies" (see [14]). Instead, he suggested the appointment of a "consumer advocate" within the federal trade practices agency proposed by his Advisory Council on Executive Reorganization (see GOVERNMENT REORGANIZATION). Since the council's agency overhaul plan would not reach Congress until sometime after April 20, the President urged that the advocacy function be placed under the FTC in the interim.

[6] **Lye regulation.** The FDA announced June 9 that liquid drain cleaners that contained more than 10% lye would be banned in 60 days unless sold in a government-approved "child-proof" package. The action followed reports of at least 271 incidents of children swallowing drain cleaners in the last four years, with 114 hospitalizations and three deaths. In a similar development reported Sept. 7, the FDA proposed a rule requiring furniture oil polishes containing 10% or more petroleum distillates to be sold in child-proof packages. Commissioner Edwards said that between 1965 and 1970, 54 children died after swallowing furniture polish.

[7] **FDA acts on labels.** The FDA June 13 proposed a regulation, effective after 90 days, that required processed-food manufacturers to list the source of animal or vegetable fat in a product. The regulation also allowed labels to cite the percentage of unsaturated fats, but the agency refrained from endorsing

the disputed view that saturated fats contribute to heart disease. In another labeling development, the FDA had announced June 4 a voluntary agreement by which citrus growers and producers of diluted orange beverages agreed to label products according to the percentage of pure orange juice in the drinks. Products called "orange juice drink" would have to contain at least 35% pure orange juice, "orange drink" at least 10% and "orange flavored drink" less than 10%.

[8]   Poisoning leads to soup recalls. The FDA July 7 ordered the recall of all soups, sauces and other canned products made by Bon Vivant Soups, Inc. of Newark, N.J. The action came after the June 30 death by botulism poisoning of Samuel Cochran Jr. of Westchester County, N.Y. after he ate canned vichyssoise made by the company. The toxin from Clostridium botulinus bacteria, which also caused the serious illness of Cochran's wife, causes paralysis and death, usually from respiratory failure, by attacking the central nervous system. Although the bacteria are normally harmless, they can grow and produce toxin in the airless atmosphere of improperly processed canned foods. Tests completed July 2 confirmed that botulism of the type fatal in 70% of all cases was present in the can of vichyssoise eaten by the Cochrans. The total recall was ordered after four additional cans in the same lot were discovered contaminated from botulism. The FDA said July 9 that the contamination was the result of "human error" and was probably caused by the improper heating of the cans. The agency acknowledged July 20 that the plant had not been inspected since May 1967 (*see* [12]).

**[9]   **The FDA began seizing Bon Vivant products Aug. 11 because, it charged, Bon Vivant (which had filed for bankruptcy July 26) and the National Canners' Association (NCA) had failed to meet the recall agreement. The recall had been accelerated July 23 as more underprocessing of Bon Vivant products was discovered. Joseph Walsh, the receiver appointed in the company's bankruptcy proceedings, had begun court proceedings Aug. 2 in an attempt to halt the recall. He said he was not bound by the voluntary recall agreement made by Bon Vivant. The NCA said Aug. 13 that in view of Walsh's actions it had "no choice but to hold in abeyance all voluntary recall efforts." Walsh's court action was lost in August and Walsh began negotiating with the FDA to determine means of testing the embargoed cans. By Sept. 18, the FDA had filed 106 separate suits in as many courts to seize stocks of Bon Vivant products held in storage by retailers and distributors. The individual orders were necessitated by the FDA's lack of authority to order national recalls.

**[10]   **In another development, Campbell Soup Co. announced Aug. 22 that it was recalling chicken vegetable soup from 16 Southern and Western states because it had discovered botulism contamination. The company said contamination had been discovered through its own inspection facilities and no illness resulting from it had been reported. The recall was accelerated Aug. 21 after the FDA made a conclusive identification of botulism contamination in the soup. The recall was completed Sept. 19.

[11]   Flammable sleepwear ban. Commerce Secretary Maurice H. Stans July 28 announced regulations to ban by July 1973 the sale of flammable sleepwear for children up to six years of age. The rules required garments that failed fireproofing tests by June 1972 to be labeled as not meeting government standards. The sale of such garments would be prohibited the following year. Health, Education and Welfare Department statistics estimated that 3,000-5,000 deaths and 150,000-250,000 injuries each year resulted from burns due to flammable garments and indoor furnishings.

[12]   Increased FDA funds sought. Commissioner Edwards Aug. 3, in testimony before a House subcommittee, said the FDA would need five or six times as many food inspectors and funds to bar adulterated, contaminated or mislabeled foods from the consumer market. Edwards said that the FDA's 210-man force inspected each of the nation's 60,000 food plants on an average of once in six years and that lack of resources prevented inspections every two years as specified in agency rules. He said that the Bon Vivant "emergency" (*see* [8-9]) would probably prevent the planned inspection of about 2,300 food plants, one-fifth of the total scheduled to be inspected in the fiscal year ending June 1972. Edwards estimated that about 20% of these plants would be found defective in some respect if they were inspected. Edwards said the FDA inspected 51,000 imported food products in the fiscal year ended June 30, but that there should be a "minimum" of 75,000-100,000 such inspections. He said the agency had a staff of 43 to check imports of both food and drugs.

[13] **Business-consumer council.** President Nixon Aug. 5 established the 80-member National Business Council for Consumer Affairs and named Robert E. Brooker, executive committee chairman of Marcor, Inc., as council chairman. The council, appointed by the secretary of commerce, would serve as a forum to deal with valid consumer complaints and to recommend solutions for "current and potential consumer problems." Rep. John E. Moss (D, Calif.), chairman of a House Commerce subcommittee overseeing consumer legislation, noted Aug. 7 that several council members represented manufacturing firms whose products had been categorized as hazardous by the National Commission on Product Safety.

[14] **House OKs consumer agency bill.** The House, by a 344-44 vote Oct. 14, approved a bill to set up an independent Consumer Protection Agency after defeating attempts by consumer advocates to strengthen the agency's powers. (The Senate had approved similar legislation in 1970.) The bill—criticized by Ralph Nader and by its original sponsor, Rep. Benjamin Rosenthal (D, N.Y.), as disastrously weakened—would empower the new agency to intervene in formal proceedings of federal regulatory agencies, to conduct or sponsor tests and surveys and to maintain public files on consumer complaints. An amendment proposed by Rep. William Moorhead (D. Pa.) and sponsored by Rosenthal and 16 other members of the Government Operations Committee (which had reported the bill Sept. 27), which would have enabled the agency to intervene in informal proceedings and in cases where agencies were considering specific fines or penalties, was defeated by a 160-218 vote. An amendment to further weaken the proposed agency by limiting it to advisory functions and to entering court suits on an *amicus curiae* (friend of the court) basis was defeated 149-240.

[15] **Lead in paints curbed.** The FDA announced new rules Oct. 29 limiting lead content to .5% in all paints with which children might come into contact. Included were paints for interior walls, toys, pencils and furniture. The November issue of the magazine Consumer Reports had reported that 400,000 children a year contracted lead poisoning, of whom 200 died, usually after eating 30-year-old paint from peeling slum walls.

[16] **State meat law upheld.** U.S. District Court Judge Noel P. Fox ruled Nov. 12 that meat processors selling in Michigan must comply with a state packaging law tougher than federal regulations. Armour & Co. of Chicago, Wilson & Co. of Phoenix, Ariz. and George A. Hormel & Co. of Austin, Minn. had challenged the state law on grounds that the U.S. Wholesome Meat Act of 1967 had been designed to unify standards. The Michigan law mandated 12% protein content and barred organ meats in hot dogs, sausages and similar products.

[17] **FCC drops AT&T study.** The Federal Communications Commission (FCC) announced Dec. 23 that it had decided by a 4-2 vote to drop a full-scale investigation of the American Telephone & Telegraph Co. (AT&T), for lack of staff and funds. The investigation would have determined whether the FCC should accept AT&T's expense figures in ruling on a requested long distance rate increase. The investigation would have covered prices and profits of Western Electric Co., an AT&T subsidiary, investment practices and overall efficiency. The FCC would now accept AT&T's own cost estimates, but said it would await Price Commission guidelines on regulated industries before making a final decision on the rate request.

See also AUTOMOBILES [2-4, 9-12]; CANADA [19] ; CIVIL RIGHTS [24]; GOVERNMENT REORGANIZATION; POLLUTION [9, 13]; TAXES

CONTRACEPTIVES—*See* BIRTH CONTROL; POPULATION
COPPER—*See* CHILE [4-5, 8, 17]
COPTIC ORTHODOX CHURCH—*See* CHURCHES [16]

COPYRIGHTS, INTERNATIONAL—A 46-nation diplomatic conference, which began in Paris July 5 under the auspices of the U.N. Educational, Scientific and Cultural Organization, agreed to revision of the Universal Copyright Convention, adopted at Geneva in 1952, according to a July 23 U.N. press release. The revisions constituted a compromise reconciling the views of industrialized and non-industrialized countries. Three new articles were inserted into the 1952 Convention: one defined "non-industrialized countries" as well as the period of preferential treatment from which they could benefit; another concerned the right of translation from the national language (in non-industrialized countries) into international languages; and the third article dealt with the right of reproduction.

COSTA RICA—U.S. CIA official recalled. The U.S. State Department confirmed Feb. 10 that it was recalling Earl J. Williamson, chief of the Central Intelligence Agency office in Costa Rica. Williamson's withdrawal followed rumors and charges in Costa Rica that he was involved in a U.S. attempt to overthrow President Jose Figueres Ferrer, though such involvement and any U.S.-supported coup were denied by the State Department and by Figueres. Reports had indicated that Williamson was upset over Costa Rica's plans to renew diplomatic relations with the Soviet Union.

See also HIJACKING [10]

COST-OF-LIVING COUNCIL—*See* ECONOMY, U.S. [11-16, 20]
COUNCIL FOR MUTUAL ECONOMIC AID (COMECON)—*See* COMMUNISM, INTERNATIONAL
COUNCIL OF ECONOMIC ADVISORS (CEA)—*See* ECONOMY, U.S. [4, 7] ; NIXON, RICHARD MILHOUS [9]
CREDIT CARDS—*See* CONSUMER AFFAIRS [2]

CRIME—1970 statistics. The Federal Bureau of Investigation (FBI) Aug. 31 released statistics showing that the national crime rate rose 11% in 1970. (Robbery rose 17%, rape 2%, murder 8%, aggravated assault 8%, burglary 11% and automobile theft 6%.) The statistics also showed that the number of serious crimes reported in 1970 (5,568,200) rose substantially from 1969 figures of 4,989,760 major crimes reported. In a statement accompanying the FBI report, Attorney General John N. Mitchell pointed out that the 11% overall increase was slightly less than the rise in 1969. Mitchell also noted that crime in large cities rose only 6% in 1970 after rising 9% in 1969 and 18% in 1968.

[2]   Crime control act signed. The Omnibus Crime Control Act of 1970, cleared by both houses of Congress Dec. 17, 1970, was signed by the President Jan. 2. The bill authorized $3.55 billion for federal law enforcement aid to states and com-munities in fiscal 1971-73. Designed to help local police forces increase their effectiveness, the act refocused the aid to concentrate more on urban high-crime areas.

[3]   Criminal code overhaul. The National Commission on Reform of Federal Criminal Laws, mandated by Congress in 1966 to study overhaul of the federal criminal code, Jan. 7 submitted a 366-page draft of a new criminal code. Among the recommendations of the draft: capital punishment should be abolished for all federal crimes; marijuana possession should be made punishable only by $1,000 fines, and penalties for use of heroin and other dangerous drugs should be lessened, while penalties for selling dangerous drugs would remain severe; federal jurisdiction should be broadened to include, in certain circumstances, crimes such as murder, burglary and sexual offenses, all of which previously had been under state jurisdiction; the federal government should be able to prosecute for crimes committed while in the act of violating federal law; federal courts should try certain cases involving servicemen and some U.S. and foreign civilians overseas; all handguns, except those owned by military or police officials, should be outlawed; all firearms should be registered; the hoarding of weapons or the training of "paramilitary" groups for political purposes should be illegal; laws against the sale and distribution of pornographic material should be retained; homosexuality and other deviate sexual activity among consenting adults should not be considered criminal; crimes by corporations or their officials, often subject only to minor fines, should have tougher penalties; the system of penalties should detail maximum penalties for three classes of felonies and two classes of misdemeanors.

[4]   The commission, headed by former California Gov. Edmund G. Brown, presented its recommendations in consensus form in the hope that de-emphasizing differences over volatile issues would gain Congressional approval for overhaul of the existing "hodge-podge" of federal criminal laws. The recommendation to abolish capital punishment was the only one to which minority members specifically made objections known. Sens. Sam J. Ervin Jr. (D, N.C.) and John L. McClellan (D, Ark.) said they believed the death penalty should be retained. Other commission members were: U.S. Appeals Court Judge George C. Edwards Jr. of Michigan; U.S. District Court Judges A. Leon Higginbotham Jr. of Pennsylvania and Thomas J. MacBride of California; Sen. Roman L. Hruska (R, Neb.); Reps. Robert W. Kastenmeier (D, Wis.), Abner J. Mikva (D, Ill.) and Richard H. Poff (R, Va.); and attorneys Donald S. Thomas of Texas and Theodore Voorhees of the District of Columbia.

[5]   **Drive on juvenile delinquency urged.** President Nixon March 22 sent Congress a report urging "a new national program strategy" against juvenile delinquency with emphasis on prevention rather than punishment. (Richard W. Velde, associate administrator of the Law Enforcement Assistance Administration [LEAA] March 31 said that nearly half of the nation's major crimes were com-mitted by juveniles and that the rate of crime by juvenile offenders was rising at a rate almost four times that of the youth population.) A key part of the Nixon strategy would be an attempt to meet the needs of disadvantaged groups and individuals through family and community institutions. Major stress also was placed on efforts to combat group conflict and to divert juveniles from the correctional system to "community-based treatment" outside the system. The report also called for task forces on "model systems" for prevention and rehabilitation in four social environments—the inner city slum area, suburbia, rural areas and college campuses.

[6]   **Pretrial detention bill proposed.** The Justice Department submitted to Congress May 14 legislative proposals for adoption of a national pretrial detention procedure and for reversal of the presumption of innocence in cases where a person convicted of a felony was seeking release pending an appeal. In the latter case, the proposed legislation would put on the person convicted the burden of proving that he was not likely to flee or to pose a danger to other people or their property in order to gain release. The pretrial detention proposal would extend to all federal courts a procedure enacted for the District of Columbia in 1970 and in effect since February. It would allow federal judges to jail for 60 days defendants charged with "a dangerous or organized crime act" (loan sharking, racketeering, sale of narcotics, assault related to aircraft hijacking, bombing, kidnaping and robbery) and found by the judge to constitute a threat to the safety of the community.

Criminal Prosecutions & Indictments

[7]   **Manson, 3 women found guilty.** The longest trial in California history (41 weeks long) came to a close April 19 in Los Angeles when presiding Superior Court Judge Charles H. Older sentenced Charles Manson, leader of a band of nomadic youths, and three of his female followers to be executed in the gas chamber for murder. The trial had begun July 24, 1970. Manson, Patricia

Krenwinkel (23), Susan Atkins (22) and Leslie Van Houten (21) had been convicted Jan. 26 of first degree murder and conspiracy to murder in the 1969 slaying of actress Sharon Tate, Abigail Folger, Thomas John Sebring, Voyteck Frykowski, Steven Parent, and Mr. and Mrs. Leno LaBianca. The seven men and five women who had found the four guilty rec-ommended March 29 that they be executed in the gas chamber. (Under California law, conviction of murder in the first degree carried an automatic penalty of life imprisonment or death in the gas chamber. The judge had the option of reducing the death penalty to life imprisonment.) Manson, Miss Atkins and Miss Krenwinkel were convicted on seven counts of first degree murder, each count carrying the death penalty. Miss Van Houten, charged only with participating in the LaBianca murders one night after the Tate murders, was convicted on two counts of first degree murder.

[8]   The state had called 84 witnesses to the stand. The key prosecution witness, Mrs. Linda Kasabian, a former Manson "family" member, testified that she had accompanied the killers to the Tate home on the night the murders were committed there. She also testified that Manson had ordered the Tate and the LaBianca slayings. Other state witnesses testified that Manson had ordered the murders in hopes of triggering a race war between blacks and whites, believing that the blacks would be the victors and turn to him for leadership. The penalty phase of the trial was highlighted by the admissions of the three girls that they had participated in the murders under the influence of LSD. The three insisted, however, that Manson had nothing to do with the killings. Miss Atkins testified Feb. 2 that she had personally killed Miss Tate under the orders of Mrs. Kasabian. Mrs. Kasabian had been granted immunity for testifying for the state. In further developments, Charles (Tex) Watson, one of the members of the Manson band, admitted at his trial in Los Angeles Sept. 2 that he had participated in the Tate and LaBianca murders on Manson's orders. Watson was convicted Oct. 12 and sentenced to death Oct. 21. Manson was also sentenced to life imprisonment Dec. 13 for the 1969 murders of Gary Hinman, a musician, and Donald Shea, a ranch hand.

[9]   **Alioto indicted on fee split.** Mayor Joseph L. Alioto of San Francisco was indicted March 23 in Seattle along with three others for violating a federal statute against interstate racketeering. The federal grand jury accused Alioto of conspiring to bribe John J. O'Connell, former Washington state attorney general; George Faler, formerly O'Connell's deputy attorney general; and John McCutcheon, a former Washington state county prosecutor. The three were indicted, along with Alioto, under a 1964 law that forbade interstate transportation of money gained through bribery or extortion in violation of the law of the state in which the act was committed. The indictment was tied to Alioto's splitting of a $2.3 million legal fee with O'Connell and Faler. Subsequently, the indictment charged, McCutcheon received money from O'Connell. According to the charge, Alioto paid $540,400 to O'Connell and $272,413 to Faler. McCutcheon alledgedly received $39,000. The $2.3 million fee to Alioto was payment for representing a group of Washington▸public utilities in antitrust actions before he became mayor of San Francisco. If the four were found guilty, they faced fines up to $10,000 and jail terms up to five years.

[10]   **24 slain in California.** Juan V. Corona, a 37-year-old farm labor contractor with a history of mental illness, was arraigned June 2 in Yuba City, Calif. on murder charges in connection with the slaying of 24 men whose bodies were found buried in peach orchards on the outskirts of Yuba City. Corona pleaded not guilty to 10 counts of murder at the arraignment. The charges listed the 10 bodies dug up by sheriff's deputies May 26, the day Corona was arrested. Almost all of the bodies were believed to be those of itinerant farm workers who drifted in and out of the Sacramento Valley during the farming season. A few were identified as members of Yuba City's Skid Row community. The murdered men were middle-aged, ranging from 40 to 60, and most had been clubbed in the back of the head. Corona was linked to the slayings by two

sales receipts found in the grave of a victim who had been dead less than 48 hours. Corona also had been questioned in connection with the disappearance of one of the murdered men. Corona had been committed to a state mental hospital near Yuba City for three months in 1956 at the request of his brothers. He had been diagnosed as a schizophrenic but discharged as cured.

[11] **New Jersey officials convicted.** A federal jury in Newark, N.J. convicted Jersey City Mayor Thomas J. Whelan and seven other Hudson County public officials July 5 of conspiring to extort an estimated $3.3 million from local contracting firms. Seven of the officials were sentenced Aug. 10 to prison terms. Those convicted (prison sentences in parentheses): Whelan (15 years); Thomas M. Flaherty, president of the Jersey City council (15 years); Bernard G. Murphy, purchasing agent for Jersey City (15 years); William A. Sternkopf, chairman of the Port of New York Authority (10 years and a fine of $20,000); Fred J. Kropke, Hudson County police chief (five years); Joseph B. Stapleton, Hudson County treasurer (six months and ordered to cease all political activity); Philip Kunz, Jersey City business administrator (six months); and Walter W. Wolfe, Hudson County Democratic chairman (no sentence). Only Kunz was found not guilty of some counts of the indictment. The jury acquitted him of 12 counts of the 29-count charge. The trial had opened May 17. Also indicted in the original charge, handed down November 1970, were: John V. Kenny, former Hudson County Democratic boss, who had his case severed June 10 because of illness; James R. Corrado, a Jersey City hospital official, who pleaded guilty May 20 to one of the counts of the indictment and was awaiting sentencing; John J. Kenney, former Hudson County freeholder; and Frank G. Manning, a Hudson County engineer. Kenney and Manning had been severed from the trial in exchange for their testimony under immunity.

[12] **2 New Jersey figures indicted.** A federal grand jury in Newark Aug. 11 separately indicted State Sen. William B. Knowlton and former Democratic State Chairman Robert J. Burkhardt on charges of bribery and extorting a New York construction company. Knowlton was charged in a 34-count indictment with extorting $181,000 from J. Rich Steers, Inc., of New York, in exchange for help in obtaining contracts from the New Jersey Turnpike Authority and the Delaware River Port Authority in 1968 and 1969. Burkhardt, an aide to former N.J. Gov. Richard J. Hughes, was charged with bribery in connection with Hughes's 1965 re-election campaign, and with six counts of extorting $30,000 from the Steers firm for his help in getting them a construction contract for work on the Delaware River Memorial Bridge. Named in both indictments as co-conspirator was Eugene Rau, president of the Steers company. A federal official said the charges against Knowlton and Burkhardt were unrelated and the alleged conspiracies were conducted separately.

[13] **Judge Kerner indicted.** Former Illinois Gov. Otto Kerner, a judge of the 7th U.S. Circuit Court of Appeals since his appointment in April 1968, was indicted by a federal grand jury in Chicago Dec. 15 on a 19-count indictment charging him with bribery, conspiracy, mail fraud, perjury and income tax evasion. All of the charges grew out of stock transactions involving Illinois racetracks between 1962 and 1968, while Kerner was governor. Immediately after the indictment was made public, Kerner was relieved of his duties as a judge. Also named in the indictment were Theodore J. Isaacs, Kerner's director of state revenue and chief political adviser during his first term as governor; William S. Miller, chairman of the Illinois Racing Board in 1961-67; Joseph Knight, director of Illinois's financial institutions from 1962-68; and Faith McInturf, a business associate of Miller. According to the indictments, Kerner and Isaacs bought $356,000 worth of racetrack stock for $70,158. In return, the indictments alleged, racetrack owners were given favorable treatment in the assignment of dates for races. The grand jury stated that the stock transaction constituted a bribery. Kerner was also charged with lying to a U.S. grand jury when he testified that he had never talked to members of the Illinois Racing

Commission about setting racing dates. In addition, the grand jury charged that Kerner had made a false statement to the Internal Revenue Service in 1967 when he insisted that an entry in his tax return was the name of a Chicago company and not a listing for Illinois racetrack stock. The indictment further charged that he failed to pay $147,000 in taxes in 1966 and lied to IRS agents about his ownership of racetrack stock. If convicted, Kerner faced a maximum sentence of 83 years in prison and a fine of $93,000.

Court Procedural Decisions

[14] **Speedier criminal trials ordered.** The U.S. Court of Appeals for the Second Circuit issued rules Jan. 5 designed to bring criminal cases to trial within six months after the arrest of the suspect. The rules, which applied to federal district courts in New York, Connecticut and Vermont, went into effect in July.

[15] **Domestic wiretaps limited.** U.S. District Court Judge Warren J. Ferguson ruled in Los Angeles Jan. 11 that the government could not conduct wiretaps without warrants in domestic cases, even if national security were involved. The ruling took effect in 30 days. Ferguson's decision was echoed Jan. 25 by U.S. District Court Judge Damon J. Keith in Detroit. The government had long claimed the right to eavesdrop without a warrant in national security cases involving foreign subversives. In 1969, in connection with the Chicago conspiracy trial, Attorney General Mitchell had said the government could use wiretaps without prior court approval in cases involving domestic groups if the national security were threatened. The Los Angeles decision came in the case of Black Panther Melvin Carl Smith, convicted in October 1969 on charges of being a felon and possessing firearms; the Detroit decision (upheld April 8 by the 6th Circuit Court of Appeals) came in the case of Lawrence R. (Pun) Plumondon, accused of conspiracy in the Sept. 29, 1968 bombing of a Central Intelligence Agency building in Ann Arbor. In a further wiretapping development, the Supreme Court ruled 5-4 April 5 that wiretapping without a warrant was legal with the consent of one of the parties in the tapped conversation. The justices overturned a lower court ruling that banned the use of a wired informer without court authorization. The Supreme Court ruling reinstated the narcotics conviction and 25-year sentence of James A. White of Chicago.

[16] **Crime act immunity provision voided.** U.S. District Court Judge Constance B. Motley ruled in New York Jan. 29 that an immunity provision of the 1970 Omnibus Crime Control Act (*see* [2]) was unconstitutional in that it provided insufficient protection against self-incrimination. Immunity protection under the new act applied only to use of the witness's testimony against himself, and the witness could still be prosecuted for the crime he testified about if evidence came from "untainted" sources. Judge Motley ruled the 1970 provision "is really giving up nothing in return for the witness's forced waiver of the privilege" of protection from self-incrimination. The ruling came in the case of Joanne Kinoy, whom federal prosecutors had sought to force to testify before a grand jury investigating Patricia Swinton in connection with the bombing of a federal building.

[17] **Nebraska self-defense rule voided.** The Nebraska Supreme Court held unconstitutional Jan. 29 a controversial self-defense law passed by the state legislature in 1969. The law, which was the only one enacted over the veto of former Gov. Norbert T. Tiemann, authorized a person to "use any means necessary" to defend himself or his property from attack. The ruling affirmed the second-degree murder conviction of Mrs. Judith W. Goodseal, who had argued that the trial judge refused to accept jury instructions citing the then newly enacted law.

[18] **Journalistic secrecy of sources.** The Wisconsin Supreme Court Feb. 2 upheld the contempt sentence of Mark Knops, editor of an underground newspaper, for refusing to testify before a grand jury investigating a bombing at the University of Wisconsin Aug. 24. Knops had refused to answer the grand jury on the ground that he could keep secret his journalistic sources. The court said the public's "overriding need to know" what Knops might be able to tell the grand jury outweighed his right as a journalist to conceal his sources. In other decisions, an appeals court in Frankfort, Ky. ruled Jan. 22 that newsman Paul Branzburg could keep a source of information secret, but would have to disclose the information itself before a Jefferson County grand jury. The Massachusetts Supreme Court Jan. 29 ruled, in the case of TV newsman Paul Pappas, who had refused to answer certain questions concerning Black Panthers before a grand jury investigating July 1970 racial disturbances in New Bedford, that Massachusetts had created no statutory privilege protecting news sources.

[19] **Miranda ruling limited.** The Supreme Court ruled 5-4 Feb. 24 that illegally obtained evidence generally inadmissible in a criminal trial could be used by the prosecutor to contradict a suspect's testimony if the suspect chose to take the stand in his own defense. The ruling, which upheld the 1966 narcotics conviction of Viven Harris of New Rochelle, N.Y., limited the defendant's protection resulting from the court's 1966 Miranda decision, which declared inadmissible incriminating statements taken by policemen before a prisoner had been fully warned of his rights.

[20] **Death penalty developments.** The Supreme Court, ruling on two major challenges to capital punishment May 3, upheld 6-3 the procedures by which juries in federal courts and in 38 states were empowered to impose the death penalty. The ruling affirmed the murder convictions and death sentences of Dennis C. McGuatha of Los Angeles and James E. Crampton of Toledo, Ohio. The majority, in an opinion written by Justice Harlan, rejected the defendants' claim that the death penalty was unconstitutional because juries arbitrarily decided on the death sentence without detailed standards to guide them. The court also rejected Crampton's argument that the death penalty was unconstitutional unless there were separate hearings on guilt and punishment, a procedure used in only six of the states with capital punishment. The court June 28 agreed to hear four appeals to decide on the third constitutional challenge to the death penalty—that it was "cruel and unusual punishment" as prohibited by the Eighth Amendment. The four cases, slated for argument in the court's next term, were those of: John Henry Furman of Savannah, Ga.; Earnest James Aikens Jr. of San Francisco; Lucius Jackson Jr. of Savannah; and Elmer Branch of Vernon, Tex. The court also set aside the death sentences, but not the convictions, of 39 persons on grounds that jurors opposed to capital punishment were automatically excluded from their trials. The decision, based on the court's 1968 decision in *Witherspoon v. Illinois,* lifted the death sentence of Richard Speck, sentenced for the 1966 murder of eight nurses in Chicago. Illinois prosecutors said they would try to reimpose Speck's death sentence. (In a further development, U.S. District Court Judge Francis J. W. Ford Jr. Oct. 4 upheld an order by U.S. Magistrate Willie Davis that convicts in Massachusetts could not be kept on death row for more than 10 days prior to their scheduled execution. According to court sources, the decision, in effect, abolished death row in Massachusetts.)

[21] **Juveniles' right to jury opposed.** The Supreme Court ruled 6-3 June 21 that the Constitution did not guarantee juvenile defendants the right to trial by jury. Justice Harry A. Blackmun, in the majority opinion, said that there were imperfections in the juvenile court system, but that a requirement for jury trials could "put an end to what has been the idealistic prospect of an intimate, informal protective proceeding." The decision came in the cases of Joseph McKeiver of Philadelphia, charged in 1968 with robbery and placed on probation; Edward Terry of Philadelphia, accused of assaulting a policeman in

1969 and committed to a youth center; and 46 black teenagers charged with impeding traffic in a demonstration against school consolidation in Hyde County.

[22]   Gun law held too vague. The Supreme Court held by a 5-2 vote Dec. 2 that the section of the Crime Control and Safe Streets Act of 1968 that made it a federal offense for a convicted felon to possess a firearm applied only when the gun had some connection with interstate commerce. In the majority opinion, written by Justice Thurgood Marshall, the court "refused to adopt the broad reading" of the 1968 law "in the absence of a clearer direction from Congress."

See also BLACK MILITANTS; BUDGET; DRAFT & WAR PROTEST [5]; FEDERAL BUREAU OF INVESTIGATION [2, 4]; ITALY [10-11]; LABOR [4-5]; MILITARY [3]; MINES; NIXON, RICHARD MILHOUS [1]; POVERTY; PRISONS; STATE & LOCAL GOVERNMENTS [2]; TAXES; UNION OF SOVIET SOCIALIST REPUBLICS [14-15]

CUBA—Vagrancy law announced. Radio Havana announced the terms of a new vagrancy law under which vagrants or chronically absent workers could be sentenced to from six months to two years forced labor. The law, according to report Jan. 13, stated that all physically and mentally capable male persons (except full-time students) between the ages of 17 and 60 had a "social duty to work." The law went into effect March 17. Premier Fidel Castro, in a year's end speech Dec. 31, 1970, had announced that the government planned a major campaign to decrease absenteeism and vagrancy and increase productivity.

Repatriation flights halted. It was reported March 4 that the Cuban government had apparently canceled a monthly airlift flying U.S. citizens of Cuban descent and their relatives from Cuba to Matamoros, Mexico. The last repatriation flight took place in August 1970. About 2,000 Cuban-Americans and their relatives reportedly had left Cuba on the 33 flights which had covered a period of four years. About 819 American citizens and 1,400 relatives of Americans were reportedly still in Cuba and had applied to leave the country on the repatriation flights. In a later development, Cuba informed the U.S. Aug. 31 that it intended to terminate the airlift that had brought 246,000 Cuban refugees from Havana to Florida since December 1965. The airlift was halted Sept. 1 but resumed for a week beginning Sept. 27. (The lift had been suspended Aug. 6 and resumed Aug. 16 after the Cuban government's "administrative difficulties" had reportedly been resolved.) According to a news report Sept. 1, U.S. officials believed that the Cuban government, which had previously decided that all those who were dissatisfied with the regime except those of military age could leave the country, reversed its decision due to the emigration of greatly needed skilled workers. According to the termination announcement, the airlift could be resumed when Cuban authorities had processed the names of the last group of refugees permitted to leave. A "master list" of Cubans registered to leave and approved by both the U.S. and Cuba reportedly contained 33,000 names. Another list of 1,000 was to be submitted by the Cubans for U.S. approval, and the U.S. had also approved the entry of 94,000 Cubans whose names were registered by their relatives in the U.S.

13 Americans held. The government announced June 10 that it was holding 13 Americans from three vessels and would try at least five in "revolutionary tribunals." Of the 13 detained, Fritz Sprandel of Allentown, Pa. was forced ashore in his canoe by poor weather en route to Mexico; four people were on a 58-foot yacht, and eight were on a disabled tugboat. It was reported June 15 that five of the Americans had been fined $20,000 each after trials by a revolutionary tribunal. All the accused reportedly admitted entering Cuban territorial waters and landing illegally on Cuban soil. Sprandel was released July 6; the others were released July 7. The arrests were, according to a statement by Premier Castro, closely related to the capture and arrest by the U.S. of four Cuban fishermen (see TERRITORIAL LIMITS).

Sugar harvest completed. Cuba's 1971 sugar harvest was completed July 20 with a total production of over 5.92 million metric tons. The government had originally set a goal of 7 million metric tons, altered May 1 to 6.65 million metric tons.

Spanish relations. The 15-man Cuban diplomatic mission in Madrid left Spain abruptly with their families Aug. 2, leaving only one first secretary in the embassy. No immediate explanation was given, but informed sources attributed the departure to the Spanish demand that Cuba reduce the number of diplomats in Madrid to six or seven, the same number Spain retained in Havana. The Spanish government had also threatened to impose restrictions on the Cubans similar to those Cuba had imposed on Spanish diplomats in Havana, according to an Aug. 3 report. The departure came as the two countries reached a deadlock on negotiations dealing with trade and payment by Cuba for the property of Spanish citizens nationalized when Castro came to power. Following the breakoff in negotiations, relations between the two countries deteriorated, with Cuba suspending tobacco shipments to Spain in September. A trade pact guaranteeing repayment of Cuban debts to Spain and providing mutual recognition for trade purposes as "most favored nations" was signed by Spain and Cuba Dec. 18.

Kosygin's Cuban tour. Soviet Premier Aleksei N. Kosygin arrived in Havana Oct. 26 for a four-day visit which ended with a reaffirmation of Soviet readiness to continue support of Castro's regime. Details of the substantive discussions by Castro and Kosygin were not released, but the two leaders issued a joint communique Nov. 1. The communique expressed support of the two for leftist regimes in Chile and Peru, as well as for non-Communist Latin regimes that asserted their independence from the U.S., and reasserted Soviet support for the Castro government.

Technicians enter U.S. illegally. Nineteen Cuban sugar cane technicians and three airplane crew members returned to Havana Nov. 5 after a series of events which began with their illegal and unannounced arrival in New Orleans Oct. 26 to attend the 14th Congress of the International Association of Cane Sugar Technologists. (The Cubans had paid $17,000 in fees to attend the conference.) The Cubans said Nov. 5 that they were leaving the U.S. voluntarily, but the U.S. said the Cubans were leaving under expulsion orders handed down by the U.S. Immigration Service Nov. 2 and upheld by the Board of Immigration Appeals Nov. 4. The U.S. State Department Sept. 24 had denied the Cuban group authorization to attend the congress on grounds that the meeting was not sponsored by an official international body. The Cubans arrived without notifying Federal Aviation Administration officials that they intended to land in New Orleans until the plane had already taken off from Havana. Soon after their arrival, the Cubans rejected a State Department order relayed through the Czechoslovak embassy in Washington requesting the Swiss embassy in Havana to ask the Cuban government to order the group home. The Cubans announced that they would not leave until Nov. 5, the close of the congress. The State Department gave the group permission to spend the night in a motel near the airport under the supervision of immigration officials, but transferred the Cubans to a naval air station in Belle Chasse, La. Oct. 28.

Cuba attacks U.S.-based freighter. A Cuban gunboat Dec. 15 attacked the Miami-based Johnny Express and wounded Jose Villa, captain of the freighter, in international waters 100 miles off Cuba's east coast. Cuba charged the Panamanian-registered ship was engaged in counter-revolutionary activities against Cuba. The Cuban government Dec. 16 called the Johnny Express "a pirate ship" in the service of the U.S. Central Intelligence Agency (CIA), employed in transporting arms and men to Cuba. (Premier Castro said Dec. 22 that Villa had confessed to being an agent for the CIA.) Cuba also accused the Babun family, operators of the Johnny Express and its sister ship the Lyla Express (seized by the Cuban Navy Dec. 5 on charges that some of its crew members were counter-revolutionaries), and prominent anti-Castro exiles in Miami, of being "well-known counter-revolutionary agents in the service of the U.S. government." Teofilo Babun Dec. 16 denied any connections with the CIA and claimed the attack on the Johnny Express was part of a personal vendetta against the Babun family by Premier Castro.

The U.S. protested to Cuba Dec. 16 for the seizure and demanded the immediate return of Villa, a Cuban exile and naturalized U.S. citizen, "as soon as his physical condition permits." In further response to the action, the State Department Dec. 17 issued a warning to Cuba that it would take "all measures under international law" to protect American and other ships in the Caribbean from any new attacks by the Cubans. It was reported the same day that orders had been issued to naval and air units in the Caribbean to provide armed assistance to any vessel that might be attacked by Cubans. Cuba Dec. 27 released the 26 crewmen of the Lyla Express and the Johnny Express, but continued to hold Villa on espionage charges. The 26 men returned to Panama Dec. 27 with a three-man Panamanian commission that had been sent to Cuba to investigate the boat seizures. The commission reported Dec. 30 that the ships' logs revealed they had participated in armed attacks on eastern Cuba in 1968 and 1969.

See also AVIATION [8]; CHILE [19]; COLOMBIA; COMMUNIST CHINA-U.S. DETENTE [2, 5]; EUROPEAN ECONOMIC COMMUNITY [5]; FOREIGN POLICY; HIJACKING [1,9]; LATIN AMERICA; PENTAGON PAPERS [17]; PERU; PORTUGAL; SPACE [24]; SPORTS; TERRITORIAL WATERS

CULEBRA—*See* PUERTO RICO

CYPRUS—U.N. troops on alert. The United Nations peace-keeping force on Cyprus was placed on low-level alert to "forestall possible problems" resulting from deteriorating relations between the Greek and Turkish Cypriot communities, a U.N. spokesman announced July 28. (The U.N. Security Council had voted unanimously May 26 to extend the force on Cyprus to Dec. 15.) The situation had been exacerbated by accusations exchanged by the two communities of "feverish" military preparations.

The Cyprus government (dominated by Greek Cypriots) reported that Turkish and Greek Cypriots exchanged gunfire July 28 for the first time in four years. The incident reportedly occurred when two Greek Cypriot sailors in a military vehicle were fired on by the Turkish Cypriot police near Kyrenia, and the Greeks returned fire. There were no casualties. Violence had also erupted July 22 when a Greek Cypriot national guardsman shot and wounded a Turkish Cypriot shepherd. The Turkish Foreign Ministry issued a strong protest July 23 and called the situation "delicate and tense." It was reported July 20 that the Cyprus government had called up 2,500 civil defense volunteers the week before "to answer any emergency call."

Rift between Greece and Cyprus. The deterioration of the situation on Cyprus came at a time when the three-year intercommunal talks between Turkish and Greek Cypriots were deadlocked and Greece and Turkey were actively promoting a settlement to pave the way for improved relations between them. At the same time, news reports indicated a growing rift between the Greek regime and Cypriot Archbishop Makarios, president of Cyprus. Reconciliation efforts between Greece and Turkey were bolstered when Greek Deputy Foreign Minister Christian Xanthopoulos-Palamas and Turkish Foreign Minister Osman Olcay conferred in Lisbon June 2 about the Cyprus problem prior to a NATO Ministerial Council meeting. According to a June 12 report based on an Ankara source, the two ministers agreed to seek a solution to the Cyprus problem between themselves if the intercommunal negotiations were not successfully concluded by September.

The Greek Cypriots agreed June 26 in a session of the intercommunal talks (following a visit to Cyprus by Greek Foreign Ministry official Dimitri Horofas June 19) to "discuss" the possibility of separate municipal authorities for Cyprus' five largest towns and to seek passage of a special law that would give Turks effective control of their government at the village level and slightly above. However, Makarios rejected a significant compromise proposal by

Greece calling for creation of a Cabinet post for a Turkish Cypriot minister or undersecretary with broad powers for local administration, according to a London Times report July 12. Makarios had argued that such a post would create a state within a state. Xanthopoulos-Palamas July 10 implicitly warned Cyprus to settle the conflict or face the consequences alone. He said any procedure other than successful inter-Cypriot talks would "produce hazards and defects which must be weighed in good time." He added that Greece was "abandoning the method of confrontation with Turkey and entering a phase of negotiation." Newspapers in Nicosia July 13 published the text of a letter allegedly written to Makarios by Greek Premier George Papadopoulos June 11 accusing Makarios of "breaking our common front." He allegedly said Greece would take "such measures as the national interest dictates, no matter how painful they may be."

Turkish Cypriot negotiator Rauf Denktash, returning to Nicosia from consultations in Ankara July 19, said there was "no basis for continuing local talks" because of the Greek Cypriot refusal to guarantee Cyprus' independence, with a recognition and definition of the status of the two communities. He added his side would not take the initiative in breaking off talks.

Intercommunal talks broadened. Acceptance by Greece and Turkey of a proposal by U.N. Secretary General U Thant for the appointment of a U.N. representative at the intercommunal talks was announced by Xanthopoulos-Palamas Nov. 27. He said Greece and Turkey would each appoint a "technical" consultant to participate in the talks. The new formula was presented by Thant Oct. 18 after Greek-Turkish consultations at U.N. headquarters in New York. It was reported Nov. 29 that Cyprus, after initial wariness, apparently had accepted the new procedure. Bibiano F. Osorio-Tafall, the U.N.'s special representative in Cyprus, would participate in the talks. Osorio-Tafall had previously said Oct. 2 he would resign his post because his peacemaking efforts had been rejected.

U.N. force extended. The United Nations Security Council Dec. 13 voted 14-0 (China abstaining) to extend the U.N. peacekeeping force in Cyprus to June 15, 1972. The resolution said it was expected that "by then sufficient progress towards a final solution will make possible a withdrawal or substantial reduction of the force."

CZECHOSLOVAKIA—1970 economic results. The Czechoslovak news agency CTK Jan. 28 announced the results of the 1970 economic development plan. The following major items were reported as increases over the figures for 1969: industrial production 7.7% (consumer goods 8%, producer goods 7.5%), retail trade turnover 2.2%, exports to Socialist countries 17%, exports to capitalist countries 10%, gross agricultural output 1.3%. Coal output totaled 28,183,000 tons, pig iron 7,548,000 tons, crude steel 11,480,000 tons.

[2] Federal ministers named. President Ludvig Svoboda Jan. 3 appointed eight new federal officials: federal deputy premiers—Jundrich Zahradnik, former chairman of the federal industrial board, and Jan Gregor, former Slovak industrial minister; federal transport minister (replacing Jaroslav Knizka)—Stefan Sutka, former Slovak transport, post and telecommunications minister; federal minister of metallurgy and engineering—Josef Simon, former Czech state industry minister; federal fuel and power minister—Jaromir Matusek; chairman of federal control committee—Drahomir Kolder; head of state planning committee—Vaclav Hula, a federal deputy premier; deputy to Hula—Karol Martinka, a minister without portfolio.

[3] National Front ousts Erban. The Czechoslovak National Front, representing all legal political organizations, Jan. 27 elected as its chairman Communist Party First Secretary Gustav Husak. The election bypassed former chairman Evzen Erban, a member of the CP Presidium and one of Husak's supporters. CTK gave no reasons for the change in leadership. The front also elected Tomas Travnicek as acting deputy chairman and Miloslav Vacik as central secretary.

[4] Refugee dunning ends. A campaign begun in 1970 under which Czechoslovak refugees in the West were required to pay the cost of their legal defense in Czechoslovak courts was ended Feb. 16. First Secretary Husak declared that day that, although neither he nor Premier Lubomir Strougal had known about the practice at first, "the whole matter has been stopped."

[5] Czech government changes. The Czech National Council Feb. 11 appointed Jaroslav Prokopec as Czech Republic minister of health, replacing Vladislav Vlcek. The council also named Vaclav Svoboda minister of agriculture and Antonin Pospisal as minister without portfolio. Jaromir Hrbek, minister of education, was relieved of his functions by the council July 8, "at his own request," and was replaced by Deputy Minister Josef Havlin.

[6] Prague radicals sentenced. A group of 15 Czechoslovak intellectuals charged with "subverting the Republic" were sentenced March 19 in Prague to prison terms ranging from one to two and a half years. Peter Uhl, the principal defendant, was sentenced to four years imprisonment. Two others accused were given suspended sentences and one was acquitted. The 19 had been charged with membership in the Revolutionary Socialist party and with preparing and distributing leaflets based on the writings of Leon Trotsky and Milovan Djilas, the former Yugoslav vice president. The group was also said to have opposed "consolidation of the political and economic conditions" in Czechoslovakia by joining demonstrations on the first anniversary of the Soviet invasion. The sentencing judge confirmed March 23 that Frantisek Stilip, the prosecuting attorney, had urged stricter penalties for at least 13 of the defendants.

[7] Slovak party meets. The Slovak Communist party ended a three-day congress May 15 in Bratislava with election by the Central Committee of the following 11 persons to the Presidium: Ladislav Abraham, Peter Colotka, Herbert Durkovic, Jan Janik, Ondrej Klokoc, Jozef Lenart, Elena Litvajova, Ludovit Pezlar, Gejza Slapka, Vaclav Vacok and Miroslav Valek. The names of Litvajova and Slapka were new. The Congress re-elected Lenart as first secretary and ousted Egyd Pepich as Slovak interior minister.

[8] Party congress approves changes. The 14th Czechoslovak Communist party congress, held May 25-29 in Prague, approved changes brought about by the Soviet-led invasion of the country in 1968, adopted draft directives for the 1971-75 economic development plan and elected party officials. The congress was attended by 1,200 delegates and 1,500 guests and foreign CP leaders. The Spanish party, which had opposed the 1968 invasion, did not send a delegation; and it was reported May 30 that the congress had refused to hear a condemnation of the invasion by the Italian party representative. Premier Strougal reported May 26 on the economic development plan. He said the volume of investment during 1971-75 would increase 35%-37% and that national income would rise 28% and foreign trade 38%. The final session of the congress May 29 adopted three changes in the party's statutes: congresses were to be convened every five years instead of every four, a two-year period of candidate membership was restored prior to admission into the party and the party leader's title was changed from first secretary to general secretary. Husak was re-elected general secretary May 29 and a Central Committee of 115 members was chosen, replacing a body of 132 members. The committee elected the following nine-member Presidium: Husak, Svoboda, Strougal, Vasil Bilak, Peter Colotka, Karel Hoffman (replacing Erban), Alois Indra, Antonin Kapek and Jozef Lenart. (It was reported June 3 that Antonin Novotny, former CP first secretary and Czechoslovak president expelled in May 1968, had been readmitted to party membership as a result of a compromise reached at the congress by which Novotny was restored to membership in return for agreement on the part of conservative forces not to demand strict punishment for Alexander Dubcek, Novotny's discredited successor.)

[9]   Polednak, others sentenced. Alois Polednak, former head of the Czechoslovak film industry, was sentenced July 9 in the Prague city court along with five other persons, including foreign nationals, to two years in jail for "undermining the Republic" and "endangering official secrets" between 1968 and the time of his arrest in 1970. Sentenced with Polednak were Jaroslav Sedivy, historian and former member of the Institute of International Politics and Economics in Prague (18 months), and Edita Cerenska, former secretary of the Federal Assembly (one year). Three other persons were given lengthy terms for espionage as well as for undermining the republic. They were: Vaclav Cerenska, Edita's husband and a retired army colonel (seven years); Milada Kubiasova, an interpreter at the French embassy (10 years); and Hubert Stein, an interpreter at the Dutch embassy (12 years). Polednak was freed Nov. 12 after declaring on national television that he had been "rightly sentenced."

[10]   General elections held. The country Nov. 26-27 held its first general elections since 1964 in the absence of major efforts at disruption by opponents of the government. (Leaflets urging an election boycott had been widely distributed in Prague Nov. 9.) Official results of the elections, announced Nov. 29, claimed that 99.45% of the nation's 10,253,796 registered voters had cast ballots to fill 350 Federal Assembly seats and some 200,000 regional and local council posts. A total of 99.8% of those participating had voted in favor of official candidates named by the National Front. There were reportedly 40,000 invalid ballots.

[11]   Revision of Cabinet. In a revision of the Cabinet Dec. 9, following the November elections, Foreign Minister Jan Marko resigned to become first deputy chairman of the Federal Assembly. Marko succeeded Mrs. Sona Penningerova, who had also been chairman of the House of the People, the lower chamber. That post was taken over by Vaclav David, also a former foreign minister. Marko was replaced as foreign minister by Bohuslav Chnoupek, until recently ambassador to the Soviet Union. Alois Indra (*see* [8]) was named chairman of the Federal Assembly, succeeding Dalibor Hannes, who became deputy chairman along with David, Bouslav Kucera, a former minister without portfolio, Antonin Pospisal and Ludoviet Hanusek. The only other change in the new Cabinet was the replacement of Ignac Rendek, minister in charge of the Federal Price Office, by Michal Sabolchik.

See also DISARMAMENT; DRUG USE & ADDICTION [9]; GERMANY, WEST [1]; SPACE [24]; UNION OF SOVIET SOCIALIST REPUBLICS [3]

DAHOMEY—Michel Ahouanmenon, ambassador to France, was named foreign minister July 4, replacing Daouda Badarou, who succeeded to Ahouanmenon's former post.

DALEY, RICHARD J.—*See* ELECTIONS [2]

DAVIS, ANGELA—*See* BLACK MILITANTS [3-4]
DAVIS, RENNIE—*See* DRAFT & WAR PROTEST [13]
DDT—*See* AGRICULTURE [8]; PESTICIDES
DEATH PENALTY—*See* CRIME [3-4, 20]
DEATH SQUADS—*See* ARGENTINA [14]; BRAZIL; DOMINICAN REPUBLIC

DEFENSE—Lockheed, C-5A developments. The Lockheed Aircraft Corp., beset with economic troubles, announced Feb. 1 that it was accepting a Defense Department demand, originally rejected by the company Jan. 6, that Lockheed take a fixed $200 million loss on its C-5A jet transport fleet in return for an estimated $781 million in federal funds as settlement for unresolved contracts. By Lockheed's unofficial estimate, the settlement with the Pentagon cost the corporation $480 million before taxes. By government estimates, the company would have exhausted money for C-5A production by March without the agreement. In rejecting the offer Jan. 6, Lockheed had said it would accept a Pentagon alternative proposal by which the government would pay $758 million and the issue of repricing in the contract would be settled in the courts. Lockheed had said, however, that litigation should not be restricted to the repricing factor but extended to other "major issues" of the contract. The Pentagon estimated that the costs of the program had soared from an original ceiling price of $2.3 billion for 115 planes to about $3.7 billion for 81 planes. Three other programs in the Pentagon-Lockheed dispute had been discussed Jan. 6: Lockheed accepted a proposal to end litigation on a contract, canceled in 1969, for the Army Cheyenne attack helicopter and accepted a $120 million loss in exchange for the government's absorption of another $141 million in costs; Lockheed rejected the Navy's offer of $58 million against claims of $159.8 million on several shipbuilding projects but urged continued negotiation; Lockheed agreed that a dispute involving short-range attack missiles (SRAMs) had been resolved when the company agreed in October 1970 to take $20 million against its claim of $54 million.

[2] *C-5A fleet grounded.* The Air Force grounded its entire fleet of 47 C-5A jets Oct. 12 because of technical difficulties with the plane's engine mounting. The order came to ground the fleet after cracks were discovered in a C-5A engine mounting in the same area as was involved in an accident Sept. 29 at the Altus (Okla.) Air Force Base in which an engine fell from its mounting as the pilot was preparing for takeoff. The Air Force had shelved 22 of its C-5As Oct. 7 pending an investigation of the Altus incident. The Air Force said Oct. 30 that the investigation had turned up cracks in the underwing structures of seven of the planes.

[3] **False 'alert' sent.** A number of radio and television stations across the U.S. went off the air Feb. 19 after a teletype operator at the National Emergency Warning Center at Cheyenne Mountain, Colo. sent by mistake a message containing the code word "hatefulness," which was to be used by the center only in the event of a nuclear strike against the U.S. It took employees at the center 40 minutes to find the code word ("impish") to indicate that the transmission was canceled. The original warning, which was pretaped and sent out at 9:33 a.m. EST, said the President had declared a national emergency and that normal radio and television broadcasting was to cease "immediately."

[4] **New U.S. deterrent strategy.** U.S. Defense Secretary Melvin R. Laird March 9 presented to Congress a "defense posture" statement outlining a "strategy of realistic deterrence." Laird said his "new" policy, which would limit defense spending to 7% of the nation's gross national product and reduce conventional forces from 2.8 million to 2.5 million, would steer "a prudent middle course between two policy extremes—world policeman or new isolationism." The overall strategy was based on providing enough force to fight one major and one minor war, or a 1.5-war strategy, compared with the 2.5-war strategy under the two previous administrations. The new concept would eliminate maintenance of large U.S. ground combat forces in Asia, where reliance would be put on strong air, naval and support capabilities and mobilization, in case of emergencies, for transport to the affected area of non-NATO-committed forces or the NATO reserve forces based in the U.S.

[5] Under the plan, the U.S. nuclear deterrent would remain the core of defense policy, but new emphasis would be placed on modernizing the defense forces of U.S. allies, coordinating them with U.S. forces, and on utilizing diplomacy to merge them into "regional security agreements." Stress would be placed on the value of negotiations to lessen chances of major confrontations. Increased emphasis would also be placed on research in weaponry to guard against technological surprise by adversaries. Weapons reserves were to be studied in relation to a unified allied effort.

[6] **Air Force shelves F-111s.** The Air Force reported April 30 that it was putting its 257 operational F-111 fighter-bombers on "suspended" status (to be flown only in emergencies) pending the outcome of an inquiry into the 18th crash of the swing-wing jet. The decision marked the second time in 18 months and the sixth time since they became operational in 1967 that the planes had been ordered on suspended status. The latest decision came seven days after one of the planes crashed near a gunnery range on the Edwards Air Force Base in Barstow, Calif., killing its two crewmen Maj. James W. Hurt and Maj. Robert J. Furman. The two were the 14th and 15th to die in F-111 accidents. (The last fatal crash was in Louisiana in January.) Early findings indicated that a capsule which should have separated from the plane and parachuted to the ground failed to do so. (The Air Force had announced March 26 that unforeseen rising costs and technical problems had forced it to cut 12 more planes from its planned purchase of 82 F-111s. Each of the F-111s cost about $8.6 million, making the cutback worth about $103 million in savings.)

[7] **Command setup revised.** The Pentagon July 8 announced a reorganization of its command structures around the world. The reorganization would leave the command superstructure with seven command units: North American Air Defense Command, European Command, Alaska

Command, Pacific Command, Atlantic Command, Southern Command and the Readiness Command. Under the new setup, the European Command at Stuttgart, West Germany would replace the Strike Command at MacDill Air Force Base in Florida as the nerve center for charting possible U.S. military moves in the Middle East. The Strike Command was to be dismantled, with most of its functions transferred to the Readiness Command at the MacDill base. The Pacific Command would assume responsibility in the Bering Sea and the Aleutian Islands (both previously under the Alaska Command).

[8] **U.S.-Soviet accords signed.** Soviet Foreign Minister Andrei A. Gromyko and U.S. Secretary of State William P. Rogers signed in Washington Sept. 30 two agreements on preventing nuclear accidents and on modernizing the Washington-Moscow "hot line" for emergency messages. The first pact obliged each party to notify the other "in the event of detection by missile warning system of unidentified objects" or "an accidental, unauthorized or any other unexplained incident involving a possible detonation of a nuclear weapon which could create a risk of outbreak of nuclear war." Each party agreed to notify the other "in advance of any planned missile launches if such launches will extend beyond its national territory in the direction of the other party." The "hot line" accord was to replace the existing line with a satellite that would provide instantaneous voice and teletype communication. It required the U.S. to build and operate on its territory a station for the Soviet Molniya II system while the U.S.S.R. was to do the same for the U.S. Intelsat system. Construction of the Soviet station in the U.S. was expected to take two years and to cost $5-6 million.

[9] **Navy orders 48 F-14s.** The Navy Sept. 30 put through an order for 48 more F-14 swing-wing jetfighters from the Grumman Aerospace Corp. The planes had been ordered under a contract which made it mandatory for the Navy to exercise its option by Sept. 30. The purchase had been delayed while a team of Navy cost specialists and engineers completed a review of three Grumman projects, among them the controversial F-14, because of a rise in costs from $11.5 million to $16.7 million per plane. The review, which began July 26, was held under orders of Secretary of the Navy John H. Chafee, acting under the instructions of Deputy Defense Secretary David Packard. Packard had announced June 1 that Pentagon defense planners were considering major changes in the contract for the development of the F-14. The development of the plane had been halted in December 1970 when the first F-14 crashed and burned on its second test flight. It was resumed May 24. The Navy had made final arrangements for its purchase of 48 planes after the Senate voted 61-28 Sept. 29 to allow the Navy to buy the aircraft. A House bill did not include comparable funds for the fighter.

[10] **New command directive issued.** The Defense Department made public Dec. 16 a new directive designed to make the nation's military chain of command better equipped to respond to crisis situations. The key feature of the new order was a directive authorizing the chairman of the Joint Chiefs of Staff (JCS) to act alone in place of the five top military commanders in emergencies when time was a critical factor. Under the present setup, the JCS passed its recommendations for military action to the President and secretary of defense only after meeting as a group. The new directive would permit the chairman of the JCS, currently Navy Adm. Thomas H. Moorer, to bypass the usual channels to send his recommendation to the White House either at the start of a nuclear war or more conventional crises. In addition, the new setup gave the JCS chairman the authority to overhaul the country's worldwide command communications system to give high priority to informing civilian leaders of major developments and transmitting their orders to commanders in the field.

[11] **$70 billion appropriations bill passed.** Congress Dec. 15 passed a bill appropriating $70,518,463,000 for defense in fiscal 1972. The bill, signed by President Nixon Dec. 18, was the second largest defense appropriation ever enacted by Congress (second only to the fiscal 1969 bill), but still $3 billion less

than had been requested by the Administration. The bill was the result of a House-Senate conference reconciling differences between a House bill, approved Nov. 17, for $71 billion in appropriations and a Senate bill, passed Nov. 23, for a $70.8 billion appropriation. Allotment of the funds by service was: Navy $22,470,795,000; Air Force $22,244,570,000; Army $20,211,446,000.

Criticism of Spending

[12] **Arms buying scored.** The General Accounting Office (GAO) March 17 released the third and what it described as the final version of a report accusing the Pentagon's defense planners of widespread inefficiency. The Pentagon planners' poor judgment, according to the study, contributed to high arms profits by defense contractors. The new report followed March 1 and March 16 reports which had offered similar criticism but used harsher language. The first report had contained the harshest criticism, concluding that Pentagon methods in negotiating arms contracts in effect rewarded cost overruns. Data seen as critical of negotiating methods was not suppressed in the second report, but was rewritten into often less conspicuous places. The first report said the average rate of return on contractors' pretax capital was 56.1% for 146 completed defense contracts. In the second report, using statistics supplied by 74 businesses doing defense work for the U.S., the GAO said the contractors' pretax profit was about 21.1%. The third report used both sets of statistics to determine how big a profit contractors were making. As a result of these figures, the GAO concluded that defense contractors continued to disregard cost factors, thus wasting money. The agency called on the government to reorganize the Defense Department's procedures of awarding contracts to eliminate the money drain by establishing uniform guidelines on profit objectives on all U.S. contracts.

[13] The GAO submitted its findings for comment to five contractors' associations. Two agreed with the conclusion that investments should be considered in determining profits. Two others, however, said the agency had failed to consider the "real world" of competition in the current defense contracting business. The fifth organization did not comment on the report.

[14] **Navy cost expert assails claims.** Gordon Rule, chairman of the Navy's Contract Claims Control and Surveillance Group and the Navy's top cost expert, said May 24 that Rear Adm. Nathan Sonenshein, head of the Naval Ship Services Command, had awarded to contractors $135.5 million in claims without first determining whether the government was obligated to pay the firms at all. Rule made his disclosure before a Congressional Joint Economic Subcommittee looking into defense profits. He told the subcommittee that Sonenshein was now "having trouble justifying" the claims in the face of an audit by Rule's group. Rule said that Sonenshein had neglected to obtain a memorandum of legal entitlement (a document that established the government's liability) before settling claims with Lockheed Shipbuilding and Dry Dock Corp., a subsidiary of Lockheed Aircraft, and with Avondale Shipyards, Inc., of New Orleans, a subsidiary of the Ogden Corp. Lockheed billed the Navy for $159.2 million in added costs to build a new model destroyer and portable docking apparatus. The claim was reportedly settled for $62 million. Avondale billed the Navy for $147.5 million in extra claims for two classes of destroyer escorts, and was awarded $73.5 million in a settlement. Noting that the money had not yet been paid to the firms, Rule promised that his group, which was responsible for issuing checks for added claims, would not give any awards until "every dollar is factually supported and legal entitlement is found."

See also ARMAMENTS, INTERNATIONAL; BUDGET; CANADA [20]; DISARMAMENT; PENTAGON PAPERS; TARIFFS & WORLD TRADE [8]; TELEVISION & RADIO

DENMARK—Cabinet changes. Three cabinet changes were reported in March. According to a March 19 report, Erik Ninn-Hansen, defense minister and a member of the Conservative party, was named minister of finance, succeeding Poul Moeller, who had resigned March 16 for reasons of health. Knud Oestergaard, a conservative member of Parliament and a former career officer, took over Ninn-Hansen's defense post. According to report March 26, Lars Nordskov Nielsen, director of prisons, was named ombudsman, effective in July, replacing Stephan Hurwitz, who retired.

Bank rate cut. The National Bank lowered its discount rate from 9% to 8% Jan. 20 and from 8% to 7.5% April 14.

New government. Premier Hilmar Baunsgaard resigned Sept. 27, six days after his three-party center-right coalition lost its parliamentary majority in elections. Baunsgaard headed a caretaker government until Oct. 11, when a minority government under Social Democratic leader Jens Otto Krag, 57, was sworn in. Krag had been asked by King Frederik Oct. 6 to form a government after Krag rejected a recommendation by Baunsgaard for the creation of a broadly based four-party "Common Market" coalition comprising the Moderate (Agrarian) Liberal, Conservative, Radical Liberal and Social Democratic parties. Krag had served twice as premier, once at the head of a minority government. Krag said Oct. 9 that his government would introduce legislation to prepare for Danish membership in the European Economic Community (EEC). He also attached high priority to establishment of diplomatic relations with North Vietnam. On the domestic front, he said that his government would focus on policies to improve the economy. Other members of the Cabinet: foreign—Knud Boerge Andersen; finance—Henry Gruenbaum; budget and wages—Per Haekkerup; labor—Erling Dinesen; housing—Helge Nielsen; fisheries—Christian Thomsen; defense—Kjeld Olesen; commerce—Erling Jensen; home affairs—Egon Jensen; church affairs—Dorte Bennedsen; agriculture—Ib Frederiksen; Greenland—Knud Hertling; justice—K. Aksel Nielsen; culture—Niels Matthiasen; transport and environment—Jens Kampmann; social affairs—Eva Gredal; education—Knud Heinsen; and foreign economy—Ivar Noergaard.

The April 21 elections, which centered on the issue of the Danish economy, had given the coalition of Baunsgaard's Radical Liberals, the Moderate Liberals and Conservatives 88 seats—46.6% of the vote—in the 179-member Folketing (parliament), a loss of 10 seats from the 1968 elections. The Social Democrats won 70 seats, an increase of 8; the Socialist People's party won 17 seats, a gain of 6. In addition, Greenland's two parliamentary seats went to a Social Democrat and a leftist independent, and the Faeroe Islands' two seats followed the same split. (Formation of the new government had been postponed pending the Oct. 5 elections in the Faeroe Islands.) Krag's new government coalition held 89 seats in the Folketing.

10% import surcharge. The Folketing Oct. 20 approved, by a vote of 90-88, a temporary 10% import surcharge proposed the previous day by the Krag government. The surtax would be applied to all imports except most raw materials and unprocessed foods, newsprint, fuel oils, medicines, fresh fruit and vegetables, tea, coffee, cocoa and a few other products. Government officials explained the action was taken to strengthen the nation's currency and improve the balance of payments before Denmark's entry into the EEC, expected in 1973. The surcharge would be reduced to 7% in June 1972, to 4% in January, 1973, and abolished at the end of March 1973.

See also EUROPEAN ECONOMIC COMMUNITY [1, 16]; JAPAN [10]; PAKISTAN [35, 39]; SCANDINAVIA; VIETNAM, NORTH

DESEGREGATION—*See* CIVIL RIGHTS; SUPREME COURT
DEVALUATION—*See* ECONOMY, U.S. [8]; EUROPEAN ECONOMIC COMMUNITY [11]; INTERNATIONAL BANK FOR RECONSTRUCTION & DEVELOPMENT; INTERNATIONAL MONETARY DEVELOPMENTS [1, 8-9, 14, 16-18]

DEVELOPING NATIONS—*See* EUROPEAN ECONOMIC COMMUNITY [5, 11];
TARIFFS & WORLD TRADE [14]
DIEM, NGO DINH—*See* PENTAGON PAPERS [19-22]

DISARMAMENT—Seabed treaty signed. A treaty prohibiting installation of
nuclear weapons on the ocean floor was signed Feb. 11 by 63 nations in
ceremonies in Washington, Moscow and London. The treaty, approved by the
United Nations (U.N.) General Assembly in December 1970, barred from the
seabed beyond any nation's 12-mile coastal zone "any nuclear weapons and
launching installations or any other facilities specifically designed for storing,
testing or using such weapons." The treaty was not signed by France and
Communist China. It would be in effect upon ratification by 22 nations.

    Nuclear pact safeguards set. The U.N. International Atomic Energy
Agency (IAEA) announced March 11 that its safeguards committee,
responsible for insuring enforcement of the Nuclear Non-Proliferation Treaty,
had concluded work on a draft agreement to be negotiated with the treaty's
signatory powers. In recommending a compromise settlement of the dispute
about payment of the costs of safeguarding the treaty, the committee advised
that payments continue to be met from the IAEA's ordinary budget but that
assessments be changed to ease the burden on countries with low per capita
incomes.

    U.S.S.R. proposes nuclear parley. The Soviet Union June 15 formally
proposed a five-nation conference to discuss nuclear disarmament. The Soviet
proposal, first contained in a March address by Communist party General
Secretary Leonid I. Brezhnev, was delivered to the U.S. and France June 15
and to Great Britain June 17. It was not known when Communist China was
approached with the proposal, but it was reported July 3 that China had
rejected the plan. China July 2 repeated its proposal that "a conference of all
nations, big and small," meet to discuss a nuclear ban. Great Britain Aug. 18
rejected the proposal because China would not participate. The U.N. General
Assembly Dec. 16 unanimously agreed to postpone consideration of the Soviet
proposal until 1972. The delegates accepted a Mexican-Rumanian resolution,
intended as a substitute for the tabled Soviet version, which left the date, place
and agenda for the conference to be fixed by the next General Assembly
session.

    SALT talks. The strategic arms limitation talks (SALT) between the
Soviet Union and the U.S. continued through 1971, with a breakthrough in the
talk deadlock. The two countries announced May 20 that they had decided to
discuss an agreement on defensive nuclear weapons. The disclosure was made
simultaneously by Moscow Radio and by President Nixon in a brief televised
address. Armaments specialists considered that the effect of the understanding
was to relieve SALT delegates temporarily of the need to consider land-based
ICBMs, an area of Soviet strength, and missiles delivered by submarines and by
bombers, an area of U.S. dominance. According to a report July 22 using
unattributed testimony of Nixon Administration officials, the U.S. July 20
made oral proposals at the talks to limit both defensive and offensive weapons.
According to the report, each of the two countries would be able to choose
between protecting its capital with 100 antiballistic missiles (ABMs) or
protecting its offensive missiles with up to 300 ABMs at three sites. (The Soviet
Union was expected to choose the first option, since it already had a defensive
ring around Moscow, while the U.S. was believed likely to complete work
already begun on installing ABMs at offensive missile sites.) A companion
proposal regarding offensive weapons reportedly would establish a date beyond
which no missile silos or missile submarines could be begun or completed,
although the plan would allow either side to modernize existing weapons with
multiple warheads. (Charles W. Bray 3rd, a spokesman for the State
Department, July 23 called the July 22 report "an unfortunate breach of
security" and "a violation of our understanding with the Soviet Union that
neither side will discuss those talks while they are in progress." Bray did not

deny the accuracy of the report.) No agreement was reached by the end of 1971.

U.S.S.R. backs biological ban. In a major policy change at the U.N. Conference of the Committee on Disarmament March 30, the Soviet Union proposed a draft treaty banning biological weapons of war. (The Soviet Union previously had asked for a prohibition of both chemical and biological weapons, opposing a U.S.-supported British draft to renounce only biological weapons.) The Soviet Union was joined in sponsoring the convention by Bulgaria, Czechoslovakia, Hungary, Poland, Rumania and Mongolia. The 14-article draft prohibited the development, production, stockpiling or other acquisition of microbiological "or other biological agents or toxins" except those "designed for the prevention of disease or for other peaceful purposes." Signatory nations would be required to destroy or divert to peaceful uses all existing stocks of biological weapons within three months after the convention came into force. All parties to the treaty would be required to "conduct negotiations in good faith on effective measures for prohibiting ... chemical weapons." Violations of the treaty would be investigated by the U.N. Security Council.

The U.S. and the Soviet Union Aug. 5 presented to the conference a draft treaty combining the 1969 British proposal and the March Soviet proposal. The final draft of the joint treaty was submitted to the conference Sept. 28 and was passed by the conference and sent to the U.N. Sept. 30. The final draft of the 14-point plan strengthened the definition of toxins by adding the words "whatever their origin or method of production, of types and in quantities that have no justification for prophylactic, protective or other peaceful purposes." It contained a controversial provision which would take suspected cases of violation before the Security Council, where investigations could be vetoed. The treaty was to come into force when it had been signed by 22 countries, including the depository governments, which had not yet been named. Countries signing the treaty were to have destroyed or diverted to peaceful uses within nine months after the treaty came into force all stocks of biological weapons in their possession. Like the original Soviet proposal, the draft called for a ban on development, production, stockpiling and acquisition of biological weapons and called on signatory powers to conduct negotiations to achieve a ban on chemical weapons. The joint text did not contain a provision specifically banning the use of biological weapons. The U.S.S.R. considered such a ban unnecessary since the use of such weapons was made illegal in the Geneva Protocol of 1925, which the U.S. Congress had not yet ratified.

Test ban discussions. Other discussions at the Conference of the Committee on Disarmament centered on a prohibition of underground nuclear testing. The talks remained deadlocked due to American insistence on onsite inspection to maintain enforcement of such a ban. Although evidence at the conference and in the U.S. Senate indicated that technological advancements in satellite surveillance and in differentiating between earthquakes and underground nuclear explosions could make onsite inspection unnecessary, the U.S. continued to insist on an unspecified number of onsite inspections.

See also CANADA [22]; DRUG USE & ADDICTION [23]; FOREIGN POLICY; FRANCE [17]

DISASTERS—Nixon orders migrant relief. President Richard Nixon acted March 15 to extend disaster relief to migrant workers in Florida who were unemployed as a result of freeze and drought that ruined commercial tomatoes and other crops. The President declared the crop failure a disaster and allocated $2.5 million to pay unemployment compensation to the workers, who were ineligible for state benefits. The emergency declaration would also permit additional relief to the migrants under the federal food stamp program. Florida Gov. Reubin Askew had asked the President for federal disaster relief March 11. (In the past, disaster relief had applied only to occurrences such as floods, hurricanes and earthquakes.)

U.N. relief program approved. The United Nations General Assembly Dec. 14 approved, by an 86-0 vote with nine absentions, a program for relief to countries stricken by disaster and for assistance in disaster planning. The relief program, proposed by Secretary General U Thant in July, would also deal with man-made disaster situations. The program would be headquartered in Geneva.

Explosions. At least 25 persons were killed and 100 injured Feb. 3 in an explosion and ensuing fire in the Thiokol Chemical Corp. complex 25 miles south of Brunswick, Ga. The building in which the explosion occurred was used for the manufacture of magnesium trip flares for use in Indochina. Seventeen workmen drilling a water tunnel 250 feet below the Los Angeles suburb of Sylmar were killed June 24 when a fire, sparked by an explosion, roared through the shaft. Four men had been injured in a blast in the tunnel the day before. Twenty-two men building a water tunnel 250 feet below Lake Huron, Michigan were killed Dec. 11 as a natural gas explosion ripped through the shaft. Sixteen men escaped.

Other disasters. A government exhibit hall under construction in Belo Horizonte, Brazil collapsed Feb. 4 on about 200 workers during their lunch period. The death toll reached 63 March 2 and rescue workers said more bodies would probably be uncovered in the debris. At least three persons were killed and 28 were reported missing in a cave-in in Quebec May 5 in which a section of earth a quarter-mile long and 70 feet wide collapsed under the village of St. Jean de Vinney. The cave-in formed a crater with sheer walls as deep as 100 feet. Thirty-five homes, several cars and a bus were engulfed in the cave-in, which was caused by heavy rains.

See also AVIATION [13-14]; CHINA, COMMUNIST; EARTHQUAKES; FLOODS; MINES; SHIPS & SHIPPING; SOCCER; STORMS

DISTRICT OF COLUMBIA—President Nixon sent Congress a message on the District of Columbia April 7, calling for a voting member of Congress and a commission to study feasibility of home rule. He urged intensification of the anticrime campaign, a sharing of federal funds to develop rapid transit, more help for higher education and establishment of a development bank for the city's economy. "Federal effort should contribute wherever possible," he said, in "making this a city unexcelled in quality of life, urban grace and efficiency and economic opportunity."

Presidential primary. A bill establishing a presidential preference primary in May of presidential election years for the district was cleared by both houses of Congress Dec. 15 and signed Dec. 23.

See also ABORTION; CRIME [6]

DIVORCE—*See* CHURCHES [9]; DOMINICAN REPUBLIC; GERMANY, WEST [7]; ITALY [13]; POVERTY; ROMAN CATHOLIC CHURCH [3]
DOMINICA—*See* CARIBBEAN

DOMINICAN REPUBLIC—**Divorce veto overriden.** Both the Senate and the House of Deputies voted overwhelmingly to override President Joaquin Balaguer's veto of the country's controversial "quickie" divorce law, according to a report June 5. The law, which Balaguer had vetoed after strong opposition emerged from church and legal groups, would allow foreigners and non-resident Dominican citizens to get a divorce within a week if the action was uncontested. The law was expected to attract tourist revenue.

Coup aborted. President Balaguer announced June 30 that his government had put down an attempted right-wing coup headed by former Gen. Elias Wessin y Wessin, who was immediately put under arrest. At least 41 military men were reported to be under arrest for complicity in the conspiracy. A court-martial decided July 1 to deport Wessin y Wessin, who arrived in Spain July 5. In an apparent reaction to the abortive coup, Balaguer announced new military appointments and Cabinet changes. According to a report June 14, Balaguer appointed Col. Ramon Emilio Jiminez as the new head of the armed forces, replacing Gen. Joaquin Abraham Mendez Lara, and Gen. Salvador Llueberes

Montas as the new interior minister, replacing Gen. Juan Rene Beauchamps, who was named secretary of state and inspector general of the army. (Beauchamps had been appointed interior and police minister Jan. 1, replacing Gen. Enrique Perez y Perez, who had become chief of the national police.)

La Banda developments. The country suffered an increase in terrorism with the formation in April of an anti-Communist terrorist organization known as La Banda. La Banda, which appeared similar to the "death squads" of Brazil, Uruguay and Guatemala, was reportedly organized by Perez y Perez, on instructions from Balaguer, to conduct an offensive against the extreme left and eradicate the Communist leadership in the country. The main targets were reported to be the Marxist Popular Dominican Movement and the smaller Maoist Communist party, although other, more moderate, government opponents were also targets of La Banda's campaigns. By Aug. 28, it was reported that at least 50 leftists had been murdered and others jailed and beaten in La Banda campaigns. The same report said that the organization had 400 members in Santo Domingo under the command of Lt. Oscar Nunez Pena, a close friend of Perez y Perez. Members were described as youths in their late teens and early 20s who were trained in the use of arms.

Reportedly as a result of negative publicity abroad, the government, according to an account Sept. 14, announced a major crackdown against the group. Gen. Perez y Perez said members of the group would be tried on charges of association to commit crimes. Balaguer also forced the resignation of Nunez Pena. Balaguer Sept. 17 ordered dissolution of La Banda and Oct. 15 replaced Perez y Perez as national police chief. Gen. Neit Nivar Seijas, commander of the 1st Army Brigade, was named to succeed Perez y Perez.

See also VENEZUELA

DRAFT & WAR PROTEST—The invasion of Laos Feb. 4-15 set off a chain of protests during the early part of 1971 that was the most widespread since the reaction to the invasion of Cambodia in May 1970. Among actions springing from the invasion of Laos and increasing dissatisfaction with continuation of the war were the bombing of the Capitol building March 1 [4-5] and a series of Washington, D.C. protests in late April and early May which culminated in the arrests of 12,000 persons in disturbances May 3-5. The Washington protests began with five days of demonstrations April 19-23 by Vietnam veterans [7-8], followed by a mass march April 24 [9], protests by the Peoples Lobby April 26-30 [11] and the massive attempt to close down the nation's capital May 3-5 [12-17]. Following the May disturbances, the pace and intensity of war protests eased. A projected "fall offensive" against the war failed to result in mass demonstrations.

[2] Laos invasion protested. Antiwar demonstrators protested the invasion of Laos Feb. 4-15 with nationwide demonstrations Feb. 10 that were the most widespread since the reaction to the invasion of Cambodia in May 1970. However, the protests did not reach the level of dissent in past years. Among demonstrations across the country: 2,000 protesters demonstrated peacefully in New York City; 14 demonstrators were arrested in Boston after windows were broken and two policemen injured in a march and protest by 4,000 demonstrators; 23 persons were arrested in Baltimore when a protest by 300 demonstrators ended in rock and bottle throwing which resulted in injuring six policemen; two persons were arrested as some protesters in a demonstration of 1,500 persons near the Berkeley campus of the University of California clashed with police; several hundred protesters occupied the Social Science Building at the University of Wisconsin for several hours; six persons were arrested and some windows broken during a march by 1,000 protesters from George Washington University to the White House; several thousand persons, including Ann Arbor Mayor Robert Harris, demonstrated near the University of Michigan; peaceful protests were held in San Francisco, Chicago and Des Moines, Iowa.

[3] Antiwar teach-ins begin. A speech by former Sen. Eugene J. McCarthy Feb. 22 in Boston launched a new effort to mobilize antiwar sentiment on the campuses. McCarthy spoke at a preliminary session before an antiwar teach-in began at Harvard University. Other teach-ins were scheduled at Yale and were being organized at 10 other universities. At the Harvard meeting, attended by 1,500 students, speakers urged the students to avoid violence and to organize political pressure campaigns against the war.

[4] Bomb explodes in Capitol. A powerful bomb exploded in the Senate wing of the Capitol at 1:32 a.m. March 1, 33 minutes after a telephone warning that the blast would occur as a protest against the invasion of Laos. The explosion, in an unmarked, out-of-the-way men's lavatory, damaged seven rooms. A preliminary estimate by the Capitol architect's office calculated damages at more than $300,000. No one was injured. A conspiracy theory developed early, supported by a report from Leonard H. Ballard of the Capitol police force that two telephone callers from Chicago and Spokane, Wash., within an hour of the explosion, asked about damage. "That was almost before it was on the air and before it was known nationally," Ballard contended. In letters postmarked March 1 after the bombing and sent to the New York Times, the New York Post and the Associated Press, a group calling itself the Weather Underground claimed responsibility for the bombing. The letters were mailed from Elizabeth, N.J. (The signature Weather Underground had been used before by members of the Weatherman breakaway faction of the Students for a Democratic Society.)

[5] *Girl seized in blast.* Leslie Bacon, 19, was arrested in Washington, D.C. April 27 as a material witness "with personal knowledge" of the March 1 bombing. After her arrest, Miss Bacon was flown to Seattle April 29 where she appeared before a federal grand jury, which Justice Department officals said was investigating the bombing and other matters "relating to national security." The arrest came in a Federal Bureau of Investigation (FBI) raid of a youth commune where Miss Bacon lived with members of the Mayday Tribe, which was organizing antiwar protests in the capital (*see* [12-17]). Miss Bacon was sent to jail May 19 for contempt when she refused to answer questions about her movements March 1, despite a government offer of limited immunity under the 1970 Organized Crime Control Act. Federal District Court Judge William N. Goodwin turned her over to a U.S. marshal when she refused to obey a court order to testify. She was to be held until she agreed to answer questions or until the jury's term ended in March 1972. The immunity offered by the government was protection from prosecution based on her own testimony (*see* CRIME [16]). Miss Bacon's attorneys May 21 sought her release on grounds that the immunity was insufficient. The U.S. Court of Appeals for the 9th Circuit June 16 released Miss Bacon in the custody of her lawyers and Sept. 30 ruled that her arrest April 27 had been illegal. In response to a habeas corpus petition, the court ruled that Miss Bacon should have been given a chance to appear voluntarily before the grand jury.

[6] (During the grand jury proceedings, Miss Bacon was also questioned about her participation in a Dec. 4, 1970 attempt to bomb a New York City bank—an attempt that was thwarted when undercover policemen arrested six persons, allegedly as they were planting the bomb. Miss Bacon had pleaded the Fifth Amendment during questioning on the 1970 bombing, but was ordered by U.S. District Court Judge W. Boldt May 6 to answer questions about the bombing. Boldt said she had waived her Fifth Amendment rights in the matter when she previously testified willingly about her part in the bomb plot. Miss Bacon was arraigned in federal court in New York June 29 on charges of conspiring with the six others to bomb the bank. She had testified May 6 before the Seattle grand jury that she had taken part in the early planning of the bombing but "withdrew from all plans more than a month before the actual attempt." The other six charged in the bombing—Richard R. Palmer, identified as a Weatherman "recruiter"; Sharon Krebbs; Martin Lewis; Joyce Plecha; Claudia

Conine, and Christopher Trenkle—pleaded guilty to the crime March 18. New York State Supreme Court Justice Harold Burns May 7 sentenced Palmer, Krebbs and Lewis to the maximum sentence of four years each and Plecha and Conine to three years each. Trenkle was ordered to take a psychiatric examination before sentencing.)

[7] **Antiwar veterans demonstrate.** About 1,000 antiwar veterans held five days of demonstrations in Washington April 19-23. The demonstrations, organized by the Vietnam Veterans Against the War (a group of about 12,000 formed in 1967), included rallies, lobbying in Congress and guerrilla theater protests. The demonstrators called the protest Operation Dewey Canyon III and described it as a "limited incursion into the District of Columbia." (Dewey Canyon II was the code name used for the Laos invasion.) The protests began with a march to the Capitol April 19, after which the veterans held a rally demanding Congressional action on a 16-point program to end the war. Among their demands, the protesters asked "immediate, unconditional and unilateral" withdrawal of U.S. military and intelligence forces from Vietnam; a formal war crimes inquiry (see WAR CRIMES); amnesty for all Americans who had refused to serve in Vietnam; and improved benefits for returned veterans. The group then split up for lobbying efforts. Delegations of veterans attended Senate Foreign Relations Committee hearings April 20 and 22 and a Senate Judiciary Subcommittee hearing on Vietnam refugees and civilian casualties April 21. Several Congressional panels provided a forum for the veterans. One hundred and ten veterans were arrested on the steps of the Supreme Court April 22 as they demanded a ruling against the war as unconstitutional. The city prosecutor dropped disorderly conduct charges against those arrested after Superior Court Judge William Stewart found April 23 that there was "no evidence of any violent act." The veterans, joined by supporters, held a candlelight march to the White House the night of April 22. The high point of the protest came April 23 when 700 veterans discarded their military medals and ribbons at a demonstration at the Capitol. The demonstrations were called by Sen. George McGovern (D, S.D.) "the most effective protest to date" against the war in Indochina.

[8] The veterans began their demonstrations under the cloud of a government-sought court injunction against their use of the Mall area near the Capitol as a campground. The Justice Department, citing Interior Department rules against overnight camping on the park land, obtained a preliminary injunction against the veterans April 16 from U.S. District Court Judge George L. Hart Jr. A three-judge appeals court April 19 modified the injunction after former Attorney General Ramsey Clark, representing the protesters, argued against "judicial tailoring in advance of opportunities for free speech." Citing the precedent of National Boy Scout Jamborees and others allowed to sleep in the parks, the court said the veterans could use the Mall if they refrained from building fires or breaking ground. U.S. Supreme Court Chief Justice Warren E. Burger April 20 reinstated the original preliminary injunction, and his decision was upheld by the Supreme Court April 21. The protesters, meeting in state caucuses April 21, voted 480-400 to defy the injunction. The injunction was dissolved by Judge Hart April 22. Hart rebuked the Justice Department, which had asked that the order be dissolved, for seeking the injunction and then failing to enforce it.

[9] **Marchers demand 'out now.'** Hundreds of thousands of marchers massed in Washington and San Francisco April 24 and held peaceful rallies urging Congress to bring an immediate end to the war in Indochina. There was none of the violence and large-scale arrests that marred some of the previous mass protests against the war. In Washington, the turnout was at least double the expectation of the Justice Department and Washington police officials. Police Chief Jerry V. Wilson said 200,000 attended the rally, but the National Peace Action Coalition (NPAC), chief sponsor of the march, estimated the crowd at 500,000. Marchers accepted fellow demonstrators walking under banners

promoting women's liberation, gay liberation and a variety of radical causes. Students for a Democratic Society (SDS) organizers used bullhorns to urge protesters to abandon the "so-called liberal politicians" and attend a counter rally. Later SDS led an uneventful march to Dupont Circle, the scene of a police-protester clash during November 1969 antiwar protests. At the main rally, protesters heard former Navy Lt. (j.g.) John F. Kerry (a spokesman for the veterans' protests), Congressmen, civil rights and labor leaders and spokesmen for women's rights and Puerto Rican independence. Only 25 arrests were made in connection with the Washington march, all for minor offenses.

[10] In San Francisco, the scheduled program at the peace rally was disrupted when militant Chicanos and radicals seized the platform and held the stage for more than an hour. Led by Abe Tapia, president of the Mexican American Political Association and a scheduled speaker, dissidents including Chinese, Japanese and Indian protesters charged that the ralliers ignored "third-world" issues. Scheduled speakers left the rally without delivering addresses. The march and rally was the largest peace demonstration ever held on the West Coast. Police estimated the rally crowd at 156,000, more than three times higher than their figure for the November 1969 war protest. The NPAC claimed 300,000 participants. The marchers, led by servicemen on active duty, had the backing of San Francisco Mayor Joseph Alioto, who called the demonstrators loyal Americans. Earlier in the week, the city's Board of Supervisors had passed a resolution establishing April 24 as "a day of public determination to end the war in Vietnam."

[11] **Peoples Lobby protests.** Demonstrators lobbied in Congress April 26, and April 27-30 brought specific demands to various government agencies. Focusing on the issues of the draft, war taxes, poverty and repression, the lobbyists visited Selective Service headquarters April 27, the Internal Revenue April 28, the Health, Education and Welfare (HEW) Department April 29 and the Justice Department April 30. Joining in the lobbying effort were the Southern Christian Leadership Conference (SCLC), the National Welfare Rights Organization (NWRO) and the National Action Group (NAG). The lobbyists engaged in limited acts of civil disobedience, such as sitting in at the offices of Congressmen who refused to talk to them and blocking the doors of federal agencies. Arrests were kept to a minimum April 26 and 27, but began on a larger scale April 28 when police detained more than 200 protesters who had conducted an all-night vigil outside draft headquarters. A similar number was arrested April 29 during an attempted march from HEW to the White House. (Charges against the 200 were dropped May 7.) The marchers followed an SCLC mule train that had arrived in Washington that day after leaving New York City April 2. Some 370 demonstrators, including Hosea Williams of the SCLC, were arrested April 30 for blocking entrances to the Justice Department.

[12] **Mayday protests.** Thousands of antiwar protesters were arrested in Washington May 3-5 as demonstrators attempted massive traffic disruptions combined with marches on the Pentagon May 3, the Justice Department May 4 and the Capitol May 5. The protests, designed to close down the capital, were organized by the Peoples Coalition for Peace and Justice and particularly the coalition's radical Mayday Tribe constituent. The protests seemed at an end May 6 when a scheduled march on the South Vietnamese embassy drew only about 60 demonstrators. Washington police prepared for the threatened disruptions by ordering 30,000 protesters out of West Potomac Park in a pre-dawn raid May 2. The demonstrators' permit to use the park was canceled, according to Police Chief Wilson, because of "numerous and flagrant" violations of the permit and "rampant" use of drugs. Later, government and city officials and demonstrators alike credited the failure of the demonstrators to close down the city to the clearing of the park and dispersal of the army of demonstrators. With a mandate from President Nixon to keep the city "open

for business," police were joined by 4,000 federal troops, 1,400 National Guardsmen, and Park and Capitol police.

[13]   Police used tear gas and mass arrests May 3 to keep traffic moving and to prevent the demonstrators from reaching their announced target—the Pentagon. By 8 a.m., 2,000 of the protesters were arrested, successfully stifling their attempt to tie up traffic at targeted bridges leading into Washington and at downtown traffic circles. Lacking jail facilities, police detained thousands outdoors in the Washington Redskins football practice field near Robert F. Kennedy Memorial Stadium. Throughout the day, protesters, splintered into small groups, roamed through the city and blocked intersections, using their bodies, trash cans and disabled or parked cars. Chased by police, they regrouped on other corners. There were no reports of looting or window-breaking, but demonstrators slashed the tires of cars. In a few incidents, rocks were thrown at police, but such violence was rare. There were 155 reported injuries of police and protesters. Police used their nightsticks, aimed mostly at protesters' legs, but some of those imprisoned at the Redskin field were treated for head injuries. Mayday leader Rennie Davis was arrested May 3 on charges of conspiracy, and John Froines was arrested on similar charges May 4. Abbie Hoffman, who along with Davis and Froines was a "Chicago Seven" defendant on conspiracy charges arising from riots at the 1968 Democratic National Convention in Chicago, was arrested in New York May 5 on charges connected with the D.C. protests. (Hoffman was indicted May 13 by a grand jury in Washington.)

[14]   The protesters changed their tactics May 4 and did not attempt to block the heavily guarded bridges leading into Washington. Two thousand were arrested during the day—most during a rally at the Justice Department. Others were arrested in incidents throughout the day as police scattered groups of protesters, but without the sweeping arrests and tear gas used the day before. Protesters marching to the Justice Department cooperated with authorities by stopping for traffic lights and keeping to sidewalks. The arrests at the Justice Department were peaceful, with protesters sitting in the street, then rising to be arrested. More than 1,000 demonstrators were arrested May 5 on the steps of the House of Representatives after they had forced officials to close the Capitol to visitors. Meanwhile, 500-1,000 government workers gathered in Lafayette Square, across from the White House, in a protest organized by Federal Employees for Peace.

[15]   The suspension of standard "field arrest procedures" by the Washington police and the mass arrests of about 12,000 persons provoked widespread controversy. (The suspension meant that specific offenses were not cited in making arrests.) Public defenders, representing thousands detained in the Redskin field, May 3 filed a habeas corpus petition charging that many of those detained were non-demonstrators. Superior Court Judge Harold H. Greene May 4 ruled that the police had illegally detained protesters and that those arrested but not charged with a specific offense must be released. A federal appeals court, ruling May 5, reversed Greene's order that fingerprints and photos of those arrested but not charged be destroyed rather than turned over to the FBI. Superior Court Judge James A. Belson ruled May 7 that 600 of the demonstrators were being held in jail under circumstances constituting "cruel and inhuman punishment." Belson said the conditions under which the protesters were being held "grossly violate the minimum standards properly applicable even to temporary detention facilities." He ordered immediate court proceedings for the remaining prisoners and, by the end of the day, fewer than 200 were left in jail. An emergency appeal by the American Civil Liberties Union (ACLU) that most of the 12,000 arrested had been illegally detained, resulted in a court of appeals ruling May 26 that the Washington corporation counsel suspend prosecution unless there was "adequate evidence to support probable cause for charge and arrest." The ACLU argued that many Mayday defendants had been forced needlessly to undergo "economic and physical hardship in returning to Washington" to find their cases dismissed at the last

minute. The city prosecutor said May 27 that about 2,500 of the remaining cases would be dropped. Most of those affected by the ruling were persons arrested under the suspension of field arrest procedures. Corporation Counsel C. Francis Murphy argued May 27 that it would be "burdensome and expensive" to notify the defendants whose cases were being dropped and the ACLU offered to undertake the job. The ACLU said June 1, however, that many names on the list provided by the corporation counsel were illegible and that addresses were not supplied for more than half the names. Superior Court Justice Eugene N. Hamilton ruled May 27 that $10 collateral posted by arrested protesters would no longer be forfeited automatically if defendants failed to appear for trials in those cases the city chose to prosecute. Hamilton said if the city would certify "probable cause" for prosecution and the defendant failed to appear, the case would have to be continued until July and the defendant formally notified of his new trial date.

[16] Eight protesters, arrested May 5 on the steps of the House of Representatives, were acquitted in a Washington Superior Court jury trial July 27. (Charges had been dropped June 16 against 17 protesters because government prosecutors said they were "not ready" for trial. The 17 had not been informed that their cases were postponed.) The government had reportedly considered the May 5 arrests the most likely to result in convictions, since field arrest forms were filled out with proper identification and criminal charges. As a result of the acquittal, the federal government entered a motion Aug. 26 to drop criminal charges against 800 of the approximately 1,000 persons arrested May 5.

[17] In a ruling on an ACLU case in behalf of arrested protesters, the U.S. District Court of Appeals for the District of Columbia ruled Oct. 1 that police must refund collateral to almost all of the protesters who had forfeited it by not appearing in court to contest charges against them. The ruling also: warned that, unless prosecutors could show "legitimate governmental interests" against such procedure, the court might order all Mayday arrest records completely expunged except for those of persons convicted after trial; totally banned dissemination of Mayday arrest records, even to the FBI, except in cases of convictions; ordered the D.C. corporation counsel to trace any copies of arrest records already given to other agencies and retrieve them for metropolitan police files; and enjoined further prosecution of the estimated 325 cases still pending until the cases had been thoroughly screened by the corporation counsel. (Official court records were not available, but it was estimated that only about 200 of the 12,000 arrested had been convicted.)

[18] *War protests staged nationwide.* Protesters estimated at 20,000-40,000 gathered in Boston and 10,000 rallied in New York City May 5 in the largest of numerous antiwar protests held outside of Washington in a "moratorium" on business as usual declared by the Peoples Coalition and other antiwar groups. While most of the protests were peaceful, police used tear gas to disperse thousands of University of Wisconsin protesters in Madison and thousands of University of Maryland students who blocked traffic near their College Park, Md. campus. In San Francisco, protesters clogged the streets, and 76 demonstrators were arrested after a confrontation between police, armed with nightsticks, and protesters, armed with rocks. In Seattle, a protest march by 3,000 youths was dispersed by police. Other disruptions and arrests occurred during protests in Waukegan, Ill., Lakewood, Colo., Rochester, N.Y. and in Minneapolis, where 10 students and the chaplain from Macalester College (St. Paul) were arrested for blocking the entrance to the federal building.

[19] **Victory marchers rally in capital.** The Rev. Carl McIntire led an estimated 15,000 demonstrators, calling for a military victory in Vietnam, in a march and rally at the Washington Monument May 8. The marchers, armed with American flags and Bibles and marching behind a "victory" band of members of the Veterans of Foreign Wars, were considerably fewer in number than the 20,000 drawn by McIntire's second victory march in October 1970. In

addition to protesting what McIntire called the policy of retreat in Vietnam, the marchers carried placards calling for prayer in schools, an end to abortions, and freedom for Lt. William Calley, convicted of murdering South Vietnamese civilians at Mylai (see WAR CRIMES [3-4]).

[20] Antiwar vets march in Boston. About 400 Vietnam veterans marched from Bunker Hill (Charlestown, Mass.) to the Boston Common May 31 on the last leg of a 20-mile trek to protest the war in Indochina. The march, organized by the Vietnam Veterans Against the War, had started from Concord May 29, tracing in reverse the route of Paul Revere's ride, to "spread the alarm" against the current war. Arthur Johnson, the group's New England coordinator, said May 28 that the march, named "Operation POW" (to point out "that all Americans are prisoners of war"), was intended to "publicize the parallels between the actions of the revolutionary citizen-soldiers and our actions." About 100 of the veterans and more than 300 sympathizers were arrested May 30 for violating curfew in Lexington after a meeting May 29 of Lexington selectmen refused to suspend the curfew for the veterans camping on Lexington Green. Townspeople who opposed the decision left the meeting to join the veterans. State and local police moved in at 3 a.m. to clear the green.

[21] Lawyers lobby against the war. Hundreds of lawyers gathered in Washington June 7 for several days of lobbying and rallies sponsored by the National Convocation of Lawyers to End the War. The group backed legislation to withdraw U.S. troops from Vietnam by the end of the year (see INDOCHINA WAR [66-68]).

[22] FBI seizes draft raiders. FBI agents and local police foiled Selective Service office raids in Buffalo, N.Y. and Camden, N.J. with arrests of 25 persons late Aug. 21 and early Aug. 22. Both groups were connected with the Catholic left, but FBI officials made no direct connection between the two planned raids. In Buffalo, FBI agents, who were on the scene reportedly "checking the security of the building," arrested five young people who ransacked files in both the draft and U.S. Army Intelligence offices in the federal building. A statement by the Buffalo defendants (Charles Lee Darst, Jeremiah Horrigan, James Martin, Ann Masters and Maureen C. Considine), made public Aug. 23, indicated that their aim was to confiscate military intelligence and draft records. In Camden, 40 FBI agents were stationed at the Camden Post Office for hours preceding the 4 a.m. arrests Aug. 22. Twenty were arrested at the time of the raid, some still on the premises of the federal building, which included offices of the Selective Service Board, Army Intelligence and the FBI. Those arrested were: John Peter Grady, described as the "ringleader and mastermind" of the plot; Rev. Peter D. Fordi, a New York City Jesuit and member of the East Coast Conspiracy to Save Lives; Rev. Michael J. Doyle, assistant pastor of St. Joseph's Pro-Cathedral in Camden; Rev. Milo M. Billman, a Lutheran Minister; Rosemary Reilly; Robert Glenn Good; Paul Bernard Couming; John Swinglish; Michael John Giocondo; Joan Reilly; Kathleen Mary Ridolfi; Robert W. Williamson; Terry Edward Buckalew; Anne Cunham; Lianne Moccia; Francis Mel Madden; Barry James Mussi; Sarah Jane Tosi; Margaret Mary Inness; and Keith William Forsyth. A 21st defendant, Dr. William A. Anderson, surrendered Aug. 23. The government complaint alleged that the conspirators had met in his home.

[23] A grand jury in Camden Aug. 27 indicted 28 persons for the Camden raid. Bench warrants were issued for the seven not already arrested: Rev. Edward J. Murphy, Rev. Edward J. McGowan, Martha Shemeley, Anita Ricci, Eugene F. Dixon, Frank Pommersheim, and a woman identified as "Jamette" or "Jane Doe." All the defendants were charged with conspiracy to burglarize a government office, steal public records and interfere with the Selective Service System. Twenty-one were also charged with actually breaking into the building.

[24] War challenge review refused. The Supreme Court Oct. 12 declined to review a 2nd Circuit U.S. Court of Appeals decision upholding the constitutionality of the Vietnam war. Only two justices—William O. Douglas and William J. Brennan Jr.—voted to hear the case by the New York and American Civil Liberties Unions who argued that the conflict was unconstitutional because Congress had never formally declared war. The appeals court in April had held that Congress, through the Tonkin Gulf resolution and appropriations, implicitly condoned the war. The case was viewed as the most important constitutional challenge to the war to reach the court. In another court action, the U.S. Court of Appeals for the 1st Circuit in Boston ruled that the war was not illegal, upholding a U.S. district court dismissal June 1 of a Massachusetts state suit. The court ruled that the President had acted constitutionally "in the situation of prolonged and undeclared hostilities" and "with steady Congressional support."

[25] D.C. protesters arrested. About 300 antiwar protesters, on their way from a Washington Monument rally to the White House to deliver an "eviction notice" to President Nixon, were arrested Oct. 26 after sitting down in the middle of Pennsylvania Avenue during the evening rush hour. Police filled out field arrest forms and photographed each of those arrested, who were charged with disorderly conduct and blocking the street (see [15-17]). Bail was set at $50. Over 1,000 police had been deployed, and city officials had prepared a "demonstration contingency plan" for the first time. The plan provided for federal-city enforcement coordination and first aid, food, amenities, psychiatric help and a 100-lawyer Legal Defense group for arrested demonstrators.

[26] Monuments occupied. Fifteen members of Vietnam Veterans Against the War barricaded themselves inside the Statue of Liberty in New York harbor Dec. 26-28 to protest continuation of the war. The veterans left after a U.S. district court judge ordered them to open the doors. In Philadelphia Dec. 27, 25 protesters, most of them members of the veterans group, were held after occupying the Betsy Ross House for an hour. In Washington Dec. 28, 87 veterans were arrested for blocking the entrance to the Lincoln Memorial.

Military Protest

[27] U.S. officer seeks Swedish asylum. 1st Lt. John R. Vequist, a West Point graduate who was scheduled to go to Vietnam in November, June 9 became the first U.S. military officer to ask political asylum in Sweden to protest the Indochina war. Vequist, who had been missing from his unit in West Germany since May 20, was also believed to be the first West Point graduate to go absent without leave (AWOL) or desert since the beginning of U.S. involvement in Indochina. Swedish officials announced July 8 that Vequist, his wife and daughter had been given a residence permit to stay in the country. The Army had listed Vequist as a deserter.

[28] Antiwar officer court-martialed. A U.S. Air Force court-martial at a base near London July 13 found Capt. Thomas S. Culver guilty of organizing and taking part in an antiwar demonstration in violation of military regulations. Culver was sentenced to reprimand and a $1,000 fine July 14. (The charges carried a maximum penalty of four years imprisonment, a dishonorable discharge and forfeiture of pay.) Culver was charged with violating military regulations by participating in a demonstration in a foreign country and soliciting other servicemen to demonstrate. The charges involved a protest May 31 by some 300 off-duty U.S. servicemen in civilian clothes. After gathering in Hyde Park, the men had walked to the U.S. embassy to present petitions bearing 1,000 signatures of Air Force and Navy personnel protesting the "American war in Indochina." The defense at the court-martial argued that the protest was not a demonstration and that it was legal under military regulations to petition or present grievances to members of Congress without fear of reprisal. (About 100 U.S. servicemen and civilians carried petitions against the regulations on demonstrations abroad to the U.S. embassy in

London Aug. 1. Many of the servicemen wore disguises to make identification difficult.)

[29] Carrier sails despite protests. The carrier USS Constellation and its 80-plane bomber wing sailed from San Diego for Vietnam Oct. 1 after a six-month "Connie, Stay Home for Peace" campaign launched by a coalition of antiwar groups (Attorneys for Nonviolent Action, People's Union of Palo Alto, the local unit of the Concerned Officers Movement and the Radical Action Tribes). The protest culminated in a five-day straw ballot Sept. 17-21 in which more than 54,000 San Diego citizens and military personnel voted almost 5-1 against the carrier's return to Southeast Asia. The carrier sailed without nine young sailors who had taken refuge in a Roman Catholic church. In a predawn raid Oct. 2, the sailors were arrested and flown to the Constellation, which was 250 miles at sea, and placed in the ship's brig. Eight of the nine were given "general discharges under honorable conditions" by the Navy Dec. 6. The ninth protester decided to remain on the ship. Four crew members on the ship had sought an injunction to stop the carrier's return, alleging that the carrier was on "an illegal mission, including murder of civilians" and should be stopped pending a vote by the crew on whether they wished to return to Vietnam. Federal Judge Howard B. Turrentine rejected the petition Oct. 1.

[30] Berkeley offers sanctuary. The Berkeley, Calif. city council Nov. 10 voted to offer sanctuary to military deserters and ordered city police not to cooperate in arresting AWOL servicemen. The 6-1 vote was in response to a campaign to prevent the aircraft carrier USS Coral Sea from sailing from Alameda Naval Station to Vietnam. The Coral Sea sailed as scheduled Nov. 12. Apparently, no sailors took advantage of the sanctuary offer, despite claims by antiwar leaders Oct. 12 that over 1,000 of the 4,500 crewmen had signed a petition asking Congress to keep the ship from sailing.

See also CONGRESS [12]; FEDERAL BUREAU OF INVESTIGATION [2]; HIJACKING [15-16]; INDOCHINA WAR; PENTAGON PAPERS [10, 14, 28]; POLITICS [4]; RACIAL & MINORITY UNREST [1]; SECURITY, U.S.; SELECTIVE SERVICE SYSTEM [5-6, 11-16]; WAR CRIMES [12]; WELFARE; WOMEN'S RIGHTS; YOUTH

DRUG USE & ADDICTION—Nixon seeks wider drug fight. Describing the problem of drug addiction as having "assumed the dimensions of a national emergency," President Nixon June 17 asked Congress for an additional $155 million to help stem drug abuse. The additional funds would bring the total spent for programs to control drug abuse in the U.S. to $371 million. Nixon said the additional money would be used for a campaign of rehabilitation, research, education, enforcement and international control of illicit drug traffic. The President's message to Congress was seen as the first step in a "national offensive" against drugs announced at a Presidential news conference June 1. Shortly after asking for the funds, Nixon named Dr. Jerome H. Jaffe, director of the Illinois drug abuse control program, to head a new U.S. Special Action Office of Drug Prevention. Jaffe's primary responsibility would be to coordinate the activities of nine federal agencies now involved with research, rehabilitation and education. He was also to oversee the compulsory testing of all veterans returning from abroad and compulsory detoxification of those found to be addicted to drugs. Nixon said Jaffe's agency would have the authority to refer servicemen for treatment in Veterans Administration (VA) or private hospitals even if they had dishonorable or bad conduct discharges. Under existing regulations, servicemen with such discharges could not be referred to VA facilities. (*See* [19].)

[2] Congressional action. The Senate Dec. 2 passed by a 92-0 vote a bill authorizing the expanded powers to be wielded by Jaffe's agency and approving a $1.5 billion fund to be administered by the National Institute on Drug Abuse in the Department of Health, Education and Welfare. The money was to be allotted in grants to cities and states and for special programs operated by public and private groups. Funding was to be through fiscal 1975.

In the House, a different version of the bill, authorizing the creation of Jaffe's office and approving $411 million in funds to be used over three years, was cleared by the Commerce Committee's Subcommittee on Public Health Dec. 7.

International Control Efforts

[3] **U.S. signs world drug pact.** The U.S. and 20 other United Nations (U.N.) members Feb. 21 signed a new international treaty designed to put a stop to the multi-million dollar business of illegal stimulants, tranquilizers and hallucinogenic drugs such as LSD. The accord, concluded Feb. 19 in Vienna, had to be ratified by 40 governments before it went into effect. The agreement covered drugs not included under the 1961 Single Convention on Narcotics Drugs. The new accord, called the Convention of Psychotropic Substances, required governments to maintain strict licensing over the manufacture and supply of 32 substances, restrict their use to scientific and medical purposes and keep track of their export and import. The 32 substances were grouped in four divisions, with the strictest controls applied to the first grouping. The first group, which included LSD and mescaline, was covered by controls which prohibited all use of the substances except for scientific and very limited medical purposes and required that such use be restricted to government-run or government-sanctioned facilities. The accord also asked governments to crack down on illegal drug sales as a serious offense, punishable by prison terms, and proposed that users of the drugs be compelled to undergo treatment and rehabilitation.

[4] **U.S., France sign antidrug pact.** The U.S. and France Feb. 26 signed a protocol pledging the full cooperation of their police agencies in a crackdown against organized narcotics trafficking. Under the terms of the protocol, which formalized an agreement negotiated in January 1970, the French were to open a narcotics police bureau in New York to be staffed by French officials. The U.S. Bureau of Narcotics and Dangerous Drugs had already opened offices with American personnel in Paris and Marseilles. The pact also called for the regular exchange of information and techniques between the U.S. and French-based offices. In a related event, French police announced Oct. 9 that they had seized nearly 233 pounds of pure heroin—the largest drug haul ever made in France—bound for the American market. Andre Labray, a French businessman with textile interests in Haiti and the principal figure in the case, was arrested Oct. 6 as he was getting out of a car in front of his home. When police searched the car, they found five suitcases packed with heroin. The car was to have been shipped to New York. Three of Labray's associates were apprehended in Paris and a fifth suspect arrested in New York.

[5] **Turkey to set opium poppy ban.** President Nixon in Washington and Turkish Premier Nihat Erim in Ankara June 30 announced simultaneously that Turkey had agreed to halt by June 1972 the cultivation of opium poppies, from which almost two-thirds of the heroin reaching the U.S. was derived. Nixon said the U.S. would provide financial and technical assistance in helping Turkish farmers shift from production of opium poppies to other crops. (The U.S. had already committed $3 million to Turkey to deal with the heroin problem.) Following Nixon's announcement, Secretary of State William Rogers, who helped work out the agreement with Turkish officials, said the Turkish government was also "undertaking a very extensive program to license and control the growth of poppies during the 1971 season." In Turkey, as in several other Middle Eastern countries, the opium poppy was a legitimate cash crop.

[6] **U.S., Thais set up control unit.** The State Department announced Aug. 25 that the U.S. and Thailand had agreed to set up a joint planning group to examine the drug problem with the aim of eliminating production, trafficking and smuggling over Thai borders.

[7]　**U.S. sets up new panel.** The Nixon Administration Sept. 7 announced creation, under orders from the President, of a new Cabinet committee on international narcotics control. Secretary of State Rogers would head the committee, which would be composed of Attorney General John .Mitchell, Treasury Secretary John B. Connally Jr., Defense Secretary Melvin Laird, Central Intelligence Agency (CIA) Director Richard Helms and U.S. Representative to the U.N. George Bush.

[8]　**West Germany stiffens penalties.** West Germany's Lower House of Parliament Oct. 15 revised the country's 62-year-old Opium Law, raising the maximum penalty for drug misuse and illegal trafficking in drugs from three to 10 years imprisonment. Under the rewritten law, the maximum sentence could be applied to cases in which life or health had been endangered by drugs, trafficking for profit, the passing of drugs to minors and illegally importing large supplies of drugs.

[9]　**Drug pact concluded.** The U.S. Treasury Department said Dec. 20 that 14 European nations had agreed to join the U.S. in a concerted effort to tighten customs controls and increase the exchange of information between European and U.S. narcotics agents. The European nations which joined the pact were Austria, Belgium, Britain, Bulgaria, Czechoslovakia, Hungary, Ireland, Italy, Luxembourg, the Netherlands, Spain, Switzerland, West Germany and Yugoslavia.

National Enforcement Efforts

[10]　**New York crackdown expanded.** The government Feb. 27 announced plans to step up its drive to curb illicit drug traffic in the New York area by empowering federal prosecutors to look into the tax records of suspected narcotics dealers. Whitney N. Seymour Jr., U.S. attorney for the southern district of New York, said in announcing the expansion that the U.S. narcotics unit attached to his office had been reorganized, getting broader jurisdiction and a new director—Andrew J. Maloney. In a further development, the Justice Department announced June 4 that New York City would receive a $7.5 million federal grant for a special force of investigators, prosecutors, defense services and probation and correction officers to handle drug cases in special narcotics courts planned for the city. New York State was expected to give the city $2.5 million for the program.

[11]　**Heroin plot.** The indictment by a U.S. grand jury Nov. 15 of Col. Paul Fournier (later identified as Paul Ferrer) and the indictment May 12 of one of his former aides, Roger Delouette, uncovered a narcotics operation that had smuggled $12 million worth of heroin into the U.S. Fournier was a colonel in the French Service of Exterior Documentation and Counterespionage. The U.S. had no legal authority to arrest Fournier and bring him to the U.S. for trial without approval of the French government. Details of the smuggling plot began to evolve April 5 when a U.S. customs agent at a New Jersey pier found 96 pounds of heroin in a camper bus claimed by Delouette. Delouette was indicted May 12 in New Jersey. He pleaded guilty to the smuggling charge Nov. 16 and asserted that he had a "contact" in the French consulate in New York City. In the Nov. 15 indictment, Fournier was accused of masterminding the smuggling plan and of recruiting Delouette to carry it out. The French Interior Ministry Nov. 14 announced that it was conducting its own inquiry into the affair but suggested that Delouette had implicated Fournier to lighten his own sentence.

[12]　France and the U.S. became embroiled in a dispute over Delouette's testimony, with France demanding an official statement from Delouette before proceeding against Fournier and the U.S. insisting on a pledge that the statement would not be used to prosecute Delouette in France. (The French legal system did not protect citizens against self-incrimination.) The U.S. Nov. 21 sent French investigating magistrate Gabriel Roussel a transcript of Delouette's arraignment proceedings, and Roussel Dec. 1 transmitted to U.S.

officials a subpoena informing Delouette that the French government had indicted him for drug violations on French territory. Fournier Nov. 16 gave five hours of secret testimony to Roussel.

[13] **6 tons of heroin seized in 1971.** The U.S. State Department said Dec. 28 that efforts by U.S. narcotics authorities had contributed to the seizure of six tons of heroin and heroin ingredients worth nearly $3 billion in 1971. The amount would have been enough to supply addicts in the U.S. for one year.

Military Developments

[14] **Addiction probed.** Concern rose during the year over the increasing use of narcotics by servicemen, particularly in Vietnam. Although American military officials had acknowledged that the use of narcotics by soldiers was increasing, the extent was not known until a number of Congressional fact-finding teams issued reports and Congressional committees conducted hearings. A special House Armed Services Committee subcommittee, after an eight-month study of drug abuse, issued a report April 28 that "up to 10%" of the GIs in Vietnam were using hard narcotics and as many as 20% were using marijuana regularly. The report said attempts by the South Vietnamese government to control drug trafficking were "almost completely ineffective" because of corrupt public officials and ineffective police measures. The subcommittee said a solution to the drug problem could come only with the withdrawal of U.S. troops from South Vietnam. A Congressional investigating team, reporting to the House Foreign Affairs Committee May 25, repeated the earlier conclusion that, because of corruption and bribery in South Vietnam, the only effective solution to the military drug problem was withdrawal of U.S. troops. The team estimated that there were 26,000-39,000 American heroin addicts in South Vietnam. Dr. Jaffee (*see* [1]), testifying July 30 before a special subcommittee of the Senate Government Operations Committee, said that 5.5% of servicemen in South Vietnam showed some signs of heroin addiction. His figure was one percentage point higher than the 4.5% figure he reported to President Nixon July 17 on completion of a 10-day tour of South Vietnam, Japan and Hong Kong; but the figure was still lower than a 10% figure estimated by the Department of Defense June 21. Jaffe told the House Special Subcommittee on Drug Abuse Oct. 12 that the rate of drug abuse among U.S. soldiers in Vietnam seemed to be leveling off at 5.1%.

[15] **Army response to addiction and use.** The U.S. military command in Saigon Jan. 6 made public plans for a program to combat the spread of drug abuse among American military personnel in Vietnam. The drive, ordered by Gen. Creighton W. Abrams, commander of U.S. forces in Vietnam, directed commanders throughout Vietnam to make ground and air search operations to locate fields where marijuana was being grown. The commanders were ordered to "utilize their resources, equipment and personnel in assisting the South Vietnamese government in eradicating the unlawful growth of marijuana"; but the fields were not to "be destroyed by United States forces." The order also instructed field commanders to set up programs to curb drug abuse, including "identification and reduction of morale and welfare factors such as idleness, loneliness, anxiety and frustration." Councils were to be created to monitor all aspects of any drug problems within a command. In addition, the Army ordered its commanders to set up education programs to better acquaint GIs with the dangers of drug abuse. The directive also said programs of amnesty and rehabilitation presently underway in some commands would be extended to those "who demonstrate a sincere desire to reform." (An amnesty program was announced by the Air Force March 8 and another was announced by the Navy May 30.) In further action, the military command declared May 25 that all Vietnamese pharmacies were off limits to American military personnel. The decision was prompted by the availability without prescription of barbiturates and amphetamines that would require prescriptions in the U.S.

[16]   GI testing. The Army June 19 began a program of testing servicemen in Vietnam for heroin addiction by urinalysis. The program began by testing servicemen in Vietnam two days before they were to be shipped home after completing their tour of duty. In July and early August, however, the program was expanded. The Army announced July 11 that the testing would be expanded to include groups of American military personnel in the U.S. and Europe. The program in the U.S. would at first apply only to servicemen passing through hospitals of the First and Third Army districts as they were separated from the Army, entered the Army, were scheduled to be sent to Vietnam or were returning to overseas duty anywhere. In the European sector, the plan provided for urinalysis on a spot check basis of 2% to 5% of all soldiers in Europe before Aug. 1. The program was again expanded July 28 to include all U.S. servicemen in Vietnam, not just those leaving for the U.S. According to report, the expansion was planned after the military command learned that some GIs were extending their tour of duty to remain in Vietnam because of their addiction and the ease with which they could obtain heroin. The command said it would refuse to extend tours of duty for drug users or drug dependents. In testimony Aug. 2 before the House Public Health and Environment subcommittee of the Interstate and Foreign Service Committee, Dr. Jaffe announced that periodic urinalysis checks would begin 30 days before servicemen were due to be shipped home. The change was to prevent soldiers from avoiding detection by quitting their heroin habit a week before the drug test.

[17]   South Vietnamese government actions. Responding to U.S. threats that continued apathy in dealing with drug traffic could imperil requests for increased U.S. aid, the South Vietnamese in May began to take steps to curb the supply of drugs to American GIs. Premier Tran Thien Khiem May 7 issued an order to have all customs and police officials suspected of corruption transferred or dismissed from the Tansonnhut Airport near Saigon. The airport was held to be the main point of entry for narcotics smuggled into Vietnam. By May 23, nearly 300 customs and police officials, including airport Police Chief Mai Van Phu and his deputy, had been dismissed from their Tansonnhut posts. Police in Saigon were also ordered to step up their arrests of narcotics peddlers. In later action, President Nguyen Van Thieu sent a bill to the South Vietnamese National Assembly Aug. 10 that would make dealing in narcotics a wartime crime and would decree the death penalty for narcotics traffickers belonging to organized rings. (Thieu and Vice President Nguyen Cao Ky had been accused July 15 on U.S. television of using funds from illicit drug traffic to finance their presidential campaigns. Maj. Gen. Ngo Dzu, commander of South Vietnam's Military Region II, was accused July 7 of being one of the chief heroin traffickers in Southeast Asia. The charge was made by U.S. Rep. Robert H. Steele [R, Conn.] in testimony before a House Foreign Affairs Committee subcommittee.)

[18]   Customs sets up drug check. The U.S. Customs Bureau disclosed May 6 that it had ordered its agents to intensify their investigations of American servicemen returning from overseas as part of a drive to stem the flow of hard narcotics into the U.S. Customs agents were also directed to check more closely packages sent into the country by American GIs stationed in Southeast Asia.

[19]   U.S. to expand addiction centers. The Veterans Administration June 22 announced plans to open, by Oct. 1, 27 new drug addiction facilities to deal with the rising number of addicted servicemen returning from abroad. The VA already maintained five such facilities. Donald E. Johnson, VA administrator, said the 32-center system would be able to rehabilitate more than 6,000 addicts a year. (The House of Representatives July 19 voted unanimously to expand the VA program to include men now in the armed forces and veterans who had been given dishonorable discharges for drug use. Expansion of the program was expected to cost $5 million in fiscal 1972 and $89.3 million over the next five years.)

Other Actions

[20] **HEW submits marijuana report.** The Department of Health, Education and Welfare Feb. 1 submitted to Congress a report on the smoking of marijuana by Americans. The report concluded that not enough was known about marijuana and its effects to make conclusive final judgments. The report's major interim findings: there is no evidence that smoking marijuana leads to birth defects; smoking marijuana is not a serious cause of crime; there is no evidence to link marijuana to a loss of interest in conventional goals; and there is little evidence of progression from use of marijuana to use of more dangerous drugs. Included in the report was a survey conducted for the National Institute of Mental Health that showed: 31% of a 10,000-student sample at 50 colleges said they had tried marijuana at least once; 14% used marijuana every week or so; and use of marijuana had risen sharply in 1968 and 1969 but appeared to be dropping off.

[21] **FTC cites song selection.** The Federal Communications Commission (FCC) March 6 warned the nation's broadcasters that they faced punitive action if they failed to keep off the air song lyrics "tending to promote or glorify the use of illegal drugs." The order, approved by a 5-1 vote Feb. 24, said that the Commission expected broadcasters "to ascertain, before broadcast, the words or lyrics of recorded musical or spoken selections" to be broadcast on their stations.

[22] **Peace drug proposal stirs dispute.** Dr. Kenneth B. Clark, president of the American Psychological Association, touched off a dispute within America's scientific and medical community Sept. 4 when he proposed the creation of new mind-affecting drugs that could be given to the world's political leaders to subdue and curb their aggressive and hostile tendencies. Clark described his plan as a type of psychological disarmament, to be negotiated among nations as military disarmament is discussed. He said that conventional means of trying to prevent inhumane acts and the threat of nuclear holocaust were too slow to insure the survival of man. Clark's view was challenged Sept. 6 by a wide range of prominent psychologists who said they doubted that the drugs could be developed. They added that there would be enormous social and political problems over the control of the use of the drugs, if they could be developed.

[23] **Mood drugs curbed.** The Justice Department Dec. 2 proposed federal production quotas to hold down the total of amphetamine and methamphetamine stimulants to be made in the U.S. in 1972. Imposing the quota on the "mood drugs"—commonly known as speed, pep pills or ups-and-downs—the department's Bureau of Narcotics and Dangerous Drugs said it would allow 5,870 kilograms of amphetamines to be produced in 1972, down from 9,356 kilograms produced under no quota in 1971. For methamphetamines, the bureau proposed a quota of 2,782 kilograms, down from 4,926 kilograms in 1971.

See also BUSINESS [6-7]; CONSUMER AFFAIRS [3]; CRIME [3, 6]; STUDENT UNREST [5]; YOUTH

DUVALIER, FRANCOIS (PAPA DOC)—See HAITI
DUVALIER, JEAN-CLAUDE—See HAITI

EAGLES—*See* CONSERVATION
EARTH DAY—*See* FEDERAL BUREAU OF INVESTIGATION [5]

EARTHQUAKES—Quakes destroy Italian city. Twin earthquakes, one at 7 p.m. and another three hours later, virtually destroyed the ancient Italian city of Tuscania Feb. 6 and killed at least 22 people. About 4,000 of the town's 7,500 residents were left homeless. An official estimated that no more than 80 buildings were habitable. Art treasures, many dating back to the Etruscan era, were damaged. The quake measured about 6 on the 12-point Mercalli scale.

    62 dead in California quake. A violent earth tremor shook southern California Feb. 9, killing at least 62 people, injuring hundreds and causing property damage in Los Angeles and surrounding areas estimated in excess of a billion dollars. Officials reported that 944 buildings had suffered major damage and 139 were unsafe for occupancy. The earthquake's heaviest blows were felt at the Veterans Administration hospital in Sylmar, where the walls in two wings crumpled, killing at least 40 patients and staff members. The 45-year-old facility was described the next day as "looking like a quarry operation." One mile west, the walls of the Olive View Sanitarium were also collapsed by the quake and three persons were killed.

    The quake struck at 6 a.m. with an intensity of 6.5 measured on the Richter scale. Although tremors lasted for only a minute, weaker aftershocks were reported for 25 minutes and another single shock was reported at 8 a.m. The point of origin was officially identified Feb. 13 as a fault within the San Andreas fault system, 20-25 miles south of the San Andreas fault. Aftershocks continued for more than a week, with magnitudes as high as 5.7 on the Richter scale, but no further damage was reported.

    President Nixon declared the earthquake zone a major disaster area Feb. 9 and dispatched Vice President Spiro T. Agnew to meet with California Gov. Ronald Reagan and Los Angeles Mayor Samuel W. Yorty to speed relief efforts.

    Turkish quake. The eastern Turkish province of Bingol was ravaged by an earthquake May 22 that destroyed 90% of the city. The death toll May 25 had risen to 995. In an earlier tremor May 12 in the province of Burdur, 225 miles southwest of Ankara, at least 100 people were reported killed.

    Earthquake shakes Chile. A severe earthquake, felt for 1,400 miles along the spine of the Andes, struck the populous north-central region of Chile July 9, causing widespread damage in the provinces of Santiago, Valparaiso and Aconcagua. The Interior Ministry reported at least 90 persons dead and 250 injured. The estimates of persons left homeless ranged from 15,000 to 100,000. President Salvador Allende, who toured the region by helicopter July 10, declared a state of emergency in the three provinces and said that 60% of the homes in the area were uninhabitable. Landslides isolated some communities and many regions were without electricity or communications. Relief efforts were hampered by rain that fell for some 48 hours. The government reported that the quake registered an intensity of 10 on the Mercalli scale of 12, but there was speculation that the readings were too high.

See also ATOMIC ENERGY [14]; ENVIRONMENT

EARTH WEEK—See ENVIRONMENT
EAST AFRICAN COMMUNITY—See UGANDA
EAST-WEST RELATIONS—See COMMUNIST CHINA-U.S. DETENTE; DEFENSE [8]; ESPIONAGE; EUROPEAN SECURITY; FOREIGN POLICY; GERMAN CONSULTATIONS; GERMANY, EAST; GERMANY, WEST; KOREAN RELATIONS; NOBEL PRIZES; TARIFFS & WORLD TRADE [7] UNION OF SOVIET SOCIALIST REPUBLICS [14-15]
ECOLOGY—See ATOMIC ENERGY [16-18]
ECONOMICS—See NOBEL PRIZES
ECONOMIC STABILIZATION ACT OF 1970—See ECONOMY, U.S. [6, 9-10, 13, 16]

ECONOMY, U.S.—Faced with spiralling inflation and unemployment rates, President Nixon unexpectedly ordered Aug. 15 a 90-day freeze on wages, rents and prices and ended the traditional convertibility of the dollar into gold. The freeze, the first since 1951, was followed Nov. 14 by what the Administration named "Phase Two"—a period of economic controls tapering from the absolute restrictions of the freeze.

[2] **Prime rate changes.** U.S. banks lowered their prime lending rate (the minimum rate, charged on corporate loans) from 6.75% at the beginning of the year to 5.25% by the end of the year. The changes: Jan. 6 from 6.75% to 6.5%; Jan. 15 to 6.25%; Jan. 16 to 6%; Feb. 16 to 5.75%; March 11 to 5.25% at the Chase Manhattan Bank in New York; March 12 to 5.5% for other major banks and April 22 to 5.5% for the Chase; June 14 to 5.75% at the First Pennsylvania Banking and Trust Co.; June 15 to 6% at San Francisco's Bank of California; July 7 to 6%; Oct. 20 to 5.75%; Nov. 4 to 5.5%; and Dec. 13 to 5.25% at some major banks. The First National City Bank, the nation's second largest and New York's largest bank, announced Oct. 21 that it would replace the fixed prime rate with a weekly floating "base rate," keyed half a point above the effective rate for 90-day commercial papers (unsecured corporate notes sold over the counter to investors in the open market).

[3] **Federal Reserve discount rate changes.** During 1971, the Federal Reserve Board (FRB) trimmed its discount rate (rate of interest on loans to commercial banks) from 5.5% to 4.5%. The changes: Jan. 7 from 5.5% to 5.25%; Jan. 18 to 5%; Feb. 12 to 4.75%; July 15 to 5%; Nov. 10 to 4.75%; and Dec. 10 to 4.5%.

[4] **Annual economic report.** President Nixon, in his annual economic report to Congress, Feb. 1 stressed "orderly expansion" as the key to economic policy in 1971 and set new goals for lower levels of unemployment and inflation by mid-1972. The last of the President's three major messages to Congress, required of him by the Employment Act of 1946, was accompanied by the more detailed annual report of the President's Council of Economic Advisors (CEA). Both reports emphasized the key issues of inflation and unemployment. The President was optimistic about the economy in 1971 and 1972, but tempered his optimism by saying: "We are facing the greatest economic test of the postwar era. It is a test of our ability to root out inflation without consigning our free economy to the stagnation of unemployment." The formal report of the CEA was more extensive than the President's report and served to defend the Administration's "ambitious" economic goals and projections. However, the report departed from its usual detail in terms of supporting forecasts for the

economy, such as the numerical forecast of consumer spending. The report explained the lack of heavy statistical projections on the basis that the economy's vigorous or gradual recovery depended on variables over which the government had no control, such as the extent to which people and businesses preferred to save money rather than spending or investing it.

[5] **Construction industry controls.** Concern by the Nixon Administration over the wage and salary increase rate in the construction industry and over unemployment in the industry led to restrictive government moves during February and March. (Construction wage pacts in 1970 had called for first-year increases of 18.3% compared with an 8.1% increase for manufacturing, and unemployment in the construction industry had reached 11.1% in January—double the national average.) Feb. 23, the President suspended provisions of the 1931 Davis-Bacon Act that required contractors on federal or federally assisted construction projects to pay prevailing wage rates. The move was taken after the industry rebuffed the Administration's extended effort to gain a voluntary, anti-inflationary formula from labor and management. The President acted under authority in the Davis-Bacon Act to so act if an "emergency" existed in the industry. The Administration Feb. 23 sent letters to the states informing them that it regarded state laws governing construction wages on federal projects to be no longer in effect because of the suspension of the federal act. The President March 29 rescinded his suspension of the act and signed an executive order setting up a primarily industry-regulated system of "constraints" to stabilize wages and prices in the construction industry. It was reported that construction union leaders, who had failed to submit their own plans for controls, had made their cooperation conditional on reinstatement of the act.

[6] The objective of the constraint plan was to keep wage increases in the industry in approximate alignment with 6% annual increases given workers in the mid-1960s. Other criteria would include productivity and cost-of-living trends, as well as allowances for "equity adjustments" to maintain traditional wage level differences among crafts in a single locality or with the same craft in nearby localities. Under the order, 16-18 labor-management "craft dispute boards" would review collective bargaining agreements in each of the construction crafts. Any wage settlement found unacceptable by the boards would be further reviewed by the new tripartite Construction Industry Stabilization Board, to be appointed by the Secretary of labor. The board would make the final decision within a 15-day period as to whether the settlement violated the plan's criteria. In cases of violation: the violation would be widely publicized; the secretary of labor would be authorized to notify other government agencies of the violator's identity to discourage and possibly suspend government procurement in the area in which the violation occurred; and the secretary of labor would, in effect, be able to suspend the Davis-Bacon Act on a selective basis. The President issued the executive order under the Economic Stabilization Act of 1970 which gave him standby authority to use either general or selective wage and price controls. (The wage-price control authority of the act was extended for two months by the Senate March 4 and by the House March 29.)

[7] **Third inflation alert.** The CEA April 13 issued its third inflation alert, warning the steel industry against exacerbating its competitive position by excessive wage or price increases. It was the first alert to focus on future, rather than past, wage and price decisions, although the carefully worded statement did not make any threats or specify particular actions that the government might take. On the economy in general, the report said that the rise in prices had been "distinctly more moderate" since the second alert in December 1970, but wage increases had not exhibited a comparable slackening.

[8] Emergency measures imposed. Without warning, President Nixon Aug. 15 announced in a nationally televised address that he was ordering an immediate 90-day freeze on wages, rents and prices and was ending the traditional convertibility of the dollar into gold—in effect freeing the dollar for devaluation against other currencies. The imposition of an economic freeze, a decision Nixon had repeatedly denied he would take, also included the imposition of a 10% surcharge on dutiable imports, a $4.7 billion reduction in federal expenditures, a 5% reduction in federal personnel and a request for Congress to end automobile excise taxes and enact tax incentives for industry. The price-wage freeze was the first to be imposed in the U.S. since the ceiling ordered by the Truman Administration Jan. 26, 1951 to cope with the inflationary spiral generated by the first six months of the Korean War. The suspension of the dollar's ties to gold, ordered after massive speculation against the dollar and deficits in the American balance of payments, ended the world monetary system based on the dollar and its convertibility into gold at a fixed $35 an ounce. The President's new program was a total reversal of past Administration economic policies, particularly the "game plan" that had been played against inflation and unemployment but had failed to score. Labor leaders immediately opposed the President's program, but leaders of business applauded it. In Congress, the reaction was mixed, with most opposition coming from Democratic Presidential contenders.

[9] The major parts of the new policy became effective Aug. 16 when the President signed two documents—Executive Order 11615, entitled Executive Order Providing for Stabilization of Prices, Rents, Wages and Salaries, and Proclamation 4074, entitled Proclamation Regarding Imposition of Supplemental Duty for Balance of Payments Purposes. The executive order was issued under the Economic Stabilization Act. According to Administration estimates released Aug. 15, the government would realize a net gain of $500 million as a result of the new program. The gain resulted from preliminary reductions of $3 billion in accelerated investment tax credit, $1 billion in the anticipated increase in personal income tax exemptions and $2.3 billion in elimination of the 7% excise tax on autos; and preliminary increases of $2.1 billion in import surcharges, $1.3 billion due to the freeze of federal pay increases for six months effective Jan. 1, 1972 (submitted to Congress Sept. 1, approved by the House Oct. 4 and by the Senate Oct. 7), $1.1 billion from the deferral of general revenue sharing plans, $500 million from reduction in federal employment, $700 million from deferral of some special revenue sharing programs and $1.1 billion from deferral of welfare reform and other federal programs.

[10] _Court upholds legality of freeze._ A three-judge federal district court in Washington Oct. 22 upheld the constitutionality of the Economic Stabilization Act of 1970. The challenge was brought by the AFL-CIO Amalgamated Meat Cutters and Butcher Workmen on the grounds that the law constituted an improper delegation of power by Congress to the President and violated the separation of powers doctrine. The court held that the statute was not unconstitutional "as an excessive delegation of power by the legislature to the executive for the limited number of months contemplated by Congress to follow the initiating general freeze."

[11] _Implementation of freeze._ In his Aug. 15 address, the President established a government Cost of Living Council (CLC), to be headed by the secretary of the Treasury, "to work with leaders of labor and business to set up the proper mechanism for achieving continued price and wage stability after the 90-day freeze is over." Functioning as the operating arm of the CLC was the Office of Emergency Preparedness (OEP), created in 1962 as an arm of the executive branch to coordinate civil defense planning after natural disasters and to oversee the "stabilization of the civilian economy" in event of nuclear attack. The OEP Aug. 16-18 began setting up the organizational superstructure responsible for administering the freeze. The OEP, with its key command post in Washington, opened "regional service centers" in Atlanta, Boston, Chicago, Dallas, Denver, Kansas City (Mo.), New York, Philadelphia, San Francisco and Seattle. Under the expanded setup, each of the 10 offices would be under a regional director and would have two or more public information specialists and one or more economic stabilization experts. The offices were to report freeze violations to the Justice Department. To help the OEP administer the freeze, other government experts were shifted from their agencies to work with the 325-man OEP staff.

[12]   The CLC itself, in a series of guidelines, indicated that the wage-price freeze would be a thoroughgoing, across-the-board restriction. Council directives were issued Aug. 17 (placing federal, state, municipal and county employees under the freeze), Aug. 19-20, 23-28, 30-31, and Sept. 1 and 4. The directives were in the form of questions and answers about the freeze. The CLC Aug. 20 requested the Justice Department to "take prompt action" to insure Texas compliance with the wage freeze as it applied to state employees and teachers, and the department shortly afterwards announced plans to initiate court action. Texas Gov. Preston Smith (D) Aug. 19 had defied such application of the freeze as in conflict with state law, but he accepted Aug. 23 the Texas attorney general's ruling that the President's authority in the matter superseded that of the governor. Texas (Aug. 24), Louisiana (Aug. 20) and South Carolina (Aug. 24) all sought exemptions from the CLC for state employees and teachers. In other action, the CLC Sept. 7 met with executives called to Washington to explain why they raised dividends after the wage-price freeze had been invoked. The CLC announced Sept. 9 that three of the companies (Briggs and Stratton Corp., Martin Yale Industries, Inc. and Selas Corp.) had agreed to retract their increases; two (National Propane Corp. and Volume Shoe Corp.) had been excused from censure; and the sixth (Florida Telephone Co.) had refused to compensate a dividend increase or communicate with the council. In addition to the CLC, the Interstate Commerce Commission, the Treasury Department, the U.S. Postal Service and the Federal Home Loan Bank Board announced implementing decisions on the freeze.

[13]   **Phase Two begins.** The 90-day price-wage freeze ended at midnight Nov. 13 and the nation entered "Phase Two" of the economic stabilization program. President Nixon, in a nationally televised address Oct. 7, had outlined his plans for Phase Two. According to the plans, the program of wage and price restraints would be continued, with no calendar deadline for the end of Phase Two controls. However, the President pledged not to make controls "a permanent feature of American life. When they are no longer needed, we will get rid of them." The CLC was to continue to operate, assisted by a Price Commission, a Pay Board and a Government Committee on Interest and Dividends. Nixon also asked Congress for a one-year extension of the Economic Stabilization Act, due to expire April 30, 1972, in order to have the government prepared to act against those not cooperating with the stabilization program. The President Oct. 15 issued an executive order establishing the additional machinery for Phase Two, extending the life of the CLC and providing for the new post of executive director. (Donald Rumsfeld was appointed to the post.)

[14]   Organized labor indicated its cooperation and willingness to sit on the proposed Pay Board immediately after Nixon's address. However, a problem arose over the role of the Pay Board and the CLC, and labor agreed to support the board Oct. 12 only after receiving President Nixon's personal assurances that the Pay Board would be "completely autonomous" and that the CLC would not have veto power over its decisions as to either standards or cases. The President's statement said that the CLC would "serve as a policy review group" and would not "approve, revise, veto or revoke specific standards or criteria" developed by the Pay Board or Price Commission. The statement outlined the functions of the two bodies: establishing standards and criteria and procedures for their implementation; rendering final decisions on individual cases;

recommending legal action to assure compliance to the Justice Department; and providing mediation as needed to augment federal mediation.

[15] The White House Oct. 7 issued a text of explanation of the Phase Two program. It revealed that the CLC proposed an interim goal of a 2%-3% inflation rate by the end of 1972 (about half the pre-freeze rate) and disclosed additional Phase Two machinery. The new machinery: a 21-member Committee on Health Services Industry, with representatives of the medical professions, the insurance industry, consumer interests and the public, to advise the CLC on ways to apply standards and to enlist "the full voluntary cooperation" of the industry; a 17-member Committee on State and Local Government Cooperation, with membership from state and local governments and employee organizations, to advise the CLC, assist the pay and price boards and stimulate voluntary cooperation. The Construction Industry Stabilization Board (see [6]) would continue to operate within the standards issued by the Pay Board. The Productivity Commission, established in 1970 with members from labor, management, the federal government and the public, would be expanded to include representatives of agriculture and state and local governments and would consult with the CLC. A task force within the CLC was to be set up to recommend steps to assure that the stabilization program was "not unnecessarily prolonged." A national system of regional and local service and compliance centers was to be established, drawn primarily from the Internal Revenue System, to support administration of Phase Two.

[16] *Congressional action.* President Nixon Oct. 19 sent Congress legislation to carry out Phase Two. The proposals would: (1) extend the President's authority to regulate prices, rents and wages until April 30, 1973, and give new authority to hold down interest rates and dividends; (2) authorize civil penalties of up to $2,500 in addition to the $5,000 criminal fine for violation provided under the current legislation; and (3) establish a Temporary Emergency Court of Appeals, to be selected by the chief justice of the Supreme Court from among federal district or circuit court judges, to review federal court injunctions in wage-price cases and to hear appeals from decisions of the Pay Board and Price Commission. Both houses of Congress Dec. 14 approved, and the President Dec. 22 signed, a compromise bill on the President's legislation after the House Dec. 10 and the Senate Dec. 1 voted differing versions of the bill. The legislation, incorporating proposals (1) and (2) of the President's request, also: made all rent-controlled apartments (exempted by the Price Commission Nov. 22) subject to federal guidelines; contained a plan to provide, in some instances, retroactive pay increases that had been scheduled to become effective after Aug. 15 but were barred by the freeze; called for federal civilian and military employees to receive a 5.5% pay rise as of Jan. 1, 1972 (approved Nov. 12 by the CLC only for military employees) instead of being deferred until July 1, 1972, as requested by President Nixon; required mass transit systems not subject to federal or state regulation to seek permission of the Price Commission before raising fares; required Senate confirmation within 60 days of the pay and price board chairmen and confirmation of all future appointments to the boards; gave subpoena power to the two boards for witnesses and documents; permitted consumer suits against merchants or landlords increasing prices or rents above guidelines, with triple damages allowed on the amount of overcharge; and called upon the Pay Board not to include fringe benefits in decisions on pay raises.

[17] *Pay, Price Boards appointed.* President Nixon's appointments to the Pay Board and Price Commission were announced Oct. 22. U.S. District Court Judge George H. Boldt of Washington state was named chairman of the Pay Board. C. Jackson Grayson Jr., dean of Southern Methodist University's school of business, was selected as chairman of the Price Commission. Outgoing CLC Executive Director Arnold R. Weber was named as one of the public members of the Pay Board. His resignation from the CLC post was announced at the same time. (The position for the duration of Phase One, the 90-day freeze

period, would be filled by Edgar R. Fiedler, who was head of the CLC's policy review staff. Rumsfeld would assume direction of the CLC operation for Phase Two.)

[18]   Other public members of the Pay Board, in addition to Boldt and Weber, were Kermit Gordon, president of Brookings Institution and former director of the Budget Bureau; William G. Caples, Kenyon College president and a former vice president for industrial relations for Inland Steel Co.; Dr. Neil H. Jacoby, professor of business economics and policy at the University of California, Los Angeles, and a member of the Council of Economic Advisers under President Eisenhower. He was also a former U.S. representative on the United Nations Economic and Social Council. The five business members of the Pay Board were Rocco C. Siciliano, president of the T. I. Corp., a holding company, and a former Commerce Department undersecretary; Virgil B. Day, vice president for business environment of the General Electric Co.; Robert C. Bassett, chairman and president of Bassett Publishing Co. and Vertical Marketing, Inc.; Leonard F. McCollum, chairman of the Continental Oil Co.; and Benjamin F. Biaggini, president of the Southern Pacific Co. The Pay Board's labor members were AFL-CIO President George Meany; Leonard F. Woodcock, president of the United Automobile Workers; I. W. Abel, president of the AFL-CIO United Steelworkers; Frank E. Fitzsimmons, president of the International Brotherhood of Teamsters; Floyd E. Smith, president of the AFL-CIO International Association of Machinists and Aerospace Workers.

[19]   The seven-member Price Commission, composed of public members only, included one black, William T. Coleman Jr., a partner in a Philadelphia law firm, and one woman, Dr. Marina von Neumann Whitman, professor of economics at the University of Pittsburgh. Other members, in addition to chairman Grayson, were William W. Scranton, president of the National Municipal League and former governor of Pennsylvania; John W. Queenan, retired as a managing partner in the accounting firm of Haskin & Sells; J. Wilson Newman, vice chairman of the National Bureau of Economic Research; Robert F. Lanzillotti, professor of economics and dean of the college of business at the University of Florida.

[20]   *CLC on monitoring.* The CLC Nov. 10 announced a "three-tiered" system for monitoring Phase Two pay and prices. Companies in the first tier—those with sales of $100 million or more—were required to notify the Price Commission and Pay Board of proposed price or wage increases and receive approval on such increases. Companies in the second tier—those with sales in the $50-100 million range—did not have to give previous notification to the boards or get approval of increases, but were required to report price increases quarterly (as were those in the first tier) and to report wage increases when they became effective. Those in the third tier—all others—did not have any reporting requirements, but would be subject to all Price Commission and Pay Board regulations and to spot checks.

[21]   *Pay Board actions in Phase Two.* The Pay Board Nov. 8 adopted a 5.5% guideline for new pay increases under Phase Two. The board vote was 10-5 with the labor members unanimously opposed. Prior to adoption of the criterion, regarded as an initial one subject to review, the board rejected a proposal by labor members to estab-lish a 6% guideline and to honor existing contracts except those providing for wage increases open to a challenge of inconsistency with the board's criteria or in excess of 8% annually. In setting the 5.5% guidelines for pay increases concluded "on or after Nov. 14," the board defined "permissible aggregate increases" as "those normally considered supportable by productivity improvements and cost of living trends." In later developments on the 5.5% guideline: the board Dec. 3 issued a statement providing that "an aggregate increase in wages and salaries under any merit or salary administration plan, where no labor agreement exists, is subject to the 5.5% standard"; the Committee on State and Local Government Cooperation recommended to the board Dec. 9 that state and local government employees

hew to the guideline; the board Dec. 17 applied the guideline to executive salary increases and issued a rule for exemptions which would permit some wage increases to reach a ceiling of 7% (if wage levels were closely related to others in the same industry, if jobs were unfilled and there was difficulty in filling them at a set wage level or if aggregate pay rises of the previous three years averaged less than 7% annually).

[22]   In other Pay Board policy decisions, the Board ruled Nov. 8 that future pay increases, set under existing contracts, would be permitted unless challenged by a "party of interest" (presumably management) or by at least five Pay Board members. The board also ruled Nov. 8 that retroactive increases for pay raises denied during the freeze would be condoned if: prices were raised in anticipation of wage increases scheduled to occur during the freeze; retroactivity was "an established practice or had been agreed to by the parties" in a post-freeze wage agreement replacing one that expired before the freeze; or the increases were covered by future criteria established by the board "to remedy severe inequities." The board voted Nov. 17 9-5 to rule out retroactive payment of raises deferred by the freeze, except in special cases in which there was a well-established and consistent practice of relating increases in compensation at one level to increases at another, or unless challenged by five or more members of the board. In a decision Dec. 17, the board ruled that executive stock options granted before Nov. 14 could be exercised, and that new ones could be granted if the number of shares and the option price were not less than 100% of market value. The total number of stock options granted could not exceed the average granted over the past three years.

[23]   *Price Commission actions in Phase Two.* The Price Commission announced Nov. 11 a guideline to limit price increases to an average of 2.5% a year. The commission held that prices might not exceed freeze period levels except as changed by the commission's regulations or orders. The basic policy, it said, was "that price increases will not be allowed," except those justified by cost increases in Phase Two and reduced to reflect productivity gains, or output per manhour. The Commission stressed that the 2.5% guideline would be applied in the aggregate, that some individual pricing would be less and some more and that its standards could be modified "by considerations of equity."

[24]   In other Price Commission rulings, the commission also acted Nov. 11 to curb profits accruing from price increases, ruling out any increase in pre-tax profit margins (as a percentage of sales) as a result of price adjustments. There was no limit on the total amount of profits. The Commission Dec. 15 imposed ceilings of 2.5% on increases in doctors' fees and of 6% on increases in hospital charges. Medical services would also be required to maintain price lists revealing any changes and to make them available to patients. Hospitals could increase their charges up to 2.5% on their own and up to 6% after reporting the increases to the Internal Revenue Service. Increases over 6% required an "exception" obtained from a state advisory board, to be appointed by governors or by the IRS or the Price Commission. The Commission Dec. 20 reaffirmed an earlier decision to leave rent control with existing local control agents, but stressed that rent-controlled units were not exempt from regulations and that rent increases were subject to review. New rent regulations, issued by the commission Dec. 22, indicated that controlled rent increases of 3%-3.5% annually would be permitted. Landlords with units not covered by state or local controls would be permitted to raise base rents 2.5% to cover operating costs plus an additional amount (estimated as .5%-1%) to offset state and local property taxes and fees. The increases for taxes and fees were to be applied on a weighted basis, with expensive units in a building paying more than others. Increases were also allowable for capital improvements. (The IRS Dec. 3 had cautioned landlords not to raise rents, even within current guidelines, unless they had complete records on rental practices and made them available to tenants facing increases.) In another decision Dec. 22, the commission limited insurance premium rate increases for all insurance except life. The guideline

would be applied by a formula with factors for the insurer's past losses on the insurance involved, administrative expenses (held to the 2.5% guideline) and allowance for inflation (held to 62.5% of the current prediction for that premium).

[25]   *Dividend guideline of 4% set.* The Committee on Interest and Dividends announced Nov. 2 a guideline limiting increases in corporate dividends to 4% during Phase Two. (President Nixon decided Dec. 28 that controls on interest were not necessary at the present time.) The panel said the 4% guideline was "the general principle" to be observed voluntarily by corporations in paying dividends after Jan. 1, 1972. Dividends paid before that fell under the Administration's request for no increases. The base for the 4% ceiling could be taken from dividends paid in any of the fiscal years 1969-71. The committee Nov. 15 exempted mutual funds and other regulated investment companies from the guideline and Dec. 21 exempted companies newly turning to public ownership and companies with fewer than 500 common stockholders. The panel ruled Nov. 15 that companies that paid little or no dividends in the base period would be allowed to pay 1972 dividends of up to 15% of earnings after taxes and after payment of dividends on preferred stock. It announced a revision Dec. 21 that would allow companies that declared a higher regular dividend in 1971 prior to the freeze to count the higher dividend as its base for calculating the additional 4% allowed in 1972.

[26]   *Construction pay hikes.* The Construction Industry Stabilization Committee announced Nov. 26 approval of 48 contracts containing pay increases, many of which exceeded the 5.5% annual guideline approved by the Pay Board. CISC Dec. 3 announced approval of more settlements calling for pay increases ranging from 9.9% over one year to 56.2% over two years. The committee was told Dec. 2 by Pay Board Chairman Boldt to postpone approval of new construction settlements until its representatives consulted with the board. The consultation was held Dec. 8. The Pay Board Dec. 9 assigned three of its members to a subcommittee to devise "specific procedures" on future pay increases with a three-member group from the committee. Dec. 17 the board authorized the CISC to continue passing on labor contracts settled in the freeze period but deferred any action on retroactive payment of frozen wages pending policy on construction raises.

[27]   *Nixon confronts AFL-CIO.* President Nixon Nov. 19 appeared before the AFL-CIO in convention at Bal Harbour, Fla. and appealed for support of Phase Two. Mr. Nixon appealed for labor's support but said, "whether we get that participation or not," it was his obligation as President "to make this program of stopping the rise in the cost of living succeed, and to the extent that my powers allow it, I shall do exactly that." The President received a cool reception from the convention. He received polite, brief applause when he entered and left the convention, and some of his phrases provoked derisive laughter from the delegates.

[28]   Nixon's appearance came one day after the federation had adopted a policy of non-cooperation on Phase Two and AFL-CIO President George Meany had denounced the President's economic policies and challenged Nixon personally on the issue. The policy of non-cooperation called for labor's representatives to remain on the Pay Board "only so long as a reasonable hope exists of securing recognition of the validity of contracts and of achieving justice for working people generally—including most particularly, those with low or substandard incomes and those without the protection of strong bargaining representatives." The policy called for the three AFL-CIO representatives on the board not to vote on issues before them unless their votes were decisive for labor's side. The policy also encouraged strikes by affiliated unions to gain contracted pay increases denied during the freeze. In Meany's speech to the convention Nov. 19, he charged the board had tried to goad labor into quitting and to divide the five labor members (including representatives of the Teamsters Union and the United Auto Workers) by offering separate

"under-the-table deals." Meany accused Nixon of wanting to "make the fat cats a little fatter." He challenged Nixon, saying "If the President of the United States doesn't want our membership on the Pay Board on our terms, he knows what he can do."

[29] 3rd quarter payments deficit soars. The Commerce Department, on the basis of preliminary figures, reported Nov. 15 the largest balance of payments deficit in U.S. history in the third quarter—a staggering $12.1 billion after seasonal adjustment. The resulting $23.4 billion payments deficit for the January-September period topped any annual deficit, including the $9.8 billion in 1970, and was the equivalent of a $31 billion annual rate for 1971 as a whole. The $12.1 billion deficit, measured on the "official settlements" basis, occurred mainly in July and early August, and, according to Assistant Commerce Secretary Harold C. Passer, was one of the chief reasons for the Administration's 10% import surtax and halting gold sales to other governments.

See also BUDGET; CANADA [25-26]; CONGRESS [11]; INTERNATIONAL BANK FOR RECONSTRUCTION & DEVELOPMENT; INTERNATIONAL MONETARY DEVELOPMENTS [1-2, 9, 11, 14]; LABOR [8]; LATIN AMERICA; NIXON, RICHARD MILHOUS [1, 3]; POLITICS [4, 13]; POPULATION; POVERTY; SELECTIVE SERVICE SYSTEM [5]; TARIFFS & WORLD TRADE [4, 8-12, 14]; TAXES

ECUADOR—Army rebellion fails, but achieves goals. Gen. Luis Jacome Chavez April 1 surrendered to Army Commander Julio Sacoto Montero, ending an abortive one-day military revolt. Jacome Chavez and 50 officers of the nation's War Academy were arrested but were released early in April. Jacome Chavez had announced the revolt March 31, demanding the resignation of Defense Minister Jorge Acosta Velasco (President Jose Maria Velasco Ibarra's nephew) and Sacoto. Jacome Chavez had been dismissed from the army and fired as head of the War Academy March 30 after he demanded the two resignations, but he refused to leave his post. He was supported by the 50 college officers and claimed the support of the army's training school, the airborne battalion and "military units throughout the country, with the exception of one in Quito." Despite the failure of the rebellion, however, President Velasco April 6 yielded to army demands and fired Acosta Velasco and Sacoto. President Velasco threatened to resign if Jacome Chavez was reinstated as head of the War Academy; but the new defense minister, Luis Robles Plaza, named April 6, announced April 7 that the rebellious general had reassumed his post and would not be tried. (Col. Hector Jacome Castillo was named army commander April 6, but resigned the same day and was reported to have been arrested.)

Martial law declared. Martial law was declared May 27 in the northern province of Carchi after street clashes between police and citizens the previous day left five persons dead and 30 wounded. The clashes took place in Tulcan, capital of the province bordering Colombia, after a tax had been levied on any person crossing the border. The demonstration reportedly turned into a political protest on behalf of a return to constitutional rule. The government agreed to eliminate the border tax.

Strike fails. A 48-hour strike beginning July 28, called by the Confederation of Ecuadorian Workers and other leftist labor groups, failed when the government jailed all union leaders. (Three Soviet officials had been expelled July 6, allegedly for helping in preparations for the strike.) The army was directed to take over positions in public utilities to insure continuity of service. The unions had been demanding an increase in salaries to $250 a year, effective agrarian reform measures and increases in pension benefits.

See also LATIN AMERICA; TERRITORIAL WATERS

EDUCATION—Coeducation developments. Holy Cross College (Worcester, Mass.) Jan. 11 said it would begin admitting women students in September, 1972. The action made Holy Cross, founded by the Society of Jesus in 1843, the last of the 28 Jesuit colleges in the country to become coeducational. A special commission at Wellesley (Mass.) College recommended that the college accept a limited number of male students, according to a report March 23; but Wellesley announced April 16 that its trustees had rejected the plan. The trustees, however, reaffirmed support for a cross-registration program with the Massachusetts Institute of Technology and for student exchange programs with 11 colleges. Notre Dame University (South Bend, Ind.) announced Nov. 31 that it would begin admitting women undergraduates in 1972, aiming for a female enrollment of 1,000 in four years. The announcement was made simultaneously with an announcement that plans to merge Notre Dame and neighboring St. Mary's College were dropped for financial and administrative reasons.

[2] Yale deferred tuition plan. Yale University Feb. 5 announced adoption of a plan whereby students could defer as much as 18% of their tuition for up to 35 years. The plan, which went into effect in the fall, allowed a student to defer as much as $800 of his 1971-72 tuition to be paid back after graduation at a rate of 4% of his yearly salary for every $1,000 deferred. Students graduating in any year would be treated as a group and would have joint payment obligations totaling 150% of their deferred tuition plus administrative and interest charges. Since repayment would depend upon an individual's salary, graduates with high earnings would pay more than they theoretically owed while low-income graduates would pay less. If the total obligation was not met in 35 years, Yale would absorb the loss. Yale officials estimated that as much as 50%-60% of its enrollment would participate in the program at its outset. They said $25 million to $30 million in private funds would be needed to finance the plan in its first five years.

[3] *Other plans.* Duke University (Durham, N.C.) announced March 13 that it was adopting a limited tuition-deferment plan to begin in the fall for about 2% of Duke's students, selected from among undergraduate juniors and seniors and graduate students in the law, medical and business schools. Under the plan, a maximum of $1,000 could be deferred per undergraduate year and $1,500 per graduate year. For most participants, the repayment period would be 30 years. Duke hoped to expend the plan to all its students within two or three years. Ohio Gov. John J. Gilligan (D) March 22 introduced legislation to provide a deferred tuition plan for students in Ohio's four-year public colleges. The "Ohio Plan" would affect all students at state universities. Under the proposal, an entering student would sign an agreement to pay back the state subsidy for his education, without interest charges, beginning at a rate of $50 annually for graduates earning at least $7,000 a year and reaching a maximum of $1,000 a year for graduates earning $100,000. (The repayment was to be in addition to the current $660 in fees at the state's public colleges.) Graduates who never earned as much as $7,000 a year would never make payments. Students who dropped out before graduation would pay a portion of the subsidy. Students who made a $1,500 payment before graduation would be released from further obligation, although the four-year subsidy costs were estimated at $3,200. To relieve pressure on the state's four-year colleges, no tuition-deferred payments would be required for students at the state's two-year community colleges.

[4] Carnegie Commission reports. The Carnegie Commission on Higher Education, chaired by Dr. Clark Kerr, issued five interim subject reports (its sixth through 11th) on its five-year study of U.S. higher education to be completed by June 1972. During 1971, the Commission issued: Feb. 17 a report calling for the tripling of federal aid to the country's 105 black colleges and universities and for an increase in funds from states, corporations and foundations to allow Negro colleges to double their current enrollment of 150,000; March 13 a report urging that universities establish a bill of rights and responsibilities to apply to faculty, administrators and trustees as well as students and recommending development of contingency plans for dealing with campus disruption; April 5 a report urging state governments to remain the primary source of public funds for colleges and universities and suggesting that state governments increase their spending level for higher education from the present .7% of personal per capita income to about 1%; Oct. 7 a report predicting that the nation would need 80-105 new four-year colleges and 175-235 new community colleges by 1980; and Nov. 4 a report warning that many of the nation's small private, four-year colleges faced extinction through inadequate funds and declining enrollment.

[5] *School finances surveyed.* The Association of American Colleges Jan. 10 issued a report showing that, in a financial survey of 540 private, four-year colleges and universities, nearly half expected operating deficits in the current fiscal year. The association, which received responses from 75% of the nation's 762 accredited private institutions, said that 261 schools predicted deficits totaling $87 million for the 1970-71 fiscal year. According to the survey, the "average" institution finished the 1967-68 year with a $39,000 surplus, while the year ending in 1969 showed a $20,000 deficit. Estimates for the 1970-71 year showed an expected deficit of $115,000 for the "average" institution. The report said the institutions generally tried to reduce deficits by borrowing and transferring unappropriated surplus funds. The most popular method of heading off deficits was tuition increases. In a later report Sept. 23 the association reported that about 175 private, four-year colleges had exhausted their liquid assets by 1971. The number would reach 365 in 10 years if current deficits continued.

[6] The picture in public-supported universities was not much brighter. The National Association of State Universities and Land Grant Colleges, in a survey released July 5, said that such universities were being forced to raise student charges at an "alarming" rate of more than 30% in the last five years. Of the 78 institutions responding to the association's survey, nine expected to run deficits in the 1970-71 academic year and 60 others reported various economy measures they had been forced to adopt. The most often used stopgap measure reported in the survey was "deferment of maintenance."

[7] **Break from 'conventional wisdom' urged.** A national study group March 8 urged that "higher education break free from the conventional wisdom" about who should attend college, who should teach and how students should be trained. The report, released by Health, Education and Welfare Secretary Elliot L. Richardson, was the result of an 18-month study funded by the Ford Foundation. The report said that standard instruction methods were not meeting the needs of students and asked for alternatives to the method of reading assignments, class attendance, lectures and examinations. It suggested that many of the students who stayed in school (a minority of students entering college as freshmen) did so mainly because it was the accepted activity for persons their age. To break through the conventional patterns, the panel said off-campus education should be encouraged, with equivalency exams used to credit experience gained outside the classroom, and the use of educational television should be expanded. The group recommended alternatives—such as internships—to college for the young and urged that colleges actively recruit and encourage older students. It said that persons with wide experience in society should be used as teachers. The report also criticized the tendency toward "maximum coordination" in state university systems and said separate campuses should retain independence. It also advocated the development of "distinctive missions" for two-year community colleges.

[8] **Newark teachers' strike settled.** The Newark (N.J.) Teachers Union (NTU) and the city's board of education April 18 agreed to a contract settlement proposed by Mayor Kenneth A. Gibson, ending an 11-week teachers' strike. The strike, which began Feb. 1, was the second in less than a year in Newark and the longest in the history of any major American city. The board

had kept the city's 84 schools open to almost 80,000 students in the system, but attendance was reduced by 50% throughout the strike. The strike raised racial tensions in the city, although both black and white teachers were among the 50% of Newark teachers who remained out of class. NTU President Mrs. Carole Graves, herself a black, charged that the racial issue was being exploited by Jesse Jacob, president of the board of education, and Imamu Amiri Baraka (LeRoi Jones) a leading black playwright who headed the Committee for a Unified NewArk. The five-man black and Puerto Rican majority on the board of education opposed union demands for binding arbitration and release from certain nonclassroom duties such as supervising children in the halls and lunchroom. They charged that the teachers were unsympathetic to the needs of black children. (White enrollment in the schools was about 15%, but about 60% of the teachers were white.) From the beginning of the strike, violence exacerbated the tension. Mrs. Graves charged Feb. 1 that her car had been firebombed and windows in her home broken. About 15 men and women strikers, both black and white were beaten with clubs and fists Feb. 2 by about 25 black youths. The Organization of Negro Educators, which had been blamed for the Feb. 2 beatings, charged Feb. 15 that black non-striking teachers had been verbally and physically harassed when they tried to enter their schools.

[9] Mrs. Graves and two other union officials were jailed March 4 for violating a court injunction against the strike, but were released April 14. Some picketing teachers were arrested during the strike, and the board suspended 347 of the strikers March 30. Mayor Gibson's contract proposal came after two tumultuous public board meetings April 6 and 7 when the board rejected a settlement which it had informally agreed to earlier. Under Gibson's plan: the board agreed to reinstate the suspended teachers; both sides agreed to establishment of a three-man grievance arbitration team; teachers were to perform certain non-classroom duties and would also "voluntarily accept" other non-professional duties assigned by school principals; a "special task force of concerned citizens" was to be appointed to review the city's education problems; and teachers would be given $500 raises in the second year of the contract. (Wages were never a primary issue in the strike.)

[10] **Other strike actions.** In other strike actions in U.S. schools: striking members of the Pittsburgh Federation of Teachers voted Jan. 10 to accept a $900 annual pay raise in a pact ending a walkout that began Jan. 4; members of the Chicago Teachers Union, whose strike Jan. 12 closed the nation's second largest school system, agreed Jan. 17 to accept a two-year contract making them the highest-paid teachers in any large city in the nation, with 8% pay raises in 1971 and again in 1972; in the first major parochial school strike in the country, the New York Federation of Catholic Teachers voted Dec. 21 to accept a contract offer by the Association of Catholic Schools, ending a strike begun Nov. 22 against the 329 schools run by the Roman Catholic Archdiocese of New York.

[11] **Parochial school aid voided.** The Supreme Court, ruling 8-1 June 28, declared unconstitutional state programs to underwrite nonreligious instruction in Roman Catholic and other church-related schools. However, in a 5-4 vote, the court upheld federal legislation authorizing construction grants to private colleges, including sectarian institutions. In ruling the state programs unconstitutional, the court held that direct state grants for instruction in parochial schools violated the court's dictate against "excessive entanglement between government and religion." The rulings struck down a 1969 Rhode Island statute providing 15% of secular teachers' salaries at private schools and a 1968 Pennsylvania law under which the state contracted with parochial schools and paid them to teach certain subjects. Chief Justice Warren E. Burger, who wrote the majority opinion, said that the programs presented "excessive entanglement" because the state had to oversee a school's curriculum to assure that funds were not used for religious training. In upholding federal

EDUCATION 153

construction grants, the court gave weight to the argument that college
students were less susceptible to religious indoctrination than younger students
and said that "excessive entanglement" was avoided because the grants were
"one-time, single-purpose" grants. The program at issue in the case was
authorized under the Federal Higher Education Facilities Act of 1963 and had
provided $240 million in funds to private colleges. The court did strike down a
minor provision of the act which permitted facilities built under the grant to be
used for any purpose, including religious ones, after 20 years. (In a later
development, the Ohio Supreme Court Nov. 24 upheld a state law providing
educational materials and special services to parochial schools.)

[12] **Education aid bill signed.** President Nixon July 11 signed a $5.15 billion
education appropriation bill (HR 7016), the largest of its kind in the history of
the Office of Education. It was the first education aid bill passed by Congress
that Nixon had not vetoed. The legislation was a compromise, worked out in a
House-Senate conference, between a $5 billion bill passed by the House April 7
and a $5.6 billion bill passed by the Senate June 10. The final bill, $375 million
above the President's request, was passed by both houses June 30. Congress
added $173 million to the President's request of $440 million for areas
"impacted" by families from federal facilities, $138 million to his request of
$1.85 billion for general aid to elementary and secondary education, $100
million to his request of $469 million for vocational and adult education and
$288 million to his request of $5 million for direct loans to students under the
National Defense Education Act. The bill also provided funds for education of
the handicapped, libraries and communications, research and development,
overseas educational activities, salaries and expenses and the Corporation for
Public Broadcasting. The bill barred use of the funds for loans, loan
guarantees, salaries or other pay for any persons at higher education facilities
who had been involved since Aug. 1, 1969, in any threat of force or seizure of
property to interfere with activities or curriculum of the institutions. The bill
also prohibited the use of funds to force schools or school districts, considered
already desegregated under the 1964 Civil Rights Act, to bus students, abolish
schools or set attendance zones either against parents' choice or as a stipulation
for obtaining federal funds.

[13] **Senate, House pass college aid bills.** The Senate Aug. 6 and the House
Nov. 5 approved authorization bills for higher education aid that would provide
for the first time direct, no-strings grants to colleges and universities. The bills
faced a House-Senate conference. The House bill would authorize up to $1
billion a year in direct institutional aid to all colleges distributed two-thirds
according to the total number of students in the school and one third according
to the number of students in the school receiving federal grants and loans. It
continued the system of student aid, called opportunity grants, which channeled
scholarship funds through state governments on the basis of the total number of
students and poor people in the state and allowed college financial officers to
determine which students would receive the funds. The House bill included a
provision barring discrimination against women in employment and graduate
programs, but rejected a similar provision for undergraduates in coeducational
colleges. The bill would authorize a five-year total of $23 billion. The Senate
bill, preferred by the Administration, differed somewhat from the House
measure. The Senate version based all institutional aid (up to $700 million a
year) on the number of federally assisted students in each school; it provided a
uniform federal standard of need for student aid and would pay students
directly; it authorized a $18 billion total over three years.

[14] **NEA adopts charter revision proposal.** The 1.1 million-member
National Education Association (NEA), in its annual convention which ended
Aug. 6, approved a proposed charter revision to dilute the influence of
administrators in the association. The revision would, in some cases, ban
education administrators from membership. If the proposal passed a 1972
representative assembly and votes by state and local affiliates, educators who

negotiated for school boards would be excluded from the NEA. (In an earlier NEA development, the association and the AFL-CIO American Federation of State, County and Municipal Employees announced a coalition of the two groups March 24. Jerry Wurf, president of the public employees union, said "I hope the American Federation of Teachers [AFT, the chief rival of the NEA] will join." However, AFT President David Selden March 30 labeled the coalition "a publicity stunt.")

[15]   **U.S. seeks return of misspent funds.** Dr. Sidney P. Marland Jr., U.S. education commissioner, said Sept. 5 that the federal government was seeking the return of more than $5 million in "misspent funds" authorized under Title I of the 1965 Elementary and Secondary Education Act to improve the quality of education for underprivileged children. Marland said that government audits had turned up mistakes on the part of the states in following government guidelines. The $5 million was sought from the following school systems: District of Columbia, $1.6 million; Arizona, $1.4 million; California, $1.1 million; Michigan, $928,640; Pennsylvania, $355,479; Washington, $189,628; and Wisconsin, $33,336. (In fiscal 1971, $381,497 in misused funds had been recovered from Illinois, Wisconsin, Ohio, Oregon and Utah.) It was reported Sept. 19 that California, Washington and Arizona had challenged the Office of Education demand, claiming they would stand by their own audits. Despite the unexpected challenge, the office said it would move to recover misspent funds from seven additional states. Marland said that, when audits were completed in all states, the government might move to recover $20 million-$30 million in misused funds.

[16]   **$100 million minority college grant.** The Ford Foundation announced Oct. 9 that it was funding a six-year, $100 million program to aid minority education. The grant would involve almost 80% of the foundation's spending for general higher education in 1973-78. Almost half of the program's funds was to be used in assisting up to 10 predominantly Negro private schools with aid for students, curriculum and instructional changes, salaries for faculty, endowment and special programs. (Benedict College in Columbia, S.C., Fisk University in Nashville, Tenn., Hampton University in Hampton, Va. and Tuskegee Institute in Tuskegee, Ala. were selected as the first schools to receive the "developmental" grants.) About $40 million of the grant would be used to support scholarships and fellowships for blacks, Puerto Ricans, Mexican-Americans and American Indians at the upperclass and graduate level. The program also provided that about $10 million would be spent for the development of ethnic studies and curriculum materials, particularly at graduate schools. Part of that $10 million was also to be used to develop special programs at other "ethnic colleges" and Negro schools not included in the main foundation effort.

[17]   **Local school taxes called unfair.** The U.S. Office of Education Nov. 2 released a four-year study of the nation's school financing system that called for the federal and state governments to assume almost all public school costs. The report, by the National Educational Finance Project, contended that the property tax, now supplying nearly all the 52% of school costs raised locally, was unfair and already near exhaustion. It asked the federal government to raise its contribution from about 7% to 22% of the costs, which were expected to rise from $36 billion to as much as $73 billion by 1980, if early and remedial education programs were adopted. According to the study, federal funds would be distributed in broad-purpose block grants rather than for specific programs, and states would take into account the needs of cities with a high proportion of disadvantaged students in determining per-pupil aid. In earlier attacks on the property tax, the California Supreme Court Aug. 30 had ruled 6-1 that the state's school financing system based on property taxes favored affluent districts and discriminated against children in poorer neighborhoods. The ruling, which sent the case back to lower courts for hearings to find a more equitable financing system, held that the property-tax system "must fall before

the equal protection clause" of the 14th Amendment, which guaranteed every citizen "the equal protection of the laws." President Nixon Oct. 3 ordered a study, in light of the California decision, of the role of local property taxes in financing the nation's schools. In a preliminary ruling similar to the California decision, a federal district court judge ruled Oct. 16 that Minnesota's school financing system, based on local property taxes, was unconstitutional, and asked the state legislature to revise it.

[18] **House kills school prayer.** The House Nov. 8 rejected a proposed constitutional amendment that would have permitted "voluntary" prayers in public schools. Supporters outnumbered opponents, but the 240-162 vote failed to reach the necessary two-thirds margin. The bill had been brought to the floor Sept. 21 by a discharge petition, signed by a majority (218) of representatives, to bypass the opposition of Rep. Emanuel Celler (D, N.Y.), chairman of the Judiciary Committee, who had kept the bill in committee. The vote climaxed a nine-year campaign to overturn 1962 and 1963 Supreme Court decisions banning religious exercises in the schools. The amendment had been opposed by the U.S. Catholic Conference and the leaders of most major Protestant and Jewish bodies.

See also AGRICULTURE [7-8]; BUDGET; BUSINESS [8]; CIVIL RIGHTS [1-19]; HEALTH CARE; HUNGER; INDIANS, AMERICAN; NEGROES; STATE & LOCAL GOVERNMENTS [7]; STUDENT UNREST; WOMEN'S RIGHTS; YOUTH

EDWARDS JR., CHARLES C.—See POLLUTION [8-9, 13]
EGYPT—See UNITED ARAB REPUBLIC
EISENHOWER, DWIGHT DAVID—See PENTAGON PAPERS [19]

ELECTIONS, U.S.—Special Congressional Elections. Four special Congressional elections were held in 1971 to fill the House of Representative seats left vacant by the deaths of Rep. L. Mendel Rivers (D, S.C.), John C. Watts (D, Ky.) and Robert J. Corbett (R, Pa.) and by the appointment Jan. 29 of Rep. Rogers C. B. Morton as interior secretary. A special election April 27 for Rivers's seat was won by his godson and namesake Mendel J. Davis (D), who defeated Dr. James B. Edwards (R), a dentist, and Mrs. Victoria DeLee, a black civil rights activist. Davis pledged during the campaign to preserve the federal defense facilities implanted in the district during Rivers's tenure as chairman of the House Armed Services Committee. In a special election May 25 to fill Morton's seat, William O. Mills (R), who had been an administrative assistant to Morton, won 53% of the vote to defeat State Sen. Elroy G. Boyer (D). In a special election Dec. 4 to fill Watts's seat, State Rep. William P. Curlin Jr. (D) defeated Ray Nutter, a retired Army lieutenant colonel. An American Party candidate and a black independent in the race trailed far behind the leaders. In an election Nov. 2 to fill Corbett's seat, H. John Heinz 3d (R), grandson of the founder of the H. J. Heinz food company, defeated millionaire John E. Connelly (D) and John E. Backman (Constitutional party). Connelly was defeated by a 2-1 margin and Backman received few votes. Heinz, 33, would be the youngest member of the House.

Mayoral Elections

[2] **Daley wins fifth term.** Richard J. Daley (D) was elected to his fifth term as mayor of Chicago April 6, winning 70% of the vote to defeat Richard E. Friedman, an independent Democrat running as a Republican. Daley had served 16 consecutive years in office, longer than any other man in the city's 134-year history. (The Supreme Court Feb. 22 had refused an emergency plea by civil rights leader Rev. Jesse L. Jackson to order Illinois to place his name on the ballot for the Feb. 23 mayoral primary.)

[3] 'Radicals' win in Berkeley. Warren Widener, a black Berkeley, Calif. councilman, was elected mayor of Berkeley April 6, defeating moderate black candidate Wilmont Sweeney by 56 votes. Also elected April 6 were three "radical" candidates, considered to be aligned with Widener, to seats on the City Council. The winning coalition-backed candidates were Mrs. Ilona Hancock, a housewife associated with the women's liberation movement, and two black lawyers—D'Army Bailey and Ira T. Simmons. Control on the council was expected to be split evenly between the radicals and the moderates.

[4] Minneapolis mayor re-elected. Mayor Charles V. Stenvig of Minneapolis, who first won his post with a firm law-and-order stance, was re-elected June 8 to a second two-year term by a 2.5-1 margin over W. Harry Davis. Davis, a Negro and president of the Urban Coalition of Minneapolis, was supported by the Democratic-Farmer-Labor organization. Stenvig was backed by labor and a tax-payers group.

[5] Boston mayor re-elected. Mayor Kevin D. White (D) was re-elected Nov. 2 to a second four-year term by a surprisingly wide 42,000-plus margin over Rep. Louise Day Hicks (D), his only opponent in the nonpartisan election. White's support cut across ethnic, economic and racial lines and was surprisingly strong in white ethnic neighborhoods which had been the wellspring of Mrs. Hick's political power.

[6] Cleveland elects Republican. Ralph J. Perk, the Cuyahoga County auditor, Nov. 2 became the first Republican mayor of Cleveland in 30 years, defeating James M. Carney (D) and Arnold R. Pinkney (Ind.), retiring Mayor Carl B. Stokes's handpicked black candidate. The key to Perk's upset victory was his appeal to voters in Cleveland's white ethnic neighborhoods, where he had concentrated his campaign. The victory was seen as a severe blow to the political fortunes of Stokes, who had hoped to carry Pinkney into office.

[7] Philadelphia supports law-and-order candidate. Frank L. Rizzo (D), a former Philadelphia police commissioner who billed himself as the "toughest cop in America," Nov. 2 was elected mayor over Thacher Longstreth (R). Rizzo, who concentrated his campaign in the city's laboring white neighborhoods, won despite the defection of thousands of black Democratic voters who feared his law-and-order sentiments were a disguise for racist attitudes. Philadelphia's two largest daily newspapers had opposed Rizzo.

[8] San Francisco re-elects Alioto. Mayor Joseph L. Alioto (D) was re-elected Nov. 2 to a second four-year term over Harold S. Dobbs (R), a wealthy restaurant owner, and Mrs. Dianne Feinstein (D), president of the city's Board of Supervisors. Alioto, who was under indictment for violating a federal statute against interstate racketeering (*see* CRIME [9]), called his victory "a vote of confidence." Final returns showed that he won with nearly twice the plurality of his first campaign in 1967.

Gubernatorial Elections

[9] Lt. governor elected in Kentucky. Lt. Gov. Wendell Ford (D), campaigning on a "dump Nixon" theme, was elected governor Nov. 2 over lawyer Thomas Emberton (R), former Gov. A. B. (Happy) Chandler (Ind.) and William E. Smith (American party).

[10] Moderate elected in Mississippi. William Waller (D), a former Jackson district attorney who campaigned as a moderate dedicated "to every person in this state," Nov. 2 won 77% of the vote to defeat black independent Charles Evers, mayor of Fayette. Evers won only 21% of the vote despite the expected support of Mississippi's more than 300,000 black registered voters—almost 30% of the total electorate. There were an unprecedented 284 blacks running for office in the elections, but only 32 won. Evers announced Nov. 3 that a court challenge was being planned for some locations where blacks lost to whites in black areas. There were widespread reports that hundreds of out-of-state poll watchers had been barred from watching the voting or the vote-counting.

Federal observers had been sent into 16 counties and examiners into about 36 counties to handle complaints during the elections.

See also POLITICS [1, 4, 8-10, 12-13]; POSTAL SERVICE, U.S.; PUERTO RICO; TAXES; VOTING RIGHTS; WOMEN'S RIGHTS

ELLSBERG, DANIEL—*See* PENTAGON PAPERS [1, 11, 14-15]
ELIZABETH, QUEEN OF ENGLAND—*See* ARGENTINA [11]

EL SALVADOR-HONDURAS CONFLICT—The foreign ministers of El Salvador and Honduras, meeting at a conference of the Organization of American States, agreed April 23 to resume substantive negotiations May 20 on a peace accord between the two countries. The agreement was marred April 25 when one Honduran soldier was killed and a Salvadorean soldier wounded in a border dispute at the village of Las Tablas. According to OAS military observers, both sides opened fire April 24 when Honduran soldiers entered the village to remove Salvadoreans who had been farming there since February. The farmers were supported by Salvadorean soldiers stationed at Cerro Lagunetas. New clashes were reported April 27 along the border between Honduras and El Salvador. A Honduran communique charged that Salvadorean troops attacked three Honduran border towns and fired a mortar barrage at the town of La Virtud.

EMERGENCY DETENTION ACT—*See* SECURITY, U.S.
EMMY AWARDS—*See* TELEVISION & RADIO

ENERGY—Message on 'clean energy.' Warning that the U.S. faced an increasing shortage of electrical energy, President Nixon June 4 sent to Congress a message stressing the necessity of developing a program for "an adequate supply of clean energy." In his message, the President chose the "fast breeder" atomic power reactor, with its efficient use of nuclear fuel, as the best means to provide cheap, clean energy and asked Congress to increase development funds by $27 million to $130 million for fiscal 1972. He also favored federal support for the first demonstration breeder plant, which was expected to be in operation before 1980 and would cost at least $500 million. The message also proposed an accelerated program for leasing federal oil lands. The program for leasing off-shore oil lands, currently restricted to as far east as Louisiana in the Gulf of Mexico, was to be extended into waters off Alabama, Mississippi and Florida and possibly within the next five years along the East Coast. Oil shale lands in Colorado, Utah and Wyoming were to be opened for the first time to drilling operations and, later, land bids, in a limited way. Congress also was requested to provide $15 million more to find ways to scrub sulphur dioxide out of coal and oil stack gases and $10 million to augment the program to extract natural gas from coal.

Federal power reserves up. The Federal Power Commission (FPC) Nov. 26 said the nation's electrical power generating capacity was about 26% higher than expected winter needs—well above the generally accepted 20% safety margin. The FPC warned, however, that reserves were low in the East Central and Pacific Northwest areas. Although winter demand had risen 7.4% over 1970, capacity had increased by 8.4% to 351,317 megawatts.

Siberian power plant. The U.S.S.R. Dec. 12 announced completion of the world's largest hydroelectric power station at the new town of Divnogorsk on the Yenisei river in Siberia. The complex, with an estimated generating power of six million kilowatts, was to be used primarily to provide power to nearby aluminum plants.

See also ATOMIC ENERGY; GREAT BRITAIN [17]; OIL

ENVIRONMENT—Interior study OKs Alaska pipeline. The Interior Department Jan. 13 released a staff study stating that, despite "unavoidable" environmental consequences, a proposed 800-mile oil pipeline across Alaska should be built to meet the crucial oil needs of the nation. The report, described as "tentative" pending public hearings in February, was required under an Environmental Policy Act provision for a statement on the possible impact on the environment of government agency proposals. The report said that construction of the pipeline, held up in 1970 by a court injunction granted in a suit by environmentalists, was "essential to the strength, growth and security of the United States." It noted that U.S. security would be threatened if the country became overly dependent on oil from the troubled Middle East. The report said that the project would disturb the area's ecology but that the pipeline would be constructed under the "most stringent environmental and technical stipulations ever imposed upon industry for a project of this nature." The staff stated that only 52% of the pipeline (as opposed to 90-95% planned by oil companies) could be laid underground without causing serious erosion through melting the permafrost, a situation that could cause breaks in the pipeline and severe oil spills. The staff also suggested crossings for wild animals, protection of fish spawning areas and air and water pollution controls. Despite safeguards, however, the report said "there is a probability that some oil spills will occur even under the most stringent enforcement." The study said oil companies would be required to bear the cost of repairing oil spill damage.

Response to the department report was generally critical. In a report released March 6, the Army Corps of Engineers said environmental safeguards proposed in the report "are too general to support the positive assurances ... that ecological changes and pollution potential will be eliminated or minimized." Calling for further study, the report said the corps "cannot and will not abandon its regulatory responsibility" and that it would not assure the Interior Department or Alyeska Pipeline Service Co. (the oil companies' consortium) that it would issue the necessary permits. In a letter released March 14, William D. Ruckelshaus, administrator of the Environmental Protection Agency (EPA), urged the Interior Department to delay granting a permit for the pipeline pending study of an alternative route through Canada. The statement came in a detailed assessment of the Interior Department report, which Ruckelshaus criticized for giving only "cursory" consideration to the alternative Canadian route. Ruckelshaus said the Canadian route might be safer for the environment since it bypassed Alaska's earthquake belt and the dangers of shipping the oil by tanker through hazardous waters along the west coast of Canada and the U.S. Pointing out that a natural gas pipeline would almost certainly be built through Canada, Ruckelshaus said "it would seem preferable" to use a single route for multiple pipelines. He also said that the supply of oil from Alaska's North Slope would exceed projected West Coast demands and would have to be transported by pipeline east from Seattle. The Canadian route would pump oil directly to markets in Chicago and Toronto. (At a news conference March 11, Interior Secretary Rogers C. B. Morton had said it would be "appropriate" for Alyeska to consider the advantages of the Canadian alternative. However, in addition to the oil companies' reluctance to give up the Alaska project because of investments and plans already made, the Canadian route would be three times as long and cost an estimated $2 billion—twice as much as the projected Alaska pipeline cost.)

Nixon blocks Florida canal. President Nixon Jan. 19 ordered a halt to further construction of the Cross-Florida Barge Canal in order to "prevent potentially serious environmental damage." The President's action came after environmental groups (the Environmental Defense Fund, Inc., joined by the Florida Defenders of the Environment) won a preliminary court injunction against the project Jan. 15. The environmental groups charged that the canal, begun in the mid-60s and about 30% completed, could cause "irrevocable" injury to the Florida swamps and the Oklawaha River. They stated that work on the canal had already destroyed nearly 20 miles of river, that a 13,000-acre hardwood forest had been flooded and that fresh water sources for several cities had been threatened. Congress had authorized the 107-mile-long canal in 1942 as a shipping passage from the Atlantic to the Gulf of Mexico that would be safe from attack by German ships.

Presidential message to Congress. President Nixon Feb. 8 presented a special message to Congress calling upon Americans to dedicate themselves to a decade of "restoring the environment and reclaiming the earth." To encourage industrial participation, the President proposed imposition of a fee against polluters emitting sulphur oxides into the air. He reiterated his proposals to tax lead additives in gasoline, to allocate $2 billion a year for three years, matched by recipient states and localities, for a $12 billion program to improve waste treatment facilities, and to develop a national land-use policy. For the land-use program, Nixon proposed spending $20 million in each of the next five years to help states develop plans for protection of critical land areas, control of large-scale development and improvement of property around new communities and major facilities. The President suggested donation of surplus federal properties usable for parks to states and localities and said he would send to Congress a request for a change in the Internal Revenue Code to ease the procedure for citizens to donate land for parks. Tax incentives were also proposed as a way to encourage rehabilitation of historic landmarks. Under the Administration's "legacy of parks" program, $200 million was to be allocated for acquisition and development of new park areas in urban communities, and the park development program of the land and water conservation fund was to be fully funded at the $380 million level.

Nixon also proposed: (a) federal guidelines for state regulation of strip and underground mining; (b) authority for the EPA to set standards for noise levels on transportation and construction equipment; and a requirement for the labeling of consumer products to reveal noise characteristics; (c) a national ban on unregulated ocean dumping, and EPA authority to regulate disposal of harmful substances; (d) registration of pesticides under three categories—"general use," "restricted use" and use "by permit only"; (e) restriction of the use of chemicals and metals the EPA deemed hazardous to humans or the environment; (f) establishment of a single agency in each state, or by regions, for supervision of the location and development of power supply, to avoid the "growing number of confrontations" between power suppliers and environmentalists; (g) development of a nonprofit institute supported by the government and private foundations to study ways to combat environmental problems; and (h) establishment of a world heritage trust to extend international recognition to areas of natural, historical or cultural importance for preservation.

Local actions mark Earth Week. A single day devoted to the environment in 1970 was expanded to a week-long observance of Earth Week April 18-24. Instead of the large rallies and protests that drew attention to April 22, 1970, activities during the '71 Earth Week were calmer, localized and often directed to particular problems and issues rather than improvement of the environment in general. Among various Earth Week activities were clean-up drives in many communities, a Bike Day in Seattle and a Walk-to-Work Day at Urbana, site of the University of Illinois. In New York City, Madison Avenue was closed to traffic during the middle of the day all week, creating a pedestrian mall. President Nixon, who had taken no official notice of Earth Day '70, had issued an Earth Week proclamation April 2, which called for a "conscious, sustained effort by every American" to improve the environment. Nixon said, "I call upon the governors of the several states to encourage observance of this period and its purposes." The governors of 38 states also officially proclaimed Earth Week. In Congress, more than half the Senate had co-sponsored a resolution introduced Jan. 25 by Sen. Gaylord Nelson (D, Wis.) to make Earth Week a yearly occurrence. Rep. Paul N. McCloskey Jr. (R, Calif.) had introduced a similar resolution in the House Jan. 22.

Fights against dams. Govs. Cecil D. Andrus (D) of Idaho, Tom McCall (R) of Oregon and Daniel J. Evans (R) of Washington joined conservationists, according to a report Aug. 1, to prevent construction of the Mountain Sheep and Pleasant Valley hydroelectric dams on the Snake River in Hells Canyon. The three governors opposed the projects, first criticized by conservationists who feared the destruction of wildlife and fish habitats, in a letter to the Federal Power Commission (FPC). An FPC examiner had recommended in February that a license to build the dams be granted in order to develop the hydroelectric potential of the area. In other controversy over the projected construction of dams: the Conservation Council of North Carolina, ECO Inc. and three North Carolina residents filed suit Aug. 10 in federal court to halt further construction of the $40 million New Hope Dam in Chatham County, which the plaintiffs said would destroy wildlife and woodland and cause the loss of $1 million in farm and timber revenues; the Army Corps of Engineers, in an environmental impact statement reported Oct. 5, recommended construction of the $259 million Tocks Island Dam project on the Delaware River, despite objections by conservation groups. (The corps disclosed Oct. 22 that it would delay the start of construction on the dam after receiving a request by the Council on Environmental Quality for further information on the project's environmental impact.)

Southern waterway halted. U.S. District Court Judge John Lewis Smith Jr. issued a preliminary injunction Sept. 21 ordering the Army Corps of Engineers to halt construction of the $386.6 million Tennessee-Tombigbee Waterway pending a ruling on the environmental impact of the project. The order came in a suit brought by several environmental groups which argued that the 253-mile channel, linking the Gulf of Mexico with the Ohio River Region, would destroy the environment. The corps had announced June 4 that it would undertake a study of the environmental effects while planning and building the project. The channel, authorized 25 years before to provide a direct water route to the Gulf of Mexico at Mobile, Ala., had been initiated by President Nixon May 25. It would involve rechanneling of the Tombigbee and construction of 10 locks, a 12-mile-long reservoir and a canal.

TVA tightens strip rules. The Tennessee Valley Authority (TVA) Dec. 6 issued new rules tightening environmental requirements on strip (surface mining) coal purchase contracts, as part of its first annual environmental impact statement. But the TVA rejected demands that each of its 30-40 annual strip mine contracts include impact statements. (The TVA had been sued by environmental groups March 2 for violating environmental protection legislation in contracting for strip-mine coal in eastern Kentucky and Tennessee.) Under the new rules, the TVA would prohibit mining by suppliers on mountain slopes with more than 28-degree inclines, "scenic" and "wilderness" areas, and areas where stripping would dangerously pollute streams or water supply systems. In addition, 2% of contract payments would be withheld until reclamation work was completed. The TVA claimed that individual impact statements, which would take up to six months of study each, would make competitive bidding on coal purchasing "practically impossible."

See also ATOMIC ENERGY [8-9, 12] AVIATION [2]; BUDGET; CONSERVATION; FEDERAL BUREAU OF INVESTIGATION [5]; NIXON, RICHARD MILHOUS [1]; PESTICIDES; POLITICS [4]; POLLUTION; PUBLIC LAND; STATE & LOCAL GOVERNMENTS [8]; SWITZERLAND; WOMEN'S RIGHTS

ENVIRONMENTAL PROTECTION AGENCY (EPA)—See ENVIRONMENT; PESTICIDES; POLLUTION [1, 5, 8, 12, 14-21]

EQUAL EMPLOYMENT OPPORTUNITY COMMISSION (EEOC)—See CIVIL RIGHTS [22-24]; WOMEN'S RIGHTS

ESPIONAGE—**Army surveillance suit dismissed.** Judge Richard B. Austin of the U.S. District Court in Chicago Jan. 5 dismissed a suit which sought an injunction to halt Army domestic surveillance operations and an order to destroy files collected during the alleged spying. The suit was brought by the American Civil Liberties Union on behalf of Jay Miller, head of the Chicago ACLU; the Rev. Jesse Jackson, a civil rights leader; and Gordon B. Sherman, who had organized Business Executives Move for Peace in Vietnam. Referring to testimony that much of the Army activity was in clipping and filing newspaper stories about their "targets," Austin said, "the chief beneficiary of Army intelligence has been newspaper circulation." Although he referred to the intelligence unit that was the subject of the hearings as an "assemblage of Keystone Cops," Austin said the federal government was "well within its rights" to use any available facilities to prepare for civil disturbance emergencies.

Civilian panel to check Army investigations. Defense Secretary Melvin Laird Feb. 18 announced formation of a civilian-dominated board to directly control military intelligence investigations in the U.S. The five-man Defense Investigative Review Council, to be headed by Assistant Secretary of Defense Robert F. Froehlke, would also include Undersecretary of the Army Thaddeus R. Beal, Undersecretary of the Navy John W. Warner, Undersecretary of the Air Force John L. McLucas and Defense Intelligence Agency Director Lt. Gen. Donald V. Bennett.

Swiss engineer jailed for jet plane sale. The Federal Tribunal in Lausanne April 23 sentenced Alfred Frauenknecht, a Swiss engineer, to four and a half years in prison for selling to Israel the blueprints and specifications for the jet engine of the French Mirage 3 fighter. The court found Frauenknecht, who had headed the jet engine division of the Sulzer engineering works at Winterhur (authorized to build the engines for the Swiss air force on the condition that the blueprints be destroyed after they were microfilmed), guilty of violating military secrecy and of industrial espionage but innocent of military espionage. Frauenknecht admitted that he had sold 200,000 documents out of sympathy to Israel. (The French government had imposed an embargo on arms sales, including Mirage jets, to Israel after the June 1967 Middle East war.) The prosecution had asked for a seven-year sentence, arguing that the espionage activities threatened Swiss neutrality.

Lyalin affair. Information reportedly supplied by an official of the Soviet secret police (KGB) who defected to Britain early in September, bringing with him the names of Soviet citizens engaged in intelligence activities in Britain and "plans for infiltration of agents for the purpose of sabotage," led to the expulsion of 90 Soviet citizens from Britain Sept. 24. Britain also Sept. 24 prevented the return of 15 other Soviet citizens temporarily away, charging them and the 90 others with engaging in "operations against the security of this country." The British Foreign Office note detailing the ouster said the number of officials in all Soviet organizations would "not be permitted to rise above the levels at which they will stand after the withdrawal of persons named in the attached list." The informant was identified Sept. 30 as Oleg Lyalin, a member of the Soviet trade delegation believed to have held the KGB rank of captain. In later developments in Britain, three men (Sirioj Husein Abdoorcader, a Malaysian civil servant, and Kyriocos Costi and Constantinos Martianou, Greek Cypriot tailors) were accused Oct. 25 of conspiring with Lyalin to obtain information prejudicial to the state. Costi and Martianou were found guilty Dec. 7. Martianou was sentenced to four years in prison, and Costi was given a six-year sentence.

Soviet response. The Soviet Union Sept. 26 delivered a note of protest to Sir John Killick, the British ambassador in Moscow, asking Britain to revoke the Sept. 24 ouster. The note said that, if Britain left the expulsion order in force, "the Soviet Union will have no choice but to take corresponding measures in reply." The U.S.S.R. Oct. 8 expelled four British diplomats (Philip Hanson, Ann Lewis, Anthony Wolstenholme and Alan Holmes) and one British businessman (Vladimir Haltigan of Rank Xerox), denied re-entry to three businessmen with valid visas and refused to allow the return to the Soviet Union of 10 academics and career diplomats who had formerly been attached to the British embassy but who had not applied for visas in recent years. The order did not forbid the British government to replace the expelled diplomats. The order also suspended the operations of three Soviet-British commissions in economic and cultural fields and canceled the scheduled 1972 visit to Moscow of British Foreign Secretary Sir Alec Douglas-Home.

Defector details Soviet espionage in Belgium. Anatoly K. Chebotarev, a former Soviet trade mission employee in Brussels missing since early October, supplied Belgian police with a list of 30-40 Soviet espionage agents operating in Belgium. Belgian police sources reported Oct. 17 that they had given the Foreign Ministry the list, which allegedly involved the monitoring of telephone conversations at North Atlantic Treaty Organization (NATO) headquarters in Belgium and at Supreme Headquarters Allied Powers Europe. A Belgian source said Nov. 4 that the government would expel the alleged spies named by Chebotarev, but there would be no mass expulsion. About a third of the alleged agents had already left Belgium. (Chebotarev asked for asylum in the U.S. and was granted it Oct. 18. Following a meeting Dec. 21 at the State Department with a Soviet embassy official who gave him "a number of pieces of correspondence from his family," Chebotarev disappeared and returned to the U.S.S.R. Dec. 26.)

Chinese free two Americans. Communist China Dec. 12 released American prisoners Richard G. Fecteau and Mary Ann Harbert. The two arrived in the U.S. Dec. 13. The Communist Chinese press agency Hsinhua said Dec. 13 that Fecteau and John T. Downey had been shot down in a military aircraft over China in 1952 after dropping espionage agents trained in Japan into Manchuria. Downey's life sentence was being reduced to five more years because "both men had admitted their crimes during the trial and their behavior was not bad while serving their terms." Fecteau Dec. 14 replied with "no comment" when asked by newsmen if he and Downey had worked for the Central Intelligence Agency (CIA). (In a news conference Dec. 13, Fecteau's divorced wife Margaret said: "He was a civilian working for the U.S. government. I know what he was doing, but I can't say. Let me put it this way—the Chinese haven't been lying." She retracted her statement Dec. 14.) Miss Harbert had strayed into Chinese waters off southern Kwangtung Province in 1968 while sailing from Hong Kong in a yacht with Gerald R. McLaughlin, a family friend. Hsinhua said McLaughlin had "committed suicide on March 7, 1969."

See also COMMUNIST CHINA-U.S. DETENTE [11]; CUBA; FEDERAL BUREAU OF INVESTIGATION; PENTAGON PAPERS [2-3, 7, 14]; WAR CRIMES [8]

ETHIOPIA—U.S. soldier killed. A U.S. Army soldier was shot and killed Jan. 11 while delivering Army mail in Eritrea Province, according to the New York Times Jan. 21. The soldier, identified as Spec. Ricardo Echeandia of New York City, reportedly had driven along the Massawa-Asmara road to Ghinda, where he had exchanged packages with another Army courier. Echeandia had been attached to the U.S. military communications center at Kagnew near Asmara, the provincial capital. The area in which the shooting occurred was a center for activities of the Eritrean Liberation Front, a Moslem-led secessionist group opposed to the central government.

Cabinet changes. Emperor Haile Selassie Aug. 19 appointed Foreign Minister Ketema Yifru to the post of minister of commerce, industry and tourism. Yifru was replaced by Manasse Haile, former ambassador to the U.S. Yilma Deressa, finance minister, was named adviser to the Imperial Council.

See also AGNEW, SPIRO THEODORE; HIJACKING [3]; MIDDLE EAST [7]; SOUTH AFRICA [2]; TRACK & FIELD

EUROCURRENCY MARKET—*See* INTERNATIONAL MONETARY DEVELOPMENTS [6]

EURODOLLARS—*See* INTERNATIONAL MONETARY DEVELOPMENTS [2, 6]

EUROPEAN ATOMIC ENERGY COMMUNITY (EURATOM)—*See* ATOMIC ENERGY [13]

EUROPEAN COMMISSION ON HUMAN RIGHTS—*See* NORTHERN IRELAND [10]; SWITZERLAND

EUROPEAN ECONOMIC COMMUNITY (EEC OR COMMON MARKET)—The

six members of the EEC (France, West Germany, Italy, Belgium, Luxembourg and the Netherlands) moved toward increased unification during 1971 with agreements on harmonization of economic and monetary affairs [2], talks on integration between the EEC and the European Free Trade Association [10] and negotiations on enlargement of the community to include Great Britain, Norway, Denmark and Ireland [13-17]. By the end of the year, Great Britain had set a date for signing its treaty of accession to the community and the three other applicants had progressed significantly toward membership.

[2] **Plans for economic union set.** Foreign and finance ministers of the EEC Feb. 9 concluded a loose agreement providing for the creation of an economic and monetary union within the next decade. The agreement followed a German-French compromise postponing specific decisions on the nature of supranational institutions to control EEC members' monetary and economic affairs. (France refused to commit itself on giving up any of its national economic sovereignty.) The agreement provided for a three-stage plan. The first stage, retroactive to Jan. 1, 1971, included a narrowing of the exchange rate margins among EEC currencies, progressive tax harmonization, closer coordination of economic policies through central banks and other institutions, regular meetings of economic ministers to discuss harmonization of national budget policies, and measures to ease movement of capital within the EEC. Decisions on measures to be taken during the second stage were to be made before the end of the first stage. West Germany insisted, however, on inserting a five-year "prudence clause" which stipulated that, if agreement on successive stages had not been reached by the end of the first stage, then all actions taken up to that point would be dropped within another two years.

[3] **Farm price rises set.** Agriculture ministers of the EEC agreed March 25 on a controversial plan for higher farm prices. Agreement came after three days of tense debate accompanied by a demonstration by over 80,000 farmers demonstrating for higher farm prices. (The demonstration left one person dead and more than 150 injured.) Under the plan, target prices (those set as fair by the EEC) were increased for wheat and rye (3% average), barley (5%), milk (6%) and beef (6% in 1971 and an additional 4% in 1972). The prices were to rise beginning April 1. The increases were higher than those originally proposed by the EEC Commission, under the direction of Commission Vice President Sicco Mansholt, but less than the average 15% increase demanded by farmers' organizations in the six member states.

[4] Also approved March 25 was a $1.48 billion plan for modernization of the agricultural sector. The plan was passed at the insistence of Italy, which stood to gain little from the actual price increases. The reform plan was less extensive than one suggested in the Mansholt plan. The agriculture ministers, meeting Oct. 25-26, however, failed to agree on measures to implement the reform plan and referred the matter back to the Executive Commission's special agricultural committee for further discussion. The talks bogged down on two Commission directives on farm modernization and a reform proposal to grant farmers between the ages of 55 and 65 a pension of up to $600 per year if they would leave the land. Under the reform plan, EEC funds would be used to pay up to 65% of the cost of the pensions in the less developed regions of the EEC (Italy) and 25% in the other areas, with the remainder coming from national governments.

[5] **Preference plan set.** The governments of the six EEC members agreed March 30 to introduce a system of generalized trade preferences for 91 developing countries (members of the so-called "group of 77" developing nations) beginning June 1. The decision authorized duty-free entry for manufactured and semi-manufactured goods from developing nations while keeping the current tariffs on the same goods from developed nations. The amount of trade involved would total about $1 billion yearly and the six members would lose about $100 million in tariffs. Not included in the plan were

eight developing nations: Cuba, Israel, Taiwan, Spain, Portugal, Greece, Turkey and Malta. France reportedly had refused to extend preferences to the eight.

[6] Tariff on U.S. orange exports cut. The EEC Council of Ministers, acting on a recommendation by the Executive Commission, decided in Brussels July 27 to unilaterally reduce tariffs from 15% to 8% for a one-year period on U.S. orange exports to Common Market members. Continuation of the tariff cut would be contingent on the final agreement and implementation of a reciprocal halt of U.S. and EEC subsidies on poultry exports to third countries and of an end to U.S. subsidies on lard exports to Britain. The EEC had originally offered to cut the tariff on oranges only as part of a package deal that would reduce U.S. subsidies on poultry and lard exports. The one-year limitation, not in the original package, was added at the insistence of Italy.

[7] Investment aid curb set. The Council of Ministers agreed Oct. 20 to restrict governmental investment aid in the market's most industrialized areas—called "central areas"—to 20% of the total investment involved in any specific project. The curb, to go into effect Jan. 1, 1972, would work on a trial basis in.1972 and would be re-examined in 1973. It was designed to halt cutthroat competition to attract foreign investment.

[8] Argentine trade pact signed. Argentina and the EEC Nov. 8 signed the first nonpreferential trade agreement between the EEC and a Latin American nation. The accord, signed in Brussels, provided for reciprocal trade liberalization between the two nations, including agreement by the EEC to lower tariffs on imports of Argentinian frozen meat.

[9] Civil servants strike. The EEC's civil servants staged a series of strikes Nov. 17-Dec. 6 in Strasbourg, Brussels and Luxembourg to support claims for salary increases and for direct wage negotiations with the EEC authorities. The finance ministers agreed in principle early Dec. 7 on a $4 billion community budget for 1972, providing average salary increases of 9.5% for the civil servants. Final adoption of the budget was postponed pending agreement by science ministers on the budget for the European Atomic Energy Community. Talks by the science ministers in Brussels had ended in deadlock Dec. 6 with France's refusal to participate in a number of joint Euratom research programs.

[10] EFTA trade talks start. Negotiations on industrial free trade arrangements between the EEC and the six members of the European Free Trade Association (EFTA) who had not applied for EEC membership began Dec. 3. The six nations were Austria, Finland, Iceland, Portugal, Sweden and Switzerland. Discussions on negotiations between the EEC and EFTA had bogged down July 26 over the extent to which agricultural goods of the six noncandidates should be allowed into the Common Market and on the length of a transition period and provisions for revising any agreement ultimately reached. The EEC foreign ministers, at a meeting Nov. 8, had completed a draft of the joint negotiating position to be taken with the EFTA members. The terms provided for an offer of free trade in industrial goods, with reductions in tariffs to take place at the same rate as those between the EEC and the four new market members (see [13-17]). Special arrangements could be extended to non-industrial sectors later, a concession to Sweden and Switzerland, who wanted closer economic ties than simply free trade in industrial goods. Details of the arrangements for agricultural and sensitive industrial products were to be left to the actual negotiations.

[11] EEC rebuffs U.S. The Council of Ministers Dec. 11 refused to give the executive commission a mandate to continue talks with the U.S. on trade and currency realignments and canceled plans for further trade talks during December. The rebuff was at French insistence, reportedly in reaction to a list of demands for short-term trade concessions presented by the U.S. Dec. 9. The U.S. demands were not disclosed, but press sources said they included a freeze on import duties on farm products if the dollar were devalued, a grain stockpile agreement to help U.S. sales, special concessions for U.S. citrus fruits and tobacco and compensation for trade lost from preferential agreements between the EEC and the four candidate nations (*see* [13-17]). The demands also reportedly attacked preferential agreements with developing nations (*see* [5]). The EEC foreign ministers Dec. 11 issued a declaration of intent that trade concessions should be reciprocal and negotiations should not begin until after currencies were realigned and the U.S. devalued the dollar against gold.

[12] **Italy accepts border tax on food.** Italy Dec. 28 provisionally reversed its refusal to impose a border tax on imported food products, thus yielding to the view of the other EEC members that the levies were necessary to prevent an influx of cheap agricultural imports in the wake of the recent world currency realignment (*see* INTERNATIONAL MONETARY DEVELOPMENTS [xxx]). EEC authorities in Belgium Dec. 29 announced temporary border taxes on farm imports, effective Feb. 3, 1972, to replace the rates previously imposed individually by all the members except Italy. The tax rates would be 9.5% for the Benelux countries, 5.9% for France, 4.9% for Italy and 10.8% for West Germany.

Membership Developments

[13] **British parliament votes entry.** The House of Commons Oct. 28 approved the principle of Britain's membership in the EEC on terms negotiated by the Conservative government. The vote was 356-244 with 22 abstentions. The unexpectedly large majority—112 votes—was a personal and political victory for Prime Minister Edward Heath and a historic turning point in Britain's 10-year effort to join the Common Market. (In an earlier vote Oct. 28 the House of Lords had voted 451-58 in favor of market membership.) The Commons vote was notable for the considerable vote across party lines. In defiance of the party's strictest orders—the "three-line whip"—69 Labor members of Parliament voted in favor of entry. Thirty-nine Conservatives, who had been freed from party discipline for the vote, crossed party lines to oppose entry. Britain and the EEC agreed Dec. 17 that the date for signature of Britain's treaty of accession to the market would be Jan. 22, 1972 at the Egmont Palace in Brussels. Before the admission of Britain to the EEC, expected in 1973, the government had to secure passage of specific legislation to harmonize British laws with EEC regulations.

[14] ***EEC negotiations.*** Negotiations on Britain's entry to the EEC took place throughout the year. Negotiations between the EEC Council of Ministers, presided over by French Foreign Minister Maurice Schumann, and British chief negotiator Geoffrey Rippon and deputy negotiator Sir Con O'Neill resulted in accords May 10 on British-Commonwealth sugar policy (accepted by the Commonwealth June 3); May 12-13 on a five-year transition period for British adaptation to EEC farm policy, the granting of full "community preference" by Britain to EEC products from the date of market entry and the adjustment of British tariffs; June 7 on a gradual phasing-out of sterling's role as an international reserve currency; June 22 on the reduction of New Zealand's guaranteed dairy exports to Britain, British contributions to the EEC budget (8.64% in the first year, increasing progressively to 18.92% in 1977), integration of Britain's coal and steel industries into the EEC, the continuance of Britain's system of welfare aid to 17,000 hill farmers and the equalization of voting weight of Britain, France, West Germany and Italy in European institutions; July 12 on a plan to give Britain two years to remove restrictions on direct investments in EEC countries by British companies, two and a half years to lift the restrictions on personal capital movements and five years to end restraints on portfolio investments in EEC countries; July 19 on an exemption of Northern Ireland and the Irish Republic from the community's rules on the free movement of workers for a five-year period after entry of Britain and Ireland; Oct. 27 on the expansion of the EEC Court of Justice for

the addition of one British judgeship and one British advocate generalship; Dec. 12 on the barring of member nations from coastal waters of the applicant countries for ten years after their entry to the EEC; and July 28 (accepted by the Channel Islands Dec. 14-16) on the status of the Channel Islands of Alderney, Guernsey, Jersey and Sark after Britain's entry. (The islands were to be considered as integral parts of the EEC, but exempted from EEC rules other than free trade in industrial and agricultural goods.)

[15] *British debate over entry.* British Prime Minister Heath had planned to have the parliamentary vote on entry to the EEC during the summer, but postponed it June 17 until October in the face of rising opposition to EEC membership. The government July 7 launched a campaign to win approval for entry with the presentation of a White Paper which stressed the disparity between Britain's limited economic progress over the last decade and the far better performance of EEC members. Despite the government's campaign, however, the opposition Labor party's National Executive Council July 28 voted 16-6 in favor of a recommendation by party leader Harold Wilson to oppose entry on the terms negotiated by the Conservative government. (Wilson, as a former prime minister, had originally launched Britain's third bid for entry in 1967, but had gradually turned against entry as negotiated by the Conservatives in order to accommodate majority anti-Market feeling in the Labor party.) The recommendation against support for entry was approved Oct. 4 by a 5-1 margin at the Labor party's annual conference. The conference asked all Labor members of Parliament to vote against entry in the Commons, but stopped short of a demand for a pledge that a future Labor government would take Britain out of the EEC. (Roy Jenkins, deputy Labor party leader, aroused the wrath of his party by continuing to back British membership in the EEC.) The leaders of the Trades Union Congress (TUC) also voted (15-11) July 28 to oppose entry. The Conservative party, at its annual conference, Oct. 13 endorsed, by a 2,474-324 vote, entry into the EEC on terms negotiated by the government. In an unexpected move, Heath Oct. 18 freed Conservative members of Parliament to vote according to their conscience, without formal party orders, in the Oct. 28 vote.

[16] **Denmark approves membership.** The Danish Folketing (parliament) Dec. 16 approved, by a 141-32 vote with two abstentions, a mandate for Premier Jens Otto Krag to sign Denmark's treaty of accession to the EEC. The parliament would vote again on the treaty's ratification in May 1972, to be followed by a binding referendum on the issue.

[17] **Status on Ireland and Norway.** By the end of 1971, Ireland and Norway had not yet accepted a date for signing their treaties of accession to the EEC. Norway's rejection of the fishing agreement (*see* [14]) made its signature uncertain. Norwegian Premier Trygve Bratteli said Dec. 16 that Norway would prefer to wait for a satisfactory solution to the fisheries problem rather than push for hasty conclusion of its negotiations. (Norway had rejected the fishing agreement on the ground that it did not provide a "reasonable assurance" for Norwegian fisheries. The government wanted firmer assurances for continued special arrangements after the 10-year exempt period.)

See also BELGIUM; DENMARK; FRANCE [6]; GREAT BRITAIN [13]; INTERNATIONAL MONETARY DEVELOPMENTS [1, 3, 5, 9-10, 14, 16-17]; MALTA; NETHERLANDS ANTILLES; NOBEL PRIZES; NORWAY; TARIFFS & WORLD TRADE [12, 14]

EUROPEAN FREE TRADE ASSOCIATION (EFTA)—*See* EUROPEAN ECONOMIC COMMUNITY [1, 10]

EUROPEAN LAUNCHER DEVELOPMENT ORGANIZATION (ELDO)—*See* SPACE [17]

EUROPEAN SECURITY—Troop cut activities. Soviet Communist party General Secretary Leonid I. Brezhnev May 14 offered to begin exploratory negotiations with the U.S. and the North Atlantic Treaty Organization (NATO) countries on mutual troop reductions in Central Europe. The move was welcomed by the Nixon Administration May 17 and by the NATO foreign ministers at the end of a two-day meeting June 4. The foreign ministers expressed their desire to begin negotiations "as soon as may be practical," and said that the proposals were "receiving the closest attention." However, the ministers also indicated that they thought the Soviet proposals were in need of "further clarification." The NATO communique distinguished clearly between talks on the reduction of troops and the convening of an all-European security conference, a project also mentioned by Soviet leaders. NATO deputy foreign ministers, following a two-day session near Brussels, Oct. 6 appointed Manlio Brosio, former NATO secretary general, to begin exploratory talks on the reduction of troops. Brosio was to sound out Warsaw Pact leaders on the reductions before Nov. 15, but by Dec. 10, Brosio had still not been invited to Moscow to begin exploratory talks.

In the U.S., the May 14 Soviet proposal was one of the major factors in the defeat May 19 of a Senate proposal to cut U.S. troops in Europe. The proposal, made by Senate Democratic Majority Leader Mike Mansfield (Mont.), to halve the 310,000-man U.S. force in Europe by the end of 1971 was defeated by a 61-36 vote. Administration supporters in the Senate repeatedly emphasized during debate that approval of the troop reductions would destroy allied bargaining power and reduce NATO forces without gaining reciprocal reduction of opposing forces from the Communist bloc.

Security conference developments. The Warsaw Pact nations throughout the year called for a European security conference, but the beginning of negotiations on the conference was delayed by the insistence of NATO countries that some settlement be reached on Berlin before security talks started (*see* GERMAN CONSULATIONS). The foreign ministers of the Warsaw Pact countries met Nov. 30-Dec. 1 in Warsaw to discuss "problems involved in preparing" for the security conference. In a communique issued Dec. 2, the ministers said they had decided to appoint representatives for "multilateral consultations." The ministers urged "all European states" and the U.S. and Canada to make "practical preparations" for the conference. The communique also said that preliminary discussions would decide "the content of the agenda of the European conference, the procedure of its work, concrete dates and the procedure of convening it." The NATO Ministerial Council ended a three-day winter session Dec. 10 in Brussels without responding directly to the Soviet proposal that the western states make "practical preparations" for the conference, but issued a communique Dec. 10 in which the ministers expressed their willingness to begin multinational planning sessions "as soon as the negotiations on Berlin had reached a successful conclusion."

The NATO communique apparently acknowledged a division of opinion among the ministers as to when the Berlin accord could be regarded as complete. France and a number of the smaller countries considered that the accord would be complete, and a security conference possible, when the two German supplementary agreements had been reached. The U.S., Britain and West Germany reportedly believed the accord would be incomplete until signed by the four powers (the U.S., Great Britain, France and the U.S.S.R.) which had negotiated its main provisions. The division among NATO members was further reflected in the communique's treatment of a Finnish government invitation to heads of mission in Helsinki to begin exploratory talks for a European conference. The French text said NATO governments were "favorable" to the initiative; the British said they "appreciated" it.

See also CANADA [22]; FOREIGN POLICY; FRANCE [17]; NORTH ATLANTIC TREATY ORGANIZATION; NORWAY; PENTAGON PAPERS

EXPORT-IMPORT BANK (EXIMBANK)—*See* CHILE [8]; FOREIGN AID; TARIFFS & WORLD TRADE [7]

FAMILY ASSISTANCE PROGRAM (FAP)—*See* WELFARE
FAULKNER, BRIAN—*See* NORTHERN IRELAND [1, 4-6, 8, 11-13, 15, 17, 19]
FEDERAL AVIATION ADMINISTRATION (FAA)—*See* CUBA

FEDERAL BUREAU OF INVESTIGATION (FBI)—Stolen files disseminated. A group calling itself the Citizens Commission to Investigate the FBI broke into the FBI office at Media, Pa. March 8 and stole 800-1,000 documents from the bureau's files. Following the theft, the group, which admitted stealing the documents, disseminated the papers to the press, Sen. George McGovern (D, S.D.), Rep. Parren J. Mitchell (D, Md.) and the American Friends Service Committee. Some of the stolen records were received March 22 by McGovern and Mitchell, both of whom returned them immediately. McGovern said he refused to be associated with "this illegal action by a private group" and that he favored a Congressional investigation of the bureau. Mitchell said March 23 that burglary was a crime and should be dealt with as such. Attorney General John Mitchell said March 23 that copies of the records had also been distributed to the press and he urged that the information be withheld so as not to "endanger the lives or cause other serious harm to persons engaged in investigative activities on behalf of the United States." The Washington Post published a description of the files in its March 24 editions but omitted most names and specific locations. Copies were also received by the New York Times and the Los Angeles Times. Copies of the documents were also sent to the press April 5, April 10, April 23-27, May 8 and May 15. Over 60 of the documents were made public.

[2] The Citizens Commission May 8 sent out an analysis of the stolen documents. The group said that 40% of the papers revealed political surveillance while only 1% concerned organized crime. Included in the 40% listed as evidence of political surveillance were two documents concerning what the group defined as right-wing groups (the militant Jewish Defense League or JDL and the Ku Klux Klan), 10 concerning immigrants and more than 200 about "left or liberal groups." Besides the 40% dealing with political groups and the 1% concerned with organized crime, the breakdown on the documents was reported as follows: 25% involved bank robberies; 20% involved murder, rape and interstate theft; 7% on draft resistance; and 7% on military desertion or absent without leave (AWOL) cases. The group said the analysis did not include about 30% of the documents dealing with procedural matters.

[3] **Boggs demands Hoover ouster.** House majority leader Rep. Hale Boggs (D, La.) April 5 accused the FBI of tapping telephones of congressmen and asked that FBI Director J. Edgar Hoover be fired. Attorney General Mitchell April 5 "categorically" denied that the FBI had ever tapped a congressman's phone. Boggs, however, repeated his charges April 6, and April 22 attempted to back up his case in an hour-long House speech. Boggs said that the telephone line in his private home had been tapped in 1970, that a Chesapeake and Potomac Telephone Co. investigator had determined that his line had been tapped but that the tap had been removed, and that an official report had stated that no taps were discovered. Boggs said he learned subsequently that the company's policy was to deny the existence of a tap if it had been placed by the FBI. Boggs also suggested that an electronic surveillance device had been used at the home of Sen. Charles Percy (R, Ill.) and that listening devices had been placed in the offices of former Sen. Wayne Morse of Oregon and Sen. Birch Bayh (D, Ind.). However, Boggs did not accuse the FBI of installing the surveillance devices. In response to Boggs's charges, Rep. Bella Abzug (D, N.Y.) April 7 introduced a resolution calling on the House Judiciary Committee to conduct "a full and complete investigation" of the FBI, including "investigation of the ability of the director." Rep. Charles H. Wilson (D, Calif.) introduced a bill to limit the tenure of the head of the bureau to 10 years and to set a mandatory retirement age of 65. (Hoover, 76, has been director of the bureau since 1924.)

[4] *Bugging of Dowdy revealed.* Documents released April 16 by U.S. District Court Judge Roszel C. Thomsen in Baltimore revealed that the FBI had recorded four telephone conversations between Rep. John Dowdy (D, Tex.) and an FBI informant. According to the court papers, Dowdy's conversations had been monitored only at the informant's end of the line. The documents also showed that agents had escorted the informant to Dowdy's Capitol Hill office where a conversation with the congressman was recorded by a tape machine concealed on the informant's person. The FBI actions, connected with a bribe conspiracy charge against Dowdy, had been reported April 16. The recording activity had been approved in a court warrant and had been undertaken with the knowledge of Attorney General Mitchell. When asked to explain the Dowdy incident in relation to his statement April 7 that the FBI had not used "electronic surveillance or the tapping of telephones of senators and congressmen" even in criminal investigations, Deputy Attorney General Richard G. Kleindienst said that the Dowdy recordings did not constitute "surveillance" as defined by the Justice Department. Kleindienst said April 17 that "surveillance" occurred when neither party knew that it was being recorded.

[5] **Muskie charges Earth Day spying.** Sen. Edmund S. Muskie (D, Me.), in a Senate speech April 14, charged that the FBI spied on 40-60 Earth Day conservation rallies April 22, 1970. In support of his charge, Muskie made public an FBI intelligence report on the Washington rally. He said, "If there was widespread surveillance over Earth Day last year, is there any political activity in the country which the FBI does not consider a legitimate subject for watching? If antipollution rallies are a subject of intelligence concern, is anything immune? Is there any citizen involved in politics who is not a potential subject of an FBI dossier?" The senator proposed establishment of a domestic intelligence review board to oversee the surveillance activities of the FBI and other agencies. He said the board, to be composed of members of government intelligence agencies, Congress, the judiciary and the bar, could recommend actions and legislation "required to curb the unnecessary use of surveillance in our society." In response to Muskie's charges, Attorney General Mitchell April 15 said that FBI agents had attended the Earth Day rally because of "advance information" indicating that individuals with records of violence would be present. Mitchell said, "The FBI has no interest with an Earth Day meeting as such, but it does have a most legitimate interest in the activities of persons

whose known records reveal a likelihood of violence, incitement to riot or other criminal behavior."

[6] Probe at State Department. A State Department spokesman Sept. 22 confirmed that FBI agents had questioned department personnel in a probe of unauthorized news leaks. Secretary of State William P. Rogers said Sept. 3 that the investigation had been launched because "it looked on the surface as if there might be" a crime. The investigation, which had been extended to Defense Department officials, reportedly caused distress among some personnel at the State Department, where the FBI had not been involved since the wholesale loyalty-security investigations of the 1950s on charges of Communist infiltration raised by the late Sen. Joseph R. McCarthy. The department had its own division empowered to investigate security leaks.

[7] TV report stirs debate. A report prepared by National Educational Television (NET), containing interviews with three youths who said they had been paid by the FBI to infiltrate radical groups and encourage illegal acts that could lead to prosecution, was deleted by the Public Broadcasting System (PBS) shortly before its scheduled showing Oct. 6 as part of the *Great American Dream Machine* program. It was broadcast Oct. 9 in most major areas, amid charges of censorship and reports of FBI displeasure. FBI Director Hoover, in a letter sent after press screenings of the show, called the charges "totally and absolutely false." He added that the bureau had "referred this matter to the Department of Justice." Responding to charges by NET officials that PBS had exercised "censorship" in its cancellation decision, PBS President Hartford N. Gunn Jr. said the report had lacked on-screen "documentation," and that PBS had wanted the subject presented in greater depth as a separate program.

[8] CIA ties strained. It was reported Oct. 10 that Director Hoover had prohibited all personal contacts between FBI agents and the Central Intelligence Agency (CIA) early in 1970. (The FBI was responsible for counterespionage work within U.S. borders, while the CIA handled foreign activities.) According to the report, all regular contact between the agencies was conducted by mail or telephone. Hoover's order reportedly came after the CIA backed one of its agents who had refused to divulge the identity of an FBI agent who had passed confidential information to him. The information had concerned the disappearance of a Czechoslovak-born Russian history professor at the University of Colorado. The CIA agent had informed the university that no foul play had been involved after the FBI, which had made the investigation, refused to reveal the information.

[9] Pro-FBI group sets study. Responding to criticism of the FBI, a group called Friends of the FBI announced Nov. 10 that it was commissioning a $70,000 study of the bureau "as an institution protecting the public from militant, radical aims." The study was to be conducted by Americans for Law Enforcement, a Chicago group established as a counterweight to the American Civil Liberties Union (ACLU) and endorsed by Attorney General Mitchell.

[10] Probe of newsman disputed. White House Press Secretary Ronald Ziegler Nov. 11 admitted that the White House had ordered an FBI investigation of Columbia Broadcasting System (CBS) correspondent Daniel Schorr, but denied that the probe was related to criticism of Schorr's reporting by President Nixon and Administration aides. Ziegler and Frederick V. Malek, White House personnel aide, said Schorr had been under consideration in August for an unspecified federal job, which occasioned the investigation. Schorr said Nov. 10 that he had never been told of any job offer, even when he questioned Malek about the probe in October. Ziegler said the investigation had been started in accord with a "tightly administered procedure," which he said he was unable to explain, with Malek's knowledge. Malek, however, said that the investigation had been "kicked off" by an assistant without his knowledge.

172 FEDERAL BUREAU OF INVESTIGATION

See also BLACK MILITANTS [1, 7]; BOLIVIA [7]; CIVIL RIGHTS [9];
CRIME [1]; DRAFT & WAR PROTEST [5, 15, 17, 22]; GOVERNMENT
REORGANIZATION; HOUSING; PENTAGON PAPERS [14]; PRISONS [5];
SECURITY, U.S.; STUDENT UNREST [2, 10]; SUPREME COURT; YOUTH

FEDERAL COMMUNICATIONS COMMISSION (FCC)—*See* CIVIL RIGHTS [24];
CONSUMER AFFAIRS [17]; DRUG USE & ADDICTION [21]; GOVERNMENT
REORGANIZATION
FEDERAL HOUSING ADMINISTRATION (FHA)—*See* CIVIL RIGHTS [26];
HOUSING
FEDERAL MARITIME COMMISSION—*See* GOVERNMENT REORGANIZATION
FEDERAL POWER COMMISSION—*See* ENERGY; ENVIRONMENT;
GOVERNMENT REORGANIZATION
FEDERAL RESERVE BOARD (FRB)—*See* BANKS; BUSINESS [1, 3]; ECONOMY,
U.S. [3]; INTERNATIONAL MONETARY DEVELOPMENTS [11]
FEDERAL TRADE COMMISSION (FTC)—*See* BUSINESS [6-7]; CONSUMER
AFFAIRS [1-2, 5]; GOVERNMENT REORGANIZATION; HEALTH [8-9];
POLLUTION [7]
FEDERATION OF ARAB REPUBLICS—*See* MIDDLE EAST [1,16]; UNITED
ARAB REPUBLIC
FERTILITY—*See* POPULATION
FIJI—*See* SOUTH PACIFIC FORUM
FILIBUSTER—*See* BUSINESS [4]; CONGRESS [10]; SUPREME COURT

FINLAND—Coalition cabinet omits Communists. Premier Ahti Karjalainen
formed a new center-left coalition government March 26 that excluded the
Communists for the first time since 1966. The change ended a crisis that had
begun March 17 with the resignation of Karjalainen's eight-month coalition
cabinet after the Communists, one of the coalition partners, refused to sanction
the removal of certain price controls. The three cabinet posts of the People's
Democratic League (Communists) were given to the Social Democrats,
bringing their cabinet representation to eight. The new appointments were
Mikko Laaksonen, minister of justice; Olavi Salonen, second minister of trade
and industry; and Pekka Kuusi, minister of social affairs. In another cabinet
change, Kalervo Haapasalo, former second minister of trade and industry, was
named minister of communications, to succeed a Communist minister. The
three non-Socialist parties—the Center, Liberal and Swedish People's—retained
nine cabinet posts, and non-affiliated ministers held two. The four-party
coalition retained 108 of the 200 parliamentary seats. The Communists, with 36
seats, became the chief opposition party.

The crisis began March 17 when the Communists voted against a
government bill to remove price controls from 15 items, including coffee, sugar
and cigarettes. The bill was approved 131-51, with seven abstentions, but
Karjalainen had warned before the vote that he would resign if the Communists
insisted on a general price freeze. He said the government could not function
with such a split in its ranks. The decision of the Communists to go into
opposition was seen as a victory for the party's Stalinist wing, which opposed
the government policy of "stabilized growth" in incomes and prices. The policy
had been in effect since 1968.

The political crisis came amid Finland's worst labor and social crisis in 15
years. About 70,000 metal workers went on strike Feb. 8 (ended March 26);
about 10,000 of the 80,000 workers in the construction industry began a strike
March 11 (ended April 3). (Spurred by the Communists, the trade unions
representing the strikers had opposed collective bargaining contracts based on a
compromise proposal offered by President Urho Kekkonen in December 1970.
The compromise had called for substantial wage increases that still fell within
the stabilization program.)

Finland may recognize German states. Finland Sept. 10 sent to the governments of East and West Germany a draft treaty designed to effect the "comprehensive ordering of relations between Finland and the two Germanys" which would "come into force simultaneously." A communique accompanying the document said one of the objects of the proposed treaty would be to settle accounts arising from the "destruction caused by the forces of the German Reich in Finland [principally in Lapland] in 1944-45." In a radio and television broadcast Sept. 11, President Kekkonen said the treaty would be "a kind of package deal" and that among its provisions would be "recognition of the neutrality of Finland and ... rejection of the use of force, whether this involves the actions of the other party itself or actions by a third party from the territory of the other party...."

The London Times said Sept. 13 that East Germany had accepted the Finnish invitation. However, the Bonn government Sept. 11 cautioned against "premature establishment of diplomatic relations with East Germany" in view of the "difficult negotiations ahead in the case of the Berlin regulations." (*See* GERMAN CONSULTATIONS.)

Government resigns. The Karjalainen government resigned Oct. 29 and was replaced by a caretaker government, consisting mainly of civil servants, to hold office until elections were held in January 1972. The government resigned over its failure to resolve a dispute over agricultural policies, with Centrists backing farmers' demands for payments and for new legislation regulating agricultural prices and Social Democrats opposing the demands. President Kekkonen had given the government Oct. 26 an ultimatum to settle the dispute by Oct. 29 or he would dissolve parliament. The caretaker government: premier—Teuvo Aura; deputy premier and finances—Paivio Hetemaki; foreign affairs—Olavi J. Mattila; foreign commerce—Reino Rossi; justice—Karl-Johan Laang; defense—Lt. Col. Arvo Pentti; second finance minister—Jorma Uitto; national education—Matti Lauerkoski; second national education minister—Jouko Tyyri; interior—Heikki Tuominen; agriculture—Samuli Suomela; transport—Esa Timonen; commerce and industry—Gunnar Korhonen; social affairs and public health—Mrs. Alli Lahtinen; labor—Keijo Liinamaa.

See also ATOMIC ENERGY [10]; EUROPEAN ECONOMIC COMMUNITY [10]; EUROPEAN SECURITY; SCANDINAVIA

FIRES—1970 toll. Fires in the U.S. in 1970 killed 12,200 persons, 100 more than in 1969, the National Fire Protection Assn. reported Jan. 5. Property damage was estimated at $2.7 billion, an increase of $262.4 million over the 1969 loss.

Oil fires abate. The last of 12 oil well fires in the Bay Marchand area of the Gulf of Mexico—probably the longest and costliest offshore blazes in U.S. history—was extinguished April 16 by the Shell Oil Co. at a cost of about $26 million. The fires, which began mysteriously Dec. 1, 1970, destroyed one of the world's busiest offshore platforms.

See also CIVIL RIGHTS [9]; RACIAL & MINORITY UNREST [5-9, 12]; STUDENT UNREST [4, 6, 10]

FLOODS—Malaysia. A state of national emergency was declared Jan. 5 following days of torrential rains which brought heavy flooding in eight of the nation's 11 states. The death toll was estimated at 33-60 Jan. 7 with 114,000 persons reported evacuated. Six U.S. helicopters were diverted from South Vietnam Jan. 6 for use in the heavily flooded east coast area. A British navy supply ship rushed to the east coast Jan. 5 with food supplies for 150,000. Six British air force helicopters were offered but declined Jan. 7 by the Malaysian government.

Mozambique. Floods devastated huge areas in the northeastern portion of the territory Jan. 29, killing at least 60 persons and forcing 20,000 to flee to refugee centers.

Brazil. A flash flood swept through Rio de Janeiro early Feb. 26 leaving thousands homeless and killing more than 130 persons. Large sections of Salvador, a city of more than 890,000 on the northeastern coast, were engulfed in floodwaters April 26-28, leaving more than 140 dead and 10,000 homeless, according to army estimates. The flood followed more than 13 inches of rain in four days. Damage was estimated at $6 million.

Middle East. Violent floods struck widespread areas of the Middle East April 13-14. In Jordan, nine persons were reported dead. In Syria, the northeastern town of Bukamel was cut off by the floodwaters.

North Vietnam. North Vietnam's food crop and industry suffered heavy damage in floods that began to sweep the northern part of the country in early July. A Hanoi broadcast Sept. 2 said food crops were destroyed, roads washed out and communications destroyed. Premier Pham Van Dong did not give casualty or damage estimates but conceded that the flood was bigger than one in 1945 in which an estimated one million persons died. South Vietnam Sept. 6 offered $50,000 for the flood victims, but was rejected Sept. 8. Private relief efforts were reported underway in Saigon Sept. 10 to aid the flood victims.

India. A savage tidal wave struck the eastern coast of India Oct. 30-31 wreaking destruction. Estimates of deaths ranged as high as 30,000, but reports varied widely. About five million people were affected.

See also STORMS

FOOD & DRUG ADMINISTRATION (FDA)—*See* CHEMICAL & BIOLOGICAL WARFARE; CONSUMER AFFAIRS [3-10, 12, 15]; MEDICINE; POLLUTION [8-9, 13]

FOOD STAMPS—*See* AGRICULTURE [7]; POVERTY; WELFARE

FOOTBALL—**Colts win Super Bowl.** The Baltimore Colts of the American Football League (AFL) defeated the National Football League's (NFL) Dallas Cowboys, 16-13, to win the fifth Super Bowl game Jan. 17 before 80,055 fans in Miami's Orange Bowl. Cowboy linebacker Chuck Howley was named the game's outstanding player. The Colts, coached by Don McCafferty, received $15,000 each, while the Cowboys, coached by Tom Landry, received $7,500 each.

1971 bowl games. Jan. 1: Cotton Bowl (Dallas, Tex.)—Notre Dame 24, Texas 11; Rose Bowl (Pasadena, Calif.)—Stanford 27, Ohio State 17; Orange Bowl (Miami, Fla.)—Nebraska 17, Louisiana State 12; Sugar Bowl (New Orleans, La.)—Tennessee 34, Air Force 13; Gator Bowl (Jacksonville, Fla.)—Auburn 35, Mississippi 28.

Giants to leave New York. Gov. William T. Cahill of New Jersey and Wellington Mara, owner of the National Football League's New York Giants, announced Aug. 26 that the club would move out of New York City to play football in a new 75,000-seat stadium in the Hackensack Meadowlands in northern New Jersey in 1975. Mara signed a 30-year lease, beginning at the start of the 1975 season, to play in New Jersey. Under the agreement, the Giants were to be one of the featured attractions of a $200-million sports complex.

Lions' receiver dies. Chuck Hughes, a wide receiver for the Detroit Lions, collapsed on the field Oct. 24 during the Lions-Chicago game in Detroit and died soon after. An autopsy disclosed Oct. 25 that Hughes, 28, had suffered a heart attack. Hughes was believed to have been the first professional football player to collapse during a game and die without regaining consciousness. Five other professional football players had died from game-related ailments or injuries. The last, Mack Lee Hill, died in 1965. In the closing minutes of the game, Hughes caught a pass. Three plays later he fell to the ground while on his way back to the huddle. Resuscitation efforts failed.

Colts top All-Stars. The Colts combined a sticky defense and a potent aerial game July 30 to defeat the College All-Stars, 24-17, in Chicago in the 38th clash between professionals and the collegiate stars. Colt quaterback Earl Morall passed for 329 yards, including three touchdown tosses.

FOREIGN AID—Nixon proposes revision. President Nixon April 21 submitted to Congress a plan for major revision of the foreign aid program. The funds sought for fiscal 1972 totalled about $3.2 billion, almost $80 million more than was appropriated for fiscal 1971. The plan called for the elimination of the Agency for International Development (AID) and for establishment of two new bodies: an International Development Corp. (started with an authorization of $1.5 billion, authority to borrow $1 billion more and a first-year funding of $655 million) to provide loans to developing nations; and an International Development Institute (with a three-year authorization of $1.27 billion and an initial funding of $385 million) for research on development problems in developing countries and for training technicians and providing advisors. A single coordinator of development assistance, responsible directly to the President, would be chairman of the boards of both bodies, as well as of the Overseas Private Investment Corp., which was to continue to handle overseas private investment with guarantees and insurance for the investors. Military aid, to be renamed international security assistance, would encompass a $1.99 billion program. The military aid programs were to be regrouped into one operation under State Department direction and coordinated with the economic assistance programs. Humanitarian assistance programs were to be under the direction of a new assistant secretary of state.

Continuation refused by Senate. In a surprise of major proportions, the Senate voted 41-27 Oct. 29 to refuse authorization for continuation of the foreign aid program. (Faced by a statement by the House Foreign Affairs Committee that the reform proposal could not be cleared before the current aid program's authorization expired June 30, the Administration June 10 had submitted a request for a one-year extension of the fiscal 1971 aid program. The Congress did not act on the extension before the June 30 deadline, but passed a continuing resolution for the aid program until Nov. 15.) It was the first Senate rejection of a foreign aid authorization since the program began more than two decades before. As a result, there was no bill to be sent to conference with the House, which had approved a two-year, $6.9 billion foreign aid authorization Aug. 3. The defeated bill covered military aid for the fiscal 1972 year and economic aid for fiscal 1972 and 1973. However, there was approximately $4.7 billion in the foreign aid "pipeline," and there was an immediate movement by the Administration and some members of Congress to work out a temporary aid program pending development of a new one.

The defeat of the program came in the wake of the U.S. rebuff involved in the United Nations vote Oct. 25 to seat Communist China and expel Nationalist China (see UNITED NATIONS [7]). Congressional reaction, augmented by President Nixon's denunciation of the anti-U.S. behavior of some U.N. delegates after the China vote, was seen as a factor in the Senate vote. (Before killing the aid bill, the Senate rejected several proposals to cut U.N. funding.) The vote to kill the aid program came from a coalition of conservatives opposed to aid, Senators who resented the U.N. rebuff, and Senate liberals, who resented the Administration position taken during the debate on the aid bill—its fight against end-the-war amendments coupled with apparent indifference toward anti-U.N. proposals. In addition, many liberals favored replacement of the existing bilateral aid program with a multilateral program administered through international agencies such as the U.N.

The authority for the foreign aid program expired at midnight Nov. 15 without Congressional resolution of the impasse. The Senate Nov. 10, by a 61-23 vote, approved a bill authorizing $1.14 billion in foreign economic and humanitarian assistance. That, together with a bill passed by a 65-24 vote Nov. 11 authorizing $1.5 billion in military aid, went to the House for consideration. The total authorization under the two bills was $1.2 billion less than the Administration request. Meanwhile, the House approved by voice vote Nov. 10 a resolution to continue the foreign aid program at its $2.6 billion fiscal 1971 level until adjournment of the current Congress. However, the House move was stymied by the refusal of Sen. Allen J. Ellender (D, La.) to convene his appropriations Committee to handle it.

Both Houses of Congress Nov. 18 approved legislation to extend the spending authority for the program to Dec. 8. The legislation was signed by the President Nov. 22. A spending rate of $2.68 billion was set under the continuing resolution. A stopgap resolution to permit foreign aid spending through Feb. 22, 1972 at an annual rate of $2.84 billion was approved Dec. 17 by both houses of Congress. The resolution provided $350 million in aid to Israel, of which $300 million was for purchase of military equipment on credit. Other funds carried in the resolution were $500 million in military assistance, $600 million in supporting assistance, $400 million for economic development loans (of which $150 million was for the Alliance for Progress), $225 million for technical assistance ($75 million for the Alliance), $400 million for military credit sales (three-fourths for Israel), $100 million for East Pakistan refugee relief, $150 million for the Inter-American Development Bank and $72 million for the Peace Corps. Export-Import Bank programs also were continued.

The Senate Dec. 17, by a 33-21 vote, passed a foreign aid authorization bill setting a $2.75 billion funding level for fiscal 1972. It was to be considered in the next session of Congress by the House, which had approved Dec. 8 a $3 billion appropriations bill for the foreign aid program. The aid legislation passed by the Senate had been delayed in a Senate-House conference on the Senate's two separate bills and the House's Aug. 3 bill because House conferees refused to accept an amendment by Senate Majority Leader Mike Mansfield (D, Mont.) to end the war in six months and Mansfield refused to have the amendment dropped without a direct House vote on it. In the meantime, the Senate would not consider the House appropriations measure. The impasse was broken Dec. 16 by Rep. William Fitts Ryan (D, N.Y.), who requested the appointment of new conferees to accept Mansfield's proposal. The suggestion was killed by a tabling vote, 130-101, which Mansfield accepted as satisfying his condition. The aid conferees later Dec. 16 eliminated the amendment and approved the $2.75 authorization bill, which the Senate passed Dec. 17.

(The authorization bill awaiting action by the House carried other restrictive policy amendments. It would bar aid to Pakistan until the refugee situation was resolved, authorize $250 million for Pakistani refugee relief through international organizations, bar aid to Greece without a presidential declaration that it was in the national interest, set a $341 million ceiling on aid to Cambodia, require a 15% reduction in military aid mission personnel, periodic authorizations of State Department operating funds and release of more than $2 billion in domestic program funds "impounded" by the Nixon Administration. The funds were for housing, agriculture, health, education and welfare programs. The conferees eliminated from the legislation Senate amendments requiring annual authorizations for contributions to the United Nations, increasing development loan fund interest rates and removing presidential discretion to cut off aid to countries expropriating U.S.-owned property.)

Arms aid ceiling lifted. President Nixon informed Congress May 5 of his April 9 decision to waive the $75 million ceiling set by Congress in 1967 on annual U.S. aid to Latin America. The President also recommended a $150 million ceiling for fiscal 1972. Waiver of the ceiling was executed on the recommendation of Secretary of State William P. Rogers that it was "important to the security of the United States." Helping to arm friendly Latin countries, he said, "diminishes the prospects of powers unfriendly to the United States advancing their influence and objectives in this hemisphere." The intention of some Latin American countries to buy arms elsewhere reportedly was a factor in the decision to expand the ceiling.

Aid plans denied Senate panel. President Nixon Aug. 31 invoked executive privilege to deny the Senate Foreign Relations Committee the Administration's five-year plans for foreign military assistance. The President's action averted a Sept. 1 cutoff of such funds unless the material requested by Congress was supplied within 35 days or the President intervened. The procedure was required under the provisions of the 1961 Foreign Assistance Act, under which the committee had requested the documents from the Defense Department. Defense Secretary Melvin R. Laird had refused the documents in an Aug. 7 letter denying the existence of such long-range plans or documents. In invoking executive privilege, the President said the basic planning data and "internal staff papers" requested did not "reflect any approved program" but "only tentative intermediate staff-level thinking." Unless privacy could be maintained in such areas, he said, "the successful administration of government would be muted."

See also CHILE [4]; DRUG USE & ADDICTION [17]; GREECE [4]; HAITI; TARIFFS & WORLD TRADE [10]; TERRITORIAL WATERS

FOREIGN POLICY—State of the World message. President Nixon, in his annual State of the World message sent to Congress Feb. 25 and in a radio speech the same day on the major themes of the message, stressed the necessity for the U.S. to steer "a steady course between the past danger of overinvolvement and the new temptation of underinvolvement." In his speech, Nixon reaffirmed the Nixon Doctrine—that the U.S. would maintain its treaty commitments but would help allies to assume primary responsibility for their own defense—but emphasized "that we cannot transfer burdens too swiftly. We must strike a balance between doing too much and preventing self-reliance and suddenly doing too little and undermining self-confidence. We intend to give our friends the time and the means to adjust, materially and psychologically, to a new form of American participation in the world." The Nixon Doctrine was a basic theme of the President's first State of the World message, as well as the second, but the emphasis had shifted from the 1970 message's insistence on disengagement with honor to the "grave risk" of underinvolvement. A corollary theme was that the process of implementing the Nixon Doctrine may be lengthy and arduous.

In the message itself, Nixon claimed great results from, and great hopes for, the Vietnamization process in Indochina, but conceded that Vietnamization "cannot, except over a long period, end the war altogether." He also stated that the negotiating stalemate in the Paris peace talks and the problem of a lessened U.S. role in settlement due to lessened participation in the war remained "substantial problems" in the way of the Vietnamization process. In commenting on U.S.-Soviet relations, the President cited encouraging developments (negotiations in the strategic arms limitation talks or SALT, a treaty signed to bar nuclear weapons from seabeds, ratification of a nuclear nonproliferation treaty, the beginning of negotiations over Berlin and a first step toward practical cooperation in outer space), but tempered his optimism by noting the Soviet buildup of strategic force capability and Soviet actions in the Middle East, Berlin and Cuba, which he said were "not encouraging."

In discussing the Middle East, Nixon said the U.S. would not try to set the terms of a peace settlement, did not seek a dominant position in the area and "cannot allow" other major powers to establish dominance there. He said that the U.S. desire to limit the arms race in the Middle East, on a reciprocal basis, had been made clear repeatedly to the Soviet Union, as had the U.S. stand that the military balance between Israel and the Arab states "must be maintained." "The Soviet Union's disregard for this essential foundation for peace talks raised serious doubts about its readiness to cooperate in the effort to achieve peace," according to the President.

Nixon also said: that he favored establishing "a dialogue" with Communist China (which he referred to by its official name—the People's Republic of China), while maintaining normal relations with Nationalist China; that he favored "a European detente," but that the U.S. would maintain and improve its forces in Europe and "not reduce them without reciprocal action by our adversaries"; that the U.S. opposed a U.S.S.R. proposal for a general conference on European security (see EUROPEAN SECURITY) unless "a political basis for improving relations" was created through specific current negotiations; that the U.S. was "prepared to have the kind of relationship with the Chilean government that it is prepared to have with us," but that those governments which "display unremitting hostility cannot expect our assistance," and those intervening in their neighbors' affairs or facilitating intervention by non-hemispheric powers also should not expect to share in the benefits of the inter-American system; and that the U.S. could not be indifferent to apartheid in South Africa and would participate in economic sanctions against the Rhodesian white minority regime, but would not associate with any advocacy of a violent situation.

Kissinger's role protested. Sen. Stuart Symington (D, Mo.) charged in a Senate speech March 2 that Henry A. Kissinger, President Nixon's advisor on national security, had become "secretary of state in everything but title." Symington said that, as a result, Secretary of State William P. Rogers was being "laughed at" in Washington circles. Symington said the situation was upsetting the balance of power between Congress and the executive branch since Kissinger refused to testify before Congress under the protection of "executive privilege." Congress and the public, according to Symington, were "being increasingly denied access to pertinent facts about major foreign policy decisions" and lacked "any real knowledge, let alone a voice, in the formulation of policy decisions which could well determine the nation's future." The White House later March 2 issued a statement denouncing Symington's charges about Rogers and upholding him as "the President's chief advisor on foreign policy." The State Department also came to Rogers' defense March 3.

See also NIXON, RICHARD MILHOUS [1]; NORTH ATLANTIC TREATY ORGANIZATION; RACIAL & MINORITY UNREST [1]

FRANCE—Cabinet changes. President Georges Pompidou Jan. 7 announced a Cabinet shuffle and the creation of a new ministry for the protection of the environment, to be headed by Robert Poujade, secretary-general of the Gaullist party (the Union of Democrats for the Republic or UDR). The cabinet shuffle—made necessary by the deaths of Edmond Michelet, minister of culture, and Raymond Mondon, minister of transport; and by the illness of Jacques Duhamel, minister of agriculture—left the major posts, except for agriculture, untouched. Duhamel was named minister of culture; Michel Cointat assumed the post of agriculture minister; and Jean Chamant was appointed transport minister. Other changes included the promotion of Jacques Chirac, Gaullist state secretary for the budget, to the post of minister of state charged with parliamentary relations, succeeding Roger Frey, who was appointed minister for administrative and regional reform. Jean Taittinger became state secretary for the budget. While the other Cabinet parties retained the same number of posts as before, the UDR increased its representation by gaining the agriculture and environment ministries. The total number of ministries increased to 41, the highest number under the Fifth Republic. (In a later Cabinet change, Pierre Messmer, a former armed forces minister, was appointed Feb. 25 as minister of state for overseas development, replacing Henry Rey.

[2]   Police developments. The Paris police March 4 staged a "day of action" to counter criticism of alleged police brutality, particularly during student demonstrations. They distributed leaflets and held street-corner discussions to justify their behavior. Criticism of the police had intensified after the arrest Feb. 9 of a student who was acquitted Feb. 19 of charges that he struck a policeman. (The student, Gilles Guiot, had been sentenced Feb. 10 to six months of imprisonment—three of them suspended—after he was convicted without counsel on the sole evidence of two policemen who testified that he had punched one of them. Guiot said he had not participated in the protest, and witnesses said the actual assailant had fled. The case had become a cause celebre and had led to the largest student protests since May 1968, with a student strike observed by nearly all Paris high schools and by many schools in the suburbs and provinces. A Paris appeals court reversed the conviction Feb. 19.)

[3] *Personnel changes.* The government March 31 ended the Paris police chief's responsibility for three suburban departments around Paris and replaced police chief Maurice Grimaud with Jacques Lenoir, director of police intelligence in the Interior Ministry. Following rioting in the Latin Quarter June 5 in which a group described as "part rowdies and part leftists" smashed shop windows and stole or destroyed merchandise, a Paris district police chief, Rene Degranger, was removed from his post June 7 for "an error in judgement." Police had not arrived at the scene until two hours after the rampage had begun, despite calls from beleaguered store owners. The government Sept. 14 dismissed five senior police officials, leaders of the National Union of Uniformed Police, following the union's threat to occupy government offices to protest what they considered inadequate wage offers. Those dismissed were Roger Daurelle (secretary-general of the union), Henri Buch (deputy secretary-general) and three national secretaries. Gerard Monate, head of the Independent Federation of Police Unions, declared that his organization would boycott the current wage negotiations unless the dismissals were rescinded. It was the most serious dispute between the government and police since a 1958 police march on the National Assembly. It had begun with a resolution by the National Union Sept. 9 calling for a mass demonstration in Paris, including the occupation of the Finance Ministry and the premier's residence, if police wage demands were not met. The discontent of the union had erupted after Interior Minister Raymond Marcellin had announced a plan, reported Sept. 8, calling for wage increases and promotions, modernization of equipment and a 2,700-man increase in the police force. The union scored the plan, protesting that the largest pay increases would go to senior officers and that working hours would not be reduced. (The union represented 23,000 of the lowest-ranking urban policemen, mainly from cities in the provinces.)

[4] **Censure motion fails.** The government of Premier Jacques Chaban-Delmas April 21 survived a Socialist-sponsored censure motion that received only 95 of the 244 votes needed to win. The censure motion—the first to be pressed in parliament since May 1968—was presented to force a vote on a major policy statement made to the National Assembly April 20 by Chaban-Delmas. The premier had ruled out a vote on the question. In his speech—the government's first major statement of policy following months of student, worker and farmer unrest—Chaban-Delmas assured a government law and order campaign without "unnecessary brutality," and warned against attempts to exploit the current social unrest and to transform the government coalition, "in the name of order, into a force of conservatism and immobilism." Chaban-Delmas also promised that the government would introduce legislation to implement reforms promised in 1968 (*see* [9]).

[5] *Student unrest.* Demonstrations and strikes by leftist students throughout France in March and April led to the closing of 15 schools and colleges. The elite Ecole Normale Superieure in Paris, training ground for the nation's political leaders and intellectuals, was closed April 4 for the repair of damages incurred the night of March 20-21 when a "revolutionary festival" staged by leftist students turned into a riot. The director of the school, Robert Flaceliere, April 1 disclosed his resignation, effective the following year. Flaceliere said that Maoists had turned the school into "a sort of Red base" in control of a leftist "action committee." The school was reopened April 23. In other disturbances: students Feb. 16 locked up the president and rector of the University of Poitiers; students in Grenoble March 17 occupied a building of their school, held illegal demonstrations and clashed violently with police; leftist students clashed with teachers at the University of Nanterre March 25 after the militants had disrupted a class in an attempt to revive student agitation on the campus. In a later development, several thousand high school students staged protest marches and sit-ins Nov. 29-30 in Paris against a memorandum by

Education Minister Olivier Guichard, instructing school principals to be firm in disciplinary matters, and against the expulsion of three students at the Montaigne Lycee Nov. 29 for agitation at a banned meeting to protest the memorandum. (*See also* [2].)

[6] *Labor developments.* The French economy was plagued throughout 1971 by a series of debilitating strikes and demonstrations by workers and farmers. Among the most widespread labor actions: About 40,000 wine growers in southern France, hurt by a surplus in wine brought about by imports of foreign wine and a bumper French harvest in 1970, demonstrated Jan. 21 and Feb. 18 in protest over imports of wine from Algeria and Italy. About a quarter of France's 300,000 postal workers went on strike Feb. 3-6 for salary increases and a 40-hour work week. About 6,000 farmers in Toulouse and 2,000 in Neufchatel March 6 staged peaceful demonstrations to demand higher beef prices in the European Economic Community. A lockout (instituted after a three-day strike) that grounded French airliners for three weeks ended March 16 with a contract agreement between the three major French airlines (Air France, Air Inter and Union des Transports Aeriens) and the unions representing pilots, crews and flight engineers. Work resumed May 25-26 in all state-owned Renault auto plants, where some 93,000 workers in assembly plants had been locked out by management May 5 in an effort to stop strike action at a plant in Le Mans, after the specialized transmission workers in Le Mans accepted management offers on promotions and bonuses. Much of French industry in Paris and the provinces halted as more than 30,000 workers marched in downtown Paris May 27 to back trade union demands for a lowering of the retirement age from 65 to 60 and for greatly increased pensions. Between 20,000 and 100,000 state employees staged a nationwide strike June 4 and a march in downtown Paris the same day to demand higher pay increases to compensate for a sharp rise in the cost of living. (Following union rejection March 10 of a government-offered contract providing for increases totaling 7.15%, the government had arbitrarily decreed periodic wage increases totaling 5.7% for 1971.) An agreement, providing for the payment of pension benefits to physically unfit dock workers at age 60 and doubling daily unemployment compensation guarantees, was reached June 9 in a dock dispute which had led to about 15 strikes since September 1970. A two-week wildcat strike against the state railways, in protest that contract provisions (signed Jan. 11) for a 6% wage increase in 1971 would not keep pace with increases in the cost of living, ended June 23. Growing pressure from the public and the government forced unions representing Paris subway motormen to recommend that the motormen, on strike since Oct. 5 over demands for change in a new government pay schedule, return to work. (The recommendation was obeyed Oct. 14.) More than 20,000 persons paraded through Paris Dec. 1 to demand retirement at age 60 with full pensions. (The National Assembly Dec. 2 adopted a draft bill to increase old-age pensions by 25% by 1972 and to allow retirement at 63 with full benefits. The bill would also allow retirement at age 60 at full pension for those who were unable to work or were dismissed.) (*See also* [3].)

[7] **5-year plan approved.** The Council of Ministers April 28 approved the draft of the sixth state economic five-year plan (1971-75). The plan, approved by the National Assembly June 18, envisaged an annual growth rate of 5.8%-6%, with emphasis on collective investments—roads, telephones, housing, health, education and technical training. Expenditures on those items were estimated to increase by about 9% annually. Industrial productivity was due to rise by about 7.5% annually.

[8] **Municipal reform.** The National Assembly June 3 approved the first major municipal reform bill since 1884. The bill provided for the reduction of municipalities from the present 37,708 through mergers. To stimulate mergers, the bill would authorize a 50% increase over five years in subsidies for public works to the new municipalities.

[9]   **Education reform bills.** The National Assembly June 8-9 approved four education reform bills which provided for: improved technical training in an attempt to place it on the same level as the more prestigious liberal arts education; apprenticeship reform, including guaranteed minimum pay for apprentices; a new special tax on wages to help pay the cost of education reforms; and an undertaking by the government to provide each wage earner the continuing opportunity to improve his skills and promote his position after completion of formal schooling. (The last measure, which would apply particularly to wage earners threatened by economic and technological change and to mothers who wished to learn a skill, would guarantee income during the training period.) In other reforms, reported July 3, the National Assembly gave final approval to a bill amending education reforms legislated in 1968. The bill introduced the principle of selection of students for medical schools to reduce their numbers. (Fourth-year students were required to begin their hospital service and there were only 23,000 hospital openings available for the 29,000 students eligible.) The bill also authorized elected student-teacher councils to decide, in some cases, whether students should take final examinations or ad hoc tests to verify academic achievement.

[10]   **Political developments.** The Socialist party, the association of Socialist clubs known as the Convention of Republican Institutions (led by Francois Mitterrand) and other Socialist splinter groups decided June 11-13 at a "congress of unity" to merge into a new Socialist party. The new grouping, which claimed about 85,000 members, June 16 elected Mitterrand first secretary of the new party. In another action, three left-wing Gaullist factions (the Union of the Left 5th Republic, the Democracy and Labor and the Labor Front) agreed Nov. 13-14 to unite into a Movement for Socialism through Participation to press for social reforms. The new movement, to remain within the UDR, elected Pierre Billotte (a parliamentary deputy) as president and former Premier Edgar Faure as honorary president. (Faure supported the UDR but was not a member.) The merger won the government's sanction, symbolized by the presence of Minister Chirac, who urged the group to stay within the bounds of the Gaullist majority. Four other leftist Gaullist factions had agreed to merge into the Labor Front Oct. 2-3.

[11]   **Real estate scandal.** Robert Frenkel and his wife Nicole were arrested and jailed July 8 for swindling in connection with a housing investment company, La Garantie Fonciere, which Frenkel had founded in 1967. The fraud involved the use of subscribers' funds by the company—and other similar firms—to purchase property from associated companies at inflated prices, with company officers pocketing the difference. The arrests plunged the nation into a series of financial scandals that implicated several other real estate firms, leading financial figures and the UDR. Among those indicted in the case were: Andre Rives-Henrys de Lavaysse, a UDR deputy from Paris (suspended from the UDR July 21 pending the outcome of the case), indicted July 19; Victor Rochenoir, a lawyer closely associated with the UDR and the lawyer for the company and two other real estate groups under investigation (the Patrimoine Fonciere and the Agache-Willot company), jailed Aug. 3 for complicity in fraud and in the abuse of an official title as a member of an economic consultative committee; Andre Roulland, a former Gaullist deputy who also served in the cabinet when President Pompidou was premier, indicted Sept. 28 as manager of an associated company of Patrimoine Fonciere; Paul Reynauld, director of a firm associated with another company under investigation (Pontet-Clauzure), indicted Oct. 1; Jacques Brunet, head of the Finanpar real estate company, indicted, according to report Oct. 1, for false advertising. Arrest warrants were ordered Sept. 20 against Claude Lipsky, Patrimoine's financial director, and Georges-Walter Huc, head of the Kauffman company, associated with Patrimoine. Both had disappeared, Lipsky fleeing to Israel Sept. 29. France demanded his extradition but the absence of an extradition treaty with Israel delayed action in the case. (The Senate Nov. 10 approved a

1958 Franco-Israeli convention on extradition, approved by the National Assembly 11 years before.)

[12] In reaction to the scandal and Rives-Henrys's implication in it, the National Assembly Dec. 21 gave final approval to a Senate-amended bill tightening existing legislation on members' conflicts of interest involving private companies. (Rives-Henrys Nov. 29 had accused top Gaullist leaders of trying to destroy him. He resigned from the UDR Nov. 29 in the face of an upcoming party investigation.) The bill prohibited parliamentary deputies and senators from holding positions of responsibility in companies promoting real estate or building apartments. It also stipulated that members of parliament must declare their business activities when elected and seek authorization from the Constitutional Council or from their parliamentary house before accepting professional responsibilities while in office.

[13]   Council rejects bill restricting groups. The Constitutional Council July 16 declared unconstitutional a law that restricted the right of free association by requiring police permission to form new groups. The Gaullist-dominated Council, in its first decision against the government, said that the measure conflicted with the 1789 Declaration of the Rights of Man. The new law, which was aimed at preventing the reorganization of banned leftist groups under different names, would have amended guarantees provided in the 1901 law of associations, which enabled any group to declare itself to the prefecture of police. The prefect automatically issued a "receipt" that served as recognition of the group's legal status. The amendment, advocated by Interior Minister Marcellin, would have permitted the prefecture to deny the receipt to groups considered dangerous or subversive. The amendment had been passed by the National Assembly June 24. The Senate subsequently refused to vote on it, but the Assembly then overrode the Senate.

[14]   Industry agrees to curb prices. In response to government pleas for voluntary wage and price restraint designed to curb inflation, the Conseil National du Patronat Francaise (CNPF)—the equivalent of the National Association of Manufacturers—agreed Sept. 14 to restrict price increases on manufactured goods to not more than 1.5% between Oct. 1 and April 1, 1972. Commercial profits would also be blocked. The government would draw up anti-price rise contracts with each industry to take into account the difficulties faced by individual industries. In exchange, the government promised not to increase prices of telephone, electricity and transport and not to change the tax structure. The pledge not to raise prices of public services was a minor concession since the government had recently increased these prices.

[15]   1972 budget stresses growth. The Council of Ministers Sept. 15 approved a draft budget for 1972 that anticipated a 5.2% increase in industrial production, a 9.3% increase in the gross domestic product, and price increases totaling 3.9%. The rise in prices over the next six months would be held to .3% a month, compared with the .5% increase registered in July. Expenditures were estimated at 192.7 billion francs (about $34.7 billion), a 9.74% rise over 1971. Revenues were projected at a slight surplus of 110 million francs ($19 million), a 9.8% increase over the previous year. The government pledged to cut 200 million francs from expenditures before March 1, 1972. Budget priorities were expenditures for public works—especially roads, telephones and public transport—and factory equipment. Military expenditures were scheduled to rise by 8.1%, compared with 6.1% in 1971. Also included in the budget was an increase of $108 annually in old age pensions. The budget provided for an increase in taxes on tobacco and alcohol and a 12-month postponement of a 3% tax reduction on the earned income of non-salaried persons. The government said it would, if necessary, ease the value-added tax rate in order to insure economic growth. The value-added tax was a levy imposed on each stage of production of an item.

[16]   **Senate elections.** Elections for one-third of the Senate's 283 seats were held Sept. 26. The government claimed a gain of 14 seats by its Gaullist, Independent Republican and moderate supporters, a claim disputed by the opposition because of the ambiguity of many of the political labels. Forty senators were new. Voting was done by a 40,000-member electoral college composed of local and national government officials. The Senate Oct. 2, by a 199—26 vote, re-elected Alain Poher Senate president. Poher, a centrist, had been a candidate in the 1969 presidential elections.

[17]   **Brezhnev visit.** In his first visit to a Western nation since he became the Soviet Communist party leader, Leonid I. Brezhnev visited France Oct. 25-30. The visit, marred by several relatively minor disturbances by Jewish and extreme rightist groups, resulted in the signing Oct. 30 by Brezhnev and President Pompidou of two major documents of Franco-Soviet and European relations. The first document, a joint declaration, expressed hope that a final settlement on Berlin would be reached soon (*see* GERMAN CONSULTATIONS), paving the way for ratification of West Germany's nonaggression treaties with Poland and the Soviet Union (*see* GERMANY, WEST [1-2].) A "statement of principles," which accompanied the joint declaration and completed the protocol signed by Pompidou in Moscow in October 1970, declared French-Soviet cooperation to be "a permanent factor of international life." It cited five principles on which peaceful cooperation in Europe was to be based; the inviolability of present frontiers; noninterference in other nations' internal affairs; equality; independence; and nonrecourse to force or threats. The statement noted that French-Soviet cooperation did not affect "commitments assumed by the two countries with regard to third states." It also called for: the convening of a European Security conference (*see* EUROPEAN SECURITY) in 1972, with preliminary talks to be held in Helsinki "as soon as possible"; the resumption of the peace mission of United Nations Middle East mediator Gunnar V. Jarring; an end to foreign intervention in Indochina; support for a conference of the five nuclear powers to work toward "general and complete disarmament"; backing for a Soviet proposal for a worldwide disarmament conference; and the maintenance of peace between India and Pakistan and "understanding" for the problems of the Indian government in caring for Pakistani refugees.

[18]   In addition to the two major documents, a 10-year economic agreement was signed by the French finance minister and the Soviet trade minister Oct. 27. The agreement was designed to increase French-Soviet trade through participation in each other's industry. Another agreement was signed the same day for engineering studies and the supply of machinery by the state-owned Renault automobile firm for construction of a diesel engine plant at the Soviet Union's Kama River truck manufacturing complex.

[19]   **Bourse reforms announced.** Finance Minister Giscard d'Estaing announced Nov. 24 reforms of the French Bourse (stock exchange) based on recommendations of the Baumgartner Commission. The government rejected the commission's proposal for an increase in individual tax rebates on dividends but granted tax benefits to certain institutional investors, including insurance companies and mutual funds. Among the reforms announced were improved information for stockholders and eased rules for issuing new stock.

See also ALGERIA; ARMAMENTS, INTERNATIONAL; ATOMIC ENERGY [5, 11, 13]; AVIATION [2, 4]; CHURCHES [4]; COMMUNIST CHINA-U.S. DETENTE [8]; DISARMAMENT; DRUG USE & ADDICTION [4, 11-12]; ESPIONAGE; EUROPEAN ECONOMIC COMMUNITY [1-2, 5, 12, 14]; EUROPEAN SECURITY; GERMAN CONSULTATIONS; GERMANY, WEST [12]; INDOCHINA WAR [72]; INTERNATIONAL BANK FOR RECONSTRUCTION & DEVELOPMENT; INTERNATIONAL MONETARY DEVELOPMENTS [1, 3, 5, 7-9, 13, 15, 17-18]; JAPAN [4, 10]; MIDDLE EAST [25, 31]; PAKISTAN [35, 39, 42]; PENTAGON PAPERS [16, 18-19, 22]; SPACE [17-18]; TERRITORIAL WATERS; UNITED NATIONS [8, 13]

FRANCO, GENERALISSIMO FRANCISCO—*See* AGNEW, SPIRO THEODORE; SPAIN [1-2, 4, 6-7, 9-10]
FROEHLKE, ROBERT F.—*See* MILITARY [12]; SELECTIVE SERVICE SYSTEM [8]; WAR CRIMES [10]
FROINES, JOHN—*See* DRAFT & WAR PROTEST [13]
FRONT DE LIBERATION DU QUEBEC (FLQ)—*See* CANADA [2-4]

GABON—President Albert Bernard Bongo reorganized his government June 29. Bongo retained his former portfolios, but relinquished the Ministry of Mines, which was taken over by Jean-Baptiste Obiang-Ekomie. Georges Rawiri, previously ambassador to France, became foreign minister, replacing Jean-Remy Ayoune, who was named minister of justice.

GANDHI, INDIRA—*See* INDIA; PAKISTAN [12, 15, 20, 32, 40]

GENERAL AGREEMENT ON TARIFFS & TRADE (GATT)—*See* TARIFFS & WORLD TRADE [2, 4, 10, 12, 14]

GENEVA CONVENTION—*See* CHEMICAL & BIOLOGICAL WARFARE; DISARMAMENT; PAKISTAN [18, 21]; PENTAGON PAPERS [18-20]

GENOCIDE—*See* AFRICA

GERMAN CONSULTATIONS—**Berlin accord reached.** Negotiators for the U.S., Britain, France and the Soviet Union reached agreement Aug. 23 on a draft of principles for a Berlin settlement, ending the first phase of negotiations begun in March 1970. The four envoys—U.S. Ambassador to West Germany Kenneth Rush, British Ambassador to West Germany Sir Roger Jackling, French Ambassador to West Germany Jean Sauvagnargues and Russian Ambassador to East Germany Pyotr A. Abrasimov—signed the accord Sept. 3 after it had been approved by the governments of the Big Four, the countries with responsibility for the future of Berlin. The signing, which had been delayed 24 hours because of difficulties in textual translation and because of the illness of Ambassador Rush, took place in the former Allied Control Council building in West Berlin.

The "quadripartite agreement" was composed of three parts, four annexes, one note and two "agreed minutes." The first part pledged the signatory powers to "strive to promote elimination of tension and prevention of complications" in "the relevant area" (Berlin). It also obliged the signers to give up the "use or threat of force" in solving problems relating to Berlin and to see that the document was not "changed unilaterally." The text contained the first promise by the Soviet Union to share responsibility for "unimpeded" access to Berlin. (The undertaking was believed to have cancelled a 1955 agreement transferring control of the access routes to East German authorities. *See below.*) Goods were to be sealed in their carriers by a process to be agreed upon by East and West German officials and road tolls were to be collected annually rather than from individual drivers. West Berliners were to be allowed to travel in Communist countries on West German passports and to enjoy West German consular protection while abroad. The cultural, economic and juridical ties between West Germany and West Berlin were to be upheld, with the exception that West German houses of parliament would be forbidden to hold full sessions in West Berlin or to perform "constitutional acts" there. The Soviet Union was to be allowed to establish a consulate general in West Berlin. The agreement affirmed that, although West Berlin would "continue not to be a constituent part of" West Germany, its ties with West Germany would "be maintained and developed." The Soviet Union promised to improve "communications" between the two halves of Berlin and between West Berlin and East Germany and to allow visits "for compassionate, family, religious, cultural or commercial reasons, or as tourists."

The agreement was generally greeted with acclaim. U.S. Secretary of State William P. Rogers Sept. 3 said the accord "embraces not only a promise of a better way of life for Berliners but enhances the prospects for greater peace and security in Europe." The Soviet Communist party newspaper Pravda said in a front page editorial Sept. 4 that the accord was an "important landmark" whose signing meant "an effective foundation has been laid for normalizing and improving the situation in West Berlin and related issues." Pravda noted that the accord "removes a serious obstacle in the path of reducing tension in Europe and puts in a difficult position the opponents of the ratification of the Soviet-West German and Polish-West German treaties" (see GERMANY, WEST [1-2]). Erich Honecker, the East German Communist leader, Sept. 4 called the agreement "a success of East German foreign policy." In a television address Sept. 3, West German Chancellor Willy Brandt welcomed the agreement but added that more could have been accomplished. In West Germany, the opposition Christian Democratic Union (CDU) and its coalition partner the Christian Social Union (CSU) issued a statement Sept. 4 declaring that Western concessions in the accord "cause us special doubts." CSU leader Franz Josef Strauss called the accord a "rubber treaty" which could only benefit the Soviet Union.

German talks. The second phase of negotiations on Berlin—talks between the two Germanies over the questions of access to West Berlin and procedures for visits to East Berlin and East Germany—began Sept. 6 in Bonn and West Berlin. In the Bonn talks, West German State Secretary Egon Bahr and his East German counterpart, Michael Kohl, who had held meetings on the normalization of relations throughout the year, reached agreement on access to Berlin Dec. 4. The accord was initialed by Bahr and Kohl Dec. 11 and was signed Dec. 17. The talks in West Berlin between Ulrich Mueller, an official of the West Berlin city government, and Gunter Kohrt, an East German state secretary, on the easing of visit procedures were deadlocked until Dec. 8. The visit accord was also initialed Dec. 11 and was signed Dec. 20.

Under the access agreement, West German travelers would be hindered only by identity checks in their movement across East German territory to West Berlin, and land-route carriers would be done in sealed carriers that would remain unopened until they reached their destination. East German officials could detain or ban travelers who disobeyed traffic laws, picked up hitchhikers or gave sufficient reason to suspect that they were misusing the transit routes for purposes not relating to direct travel to and from West Berlin. Bonn agreed to pay East Germany approximately $72.2 million annually for the first four years of the agreement's operation to cover East German visas and· road tolls. The accord governing visits allowed West Berliners to visit the East for up to 30 days a year, provided they used public transport unless they were handicapped, accompanied by children under three years of age or traveling beyond East Germany. Visas for one-day visits could be obtained on demand at five offices in West Berlin·to be operated by East German officials seven hours a day on weekdays. Two of the offices were to remain open three hours a day on Saturdays, Sundays and holidays. Under the agreement, 1,710 acres of East German territory were to be exchanged for 1,560 acres of West Berlin, with West Berlin paying $1.2 million to cover the difference. A link was established between West Berlin and Steinstucken, an outlying area of the city surrounded by East Germany. The accord on visits appeared to have been reached when Kohrt, reportedly ill, was replaced by East German Deputy Foreign Minister Peter Florin, who negotiated for several hours with Mueller and reached a compromise but then rejected it. According to West Berlin Mayor Klaus Schutz, the negotiating problems had been caused by the provision in the September four-power agreement that stipulated that visits of West Berliners to East Berlin and East Germany be arranged "under conditions comparable to those applying to other persons." (West Germans were allowed to visit East Berlin every day of the year.)

Pre-accord developments. *Traffic delays.* Soviet officials detained U.S., British and French military vehicles Jan. 11 and 12 on the autobahn between West Germany and West Berlin. Delays of up to 10 hours were caused when the Soviets informed allied military personnel that their "movement papers" required an official stamp from Allied commanders. Such stamps had not been previously required. The flow of traffic returned to normal Jan. 13 after an Allied oral protest the previous day. East German authorities Jan. 27-Feb. 1 delayed civilian traffic on the West Berlin access roads to protest planned visits by West German President Gustav Heinemann Jan. 27 and by Chancellor Brandt and parliamentary representatives of the Free Democratic party Jan. 30. The West German leaders made their trips as planned and traffic was reported returning to normal Feb. 1.

Berlin phone links. Direct telephone service between East and West Berlin was restored Jan. 31 for the first time since 1952. The installation of five lines in each direction had been agreed upon under terms of a pact signed Jan. 25 between West Berlin postal authorities and East German officials. Ten more lines were installed at Easter and another 10 June 5.

Bonn accedes to 'GDR.' The West German government July 12 ordered that in all official correspondence East Germany should be referred to as the "German Democratic Republic" rather than as the "Soviet Occupied Zone," the name by which West Germany had previously referred to East Germany.

See also EUROPEAN SECURITY; FINLAND; FOREIGN POLICY; FRANCE [17]; GERMANY, EAST; NIXON, RICHARD MILHOUS [3]; SINO-SOVIET DEVELOPMENTS

GERMANY, EAST, (GERMAN DEMOCRATIC REPUBLIC)—Ulbricht resigns.
Walter Ulbricht, 77, who had helped to form the German Socialist Unity party (an amalgam of the Communist and Social Democratic parties) in 1946, resigned as first secretary of the party May 3. Ulbricht cited age and ill health as reasons for his resignation and recommended Erich Honecker, 58, as his successor. Honecker, a member of the party's Central Committee, was unanimously elected to replace Ulbricht. Ulbricht was to remain East Germany's head of state as chairman of the Council of State, a post he had held since 1960. He was also named honorary chairman of the party. Both positions were considered essentially ceremonial. Observers noted the smooth transition of power and generally concluded that Ulbricht had not acted under pressure. He had been known to be ill during the previous year.

Congress marked by Ulbricht's absence. The eighth East German Socialist Unity party congress, held June 15-19 in East Berlin, was marked by the unexpected absence of Ulbricht. Ulbricht was officially reported absent because of health reasons; the East German press agency ADN reported June 17 that Ulbricht had suffered "an acute circulatory disturbance" June 14 and had been confined to bed. However, rumors attributed his absence to his virtual loss of power within East Germany and to his anger over an early reading of Honecker's keynote address, which obliquely accused Ulbricht of "abuse of the collective" leadership. East German sources attributed Ulbricht's fall to overambitious economic projects, his attempt to conduct a policy on West Germany independent of the Soviet Union and to the creation of "a personal apparatus above the apparatus of the Central Committee."

The Congress, which was delayed one day without official explanation but reportedly to iron out policy differences with the Soviet Union, was attended by 94 delegations from 83 countries and included attendance by foreign Communist party leaders Leonid Brezhnev of the Soviet Union, Edward Gierek of Poland, Gustav Husak of Czechoslovakia, Janos Kadar of Hungary and Todor Zhivkov of Bulgaria. On domestic policy, Honecker in his keynote stressed the need for greater industrial output and promised production of more consumer goods. The Congress June 19 approved draft directives of the economic plan for 1971-75. Premier Willi Stoph, who presented the plan, promised high priority to consumer benefits: an increase in real wages of between 21% and 23%, a 36% increase in the production of industrial goods and construction of 500,000 housing units. Industrialization investments would be centered on electric power, soft-coal mining, chemicals and electronics. (A price freeze on consumer goods for the duration of the 1971-75 plan was announced by ADN Nov. 18.) Stoph acknowledged that the 1966-70 plan had not met important targets in the fields of energy, in the chemical industry, in branches of supply industries and in construction.

On foreign policy matters, Honecker stressed the "ties of socialist brotherhood" that bound East Germany to the Soviet Union and to other socialist nations. He called for "the establishment of normal relations" with West Germany "in accordance with the rules of international law." This wording was thought to indicate a softening of East Germany's previous demand for full diplomatic recognition by Bonn. However, Honecker stipulated that the normalization of relations could be only on the basis of relations between two separate nations. Honecker backed the Soviet call for a European security conference and supported the signing of treaties by West Germany with the Soviet Union and Poland in 1970. He criticized Bonn for tying the conference and ratification of the treaties to a prior agreement on Berlin and expressed a willingness to normalize relations with West Berlin as long as the city was not considered a part of West Germany. He referred to West Berlin as "a city with a special political status," dropping a previous designation—unacceptable to the West—of a "separate political entity." He also wished "success" for the Big Four negotiations on Berlin, which was thought to indicate a more positive approach than Ulbricht's hardline position.

Honecker was confirmed as first secretary of the party June 19 and Ulbricht was elected chairman of the party "in honor of his services" and chairman of the Council of State. The 100-member Central Committee enlarged slightly. The Central Committee re-elected all 14 members of the Politburo and two new members: Werner Krolikowski, secretary of the Dresden Communist party, and Werner Lamberz, a candidate member of the Politburo.

Ulbricht loses defense post. The Volkskammer (parliament) unanimously appointed Honecker chairman of the National Defense Council June 24, succeeding Ulbricht, whose name was not mentioned in the change. An official communique did not say Ulbricht had given his resignation, implying that he had been stripped of the post.

Americans freed. The East German government July 16 released and delivered to the West Berlin border six U.S. citizens previously held in its prisons on a variety of charges. The action was reportedly taken after the U.S. promised to lift its ban on visas to East Germans, imposed following the arrests of the six in 1969 and 1970. Those released were Mark Huessy, 22, of Jericho, Vt., convicted for statements hostile to the government; Lyle Jenkins, 31, Cambridge, Mass; and Jack Strickland, 28, Santa Barbara, Calif., convicted of trying to help refugees escape; Frank King, 25, Highland Park, Mich., accused of circulating anti-government propaganda; Ronald F. Mudd, 24, Columbus, Ohio, charged with assaulting a border guard; and Ronald Balch, 24, Huntsville, Ala., listed by the U.S. Army as a deserter and convicted by East Germany of trying to leave that country for Poland. With the release of the six, according to the New York Times July 16, no other Americans were known to be in East German hands.

Economic report. First Secretary Honecker told a plenary session of the party's Central Committee Sept. 16 that serious industrial "distortions" had contributed to economic deficiencies amounting to 1.2 billion marks in 1971 ($300 million at the official exchange rate). He warned that "in some cases we will need several years to overcome certain of the distortions." Honecker also reported that because of poor weather conditions, mainly drought, the 1971 harvest was 20% lower than planned. As a result, the government had to import grain to avoid slaughtering cattle. The economic shortcomings amounted to an indirect indictment of Ulbricht's policies.

Volkskammer elects officials. The new Volkskammer, elected Nov. 14 with 99.8% (11,207,235) of the valid votes cast for the official Communist National Front, Nov. 26 elected government officials. Walter Ulbricht was re-elected chairman of the Council of State, indicating that he still maintained some status within the regime. Also re-elected were Stoph as chairman of the Council of Ministers (premier) and Honecker as chairman of the National Defense Council. Honecker and Paul Verner, chairman of the Volkskammer's defense commission, were given seats on the Council of State, while Gunter Mittag, a Communist party Politburo member, was dropped from the council. The Volkskammer unanimously approved Premier Stoph's new government Nov. 29. Deputy Premiers Alexander Abusch and Max Sefrin left the government for health reasons.

See also FINLAND; GERMAN CONSULTATIONS; SPACE [24]

GERMANY, WEST (FEDERAL REPUBLIC OF GERMANY)—Eastern detente.
The West German government of Chancellor Willy Brandt continued its policy of detente with Eastern Europe, established by the signing of treaties with the Soviet Union and Poland in 1970 (submitted to the upper house of parliament Dec. 13 for endorsement), but opposition to the policy within Germany also continued during 1971. Talks were held between Soviet and German representatives on a mutual trade agreement. The U.S.S.R. and Germany agreed July 22 to the establishment of consulates general in Leningrad and Hamburg and agreed Oct. 5 to the establishment of a direct air connection between the two countries, to be flown by their respective national airlines, Aeroflot and Lufthansa. Following 1970 preliminary talks on normalization between German and Czechoslovak officials, discussions at a higher level were begun March 31 and April 1 in Prague. Germany was represented at the talks by Foreign Ministry State Secretary Paul Frank, and Czechoslovakia was represented by Deputy Foreign Minister Milan Klusak.

[2] Within Germany, Kurt Georg Kiesinger, leader of the opposition Christian Democratic Union (CDU), Jan. 25 accused the Brandt government of plunging "into the hectic adventure of its Eastern policy, which the whole world and the Soviet Union itself judge to be a great political success for Moscow." Referring to the 1970 treaties, Kiesinger said: "No easing of tensions is visible despite the fact that German political positions have been given away." The Deutsche (German) Union was formed June 12 to oppose the East European policies of Chancellor Brandt. The membership of the party was primarily composed of members of the National Liberal Action, a group that had defected from the Free Democratic party (FDP) in April 1970 to protest the leadership of the party chairman, Foreign Minister Walter Scheel. A right-wing extremist, Karsten Eggert April 9 confessed that he intended to murder President Gustav Heinemann to protest the Eastern policy.

[3] **Arms sales limited.** Government spokesman Conrad Ahlers announced Jan. 22 that West Germany would send no more arms to Portugal or Greece. Contracts with both countries had expired and would not be renewed. In an extension of the policy of arms control, the Cabinet June 16 decided to limit the sales of arms and war materials to all nations except NATO members. The ban applied to sales by government and by private firms.

[4] **West Berlin SDP rejects coalition.** The West Berlin Social Democratic party (SDP) decided April 1 to abandon its coalition government with the liberal FDP and to administer the city alone with the bare parliamentary majority (73 of 138 seats) it won in elections March 14. The SDP rejected the FDP claims for three ministerial posts (compared with their former one) and for policy changes regarding university and police administration. The federal government in Bonn had urged the Berlin SDP to reconstitute the coalition.

[5] **Economic stability program.** As part of a new economic stability program, the government May 10 ordered a freeze of 1.5 billion marks (nearly $500 million) on federal and state spending. To curb foreign capital and currency inflow, the government decreed that foreign investments in Germany would require government authorization to be eligible for interest earnings.

[6] **Moeller resigns.** Finance Minister Alex Moeller resigned from the cabinet May 13 because of conflicts over the federal budget (see [9-10]). Government spokesman Ahlers said Moeller felt physically incapable of fighting for an austerity budget in the face of heavy financial demands by various ministries. (Ministers of defense, transport and science had demanded more funds for expensive reform programs.) Economics Minister Karl Schiller was appointed immediately to assume control over a newly merged Finance and Economic Ministry, assuring his complete control over all economic matters.

[7] **Divorce reform.** The Cabinet May 19 approved reform legislation that would base divorce on the concept of "deterioration" of a marriage, rather than require establishment of guilt. A three-year separation of marriage partners would serve as proof of deterioration—and grounds for divorce—while a one-year separation would suffice in cases where both partners wanted the divorce. The legislation would also liberalize alimony regulations. It would also permit couples getting married to take either the last name of the husband, or that of the wife, or a joint name.

[8] **Tax reform.** Economics and Finance Minister Schiller June 11 announced plans for a major tax reform that would bring "justice and simplicity" to the tax system. The reform would provide for an increase in the basic deduction for all taxpayers from 1,680 marks (about U.S. $470) to 2,040 marks ($571) and a doubling of the basic deduction for employes to 480 marks ($134); an increase in the minimum income tax rate on low-income earners from 19% to 20% and in the maximum rate on the highest income group from 53% to 56%; a simplification of tax deductions, including elimination of expense account, gift benefit and certain other deductions; replacement of the double tax for shareholders with a unitary tax on income from capital of 56%; a rise in the tax on large inheritances; an increase in automobile taxes; and tax inducements to encourage environmental protection. The program would encourage saving and investment through a 30% expansion of the 1970 legislation known as "property formation," under which the federal government paid workers 640 marks for saving an equal amount. To compensate for reduced tax receipts, the government would increase the value-added tax (a tax imposed on each stage of production of an item) from 11% to 12%, effective Jan. 1, 1974.

[9] **Purchase of U.S. Phantoms announced.** An agreement under which West Germany would purchase 175 Phantom F-4 jet fighters from the U.S. firm of McDonnell Douglas was announced Sept. 1 by U.S. Secretary of Defense Melvin Laird. The $750 million contract was the biggest sale of Phantom jets yet made by the U.S. Pentagon spokesman Brig. Gen. Daniel James announced the following day that delivery of the Phantoms would not begin until early 1974. He disclosed the sale price did not include the cost of the two jet engines per plane. The planes would replace the air force's Lockheed Starfighter F-104s and Fiat G-91s and would be used until the European Multi-Role Combat Aircraft—to be built by Germany, Britain and Italy—went into service.

[10]   1972 'stability budget' adopted. The Cabinet Sept. 10 adopted what was called a "stability budget" for 1972, with expenditures estimated at 106.57 billion Deutsche marks (about $31.9 billion), an 8.4% increase over 1971. The budget for 1971 had provided for increased expenditures of 12% over the previous year. Economics and Finance Minister Schiller defined the budget as one of "consolidation," designed to curb inflationary trends and, at the same time, to prevent recession. Schiller said the Cabinet had approved his projected "eventual budget" of an additional 2.5 billion DM ($750 million) to be used in case of recession.

[11]   The largest quantitative increases were earmarked for defense, transport and social security, while education and housing each received the largest percentage increases—almost a third more than for 1971. Defense expenditures were estimated at $5 billion. Higher excise taxes on gasoline, tobacco and liquor were expected to yield the government almost $30 million in additional revenue in 1972. A longer-term government finance program anticipated a 7.5% average annual increase in federal expenditures during 1972-75, based on an average annual increase of 7% in the gross national product and of 3.5% in prices.

[12]   **Barzel elected CDU chairman.** Rainer C. Barzel, parliamentary leader of the CDU, was overwhelmingly elected party chairman Oct. 4 to succeed Kiesinger, who had said July 5 he would not seek the chairmanship. Barzel defeated his only rival, Helmut Kohl, minister-president (governor) of the state of Rhineland-Palatinate, by a 344—174 vote on the first day of the two-day party conference in Saarbrucken. Barzel's victory apparently assured him of his party's candidacy for the chancellorship in the 1973 federal elections.

[13]   **Nazi developments.** France and West Germany Feb. 2 signed an agreement allowing West German courts to try Nazis who had been convicted in absentia in France but not brought to trial in Germany. A West Berlin court March 23 released from jail Dr. Karl Werner Best, a former general in the Nazi SS Elite Guard implicated in the killing of 11,000 Polish civilians. The court ruled that there was insufficient evidence to try Best, who was placed under investigative arrest in 1967. In a retrial April 6, a West Berlin Court confirmed a 12-year jail sentence for Fritz Woehrn, a former SS captain, for having sent thousands of Jews to the Auschwitz concentration camp and for having contributed to the death of five Jews. A Frankfurt court April 6 sentenced Dr. Bruno Berger, a former aide to SS leader Heinrich Himmler, to three years in jail for aiding in the murder of 86 Jews whose skeletons were sent to a Nazi institute. Wolf-Dieter Wolff was freed of the same charge because charges had been brought against him too late. A Frankfurt court April 14 declared Horst Schumann, a former concentration camp doctor, physically unfit to stand trial and suspended proceedings against him on charges of murdering 15,314 persons. Schumann admitted to personally opening gas valves at two "mercy killing" institutes but denied having selected weak and sick inmates for death. The Munich public prosecutor June 22 closed the dosier of Klaus Barbie, former Gestapo chief of Lyons in France, condemned in absentia to death in 1954 in France, for lack of evidence of his role in the execution of Jews after their deportation from Lyons. The decision provoked strong protests from former French Resistance members, who submitted documents to back up their demands to reopen the case. (Barbie had disappeared from Germany in February, following signing of the French-West German pact.) Engelbert Kreuzer, a former Nazi police official, was sentenced by a Regensburg court Aug. 5 to seven years in prison for his part in organizing the executions of Jews at Babi Yar in the Kiev area. Rene Rosenbauer and Martin Besser, also accused, were excused from the trial for poor health. A Hanover court Oct. 14 sentenced Erhard Grauel, a former S.S. officer, to six years in detention on charges of participating in the murder of 250 Jews and Communists in Latvia during World War II. Five other persons were sentenced to jail terms ranging from 18 months to seven years. Hans Sobotta, a former S.S. commander, was

sentenced to life imprisonment Dec. 2 by a Munich court for the murder of three Jews in concentration camps in Galicia.

[14] Metalworkers end strike. The worst labor dispute in Germany's post-World War II history ended Dec. 15, one day after striking metalworkers in northern Baden and Wurttemberg voted to accept a compromise wage package which involved a 7.5% wage increase over twelve months. (Employers had originally offered a 4.5% increase, and the union had demanded an 11% increase.) The dispute had begun Nov. 22 when the metalworkers' union, Industriegewerkschaft Metall, struck six plants belonging to the automobile and truck assembly manufacturers of Audi-N.S.U. and Daimler-Benz after wage talks had been deadlocked. The strike spread to 75 smaller supplier firms in southwest Germany. Stressing solidarity with the struck plants, employers responded Nov. 25 with a regional industrywide lockout of blue collar workers in nearly every plant employing more than 100 workers. The number of those out of work rose to nearly 600,000 when companies halted production because of a lack of spare parts manufactured by the struck plants. Chancellor Brandt had intervened in the deepening deadlock Dec. 7 when he met with union and management negotiators after special arbitration talks had reached a stalemate.

See also ATOMIC ENERGY [13]; AVIATION [9-11, 14]; BOLIVIA [5]; CHURCHES [2]; COMMUNIST CHINA-U.S. DETENTE; DRUG USE & ADDICTION [8-9]; EUROPEAN ECONOMIC COMMUNITY [1-2, 12, 14]; FINLAND; FRANCE [17]; GERMAN CONSULTATIONS; GERMANY, EAST; GUINEA; HEALTH [7]; INTERNATIONAL MONETARY DEVELOPMENTS [1-5, 8-10, 13, 15, 18]; JAPAN; NOBEL PRIZES; PAKISTAN [35, 39]; PESTICIDES; RACIAL & MINORITY UNREST [15, 19]; SPACE [17]; SUDAN

GHANA—Prime Minister Kofi Busia Jan. 27 made the first major government changes since coming to power in 1969. The new cabinet: William Ofori-Atta—foreign affairs; S. D. Dombo—health; R.R. Amponsah—education and sports; Victor Owusu—justice and attorney general; T. D. Brodie-Mends—lands and mineral resources; Jato Kaleo—transport and communications; N.Y.B. Adade—internal affairs; W. Bruce Konuah—labor; B. K. Adama—defense; Joseph Mensa—finance; S. W. Awuku Darko—housing and works; Richard Quarshie—trade, industry and tourism; K. G. Osei-Bonsu—minister of state and head of protocol; Kwame Safo-Adu—agriculture; A. A. Munifie—rural development and social welfare; J. Kwesi-Lamptey—minister responsible for parliamentary affairs.

TUC illegal. The National Assembly Sept. 10 passed a bill classifying the Trade Union Congress (TUC) as an "illegal institution" in its present form. The bill, requiring presidential approval, freed individual trade unions from the obligation of joining a federative body, although another such umbrella organization could be formed. (Sixteen unions Sept. 10 formed a new congress under the leadership of Benjamin Bentum, the TUC secretary general.) Labor Minister William Bruce Konuah said the new legislation guaranteed the rights of individual workers, who could now choose whether to belong to a union. Konuah said that the old TUC, part of former President Kwame Nkrumah's Convention People's Party, had continued to exist "by oversight" after the 1966 coup deposing Nkrumah and his party.

GOLD—*See* INTERNATIONAL MONETARY DEVELOPMENTS [8, 11, 14, 17-18]

GOLF—**Masters.** Charles Coody withstood a third-round challenge by Jack Nicklaus and a closing-round 68 by John Miller to win the Masters golf title April 11 at the Augusta National Golf Club in Augusta, Ga. Coody, 33, carded a final-round 70 to finish with a 72-hole total of 279, nine strokes under par. His other round scores were 66, 73 and 70. Coody's triumph earned him $25,000. Miller and Nicklaus tied for second with 281s.

U.S., British Opens. A cloudburst and lightning storm forced Lee Trevino and Nicklaus off the Merion course in Ardmore, Pa. June 21, but when they returned 35 minutes later Trevino nailed down the U.S. Open Golf championship with a 68 in their head-to-head match for the title. Trevino and Nicklaus had finished regulation play over Merion's East course with 72-hole total scores of 280. The triumph was worth $30,000 to Trevino.

In the British Open in Southport, England July 10, Trevino, comfortably ahead of his nearest challenger with a five-stroke lead, almost blew the title with a double bogey on the 17th hole. But he sewed up the title with a birdie on the 18th to finish one stroke ahead of Lu Liang Huan of Taiwan. Trevino joined Bob Jones (1930), Gene Sarazen (1932) and Ben Hogan (1953) as the only golfers to win the U.S. and British championships in the same year. Trevino's first-place prize was $13,200.

GOVERNMENT REORGANIZATION—Volunteer agency plan cleared. The Senate, voting 54—29 June 3, and the House, voting 224—131 May 25, rejected motions to block President Nixon's volunteer agency reorganization plan. The absence of a Congressional veto cleared the way for the plan to take effect automatically, creating an agency called Action to take over the activities of the Peace Corps, VISTA (Volunteers in Service to America) and several smaller volunteer units. The agency headed by Joseph Blatchford, was inaugurated July 1. It had been proposed by the President March 24.

Opposition to the reorganization was led by supporters of VISTA in Congress and in the National VISTA Alliance, representing a large number of VISTA volunteers. They argued that the merger was designed by the Administration to downgrade VISTA and submerge its activity on behalf of the poor in a broad, multipurpose agency dominated by the Peace Corps. To gain support for the merger, the Nixon Administration made various promises to continue the VISTA program. Rep. Ogden R. Reid (R, N.Y.) said May 25 the Administration had agreed to raise VISTA's budget from $33 million to $45 million in fiscal 1972, beginning July 1. George P. Shultz, director of the Office of Management and Budget, wrote May 19 to Sen. Jacob Javits (R, N.Y.) that there would be two associate directors of Action, one for poverty and domestic activities—for VISTA affairs—and another for the Peace Corps. Shultz also promised that VISTA volunteers and poor people who were participants in VISTA programs would serve on task forces to plan the organization of Action.

Besides the Peace Corps and VISTA, Action would incorporate other special volunteer programs in OEO; Foster Grandparents and the Retired Senior Volunteer Program from the Department of Health, Education and Welfare; Service Corps of Retired Executives and Active Corps of Executives from the Small Business Administration; and the Office of Volunteer Action from the Department of Housing and Urban Development. The formal merger of the Peace Corps and the HUD program into Action was to take place by executive order after Action went into effect.

Regulatory agency overhaul asked. President Nixon Feb. 11 released details of a plan to overhaul the commissions regulating the securities, transportation and power industries, and consumer affairs. The key recommendation of the 125-page report prepared by the Advisory Council on Executive Reorganization was a proposal to abolish most of the independent multi-member commissions in favor of one-man administrators of new agencies. The report said the regulatory commissions had been inflexible and ineffective in developing consistent policies. To replace them, the report suggested that single administrators be appointed without fixed terms but who would be subject to Senate confirmation and responsible to the White House and the public. The report said the present commission structure heightened unaccountability and theorized that single agency heads would not only be better administrators but would be more clearly accountable for regulatory decisions.

Among the structural changes proposed by the council: replacement of the five-member Federal Trade Commission by a new federal trade practices agency under a single administrator with the FTC's antitrust functions shared by a federal antitrust board, composed of a chairman and two economist members, and the Department of Justice; the Interstate Commerce Commission, the Civil Aeronautics Board and the Federal Maritime Commission would be merged into a new transportation regulatory agency under a single administrator; the Federal Power and the Securities and Exchange Commissions would each be replaced by new agencies with single administrators; the Federal Communications Commission would be reduced from seven to five commissioners, retaining its multimember composition because the FCC's "subjective" decision on program content required more than one viewpoint; appeals from final decisions of the transportation, securities and power agencies would be heard by a new 15-member administrative court instead of by federal courts.

Cabinet reorganization. President Nixon submitted to Congress March 25 his plan for reorganizing the cabinet by establishing four new departments—Human Resources, Economic Affairs, Community Development and Natural Resources—that would absorb the present departments of Labor, Agriculture, Commerce, Transportation, Housing and Urban Development (HUD) and Health, Education and Welfare (HEW). The Departments of State, Treasury, Defense and Justice would remain largely unchanged. (Nixon announced Nov. 11 that the Agriculture Department would also remain unchanged.) The proposals largely followed recommendations of Nixon's Advisory Council on Executive Reorganization, which was headed by Roy L. Ash, president of Litton Industries. However, the President made some departures from the Ash plan—preferring to keep the Tariff Commission as a separate entity instead of placing it in the Economic Affairs Department; retaining the Agriculture Department's Soil Conservation Service instead of splitting it up; and transferring the planning, funding and evaluation operations of the Army Corps of Engineers to the Natural Resources Department while keeping its construction personnel in the Defense Department. The proposed four new departments would have a total employment of 423,400 and total budget for fiscal 1971 of $49.2 billion.

Under the Nixon plan, the Human Resources Department would consist of three administrations for health, human development and income security. The department would take over most of the present HEW operations; the Labor Department's manpower, income maintenance and security operations; HUD's college housing programs; Agriculture's economic and agricultural research and meat, egg and poultry inspection; and Office of Economic Opportunity (OEO) programs for alcoholism, family planning, drug rehabilitation, migrants and nutrition. The Economic Affairs Department would assume Labor Department programs on labor relations, statistics, occupational health and safety; Agriculture's farmers' operating loans, cooperative service, commodity exchange and credit and marketing services, statistics, export marketing and crop insurance programs; Transportation's car and highway safety programs, the Railroad Administration, the Federal Aviation Agency and the Coast Guard; all of the Commerce Department's activities except those transferred to the Departments of Community Development and Natural Resources; the Small Business Administration (SBA), except for disaster loans; the Federal Mediation and Conciliation Service, and the nonregulatory functions of the National Mediation Board.

The Community Development Department would have four divisions: a Housing Administration, Community Transportation Administration, Urban and Rural Development Administration and Federal Insurance Administration. It would take over HEW's program for construction grants for libraries; HUD's programs except for college housing programs; Agriculture's rural electrification, farmers' housing loans and water and waste disposal grants; Transportation's highways and urban mass transit programs;

Commerce's Economic Development Administration and regional commissions; the OEO's Community Action Programs and Special Impact Programs; and the SBA's disaster loans. The Natural Resources Department would have five divisions: Land and Recreation Resources, Water Resources, Energy and Mineral Resources, Indian and Territorial Affairs and Oceanic, Atmospheric and Earth Sciences. It would assume Agriculture's Forest Service, soil and water conservation and watershed loans; Transportation's Oil and Gas Pipeline Safety Programs; Commerce's Oceanic and Atmospheric Administration; the Interior Department; and the Atomic Energy Commission's Uranium Raw Materials, Uranium Enrichment and Civilian Nuclear Power Reactions programs, as well as funding and some planning operations of Plowshare.

Nixon proposes legal aid corp. President Nixon sent a message to Congress May 5 proposing an independent legal services corporation that he said would protect the program from "unusually strong political pressures." The principle of an independent corporation to replace the OEO legal services program had been embodied in bipartisan bills introduced in the House and Senate in March. Commenting on the political pressures inherent in the OEO program, Nixon said, "Much of the litigation initiated by legal services has placed it in direct conflict with local and state government." The independent, nonprofit corporations envisioned in both the Administration proposal and the Congressional legislation would be free from the veto power that governors could exercise over the present OEO program. However, under the Administration plan the corporation would have to give 30 days' notice to governors of proposed grants. Rep. William A. Steiger (R, Wis.), a principal sponsor of the House bill, argued that the notification requirement would insure "that powerful state interests will continue to have a substantial voice" in the operation of legal services. The White House proposal also differed from the Congressional legislation in that it called for all 11 members of the board of the corporation to be appointed by the President. The Congressional version would provide a 19-member board with five Presidential appointees. Others would be chosen by the U.S. chief justice and the organized bar, with six members representing poverty lawyers and their clients.

Intelligence work realigned. The White House announced Nov. 5 a reorganization of U.S. intelligence activities to improve efficiency. An "enhanced leadership" role was assigned to Richard Helms, director of the Central Intelligence Agency (CIA). In addition to his operations duties at CIA, he was to have broad supervision over all foreign intelligence activities, which were carried on, in addition to the CIA, by intelligence units within the Defense and State Departments, the Atomic Energy Commission (AEC) and the Federal Bureau of Investigation. Two new units were to be established within the National Security Council. One, headed by Henry A. Kissinger, presidential adviser for national security affairs, would review intelligence operations; another, a "net assessment group," would evaluate all intelligence.

AEC reorganized. The AEC Dec. 7 announced its first major structural reorganization in 10 years. The streamlining operation involved reduction of the number of general program areas from nine to six, with each headed by an assistant general manager. The six areas were national security, environment and safety, energy and development programs, research, production and administration. Three program areas dealing with military and international affairs were consolidated into the one area of national security.

See also BUDGET; CONSUMER AFFAIRS [5, 14]; MEDICINE; NIXON, RICHARD MILHOUS [1]; POSTAL SERVICE, U.S.

GOWAN, MAJ. GEN. YAKABU—*See* NIGERIA

GRAMMY AWARDS—*See* RECORD INDUSTRY

GRAVEL, MIKE—*See* PENTAGON PAPERS [10, 13]

GREAT BRITAIN—The British government concentrated its efforts in 1971 on attempts to stimulate Britain's lagging economy and reduce spiraling unemployment without increasing the country's rising inflation. In such attempts, the government issued a deficit budget for fiscal 1972 [14], cut taxes and made concessions to business in return for an industry promise to hold price increases to 5% [19] and announced a program of accelerated public spending to decrease unemployment [22]. The government also attempted to reduce its role in the economy—announcing plans to sell parts of nationalized concerns to private industry [2] and refusing to bail out failing British companies [5-7], including Rolls-Royce, Ltd. [5]. Strikes against industry [11-12], however—including a 47-day postal strike [11]—hampered government efforts to restrain inflationary wage settlements. Several strikes and other protests were held against a proposed labor bill, passed by Parliament Aug. 5 [20].

[2] **Robens resigns as coal chairman.** Lord Robens resigned Jan. 4 as chairman of the National Coal Board in protest against the government's rumored plans to sell to private industry the more profitable side of operations of the nationalized coal industry. The government officially announced the resignation Jan. 5. Robens declined to serve another five-year term after his current term expired Jan. 31, but agreed to serve another six months while the government sought a successor. In other developments in the government's campaign to sell parts of nationalized industries to private concerns (*see also* [5]), the government Jan. 27 confirmed plans to sell Thomas Cook & Son, Ltd., owned by the government since World War II, and two other publicly owned travel agencies to private enterprise. (The Cook agency reported profits before taxes of only $2.6 million in 1969.) The government April 2 announced that it would conduct a "profound review" of the nationalized British Steel Corp. (BSC). It was believed that the government wished to sell some parts of the company to private industry. (Some opposition Labor party members credited that wish as the cause of BSC Chairman Lord Julian Melchett's April 2 announcement that he would relinquish control of daily production operations to his deputy chairman, H. M. Finniston, and would himself concentrate on policy matters.) The government's announcement accompanied an order that BSC reduce by half a 14% price increase announced earlier the same day. The BSC contended the increase was necessary to offset current losses—estimated at $6 million weekly—stemming from cost inflation and reduced orders. It had informed the government Feb. 17 of the proposed increase, but the government had postponed a final decision.

[3] **Dutschke expulsion upheld.** A special immigration appeals tribunal recommended Jan. 8 that Rudi Dutschke, a West German radical student leader, should not be allowed to remain in Britain for academic studies. Dutschke, who had gained worldwide recognition as a radical student leader at the Free University of West Berlin, had moved to Britain in December 1968 for treatment of head wounds suffered from an assailant in Berlin. He had applied in the summer of 1970 for a change in his legal status to that of full-time postgraduate student at Cambridge University, but Home Secretary Reginald Maudling turned the application down and ordered him to leave the country. The tribunal decision Jan. 8 was to reject Dutschke's appeal against the deportation order. The five-man body ruled that Dutschke had violated his pledge (given in 1968 when he entered Britain) not to engage in political activity. Dutschke denied that he had engaged in "direct political or organizational activity in Britain." The tribunal's decision was criticized sharply by the opposition Labor party and by British civil libertarians, but Dutschke left Britain Feb. 19 to assume a teaching post at Aarhus University in Denmark.

[4] **Bomb attacks.** A group of young revolutionaries calling itself "The Angry Brigade," claimed responsibility for several bomb attacks during 1971. The attacks included: the explosion of two bombs Jan. 12 at the suburban Hadley Green home of Minister of Employment Robert Carr; the explosion

May 22 of a bomb which damaged brickwork and shattered windows at a police computer center in London, but caused no injuries; the explosion July 31 of a bomb which damaged the London apartment of Secretary of State for Trade and Development John Davies; a bomb explosion Oct. 31 which severely damaged the top floors of the Post Office Tower in London; and the explosion Nov. 1 of a bomb which caused minor damage to an army drill hall a quarter of a mile from Parliament. (A man with an Irish accent telephoned a British news agency six hours after the Oct. 31 blast and claimed that a London branch of the Irish Republican Army was responsible for the bombing. Both the "official" and "provisional" branches of the IRA issued statements in Dublin denying responsibility for the explosion.)

[5] Rolls-Royce declares bankruptcy. Rolls-Royce, Ltd., saddled with the spiraling costs of developing the RB-211 engine for Lockheed Aircraft Corp.'s new Tri-star airbus, declared bankruptcy Feb. 4. Minister of Aviation Supply Frederick Corfield, in an address to the House of Commons the same day, announced that the government would nationalize the Rolls airplane engine, marine and industrial gas turbine operations deemed essential for national defense. (The Royal Air Force, as well as the air forces of many other nations, was powered by Rolls-Royce engines and depended on Rolls for spare parts.) The nationalized divisions, which would continue work on all aircraft engine projects except the RB-211, would be established as a government-owned company, with about 50,000 of Rolls's more than 80,000 employees kept on the payroll. E. Rupert Nicholson, a British accountant named as receiver Feb. 4, said his "main objective would be to preserve as much as I can of the company." It was reported Feb. 5 that the firm's profitable car division, its oil division and its computer complex would be sold to private enterprise. (The prestigious, high-priced automobiles accounted for only 5% of Rolls's 1969 sales of $723 million.) Corfield said the government was conferring with the U.S. and Lockheed on the future of the RB-211 engine (see BUSINESS [3-4]). The labor government had granted Rolls $113 million of the original estimated development costs ($156 million). A doubling of expenditures to $360 million led the Conservative government in November 1970 to promise $100 million in additional aid, backed up by $43 million in loans from private banks, contingent on an independent auditing inspection. The negative audit results led the Conservative government to refuse the loan.

[6] *Other ailing industry developments.* The Vehicle and General Insurance Co., one of Britain's largest automobile insurance firms, declared itself insolvent March 1, leaving its 700,000 auto policyholders without insurance overnight. The British Insurance Association, of which the firm was a member, said it would cover only third-party bodily injury claims. Secretary for Trade and Industry Davies told the House of Commons March 2 that the government had known of the company's financial problems since July 1970, but had not acted publicly for fear of undermining confidence in the company.

[7] Adhering to its policy of not rescuing failing private industries, the government June 14 refused to provide a $14.4 million subsidy to the Upper Clyde Shipbuilders consortium in Scotland, the nation's largest shipbuilding yard and builders of prestigious transatlantic ocean liners. The decision forced the firm to begin liquidation proceedings. Robert C. Smith was confirmed June 15 as provisional liquidator—the Scotch equivalent of a receiver—for the company. Secretary Davies June 15 appointed a three-man team to aid in reconstruction of the consortium. The team recommended a plan, announced by Davies July 29, calling for temporary government financial assistance pending a reorganization of the shipyard's management and the conclusion of new working agreements with unions. Davies indicated the reorganized company would close two of its four shipyards and probably assure jobs for only about 2,500 of the firm's more than 8,000 workers. He said many of the laid-off workers would find jobs in other shipyards. (Unemployment in Scotland had already reached a high level.) Following the announcement, militant workers

July 30 seized control of the John Brown shipyard of the consortium and declared their "work-in" an experiment in industrial democracy. Six thousand workers at Upper Clyde's three other shipyards voted Aug. 9 to join the takeover.

[8] Decimal currency system adopted. Britain switched to a decimal currency Feb. 15, ending a 1,000-year existence for one of the most complicated currency systems in the world. (The Republic of Ireland also switched to the decimal currency system Feb. 15.) According to Lord Fiske, chairman of the Decimal Currency Board, the transition from 240 pence per pound to 100 new pence per pound might be completed by 1972. Meanwhile, the old currency would be accepted in some places along with three new copper coins: the 2 penny piece, a penny and a halfpenny.

[9] Immigration bill introduced. The government Feb. 24 proposed a new immigration bill that would restrict the right of non-white Commonwealth citizens to settle in Britain after July 31. The bill would distinguish between two categories of Commonwealth immigrants: patrials (persons born or naturalized in Britain, or with one parent or grandparent who was) and nonpatrials. Patrials, mainly Canadians, Australians, New Zealanders and other white settlers in the old British empire, as well as Irish citizens, would maintain automatic right of entry to Britain and would be exempt from restrictions once settled. Nonpatrials would receive the same treatment as aliens: they would be admitted only as workers with permits, renewed annually, for specific jobs; once in Britain, they would have to register with the police and would need government authorization to change jobs; after five years residence, they could apply for citizenship and permanent unrestricted residence in Britain. Under the bill, the government would finance voluntary repatriation of persons who wanted to leave Britain. The new legislation would remove the previous quota limitation on work permits—8,500 annually—and would leave discretion for the number of permits to the Department of Employment. The bill would not change the volume of immigration, already subject to controls.

[10] In another immigration development, Secretary Maudling announced in the House of Commons May 26 that the quota of immigrants from Britain's former East African colonies would be doubled from 1,500 heads of family to 3,000, effective June 1. Maudling also announced abolition of work permits issued to Commonwealth countries other than Malta for unskilled or semi-skilled employment and a reduction in the annual issue of permits for persons with certain specified skills.

[11] Postal strike. Britain's longest major strike since 1926 ended March 8 as postal workers resumed work after branches of the Union of Post Office Workers voted to submit the dispute to a three-man nongovernmental arbitration board and end the 47-day strike which had begun Jan. 20. The union, which included postmen, mail sorters, counter clerks and telephone operators, voted for the strike Jan. 15 to support their demands for a 15% wage increase. The government had offered an 8% increase, claiming that the government could not "find the money for a larger wage increase." Both sides in the strike were hampered by finances: the post office was saddled with a heavy deficit (increased by a strike loss of $64.8 million in revenue), and strikers received no money during the strike because the union strike fund was depleted. The end of the strike was seen as a defeat for the union, since the post office only offered an additional 1% increase for productivity to its original offer. Union leadership recommended settlement because the union treasury lacked funds to continue the strike. Britain weathered the strike with comparatively little deprivation. Although the delivery of mail was halted, about 50% of the post office's telecommunication workers did not strike. Automatic dial telephone systems continued to function, and private mail and messenger services were organized.

[12]*Other strike and labor action.* About 2,500 engineering and maintenance workers struck British European Airways (BEA) Jan. 26-29 in protest over the dismissal of a maintenance staff which had refused orders to service two engines. The strike cost BEA $600,000 a day. A nine-week strike that began Feb. 1 at the Ford Motor Co.'s 21 plants in Britain was settled March 31 after union acceptance of a new two-year wage contract providing for wage increases of nearly 33%—about 16% retroactive to March 1, and about 8.5% effective Dec. 1 and again Aug. 1, 1972. The contract, seen as a defeat for the government's drive to restrain inflationary wage settlements, also contained a unique no-strike pledge and a freeze on occupational grading and wage structure for the duration of the pact. Following union ratification, work resumed April 5 at 17 plants, with wildcat stoppages continuing until April 8 at three plants near Liverpool and one in South Wales. The final settlement was opposed by militant shop stewards who claimed the union's leaders had backed down from the workers' original demand: parity with the best-paid United Kingdom auto workers. The strikers had originally asked for increases nearly four times higher than those accepted in the settlement. (William B. Batty, managing director of Ford's British subsidiary, disclosed Feb. 23 that Ford had decided against building a $72 million engine plant in Britain because of persistent labor troubles.) In another strike action, 12,000 steel blast furnacemen employed by the nationalized BSC struck the corporation June 1-4. The executive board of the National Union of Blastfurnacemen voted by a slim majority June 4 to allow negotiations to reopen on its claim for a 35% wage increase. (*See also* [20].)

[13]   **Farm policy changes announced.** British Agriculture Minister James Prior told the House of Commons March 17 that the change of Britain's system of agricultural supports from government subsidies to import levies would go into effect in July. The change, amending Britain's system to conform with that of the European Economic Community (EEC), would institute levy arrangements for cereals, beef and veal, mutton and lamb, and milk products (excepting butter and cheese), as well as increasing minimum import prices for eggs.

[14]   **1972 budget sets tax cuts, reform.** In an effort to stimulate the country's lagging economy, without adding to its high inflation rate, Chancellor of the Exchequer Anthony Barber presented a deficit budget for fiscal 1972 (April 1, 1971-March 31, 1972) to the House of Commons March 30. It was approved by the Commons April 5. The budget provided for a wide range of tax cuts and for the most fundamental reform of Britain's tax system in decades. The tax changes were expected to reduce government revenues by about $1.5 billion annually and increase demand by about $600 million in 1971. Barber halved the rate of the selective employment tax (essentially a payroll tax on services), reduced the top rate on incomes over $48,000 from nearly 89% to 75%, cut the corporation tax by 2.5% to 40%, reduced the short-term capital gains tax and real estate taxes and eliminated various taxes on savings and loans. Other aspects of the budget: the annual income tax exemption for each child was increased by $96; old-age pensions for single persons were increased from $12 to $14.40 a week and for married couples from $19.94 to $23.28; the purchase tax on luxury goods and the selective employment tax would be abolished in 1973 and replaced by the value-added tax (in which a form of sales tax was levied on each step of production of an item); in 1973, the present income tax and surtax system would be replaced by a single graduated personal tax at a basic rate of 30%.

[15]   **Government reorganization.** In a minor governmental reorganization announced April 7, Minister of Aviation Supply Corfield was appointed to the newly created post of minister for aerospace at the Department of Trade and Industry, effective May 1. Lord Carrington, secretary of state for defense, was named minister of aviation supply, with responsibility for defense procurement. (Under a new system, to be fully operational in April 1972, all defense

procurement activities would be concentrated at the Ministry of Defense.) In other appointments: William Ryland, acting chairman of the Post Office Corp. since November 1970, was appointed chairman April 22; Richard Marsh, a Labor member of Parliament and former transport minister, was appointed in April to be director of railroads, effective in September.

[16]   New airport on coast. Secretary of State for Trade and Industry Davies announced April 26 that London's third airport would be built at Foulness, a sparsely populated coastal site 55 miles east of London. Davies attributed rejection of an inland site to environmental considerations. He said the government would use a combined system of charge incentives and flight rationing to assure that airlines used the Foulness airport, which would be less conveniently located than London's two other airports. The cost of an airport at Foulness with access facilities was officially estimated at $1.2 billion—$360 million more than the cost of the inland alternatives. The first runway was expected to be operational by about 1980.

[17]   Oil auctions. The government June 22 announced plans for auctioning the 15 most promising oil and gas areas of the North Sea continental shelf. The 15 were part of an offering of production licenses covering 436 blocks. Applicants submitting tenders for licenses would also have to satisfy the government as to their capability to exploit their blocks. (Britain's previous system allocated licenses solely on the basis of the financial and technical capability to fulfill an exploration program.) The oil auction, held Aug. 20, brought in bids of $326 million.

[18]   India trade accord to end. The government, in a Parliamentary written answer June 30, announced it would terminate the Anglo-Indian trade agreement of 1939 at the end of the year and would impose a 15% duty on Indian cotton textile imports. The decision was made because of the Indian government's refusal to modify the agreement in line with Britain's decision to switch from quotas to tariffs on cotton textile imports from Commonwealth nations. The changeover—recommended in a report issued in 1969 by the Textile Council—was designed to stimulate the British textile industry.

[19]   Economic expansion program. In response to a July 15 offer by the Confederation of British Industry (CBI) to restrain price increases to 5% (half that of 1970) if the government should act to stimulate the economy, Chancellor of the Exchequer Barber announced July 19 an economic program that would reduce taxes by about $564 million a year, increase investment incentives and eliminate all consumer credit controls. The total program was designed to increase national output to 4%-4.5% from the current rate of slightly more than 3%. It virtually amounted to voluntary wage-price controls and was thought to represent a significant shift for the Conservative government. Under the program, purchase (excise) taxes on consumer goods would be reduced by about 18%, effective immediately. It was the first such purchase cut in eight years and the largest in 20 years. All controls on hire-purchase, credit sale and rental agreements would be eliminated. Tax deductions would be increased from 60% to 80% on first-year expenditures for capital equipment over a two-year period. Service industries in depressed regions would be permitted to write off total investment in fixed plant and equipment. Following Barber's announcement, the CBI pledged to limit price increases over the next year to 5%.

[20]   Labor bill enacted. After eight months of debate, amendments and protest strikes, Britain's most comprehensive labor relations bill was enacted Aug. 5. Earlier the same day, the House of Commons had approved by a vote of 254-217 amendments by the House of Lords. (An earlier version had been approved by Commons March 24.) The bill then received royal assent. In accord with the bill's provisions, after enactment a code of industrial practice was to be drafted banning wildcat strikes and the closed shop. The code was also to provide 60-day cooling-off periods in strikes involving national interest and to require that employers recognize unions approved by a majority of workers. Left-wing militant union leaders Jan. 12 had organized a one-day protest against the bill. The protest was opposed by the Trade Unions Congress (TUC). The TUC had staged a peaceful march and rally in central London Feb. 21 to express its opposition to the bill. The Amalgamated Engineering Union March 21 staged a one-day strike (condemned by the TUC) against the bill which closed auto plants, shipyards and newspapers, disrupted engineering firms and resulted in unofficial estimates of nearly $24 million in production loss. The engineering union and the Transport and General Workers Union March 18 staged another one-day strike (again opposed by the TUC) which shut down most engineering plants, docks, newspapers and automobile and aircraft factories and cost an estimated $170 million in lost production.

21] Police urge tougher anti-crime action. Two senior Scotland Yard officials (later identified as Assistant Commissioner Peter Brodie and Deputy Assistant Commissioner Peter Chittie) condemned Parliament, the courts, the government and the "do-gooders" for leniency toward violent criminals in an anonymous interview published Aug. 24. The two urged abolition of parole and suspended sentences for persons convicted of violent crimes. They also advocated harsher jail sentences and harsher treatment in prison of violent criminals. The interview was believed to be the first step in a police campaign aimed at toughening penal codes. (Figures released by the Yard Aug. 26 documented a 4% increase in violent crime in London in the first six months of 1971. During that period of time, 54 homicides occurred in London, compared with 51 in all of 1970. Cases of violent robbery totaled 258 in the period, an increase of 11.3% over the equivalent 1970 period.)

[22] Public funds to spur employment. In an effort to stem spiraling unemployment, Chancellor of the Exchequer Barber announced Nov. 23 that the government would accelerate public spending of more than $384 million over the next two years. The program would involve accelerated capital spending by nationalized industry and increases in public work expenditures. The program was announced in the House of Commons during debate on an opposition Labor party motion (defeated 311-289) to censure the government for failing to alleviate rising unemployment. (Workers clashed with police outside the Commons Nov. 24 after a mass protest, involving 10,000-20,000 persons, against rising unemployment. At least eight people were arrested during a melee of fist fights and window smashing. The police had sought to prevent some of the demonstrators from gathering outside Parliament.)

See also AFRICA; ANGUILLA; ARGENTINA [9, 13]; AVIATION [2, 4]; BAHRAIN; CARIBBEAN; CEYLON; CHILE [17]; CHURCHES [3-4]; COMMUNIST CHINA-U.S. DETENTE [3, 8, 12]; DISARMAMENT; DRUG USE & ADDICTION [9]; ESPIONAGE; EUROPEAN ECONOMIC COMMUNITY [1, 6, 13-15]; EUROPEAN SECURITY; GERMAN CONSULTATIONS; HEALTH [4]; INDOCHINA WAR [72]; INTERNATIONAL MONETARY DEVELOPMENTS [9, 13, 15-16, 18]; IRAN; JAPAN [4, 10]; JORDAN [12]; MALAGASY REPUBLIC; MALAYSIA; MALTA; MIDDLE EAST [31]; NORTH ATLANTIC TREATY ORGANIZATION; NORTHERN IRELAND; PACIFIC ISLANDS; PAKISTAN [35, 39, 42]; PENTAGON PAPERS [19]; PERSIAN GULF STATES; QATAR; RHODESIA; SIERRA LEONE; SOUTH AFRICA [4-7]; SPACE [17, 19]; TARIFFS & WORLD TRADE [14]; UNITED NATIONS [4, 13]

GREECE—15 basic laws promulgated. The military-backed regime Jan. 5 promulgated 15 "institutional laws" embodying still-suspended articles of the 1968 constitution. Six of the laws entered into force immediately: one authorizing judges to suspend the secrecy of the mails in cases involving national security and public order; another authorizing only those public assemblies organized and announced to the police in advance; and others dealing with the right to petition, commissions of inquiry, the National Education Council and ministerial penal responsibility. A six-month schedule for the implementation of four basic laws was planned, beginning Jan. 10 with a law regulating the designation of members of a Constitutional Tribunal which would regulate political parties and supervise application of the constitution. The other laws in this group dealt with expropriations, labor unions and associations and civil tribunals (*see* [5]). The government did not fix a date for implementation of the suspended constitutional articles on the formation of political parties, lifting of martial law or defining procedures for the regency.

[2] Prison visits ended. Following ten weeks of negotiations on a new procedure for visits to political prisoners, Christian Xanthopoulos-Palamas, undersecretary of foreign affairs, disclosed Jan. 9 that the government would deny the International Committee of the Red Cross access to the prisoners. Negotiations were reportedly ended because of government insistence that visits be only at the government's request. Xanthopoulos-Palamas maintained that negotiations were no longer necessary following the release of 305 prisoners at Christmas of 1970 and the government's pledge to liberate 400 other prisoners by April. (The prison camps on Leros Island and at Oropus were dismantled beginning April 10. The Public Order Ministry announced April 7 that 234 Communist political prisoners detained in the camps had been freed and that about 50 "dangerous and unrepentant Communists" would be committed to "enforced residence" in remote villages. According to report April 15, 450 non-Communist persons convicted of alleged subversive activities remained in prison.) (*See also* [18].)

[3] Regime criticized in U.S. A Senate Foreign Relations Committee staff report on the Greek regime, released March 4, concluded that the U.S. "policy of friendly persuasion has clearly failed" and that the regime "seems to have been able to exert more leverage on us with regard to military assistance than we have been able to exert on the regime with political reform." Also included in the report: (a) the regime continued a course of "intimidation" through political arrests and brutality; (b) the U.S. diplomatic stance was the regime's "greatest asset" in that it indicated U.S. support; and (c) generally, the regime was supported by the business community, much of the army and the church hierarchy and was opposed by intellectuals, students, civil servants and professionals.

[4] Opposition unites. Leaders of the nation's two largest opposition parties—Panayotis Kanellopoulos, head of the National Radical Union, and George Mavros and Ioannis Zigdis, members of the Central Union—joined for the first time to denounce the regime March 23. The joint statement declared their "unshaken belief in the democratic institutions" and determination "to devote all our strength to the reinstatement of democracy in its own birthplace." Kanellopoulos March 25 said of the statement: "It is important for the people in Greece and the policymakers in Washington who have said until now that there is no alternative to the present regime. The declaration shows that the two big parties are united and ready to assume responsibility."

[5] Military courts curbed. The office of Premier George Papadopoulos April 17 announced the transfer of five categories of offenses (crimes against the security of the state and crimes of insulting the king and the head of state) from the jurisdiction of military tribunals to civil courts. Thirteen offenses—including attempts to overthrow the regime, instigation to mutiny, formation of armed bands, illegal possession of explosives, causing an explosion and spreading false rumors and reports—would still be tried by military tribunals. In addition, the military courts would continue to try violations of five prohibitions under martial law, including unauthorized possession and operation of radio transmitters and printing machines, spreading propaganda against the established constitutional order, transmission of music by Mikis Theodorakis (an anti-regime composer living in Paris) and the sale of records by expatriate actress Melina Mercouri.

[6]   **Greece, Albania set diplomatic ties.** Greece and Albania, still technically at war because of their failure to sign a peace treaty after World War II, announced May 6 their agreement to resume diplomatic relations broken in 1940 when Italy invaded Greece from Albanian soil. Full diplomatic relations were restored Nov. 16.

[7]   **European action group formed.** A European-Atlantic Action Committee on Greece was formed June 1 in London. The committee was composed mainly of parliamentarians from Britain, the U.S. and European nations. The group's main purpose was to pressure their governments to force the Greek regime to restore democracy. The committee's formation was hailed June 2 in Athens by the first joint declaration to be issued by all Greek opposition leaders since the 1967 coup. Those signing the declaration were Kanellopoulos, Mavros, Zigdis and Demetrios Papaspyrou, president of the last Greek parliament and a Liberal.

[8]   **Accords with Rumania, Bulgaria.** The government's efforts to improve relations with its East European neighbors were furthered by a Greek-Rumanian agreement June 15 to create a joint commission to promote cooperation and the conclusion of tourism and judicial agreements between the two. A joint committee to study economic, technological, industrial and scientific cooperation between Greece and Bulgaria was announced July 2 in a joint communique. The communique envisaged a long-term increase in Greek-Bulgarian economic relations and tourism.

[9]   **18 acquitted of sedition.** In the first trials since sedition cases were removed from the jurisdiction of military courts (*see* [5]), an Athens civil court Aug. 6 acquitted 18 of 25 defendants accused of sedition. In the two cases (the first involving membership in the leftist clandestine student organization Righas Ferraios and seditious activities, and the second involving plans to overthrow the government and membership in the illegal Communist Organization of Athens), five defendants received sentences ranging from 10 months to three years in jail. Two persons received suspended sentences. The sentences were considered much lighter than those given by military tribunals.

[10]   **6 stripped of citizenship.** The government deprived six expatriates of their Greek nationality in July and August. Mrs. Helen Vlachos, former publisher of conservative Athens newspapers who had fled to London after the 1967 counter-coup by King Constantine, was deprived of her nationality July 20 because she had allegedly taken part in anti-regime activities. (The government reportedly regarded her as the prime mover in the creation of the European-Atlantic Action Committee on Greece. See [7].) The government Aug. 9 stripped of their citizenship two retired Greek army officers and George Plytas, former mayor of Athens who fled to London after the counter-coup and published there a magazine critical of Greek government leaders. Andreas Papandreou, leader of the Panhellenic Liberation Movement (PAK) who lived in exile in Toronto, Canada, was deprived of his Greek nationality Aug. 13. The same day, George Vandalis, a former Greek diplomat, was also stripped of his nationality.

[11]   **Government reorganization.** Premier Papadopoulos named a new cabinet Aug. 26 following a major government reorganization plan decided upon Aug. 24. The move abolished nine ministries, created four new ones, reduced the power of Stylianos Patakos and Nikolaos Makarezos (two of Papadopoulos's closest collaborators) and divided the nation into seven administrative districts under the authority of undersecretaries. Observers saw the reorganization as a further "demilitarization" of the government.

[[12]   The cabinet ministers were mainly technocrats without political affiliation. In the cabinet changes: Papadopoulos, in addition to keeping his post as premier, retained the Ministries of Defense and Foreign Affairs and would supervise a new Ministry of Government Policy, which would centralize all policy making and would replace the Ministry of the Premier and the Economic Coordination Ministry; Patakos was retained as first deputy premier but was replaced as interior minister by Adamandios Androutsopoulos, former finance minister; Makarezos was appointed second deputy premier but lost control of the abolished Economic Coordination Ministry; George Pezopoulos was appointed to head the newly created Ministry of National Economy, which replaced the Ministries of Labor, Industry, Agriculture and Commerce; Constantine Panayotakis was named to head the newly created Ministry of Civilization and Sciences. The other new ministers: Education and religion—Gerasimos Frangatos; social welfare—Antonios Bernaris; marine, transport and communications—Orestis Giakas; public order—Spyridon Velianitis; finance—Ioannis Koulis; minister assistant to the premier—Ioannis Agathanghelou; and minister without portfolio—Emmanuel Fthenakis. Two alternate ministers were also named. Fifteen secretaries-general of existing ministries—all former military officers—resigned their posts by request of the premier Aug. 24. Twenty under-secretaries were appointed Aug. 26. Patakos was authorized by a law published Sept. 4 to act as premier in the absence of Papadopoulos or in case the premier was unable to fulfill his duties. Makarezos was named second in line to the premiership.

[13] **Lady Fleming, others sentenced.** Lady Amalia Fleming, Greek-born widow of the British discoverer of penicillin, was sentenced Sept. 28 by an Athens military court to 16 months in prison for her admitted participation in an abortive attempt during August to aid in the escape of Alexandros Panaghoulis, the convicted would-be assassin of Premier Papadopoulos. Lady Fleming said she had been prepared to hide Panaghoulis, but denied taking part in the actual execution of the plan. Lady Fleming's sentence was suspended by a civil court Oct. 21 for eight months because of her ill health, but she was stripped of Greek nationality and forcibly deported to Britain Nov. 14. Also convicted in the plot were Constantine Androutsopoulos, a lawyer sentenced to 15 months in jail after he admitted in court that he had organized the August attempt and another in June; Constantine Bekakos, a prison guard who received a 13-month term for failing to report the June escape attempt; Mrs. Athena Psychoghiou, a Greek-American housewife who was sentenced to a 14-month term; and John Skelton, a U.S. theology student in Athens. The escape attempt had been thwarted Aug. 31 when military police arrested Skelton, Androutsopoulos and Mrs. Psychoghiou before dawn as they waited in a car near the military police training camp in Athens where Panaghoulis was being held. Lady Fleming was arrested a few hours later.

[14] **Press law issued.** The government promulgated a revised press law Oct. 12 imposing government restrictions on Greek and foreign journalists. The law was scheduled to go into effect Nov. 1. The revised law demanded journalistic accuracy and truthfulness, and condemned defamation and plagiarism. It also decreed punishment for newsmen who used indecorous language, led an "undignified" private life, or deviated from what was cited as "the public mission of the press." Penalties for infractions of the law would range from a reprimand and a fine to temporary or permanent expulsion from journalism. Permanent suspension was decreed for any journalist condemned twice in five years for violating the press law or who had been convicted for such offenses as disclosing military secrets or promoting or disseminating the ideas of outlawed organizations. The promulgated law was thought by observers to be stricter than the revised draft issued Aug. 18.

[15] **Security roundup.** The government announced Oct. 25 the arrest of 36 persons as members of two anti-government organizations. Among those arrested were two leaders of a dissident group of the outlawed Moscow-oriented Greek Communist party, Demetrios Partsalidis, 67, who had been premier of the Communist rebel Greek government in 1949, and Haralambos Drakopoulos, 54, secretary general of the dissident party. Both men had entered Greece on false passports in order, according to the government, "to organize the Communist underground." Arrested as members of the Communist network organization were 29 Greeks and one German woman. The security forces

claimed to have seized a clandestine printing plant as well as "the party's archives." Four other persons were arrested as members of what was described as a "branch of the Paris-based illegal terrorist organization named 'October 20 Movement.'" They were accused of planting 11 time bombs in the Athens area. In a move reported Nov. 2, the government during October arrested 10 persons allegedly linked with an anti-regime organization located in Italy.

[16] **Onassis contract canceled.** The government announced Nov. 8 that it had agreed to cancel the $600 million investment contract of shipowner Aristotle Onassis. Under the mutual agreement, Onassis relinquished his $20 million compensation claim for expenses and the government returned to Onassis his $7 million performance guarantee. Onassis also agreed to abandon arbitration proceedings in which he had claimed more than $1 billion in damages if arbitration compelled him to fulfill his contract commitments. The contract had awarded Onassis a concession to supply 64 million tons of crude oil to Greece in exchange for his construction of a giant industrial complex. A sharp increase in oil prices and freights after the signing of the contract in January 1970 led Onassis to demand a drastic revision or annulment of the agreement.

[17] **Consultative committee elected.** Sixty members of the "consultative committee on legislation" (formed in 1970 to act as an advisory body on draft legislation and as a political training ground) were elected Dec. 12 by 10,670 voters—mainly government-appointed mayors and city councilmen, as well as the principal labor, farmer, trade and professional unions. Premier Papadopoulos was to appoint 15 other members. In an effort to improve the stature of the committee, the government made the elections more direct in 1971 and doubled the committee members' tenure to two years. The electoral college was eight times larger than the one in 1970.

[18] **Martial law eased.** Premier Papadopoulos announced in his annual year-end message Dec. 18 that, beginning Jan. 1, 1972, martial law would be restricted to the area of Attica, which included Athens and Piraeus, and to Salonika and the Aegean Islands. He also announced broader duties for the consultative committee, assuring that draft bills rejected by a simple majority of the body as "not in the state's interest" would be withdrawn unless the government publicly explained why it overruled the vote. Papadopoulos also announced income tax cuts and special family allowances to spur population growth and the release, effective Dec. 20, of what he said were the remaining 69 political opponents banished to remote villages. (About 50 of the prisoners were reportedly "unrepentant" Communists, and the remainder were mainly Royalist officers who had participated in King Constantine's abortive coup in 1967.)

See also AGNEW, SPIRO THEODORE; CHURCHES [3]; CYPRUS; EUROPEAN ECONOMIC COMMUNITY [5]; FOREIGN AID; GERMANY, WEST [3]; ITALY [7]

GRENADA—*See* CARIBBEAN
GROSS NATIONAL PRODUCT (GNP)—*See* BUDGET; NOBEL PRIZES
GROUP OF 77—*See* EUROPEAN ECONOMIC COMMUNITY [5, 11]; LATIN AMERICA
GROUP OF 10—*See* INTERNATIONAL MONETARY DEVELOPMENTS [1, 14-16]
GUAM—*See* STATE & LOCAL GOVERNMENTS [5]

GUATEMALA—The undeclared civil war between rightists and leftists continued in 1971. The state of siege imposed in November 1970 was continued until Nov. 23, although the government of President Carlos Arana Jan. 30 lifted the curfew imposed with the state of siege. The World Confederation of Labor, meeting in Brussels, issued a communiqué Feb. 9 charging that "since individual and collective guarantees had been suspended in Guatemala ... the 'forces of order' had assassinated by their own hands more than 600 persons."

According to a report July 29, the International Commission of Jurists denounced what it called "the reign of terror" in the country, "where, after five years, more than 8,000 persons have been assassinated." According to the commission, more than four assassinations were committed each day by rightist terrorist groups. Guatemala, according to a report Oct. 6, expelled U.S. Episcopal Bishop William G. Frey and the Rev. Jose Marin, a Spanish Roman Catholic priest, after the two had signed a document calling for an end to the rightist-leftist conflict. The government said that the two were expelled because they violated a constitutional prohibition against foreigners becoming involved in internal politics and broke a standing law on public order "by making comments of a political nature about the government." Frey said that the document merely called for a cease-fire. He commented that "an average of 20-25 bodies are found strewn along the streets every week" and that the government was "forcing those with different opinions to resort to violence." The high level of violence in the country also prompted Oct. 9 an indefinite strike by more than 12,000 students in the University of San Carlos.

Among the incidents of terror: two members of the current congress—Mijangos Lopez, leader of the opposition coalition made up of the Democratic Revolutionary Union and the Christian Democratic party, and Jose Luis Arriaga Arriola, a member of the Revolutionary party—were killed Jan. 13 and July 6, respectively; labor leader Tereso de Jesus Oliva, head of the Confederation of Guatemalan Workers, was shot and killed Jan. 17; former provincial police chief Roberto Orellana was shot and killed by terrorists according to report March 17; Jose Manuel Aguirre Monzon, a political prisoner who had been sent to Mexico in 1970 as a ransom for the release of kidnapped U.S. embassy official Sean Holly, was shot and killed in a police raid on a suspected terrorist hideout, according to a report March 18; Victor Kaire, an important bank director was kidnaped in July and released in early August after an intense shoot-out in which three kidnapers, members of the National United Revolutionary Front, were reportedly killed by armed troops; Robert Alejos, a wealthy businessman and former presidential candidate, was kidnaped in Guatemala City Aug. 4; police announced Aug. 27 that two policemen and a student who had been searching for Alejos were assassinated on the outskirts of Guatemala City and a second student with them abducted by the killers; Rudy Huarte, second in command of the secret police, and his assistant were assassinated according to a report Sept. 14.

Inco mine agreement. International Nickel Co. of Canada (Inco) reached agreement with the Guatemalan government during the last week of February on a plan for Inco to construct a strip mine at a cost of $250 million (more than Guatemala's annual budget), it was reported March 2. The plan, designed to exploit about 60 million pounds of ore (composed of nickel oxides) per year, was contingent on Inco's ability to finance it. The final plan, which had been in the bargaining stage for 10 years, provided for Guatemalan acquisition of a 30% interest in the mine by purchasing stock from its tax receipts. In addition, a majority of Guatemalan nationals were to be trained and employed at the mine.

See also ARGENTINA [15]; DOMINICAN REPUBLIC; HIJACKING [2]; LATIN AMERICA

GUEVARA, ERNESTO "CHE"—*See* BOLIVIA [12]

GUINEA—Plotters hanged. The government hanged an unknown number of persons in various parts of the country after condemning them to death Jan. 24 for alleged complicity in the November 1970 invasion of Guinea. The number of persons hanged in the executions, carried out Jan. 25-28, could not be determined. Diplomatic sources in Washington and Conakry could confirm the deaths of only five persons, all believed to be former officials. Among those sentenced to death were three state secretaries, Ibrahima Barry (Financial Control), Ousmane Balde (Planning) and Loffo Camara (Social Affairs), two former state secretaries, Sekou Camara (Trade) and Magassouba Moriba (Defense), and Habib Tall, former director of the presidential office. Radio

Conakry declared the executions had been "a carnival" in which "people spat on those hanged and stoned their bodies."

The National Assembly Jan. 24 had condemned to death a total of 92 persons, 34 of them in absentia, and had decreed life imprisonment sentences for 72 others. Those given life sentences included Raymond-Marie Tchidimbo, the Roman Catholic archbishop of Conakry, two West Germans, three Frenchmen and 10 Lebanese. According to a report Jan. 20, Tchidimbo's sentence had resulted from his refusal to issue a pastoral letter in support of President Sekou Toure's police during the November invasion. (According to reports reaching Senegal Jan. 31, Tchidimbo had been beaten and all those given life sentences were being kept in cells too small to lie down in.) Informing the National Assembly Jan. 18 of his intention not to grant clemency, President Toure said of the accused plotters: "Slit the throats of the enemies of the people. Kill the mercenaries first and report to the authorities later. Let the people kill their enemies wherever they find them. I repeat: Slaughter all members of the fifth column, cut them into pieces and burn them."

Finance Minister Ismael Toure announced Jan. 19 that Hermann Siebold, a church leader working at a vocational training school in the country and one of the two West Germans later sentenced to life imprisonment, had committed suicide in his cell. (One hundred West Germans, including Siebold's wife, had been expelled from Guinea Jan. 4.) The West German charge d'affaires in Conakry asked government authorities Jan. 20 to hand over Siebold's body, and West German President Gustav Heinemann telephoned President Toure Jan. 21 and urged him not to allow anything "which could not be undone" to happen to Adolf Marx, director of a French brewery in Guinea and the other West German being held. Guinea announced Jan. 29 its intention to break "all diplomatic relations" with West Germany. It claimed to have established "irrefutably the existence of a subversive network armed by West German experts." A spokesman for the West German Foreign Ministry said Jan. 29 that the charges were "pure nonsense" and were made with the help of documents forged by the East German government.

In a further development in the attempt to determine local responsibility in the invasion, Bangoura Karim and Fadiala Keita, successive ambassadors to the U.S. and both arraigned under sentence of death, accused William Attwood, publisher of the U.S. newspaper Newsday and former U.S. ambassador to Guinea, of paying them to help the Central Intelligence Agency (CIA) and U.S. mining firms to gain access to bauxite and iron ore deposits in the country. The accusations were made in confessions at trials beginning July 29. Attwood and Thomas H. Wright Jr. of the Ford Foundation, also accused by Karim of making payoffs, both denied the charges.

Cabinet changes. Government personnel changes were announced Feb. 22 by Radio Conakry. The new Cabinet: Marcel Mato Bama—minister-delegate to Upper Guinea; Conde Soumany—minister-delegate to the forest region; Mamady Kaba—secretary of state for internal trade; Fode Mamadou Toure—financial control; Salifou Toure—civil service and labor; Gingiya Mamadou Beyla—budget; Kouyate Diribaka—foreign trade; Alioune Drame—planning; Mouktar Diallo—posts and telecommunications; Moricandia Savane—transport; Sidi Sissoko—secretary-general at the presidency; Sory Barry—secretary-general of the government.

See also AFRICA; SIERRA LEONE

GUN CONTROL—*See* CRIME [3, 22]

GUYANA—Cabinet changes. The January newsletter of the Guyana embassy in Washington, D.C. reported that Prime Minister Forbes Burnham Dec. 31, 1970 had made the following changes in the cabinet: Burnham was to head the newly created Public Corporations Ministry; Hubert O. Jack was to head the newly created Mines and Forests Ministry; Ptolemy A. Reid was named agriculture minister; Hugh Desmond Hoyte was appointed finance minister;

Oscar Clarke was named to take over the Home Affairs Ministry, and Vibert Mingo took over the Local Government Ministry.

Bauxite nationalization. Burnham announced Feb. 23 that the Canadian-owned Demerara Bauxite Co. would be nationalized "with reasonable compensation." Burnham introduced a bill into Parliament Feb. 26 calling for such action. Guyana July 14 agreed to pay the company $53.5 million over a period of no more than 20 years. Talks between the government and representatives of the firm, owned by Canada's Alcan Aluminum Ltd., begun in December 1970, on plans for Guyana's acquisition of a majority share in the company reportedly broke down the weekend of Feb. 20. According to Burnham, company officials indicated they were unwilling to make further investments in Guyana. Burnham explained that two unidentified European countries had indicated a desire to purchase more than half the bauxite produced by the firm.

See also CARIBBEAN

HAITI—Duvalier names son as successor. President Francois (Papa Doc) Duvalier officially named his only son, Jean-Claude, as his successor Jan. 22. The appointment of Jean-Claude, hinted Jan. 2 by his father, was overwhelmingly approved in a referendum held Jan. 31. Results of the referendum showed 2,319,916 in favor of the succession and apparently none against. The Chamber of Deputies had unanimously approved a total of 13 constitutional amendments Jan. 14 to allow Jean-Claude to become Haiti's next president. Under the amended constitution, Papa Doc was authorized to choose his successor and the age requirement for the presidency was lowered from 40 to 20. (Estimates of Jean-Claude's age ranged from 19 to 22 years.)

Duvalier dies. President Duvalier, 64, died April 21 after a long illness attributed to heart disease and diabetes. Jean-Claude was sworn in April 22 as president for life and pledged to carry on the government in the traditions of his father. Duvalier named a cabinet of 12 ministers, including four carried over from his father's government. Those expected to exert an important influence on the formation of Haitian policy were Lt. Col. Luckner Cambronne, named secretary of defense and of the interior, and Brig. Gen. Claude-Louis Raymond, chief of the army staff, whose brother Adrien was appointed foreign minister. Papa Doc's body lay in state April 23 and was buried the following day in the national cemetery in Port-au-Prince. U.S. warships displayed their presence in the waters around Haiti April 22, reportedly to gather information on "the circumstances in the area."

Armed forces developments. The semi-official newspaper, Le Nouveau Monde, reported May 14 that Astrel Benjamin, commandant of the Ton Ton Macoute, an armed unit created by the late president and based in the Les Cayes district of southern Haiti, was dismissed in a campaign to curb the power and autonomy of the organization. Minister of Interior, National Defense and Police Cambronne announced plans for a special anti-Communist armed force of 567 men, to be called the "Leopards," according to report May 27. The new unit was to be placed under the direct command of the president.

Duvalier survives political crisis. Duvalier was reported Aug. 20 to have survived a power struggle between his sister, Mrs. Marie-Denise Dominique, and her husband, Col. Max Dominique, on the one side, and Cambronne and Duvalier's mother, Mrs. Simone Duvalier, on the other. Diplomatic sources said Aug. 7 that the dispute came into the open when Mrs. Dominique resigned Aug. 5 as personal secretary to her brother. Mrs. Dominique had been influential in Haitian politics, especially in her brother's succession. She reportedly desired a rapid liberalization of the Haitian regime, a position which placed her in direct opposition to Cambronne. Sources reported that the immediate confrontation arose out of Cambronne's jailing of her husband's cousin, Gaston Daniel, on charges of passport forgery. Mrs. Dominique reportedly demanded that her brother choose between her and Cambronne. On the advice of his mother, Duvalier chose Cambronne. Brig. Gen. Raymond concurred in the decision, and Mrs. Dominique returned to Paris Aug. 12 to rejoin her husband, Haiti's ambassador to France.

One of Mrs. Dominique's projects had been an attempt to obtain substantial aid for Haiti. According to a report Aug. 20, a high-level delegation of the Inter-American Committee on the Alliance for Progress which visited Haiti in June reported that foreign aid resumptions could not yet be justified due to administrative inefficiency. However, it was reported Aug. 15 that the State Department was planning to accede to Haiti's request for U.S. technical advisers to reorganize the country's customs and postal services. The U.S. government was also reported to be ready to permit Haitian purchase of small arms and material to equip the Leopard battalion.

Guarantees for exiles. President Duvalier promised July 24 "absolute guarantees" for Haitian exiles who wished to return to form opposition parties. (He had declared an amnesty April 29 for all political exiles, excluding Communists and other "subversives.") In his July 24 announcement, the president warned that the formation of Communist or "revolutionary" parties that would attempt to undermine the government or "interrupt 14 years of nationalist effort" would not be tolerated. The "guarantees" were modified in a July 27 report when Gerard de Catalogne, minister of information and tourism, said Duvalier had put aside a general amnesty for political prisoners. It was estimated that more than 1,000 persons were imprisoned in Haitian jails for political crimes. (Catalogne, a long-time friend of Papa Doc Duvalier, was replaced as the country's minister for tourism and official spokesman for President Duvalier, according to a Sept. 3 report. Catalogne resigned after the tourist department was placed under the control of the finance ministry. He was reportedly named ambassador to Holland. He was succeeded as tourist director by former Haitian Ambassador to the U.S. Andre Theard.)

See also LATIN AMERICA

HAMPTON, FRED—*See* BLACK MILITANTS [13-14]
HARDIN, CLIFFORD M.—*See* AGRICULTURE [11-12]; HEALTH [3]; PESTICIDES
HARLAN, JOHN M.—*See* OBITUARIES; SUPREME COURT
HARLEM FIVE—*See* BLACK MILITANTS [6]
HARRIS, FRED R.—*See* POLITICS [8-9]; SUPREME COURT

HEALTH—Cholera pandemic. The cholera pandemic which began in 1961 in the Celebes Islands of Indonesia—the seventh cholera pandemic since 1817—continued in Asia and Africa during 1971 and even made an appearance in Spain. In Nigeria, health officials announced Jan. 6 that cholera had spread from Lagos to the Western State capital of Ibadan. By Feb. 20, cholera had spread through Lagos State, the Western State and the Midwest State; but the Health Ministry announced April 8 that the incidence of the disease was declining in most parts of the country. The April dispatch said that 3,000 cases had been identified since the disease was first reported and that 481 persons had died. The Kenya Ministry of Health March 8 confirmed an outbreak of cholera in the Gaole district on the Tana River. Unusually severe drought conditions in Kenya were reported March 20 to have aided the spread of the disease and to have placed an estimated 140,000 persons on famine relief. The epidemic of cholera in Chad, which had taken 400 lives in the first week of June, was reported June 8 to have broken out in two separate areas of a zone in which vaccinations were administered. The outbreak was reported July 28 to be waning after killing 2,369 persons of 7,888 stricken by cholera. The Uganda Ministry of Health confirmed June 4 that an outbreak of cholera in the northern part of the country had produced 45 cases, of which five were fatal. Indian Health Minister Uma Shankar Dixit reported to the Indian Parliament June 7 that the cholera death toll among East Pakistani refugees in India had reached 1,250 with another 9,500 East Pakistanis hospitalized. (Informed sources in Calcutta had reported June 5 that about 8,000 refugees had died of the disease. The World Health Organization [WHO] June 7 placed the death toll at 3,000.) India had appealed May 31 for international assistance to help combat the cholera outbreak and to cope with the refugee problem in general (*see* PAKISTAN [32-36]). Various governments and private charitable organizations were reported June 8 to have provided or pledged to donate aid for the refugees. An Indian health official in the Nadia district of West Bengal State said June 5 that "there is growing evidence that the cholera epidemic is raging on the other side of the border" in East Pakistan, where medical facilities were said to be virtually nonexistent. Indian border security forces June 5 sealed off the border in the Nadia district where cholera victims had been crossing into India in the previous few days. Officials in Spain announced July 26 that the WHO had pronounced the country free of a mild outbreak of cholera that had occurred in the northeastern province of Zaragoza. Seven cases had been reported in two small villages in the Jalon Valley. All had recovered. Health authorities in Portugal reported Oct. 23 that two persons had died and five were hospitalized in an outbreak of cholera in Lisbon and outlying areas. It was announced Oct. 30 that 64 cases had been identified over a 40-day period.

[2] **Virus kills 1,000 horses.** More than 1,000 horses in Texas died July 5-22 after contracting Venezuelan equine encephalomyelitis, a sleeping sickness virus spread by marsh mosquitoes. Nearly 1,500 other horses in the Southwest were affected by the disease that had swept northward into Texas from Mexico. As of July 27, the virus remained unchecked. The disease also affected humans. Texas health officials reported July 22 that more than 100 Texans had been hospitalized with its symptoms. Texas medical officials said there had been no human deaths directly attributable to the virus. According to a United Press International report July 19, Mexican health authorities said 779 persons had been taken ill by the disease.

[3] Secretary of Agriculture Clifford M. Hardin called the spread of the encephalomyelitis a "national emergency" July 16 and promised immediate federal aid and assistance to try to halt the disease. Hardin's action enabled the department to use money from other agricultural programs to fight the virus. Massive inoculation programs were under way in Texas, Oklahoma, Louisiana, Arkansas, New Mexico and Mexico as part of the drive to curb the spread of the virus. In another step, the Air Force began spraying coastal marshes along the Texas Gulf Coast, the main breeding area for the mosquito believed to be carrying the encephalomyelitis.

Smoking & Health

[4] **British doctors condemn smoking.** Great Britain's Royal College of Physicians, in a sweeping condemnation of cigarette smoking, said Jan. 5 that nearly 28,000 English men and women died prematurely each year as a result of smoking. The College, England's leading body of physicians, likened smoking to epidemic diseases and said that by the 1980s the death toll could rise to as many as 50,000 Britons. In the College's report, prepared by 13 members under the direction of Lord Rosenheim, a neurologist and the College's president, the physicians stated that the average smoker could expect to lose 5.5 years of his life compared with a non-smoker, that smokers were about twice as likely to die in middle age as non-smokers and that two smokers out of every five were likely to die before 65, compared with one out of every five non-smokers. The report said that women who smoked during pregnancy were more likely to have smaller babies and were more likely to lose their babies from miscarriages. The study was the second on smoking issued by the group. It recommended that the

government prohibit all forms of cigarette advertising, ban vending machine sales of cigarettes in public places and require the printing of warning statements on all cigarette packages. The physicians also urged the government to launch a permanent anti-smoking campaign. (Sir Keith Joseph, secretary for social services, announced March 16 that British tobacco manufacturers had voluntarily agreed to include on all cigarette packages by summer the following: "Warning by H.[er] M.[ajesty] Government: Smoking can damage your health.")

[5] Women find smoking hard to give up. U.S. doctors and psychologists overseeing a governmental study on the behavioral patterns of smokers in San Diego, Calif., and Syracuse, N.Y., said Jan. 9 that early findings showed women were less successful than men at breaking the cigarette habit. The five-year study, sponsored by the U.S. Public Health Service, still had a year to run. The researchers were at a loss to explain "a consistent phenomenon" of women's resistance to giving up cigarettes and—among those women who do give it up—a relapse rate that was 38% higher than that of men. One staffer suggested that women tended to rely far more than men on cigarettes as a means of controlling their anger and frustration. (In the previous 15 years, the number of women smoking cigarettes had nearly doubled while the number of men who smoked dropped.)

[6] Japan warned on smoking. Dr. Takeski Hirayama of Japan's National Cancer Center warned Jan. 11 that the annual death toll from lung cancer in Japan would double to more than 20,000 by 1977 unless the government took steps to discourage cigarette smoking. Hirayama, who has been investigating smoking and lung cancer since 1965, said that his work has shown that the lung cancer death rate was 30% higher among smokers than among non-smokers. (In the years between 1950 and 1969, lung cancer deaths in Japan had increased tenfold from 1,119 in 1950 to 10,130 in 1969.)

[7] German cigarette ad accord. A West German health Ministry official confirmed March 16 that the government and the country's cigarette industry had agreed on new curbs on cigarette advertising, including a "step-by-step" discontinuance of television advertising. The agreement called for a total phaseout of cigarette television advertising by the end of 1972.

[8] Tobacco firms agree to ad pact. The Tobacco Institute, Inc., a trade association representing U.S. cigarette companies, said April 15 that seven of the nation's nine cigarette companies had agreed to display a health warning in advertisements of their products. The agreement was widely viewed as a compromise measure to head off possible action by Congress or the Federal Trade Commission (FTC) to require stiff health warnings in all cigarette ads. In a letter made public March 14, Miles Kirkpatrick, chairman of the FTC, raised the possibility that the agency might soon require all cigarette ads to carry the following statement: "Warning: Cigarette smoking is dangerous to health and may cause death from cancer, coronary heart disease, chronic bronchitis, pulmonary emphysema and other diseases." Under the accord, the companies agreed to depict in all future newspaper, magazine and billboard ads their brands' packages "Legibly showing the health warning that Congress requires on the packages"—"Warning: The Surgeon General has determined that cigarette smoking is dangerous to your health." The seven firms accounted for 74% of the nation's cigarette sales. Those participating were: Brown & Williamson Tobacco Corp., Larus & Bros. Co., the Lorillard Division of Loew's Theatres, Inc., Philip Morris, Inc., The R.J. Reynolds Co., Stephano Brothers, Inc., and the United States Tobacco Co. The two non-participating companies were American Brands, Inc. and Liggett & Myers, Inc.

[9] The FTC warned Brown & Williamson, Lorillard, Philip Morris, R. J. Reynolds, American Brands and Liggett & Myers July 1 that it would take them into court unless they agreed to include "clear and conspicuous" health warnings in their ads. The FTC contended that the warnings resulting from the cigarette companies' agreement were not sufficiently clear and conspicuous.

The agency said that the lack of adequate warnings constituted a false, misleading, unfair and deceptive practice in violation of the Federal Trade Commission Act.

[10] **Canadian advertising code.** The Canadian Council of Tobacco Manufacturers, which represents the country's four major cigarette-makers, announced Sept. 1 an industry-wide agreement to voluntarily end radio and television advertising Jan. 1, 1972. The Council said it would continue to advertise in newspapers and magazines and on billboards. The new code would freeze overall advertising spending at existing levels of $25 million and would require that, after April 1, 1972, cigarette packages would be manufactured with the printed warning that "excessive cigarette smoking may be dangerous to your health." The code also required that the average tar and nicotine content of smoke should not exceed 22 milligrams of tar and 1.6 milligrams of nicotine per cigarette.

[11]   Health and Welfare Minister John Munro had introduced a bill June 10 in the House of Commons that proposed a total ban on all forms of cigarette advertising. The Jan. 1, 1972 target date originally expected by Munro had been postponed due to the legislative timetable and some opposition by the ruling Liberal party. Munro said he was "very pleased" by the industry code but indicated that it did not go far enough, especially with the continuation of newspaper advertising and the tar and nicotine ceilings.

[12] **Smoking linked to cancer recurrence.** Cigarette smokers who continued to smoke after being successfully treated for cancer faced a much greater risk of developing another malignancy than did smokers who stopped after treatment for cancer, according to a report by Dr. Condut Moore of the University of Louisville Medical School. In his study, Moore worked with 203 cigarette smokers who had been successfully treated for cancer by surgery or X-rays. Moore said that 40% who continued to smoke suffered a recurrence of cancer in their mouths, throats, voice boxes or lungs. Only 6% of those smokers who stopped developed new cancers in areas exposed to smoking.

See also ATOMIC ENERGY [1-3]; BUDGET; HEALTH CARE; HUNGER; NIXON, RICHARD MILHOUS [1]; PAKISTAN [32]; POLLUTION [3, 8, 13, 19]; STATE & LOCAL GOVERNMENTS [8]

HEALTH CARE—Broad changes proposed. President Nixon Feb. 18 submitted to Congress his proposals for "a comprehensive national health insurance program." (The proposals were designed to cover private sector workers and welfare families, and would exclude Armed Forces personnel and civilian federal employees, who "would continue to have their own insurance programs," and the elderly, who would "continue to have Medicare.") The new plan proposed passage of a National Health Insurance Standards Act and establishment of a Family Health Insurance Plan (to cover poor families not included under the proposed act). Passage of the National Health Insurance Standards Act would require all employers, beginning July 1, 1973, to provide "basic health insurance coverage for their employees." The minimum coverage of $50,000 over the life of the agreement substantially exceeded most programs in effect and would "pay for hospital services—both in the hospital and out of it—for full maternity care, well-baby care (including immunizations), laboratory services and certain other medical expenses." Chronic psychiatric or extended nursing home care would not be included. After the $50,000 coverage had been exceeded, a patient could still collect benefits of at least $2,000 yearly or, if healthy, accumulate $2,000 yearly in future credits. Premiums and deductibles would vary according to circumstances and geographical regions, and workers would be allowed to purchase membership in a Health Maintenance Organization (HMO) under the insurance plan. Under the plan, employees could be asked to contribute up to 35% of costs during the first 2.5 years of operation and up to 25% thereafter, with employers paying the remainder.

The Family Health Insurance Plan advocated by Nixon would be "fully financed and administered by the federal government" and would cover "all poor families (with children) headed by self-employed or unemployed persons whose income is below a certain level" ($5,000 for a family of four). Charges would be based on income, with no charges for the poorest families. Under the plan, which would also go into effect July 1, 1973, expanded insurance would be coupled with an increased use of prepaid HMOs. The plan would eliminate the parts of the Medicaid program designed to help most welfare families; the Medicaid provisions covering the aged, poor, the blind and the disabled would continue.

Also recommended in the plan: that each state be required to set up "special insurance pools which would offer insurance at reasonable group rates to people who did not qualify for other programs; that Medicare regulations be changed to allow beneficiaries to join HMOs and to consolidate financing of Parts A and B of Medicare, which provide for hospital and outpatient care, respectively; that the current $50 deductible under Part B be increased and that the amount that the elderly had to pay for hospital care be increased; that HMOs hold direct federal contracts as a means of overriding total or partial legal barriers against contract practice or practice by non-doctors in more than 20 states; that federally financed family health centers be created in urban or rural centers with a scarcity of medical care and linked to hospitals or HMOs for comprehensive care; that centers be established in scarcity areas for the training of doctors and other medical workers; that medical, dental and osteopathic schools be given $6,000 in federal aid annually for each student graduated; that a "National Health Service Corps" be created to serve in areas of scarce medical manpower; and that "allied health personnel training programs be expanded by 50% over 1971 levels, to $29 million, and that $15 million of this amount be devoted to training physicians' assistants."

HEW moves to curb Medicaid fraud. The Department of Health, Education and Welfare issued final regulations March 26 to prevent fraud by doctors, dentists and other dispensers of medical services under Medicaid. Under the regulations, first proposed in 1969, states would have to spot-check clients from among the 17 million participants in the $6 billion Medicaid program to determine whether reported services had actually been received. States would also have to file annual information returns with the Internal Revenue Service showing amounts paid to providers of Medicaid service, who would be identified by name, address and Social Security number. The regulations also provided for state and federal prosecution for Medicaid fraud.

Nursing home improvement sought. President Nixon announced Aug. 6 steps to improve nursing homes. A federal training program for state nursing home inspectors was to be expanded, and a program for "short-term training" of health workers slated to work in nursing homes was to be established by HEW. The department also would conduct a review of standards and practices of nursing homes.

Congress clears manpower bill. The House Nov. 9 approved by voice vote and sent to the President two health manpower training bills (approved by the Senate Oct. 19). The bills, signed by President Nixon Nov. 18, authorized $3.7 billion over three years and were designed to raise the number of practicing physicians by 30% to 436,000 in 1978 and the number of nurses by over 50% to 1,100,000. The bills provided for: construction grants for new and expanding medical, dental, veterinary, pharmacy and osteopathic schools; per capita yearly grants of $2,500-$4,000 for schools expanding their enrollment, with further incentives for allowing students to graduate in three years; grants of $1,000 to professional schools for each student training as a physicians' assistant or dental therapist; grants totaling $885 million to nursing schools; incentives to make more doctors available for family practice and for service in rural and central city areas; encouragement of increased enrollment of minority and disadvantaged students; and prohibitions against sex discrimination by recipient schools.

Child care ordered. HEW Nov. 9 ordered the 48 states in the Medicaid program to provide routine medical screening of all needy children, and to treat all hearing and eye defects and some dental problems uncovered in the tests. (Alaska and Arizona were not participants in Medicaid.) The order, which would aid about 13 million children up to age 21 by 1974, would cost $200 million, 54% in federal and 46% in state funds. Congress had mandated that the regulations be effected by July 1, 1969, but HEW Secretary Elliot Richardson said state budgetary problems had caused the two-year delay.

See also AGING; AGRICULTURE [7]; BUSINESS [8]; ECONOMY, U.S. [15, 24]; MEDICINE; POLLUTION [3]; WOMEN'S RIGHTS

HEATH, EDWARD—*See* CHURCHES [4]; EUROPEAN ECONOMIC COMMUNITY [13, 15]; MALTA; NORTHERN IRELAND [8, 10-13, 15, 17]

HEPATITIS—*See* MEDICINE
HERBERT, ANTHONY—*See* WAR CRIMES [10]
HERBICIDES—*See* CHEMICAL & BIOLOGICAL WARFARE; PESTICIDES
HEROIN—*See* DRUG USE & ADDICTION [4-5, 11-14, 16-17]

HIJACKING—U.S. Nine U.S. planes were hijacked to Cuba during 1971. In the first hijacking of the year, a National Airlines plane with 96 persons aboard a flight from Los Angeles to Miami was diverted to Havana Jan. 3. The two hijackers, their wives and four children remained in Cuba. A Northwest Airlines jet carrying 61 persons from Milwaukee to Washington was hijacked Jan. 22 by a man tentatively identified as Gerald Grant. Grant demanded to be flown to Algeria, but agreed on Cuba when he was told the Boeing 727 was incapable of flying that far. He remained in Cuba. A Delta Airlines jet flying 27 persons from Chicago to Nashville was diverted to Cuba Feb. 4 by a single hijacker. An Eastern Airlines jet with 82 persons aboard a flight from New York to San Juan, Puerto Rico, was hijacked March 31 and flown to Havana. A hijacker, identified as Ivan Gustavo Garcia Landaetta of Venezuela, diverted a Pan American Airways jet, en route from Caracas to Miami with 68 persons aboard, to Havana May 29. The passengers and crew of the plane were held four days—longer than any previous group of hijack victims. A National Airlines jet en route from Miami to Houston with 83 persons aboard was diverted to Cuba July 24. One stewardess and a passenger were wounded when the hijacker panicked and fired a gun. Ex-convict Frederick Dixon, stopped for questioning before boarding an Eastern Airlines flight at Detroit, pulled a gun and ordered the plane to fly to Havana Oct. 9. The plane, en route from Detroit to Miami and San Juan, had 46 persons aboard. An American Airlines 747 jet en route from New York to San Juan was hijacked to Cuba Oct. 25 by a single hijacker. The plane had 236 persons aboard. three armed men, who identified themselves as members of a black militant group called the Republic of New Africa and who were wanted in the slaying of a New Mexico state policeman, hijacked a Trans World Airlines plane Nov. 27 in Albuquerque, N.M. and ordered it to Cuba. The 43 passengers aboard were left behind during a fueling stop at Tampa (Fla.) International Airport the same day. The men had wanted to go to Africa, but were told the plane would not make it. (Outgoing Swiss Ambassador to Cuba Alfred Fischle said Jan. 1 that hijackers to Cuba were "sent to prison or to mental hospitals.") (*See also* [9].)
[2] In other U.S. hijackings: a U.S. Army draftee, Chappin S. Paterson, hijacked a Western Airlines jet, en route from Ontario, Calif. to Seattle with 92 passengers aboard, to Vancouver Feb. 25 to avoid military service; James Bennett, a former New York policeman, hijacked an Eastern Airlines 727 jet en route from New York to Miami May 28 and, after allowing all 128 passengers and five crewmen to leave, ordered the cockpit crew to fly him to the Bahamas, where $500,000 ransom, to be given to the Irish Republican Army, was to be waiting. Bennett was seized in the Bahamas as he stepped off the jet and was ordered by a federal court in New York to be held in $50,000 bail for a mental examination. Robert Lee Jackson surrendered to Argentine officials July 4

after hijacking a Braniff Airways Boeing 707 jet, en route from Acapulco to San Antonio, Tex. July 2. The hijacking ended in Buenos Aires when officials refused to allow the jet to refuel and be cleared to fly to Algeria. Jackson allowed 100 passengers and three stewardesses to disembark in Monterrey, Mexico, after receiving $100,000 ransom from one of the passengers. Argentina refused extradition requests from the U.S. for Jackson and sentenced him Dec. 16 to five years in prison for the hijacking. An accomplice, Lydia Sanchez of Guatemala, was sentenced to three years in jail. A middle-aged man parachuted from a Northwest Airlines 727 jet into the Washington state wilderness Nov. 25 after collecting $200,000 in ransom money—the largest amount ever delivered to a hijacker of a U.S. commercial plane—by threatening to blow up the plane with 36 passengers and a crew of six. The hijacker allowed the plane, en route from Portland, Ore. to Seattle, to land in Seattle, where he collected the ransom from the airline and permitted the passengers to deplane. The crew then flew him south. Shortly after the plane was airborne, he bailed out. It was the first time a hijacker had parachuted from a plane.

[3] **Ethiopia.** An Ethiopian Airlines DC-3 on a domestic flight from Bahar Dar to Gondar was hijacked to Banghazi, Libya, with fuel stops in Khartoum and Cairo, by four unidentified men Jan. 21. The aircraft's 16 passengers were allowed to disembark at Cairo. The hijackers were detained in Libya.

[4] **Korea.** A South Korean attempting to hijack an airliner to North Korea Jan. 23 was shot and killed by a steward. The co-pilot was fatally injured when grenades carried by the hijacker exploded. Fifteen other persons aboard were injured by the blasts. The plane, en route from Sokcho to Kangnung, was fired upon by South Korean jet fighters and shore batteries as a warning not to fly to North Korea. The aircraft crashlanded near Kansong, 20 miles south of the border. The police chief at Sokcho was dismissed and three of his men were arrested for suspected negligence in making security checks before the plane's departure.

[5] **India.** Two armed Kashmiri nationalists Jan. 30 hijacked an Indian Airlines plane en route from Srinigar to Jammu in Kashmir and forced it to fly to Lahore, Pakistan where they blew it up with hand grenades Feb. 2. The hijackers were members of the National Liberation Front in Indian-held Kashmir. All 26 passengers and four crewmen were permitted to leave the plane, but the two men refused to get off until they were guaranteed freedom from prosecution. They were granted asylum Jan. 31. The hijackers blew up the aircraft following India's rejection Feb. 1 of their demand for the release of 36 political prisoners in Kashmir. They suffered only slight injuries and surrendered to police.

[6] India accused Pakistan Feb. 3 of being directly involved in the hijacking. A note handed Pakistani High Commissioner Sajjad Hyder in New Delhi charged that his government's encouragement and support of the two nationalist Kashmiri hijackers led to the plane's destruction. In further protests to the high commissioner, India Feb. 5 demanded return of the two hijackers, who had been granted asylum in Pakistan, and—it was reported Feb. 9—requested compensation for the destroyed aircraft. New Delhi Feb. 4 had banned all Pakistani civil aircraft from flying over India as a retaliatory measure. The Pakistan High Commission building in New Delhi was a target of violent anti-Pakistani demonstrations Feb. 3-5. Police clashed with an estimated 4,000 students who attempted to storm the building Feb. 5 and 200 persons were injured. In Bombay, dock workers boycotted all Pakistani ships in a protest action.

[7] **Philippines.** A Philippines Air Lines passenger plane, en route from Manila to the southern city of Davao with 38 passengers and a crew of five, was hijacked March 30 by six armed students and forced to fly to Canton, Communist China after a refueling stop at Hong Kong. Nineteen passengers were permitted to leave the plane in Hong Kong, and the remaining passengers

and crew were released by the Chinese and flown back to Manila March 31. The six students were detained in Canton.

[8] **Bolivia.** Eleven Bolivian political prisoners, who Nov. 3 hijacked an Army plane bringing supplies to a jungle encampment where they were detained, sought asylum in Chile Nov. 7. The prisoners, who were accompanied by five mutinous guards, had first sought asylum in Peru. Peruvian authorities transferred them to the Chilean port of Arico.

[9] **Canada.** The pilot of an Air Canada jet knocked out a hijacker Nov. 13 as he prepared to bail out of the plane over Calgary, Alberta. The gunman, claiming to be a member of the Irish Republican Army, hijacked the plane with 124 persons aboard in flight over Winnipeg. He demanded $1.5 million in ransom and demanded that the jet fly to Ireland. (Air Canada officials made arrangements with local banks in Great Falls, Mont. to raise about $50,000, which was paid when the jet landed at Great Falls.) In a later development, Patrick Dolan Critton, a U.S. citizen who said he was going to Cuba because of his involvement in a December New York bank robbery, Dec. 26 hijacked an Air Canada jetliner, en route from Thunder Bay, Ont. to Toronto, to Cuba. Critton allowed the 83 passengers to deplane in Toronto while the plane was refueled. The plane and six crew members returned to Toronto from Havana Dec. 27.

[10] **Costa Rica.** Carrying a sub-machine gun, Costa Rican President Jose Figueres led more than 200 civil guards in the capture Dec. 12 of a Nicaraguan plane being hijacked to Cuba at El Coco Airport in San Jose, the capital of Costa Rica. The plane had been hijacked by three men during a flight from Managua, Nicaragua to Miami. Shooting broke out, injuring Alfonso Lobo, the son of Nicaragua's agriculture minister, and the pilot radioed the airport to land for refueling. Figueres, who had been visiting the Costa Rican interior, went to the airport and offered the hijackers safe conduct to a country of their choosing if they would free the passengers and crew. The 54 passengers were freed, but the hijackers refused to let the crew go. Under Figueres' orders, the guardsmen stormed the aircraft, freeing the crew and capturing two hijackers and killing one, Raul Arana, 20, a member of a Nicaraguan guerrilla group called "Frente Sandinista." The two surviving hijackers were returned to Nicaragua.

[11] **Rumania.** A Rumanian national airlines plane, on a domestic flight from Oradea to Bucharest, was hijacked May 27 by five men and one woman and ordered flown to Munich. At a refueling stop in Vienna, the front wheel tire burst and police equipped with machine guns surrounded the craft. The hijackers released the 16 passengers and four crewmen and surrendered. The hijackers asked for political asylum.

[12] **Measures against hijackers.** Vitautas Simokaitis was sentenced to death Jan. 14 by the Lithuanian Supreme Court for attempting to hijack a plane November 1970. However, according to a Jan. 31 report, his sentence was commuted by the Supreme Soviet of the Lithuanian Republic to 15 years in a labor camp. Simokaitis and his wife Grazina, sentenced to three years in a prison camp, had attempted to seize an Aeroflot plane Nov. 9, 1970 while it was flying between the Lithuanian towns of Vilnius and Palanga. The plane's navigator overpowered Simokaitis, reportedly armed with a gun. The pilot, a friend who had let the couple aboard without tickets, was scheduled for a separate trial.

[13] The Iranian parliament approved a bill Feb. 23 providing the death penalty for any hijacker who damaged a plane or caused the death of any passenger or crewman. The measure also provided a 3-15 year prison term for any hijacker arrested in Iran.

[14] Raffael Minichiello, a U.S. Marine corporal who had hijacked a Trans World Airlines plane at gunpoint from California to Rome in 1969, was released from prison in Rome May 1 after spending 18 months in jail. He had been convicted and sentenced to a $7\frac{1}{2}$-year prison term in November 1970. An

appeals court in April reduced the sentence to 3½ years. A presidential amnesty, which reduced prison terms for most convicts by two years, shortened Minichiello's sentence to 18 months. Minichiello had become a cause celebre in the Italian press and among a substantial portion of the population.

[15] Canada, U.S. sign hijack pact. The U.S. and Canada signed an extradition treaty in Washington Dec. 3 covering hijackers of aircraft and assailants of diplomats for the first time. The treaty would not apply to draft dodgers or military deserters. The treaty denied hijackers and those committing crimes against foreign diplomats the privilege of claiming that their acts were political in character. The pact, which listed 30 extraditable offenses, carried the usual provision that a person could not be extradited for a political offense. The treaty placed emphasis on conspiracy to commit an extraditable offense, which would make possible the extradition of persons who conspired to commit a crime as well as those who did commit crimes.

[16] Canada was the first country to accept the U.S. argument that hijacking should be exempted from the political protection clauses found in standard extradition treaties. Draft evaders and deserters could be extradited only if they had hijacked aircraft to flee, or in specific cases, if they were guilty of common criminal offenses. If extradited, they could be tried only for these offenses, but not for draft evasion or desertion. The treaty replaced an existing 82-year old convention and would come into force when Canada and the U.S. exchanged ratifications by their respective legislatures.

See also ARGENTINA [10]; AVIATION [8]; CHINA, COMMUNIST; COLOMBIA; CRIME [6]; UNION OF SOVIET SOCIALIST REPUBLICS [9-12]

HILLIARD, DAVID—*See* BLACK MILITANTS [8, 10]
HIT & RUN—*See* AUTOMOBILES [14]
HO CHI MINH—*See* PENTAGON PAPERS [16, 18]
HO CHI MINH TRAIL—*See* INDOCHINA WAR [1, 18-20, 22-27, 35, 43, 49]

HOCKEY—West wins All-Star game. The National Hockey League's (NHL) West Division All-Stars scored two opening period goals and went on to top the East's All-Stars Jan. 19, 2-1, in Boston. The West was paced by Chicago's Bobby Hull and Chico Maki who swatted home the team's scores. The East's Yvan Cournoyer of Montreal scored in the first period. The West was coached by Scotty Bowman of St. Louis. Harry Sinden, who coached the Boston Bruins to a Stanley Cup triumph in 1970 and then quit hockey, returned for one night to coach the East.

Canadiens win Stanley Cup. Behind the spectacular goaltending of Ken Dryden, the Montreal Canadiens rallied to defeat the Chicago Black Hawks, 3-2, May 18 and win the seventh and deciding game of the NHL's Stanley Cup playoff in Chicago. It was the Canadien's 16th Stanley Cup triumph since the formation of the NHL in 1917 and their 11th in the last 19 years. Montreal was coached by Al MacNeil. Chicago was coached by Billy Reay.

Detroit shuffles front office. The Detroit Red Wings reshuffled their front office Jan. 6-8 as players and club officials expressed bitterness over coaching methods, training rules and executive decisions. Sid Abel, Wing's general manager for eight years, quit Jan. 6 after the club's owner refused to back his decision to fire coach Ned Harkness, who had come under fire from Abel after players complained of the coach's training methods. Harkness was named to replace Abel as general manager Jan. 8 and relinquished his coaching position. Doug Barkley, a former NHL player, was named to replace Harkness as coach.

Canadiens change coaches. The Canadiens announced June 10 that coach Al MacNeil had resigned and that Scotty Bowman had been signed to replace him. MacNeil was appointed by the Montreal front office as coach and general manager of the Nova Scotia Voyageurs in the American Hockey League. He stepped down as Montreal coach after being publicly criticized by his players. Bowman was signed by Montreal nearly a month after he resigned as coach and general manager of the St. Louis Blues. (He had returned to coaching the

Blues Feb. 2, replacing Al Arbour, who returned as a player. Bowman had resigned as coach of the Blues in June 1969 to devote full time to his role as club manager.)

New league organized. A new professional hockey league, to be known as the World Hockey Association (WHA), was organized Sept. 13. Fourteen groups made bids for teams. The WHA, which said it hoped to begin play by October 1972, awarded 11 franchises: Chicago, New York, Los Angeles, Miami, Milwaukee, San Francisco, Dayton (Ohio) and St. Paul (Minn.) in the U.S. and Winnipeg, Calgary, Alberta and Edmonton in Canada. (Each group accepted had to post $100,000 bond and show a bank account with a minimum of $2 million.)

NHL to add 2 new clubs. The NHL announced Nov. 9 that it had awarded new franchises to Atlanta and Long Island, with the teams scheduled to begin play in the 1972-73 season. (The board of governors also announced Nov. 11 that it would add two teams for the 1974-75 season.) Entrance for each club was set at $6 million. Additionally, the Long Island franchise owners were to pay extra compensation to the New York Rangers to offset the potential losses to the Rangers from a new team in the New York area. The entrance of a Long Island team would give the NHL two clubs in the same area for the first time since 1942.

HODGSON, JAMES D.—*See* LABOR [10]; UNEMPLOYMENT; WOMEN'S RIGHTS
HOFFA, JAMES R.—*See* LABOR [4-5]
HOFFMAN, ABBIE—*See* DRAFT & WAR PROTEST [13]

HONDURAS—Cruz elected president. Ramon Ernesto Cruz and his National party won a narrow but decisive victory over Jorge Bueso Arias and his Liberal party in presidential elections March 28. Cruz, 68, the first president freely elected in Honduras since 1949, received about 258,000 votes. Bueso Arias received 242,900 votes. Almost 45% of the 900,000 eligible voters abstained. Rumors that the army would prevent the election, as it had done in 1963, proved unfounded.

President-elect Cruz said March 29 that he would work for solution of the nation's border problems with El Salvador, but added that he hoped the Organization of American States (OAS) observer force would continue to patrol the border. Cruz, a lawyer, diplomat and teacher known to most Hondurans as Monchito, generally took a hard line position on Honduras' virtual withdrawal from the Central American Common Market (CACM). Cruz had blamed Bueso Arias, who as economy minister in a previous administration, had helped draft the terms of Honduras entry into the CACM, for allowing Honduras to join under unfavorable terms. The president-elect told reporters March 29: "We would like to take Honduras back into the Central American Common Market, but we have to develop our economy first."

Cruz took office June 6 for a six-year term. Cruz headed a bipartisan coalition of both Nationalists and Liberals under a national unity plan adopted by Cruz and Bueso in January. The outgoing president, Osvaldo Lopez Arellano, retained the key post of chief of the armed forces and was expected to wield considerable power in the government. The new cabinet, as reported June 8: interior & justice—Ricardo Zuniga Agustinas; foreign affairs—Andres Alvarado Puerto; economy—Ruben Mondragon; national defense—Col. Raul Galo Soto; education—Tula Bogran de Guel; public safety & social welfare—Dr. Gilberto Osorio Contreras; finance—Elio Ynestroza; communications—Roberto Cantro; public works—Jorge Valle; labor—Gautama Buda Fonseca; natural resources—Edgardo Sevilla Idiaquez; minister attache to the president—Guillermo Lopez Rodezno.

See also EL SALVADOR-HONDURAS CONFLICT

HONECKER, ERICH—*See* GERMAN CONSULTATIONS; GERMANY, EAST
HONG KONG—*See* CHINA, COMMUNIST; ESPIONAGE; HIJACKING [7];
STORMS; TARIFFS & WORLD TRADE [3, 5]
HOOVER, J. EDGAR—*See* FEDERAL BUREAU OF INVESTIGATION [3, 7-8];
SECURITY, U.S.; YOUTH

HORSE RACING—Canonero II wins Derby, Preakness. Canonero II, with
Gustavo Avila riding, became the fourth field horse (nonfavorite in a large
field) in history to win the Kentucky Derby, outrunning 19 other colts May 1 at
the 97th running of the Derby at Churchill Downs in Louisville. (The Derby
favorite, Hoist the Flag, had broken a leg March 31 during a workout.)
Canonero II's triumph also marked the first time a foreign thoroughbred had
won the Derby. He had been bred in Kentucky but had spent most of his racing
career in Venezuela. Again ridden by Avila, he won the second jewel in racing's
triple crown (Derby, Preakness, Belmont Stakes) May 15 with a victory in the
Preakness Stakes in Baltimore. He set a record in the process as he covered the
one and three-sixteenths-mile track in 1:54—three-fifths of a second faster than
the old track mark.
   Belmont. Canonero II lost his chance at the triple crown June 5 in New
York, as unheralded Pass Catcher won the 1.5 mile Belmont Stakes. Pass
Catcher went off as a 34-1 longshot with Canonero II the 3-5 favorite.
Canonero II finished fourth.
   Off-track betting in New York. New York City April 7 opened the
country's first legalized off-track betting system (OTB) that enables
horseplayers to bet on their choices at city-operated betting windows at two
sites away from the track. OTB, designed to raise revenue for New York City,
went into operation after months of labor disputes, contractual arguments with
racetrack officials and failure to install by opening day a computerized
wagering operation. OTB encountered difficulties at both sites with the manual
ticket-selling procedure and the number of horseplayers seeking to place bets.
Until the early wrinkles were straightened out, OTB limited the wagering to
the trotters at Roosevelt Raceway. Under the OTB operation, off-track
wagerers were taxed at the same 17% as those who bet at the tracks. The split
of the take, however, was different. With OTB, .5% off the top of the take
went to the state, 1% to the track and the remaining 15.5% to OTB. After
OTB met its expenses, 80% of the net revenue went to the city and 20% to the
state. The OTB system hoped ultimately to have 200 betting windows in
operation throughout the city.
   See also CRIME [13]

HOUSING—Mortgage aid suspended. George Romney, Secretary of the
Department of Housing and Urban Development (HUD), said Jan. 14 that the
federal government was suspending a major home ownership program
(authorized under Section 235 of the 1968 Omnibus Housing Act) for lower
income families. The House Banking and Currency Committee Jan. 5 had
released a report on the program denouncing the Federal Housing
Administration (FHA) for allowing speculation and "sheer fraud" under
Section 235. Romney had described the report as "inaccurate" and
"misleading," but said Jan. 14 that "it is apparent that abuses ... are more
prevalent and widespread than had previously been evident." He denied Jan. 14
that the program was a scandal, but said he would suspend the part of the
program dealing with existing housing until he was assured that the condition
of the houses to be purchased would be adequately inspected and until steps
could be taken to eliminate "incompetence, impropriety or fraudulent practices
that might have existed." The suspension did not affect the buying of new
homes with mortgage subsidies supplied under the program, but Romney said
he was studying possible improvements in the new home program. Romney
cited defects in the law and in administration of the program as underlying
problems. He said many families who were aided by the program lacked home

ownership experience, and he blamed Congress for failing to provide funds to give counseling services.

Romney announced Feb. 5 that the program was being resumed in 21 selected areas throughout the country. The suspension remained in effect for the rest of the country. The 21 regional HUD and FHA offices which would resume issuance of mortgage commitments served: Maine, Rhode Island, New Mexico, Iowa, Nebraska, Montana, North and South Dakota, Utah, Wyoming, Idaho, Puerto Rico, parts of New York (Albany, Hempstead and New York City), parts of Texas (Houston and Lubbock), Tampa (Fla.), Memphis (Tenn.), Shreveport (La.) and Tulsa (Okla.). HUD announced April 2 that seven more HUD-FHA offices would resume operation of the program. The seven offices served Maryland, Delaware, Nevada, Hawaii, parts of California (Sacramento and Santa Ana) and Pittsburgh (Pa.). In reporting to the House Banking and Currency Committee March 31, Romney reported that a HUD examination of the program had led to the referral to the Federal Bureau of Investigation (FBI) of 86 cases for possible statute violations and false certifications. He said that nine FHA appraisers were under FBI investigation and that five had been given administrative punishment.

Funds to New York, Newark frozen. HUD announced Feb. 11 an immediate "embargo" of federal contributions to New York City's slum clearance programs because of what the department said was the city's failure to provide "decent, safe and sanitary" housing for persons displaced by urban renewal. The department announced April 15 that $400,000 in aid due the Newark Housing Authority (fourth largest housing authority in the U.S.) would be withheld because the agency had refused to reorganize itself as ordered in January. HUD said that the aid would be withheld until the agency agreed to separate the functions of administering public housing and urban renewal.

Housing abandonment studied. The National Urban League and the Center for Community Change, in a survey reported April 21, warned that the abandonment of housing by landlords in inner-city ghetto neighborhoods threatened to create "ghost towns." The report said a massive commitment by all levels of the government was needed to fight the problem. The study found St. Louis—with two neighborhoods where 16% of all housing was abandoned— had the highest level of abandonment of the cities studied. Cleveland was also found to have a high level of abandonment. The least abandonment was found in Detroit and Atlanta. (Economic integration of the neighborhoods, substantial home ownership and the availability of mortgages were cited as factors in the low level of abandonment in those two cities.) Chicago, Hoboken (N.J.) and New York were also included in the survey.

Housing project veto sustained. The Supreme Court April 26 upheld the constitutionality of state referendum laws that allowed a majority of voters in any state, city or county to block low-rent public housing in their community. By a 5-3 vote, the court sustained California's referendum law, on the books since 1950, which required public approval of the low-rent projects before they could be built. California voters had used the law to block construction of almost half the low-rent housing proposed for the state since its passage. The law was challenged in a suit brought by 41 welfare families in San Jose after the city's voters reversed a decision by the city council in 1968 to build 1,000 low-rent apartments. A three-judge federal district court in San Francisco struck down the law as violative of the 14th Amendment because it discriminated against the poor. In the Supreme Court majority opinion, Justice Hugo L. Black said that the 14th Amendment's principal thrust was to outlaw legal distinctions based on race and that there was no evidence that the California law was prejudicial against any racial minority. The court had also been asked in a host of friend-of-court briefs (including briefs by the National Urban Coalition, the National Association of Home Builders, the American Institute of Architects and the Justice Department) to strike down the law on the ground that it frustrated efforts to erect low-rent public housing for the poor.

HUD acts to disperse housing. HUD Sept. 29 announced proposed guidelines that would disperse subsidized housing in metropolitan areas and prevent its concentration in inner-city ghettos. According to Secretary Romney, the guidelines were designed "to pursue the Administration policy of not contributing to minority concentration of housing and to obey the orders of federal courts which have ruled on these questions." The guidelines would give priority to projects that avoided concentration of minorities and that provided housing for low-income families in areas where services and jobs were available. The proposal allowed exceptions if the project was to be located in an area of minority concentration but "was necessary to meet overriding housing needs which cannot otherwise feasibly be met in that housing market area." Projects could also be built in areas where the prospective residents had "strong cultural, social or economic ties."

HUD ruled guilty of bias. The U.S. Court of Appeals for the 7th Circuit Sept. 10 judged HUD and Secretary Romney to be guilty of racial discrimination in funding construction of segregated public housing in Chicago between 1950 and 1969. The three-judge panel, overturning a 1970 decision by U.S. District Court Judge Richard B. Austin that his 1969 injunction against segregated site selection and discriminatory tenant assignment by the Chicago Housing Authority had provided adequate relief, said that HUD and Romney had violated the rights of the plaintiffs (represented by the American Civil Liberties Union) by not insisting on dispersal of public housing projects in all parts of the city, including white neighborhoods. Attorney Alexander Polikoff, who argued the case for the ACLU, said the decision would work against President Nixon's December 1970 statement that his Administration would avoid using federal funds to force racial or economic integration in the suburbs. The appeals court, however, refused to order HUD to deny financial aid to suburbs which exclude public housing, instead leaving the remedy to the discretion of Judge Austin.

Romney OKs NYC project. Secretary Romney Nov. 22 gave final approval to plans to build a federally subsidized low-income housing project in a white middle-class section of New York City. He had promised an "immediate and thorough review" of the project Nov. 16, one day after HUD had issued final approval of construction contracts and three years after the department had authorized acquisition of the site in Forest Hills. Construction began as scheduled Nov. 22, but opponents vowed to block the project through "legal avenues." Sen. James L. Buckley (R-Conservative, N.Y.) had requested a review of the project Nov. 16 after widespread community opposition developed. Critics cited cost overruns and inadequate school facilities for the expected 840 families. Residents of the neighborhood, expressing fears of increased crime and demanding "community control," repeatedly demonstrated at the construction site, amid charges of racism by the project's supporters. A state supreme court judge issued an injunction Nov. 19 barring interference with construction, after protesters broke windows and threw torches at the site the previous night.

See also AGING; AGRICULTURE [7-9]; BUDGET; CIVIL RIGHTS [1, 15, 25-29]; ECONOMY, U.S. [16, 24]; INDIANS, AMERICAN; NEGROES; STATE & LOCAL GOVERNMENTS [4]

HUGHES HAROLD E.—*See* POLITICS [8-9]
HUMPHREY, HUBERT H.—*See* POLITICS [8]

HUNGARY—1970 economic results. The Central Statistical Board announced the results of the 1970 economic development plan Feb. 6. Measured as increases over the figures for 1969, the following major items were reported: national income 5%, exports 11%, imports 30% (attributed to a fall in meat production), wages 7%, investments in the Socialist sector 14%-15%, industrial production 8%, building materials 6%, coal 5%, mineral oil 11%, natural gas 7%, crude steel 3% and cement 8%. The following decreases in production were reported: sugar beets 34%, vegetable and potato crops 5%-10% and wine and fruit 20%.

General elections. In elections to the Hungarian parliament April 25, eight incumbents were unseated and two deputies forced into runoffs. A total of 49 of 352 National Assembly seats and 3,016 of 70,000 local council seats were contested by candidates supporting the Communist party program. Government and party leaders ran unopposed. Approximately 98% of the electorate cast ballots. The elections had been set Feb. 19 by the Presidential Council. Under amendments to the election laws approved in 1970, any candidate receiving 30% of the vote at nomination meetings in streets or factories was entitled to a place on the ballot.

Government changes. A session of the National Assembly May 12 approved changes in government personnel. Antal Apro was named president of the National Assembly, replacing Gyula Kallai. Peter Valyi became a deputy premier and was succeeded as minister of finance by Lajos Faluvegi, formerly deputy minister. Mrs. Janos Keserue moved from minister of internal trade to minister of light industry, taking over from Jozsef Nagy. Istvan Szurdi became minister of internal trade. Ferenc Levardi was replaced as minister of heavy industry by Gyula Szeker.

See also DISARMAMENT; DRUG USE & ADDICTION [9]; ROMAN CATHOLIC CHURCH [8]; SPACE [24]

HUNGER—Senators hear plight of migrants. In testimony before the Senate Select Committee on Nutrition Feb. 23, Colorado pediatrician Dr. H. Peter Chase said malnutrition among the children of migrant workers was 10 times greater than among the nation's children generally. Dr. Chase, of the University of Colorado medical center, was conducting his third study of Mexican-American migrant children in Texas and Colorado. He reported instances of severe malnutrition and disease among the children he examined. He said that, while extreme cases were rare, malnutrition serious enough to stunt growth and endanger mental development "definitely exists in this [migrant] population and must be corrected."

Inaction on hunger charged. Seventy-nine panel chairmen and vice chairmen of the 1969 White House Conference on Food, Nutrition and Health, at a one-day followup meeting in Williamsburg, Va. Feb. 5, said that, despite "very real progress" in the fight against hunger in the U.S., the Nixon Administration's response to the conference's recommendations had been inadequate. Mrs. Patricia Young, who had chaired the Women's Task Force at the 1969 conference, said: "I assumed this job with the understanding that our real work would begin after the first conference ended—to press for public, private and governmental action against hunger. But we've had almost no support at all for this from the Administration." She said the delegates had "to put pressure on the White House even to have the followup meeting."

Hunger session held. Witnesses from 12 states testified at a public meeting in Washington Feb. 16 staged to call attention to hunger in the U.S. by the Citizens Board of Inquiry into Hunger and Malnutrition. Leslie W. Dunbar, executive director of the Field Foundation and chairman of the meeting, said testimony from the 100 participants demonstrated "a pattern of official lawlessness, at that point where government most comes into contact with poor people." Many of the witnesses recounted incidents of official callousness and bureaucratic bottlenecks confronting persons seeking relief.

Wider school lunch aid passed. The House, by a 353-0 vote Oct. 18, and the Senate, by unanimous voice vote Oct. 20, passed and sent to the President a school lunch aid bill prohibiting Administration cutbacks in the number of eligible children and increasing the federal per-meal subsidy to a minimum (rather than an average) of 46¢ for each needy child. The bill also would restrain the Agriculture Department from restricting the growing school breakfast program, designed for severe poverty areas. (The department had reported Oct. 13 that it had ordered states not to add to the 952,000 children who received breakfast aid in 1970.)

The Agriculture Department Oct. 18 revoked an Oct. 6 order which had ended subsidies for lunch aid to children of families above the official poverty line. The order would have eliminated between 584,000 and 1.5 million children in states with eligibility limits above the federal poverty guideline of $3,940 for a family of four. The cutback had been designed to compensate for a per-meal subsidy rise to 45¢ from the previously issued figure of 35¢. (1970-71 payments had averaged 42¢ for each of the 7.3 million children receiving free or reduced-price meals.) Congress had reacted to the Oct. 6 move as an attempt to circumvent the intent of the 1970 law funding the program. In an Oct. 15 letter to President Nixon, 59 Senators of both parties asked him to overrule the department's order. Two days later a White House spokesman reported that Nixon had ordered the department to "clarify its regulations."

See also CHURCHES [14]; MEDICINE; POVERTY; WOMEN'S RIGHTS

I

ICELAND—Leftist government installed. A leftist coalition government headed by Olafur Johannesson, 58, leader of the agrarian Progressive party, was sworn in July 14. It replaced the coalition of Premier Johann Hafstein's conservative Independence party and the Social Democrats, which lost its majority in elections June 13 and resigned June 14. The new coalition— controlling 32 of the 60 parliamentary seats—was formed by three members of the Progressive party, two members of the Liberal Left (a leftist splinter group), and two members of the Communist-led Labor Alliance. The new Cabinet: Premier, minister of justice and ecclesiastical affairs—Johannesson; foreign—Einer Agustsson; finance and agriculture—Halldor Sigurdsson; transportation and social affairs—Hannibal Valdimarsson; education— Magnus Torfi Olafsson; industry and health—Magnus Kjartansson; fisheries and commerce—Ludvik Josefsson.

See also EUROPEAN ECONOMIC COMMUNITY [10]; RACIAL & MINORITY UNREST [17]; SCANDINAVIA; TARIFFS & WORLD TRADE [2]

ILLEGITIMACY—See POPULATION
IMMIGRATION—See NIXON, RICHARD MILHOUS [8]

INDIA—New Congress party wins victory. Prime Minister Indira Gandhi's ruling New Congress party won a landslide victory in national elections held March 1-10 for the Lok Sabha, India's lower house of parliament. New Congress gained 350 of parliament's 521 seats, two more than a two-thirds majority. The principal four-party opposition received only 49 seats. They were the Old Congress party, the conservative faction that had broken away from the original Congress party in 1969; Swatantra, a right-wing free-enterprise party; Jan Sangh, a militant Hindu party; and the Samyukta Socialist party. The remaining seats went to other parties and independents sympathetic to Mrs. Gandhi's policies.

Mrs. Gandhi was re-elected leader of the New Congress party March 17 and President V.V. Giri asked her to form a new cabinet. Her previous cabinet had resigned earlier in the day in accord with the constitution. A new 36-member cabinet was sworn in March 18 by Mrs. Gandhi. It included 13 ministers, 15 ministers of state and eight deputy ministers. The cabinet was smaller than the previous one, which had 53 members. Mrs. Gandhi retained four senior ministers, who, with her, formed the "inner cabinet." They were Defense Minister Jagjivan Ram, who had resigned as president of the New Congress party, Finance Minister Y. B. Chavan, Foreign Minister Swaran

225

Singh and Food Minister Fakhruddin Ali Ahmed. Five new ministers, all elected in the March 1-10 parliamentary balloting, were Mohan Kumaramangalam, Siddarth Shankar Ray, Moinul Huq Chaudhuri, Raj Bahadur and H. R. Gokhale. Seven former cabinet ministers were dropped. They were Education Minister V. K. Rao, Industries Minister Dinesh Singh, Petroleum and Chemicals Minister Triguna Sen, Railway Minister Gulzarilal Nanda, Steel Minister B. R. Bhagot, Parliamentary Affairs Minister Kotha Raghuramiah and Labor Minister Damodaram Sanjivayya.

The elections had been preceded by a wave of violence and unrest. The Kashmiri government Jan. 8 arrested more than 500 workers of the Plebiscite Front (PF) on the ground that the PF had planned to use the elections as a "cover for subversion and for pro-Pakistani secessionist activities." (The front had planned to contest the elections.) The Kashmiri government Jan. 9 also barred Moslem leader Sheik Mohammed Abdullah and two of his aides from returning to Kashmir after a week's visit in New Delhi. The three were members of the PF, which sought self-determination for Indian-controlled Kashmir. Eight persons were killed in West Bengal state Feb. 22 at the start of a 24-hour general strike called by all political parties to protest the Feb. 20 slaying in Calcutta of Hemanta Kumar Bose, a candidate for the state legislature. Violence again erupted in West Bengal March 1-7, with at least 40 persons slain in disturbances. Bejoyyananda Chattopadhyay, vice president of the state's Old Congress party, was found stabbed to death in Calcutta March 5. Twenty-five persons were injured Feb. 22 in the Hindu holy city of Allahabad in battles between Hindus and Moslems following a clash between two rival candidates. In Punjab state, three leaders of the extreme left-wing Naxalite movement were killed in a clash with police Feb. 20.

Council of Ministers formed. Prime Minister Gandhi May 2 formed a new Council of Ministers comprised of 18 cabinet or subcabinet members. Mrs. Gandhi also appointed Umashankar Dixit as works and housing minister with full cabinet rank.

20-year friendship treaty signed. India and the Soviet Union signed a 20-year friendship treaty Aug. 9. The pact was initialed in New Delhi by Soviet Foreign Minister Andrei A. Gromyko and Indian Foreign Minister Singh. The treaty, ratified by India Aug. 11 and by the Soviet Union Aug. 13, was seen as aimed at strengthening India's hand in its current dispute with Pakistan resulting from the civil war in East Pakistan. The accord committed India and the Soviet Union to noninterference in each other's internal affairs, to nonaggression against each other, to efforts "to strengthen peace in Asia and throughout the world" and to widening Soviet-Indian contacts and cooperation. A key clause said both sides would "abstain from providing assistance to any third party that engages in armed conflict with the other party. In the event of either party's being subject to such an attack or a threat thereof," mutual talks would be held to remove the threat and insure future peace and security of the two countries.

Indian embassy officials in Moscow disclosed Aug. 13 that the treaty had been negotiated in 1969 but its signing had been delayed at Prime Minister Gandhi's request because she feared it would arouse domestic opposition. The embassy officials said the decision to put the treaty into effect had been taken in the previous two weeks when India feared a Pakistani attack supported by China.

China charges intrusion. Communist China Dec. 16 and Dec. 27 protested to New Delhi against incursions into China's Tibet Province. The Dec. 16 protest said that seven Indian soldiers had crossed into the province from the Indian protectorate of Sikkim Dec. 10 to carry out reconnaissance. The Indian Foreign Ministry Dec. 16 called the charge "totally without foundation." The Dec. 27 statement said that eight Indian soldiers had crossed into Tibet from Sikkim Dec. 15 and carried out reconnaissance "for as long as half an hour." The statement also contended that Indian planes that day had flown over the

Chayul area of Tibet, penetrating 13 miles north of the line on which Chinese and Indian troops established themselves after their 1959 border disputes.

See also CEYLON; FLOODS; FRANCE [17]; GREAT BRITAIN [18]; HEALTH [1]; HIJACKING [5-6]; INTERNATIONAL BANK FOR RECONSTRUCTION & DEVELOPMENT; PAKISTAN [1, 5, 7-10, 12-21, 23, 30-38, 40-43]; PENTAGON PAPERS [19]

INDIANS, AMERICAN—Misuse of school funds charged. The NAACP (National Association for the Advancement of Colored People) Legal Defense and Educational Fund Inc. charged Jan. 12 that federal funds appropriated for the education of Indian children were being used for "every conceivable school need except" aiding the 177,000 Indian children in public schools. The charges were based on a 10-month study (of 60 school districts in eight states) investigating the use of $66 million in annual federal aid appropriated for Indian public school students through the 1934 Johnson-O'Malley Act, the impact aid program and Title I of the Elementary and Secondary Education Act, providing extra funds for poor children. The NAACP group said that local officials used the funds for "fancy equipment" for white schools and to reduce the taxes of white property owners. The group threatened court action if the abuses were not corrected and demanded the resignation of two officials in the Bureau of Indian Affairs (BIA) who administered funds under the Johnson-O'Malley Act, charging that federal officials allowed misuse of funds with full knowledge.

Army base given to Indians. The federal government Jan. 14 granted custody of an old Davis, Calif. Army base to Indians who had occupied the 640-acre site in November 1970. Jack Forbes, a Powhatan Indian, said a university for Indians and Mexican-Americans would be developed on the site. In other developments resulting from what Indians claimed was a treaty privilege giving them unused federal lands: 35 U.S. marshals June 11 removed 15 Indians from Alcatraz Island in the San Francisco Bay, ending a 19-month occupation of the former prison island. The Indians had been negotiating with the government on plans to convert the island to an Indian cultural center. Indian leader John Trudell said June 11 that the government had broken its promise to take no action while negotiating with the Indians. Trudell and a group of 50 Indians took over an abandoned Nike missile site near Richmond, Calif. June 14, but were removed by some 100 law enforcement officials early June 17.

About 100 Indians who had occupied several buildings at a former Nike site near Chicago June 14 were removed July 1 by 150 policemen armed with rifles and tear gas. The Indians had occupied the buildings in protest against the lack of housing available in Chicago. About 75 Indians, reportedly the same group, peacefully occupied buildings of an abandoned Nike site in Hinsdale, a Chicago suburb, July 30. Twenty Indians, demanding that the government honor an 1868 Sioux treaty that declared all land in South Dakota west of the Missouri River belonged to the Indians, were arrested June 6 about 12 hours after a group of 40 set up camp on the top of the Mount Rushmore National Memorial. Those arrested were charged with climbing the monument—a misdemeanor. Federal marshals and Hennepin County, Minn. sheriff's officers evicted about 35 Indians from a building at the Twin Cities Naval Air Station May 21 and jailed 25 on charges of trespassing on federal property. The naval base had been closed as a permanent station in 1969 but was still used for weekend duty by the Naval Reserve. Twenty-five members of the American Indian Movement (AIM) took control of an abandoned Coast Guard lifeboat station in Milwaukee Aug. 14 to protest insufficient housing, employment and education opportunities for urban Indians. They said they would stay at the station until Coast Guard officials agreed to turn it over to them.

OEO announces urban Indian centers. Frank Carlucci, director of the Office of Economic Opportunity (OEO), said May 26 that the government would provide $880,000 in grants to set up a Model Urban Indian Center program, to be administered by OEO and funded by OEO and the departments of Labor, Housing and Urban Development, and Health, Education and Welfare. A network of Indian centers would be established in Los Angeles, Minneapolis, Gallup (N.M.) and Fairbanks (Alas.), and there would be a coordinating office in New York. Carlucci said the centers would serve as models to improve services in some 40 existing urban service centers for Indians.

BIA-Indian conflicts. Indian spokesmen clashed with the BIA over personnel changes during July-September. Interior Secretary Rogers C.B. Morton July 23 issued an order (reported Aug. 15) reviving the post of deputy commissioner of Indian affairs and transferring most of the administrative duties and responsibilities of BIA Commissioner Louis R. Bruce to the position. John D. Crow, a BIA career employee viewed as a traditional bureaucrat by Indians, was appointed to the position. Morton said Aug. 15 that the change had been made to "upgrade the entire secretariat" of the bureau and to free Bruce for "creative" efforts among the Indians. The order was amended Aug. 17 to restore powers to Bruce. The controversy came to the attention of the press over an alleged ultimatum given to William V. Veeder, a BIA water rights expert, to transfer from Washington to Phoenix, Ariz. Veeder formally rejected the transfer Sept. 9 and was notified Sept. 17 that it was suspended pending hearings. Indian activists held Crow responsible for the Veeder transfer order and charged that it, and other personnel changes, were Interior Department attempts to silence staff members who were champions of Indian rights. The National Congress of American Indians and 10 other Indian organizations wrote President Nixon Aug. 28 asking for reconsideration of the Veeder transfer and complaining about the appointment of Crow and of Wilma Victor as Morton's assistant for Indian affairs. The National Tribal Chairmen's Association Sept. 21 asked for the transfer of the BIA to a "receivership under the Executive Office of the President" in order to keep BIA reforms from being "subverted" by Interior Department bureaucrats.

Morton pledges reforms. Secretary Morton pledged Oct. 4 to implement a series of reform programs to meet Indian criticism of the BIA. He called for a new Indian water rights office, with a $2 million first-year budget, to protect reservations against competing federal and commercial water resource demands. The office would prepare suits for prosecution by the Justice Department. He promised to fight for BIA budget requests for an expanded road building plan for economically isolated communities. The bureau's program of contracting with Indian tribes for services in schools and housing would be encouraged by a full-time training program. Morton also said that he planned to create a 15-man advisory board, including representatives of national Indian organizations, to insure better communications between the bureau, his own office and the community.

Alaska land bill signed. President Nixon Dec. 18 signed an Alaska native land settlement bill, after the Alaska Federation of Natives voted its approval 511-56. Congress passed the measure Dec. 14, the House 307-60, the Senate by voice vote. Signing of the bill lifted the freeze on Alaska state land acquisition set during the previous Administration. The bill granted a total of $962.5 million ($462.5 million of that amount over 11 years from the federal government and the remainder from state mineral revenues at a rate of 2% a year). Forty million acres of land and mineral rights were to be selected by the natives, mostly surrounding their villages. The land and money would be administered by 12 regional native corporations. The secretary of the interior was authorized to designate 80 million acres for potential recreation and conservation use, subject to Congressional approval within five years, and to set aside an 800-mile corridor should he approve a proposed oil pipeline (*see* CONSERVATION). A federal-state land planning advisory commission was established. Critics of the bill included the Arctic Slope Native Association, representing 4,500 Eskimos from the North Slope area who were allowed only surface rights to their oil-rich lands, with compensating subsurface rights elsewhere. (The association had filed a suit Oct. 5, claiming full rights to the

North Slope.) Nonresident natives protested their exclusion from land rights and mineral revenues, although they were included in the federal grants.
See also EDUCATION [16]; POPULATION; YOUTH

INDOCHINA WAR—U.S. participation in ground fighting in Indochina declined during 1971 as President Nixon continued his plans for troop withdrawals. Further increases in the rate of withdrawal were announced April 7 and Nov. 12. However, as the participation in ground fighting decreased, U.S. bombing of North Vietnamese installations and troop concentrations in the demilitarized zone remained heavy, with massive strikes coming Dec. 26-30. U.S. bombing was greatly increased over the previous year's rate in Laos and Cambodia. U.S. air forces provided support to a South Vietnamese incursion into Laos Feb. 8 to break Communist supply lines along the Ho Chi Minh Trail. The South Vietnamese drive into Laos was scheduled to last till around May 1, but was terminated suddenly March 24 with heavy South Vietnamese losses. The U.S. Congress approved the Mansfield end-the-war amendment which called for withdrawal of all American troops from Indochina at a "date certain," conditional on release of American prisoners of war. President Nixon signed the military procurement bill containing the amendment Nov. 17, but said he was not bound by provisions of the amendment. The Paris peace talks remained deadlocked throughout the year, despite the submission to the talks July 1 of a Viet Cong peace proposal. Negotiators at the talks failed to reach agreement over the issue of American prisoners of war.

Fighting—Cambodia

[2] **Drive to clear Route 4.** Cambodian and South Vietnamese troops during January wrested control of the 115-mile-long Route 4, linking the Cambodian capital of Pnompenh with the country's only port of Kompong Som. The road had been blockaded by Communists since Nov. 20, 1970, creating a serious gasoline shortage in Pnompenh. A force of 3,500 Cambodian troops moved southward Jan. 4 to attack the heights of Pich Nil Pass, commanding the highway about 60 miles southwest of the capital. Little enemy resistance was encountered at first, but Communist assaults later stalled the Cambodian push. The Cambodians and South Vietnamese were given air support during the fighting by U.S. helicopter gunships believed to have flown from two American helicopter carriers stationed off the Cambodian coast in the Gulf of Siam. (The U.S. Command Jan. 18 confirmed the presence of the two carriers and said they were part of the 7th Fleet "amphibious readiness group" used for the "interdiction" of enemy lines and the supplying of allied forces fighting in Cambodia.) More than 1,000 South Vietnamese troops and artillery were helicoptered Jan. 19 to the Cambodian garrison of Kompong Seila, just below the southern approaches to Pich Nil. Another South Vietnamese group of over 1,000, which had left Pnompenh Jan. 12 to aid the Cambodian troups, Jan. 18 had relieved enemy pressure on Kompong Seila and Jan. 16 had captured another strategic point—Stung Chhay Pass, 95 miles southwest of Pnompenh. Advance elements of the South Vietnamese force reached the Cambodians stalled at Pich Nil Pass Jan. 20, and the main bodies of the forces linked Jan. 22 three miles from the northern end of the pass. The road, unusable because it was scarred by bomb craters and many of its bridges were destroyed, was considered to be in allied hands, although a South Vietnamese spokesman said Jan. 23 that about 1,800 enemy troops remained in the Pich Nil area. (The U.S. announced Jan. 25 the withdrawal that day of the two helicopter carriers from the Gulf of Siam. South Vietnam announced Jan. 25 that 1,500 of its troops involved in the Route 4 operations had been pulled out. A Saigon spokesman said an additional 3,800 troops returned to South Vietnam that day.)
[3] North Vietnamese and Viet Cong troops March 30 captured a 10-mile stretch of Route 4. (They had destroyed 80% of oil storage facilities at Kompong Som with shelling March 2 and 4.) The new fighting erupted March 29 when a Cambodian convoy of several battalions, moving down the road

about 58 miles from Pnompenh, was ambushed by a Communist force. About 50 government soldiers were said to have been killed. The Cambodian convoy again came under attack the following day and retreated three miles to a fortified camp. The Communists were reported April 8 to have widened control of Route 4 by seizing another two-mile section. Throughout April, fighting flared along the road, centering around Pich Nil Pass, where a government force holding defensive positions was under North Vietnamese attack. An 8,000-man Cambodian force, attempting to relieve the besieged garrison, reached within two miles of the surrounded government soldiers April 28. The Cambodian government May 20 announced the opening of a new drive to establish an alternative route from Pnompenh to the Gulf of Siam. One government column was moving down Route 3 (roughly parallel to Route 4) and another was moving north.

[4]   South Vietnam-Cambodian relations. Relations between Cambodia and its South Vietnamese allies degenerated during 1971, despite agreements signed by South Vietnamese officials and Cambodian Premier Lon Nol Jan. 20-21 to expand relations and reduce tensions between the two countries. (According to Lon Nol, both sides agreed to recognize a common border and expand telecommunications, transport, tourism and joint use of the Mekong River. A mixed commission was to be established to inspect the treatment by each nation of the other's nationals.) Cambodian and South Vietnamese forces fought each other in two separate clashes June 30, for undetermined reasons. A civilian bystander was killed and 14 wounded as South Vietnamese sailors and Cambodian soldiers exchanged mortar and machine gun fire in Pnompenh for 15 minutes until stopped by Cambodian tanks and troop reinforcements. In the second clash, South Vietnamese marines attacked a Cambodian outpost at Vealthhom, later attacked by Viet Cong forces. Three Cambodians were killed and seven wounded, but it was not known if the casualties were inflicted by the South Vietnamese or Viet Cong. A joint Cambodian-South Vietnamese report, signed March 6 and made public March 20, and a Cambodian Foreign Ministry document (covering the period since March), made public July 15, both accused South Vietnamese troops of violence against Cambodian civilians. The crimes of violence included theft, plunder, rape, torture, gunfire attacks and rocket attacks. The report issued in March proposed the creation of a joint commission in Pnompenh consisting of two high officials from each side and the establishment of permanent subcommissions in each province in which Saigon troops might be operating. Protests following the issuance of the July report led the Cambodian high command Aug. 15 to demand the evacuation of most of South Vietnam's troops from Cambodia and the closing of the South Vietnamese military base at Neak Luong. The Neak Luong area was said to have been the scene of alleged South Vietnamese atrocities committed against civilians.

[5]   Attacks on Pnompenh. Striking at Pnompenh for the first time in the Indochina war, Communist forces Jan. 22 carried out a devastating shelling attack on the city's Pochentong international airport and nearby installations, virtually wiping out Cambodia's tiny air force and causing widespread damage. The raid was followed by a series of smaller enemy assaults on the capital, prompting the government to impose a dusk-to-dawn curfew throughout Pnompenh Jan. 25. At least 15 soldiers and 26 civilians were killed and at least 170 wounded in the shelling of the airport. About 10 Cambodian air force and civilian planes and four helicopters were reported destroyed. Two ammunition dumps near a military housing area occupied by civilians were blown up, as were field dumps. Three of the airport's hangars were destroyed and the civilian control tower was damaged. The 10 Communist infiltrators were reported to have entered the airport behind a mortar barrage. They ran from plane to plane attaching explosive charges. Three of the attackers were reported killed. Other guerrillas fired 30 rocket and mortar shells at the Chran Changvar Naval Base across the Tonle Sap River from Pnompenh. Some

enemy shells also landed in the center of the city. Within the city, bombs shattered the Cambodian immigration office and rocked the home of South Vietnamese Ambassador Tran Van Phouc (injuring him slightly) Jan. 23, and destroyed the headquarters of the city's power utility Jan. 24, wounding 10 employees. The airport came under fresh mortar and rocket attack Jan. 24. Meanwhile, sharp clashes between Cambodian and Communist forces occurred on the outskirts of Pnompenh Jan. 24-25. Raids against the city continued on a small scale Jan. 26-27. More than 20 Cambodian battalions Jan. 27 launched a major drive to wipe out Communist troop concentrations west and northwest of Pnompenh.

[6]   Heavy attacks around the capital resumed in late May and June. North Vietnamese forces May 25 launched 10 days of heavy attacks along a 10-mile front across the Mekong River from Pnompenh, in an attempt to seize a marshy area near the village of Vihear Suor that was part of the city's outer defenses. (Enemy seizure of the strongpoint would bring the capital within range of heavy mortar fire, according to Cambodian military sources.) About 400 Communists and 200 government troops were reported killed in the clashes. Following a Communist ambush of a government column in the center of the Vihear Suor marshes, four government strongpoints in the marshes (Prey Bang, Kompong Chamland, Kompong Ampil and Vihear Suor) were struck by Communist mortar and rocket fire June 9. Heavy fighting continued in the area, and Cambodian authorities ordered a news blackout on the battle June 11. Heavy clashes re-erupted in the area June 23 as government troops overran a North Vietnamese regimental headquarters within 15 miles of Pnompenh, resulting in the death of 120 North Vietnamese.

[7]   Pnompenh came under heavy shelling Nov. 10 and Dec. 7. In the Nov. 10 attack, 25 persons were killed, 30 wounded and nine aircraft damaged by a Communist rocket barrage on the airport. In the Dec. 7 shelling, the city was struck by three rockets (wounding four civilians), and the airport was struck by eight rockets (killing two soldiers and wounding two). The second attack followed the virtual collapse Dec. 2 of Cambodian defenses northeast of the capital in the face of heavy North Vietnamese assaults. Half of the 20,000-man government force in the area, attempting to reopen Route 6 to the northern provinces, was said to have fled in disarray following Cambodian abandonment of Baray and Kompong Thmar (six and 12 miles north of Pnompenh). North Vietnamese troops reoccupied a 30-mile stretch of the highway after the Cambodian retreat. Hundreds of Cambodian troops were reported killed in the attacks. In the wake of the government pullback, 10,000 Cambodian troops and thousands of refugees were reported cut off in the Kompong Thom area to the north. At least 100 Cambodian soldiers were reported killed or wounded Dec. 5 in continued fighting in the northeastern sector—nearly half of the casualties in a clash near Bat Doeung, 16 miles north of the capital. (The village was abandoned by the Cambodians Dec. 6.) Fighting raged within nine miles of the capital Dec. 8 as 1,000 government troops moved to block a North Vietnamese advance near the hamlet of Sre Ngei. The Communist troops this time were moving in from the south in an attempt to encircle the city. (See also [13, 16].)

[8]   **Saigon opens new border drive.** A force of 2,500 South Vietnamese troops crossed the border into the Fishhook area of Cambodia to join 7,500 other Saigon troops there in the start of a new campaign to clear out what were described as Communist border sanctuaries, it was announced Feb. 3. The sweep, which had begun the previous week, was assisted by 7,500 Cambodian troops and U.S. air support. The new operation centered in Kompong Cham Province. (No major Communist activity had been detected in the area.) A Cambodian military spokesman said the first objective of the Pnompenh troops was to attack the command post of the 9th North Vietnamese Division at Chup. In an initial encounter with the enemy Feb. 4, Saigon reported that allied forces had killed 69 Communist soldiers. South Vietnamese losses were placed at seven dead and 28 wounded.

[9] *2 allied generals killed.* The new allied offensive was virtually halted following the Feb. 24 death of South Vietnamese commander Lt. Gen. Do Cao Tri, as Tri's successor, Gen. Nguyen Van Minh, developed his battle plans. Tri and nine other persons had died when their helicopter crashed shortly after taking off from Tayninh, South Vietnam, for Kompong Cham. Cambodian Brig. Gen. Neak Sam, the first Cambodian general killed in the fighting in that country, was killed with 14 other government soldiers Feb. 12 in a clash with Communist troops 65 miles south of Pnompenh. Twenty-seven Communists were slain in the action.

[10] **2 new drives begin.** South Vietnamese forces launched two separate drives against Communist concentrations in Cambodia May 11 and 15. Field commanders said the purpose of the offensive was to disrupt a complex of "Communist command and control facilities, headquarters and training areas" in eastern Cambodia that were being used to attack the two adjacent South Vietnamese provinces of Haunghia and Longan, west of Saigon. In the first action, a force of about 5,000 South Vietnamese troops, assisted by American air support, swept a 25-mile stretch from the Cambodian town of Kandol Chrum on Route 7 southward to Kompong Trach, an area ranging 75-100 miles northwest of Saigon. Operating up to 12 miles inside Cambodia, two task forces were moving southward from Kandol Chrum to meet a task force heading northward from Kompong Trach. The second drive was concentrated in the Parrot's Beak of eastern Cambodia to the south of the first operation. More than 1,000 Saigon troops were participating, assisted by U.S. and South Vietnamese air support.

[11] The heaviest fighting in the first drive occurred at the end of May in Snoul, a rubber plantation town 15 miles from Kandol Chrum. About 1,000 North Vietnamese struck at the South Vietnamese-held town May 26 and fought their way into the town the following day. They were first thrown back by the defenders with the help of U.S. air support. The North Vietnamese launched a heavy attack about a quarter of a mile west of the town May 27, but were stopped again by government troops. The Saigon command reported May 29 that the fighting was over and its forces were in complete control of Snoul, but the battle flared again the following day and the North Vietnamese captured the town May 31. (A Saigon military spokesman said June 1 that the pullout by defenders was a "preplanned" "realignment" to cope with the coming rainy season.) Maj. Gen. Nguyen Van Hieu, who had commanded the 2,000-man 5th Division at Snoul, said June 3 that his forces had lost 37 killed, 167 wounded and 74 missing. He said that North Vietnamese casualties were 1,043 killed. However, Saigon military sources June 3 claimed that the South Vietnamese had lost 100-200 killed and 400-500 wounded. About 380 were evacuated and 200 were missing, according to the report. The retreating government forces were said to have left behind 50 trucks, 10 tanks, 14 armored personnel carriers and 22 mortars. Most of the equipment was in operating condition. Some of the artillery was said to have been turned against the South Vietnamese by the Communists. Hieu was reported June 9 to have been relieved of his command. The North Vietnamese capture of Snoul gave them control of parts of Routes 7 and 13 leading into the northern provinces of South Vietnam's Military Region III, which included Saigon and 11 surrounding provinces.

[12] **4 new drives open.** South Vietnamese forces launched four separate drives in Cambodia July 19, 21, 26 and 28. This raised the South Vietnamese force in Cambodia to more than 12,000 men. The new offensives followed a previous South Vietnamese thrust into Cambodia July 8 that was called off July 15 after a fruitless search for Communist troops. In the July 19 effort, 2,000 government rangers searched the flatlands in the southeastern part of Cambodia to stem North Vietnamese infiltration into South Vietnam's Mekong Delta. (An estimated 2,200 Communist soldiers were reported in recent months to have moved into the delta's U Minh Forest, long a stronghold of the Viet

Cong.) The July 21 drive was described as the largest in six months, reportedly employing 10,000 men already positioned in Cambodia, reinforced by an armored brigade and spearheaded by 200 armored vehicles. The assault was centered 100 miles northeast of the first announced attack. The July 26 drive was centered 10 miles inside Cambodia and 90 miles north of Saigon. About 1,000 troops were participating in the sweep, with another 1,000 in reserve. The July 28 offensive centered about eight miles north of Kompong Trabek near Route 1, the road connecting Pnompenh with Saigon. About 3,500 troops and 80 armored vehicles participated in the drive.

[13] **Oil tanks attacked.** Cambodia lost 40% of its civilian fuel supply Sept. 20 when Communist forces fired rockets into big storage tanks on the Tonle Sap River in Pnompenh. North Vietnamese or Viet Cong gunners were said to have ignited millions of gallons of gasoline, diesel oil and fuel oil. Other tanks were set afire by blazing fuel from punctured tanks. Three persons were reported killed. Tanks owned by Shell Oil and Esso were struck, but tanks belonging to the Cambodian government escaped damage. Fires in the storage dumps were finally extinguished Sept. 21.

[14] **Fighting intensifies.** Sharp fighting erupted along the Cambodian-South Vietnamese frontier Sept. 26 and continued through October. The fighting broke out Sept. 26 as North Vietnamese attacked South Vietnamese positions along the border. U.S. and South Vietnamese troops Sept. 29 launched a counteroffensive to reopen the 30-mile stretch of road leading north along Route 22 from Tayninh, in South Vietnam, to Krek, just over the border in Cambodia. The road had been cut by the Communists in an apparent threat to overrun about six allied bases in the area. About 4,000 government troops were rushed into the area to reinforce 20,000 South Vietnamese soldiers already there on both sides of the frontier. The U.S. reported moving 1,500 Americans and armored vehicles to the front, but they stayed inside South Vietnam. Saigon estimated that 259 enemy soldiers were killed in the allied counter strikes. Meanwhile, U.S. B-52 bombers Sept. 29 struck at North Vietnamese positions in Tayninh Province and at rear Communist bases in the Krek region. The counteroffensive was also marked by the lifting of sieges of the South Vietnamese bases of Firebase Tran Hung Dao (lifted Oct. 1) and artillery base Alpha (lifted Oct. 4). Both had been surrounded since the start of the North Vietnamese drive. Alpha was again besieged and the siege was again lifted Oct. 9. In the heaviest raid on North Vietnamese positions in more than a year, U.S. B-52s Oct. 7 dropped about 1,000 tons of bombs on North Vietnamese bunkers and gun emplacements near Krek and around Tayninh City. (A U.S. fighter-bomber Oct. 18 accidentally attacked a South Vietnamese position near the Cambodian border, killing 18 government soldiers and seriously wounding seven others.)

[15] *Fighting in northeast causes heavy losses.* Cambodian forces engaged in heavy combat with North Vietnamese and Viet Cong forces northeast of Pnompenh beginning in late October and sustained heavy losses. Major clashes broke out Oct. 27-29 around the provincial capital of Kompong Thom and Rumlong, 50 miles northeast of the capital. The fighting broke out after Communist frogmen blew up a bridge on Route 6, cutting off supplies and reinforcements for the 20,000 government troops on the northeastern front. In an effort to reinforce the beleaguered garrison at Kompong Thom, more than 300 Cambodian soldiers were killed in a week of fighting. Heavy casualties were suffered by government troops at nearby Rumlong. The town was abandoned to the Communists Nov. 13. The Cambodian high command said 30 of the defenders escaped and the rest of the 400 men in the town were killed or captured. Two other battalions left 400 dead or wounded behind when they retreated after an unsuccesful attempt to lift the siege. The Communist siege of another town in the area, Prakham, was lifted Nov. 2 when a Cambodian relief force broke into the village. The North Vietnamese and Viet Cong, who had encircled Prakham for more than a week, pulled back, losing 291 men,

according to the Cambodian government. Prakham and Taing Kauk, 12 miles further north, were surrounded by Communist forces Dec. 16. It was reported Dec. 21 that a Cambodian task force had broken through to Prakham Dec. 21.

[16] **New drive in eastern Cambodia.** In a move aimed at relieving North Vietnamese pressure around Pnompenh (*see* [5-7]), [5-7]), South Vietnamese forces launched a major drive into Cambodia Nov. 22. The drive, which lasted until Dec. 30, was ex-tended Nov. 24 by the airlift of several thousand paratroops from Krek to Chup, both about 60 miles northeast of Pnompenh and both principal targets in the offensive. The key objectives of the new thrust (launched after a Nov. 19 appeal for assistance by Cambodian officials) were the rear headquarters and supply depots of three North Vietnamese divisions near Chup, from which the Communists had been launching attacks against Pnompenh. The operation was also intended to thwart possible North Vietnamese plans for attacks on Tayninh Province. With the extension of the offensive Nov. 24, a total of 25,000 men were committed to the fighting, but little enemy resistance was reported. South Vietnamese forces Dec. 14 captured Chup without opposition. The attack against Chup, strongly supported (as was the entire offensive) by U.S. bomber attacks, was launched Dec. 13. The capture failed to find a trace of an estimated 9,000 North Vietnamese troops reported to be hiding in the area. The town was abandoned by the South Vietnamese Dec. 17. In the only area in which the South Vietnamese encountered strong enemy resistance during the offensive, it was reported that South Vietnamese forces had killed 167 Communists in fighting around the hamlet of Dam Be Dec. 8-10. South Vietnamese losses in the town (on a supply route near Chup) were placed at 10 soldiers and four airmen killed. The Viet Cong radio Dec. 14 announced that 500 South Vietnamese had been killed at Dam Be. The Saigon command Dec. 30 gave the following figures on the 39-day offensive: 1,336 North Vietnamese killed; 195 enemy weapons captured; 86 South Vietnamese soldiers killed and 226 wounded; and 17 South Vietnamese armored vehicles destroyed or damaged.

Fighting—Laos

[17] **Communists start drive.** Laotian Defense Minister Sisouk Na Champassak announced Feb. 3 that North Vietnamese troops had captured key towns in northern Laos in what appeared to be the start of a major offensive.The strategic towns of Muong Soui and Phou So had been seized Feb. 2 and two adjacent government positions on the western edge of the Plaine des Jarres fell into Communist hands, the minister disclosed. Enemy forces had also overrun four small positions guarding the royal capital of Luang Prabang, he said. Muong Soui, 100 miles north of Vientiane, had been abandoned by government defenders after it came under enemy shelling. Contact with the 5,000 government troops there had been lost. Government forces had occupied Muong Soui since its recapture from the North Vietnamese in October 1970. In another successful foray, North Vietnamese troops Jan. 27 had captured the town of Phalane, 54 miles from Savannakhet, a strategic village on the Mekong River border between Thailand and Laos.

[18] **Dewey Canyon II.** Sweeping across the border from the northwestern corner of South Vietnam, an estimated 5,000 South Vietnamese troops invaded Laos Feb. 8 in a drive codenamed Dewey Canyon II or Operation Lam Som 719. The drive was ordered to smash North Vietnamese supply bases along the Ho Chi Minh Trail and, according to official statements by South Vietnamese President Nguyen Van Thieu Feb. 7 and the U.S. State Department Feb. 8, to deprive the Communists of sanctuaries close to the South Vietnamese borders. The first stage of the drive started Jan. 30 when 20,000 South Vietnamese and 9,000 U.S. soldiers reactivated the former American base at Khesanh and pushed west to the frontier, preparatory to crossing. The U.S. command Feb. 4 lifted a six-day blackout on news with an announcement that the drive was underway. The American role in the first stage consisted of clearing roads

leading to the frontier, repairing abandoned air strips, providing air cover and highway security and airlifting South Vietnamese troops to the area. A Congressional ban on the use of American ground forces in Laos prevented the U.S. troops from crossing the frontier. (Some U.S. soldiers and newsmen during February reported that U.S. ground troops were being used in Laos, but the White House denied the allegations. U.S. officials announced Feb. 26 that small groups of American infantry could be sent into Laos to rescue downed American airmen. The officials said that the "protective encirclement" groups would be regarded as "rescue forces, not combat troops.")

[19] Although it was predicted at the start of the incursion that the operation would end shortly before the start of the rainy season (normally 10 days to two weeks before or after May 1), the drive came to an abrupt end March 24 as the last of the invading force fought its way back across the border into South Vietnam with Communist soldiers and tanks in hot pursuit. Saigon's troops were forced March 12 to start pulling back in the face of heavy enemy assaults. They began leaving Laos March 18, and virtually the entire invading army (grown to 21,000 troops) completed the pullback March 24. Almost all available American helicopters were utilized in rescuing the battered Saigon troops from the battle zone and transferring them to the staging base at Khesanh. About 500 South Vietnamese marines remained behind in Laos on Co Roc Mountain, two miles from the border just south of Route 9, to defend Khesanh. U.S. Defense Department sources were reported to have said March 24 that President Thieu had decided to end the operation—rejecting American suggestions to send in replacements and continue the incursion—in order to cut his army's costs. The operation was officially ended April 9. Despite its premature termination, U.S. and South Vietnamese authorities said the operation's objective of disrupting enemy supply lines on the Ho Chi Minh Trail had been accomplished. However, American pilots April 7 reported that North Vietnamese supplies along the trail were moving freely once again.

[20] A Saigon command spokesman March 29 reported a revised count of total South Vietnamese losses in the campaign. (The command had issued a lower count March 25.) According to the report: 1,160 government troops were killed, 4,271 wounded and 240 missing. (The spokesman denied reports that half of the 21,000-man force had been killed or wounded or were missing.) In its March 25 report, the command had estimated North Vietnamese deaths at 13,668, but U.S. military authorities believed the count was exaggerated. The U.S. command reported March 25 that 89 American helicopters had been destroyed, many of them shot down during the process of withdrawing from Laos. The command said 51 American 'copter crewmen had been killed and 28 were missing. Many other helicopters, not included in the official count, had been damaged or shot down and recovered.

[21] **Laos declares emergency.** The Laotian government Feb. 12 declared a state of emergency, giving armed forces commander Gen. Ouane Rathikoune power to take measures for general security throughout the country. The cabinet had adopted the decision Feb. 11. It had also adopted a communique calling the South Vietnamese incursion and the continued presence of North Vietnamese troops in Laos a violation of the 1962 Geneva Convention, which guaranteed Laos neutrality. In another protest against the incursion, Communist China Feb. 12 issued a stern warning that it could not tolerate the action, but U.S. officials discounted the possibility of Chinese military intervention.

[22] **Ho Chi Minh Trail cut.** Inclement weather, U.S. bomb craters on the invasion route of Highway 9 and what the South Vietnamese described as "the discovery of so many supply caches we have to have time to search" slowed the westward drive into Laos during the first half of February, although little enemy ground resistance was met. However, Saigon military officials claimed Feb. 15 that the government forces had severed all but two key sections of the Ho Chi Minh Trail.

[23] *Communists slow drive.* Mounting North Vietnamese ground resistance beginning Feb. 18 stalled the South Vietnamese drive about 17 miles inside Laos. At the same time, intense Communist antiaircraft fire continued to take a heavy toll of U.S. helicopters. It was reported that 298 South Vietnamese were killed or wounded in a seige by North Vietnamese of a hilltop patrol and artillery base a few miles west of Phu Loc (six miles inside Laos and nine miles north of Route 9). Survivors of the siege, which started Feb. 18, were said to have brought out 108 wounded when they were driven from the base Feb. 20, but left 60 others behind with the bodies of 130. North Vietnamese losses were put at 639 killed. The North Vietnamese overran the base despite large-scale U.S. air strikes. An American helicopter crew chief, Spec. 5 Dennis Fujii, had taken virtual command of Phu Loc defense. He had been participating in a medical-evacuation mission at the base and had remained after giving up his seat to a wounded South Vietnamese. Since that time, till he was wounded and airlifted to safety Feb. 23, he had been directing air and artillery strikes against the Communist attackers.

[24] South and North Vietnamese troops fought one of the fiercest battles of the Indochina war Feb. 25-27 around two South Vietnamese artillery bases six miles inside Laos. The heaviest action took place at Hill 31, north of Route 9, where North Vietnamese forces, using tanks for the first time in the Laotian fighting, were reported to have driven South Vietnamese troops from their positions Feb. 25. The 500 defenders withdrew with heavy losses after coming under attack by 20 light Soviet-made tanks. Following intensive American air strikes on the 2,000 attackers and the moving in of troop reinforcements, it was reported Feb. 27 that Saigon soldiers had regained control of the hill. U.S. helicopter pilots reported March 1 that both sides occupied opposite slopes of the hill, with the top a no-man's-land. Other fighting took place at an artillery base on Hill 30, four miles away and just south of Route 9. The base, at Hong Ha Ha, was reported March 1 to have been evacuated because of heavy North Vietnamese pressure.

[25] *Tchepone captured.* Reinforced South Vietnamese troops March 6 pushed westward and captured Tchepone, the main North Vietnamese supply base on the Ho Chi Minh Trail—about 25 miles inside Laos. (Over 2,000 additional South Vietnamese troops were moved into Laos March 2-4.) More than 2,000 Saigon troops pushed into Tchepone, which was found almost destroyed after days of American air attacks. About 200 enemy bodies were discovered in the town. A South Vietnamese spokesman said the troops had found large quantities of ammunition and food and 15 antiaircraft guns and other weapons. After taking Tchepone, South Vietnamese troops began to set up a ring of helicopter landing zones and at least two artillery bases two and a half miles south and west of the town to prepare for a possible North Vietnamese counterattack. The first counterstrikes against the new forward positions came March 7 at an artillery base called Lolo, about six miles southeast of Tchepone. A force of about 2,500 South Vietnamese March 8-9 established positions in the hills surrounding Tchepone because the valley was vulnerable to enemy attacks. A North Vietnamese offensive, launched March 12, forced the government troops to pull out of those positions and out of Tchepone. The South Vietnamese then established five or six new combat bases on a mountain ridge 5-15 miles southeast of Tchepone. Lolo was evacuated by the South Vietnamese March 15-18 under a Communist tank and artillery assault launched March 14. Bad weather and intense antiaircraft fire had prevented U.S. helicopters from bringing supplies into the base. About 1,500 South Vietnamese retreated five miles eastward and established positions March 16 at Landing Zone Brown, an artillery base three miles south of Route 9. The base came under attack the following day and was abandoned by the South Vietnamese March 20 after four days of fighting. The South Vietnamese were also forced March 20 to abandon their main base of Aloui (just to the

north on Route 9), despite strikes that day by about 300 American jets attempting to stem the North Vietnamese advance.

[26] *Aftermath.* At the end of the operations in Laos, allied troops began to withdraw from bases on the South Vietnamese border that supported the incursion. The pullback was carried out amid growing concern over a possible North Vietnamese attack on allied installations in the area. The Communists had begun a series of harassing raids against allied positions in the Khesanh area March 25-30 (preceded by shelling of Khesanh throughout the Laos operation and a ground assault on the base March 14) and struck further south near Danang March 28, killing 33 Americans. Meanwhile, several hundred South Vietnamese marines were sent to patrol the Laotian frontier while a small force of other marines moved back into Laos to reoccupy a hill position two miles across the border and just south of Route 9. The mission of the troops was to protect the continued withdrawal of the allied forces from the northernmost part of South Vietnam. Despite the end of operations in Laos, American planes continued to bomb the Ho Chi Minh Trail. South Vietnamese commandos March 31 and April 6 carried out raids into Laos. The strikes reportedly destroyed Communist storage huts and military and food supplies.

[27] **Boloven Plateau fighting.** Laotian forces began in early March to lose their hold on the strategic Boloven Plateau area in the southern part of the country as North Vietnamese forces launched heavy attacks on bases used by the government for surveillance and raids against the Ho Chi Minh Trail. Government troops March 9 were driven from Position 22 (the strongest Laotian base in the Boloven area) and three smaller positions on the eastern edge of the plateau following two days of Communist rocket, mortar and ground attacks. Eight battalions of North Vietnamese May 16 captured Paksong and Ban Houei Sai to take virtual control of the plateau. The defenders of the two adjacent towns, totaling about three battalions, were said to have lost about 50 men and large quantities of materiel. North Vietnamese forces May 19 captured the last stronghold on the plateau—Houei Kong. Laotian troops July 28 captured the provincial capital of Saravane on the northern edge of the plateau. Government soldiers were airlifted into Saravane and met no significant resistance. The town, guarding a main junction on the Ho Chi Minh Trail, was reported devastated by American and Laotian air strikes. It was reported Aug. 2 that Laotian forces had launched a major drive to recapture Paksong. After a two-day battle Sept. 15-16, government forces recaptured the town. Two of seven government battalions were put out of action in the fighting, with casualties totaling 202 killed, 745 wounded and 195 missing. North Vietnamese losses were estimated at 279 killed and about 600 wounded. Following an attack by two North Vietnamese battalions, Laotian forces Dec. 6 abandoned Saravane and the air strip at Ban Khot, six miles northeast of Saravane. North Vietnamese forces Dec. 28 recaptured Paksong, but Laotian forces reoccupied the town Dec. 29 after enemy forces withdrew.

[28] **Battle near Luang Prabang.** Heavy fighting erupted March 22 around the royal Laotian capital of Luang Prabang, with a force of 3,000 North Vietnamese and Pathet Lao troops attacking in an area between one and five and a half miles north of the city. The attack was preceded by extensive shelling of the city's airport March 20-22. The 150 rocket and mortar shells fired reportedly killed at least six persons, destroyed or damaged five planes and caused widespread damage to airport structures. Six Communist battalions followed up the shelling with assaults on six government positions between Luang Prabang and Pak Ou, a town 22 miles to the northeast. A Pathet Lao broadcast March 24 said the rebels had no intention of capturing Luang Prabang, but were merely warning Premier Souvanna Phouma not to abandon his neutrality. The threat to the capital was eased March 24 when three battalions of government reinforcements pushed the Communists from the edge of the city. However, March 26-April 6 government forces abandoned several strategic hill positions near the city as Communist attackers drove to within four to five miles of the city. The Laotians used air and artillery strikes in an effort to stem the advance. By April 5, the North Vietnamese were reported to be reinforcing their positions and bringing in antiaircraft guns.

[29] **Plaine des Jarres fighting.** Laotian Meo tribesmen were reported July 13 to have seized complete control of the Plaine des Jarres in northern Laos in a drive begun July 7. No significant resistance was met in the recapture of the strategic heights formerly held by North Vietnamese, Viet Cong and Pathet Lao forces. (The Communists captured the plain in February 1970, but were said to have abandoned it the following month.) Laotian officers said the drive was coordinated by the U.S. Central Intelligence Agency (CIA) and that some of the tribal commandos were led by American advisers. The U.S. State Department July 9 denied that any U.S. advisers were accompanying Laotian forces. U.S. officials in Vientiane July 9 said the drive was to destroy Communist supplies, not to occupy the plain. Large caches of enemy munitions, food, medicines and other supplies were said to have been found by advancing forces. Six Meo battalions were said to be participating in the offensive with two Thai battalions.

[30] About 15,000 North Vietnamese troops, according to report Dec. 20, recaptured the plain. The Communist advance was supported by tanks and heavy artillery. According to a government report, 1,500 of the attackers were killed. The government's 6,000-7,000 men on the plain and the Thai irregulars assisting them were reported to have suffered heavy casualties. With the capture of the plain, the Communists launched a new drive Dec. 21, posing a threat to the pro-government base of Long Tieng, 30 miles to the southwest. The base, defended by a CIA-sponsored Meo army, was attacked by 20 Communist commandos Dec. 21. The raiders were driven off. Government forces Dec. 25 abandoned two strongpoints 14 miles northwest of Long Tieng to the advancing Communist attackers.

[31] **Thais build bases.** It was reported July 20 that Thai troops, with the aid of the CIA, had constructed several permanent bases in Laos. The bases had been erected in a large area of Sayaboury Province, which bordered northeastern Thailand, and were built parallel to a complex of CIA-maintained Laotian bases extending eastward from Xieng Lom in a 40-mile arc to Hong Sa. The Thai unit had entered Laos from Nan Province in Thailand during a sweep against Thai guerrillas. The U.S. State Department Aug. 9 insisted that the Thai troops were volunteers, although a U.S. newspaper report the same day said the Thai units serving in Laos with irregular forces were regular Thai troops. The department said it was entitled to withhold complete compliance with the Geneva agreement on Laos since North Vietnam was already violating that neutrality with the presence of 80,000 troops in that country.

[32] **CIA force in Laos acknowledged.** The Nixon Administration Aug. 2 officially confirmed for the first time that the CIA was maintaining an "irregular" force of 30,000 fighting men engaged in battle throughout Laos. According to the report containing the acknowledgement, the CIA-backed force had become "the main cutting edge" of the Royal Laotian army. Thai "volunteers" recruited and paid by the CIA were among those in the 30,000-man force.

[33] **MiGs challenge U.S. jets.** The U.S. State Department confirmed Dec. 1 that a North Vietnamese MiG-21 fighter had attacked a U.S. B-52 bomber over the Ho Chi Minh Trail in southern Laos in late November, but its air-to-air missile missed. There had been at least 10 reported incidents of MiG passes at American planes, but the department's statement was the first official confirmation of such an attack. Reports in previous weeks had told of increased North Vietnamese MiG activity and the improvement of three airfields (Donghoi, Vinh and Quanglang) from which the planes operated in southern North Vietnam near the Laotian border. The Defense Department had warned Dec. 1 that the continued use of the MiGs could lead to retaliatory strikes at the three airfields (*see* [35])

Fighting—Vietnam

[34] **New Year's truces end.** The Viet Cong's three-day New Year's cease fire ended at 1 a.m. Jan. 3 amid reports that fighting had continued through most of the period. By contrast, the allied 24-hour truce begun at 6 p.m. Dec. 31, 1970 had been the quietest of the holiday fighting pauses since their inception in 1967. The heaviest fighting of the three-day cease-fire occurred Jan. 2 when South Vietnamese forces swept into the southern half of the demilitarized zone (DMZ) to pursue North Vietnamese troops that had attacked a Saigon unit patrolling just below the DMZ. The South Vietnamese withdrew from the zone after engaging the North Vietnamese for 10 hours.

[35] **Protective reaction strikes.** During 1971, U.S. planes carried out numerous "protective reaction" bombing strikes against missile and antiaircraft installations and oil storage tanks in North Vietnam. The strikes were made primarily in the area north of the DMZ and near the Mugia Pass at the Laotion border. They were made for a variety of reasons: because radar at enemy installations had locked in U.S. bomber escort planes preparatory to firing on them; because of antiaircraft or artillery attacks against U.S. bombers or observation planes flying over Laos or North Vietnam; or because of firing passes made at U.S. planes by North Vietnamese MiG-21s. By Nov. 21, 80 protective reaction strikes had been made, with the heaviest attacks coming Feb. 20-23, March 21-22 and Sept. 20. The heaviest attack, however, took place Dec. 26-30 as U.S. Air Force and Navy planes carried out massive sustained attacks on military installations in North Vietnam, involving 1,000 strikes. The raids were in retaliation for what allied commanders charged was a huge buildup of military supplies by North Vietnam in preparation for a possible offensive against Cambodia and South Vietnam and for a sudden upsurge in North Vietnamese air and missile attacks on American planes that bombed the Ho Chi Minh Trail in Laos. The U.S. command withheld information on the bombing until its termination Dec. 30. It said then that the strikes "were directed against surface-to-air missiles, antiaircraft artillery units, air-defense radar sites, the enemy's logistics and P.O.L. [Petroleum-Oil-Lubricant] buildup north of the DMZ and particularly opposite major passes into Laos." Also included in the targets, according to the statement, "were certain airfields [believed to be Baithuong, Quanglang and Donghoi] south of the 20th Parallel from which there has been increasing aircraft activity in recent weeks." Hanoi claimed that 19 American jets were downed in the raids and that "a number" of pilots were killed and three captured. The U.S. command acknowledged the loss of only three aircraft and reported one Navy pilot was rescued and three were missing. (*See also* [47, 65].)

[36] **Tet truce.** Sporadic fighting continued in South Vietnam during separate truces declared by allied forces Jan. 26-27 and by Communist troops Jan. 26-30 in observance of Tet, the lunar new year. The U.S. and South Vietnamese commands reported Jan. 27 at least 53 enemy troop violations during the allied truce, but called it the quietest in recent years. The U.S. command reported no American deaths, but South Vietnam said seven of its soldiers had been killed and 28 wounded. The enemy death toll was listed at 22. The allied command said the Viet Cong and North Vietnamese had committed a number of violations during their own cease-fire, directing attacks against civilians. In Binhdinh Province, a Communist grenade ripped through a theater, killing 10 South Vietnamese. About 80 miles north, nine civilians were reported killed when a bomb exploded in a market place.

[37] **Fight for Fire Base 6.** Beginning March 31, North Vietnamese troops launched a heavy attack on South Vietnamese-held Fire Base 6 in the Central Highlands near Dakto, six miles from the Laotian border. The South Vietnamese were driven from the base March 31 and reoccupied it the following day before the enemy launched another attack. The installation was defended by 5,000-6,000 men, but its artillery pieces were destroyed in the initial Communist ground assault. Waves of U.S. bombers dropped explosives and

napalm on enemy troops April 9 within two to three miles of the base, setting off jungle fires; but North Vietnam commandos, defying the raids, attempted to infiltrate the base April 10. They were repulsed; and, after they were thrown back, South Vietnamese planes joined the U.S. B-52s in pounding enemy forces around the base. The Communists shot down one American helicopter attempting to bring supplies into the base April 11 and forced 11 other supply aircraft to turn back. In a determined effort to break the siege, U.S. planes April 12 began dropping seven-and-a-half ton bombs (normally used to blast out heavy jungle growth to clear landing space for helicopters) on North Vietnamese troop concentrations around the base. Enemy pressure on the base began to ease April 13-14 with the arrival of four South Vietnamese infantry battalions, airlifted by American helicopters to a landing zone two miles south of the base. The South Vietnamese, making their way to the base on foot, encountered heavy fighting about one-half mile from the base April 14. The arrival of the troops at the base April 16 prompted the Saigon commander in the area to declare the siege broken. However, 6,000-10,000 North Vietnamese troops continued to surround the base, making it difficult for reinforcements to reach the base on foot. Meanwhile, an American helicopter April 14 lifted out four of the five U.S. military advisers at the base. No reason for the evacuation was given. As of April 16, Saigon claimed to have killed more than 3,000 North Vietnamese in the fight, while suffering casualties of 195 killed, 442 wounded and 32 missing.

[38] **Pacification drive.** A new pacification program, aimed at exerting greater effort in an attempt to smash the Viet Cong political apparatus in South Vietnam, was instituted March 1 and endorsed by the U.S. and South Vietnamese commands. Because of its increased scope, the plan was said to be the most expensive one to date, costing the U.S. more than $1 billion and Saigon an undisclosed sum. The program called for: expansion of the People's Self-Defense Force, made up entirely of civilians operating in rural areas, from 500,000 to four million (with women enlisted in combat units and children over the age of seven placed in supporting units); the slaying or capture of 14,400 Viet Cong agents under an expansion of Operation Phoenix, an intelligence-gathering operation supported by the U.S. military; and the establishment of a complex "people's intelligence network" to spy on the Communists.

[39] **Allies probe Ashau Valley.** U.S. and South Vietnamese forces April 14 launched a probe of the Ashau Valley, a 30-mile long area used by the North Vietnamese as an infiltration corridor and transshipment point from Laos into northern South Vietnam. About 400 U.S. and 5,000 South Vietnamese soldiers were reported initially committed to the sweep, codenamed Lam Son 720 and described as a follow-up to the February-March thrust into Laos (*see* [18-26]). According to South Vietnamese newspaper reports, the operations were a "training exercise" for the many fresh troops that were sent to the 1st South Vietnamese Infantry Division to replace those lost in the Laos fighting. U.S. helicopters flew about 1,500 marines to landing zones 20-25 miles north of the valley April 21, flew in another 525 government troops to a mountain artillery base 18 miles north of the valley April 23 and airlifted a battalion of 1,600 troops into the valley July 26. Little resistance was met in the drive. The first major battle occurred May 12 as North Vietnamese troops attacked two South Vietnamese positions, but were repelled with heavy losses. In the first engagement, about 400 Communists struck at a night bivouac of a 500-man Saigon marine battalion and lost 23 men. Six South Vietnamese marines were killed and 48 wounded. In the second assault, the same battalion fought off another North Vietnamese thrust, reportedly killing 177 while suffering casualties of 36 killed or wounded. (Five U.S. soldiers had been killed and 10 wounded April 30 in a Communist ambush just east of the valley. They were the first American ground losses of the campaign. U.S. B-52 bombers carried out raids May 1 in an attempt to strike at the North Vietnamese troops responsible for the ambush.) Sporadic fighting flared in and around the valley May 19-23,

with South Vietnamese claiming Communist losses of 115 killed in several battles. South Vietnam also claimed that 28 Communist bunkers were captured May 20 and that 50 enemy huts were destroyed and large quantities of ammunition were captured May 21. Communist ground fire downed an American helicopter and damaged two other 'copters and a reconnaissance plane during a six-hour battle May 19. (*See also* [42].)

[40] **Communists hit allied bases.** North Vietnamese troops carried out sharp attacks on allied bases and installations throughout South Vietnam April 24-27 and again May 19-23 and May 29-30, inflicting heavy casualties. Reports listed 54 South Vietnamese killed and 185 wounded and seven Americans killed and 60 wounded in the April fighting. The South Vietnamese suffered their heaviest casualties April 24 when Communist commandos overran part of the Hoanganh combat base 15 miles northwest of the coastal city of Quangngai. Of the estimated 400 defenders, 22 were killed and 52 wounded. Saigon said that 21 North Vietnamese had been killed. In attacks May 19-22 all along the DMZ, the heaviest losses were suffered May 21 when 30 Americans were killed and 50 wounded in three rocket and mortar attacks, primarily on a position called Charlie 2, four miles southwest of the DMZ. The base was hit by 15 100-pound rockets. The casualties were said to be the heaviest from shelling of U.S. units in at least 17 months. In an attack May 23, about six Viet Cong demolition experts slipped into the American air base at Camranh Bay, planted satchel charges on six fuel tanks and blew them up, setting huge fires and destroying 1,500,000 gallons of aviation fuel. Two Americans were injured. All six infiltrators escaped. Six hours after the explosion, enemy gunners fired 30 mortars into another part of the base, but caused no casualties or damage. (*See also* [48].) In the May 29-30 fighting, Communist forces carried out 48 attacks, killing at least 20 government soldiers and 12 civilians and wounding 101 soldiers and 18 civilians. One American was killed and eight wounded. North Vietnamese and Viet Cong losses during the attacks were placed at 85 killed. The Communist strikes included 30 rocket and mortar attacks against South Vietnamese positions. Among the targets of the assaults were the U.S. air base at Danang, the city of Danang and four allied bases guarding the DMZ.

[41] **Cease-fires violated.** U.S. and South Vietnamese forces observed a 24-hour battlefield truce May 8-9 to mark the birth of Buddha. Viet Cong and North Vietnamese troops unilaterally declared a similar cease-fire but extended it another 24 hours until 7 a.m. May 10. The allied commands claimed May 10 that the Communists had violated both cease-fires, initiating 66 attacks with a heavy loss of South Vietnamese lives. Saigon headquarters said 56 South Vietnamese soldiers and civilians had been killed and 36 wounded. A total of 34 North Vietnamese and Viet Cong soldiers were reported slain. American casualties were placed at two killed and six wounded. The South Vietnamese fatalities included 41 civilians, 36 of whom had died May 9 in a mine explosion on a ferry boat on a river in northernmost Quangtri Province, three miles northeast of Dongha.

[42] **DMZ attacks increase.** Communist guns inside North Vietnam shelled allied positions along the DMZ from the end of May through August. Meanwhile, sharp ground clashes were fought in the DMZ vicinity. Among the most significant events in the area: South Vietnamese forces May 31 launched a sweep 15-20 miles south of the DMZ to smash a North Vietnamese buildup and to clear and block Communist infiltration routes in western Quangtri Province. The operation was supported by U.S. helicopters. Little contact was made with the enemy, with the only significant action occurring June 2 when enemy gunners shelled a South Vietnamese batallion near Khesanh for 10 hours, killing six government soldiers. The 6,000-man Saigon force operating in the Ashau Valley (*see* [39]) June 12 moved 35 miles north toward the DMZ to join the two government marine brigades blocking infiltration south of the buffer strip. (It was reported June 27 that at least two North Vietnamese regiments had infiltrated across the DMZ into South Vietnam in the first large

Communist thrust through the zone in three years. Infiltration seemed to have been rerouted into the buffer zone because monsoon rains had made travel difficult on the Ho Chi Minh Trail.)

[43] Heavy fighting raged during June around Fire Base Sarge, a government stronghold 12 miles northeast of Khesanh. Allied forces claimed to have killed 241 North Vietnamese in the area June 5-6. A force of about 400 North Vietnamese reopened attack on the base June 17, but were repelled by the 200-man South Vietnamese garrison, with a loss of 95 Communist lifes and 13 South Vietnamese lifes. The defenders were aided by American jet and helicopter strikes. About 1,800 government reinforcements were sent to the base June 18, and the expanded Saigon force seized the initiative. Enemy attacks tapered off later in the day.

[44] A major confrontation between North and South Vietnamese forces erupted June 22 with an enemy attack on Fire Base Fuller, a government outpost four miles south of the DMZ. Communist forces overran the base June 24, but Saigon claimed June 28 that 120 of its forces had reoccupied the outpost after the Communists left it unoccupied. The North Vietnamese 1,500-man assault had been preceded by heavy rocket and mortar shelling of the base June 19. U.S. B-52s dropped 60 tons of explosives around the base June 21 in an attempt to smash enemy concentrations. The garrison's 500 defenders were reinforced June 24 by 800-1,000 government troops, but enemy bombardment had destroyed up to 80% of the bunkers, leaving the defenders with little protective covering. Saigon said it had "no intention of rebuilding the fortifications of the base." South Vietnamese forces June 25 conducted a sweep near the base for the enemy rocket and mortar emplacements that had contributed to the fall of the position. About 38 North Vietnamese were said to have been killed in a flareup of fighting around the base June 30. Fighting around the base continued July 1 as the defenders beat off an assault by 300 enemy troops. The defenders, reinforced that day by 150 men, were aided by U.S. and South Vietnamese planes and helicopter gunships.

[45] After a lull of more than three weeks, North Vietnamese artillery July 21 shelled four South Vietnamese bases just south of the DMZ. No casualties were reported. The North Vietnamese again stepped up their attacks Aug. 12, killing at least 15 South Vietnamese in three ground assaults against government positions. The hardest hit bases were Alpha 1 and 2, which were struck by 300 shells Aug. 13. Government casualties were light. The Saigon command acknowledged Aug. 16 that the marine post of Baho, two miles north of the DMZ, had been overrun by North Vietnamese forces Aug. 15. The 180 government defenders were believed to have suffered heavily, most being killed, wounded or missing. Enemy losses were placed at 200 dead.

[46] *U.S. ends DMZ role.* South Vietnamese troops July 9 assumed complete responsibility for defense of the area just below the DMZ when they replaced American forces at Fire Base Charlie 2, four miles south of the zone. About 500 U.S. troops of the 1st Brigade, 5th Mechanized Division, pulled out of the stronghold, and soldiers of the South Vietnamese First Division moved in. The American withdrawal from Charlie 2 completed a turnover of border responsibilities begun in 1969. Another stronghold nearby, Fire Base Alpha 4, had been turned over to South Vietnamese forces by American troops July 8. About 50 American artillerymen and technicians remained at Charlie 2 to operate a battery of guns and to monitor radar equipment. A similar U.S. contingent remained at Alpha 4. The last American combat unit just below the zone—a 920-man force of the 1st Brigade, 5th Mechanized Division—pulled out July 22.

[47] *U.S. forces bomb DMZ.* The U.S. command Aug. 17 acknowledged for the first time that B-52s had been bombing North Vietnamese targets in the DMZ "over a period of the last several months." A command spokesman said that American planes had flown no further than the Ben Hai River, which divided the six-mile buffer zone. The spokesman pointed out that, since the southern part of the zone was South Vietnamese territory, the raids on it were not a violation of the 1968 U.S. halt in bombing on North Vietnam except for retaliatory attacks. The report was followed by another command disclosure Aug. 19 that ships of the U.S. 7th Fleet had also been pounding North Vietnamese rocket and mortar positions in the southern sector of the DMZ for the past six days. The report said guns of a guided missile destroyer had touched off fires and explosions, indicating hits on ammunition dumps. The air and naval attacks were said by the command to be in response to the recent acceleration of North Vietnamese attacks against South Vietnamese positions just south of the DMZ.

[48] Election disruption attacks. Communist forces launched widespread attacks on civilian and military targets throughout South Vietnam Aug. 25-30 in an apparent attempt to disrupt the Aug. 29 National Assembly elections (*see* VIETNAM, SOUTH). The Saigon command reported Aug. 31 that Communists had carried out 96 attacks Aug. 28-30, mostly in the northern section of the country from the Central Highlands to the DMZ. According to official reports, at least 41 South Vietnamese soldiers and eight civilians were killed. The U.S. and Saigon commands said 347 Communist soldiers had been killed Aug. 28-29, many in air raids and artillery barrages. At the start of the enemy attacks, a 13-hour long series of explosions swept a huge ammunition dump at Camranh Bay, wounding five American servicemen and destroying about 50% of the ammunition dump (*see also* [40]). The Danang base, Camp Faulkner (just south of Danang), the Lakhe base camp (30 miles north of Saigon) and a number of installations 40 miles east of Saigon also came under attack Aug. 25. In other developments in the Danang area during the attacks: North Vietnamese gunners Aug. 25 struck a hamlet on the outskirts of the city, killing five civilians and destroying 100 homes; South Vietnamese forces Aug. 25 launched a general sweep 35 miles south of the city to head off enemy assaults against district towns in the area; and five Americans were killed Aug. 26 when North Vietnamese troops assaulted a unit of the American Division bivouacked 16 miles southwest of Danang. (In the first attack of its kind since Dec. 19, 1970, Communist gunners Oct. 3 fired at least three rockets into Saigon in an attempt to disrupt that day's presidential elections, killing two civilians.)(*See*VIETNAM, SOUTH. [1])

[49] Allied drive near Laotian border. A South Vietnamese force of 12,000 men (increased Sept. 9 to 13,500), supported by 1,500-2,000 U.S. soldiers (not ground troops), made a major sweep Sept. 6-18 against 30,000 North Vietnamese troops believed deployed below the western end of the DMZ near the Laotian border. No significant contact with the enemy was made during the drive. The commander of the northern Military Region I, Lt. Gen. Hoang Xuan Lam, said Sept. 16 that half of the North Vietnamese had withdrawn across the DMZ and the Laotian border because of an apparent lack of supplies. The allied mission, called Operation Lam Son 810, was launched to destroy enemy supply bases, halt troop and supply movements into the northwest section of South Vietnam over roads of the Ho Chi Minh Trail and stave off attacks aimed at disrupting the Oct. 3 South Vietnamese presidential elections (*see* [48]). The American military commitment in the sweep involved troop-carrying helicopters, artillery and air strikes and transport of war supplies. B-52 raids against the southern part of the demilitarized zone (*see* [47]) mounted in intensity as the South Vietnamese drive progressed, with the heaviest assault launched Sept. 9.

[50] Mekong Delta fighting. South Vietnamese forces, aided by U.S. air and artillery fire, Sept. 14 launched a drive against a Communist stronghold in the U Minh Forest of the Mekong Delta. According to government estimates, 623 Communists were killed. Government losses through Sept. 21 were placed at 113 killed and 183 wounded. Eleven U.S. helicopters were shot down by North Vietnamese gunners Sept. 14-21.

[51]   Saigon opens two new drives. South Vietnamese forces launched two new operations—one in the Mekong Delta Nov. 22 and the other in the Central Highlands Nov. 27. A force of 25,000 South Vietnamese was committed to the Mekong Delta drive, which was aimed at destroying an estimated force of 5,000 enemy troops in the area stretching from the U Minh Forest to the Camau Peninsula in the south. Only light fighting was reported. The Central Highlands offensive, involving 15,000 troops, was aimed at weakening enemy base areas in the region where South Vietnamese, Laotian and Cambodian borders met. The U.S. was providing air and artillery support, and three of its helicopters were shot down in the area after the start of the attack.

[52]   Holiday truces. Ground fighting in South Vietnam was relatively stilled by a 24-hour allied Christmas truce Dec. 24-25. The Communists had unilaterally declared a 72-hour Christmas truce Dec. 23-25. Another 24-hour truce for New Year's went into effect Dec. 31. The U.S. continued its air war over Indochina during the holiday truces. The Saigon command announced on the expiration of the Christmas truce at 6 p.m. Dec. 25 that Viet Cong forces had committed 49 violations; the Viet Cong charged 170 truce breaches by allied forces.

Prisoner of War Releases

[53]   Communist prisoners freed. South Vietnam Jan. 24 released 37 ill and disabled North Vietnamese prisoners of war (POWs). The captives rowed themselves across the Benghai River in the DMZ and were greeted by North Vietnamese troops on the opposite shore. South Vietnamese officials said 40 North Vietnamese prisoners had been chosen to be freed, but three of them "changed their mind at the last minute" and decided not to return.

[54]   Hanoi bars POW acceptance. North Vietnam June 3 officially refused to accept the return of 13 sick and wounded North Vietnamese POWs held in South Vietnam. The rejection was announced as a U.S. Navy ship was on its way to a prearranged rendezvous with a North Vietnamese barge off the coast of the DMZ to transfer the captives. The American vessel returned to Danang June 4 with the prisoners. Hanoi had agreed May 14 to a Saigon offer to release 570 sick and wounded North Vietnamese prisoners. South Vietnam added another 90 to the list of potential returnees, but announced May 31 that only 13 of the 660 POWs screened by International Red Cross officials wished to be repatriated. Hanoi June 3 cancelled the transfer accord, saying "because the U.S. and puppets have treacherously gone back on the decision to send 570 persons to the North, the stipulations for the scheduled June 4 reception are considered annulled." South Vietnamese Foreign Minister Tran Van Lam said June 2 that most of the prisoners who had refused to be freed fear "dread reprisals" and "violence against them."

[55]   2 prisoners released. The Viet Cong released American POW S. Sgt. John C. Sexton Oct. 8, and the U.S. reciprocated Oct. 11 by freeing a North Vietnamese captive in Cambodia. Sexton, the 24th American released by the Viet Cong and the first in 22 months, had been captured Aug. 12, 1969. He made his way to an allied base camp at Locninh, 70 miles north of Saigon.

[56]   Saigon frees Viet Cong. In honor of President Thieu's inauguration (*see* VIETNAM, SOUTH), the south Vietnamese government Oct. 31 began releasing 2,938 Viet Cong POWs. It was the largest such amnesty of the war. Of the total number freed, 618 prisoners were being returned to their villages in South Vietnam. The others were being assigned to the government's Chieu Hoi (Open Arms) program, which called for a two-three month indoctrination period. On completion of their "political rehabilitation," the men were to be released but were subject to future military service.

[57]   Hanoi pressed on U.S. POWs. U.S. entertainer Bob Hope met with North Vietnamese officials in Vientiane, Laos Dec. 23 in an attempt to negotiate the release of American POWs. Hope, who was in Indochina for his annual Christmas show for GIs, said he had proposed freeing the American

captives in exchange for a $10 million contribution to a North Vietnamese children's charity. Hope said he would raise the money through a charity show he would put on in the U.S.
(*See also* [59-60, 67-68, 71, 73-75, 79].)

American Withdrawals

[58] **Nixon increases pullout rate.** President Nixon announced in a televised address April 7 his decision to increase the rate of American troop withdrawals from Vietnam in order to bring home 100,000 more troops between May 1 and Dec. 1. Utilizing charts, the President pointed out his record of withdrawing troops: 265,000 by May 1, "almost half of the troops in Vietnam when I took office," and 365,000 by Dec. 1, over two-thirds of the number in Vietnam when he assumed office. The authorized force level when troop withdrawals were initiated June 15, 1969, was 544,000. It was 302,000 April 1. By Dec. 1, the target was 184,000. To achieve that, withdrawals would average 14,300 men a month compared to a 12,500 average over the previous year.

[59] **Total pullout conditions cited.** President Nixon April 16 conditioned a total U.S. withdrawal from Vietnam on release of all U.S. POWs and on South Vietnam's capacity to defend itself. (He reiterated the conditions April 29 at a news conference.) The President said that, while total withdrawal was the U.S. goal, it would be necessary for the U.S. to maintain a residual force and "an air presence" until those two conditions were met. Speaking of the POW issue, Nixon castigated the North Vietnamese for having been "the most barbaric in their handling of prisoners of any nation in modern history." He said no American president "could simply remove our forces" from Vietnam "as long as there's one American being held prisoner." There was some responsibility, he said, "to have some incentive on our side to get that man released." As for South Vietnam's ability to defend itself, Nixon defined that ability as "not the sure capacity, but at least the chance." Nixon defended his position by contending that it would save many more Asian lives than were lost by U.S. bombing and combat supply missions. If the U.S. "were to fail in Vietnam," he said, "if the Communists were to take over, the bloodbath that would follow would be a blot on this nation's history from which we would find it very difficult to return."

[60] **Further U.S. cut announced.** President Nixon, in an unscheduled appearance at a regular White House news briefing, announced Nov. 12 that 45,000 more U.S. troops would be withdrawn from South Vietnam by Feb. 1— 25,000 in December and 20,000 in January. The reduction in the authorized troop-level ceiling would be to a force of 139,000 men. As for future withdrawals, the next announcement would be made before Feb. 1, 1972, Nixon said, and would be based on: the level of enemy activity, particularly the infiltration rate; progress in the Vietnamization program; and progress "that may have been made" on gaining release of U.S. POWs and obtaining a cease-fire "for all of Southeast Asia." If a negotiated settlement of the war were attained, he said, it would mean total U.S. withdrawal from Southeast Asia, including the Asian theater supporting the Vietnam effort, and an end to air strikes. "If we do not get a negotiated settlement," Nixon said, "then it is necessary to maintain a residual force" in order to maintain a negotiating position and to work toward a South Vietnam capable of defending itself.

[61] **Allied withdrawals.** The U.S., Australia, South Korea, South Vietnam and New Zealand agreed April 23 to maintain support forces in South Vietnam as combat soldiers were withdrawn. In other developments: Australia and New Zealand announced Aug. 18 that they would withdraw their combat forces from South Vietnam by the end of 1971. Australian Prime Minister William McMahon said the majority of his country's 6,000 troops would be home by Christmas. New Zealand Prime Minister Sir Keith Holyoake said New Zealand's small force of 264 men would be pulled out by "about the end of this year." (New Zealand had announced March 17 that it would withdraw an

artillery battery of 131 men from South Vietnam in May.) Australia officially ended its combat role Nov. 7 by turning over to South Vietnamese forces its main base at Nuidat. South Korean Defense Minister Yoo Jae Heung announced Sept. 9 that withdrawal of an unspecified number of South Korea's 48,000-man force in South Vietnam would begin in December and be completed by June 1972.

Nixon Administration Policy

[62] **Nixon refuses to rule out invasion.** President Nixon refused to rule out the possibility of a unilateral South Vietnamese military move into North Vietnam, or any South Vietnamese operation which did not require U.S. cooperation. The President also declined to set any limits on the use of U.S. air power in the Indochina war except to bar the use of tactical nuclear weapons, but he reiterated that the U.S. would not use ground forces or advisers in Laos or Cambodia. Nixon refused to speculate on any South Vietnamese decision on a possible incursion into North Vietnam; and he repeated his frequently asserted policy to "take strong action," specifically including the use of air power, against any enemy action that would threaten U.S. troops remaining in Indochina. As for U.S. reaction to any incursion across the DMZ by North Vietnam, Nixon said, "I think the very fact that the North Vietnamese know that I intend to take strong action to deal with that incursion means that they are not going to take it. If they do, ... I would not be bound ... by any so-called understandings which they have already violated at the time of the bombing halt."

[63] A statement Feb. 25 by President Thieu that an invasion of North Vietnam was only a matter of time, and a charge the same day by Hanoi that the U.S. was planning a ground attack on North Vietnam, led to a barrage of statements by Administration officials aimed at discounting the possibility of extending the war into the North. U.S. Presidential adviser Henry A. Kissinger said Feb. 26 that the U.S. had no plans to invade North Vietnam, but he refrained from categorically denying that South Vietnamese forces would do so.

[64] **Report on U.S. air war.** A six-month survey sponsored by Cornell University's Center for International Studies, made public Nov. 7, said the U.S. was increasing the air war in Laos and Cambodia and maintaining a high level of bombing in South Vietnam as it reduced the American ground combat role in Indochina. The survey said the heavy use of American airpower was not impeding the Communist advance in Indochina and was imperiling prospects for peace because it was destroying the societies of the target countries. According to the report, the current level in bombing averaged about 70,000 tons a month, about the same level as in 1967, though only about half the rate of the peak period of 1968-69. By the end of 1971, the U.S. would have dropped on Indochina six million tons of bombs and other aerial ammunition—three times the tonnage used in World War II. The report also said that the rate of bombing in Laos and Cambodia had been increasing steadily—with about 400,000 tons of explosives being dropped during a year in Laos and about 90,000 tons a year in Cambodia. The high level of bombing in South Vietnam was being maintained with an average of 300,000 tons annually, according to the report, but the explosives were being dropped largely by the expanded South Vietnamese air force.

[65] **Laird explains bombing raids.** U.S. Defense Secretary Melvin R. Laird Dec. 27 declared that massive bombing raids on North Vietnam Dec. 26-30 (*see* [35]) had "the primary emphasis of protecting the remaining forces of Americans" in South Vietnam. He warned that the attacks would be repeated whenever necessary to protect the U.S. forces still in Vietnam. He also linked the raids to North Vietnam's alleged violation of the so-called understanding that led to the U.S. bombing halt in 1968, an understanding whose existence Hanoi had repeatedly denied. The Secretary said North Vietnam had violated

that understanding by shelling cities in the South, by constructing a road through the DMZ, by failure to engage in serious negotiations at the Paris peace talks (see [73-79]), by carrying out ·"very heavy attacks" on unarmed American reconnaissance aircraft and by using North Vietnam as a sanctuary for attacks by MiG fighters against American planes operating in Laos. Laird said the attacks were of "limited duration" and did not represent a basic change in U.S. bombing policy.

Congressional Action

[66] **Senate, House reject deadlines.** The Senate June 16 rejected two attempts to set a deadline for the withdrawal of American troops from Indochina. In the House, representatives voted 254-158 June 16 to defeat legislation setting a Congressional deadline for the withdrawal of U.S. forces by Dec. 31. The House action came on an amendment—offered by Reps. Lucien N. Nedzi (D, Mich.) and Charles W. Whalen Jr. (R, Ohio)—to a military procurement bill. The amendment was the counterpart of the (George S.) McGovern (D, S.D.)-(Mark O.) Hatfield (R, Ore.) amendment to the Selective Service bill defeated by a 55-42 vote in the Senate June 16. In an earlier vote June 16, the Senate had rejected, by a 52-44 vote, a compromise amendment to the same draft bill that would have set a withdrawal deadline of June 1, 1972. That proposal was sponsored by Sen. Lawton Chiles (D, Fla.).

[67] **Mansfield amendment.** The Senate June 22 adopted, by a 57-42 vote, an end-the-war amendment sponsored by Senate Majority Leader Mike Mansfield (Mont.) to the Selective Serv-ice bill. The amendment called for the withdrawal of all U.S. forces in Indochina within nine months in return for the phased release of American POWs. Although it was provisional, it was the first time the Senate had set a deadline for the disengagement of U.S. troops from Indochina. The Mansfield amendment, viewed as a moderate plan because it did not cut off funds to require a withdrawal by a certain date as other amendments had been designed to do, would establish the policy that the U.S. should "terminate at the earliest practicable date all military operations" in Indochina and "provide for the orderly withdrawal" of all U.S. forces within nine months after enactment of the amendment. The disengagement would be contingent on the release of all American prisoners. The amendment called on the President to establish a final date for troop withdrawal and to negotiate with North Vietnam an immediate cease-fire to be followed by "phased and rapid" withdrawal of U.S. troops in return for phased release of American prisoners. After five weeks of House-Senate conference on the Selective Service bill, during which House conferees refused to accept the Mansfield amendment, the amendment was diluted and the deadline for withdrawal was rewritten as a "sense of Congress" declaration that the war be ended at the "earliest practicable date." Backers of the amendment tried to send the bill back to conference to get the stronger measure reinstated, but the Senate rejected the recommittal motion by a 47-36 vote Sept. 17.

[68] The Senate, by a 57-38 vote Sept. 30, again approved a modified form of the Mansfield amendment as an amendment to a defense procurement bill. The modification in the amendment was in a change from withdrawal in nine months to withdrawal in six months. The other requirements of the bill remained the same. The House of Representatives Oct. 19 rejected, by a 215-192 vote, a motion by Leslie C. Arends (Ill.), senior Republican on the Armed Services Committee, to have House conferees in a House-Senate conference on the military procurement bill refuse to accept eight Senate amendments (including the Mansfield amendment) as nongermane to the bill and thus in violation of House procedure. The House Nov. 10 passed the military procurement bill, including the Mansfield amendment in a conference version which deleted the six-month deadline in favor of withdrawal by a "date certain" on condition of the release of the POWs. President Nixon signed the

procurement bill Nov. 17, but said that he would disregard the Mansfield amendment as having "no binding force or effect."

Peace Moves

[69] **Cambodia urges talks.** Cambodian Chief of State Cheng Heng May 31 proposed talks to end the fighting in Cambodia if the Viet Cong and North Vietnamese withdrew all their troops from the country. Government sources said that the proposal was not new but that it was the first time Cambodia had voiced the suggestion since the ouster of Prince Norodom Sihanouk in March 1970. Representatives of the North Vietnamese and Viet Cong at the Paris peace talks rejected the suggestion. In rejecting the proposal, a spokesman of the Viet Cong said: "We support the struggle waged by Prince Norodom Sihanouk and the Khmer people and will never have anything to do with the present Pnompenh administration."

[70] **Proposals on Laos.** Laotian Premier Souvanna Phouma May 26 proposed peace talks with the Pathet Lao "without delay" to halt the fighting in Laos. The proposal was contained in a letter sent to Pathet Lao leader Prince Souphanouvong. Souvanna Phouma June 30 called for holding peace talks in Vientiane without preconditions. He also indicated that withdrawal of foreign troops from Laos was his condition for acceptance of a Pathet Lao proposal sent by Souphanouvong June 22 and repeated June 25. The Pathet Lao June 30 refused his suggestion. On the Pathet Lao side, the plan submitted June 22 and 25 called for an "immediate cease-fire on the whole of the Laotian territory, which would include the end of American bombing and a cease-fire on the spot by the armed forces of Laos, with an end to all military activities on land and in the air, all acts of violation or encroachment against the area under the control of the other side." The cease-fire would be followed by negotiations to bring about "peace and national agreement." A new element in the Pathet Lao plan was the inclusion of a halt to the American bombing as part of the truce proposal; they had previously demanded the bombing halt as a precondition for a truce.

[71] **Clifford offers peace plan.** Clark M. Clifford, secretary of defense under former President Lyndon B. Johnson, proposed a plan June 8 for ending American involvement in Indochina by the end of 1971. He said his formula was based on a "number of conversations and meetings I have had in recent weeks with different people, some of them Americans and some of them not." He declined to say whether he had been in direct contact with North Vietnamese, Viet Cong or Soviet officials. Clifford suggested withdrawal of all American troops and an end to U.S. military activity in Vietnam by Dec. 31. All American POWs held by North Vietnam were to be released within 30 days of a joint Washington-Hanoi announcement of the accord. The Viet Cong and North Vietnamese in turn would agree to refrain from attacking U.S. soldiers during the withdrawal period. U.S. obligation to remove its troops would be suspended if the Communists failed to release the captives within the specified 30 days.

[72] **Peking for Asian parley.** The Australian embassy in Washington July 14 informed the U.S. State Department that Communist China had expressed interest in participating in a new international conference on Indochina. (Australian opposition Labor party leader Gough Whitlam had discussed the matter with Premier Chou En-lai in Peking during a visit to China in July and had communicated the substance of the conversations to the Australian government.) According to the Australian notice, the Chinese wanted the "administrative arrangements" of such a conference "to be more in an Asian framework than the framework set up in 1954" for the Geneva conference which had ended French-Communist fighting in Indochina. The 1954 parley had been attended by China, the Soviet Union, Laos, Cambodia, South Vietnam, the U.S., Britain and France. China's readiness to take part in a new

conference evoked counterstatements July 17-20 by the Viet Cong and North Vietnamese, who insisted the problem be handled by the Vietnamese themselves.

[73] Paris peace talks. The Paris peace talks remained deadlocked during 1971 as they entered their fourth year. The talks were suspended March 18-April 8 by the North Vietnamese and Viet Cong delegations in protest over U.S. air strikes against North Vietnam (*see* [35]). North Vietnamese chief delegate Xuan Thuy boycotted the talks March 4-April 15 over the same issue. North Vietnam April 29 proposed negotiating a date for the total withdrawal of U.S. troops from South Vietnam, but President Nixon rejected the offer the same day by reiterating his insistence that he would not set a definite date for a complete pullout until Hanoi made "a commitment to release our prisoners." David K. E. Bruce, chief American delegate to the talks, July 28 formally announced his resignation for reasons of health. He attended his last session of the talks July 29. Bruce was replaced by William J. Porter, U.S. ambassador to South Korea. Philip C. Habib, senior adviser to Bruce, acted as head of the American delegation until Sept. 9 when Porter assumed the post. Porter Sept. 9 renewed a U.S. offer to hold secret talks, but the Communists rejected the suggestion. At the 138th session of the talks Dec. 9, allied and Communist delegations failed to agree even on when to hold their next meeting. Porter proposed that the next session be Dec. 23 rather than Dec. 16 as would be the normal pattern. Porter suggested the delay to allow the Communists "more time to develop a constructive approach here." The Communists rejected Porter's suggestion and inquired Dec. 14 if the allied side was prepared to meet Dec. 16. Porter Dec. 15 said he would not meet Dec. 16 and was also canceling the proposed new date. He suggested the meeting be held Dec. 30. The scheduled Dec. 30 talks were canceled by the U.S. and North Vietnamese Dec. 28 in reaction to the massive air attacks on North Vietnam (*see* [35]). The North Vietnamese proposed that the next session be held Jan. 6, 1972, but the U.S. and South Vietnamese did not respond to the offer.

[74] POW discussions. Throughout the year, American delegates to the talks requested clear and complete figures on American servicemen being held prisoner by the North Vietnamese and Viet Cong. The Communists repeatedly insisted that a list of 339 American prisoners (listing 20 as dead) released December 1970 was "complete and definitive." In an interview July 30, Mrs. Nguyen Thi Binh, head of the Viet Cong delegation, offered to identify all American POWs as soon as the U.S. set a deadline for the total withdrawal of its troops from Indochina. U.S. spokesman Stephen Ledogar Oct. 7 said that 1,618 American servicemen were missing, only a third of them believed to be still alive.

[75] New Viet Cong plan. Mrs. Binh July 1 submitted to the talks a seven-point peace plan (approved by the North Vietnamese) which proposed the release of all American and allied POWs in North and South Vietnam by the end of 1971 if all U.S. troops were withdrawn by that date. Both procedures were to start and end simultaneously. The plan contrasted with a previous Communist proposal that merely called for a start of immediate discussions of the POW issue as soon as Washington set what the Communists regarded as a reasonable date for a pullout. The troop withdrawal-POW issue was the first of the seven points of the plan. The first point also said that the U.S. "must put an end to its war of aggression and stop the policy of 'Vietnamization' of the war" and that all American and other non-Vietnamese troops be pulled out of South Vietnam and their bases in the country be dismantled "without posing any condition whatever." The statement said "a cease-fire will be observed" between the Viet Cong and U.S. forces "as soon as the parties reach agreement" on the withdrawal proposal.

[76] The remaining six points dealt with the political aspects of the problem: 2. The U.S. must "put an end to its interference in the internal affairs of South Vietnam, cease backing the bellicose group headed by Nguyen Van Thieu, ... and stop all maneuvers, including tricks on elections, aimed at maintaining"

Thieu in power. Viet Cong and Thieu administration officials would hold immediate talks on forming "a broad three-segment government of national concord that will assume its functions during the restoration of peace and the holding of general elections...." A truce was to be observed as soon as the new government was formed. 3. The Vietnamese themselves would "settle the question of Vietnamese armed forces in South Vietnam ... without foreign interference...."

[77] 4. The reunification of Vietnam was "to be achieved step by step by peaceful means, on the basis of discussions and agreements between the two zones, without constraint and annexation from either party, without foreign interference." "Pending the reunification of the country, the North and the South zones will re-establish normal relations, guarantee free movement, free correspondence, free choice of residence, and maintain economic and cultural relations on the principle of mutual interests and mutual assistance. All questions concerning the two zones will be settled by qualified representatives of the Vietnamese people in the two zones on the basis of negotiations, without foreign interference. In keeping with the provisions of the 1954 Geneva agreements on Vietnam, in the present temporary partition of the country into two zones, the North and the South zones of Vietnam will refrain from joining any military alliance with foreign countries, from allowing any foreign country to have military bases, troops, and military personnel on their soil, and from recognizing the protection of any country, of any military alliance or bloc."

[78] 5. South Vietnam must "pursue a foreign policy of peace and neutrality." 6. The U.S. "must bear full responsibility for the losses and the destruction it has caused to the Vietnamese people in the two zones." 7. The "parties will find agreement on the forms of respect and international guarantees of the accords that will be concluded."

[79] The plan was first officially criticized July 8 by Ambassador Bruce, who proposed at that time further discussion of the proposal in a secret meeting the following week. The suggestion was rejected by the Communists. Bruce objected to the Viet Cong demand for unconditional withdrawal of American troops as "so sweeping and categorical in nature that we cannot possibly accept" it "without any discussion or negotiation." He disapproved of the Viet Cong proposal (clarified July 6) for dealing only with the release of prisoners taken in Vietnam and not with those captured in Laos and Cambodia. He objected to the Communist call for a transitional Saigon regime that would exclude President Thieu and said: "We will not impose any government on the people of South Vietnam who must be allowed to determine for themselves their future." At the July 15 session, Bruce continued to press for clarification of the plan. He called on the Communists to answer five questions concerning the plan. The questions dealt with: whether the plan was the only basis for negotiation; whether the allies had to agree to the Viet Cong's "arbitrary demands [in point one] without any discussion or negotiation on them"; if point one meant that the U.S. must fix its date of withdrawal without negotiations beforehand; if the POW release would include prisoners taken in Laos and Cambodia; and if the "military and political questions" were to be "dealt with separately." Xuan Thuy called Bruce's questions an attempt "to stall negotiations by refusing to answer the seven points."

See also AUSTRALIA [1, 12]; BUDGET; BULGARIA; CAMBODIA; CHURCHES [11, 13-14]; COMMUNIST CHINA-U.S. DETENTE [8, 10, 13]; DRAFT & WAR PROTEST; DRUG USE & ADDICTION [14-19]; FOREIGN AID; FOREIGN POLICY; FRANCE [17]; PENTAGON PAPERS; POLITICS [4, 13]; RACIAL & MINORITY UNREST [1]; SECURITY, U.S.; SELECTIVE SERVICE SYSTEM [5-6, 13]; SUDAN; UNEMPLOYMENT; VIETNAM, NORTH; WAR CRIMES; YOUTH

INDONESIA—Ruling coalition wins. The government's ruling Sekber Golkar coalition won a sweeping victory in the July 3 parliamentary elections, according to the official results announced Aug. 7. The party captured 227 of the 351 contested seats of the 360-member House of Representatives. Sekber Golkar was expected to win all nine seats from West Irian when the tally in the New Guinea province was completed. The seats won by the opposition parties: Moslem Scholars—60; Parmusi, another Moslem party—23; and the Indonesian Nationalist party, founded by the late President Sukarno—20. The remaining seats were split between the four minor parties. It was Indonesia's first national election in 16 years.

Prisoners to be freed. Foreign Minister Adam Malik announced Aug. 28 that Indonesia would release 22,000 Communist detainees by the end of 1971. He said 6,000 would be freed by the end of September. Malik placed the number of Communist prisoners at 45,000 and said the government would release those not criminally involved in anti-government unrest during 1965-66.

See also OIL

INFLATION—See ECONOMY, U.S.; POVERTY
INSURANCE—See AUTOMOBILES [6-7, 13]; ECONOMY, U.S. [24]; HEALTH CARE; MEDICINE
INTEGRATION—See CIVIL RIGHTS
INTELSAT—See DEFENSE [8]
INTER-AMERICAN COMMITTEE ON THE ALLIANCE FOR PROGRESS (CIAP)—
See LATIN AMERICA
INTER-AMERICAN DEVELOPMENT BANK—See FOREIGN AID; LATIN AMERICA
INTERNAL REVENUE SERVICE (IRS)—See CIVIL RIGHTS [13]; ECONOMY, U.S. [15, 24]; HEALTH CARE; TAXES
INTERNATIONAL ATOMIC ENERGY AGENCY (IAEA)—See ATOMIC ENERGY [10, 13]; DISARMAMENT

INTERNATIONAL BANK FOR RECONSTRUCTION & DEVELOPMENT (IBRD OR WORLD BANK)—The governors of the 116-nation World Bank Group and the 118-country International Monetary Fund met in Washington Sept. 27-Oct. 1 for their 26th joint annual conference. The meeting, attended by most of the world's finance ministers and central bank chiefs, centered on the need to restructure the world monetary system and to deal with the dislocations stemming from the new economic policy adopted by the Nixon Administration Aug. 15. Existing monetary and trade problems had been heightened by the U.S. action Aug. 15 ending the dollar's convertibility to gold and imposing a 10% surcharge on nonquota imports. (See ECONOMY, U.S. [8].)

Despite an early atmosphere of divisiveness, the IMF governors reached agreement Oct. 1 on broad outlines of the measures needed to reform the monetary system and deal with the differences between the U.S. and its trade partners. The board voted a resolution calling on member governments to: "Establish a satisfactory structure of exchange rates, maintained within appropriate margins, for the currencies of members, together with the reduction of restrictive trade and exchange practices, and facilitate resumption of the orderly conduct of the operations of the fund." Collaborate in efforts to bring about "A reversal of the tendency in present circumstances to maintain and extend restrictive trade and exchange practices, and satisfactory arrangements for the settlement of international transactions which will contribute to the solution of the problems involved in the present international monetary situation."

The highlight of the conference was a conditional offer by U.S. Secretary of the Treasury John B. Connally Jr. Sept. 30 to remove the surtax if other nations (1) made "tangible progress toward dismantling specific barriers to trade" (he did not specify the nations or items involved) and (2) allowed "market realities freely to determine exchange rates for their currencies for a transitional period." Connally presented his offer as a "more timely and constructive" way to remove the surtax than as part of lengthy and arduous negotiations over specific new currency exchange rates. A government official later said the proposal was submitted as an "alternative" to, but not necessarily a substitute for, direct negotiations. The proposal was warmly applauded at the meeting as the first U.S. step toward breaking the international economic stalemate.

Connally proposed a "clean float" be authorized to permit currency rates to fluctuate in response to market forces uncurbed by intervention or restrictive measures by national governments and central banks. The idea of a free float was welcomed by some nations, but described as unrealistic by others. Although Connally's speech implied flexibility on issues of immediate negotiation, it expressed determination to secure a binding solution to the inequities of the U.S. position abroad.

In an earlier development, France, Italy, Canada, Japan, India, Belgium, Holland and Australia, led by West German Economics and Finance Minister Karl Schiller (chairman of the meeting) and IMF Managing Director Pierre-Paul Schweitzer Sept. 27, supported proposals for replacing the dollar with the IMF's Special Drawing Rights (SDR or paper gold) as the major reserve unit. (Several countries earlier had called for the devaluation of the dollar as part of a general currency realignment.) Although most countries only endorsed the concept, British Chancellor of the Exchequer Anthony Barber Sept. 28 presented a detailed plan to implement it. The core of the Barber plan was to phase out national currencies as reserve currencies in order to create a system not dominated by a national currency. The three central points of the plan were: use of the SDRs as the pivotal measure of the monetary system and its main reserve unit; controls for adequate but not excessive world liquidity without reliance on the deficit position of one or more countries; and expanded use of national currencies for trading and market intervention. Most delegations supported the proposals for increased reliance on SDRs.

See also COMMUNISM, INTERNATIONAL; PAKISTAN [35, 39]

INTERNATIONAL BROTHERHOOD OF TEAMSTERS—*See* LABOR [2, 4-5, 9-10]
INTERNATIONAL COURT OF JUSTICE—*See* ITALY [15]; SOUTH AFRICA [2, 12]; TERRITORIAL WATERS; UNITED NATIONS [3]
INTERNATIONAL INVESTMENT BANK—*See* COMMUNISM, INTERNATIONAL
INTERNATIONAL JOINT COMMISSION (IJC)—*See* POLLUTION [11]
INTERNATIONAL LABOR ORGANIZATION (ILO)—*See* UNITED NATIONS [10]

INTERNATIONAL MONETARY DEVELOPMENTS—A hugh dollar outflow from the U.S. to Europe in April and early May resulted in a massive wave of speculation against the dollar and the revaluation or flotation of five European currencies. In response to the monetary crisis, West Germany urged the flotation of all currencies in the European Economics Community (EEC), but the move was opposed by France and Italy. The dollar weakened in international trading and European countries and Japan were forced to pass measures to reduce speculation. President Nixon's decision Aug. 15 to float the dollar (*see* ECONOMY, U.S. [8]) caused foreign exchange markets to close and resulted in further weakening of the dollar. Following a "mini-summit" between President Nixon and French President Georges Pompidou Dec. 13-14 and a meeting of finance ministers of the Group of 10 Dec. 17-18, the U.S. Dec. 18 announced the devaluation of the U.S. dollar by 8.57%.

[2] Some European currencies shift. A massive wave of speculation against the dollar swept through European money markets beginning May 4 and resulted, by May 9, in the upward revaluation of the Swiss franc and the Austrian schilling and the flotation of the West German mark and the Netherlands guilder. The shift amounted to a partial devaluation of the dollar. Underlying causes of the crisis of confidence in the dollar were enmeshed in a variety of interrelated factors: continued and growing deficits in the U.S. balance of international payments ($10.68 billion in 1970 when calculated on an official payments basis); monetary inflation in the U.S., coupled with declining interest rates in a recessive economy at a time when West Germany was raising interest rates to cope with its own inflationary pressures; the spectacular recent growth in Euro-dollars (dollars held by Europeans and U.S. banks and firms doing business in Europe), flowing freely through the West's capital markets and adding mass to the wave of speculation; and dwindling U.S. reserves of gold and foreign currencies. (Some U.S. and European news sources attributed the latest run on the dollar to the publication May 3 of a group of West German economic studies urging that the mark be freed from its current dollar parity to float to a new and higher value.) The flood of dollars into European markets forced European central banks to intervene and absorb them to prevent the dollar's value from falling below its "floor"—1% below its official fixed parity with the specific country's currency. The West German Central Bank alone was reported to have bought $1 billion in U.S. dollars May 4. On the morning of May 5, West Germany's Bundesbank—followed by the central banks of Switzerland, Belgium, the Netherlands and Austria—unexpectedly withdrew support of the dollar and refused to accept more U.S. currency. The five countries suspended foreign exchange markets for the rest of the week. Later in the day, Portugal and Finland also closed their foreign exchange markets.

[3]   West Germany won the grudging permission of its EEC partners May 9 to free the mark from its fixed parity and permit it to float within a certain range. Following a marathon 20-hour meeting of the EEC's finance ministers, a compromise communique was issued that enabled the West German Cabinet to take independent action. (West Germany had sought agreement at the meeting on a plan to float all EEC currencies together to create a new and flexible parity base that would result in common increases in value against the dollar. France and Italy had been opposed to the plan, arguing that it would bring devaluation of their currencies against those of other EEC members.) The May 10 decision to float the mark freed the West German currency to find a new value in the competitive market, but within a predetermined and undisclosed range. The secrecy of the new margins and their duration was intended to conceal from speculators the point at which the Bundesbank would intervene and sell marks to maintain a secret ceiling on its value. In a supplementary action, the government introduced a series of tough new controls on capital movements designed to assist the Bundesbank in managing the float.

[4]   West Germany's close trading partners—Switzerland, the Netherlands, Austria and Belgium—all acted May 9 to control the tide of excess dollars in their countries. Switzerland raised the value of its franc 7% against the dollar in the first parity change in the gold-backed franc since 1936. Austria raised the value of the schilling 5.05%. The Netherlands floated the guilder. Belgium, the only EEC country with a two-tier (free and official) foreign exchange market, announced that it would float its franc in free market transactions (into which excess capital inflows would be funneled). (Belgium decided May 11 not to float the franc or to widen its permitted fluctuation from parity.) The International Monetary Fund (IMF) May 9 officially approved the revaluation of the schilling, but noted that the flotation of the mark and the guilder was a violation of an IMF rule that the market price of a member's currency be held to within 1% of its official parity. Germany and the Netherlands reportedly had assured the IMF that they would float their currencies only temporarily and would return to a fixed parity. (As foreign exchange markets opened May 10, the mark's value rose by 3.3%—a narrower rise than expected. The dollar displayed firmness against the mark and most other currencies.)

[5]   *EEC stalemate.* The May 9 currency changes produced a stalemate in the EEC which brought a meeting of finance ministers to a standstill on monetary reform July 2. France refused to back proposals by the EEC's Executive Commission on greater currency flexibility in member nations unless Germany and the Netherlands detailed the date on which their currencies would return to

a fixed parity. Germany said that the mark would continue to float until the IMF adopted new rules widening the permissible margins of fluctuation in exchange rates to 2% or 3% from the authorized 1%. Two days of French-West German summit talks July 5-6 in Bonn between President Pompidou and German Chancellor Willy Brandt failed to break the deadlock. The summit resulted only in a promise from Brandt that the mark would not float indefinitely.

[6] *BIS meeting.* The Bank for International Settlements (BIS) June 14 announced an agreement by member central banks on joint action to control the Eurocurrency market (an unregulated pool of currency on deposit, including an estimated $1 billion in Eurodollars, held by institutions outside their country of origin). The Eurocurrency poll was believed to have been a principal source of the "hot money" capital flows that had fueled the run on the dollar. With about $3 billion of surplus BIS funds in the Eurocurrency market, the central bankers agreed to temporarily refrain from placing BIS funds in the market and to withdraw funds "when such action is prudent in the light of market conditions."

[7] **France checks dollar intake.** The Bank of France inadvertently touched off a burst of speculation against the dollar Aug. 4 when it became known that the bank had issued instructions the previous day banning all purchases of dollars except for commercial transactions. Rumors of an impending revaluation of the franc, fanned by the central bank's action, sent European currencies soaring and the dollar falling on the Zurich, Frankfurt and London money markets. The dollar dropped below its floor in Brussels and Paris. The French central bank took stronger measures to stem the inflow of dollars Aug. 6, and pressure on the dollar subsided. The bank announced that French banks would no longer pay interest on foreigners' deposits of French francs for less than 91 days. Banks were also expected to adhere unofficially to a proposed $500,000 ceiling for deposits not requiring authorization.

[8] **Devaluation report causes dollar weakening.** The Congressional Joint Economic Subcommittee on International Exchange and Payments, in a report Aug. 7 based on hearings held in June, in effect recommended devaluation of the U.S. dollar. The report said that international exchange rates should be readjusted to compensate for an unspecified overvaluation of the dollar. It urged the IMF to pressure certain of its members to revalue their currencies upward against the dollar. If the IMF should fail to comply, the report suggested that the U.S. should consider a unilateral action to achieve the same result. The subcommittee's chairman, Rep. Henry Reuss (D, Wis.) said Aug. 7 that a total devaluation of the dollar by raising the price of gold would be unacceptable because it would give gold-producing countries "windfall profits" but would not assure a shift in the dollar's relative exchange rate with other countries. The congressional report was blamed for a new round of speculation against the dollar and a sharp rise in the price of gold on European markets Aug. 9. The Swiss Central Bank Aug. 9 suspended convertibility of the dollar to stem a speculative tide of "hot money" into Switzerland. (The suspension was to last until Aug. 20, when a gentlemen's agreement between the central bank and the Swiss Bankers Association would become effective, enabling the central bank to fix reserve requirements as high as 100% on foreign-owned franc deposits in excess of normal business transactions and to limit or forbid interest payments on funds entering Switzerland.) In Frankfurt, the dollar closed at 3.4090 marks to the dollar, in effect a 7.5% devaluation of the dollar in terms of the mark's value before it was floated. The dollar briefly dropped through its floor of 620.50 lira in Milan. In Brussels and Tokyo, central banks intervened to keep the dollar from falling below its limits. In Paris, the dollar fell to its floor of 5.5125 francs to the dollar. On the London bullion exchange, gold rose Aug. 9 from $42.90 an ounce to $43.95—its highest level since the two-tier system for gold dealing was introduced in March 1968.

[9] **Dollar floated.** President Nixon's Aug. 15 decision to float the dollar (*see* ECONOMY, U.S. [8]) caused most European governments to close their foreign exchange markets Aug. 16 with no clear idea of when normal currency dealings would resume. The IMF recognized the dollar as a floating currency Aug. 20. The EEC Council of Ministers, at a 16-hour meeting in Brussels Aug. 19-20, agreed to an opening of their exchange markets, but failed to agree on a joint monetary policy toward the newly freed dollar. Each member nation was to decide for itself how much the dollar would be allowed to depreciate against its currency. The talks stalled over the same issue that had arisen after Germany devalued the mark (*see* [3]). After an emergency Cabinet meeting Aug. 18, France proposed the system it adopted Aug. 23, a two-tier exchange system like that in Belgium. Germany had traditionally opposed the system because government intervention would be required in the free market. European exchange markets reopened Aug. 23. None of the major nations followed President Nixon's suggestion Aug. 15 that they raise the value of their currencies against the dollar. Instead, they adopted controlled floats (in Britain, Switzerland, Belgium and Italy), widened bans of fluctuation from parity, two-tier systems and, in Israel's case, outright devaluation.

[10] Swiss money markets remained offically closed Aug. 23, but in interbank trading where the Swiss franc was allowed to float unofficially, the dollar was quoted at just below the official support level of 4.01 francs to the dollar. A Cabinet meeting Aug. 23 failed to reach a decision on policy toward the monetary crisis, but the gentlemen's agreement went into effect Aug. 13. Another decree by the central bank banned interest payments on deposits made by nonresidents after July 31, except those that could not be withdrawn before six months. Belgium, which permitted the franc to float in both tiers of its system, Aug. 21 reached agreement with the Netherlands and Luxembourg to form a provisional monetary bloc within the EEC to coordinate a common float against the dollar. In Milan, the Italian lira was permitted to float above the mandatory support level for a rise in value of just over 1%. West Germany continued to float its mark. Austria waited until Aug. 24 to reopen its exchanges. It supported the official parity of 26 schillings to the dollar, but widened the margins from parity. Norway's central bank Aug. 23 floated the crown in relation to the dollar. The Bank of Sweden announced Aug. 22 that it would not alter the exchange rate of the kroner, but would let the dollar decline without imposing a lower limit.

[11] *IMF informed of U.S. action.* The U.S. formally notified the IMF Aug. 16 that it "no longer freely buys and sells gold for the settlement of international transactions." This meant that the U.S. would no longer honor its agreement to pay out gold for foreign-held dollars at the rate of $35 an ounce. According to the Treasury's Public Affairs Department, U.S. gold reserves stood at $10,132,144,053.74 when payments were suspended Aug. 16. The Treasury was instructed to limit further use of all reserve assets to settlement of outstanding obligations and, in cooperation with the IMF, "to other situations that may arise in which such use can contribute to international monetary stability and the interests of the U.S." In another move, the Federal Reserve Board (FRB) was asked by the White House to suspend use of its "swap" network for converting dollars into other foreign currencies. (The FRB July 12 had increased its swap lines in order to temporarily borrow back excess dollars from other countries.)

[12] *Japan floats yen.* Following an emergency meeting at the Finance Ministry Aug. 27, the Japanese government announced that it would float the yen within undisclosed parity bands against the U.S. dollar. The present value of 360 yen to the dollar would be maintained, avoiding outright revaluation of the yen. The float was accomplished by a temporary suspension, effective Aug. 28, of IMF 1% fluctuation rules. The Finance Ministry statement said that the competitive strength of the yen had become so "enhanced" over the previous two decades that the IMF margins were "no longer wide enough to ensure the

smooth functioning of trade and other external transactions." Japan Aug. 31 tightened its currency exchange controls against a runaway rise in the yen's value. The controls were imposed after the yen floated upward to a quotation of 339 yen to the dollar, representing a 5.8% upward revaluation. The measures prohibited advance payments for Japanese exports, sharply restricted "free yen" accounts by non-Japanese residents and insured strict observance of unofficial guidelines set down by the Bank of Japan requiring each foreign exchange bank to have on reserve a certain number of dollars.

[13] **Europe tightens money curbs.** Among actions taken, following the floating of the dollar, by European governments to cope with speculative inflow of dollars: Great Britain, following a record $1.56 billion capital inflow in August, Aug. 27 imposed controls, effective Aug. 31, prohibiting interest payments on new pound holdings by nonresidents and Sept. 2 lowered its bank rate from 6% to 5% to discourage further transfers; West Germany July 21 announced plans to freeze without interest part of the foreign credits accrued there by nonbanking corporations, thus making it less economic for companies to borrow abroad; the Swiss central bank acted Aug. 27 to abolish interest on capital entering Switzerland since July 31 in Swiss francs for longer than six months (see [10]); the Netherlands Sept. 6 introduced a series of currency controls requiring nonresidents to buy bonds with what were designated as "O" guilders obtained from a revolving pool of "O" guilders fed by the sales of the bonds. (If foreign demand became heavy, the "O" guilders could be obtained only at a premium, making them progressively more expensive for speculators.) France announced Dec. 3 strict new foreign exchange controls to block, beginning Dec. 10, the conversion back to other currencies of nonresident franc holdings accumulated from Nov. 30. The move was designed to prevent foreigners from speculating in the commercial franc—the franc maintained at the old parity rate in France's new two-tier system.

[14] **Dollar devalued.** Finance ministers and central bank governors of the Group of 10 industrial nations, meeting in tight security in Washington, D.C. Dec. 17-18, reached agreement on a general realignment of currency exchange rates that included an 8.57% devaluation of the dollar against gold. The chief monetary aspects of the agreement, including an enlargement of parity fluctuation margins to 2.25%, were approved by the executive directors of the IMF in Washington Dec. 19. The agreement—said to be the first genuinely multinational negotiation of exchange rates—ended the flotation of major currencies. The accord was announced by President Nixon Dec. 18. Nixon confirmed that, for its part, the U.S. had agreed to official devaluation of the dollar and swift removal of the 10% surcharge (see TARIFFS & WORLD TRADE[8-12]). The agreement included a proposed increase in the official price of gold from $35 an ounce to $38—to be authorized by the U.S. Congress only when undisclosed short-term trade concessions to the U.S. (presumably from Japan, Canada, and the EEC) were "available for congressional scrutiny." Restoration of the dollar's convertibility into gold (see [11]) was not immediately envisaged. In the interim, exchange rates would be fixed as if the new gold price were already effective. The higher gold price formally devalued the dollar by 8.57% in terms of converting dollars into foreign currencies, or 7.89% when converting foreign currencies to dollars. The devaluation and realignment amounted to an average depreciation of 12% in the dollar's value when weighted for differing parties and varying levels of trade with the other countries concerned.

[15] Most of the member nations, plus Switzerland (a participating member at the Group of 10 meeting), agreed to further revalue their currencies by varying amounts. The exceptions were France and Britain, whose rates remained unchanged in terms of their relation to gold but not to the U.S. dollar, and Canada, whose dollar continued to float. Although the new rates were not disclosed by the Group of 10 communique in order to permit individual announcement by the members, it was revealed that, compared with the rates

prevailing before May, they would include upward revaluations of the mark by 12.89%, the yen by 16.89%, the Belgian franc by nearly 11% and the Swiss franc by 14.89%. Upward revaluations for the British pound and the French franc would be 8.57%—the equivalent of the U.S. devaluation. The Italian lira and the Swedish kroner would be devalued by 1%-2%.

[16] *Background to decision.* The U.S. first showed a willingness to devalue the dollar, rather than insisting on an upward revaluation of other currencies, at a Group of 10 meeting Nov. 30-Dec. 1. The delegates to the meeting Nov. 30 rejected a U.S. proposal for an overall 11% upward revaluation of major currencies against the dollar in exchange for the removal of the 10% surtax. The U.S. proposal also called for 3% fluctuation margins in any new parity system. The U.S. apparently altered its devaluation position after the delegates of the EEC and Britain refused to present their proposed parity changes unless the U.S. accepted dollar devaluation "in principle." The U.S. Dec. 1 reportedly asked the delegates in a closed executive session what the other nations would do if the dollar was devalued by 10%. A recess was called and, when the talks resumed later that day, the U.S. was reportedly told that 10% would be too high.

[17] The first concrete statement that devaluation would occur came Dec. 14, after about 12 hours of talks Dec. 13-14 in a "mini-summit" in the Azores between Presidents Nixon and Pompidou. In the communique issued Dec. 14, the two presidents agreed to "work toward a prompt realignment of exchange rates through a devaluation of the dollar and revaluation of some other currencies." (Pompidou did not agree to revalue the franc.) The U.S. agreement in principle, which openly committed the Nixon Administration to the first official change in the dollar value of gold since 1934, marked a major concession to Europe—and to France in particular—which had long insisted on the move as a way to alleviate the world monetary crisis. The two presidents agreed that the realignment could "be accompanied by broader permissible margins of fluctuation around the newly established exchange rates." This marked a concession by France to the U.S. France previously had insisted that the existing rate margins remain untouched. France's main concession in the accord was to agree to work with other members of the EEC to prepare "a mandate which would permit the immediate opening" of trade negotiations with the U.S. France had previously refused to let the EEC open negotiations pending U.S. concessions toward monetary settlement. No specific figures were disclosed for the devaluation of the dollar.

[18] The Nixon-Pompidou announcement sent the dollar plunging on most international monetary markets Dec. 14-15. The French central bank intervened to support the dollar against the commercial franc but then withdrew, letting the dollar slip to 5.51 francs to the dollar. The floating financial franc rose to 5.29-5.31 francs to the dollar Dec. 15, up from 5.38-5.39 francs to the dollar Dec. 14—in effect a 3.14% upward revaluation of the franc. After quiet trading, marked by the intervention of the Bundesbank, the dollar closed in Frankfurt Dec. 14 and 15 at 3.25 marks to the dollar. In London, the pound held Dec. 15 at about $2.51, almost 5% above the parity of $2.41 to the pound. The Japanese yen reached a 12% upward revaluation since it was floated, as the dollar fell to a new low of 321.39 yen Dec. 15. Gold prices on the bullion markets showed little reaction to the decision to devalue the dollar.

See also AFRICA; COMMUNISM, INTERNATIONAL; COMMUNIST CHINA-U.S. DETENTE [5]; ECONOMY, U.S. [8]; EUROPEAN ECONOMIC COMMUNITY [2, 11-12]; GREAT BRITAIN [8]; INTERNATIONAL BANK FOR RECONSTRUCTION & DEVELOPMENT; TARIFFS & WORLD TRADE [8-9]

INTERNATIONAL MONETARY FUND (IMF)—*See* INTERNATIONAL BANK FOR RECONSTRUCTION & DEVELOPMENT; INTERNATIONAL MONETARY DEVELOPMENTS [4-5, 8-9, 11-12, 14]; TARIFFS & WORLD TRADE [1]

INTERNATIONAL RED CROSS—*See* GREECE [3]; INDOCHINA WAR [54]; KOREAN RELATIONS; PAKISTAN [34]
INTERNATIONAL TELECOMMUNICATIONS SATELLITE CONSORTIUM (INTELSAT)—*See* SPACE [20]
INTERNATIONAL TELEPHONE & TELEGRAPH (ITT)—*See* CHILE [11]
INTERSPUTNIK—*See* SPACE [24]
INTERSTATE COMMERCE COMMISSION (ICC)—*See* GOVERNMENT REORGANIZATION; RAILROADS
INVESTORS OVERSEAS SERVICES (IOS)—*See* BUSINESS [2]

IRAN—2,500-year anniversary celebration. Shah Mohammed Riza Pahlevi staged an elaborate celebration Oct. 12-14 to honor the 2,500th anniversary of the founding of the Persian Empire by Cyrus the Great. To accommodate the long list of illustrious guests, the shah built a tent city in the desert at Persepolis. Cost of the celebration was reported to be about $100 million, a figure many thought to be too extravagant for Iran's developing economy. Guests included Emperor Haile Selassie of Ethiopia, President Nikolai V. Podgorny of the Soviet Union, Marshal Tito of Yugoslavia, U.S. Vice President Spiro Agnew, Kuo Mo-jo, a representative of Communist China, President V. V. Giri of India, President Agha Mohammed Yahya Khan of Pakistan, King Frederik and Queen Ingrid of Denmark, King Baudouin of Belgium, King Constantine of Greece, and Prince Philip and Princess Anne of Great Britain.

Iran seizes Persian Gulf islands. Iranian troops Nov. 30 seized the three Persian Gulf islands of Greater and Lesser Tunb and Abu Musa. The action prompted Iraq to sever diplomatic relations with Britain and Iran. The Iranian move also evoked a protest from the Trucial State of Ras al Khaima, which claimed the islands, and from Libya, which Dec. 7 nationalized all holdings of the British Petroleum Co., Ltd for what Libya termed Britain's "conspiracy" in the seizure. Britain, which had been planning to withdraw its forces from the gulf area by the end of 1971, had been trying to arrange a settlement of the disputed territory.

Iran said its landing force encountered resistance on Greater Tunb as police of Ras al Khaima opened fire, killing three Iranians. According to Teheran, the Iranians returned the fire, killing four policemen. The takeover of Abu Musa was peaceful since it had been agreed to under an accord announced Nov. 29 by Iran and Sheik Khalid Qasimi, ruler of the Trucial State of Sharja. The pact permitted Iranian troops to occupy specified areas of Abu Musa while Sharja authorities were to retain authority over the rest of the island. The agreement was assailed Nov. 30 by the National Assembly of Kuwait. In a protest to Britain, Iraq charged Nov. 30 that Iran's seizure of the islands was an act of aggression that posed a threat to the peace and security of the region and violated "Arab sovereignty" of the islands. The Teheran government reported Dec. 30 that, seemingly as a result of the seizure, Iraq had expelled 60,000 Iranians in the previous few days.

See also AGNEW, SPIRO THEODORE; HIJACKING [13]; MIDDLE EAST [7]; OIL

IRAQ—A decree issued Sept. 28 by President Ahmad Hassan al-Bakr dismissed Vice President Saleh Mahdi Ammash and Foreign Minister Abdel Kerim Shaikhaly from their posts and as members of the ruling Revolutionary Command Council. Ammash was transferred to the Foreign Ministry with the rank of ambassador. Shaikhaly was appointed to Iraq's delegation to the U.N. The Lebanese press reported that the men may have been shifted in connection with a power struggle in Iraq's Baathist party regime as a result of the ill health of President Bakr.

See also JORDAN [6, 9]; OIL; SUDAN

IRELAND—Arms curb voted. As part of a campaign to curb the activities of the outlawed Irish Republican Army (IRA), the Dail Eireann (parliament) unanimously approved a bill June 9 restricting the purchase and carrying of arms. The law specifically banned the holding of arms designed to be used beyond Ireland's frontier (viewed as an attempt to halt the illicit traffic of arms to Northern Ireland). The bill provided for an amnesty to arms holders who yielded their weapons before enactment of the bill.

Boland quits Fianna Fail. Kevin Boland, former minister for local government and social welfare, announced his resignation from the ruling Fianna Fail party of Prime Minister John Lynch May 3. He said that he had lost faith in the possibility of changing the party's present policies, particularly its moderate policy toward ending Irish partition. (Boland had resigned his Cabinet post in May 1970 because of his opposition to the dismissal of two Cabinet colleagues accused of attempting to ship arms to the IRA in Northern Ireland.) Boland Sept. 19 formed the Republican Unity party in Dublin. Two members of parliament quit the Fianna Fail to join Boland's new party.

Lynch wins confidence vote. Prime Minister Lynch won what was essentially a parliamentary confidence vote Nov. 10 when the Dail defeated 72-69 a motion to censure Minister of Agriculture James Gibbons. Gibbons was accused of deceiving the Dail when he was defense minister by denying knowledge of the 1970 conspiracy to supply the IRA with arms and ammunition. Lynch treated the issue as a vote of confidence for his government. Prior to the vote Lynch had said he would expel from the Fianna Fail any member refusing to vote with him. Two party members—Neil T. Blaney, a former minister who had been dismissed from Lynch's Cabinet for his alleged role in the conspiracy, and Paudge Brennan—abstained. They were expelled Nov. 17. Charles Haughey, another former minister who had been acquitted in a court trial of his alleged role in the conspiracy, backed Lynch in the vote. Defections from the party over the conspiracy issue and over Lynch's policy toward Northern Ireland reduced the government's majority to 70, compared with 68 for the opposition Fine Gael party, with six independents.

See also BIRTH CONTROL; CHURCHES [3]; DRUG USE & ADDICTION [9]; EUROPEAN ECONOMIC COMMUNITY [1, 14, 17]; GREAT BRITAIN [8-9]; HIJACKING [9]; NORTHERN IRELAND [1, 10-13, 15, 17]; TARIFFS & WORLD TRADE [2, 14]

IRISH REPUBLICAN ARMY (IRA)—*See* GREAT BRITAIN [4]; HIJACKING [2, 9]; IRELAND; NORTHERN IRELAND [2-3, 15, 17-19]

ISRAEL—Arab gets high post. An Israeli Arab, Abdul Aziz el-Zuabi, 45, was appointed deputy minister in the Israeli government May 16. He was to serve as deputy to Health Minister Victor Shemtov. This was the highest office ever reached by an Israeli Arab. Zuabi was a member of the left-wing Mapam party. He had served for various periods as deputy mayor of Nazareth and had been a member of the Knesset since 1965.

Civil unrest. Police in Jerusalem May 18 clashed for six hours with members of the Black Panthers, a group of Jews of African and Asian origin who were staging a demonstration to protest alleged economic and educational discrimination. Police arrested 74 persons. Ten policemen and several demonstrators were injured. The fighting started when the protesters left an approved rally site and held their demonstration at an unauthorized location.

Strike ban sought. The government decided Sept. 12 to draw up proposals to halt a wave of strikes by civil servants that had plagued the country since June. The Cabinet approved projected legislation that would bar walkouts by government employees during the life of a contract. Under the proposal, workers who violated the contract would be fined and dismissed. Sporadic walkouts and labor agitation in June had involved hospitals, electricity plants, port facilities and other public services. Doctors had gone on strike in August and a wildcat work stoppage at Lydda airport Sept. 7 ended Sept. 12 as baggage examiners returned to their jobs in compliance with a government injunction.

Blacks deported. The government Oct. 7 deported a group of 21 black Americans who had arrived at Lydda airport the previous day to join the 200-member "Black Israelite" community in Dimona, an immigrant town in the Negev. The new arrivals were turned away because it was decided they were not tourists although they arrived on visitors' visas. The first Dimona group arrived in Israel in 1969 on visitors' visas but were given immigrant status. Later arrivals joined them illegally. They claimed they were descended from the Hebrew patriarchs and were thus entitled to settle in Israel under the Israeli law of return, which granted every Jew the right to live in the country. The Interior Ministry said the government would decide whether the blacks could remain in Israel when their visas expired.

See also ARMAMENTS, INTERNATIONAL; ESPIONAGE; EUROPEAN ECONOMIC COMMUNITY [5]; FOREIGN AID; FOREIGN POLICY; INTERNATIONAL MONETARY DEVELOPMENTS [9]; JORDAN [1, 3, 6-9, 11]; MIDDLE EAST; TURKEY [6]; UNION OF SOVIET SOCIALIST REPUBLICS [13]; UNITED ARAB REPUBLIC

ITALIAN SOCIAL MOVEMENT (MSI)—*See* ITALY [3, 12, 21]

ITALY—Rioting in Reggio. Violence which had erupted in July 1970 in the south Italian city of Reggio Calabria again broke out during January and February, with sporadic disturbances in April and September. The rioting was in protest over the national government's decision to name the rival town of Catanzaro, rather than Reggio, as capital of the newly formed region of Calabria. In developments during the serious January-February disturbances: Francesco Franco, a neo-Fascist labor organizer, organized a general strike Jan. 20-Feb. 9 to back demands that Reggio be named the capital of Calabria. The work stoppage cut off railroad and mail service and closed down most stores, banks, public offices and schools. (A warrant was issued for Franco's arrest Jan. 31.) Fire bombings swept the city Jan. 23. Police fought stone-throwing demonstrators—mostly teenagers—Jan. 27 with tear gas, and dismantled barriers erected by the protesters. The unrest intensified Jan. 27 after a parliamentary constitutional commission in Rome announced it was not competent to designate the capital of Calabria and returned the issue to the regional assembly, located in Catanzaro. (Reggio's representatives refused to attend meetings there.) Hundreds of police were sent from Rome to reinforce local police in quelling the protests Jan. 28. According to news reports the same day, army armored car detachments were also deployed outside the city. The army strengthened its patrols along the north-south railroad leading to Reggio Jan. 31 following several bombings of state railroad installations. Police Jan. 31 arrested four members of an "Action Committee"—including millionaire coffee merchant Demetrio Mauro—on charges of instigating the violence. Police Feb. 8 arrested wealthy shipowner and publisher Amadeo Matacena on charges of instigating armed rebellion and disobedience of the law. He was accused of financing right-wing groups that had participated in the disorders. He was also accused of publishing in his Reggio newspaper a letter he had sent the previous week to President Guisseppe Saragat denouncing police behavior during the riots.

[2] Renewed Reggio violence and demonstrations greeted the confirmation by the regional assembly Feb. 16 of Catanzaro as capital of Calabria. The assembly voted 21-12 to confirm Catanzaro as the capital and to accept a compromise proposed by Premier Emilio Colombo to make Reggio the seat of the assembly. In addition, Calabria Province was to be the site of a new steel mill which would provide about 12,000 jobs in an area of high unemployment. Residents of Reggio, however, were dissatisfied with the compromise, since the regional assembly would be allowed to meet in Catanzaro, as well as in Cosenza, a third city in Calabria. Reggio residents were also dissatisfied because the executive offices of the regional government would be located in Catanzaro.

Rioting broke out again in Reggio Feb. 16 as citizens from the Sbarre working class district battled police with stones, fire and sporadic gunfire. Police tore down barricades in the rebel Santa Caterina district Feb. 18 and in Sbarre Feb. 23 in an attempt to quell the rioting. Leftists and rightists fought violently in Reggio April 4 in connection with ceremonies proclaiming the regional status of Calabria. Four regional legislators were slightly injured when demonstrators overturned their cars. One man was killed in a fresh outbreak of violence in Reggio Sept. 17, the first anniversary of a violent clash in 1970. Several persons were injured Sept. 19 in rioting during the funeral of the man who was killed.

[3] *Police clash with anti-Fascists.* A fatal grenade attack in Catanzaro Feb. 4 (believed related to the Reggio dispute) precipitated clashes between police and demonstrating anti-Fascists in Rome Feb. 5 as a crowd of 6,000 left-wing students staged a march protesting the Catanzaro violence which had killed one man and wounded 13. (Three hand grenades had been tossed into a crowd of left-wing demonstrators outside the headquarters of the neo-Fascist Italian Social Movement.) Police in Rome clashed with the students after fire bombs were thrown in the central plaza where the police were confronting the demonstrators. The students then carried out violent acts in other parts of the city, overturning cars and setting fire to the office of a neo-Fascist party. At least seven persons were injured and about 50 were arrested.

[4] *L'Aquila riots.* Violence erupted in L'Aquila Feb. 27 in a regional dispute similar to that in Reggio. Protesters broke up a regional assembly meeting Feb. 26 that had agreed to a plan to retain the assembly seat in L'Aquila but place the Abruzzi regional offices in both L'Aquila and Pescara, a rival town. (Riots had erupted in Pescara in June 1970 after it was first learned that the Abruzzi regional assembly would be located in L'Aquila.) Clashes between police and demonstrators continued in L'Aquila through March 1 and the city was in the grip of a total strike. Police moved armored vehicles into the city's center March 1 and Italian national police chief Angelo Vicari asserted that "extremist fringes" were causing the disorders. After agreements reached late March 1, shopkeepers ended the general strike. Police riot squads withdrew from the center of the city March 2.

[5] **Colombo wins vote of confidence.** The seven-month-old government of Premier Colombo received a vote of confidence in the Chamber of Deputies March 4 and in the Senate March 5. Colombo had called for the vote after the Republican party, criticizing disunity in the government, withdrew from the ruling four-party (Colombo's Christian Democratic party, the Social Democratic party, the Socialist party and the Republican party) coalition Feb. 26 and withdrew its single cabinet minister, Justice Minister Oronzo Reale, and its two under-secretaries. The Republican party had pledged to continue supporting the Colombo coalition in Parliament. Colombo temporarily assumed the post of justice minister. One of the major issues in the parliamentary debate over the vote of confidence was the degree of participation of the Communist party in the coalition. The Social Democratic party was opposed to further Communist support, while the Socialist party favored increased Communist participation.

[6] **Alleged rightist coup plot.** Interior Minister Franco Restivo March 17 disclosed to Parliament a police inquiry into an alleged right-wing coup conspiracy in December 1970. He said police in Rome, Genoa, Milan, Naples and Bari had conducted raids on the homes or offices of 32 persons belonging to right-wing extremist groups suspected of plotting the coup. A judicial inquiry into the alleged coup March 18 summoned Prince Junio Valerio Borghese, a neo-Fascist leader of an extremist extra-parliamentary movement, the National Front. The following day, Borghese, who had gone into hiding, was charged, in absentia, with political conspiracy and attempted armed insurrection. Followers of Borghese were detained for questioning March 18-19. According to reports of the findings of the judicial inquiry, several hundred of the prince's followers, including many aged pensioners and war veterans, had gathered at three different places in Rome Dec. 7, 1970, under the pretext of viewing a film. People at the rallies allegedly believed they would participate in the arrest of politicians and occupation of key installations by sympathetic army units. For unknown reasons, the prince allegedly called off the plot at the last minute. Lawyers for the prince March 21 denied the coup charge and said the Dec. 7 meeting was planned to organize a demonstration against the proposed visit of Yugoslav President Tito.

[7] *Leftist-rightist polarization.* Meanwhile, conspiracies on the left were adding to the growing polarization of Italian extra-parliamentary groups. In Genoa March 26, a bank was robbed and a cashier killed. A raid on the residence of one suspect in the robbery revealed clandestine radio stations, arms and explosives and booklets on urban guerrilla techniques. The week before, Milan police had seized weapons and bomb parts traced to an ultra-leftist underground group known as the "Red Brigades," which had claimed responsibility for a series of explosions in the city. On the rightist side, more than 2,000 right-wingers marched through Rome March 14 defending the army and calling for a military government such as that in Greece. Similar rallies had been staged by related groups in Turin March 7 and in Milan March 13. Thirty-three persons were injured, eight arrested and 79 detained for questioning April 17 as police clashed with extreme rightists in Milan. The clash occurred when police tried to disperse an unauthorized neo-Fascist meeting, banned after unidentified terrorists (believed to be neo-Fascists) bombed the headquarters of the Socialist and Communist parties April 16. Mass protests against the reported resurgence of fascism took place March 21 in Bologna (100,000 marchers) and Nov. 28 in Rome (100,000-200,000 marchers) and in other cities Nov. 27-28.

[8] **Labor, social unrest.** Italy's three major labor unions (the Italian Confederation of Labor [Communists and Socialists], the Italian Confedertion of Workers Syndicates [Roman Catholic] and the Italian Union of Labor [left-of-center]) staged a nationwide general strike—the first since 1969—April 7 to show dissatisfaction with what they considered an inadequate housing bill and with what they charged were insufficient reforms in health services and taxation. The strike paralyzed major industries, but had little impact on the nation's daily life. Stores, restaurants and cafes generally remained open. Adherence to the strike was strongest in the North, where participation was estimated at 80%-90%. The three unions March 4 had begun talks with the Christian Democratic and Social Democratic parties in an effort to implement the social reforms. More than 100,000 workers from across the nation marched in Rome May 30 in a demonstration, organized by the three unions, to put pressure on the government to stimulate the economy, particularly in the South, and to implement the social reforms. In a later development, the three unions agreed Nov. 21 to merge into a single labor federation, with a membership of five million-seven million, by February 1973. The merger was expected to strengthen the unions' campaign for social reforms. About 380 officials of the groups met in Florence Nov. 22-24 and agreed to hold separate conventions for the three unions Sept. 21, 1972 to vote for dissolution. A congress representing the new labor organization would be convened by February 1973.

[9] *Other labor activities.* In other major labor activities: about 1.5 million workers in the building industry struck Jan. 26 to support their demands for improved pay and working conditions and to protest delays in the government program of social reform announced in August 1970; labor unions staged a general strike in Naples March 11 to protest the economic stagnation of the South; the Postal Workers' Union struck April 14-15 and continued partial strikes and slowdowns in postal, telephone and telegraph operations until April 23 when agreement was reached with the government on wage demands and readjustment of civil service gradings; sanitation services were halted as Rome's 24,000 municipal workers struck May 5-11 for higher pay and revised civil service gradings; national telephone company technicians staged a 24-hour

strike May 10-11 to support their demands for improved salaries and working conditions; a wage agreement between the management of Fiat Motor Co. and the metallurgical unions was signed June 19, ending months of staggered strikes, work slowdowns and violent demonstrations; agreement on a new national labor contract (increasing pay and reducing working hours) between hotel workers and management was reached July 9, ending nearly five months of strikes and negotiations; longshoremen Nov. 20 ended a 48-hour strike, called to back demands for a guaranteed minimum wage and a 40-hour workweek; the employees of the state-owned railroads Nov. 20 began a 24-hour strike after negotiations broke down over union demands for higher pay, hiring of more workers and better working conditions; about 44,000 civil service executives staged a 48-hour strike Nov. 29-30 to demand higher pay, improved promotion opportunities and bureaucratic reforms.

[10] Palermo prosecutor slain. The chief prosecutor of Palermo, Pietro Scaglione, was assassinated May 5 by unidentified gunmen. His chauffeur was also killed. A special parliamentary commission investigating the Mafia May 6 attributed the assassination to the Mafia. Various members of the commission thought that Scaglione had been in secret collusion with the Mafia and had been killed for his knowledge of its secrets. (Scaglione had been cleared of connivance with Mafia figures in a 1970 disciplinary investigation by the Superior Council of the Judiciary in Rome.) Following the slaying, the government embarked on a wide-ranging roundup and exile to isolated islands of suspected Mafia chiefs. According to varying reports, 16-18 reputed Mafia leaders were deported May 18 to Linosa (a small island south of Sicily with a population of 387) in the biggest deportation operation since World War II. The deportation was followed May 26 by the exile of about 15 suspected Mafia chiefs to the island of Filicudi, one of the Aeolian Islands off Sicily's north coast. The exiles included major figures such as Giovanni Bonventre, a one-time New York Mafia leader, and Antonio Buccellato. (Some of Filicudi's 270 inhabitants clashed with police May 26 in an attempt to prevent the Mafia from settling on the island. The demonstrators feared the exiles would spoil a burgeoning tourist trade. The government contended, however, that small islands with poor communications like Filicudi would facilitate the isolation of the Mafia chieftains. By May 31, all of the inhabitants of Filicudi had abandoned their homes for the island of Lipari—the administrative center of the Aeolians—and vowed they would not return until the Mafia exiles were removed. Sicilian justice authorities June 22 ordered transfer of the alleged Mafia leaders from Filicudi to the island of Asinara, northwest of Sardia. Police announced July 10 that 10 more suspected Mafia leaders were being exiled to Asinara.)

[11] *Other Mafia developments.* A group of parliamentary deputies June 23 presented a motion urging the government to conclude cooperation agreements with the U.S., Canada and various Mediterranean nations to combat the Mafia. Twenty-three suspected Mafia members were arrested July 23 throughout Italy, bringing to 56 the number arrested recently on charges of association to commit crime. The parliamentary commission investigating the Mafia July 13 released a report identifying 13 Mafia leaders and describing their criminal activities and their ties with political figures. The report said Mafia members had enjoyed "powerful and authoritative protections and political complicity" from police, judges, politicians and civil servants. Among the Mafia leaders identified, only Vincenzo di Carlo was in jail, serving a life sentence for murder. Four others had been shot to death and five were missing. One of the leaders—Tomaso Buscetta—had been arrested in New York in August 1970 and charged with illegal entry into the U.S. He was released on bail in September 1970 and was awaiting grand jury action.

[12] Gains for neo-Fascists. The neo-Fascist Italian Social Movement (MSI) June 13 captured 13.9% of the more than seven million votes—one-fifth of the national electorate—cast in scattered regional and local elections in Sicily, Rome, Genoa, Bari and other cities. Compared with the 5.2% the party won in more extensive regional elections in 1970, the MSI emerged as the most significant winner at the expense of Premier Colombo's Christian Democrats. The elections were not necessarily representative of all of Italy since the elections were mainly in the center and south of the contry—traditionally more conservative than the industrialized north—and because 4.8 million of the voters were concentrated in Sicily and Rome. The governing three-party coalition won 49.8% of the vote, compared with 58.2% in the regional elections in 1970. The percentage results of the total vote (1970 regional percentages in parentheses): Christian Democrats 31% (38.8%); Socialists 11% (10.4%); Social Democrats 7.8% (7%); Communists and their ally, the Socialist party of Proletarian Unity, 25.3% (31.1%).

[13] Divorce law upheld. The Constitutional Court published a ruling (made June 28) that upheld the constitutionality of the controversial divorce law. Conservative Roman Catholics had challenged the law as a violation of Italy's 1929 Concordat with the Vatican and the 1948 constitution. The concordat had given the Roman Catholic Church jurisdiction over dissolving marriages; the constitution upheld the church-state relations provided in the concordat. Divorce opponents pushed their campaign for repeal of the law by submitting to a federal court petitions signed by 1,370,134 persons in favor of a popular referendum on the issue. Half a million signatures were required to authorize the referendum.

[14] Economic expansion program. In an effort to stimulate lagging production and to increase investments, the Cabinet July 3 approved a series of measures providing for government financial aid to medium and small firms in industry, commerce and agriculture. The program called for creation of low-interest investment credit facilities; increased funds for industrial research; specific financial aid for shipbuilding, the fishing industry, exporters, and for contracts with developing nations; and extended exemptions of social security charges for industrial companies in the economically depressed South. The measures—unofficially estimated to cost over $1 billion—were effective immediately unless rescinded by Parliament within 60 days.

[15] South Tyrol pact with Austria. Italy and Austria signed a treaty in Rome July 17 under which both nations agreed to refer to the International Court of Justice at The Hague any future disputes arising out of the 1969 accord on the predominantly German-speaking South Tyrol (Alto Adige) section of Italy's northern Bolzano Province. The accord was complemented by the signing of two other agreements on minor border questions. Italy also pledged support for Austria's bid for a special association agreement with the European Economic Community that would leave Austria's neutrality intact. Under the 1969 agreement—major provisions of which were ratified by the two parliaments as a constitutional amendment Oct. 22—Italy would give South Tyrol more legislative and administrative autonomy and Austria would pledge noninterference in the region's affairs.

[16] Housing, tax reforms approved. The Senate Aug. 7 and the Chamber of Deputies Oct. 7 approved two major reform bills designed to provide low-cost housing to workers (see [8]) and to revise and streamline the complicated tax system. The bills had originally been approved by the Chamber in March but had been stalled in the Senate by the opposition of neo-Fascists and some right-wing Christian Democrats (both of whom boycotted voting on the bills) and by Communists (reportedly because tax reforms would hit the middle-income bracket hardest and because the housing reform had been drastically weakened). The passage of the bills by the Senate alleviated a government crisis in which Premier Colombo had threatened to resign if the bills were not passed. The tax bill introduced Italy's first general income tax with deductions on a sliding scale from 10% to 72%, replacing seven taxes. Four other taxes introduced were: a tax on corporate revenues, a local tax on self-earned and unearned personal income, a local tax on the increase of real estate value and a value-added tax. The reform also initiated a centralized register in which the name and earnings of each citizen would be recorded under a code number to reduce income tax evasion. The housing bill provided for the expropriation of private properties by municipalities for low-rent housing and public utilities. To curb land speculation, compensation would be calculated on the value of farmland rather than on the real estate market price. A permanent committee for housing construction, to be created within the Ministry of Public Works, would be responsible for drafting and overseeing the execution of regional low-rent housing plans and centralizing funds. The Socialists in the Senate had resisted amendments to the bill offered by the Christian Democrats, who feared the bill had alienated conservatives. The Socialists finally accepted Colombo's compromise, which included authorization for municipal officials to appropriate 60% of the lands encompassed by the housing plans and 20% outside the plans. Both bills were to be implemented by Jan. 1, 1972, but the implementation date was changed to Jan. 1, 1973 according to a report Nov. 2.

[17] Price controls imposed. The government Sept. 22 imposed price controls to halt a sudden increase in the cost of food and other basic supplies in previous weeks. Under authority derived from a 1944 decree against black marketeering, the government hoped to freeze prices of most major items at the present level and to cut back excessive increases.

[18] Municipal elections postponed. The government Oct. 11 postponed municipal elections, scheduled for Nov. 28, until March 1972. The government attributed the delay to organizational problems because a nationwide census would have been held at the same time. Neo-Fascist officials charged the government feared further election losses similar to those suffered by the coalition in June (see [12]).

[19] Anti-pollution bill presented. The Ministry of Merchant Marine Nov. 4 proposed a bill to Parliament which, in accordance with the London Convention of 1954, would authorize one year in prison and fines ranging from $833 to $8,333 for the owner or captain of a ship discharging oil or other substances into Italy's territorial waters. In previous pollution developments: a Rome court May 18 ordered police to impound two oil tanker terminals three miles off the coast of Fiumicino, near Rome, and closed the pipelines linking the platforms to an oil refinery inland. The offshore tanker operations were thought to have contributed to beach and water pollution. The judge also ordered the director of Rome's international airport to clean and overhaul its drainage system, a major polluter. Nearly all the fish in a 25-mile stretch of the Tiber River, from near Fiumicino to Rome's northern outskirts, died May 13-18 after wastes accumulated for four-days were flushed into the river. (Rome's municipal authorities had shut off about half the running water for four days to connect a new aquaduct with the city network.) The National Research Council's Water Institute reported June 4 that major areas of the Italian coastline around Rome, Naples, Genoa and Venice were seriously polluted.

[20] Leone elected president. Giovanni Leone, a lawyer, senator and moderate member of the Christian Democrats, was elected president of Italy Dec. 24 by the electoral college of the National Assembly after the longest deadlock in postwar Italian history. Leone was sworn in Dec. 29 to succeed Saragat, whose term expired. Premier Colombo agreed the same day to Leone's request that he remain in office. He withdrew his Cabinet's resignation, offered according to constitutional tradition, but later said through a spokesman that a "thorough analysis" of the political situation was necessary. The Christian Democrats and the Socialists had clashed bitterly during the election. Leone won on the 23rd ballot of an election that had begun Dec. 9. He received 518 votes, only 13 more than the required majority of 1,008 senators, deputies and regional representatives voting. The runner-up was Pietro Nenni, the veteran Socialist leader, who received 408 votes from a coalition of Communists, Socialists and other left-wing groups. Alessandro Pertini, the president of the Chamber of Deputies, received six votes. Saragat, who had dropped out of the race Dec. 18, received seven votes, and the remainder were accounted for by blank votes, abstentions and votes for diverse candidates.

[21]   The Christian Democrats had switched to Leone Dec. 21 after their first candidate, former Premier Amintore Fanfani, failed to win a majority because 30-50 Christian Democrat dissenters withheld support from him. The party abstained on 14 of the 23 ballots while they sought additional support, first for Fanfani and then for Leone. (Wild shouting and near fistfights had erupted in the Chamber of Deputies Dec. 22 when the Christian Democratic leadership, acting for tactical reasons, instructed their delegates to abstain in a vote on Leone, one day after they had selected him as their new candidate.) Leone finally won the backing of the right-of-center Liberal party, the Social Democratic party and the Republican party. Nenni was chosen as the left-wing candidate Dec. 23 after their first candidate, Deputy Premier Francesco de Martino, withdrew. After the election, the Communists condemned the "formation of a center-right front extending to the fascists," a reference to reports that Leone had won with the backing of the neo-Fascist MSI.

See also ABORTION; ATOMIC ENERGY [13]; BIRTH CONTROL; DRUG ABUSE & ADDICTION [9]; EARTHQUAKES; EUROPEAN ECONOMIC COMMUNITY [1, 4, 6, 12, 14]; FRANCE [6]; HIJACKING [14]; INTERNATIONAL BANK FOR RECONSTRUCTION & DEVELOPMENT; INTERNATIONAL MONETARY DEVELOPMENTS [1, 3, 8-10, 15]; MIDDLE EAST [11]; PAKISTAN [35, 39]; SPACE [17, 21]; TARIFFS & WORLD TRADE [6]

IVORY COAST—Cabinet changes. President Felix Houphouet-Boigny assumed the portfolio of national education June 8 following closure of the University of Abidjan in April due to student disturbances. (Students had been required April 15 to sign an agreement to observe the university's rules and to refrain from political activity outside the Democratic party, the country's only political party.) Former National Education Minister Guede Jean Lorougnon was appointed minister of scientific research, a new ministry. The Tourism Ministry came under the control of Mathieu Ekra, a minister of state; former Tourism Minister Loua Diomande was named minister of state in charge of relations with the national assembly.

See also AFRICA; SOUTH AFRICA [12]

JACKSON, GEORGE—*See* PRISONS [4-5]
JACKSON, HENRY M.—*See* POLITICS [8]
JACKSON, JESSE L.—*See* ELECTIONS [2]; ESPIONAGE; NEGROES
JAFFE, JEROME H.—*See* DRUG USE & ADDICTION [1-2, 14, 16]
JAILS—*See* PRISONS [1, 3]

JAPAN—Korean repatriation accord. Representatives of Japanese and North Korean Red Cross organizations Feb. 5 reached agreement on repatriation of 15,000 (out of about 600,000) Korean residents of Japan to North Korea. The emigration move was to start in May and be completed within six months. The South Korean government Feb. 4 had urged the Japanese government to block the action, but Tokyo was said to have replied that it had "no direct responsibility" for the repatriation plan.

[2] Student developments. Tokyo police Feb. 2 raided offices and meeting places of various new left student groups, arresting five students and confiscating 1,366 weapons. The raids reportedly were aimed at forestalling an alleged plot by the Sekigun (Red Army) student faction to kidnap government and business leaders. In another development, the dissolution of the Shield Society, the private army of right-wing university students formed by the late author Yukio Mishima, was announced by the organization Feb. 28 at a Shinto service for Mishima and his chief follower, Masakatsu Morita. A society member said the dissolution had taken effect as of Nov. 25, 1970, the day Mishima and Morita had committed ritual suicide.

[3] Tokyo airport clashes. Police Feb. 22-March 2 fought a group of more than 1,000 squatters and student supporters at the proposed site of Tokyo's new international airport at Narita, 26 miles northeast of the city. The police sought to evict farmers who refused to sell their land for the project. Students joined the farmers in resisting the police by building barricades. The worst rioting occurred Feb. 25 when hundreds of helmeted students hurled rocks and charged at police with bamboo spears. Police said 141 students were arrested and 12 policemen injured. Police smashed the demonstrators' barricades March 5. Three policemen were killed and 150 persons injured Sept. 16 as clashes again broke out. Both sides, numbering about 5,000 each, fought with clubs, shields, gasoline-filled bottles, stones and spears. About 34 policemen were hospitalized. Police Sept. 17 cleared the airport site of the students and farmers following another round of sporadic fighting.

[4] Defense expansion plans. The government Defense Agency April 27 announced that $14.4 billion would be spent on expanding the country's armed

267

forces for the five-year period beginning April 1, 1972. This represented a 220% increase over the current five-year program, the agency said. The increased outlay, which would make Japan the seventh largest defense spender in the world (after the U.S., the U.S.S.R., Communist China, West Germany, France and Great Britain), would provide for: an increase in the number of armed forces personnel from the current 260,000 men to 271,000 and expansion of the tank force to 990; construction of two 8,000-ton destroyers equipped with helicopters, submarines, 14 high-speed missile carriers and 61 other naval craft (these ships, totaling 103,000 tons, would increase Japan's naval strength to 200 ships with a total tonnage of 247,000); addition of 76 F-4 Phantom jet fighters and 920 other new planes, which would increase air force strength to 1,740 planes by the end of 1977; and movement of 6,000 troops to Okinawa when the U.S. turned the island over to Japan in 1972. (*See* [5-6].)

[5] Okinawa pact. At separate ceremonies in Washington and Tokyo June 17, U.S. Secretary of State William Rogers and Japanese Foreign Minister Kiichi Aichi signed a treaty committing the U.S. to return to Japan at an unspecified date in 1972 the island of Okinawa, the other islands in the Ryukyu group and the Daito Islands. The treaty was approved by the Japanese House of Representatives by a 285-73 vote Nov. 24, and by the U.S. Senate by an 84-6 vote Nov. 10. (The voting in Japan was boycotted by Socialist and Communist party members of the House of Representatives.) In giving up control of the Ryukyus, the U.S. agreed "to relinquish in favor of Japan all rights and interests" under Article III of the U.S.-Japanese Peace Treaty of 1951, except where such rights had been given up by previous agreements. The U.S. was to retain 88 military installations on Okinawa, including the Kadena Air Base, and 46 smaller facilities were to revert to Japan. Japanese courts were to assume jurisdiction over all civil and criminal cases on the islands except for legal claims by Japanese nationals applicable during the years of U.S. administration. The Japanese government was to pay the U.S. $320 million for "extra costs" incurred by the U.S., "particularly in the area of employment after reversion," and three Ryukyu firms were to become Japanese property. The Voice of America relay station on Okinawa would be allowed to broadcast for five years after the date of entry into force of the treaty. The treaty did not directly mention nuclear weapons, believed to have been installed by the U.S. on Okinawa. In a later development, the U.S. and Japan June 29 signed an agreement requiring Japan to assume the major defense role on Okinawa by July 1, 1973. Under the agreement, within six months after reversion, Japanese jet fighters were to be ready for action on Okinawa and 3,200 men of the Self-Defense Forces were to be stationed on the island. Japan was to complete an air-defense missile system on the island by July 1, 1973.

[6] *Protests over Okinawa.* Demonstrators protesting the retention of American bases on Okinawa staged violent demonstrations in Tokyo and other cities Nov. 14-24. The worst rioting occurred in the capital Nov. 19, when about 96,000 persons fought with police in clashes throughout the city. One person was killed, 15 policemen and 10 civilians injured and 1,785 arrested. Damage was extensive. Protests over the retention of the bases had also erupted Nov. 10 as huge rallies were held in Tokyo and 100,000 workers staged a general protest strike leading to riots that caused the death of one policeman and injuries to many others in Naha, the capital of Okinawa. The Naha rioting erupted as demonstrators, marching on the buildings of the U.S. Civil Defense Administration, were intercepted by police.

[7] Cabinet reorganized. Premier Eisaku Sato appointed a new Cabinet July 5. At his first meeting with the new ministers, Sato instructed them to "tackle difficult internal and external problems with courage, and to work to improve friendly relations with the United States." Sato's emphasis on ties with Washington stemmed from Japan's growing concern with American criticism of rising Japanese exports to the U.S. and American impatience with Tokyo's repeated promises to carry out "orderly marketing" or liberalize Japan's highly protectionist policies on trade and capital imports. The new Cabinet: premier—Sato; justice—Shigesaburo Maeo; foreign—Takeo Fukuda; finance—Mikio

Mizuta; education—Saburo Takami; health and social security—Noboru Saito; agriculture and forests—Munenori Akagi; international trade and industry—Kakuei Tanaka; transport—Kyoshiro Niwa; labor—Kenzaburo Hara; construction—Elichi Nishimura; interior—Motosaburo Tokai; Cabinet secretary—Nobutu Takeshita; director of the premier's office—Sadanori Yamanaka; defense—Keikichi Masuhara; economic planning—Toshi Kimura; science and technology—Wataru Hiraizumi; and environment (new ministry)—Buichi Oishi.

[8] House elections. Premier Sato's ruling Liberal-Democratic party suffered a slight setback and the Communists scored large gains in elections held June 27 for half of the 252-seat House of Councilors, Japan's upper house of parliament. According to complete returns released June 29, the Liberal-Democrats won 63 seats, the Socialists 39, the Komeito (Clean Government party) 10, and the Democratic Socialists and Communists six each. Composition of the new House of Councilors: Liberal-Democrats 136, Socialists 66, Komeito 23, Democratic Socialists 13, Communists 10 and four independents. The Liberal-Democrat popular vote dropped to 44.6% from 46.7% in 1968. The Communist tally increased from 5% to 8%.

[9] *Komeito widens appeal.* The Komeito party Sept. 21 adopted a new program at the conclusion of its three-day annual convention aimed at transforming it from a religious to a national party with wide appeal. (Yoshikatsu Takeiri, chairman of the party, was stabbed twice and seriously wounded in Tokyo Sept. 21 as he returned from the opening session of the convention. His arrested assailant, Takaari Yajima, said he attacked Takeiri because he opposed Komeito's policy of advocating closer relations with Communist China.

[10] Hirohito visits Alaska, Europe. Emperor Hirohito became the first Japanese monarch to leave his native land as he toured Europe Sept. 27-Oct. 13, with a stopover in Anchorage, Alaska Sept. 26, where he was greeted by President Nixon. Hirohito had last visited Europe in 1921 as crown prince. The emperor's itinerary took him to Denmark Sept. 27-28; Belgium Sept. 29-Oct. 1; France Oct. 2-4; Britain Oct. 5-7; the Netherlands Oct. 8-10; and West Germany Oct. 11-13. He encountered some hostility in Britain, Holland and West Germany, where a number of demonstrators, mindful of Japan's World War II role, protested his visit. In one incident, an unidentifed man threw a stone through the windshield of the emperor's car near The Hague Oct. 8. No one was injured. The emperor's party included Empress Nagako and Foreign Minister Fukuda.

[11] $810,000 court judgment against firm. In Japan's first court settlement of a major pollution case, Showa Denko, a leading chemical firm, lost an $810,000 court judgment Sept. 29 in a suit brought four years before on behalf of 77 victims of mercury poisoning. The settlement was about half the amount asked by the plaintiffs. The court found that the victims, seven of whom died, had been poisoned after eating fish caught downstream from the company's plant at Niigata and that the sickness was due to mercury discharges by the company. Showa Denko said the mercury was due to the accidental release of chemical fertilizer during a 1964 earthquake.

[12] No-confidence motion defeated. The House of Councilors Oct. 28 rejected, by a 132-106 vote, an opposition motion to censure the Sato government for the failure of its efforts to block the United Nations General Assembly resolution Oct. 25 admitting Communist China and ousting Nationalist China (*see* UNITED NATIONS [7]). Japan had joined the U.S. in its attempt to save the Nationalists from expulsion. In a statement to the house, Sato acknowledged the widespread diplomatic support received by the Peking regime, but he insisted that Japan had obligations to the Chinese Nationalists, with whom it had concluded a peace treaty in 1952.

[13]   China spurns ties. Japan was reported Nov. 11 to have made its first official move to establish diplomatic relations with Communist China, but Chinese Premier Chou En-lai was said to have unofficially rejected the overture. Shigeru Hori, secretary general of the Liberal Democratic party, said he had proposed in a letter to Chou (sent prior to the Oct. 25 U.N. vote) that bilateral talks be held to normalize ties between the two countries. Premier Sato had also expressed interest in visiting Peking. At a meeting Nov. 10 with a Japanese delegation, Chou was reported to have spurned the idea of a Sato visit and to have stated that there could be no Chinese-Japanese negotiations until Tokyo accepted three conditions: that Peking was the only legal government of China; that Taiwan's "independence" or "self-determination" drives were unacceptable; and that the 1952 treaty with Nationalist China was abrogated.

See also ATOMIC ENERGY [11]; AVIATION [13-14]; CHEMICAL & BIOLOGICAL WARFARE; COMMUNIST CHINA-U.S. DETENTE [8]; ESPIONAGE; HEALTH [6]; INTERNATIONAL BANK FOR RECONSTRUCTION & DEVELOPMENT; INTERNATIONAL MONETARY DEVELOPMENTS [8, 12, 14-15, 18]; NIXON, RICHARD MILHOUS [2]; PAKISTAN [35, 37]; PENTAGON PAPERS [19]; POLLUTION [4]; SOUTH PACIFIC FORUM; SPACE [22]; SPORTS; TARIFFS & WORLD TRADE [3-4, 8-9]; UNION OF SOVIET SOCIALIST REPUBLICS [5]; UNITED NATIONS [8]

JARRING, GUNNAR V.—See FRANCE [17]; MIDDLE EAST [1, 27-30, 34, 37, 39]; UNITED NATIONS [12]

JET PROPULSION LABORATORY (JPL)—See SPACE [10-11]

JEWISH DEFENSE LEAGUE (JDL)—See FEDERAL BUREAU OF INVESTIGATION [2]; UNION OF SOVIET SOCIALIST REPUBLICS [13, 15]

JEWS—See CANADA [22]; CHURCHES [7]; GERMANY, WEST [13]; ISRAEL; UNION OF SOVIET SOCIALIST REPUBLICS [9-15]

JOHN BIRCH SOCIETY—See SUPREME COURT

JOHNSON, LYNDON BAINES—See PENTAGON PAPERS [2, 20, 22-28]

JOINT CHIEFS OF STAFF (JCS)—See DEFENSE [10]; PENTAGON PAPERS [5, 20, 23-28]; WAR CRIMES [4]

JORDAN—Anti-commando drive. Jordanian troops launched a major attack against Palestinian commando bases north of Amman Jan. 8. The fighting broke out around the towns of Jarash, Salt and Ruseifa. The government said the clashes in the Jarash area followed the commando kidnaping Jan. 7 of two noncommissioned army officers and the killing of a government soldier. The commandos asserted that government forces had shelled their bases and confiscated their arms. The most powerful of the commando groups, Al Fatah, claimed that a hospital at El Rumman had been shelled and that the al-Baqaa refugee camp, a few miles west of Amman, had been bombed. Brig. Ahmed Hilmi, the Egyptian head of the inter-Arab truce team created after the Jordanian civil war in September 1970, blamed the Jordanians for starting the latest round of fighting. Hilmi said he and other observers had been barred from the scene of the clashes and, as a result, would suspend their truce work until further notice. Heavy fighting continued in the area and in the capital itself until Jan. 13, when a truce was agreed to by both sides. An estimated 60 persons were killed or wounded in the fighting. Ibrahim Bakr, a member of the Central Committee (the coordinating group of the 10 guerrilla organizations in Jordan), said Jan. 11 that the latest Jordanian attacks had paralyzed the commando movement and made it impossible for commandos to mount raids against the Israelis.

[2]   Government and commando representatives, assisted by the inter-Arab truce team, met Jan. 12 to negotiate a truce that was agreed to Jan. 13. The 13-point agreement, effective Jan. 14, reportedly contained nothing new except a timetable to implement the unfulfilled pledges contained in the pact that had ended the 1970 civil war. The latest treaty, signed by Premier Wasfi Tell, Bakr and Hilmi, called on guerrillas to withdraw to bases outside the cities and towns and for both sides to release all prisoners by Jan. 20. (About 400 guerrillas were

said to be in government hands.) Other points of the agreement: the government was to return guerrilla weapons and provide for free commando movement; the government was to return the office of the Palestine Armed Struggle Command at Ramtha, seized during the September fighting; and the commandos were to be allowed to reopen within a month their closed offices and bases specified under previous agreements. As the pact went into effect, commando leaders began collecting weapons from their armed followers.

[3] *Other winter-spring clashes.* Jordanian troops and commandos fought another round of clashes in and around Amman Feb. 11-15. No casualty figures were given, but the number of killed and wounded was reported to be high. Both sides had agreed to a truce Feb. 12, but sporadic fighting continued through the next four days. Government troops and commandos engaged in sharp fighting in the capital and in the northern sector around Irbid March 26-April 6. Fighting also broke out for the first time along the border with Syria, from which some guerrilla units were believed to have moved into Jordan. The commando force displayed its most aggressive stance since the civil war, initiating offensive actions and carrying out widespread acts of sabotage against government facilities, including railroad tracks and an oil pipeline. A guerrilla announcement April 2 declared that the fedayeen were fighting to force King Hussein to replace Tell as premier and to oust the high-ranking officers whom they regarded as responsible for starting the latest round of fighting. Syria was reported April 4 to have warned Jordan that the 6,000 regular troops of the Palestine Liberation Army stationed south of Damascus would be permitted to move into Jordan "unless harassment of guerrillas was quickly stopped." An agreement to end the fighting was reached April 9. Under the accord, arranged through the mediation of Syria, a six-member committee was to be established to supervise the 1970 peace agreements. The committee was to be formed of two men each from Jordan, Syria and the commandos. The new body would, in effect, supersede the now-defunct 100-member pan-Arab truce team. Commando sources said April 12 that their agreement to appoint representatives to the new truce committee was contingent on ratification of the 1970 peace plan by delegations of nine Arab states that had opened a meeting in Damascus April 10. Despite the peace accord, Jordan April 12 reported more clashes between government and commando forces in the northern part of the country. One of the attacks had come from Syrian territory. Jordanian troops and Palestinian commandos fought a battle for more than six hours near Jarash May 29. An Al Fatah spokesman said June 1 that the commando bases of Jarash and Salt were under army siege and had been shelled in the previous three days, with heavy losses. The spokesman said that Israeli and Jordanian forces were cooperating with each other in firing on commandos entering or leaving the Israeli-occupied west bank.

[4] **Cabinet revised.** Premier Tell May 22 revised his Cabinet following the resignation of Interior Minister Mazen Ajlouni, Rural Affairs Minister Fouas Kakich and Public Works Minister Mounib Masri. The revamped Cabinet: premier & defense—Tell; reconstruction & development—Sobhy Amine Amr; interior—Ibrahim Habachneh; finance—Ahmed el Louzi; foreign—Abdallah Salah; information, culture, tourism & antiquities—Adnan Abou Audeh; health—Mohammed el Bechir; rural affairs—Yakoub Abou Ghosh; economy— Onar Naboulsi; agriculture—Omar Abdullah; communications—Mohammed Khalaf; transport—Anis al Mouacher; education—Ishac Farhane; labor— Mustafa Daoudine; and public works—Mohammed al Farhan.

[5] **Hussein orders commando purge.** King Hussein June 2 ordered a "final crackdown" against the commandos, whom he charged with attempting "to establish a separate Palestinian state and destroy the unity of the Jordanian and Palestinian people." Hussein's directive, given to Premier Tell, demanded "bold, decisive action against the handful of professional criminals and conspirators who use the commando movement to disguise their treasonable plots." In an earlier statement, issued by the central committee of the Palestine Liberation Organization in Beirut June 1, the commandos had accused Jordan

of mounting an offensive against commando bases "in a conspiracy against the Palestine revolution." The statements by Hussein and the PLO came after three and four days, respectively, of renewed fighting between government and guerrilla forces and were followed by a fresh outburst of clashes. Premier Tell June 6 blamed the commandos for the latest flare-up in a bid to establish a Palestine government in exile. Tell charged that Arab states were exaggerating reports of the clashes to suggest that Amman wanted to exterminate the guerrilla movement and "to show that conditions were unstable" in Jordan.

[6]   **Government claims commandos crushed.** Jordanian forces launched an all-out attack against Palestinian commandos in the Ajlun-Jarash area, stronghold of the commando movement, July 13. After several days of heavy fighting, the government claimed that the guerrillas had been crushed and that 2,300 were captured, leaving only about 200 still at large. Two thousand of those captured were released July 21. Israeli officials reported July 19 that 72 guerrillas had fled across the Jordan River into Israeli-occupied territory to escape Jordanian troops and had surrendered to Israeli authorities. Prior to Jordanian suppression of commando resistance, Syria had begun mediation efforts to end the fighting, but its July 15 intercession apparently had no effect. The new outbreak in clashes caused a further deterioration in relations between Amman and Egypt, Syria and Iraq, which assailed the crackdown against the guerrillas. Iraq closed its borders with Jordan July 19 and said it planned to withdraw its ambassador to Amman. Syria and Jordan reported exchanging artillery fire July 19.

[7]   **Arab leaders warn Jordan.** The leaders of five Arab states (Presidents Muammar el-Qaddafi of Libya, Anwar Sadat of Egypt, Hafez al-Assad of Syria, Salem Ali Rubaya of Southern Yemen and Abdul Rahman al-Iryani of Yemen) conferred in Tripoli, Libya July 30 on joint action to prevent Jordan's suppression of commando groups. The meeting produced agreement on what were described as "practical measures" against Jordan, but none of the measures was specified. A communique issued following the four--hour meeting declared that, unless Jordan halted its campaign against the guerrillas, "it will be the duty of all Arab governments to take whatever practical measures they may deem necessary ... to protect the rights of the Palestinian people to self-determination." The statement warned Jordan against any attempt to make a separate peace with Israel. Qaddafi, who had called the meeting as an Arab summit, said Aug. 1 that the conferees had adopted "secret resolutions" for actions "which will be carried out in due course depending on the events in Jordan."

[8]   *Syria breaks ties with Jordan.* Syria Aug. 12 severed diplomatic relations with Jordan after a day of heavy border fighting between the military forces of both countries. A Damascus communique accused Jordan of "continuing to engage in a policy inconsistent with Arab character and with joint Arab confrontation against the common enemy [Israel]." The statement held Jordan responsible for "continued provocations against Syrian forces and aggression against Syrian territory." In ending its ties with the Amman government, Damascus also barred Syrian airspace to Jordanian planes. Fighting along the border eased Aug. 14, but Jordan charged the following day that Syria was massing troops and tanks along the border. A report from Ramtha said the Syrians had deployed 30 Soviet-made tanks in the area and that "a large infantry force" was dug into hill positions.

[9]   **Forces, politics revamped.** Jordan was reported Sept. 4 to be reorganizing its armed forces into a hard-hitting mechanized force, deploying a major portion of it in the northern part of the country along the Syrian and Iraqi borders to cope with a possible threat there. The Israeli front to the west was reported guarded largely by infantry with artillery and antitank weapons. The transformation of the army from an emphasis on infantry to one on armor was reported to have been made possible by an American decision to provide Jordan with 90 M-60 tanks, 200 M-113 armored personnel carriers and about

40,000 automatic rifles. In an announcement Sept. 7, King Hussein also reorganized the political structure of the country. According to the announcement, a National Union was formed as Jordan's only authorized political party. Communists were barred from all political activity. According to Hussein, the National Union would apply to Arabs both on the east bank of the Jordan River and on the Israeli-occupied west bank.

[10] Peace talks. Representatives of Jordan and the guerrillas opened a meeting in Jidda, Saudi Arabia Sept. 20 to discuss a possible resolution of their long-standing feud. However, the talks collapsed Nov. 26 with no agreement. The meeting, arranged by Egypt and Saudi Arabia, had been called to consider a "working paper" drawn up by Egypt and Saudi Arabia in August that would permit the guerrillas to re-establish some bases in Jordan under Jordanian sovereignty. The conference had been scheduled to open in Jidda Sept. 6, but the Jordanian delegation had returned to Amman Sept. 9 after being informed that the commandos would not attend. Both delegations were in Jidda Sept. 15, but sharp differences prevented the start of the conference. King Faisal of Saudi Arabia was said to have intervened Sept. 19 to pave the way for the discussions. Both sides were reportedly warned by Egypt and Saudi Arabia Sept. 13 that action would be taken against them if they did not appear at the conference table Sept. 15. (Saudi Minister of State for Foreign Affairs Omar Saqqaf said his country would close its border with Jordan and discontinue aid to the Jordanian government if the government delegation did not participate in the conference and would "stop all our aid" to Al Fatah—the only Palestinian group Saudi Arabia recognized—if its delegation boycotted the meeting.)

[11] Premier assassinated. Premier Tell was shot to death by three Palestinian gunmen while entering a hotel in Cairo Nov. 28. Jordanian Foreign Minister Sallah was slightly injured and an Egyptian policeman accompanying the two men was seriously wounded. At least 10 shots were fired. The three gunmen (Monzer Suleiman Khalifa, Gawad Khali Boghdadi and Ezzat Ahmad Rabah) and an unidentified Palestinian acting as lookout were arrested and charged with premeditated murder and other crimes in a Cairo court Nov. 29. The gunmen described themselves as members of a Palestinian commando group called the Black September Organization, formed in July to avenge the slaying of guerrillas in the 1970 civil war. Tell was assassinated as he was returning to his hotel from a meeting of the Arab League's Joint Defense Council discussing strategy against Israel. King Hussein Nov. 28 proclaimed seven days of national mourning and a 40-day mourning period for the palace court in Amman. Tell was buried in Amman Nov. 29. The government radio later reported that thousands of persons demonstrated in the capital and in other cities in support of demands that "the assassins and subversive elements be struck with an iron fist." Ahmed el-Louzi, Tell's finance minister, Nov. 29 was appointed premier and defense minister.

[12] Aides attacked. The Jordanian ambassadors to Britain and Switzerland were the targets of assassination attempts Dec. 15 and 16. The Black September Organization claimed credit for the attempt on the life of Zaid al-Rifai, ambassador to Britain. However, the Jordanian government charged that the Black September group did not exist and was "only a mask used by [Al] Fatah to hide its treacherous schemes." Rifai was shot and wounded in the hand Dec. 15 when his car was ambushed by a gunman near a London street intersection. A witness said the assailant fired 30-40 rounds from an automatic weapon. Police were searching for two suspects. In Geneva, two Swiss policemen were seriously injured Dec. 16 when a package left at Jordan's United Nations mission and addressed to Ambassador Ibrahim Zreikat exploded as they were opening it. Zreikat was in another room and escaped unhurt. Police and firemen had been called by mission authorities to examine the parcel.

[13] Air chief ousted. Jordan's air force commander, Maj. Gen. Saleh al-Kurdi, was ousted from his post and assigned to the Foreign Ministry as ambassador, it was reported Dec. 19. Kurdi was regarded as Hussein's most trusted officer.

See also FLOODS; MIDDLE EAST [8, 11-12, 19, 21, 27-28, 32]; UNITED ARAB REPUBLIC

JUAN CARLOS DE BORBON—*See* SPAIN [9-10]
JUDAISM—*See* CHURCHES [4, 7]
JUDICIAL CONFERENCE OF THE UNITED STATES—*See* JUDICIARY [4, 6, 11]

JUDICIARY—Contempt power limited. In an unanimous decision Jan. 20, the Supreme Court ruled that, if a judge waits until the end of trial to consider contempt of court charges, he should let another judge preside over the hearing. The court, however, reaffirmed a judge's broad power to deal immediately with courtroom disruption, as set down in a March 1970 ruling. (The court's Jan. 20 decision came in the case of Richard O. Mayberry, a convict tried in Pittsburgh in 1966 for a prison break. Mayberry had disrupted the trial and, according to the Supreme Court, "cruelly slandered" the judge, who sentenced Mayberry at the end of the trial to up to 22 years in prison for contempt.)

[2]   Rules for magistrates issued. The Supreme Court Jan. 28 issued the text of new rules to govern trials by federal magistrates. Justice Hugo L. Black, in a dissent joined by Justice William O. Douglas, argued that the court had exceeded its power and that the rule-making amounted to "judicial legislating," a function that should be left to Congress. Specifically, Black and Douglas argued that the rules prejudged a major constitutional issue—the right to free counsel and trial by jury for "petty" offenses. The majority said that for "minor offenses"—punishable by up to a year's imprisonment and $1,000 fines—the magistrate must instruct the defendant of his right to jury trial and to free counsel if he is poor. For "petty offenses"—carrying sentences of up to six months and $500 fines—the court said the magistrate must inform the defendant of his right to have counsel present but need not mention his right to free counsel or jury trial. The dissenters said the Sixth Amendment guarantees of counsel and jury trials "make no exception for so-called 'petty offenses.'"

[3]   U.S. court interference curtailed. The Supreme Court ruled Feb. 23 that federal judges should not interfere with on-going state criminal trials unless there was a strong showing of bad faith and abuse on the part of the state prosecutor. The ruling came in six cases, producing 16 separate opinions. Only Justice Douglas dissented to the central decision in the rulings. Writing for the majority, Justice Black said, "Our federalism," involving "proper respect for state functions," must be protected and that "national policy" on the issue was set in 1793 when Congress banned federal injunc-tions in state cases. Douglas argued that there had been "a revolution" after the Civil War when Congress authorized federal court lawsuits to protect civil rights. The rulings were expected to curb a rising number of injunctions and declaratory judgments issued by three-judge federal panels with authority from a 1965 Supreme Court ruling, Dombrowski v. Pfister. The 1965 ruling suggested that federal panels could strike down apparently unconstitutional state laws that were invoked against dissident groups to discourage protests.

[4]   Moves to cut jury size. Supreme Court Chief Justice Warren E. Burger March 16 announced that the Judicial Conference of the United States (the administrative and policy-making arm of the federal judiciary) had approved "in principle" a plan to reduce the size of juries in federal civil trials to an unspecified number below 12. (Federal district courts in Minnesota, New Mexico, Southern Illinois, Southern Florida and Indiana in recent months had used six-man civil juries.) The 12-man conference, meeting in Washington March 15-16, had commissioned two of its committees to consider "the best means of effectuating the recommendations for reduction in the size of civil juries."

[5] Group legal services backed. The Supreme Court, in a 5-3 ruling April 5, upheld the right of the United Transportation Union to provide group legal services to its members. The justices reversed a ruling by the Michigan Supreme Court that the union's program constituted illegal solicitation and control of lawyers' fees. Justice Black, writing for the majority, said "Collective activity undertaken to obtain meaningful access to the courts is a fundamental right within the protection of the First Amendment."

[6] Ethics code proposed. A special committee of the American Bar Association (ABA), formed in 1969 to revise the 1924 ABA judicial code, May 22 released a draft of a proposed new code of judicial ethics. The code, to be finally considered in August 1972, rejected a system of complete financial disclosures by judges to guard against conflict of interests. The code said that judges should disclose income received for such activities as lecturing and writing, but that complete reports of investments and debts were unnecessary. The code, however, warned judges to "avoid all impropriety and appearance of impropriety" and said a judge "must expect to be the subject of constant public scrutiny" and "must therefore accept restrictions on his conduct that might be viewed as burdensome by the ordinary citizen." The code would allow judges to perform legal and financial services only for family members and would prohibit service on corporate boards. It said judges should avoid serving on outside bodies except those furthering "the administration of justice." On disqualifications, the code said the ownership of one share in a company was sufficient to disqualify a judge from sitting in a case involving that company, but that a judge with "unsubstantial" holdings in a party to a case could disclose those holdings and sit in the case if requested in writing by both sides. (Under former Chief Justice Earl Warren, the U.S. Judicial Conference had required federal judges to file investment reports and obtain permission for extra-judicial activities. The rules were suspended under Chief Justice Burger, who had appointed an interim committee to handle questions of judicial ethics pending approval of a new code by the ABA.)

[7] State of the Judiciary. Chief Justice Burger made his second annual State of the Judiciary Address July 5 to the opening meeting of the ABA convention in New York. Burger called for "more stringent discipline" to protect the public from "a small minority of lawyers who have exploited uninformed laymen and abused the trust implicit in the franchise to engage in practice." He warned that, if the legal profession wanted to "avoid regulation from the outside, it must sternly regulate itself from within." Noting that nothing had been done about his 1970 recommendation that Congress authorize a joint judiciary body to advise on the effect of proposed legislation on the courts, Burger urged the ABA to set up a committee to convince Congress of the need for such a body. He said that he was pleased that another of his recommendations, for efforts to coordinate state and federal courts, had resulted in the establishment of state-federal judicial councils in more than 40 states. Burger also warned of the over-burdening of federal courts and said that a reduction in jury size could lead to savings of time and money for the federal judiciary. He cited progress for streamlining the federal court system through an experiment in which appellate courts selected some appeals to be heard soon after trial, without the usual time for preparation of written transcripts or briefs.

[8] Black judges organize for reform. The formation of a Judicial Council was announced Aug. 4 to organize the nation's black federal, state and municipal judges to work for judicial reform. The council was announced at an Atlanta news conference during the 46th annual meeting of the predominantly black National Bar Association (NBA). Judge Edward F. Bell of Detroit, president of the NBA, said the job of the new council "is to return to the idea that the courts belong to all of the people, not just the rich people, but the poor people as well, not to just white people but to black as well." The judges spoke of the absence of black federal judges in the South. There were 285 blacks serving on federal, state and local benches, representing only slightly more than 1% of the 20,000 judges in the nation.

[9] Panel urges uniform treatment. The President's Advisory Commission on Intergovernmental Relations advised Aug. 25 that states assume all costs for providing adequate defense counsel for indigent defendants and also take on the costs of local courts. In both proposals, the panel emphasized that state rather than local financing would provide more equal treatment in the nation's criminal justice system. The commission cited what it called a "patchwork response" to Supreme Court rulings requiring public-financed defense for poor persons charged with crimes. It also opposed the present system of shared court expenses by state and local governments. "Variations in local levels of financing," said the panel, "produce wide disparities in the performance of the courts." Another recommendation made to the President was a proposal to downgrade the role of grand juries in prosecutions. It said prosecution proceedings should be allowed by filing of criminal informations, the case in all but 21 states, and grand juries should be used primarily for investigating alleged official corruption. The panel also urged states to develop machinery for removing unfit judges. It recommended a system, begun in California and adopted in 17 other states, employing a commission of judges, lawyers and laymen to investigate complaints against judges. The system gave the state's highest court the power to force retirement of an unfit or incapacitated judge.

[10] Coercion of deadlocked jury barred. The U.S. Court of Appeals for the District of Columbia ruled 5-4 Sept. 14 that judges could not force a deadlocked jury to continue deliberations until it reached a verdict. The court ruled against versions of the traditional "Allen charge" used by judges to persuade minority jurors to reconsider their views. (The ruling overturned the 1968 armed assault and robbery conviction of Anthony C. Thomas.) With the ruling, the D.C. circuit joined the U.S. Courts of Appeals for the 3rd and 7th circuits in disallowing any version of the Allen charge, named after an 1896 Supreme Court case, except a mild form drafted by the ABA which said it was the jurors' "duty to consult with one another and to deliberate with a view to reaching an agreement, if it can be done without violence to individual judgment." The supreme courts of Arizona and Montana had also banned the Allen charge.

[11] Judges seek speedier trials. Chief Justice Burger said Oct. 30 that the U.S. Judicial Conference had asked the Supreme Court to amend court rules of procedure to require all U.S. courts to set up "speedy trial" timetables for criminal cases. The conference asked the court to adopt its proposal without waiting for Congress to act on a pending bill that would provide for speedier trials of criminal cases in federal courts. If the Supreme Court accepted the group's recommendation, the new measure would become part of the Federal Rules of Criminal Procedure unless Congress objected. The conference's recommendation would require each federal district court to set its own time schedule within which defendants would have to be tried and sentenced.

See also BUSINESS [8]; CIVIL RIGHTS [22]

JUVENILE DELINQUENCY—*See* CRIME [5]

KAHANE, MEIR D.—*See* UNION OF SOVIET SOCIALIST REPUBLICS [13, 15]
KENNEDY, EDWARD M.—*See* POLITICS [8]
KENNEDY, JOHN F.—*See* MICRONESIA; PENTAGON PAPERS [20-21]
KENNEDY ROUND—*See* TARIFFS & WORLD TRADE [2]
KENT STATE UNIVERSITY—*See* STUDENT UNREST [1-3]

KENYA—12 sentenced in plot against Kenyatta. A Nairobi magistrate June 8 sentenced 12 Kenyans to a total of 91½ years in prison for plotting to overthrow the government of President Jomo Kenyatta. An unspecified number of other persons were mentioned in connection with the plot and their indictment was expected. Joseph Daniel Owino, a former army officer considered to be the group's organizer, was sentenced to nine and a half years in prison. Joseph Muga Ouma, a lecturer in geography at Makerere University College in Kampala, and four other persons were given eight years apiece. Those sentenced to the same term as Ouma were Apollo Wakiaga Odare, a government marketing board executive; Juvenalis Benedict Aoko; Joshua Silvano Ooko, a trade unionist and former personal secretary to Tom Mboya, the Kenyan politician assassinated in 1969; and Sylvanus Okech Oduor. The remaining six accused were each sentenced to seven years in prison. The name of a 13th defendant was withdrawn from the proceedings June 8 at the request of James Karugu, the public prosecutor. Many of the accused were understood to be members of the Luo and Somali tribes and supporters of the Kenya People's Union, a banned opposition party. All pleaded guilty as charged.

According to Karugu's presentation June 4, the group had deputized Ouma to approach Tanzanian President Julius K. Nyerere with a request for money, weapons and a Tanzanian "military presence" near the Kenya frontier. Nyerere was said to have replied: "If it was Malawi I might think about it, but not with Kenya and definitely not while Mzee [Kenyatta] is alive." (The Washington Post reported June 5 that Nyerere had waited nearly a month before informing Kenya authorities of Ouma's request.) The prosecutor said Ouma had been introduced to Nyerere by Sam Odaka, foreign minister in the government of former Ugandan President Milton A. Obote, who was overthrown in January. Karugu implicated two prominent national figures June 4 when he argued that Gideon Mutiso, a member of parliament and known critic of the government, acted as liaison between the plotters and Maj. Gen. J. M. L. Ndolo, commander of the Kenyan armed forces. Mutiso and Ndolo were both of the Kamba tribe, a group whose members held influential positions in the army. Karugu said June 7 that those collaborating with the plotters included "a few individuals in high places. The identities of most, if not all of them, are known."

Bank merger. President Kenyatta announced June 1 that the government would take 50% of the shares of a new bank to be formed from the merger of two British firms, Barclays Bank and the Standard Bank. In explaining the move, Kenyatta said: "In Kenya we consider that a 50% shareholding partnership would be an ideal solution to various key sectors or economic activities. This allows continuing incentive for international skills, resources and ideals. It also lays proper claim to, and provides effective outlet for, the rights and aspirations of our people."

See also AGNEW, SPIRO THEODORE; HEALTH [1]; SPACE [21]; TRACK & FIELD; UGANDA

KERNER, OTTO—See CRIME [13]

KHRUSHCHEV, NIKITA—Nikita S. Khrushchev, 77, who was deposed in 1964 as leader of the Soviet Communist party and government, died Sept. 11 in a Moscow hospital following a heart attack. Khrushchev, who had suffered from heart trouble in recent years, reportedly had an attack about Sept. 7. He had lived in obscurity for most of the previous seven years at Petrovo-Dalneye near Moscow, making a public appearance June 13 to vote in elections for the Supreme Soviet of the Russian Republic. A volume of memoirs of disputed authenticity had been published abroad under Khrushchev's name in 1970.

The burial ceremony took place Sept. 13 in a small cemetery adjoining the Kremlin. It was attended by about 150 persons including Khrushchev's wife, Nina Petrovna, his daughters Yulia, Rada and Yelena, his son Sergei, his son-in-law Aleksei S. Adzhubei, former editor of the government newspaper Izvestia, and a number of foreign newsmen. No Soviet officials were present, although the Communist party Central Committee and the government sent a large funeral wreath. The first official government confirmation of Khrushchev's death came Sept. 13 when the Soviet press agency Tass carried a one-sentence announcement in which the Communist party and government noted "with sorrow" the death of "special pensioner" Khrushchev after "a severe and long illness."

KIDNAPING—See ARGENTINA [11]; BRAZIL; CANADA [2-4]; COLOMBIA; CRIME [6]; LATIN AMERICA; MEXICO; PANAMA; SECURITY, U.S.; TURKEY [1, 6]; URUGUAY [9-12]; VENEZUELA

KINSHASA—See CONGO, DEMOCRATIC REPUBLIC OF THE

KISSINGER, HENRY—See COMMUNIST CHINA-U.S. DETENTE [6-7, 13]; FOREIGN POLICY; GOVERNMENT REORGANIZATION; INDOCHINA WAR [63]; NIXON, RICHARD MILHOUS [3]; PAKISTAN [37]; SECURITY, U.S.

KLASSEN, ELMER T.—See POSTAL SERVICE, U.S.

KOREA, NORTH (DEMOCRATIC PEOPLE'S REPUBLIC OF KOREA)—Military aid. Under an agreement signed in Peking Sept. 6, Communist China was to provide North Korea free military assistance for the first time since the Korean War. The agreement, details of which were not made public, was signed by Gen. Huang Yung Sheng, Chinese armed forces chief, and his North Korean counterpart, Gen. O Jin U. The Chinese-North Korean mutual defense treaty of 1961 had been reaffirmed in a Chinese message sent to Pyonyang's leaders in July.

See also COMMUNIST CHINA-U.S. DETENTE [2, 5]; HIJACKING [4]; JAPAN [1]; KOREAN RELATIONS; KOREA, SOUTH; MEXICO; PENTAGON PAPERS [18]; UNITED NATIONS [6]

KOREAN RELATIONS—Red Cross talks. Red Cross officials of North and South Korea met briefly in Panmunjom Aug. 20 for the first bilateral meeting between representatives of the divided nation since the Korean War. Following five meetings between liaison officers, preliminary discussions opened Sept. 20 to arrange a formal conference to deal with the problem of reuniting families divided by the 1950-53 conflict. In opening statements Sept. 20, the leaders of both of the five-man delegations expressed hope that their negotiations would help lead the way to the eventual reunification of Korea. Both sides agreed to establish a permanent liaison office at the Panmunjom armistice conference site. South Korean Red Cross President Choi Doo Sun had proposed the meetings in a letter sent Aug. 12 to his North Korean counterpart, Son Song Pil. In response to the negotiations, the North Korean Communist party newspaper, Worker's Daily, Aug. 21 proposed the unification of Korea and offered Seoul three choices: the establishment of a confederation of the North and South, leaving the political systems of both intact, as a transitional step for reunification; a program of economic and cultural exchanges and mutual visits; or, at least, "the humanitarian measure for the exchange of letters between the North and South Korean people."

Chinese rejoin armistice group. Communist China rejoined the Korean Military Armistice Commission at Panmunjom after an absence of nearly five years, it was reported June 19. China had withdrawn its senior delegate from the commission after North Korea declared its "independence" from both Moscow and Peking in August 1966. China, however, continued to be represented by three junior officers as observers. Peking's new delegate, Ho Chu-jo, had arrived in Pyonyang, North Korea June 8.

Military developments. Under an agreement concluded Feb. 6 between the U.S. and South Korea, South Korean forces completed the replacement of U.S. troops on the armistice border with North Korea, according to report March 12. The South Koreans thus became responsible for the entire 151-mile border. The Americans, who had previously guarded an 18-mile stretch of the buffer zone, pulled back about 20 miles. The U.S.-Korean agreement called for the American military force to be reduced by 20,000 to 43,000 by June 30. The only role of the remaining U.S. soldiers would be to stand guard at Panmunjom. In clashes between the North and South Koreans: a North Korean ship was sunk May 14, and all 15-17 men aboard the vessel drowned, in a clash with a South Korean navy ship and jet fighters in the Yellow Sea 100 miles northeast of Seoul; one South Korean policeman was killed and another seriously wounded in an exchange of gunfire May 4 between a South Korean police vessel and a North Korean spy boat off Inchon, 20 miles west of Seoul; South Korea claimed June 1 that its forces that day had sunk a 70-ton North Korean spy ship, drowning all 15-17 men aboard, in a clash in which a South Korean transport plane with seven men aboard plunged into the sea; one North Korean was killed in a clash with a South Korean border patrol in the demilitarized zone (DMZ) June 16; South Korean forces June 18 killed two members of a three-man North Korean infiltration team and June 22 killed the third; five North Koreans and one South Korean were slain in a series of fire fights Aug. 16 along the eastern sector of the DMZ; three of four North Korean infiltrators, five South Korean marines and three South Korean civilians were killed Sept. 17-18 in clashes following the infiltrators' seizure of a South Korean village 25 miles northwest of Seoul.

See also KOREA, SOUTH; UNITED NATIONS [6]

KOREAN WAR—*See* PENTAGON PAPERS [17-18]; SUDAN; UNITED NATIONS [6]; WAR CRIMES [10]

KOREA, SOUTH (REPUBLIC OF KOREA)—President Park re-elected. Chung Hee Park was re-elected to his third and, according to his own statement, last four-year term as president in nationwide balloting April 27. He was sworn in July 1. Park had a plurality of 946,928 votes over his principal opponent, Kim Dae Jung of the New Democratic party. Three other rival candidates represented minor splinter groups.

Cabinet shifts. Paik Too Chin, premier of South Korea, and his entire 18-member cabinet resigned June 3 to give Park a free hand in choosing a new government following National Assembly elections May 25 in which Park's ruling Democratic Republican (DR) party had its majority reduced by 56 seats.

Park replaced nine ministers and retained 10 others. The new cabinet members were: prime minister—Kim Chong Pil, vice president of the ruling Democratic Republican party; foreign—Kim Yong Shik; home affairs—Oh Chi Song; justice—Sin Chik Su; education—Min Kwang Shik; construction—Tae Wan Son; health and social affairs—Yi Kyong Ho; culture and public information—Yun Chu Yong; and science and technology—Choe Hyong Sok. Reappointed ministers were: deputy prime minister—Kim Hak Yol; finance—Nam Tok U; national defense—Chong Nae Hyok; agriculture and forestry—Kim Po Hyon; commerce and industry—Yi Nak Son; transportation—Chang Song Hwan; communications—Sin Sang Chol; government administration—So Il Kyo; national unification—Kim Yong Son; and minister without portfolio—Yo Pyong Ok.

Prison mutiny. Thirty-eight persons were killed following the mutiny and escape of 23 "special criminals" (not military men) Aug. 23 from a South Korean air force stockade on the island of Silmi, 15 miles off the west coast port of Inchon. The escapees were erroneously identified at first as North Korean infiltrators. Sixteen of the prisoners were among the dead. After breaking out of the stockade, the inmates seized guns and hand grenades, killed 12 prison officials and fled the island to Inchon. There they commandeered a bus and headed for Seoul. The vehicle crashed into a tree after being intercepted in the southwestern part of the city by soldiers and police. Minutes later the bus' occupants set off hand grenades, killing 15 of them. Defense Minister Chong assumed responsibility for the incident and resigned Aug. 23 as did Gen. Kim Doo Man, air force chief of staff. Chong was succeeded Aug. 24 by Yoo Jae Heung, a special presidential assistant on defense affairs. Lt. Gen. Ok Man Ho, deputy air force chief of staff, was appointed as Kim's replacement Aug. 25.

Party dispute. Two chief rivals of Premier Kim were forced to resign from the DR Oct. 5. Three others were suspended. The two key officials were Kil Chae Ho, chairman of the party's policy committee, and Kim Sung Kon, head of its central committee. Their departure was linked to an intraparty dispute that had resulted in 16 party members joining the opposition in the National Assembly Oct. 2 in approving a resolution calling for the dismissal of Home Affairs Minister Oh. Oh, who resigned after the assembly vote, had been criticized because of recent domestic disturbances. He also was suspended from the party. DR unity was further fragmented when all 13 members of the party's executive committee submitted their resignations to President Park.

Student unrest. Thousands of university students staged demonstrations and clashed with police Oct. 11-15 in protest against alleged government corruption and student military training. In a move to quell the growing unrest, troops Oct. 15 occupied six universities in Seoul. The soldiers withdrew Oct. 23 following demands by the opposition New Democratic party for their removal. They were replaced with policemen who barred students from entering the campuses. Thirteen universities remained closed.

National emergency declared. President Park declared a national emergency Dec. 6. He said the action was necessary to cope with a possible invasion by North Korea and to "make the South Korean people look at the rapid changes in the international situation." The U.S. State Department Dec. 6 said it saw no evidence of a crisis. The department said Washington did not "altogether share the views of the South Korean government on the present military situation in North Korea and have no information that an attack is imminent." Park's announcement was coupled with the issuance of a six-point emergency program that did not provide any specific measures. It merely prohibited "all social unrest that might weaken national security," barred "irresponsible arguments on national matters" and demanded that, in critical situations, every citizen "conceded some of the freedom that he enjoys for the sake of national security." Park took issue with President Nixon's contention that he sought to replace confrontation by negotiations with the Communist powers. Asserting that Nixon's policy was not reflected "in our Korean peninsula," Park said "local tension" was mounting with the North Koreans "busily occupied in mass production of war weapons." He claimed North Korea had "nearly completed the preparations for invasion" of the South. Park said infiltration of North Korean armed espionage agents had increased.

Park gets emergency powers. The National Assembly Dec. 27 approved the Special Measures Law for National Security and Defense, signed into law by President Park later the same day. The law gave the president authority to impose economic controls, curtail freedom of the press, issue a national mobilization decree, ban outdoor gatherings and demonstrations, curb labor unions, and change the national budget, when necessary, to cope with emergency conditions. Submitted to the assembly Dec. 21, the law was aimed at providing legal grounds for the state of national emergency declared earlier. The National Assembly session that passed the bill was held in an annex building of the legislature and was attended only by members of the DR and two independents. The site of the meeting was shifted after opposition New Democratic party members had begun a sit-in at the regular assembly building Dec. 21 to block passage of the bill. They were not notified of the session being held in the annex. When some New Democratic members learned of the meeting, they rushed the building, but were blocked from entering by a cordon of police.

See also AGNEW, SPIRO THEODORE; HIJACKING [4]; INDOCHINA WAR [61]; JAPAN [1]; KOREAN RELATIONS; PENTAGON PAPERS [18]; TARIFFS & WORLD TRADE [3, 5]; UNEMPLOYMENT; UNITED NATIONS [6, 8]

KOSYGIN, ALEKSEI—*See* CANADA [16, 22]; CUBA; UNION OF SOVIET SOCIALIST REPUBLICS [5]

KU KLUX KLAN—*See* CIVIL RIGHTS [9]; FEDERAL BUREAU OF INVESTIGATION [2]; SUPREME COURT

KUWAIT—Elections. In elections held Jan. 23 for the 50-seat Kuwait National Assembly, the Nationalist party won 10, the Merchant and Bedouin parties 17 each and the remaining six were captured by six independent candidates. The Nationalists, led by Ahmedal Khatib, previously held no seats.

Chinese relations. Communist China and Kuwait established diplomatic relations March 22, it was announced in Peking March 29. A joint communique signed in Kuwait said both countries would exchange ambassadors soon. Nationalist China March 29 assailed Kuwait's action as a "most unfriendly act" and severed relations with the Persian Gulf state.

See also AGNEW, SPIRO THEODORE; OIL

KY, NGUYEN CAO—*See* DRUG USE & ADDICTION [17]; VIETNAM, SOUTH

LABOR—Nixon asks for transport strike legislation. President Nixon Feb. 3 renewed his request to Congress for stronger procedures to handle major strikes in the transportation industry. He requested: elimination of the emergency strike provisions of the Railway Labor Act (applicable to both railroads and airlines) under which strikes could be delayed 60 days by appointment of an emergency board to study the case and recommend a settlement; extension of the Taft-Hartley Act emergency provisions to the railroad and airline industries; and broadening the options under Taft-Hartley to include a "final-offer-selection." The final-offer-selection required agreement by both sides in a dispute to abide by the decision of a special panel in its choice of the last, best offer of either management or labor. (A similar proposal by Nixon in the previous Congress was not considered.) Special legislation imposing a settlement was the only present recourse under the Taft-Hartley Act following expiration of an 80-day cooling-off period.

[2] Chavez-Teamsters dispute ends. Cesar Chavez, leader of the AFL-CIO United Farm Workers Organizing Committee (UFWOC), March 26 announced an accord with the International Brotherhood of Teamsters on their jurisdictional dispute over organizing workers employed by growers. Under the agreement, signed March 26 by AFL-CIO President George Meany and acting Teamsters President Frank Fitzsimmons, the UFWOC would take the organizing initiative among field workers and the Teamsters among drivers and food processors. Jurisdictional disputes, if unresolved within five days, were to be submitted for an attempt at solution, first to the U.S. Catholic Bishops Committee on Farm Labor and, remaining unresolved for 15 days more, next to Meany and Fitzsimmons or to an arbitrator appointed by them for final and binding arbitration. The accord could lead to the end of a national boycott of lettuce begun by the UFWOC Sept. 16, 1970, but the intention of the Teamsters concerning their contracts with growers remained unclear.

[3] Chemical union joins AFL-CIO. The 104,000-member International Chemical Workers Union reaffiliated with the AFL-CIO May 12. The Chemical Workers Union had been ousted by the federation in 1969 after it voted to join the Alliance for Labor Action (ALA), set up by the late United Automobile Workers (UAW) President Walter P. Reuther after the UAW left the AFL-CIO in 1967 over policy differences. (In announcing the reaffiliation, President Meany said the UAW could also reaffiliate if they desired.) Chemical Workers President Thomas Boyle said he was satisfied with the ALA's community action effort but disappointed with its costly organizing program.

He said a primary reason for re-entry into the AFL-CIO was the need for a united organized labor effort to combat unemployment and exert pressure upon the Nixon Administration to develop job programs.

[4] Hoffa sentence commuted President Nixon Dec. 23 commuted the prison term of James R. Hoffa, former president of the Teamsters. Hoffa was freed that day after serving four years, nine months and 16 days of a 13-year sentence. The sentence was commuted to six and one-half years, which made Hoffa eligible, with time taken off for good behavior, for release. The commutation was conditional on a requirement that Hoffa "not engage in the direct or indirect management of any labor organization" until March 6, 1980, the date when his full prison sentence would expire. He was to report regularly to a federal probation officer until 1973. According to Justice Department and parole board sources, Hoffa could express his opinions on national union issues without violating parole, could have limited contact with his former associates, could appear on national television talk and news programs and could participate in rank-and-file meetings of his Detroit Teamsters local.

[5]   In preceding events during the year: the Supreme Court Jan. 11 declined to hear a Hoffa petition to set aside a five-year sentence (to be added to his current eight-year term for jury-tampering) for conspiracy to use the mails to divert union pension funds; the U.S. Board of Parole March 31 denied Hoffa parole and said it would not consider any other application for his parole until June 1972; U.S. District Court Judge Richard B. Austin in Chicago May 10 denied a plea to permit Hoffa to serve his five-year mail fraud sentence concurrently with his eight-year jury-tampering sentence; Hoffa announced from prison June 3 that he was not a candidate for re-election as president of the Teamsters, and instead endorsed Fitzsimmons for the presidency; Fitzsimmons was elected president July 8, at which time Hoffa was made president emeritus for life; Hoffa June 24 resigned as head of Detroit Local 299, the Central Teamsters Conference, Joint Council 43 in Detroit and the Michigan Conference of Teamsters; the U.S. Board of Parole again rejected Hoffa's bid for parole Aug. 20, after a special hearing was granted to consider "new and substantial information" (presumably Hoffa's resignation from his Teamsters posts).

[6] 1970 strike data. The Labor Department reported Jan. 11 that 3.3 million workers were involved in strikes in 1970 and the amount of work time lost by strikes was at the highest level in more than a decade. Man-days of work lost through strikes in 1970 totaled 62 million, or .34% of estimated working time (34 days out of every 10,000 worked). This was the highest total since 1959 when 69 million man-days were lost, or .5% of estimated working time. The 1969 totals were 42.7 million man-days lost (.24%) and 2.5 million workers involved.

[7] New York police strike. About 21,000 New York City patrolmen—85% of the city's force—engaged in a wildcat strike Jan. 14-19 without resolution of the pay dispute involved. The city announced June 9 that the strikers had been found in violation of the state's Taylor Law forbidding strikes by public employees and would be fined two days' pay for each day of absence and be put on probation for a year. The strike action was opposed by the Patrolmen's Benevolent Association (the policemen's union), but spread to 85% of the force and drew sympathy walkouts by security officers in transit, housing and social service work. It ended Jan. 19 when PBA delegates voted resumption of customary duties. Essential service was maintained during the strike, and there was no evidence of an upsurge in crime. The pay dispute involved the salary ratio between sergeants, who had received a pay raise, and patrolmen, who demanded retroactive $100-a-month raises to maintain the 3.5-3 ratio they contended was written into their contract which expired Dec. 31, 1970. (A state Supreme Court justice ruled Feb. 5 that the patrolmen were entitled to the retroactive pay.)

[8] **Steelworkers settlements.** A 28-day strike against three major can manufacturers (Continental Can Co., the American Can Co. and the Crown Cork and Seal Corp.) ended March 14 with union ratification of a March 12 negotiators' agreement on three-year contracts calling for a package increase per worker of $1.50 an hour in wages and fringe benefits. The strike, by 33,000 workers represented by the AFL-CIO United Steelworkers of America (USW), began Feb. 15 against 125 plants. The settlement was found "excessive" by the President's Council of Economic Advisors (*see* ECONOMY, U.S. [7]). The USW and four major aluminum companies (Aluminum Company of America [Alcoa], Kaiser Aluminum and Chemical Corp., Reynolds Metal Co. and Ormet Aluminum Co.) reached agreement May 31 on new three-year contracts that would provide wage increases of about 31% over the three-year period. A similar package was signed with nine major steel companies Aug. 2. The White House reported that President Nixon was displeased over the size of the settlements. (*See also* [12].)

[9] **New York struck by city employees.** About 8,000 municipal employees struck June 7-8 on behalf of a pension plan negotiated with the city in 1970 but not passed by the state legislature. The plan would have enabled the 122,000 members of the AFL-CIO International Brotherhood of the American Federation of State, County and Municipal Employees (AFSCME) to retire at half-pay after 20 years or at full pay after 40 years. The strike action, called by the AFSCME, ended with an agreement to submit the pension plan to the 1972 state legislature and, failing action there, to negotiation and an impartial panel. The strike action was joined June 7 by Local 237 of the Teamsters and its 318 bridge tenders. Commuting motorists that day were faced with open drawbridges and city trucks abandoned in key lanes. Massive traffic tie-ups resulted. The Teamsters returned to work June 8; but that day other workers (sewage and incineration workers, park workers and drivers delivering food for school lunch programs) joined the action and the city's problem shifted to a pollution peril as hundreds of millions of gallons of sewage poured untreated into waterways. The city announced June 9 that the strikers would be informed of their liability to penalties for violating the Taylor Act (*see* [7]).

[10] **Dock strikes.** A break in negotiations shortly before expiration of a five-year contract at midnight June 30 precipitated the first coastwide dock strike in 23 years July 1. Oct. 1, docks on the East and Gulf Coasts were also closed as members of the AFL-CIO International Longshoremen's Association (ILA) joined the striking West Coast International Longshoremen's and Warehousemen's Union (ILWU). (The key issue in the West Coast dispute reportedly was a jurisdictional dispute between the ILWU and the Teamsters over handling of container cargo.) It was the first time in history that docks were shut down on all three coasts simultaneously. (The only exceptions were several ILA locals working on an hour-to-hour basis in areas of Texas.) President Nixon Oct. 4 invoked the Taft-Hartley Act to deal with the strikes. Nixon had directed Labor Secretary James D. Hodgson and Director of the Office of Management and Budget George P. Schultz to meet with both sides in the West Coast strike Sept. 25 and himself had met with both sides later the same day. Both sides had met daily from Sept. 28, but J. Curtis Counts, director of the Federal Mediation and Conciliation Service, reported Oct. 4 that the talks were at an impasse. Nixon invoked the Taft-Hartley Act on the grounds that the strikes would "imperil the national health and safety." Under the act, the President established a five-man board of inquiry to assess the status of dock negotiations. The board reported little imminent chance of settlement in the West Coast strike and in an ILA-local dispute which had begun in the port of Chicago Sept. 1. The board found that serious bargaining had not yet begun in the East and Gulf Coast strikes and indicated that more time should be allowed for settlement. Federal courts in San Francisco and Chicago Oct. 6 issued 10-day restraining orders against the strikes in their areas in response to Justice Department requests. The courts also scheduled hearings on the matter

of an 80-day Taft-Hartley injunction. In response to the court orders, strikers in both areas returned to work. (U.S. District Court Judge Abraham Marovitz Nov. 3 refused to grant a Taft-Hartley injunction against the Chicago strikers and vacated the temporary restraining order issued Oct. 6.) The board of inquiry reported to the President Nov. 25 that there was "little chance of a prompt settlement" in the East and Gulf Coast strikes. The Justice Department Nov. 26-29 asked for and was issued return-to-work orders by federal courts in 12 harbor districts. The full 80-day cooling-off period allowed under the Taft-Hartley Act was invoked by federal courts in New York Dec. 3 and Miami Dec. 15. The West Coast ILWU agreed Dec. 23 to extend its current contract until Jan. 10, 1972, in a continuing effort to reach agreement on a new contract.

[11] Telephone workers strike. About 532,000 telephone workers July 14 struck companies of the Bell Telephone System after a new contract was rejected by union leaders. Many other nonstriking workers honored picket lines and stayed off the job, but phone service was relatively unaffected as supervisory personnel took over the largely automated service. The strike, called by Bell's largest union, the Communications Workers of America (CWA), was joined by the International Brotherhood of Electrical Workers (IBEW) in New Jersey and two large independent unions in Connecticut and Pennsylvania. CWA contracts had begun expiring April 30 and were extended on a daily basis until July 14. After a tentative contract agreement (providing for a wage-benefit increase of 31% to over 33.5%) was reached between the CWA and the American Telephone & Telegraph Co., parent firm of the Bell System, July 20, CWA President Joseph A. Beirne ordered the members back to work. However, the presidents of 23 locals in New York state, dissatisfied with contract vacation and pension provisions, voted overwhelmingly July 20 to defy the national leadership and continue the strike. The strike resumed July 21 in New Jersey, Pennsylvania, Connecticut, California, Arizona and New York. Most of the strikers were CWA members, but others belonged to the IBEW or to small independent local unions. The IBEW was still negotiating a separate contract with AT&T. The New Jersey Bell Telephone Co. July 21 reached tentative agreement on a new contract with the 12,000-member Telephone Workers Union of New Jersey (made up of both CWA and IBEW members). The terms of the three-year contract were almost identical with those in the CWA contract. In Philadelphia, the Pennsylvania Telephone Guild, an independent union representing some 2,600 persons, also agreed July 21 to a new three-year contract; but union members planned to honor picket lines of the 13,500-member Federation of Telephone Workers of Pennsylvania, which had not reached a settlement.

[12] Copper strike. The Nonferrous Conference, a 26-union coalition led by the USW (*see* [8]), reached tentative agreement in Salt Lake City July 25 on a new three-year contract with the nation's largest copper producer, Kennecott Copper Corp. It was a major breakthrough in ending a 26-day copper strike, called against the Big Four copper producers (Kennecott, Anaconda Co., Phelps Dodge Corp. and American Smelting and Refining Co. [Asarco]) July 1 after two months of separate contract negotiations had failed. The strike had idled more than 35,000 workers in 11 states. The three-year contract, conditional on resolution of a work rules issue, provided for a 92¢-an-hour wage boost over the life of the contract—about a 28% hike. An unlimited cost-of-living escalator, one of the major obstacles to a settlement, was to go into effect during the second year of the contract. Regular pension benefits were increased 50%. An earlier tentative agreement between Anaconda and the USW, covering 6,000 workers in Montana, had been reported July 20 but had become entangled over terms of work rules changes. Another agreement covering Anaconda's Nevada Yerington mines was ratified July 21 by the Nevada Industrial Council, AFL-CIO. Phelps Dodge Aug. 1 announced tentative agreement with 15 unions in Arizona, representing 6,400 workers. As of Aug. 2, Asarco was the only major copper producer without any form of agreement.

[13]   Douglas Aircraft strikers return. UAW President Leonard Woodcock Dec. 11 issued a back-to-work order to 4,000 strikers at Douglas Aircraft of Canada Ltd. at Malton, and cut off strike benefits of up to $40 a week as of Dec. 13. The order was unprecedented in the history of the union in Canada. Although the international union sanctioned the strike, Woodcock said McDonnell Douglas, the parent U.S. firm, had made a settlement offer Nov. 13 which had corresponded to union demands. Local union membership had rejected the offer Nov. 18. The new settlement provided increases of 80¢ an hour over three years, plus improvements in pensions and other fringe areas.

See also AGING; AGRICULTURE [7-10]; AUTOMOBILES [1]; AVIATION [2, 6]; CANADA [6-10, 23]; CHILE [5, 22]; CIVIL RIGHTS [1, 20-24]; ECONOMY, U.S.; EDUCATION [8-10, 14]; FRANCE [6]; GREAT BRITAIN [11-12, 20]; ITALY [8-9]; MINES; POSTAL SERVICE, U.S.; PRISONS [7, 10]; RACIAL & MINORITY UNREST [1]; RAILROADS; STATE & LOCAL GOVERNMENTS [3]; TARIFFS & WORLD TRADE [11]; UEMPLOYMENT; WOMEN'S RIGHTS

LAIRD, MELVIN—See DEFENSE [4]; DRUG USE & ADDICTION [7]; ESPIONAGE; FOREIGN AID; INDOCHINA WAR [65]; MILITARY [7]; NIXON, RICHARD MILHOUS [10]; PENTAGON PAPERS [11]; PUERTO RICO; RACIAL & MINORITY UNREST [14]; TELEVISION & RADIO
LAOS—See DRAFT & WAR PROTEST [2, 4-5, 7]; INDOCHINA WAR [1, 17-33, 35, 39, 49, 51, 62, 64-65, 70, 72, 79]; PENTAGON PAPERS [20, 22-24, 27]
LASERS—See NOBEL PRIZES

LATIN AMERICA—OAS convention on kidnaping. The 23 foreign ministers of the Organization of American States (OAS) ended a nine-day special meeting in Washington Feb. 2 with passage of a convention condemning political kidnaping. The convention, adopted 13-1 with two abstentions, labeled as a "common crime, whatever the motives," kidnaping, murder and other acts of terror against diplomatic and foreign officials. The text also provided for denial of the right of political asylum to the kidnapers and terrorists and authorized their extradition and/or trial. However, the final text of the convention authorized any country to refuse extradition if it considered the accused person guilty of a political rather than a criminal act. Chile voted against the convention, stressing that it violated the sovereignty of Latin American nations. Peru and Bolivia abstained from voting. Brazil, Argentina, Ecuador, Paraguay, Guatemala and Haiti had walked out of the meeting Feb. 1. The boycotting nations considered the convention too weak and wanted a stronger document condemning all acts of terrorism.

Andean capital pact effective. The five nations of the Andean Common Market (Bolivia, Colombia, Ecuador, Chile and Peru) July 1 put into effect an agreement, first approved in December 1970, by which foreign investments would be put under tight controls. (According to a report Dec. 8, Venezuela agreed to enter into negotiations for its entry into the Andean group. It had sought admission as an associate member in 1970, but had been rejected by the five members.)

Canada enters inter-American system. Canada took its first step toward joining the inter-American system July 6 when it requested full membership in the Pan American Health Organization. The organization's executive committee unanimously recommended acceptance of the request by its directive council. Canada followed up the first step by informing the Inter-American Development Bank (IDB) Aug. 10 that it desired membership in the organization. Before entering the IDB, Canada must negotiate the amount of money it would commit to the bank as well as its voting rights. The bank had to amend its charter to permit membership to a non-OAS member.

CIAP report cites differing courses. The Inter-American Committee on the Alliance for Progress Aug. 15 (the Alliance's 10th anniversary) released a report prepared at its request by the General Secretariat of the OAS. The report recommended that Latin American countries be permitted to follow differing courses of development and that the U.S. accept the movement toward socialism in some Latin American nations. It emphasized that, while Latin American nations in 1961 accepted a "single path" to socio-economic development, at present "it would be impossible and unsuitable to define a uniform strategy for all countries of the region." Most of the report concentrated on the socio-economic accomplishments and failures recorded in the 10 years of the Alliance. It showed that, while Latin American nations were able to mobilize more than twice the funds anticipated toward the Alliance's social and economic goals, there was a wide degree to which individual countries moved toward specific socio-economic goals. The report also revealed that official financing terms were "harder" than expected and that the U.S. received more money from Latin America than it expended during the 10-year period. Among the failures cited by the report were: agrarian reform programs, which "did not significantly improve during the decade"; the housing shortage, which actually increased in six of nine countries for which statistics were available; the region's unemployment problem, which "perhaps even worsened"; and the international trade situation, which continued to look bleak. Among the Alliance's successes was the region's per capita economic growth rate, which reached 3.8% in 1970 and exceeded the Alliance's 2.5% goal for the previous two years. Due to the chronic unemployment problem, the study recommended a 4%-5% annual per capita growth rate target.

Report cites unemployment problem. An OAS report submitted to the Latin American Trade Union Technical Advisory Council stated that the prospects for the elimination of unemployment in Latin America were "bleak," according to a Sept. 10 report. The report cited the "large numbers of young people with more education and higher aspirations, and a greater capacity for organized protest" among the unemployed as creating a "potentially explosive situation." Capital-intensive production techniques, which required fewer workers than labor-intensive methods, were held to have contributed to the region's growing unemployment, which increased from 5.6% of the work force in 1950 to 11.1% in 1965. The greatest increase was among unskilled workers. According to the report, there had been a failure in the 1960s to generate enough jobs for the two million people who entered the labor force annually. (Three million people were expected to enter the labor force annually in the 1970s.) The report stressed that, "basically, the road to full employment in Latin America lies in the adoption of policies that would result in the development of broad, internal markets in which the great masses of Latin America can actively participate."

Meyer stresses U.S. commitment. Assistant Secretary of State for Inter-American Affairs Charles Meyer Oct. 25 said that the U.S. remained committed to President Nixon's 1969 promise of "a new kind of partnership" for Latin America, even though the U.S.'s own economic problems had prevented implementation of some main points of policy. Meyer's speech, the first policy statement on Latin America since Nixon unveiled his Western Hemisphere policy in 1969, was partly a response to growing dissatisfaction in Latin America with the 10% import surcharge imposed by the U.S. Aug. 15 (*see* ECONOMY, U.S. [8]; TARIFFS & WORLD TRADE [8-9]). Many Latins regarded the surcharge as especially unfair in light of the fact that the U.S. enjoyed a favorable balance of payments with almost all Latin countries and favored a preferential import policy toward Latin America. Admitting that the U.S. had not fulfilled its commitment "to implement a system of generalized trade preference for the developing countries," Meyer said the Administration believed it would be "unwise to submit a preference bill at this time," in view of the fact that the U.S. trade and balance of payments position had "deteriorated rapidly, creating a strong protectionist sentiment in Congress." He added that the U.S. had submitted U.S. economic policies for annual review by the CIAP, "an unprecedented step for a donor nation."

OAS to study Cuban relations. The OAS announced Dec. 8 that it would appoint a committee to study the lifting of sanctions against Cuba. (Cuba was suspended by the OAS in 1962. The OAS imposed diplomatic and economic sanctions against Cuba in 1964.) OAS Secretary General Galo Plaza said the plan would allow OAS member nations to establish individual diplomatic and trade relations with Cuba if they wished. However, he added: "We will not ask Cuba into the OAS." Peru planned to present a formal motion during an OAS meeting Dec.17 that would have allowed member nations to unilaterally restore diplomatic relations with Cuba. However, Luis Alvarado, Peruvian Ambassador to the OAS, asked that the meeting be canceled in order to bring up the matter for discussion "at a more propitious occasion." U.S. State Department spokesman Robert J. McCloskey announced Dec. 16 that the U.S. opposed the move to allow unilateral action on Cuba. (Secretary General Plaza had begun quiet consultations with member nations in November 1970 in an attempt to harmonize differing attitudes toward Cuba and to prevent a loss of prestige to the OAS from actions toward Cuba taken outside the organization. Cuba had been accepted Oct. 19 as a member of the "Group of 77"—a loose grouping of developing nations—with no objections from Latin American representatives at the meeting.)

See also BRAZIL; COLOMBIA; CUBA; FOREIGN AID; FOREIGN POLICY; TARIFFS & WORLD TRADE [8, 10, 13]

LAW & ORDER—*See* ELECTIONS [4, 7]
LAW ENFORCEMENT ASSISTANCE ADMINISTRATION (LEAA)—*See* PRISONS [1]; STATE & LOCAL GOVERNMENTS [2]
LEAGUE OF NATIONS—*See* SOUTH AFRICA [2]

LEBANON—Commandos curb forces. The Palestinian commandos in Lebanon announced a series of moves Jan. 3 designed to curb the "bourgeois appearance" of the movement in the country, to restore the secrecy of the guerrilla organization and to create greater efficiency. Al Fatah, the major commando force of the 10 guerrilla groups, said it would withdraw arms from its men in Lebanon to achieve closer cooperation with the Beirut government and close its four offices in the country's refugee camps. The Beirut office would remain open. The guerrilla decision was conveyed to Lebanese Premier Saeb Salam Jan. 4 by commando leader Yasir Arafat, also head of Al Fatah, who had arrived in Beirut the previous day.

The guerrillas were said to be concerned over a recent outbreak of violence among their followers. In one incident, an Al Fatah man had been slain by three other guerrillas in Beirut Dec. 31, 1970. Al Fatah's own military police arrested two of the three suspects and turned them over to Lebanese authorities. The alleged assailants were identified as members of the extreme Action Organization for the Liberation of Palestine (AOLP), an offshoot of Al Fatah. Al Fatah also seized AOLP leader Issam Sartawi, closed AOLP's office in Beirut and seized its arms. Sartawi was later deported to Damascus.

See also MIDDLE EAST [2, 20]; PENTAGON PAPERS [17]

LEUKEMIA—*See* MEDICINE
LIBEL—*See* NEWSPAPERS

LIBERIA—Tubman dies. William V. S. Tubman, 75, elected to a seventh term as Liberian president January 20, died July 23 in a London clinic when hemorrhaging developed after an operation to correct a prostate condition. Vice President William R. Tolbert was sworn in July 23 to succeed Tubman. The Liberian leader had been known for his extension of suffrage to women, his "open door" policy on foreign investment and his efforts to promote equality between Liberia's indigenous tribes and the country's elite of families descended from U.S. slaves.

See also SOUTH AFRICA [2]

LIBYA—Cabinet changes. The Revolutionary Command Council, Libya's military government, announced changes in the Cabinet Aug. 13. Four officers of the council were replaced by civilians in the new government and two new ministries were created. The new ministries were: information, headed by Saleh Busheir, a former foreign minister; and local government, with Mustafa Yaqubi, one of the civilians, as minister. The other civilian ministers were: Mohamed Manqus, housing; Abu Sherif Ben Amer, communications and electric power; and Mohamed Mustafa Maziq, education and national guidance. Abdel Moneim Honi became minister of the interior. No foreign minister was named, reportedly because of Libya's plans for federation with Egypt and Syria, which would result in coordinated foreign policy.

Corruption trial ends. Sixty-four persons, including 23 convicted in absentia, were sentenced Sept. 30 to prison terms ranging from six months to 15 years for election rigging between 1952 and 1969. Those on trial included Abdulhamid Bakkoush and four other ministers of the government of King Idris, which was deposed in the 1969 revolution that brought Col. Muammer el-Qaddafi to power. Bakkoush was sentenced to four years in prison. Thirty persons were acquitted. In a related development, King Idris and 20 other persons were placed on trial in absentia in Tripoli Oct. 23 and charged with corruption.

See also CHAD; HIJACKING [3]; JORDAN [7]; MIDDLE EAST [1, 16]; MOROCCO; OIL; SUDAN; UNITED ARAB REPUBLIC

LIECHTENSTEIN—Male voters in Liechtenstein Feb. 28 defeated 1,897–1,817 a proposal giving Liechtenstein women the right to vote. The proposal had been decisively approved by parliament in December 1970. The major political parties, leaders of the Roman Catholic Church, and nearly all young male voters were believed to have favored women's suffrage. The vote was much closer than a referendum on women's suffrage three years before. Liechtenstein remained the only European nation to deny women the right to vote.

MACAO—*See* CHINA, COMMUNIST
MAFIA—*See* ITALY [10-11]; UNION OF SOVIET SOCIALIST REPUBLICS [15]
MAKARIOS, ARCHBISHOP—*See* CYPRUS

MALAGASY REPUBLIC—Cabinet shift. President Philibert Tsiranana Feb. 18 announced a reshuffle of the Cabinet appointed in September 1970. Andre Resampa, one of four vice presidents, lost the post of interior minister, which was taken over by Tsiranana. Alfred Ramangasoavina, minister of commerce, industry and mines, and Cesaire Rabenoro, minister of state for public health and population, switched cabinet posts. Tsiranana said Feb. 19 that he had made the changes because of unspecified "disagreements among ministers."

30 slain in clashes. An attempted rebellion by leftist government opponents April 1 left 30 dead and six injured in Tulear Province in southern Madagascar. The uprising took the form of an attack on the military post of Soalala by followers of Monja Jaona, leader of the Monima party. The attackers, reportedly armed only with guns, slings and spears, had been promised more substantial ammunition by Jaona, who mistook two Soviet tugs anchored off the coast for Communist Chinese warships. A government communique April 3 said order had been restored in most parts of the province and that the Monima party had been banned. Jaona was arrested April 24. According to a report May 11, 500 persons involved in the events were being placed under government surveillance on the island of Nosy-Lava. A total of 250 were released June 5.

U.S. envoy withdrawn. The State Department said June 25 that Anthony D. Marshall, the U.S. ambassador to Madagascar, had been recalled along with five of his assistants; but it denied that the U.S. had interfered in the island's internal affairs. Marshall's departure appeared to be connected with the arrest June 1 of Second Vice President Resampa on charges of complicity with a foreign power. Marshall returned to Washington June 7. Arrested along with Resampa were Pierre Bora, former director of national security, and Lucien Ndriva, president of the ruling Social Democratic party's National Assembly group. (Resampa had resigned his post as SDP leader and was succeeded June 4 as agriculture minister by Raphael Jakoba, vice president of the National Assembly.)

Britain to remove navy men. The British Foreign Office announced June 24 that consultations were in progress, following a request by the Malagasy government, on fixing a date for the removal of the British naval detachment at Majunga. The group of two reconnaissance aircraft and two frigates had been patrolling the Indian Ocean in an effort to prevent the unloading of Rhodesia-bound oil at the Mozambique port of Beira.

MALAWI—Cabinet shakeup. President Hastings Banda announced a cabinet shakeup April 21. Those named as ministers were: finance, information and tourism—Aleke Banda; trade and industry—John Msonthi; transport, communications and labor—John Gwengwe; education, health and community development—Malani Lungu; local government—Richard Sembereka; ministers of state in the president's office—Albert Muwalo and Alfred Chiwanda; Northern region minister—Qabaniso Chibambo; Southern region minister—Gwanda Chakuamba; Central region minister—Jeremy Kumbweza; and parliamentary secretary in the president's office—Margaret Mlanga. Banda assumed responsibility for agriculture and natural resources.

Banda made life president. Dr. Banda was sworn in as President for Life July 6, the fifth anniversary of the Malawi republic. The oath of office was administered by Chief Justice James Skinner. A constitutional amendment creating the new position had been passed in November 1970.

MALAYSIA—Emergency rule ended. Emergency rule, in effect since the suspension of parliament following the Chinese-Malay riots of May 1969, ended Feb. 19 with the abolishment of the temporary ruling National Operations Council. Parliamentary rule was formally restored Feb. 20 and Sultan Halim Muazzam Shah was crowned as Malaysia's new king for a five-year reign. In another event related to the Malay-Chinese riots, which the government had attributed to inflammatory statements by politicians, the parliament March 3 approved a constitutional amendment making it an act of sedition to publicly discuss any subject "likely to arouse racial feelings and endanger racial peace in the country." The legislation also barred discussion of racial matters in parliament.

Singapore defense pact. Joint defense arrangements for Malaysia and Singapore were agreed to April 16 in London by defense ministers of Malaysia, Singapore, Great Britain, Australia and New Zealand. The treaty took effect Nov. 1 on expiration of an agreement under which Britain was pledged to defend the two countries against any external attacks. A key clause in the communique issued at the end of the talks said "that in the event of any form of armed attack or the threat of such an attack against Malaysia or Singapore," the signatory states "would immediately consult together for the purpose of deciding what measures should be taken jointly or separately in relation to such an attack or threat." The pact provided for a five-nation consultative council that would meet alternately on a regular basis in Malaysia and Singapore, and reduced the British military presence in the area. An infantry battalion, some helicopters and naval and reconnaissance aircraft, six frigates or destroyers and one submarine were to be attached to Australian forces and rotated in and out of the area.

Guerrilla developments. Prime Minister Abdul Razak June 30 reported an outbreak of Communist guerrilla attacks in several key sections of Malaysia. Half of Malaysia's 48,000 troops and armed police were said to be committed to anti-guerrilla operations. Officials acknowledged that more than 1,800 guerrillas were operating in west Malaysia and another 400-500 in Sarawak, on Borneo Island. Sarawak officials said 23 terrorists had been killed in fighting there during the first week of June. More than 1,500 troops and police launched a drive against guerrillas in western Sarawak Aug. 7.

Cabinet changes. Prime Minister Razak revised his Cabinet Dec. 22, adding four new ministries. The new offices included the National Unity Ministry, led by V.T. Sambanthan, an Indian who had headed the former Works, Post and Telecommunications Ministry. Lim Kheng Yaik, a Chinese, was placed in charge of a new ministry to coordinate development of about 400 villages to house Chinese resettled after the 1948-60 Communist insurgency. The Communications Ministry, headed by Inche Sardon bin Jubir, was created from the Transport and Telecommunications departments. The Commerce and

Industry Ministry was divided into a Trade and Industry Ministry and a National Resources Ministry. Ghani Gilong, former transport minister, was appointed works and power minister.

See also FLOODS

MALI—Lt. Moussa Traore, head of state and president of the National Liberation Military Committee, announced April 7 that the committee had deprived two members of their rank and dismissed them from the army after an attempted coup d'etat. Traore said Capts. Yoro Diakite, first vice president, and Malik Diallo, information commissioner, had tried to overthrow the government after "having failed democratically" to convert the committee to "their anti-national, anti-African and reactionary stand." Diakite, made premier after the coup which ousted former President Modibo Keita in 1968, had fallen out of favor with Traore.

MALNUTRITION—*See* HUNGER

MALTA—**Mintoff becomes prime minister.** Dominic Mintoff, 55, was sworn in as prime minister June 17 after his Labor party won a narrow parliamentary election victory over the Nationalist government of George Borg Olivier. Borg Olivier had been in power for nine years. The elections, which began June 13 and whose official results were announced June 17, gave the Labor party 28 parliamentary seats and the Nationalists 27. The Nationalists had held a 28-22 majority in the last Parliament. (A constitutional amendment in August 1970 had raised the number of parliamentary seats from 50 to 55.) The election was the first in which the Roman Catholic Church dropped its ban on voting for the Labor party.

The Cabinet was sworn in June 21. Mintoff took over the posts of foreign affairs and Commonwealth affairs as well as prime minister. Other members included: Anton Buttigieg—minister of justice and parliamentary affairs; Freddie Micalef-Stafrace—trade and agriculture; and Wistin Abela—finance. The resignation of Sir Maurice Dorman as governor-general was announced June 22. This followed the expressed desire of Mintoff to appoint a Maltese citizen as governor-general. Malta's Chief Justice Sir Anthony Mamo assumed Dorman's duties and was named governor-general July 3.

One of the central issues in the election campaign was Malta's ties to Great Britain and members of the North Atlantic Treaty Organization (NATO). In contrast to Borg Olivier's campaign pledge to tighten Malta's ties with Britain and NATO, Mintoff had campaigned for a revision of the 10-year defense and financial pact with Britain signed in 1964. Under the agreement, Britain paid $11.9 million annually to station troops on the island; Mintoff wanted more money for the use of Malta's military facilities by Britain, the U.S. and other NATO countries. Malta was not a member of NATO. Another issue in the campaign was a Labor party promise to try to modify Malta's associate membership agreement with the European Economic Community.

British treaty abrogated. The government June 30 declared that the defense treaty with Britain was "no longer in being" and that new arrangements would have to be made if British troops were to remain on the island. Britain rejected the move July 1. Joseph Godber, minister of state at the Foreign Office, said that "both the defense agreement, and consequently the financial agreement which is dependent on it, have always remained legally in force and still do so." Godber was replying to a Maltese contention that the treaty had been abrogated in 1967 by the government then in power on the island. Britain's defense minister, Lord Carrington, arrived in Malta July 19 for negotiations but said on his return to London (reported July 22) that "on the present basis I do not see that a settlement is possible."

Malta, Britain reach base accord. Malta's acceptance of a compromise offer from Britain and NATO for annual payments of $22.8 million for continued use of the island's military bases was announced in a joint statement issued in London and Valletta Sept. 22. NATO had announced Aug. 13 that it would close its Mediterranean headquarters on the island in accordance with a request by the Malta government.

Britain would pay half of the newly agreed upon costs, nearly double the payments prior to the negotiations. Other NATO members said they would also consider allocation of economic development assistance to Malta. A final accord of the new financial terms would be concluded within six months. Agreement followed a visit by Prime Minister Mintoff to London Sept. 17, where he conferred with British Prime Minister Edward Heath.

Britain announces pullout. The British Foreign Office said Dec. 29 that Great Britain would withdraw its forces from Malta rather than pay the amount demanded by Prime Minister Mintoff for use of military facilities there. The Foreign Office charged that Mintoff had issued an ultimatum Dec. 24 demanding the withdrawal of British troops from the island by midnight Dec. 31 unless Britain immediately paid an additional $11 million for the facilities. Mintoff Dec. 31 extended his withdrawal deadline to Jan. 15, 1972. Negotiations had broken down on the terms of a new defense agreement that would include increased rental payments by Britain for the base. An earlier reported accord in September had required an immediate British payment of approximately $12.35 million, about half the total annual rental. Britain paid the amount Sept. 30. In subsequent talks, Mintoff demanded about $47 million. (Mintoff's government Dec. 29 defeated, by a 28-27 vote, a parliamentary motion of no-confidence over the handling of the dispute with Britain.)

See also EUROPEAN ECONOMIC COMMUNITY [5]; GREAT BRITAIN [10]; SUDAN

MANSON, CHARLES—See CRIME [7-8]
MAO TSE-TUNG—See CHINA, COMMUNIST; COMMUNIST CHINA-U.S. DETENTE [1, 6]
MARIJUANA—See CRIME [3]; DRUG USE & ADDICTION [14-15, 20]; YOUTH
MARINER 9—See SPACE [11]
MARINES, U.S.—See MILITARY [1, 11, 13]; PENTAGON PAPERS [25, 27]; WAR CRIMES [12]
MARS—See SPACE [10-11]

MAURITANIA—Daddah re-elected. President Moktar Ould Daddah was re-elected Aug. 8 for a third five-year term. Daddah announced the formation of a new government Aug. 18 with himself as premier. Hamdi Ould Mouknass was reappointed foreign minister. Sidi Mohamed Diagana, formerly in charge of industrialization and mines, became defense minister. Ahmed Ben Amar was shifted from responsibility for health and labor to interior. Soumare Diara Mouna was named finance minister. (Moktar Ould Haiba, the previous finance minister, had been removed from his position Aug. 16 and arrested Aug. 30 on charges of embezzlement.)

MAURITIUS—State of emergency lifted. The government announced Jan. 6 that the state of emergency imposed prior to independence in 1968 had been lifted Dec. 31, 1970. At the same time, the government announced the Public Order Act had gone into effect Dec. 31. Approved by the Legislative Assembly late in December, the measure provided for preventive detention and a ban on public meetings while parliament was in session. The 1968 emergency rule had been imposed following Moslem-Creole clashes in which 24 persons were killed.

MAYDAY—See DRAFT & WAR PROTEST [5, 12-17]
MCCARTHY, EUGENE J.—See DRAFT & WAR PROTEST [3]; POLITICS [9]
MCCLOSKEY JR., PAUL N.—See POLITICS [4]
MCGOVERN, GEORGE—See DRAFT & WAR PROTEST [7]; FEDERAL BUREAU OF INVESTIGATION [1]; POLITICS [8-9]
MCINTIRE, REV. CARL—See DRAFT & WAR PROTEST [19]
MCNAMARA, ROBERT—See PAKISTAN [39]; PENTAGON PAPERS [2, 20, 26-28]
MEANY, GEORGE—See LABOR [2-3]
MEDICAID—See HEALTH CARE; WELFARE

MEDICARE—*See* AGING; HEALTH CARE; WELFARE

MEDICINE—Hepatitis breakthrough. Dr. Saul Krugman reported March 29 that a team of New York University Medical Center researchers operating under him had apparently succeeded in immunizing a handful of children against serum hepatitis, a highly infectious and sometimes fatal liver disease generally transmitted by blood transfusions from a carrier. Dr. Krugman emphasized that the results were preliminary, that only a few children were innoculated and that more time was needed to evaluate the length of time the protection provided. In the tests, 14 retarded children at the Willowbrook State School were innoculated with a protective serum containing Australia antigen, a virus-like particle associated with serum hepatitis. Serum containing the antigen normally would transmit the disease, but boiling apparently eliminated infectiousness without affecting the stimulation of antibodies that protect against the disease. Krugman's use of retarded children for the experiments had been criticized by some legislators and physicians. Krugman emphasized that the research team had obtained written consent from parents of the children involved and that the experiments had been reviewed with government health officials before they started. Young children were used in the tests because hepatitis tended to be a much milder disease in the young.

Malnutrition linked to brain damage in rats. A study on rats by Prof. Richard J. Wurtman and graduate student William J. Shoemaker at the Massachusetts Institute of Technology published March 12 gave evidence suggesting that severe protein malnutrition before and after the rats were born interfered with the ability of nerve cells in the brain to transmit messages. Specifically, the findings seemed to indicate that under-nourishment affected the brain's ability to produce neurotransmitters, the chemical agents that permitted communications between nerve cells. The findings, while not directly applicable to humans, were believed to constitute the first evidence explaining how malnutrition could affect the brain and learning ability.

Inroads against leukemia. Dr. Ronald Pinkel of St. Jude Children's Research Hospital in Memphis disclosed in a report published April 26 that certain combinations of drug and radiation therapy were making inroads against acute lymphocytic leukemia, a cancer of the blood-forming organs which killed more young American children than any other disease. Pinkel said that the combination therapy administered to 37 children had resulted in seven surviving for six years free of any signs of the disease. Acute lymphocytic leukemia resulted in the overproduction of a form of white blood cells which failed to mature properly and were unable to perform their normal disease-fighting task.

AMA convention ends in rift. The American Medical Association (AMA) ended its annual convention in Atlantic City, N.J. June 24 leaving unsettled a proposal to streamline the 124-year-old organization and give young doctors a greater role in determining the group's policies. The proposal was made by AMA President Dr. Wesley W. Hall of Reno, Nev. Hall called on the group's House of Delegates June 23 to convene a constitutional convention that would act to reorganize the AMA and give a greater voice to young doctors, many of whom complained that the AMA had not kept pace with the times. The proposal evoked considerable opposition from the AMA's 15-member board of trustees. The board took the position that a convention was unnecessary. Dr. Charles Hoffman of Huntington, W.Va., who was elected to succeed Hall as AMA president in 1972, refused to take a position on the constitutional issue.

The AMA June 22 voted to admit the nation's interns and residents to the association on a low-cost membership basis. But at the same time, the leadership provided that the new members, about 54,000, be permitted only one vote in the group's 246-man House of Delegates. Full representation would have given the new doctors 106 votes in the House. In other action, the AMA adopted a declaration June 23 saying that every doctor had the right "to choose whom he will serve and the conditions under which" he would serve them. Some doctors indicated that the declaration served notice that AMA members might withhold their services if they disliked the terms of a national health insurance policy system.

Human cancer virus isolated. A research team in Texas announced July 2 that it had isolated a cancer virus from cells taken from a cancer patient. Specialists saw the development as a significant new lead in the search for human cancer viruses. The research work, sponsored under a contract with the National Cancer Institute, was done at the M.D. Anderson Hospital and Tumor Institute in Houston. The medical team included Drs. Elizabeth S. Priori, Leon Dmochowski, Brooks Myers and J. R. Wilbur. The characteristics of the virus and the circumstances of its discovery by the research team indicated that the spherical C-type virus could be linked to the cause of Burkitt's lymphoma, a lymph gland cancer. The cancer link, however, had not yet been proved by the Texas team. At the present time, no human cancer had been proved to be caused by any virus, but many experts believed proof was only a matter of time. Cells containing the virus were extracted from a child suffering from a form of lymphoma. Four months after extracting the cells, the research team discovered that the cells in the laboratory tissue culture were releasing large numbers of virus particles in various stages of development. At least one virus particle was found in every cell studied.

Fracture healed by electricity. University of Pennsylvania orthopedic surgeons reported Oct. 29 that they had successfully used direct electric current to help knit a bone fracture in a woman's ankle. Their feat represented the first time electricity had been used successfully to help heal a human fracture. The surgeons said fracture healing through electricity could lead to faster healing and a reduction in muscle stiffness because of the shorter time the bone would need to be immobilized in a cast.

FDA warns on hormone drug. The Food and Drug Administration (FDA) proposed changes Nov. 9 in labeling guidelines that would advise physicians not to prescribe the synthetic hormone diethylstilbesterol (DES) for pregnant women. The drug, a synthetic estrogen hormone, had been linked to a number of cases in which young women whose mothers had taken the drug during pregnancy had been afflicted with vaginal cancer. An FDA spokesman said the agency was planning to study the effects of the DES-hormone on the daughters of women who took it during pregnancy. The reports tying the vaginal cancer in at least 60 cases to the synthetic hormone had led to the FDA's decision to change labeling requirements.

Conferees approve cancer fund. House and Senate conferees agreed Dec. 7 on legislation that authorized a $1.6 billion fund to expand efforts to conquer cancer. The legislation had been bottled up in Congress after the House and Senate passed different versions of the bill Nov. 15 and July 7, respectively. At the center of the controversy was whether a new agency would be set up to administer the expanded program or whether it should be controlled by the existing federal health apparatus. The legislation reported out by the conferees left the stewardship of the program within the National Institutes of Health, as had the House version of the bill. The main thrust of the compromise bill was directed at cancer research rather than patient care. It did, however, re-establish some public health programs for cancer detection and other control measures. As part of clinical research studies, 15 centers were to be set up to treat cancer patients. Under the legislation, President Nixon was to appoint a director of the National Cancer Institute, the existing government agency charged with overseeing the cancer research program. The agency's budget was to be prepared by the director and sent directly to the Office of Management and Budget.

See also CONSUMER AFFAIRS [3]; ECONOMY, U.S. [24]; HEALTH CARE; NIXON, RICHARD MILHOUS [1]; NOBEL PRIZES; UNION OF SOVIET SOCIALIST REPUBLICS [3]

MEDINA, ERNEST L.—*See* WAR CRIMES [6]
MERCURY CONTAMINATION—*See* POLLUTION [9-11, 20]
MERGERS—*See* BUSINESS [6-7]
METHAMPHETAMINES—*See* DRUG USE & ADDICTION [23]
METROPOLIA—*See* CHURCHES [6]
MEXICAN-AMERICANS—*See* EDUCATION [16]; HUNGER; INDIANS,
AMERICAN; RACIAL & MINORITY UNREST [3, 5, 13]

MEXICO—5 Soviet diplomats expelled. The Mexican government March 18
declared five members of the Soviet embassy in Mexico (Charge d'Affairs
Dimitri Daikonov, First Secretary Boris Kolmiakov, Second Secretary Boris
Voskovoinikov, Second Secretary Oleg Netchiporenko and Alexandre
Bochakov) persona non grata and ordered them to leave the country "as soon
as possible." All but Daikonov left the country March 21; Diakonov left March
22 after briefing the Soviet ambassador to Mexico, Igor Kolosovsky, who had
returned from leave in the Soviet Union March 20. The government gave no
reason for the expulsion, but press reports connected it with arrests announced
March 15 of 19 Mexican members of the Revolutionary Action Movement
(MAR) whose leaders, the government charged, had studied in the Soviet Union
in 1963 and traveled to North Korea in 1968 and 1969 to study terrorism and
guerrilla warfare. Following the arrests, the Mexican ambassador to the Soviet
Union, Carlos Zapata Vela, was recalled from Moscow March 17 for
consultations and what was called "a temporary diplomatic withdrawal."
   11 students die in clashes. Eleven students were killed and 160 wounded
June 10 in clashes between demonstrating students (protesting conditions at
Nuevo Leon University in Monterrey and the continued detention of some
students arrested in student demonstrations preceding the Olympic games in
October 1968) and armed right-wing extremists in Mexico City. The clashes
began when a group of 8,000 leftist students began an anti-government march
from the Polytechnic Institute in the north of the city to the downtown area.
They were soon confronted by a group of 500 right-wing youths who attacked
while police stood by. (Students said the attackers were members of the
"Hawks," who were recruited by police. The government originally contended
that they were members of the anti-government group MURO, attempting to
embarrass Mexican President Luis Echeverria Alvarez, whom they considered
too liberal.) Government sources indicated June 13 that there was evidence of
collaboration between the police force, which was given orders not to intervene,
and the Hawks, who were permitted to pass through a police cordon to attack
the students. A government opposition group, the Independent Trade Union
Front, charged that police dressed as civilians fired into the crowd. There was
speculation that the attack was a plot by conservative elements of the ruling
Institutional Revolutionary party (PRI) to weaken the position of Echeverria.
It was reported that they had the support of Mexico City Mayor Alfonso
Martinez Dominguez, who was responsible for the maintenance of order in the
capital. (Martinez Dominguez and Police Chief Rogelio Flores Curiel resigned
June 15, "in order to facilitate the official investigations" into the attack
authorized by Echeverria June 11. Octavio Senties, president of the Chamber of
Deputies and leader of the PRI's peasant wing, was appointed mayor June 17.
Most leading officials of the city turned in their resignations to Senties.)
   After 42 days of investigation into the attack, Attorney General Julio
Sanchez Vargas said July 23 that those responsible for the killings could not be
identified, although the Hawks attacked the students. Sanchez also announced
that there was no proof that the Hawks were associated with the Mexico City
government. Sanchez said city buses were used to transport members of the
Hawks to the student demonstrations. He said his office had found evidence
that police on the scene had stood by passively while the students were being
killed because they were under instructions not to stop the student
demonstrations and had therefore not intervened. Sanchez resigned Aug. 19

after admitting that the investigation had failed. He was immediately replaced by Pedro Oleja Pallada, a senior official in the office of President Echeverria.

Copper industry nationalized. The government announced Aug. 27 that Mexico's small copper industry would be nationalized. It was seen as an effort to complete the so-called "Mexicanization" of the nation's mining industry. The Anaconda Co. said the same day that it would sell 51% of the stock in its Mexican mining operation to the Mexican government and private investors in the country. Mexican National Properties Minister Horacio Flores de la Pena said the government would pay Anaconda $40 million over a four-year period. Anaconda would retain 49% ownership and said it planned to continue a mine expansion program.

New leftist movement formed. A group of prominent leftist intellectuals and labor leaders Sept. 23 announced the formation of a new political organization to challenge the one-party system of the PRI, which had ruled Mexico since 1929. Among the group's members were writers Octavio Paz and Carlos Fuentes, mining leader Manuel Santos and student leaders Herberto Castillo and Luis Cabeza de Vaca, who had both completed prison terms stemming from their roles in the 1968 student movement. Fuentes said the group would not adopt a formal name or announce a formal platform because its purpose was not to impose another structure from above, but to form an organization from below that reflected the political reality of Mexico. In addition to providing an alternative to the PRI, the group's principal aims included nationalization of banks and basic industries, strict control of foreign investments, an end to Mexican dependence on the U.S. through the opening of new export markets, union democracy, total agrarian reform and an equitable educational system.

Church issues critical report. It was reported Sept. 26 that Mexico's traditionally conservative Roman Catholic Church had published a highly controversial report (entitled "Justice in Mexico") criticizing its own lack of action in opposing the oppression of the masses and in attacking social injustice in Mexico. The document was presented to the World Synod of Bishops in Rome Sept. 30. Among the principal points made by the report were: the "marked affinity of the church towards economic power groups," which prevented it "from fulfilling its prophetic vocation"; a peasant class which suffered from "political and economic domination"; the social, economic and religious discrimination suffered by the Indians; and the U.S. hegemony over Mexico which converted the latter into a "complement of its own system as a peripheral and dominated country." It was reported Nov. 15 that Mexico's trade union leaders and conservative Catholics and politicians had launched an attack on the authors of the report, accusing them of violating the Mexican constitution, which prohibited the church from being involved in political matters.

Kidnapings. Julio Hirschfeld Almada, industrialist and director of the nation's airport system, was kidnaped Sept. 27 by three armed men and a woman. Police Sept. 28 imposed special security precautions for Mexican officials and foreign diplomats as a result of the kidnaping. All senior government officials and diplomats were put under special police protection. Hirschfeld was released unharmed Sept. 29 after the payment of $240,000. The kidnapers were originally identified as members of the MAR; but, according to report Nov. 29, the abduction appeared to have been carried out by a right-wing group—the Zapatist Urban Front (FUZ)—in order to provoke government repression of the left. A group of leftist rural guerrillas under command of Genaro Vazquez Rojas was believed responsible for the Nov. 19 kidnaping of Dr. Jaime Castrejon Diaz, rector of the State University of Guerrero and millionaire owner of the Coca-Cola bottling concession in Guerrero. Castrejon Diaz was released Dec. 1, two days after his family paid a $200,000 ransom and the government released nine political prisoners. (The prisoners were flown to Cuba.) The kidnapers had also demanded that a second group of 15 political prisoners, held incommunicado, be brought to trial. However, the government made no public response to the demand.

U.S.-Mexico border treaty. The U.S. Senate ratified Nov. 29 a treaty with Mexico to settle border differences stemming from the shifting courses of the Rio Grande and the Colorado rivers. The treaty settled three border disputes involving small tracts of land, and established a formula for avoiding future disputes.

See also AVIATION [8]; CUBA; HIJACKING [2]

MICRONESIA—Problems considered. President Nixon appointed a personal representative March 13 to negotiate with Micronesians over the future status of the Pacific territory that the U.S. had administered under United Nations trusteeship since the Japanese held the 2,141 islands and atolls 25 years ago. Nixon said Franklin Haydn Williams, 51, president of the Asia Foundation and former deputy assistant defense secretary, would hold the rank of ambassador. Williams was to be responsible for resolving conflicts within the Administration and for persuading Micronesians to accept plans that would be developed for their future political status. The Departments of Interior, Defense and State were all concerned with the trust territory. The Micronesians had rejected a U.S. offer of commonwealth status, and the U.S. had found unacceptable Micronesian proposals for a self-governing "free association" with the federal government or independence.

U.S. plans. A hitherto unpublished portion of a 1963 report which purportedly told of plans to make Micronesia a permanent American possession was being circulated by Micronesian nationalists, it was reported May 8. As administrator of the U.N. trusteeship, the U.S. was required by agreement to guide the Pacific islands toward eventual "independence or self-government." The document was based on a report to the late President John F. Kennedy by a nine-man mission to the islands headed by Anthony M. Solomon. Portions of it were published, while other sections were kept secret. The part reportedly suppressed had stated that Kennedy, in a memorandum dated April 8, 1962, "set forth as U.S. policy the movement of Micronesia into a permanent relationship with the U.S. within our political framework" for security reasons. The document continued: "In keeping with that goal, the memorandum called for accelerated development of the area to bring its political, economic and social standards into line with an eventual permanent association."

MIDDLE EAST—Most of the action in the Middle East during 1971 consisted of attempts to find a peaceful solution to the crisis in the area. There was little fighting—most occurring in the areas occupied by Israel since the 1967 war with the Arabs [5-6]—but fighting did flare up at the Suez Canal in September [3]. The truce along the Suez Canal was extended for 30 days Feb. 5. Egypt refused to again extend the cease-fire March 7, but troops along the canal still held their fire [32]. Most peace talks during the year centered around plans to attempt a reopening of the Suez Canal, but Israel refused to withdraw her forces from the east bank of the waterway to allow for the reopening unless there were assurances that Egyptian or Soviet forces would not move into areas from which the Israelis had withdrawn [33-36]. Indirect talks between Egypt and Israel, under the mediation of Gunnar Jarring and the sponsorship of the United Nations, resumed in January after a lapse of over four months. They were suspended in March, but resumed in December following a resolution passed by the U.N. General Assembly Dec. 13 calling for Israeli withdrawal from occupied territories and for the resumption of the talks [30, 39]. In another development, Egypt, Syria and Libya Sept. 1 joined in the Federation of Arab Republics [16].

Fighting

[2] Israelis raid Lebanon. In response to attacks from Lebanon by Palestinian guerrillas against Israeli settlements, Israeli forces crossed into Lebanon for attacks on commando bases Jan. 14, Jan. 31, June 28, June 29, Aug. 9 and Sept. 2. In the Jan. 14 attack, an Israeli helicopter-borne force penetrated 28 miles into Lebanon to attack a commando base at the coastal village of Sarafand. Lebanese reports said that government forces had joined guerrillas in repelling the invading force, killing or wounding 15-20. Israeli reports said that two houses and other guerrilla facilities were blown up in Sarafand and 10 guerrillas killed, while the invading force suffered only six men slightly wounded. In the Jan. 31 raids, according to Israeli reports, a building serving as a recruiting office and a base for operations against Israel were destroyed at El Kyam, four miles north of the Israeli border town of Metulla, and two other buildings were razed at Kfar Kila, one mile west of Metulla. In the June 28 raid, about 200 Israeli troops participated in an attack on a guerrilla base at Blida and allegedly blew up three houses used for attacks on Israel. In the June 29 attack, Lebanon reported that government troops fought with Israelis about one mile inside Lebanon as the Israelis attacked the villages of Taybeh and Al Adassiyae. In the Aug. 9 attack, Israeli troops pushed four miles inside Lebanon for a six-hour attack on two guerrilla bases near the villages of Hebbariye and Rashaya. In the Sept. 2 attacks, Israel said its troops had wounded six commandos but had made no contact with Lebanese soldiers or occupied Lebanese villages. Lebanon, however, reported that the Israelis had penetrated three miles inside Lebanon and attacked army positions at Kfar Hamman and adjacent areas with heavy artillery for five hours.

[3] Suez Canal flare-up. Israeli and Egyptian forces Sept. 18 exchanged heavy fire across the Suez Canal for the first time since the cease-fire went into effect in August 1970. Troops of both sides exchanged air and ground missile fire across the canal in the clashes. Israel said that Egypt had fired surface-to-air missiles at Israeli Phantom planes flying over the Sinai Peninsula, west of the truce line. Egypt said that the Phantoms had fired air-to-ground missiles at Egyptian positions on the west bank of the canal. The outburst followed the downing of an Egyptian and an Israeli plane in the area Sept. 11 and 17. The Egyptian plane downed by the Israelis Sept. 11—the first plane downed since July 30, 1970—was one of two Soviet-made Sukhoi-7 fighter bombers that had flown over the eastern bank of the canal 20 miles south of Port Said, on the Mediterranean. The plane was fired at by an Israeli machinegunner and crashed in Egyptian territory. The Israeli aircraft shot down Sept. 17 was a U.S.-made Stratocruiser transport cargo plane, flying without escort over the Sinai Peninsula 14 miles east of the canal on a routine mission, according to the Israelis. Israel filed complaints of a violation of the cease-fire in both incidents. Egyptian forces were reported Sept. 20 to have been placed on "maximum alert" to cope with a possible Israeli strike.

[4] Syria charges Israeli air breach. The Syrian army reported Oct. 14 that Israeli planes had penetrated into Syria about 35 miles southwest of Damascus, but were driven off by Syrian interceptors. Israel denied any contact between Israeli and Syrian aircraft, but declined to say whether the Israeli planes had crossed the cease-fire line. (The Syrian government charged Dec. 18 that a large number of Israeli units were being massed along the truce line in the Golan Heights in preparation for an attack on Syria before the year's end. According to the charges, Israel's aim was to capture more Arab territory to gain a better bargaining position in a final peace settlement. It was reported Dec. 19 that Syria was reinforcing its defenses around Damascus, 40 miles from the Golan Heights, through a network of underground trenches, tunnels and blockhouses.)

[5]   **Occupied area fighting.** Arab guerrillas carried out attacks against Israelis and Arab civilians in the Gaza Strip Jan. 2, 4 and 9. In the Jan. 2 incident, a civilian car in the town of Gaza was attacked and two Israeli children were killed. The action prompted Israeli military authorities Jan. 3 to dismiss Gaza Mayor Reghen el-Alami (appointed governor of the Gaza Strip by the Egyptians, but retained by the Israelis when they seized the territory in 1967) and to clamp a curfew on parts of the strip, particularly in refugee camps said to harbor guerrillas. (El-Alami was replaced Sept. 23 by Rashad Shawa, an Arab.) In Jan. 4 action, Israeli military patrols came under three guerrilla assaults in the strip and killed one guerrilla. An Israeli army patrol Jan. 9 killed three guerrillas in fighting off an attack by a unit of the Popular Front for the Liberation of Palestine (PFLP). Later in the day, the guerrillas hurled grenades at Arab civilians, injuring 12, in an attempt to intimidate Arab civilians into joining a general strike in the town of Gaza in tribute to the three dead guerrillas. The guerrillas succeeded in closing down the town's shops, schools and public transport Jan. 9-10.

[6]   Israeli forces launched a major drive against the Palestinian commandos in the strip at the beginning of July and reportedly killed 25 guerrillas through Aug. 10. In an operation aimed at facilitating the policing of suspected guerrilla hideouts, Israeli bulldozers July 30 began cutting security lanes in the Jabaliya refugee camp in Gaza. About 400 huts were demolished and 1,200 refugees were transferred to new quarters, most of them to El Arish, in the northern Sinai south of the strip. The bulldozer operations were resumed at the Jabaliya camp Aug. 2 and a similar undertaking was started at the Shatti camp. Leaflets by two commando groups, urging a general strike in protest of the Israeli action, resulted in a standstill of all commercial activity in Gaza and in the camps. Israeli troops and police Aug. 14 used force to reopen stores shut by the strike, but several of the reopened shops were targets of guerrilla grenade attacks Aug. 16. Egypt Aug. 15 urged United Nations Secretary General U Thant to use his influence with Israel to stop the bulldozing and transfer operations. Thant protested the operations in an aide-memoire sent to Israel Aug. 18. Israel announced Aug. 30 that the operations had been suspended, that commando operations in the strip had been wiped out and that violence in the area had virtually ceased. The transfers had resulted in the evacuation of 13,366 persons from the camps—about 2,000 to El Arish and about 300 others to the west bank.

[7]   **Terrorist actions.** The PFLP claimed credit for the June 12 shelling of the Israeli-chartered Coral Sea, bound for the Israeli port of Elath. Three bazooka shells hit the tanker, ripping holes in its sides and causing a number of fires which were quickly extinguished. The Coral Sea, flying the Liberian flag and carrying 70,000 tons of crude oil from Iran for transshipment to Europe, had entered the 18-mile-long Strait of Bab el Mandeb at the southern arm of the Red Sea when one of several boats in the area, with three armed men aboard, approached the tanker and started firing. No injuries were reported and the Coral Sea made her way to Elath without further incident. In a statement June 13, the PFLP said the shelling was aimed at the "alliance between the Israeli enemy and the Iranian reactionaries." The PFLP reported June 15 that four of its members landed on the Yemeni coast north of the port of Hodeida following the attack and were arrested by Yemeni authorities. The statement said the guerrillas were forced ashore after "their boat was intercepted by an unidentified naval patrol believed to be Ethiopian."

[8]   Arab guerrilla rockets July 7 struck the Israeli city of Petah Tiqva, seven miles northeast of Tel Aviv, killing four persons and wounding 30. Al Fatah, a commando group, claimed credit for the shelling. Targets of the attack were a hospital and a schoolyard. Six Arab guerrillas linked by the Israelis to the shelling were killed in an encounter with an Israeli patrol July 14. A seventh was reported to have escaped into Jordan.

[9] An Israeli military court Aug. 5 convicted and sentenced three women members of the PFLP (Nadia Bashir Bardali and her sister Marline—both Moroccans—and Evelyn Barge—a French citizen) on charges of planning to blow up hotels in Haifa and Tel Aviv during the Easter-Passover season. Each was sentenced to a prison term of at least 10 years. The three had confessed to the charges at the start of their trial July 27. They had been arrested on arriving at Lod airport April 12-13 after they were found to be carrying incendiary material.

[10] An Arab terrorist Sept. 19 hurled a hand grenade at a group of American Christian pilgrims in the Old City of Jerusalem. A four-year-old Arab girl playing nearby was killed. Five of the tourists were injured. A guerrilla broadcast in Beirut claimed credit for the attack.

Occupied Area Developments

[11] **Jerusalem housing plan.** Israel announced Feb. 15 that it would proceed with its long-delayed plans to build four huge housing projects on the hillsides surrounding Jerusalem, an area that had been seized from Jordan in the 1967 war. Jerusalem's Municipal Council approved the project Feb. 21, drawing the opposition of the U.S., Egypt and Jordan. About 35,000 units accommodating 122,000 residents would be built in the four areas: 1,700 units in Neve Yaakov to the north; up to 18,000 units in Ramot near Nebe Samuel to the west; 3,000 units in Tapiot East to the east; and 12,000 units in Sharafat in the south. During the first stage of building, 23,020 units were to be built, with the remainder being added in stages during a five-year period. More than 30 old stone houses were demolished in Nebe Samuel to make way for new buildings to house Jewish immigrants, according to report March 31. The housing plan was criticized June 9 by the U.S. State Department as being in violation of the 1949 Geneva convention which barred an occupying power from transferring part of its population into an occupied territory. The U.N. Security Council, meeting at the request of Jordan, Sept. 26 adopted a Jordanian resolution calling on Israel to halt further measures to change the character of East Jerusalem and to rescind all actions it had taken to that effect. The vote was 14-0, with Syria abstaining on the ground that the resolution was not strong enough. The council instructed Secretary General Thant to take any action in carrying out its orders, including dispatch of observers to Jerusalem. Thant was to report back to the council in 60 days. Israel said it would not abide by the council's decision. Thant, according to report Oct. 27, selected the U.N. representatives of Argentina, Italy and Sierra Leone to serve on a U.N. commission to investigate Israel's housing and population policies in East Jerusalem, but informed the Security Council Nov. 22 that Israel had barred the commission from visiting Jerusalem.

[12] **Jerusalem compensation plan.** The Israeli government June 29 introduced legislation that would compensate Arabs in East Jerusalem for property they had owned before the creation of Israel in 1948. Justice Minister Yakov Shimshon Shapiro, who submitted the plan, said most of the properties were in West Jerusalem and in the old city of Jaffa, now the Arab quarter of Tel Aviv. Payment was to begin in 1975 and extend over a period of about 20 years in government bonds. Shapiro said about 10,000 Arabs were eligible and would receive a total of $100 million. The abandoned properties would be paid for at their value as assessed in 1947, plus 25% interest. Shapiro recalled that about 80% of the Arabs living elsewhere in Israel had submitted claims, and accepted cash payments, for their properties captured by the Israelis since the 1947 war. Jordan rejected the Israeli compensation plan June 30, charging that the proposal was a plot to change the citizenship of Jerusalem Arabs from Jordanian to Israeli in order "to complete the annexation of the Holy City."

[13]   **Dayan plan.** Israeli Defense Minister Moshe Dayan suggested Aug. 19 that Israel immediately establish permanent rule of the Arab territories it had been occupying since the 1967 war instead of waiting for a peace settlement. The following day, the U.S. sharply criticized the proposal and Israeli officials, including Premier Golda Meir, dissociated themselves from it. Dayan clarified the plan Aug. 21, explaining that he did not mean that Israel should annex the Arab territories, but that it should conduct itself in the same manner as a permanent government—making and carrying out long-range plans.

[14]   **West bank elections set.** The Israeli military command on the west bank of the Jordan River Nov. 25 ordered that municipal elections be held in the towns of Jericho, Jenin, Qalqiliya and Tulkarm before April 30, 1972. The balloting, the first since 1967, would determine whether the Arabs on the west bank were ready to take part in the normalization of political life under military occupation. The voting in the four towns also would decide on the feasibility of elections in the main cities.

Arab World Developments

[15]   **U.A.R., Syria in joint command.** Syria and Egypt formed a joint military command, it was announced March 16 by Syrian President Hafez al-Assad. Diplomatic sources said the merger paved the way for establishment of Egyptian air bases in Syria, within easy striking distance of Israeli cities. Assad said Syria backed Cairo's efforts to reach a peace agreement with Israel, asserting that "diplomatic efforts are an important element in the battle for the liberation of occupied Arab lands and as such must not be ignored."

[16]   **Arab federation accord.** An agreement to form a federation of Egypt, Syria and Libya was announced April 17. The federation was to be called the Federation of Arab Republics. Egyptian President Anwar Sadat said that the federation "constitutes the decisive answer to the challenges of imperialism and Zionism. It is the way to restore our dignity, liberate our territory and eliminate all forms of imperialism, exploitation and backwardness in the Arab world." Explaining the structure of the future federation, Sadat disclosed: the union would be headed by a council comprised of the presidents of the three member-countries (Sadat, Syrian President Assad and Libyan leader Muammar el-Qaddafi); the federal president would be chosen by a majority of the three presidents; there would be a national assembly for federal legislation; the new country's ideology would be "democratic socialism"; membership would be open to any "liberated" Arab country; the federal government would have the authority to order military intervention in any of the three republics in case of "disorders from within or without." (Sudan had been envisioned as a member of the federation, but strong Communist resistance in the country was said to have discouraged it from joining.) The leaders of the three countries signed a constitution Aug. 20 for the proposed federation, and voters in the three countries overwhelmingly endorsed the charter Sept. 1. With the formal establishment of the federation, Egypt dropped the name United Arab Republic, adopted after an abortive 1958 merger with Syria, and assumed the name of Arab Republic of Egypt. In a meeting of the federation's presidential council, President Sadat was selected Oct. 4 as first president of the federation and Cairo was designated Oct. 5 as the federation's capital. Sadat Dec. 24 announced the formation of a Cabinet to supervise integration of the federation. The Cabinet was headed by Ahmed al-Khatib, speaker of the Syrian People's Assembly. The other members: foreign affairs—Mohammed Fatallah Khatib of Egypt; planning, economic and social affairs—Saml Srzelma of Syria; public services—Mohammed el-Khowaga of Libya; transport and communications—Ali el-Sayed Mohammed of Egypt; scientific research—Salah Hedayet of Egypt; information—Abdel Kader Ghoka of Syria; and culture and education—Mohammed Mustafa el-Mazak of Libya.

[17]   **Egyptian-Syrian unity agreement.** A separate Syrian-Egyptian unity agreement was announced in Damascus Oct. 14. The agreement provided for the establishment of a committee that would consider the possible integration of the Arab Socialist Union, Egypt's only political party, with the Baath party of Syria. It was disclosed in Cairo Oct. 17 that Presidents Sadat and Assad had also agreed that Egypt would lead Syrian troops facing Israel to coordinate operations with Egyptian soldiers confronting Israeli forces on the Suez Canal line. Gen. Mohammed Sadek, Egyptian minister of war, was given command of the Syrian troops.

[18]   **Sadat takes command of forces.** President Sadat Nov. 1 took personal leadership of the Egyptian armed forces. His action was followed by a meeting Nov. 3 of the National Defense Council, the first since Feb. 2. Sadat presided over the session, which discussed a new plan for political and military action. The council was Egypt's top strategic and defense planning body. Its members included Sadat, the vice president and ministers of war, foreign affairs, interior and presidential affairs, the first secretary of the Arab Socialist Union, the chief of intelligence and the military chief of staff.

[19]   **Arabs map war strategy.** The Arab League's Joint Defense Council met Nov. 27-30 in Cairo to consider united strategy against Israel. The conference, interrupted Nov. 28 by the assassination of Jordanian Premier Wasfi Tell (see JORDAN [11]), ended with the adoption of "secret resolutions." The conference was preceded by a preparatory meeting of the chiefs of staff of 13 Arab nations in Cairo Nov. 24-25. An accord announced Nov. 25 provided for a plan of military and financial cooperation for the struggle against Israel. Representatives of the Arab League met again Dec. 27-28 in Cairo to plan military and economic strategy. A brief statement issued Dec. 28 said appropriate action had been taken but gave no further details.

Arms Developments

[20]   **Arab, Soviet arms buildup.** One week after a conference between President Sadat and Soviet officials in Moscow March 1-2, Egypt began a buildup of aerial defenses along the full length of the Nile Valley, with a particularly heavy concentration in the upper regions around the Aswan High Dam. The Soviet Union began a sharp increase in its air and sea shipment of arms to Egypt sometime in March. The shipments focused on Egypt's air defense, including antiaircraft missiles, electronic and radar devices, guns and crates of unidentified equipment. The increase in arms shipments lasted through the year. Increased shipments to Syria began around the beginning of April. Lebanon Nov. 3 announced that it was to purchase its first shipment of arms from the Soviet Union. Shipments to Egypt included, according to report April 10, a small number of the U.S.S.R.'s latest jet fighter planes—either the MiG-23 or the "Flogger," both believed capable of outperforming any other fighter in the world. The Soviets also sent to Egypt large numbers of MiG-21, Sukhoi-7 and Sukhoi-11 jet fighters and TU-16 reconnaissance planes. (See also [23].)

[21]   **U.S. sends tanks to Jordan.** The U.S. sent Jordan heavy M-60 tanks during August, according to reports from State Department sources Sept. 1. The shipments were confirmed Sept. 2 by an Israeli newspaper which said that a large consignment of the tanks and ammunition had arrived in recent days at the Jordanian port of Aqaba (opposite Elath) in U.S. cargo ships.

[22]   **Israel asks for more U.S. arms.** In response to the Soviet buildup in Arab countries, Israel throughout the year asked for the U.S. to supply it with more war planes and advanced armaments to preserve the balance of power in the Middle East. The Nixon Administration disclosed April 19 that the U.S. had decided in the fall of 1970 to sell Israel 12 more Phantom F-4 fighter-bombers. Israeli Premier Mrs. Meir and Foreign Minister Abba Eban were reported to have informed the U.S. Nov. 1 that Israel would not accept an American proposal for indirect talks with Egypt on reopening the Suez Canal

unless the U.S. resumed shipment of Phantom jets to Israel (*see* [36]). (Acting on a resolution submitted by Republican Sen. Hugh Scott of Pennsylvania, 78 U.S. senators Oct. 15 had asked the Nixon Administration to resume the shipment of Phantoms to Israel.) The U.S. was reported Nov. 15 to have decided, although it had not given Israel a formal reply to its request for more Phantoms, that it would not resume sale of the fighter-bombers to Israel on the ground that the balance of power in the Middle East had not shifted in favor of the Arab states. Mrs. Meir met with President Nixon in Washington Dec. 2 to confer on the Israeli request for more Phantoms and on the conflicting approaches of their two nations on peace initiatives. A statement issued by the White House after the talks did not mention the Phantoms, but confirmed continuing U.S. assistance in Israel's military development. However, it was reported Dec. 30 that the two leaders had agreed in principle during their meeting that the sale of Phantoms would resume, with timing and details to be worked out in January 1972. It was also reported Dec. 6 that the U.S. had decided to resume the sale of A-4 Skyhawk attack-bombers to Israel, with shipment in late 1972.

Relations with Foreign Governments

[23]   **U.A.R.-Soviet pact signed.** Egypt and the Soviet Union May 27 signed a 15-year treaty of friendship and cooperation. The accord was initialed in Cairo by Presidents Sadat and Nikolai Podgorny following talks begun the previous day. The two also announced their agreement on continued Soviet assistance to Egypt and other Arab countries for the recovery of "all Arab territories occupied by Israel." The treaty barred the two countries from interference in each other's internal affairs and pledged each to respect the "sovereignty and integrity" of the other. It pledged continuing military cooperation, providing specifically for assistance in the training of Egyptian military personnel, in mastering the armaments and equipment supplied Egypt with a view to strengthening Egyptian capacity "to eliminate the consequences of aggression as well as increasing its ability to stand up to aggression in general." The two parties were to "contact each other without delay" to coordinate their positions in case of an international crisis. Under terms of the treaty, each party pledged that it would not "enter into any pacts or take part in any groupings or participate in operations or measures against the other party." The accord went into effect with its ratification in Moscow during a visit by Egyptian Foreign Minister Mahmoud Riad June 30-July 4.

[24]   **Soviet-Israeli contacts hinted.** Israel and the Soviet Union were reported June 23 to be studying possible resumption of diplomatic relations severed by Moscow in the 1967 war. Soviet officials June 25 denied that any contacts were taking place between the two countries, as did Foreign Minister Eban June 22. (Eban also said his government was ready to open a dialogue with the Soviet Union on the Middle East.) However, a report from Jerusalem June 28 disclosed that Soviet journalist Victor Louis, with the sanction of Soviet authorities, had visited Israel June 13-18 on a diplomatic mission. (Louis, believed to be connected with Soviet intelligence, said June 28 that his visit was for medical attention and personal reasons. The Israeli Foreign Ministry confirmed the same day that Louis had met with Simcha Dinitz, Mrs. Meir's political adviser, and with other persons described as "acquaintances who had served in the Israeli embassy in Moscow." Official sources said no progress had been made toward re-establishing diplomatic ties.)

[25]   **French-Israeli talks.** Israeli and French officials Nov. 12 opened talks in Paris on improving relations between the two countries, strained in the wake of the 1967 war. (French Foreign Minister Maurice Schumann had said July 31 that relations between the two countries should become "friendlier.") The discussions centered largely on the dispute resulting from France's 1967 embargo on the shipment of 50 Mirage V jets to Israel despite Israeli payment for the planes, and Jerusalem's subsequent refusal to accept reimbursement or

give up claims to the aircraft. Israel was said to have reversed its position on reimbursement but to have demanded that it be paid at current rates of $1.5 million a plane rather than the original price of $1 million each. Other Israeli proposals included: French assurances that the shipment of spare parts to Israel (currently taking place with only tacit government approval) would continue on a regular basis with official approval by the Paris government; a halt to what Israel regarded as France's anti-Israeli initiatives on the international diplomatic scene; and more French-Israeli consultations.

[26]   **U.S.S.R. offers aid to Al Fatah.** According to U.S. State and Defense Department analysts Dec. 29, the Soviet Union had offered to train Al Fatah guerrillas in the Soviet Union and to provide hospitalization for any of their members wounded in action against Israel. The Soviet offer, said to have been made to Fatah leader Yasir Arafat during his visit to Moscow in October, held as a major stipulation that the Palestinian commandos stop their feuding with each other and confine their activities to resumption of attacks on Israel. The American analysts were reported to have concluded that three factors prompted the Soviet Union to shift from its previous strategy of not getting involved with the commandos: concern that China was about to provide the commandos with military and political assistance; a desire to get the commandos to halt their campaign of assassinating Arab leaders (*see* [19]); and a wish to impose greater pressure on Israel without precipitating a major military confrontation between Israel and Egypt along the Suez Canal.

Peace Moves

[27]   **Jarring talks resume.** Israel Jan. 5 resumed indirect peace talks with Egypt and Jordan under the mediation of Dr. Gunnar V. Jarring, U.N. Secretary General Thant's special representative for the Middle East and Swedish ambassador to the Soviet Union. The U.N.-sponsored negotiations, aimed at settling the Middle East conflict, had been in suspension since Israel withdrew from the start of the discussions Aug. 25, 1970 after accusing Egypt of violating the Suez Canal cease-fire agreement, which had gone into effect Aug. 7. The resumption of negotiations coincided with the publication by Thant of a report by Jarring on his peace efforts since his appointment as mediator November 1967. According to the report, both sides had made slow but noticeable progress in reducing their differences on a number of basic issues. Israel had reversed its 1967 demand that a peace settlement could be reached only "through direct negotiations between the parties culminating in a peace treaty and there could be no question of withdrawal of [Israeli] forces prior to such a settlement." Jordan and Egypt in turn had dropped their 1967 demand that there could be no peace talks with Israel until Israel withdrew its forces from the Arab areas occupied during the 1967 war. However, Israel and the two Arab states remained at odds over their intrepretation of the Security Council's Nov. 22, 1967 resolution calling for peace, including Israeli withdrawal from the occupied Arab lands and the recognition of "safe and recognized boundaries" and the mutual recognition of sovereignty. Israel regarded the resolution as a framework for negotiations, while Egypt and Jordan held it to be a plan for a peace settlement that had to be "implemented" as such, with only the means of implementation to be discussed. The parties also were in disagreement on the resolution's withdrawal provisions. The two Arab states insisted they applied to all Arab territories occupied by Israel during the war, while Israel continued to emphasize the provisions dealing with secure and recognized boundaries.

[28]   *Israeli peace plan.* Jarring visited Jerusalem Jan. 8-9 at the request of the Israeli government. (The request reflected Israeli desires to raise the current U.N. level of the talks to a higher and more authoritative level. The Israelis were said to regard it as essential that Jarring meet with them directly and at the highest level before the indirect negotiations entered a detailed stage.) Israel gave Dr. Jarring an Israeli plan for a peace settlement, which he conveyed to

the U.N. representatives of Egypt and Jordan Jan. 11 and 12 for their consideration. The 14-point peace formula was disclosed by the press Jan. 19. It contained essentially the same conditions previously demanded by Israel for settling the dispute. The text included an allusion to Israeli withdrawal from occupied Arab territories "located beyond the positions agreed to in the peace treaty," leaving Israel's future boundaries open to negotiations. The formal rejection of the plan by Egypt and Jordan was made public by the two Arab nations Jan. 20 and 25. The two had given their formal replies to the proposal to Jarring Jan. 15 and 18. The release of the Egyptian reply was criticized Jan. 24 by Israel, which regarded the action as a breach of the principle of secret diplomacy. The Egyptians said they were making the release because Israel had leaked its original offer to the press.

[29] *Jarring peace plan.* Jarring submitted a memorandum Feb. 8 to the Egyptian and Israeli U.N. representatives, advancing his own plan for peace. The text of the memorandum was released March 9. It called for Israel to give a commitment to withdraw its forces from occupied Egyptian territory to the former international boundary between Egypt and the British Mandate of Palestine, on condition that satisfactory arrangements were made for establishing demilitarized zones and for guaranteeing freedom of navigation through the Strait of Tiran and the Suez Canal. It called on Egypt to enter into a peace agreement with Israel and to acknowledge, on a reciprocal basis, the end of "all claims on a state of belligerency," the right of the other country to live in peace within secure and recognized boundaries, its responsibility to prevent acts of hostility originating within its boundaries, and noninterference in the other country's domestic affairs. An Egyptian reply to Jarring Feb. 15 accepted the proposal, reversing a long-standing refusal by Arabs to agree to an Israeli demand for a binding peace settlement. The Egyptian acceptance, however, was conditional on Israeli withdrawal from all occupied Arab territories. Israel implied rejection of the Jarring plan and asserted that Jarring had overstepped his role as a mediator in drawing up a specific proposal. Israel Feb. 26 formally replied to Egypt's proposal. The reply was reported to state that Israel would be willing to discuss in detail territorial and other terms of a peace pact with Egypt, but would not commit itself to total withdrawal from occupied Arab lands.

[30] *Talks halt, resume.* Dr. Jarring left for Moscow March 25 to resume his duties as ambassador to the Soviet Union. His departure from U.N. headquarters in New York, a week earlier than originally planned, placed his deadlocked mediation talks in a virtual state of suspension. Jarring resumed his discussions Dec. 15 and 16 as the result of a General Assembly call Dec. 13 for reactivation of the mission (*see* [39]).

[31] **Big 4 deadlock.** Meetings of the Big Four (the U.S., the U.S.S.R., France and Great Britain), attempting to find a solution to the problems in the Middle East, were deadlocked in the first quarter of the year. The Soviet Union charged Feb. 10, and Western diplomats at the U.N. confirmed the same day, that the U.S. had rejected a proposal by the other three that would have sought to induce Israel to agree to complete withdrawal from occupied Arab territories. The U.S. rejection of the proposal at the Feb. 4 meeting was based on an American refusal to express any substantive comment that could be interpreted as outside pressure on the governments involved. Big Four representatives met March 1-5 to draw up a joint communique on the Middle East, but abandoned their efforts March 5 after a deadlocked meeting. Soviet representatives had allegedly prevented the issuance of a statement by rejecting a suggestion of the other three to endorse a plea by U Thant March 5 urging Israel to give up all Egyptian territory. The Big Four were said to have agreed on other aspects of the communique, including support for Jarring's mission, a mention of Egypt's positive reply to him and a plea for an equally positive reply by Israel. Soviet sources said the session had bogged down over U.S. refusal to call for unconditional Israeli withdrawal. U.S. and Soviet representatives to the negotiations clashed March 18 over the creation of a peace-keeping force and other aspects of the Middle East dispute. The U.S.S.R. reportedly insisted that the Big Four specify that their guarantees apply to Arab-Israeli borders that existed before the 1967 war, while the U.S. (supported by France and Britain) favored the re-establishment of the 1967 frontiers with some "insubstantial" alterations in the borders between Israel and Jordan and Israel and Syria. The U.S. and Britain wanted the Secretary General to be in charge of operations of the proposed peace force, contending that the Security Council would be slow and ineffectual. France and the Soviet Union held that, under the U.N. charter, the council must have authority over peace-keeping.

[32] Truce extended. The third 90-day Middle East cease-fire expired Feb. 5, but was extended another 30 days until March 7. Secretary General Thant had appealed for an extension of the truce in messages to Israel, Egypt and Jordan Feb. 2. Israel immediately approved Thant's appeal, saying it would observe the truce as long as the Arabs did not shoot. Egypt Feb. 4 also approved the appeal. (Egypt had said Jan. 23 that it had formally rejected a U.S. suggestion for an extension of the cease-fire.) Egyptian President Sadat March 7 refused to again extend the truce, but Israeli and Egyptian forces along the Suez Canal continued to hold their fire. Sadat, in July 5-16 talks with U.S. State Department aides Donald C. Bergus and Michael Sterner, reportedly agreed to observe the unofficial cease-fire along the canal until Aug. 15, in return for a pledge by President Nixon to press for a specific solution of the Middle East conflict. No such solution was reached, but the Aug. 15 deadline passed without incident.

[33] Suez Canal discussions. *Egyptian proposals.* In his Feb. 4 acceptance of an extension of the cease-fire, Sadat also proposed the reopening of the Suez Canal if Israel agreed on a partial withdrawal of its troops from the eastern bank of the waterway by March 7. Israel Premier Mrs. Meir Feb. 9 said that Israel supported the idea and was ready to discuss with Egypt a "mutual de-escalation of the military confrontation." However, she said she considered it "strange" that Sadat proposed the withdrawal of Israeli troops from the canal "outside a framework of agreed arrangements for the absolute termination of the war." Sadat provided further details of his proposal in an interview published Feb. 22. Sadat said that, under his plan, Israeli troops would pull back to a line behind El Arish, a town on the northeastern edge of the Sinai Peninsula, 30 miles from the Israeli-Egyptian border (thus returning most of the peninsula lost by Egypt in the 1967 war). In exchange for the withdrawal, Sadat said he would "guarantee to reopen the canal in six months to international trade. I would prolong the cease-fire to a fixed date to give Jarring time to work out the details. I would guarantee free passage in the Strait of Tiran with an international force at Sharm el Sheik." Sadat said the force could be comprised of troops of the Big Four or other nations. Asked whether Israel would be permitted to use the reopened canal, Sadat said only after Israel had "fulfilled her obligations" under the U.N. resolution of Nov. 22, 1967. This appeared to be a reiteration of Cairo's stand that a solution of the Palestinian refugee problem must precede an agreement on Israel's use of the canal. Sadat April 1 reiterated his plan as a condition for the formal reinstatement of a limited cease-fire. Israeli officials, in effect, rejected the proposal in statements April 2 and 4.

[34] *Israeli proposals.* Israel April 19 submitted to the U.S. a plan to achieve an interim peace arrangement with Egypt to permit reopening the canal. The contents of the plan were not disclosed, but reportedly insisted on three conditions for the withdrawal of Israeli troops from the eastern bank of the waterway: an end to "the state of belligerency"; an agreement to prevent the occupation of the area by "either Egyptian or Soviet forces" following Israeli withdrawal; and an agreement to continue the Jarring peace talks. Egyptian rejection of the plan was indicated by a Cairo statement April 12 that had turned down a similar suggestion made April 11 by Israeli Defense Minister

Dayan. Dayan had suggested an Israeli withdrawal provided there was a permanent truce and restrictions against movement of Soviet or Egyptian forces across the canal. In a later proposal, Israel Nov. 10 suggested to the U.S. that the canal be reopened without an agreement. Under the plan, Israel would not be required to withdraw its troops during clearance operations and Israeli ships would be permitted to use the waterway once it was opened. Israel would allow Egyptian workers, but not troops, to cross to the east bank to facilitate dredging operations. Israeli Foreign Minister Eban had also suggested Sept. 30 that he and Egyptian Foreign Minister Mahmoud Riad hold direct talks on an interim Suez agreement under U.S. auspices, or discuss a permanent settlement under Dr. Jarring's chairmanship.

[35] *Sisco plan.* U.S. Assistant Secretary of State Joseph J. Sisco July 30-Aug. 5 held talks with Mrs. Meir and other Israeli officials in a new diplomatic initiative aimed at opening the canal. Two Israeli newspapers Aug. 8 published what was purported to be a plan suggested by Sisco in his talks. According to the reports, Sisco had proposed a two-stage withdrawal from the east bank. During the first phase, the Israelis would pull back 6-7.5 miles over a six-month period and a token force of Egyptian troops would cross to the eastern bank. In the second phase, the Israelis would withdraw to the Mitla Pass, 20 miles east of the canal. The area between the Israeli and Egyptian armies would be occupied by a U.N. force.

[36] *Rogers plan.* U.S. Secretary of State William P. Rogers Oct. 4 called on Israel and Egypt to work out an interim agreement on the reopening of the canal as the first step toward resolving the Middle East crisis. Roger's call came in an address to the U.N. General Assembly. The secretary stressed that the maintenence of a cease-fire and the eventual achievement of a "permanent end to belligerency" were not "realizable in the context of an interim agreement"; but he stressed that, "with goodwill on both sides," a common understanding could be reached. Rogers took note of Egypt's demand for a military presence on the east bank, a move which Israel opposed. He said, however, that compromises could be worked out that "are not negative." He reaffirmed the U.S. intention to continue to assist Israel and Egypt "in arriving at an interim agreement." Egyptian President Sadat Oct. 10 said that Rogers's plan amounted to "giving Israel all she wants but in a diplomatic way." Israeli officials criticized the plan Oct. 6 and again Oct. 26 in a major policy address by Mrs. Meir to the Knesset (parliament). In the Oct. 26 speech, Mrs. Meir said the Rogers proposals constituted withdrawal of American support of Israel's negotiating position in favor of Egypt. The premier complained that the U.S. had made "disturbing changes" on three specific issues: favoring a limited truce rather than the permanent one demanded by Israel; allowing for the possibility of compromise on Israel's refusal to have troops of any kind move into the east bank area after Israeli withdrawal; and viewing a Suez Canal agreement as merely a step toward reconciliation of the conflict rather than an agreement not entailing other commitments, as Rogers had stated on a visit to Israel in May.

[37] **African peace mission.** Presidents Leopold Sedar Senghor of Senegal, Gen. Joseph D. Mobutu of Zaire (formerly Congo-Kinshasa), Ahmadou Ahidjo of Cameroon and Gen. Yakubu Gowan of Nigeria discussed the prospects of a peace settlement with Israeli officials in Jerusalem Nov. 3-5 and Nov. 24 and with Egyptian leaders in Cairo Nov. 5-7 and Nov. 25. The four presidents were to report on their talks to a 10-nation Middle East committee established by the Organization of African Unity June 21-23. The Africans were not seeking to mediate the Middle East dispute, but to clarify certain positions involved in a possible settlement. These positions included security guarantees, borders, demilitarized zones and freedom of shipping through the Suez Canal. (The Egyptian government announced Nov. 7 that it would postpone U.N. General Assembly debate on the Middle East to permit the African group to complete its peace mission.) At the conclusion of the mission, Presidents Senghor and

Gowan presented to President Sadat, Mrs. Meir and Foreign Minister Eban a memorandum containing proposals for breaking the Middle East deadlock. Israel's agreement to the reactivation of the Jarring mission was Jerusalem's principal response to the African mission, the Israeli state radio reported Nov. 27.

[38] **Sadat warns of war.** President Sadat warned Egyptian troops Nov. 20 that war with Israel "is at hand" because there "is no longer any hope whatever of a peaceful settlement." Sadat followed up his threat of launching a new conflict with the disclosure Nov. 21 that he had "cut off all contacts with the United States for a peaceful solution" of the crisis. Sadat charged that Washington had a predetermined position on the peace talks that was closely aligned with Israel's view. In the face of Sadat's stand, the U.S. announced Nov. 22 that it had suspended mediation efforts to promote an interim agreement in the Middle East. (Egyptian troops were placed in a state of standby alert and leaves were canceled in the wake of Sadat's declarations.)

[39] **U.N. demands Israeli withdrawal.** The U.N. General Assembly Dec. 13 approved by a 79-7 vote (36 abstentions) a resolution calling on Israel to withdraw from all occupied Arab territories and instructing Secretary General Thant to "reactivate" the Jarring mission. (Debate on the Middle East had opened in the Assembly Dec. 3.) Israel and six Latin American countries voted against the resolution. The U.S. was among the abstainers, but U.S. Deputy Ambassador to the U.N. Christopher H. Phillips said that "nothing in our abstentions should be taken as a change in American policies." Phillips said that Washington continued to support the Jarring mission, but regarded its own mediation efforts regarding reopening of the Suez Canal as the "most promising avenue" at the moment. Israel had sought to modify the African-Asian resolution, submitted Dec. 9, by supporting two proposals drafted by Barbados and Uruguay. They called for resumption of the Jarring mission, but did not mention Jarring's Feb. 8 memorandum (see [29]) calling on Israel to commit itself to ultimate withdrawal. Israel had made it clear during debate that it would not abide by any Assembly demand that called for Israeli withdrawal prior to negotiations.

See also AGNEW, SPIRO THEODORE; BULGARIA; ENVIRONMENT; ESPIONAGE; FLOODS; FOREIGN AID; FOREIGN POLICY; FRANCE [17]; ISRAEL; JORDAN; LEBANON; PENTAGON PAPERS [18]; SUDAN; TURKEY [6]; UNION OF SOVIET SOCIALIST REPUBLICS [13]; UNITED ARAB REPUBLIC

MIGRANT WORKERS—See AGRICULTURE [7-10]; DISASTERS; HUNGER

MILITARY—**Marines to retain strict codes.** The Marine Corps was reported Jan. 4 to have rejected proposals to relax the strict codes that regulated the corps' conduct and appearance. The decision was made by Gen. Leonard F. Chapman Jr., commandant of the Marine Corps, and senior officers in his command. Chapman said he and his staff had rejected proposals for easing the corps' disciplinary codes because the Marines had a mission of being prepared to be the first branch to be sent into battle. He also said that, since the corps was much smaller than the Army or Navy, getting volunteers was less of a problem. In a later, related development, according to report Feb. 20, Adm. Elmo R. Zumwalt Jr., chief of naval opera-tions, was persuaded by senior officers on his staff to rewrite or clarify some orders issued in November 1970 that relaxed personal appearance codes for sailors. Among changes in the rewritten rules: enlisted men could wear dungarees in public only on the way to and from work at Navy installations, rather than at any time while off base; and requirements were set down for "neatly trimmed" hair, beards and sideburns.

[2] **Army promotion plan set.** The Defense Department unveiled a new program Jan. 9 providing a time limit for Army enlisted men to move up in rank or face the possibility of being barred from re-enlisting. Col. William Weber, in charge of developing the program, estimated that 5,000-10,000 men might be mustered out of the service in the "first-surge" impact of the plan during 1971. Weber, who was in the Army's Promotion, Separation and Transition Division, said that, thereafter, about 1,000 enlisted men might be eliminated each year. Under the program, a private had three years to reach the rank of private first class. Time limits for reaching other ranks: corporal, eight years; sergeant, 12 years; staff sergeant, 20 years; platoon sergeant or sergeant first class, 24 years; master sergeant, 27 years; and staff sergeant major, 30 years.

[3] **Arms theft case.** Retired Maj. Gen. Carl C. Turner, who had served as the Army's chief law enforcement officer, was indicted Jan. 12 by a federal grand jury on nine counts of unlawful firearms transactions and four counts of income tax evasion. The charges grew out of a 1969 Congressional investigation of military corruption. The federal jury charged Turner with asking the Chicago Police Department for guns it had confiscated and "did represent that such gift was being solicited for the use of the United States" on five different occasions, involving 423 firearms, during 1968. It also charged him with filing false personal income tax returns from 1965-68. Turner April 9 pleaded guilty to charges of illegal gun solicitation. At the request of U.S. Attorney Brian T. Gettings, the eight other firearms counts against Turner were dismissed. Turner was sentenced May 10 to three years in prison on the gun charge. He pleaded guilty May 14 to a charge of income tax evasion in 1968 and was sentenced May 18 to three months in prison and fined $2,500. The other three counts of tax evasion were dropped on a government motion.

[4] **8 indicted in service club case.** The same Congressional investigation which resulted in the Turner indictment resulted Feb. 17 in the indictment by a federal grand jury of eight persons on charges of conspiring to defraud non-commissioned officers' clubs in South Vietnam during 1965-69. Indicted were: former Sgt. Maj. of the Army William O. Woodridge, the Army's former highest-ranking enlisted man, who had been stripped of that rank but retained his status as a sergeant and remained on active Army duty at White Sands, N.M.; M. Sgt. William E. Higdon, who also was convicted June 10 by a military jury of stealing funds and taking kickbacks while running service clubs in Vietnam; Sgt. I. C. William C. Bagby; Sgt. 1. C. Narvaez Hatcher, retired, who was also charged with four counts of giving a total of $14,000 in bribes to service club employees; Sgt. 1. C. Seymour Lazar, retired, who was also charged with the four bribery counts and with 14 counts of submitting fraudulent claims to various service clubs; Theodore Bass, a civilian who had been an Army noncommissioned officer and who was also charged with the four bribery counts; and Charles and Irene Terhune, civilians also charged with the four bribery counts. Also named as a defendant and charged with bribery was Marmed, Inc., a California corporation which sold goods to service clubs. (Lazar, Bass, Hatcher and the Terhunes were listed as stockholders of the corporation.) The conspiracy count carried a maximum penalty of five years in prison and a $10,000 fine. Each bribery count carried a possible sentence of 15 years in prison and a $20,000 fine or three times the amount of the bribe. Each count of submitting fraudulent claims carried a maximum penalty of $10,000 and five years in prison.

[5] **New Senate probe opened.** The Senate Permanent Investigations Subcommittee Feb. 17 opened hearings into reports of alleged bribery, smuggling and kickbacks in the Army's post exchange service. The hearings, which continued into March, were dominated by the names of William John Crum and Brig. Gen. Earl F. Cole. Crum, a China-born American, had provided a $2,000-a-month Saigon villa for PX officials, urged them to stock their clubs' bars with whiskeys and beers that paid him fees, and used his

influence to build a $40 million operation in Vietnam. Crum reportedly had received from the Army a "certificate of achievement" for contributing to the troops' "morale and welfare." Cole, who was allegedly paid by Crum for protection of the operation, was demoted to a colonel in July 1970, stripped of a Vietnam distinguished service medal and retired for failure to maintain "a high degree of personal and professional integrity." Cole was also linked Feb. 23 to a scheme in which PXs in Vietnam reported that they were running out of beer when they had 99,000 cases in stock and 125,000 cases arriving each month. Cole appeared before the Senate panel March 10 and asserted that the charges against him were "unprecedented, unproved, untrue and slanderous." Sen. Abraham Ribicoff (D, Conn.), chairman of the subcommittee, disclosed March 12 that the late Rep. L. Mendel Rivers (D, S.C.), chairman of the House Armed Services Committee, had sought twice in 1969 to intervene on Cole's behalf to block the Senate investigation.

[6]   The subcommittee Nov. 2 issued a report on the full three-year probe of corruption in the PX system. The report accused equally Pentagon administrators, U.S. servicemen and big business of turning the military's PX and service club operation into a system riddled with graft and corruption. Included in the report were 41 specific "findings," 15 recommendations and four legislative proposals. One of the proposals, submitted by Sen. Ribicoff, would require the service clubs to make their financial records available for audits by the General Accounting Office (GAO). Under the present PX setup, the clubs and exchanges operated on their own earnings rather than with funds appropriated by Congress. The clubs had successfully resisted GAO auditing in the past.

[7]   *Investigating procedures tightened.* Defense Secretary Melvin Laird ordered March 17 that the Army's Criminal Investigation Division (CID) be brought under tighter Pentagon control. Laird ordered the development of "a CID agency which has vertical control of all CIDs worldwide," to be similar in structure to the Air Force's Office of Special Investigations. Under present regulations, units of the CID took orders from local commanders. Under the Air Force structure, local criminal investigators were under the direction of the Special Investigations department in Washington.

[8]   *Air Force to try 7 officers.* The Air Force announced Feb. 18 that it would court-martial seven officers accused of mishandling funds used to purchase supplies for mess halls in Thailand. (The Air Force had originally said Feb. 16 that 14 men would be tried.) The seven accused officers were among 14 charged in March 1970 with corrupt and illegal practices in handling the mess hall funds. All were charged with "accepting gratuities" from companies doing business with their messes. Some were charged with accepting bribes from an entertainment booking agency, while others were accused of soliciting bribes. Trials for the seven were scheduled to begin April 15 at Clark Air Force Base in the Philippines.

Personnel Developments

[9]   **Drives for blacks.** Adm. Zumwalt announced March 31 the formation of a six-man team—including three admirals—to oversee a five-year program to recruit for the Navy more black officers and enlisted men. The aim of the recruiting drive was to bring the number of black Navy personnel up from 5.5% of the force to the level of their 12% representation in the U.S. population. Among the features of the campaign: black recruiters were to be added to the staffs of 37 recruiting stations across the country; new Naval Reserve Officer Training Corps units would be opened at Savannah State in Georgia and Southern University in Baton Rouge, La. to supplement the sole existing black Navy ROTC unit at Prairie View A & M in Texas; the number of black midshipmen at the Naval Academy at Annapolis, Md. would be increased; base facilities would be re-examined to insure that the needs and tastes of nonwhites were answered; social opportunity would be guaranteed by

a new, close examination of service clubs and of housing used by minority dependents; and the General Classification Test, which was used to assign Navy men to categories of duty, would be reviewed.

[10]   The Pentagon announced Oct. 27 new moves designed to increase the number of blacks in the National Guard from 1.7% to 4.6% of the force. The recruiting effort was described by the Pentagon as the first step in a major program to make reserve forces reflect the religious and ethnic makeup of the communities from which the units drew recruits. Under the new policy, reserve unit commanders would not have to draw recruits from the waiting lists which had been compiled in their own community. Commanders were free to step up recruiting drives in their communities, bypassing the waiting lists.

[11]   **Army ad drive halted.** The Pentagon April 6 ordered the Army to stop spending money on radio and television advertising until it had evaluated the effectiveness of the planned $10.6 million 13-week campaign to attract new recruits from among the nation's high school seniors. The Army had opened its campaign March 1 through the N.W. Ayer Agency of Philadelphia, the nation's 13th largest advertising agency. A Pentagon spokesman said the ad drive was being halted after the Air Force, the Marine Corps and the Navy complained that it was depriving them of free advertising previously given the military branches by the media. Another reason given for the order was complaints from many of the largest advertising houses in the country that only seven of them had been invited to bid for the expanded drive. (Ayer had handled the Army's advertising for several years.) The ad drive was funded primarily by increasing the Army's advertising budget from $3.1 million in 1970 to $18.1 million in 1971. The increase was in response to Nixon Administration plans for an all-volunteer Army by mid-1973. Ayer said Aug. 7 that the campaign had helped increase Army enlistments in the armor, artillery and infantry branches seven-fold during March, April and May.

[12]   **Resor resigns.** Secretary of the Army Stanley R. Resor resigned May 21 after six years in office. He said he would carry on until a successor was named. In his letter of resignation, Resor said he felt that "after six years some greater attention to my family is long overdue." President Nixon accepted the resignation with "special regret." Resor was expected to return to the New York law firm he had left in 1965 to take up the Army post. Resor was replaced as secretary by Robert F. Froehlke June 30.

[13]   **Cushman to head Marines.** President Nixon passed over two four-star Marine generals (Lt. Gen. John R. Chaisson and Gen. Raymond G. Davis) Nov. 30 and appointed Lt. Gen. Robert E. Cushman Jr. to be the next commandant of the Marine Corps. Cushman, who had been deputy director of the Central Intelligence Agency (CIA) since appointed in March 1969, would succeed Gen. Chapman, who was retiring Dec. 31. Cushman had served four years as a national security adviser to Nixon when the latter was vice president.

See also ABORTION; CONGRESS [12]; CRIME [3]; DEFENSE; DRAFT & WAR PROTEST; DRUG USE & ADDICTION [14-19]; ECONOMY, U.S. [16]; ESPIONAGE; FEDERAL BUREAU OF INVESTIGATION [2]; HIJACKING [15-16]; RACIAL & MINORITY UNREST [14-19]; SELECTIVE SERVICE SYSTEM; WAR CRIMES

MILLS, WILBUR D.—*See* POLITICS [8]
MINDSZENTY, JOZSEF CARDINAL—*See* ROMAN CATHOLIC CHURCH [20]

MINES—1970 Kentucky blast actions. The U.S. Bureau of Mines said Jan. 29 that it would ask the Justice Department to prosecute those responsible for the coal mine explosion in Hyden, Ky. Dec. 30, 1970 where 38 men died. It was the first time the 60-year-old bureau had suggested federal prosecution for criminal negligence. The bureau reported that numerous violations of the 1969 Coal Mine Health and Safety Act had been uncovered in its investigation, including the illegal use of primer cord (a high-intensity explosive banned from use in underground mines). The ignition of the primer cord, which led to a mine-wide coal dust explosion, was cited as the principal cause of the disaster. Haphazard safety practices by the mine's explosive shooter were also cited. (The explosive shooter and the day-shift foreman were charged Jan. 20 by the Kentucky Department of Mines and Minerals with inept safety practices and the use of explosives in a "non-permissible" manner.) Federal mine inspectors, who failed to make a mandatory inspection eight days before the explosion, were absolved of blame because of "priority duties" which had routed an assigned inspector to other area mines. Consumer and safety advocate Ralph Nader, according to a report Jan. 10, charged that the bureau's one-day hearing into the disaster was "a poorly enacted sham and a callous attempt to cover up" the bureau's "own guilt and failure." The House General Labor Subcommittee, which had begun its own investigation into the explosion March 9, June 19 said that the bureau's probe of the disaster was "so poorly handled it might be said to have impeded the purpose of the investigation." The subcommittee charged that the bureau had a "heavy burden of responsibility" for the deaths in the blast and was negligent in not completing follow-up inspections to insure that safety violations were corrected. The subcommittee also said that it was known in the Hyden area that illegal explosives were being used in the mine.

The Interior Department March 8 proposed a fine of $53,600 against the Finley Coal Co., owners of the mine. Attorney Gen. John N. Mitchell announced June 23 that the company had been indicted in U.S. District Court in Pikeville, Ky. for 24 violations of federal coal mine safety standards.

West Va. bars some strip mining. The West Virginia legislature approved a measure March 14 placing a two-year prohibition on issuance of state mining permits in 22 of 55 counties where such mining had not begun. An attempt to halt the spread of strip mining throughout the state, backed by conservationists and Secretary of State John D. Rockefeller 4th, was decisively defeated. The approved compromise was weakened by a Senate-House conference committee which rejected a statewide limit on new strip mining permits, gave the Department of Reclamation discretionary control regulations and deleted a provision to require public hearings on challenged permits.

Soft coal strike. The soft coal industry in 25 states (primarily in Pennsylvania, Kentucky and the Virginias) was shut down early Oct. 1 by a strike by 100,000 soft coal miners. Although there was no formal strike call, the miners, members of the United Mine Workers (UMW), walked out at, or just before, expiration of their contracts. Their major demands were a $50 daily wage, up from $37, and an 80¢ royalty, up from 40¢, paid by the operators into the union's welfare fund for each ton of coal mined. Working conditions were also unresolved. The UMW and the Bituminous Coal Operators Association, following an all-day negotiating session with Gov. Arch A. Moore Jr. (R, W.Va.) participating as mediator, signed a three-year agreement at 11:45 p.m. Nov. 13, minutes before the Nixon Administration's 90-day economic freeze (*see* ECONOMY, U.S. [8-12]) ended. The contract acceded to the miners' demand for the increase in the royalty fund—the first such increase since 1952—and called for an average package increase in wages and benefits of 39% (including the royalty increase) over the three-year period.

The contract came under the scrutiny of President Nixon's Pay Board Nov. 18 because the first-year increase exceeded the 5.5% guideline for new pay increases (*see* ECONOMY, U.S. [21]). The board, with its public members strongly objecting, voted 10-3 Nov. 19 to uphold the first-year pay raise of the contract. (No ruling was made on the second and third yearly raises.) The business members of the board said the increase was justified on the basis of a needed 4% increase in the UMW health and welfare fund, the relative wage position of the miners, difficulty of their work and a need to attract new workers to the industry. UMW President W. A. (Tony) Boyle ordered his active members to end their strike after the board approved the contract, but 15,000 miners were still off the job Nov. 23. Although the union leadership had tacitly approved the refusal by many workers to return to work following the signing of the contract and pending outcome of the board's decision, mounting rank-and-file dissidence over the new contract was responsible for continued absenteeism. Miners were angry that only a minority of highly skilled workers would receive the daily increase of up to $50.

Other Union Developments

Boyle indicted. UMW President Boyle was indicted by a federal grand jury in Washington March 2 on charges of making illegal political contributions with union funds. Indicted with Boyle were James Kmetz, head of the UMW's lobbying and political-action arm, and John Owens, UMW secretary-treasurer. According to the indictment, union funds were transferred to the union's political arm, Labor's Non-Partisan League, where checks were drawn to "cash," and the money deposited in personal checking accounts and later given as political contributions from 1967-69. The amount of such illegally channeled funds set in the indictment was $49,250, including $5,000 allegedly embezzled by Boyle. The three union leaders pleaded not guilty March 3.

Fund mismanagement found. U.S. District Court Judge Gerhard A. Gesell in Washington April 28 upheld charges of mismanagement and conspiracy against the UMW, its welfare and retirement fund and the union-owned National Bank of Washington. The ruling, on a civil suit filed in 1969 by a group of miners and widows, ordered the fund to withdraw its money from the Washington bank by June 30 and Boyle to retire by that date as a trustee of the welfare fund. The charges involved the maintenance of non-interest-bearing deposits in huge amounts from the welfare fund in the Washington bank. Gesell said the arrangement originated with the late UMW leader John L. Lewis and bilked union pensioners and beneficiaries of investment income while providing collateral advantages to special interests of the fund and bank officers. A court hearing on compensatory damages was planned.

Officials convicted. UMW District 5 President Michael Budzanoski and Secretary-Treasurer John Seddon were convicted by a federal jury in Pittsburgh May 6 on charges involving a conspiracy to use union funds, obtained by false vouchers, for the 1969 re-election campaign of President Boyle.

Antitrust settlement paid. The UMW and the Consolidated Coal Co. Oct. 15 paid an $8,907,000 antitrust damage settlement to the Southeast Coal Co. of Kentucky. The UMW's half share of the penalty was the largest antitrust penalty ever imposed on a union. The total settlement included $7.3 million of a treble-damage award made under federal antitrust laws and $1.6 million of penalty interest charged for every day the October 1968 judgment went unpaid through the appeal process. The final Supreme Court rejection of an appeal was handed down Oct. 12.

See also CHILE [2, 4-5]; ENVIRONMENT; GUATEMALA; MEXICO; PERU; RAILROADS; YOUTH

MINH, DUONG VAN—*See* VIETNAM, SOUTH
MINICHIELLO, RAFFAEL—*See* HIJACKING [14]
MITCHELL, JOHN—*See* AGRICULTURE [10]; BUSINESS [7]; CRIME [1, 15]; DRUG USE & ADDICTION [7]; FEDERAL BUREAU OF INVESTIGATION [1, 3, 5, 9]; PENTAGON PAPERS [2]; PRISONS [8]; STUDENT UNREST [2]; SUPREME COURT; VOTING RIGHTS
MONGOLIA—*See* DISARMAMENT; SPACE [24]
MOON—*See* SPACE [1-5, 12, 23]

MOROCCO—Cabinet changes. King Hassan II dismissed four ministers April 23, reportedly in connection with unspecified financial irregularities concerning investments in the tourist industry. Those dismissed were: Mohamed Jaidi (commerce and industry), replaced by Mohamed Tahiri; Abdelkrim Lazrak (finance), replaced by Mohamed Karim Lamrani; Abdelhamid Kriem (tourism), replaced by Mohamed Lazrak; and Mamoun Tahiri (secondary instruction), replaced by Ahmed Laski.

Hassan survives rebel attack. King Hassan July 10 survived an attempted coup d'etat by rebellious army officers and cadets, who stormed the king's summer palace and killed 93 guests attending festivities on his birthday. A major, five colonels and four generals—Ahmanzoun Hammou, Hassan's brother-in-law and military governor of Rabat-Kneitra; Khiati Bougrine, military governor of Taza; Abdurrahman Habibi, military governor of Marrakesh; and Amerach Mustafa, commander of military schools—were executed without trial July 13 for their part in the attempt. Major aspects of the coup attempt remained unclarified, but it appeared that the rebels had intended to overthrow the monarchy and set up an Arab Socialist regime on the Libyan model. The king was taken to a place of safety during the attack, but reappeared about three hours later and was greeted with proclamations of loyalty by the rebellious soldiers. Some accounts said the rebels faltered after Gen. Mohamed Medbouh, believed to have led the plot, was killed in unknown circumstances during the fighting. The version given by Hassan July 11 was that the cadets, believing themselves to be on a mission to free Hassan from control of the diplomats, called off the shooting when they recognized the king. He said the rebellious cadets had been drugged and that a flask of unknown liquid had been found on each of them. Hassan July 10 had charged Libya with inciting the rebellion, but said he did not "give a royal damn."

The palace fighting ended at about 6 p.m. Shortly thereafter, the rebels occupied the broadcasting station of Radio Rabat and announced that the monarchy had been overthrown and that a Socialist revolution was underway. Forces loyal to Hassan secured control of the station a few hours later and broadcast an appeal for calm from Interior Minister Gen. Mohamed Oufkir, whom Hassan had invested with all civil and military powers. Oufkir July 11 directed a house-to-house search for rebel holdouts in Rabat and there were reports that some of the captives were executed summarily. The market quarter of the town was blocked off, but elsewhere stores were open.

New government named. Apparently in a move designed to combat influences leading to the coup attempt, Hassan Aug. 4 dismissed his Cabinet and Aug. 6 appointed a new one. The new Cabinet was led by former Finance Minister Lamrani as premier, replacing Ahmed Laraki. It included Gen. Oufkir as defense minister and commander of the armed forces. (He was replaced as interior minister by his protege, Ahmed Benbouchta.) The 15-man Cabinet included 10 ministers from the previous government, but no members of the country's two major political parties. Hassan said he would delegate his executive powers to the new government, which had previously taken orders from the palace through the Directorate General of the Royal Cabinet, abolished Aug. 4.

Former ministers arrested. Hassan arrested a number of former government ministers and other key officials during November in an apparent attempt to isolate the sources of corruption believed to have been the cause of the coup attempt. Arrested Nov. 1 were Mamoun Tahiri, Mohamed Jaidi, Abdelhamid Kriem and Mohamed Lazrak, all former financial and commercial ministers. Arrested with them were Abdelaziz Benchekroun and Driss Ben Bachir, officials of the Bureau de Recherches et de Participations Minieres (BRPM), a state agency to develop the mining industry. (Nacer Belarbi, former director of the the bureau, was arrested Nov. 12.) Mohamed Imani and Yahia Chefchaouni, both former ministers of public works, were seized Nov. 6 and 8 as well as three Jewish businessmen, including David Ben Amar, secretary general of the Jewish Community Council. A warrant was issued for the arrest of Paul Ohana, a Moroccan Jew who had managed the country's largest oil refinery and was accused of manipulating crude oil purchases.

Marrakesh plotters convicted. The trial of 193 leftists accused of plotting to overthrow the government, which began June 14, ended Sept. 17 with the sentencing of five persons to death and six others to life imprisonment. Of those charged with planning to oust Hassan with financial help from the Syrian government, 59 were acquitted and the remaining 123 given sentences ranging from 18 months to 30 years. Muhammed Ajar, brought back from Spain in 1970, and Mohamed Basri, pardoned after being convicted of a plot in 1963, were among those sentenced to death. Habib el-Forkani, secretary general of the opposition Union Nationale des Forces Populaires (UNFP) for Marrakesh, was given 10 years in prison. (The International Organization of Jurists had addressed a Sept. 8 appeal to King Hassan, asking him to revoke the death penalty being demanded by the prosecutor for Forkani and 48 others.)

See also AGNEW, SPIRO THEODORE

MORTON, ROGERS C.B.—*See* ENVIRONMENT; INDIANS, AMERICAN; NIXON, RICHARD MILHOUS [5]; POLLUTION [5]

MOTION PICTURES—Nixon confers on industry. President Nixon conferred April 5 with 22 leaders of the film industry. The President, who had initiated the meeting, directed aides to study ways to help the economically depressed industry, but offered little hope for the passage of a tax relief bill before Congress. The measure would give film makers a 20% tax cut to help the industry become more competitive with subsidized foreign film makers. Industry leaders reported to the President that weekly theater attendance in the U.S. had dropped from about 80 million cinema-goers 20 years ago to 17.5 million. Charlton Heston, president of the Screen Actors Guild, said that 76% of his union members took home less than $3,000 a year, an amount well below the government-established poverty level.

Church groups repudiate ratings. Citing the unreliability of the GP rating, Protestant and Catholic motion picture review panels withdrew their support of the film industry's ratings system, according to report May 19. (The current classifications: G—all ages, GP—all ages but parental guidance suggested, R—children under 17 not admitted unless accompanied by a parent or guardian, X—no one under 17 admitted.) The Broadcasting and Film Commission of the National Council of Churches and the National Catholic Office for Motion Pictures said the GP rating had been given to several films that merited the R designation because of the nature of their subject matter. The Rev. Patrick J. Sullivan, director of the Catholic group, explained that the rating system, instituted in 1968, overemphasized overt visual sex and gave little consideration to "the implicit exploitation of sex and the overall impact of violence and other antisocial aspects of the film...."

Academy awards. *Patton* won seven awards at the 43rd annual presentation of the "Oscars" in Los Angeles April 14 by the American Academy of Motion Picture Arts and Sciences. The biography of the Army general was named the best film of 1970 and Franklin J. Schaffner drew a citation as the best director. George C. Scott, who said he would not participate in the awards, was named best actor. The film's other awards: Douglas Williams and Don Bassman for sound, Hugh S. Fowler for film editing, Francis Fred Coppola and Edmund North for best story and original screenplay and art and set direction. The other winners: **actress**—Glenda Jackson, *Women in Love;* **supporting actor**—John Mills, *Ryan's Daughter;* **supporting actress**—Helen Hayes, *Airport;* **foreign-language film**—*Investigation of a Citizen Above Suspicion;* **screenplay** (based on material from another medium)—Ring Lardner Jr.—*M*A*S*H;* **cinematography**—Fred A. Young, *Ryan's Daughter;* **short subject** (live action)—*The Resurrection of Billy Bronco;* **short subject** (cartoon)—*Is It Always Right to be Right?;* **documentary** (feature)—*Woodstock;* **documentary** (short subject)—*Interviews with My Lai Veterans;* **costume design**—Nino Novarese, *Cromwell;* **special visual effects**—A. D. Flowers and L. B. Abbott, *Tora! Tora! Tora!;* **original score**—Francis Lai, *Love Story;* **original song score**—the Beatles, *Let It Be;* **art direction**—Terry Marsh and Bob Cartwright, *Scrooge;* **song**—"For All We Know," *Lovers and Other Strangers;* **pecial award for contributions to the film industry**—Orson Welles.

See also OBSCENITY & PORNOGRAPHY

MOVIES—*See* MOTION PICTURES

MOZAMBIQUE—The Portuguese government May 25 told the White Fathers, an order of Roman Catholic priests, they had 48 hours to leave Mozambique after the order had earlier announced its intention of withdrawing from the territory. Rev. Theo Van Asten, the White Fathers' superior general, said in a May 15 letter to the order's priests in Africa that the nine parishes in Mozambique were being closed and the 40 missionaries withdrawn because of the "basic ambiguity" in being identified with Portuguese colonial rule. The White Fathers' General Council announced May 19 that dissolution of the Mozambique mission would be completed by July 1. In explaining his government's decision May 28, Portuguese Foreign Minister Rui Patricio accused two White Fathers of recruiting terrorists for FRELIMO, the Mozambique Liberation Front, of "insulting the Portuguese flag and the name of Portugal." Patricio said that after the two had been expelled and other priests supported them, the Portuguese government received notice that the White Fathers were leaving Mozambique.

See also AFRICA; FLOODS; PORTUGAL; ZAMBIA

MUKTI BAHINI—*See* PAKISTAN [10, 17, 19, 21]
MUSIC—*See* RECORD INDUSTRY
MUSKIE, EDMUND S.—*See* FEDERAL BUREAU OF INVESTIGATION [5]; POLITICS [8, 10]; POLLUTION [14]; STATE & LOCAL GOVERNMENTS [9]
MUTUAL FUNDS—*See* BANKS
MYLAI MASSACRE—*See* WAR CRIMES [1-7]

NEGROES—Statistics. The Joint Center for Political Studies reported April 28 that the number of black elected officeholders in the U.S. rose 22% (from 1,500 to 1,860) during 1970. Despite the gains, however, black public officials still represented about .3% of all officeholders in the nation. Nearly three-fifths of the blacks in office were in the South. According to the figures, 711 blacks held office in the 11 Southern states, a 26% rise above the 1970 figure of 563.

The Census Bureau reported May 18 that new figures based on the 1970 census showed that half of the nation's 22.3 million Negroes now lived in 50 cities. A further breakdown of the figures revealed that one-third of America's Negro population was concentrated in 15 cities. According to the bureau, six cities had black majorities while eight others had black populations of 40% or more. The highest proportion of blacks in all cities occurred in Compton, Calif. and Washington, each with about 71%. The other cities with black populations exceeding 50% were East St. Louis, Ill., with 69.1%, Newark, N.J., with 54.2%, Gary, Ind., with 52.8% and Atlanta with 51.3%. New York City had by far the largest black population, almost 1.7 million. The new figure represented an increase of nearly 580,000 over 1960 and raised the black proportion of New York's population to 21% from 14% in 1960. Chicago had the second largest number of blacks with slightly more than 1.1. million. Nationwide, Negroes constituted about 11% of the total population.

A study of the 1970 census by federal analysts showed that despite a decade of progress by black Americans, blacks in 1970 remained far behind whites in terms of economic prosperity, educational advancement and social gains. The study, compiled by the Census Bureau and the Bureau of Labor Statistics, and made public July 26, found that 28.9 of every 100 nonwhite families were headed by women. The percentage of fatherless white families in the 1960s remained constant at about 9%.

Another set of figures showed that blacks increased their median income by 50% during the 1960s, but that by 1970 their income was only three-fifths that earned by whites. The black median income rose from $4,000 to $6,191. The white increase was from $7,252 to $9,794. According to the report, about one-fourth of all black families had incomes of $10,000, but one-fifth of all black families earned less than $3,000. The report also showed that young blacks were enrolling with increasing frequency in colleges with a majority of white students from 1965 to the end of the decade. In 1964, slightly more than half of all black college students were in predominantly black colleges and universities. By 1970 almost three-fourths of all black students were in schools with a white majority.

The report revealed that about half of all-black occupied housing units in rural areas were substandard in 1970, compared with only 8% of white rural housing. The report also said that 5% more blacks owned their homes in 1970 than in 1960. The percentage of black dwellings lacking some plumbing facilities declined in the 1960s from 41% to 17%. There were no dramatic changes in health statistics such as life expectancy for either blacks or whites during the 1960s. The 25-year-old black in 1968 could expect to die six years sooner than a white person the same age. The same finding was reported in 1960.

Black Expo ends. More than 800,000 persons, among them the nation's leading black political and civil rights leaders, attended the third annual Black Business and Cultural Exposition in Chicago Sept. 29-Oct. 3. Better known as Black Expo, the exposition was sponsored by Operation Breadbasket, the economic arm of the Southern Christian Leadership Conference (SCLC). The exposition featured nearly 500 exhibitions of black business enterprise, art and entertainment. One of the driving forces behind Black Expo was the Rev. Jesse L. Jackson, director of Operation Breadbasket. Jackson said in the exposition's opening ceremonies Sept. 29 that government and industry could assure the economic growth of America's black communities by assistance programs similar to the ones used by the U.S. to help its Western allies.

Jackson, SCLC split. Rev. Jackson announced in Chicago Dec. 18 the formation of a new black political and economic development organization, after resigning Dec. 11 as national director of Operation Breadbasket. The new group was to be called Operation Push (People United to Save Humanity). Jackson resigned after the Atlanta-based SCLC board of directors Dec. 2 suspended him from his $12,000-a-year post for 60 days, in a dispute over disposition of $500,000 collected during Black Expo. SCLC opposed the creation of two nonprofit corporations to handle Expo and had not received any of the funds at the time of the suspension. Earlier in the year, Jackson had refused a request by the Rev. Ralph David Abernathy, SCLC executive director, to move Operation Breadbasket's national headquarters from Chicago, which had the most active of 18 Breadbasket affiliates, to Atlanta. In an attempt to avoid a damaging public split, the SCLC board Dec. 15 rejected Jackson's resignation and offered to discuss with him outstanding differences. They agreed, however, to turn over the Chicago headquarters building to Jackson if the split could not be reconciled.

Jackson, who took with him the entire leadership of the Chicago SCLC chapter, indicated in his Dec. 18 announcement that Operation Push would continue the economic emphasis of Breakbasket, since "the problems of the seventies are economic, so the solution and the goal must be economic." The new group also was reported to favor political organization, aimed especially at newly enfranchised voters. Jackson told 4,000 local supporters Dec. 18 "we must picket, boycott, march, vote and, when necessary, engage in civil disobedience. We must express our power—the judges are too slow—the courts are too corrupt."

See also AGING; AGNEW, SPIRO THEODORE; BLACK MILITANTS; CIVIL RIGHTS; EDUCATION [4, 8-9, 16]; ELECTIONS [3-4, 6, 10]; JUDICIARY [8]; MILITARY [9-10]; POLITICS [9-11]; POPULATION; POVERTY; PRISONS [2, 4, 7]; RACIAL & MINORITY UNREST [1, 4, 6-8, 10-19]; RHODESIA; SECURITY, U.S.; SOUTH AFRICA [1-3, 8-9, 11-12]; STUDENT UNREST [8]; SUPREME COURT; VOTING RIGHTS; YOUTH

NEO-FASCISM — *See* ITALY [3, 6-7, 12, 16, 18, 21]

NEPAL—Kirti Nidhi Bista resigned as premier of Nepal Aug. 26 but was reinstated by King Mahendra Aug. 29. Bista had resigned in the wake of Mahendra's criticism of parliament Aug. 25 for refusing to allow Ramraja Prasad Singh to take his seat following his election. Singh was barred after he had been found guilty earlier in August of "antistate" activities and sentenced to 2½ years imprisonment. Mahendra granted Singh a pardon Aug. 25.

NETHERLANDS—Election, government crisis. The ruling coalition government of Christian and conservative parties, headed by Premier Piet J.S. de Jong, April 28 lost its parliamentary majority in national elections that registered a significant swing toward the moderate left and an erosion of religious-based parties. The three confessional parties (the Catholic People's, Anti-Revolutionary and the Christian Historical Union), the Liberals and the Democratic Socialism '70 (DS '70) party immediately began consultations with P.A.J.M. Steenkamp, appointed as "Informator" May 15, on the formation of a new government but reached an impasse over the issues of housing, defense and social insurance. The parties reached agreement June 9 on an economic program presented by Steenkamp. The plan envisaged an economic austerity program in 1972-73 and barred tax increases for the period. The loss of the government's majority in the elections was attributed partly to inflation and the balance of payments deficit. Prices were rising by an average annual rate of 7%, and wages had been frozen in December 1970.

Twenty-eight parties competed in the election and 14 won seats. The seats won by the majority parties (1967 strength in parentheses): Catholic People's— 35 (42); Labor—39 (37); Liberals (Freedom and Democracy)—16 (17); Anti-Revolutionary party (Calvinists)—13 (15); Democracy '66—11 (7); Christian

Historical Union—10 (12); DS '70—8 (3); Radical Political party (Radical Catholics)—2 (3); Pacifist Socialists—2 (4); Communist party—6 (5); Farmers— 1 (7). The strength of the coalition parties—the confessional parties and the Liberals—fell from 83 to 74 seats in the 150-seat Tweede Kamer (second chamber or lower house) of the Dutch Staten-Generaal (parliament). For the first time since 1965, the opposition Labor party became the largest in the house.

New Cabinet installed. Barend W. Biesheuvel, leader of the Anti-Revolutionary party and a former deputy premier, was sworn in July 6 as premier of a new right-of-center coalition government. Agreement had reportedly been reached June 22 by the parties in the Steenkamp talks on a 23-point government program which placed priority on housing. The 16-member Cabinet was composed of six members of the Catholic People's party, three members of the Anti-Revolutionary party, two members of the Christian Historical Union, three Liberals and two members of DS '70. The government parties controlled 82 seats in the Tweede Kamer. The new Cabinet; premier— Biesheuvel; 1st deputy premier and finance minister—Roelof J. Nelissen; 2nd deputy premier and home affairs minister—Willem J. Geertsema; foreign affairs—W. K. Norbert Schmelzer; economic affairs—Hendrik Langman; defense—Hans J. de Koster; agriculture and fisheries—Pierre J. Lardinois; justice—Andreas A. M. Van Agt; health and environment—Lodewijk B. J. Stuyt; aid to developing countries—Cees Boertien; social affairs—Jaap Boersma; housing and planning—Berend J. Udink; education—Chris Van Veen; culture—Piet J. Engels; transportation and waterways—Willem Drees Jr.; and scientific research—Maurits L. de Brauw.

Budget designed to halt inflation. An austere 1972 budget designed to halt inflation was introduced by Finance Minister Nelissen Sept. 21. Expenditures were estimated at 37.8 billion guilders (about $11 billion), with a deficit of 3.9 billion guilders (about $1 billion). The 1971 deficit totaled $576 million. In an effort to reduce the 1972 deficit, Nelissen announced an increase of the surcharge on income and other taxes from 3% to 5%, a rise in the price of gasoline, and the introduction of excise duties on soft drinks. He also said the government would aim for a reduction in the $2.9 billion allotted for education.

See also ATOMIC ENERGY [13]; DRUG USE & ADDICTION [9]; EUROPEAN ECONOMIC COMMUNITY [1]; INTERNATIONAL BANK FOR RECONSTRUCTION & DEVELOPMENT; INTERNATIONAL MONETARY DEVELOPMENTS [2, 4, 10, 13]; JAPAN [10]; NETHERLANDS ANTILLES; PAKISTAN [35, 39]; ROMAN CATHOLIC CHURCH [1]

NETHERLANDS ANTILLES—The government was forced to resign following parliamentary failure to approve a bill increasing taxes, it was reported Jan. 1. Half of parliament's 22 members opposed the increase, which would have provided the government with the $12.5 million necessary to balance the national budget. A new Cabinet under Premier Ronchi Isa was approved Feb. 12 by Gov. Bernhard Leito, but Isa resigned after six months and was replaced June 5 by former Education Minister Ora Beaujon.

Independence study set up. Gov. Leito, official representative of the Netherlands on the island of Curacao, appointed a special commission to study the issue of independence and other relations between the Netherlands and its semi-autonomous colonies, the six Antilles islands and Surinam, it was announced Dec. 18. Parallel commissions were also to be set up in Surinam and the Netherlands. The Netherlands had provided a large amount of financial security to Surinam and the islands. Both also had become associate members of the European Common Market when the Netherlands joined, opening the European market for goods and materials from the Dutch Caribbean.

NEWSPAPERS—Libel protection expanded. The Supreme Court, in three rulings Feb. 24 and a fourth June 7, broadened the protection of the press against libel suits by public officials or by private individuals in cases of news accounts of matters of public interest. Each of the four opinions affirmed that malice must be proved in such cases. The Feb. 24 rulings held that the press could report charges of criminal behavior by politicians even though the charges were old, untrue or not related to the subject's public life. In those rulings the court: voided a $20,000 award against the Concord (N.H.) Monitor and the North American Newspaper Alliance given in a suit by 1960 Senate candidate Alphone Ray; reversed a $22,000 award to Mayor Leonard Damron of Crystal City, Fla. against the Ocala (Fla.) Star-Banner; and held that Time Magazine was not guilty of malice in reporting charges of police brutality against Capt. Frank Pape of Chicago without labeling the charges as alleged. In the June 7 ruling, the court overturned a $200,000 award won by George A. Rosenbloom, a Philadelphia magazine distributor, in a suit brought against Metromedia, Inc. The majority opinion, written by Justice Brennan, held that constitutional protection should be extended to communication involving matters of public concern, "without regard to whether the persons involved are famous or anonymous."

Agnew on media 'paranoia.' Vice President Spiro T. Agnew offered another critical assessment of the news media June 1, in a speech to radio station owners affiliated with the Mutual Broadcasting System, who were meeting in the Bahamas. Agnew said the media had reacted to the "constructive" criticism offered by himself and others in the previous 18 months with a "frenzy about intimidation and repression." But "attempts to portray the government as anxious to control or suppress the news media," he said, would "backfire" and compound the "credibility problem" faced by the media. What the criticism amounted to, Agnew said, was "to call on the free press of this country ... to police itself against excesses that on occasion have been so blatant they have undermined the confidence of the public in the credibility of the news media as well as the credibility of the government."

See also BUSINESS [8]; CANADA [23]; CHILE [10]; COMMUNIST CHINA-U.S. DETENTE [4]; CRIME [18]; GREECE [14]; PENTAGON PAPERS; PERU; PULITZER PRIZES; SPAIN [6-7]; URUGUAY [2]

NEWTON, HUEY—*See* BLACK MILITANTS [15-16]
NEW YORK STOCK EXCHANGE (NYSE)—*See* BUSINESS [10]; STOCK MARKET

NEW ZEALAND—**Budget presented.** The government presented to Parliament June 10 the budget for fiscal year 1972. Total government expenditures were estimated at $NZ1.918 billion ($2.148 billion), a 10.5% increase over the previous fiscal year. The budget envisaged a deficit, before borrowing, of $NZ62 million, compared with an actual deficit of $NZ81 million the previous year. The government also canceled the 10% income tax surcharge imposed in October 1970, authorized citizens traveling abroad to take up to $NZ600 in foreign currency each month, and raised pensions for married couples. An economic growth rate of 4.5% was predicted.

See also ATOMIC ENERGY [11]; EUROPEAN ECONOMIC COMMUNITY [14]; GREAT BRITAIN [9]; INDOCHINA WAR [61]; MALAYSIA; SOUTH PACIFIC FORUM

NICARAGUA—**Priest expelled.** The Rev. Jose Antonio Salines, a Spanish Jesuit priest, was ordered out of the country within 24 hours, it was reported Jan. 24. Salines was charged with inciting disorder among students at a Nicaraguan university. Students occupied two universities in Managua Jan. 20 and clashed with police. Government sources charged that the student occupations had been led by Spanish priests.

Congress dissolved. The Congress voted its own dissolution Aug. 31, a measure that effectively transferred President Anastasio Somoza Debayle until April 1972 when a new constitutional convention would meet to alter the country's constitution. Opposition groups criticized the measure, saying that it was a manuever designed to facilitate re-election of the president, prohibited under the present constitution. Somoza, 46, had succeeded his brother, father, grandfather and great-grandfather as president of Nicaragua.

See also HIJACKING [10]

NIGER—*See* AFRICA

NIGERIA—New budget announced. In a radio broadcast March 31, Maj. Gen. Yakubu Gowon, the Nigerian head of state, outlined the country's budget for 1971-72. He said the three most serious problems affecting the economy were "the deteriorating foreign exchange situation and the continued unfavorable balance of payments," unemployment "in the war-affected areas in particular" and inflation and a cost-of-living rise caused by trade restrictions and profiteering. In a move to lift the import restrictions brought on by the civil war which ended in January 1970, Gowon said the government would no longer require import licenses except for a few items such as rice, wheat, tobacco and some types of beverage. Gowon announced plans to introduce a decimal currency in January 1973 and said the country was continuing to lay the "necessary solid economic and social foundations" for the planned return to civilian rule in 1976.

Oil prices increased. The government April 22 reached an agreement with Western oil companies on an increase in the posted price of Nigerian crude oil from $2.36 a barrel to $3.21 a barrel. The accord, announced in Lagos and dated from March 20, chiefly affected Shell-BP (British Petroleum). It included a 2½% escalation clause to cover inflation and an annual increase of 5¢ a barrel beginning in January 1973. In a related development, the government said April 22 that Safrap, a subsidiary of the French state-owned company Elf-Erap, was to resume operations, with Nigeria taking an immediate 35% participating interest. The company had been idle since the beginning of the civil war.

Finance minister resigns. Lagos Radio announced June 17 that Gen. Gowon had accepted the resignation of Chief Obafemi Awolowo as minister of finance. The report said that Gowon had accepted Awolowo's decision with "the greatest regret and reluctance" and that Awolowo was stepping down for reasons of health.

See also AFRICA; COMMUNIST CHINA-U.S. DETENTE [3]; HEALTH [1]; MIDDLE EAST [37]

NIXON DOCTRINE—*See* FOREIGN POLICY

NIXON, RICHARD MILHOUS—State of the Union Message. President Nixon delivered before a joint session of Congress Jan. 22 his second State of the Union Message, in which he outlined proposals for a $16 billion annual sharing of federal revenues with state and local governments (*see* STATE & LOCAL GOVERNMENTS [1-9]), and for a sweeping revision of the cabinet departments—a reduction from 12 to eight (*see* GOVERNMENT REORGANIZATION). Major emphasis was also put on welfare reform, environmental cleanup, expansion of park lands and open spaces and a health program, including a $100 million campaign to find a cure for cancer (*see* MEDICINE). The address dealt only with domestic issues. The President announced he would submit a separate report later to the Congress and the nation on foreign policy (*see* FOREIGN POLICY). In his address, the President said "America has been going through a long nightmare of war and division, of crime and inflation" and was now "ready for the lift of a driving dream." He urged Congress to adopt his program and open "the way to a new American Revolution—a peaceful revolution in which power was turned back to the people—in which government at all levels was refreshed and renewed, and made truly responsive." Nixon said his program would be presented in the context of an expansionary budget (*see* BUDGET).

[2] Nixon's message was greeted with a mixed reception by Congressional leaders Jan. 22. Top Republicans warmly embraced the President's proposals and the Democratic leadership expressed mild approval coupled with cautious optimism. Many Congressmen said they would withhold judgment of the message until they had seen the specifics of the President's broad proposals.

[3] Visits planned. White House Press Secretary Ronald L. Ziegler announced Aug. 30 that President Nixon would visit Canada in the spring of 1972 and "would like to go to Japan." No specific dates were set for the visits. The Japanese trip had not yet been resolved as a firm commitment. The visits were seen as a move by the Nixon Administration to conciliate the two allies most severely affected by the President's new economic policy (*see* ECONOMY, U.S. [8]; TARIFFS & WORLD TRADE [8-10]). It was announced simultaneously in Washington and Moscow Oct. 12 that Nixon would visit the Soviet Union "in the latter part of May 1972" for discussions with Soviet leaders on "all major issues, with a view toward improving ... bilateral relations and enhancing the prospects of world peace." Nixon said that the trip had no connection with his scheduled trip to Peking (*see* COMMUNIST CHINA-U.S. DETENTE [6-10]). He said that he would be accompanied on the trip to Moscow by Henry A. Kissinger, his adviser on national security affairs, and by Secretary of State William P. Rogers. It was time for a summit meeting, Nixon said, because, in "significant areas" like biological weapons (*see* DISARMAMENT), agreements to prevent nuclear accidents and improve the Washington-Moscow "hot line" (*see* DEFENSE [8]) and in the preliminary Berlin settlement (*see* GERMAN CONSULTATIONS),there had been progress toward better relations between the two nations.

Appointments & Resignations

[4] Senate approves Connally. Former Gov. John B. Connally Jr. of Texas, President Nixon's nominee to be secretary of the treasury to replace David M. Kennedy (who resigned in December 1970), was approved Feb. 8 by the Senate without debate or opposition. Connally, originally nominated in 1970, was renominated by Nixon Jan. 25.

[5] Russell resigns. Undersecretary of the Interior Fred J. Russell suddenly resigned Feb. 17, reportedly at the request of the new secretary of the interior, Rogers C. B. Morton. Interior sources said that Russell had been fired because of his increasingly "strong pro-business" position. It was reported that as soon as Russell became acting secretary before Morton's appointment, he reversed various orders of the former secretary, Walter J. Hickel, connected with environmental protection and initiated some new ones that were said to weaken mine safety regulations.

[6] Chotiner leaves White House staff. Murray M. Chotiner, one of President Nixon's closest political aides since 1946, resigned March 4 as special counsel to the President to enter private law practice in Washington. Reports of his impending departure to prepare for Nixon's re-election campaign had circulated in January.

[7] Casey confirmed. The Senate approved by voice vote March 25 the nomination of William J. Casey, President Nixon's controversial choice as chairman of the Securities and Exchange Commission. Sen. William Proxmire (D, Wis.), who led the opposition to the nomination, was the lone dissenter of the eight senators present for a vote.

[8] Mexican-American nominated for treasurer. President Nixon Sept. 20 announced the nomination of Mrs. Romana A. Banuelos as treasurer of the U.S., to replace Dorothy Andrews, who had died July 3 (*see* OBITUARIES). Mrs. Banuelos, confirmed by the Senate Dec. 6 without opposition, was the highest ranking Mexican-American woman in the federal government. Congressional and public opposition to her nomination developed as a result of a raid by agents of the U.S. Immigration and Naturalization Service Oct. 5 on a Gardena, Calif. food processing plant owned and directed by Mrs. Banuelos. The agents arrested 36 illegal Mexican immigrants working at the plant. Mrs. Banuelos denied knowing that her firm employed the immigrants. (Federal law did not require employers to check out the residence status of employees or prohibit employment of illegal entrants.)

[9] Stein replaces McCracken. Paul W. McCracken, one of the chief architects behind the Administration's first economic "game plan" that was based on a policy of gradualism to retard economic growth as a means of slowing inflation, resigned Nov. 24, effective Jan. 1, 1972, as chairman of the President's Council of Economic Advisors (CEA). President Nixon named Herbert Stein, a CEA member since the beginning of his Administration, as McCracken's successor. McCracken said he planned to return to an economics professorship at the University of Michigan.

[10] Packard resigns. The White House announced Dec. 11 that David Packard was resigning his post as deputy secretary of defense after nearly three years as the second highest official in the Defense Department. Packard said his resignation, effective Dec. 13, was for "strictly personal reasons." The White House emphasized that Packard was not leaving because of policy differences with the Administration or with his superior, Defense Secretary Melvin R. Laird. Packard announced Dec. 14 that he was returning as chairman of the board of Hewlett-Packard, a Palo Alto, Calif.-based electronic instruments concern of which he was a co-founder.

See also ABORTION; AGING; AGNEW, SPIRO THEODORE; AGRICULTURE [4-6, 12]; ALGERIA; ATOMIC ENERGY [4, 16-17]; AUSTRALIA [8-9, 12]; AVIATION [11]; BLACK MILITANTS [10]; BRAZIL; BUDGET; BUSINESS [3, 7]; CANADA [26]; CHEMICAL & BIOLOGICAL WARFARE; CHURCHES [11]; CIVIL RIGHTS [1, 12, 14-15, 21, 27]; COMMUNISM, INTERNATIONAL; COMMUNIST CHINA-U.S. DETENTE [1, 5-11, 13]; CONGRESS [1]; CONSUMER AFFAIRS [2, 4-5, 13]; CRIME [2, 5]; DEFENSE [11]; DISARMAMENT; DISASTERS; DISTRICT OF COLUMBIA; DRAFT & WAR PROTEST [12, 25]; DRUG USE & ADDICTION [1, 5, 7, 14]; EARTHQUAKES; ECONOMY, U.S. [4-6, 8, 13, 16, 25, 27-28]; EDUCATION [12]; ELECTIONS [9]; ENERGY; ENVIRONMENT; EUROPEAN SECURITY; FEDERAL BUREAU OF INVESTIGATION [10]; FOREIGN AID; FOREIGN POLICY; GOVERNMENT REORGANIZATION; HEALTH CARE; HOUSING; HUNGER; INDIANS, AMERICAN; INDOCHINA WAR [1, 58-60, 62, 68, 73]; INTERNATIONAL MONETARY DEVELOPMENTS [1, 9, 14, 17-18]; JAPAN [10], KOREA, SOUTH; LABOR [1, 3-4, 8, 10]; LATIN AMERICA; MEDICINE; MICRONESIA; MIDDLE EAST [22, 32]; MILITARY [12-13]; MOTION PICTURES; NORTH ATLANTIC TREATY ORGANIZATION; OIL; PAKISTAN [37]; PENTAGON PAPERS [2, 9, 12, 17]; POLITICS [2-4, 8, 12]; POLLUTION [3, 5, 12]; POSTAL SERVICE, U.S.; POVERTY; PRISONS [6]; PUBLIC LAND; PUERTO RICO; RACIAL & MINORITY UNREST [1]; RAILROADS; RHODESIA; SCIENCE; SECURITY, U.S.; SELECTIVE SERVICE SYSTEM [5]; SHIPS & SHIPPING; STATE & LOCAL GOVERNMENTS [1-9]; STORMS; SUPREME COURT; TARIFFS & WORLD TRADE [3-4, 8, 12]; TAXES; UNEMPLOYMENT; UNITED NATIONS [8]; VOTING RIGHTS; WAR CRIMES [4]; WELFARE; YOUTH

NOBEL PRIZES—The 1971 Nobel Prizes, their value increased to approximately $90,000 each, were awarded Oct. 14-Nov. 2 by the Swedish Royal Academy of Science in six fields—peace, medicine, economics, literature, physics and chemistry. The winners:

Peace. West German Chancellor Willy Brandt was awarded the Nobel Peace Prize for 1971 Oct. 20 for his promotion of East-West peace initiatives. Brandt was the unanimous choice of the five-member Nobel Committee of the Norwegian Parliament. Singled out among Brandt's achievements as foreign minister since 1966 and chancellor since 1969 were the signing of the treaty to prevent the spread of nuclear weapons, the West German peace treaties with Poland and the Soviet Union and "efforts to obtain for West Berlin the fundamental human rights of personal security and full freedom of movement." His efforts to expand the European Economic Community were also cited. (Brandt had lived in Norway as a refugee from Nazism.)

Literature. The 1971 Nobel Prize for Literature was won Oct. 21 by the Chilean poet and statesman Pablo Neruda. Neruda, 67, the Chilean ambassador to France, was believed to have been considered for the award for years but excluded because of his radical political views. Neruda, a Communist, had published more than 300 works in 81 languages during the last half-century.

Medicine. Dr. Earl W. Sutherland, 55, professor of physiology at Vanderbilt University, won the 1971 Nobel Prize in Physiology or Medicine Oct. 14 for his work with hormones. Sutherland was the 43rd American to be cited by the Royal Caroline Institute since the awarding of the medicine prize began in 1901. It was the first time in 10 years that the prize had not been shared. Sutherland's research, begun 25 years ago, helped explain the general mode of action of hormones and the mechanism by which they exert control over metabolic activities throughout the body.

Physics. Dr. Dennis Gabor, 71, was awarded the 1971 Nobel Prize for Physics Nov. 2 for inventing holography, a three-dimensional imagery system. A staff scientist for the Columbia Broadcasting System and professor emeritus of the Imperial College of Science and Technology in London, Gabor developed the system beginning in 1948 using a laser beam to emit a concentrated beam of light to produce a three-dimensional image. Gabor, Hungarian-born, was a naturalized Briton.

Chemistry. The 1971 Nobel Prize for Chemistry was awarded Nov. 2 to Prof. Gerhard Herzberg, 66, of the National Research Council of Canada in Ottawa for his research in molecular structure, particularly with fragments of molecules known as free radicals, which are highly reactive and combine easily with other molecules. Herzberg's laboratory was cited as the foremost center for molecular spectroscopy in the world.

Economics. The third Alfred Nobel Memorial Prize in Economic Science was awarded Oct. 15 to Simon Kuznets, 70, a retired Harvard professor who developed the use of the Gross National Product as a means of measuring economic output.

NOISE—*See* AVIATION [2]; ENVIRONMENT
NOMINATIONS—*See* NIXON, RICHARD MILHOUS [4, 7-8]; RACIAL & MINORITY UNREST [2]

NORTH ATLANTIC TREATY ORGANIZATION (NATO)—Allies pledge spending boost.

The 10 members of NATO's Eurogroup announced Dec. 7 after a one-day meeting in Brussels that they were increasing their national defense budgets in 1972 by over $1 billion. The funds were added to a similar amount pledged in 1970 for air-raid shelters and improved communications. In revealing the group's decision, British Defense Minister Lord Carrington told newsmen: "Those who criticize European efforts sometimes are inclined to do so without all the facts," adding that European countries provided 90% of the ground forces, 75% of the air forces and 80% of the naval forces at NATO's disposal. Carrington provided a list of military equipment that would be purchased by Eurogroup members in fiscal 1972 as a result of the new appropriations.

Documents recovered. A Norwegian Defense Ministry spokesman said July 1 that top-secret documents belonging to NATO had been recovered after being sold by mistake at an army base in Oslo. The papers, some of them describing Norway's air defense installations, had apparently been left in a surplus cabinet when the Defense Ministry moved its headquarters in 1970. They were sold to Tord Boerke, a businessman, for $4.50 during an auction at the Gardermoen army base. When Boerke discovered the error, he returned the papers and signed a pledge of silence, the spokesman said.

See also AGNEW, SPIRO THEODORE; ARMAMENTS, INTERNATIONAL; CANADA [20]; CYPRUS; DEFENSE [4] ESPIONAGE; EUROPEAN SECURITY; GERMANY, WEST [3]; MALTA; NORWAY; PORTUGAL; VIETNAM, NORTH

NORTHERN IRELAND (ULSTER)—The communal fighting between Catholics and Protestants, which had erupted in 1969, continued throughout 1971. By Dec. 29, continuing violence had resulted in the death of 173 persons in 1971, bringing the toll since 1969 to 202 persons. A conflict between right-wing members of the ruling Protestant Unionist party, who wanted more extreme measures to be taken against terrorists, and the British government, which refused to accede to such measures, resulted March 20 in the resignation of Northern Ireland Prime Minister James Chichester-Clark and his replacement March 23 by Brian Faulkner [4]. The government's adoption Aug. 9 of a policy of interning suspected political terrorists without trial resulted in the worst fighting in Northern Ireland in 50 years [8-9]. The government and British soldiers were also accused of torturing and brainwashing internees [10]. Ireland's continued protests over events and policies in Northern Ireland and its continued insistence on a voice in Northern Ireland affairs led to tri-partite talks in England Sept. 27-28 between the prime ministers of Britain, Ireland and Northern Ireland; but no solution to Ulster's problems was achieved in the talks.

[2]   11 die in Belfast riots. At least 11 persons were killed in a new outbreak of clashes Feb. 3-9 between armed Roman Catholic extremists and British soldiers in the Catholic area of Belfast. Ulster officials and British army officers blamed the outbreaks on the "provisionals" of the outlawed Irish Republican Army. (The provisionals were nationalists who split in 1970 from the leftist leadership of the IRA "officials" and who advocated unification by force of Northern Ireland with the Republic of Ireland.) The upsurge in violence began Feb. 3 as Roman Catholics used submachine guns and threw bombs, grenades, stones and bottles at British troops during an arms search in the Clonard district of west Belfast. (British troops had not previously entered the Clonard district, considered a "harbor" of leaders of the provisionals.) The soldiers, retaliating mainly with water cannon and rubber bullets, also returned fire six times. Seven soldiers were injured and more than 60 people arrested. The violence continued Feb. 5 and intensified Feb. 6 when four civilians and one soldier were killed in a street battle. Gun battles raged in the Ardoyne and Crumlin districts in Belfast Feb. 7, while in Londonderry rockthrowing rioters also battled British troops. The same day, bombs exploded in the towns of Newry, Kileen and Carrickmore, near the border with the Irish Republic.

[3]   New security measures. Prime Minister James Chichester-Clark March 2 announced new security measures against IRA terrorists. The measures included the dispatch to Northern Ireland of an extra battalion of British troops, raising the number there to about 8,000; maintenance of a permanent military presence in "riotous and subversive" IRA enclaves; "hot pursuit" of terrorists who engaged in armed violence; and the cordoning of areas to prevent terrorists from fleeing. The new measures came amid continuing violence in Belfast during the end of February and in early March. The violence included the murder of three British soldiers.

[4]   Faulkner elected prime minister. Development Minister Brian Faulkner, a Protestant moderate, was elected March 23 as the sixth prime minister of Northern Ireland, replacing Chichester-Clark, who resigned March 20 in a bitter political dispute over tactics against Roman Catholic terrorists. (Militant Protestants had demanded a tougher security policy and Britain had refused to accede to the demands. Chichester-Clark had flown to London March 16 for talks with British Home Secretary Reginald Maulding. Chichester-Clark announced March 18 that Britain would send 1,300 more troops to Northern Ireland, but would not accede to Protestant demands that Catholic guerrillas be interned without trial. Chichester-Clark was reportedly angry over what he considered lack of British support.) Faulkner, by a 26-4 vote, defeated his hard-line opponent, William Craig, for leadership of the ruling Protestant Unionist party. Faulkner immediately pledged to restore confidence in Northern Ireland through a vigorous law and order campaign. He called for greater coordination between the British army and the provincial police—the Royal Ulster Constabulary (RUC)—to combat terrorism; but he ruled out repressive measures, pledged "early talks with all shades of opinion" and promised that the civil rights "program for progress" would be "energetically continued."

[5] Cabinet shuffled. Faulkner March 25 shuffled the Cabinet in order to establish what he called a "broadly based government." His major appointments were seen as an effort to heal the breach between the feuding left and right wings of the Unionist party. Faulkner said he would retain the post of minister of home affairs himself and would concentrate on security. He announced that he would establish "a small but high-powered" branch for the coordination of security. The Cabinet changes: Harry West, a Protestant hardliner, was appointed minister of agriculture; David Bleakley, a member of the opposition nonsectarian Labor party, was named minister of community relations; Roy Bradford, former minister of commerce, was named minister of development; John Taylor was named minister of state at the Ministry of Development; Robin Bailie was appointed minister of commerce; and Captain John Brooke was named chief whip and minister of state at the Ministry of Finance.

[6] Wave of terrorist attacks. Large-scale terrorist attacks that resulted in several deaths and numerous injuries occurred in the Belfast area from April through early June. Some observers thought the IRA had embarked on a new policy designed to provoke British soldiers to retaliate against civilians. (Prime Minister Faulkner disclosed May 25 that British troops had been authorized to shoot on sight anyone "acting suspiciously." He explained the next day that the order applied to circumstances in which firearms or explosives might be used.) Bomb attacks took place in the Belfast area: April 16 in the downtown area, injuring four persons; May 21 in a British ex-servicemen's hall in the suburb of Suffolk, injuring about 30 persons; May 24 in a pub in a Protestant area of the city, injuring 18; May 25 in a police station in a Roman Catholic area, killing one British soldier and injuring 20 persons; June 5-6 in various areas of the city. Unknown gunmen ambushed a British army vehicle May 15 in downtown Belfast, killing one civilian and wounding two soldiers and two civilians. A British soldier was killed and two injured in the ambush of an army night patrol in Belfast May 21-22.

[7] Opposition to boycott Parliament. The Social Democratic and Labor party (SDLP), the main opposition party, announced July 16 that it would boycott the Northern Ireland legislature, scheduled to resume in October, and would create an alternative assembly. In addition to the six SDLP parliamentary members, others of the 13-member opposition said they would boycott Parliament. The SDLP decision followed the refusal of the British government to order an independent public inquiry into the killing of two Catholic civilians by British troops in Londonderry. (George Desmont Beattie and Seamus Cusack were shot July 8 during the fifth consecutive day of rioting in Londonderry, in a riot during which rioters threw bombs and troops used live ammunition in retaliation. Catholics asserted that the two were unarmed and demanded a public inquiry. British Minister of State for Defense Lord Balneil rejected the demand and supported the army's conclusion that the two had been armed with a rifle and nail bomb and were ready to use their arms. The deaths generated more rioting July 9-10.)

[8] Internment sparks new riots. A new wave of rioting erupted Aug. 9 after the government invoked emergency powers of preventive detention and internment to crush the IRA. Under the internment order, which was authorized under the Special Powers Act applicable only to Northern Ireland, people could be arrested and held for 48 hours—longer if necessary—without being charged. Within 14 days, Prime Minister Faulkner would review the case of every arrested person and decide whether to intern the suspect for an indefinite period. (It was reported Nov. 11 that 980 persons had been seized under the act. Of those, 299 were interned, 103 detained and 443 released without detention.) At the same time as he announced the invocation of internment, Faulkner announced a ban on religious parades in Northern Ireland for six months. The prime minister said his decision on internment was made after consultation in London Aug. 5 with British Prime Minister Edward Heath and other officials. (As a result of the meeting, the British government announced Aug. 6 that it would increase British troops in Ulster to 12,000 in anticipation of increased violence threatened by the IRA.)

[9] Rioting erupted in Belfast, Londonderry, Newry and Fermanagh immediately before the first dawn arrests Aug. 9, hours before Faulkner's announcement. The fighting was reported to be the heaviest in Northern Ireland in 50 years. In Belfast, Catholics set fire to buildings, hurled nail and gasoline bombs and exchanged gunfire with British troops. Twelve buses were hijacked. The city came to a standstill as pubs and restaurants shut down and public transportation ceased to run. Protestant families in predominantly Catholic neighborhoods and Catholic families in Protestant areas fled their homes. Protestants set fire to their own homes to insure that Catholics would not occupy them. In Londonderry, four British soldiers were shot and six were injured by thrown objects. Catholics attacked a police station with machine guns and gasoline bombs. At least 21 persons were killed in the fighting by Aug. 11. In response to the rioting, all police leaves were canceled and 4,000 part-time army reservists were called into full-time duty Aug. 9. The British government sent 550 additional soldiers to Northern Ireland Aug. 11. The fighting waned Aug. 12, with only sporadic clashes occurring through Aug. 18. The two IRA factions apparently split again over a dispute on tactics to be taken against internment. The provisionals Aug. 14 said that, unless British troops ceased their "repressive measures" in support of the Ulster government, they would launch a bombing campaign in major British cities against government installations and big business companies (see GREAT BRITAIN [4]). The officials said later the same day that they would not support reprisals and instead called for an end to confrontation with the troops and for a campaign of civil disobedience. In response to the officials' call, Catholics staged a general strike Aug. 16. The campaign of civil disobedience also included a rent strike, refusal to pay income and real estate taxes and the resignation of public officials to protest internment. (More than 30 leading Londonderry Catholics resigned from public office Aug. 19. More than 100 opposition local councillors decided in Tyrone county Aug. 21 to withdraw from their elected seats and to urge all other non-Unionist councillors—about 300—to support civil disobedience. They also urged the establishment of a "rival" Ulster government.)

[10] *Torture probes.* Reports that internees had been subjected to torture and brainwashing to make them reveal information resulted in the announcement by British Prime Minister Heath Oct. 18 that he had ordered an official inquiry into the charges. The allegations would be examined by an already existing committee (established to examine whether there were adequate grounds to intern suspected terrorists), headed by Northern Ireland ombudsman Sir Edmund Compton. The Compton commission Nov. 16 presented a controversial report, concluding that internees had been subjected to "physical ill-treatment" but not to "cruelty or brutality." The commission dismissed the charges of brainwashing, third-degree methods, savage beating and torture. They said that prisoners had been hooded, subjected to "continuous and monotonous noise," fed only bread and water, deprived of sleep and forced to stand against a wall for hours. The report drew sharp criticism from Catholics in Northern Ireland. (The Irish Republic government announced Nov. 30 that it would ask the European Commission on Human Rights to investigate charges of alleged brutality against internees in Northern Ireland.)

[11] *Relations with Ireland.* The Aug. 12 call by Irish Republic Prime Minister John Lynch for replacement of the Ulster government by an

administration in which the Catholics would share power with Protestants caused a bitter political dispute to erupt between the governments of the two Irelands. Lynch also urged all Irishmen to take united political action to topple the Ulster government, which he charged had "consistently repressed" the Catholics. Following up on that statement, Lynch Aug. 19 warned that he would support the policy of civil disobedience in Northern Ireland unless Britain abandoned "attempting military solutions" in that country. Lynch also agreed to attend a summit meeting of "all the interested parties designed to promote the economic, social and political well-being of all the Irish peoples" if military action were replaced by a policy of finding solution by "political means." British Prime Minister Heath immediately said that Lynch's statement was "unacceptable in its attempts to interfere in the affairs of the United Kingdom and can in no way contribute to the solution of the problems in Northern Ireland." Lynch and Heath met Sept. 6-7, but their meeting was deadlocked over internment, the campaign to smash the IRA, constitutional changes for Ulster and Lynch's demand that he participate in direct negotiations involving Northern Ireland. Lynch suggested at the meeting an immediate conference of the Irish, British and Ulster governments, as well as representatives of the Ulster opposition, which was largely Catholic. Heath rejected the proposal and instead announced that British officials would meet with representatives of the Ulster government, the province's political opposition and members of the Protestant and Catholic communities in Northern Ireland. At the same time, Heath proposed a three-way conference of himself, Lynch and Prime Minister Faulkner. The SDLP rejected the proposed meeting unless internment was halted and the Ulster government was suspended. The Northern Ireland Labor party and the Ulster Trades Union Council, which represented Catholic and Protestant workers, accepted the invitation to join the talks.

[12]   The three prime ministers ended two days of talks Sept. 28 with an appeal for "political reconciliation" in Northern Ireland and a condemnation of "any form of violence as an instrument of political pressure." They vowed "to seek to bring violence and internment and all other emergency measures to an end without delay." They failed, however, to agree on new measures to halt the escalating violence or to reach a joint position regarding internment. The three agreed to hold another meeting (see [15]).

[13]   *Government resignations.* Desmond Boal and John McQuade, members of Parliament, resigned from the Unionist party Sept. 13 and 14, respectively, to protest Prime Minister Faulkner's decision to attend the tripartite talks with Heath and Lynch. Minister of Community Relations Bleakley resigned his post Sept. 26 to protest one-party rule, internment and what he considered inadequate political initiatives. (Bleakley would have had to resign Oct. 1 because he did not hold a parliamentary seat and was consequently limited to a six-month Cabinet term.) Faulkner Oct. 26 appointed William McIvor, a Protestant Unionist member of Parliament, as minister of community relations to replace Bleakley. James Craige and Councillor William Spence, the chairman of the Belfast transport department, resigned from the Unionist party Sept. 30 to protest what they considered the government's inadequate antiterrorist policy.

[14]   *Catholic named to Cabinet.* Dr. Gerard B. Newe, a Catholic layman with no previous political experience, was appointed Oct. 27 as minister of state in the Prime Minister's Office. He was the first Catholic ever to be named to Northern Ireland's Cabinet. Shortly after his appointment, Newe said he would work "to create as soon as possible the circumstances" in which internment could be ended. (In an earlier attempt to win support from Catholics, the government Oct. 26 had presented a document suggesting the possibilities of proportional representation in future elections, enlargement of the House of Commons by 20-30 seats from the current 52 and a proportionate increase in the Senate. The document also rejected as "fundamentally unrealistic" a system that would allot Cabinet posts in proportion to a party's parliamentary

strength. It reaffirmed that Northern Ireland must remain an integral part of the United Kingdom.)

[15] Border measures announced. British Undersecretary of the Home Office Lord Windlesham announced Sept. 23 that the army would strengthen mobile patrols and air reconnaissance at the border between Northern Ireland and the Irish Republic in an effort to halt the influx of guerrillas into Ulster. In further developments along the border: following the second meeting of Prime Ministers Heath, Lynch and Faulkner, Britain announced its decision to send 1,750 more men into Northern Ireland "to strengthen control of the border and to follow up more rapidly the action against terrorists"; British army sources Oct. 12 confirmed that troops had been authorized to shoot across the border into the Irish Republic at armed men if their lives were endangered; British troops Oct. 13 began blowing up more than 50 secondary roads between Ulster and the Irish Republic to halt the flow of arms and guerrillas across the border; Ireland Oct. 14 arrested four IRA guerrillas (the first arrested in Ireland since the outbreak of violence in Ulster) after the guerrillas had recrossed into Ireland following the ambush of a British squad destroying secondary roads in Northern Ireland.

[16] Reserve police to be armed. The government yielded Nov. 3 to police demands—backed up by the threat of a strike—and authorized the arming of the 1,000 members of the RUC reserve force. The police strike threat followed mounting terrorist attacks on policemen in previous weeks. The Northern Ireland Police Authority announced Nov. 12 that the RUC would be given machine guns when needed to protect police stations that had recently come under terrorist attack. (The RUC had been disarmed on the basis of a recommendation by a British commission in 1969, but even regular RUC forces were now often permitted to carry revolvers in trouble spots.)

[17] Wilson proposes unification plan. British opposition Labor party leader Harold Wilson Nov. 25 proposed a radical new police plan for Ulster that would lead to the creation of a united Ireland. At the same time, he backed the British Conservative government's security policy, saying that there would have to be a "military solution" to crush the IRA terrorist campaign before a political solution could be implemented. Wilson opened his political proposals with a call for interparty talks in Britain and Northern Ireland that would lead to creation of a constitutional commission representing the major parties of Britain, Northern Ireland and the Irish Republic. The commission would examine the possibility of creating a united Ireland, whose draft constitution would be ratified by the three parliaments and would go into effect 15 years from the date of agreement, "provided violence as a political weapon has come to an end." Wilson also proposed membership for the new united Ireland in the Commonwealth of Nations; maintenance of a British military force in Northern Ireland during the 15-year transitional period and possibly for five to 10 years after unification; an end to internment without trial as soon as the security situation improved; a guarantee of minority rights in both northern and southern Ireland; representation of minority views in the Ulster government during the 15-year transitional period; and alignment of social service provisions of the new Ireland, involving health, education and social security, with British policies. Wilson's suggestions were welcomed as constructive by Prime Ministers Heath and Lynch, but rejected Nov. 26 by Prime Minister Faulkner, who reiterated the determination of Ulster's Protestant majority to remain an integral part of the United Kingdom.

[18] 15 die in bomb blast. Fifteen Roman Catholic civilians, including two children, were killed Dec. 4 when a bomb exploded in a Belfast bar. It was the highest toll for a single terrorist incident in the more than two years of the province's unrest. Police hypothesized that the bar might have been used as a transfer point when the bomb exploded accidentally. Both factions of the IRA disclaimed responsibility. Catholics were said to be convinced the incident was the work of an extremist terrorist group.

[19]   **Rightist senator killed.** Sen. John Barnhill, a right-wing member of the Unionist party, was shot to death and his house was bombed by IRA terrorists Dec. 12. The official faction of the IRA Dec. 13 claimed responsibility for the killing and explosion, but said it had intended only to destroy the house in "reprisal for the destruction of working-class homes throughout the province" by the British army. The statement said that Barnhill had been shot after he attacked two IRA members who had asked him and his wife to evacuate the house because they planned to bomb it. It was Northern Ireland's first political assassination since 1922. Prime Minister Faulkner Dec. 13 accused the Irish Republic of offering a "safe haven" to the men responsible for the killing. Shortly afterward, Prime Minister Lynch condemned the killing but denied that his government had sheltered the terrorists. (A bomb set by the IRA Dec. 30 destroyed the County Down country home of Maj. Ivan Neill, the speaker of Ulster's parliament in County Down. No one was hurt in the blast.)

   See also EUROPEAN ECONOMIC COMMUNITY [14]; IRELAND

NORWAY—Premier resigns over EEC press leak. Premier Per Borten announced the resignation of his five-year-old coalition government March 2 in the wake of a political scandal involving his disclosure of a confidential report on Norway's negotiations with the European Economic Community (EEC). He told the Storting (parliament) he accepted full responsibility for the unauthorized disclosure. The resignation climaxed a growing political storm that began Feb. 15 when Borten divulged the contents of a confidential report from Norway's ambassador in Brussels to Arne Haugestad, leader of an organization called People's Resistance Movement against the EEC. Haugestad disclosed the contents to newsmen. Extracts of the report published Feb. 19 by the Oslo newspaper Dagbladet said a senior EEC official had warned that Norway's demands for special privileges for agriculture and fisheries would prevent its admission to the market. Borten, in a public statement Feb. 25, denied reports that he had leaked the report. However, he withdrew the denial Feb. 27 and admitted that he had been "guilty of an indiscretion" in making the information available to Haugestad.

   Opposition political leaders charged that Borten had leaked the report to obstruct Norway's bid for EEC membership. Borten, leader of the agrarian Center party, had opposed Norway's membership because of potential dislocation of Norway's agriculture and fisheries industries. He ultimately supported the nation's application, according to reports, in order to preserve the government coalition of four non-Socialist parties—Center, Conservative, Liberal and Christian People's. The other coalition partners, particularly the Conservatives, had favored EEC membership. Moreover, the Storting had voted overwhelmingly in favor of negotiations.

   Minority Labor government sworn in. Labor party leader Trygve M. Bratteli was sworn in March 17 as premier of a minority government after attempts to reconstruct a four-party non-Socialist coalition cabinet failed. Talks between the four non-Socialist parties on reconstruction of their coalition under the leadership of Kjell Bondevik, head of the Christian People's party, collapsed March 9 because former Premier Borten's Center party refused to change its opposition to negotiations with the EEC. Bratteli said the following day that his government would pursue the EEC talks. Premier Bratteli's Labor party held only 74 of the 150 seats in the Storting.

   The new cabinet: premier—Bratteli; minister of foreign affairs—Andreas Cappelen; finance—Ragnar Christiansen; municipal affairs—Odvar Nordli; social affairs—Odd Hojdahl; industry—Finn Lied; commerce—Per Kleppe; education and ecclesiastic affairs—Bjartmar Gjerde; fishing—Knut Hoem; agriculture—Thorstein Treholt; defense—Alf Jakob Fostervoll; justice—Oddvar Berrfjord; communications—Reiulf Steen; wages and prices—Olav Gjaerevoll; family and consumer affairs—Inger Louise Valle.

   Bratteli outlined his government's program to the Storting March 18. The major policy departure was an announcement that Norway would take steps to establish diplomatic relations with North Vietnam. Norway would be the first member of the North Atlantic Treaty Organization (NATO) to establish full diplomatic ties with Hanoi. Bratteli said the decision would not affect Norway's participation in NATO. In other policy decisions: The government would support negotiations for Norwegian membership in the EEC. It would also press for a European security conference. Oil exploration in the Norwegian sector of the North Sea would be "placed under state management and a complete measure of state control." (The former government had purchased 51% interest in Norsk Hydro in the autumn of 1970. Norsk Hydro held a 7% interest in the division of Phillips Petroleum Co. that had made promising oil finds in the North Sea in 1970.) Retirement age would be lowered to 67, effective Jan. 1, 1973. Regional committees would be created to implement government decentralization.

Oil acreage returned. In compliance with government regulations, North Sea offshore oil prospectors Sept. 1 returned 25% of the acreage granted them in 78 sectors by the Norwegian government in 1965. Another 25% of the claims had to be returned after nine years. Only one well—worked by a consortium headed by the Phillips Petroleum Company—was in production after years of competitive exploration among the leading oil firms.

See also CONSERVATION; EUROPEAN ECONOMIC COMMUNITY [1, 17]; INTERNATIONAL MONETARY DEVELOPMENTS [10]; PAKISTAN [35, 39]; SCANDINAVIA; VIETNAM, NORTH

NUCLEAR NON-PROLIFERATION TREATY—*See* DISARMAMENT
NURSING HOMES—*See* HEALTH CARE

OBITUARIES—Among noteworthy people who died in 1971:

Col. Rudolf Abel, 68, Soviet master spy who headed espionage network in U.S. while posing as artist in New York City, arrested in 1957 and sentenced to 30-year jail term, exchanged for U-2 pilot Francis Gary Powers in 1962; Nov. 15 in Moscow of lung cancer.

Dean Acheson, 78, U.S. secretary of state (1949-53), under secretary of Treasury (1933), assistant secretary and undersecretary of state (1945-47), one of the leading architects of post-World War II policy of containment through U.S. military strength and political alliances, helped formulate Truman Doctrine, Marshall Plan, North Atlantic Treaty Organization, and policies leading to United Nations intervention in Korea and arming of West Germany, adviser to Presidents Kennedy, Johnson and Nixon, awarded Pulitzer Prize for book *Present at the Creation: My Years in the State Department;* ct. 12 in Silver Springs, Md.

Joe Adonis (Giuseppe Antonio Doto), 69, Mafia and underworld chief reputed to be East Coast gambling king, returned to native Italy in 1956 to escape possible jail sentence and deportation, indicted for contempt for refusing to answer questions of Kefauver Senate Crime Investigating Subcommittee; Nov. 26 in Ancona, Italy of heart failure.

Gregory Peter Cardinal Agagianian, 75, native of the Soviet Union and member of the Sacred College of Cardinals since 1946, twice considered a leading candidate for the papacy, headed mission activities throughout world as prefect for the Vatican's Congregation for the Propagation for the Faith; May 16 in Rome.

James E. Allen Jr., 60, U.S. commissioner of education (1969-70) dismissed after 13 months in office after dispute with Nixon Administration over school desegregation and Vietnam war policies, served as New York commissioner of education (1955-69), promoted innovative, urban-oriented reforms, mediated New York City teachers' strike (1968); Oct. 16 with his wife Florence and eight other persons in the crash of a two-engine plane near Peach Springs, Ariz.

Louis (Satchmo) Armstrong, 71, jazz trumpeter who reshaped the development of American music by moving black folk music of New Orleans into mainstream of the musical world; his abrasive voice and innovational solos were trademarks of career begun in 1918 in small clubs in South, popularized scat-singing (wordless singing) in recording "Heebie Jeebies"; July 6 in New York. President Nixon eulogized him as

"One of the architects of the American art form..."

Dr. Georgi N. Babakin, 56, Soviet space scientist who designed vehicles for unmanned spacecraft and played a key role in the Lunokod program, awarded highest Soviet civilian title—Hero of Socialist Labor; reported from Moscow Aug. 3.

Ivan Bashev. *See* BULGARIA

Rabbi Israel S. Ben-Meir, 60, leader of Israel's National Religious party, served as deputy minister of welfare (1953-58) and deputy minister of the interior (1963-69); April 4 in Jerusalem after a heart attack.

Adolf A. Berle Jr., 76, one of the original members of President Franklin D. Roosevelt's "brain trust," held numerous government positions including assistant secretary of state (1938-44), ambassador to Brazil (1945-46) and chairman of the Presidential task force on Latin America (1961), chairman of New York's Liberal Party (1947-55), law professor at Columbia University (1927-64); March 17 in New York.

Peretz (Fritz) Bernstein, 80, president of Israel's Liberal party and minister of commerce, industry and supplies in Israel's provisional 1948 government; March 21 in Jerusalem.

Hugo LaFayette Black, 85, Supreme Court justice from 1935 till one week before his death, U.S. Senator (1925-35), known during his years on court for his absolute defense of rights as literally defined in the Bill of Rights and the Constitution; Sept. 25 at the Bethesda Naval Hospital of inflammation of the arteries and a stroke suffered Sept. 19.

Michael Cardinal Browne, 83, former master-general of the Roman Catholic Dominican order, became a cardinal in 1962, was the major traditionalist force during the 1962-65 Vatican Ecumenical Council; April 30 in Rome.

Dr. Ralph J. Bunche, 67, United Nations under-secretary general for special political affairs (1955-70), won 1950 Nobel Peace Prize for negotiating 1949 armistice between Israel and Arab states, directed U.N. peacekeeping efforts in the Suez (1956), Congo (1960) and Cyprus (1964), served in U.S. State Department (1944-47) prior to joining U.N. (1947); Dec. 9 in New York City.

Jaime Cardinal de Barros Camara, 76, archbishop of Rio de Janeiro since 1946, as a strict conservative and anti-Communist believed in following dictates of the Pope; Feb. 18 of a collapsed lung in Sao Paulo, Brazil.

Bennett Cerf, 73, publisher, editor, columnist, lecturer, president of Modern Library since 1925, founder (1927), president (1927-65) and chairman (1965-70) of Random House, won landmark court battle (1933) lifting censorship ban on James Joyce's *Ulysses,* publisher of numerous literary figures including William Faulkner, Eugene O'Neill and Franz Kafka, compiled and edited more than 20 anthologies of humor, regular panelist on *What's My Line?* quiz show since 1952; Aug. 28 in New York City.

Gabrielle (Coco) Chanel, 87, one of the most influential fashion designers of the 20th century; Broadway musical *Coco* (1969) was based on her life; Jan. 10 in Paris.

Lord Constantine, 69, first black man to sit in Britain's House of Lords, High Commissioner for Trinidad and Tobago to London (1962), led renowned West Indian cricket team to victory over Britain in 1928; July 1 in London.

Gladys Cooper, 82, British actress whose career spanned more than 60 years from roles as an English pin-up girl in 1906 to Broadway and film parts that included *Relative Values* (1951) and *The Chalk Garden* (1955), played opposite David Niven on *The Rogues* television show; Nov. 17 in London.

Rev. Roland de Vaux, 67, French archaeologist who directed transcribing, editing and publication of the Dead Sea Scrolls, director of the Ecole Biblique et Archeologique de Jerusalem (1945-65); Sept. 10 in Jerusalem after an appendectomy.

Thomas E. Dewey, 68, three-term governor of New York (1942-54), twice Republican nominee for president (1944, 1948); March 16 in Bal Harbour, Fla.

Roy O. Disney, 78, behind-the-scenes financial consultant to younger brother Walt Disney, chief executive officer of entertainment empire following brother's death in 1966, instrumental in development of Walt Disney World near Orlando, Fla.—world's largest entertainment center; Dec. 20 in Burbank, Calif. of a cerebral hemhorrage.

Thomas J. Dodd, 64, former Democratic senator from Connecticut who was censured by the Senate in 1967 for diverting campaign funds for his personal use, elected a representative in 1952 and won Senate seat in 1958 after unsuccessful bid in 1956, failed to gain re-election as an independent in 1970, known for his anti-Communist stand and for his promotion of stricter gun control legislation; May 24 in Old Lyme, Conn.

William J. Donaldson Jr., 78, member and superintendent of the House of Representatives press gallery for more than half a century until 1960 retirement; July 13 in Washington.

Tilla Durieux, 90, "grand old lady of the German theater," pioneered in the Eliza Doolittle role in 1913 production of Shaw's *Pygmalion,* after exile from Germany in 1933 returned to Berlin at age 71 to begin new stage career, awarded West German Legion of Merit (1970); Feb. 21.

Francois (Papa Doc) Duvalier. *See* HAITI

Dr. Rolla E. Dyer, 84, director of the National Institutes of Health (1942-50), expert on diseases caused by rickettsia—organisms categorized between bacteria and viruses, awarded 1948 Lasker Award; June 2 in Atlanta.

Cliff Edwards, 76, film voice of Jiminy Cricket in 1940 film, *Pinocchio,* where he sang "When You Wish Upon a Star," Oscar-winning song that sold more than 74 million records, appeared in more than 100 films; July 17 in Hollywood, Calif.

Walter Brian Emery, 67, prominent Egyptologist whose diggings in Egypt spanned 40 years, including eight expeditions searching for the lost tomb of Imhotep; March 11 in Cairo after a stroke.

Dr. Herbert McLean Evans, 88, discovered vitamin E in 1922, headed Institute of Experimental Biology at Berkeley (1930-52); March 6 in Berkeley, Calif.

Joseph Frazer, 79, co-founder of automobile manufacturing Kaiser-Frazer Corp., pioneered in developing low-priced cars and Jeep of World War II; Aug. 7 in Newport, R.I. of cancer.

Francesco Giunta, 84, secretary general of the Fascist party of Italy during reign of Benito Mussolini (1923), vice president of the chamber of deputies, commander of Mussolini's street fighters and enforcers; June 8 in Rome after a long illness.

Harry F. Guggenheim, 80, who with his wife founded Long Island's Newsday (1940) and turned it into the largest suburban daily newspaper in the U.S.; served as ambassador to Cuba (1929-33); Jan. 22 in Sands Point, N.Y.

Sir Tyrone Guthrie, 70, director, author, producer, noted for his adherence to technical perfection in his nearly 50-year association with theater, chancellor of Queens University in Belfast, director of Scottish National Theater (1926); May 15 in Dublin, Ireland.

Camille Gutt, 86, first managing director and chairman of the board of the International Monetary Fund (1946-51), served in several posts in post-World War II Belgium including minister of finance, national defense and economic affairs, prominent spokesman for Belgian resistance movement against Nazis; June 7 in Brussels.

John Marshall Harlan, 72, 89th Justice of the U.S. Supreme Court (1955-1971), considered a conservative who preached judicial restraint and strict interpretation of the Constitution, sought to "de-emotionalize" his decisions citing precedent and statutory language rather than social norms, voted against reapportionment of state legislatures and against warning criminal suspects of their rights in "Miranda" ruling, but authored numerous "liberal" decisions including one in 1955 to hasten school desegregation process; Dec. 29 in Washington of cancer. (President

Nixon issued a statement from Key Biscayne, Fla. in which he called Harlan "one of the 20th century's giants on the Supreme Court.)

Adm. Thomas C. Hart, 94, commander in chief of the Pacific Fleet during Japanese strike at Pearl Harbor, superintendent of Annapolis (1931-34), appointed Republican senator from Connecticut in 1945 to fill a vacancy; July 4 in Sharon, Conn.

Van Hefflin, 60, veteran Hollywood stage and film actor whose films included *Shane, Airport,* and a role in *Johnny Eager* (1942) that won him an Academy Award as best supporting actor; July 23 in Hollywood after suffering a heart attack June 6 while swimming.

Sir Alan P. (A.P.) Herbert, 81, British humorist and satirist often called "the wittiest man of his time, author of more than 60 books and 17 musicals, member of Parliament (1935-50) who helped pass radical reform of Britain's divorce laws (1937); Nov. 11 in London.

Bourke B. Hickenlooper, 75, GOP senator from Iowa (1945-69) and influential member of Senate Foreign Relations Committee, chairman of Joint Congressional Committee on Atomic Energy, co-sponsored Atomic Energy Act of 1954, authored amendment to 1962 foreign aid bill denying aid to countries expropriating U.S.-owned properties, governor of Iowa (1943-45); Sept. 4 at Shelter Island, New York apparently after a heart attack.

Dr. Bernardo Alberto Houssay, 84, Argentine physiologist who shared 1947 Nobel Prize in medicine and physiology for discovery of role of pituitary hormones in sugar metabolism; Sept. 21 in Buenos Aires.

Chuck Hughes. See FOOTBALL

Robert Tyre (Bobby) Jones Jr., 69, only golf champion ever to win the grand slam—British Open, U.S. Open, British Amateur and U.S. Amateur—in one year (1930), won 13 major tournaments between 1923-30; Dec. 18 in Atlanta.

Dorothy Andrews Kabis, 54, fifth woman treasurer of the U.S. (since 1969), active in Republican party circles and president of the National Federation of Republican Women;

July 3 in Washington, D.C. after a heart attack.

Dr. Paul Karrer, 82, Swiss chemist who won 1937 Nobel Prize in chemistry for pioneering research in vitamins; June 18 in Zurich.

Mathilde Kchessinska, 99, Russia's most famous ballerina and first international dancing star, one of only two dancers to hold title prima ballerina assoluta in history of Russian ballet, mistress of Nicholas II before he became czar; Dec. 7 in Paris.

Nikita S. Khrushchev. *See separate entry.*

Patriarch Kiril, 70, elected first patriarch of modern Bulgarian Orthodox Church in 1953 amid charges that the move was a violation of orthodox canonical law; March 7 in Sofia, Yugoslavia.

Pope Kyrollos VI, 69, Coptic Orthodox Patriarch enthroned in 1959, initiated sweeping reforms of Coptic Orthodox Church and its monasteries; March 9 in Cairo after suffering third heart attack in six months.

Nathan F. Leopold, 66, convicted with Richard Loeb of Chicago's sensational "crime of the century," senseless murder of 14-year-old Bobby Franks in 1924, paroled in 1958 after 33½ years in prison; Aug. 28 in San Juan, Puerto Rico.

Rabbi Yehuda Leib Levin, 76, spiritual leader of Moscow's Jewish community, defended Soviet Union against anti-semitism charges and criticized Jewish militants in U.S. in sensitive position as chief rabbi; Nov. 17 in Moscow.

Ted Lewis, 80, nightclub entertainer and singer, popularized such songs as "Me and My Shadow," "When My Baby Smiles at Me" and "On the Sunny Side of the Street"; Aug. 25 in New York City.

Sigmund Wilhelm Walther List, 91, Nazi field marshal known for his "blitzkrieg" tactics that played a major role in four Nazi campaigns and broke France's Maginot Line (1940), relieved of command by Hitler after refusing orders to squander troops on Russian front; Aug. 17 in Garmisch-Partenkirchen, Germany.

Charles (Sonny) Liston, 38, world heavyweight boxing champion who defeated 33 of 34 opponents before knocking out Floyd Patterson Sept. 25, 1962 to capture crown; lost title in controversial two-minute bout with Muhammad Ali, then known as Cassius Clay, in 1964; found dead Jan. 5 in Las Vegas, Nev. of lung congestion.

Harold Lloyd, 77, comedian whose portrayals of a bumbling, bespectacled youth in impossible situations made him an international silent film star and one of the highest paid screen actors in Hollywood in the 1920s; March 8 in Hollywood of cancer.

Gyorgy Lukacs, 86, one of the most influential Marxist philosophers of the century, his theories defending humanism and progressivism in Communist letters, extending Marx's ideas of alienation in industrial society and repudiating political control over artists had major impact on European Communism from its beginnings to the 1940's, served as minister of education under Bela Kun regime in Hungary in 1919 and as minister of culture under Premier Imre Nagy in 1956, expelled from Communist party for supporting Hungarian uprising, authored more than 30 books including controversial *History and Class Consciousness,* which he later repudiated, befriended Thomas Mann who modeled character after him in *The Magic Mountain;* June 4 in Budapest, Hungary.

Jim Morrison, 27, controversial rock superstar who soared to prominence in 1967 with The Doors rock group; his suggestive lyrics and frenzied movements culminated in 1969 conviction for indecent exposure during a Miami concert; July 3 in Paris apparently of heart failure.

Dr. K. M. Munshi, 83, founder and president of India's largest educational and cultural organization, Bharatiya Vidya Bhavan, minister of food and agriculture (1950-52), named governor of Uttar Pradesh in 1952, as a member of the Assembly helped frame country's constitution; Feb. 8 in Bombay.

Audie Murphy, 46, World War II serviceman whose exploits made him the most honored hero of the war, began film career in 1948 portraying characters similar to himself including the starring role in *To Hell and Back,* the story of his life; May 28 near Roanoke, Va. in a plane crash.

Ogden Nash, 68, American poet and lyricist noted for his light and pungent verse including the classic "Candy is dandy/but liquor is quicker," most of his reputation was based on his lengthy lines and strange words, often misspelled, used to create rhyme schemes; May 19 in Baltimore.

Reinhold Niebuhr, 78, Protestant theologian and political philosopher whose complex philosophy based on the fallibility of man, the absurdity of human pretensions and the Biblical precepts of love molded 20th century intellectual thought, professor at New York's Union Theological Seminary since 1928 (served as vice president from 1955), writings in more than 20 books including *The Nature and Destiny of Man,* and *Christianity and Crisis,* a journal he founded in 1941; June 1 in Stockbridge, Mass.

Gerald P. Nye, 78, Republican senator from North Dakota (1925-44), one of the nation's foremost isolationists, opposed U.S. entry into World War II and helped draft 1936 Neutrality Act barring aid to belligerents, used his seat on Public Lands Committee to expose high-level corruption in Teapot Dome oil scandals; July 17 in Washington.

Lord Oaksey, 90, presiding judge of the international war crimes tribunal at Nuremburg (1945-46) who sentenced 11 Nazi war criminals to death; Aug. 28 in London.

Gen. Emmett (Rosy) O'Donnell, 65, led numerous World War II operations, headed Air Materiel Command after Japanese surrender, commanded 15th Air Force, deputy chief of staff for personnel (1953-59), commanded Pacific Air Forces (1959-64); Dec. 26 in McLean, Va. after a heart attack.

W i n s t o n L. P r o u t y. *See* CONGRESS [13]

Lt. Gen. Lewis B. (Chesty) Puller, 73, Marine Corps Commander who, in 37 years of service, won every medal of valor awarded by U.S. except Medal of Honor, stirred national dispute following Korean War by criticizing training camp laxity in Corps; Oct. 11 in Hampton, Va.

Matyas Rakosi, 78, premier of Hungary (1952-56) and twice first secretary of the Communist central committee, exiled in 1956 to the Soviet Union; Feb. 4 in Budapest.

Michael Romanoff, 79, Hollywood personality and restaurateur, built career as self-styled Russian prince; Sept. 1 in Hollywood after a heart attack.

Sen. Richard Brevard Russell, 73, president pro tem of Senate, Democratic Georgia Senator since 1933, chairman of Senate Armed Services Committee (1951-69), chairman of Senate Appropriations Committee since 1969; Jan. 21 of a respiratory illness at Walter Reed Army Medical Center in Washington, D.C.

David Sarnoff, 80, broadcasting pioneer who helped found the electronics communications industry, president (1930) and chairman (1947-69) of the RCA Corp., guided development of NBC radio and television since 1926; Dec. 12 in New York City. (New York Gov. Nelson A. Rockefeller delivered the principal eulogy at the funeral Dec. 15.)

Lord Simonds (Gavin Turnbull Simonds), 89, speaker of Britain's House of Lords (1951-54); June 28 in London.

Franz Stangl, 63, commandant of the Nazi concentration camps at Treblinka and Sobobor in Poland in 1942-43, convicted of supervising murder of 400,000 Jews; June 28 in Dusseldorf, West Germany in prison serving an indefinite sentence.

Igor Stravinsky, 88, most influential composer of the 20th century noted for his radical avant-grade innovations, composed more than 100 works including ballets such as *The Firebird* (1910), *Petrushka* (1911) and the highly controversial *The Rite of Spring* (1913), embraced serialism in 1953 and produced about a dozen 12-tone works including *Agon* (1957) and the *Huxley Variations* (1965); April 6 in New York of heart failure; buried in the cemetery of San Michele, Venice.

Igor Tamm, 75, Nobel Prize-winning Soviet physicist (1958), specialized in quantam mechanics and nuclear energy theory, considered the "father of the Soviet hydrogen bomb," fought against the rehabilitation of Stalin and Stalinist methods; April 12 in Moscow.

Wasfi Tell. *See* JORDAN [11]

Metropolitan John Theodorovich, 83, spiritual leader of the 200,000-member Ukranian Orthodox Church of the U.S.; May 3 in Philadelphia.

Dr. Arne W. K. Tiselius, 69, Swedish biochemist who won the 1948 Nobel Prize for Chemistry for his research on serum proteins; Oct. 29 reported from London.

Sir John Tovey, 85, British admiral who commanded the pursuit and destruction of the German battleship Bismarck in 1941; Jan. 12 in Madeira.

William V. S. Tubman. *See* LIBERIA

Alexander T. Tvardovsky, 61, winner of numerous Soviet prizes for poetry, editor of literary journal Novy Mir who published Alexander I. Solzhenitsyn's anti-Stalinist novel *One Day in the Life of Ivan Denisovich;* regarded by many as the foremost defender of literary freedom for Soviet writers; Dec. 18 in Moscow of a stroke.

Joseph M. Valachi, 67, first gangster to break a blood oath and detail the inner workings of the crime organization known as the Mafia and "Cosa Nostra," identified 317 members of the organization in televised hearings before a Senate committee; April 3 at La Tuna Federal Correctional Institution in El Paso, Texas.

Jean Vilar, 59, French actor and director who shaped theater in home country for a generation, directed state-owned Theatre National Populaire; May 28 in Sete, France.

Dr. Ramon Villeda Morales, 62, president of Honduras (1957-63) overthrown in army coup and fled to Costa Rica, president of national committee of the Liberal party (1949-56), served as Honduran ambassador to U.S. and to Organization of American States, and delegate to

United Nations; Oct. 9 in New York City.

Nathan Voloshen, 73, lawyer and lobbyist convicted of conspiring to use office of House Speaker John W. McCormack to defraud agencies of federal government (1970); Aug. 23 in New York.

Mikhail K. Yangel, 60, chief designer of the Soviet Union's space program since 1966, while his work

was shrouded in secrecy; Oct. 25 after a heart attack reported from Moscow.

Whitney M. Young Jr, 49, executive director, National Urban League; March 11 in Lagos, Nigeria, while swimming. Medical examiners in Lagos listed cause of death as subarachnoid (brain) hemorrhage, but a New York autopsy said death was caused by drowning.

OBSCENITY & PORNOGRAPHY—Lewd mail laws voided. The Supreme Court, in a unanimous ruling Jan. 14, declared unconstitutional two federal laws that allowed the Post Office to refuse to handle the mail of businesses selling pornographic material. A spokesman for the Post Office said, however, that the effect of the ruling was "negligible" since the laws had only been used in recent years in the two test cases before the court. The laws allowed the Post Office to impound incoming mail to a mail-order house pending a hearing determining whether the business dealt in pornographic material. In an opinion by Justice William J. Brennan Jr., the court said the laws violated principles laid down in a movie censorship ruling in 1965. Brennan objected that the laws placed the burden on the business to prove its material was not obscene and that there was no provision for quick judicial review of the issue. The ruling involved two mail-order businesses, the Mailbox in Los Angeles and the Book Bin in Atlanta.

Maryland movie ban allowed. The Supreme Court, deadlocked over the question of whether the Swedish film *I Am Curious (Yellow)* was obscene, upheld the right of the Maryland Board of Censors to ban the film March 8. The effect of the 4-4 ruling was to affirm a lower court ruling in favor of the ban, but the decision would have no weight as a precedent. Justice William O. Douglas abstained from the case, as he had done in other cases involving Grove Press, which had published an excerpt of his book in its Evergreen Review. Noting that Douglas customarily ruled against censorship in any form, a lawyer for Grove Press said the decision meant that "anyone but Grove Press can distribute a movie like this" since Douglas would be free to participate in other obscenity cases.

Obscenity laws backed. The Supreme Court upheld two federal laws May 3 making it a crime to send obscene materials through the mails and forbidding the importation of pornographic material from abroad. Justice Byron R. White, writing both majority opinions, conceded a "developing sentiment that adults should have complete freedom" in regard to obscenity, but he said changes in the laws should be made by the legislatures rather than the courts. In the ruling on the use of the mails, the court reversed a decision by Judge Harry Preferson of Los Angeles and reinstated an indictment against Norman G. Reidel, charged with mailing a pornographic booklet to persons who answered his advertisement in an underground newspaper. Justices Douglas and Hugo L. Black dissented. The second ruling, with dissents by Justices Douglas, Black and Thurgood Marshall, reversed a Los Angeles federal court ruling and upheld a seizure by customs agents of obscene photographs brought from Europe by Milton Luros.

See also CRIME [3]

OCEANS—*See* ENVIRONMENT
OCCUPATIONAL SAFETY & HEALTH ACT—*See* POLLUTION [20]
OFFICE OF ECONOMIC OPPORTUNITY (OEO)—*See* INDIANS, AMERICAN
OFFICE OF EMERGENCY PREPAREDNESS (OEP)—*See* ECONOMY, U.S. [11];
POVERTY; WELFARE
OFFICE OF MANAGEMENT AND BUDGET (OMB)—*See* CIVIL RIGHTS [15]

OIL—Teheran negotiations begin. The 10-member Organization of Petroleum Exporting Countries (OPEC) met with representatives of 17 Western oil companies in Teheran, Iran Jan. 12 and 21 to press new demands for unspecified higher payments. The OPEC had first aired its demands for higher payments at a joint meeting in Caracas, Venezuela Dec. 28, 1970. The conferees issued a manifesto that included a demand that the oil countries' average oil-income tax rate of 55% become standard and that all posted prices be raised to the highest level. (The posted prices normally were higher than the actual market prices and were used primarily to compute oil tax and royalty payments to host countries.) The OPEC members (Iran, Iraq, Saudi Arabia, Kuwait, Qatar, Abu Dhabi, Libya, Algeria, Indonesia and Venezuela) accounted for about 85% of the world's oil production outside the U.S. and Soviet Union.

In a memorandum submitted to the OPEC Jan. 16, a group of 15 oil firms, including 12 American companies, proposed to negotiate "simultaneously" with the 10 organization members to seek a single five-year "overall endurable settlement" of their demands. Previous oil contracts had been arranged between a company and a single nation. The Persian Gulf producers—Kuwait, Saudi Arabia, Iran, Iraq, Abu Dhabi and Qatar—sought a regional settlement in line with a resolution approved at the Caracas meeting. The memorandum of the 15 firms also expressed opposition to further dealings on an individual basis with Libya, which had attempted to increase its terms beyond those granted to the Persian Gulf producers.

Persian Gulf pact signed. Representatives of 23 Western oil companies signed an agreement in Teheran Feb. 14 to pay the six Persian Gulf members of the OPEC an additional $10 billion in revenue in the next five years. (The OPEC Feb. 4 had announced that Feb. 15 was the deadline for settlement of the pact. The announcement said that, if the deadline were not met, the organization would pass legislation to unilaterally raise prices.) The pact provided increased payments of more than $1.2 billion in 1971, rising to $3 billion in 1975. (The six countries' current level of oil income was $4.4 billion.) The Gulf States reportedly had demanded $1.4 billion in increased payments in 1971, rising to $11.8 billion in 1975. The new annual raises were to start June 1 and were to be repeated at the beginning of 1973, 1974 and 1975. The pact also included a fixed rate of 55% of the companies' net income, even if other oil producing nations were to gain higher rates, and an immediate boost of 35% a barrel in posted prices for crude oil at Persian Gulf tanker terminals.

Libyan accord signed. After nearly six weeks of negotiations in Tripoli, Libya, the Libyan government and some 25 Western oil companies signed a five-year agreement April 2 increasing the posted price of Libyan oil from $2.55 to $3.45. (The talks had begun Feb. 24. In a private meeting the same day, Algeria, Iraq and Saudi Arabia agreed to be represented in the negotiations by Libyan Deputy Premier Abdel Salem Jalloud.) In announcing the pact, Jalloud disclosed the following details: the $3.45 posted price included $3.20 as a permanent price plus 25¢ as variable freight premium; the companies had "responded to an increase in the tax rate from 50% to 55% with the pledge that they pay the difference in rates from 1965 to September 1970"; the companies agreed to an annual inflation allowance of 2.5% of the posted price per barrel plus 7¢; the companies "pledged to undertake exploration, drilling and other investments in the oil sector in a specific way and satisfactory manner until 1975." (The inflation allowance percentage plus 5¢ was to become effective from March 20, the date of the agreement. The remaining 2¢ increase was to be levied from the beginning of 1972 through 1975.)

Oil import quota raised. President Nixon Dec. 21 authorized a 100,000-barrel-a-day increase in the 1972 quota of oil imports for states east of the Rocky Mountains. The increase raised the total quota for the area to 1,550,000. (The 400,000-barrel-a-day quota for states west of the Rockies remained unchanged.) Two thirds of the increase was allocated to Canada, and the announcement said discussions were "proceeding" with Canada for an agreement to permit Canadian crude oil to enter the U.S. without qualitative curbs.

See also ALGERIA; CANADA [12, 25]; ENERGY; ENVIRONMENT; FIRES; GREAT BRITAIN [17]; GREECE [19]; INDIANS, AMERICAN; NIGERIA; NORWAY; POLLUTION [4-6, 11]; VENEZUELA

OKINAWA—*See* CHEMICAL & BIOLOGICAL WARFARE; JAPAN [4-6]
OLYMPIC GAMES—*See* MEXICO; SOUTH AFRICA [11]; SPORTS
OMAN—*See* UNITED NATIONS [1]
OMNIBUS CRIME CONTROL ACT OF 1970—*See* CRIME [2,16]; DRAFT & WAR PROTEST [5]
ONASSIS, ARISTOTLE—*See* GREECE [19]
OPERATION PUSH—*See* NEGROES
OPIUM—*See* DRUG USE & ADDICTION [5]
ORGANIZATION OF AFRICAN UNITY (OAU)—*See* AFRICA; MIDDLE EAST [37]; SOUTH AFRICA [12]
ORGANIZATION OF AMERICAN STATES (OAS)—*See* CHILE [19]; COLOMBIA; EL SALVADOR-HONDURAS CONFLICT; LATIN AMERICA; TERRITORIAL WATERS
ORGANIZATION OF SENEGAL RIVER STATES—*See* AFRICA
OSCARS—*See* MOTION PICTURES

PACHECO ARECO, JORGE—*See* URUGUAY [1-3, 5-6, 9-10, 12]

PACIFIC ISLANDS—A new constitution granting substantial self-government to the British-ruled Gilbert and Ellice Islands in the Pacific Ocean went into effect April 14. The constitution required the British resident commissioner, Sir John Field, to obtain the consent of an elected legislature in most matters other than defense and security, which remained under London's control. The islands were also removed from the authority of the British high commissioner in the Western Pacific, Sir Michael Gass, based on Guadalcanal Island, the administrative seat for the British Solomon Islands Protectorate.

PAKISTAN—Unrest between East and West Pakistan, simmering for years, erupted in March into civil war [5]. Fighting between government forces and the rebels (who established the country of Bangla Desh) was marked by violence and atrocities against civilians as well as military personnel. The fighting broadened Dec. 4 into war between India and Pakistan [15]. Indian superiority in the air between India and Pakistan [15]. Indian superiority in the air paved the way for Indian ground gains, and Pakistan Dec. 16-17 surrendered in East Pakistan [18]. The surrender was followed by harsh reprisals by rebels against Pakistani soldiers and Pakistani supporters [19]. Pakistan Dec. 17 accepted a cease-fire in West Pakistan [20], and India and Bangla Desh agreed upon an Indian exit plan from Bangla Desh Dec. 27 [21]. During the war, over 10 million refugees fled East Pakistan to India, causing a drain on India's resources for their support [32-35]. A repatriation plan for the refugees was agreed on Dec. 23 [36].
[2] **Assembly opening postponed.** President Agha Mohammad Yahya Khan March 1 announced the indefinite postponement of the opening of the country's first popularly elected national assembly. The Pakistan People's party (PPP), the leading party in West Pakistan, and other parties had said they would not attend the March 3 first meeting to begin drafting a charter to return Pakistan to civilian rule. (PPP leader Zulfikar Ali Bhutto Feb. 28 had threatened to call a general strike in West Pakistan if the assembly met without his party. The PPP wanted assurances that a regional autonomy plan demanded by Sheik Mujibur Rahman's Awami League—the chief political party in East Pakistan and the dominant party in the National Assembly—was negotiable to provide greater federal power.) Yahya March 5 announced that the assembly would open March 25, but the opening was again postponed March 22.

343

[3] *Strike called.* In response to the March 1 postponement and to an action the same day which turned over the civilian administrations in East Pakistan and the four provinces of West Pakistan to martial law authorities, Sheik Mujibur March 1 called a general strike. (Although Pakistan had been under martial law since 1969, the five provinces had retained their civilian administrations.) Violence erupted March 2 in the East Pakistani capital of Dacca as thousands of youths rampaged through the city paralyzed by the walkout. In the wake of the rioting, Dacca was placed under curfew. The strike ended March 6. It was reported that 172 persons had been killed and 358 injured in the strike disturbances in Dacca and other cities of the province. Sheik Mujibur called for a partial resumption of the strike March 7, to go into effect March 8. The new protests were to close all government offices, courts and schools and to refuse to pay revenue to the central government. Complying with Mujibur's order, High Court Chief Justice B. A. Sidiqui March 8 refused to swear in Gen. Tikka Khan as the newly appointed military governor of East Pakistan. The strike was further extended March 9 as East Pakistani government officials refused to work for the martial law authorities assigned by the central regime. East Pakistan took another step closer to total independence March 15 when Mujibur announced measures assuming administrative control over the province. The measures included suspending the collection of income taxes by the central government and barring the remission of customs and excise duties and sales taxes, normally sent to the Karachi regime. East Pakistanis throughout the province March 23 displayed the new flag of Bangla Desh (Bengali homeland) to mark the celebration of "resistance day"—opposition to the martial law imposition.

[4] *Consultations.* Yahya March 3 had invited the 12 leaders of parliamentary groups in the assembly to a meeting March 10 to discuss the constitutional issues in the dispute between East and West Pakistan. Mujibur rejected the invitation and the meeting failed to materialize. Mujibur March 7 also refused to attend the proposed March 25 assembly meeting, charging that he had not been consulted beforehand. He listed four conditions that had to be met before he attended the assembly meeting: return of government troops to their barracks; an inquiry into killings in East Pakistan during the strike demonstrations; an end to martial law; and the transference of power to the elected representatives of the people. Yahya and the leaders of all major political parties in West Pakistan except the PPP March 16 began talks with Mujibur on East Pakistan's demands for self-rule. The talks continued to March 25 (joined March 21 by Bhutto), but then broke down. However, the central government March 17 acceded to one of Mujibur's demands and announced that it would establish a commission to investigate the killings of East Pakistani civilians by army troops during the strike demonstrations. Mujibur rejected the proposal March 18, taking issue with the terms of reference of the projected investigative body which read: "To inquire into the circumstances which led to the calling out of the army in aid of civil powers in East Pakistan."

Civil War—Fighting

[5] **War breaks out.** With the breakdown in talks between East and West Pakistan, civil war erupted March 25 as troops of the central government launched widespread attacks in an attempt to crush East Pakistan's autonomy movement. The rebel radio March 26 announced the proclamation of an independent nation of Bangla Desh. Reports from neighboring India quoted the rebel station as having announced that a provisional government, headed by Maj. Jia Khan, described as commander of the forces of Bangla Desh, had been installed and would function under the direction of Mujibur, who reportedly had been arrested with other Awami League leaders. Exact accounts of the armed struggle were obscured by strict news censorship imposed by the Karachi regime; but dispatches from the rebel radio, India and other sources

reported massive killings of unarmed civilians and ill-equipped forces by heavily armed West Pakistani soldiers. While the government claimed that the uprising was crushed and that life was returning to normal in Dacca and other cities, rebel broadcasts told of continued heavy fighting throughout East Pakistan.

[6] March fighting. Heavy fighting erupted March 26 in Dacca and other major cities, including the port of Chittagong, Comilla, Sylhet, Jessore, Barisal, Rangpur and Kyulna. The West Pakistani army, reinforced to a total of 70,000 men, was arrayed against a force of East Pakistani policemen and a paramilitary organization known as the East Pakistani Rifles. The resisting rebels were lightly armed with rifles and pistols, while the government soldiers were equipped with heavy guns, tanks and planes. Reports from India said civilians were engaged in the fighting, using knives, clubs and scimitars. The rebels March 28 claimed the capture of government army barracks in Comilla, Jessore and Kyulna. An Indian report that day said that the rebels had taken the northern town of Rangpur. The stiffest rebel resistance was centered in Chittagong. In Dacca, army control was claimed March 27-30. Reports of the fighting there said that government troops had surrounded two areas of the city and then set buildings aflame. Soldiers reportedly fired indiscriminately on civilians, and about 5,000-7,000 civilians were reported killed in the area.

[7] April fighting. During the beginning of April, West Pakistani government troops virtually controlled all major cities, while rebel forces held great stretches of the countryside. Meanwile, West Pakistan continued to build its strength in East Pakistan, bringing in troop reinforcements by plane. India refused to allow the airlift to fly over its territory; and, as a result, many of the Pakistani aircraft were forced to fly around the subcontinent, making refueling stopovers in Ceylon. The Ceylonese, however, denied that they were assisting the airlift. Rebel troops were said to have captured Jessore, leveled after four days of fierce fighting, April 1. Pockets of resistance were reported in at least nine cities and towns. Pakistani planes carried out bombing raids on the pockets, virtually destroying Chittagong by sea, air and artillery bombardment. Pakistani troops opened a general, three-pronged offensive in the western part of the province April 8. There was bitter fighting, with government forces claiming military successes, but other reports saying that the rebels appeared to be gaining strength in the eastern part of the province. Rebels conceded April 9 that government forces had taken Jessore April 6, but said that guerrilla forces from the city were regrouping nearby. Pakistani army convoys April 10 moved out of major garrisons, including Jessore and Dacca, and headed for towns under rebel control. Three of the convoys were ambushed by rebels on roads leading to Rangpur, in the northern tip of the province. Karachi reported April 11 that two Indian army companies had moved into East Pakistan in support of the rebels, but had been wiped out by government forces April 10. Rebel resistance was reported April 13 to be collapsing in the face of advances by federal troops as they pushed west from Dacca into the countryside. Pakistan claimed April 14 that it had destroyed rebel resistance in the key town of Rajshani, 135 miles from Dacca. Heavy government bombing on the Bangla Desh capital of Chuadanga April 16 forced members of the new government to abandon the city and move to Meherpur on the Indian border. Rebel fighters also abandoned Meherpur April 18 as the government forces continued their offensive. India and Pakistan, from April 15, accused each other of attacking the other's territory along the frontier with East Pakistan. India accused Pakistan of firing into Indian territory, and Pakistan accused India of infiltrating East Pakistan.

[8] May fighting. Accusations continued between India and Pakistan during May. About 160 Indian and Pakistani troops were reported killed in clashes along the frontier May 24-25. India charged that Pakistani troops had carried out three assaults in the northeastern Indian state of Assam and in the territory of Maghlaya, but were repulsed by Indian troops. India also reported heavy shelling by Pakistani forces of Sutarkandi in south Assam May 23 and 24. Karachi radio reported May 26 that the Pakistani navy earlier in the week had intercepted and sunk two boats carrying arms and ammunition to East Pakistan from India. India was reported May 23 to be taking further precautions against a possible widening of the conflict with Pakistan. Among the Indian moves: air defenses were being strengthened at Calcutta airport; several hundred Indian troops were reported to have moved to within 50 yards of the border in the Jessore sector; and fortifications and dugouts were being built 100 yards from the frontier. Meanwhile, the Pakistanis were said to be massing in strength along the 620-mile northern Indian-East Pakistani border.

[9] June fighting. India June 20 imposed a month-long 8 p.m.-4 a.m. curfew along its 300-mile Maghalaya State border with Pakistan to prevent the infiltration of Pakistani spies. The curfew was to be enforced to a depth of three miles. (Several Indian border villages had been evacuated following reported attacks by Pakistani troops believed to have been pursuing East Pakistani guerrillas across the frontier.) Meanwhile, continued Pakistani military buildup and repression of East Pakistanis were described in a private report from Dacca made public June 12. According to the report, Pakistani troops were executing 10-20 people a day in the town of Barisal.

[10] July fighting. Continued rebel resistance was evidenced by reports July 5 that the insurgents had knocked out electrical power in Dacca and Comilla. Dacca had reportedly been blacked out since July 3, when the main transformer had been either destroyed or badly damaged. Comilla was said to have been without power for more than a week. Rebels July 19 stormed Dacca's three power plants and bombed them, knocking them out of operation. In another action in Dacca, rebels distributed handbills July 26 warning civilians to evacuate the city by Aug. 1 in preparation for an expected insurgent drive against the army. The leaflets were signed by the Mukti Bahini (Liberation Army). They advised residents to start moving from Dacca immediately and said vehicular traffic should be off the streets at night beginning July 28. Clashes between India and Pakistan also continued during July. Pakistan charged July 4 that Indian air and ground forces had attacked the East Pakistani town of Amarkhana July 3. India July 5 accused Pakistani troops of carrying out almost daily attacks against Indian territory from East Pakistan. Pakistan charged that Indian artillery July 20 shelled Comilla, killing a number of persons and wounding "many others." Another Indian shelling of Comilla July 26 killed five civilians and wounded 13, Pakistani officials charged July 27. (Indian Foreign Minister Swaran Singh had accused Pakistan July 20 of attempting to attribute the successes of the Mukti Bahini to Indian forces as an excuse to declare war on India.)

[11] August fighting. Rebel forces continued sporadic attacks against government soldiers and major installations in East Pakistan in August. A hotel in Dacca was struck by a bomb explosion Aug. 11, reportedly killing five persons and heavily damaging the building. A rebel threat to carry out attacks in Dacca to coincide with the 24th anniversary of Pakistan's independence Aug. 14-15 prompted government troops to conduct house-to-house searches in the city those two days to head off the expected raids. Rebel forces Aug. 20 attacked and set fire to a police station and another government building at Holhajang, 30 miles from Dacca. (A Pakistani government white paper Aug. 5 charged that Bangla Desh separatists had massacred 100,000 of their fellow countrymen in a "reign of terror unleashed by the Awami League." The report said that "unmentionable brutalities were committed with the active assistance of Indian armed infiltrators.")

[12] October fighting. Indian sources indicated Oct. 14 that India and Pakistan had been strengthening their military forces along the frontier in recent weeks. The sources indicated that the buildup was begun by Pakistan in September and that Indian troops had moved in response to the buildup. It was reported Oct. 20 that almost all infantry and armored divisions in West

Pakistan had been mobilized along the Indian border. Four or five divisions were said to have been strengthened along the East Pakistani border. India was reported to have an equal number of divisions along its side of the border. Each side charged the other with attempting to provoke a war. Pakistan warned India Oct. 19 that it would take "appropriate action" if Indian aircraft continued to violate Pakistani air space. Indian Defense Minister Jagjivam Ram Oct. 11 warned Pakistan that, if that country launched a surprise attack, India would extend the war into Pakistani territory. Ram said Oct. 17 that India would not withdraw from any Pakistani territory it occupied if war were to break out between the two countries. He added that India would not withdraw its forces from the border as long as the civil war remained unresolved. Indian Prime Minister Indira Gandhi declared Oct. 19 that India would reduce its border buildup on two conditions: that West Pakistani soldiers "stop their atrocities in Bangla Desh" and that Pakistan permit freely elected representatives (of the Awami League) in East Pakistan to assume office. Heavy clashes broke out along the border Oct. 23-26, with the heaviest fighting occurring Oct. 24-25 in the Kasba area of Comilla District. According to Karachi report, 579 Indians and Bangla Desh rebels were killed in the fighting. Pakistan denied Indian claims that the Kasba area was under rebel control. Fighting was also said Oct. 24 to have erupted between Indian and Pakistani forces in Kashmir, near the West Pakistan frontier.

[13] **November fighting.** Rebel activity in East Pakistan was on the increase during November, with the guerrillas concentrating on the assassination of political officials and others suspected of cooperating with federal government authorities, and on attacking ships in East Pakistani ports. Rebel bombs exploded at three educational institutions (believed by the rebels to be controlled by the army) and at other targets in Dacca Nov. 8. Despite the increase in rebel activity, however, the most serious fighting occurred between India and Pakistan along the border. It was reported Nov. 7 that Indian troops had penetrated into East Pakistan for the first time Oct. 30-Nov. 1 to silence Pakistani guns that had been shelling India's Tripura State. India Nov. 1 had described the incident as a "counteraction," but had not indicated that Indian troops had crossed the border. A government briefing Nov. 3 insisted that the Indians had not crossed into East Pakistan and had "strict orders" not to do so. India claimed Nov. 11 that its forces had killed 135 Pakistani troops in a clash inside Indian territory in the Shikapura area. Indian casualties were reported to be light. The fighting along the border appeared to have escalated to major proportions Nov. 21. Pakistan claimed that a force of 12 Indian divisions, numbering more than 100,000 men, had launched a four-pronged attack on East Pakistan Nov. 21. New Delhi officials denied that Indian troops had driven into East Pakistan, but indicated that Bangla Desh rebels had mounted a large offensive against Pakistani troops in the western part of the province. An American newspaper correspondent reported that Indians and rebels were carrying out joint operations, with the Indians playing a large, if not a dominant, role in the latest upsurge of fighting. The Indian government radio reported Nov. 22 that the rebels were concentrating in the Jessore area and were pushing the Pakistanis back. The fighting was also marked by Indian-Pakistani air clashes Nov. 22. (India claimed that its air force had shot down three of four Pakistani planes in a dogfight over Jessore District. Karachi reported the same incident as having caused the loss of two Pakistani planes and two Indian planes.)

[14] The fighting intensified at the end of November, with India acknowledging Nov. 24 that its troops had crossed the border into East Pakistan in "defensive actions" Nov. 21 and 24. Heavy fighting between Indian and Pakistani forces broke out in the northwestern section of East Pakistan Nov. 27 at the strategic town of Hilli and continued through Nov. 30. In fighting to the south, Indian and Bengali rebels were said to have seized small pieces of territories near Jessore, Comilla, Sylhet and west of Chittagong.

Pakistan claimed Nov. 30 that 2,000 Indians had been killed and 4,000 wounded in a week of fighting, with Pakistani losses placed at 30 killed and 100 wounded in the same period. The threat of heavier battle loomed Nov. 28 as India announced that its forces would follow a policy of hot pursuit. Defense Minister Ram said that Indian troops had been given permission to move as deep into Pakistan as the range of Pakistani guns shelling them—15-20 miles. A Defense Ministry spokesman Nov. 29 explained that Indian troops would cross the border whenever the integrity of that border or the life or property of Indian citizens was endangered and would remain in East Pakistan until the threat had been removed.

[15] **War breaks out with India.** The character of the fighting in Pakistan changed early in December as Indian Prime Minister Gandhi charged Dec. 3 that Pakistan had "launched a full-scale war against us" and that the Indian government had no other choice but "to put our country on a war footing." She charged that Pakistani planes that day had struck Indian air fields in the west at Amristar, Pathankot, Sringar, Avantipur, Utterlai, Jodhpur, Ambala and Agra. Pakistani ground forces, she charged, were shelling Indian defense positions at Sulemankhi, Khemkaran, Poonch and other sectors. The Indian parliament Dec. 4 approved emergency legislation giving the government sweeping powers, including the right to detain suspected subversives for up to two years. Pakistani President Yahya vowed Dec. 4 that his country's armed forces would "strike and destroy" the enemy in his own territory. Yahya made no formal declaration of war, but the Pakistani Government Gazette said "a state of war exists" between India and Pakistan. The president charged that India had "launched a full-scale war on us."

[16] The war between the two countries began in earnest Dec. 4 in the west and in Kashmir. An Indian report Dec. 4 said that small formations of Pakistani planes had bombed eight airfields in the west, causing minor damage, and that artillery had begun shelling Indian positions along the heavily defended Punjab State border. The first Pakistani ground action reported by New Delhi was a thrust across the cease-fire line in Kashmir near Poonch. Pakistan claimed gains in the Kashmir area Dec. 4-6 and also claimed victories in air battles in the west. In the first naval engagement of the conflict, the Indian navy Dec. 5 claimed that its forces had sunk two of Pakistan's five destroyers and a merchant ship anchored off Karachi. The report also claimed the probable sinking of a Pakistani submarine in the Bay of Bengal. Indian officials indicated Dec. 5 that they would no longer honor the Kashmir cease-fire and the truce line that had divided the states since the Indian subcontinent's partition in 1948, and would keep any part of the Pakistani-controlled area of Kashmir they could capture. Pakistani forces Dec. 7 launched a major drive in Kashmir, advancing 10 miles into Indian-held territory and claiming the capture of Chhamb and the destruction of a large number of tanks. India acknowledged that its Kashmir forces had retreated five miles to prepare positions after inflicting heavy casualties on the Pakistanis around Chhamb.

[17] Indian forces in East Pakistan scored a major victory Dec. 7 with the capture of Jessore, the site of a Pakistani divisional headquarters. The capture of the city virtually assured India's control of about half of East Pakistan. Shortly after Jessore had fallen, Indian Army Chief of Staff Gen. S. H. F. J. Manekshaw appealed to the 70,000 Pakistani troops in the province to "lay down your arms before it is too late." In addition to capturing Jessore, Indian troops Dec. 7 occupied Sylhet in the northeast and encircled Comilla in the south. In the first mention of the rebel role in the widening conflict, Indian Maj. Gen. J. F. R. Jacob, chief of staff of the Eastern Command, said Dec. 7 that the "Mukti Bahini are collaborating with our troops in all sectors wherever they are." Indian mastery of the air had paved the way for Indian ground gains in the province. An Indian spokesman Dec. 5 had announced that all but four Pakistani planes in use on the eastern front had been destroyed. India reported advances in five sectors of the western front Dec. 14. Indian Defense Minister

Ram said the same day that, in the first 10 days of fighting, Indian losses had totaled 1,978 killed, 5,025 wounded and 1,662 missing. Ram said that the Indians had captured 4,102 members of the regular Pakistani armed forces and 4,066 men of the Pakistani paramilitary forces in the 10-day period.

[18] East Pakistani forces surrender. Pakistan's commander in East Pakistan, Lt. Gen. A. A. K. Niazi, surrendered to India Dec. 16 (Dec. 15 in the Western Hemisphere). Niazi, who had pledged Dec. 11 never to capitulate, called on his troops to give up. The Indians had set 9 a.m. Dec. 16 as the deadline for a Pakistani reply to their surrender demand and threatened to continue their offensive unless terms of the ultimatum were met. Gen. Manekshaw acknowledged receiving from Gen. Niazi a message through U.S. diplomatic channels Dec. 14 regarding a truce, but refused to disclose its contents. Manekshaw had ordered a suspension of Indian air raids on Dacca from 5 p.m. Dec. 14 until 9 a.m. Dec. 15 to give the Pakistanis time to consider the demand to end all resistance. The actual battle for Dacca started Dec. 14 as advance Indian units approached to within seven miles of the city and Indian bombing attacks struck parts of the city and set Government House, in the center of Dacca, afire. Niazi's Dec. 16 surrender was an agreement to end all resistance provided that he be permitted to "regroup" his forces in "designated areas." The Indians rejected the terms, taking them to mean that Niazi wanted to stop fighting but to keep his troops under arms and under control of their officers. The Indians insisted on total surrender of the Pakistan army and received that surrender Dec. 17 under terms of an agreement signed in Dacca by Niazi and Lt. Gen. Jagjit Singh Aurora, the Indian eastern commander. The papers, signed shortly after the Indian capture of Dacca earlier the same day, resulted in the surrender of Pakistan's four divisions in East Pakistan. The document referred to East Pakistan as Bangla Desh and pledged that all Pakistanis who gave up would be treated in accord with the provisions of the Geneva convention.

[19] *Atrocities and killings.* The capture of Dacca loosed pent-up Bengali hatred for Pakistani soldiers and their supporters and resulted in widespread reprisal killings and executions in the capital and elsewhere. Many of those slain were Bihari Moslems and razakars, the irregular militia that aided the Pakistanis in maintaining order in East Pakistan. Indian troops were disarming the Bengali rebels in an attempt to stop the wanton killings. Unarmed Bengali civilians in Dacca were reported Dec. 17 to have been killed in recent weeks in street fighting by the remnants of razakars. In defiance of their leaders, Bengali rebels killed two Pakistani soldiers Dec. 17. Many Bihari Moslems also were found stabbed to death in the streets of the capital. The bodies of 125 Bengali intellectuals, regarded as the future leaders of Bangla Desh, were found in a ditch outside Dacca Dec. 18. They were among 300 Bengali professionals who had been seized in recent weeks and held by the razakars as "hostages" in exchange for fair surrender terms. They appeared to have been murdered just before the Pakistani surrender Dec. 16. Their hands were tied behind their backs and they had been bayonetted, strangled or shot. The victims included doctors, professors, writers and teachers. Two captured razakars were said to have confessed to some of the killings; but it was later reported that Al-Badao, the extremist faction of the right-wing Moslem Jamaat-Islami party, had carried out the slayings with the encouragement and assistance of Pakistani army officers. An Indian source reported Dec. 19 that a few Bengalis and more than 100 Biharis had been stabbed or shot to death in clashes that followed a victory celebration in Khulna Dec. 17. A Mukti Bahini victory celebration in Dacca ended Dec. 17 with the beating and bayonetting to death of three young pro-Pakistani prisoners by Bengali rebels. At another public rally in Dacca Dec. 18 four razakars were tortured and executed as 5,000 persons looked on. No Bengali rebel leaders were present.

[20] **Western border cease-fire.** President Yahya Dec. 17 announced Pakistani acceptance of a cease-fire in the west. (Yahya had vowed Dec. 16 that he would continue the struggle despite his government's defeat in the east.) India's truce offer of a "cease-fire everywhere on the western front with effect from 8 a.m. ... Dec. 17" had been announced Dec. 16 by the Indian government and Mrs. Gandhi. In his announcement, Yahya noted that Pakistan had earlier accepted United Nations cease-fire proposals (*see* [42]), while India had rejected them. He urged India to formalize the cease-fire through the U.N. The cease-fire on the western front had been preceded by heavy fighting in the region. According to Indian reports, Pakistani troops had carried out a "heavy counterattack" Dec. 15-16 in an effort to stem an Indian advance in the Shakargarh area in West Pakistan's Punjab. Indian forces reached the west bank of the Basantar River west of Shakargarh and a heavy tank battle followed, as a result of which India was in possession of 400 square miles of Pakistani territory in a salient that jutted into India. (This brought to 1,500 the number of square miles lost by Pakistan in the west, while India conceded the loss of only 50 square miles of its own territory—all of it in the Chhamb area.)

[21] **Bengalis disarmed, India exit plan.** India and the Bangla Desh government completed an arrangement Dec. 27 on reorganizing and disarming the Bengali rebels in the next 10 days and on withdrawing Indian forces from the region in two-three months. Under the plan, the 100,000 Mukti Bahini were to report immediately to newly established camps in their home areas to turn in their arms and be trained as national militia. The Pakistani prisoners were to be shipped to India. The Indian and Bangla Desh campaign to disarm Bengalis in a move to halt reprisal killings had been defied Dec. 24 by a student group which stated that the students would not turn in their weapons until Sheik Mujibur was released from prison in West Pakistan. The Bangla Desh government Dec. 27 issued an appeal to Bengalis not to take reprisals against Pakistani collaborators. (India said Dec. 27 that it was weighing the possibility of holding trials for Pakistani military personnel charged with "heinous crimes" in East Pakistan. India held that the Geneva convention did not provide soldiers with immunity from prosecution for atrocities and other such crimes, but indicated that such prosecution was up to the Bangla Desh government. Bangla Desh radio had announced Dec. 24 that tribunals were being established to try enemy agents responsible for the killing of Bengalis during the civil war. The former governor of East Pakistan, Abdu Mutaleb Malik [*see* 27], several of his ministers and officials were taken into custody by Bangla Desh Dec. 24.)

Civil War—Political Developments

[22] **Bengalis form cabinet.** It was reported April 13 that, despite the slaying of a large number of East Pakistani secessionist leaders, several members of the movement's high command had formed a cabinet. Tajuddin Ahmed, second-in-command to Sheik Mujibur, was named prime minister and defense minister of Bangla Desh. Mujibur was named president, although he remained in detention in West Pakistan. The government of Bangla Desh proclaimed its sovereignty April 12 and appealed to "all democratic countries" for recognition and aid in the civil war. The statement said that Chuadanga had been established as the capital of Bangla Desh.

[23] **India-Pakistan diplomatic missions.** Dissident Bengali diplomats seized the Pakistan consulate in Calcutta, India April 18 and declared it would "function as the mission of Bangla Desh." Pakistan April 21 appointed Mahdi Masud as high commissioner in Calcutta to replace dissident M.V. Hosain Ali, but Indian Bengali demonstrations prevented Masud from assuming his post. In reaction, Karachi April 23 accused India of not taking action to curb the demonstrations and of failing to oust the dissidents from the Calcutta mission. It called on India to send back to Pakistan the entire Calcutta staff, including the dissidents. Pakistan also asked India to close its mission in Dacca. India

said that it would not grant diplomatic privileges to Ali and his aides or recognize Bangla Desh, but that Pakistani representation in India must be settled among the Pakistanis. The two countries closed their respective missions April 26. New Delhi charged that its diplomats in Dacca were refused permission to depart for India and April 26 imposed similar restrictions on Pakistani diplomats in India. In a further retaliatory move, India April 27 ordered "strict police vigilance" on the movement of Pakistani diplomats in Calcutta. Both sides reached a tentative agreement on repatriation May 3; but the accord bogged down May 5, the day it was to take effect, as the Pakistanis insisted that the repatriation could not take place until their representative interviewed each member of the delegation in Calcutta to determine who did not want to return to Pakistan. India held that it could not force the Bangalis to meet with any Pakistani representative individually. In a move to break the impasse, Pakistan called on Switzerland May 8 to mediate the dispute. The Swiss agreed and India accepted the arrangement May 11. A Swiss diplomat arranged and held interviews with more than 60 Bengalis at the Calcutta mission, and India and Pakistan agreed on a repatriation pact Aug. 10. More than 200 Indians and 30 West Pakistanis were repatriated Aug. 12.

[24] **Yahya vows civil rule.** President Yahya announced June 28 that he had appointed a "committee of experts" to draw up a new constitution that would return Pakistan to civilian rule "in a matter of four months or so." Yahya said, however, that "the precise timing will naturally depend on the internal and external situation at the time." He said the new charter would go into effect at the first sitting of the National Assembly. He said that he had decided "that the national and provincial governments will have at their disposal the cover of martial law for a period of time. In actual practice, martial law will not be operative in its present form, but we cannot allow chaos in any parts of the country." Although he retained his ban on the Awami League, Yahya said that party members who had won seats in the December 1970 Assembly elections would be permitted to assume their legislative posts if they were not among a list of those who had participated in "antistate" or "criminal acts."

[25] The Pakistani government announced Aug. 7 that 88 of the 167 Awami League members of the Assembly would retain their seats and the 79 others would be given an opportunity to clear themselves of charges against them. Lt. Gen. Tikka Khan announced Aug. 20 that criminal charges had been filed against 13 more Awami League members of the Assembly. The Pakistani government Aug. 19 disqualified 195 of the 288 Awami League legislators of the 310-member East Pakistan Provincial Assembly. The remaining league members were to be allowed to remain, but not under their party label. The Pakistani Election Commission announced Sept. 19 that by-elections would be held in East Pakistan Nov. 25 for 78 National Assembly seats, Dec. 9 for 105 Provincial Assembly seats and later for the remaining seats vacated by the disqualification of the 79 National Assembly members and the 195 Provincial Assembly members. (Ali Bhutto hinted Sept. 22 at possible armed action by his followers unless the by-elections were held and the National Assembly "convened by the end of this year.") Yahya Oct. 10 lifted the ban on political action imposed in March and imposed stringent curbs on the conduct of parties and politicians in preparation for the by-elections. The new rules permitted parties (though not the Awami League) and individuals to participate in politics but set limits on permitted activities. The regulations covered the contents of party propaganda and required notice to be given to local officials of any public meetings. (Yahya also announced Oct. 12 that the National Assembly would convene Dec. 27.) Pakistan announced Nov. 2 that 53 National Assembly seats taken from the Awami League would be filled without contest (including 14 to be given to the Jamaat-Islami party, which had failed to win any seats in the 1970 elections).

[26] **Mujibur trial.** Sheik Mujibur went on trial for treason in West Pakistan Aug. 11. (The trial was confirmed by Pakistan Aug. 18.) The government's Martial Law Administrator's Office in Rawalpindi had announced Aug. 9 that Mujibur would be tried in secret by a special military court for "waging war against Pakistan" and other offenses. He would be permitted to prepare his own defense and engage a lawyer, provided the attorney was a citizen of Pakistan. Mujibur was said to have rejected the offer of a lawyer (although the government announced Aug. 20 that he had accepted A. K. Brohi as his lawyer) and contended that the military tribunal was "not competent" to judge him.

[27] **Civilian governor appointed.** The Pakistani government Sept. 1 announced the appointment of Dr. Malik (*see* [21]), a civilian, to replace Lt. Gen. Tikka Khan as governor of East Pakistan, effective Sept. 3. Malik Sept. 18 administered the oath of office to nine members of a 10-man interim Civilian Council of Ministers for the province. The 10th minister was to be sworn in at a later date. The council included two members of the Provincial Assembly who had belonged to the Awami League.

[28] **East Pakistan regime resigns.** The entire East Pakistani government in Dacca resigned Dec. 14 and dissociated itself from further actions of the central government. Malik drafted a letter of resignation to Yahya and gave written orders to his council ministers to cease their official functions and take refuge in the Inter-Continental Hotel, declared a neutral zone and administered by the Red Cross. Malik, his family and the Cabinet took refuge in the hotel.

[29] **Yahya quits, Bhutto succeeds him.** Yahya resigned as president of Pakistan Dec. 20 and was immediately replaced by Ali Bhutto, who was sworn in as president and martial law administrator, assuming full powers over both civilian and military administrations and returning the government to civilian rule for the first time since 1958. (Yahya had appointed Bhutto deputy premier and foreign minister Dec. 3.) Yahya, who had been under powerful military and civilian pressure to resign following his acceptance of the Indian cease-fire (*see* [20]), had announced his decision to quit and turn over the reins of government to Bhutto Dec. 18. The Pakistani air force was said to have played a key role in forcing Yahya to resign by threatening a possible coup unless he stepped aside. Antigovernment demonstrations had been held in Rawalpindi Dec. 18 protesting Yahya's acceptance of the cease-fire. In one of his first acts as president, Bhutto Dec. 20 retired Yahya and six other high-ranking officers from the army. He also named Lt. Gen. Abdul Gul Hassan, chief of the general staff and one of Yahya's severest critics, as acting commander-in-chief of the armed forces. Bhutto Dec. 21 appointed Prime Minister Nural Amin, another critic of Yahya, as vice president. He also announced that Sheik Mujibur would soon be released from prison and placed under house arrest. (Mujibur was released from jail and placed under house detention Dec. 20.) Bhutto continued his purge of the armed forces Dec. 23 by dismissing six navy senior officers and three army generals. Bhutto appointed Commodore Hasan Hafeez Ahmed as acting commander-in-chief of the navy. Bhutto Dec. 24 swore in a new 11-member civilian Cabinet. He retained the ministries of defense, foreign affairs, interior and inter-provincial affairs. Amin was given the additional post of minister in charge of Cabinet affairs. Eight of the new ministers were members of Bhutto's PPP.

[30] **Bangla Desh leaders return.** The leaders of the provisional government of Bangla Desh returned to Dacca Dec. 22 after months of exile in Calcutta, where they had established the secessionist regime. The government had been formally installed in Dacca after the surrender of West Pakistan to Indian forces in the area. Among the Cabinet ministers listed as returning were Acting President Syed Nazrul Islam, Prime Minister Ahmed, Foreign Minister Khadker Mushtaque Ahmed, Home Minister A. H. M. Kamaruzzaman and Finance Minister Mohammad Mansoor Ali. Bengali guerrillas and their supporters in Dacca were reported Dec. 21 to have expressed strong opposition to the Bangla Desh leaders because they had remained in Calcutta during the

military struggle. A direct confrontation between the two factions had occurred when a radical wing of students and former students known as the Mujib Bahini, staunch backers of Sheik Mujibur, had seized the Dacca radio station in the aftermath of the Pakistani surrender there and began broadcasting their own policy statements. The Bangla Desh Cabinet while in Calcutta had sought jurisdiction of the station to relay its own policy statements.

[31] **Pakistan to probe defeat.** Bhutto Dec. 24 announced the appointment of a commission to investigate Pakistan's defeat in the war with India. The commission, headed by Chief Justice Hamood Dur Rahmin, was empowered "to inquire into the circumstances leading to the military debacle in East Pakistan and the cease-fire in the west." Private citizens in Lahore had filed complaints against Yahya's handling of the war and the High Court had started proceedings to determine whether any action should be taken. Yahya, accused in the complaints of murder, treason and conspiracy, had been placed under house arrest, according to a report Dec. 29, and would remain under detention during the government investigation into his wartime leadership.

Refugees and Relief

[32] **India plans refugee shift.** India announced July 11 that it would shift about 2.5 million East Pakistani refugees from its border states to the central part of the country in order to relieve the pressure on frontier regions caused by the influx of nearly seven million refugees. India was erecting 46 camps in central India to house the East Pakistanis. In previous refugee developments: India April 22 appealed to the U.N. to provide assistance for the East Pakistani refugees; the West Bengal State government reported April 22 that cholera and smallpox had broken out among the refugees (*see* HEALTH [1]); in a reversal of policy, Pakistan May 17 appealed to the U.N. to provide relief for East Pakistan; India reported May 22 that Prime Minister Gandhi had written to all heads of state informing them of the problems caused by the huge influx of East Pakistani war refugees into India; the Pakistan government June 10 urged all refugees in India to return to East Pakistan, under a general amnesty for military deserters and political dissidents.

[33] **U.N. relief program.** Nixon Administration officials in Washington July 31 disclosed agreement by the U.N. and Pakistan on an American plea for establishment of a 153-member U.N. relief and rehabilitation unit in East Pakistan. The effort was to be financed by non-U.N. funds. (Secretary General U Thant Aug. 11 and Aug. 18 appealed for more funds for the program. He said that the $51 million in cash received by the U.N. was less than 10% of the amount needed for the first phase of the relief work.) The U.N. team would include 73 monitors and another contingent of members of U.N. specialized agencies such as UNICEF, the Food and Agriculture Organization, the World Food Program and the World Health Organization. The establishment of a U.N. working group in Geneva to coordinate the U.N. relief efforts was announced by U Thant Aug. 6. The U.N. was also extending its relief program to Eastern India, it was announced July 31. UNICEF was to establish 1,000 centers in the border region Aug. 15 to distribute high-protein foods to prevent deaths from malnutrition among refugee children.

[34] *Reaction to relief.* India July 30 ordered foreign relief workers among East Pakistani refugees to cease their operations within 48 hours. It had been reported July 22 that India was planning the ouster action because it was suspected that the U.S. had planted espionage agents in charitable organizations functioning near the border. An Indian government spokesman was quoted as saying that foreign volunteer refugee relief workers were not wanted because it was a strain on the government to provide security and living quarters and because there was no lack of Indian doctors and nurses. In Pakistan, the International Committee of the Red Cross announced July 30 that President Yahya had agreed to the ICRC resumption of relief work in

East Pakistan, stopped by the Pakistanis in April. Pakistan Aug. 27 charged that India was using relief funds provided by the U.S. and U.N. to train East Pakistani guerrillas. In East Pakistan, an official of the Bangla Desh government Aug. 12 warned the U.N. against posting observers in East Pakistan, hinting that they would be killed.

[35] **India gets refugee aid.** A 13-nation (U.S., Britain, France, West Germany, Canada, the Netherlands, Belgium, Norway, Sweden, Denmark, Italy, Japan and Austria) consortium agreed at an emergency meeting Oct. 26 to provide India with a "substantial part" of the estimated $700 million for relief of the nearly 10 million east Pakistani refugees in India until March 1972. The meeting was held under the auspices of the World Bank. A communique issued by the conferees "noted that worldwide contributions pledged to date came to over $200 million."

[36] **India sets refugee return.** India Dec. 23 announced plans to repatriate the East Pakistani refugees who had fled to India. The resettlement program was expected to start Jan. 1, 1972 and would be completed in two months. At a meeting Dec. 20 between Bangla Desh and Indian officials, it was agreed that India would provide all the transportation and materials needed to transfer the refugees to transit camps in Bangla Desh.

Foreign Involvement

[37] **U.S. policy on arms to Pakistan.** The State Department announced April 15 that it had been informed by the Defense Department that no "non-lethal" military equipment or ammunition had been provided to Pakistan since the start of the civil war and that nothing was scheduled for delivery. Despite the ban, however, it was reported in June that one freighter, bearing military equipment including parts for armored personnel carriers, had sailed from New York to Karachi May 8 and that a second, with cargo including eight planes, parachutes and thousands of spare parts, had sailed June 22. State Department spokesman Charles W. Bray 3rd, responding to Indian protests and Congressional criticism, explained June 29 that the current arms shipments were not in violation of the April 15 announcement since they had been licensed prior to the outbreak of the Pakistan civil war. He said that no new licenses for military sales or for direct commercial sales had been issued since that date. In later developments: the State Department disclosed Aug. 12 that American military contracts for Pakistan had been reduced from $15 million in June to $4 million—largely in aircraft parts—scheduled to be delivered between August and March 1972; the U.S. announced Nov. 8 the cancellation (with the consent of Pakistan) of $3.6 million worth of military equipment to Pakistan and the clearance of $160,000 worth of spare parts (already cleared by U.S. Customs and awaiting shipment in New York) to be sent to Pakistan. Syndicated columnist Jack Anderson reported Dec. 30 that there had existed a secret U.S. proposal, later dropped, for the shipment of U.S. arms to Pakistan during the war with India. According to Anderson, Henry A. Kissinger, Presidential assistant for national security affairs, had said in strategy sessions at the White House Dec. 6 and 8 that President Nixon "does not want to be even-handed. The President believes that India is the attacker." (Anderson also wrote that, according to official documents, the dispatch of an eight-ship U.S. task force to the Bay of Bengal Dec. 10 was aimed at putting military pressure on India and not for the announced purpose of evacuating American citizens.)

[38] **U.S. bars arms to India.** The U.S. Dec. 1 suspended arms shipments to India in reponse to India's refusal to withdraw its troops from the borders of East Pakistan. Previously approved licenses for about $2 million worth of ammunition and ammunition-making equipment were also revoked. The U.S. said it would honor but keep "under review" contracts already authorized for $11.5 million in military communications equipment and spare parts for transport aircraft. (India purchased a relatively small amount of arms from the U.S., and the move was viewed as political rather than military.) The U.S. Dec.

3 canceled the $11.5 million licenses and Dec. 6 suspended $87.6 million in development loans to India, charging that New Delhi was the "main aggressor" in the war with Pakistan. (A report from New Delhi Nov. 8 had said that India had requested an increase in the purchase of Soviet arms in recent weeks and a speedup in the shipment of Russian military equipment ordered earlier.)

[39] International aid to Pakistan barred. A majority of a group of 11 nations (the U.S., Japan, Norway, the Netherlands, France, West Germany, Denmark, Italy, Belgium, Canada and Great Britain) meeting in Paris June 21 agreed formally to postpone indefinitely granting any new aid to Pakistan because of East Pakistan's economic and administrative turmoil. The agreement did not affect the assistance being given for the East Pakistani refugees. Most of the 11 nations formed the Aid to Pakistan Consortium, which was coordinated by the World Bank. Aid to Pakistan totaled $500 million annually. The decision to halt the economic assistance was influenced by a report delivered by Peter Cargill, director of the World Bank's South Asia department. Cargill, who had headed a mission to Pakistan in the first two weeks of June, reported economic paralysis, prospective famine, continuing unrest and the disruption of life in East Pakistan. (The partial text of the Cargill report was obtained and published by an American newspaper July 12. World Bank President Robert McNamara was reported July 20 to have sent President Yahya a letter of apology for the unauthorized publication of the report. McNamara had reportedly barred distribution of the report, fearing the document would be interpreted as a condemnation of Yahya's policies.)

[40] Thant peace plea. Secretary General Thant Oct. 21 sent personal pleas to India and Pakistan, reportedly offering his personal mediation to avert a conflict between the two countries. Mrs. Gandhi Nov. 16 rejected Thant's offer. Thant, the U.S.S.R., the U.S. and Communist China had repeatedly made pleas for peace to Pakistan and India. (China Nov. 7 had pledged to "resolutely support" Pakistan in the event of war with India. Acting Foreign Minister Chi Peng-fei of China declared that day: "Our Pakistani friends may rest assured that should Pakistan be subjected to foreign aggression, the Chinese government and people will as always support the Pakistani government and people." China and the U.S.S.R. repeatedly, during December, accused each other of inciting the conflict between India and Pakistan.)

[41] India recognizes Bangla Desh. India Dec. 6 extended recognition to Bangla Desh. Pakistan promptly retaliated by severing diplomatic ties with India. The Asian kingdom of Bhutan, which was treaty-bound to accept India's advice on foreign affairs, recognized Bangla Desh Dec. 7.

[42] U.N. urges end to fighting. The U.N. General Assembly Dec. 7 approved, by a 104-11 vote (10 abstentions) an Argentine resolution calling on India and Pakistan to end the fighting and withdraw their forces. Two similar cease-fire and troop withdrawal resolutions introduced in the Security Council Dec. 5 had been rejected by Soviet vetoes. Both were defeated by identical votes—11 for, 2 abstentions (Britain and France) and 2 against (the Soviet Union and Poland). Between the two Security Council votes, the Council had rejected by a two to one (China) vote (12 abstentions) a Soviet resolution calling for a political settlement in East Pakistan "which would inevitably result in a cessation of hostilities" and for an end to "all acts of violence by Pakistani forces." Faced with its inability to act in the crisis, the Council Dec. 6 approved by an 11-0 vote a resolution to transfer debate on the question to the General Assembly. The Council again Dec. 13 rejected, by the same vote as earlier, a U.S. resolution for a cease-fire and troop withdrawal. The resolution had been introduced after the American delegation called the Council into emergency session Dec. 12 to reconsider the Indian-Pakistani conflict. The Council Dec. 21, by a 13-0 vote (the Soviet Union and Poland abstaining) finally approved a resolution calling on India and Pakistan to withdraw their forces to their respective territories and to observe a cease-fire. The resolution had been drawn up in consultations held Dec. 17-20 between Somalia delegate Abdulrahim A.

Farrah and the Indian and Pakistani delegations. The Council had been in session since Dec. 12. (Bhutto, head of Pakistan's delegation, had walked out of the Council's Dec. 15 session to protest its failure to take effective action in halting the war.) India and Pakistan endorsed the proposal. (Pakistan Dec. 9 had accepted the General Assembly's Dec. 7 resolution; but India had, in effect, rejected it Dec. 8.)

[43] **Naval moves.** In addition to the U.S. presence in the Bay of Bengal (see [37]), it was reported Dec. 12 that the Soviet Union appeared to be increasing its naval strength in the Indian Ocean. A guided missile warship was said to have left Vladivostok naval base and was heading south. Another Soviet guided missile vessel had joined the Soviet fleet in the Indian Ocean the previous week. The Soviet armada in the area was said to total 10-12 ships, some of them weather and hydrographic survey vessels, and 10 nuclear-powered submarines. The presence of Chinese ships off the coast of East Pakistan, preparing for possible evacuation of escaping Pakistani forces from the province, was reported by Indian intelligence sources Dec. 12. The Chinese ships were said to be deployed off the Ganges estuary in the south of East Pakistan. India had repeatedly warned that it would attack and sink boats attempting to take escaping troops to West Pakistan.

See also CANADA [26]; CEYLON; FOREIGN AID; FRANCE [17]; HEALTH [1]; HIJACKING [5-6]; INDIA

PALESTINE LIBERATION ORGANIZATION (PLO)—*See* JORDAN [5]
PALESTINIAN COMMANDOS—*See* JORDAN; MIDDLE EAST [2, 5-10, 26]; TURKEY [6]; UNITED ARAB REPUBLIC

PANAMA—**Priest's kidnaping spurs controversy.** The Rev. Hector Gallego, a Colombian priest working in Santa Fe Province in central Panama, was kidnaped June 9 by two men claiming to be government agents, according to a report June 27. The government denied any involvement in the priest's disappearance. Gallego, 28, had worked with Santa Fe peasants for four years, organizing them against exploitation. He had been harassed, beaten, arrested briefly for subversion, and his home was burned May 23.

The military government of Gen. Omar Torrijos Herrera authorized the church to conduct its own investigation of the kidnaping. A government investigation exonerated two suspects who were members of the National Guard, one of them Torrijos' cousin, as well as several other persons. Both Msgr. Marcos McGrath, Panama's archbishop, and Msgr. Martin Legarra, bishop in Veraguas Province, publicly condemned the kidnaping. Legarra excommunicated all persons involved in the kidnaping, according to a July 8 report.

Canal talks reopen. Panama and the U.S. began negotiations June 29 on a new treaty governing the operation of the Canal Zone. The last discussions took place in 1967 and an agreement, calling for joint U.S.-Panamanian authority, was never acted on by either government. The U.S. representatives were former Treasury Secretary Robert Anderson and John C. Mundt. Panamanian representatives were Ambassador Jose Antonio De La Ossa, former minister of foreign relations, Carlos Lopez Guevara, and Hernando Manfredo, former minister of trade and industry. Panamanian negotiators said, according to a June 27 report, that they would not sign a treaty unless it gave Panama jurisdiction over the Canal Zone, although they were prepared to give the U.S. administrative rights and to assure safe passage through the canal. Panama placed her case for a new treaty before the United Nations General Assembly Oct. 5 after negotiations failed to result in any preliminary agreements.

It was reported Oct. 21 that the U.S. and Panama had reached general agreement on a new canal treaty that would give Panama sovereignty over the waterway but keep its operation under U.S. control. Although final agreement was not reached, it appeared that the main points at issue had been resolved. Among these points: (1) jurisdiction over the canal would be ceded to Panama;

(2) a provision of the 1903 treaty that gave the U.S. a lease on the Canal Zone "in perpetuity" would be eliminated; (3) Panama would have a higher share of the revenues of the canal; (4) administration of the canal would remain in the hands of the U.S.; and (5) the U.S. would continue to have responsibility for the military protection of the canal. As part of the agreement, the U.S. would maintain its military bases in the zone.

See also CUBA

PAN AMERICAN GAMES—See SPORTS

PAPADOPOULOS, GEORGE—See CYPRUS; GREECE [5, 11, 13]

PARAGUAY—Priest's arrest stirs controversy. The arrest in Paraguay of Uruguayan priest Uberfil Monzon Feb. 27 stirred a church-state controversy in Paraguay which resulted in the excommunication of the interior minister and the chief of police. After working only one month in Paraguay, Monzon was arrested on charges of connections with Uruguay's Tupamaros guerrillas. He was released April 5 after a confession in his name had been made public in which he admitted connection with the Tupamaros and stated that a Tupamaros-type movement could not succeed in Paraguay.

Uruguayan Bishop Andres Rubio flew to Asuncion March 8 to seek Monzon's release and was attacked at the airport by a group of women. Uruguayan and Paraguayan priests had claimed that Monzon was innocent and that his arrest was in effect a "kidnaping." Asuncion Archbishop Ismael Blas Rolon Silvero announced March 18 the excommunication of 30 persons, specifically mentioning Interior Minister Sabino Montanaro and Police Chief Gen. Granco Britez, in connection with Monzon's arrest and the attack on Rubio. The government "repudiated" the excommunications, charging that the actions were "unconstitutional interference" with governmental authority to enforce law.

Wage increase decreed. The government April 15 announced a 10% increase in the minimum wage for Paraguayan workers. Designed to meet the increase in the cost of living, the wage hike was the first since 1964.

See also LATIN AMERICA

PARIS PEACE TALKS—See INDOCHINA WAR [69, 73-79]

PARKS—See ENVIRONMENT

PAROCHIAL SCHOOLS—See EDUCATION [10-11]

PAUL VI—See CHURCHES [17]; ROMAN CATHOLIC CHURCH [1, 5, 7-9, 11]

PAY BOARD—See ECONOMY, U.S. [13-15, 17-18, 20-22, 26, 28]; MINES

PEACE CORPS—See FOREIGN AID; GOVERNMENT REORGANIZATION

PENN CENTRAL TRANSPORT CO.—See RAILROADS

PENTAGON—See ATOMIC ENERGY [14]; DEFENSE; PENTAGON PAPERS; RACIAL & MINORITY UNREST [14]; TELEVISION & RADIO; WAR CRIMES [7]

PENTAGON PAPERS—The New York Times June 13 began the publication of a series of articles based on a secret Pentagon study of U.S. involvement in Vietnam. The publication [2-4] set off a chain of events which included publication of articles based on the same study in the Washington Post [5] and other papers [8], a Supreme Court decision [6] which allowed the Times and the Post to continue publishing the articles after a hiatus caused by Justice Department requested court injunctions against publication and the indictment of Dr. Daniel Ellsberg, who admittedly had leaked the papers to the press [14]. (For a brief treatment of the contents of the parts of the study published by the newspapers, see [18-29].)

[2] Times begins publication. The New York Times June 13 began publishing a series of articles and documents based on a secret Pentagon study made during the Administration of former-President Lyndon B. Johnson (commissioned by then-Defense Secretary Robert S. McNamara) of the policy decisions made over a period ending in 1968 which drew the U.S. into military involvement in the Vietnam War. The study (3,000 pages of analysis and 4,000 pages of official documents) had been held confidential—only 15 copies reportedly were produced initially—and eventually committed by McNamara to the National Archives. The Times came into possession of 39 of the 47 book-length volumes of the study, which did not include Presidential papers, nor State Department documents except those that turned up in Defense Department files. The Nixon Administration took the position on the Times articles that they involved unauthorized release of classified defense material and that the policy decisions cataloged in the papers were not a part of President Nixon's "new Vietnam policy" developed in 1968. (The documents bore a "top secret" classification.) The Pentagon June 14 cited its concern about "the disclosure of publication of highly classified information affecting national security" and said that it had called "this violation of security" to the attention of the Justice Department. Later June 14, Assistant Attorney General Robert C. Mardian, head of the internal security division, telephoned the Times to request that publication of the series be halted and to state that court action would follow lack of compliance. The call came about two hours before press time for the edition scheduled to carry the third installment of the series. An hour before press time, the Times received a telegram from Attorney General John N. Mitchell asking it to refrain from publishing any "further information of this character" on the ground it would "cause irreparable injury to the defense interests" of the U.S. Mitchell requested a return of the documents to the Defense Department. He said that the top secret classification of the information resulted, under the provisions of the Espionage Law, in a direct prohibition of publication. The Times refused to stop publication on the ground that: "It is in the interest of the people of this country to be informed of the material contained in this series of articles." The newspaper said that it would oppose a U.S. court action, but would "abide by the final decision of the Court."

[3] The Justice Department June 15 filed a civil suit to seek permanent enjoinment against publication of the articles. At a hearing before U.S. District Court Judge Murray I. Gurfein in New York, U.S. Attorney Michael D. Hess contended that the newspaper had violated a statute making it a crime for persons having "unauthorized possession" of federal documents to disclose their contents in a way that "could be used to the injury of the United States or to the advantage of any foreign nation." The Times' attorney, Yale University professor Alexander M. Bickel, told Gurfein that the issue involved was a "classic case of censorship" that was forbidden by the First Amendment's guarantee of a free press. He said that court action to bar publication of an article was unprecedented in the U.S. and that the government's case was based on an anti-espionage law never intended by Congress to be used against the press. Gurfein urged the Times to consent to halt publication of the articles, but the Times, holding that this would be a precedent for federal action to curb news publications, refused. Gurfein agreed with the U.S. position that temporary harm done to the Times would be "far outweighed by the irreparable harm that could be done" to the interests of the U.S. He ordered the Times June 15 to halt publication of the articles for four days, and he set a hearing for June 18 on the issue of continuing the ban. He declined at that time to order the Times to return the Pentagon material but June 16 set another hearing on the Justice Department's request to have the Times relinquish its Pentagon papers for government inspection. Gurfein June 17 ruled against what he called a federal "fishing expedition into the files of any newspaper" and suggested the Times give the court and the Justice Department a list of descriptive headings of the documents in its possession. The Times complied. Gurfein June 19 denied an injunction against the Times' series but extended the restraining order against publication pending appeal. He found "no cogent reasons" advanced, aside from the overall embarrassment aspect, that public knowledge of the material would be a vital security breach; and he rejected a contention that the case constituted a violation of espionage laws. The restraining order was extended June 19 by Judge Irving R. Kaufman to permit consideration of the issue by a three-judge panel of his 2nd Circuit Court of

Appeals and again June 21 by the panel so that the case could be carried before the entire eight-member court.

[4]   The government contended before the appeals court that "national defense documents, properly classified by the Executive, are an exception to an absolute freedom of the press and should be protected by the courts against unauthorized disclosure." The government also presented a sealed list of items in the papers which the government claimed would be security impairments if disclosed. The court June 23 issued a 5-3 decision that the Times could resume publication of the series after June 25 but could not use any material that the government held vital to national security. The court instructed Gurfein to hold secret hearings to determine what part of the papers posed "such grave and immediate danger" to U.S. security as to warrant enjoinment of publication.

[5]   **Post begins publication.** The Washington Post June 18 began publishing a series of articles based on the Pentagon papers. The Justice Department June 18 sought court restraint after the Post refused to voluntarily halt such publication, but U.S. District Court Judge Gerhard A. Gesell in Washington refused the same day to sanction prior restraint of the articles with the observation that "the court has before it no precise information suggesting in what respects, if any, the publication of this information will injure" the country. Gesell suggested that the proper recourse of the government in case of a security violation would be a criminal suit. Gesell's ruling was overturned June 19 by the U.S. Court of Appeals for the District of Columbia, which held in a 2-1 decision that the articles should be barred, pending a full hearing, and that "freedom of the press, as important as it is, is not boundless." After further hearings, some parts of which were secret at the government's request, Gesell June 21 again upheld the Post against prior restraint and permitted resumption of the articles; but the appellate court June 21 continued the press curb and ordered a hearing before the entire nine-man court. Hearings before the full court, including secret sessions, were held June 22-23. U.S. Solicitor General Erwin N. Griswold entered the case for the first time June 22 and announced he had been authorized by the secretaries of state and defense and the joint chiefs of staff to offer the solution of a "joint task force" to examine the documents involved for possible declassification within 45 days. The appeals court June 23 rejected the government's contention that continued publication of the material would jeopardize security and upheld the Post's constitutional right to publish the articles, but continued the curb against the series to permit appeal. The court June 24 denied the Justice Department's request for a rehearing on the case and reaffirmed its earlier ruling that the government had not demonstrated any grounds for preventing publication of the material.

[6]   **Supreme Court rebuffs restraint.** The Supreme Court June 25 accepted the Times and Post cases. Because of the restraint imposed on the Times, the court put both papers under equal publication restraints pending an ultimate decision. It marked the first time the court had restrained publication of a newspaper article; and Justices Hugo L. Black, William O. Douglas, William J. Brennan Jr. and Thurgood Marshall dissented in favor of freeing both papers to print the articles without hearing arguments. The court's order permitted both newspapers to publish information from the Pentagon papers but proscribed items the government considered "dangerous" to national security. Both newspapers declined to resume the articles under such circumstances, which they considered tantamount to government censorship. With Chief Justice Warren E. Burger and Justices Harry A. Blackmun and John M. Harlan dissenting, the court June 26 rejected the government's request for a secret hearing for presentation of details that publication of the material would be harmful to national interest. The court June 30, by a 6-3 decision, upheld the Times and the Post against the government's restraint. Prior stays against publication were vacated.

[7] The court's brief, unsigned decision quoted precedents that "any system of prior restraints of expression comes to this court bearing a heavy presumption against its constitutional validity" and that the government "thus carries a heavy burden of showing justification for the enforcement of such a restraint. It said that the district courts in New York and Washington and the appellate court in Washington had "held that the government had not met that burden" and "we agree." The majority was divided into two groups. Three (Black, Douglas and Marshall) held that the First Amendment's guarantee of a free press was unassailable and that the courts lacked the power to suppress press publication, no matter what threat to national security were involved. A second group (Brennan and Justices Potter Stewart and Byron R. White) asserted that the press could not be curbed except to prevent immediate and irreparable damage to the nation. They held that the material in question in this case did not pose such a threat. White also said that "the newspapers are presumably now on full notice" that federal prosecutions could be brought for the violation of criminal laws, including espionage laws. He added that he "would have no difficulty in sustaining convictions" in such an event even if the security breach were not sufficient to justify prior restraint. The three dissenting justices (Burger, Blackmun and Harlan) held that the decision was too precipitous and that the issue should be returned to trial with restraints upon publication continued.

[8] **Other papers publish excerpts.** Publication of the Pentagon papers spread June 22 to the Boston Globe, which printed four and a half pages of material. A Justice Department suit to ban further articles was immediately filed with U.S. District Court Judge Anthony Julian, who issued a temporary restraining order later the same day against further publication of the articles. Julian also ordered the documents or material from which the article was drawn impounded. He revised that requirement June 23 to permit the documents to be placed by the Globe in a bank safe deposit vault with restricted access. The suit against publication of the articles was dismissed Sept. 8. Publication of the material continued to spread with publication in the Chicago Sun-Times June 23, in eight of the 11 Knight newspapers June 23, in the Los Angeles Times June 24, in the St. Louis Post-Dispatch June 25, and in the Christian Science Monitor June 29. U.S. District Court Judge James H. Meredith issued a restraining order against the Post-Dispatch June 26 at the request of the Justice Department. The department took no court action against the other papers. (The National Review, a conservative weekly magazine, July 20 published more than 20 pages of what it described as government memorandums "not published by the New York Times and Washington Post." However, William F. Buckley Jr., editor in chief of the magazine, said July 21 that the publication of the documents was a hoax to show that "forged documents would be widely accepted as genuine, provided their content was inherently plausible." Buckley said the National Review editors had composed the "documents" in their offices.)

[9] **Documents released to Congress.** President Nixon informed Senate Majority Leader Mike Mansfield June 23 that he would release to Congress the 47-volume Pentagon papers and a 1965 Defense Department study of the Gulf of Tonkin incident. The President specified that he was releasing the documents, which retained their top secret classification, with the understanding that they would not be made public until their classification had been reviewed by the executive branch. White House Press Secretary Ronald L. Ziegler said Nixon was releasing the studies because "the unauthorized publication of portions of the documents created a situation in which Congress would necessarily be making judgments in the meantime on the basis of incomplete data, which would give a distorted impression of the report's contents." Two copies of the 47-volume Pentagon papers were delivered to Congress June 28 and placed in locked vaults under 24-hour guard. The House Armed Services Committee June 29 rejected 25-2 a resolution by Rep. Bella

Abzug (D, N.Y.) that would make the study available to all House members and security-cleared staff members and permit them to take notes. Seven members of a House Government Operations subcommittee, investigating government information and security policies, June 28 acted under a 1928 law requiring any executive agency to submit requested information pertaining to matters within a committee's jurisdiction and demanded that the government give the committee copies of the Pentagon study and the report on the Gulf of Tonkin incident. The Pentagon in effect turned down the request July 1 by saying that the documents had been made available to the Congressional leadership and that individual congressmen should request the materials from that leadership.

[10] *Gravel reads papers to press.* Sen. Mike Gravel (D, Alaska) read aloud to newsmen for over three hours June 29 portions of the Pentagon study. The act was deplored by many Republican colleagues, but Majority Leader Mansfield refused to take disciplinary action against the freshman senator. Mansfield noted Gravel's sincere convictions and said he would have a "friendly talk" with Gravel. Gravel, who said he had received about half of the study June 24 from an unidentified private source, had intended to read the documents to the Senate in an all-night speech; but the Republican leadership thwarted attempts to raise the necessary quorum. Gravel hastily called a meeting of the Senate Public Works Committee, of which he was chairman, and read the papers there to gain Congressional immunity from possible prosecution. Gravel said he was convinced his action was "in no way jeopardizing this nation's security." During the reading, Gravel omitted supporting papers he considered sensitive material. The documents disclosed by Gravel contained substantial material not already published. Visibly exhausted, Gravel stopped reading at 1:12 a.m. June 30, after he had broken into tears several times during the session. He then read an impassioned speech against the war. His staff made copies of the remaining papers available to the press.

[11] **Rand security tightened.** Defense Secretary Melvin R. Laird July 1 issued orders to the Air Force to take custody of all secret documents stored at the Santa Monica headquarters and Washington substation of the Rand Corp. (The Air Force contracted with Rand for military projects.) It had been reported that Dr. Daniel Ellsberg, a former employee at the California headquarters, had copied Rand's set of the Pentagon papers and later released a copy to the press. There were, according to an Air Force statement, 170,000 documents at the two Rand locations classified as either secret or top secret. Laird's order provided that Rand researchers would still be authorized to use secret materials in the two locations, but that Air Force personnel would replace Rand security officials in assuming custody of the data. The Air Force was also directed to make an inventory of all secret documents used at Rand to determine whether it needed them for the work it was engaged in.

[12] **Limit on clearances sought.** It was acknowledged July 7 that President Nixon June 30 had ordered all government departments and agencies to compile at once lists of all persons who had authority to see top-security material. According to a newspaper report July 6, all federal departments and agencies had to submit by July 10 lists of all the government workers, outside consultants and private contractors who held clearance for top-secret information and the "various categories of compartmented intelligence data." By the end of July, the agencies were expected to supply the White House with the names of those who held security clearances and whether they were employed by the government or by outside firms.

[13] **Boston grand jury probe.** A federal grand jury in Boston was reported July 12 to be investigating possible criminal action against the Times, the Post, the Globe and Neil Sheehan (the Times reporter credited with breaking the story about the Pentagon papers) in connection with the publication of the papers. The jury, which had been sitting on other matters, was called back into session July 7 amid tight security measures. According to published reports, the grand jury was seeking to determine where the documents were copied and who

conveyed them to the newspapers. The grand jury was reported July 20 to have been dismissed because of a leak to the press. According to the reports, a new jury was empaneled at once to continue the investigation. The 1st Circuit Court of Appeals in Boston Oct. 29 suspended the jury pending a ruling on the contention by Sen. Gravel that the inquiry infringed on his Congressional immunity. Gravel sought court relief after a lower court ruled that the grand jury could subpoena Dr. Leonard S. Rodberg, one of Gravel's legislative aides, on the ground that Congressional immunity did not extend to congressmen's aides and assistants. The appeals court temporarily vacated that decision. The court Nov. 29 ruled that the grand jury investigation could continue so long as it did not touch on any aspect of the case involving Gravel, his staff or staff members of his committee.

[14] **Ellsberg indicted.** Daniel Ellsberg (see [11]) surrendered to the U.S. Attorney in Boston June 28 after admitting June 26 that he had leaked the documents to the press. Ellsberg said that his only regret was that he had not acted sooner in releasing the information to the press. Later June 26, Ellsberg said he would not have released the documents if he had thought a single page "would do grave damage to the national interests." On the advice of his lawyers, Ellsberg had eluded an intensive search by the Federal Bureau of Investigation after a warrant for his arrest had been issued in Los Angeles late June 25. The warrant charged Ellsberg specifically with possession and failure to return the secret documents, under Title 18, Section 793E, of the U.S. Code. He was not charged with transmitting the documents to anyone else. After his arrest and arraignment June 28, Ellsberg was released on $50,000 bail. Later in the day, a Los Angeles grand jury indicted Ellsberg on two counts—violation of the Espionage Act and theft of government property. The second count of the indictment cited Section 641 of the U.S. Code and charged that Ellsberg had "willfully, knowingly and unlawfully" retained the Pentagon study and had failed to deliver it to the proper recipient. Each count carried a maximum 10-year prison sentence and/or a $10,000 fine. Ellsberg Aug. 16 pleaded not guilty to the two charges in Los Angeles. U.S. District Court Judge William M. Byrne Jr. set Jan. 4, 1972 for a hearing on several defense motions, including a motion to have the proceedings moved to Boston. Ellsberg indicated that he would base his defense on the importance of the papers and on the public's right to know what they contained. He intimated that this would be the core of a political defense that would go beyond the specific charges and would include a sweeping indictment of U.S. policy in Southeast Asia. In further developments: federal agents, armed with a search warrant, Sept. 21 seized from a Los Angeles warehouse several dozen boxes of Ellsberg's personal papers and possessions—including, according to a Justice Department attorney, classified government documents; the Los Angeles grand jury Dec. 30 indicted Ellsberg on 12 additional charges including conspiracy and violation of espionage statutes.

[15] *Russo surrenders.* Anthony J. Russo, who had worked with Ellsberg at the Rand Corp., surrendered to federal officials in Los Angeles Aug. 16 to begin serving a jail sentence on contempt charges stemming from his refusal to testify before the grand jury that indicted Ellsberg. Russo had refused to talk about the leaking of secret documents even though the U.S. attorney general's office had granted him immunity from prosecution. Russo surrendered after his final attempt to have the contempt charge reversed was denied. He was to remain in jail until he decided to testify or until the grand jury ceased sitting. Russo was freed Oct. 1 after he agreed to testify if the government would give him a complete transcript of his testimony. Russo again refused to testify Oct. 18 when the Justice Department refused to give him that transcript. U.S. District Court Judge Warren J. Ferguson ruled Nov. 4 in Los Angeles that the government could not force Russo to testify unless the transcript were provided. Russo was also indicted Dec. 30 on four counts, including conspiracy, in connection with the Pentagon papers' publication. (Also named as co-

as co-conspirators with Russo and Ellsberg, though not indicted, were Miss Linda Siñay—who had testified that she had received $150 from Ellsberg for use of a duplicating machine she had rented—and Vu Van Thai, a former South Vietnamese ambassador to the U.S.)

[16] **U.S. releases study.** The government put on public sale Sept. 27 an expurgated version of the Pentagon papers. (Judge Gesell in Washington Dec. 7 denied an attempt by Reps. Ogden R. Reid [R, N.Y.] and John E. Moss [D, Calif.] to compel the government to release the entire, unexpurgated study.) The study was released after specialists from the State and Defense Departments and the Central Intelligence Agency declassified the documents. Portions of the papers which the security personnel thought would jeopardize national security or embarrass other nations were deleted. Some of the deletions (references to U.S. diplomatic contacts with the Soviet Union, data about U.S. discussions regarding relations with nations contributing troops to the Vietnam conflict and material about covert military operations ordered by the Johnson Administration against North Vietnam) had already been published by the Times, the Post and other newspapers. Four entire volumes of the original study, which dealt with secret diplomatic negotiations during the Johnson Administration, were withheld entirely. (None of those volumes had been obtained by the press.) The government's version also contained some previously unpublished material from the war study, including eight letters and cablegrams from Ho Chi Minh (then Communist leader in Vietnam and later president of North Vietnam) that went unanswered. In the correspondence, Ho appealed for help in his fight against France in 1945-46.

[17] *Declassification of documents.* The publication of the Pentagon papers caused the Administration to re-examine its classification procedures. Among the results of that re-examination: President Nixon Aug. 3 sent a request to Congress for a supplemental $636,000 appropriation to start "an immediate and systematic effort to declassify the documents of World War II." Government officials had estimated that only 5%-10% of the secret documents of the 1940-45 period still contained material that should retain its secret classification. The declassification program was expected to take five years to complete and 10 times as much money as the original appropriation. The White House announced Aug. 12 that President Nixon had ordered the early declassification of secret government documents from the Korean War, the landing of American soldiers in Lebanon in 1958 and the Cuban invasion and missile crisis of 1961-62. (At the same time, the White House announced that new rules would restrict the distribution and duplication of current classified documents in an effort to prevent leaks.) The Defense Department announced Oct. 20 that it planned to reactivate the Classification Review and Advisory Board (dormant since March 1968) as part of its program to simplify the system used to classify and declassify secret documents. As part of the change, the Pentagon said it planned to make its documents harder to classify and easier to declassify. The board was to give the Pentagon policy guidance to its security classification management program, that would rewrite the rules that governed the U.S. classification system.

Contents of Papers

[18] **Truman makes first 'crucial' move.** *(Reported in the Washington Post July 3.)* Approval by President Harry S. Truman May 1, 1950 of $10 million for French forces in Indochina was described by Pentagon analysts in the papers as the first "crucial decision regarding U.S. military involvement in Indochina." The growing U.S. concern with events in that part of Asia was reflected in a National Security Council (NSC) paper No. 64, issued February 1950, several months after Communist Chinese troops had reached the Indochina border. The document concluded that the State and Defense Departments should prepare a program of "all practicable measures designed to protect U.S. security interests in Indochina." A 1949 NSC paper had expressed concern with the Soviet

Union's efforts "to gain control of Southeast Asia" and presented what later became known as the domino theory by saying "if Southeast Asia also is swept by Communism, we shall have suffered a major political rout the repercussion of which will be felt throughout the rest of the world, especially in the Middle East and in critically exposed Australia." The North Korean attack on South Korea June 27, 1950 led to still further American involvement in Indochina. Despite the pressing needs of the Korean War, American military aid to Indochina rapidly increased and, by the time of the Geneva accords in July 1954, it had totaled $2.6 billion. According to the Post account, although the Truman Administration was reluctant to support France in recovering its lost colony in Indochina, it was nevertheless adamant in its opposition to the ascendancy of Ho Chi Minh (*see* [16]).

[19] Geneva accords undermined. *(Reported in the New York Times July 5.)* The Pentagon study concluded that the U.S. had "a direct role in the ultimate breakdown of the Geneva settlement" of the Indochina conflict in 1954. The study indicated that Aug. 20, 1954, immediately after the Geneva convention, the Eisenhower Administration decided to replace French advisers and supply direct aid to the South Vietnamese government of Ngo Dinh Diem. According to the study, "except for the United States, the major powers [France, Britain, the Soviet Union and Communist China] were satisfied" with the Geneva agreements as concluded July 21, 1954. However, the NSC, in meetings Aug. 8 and 12, concluded that the settlement was a "disaster" that "completed a major forward stride of communism that may lead to the loss of Southeast Asia." The study said that Eisenhower's decision to support Diem was taken despite intelligence warnings that Diem was too weak to prevent a further deterioration of anti-Communist forces. According to the analyst, "the U.S. decided to gamble with very limited resources because the potential gains seemed well worth a limited risk." Beside the direct aid to Diem, the U.S. sent to Saigon in June Col. Edward G. Lansdale of the Central Intelligence Agency (CIA), who headed a team of agents that began covert sabotage operations against North Vietnam soon after the close of the Geneva convention. Included in the Pentagon papers was a lengthy report in the form of a diary describing the operations of Lansdale's Saigon Military Mission (SMM) from June 1954 through August 1955. The Pentagon study concluded that, although the U.S. did not "connive" with Diem to prevent 1956 elections called for in the Geneva accords, the Eisenhower Administration did wish to postpone the elections as long as possible and these views were communicated to Diem. The analyst went on: "Without the threat of U.S. intervention, South Vietnam could not have refused even to discuss the elections called for in 1956 under the Geneva settlement without being immediately overrun by the Vietminh armies." The analyst concluded that "South Vietnam was essentially the creation of the United States." The July 5 Times report also showed the reiteration in NSC documents throughout the 1950s of the domino theory that the "loss of any single country" in Southeast Asia would lead to a loss of all the area, then Japan and India, and would finally "endanger the stability and security of Europe." The report also said that twice in the spring of 1954 the U.S. very seriously considered direct intervention of U.S. troops to help the French. (In another story published July 5, the Times reported the Pentagon analyst's conclusion that the U.S. official view that war was forced on South Vietnam because of North Vietnamese aggression was "not wholly compelling." The study cited intelligence estimates in the 1950s indicating that the war began as a rebellion in the South against Diem's oppressive regime.)

[20] The Kennedy years. *(Reported in the New York Times July 1 and in the Washington Post July 1-2.)* During the John F. Kennedy years (1961-63), the Pentagon study found a transformation from a "limited-risk gamble" of the Eisenhower Administration into a "broad commitment" to bar Communist domination of South Vietnam. The study also reported that "the dilemma of the U.S. involvement dating from the Kennedy era" was to use "only limited means to achieve excessive ends." According to the study, Kennedy resisted pressures for putting U.S. ground combat troops in Vietnam, but combat support and advisory missions were built up in a decision made "almost by default" because of the intense debate in 1961 over the question of ground combat troops—with the Joint Chiefs of Staff and the secretaries of defense and state urging a commitment of troops. Starting from a decision in the spring of 1961, not announced publicly, to send 400 Special Forces troops and 100 other military forces to South Vietnam, the American involvement grew to 16,732 men by October 1963. (The Geneva agreement cited a 685-man limit on the size of a military mission in South Vietnam.) A strange aspect of the period was a drive by Defense Secretary McNamara, when events seemed to subside in 1962 from the chronic crisis of 1961, to begin planning for American withdrawal. McNamara ordered the planning begun on July 23, 1962, the day a Laotian peace agreement was signed in Geneva. The continuing political deterioration attending the Diem struggle caused the eventual demise of all phase-out planning in early 1964. Another aspect of the period was Diem's reaction to the possibility, broached by then-Vice President Johnson during a 1961 Asian tour, of U.S. combat units being sent to South Vietnam and a defensive security alliance drawn between the U.S. and South Vietnam. As told in an embassy report, Diem was uninterested and said he wanted American combat troops only in the event of an open invasion. In a June 9, 1961 letter to Kennedy, however, Diem asked for a "considerable" buildup of U.S. troops and a 100,000-man expansion of the South Vietnamese army. By Sept. 29, 1961, according to a cablegram from the U.S. ambassador in Saigon, Diem was asking for a bilateral treaty. On the U.S. side, the study revealed the ascendancy of the domino theory.

[21] The Diem coup. *(Reported in the New York Times and in the Washington Post July 1.)* The Pentagon study detailed U.S. "complicity" in the coup that overthrew President Diem in 1963 and resulted in the death of Diem and his brother Nhu, U.S. support for the plotters and the discovery later that the war against the Viet Cong was in much worse shape than previously thought. The resultant trend, according to the Pentagon analysis, was to do more rather than less for Saigon. By supporting the coup, it said, "the U.S. inadvertently deepened its involvement. The inadvertence is the key factor." President Kennedy was kept abreast of the coup planning; and, although the White House repeatedly called for caution on the part of U.S. Ambassador in Saigon Henry Cabot Lodge if the coup showed signs that it would not succeed, Kennedy made no direct countermand to the strong hand backing the coup played by Lodge. (Lodge, in communications with the White House, opposed any effort to "put cold water" on the plot.) According to the Pentagon report, the U.S., for two months before the coup, "variously authorized, sanctioned and encouraged the coup efforts of the Vietnamese generals and offered full support for a successor government." The study held that the U.S. had faced three "fundamental choices": to back Diem, to encourage a coup or to seize the opportunity of political instability to disengage from South Vietnam. The first choice was not taken because of the consideration that "we could not win" with Diem and Nhu. The third alternative, according to the study, was "never seriously considered" because of the underlying assumption that an independent, non-Communist South Vietnam was "too important a strategic interest to abandon." The report attributed much of the impetus toward the coup to Diem and Nhu and their violent action against the Buddhist opposition, including the midnight assaults on pagodas throughout Vietnam Aug. 21, 1963 despite a public pledge of conciliation by Diem.

[22] Post-Diem years. *(Reported July 1-3 in the Washington Post.)* According to the Pentagon report, the U.S. was struggling in 1963-64 more to keep in the war than to get out of Vietnam. The weakness in Saigon following the coup was also a major problem of the war from 1964-67, when U.S. forces in Vietnam grew from 15,000 advisers to nearly 50,000 troops. The U.S.

attitude toward the Diem ouster and the January 1964 coup against his pro-U.S. successor Gen. Duong Van Minh was colored by fear that pro-French politicians and generals in Saigon might embrace French President Charles de Gaulle's August 1963 call for "neutralization" of Vietnam. Then-President Johnson March 1964 sent word to Ambassador Lodge that "your mission is precisely for the purpose of knocking down the idea of neutralization wherever it rears its ugly head." The papers indicated that the justification used by Gen. Nguyen Khanh for the Jan. 30, 1964 bloodless coup that toppled Minh was that he moved against Minh to frustrate the ambitions of "pro-French" generals in Saigon who wished to seize power and negotiate for neutralization. The political difficulties in South Vietnam following the Diem ouster were such that there were six major changes of government in 18 months, with the U.S. not being informed in advance about four major coups or coup attempts. During this period, the Pentagon papers showed the U.S. preoccupation with strengthening the Saigon government in order to successfully pursue the war in the South. The Saigon regimes, however, pressed for military action outside South Vietnam—for action in Laos and a "March North" campaign. The U.S. was drawn into increased military involvement, partially in order to encourage and improve the morale of the weak leaders in Saigon. According to the study, President Johnson, during the first year of his presidency (1964), was confronted with conflicting advice from advisers adding up to a dilemma that whatever course he chose in Vietnam would lead to a risk of nuclear war. While some advisers cautioned that inaction in Southeast Asia, leading to the loss of Vietnam, would cause the U.S. to slip into a nuclear confrontation, others warned that massive intervention could trigger a nuclear war with Communist China. According to the Post account, no adviser seemed able to guarantee just what Communist China's reactions would be.

[23] **Tonkin period.** *(Reported in the New York Times June 13.)* The Pentagon study cited three elements of a growing clandestine war against North Vietnam during the period beginning in early 1964 and continuing to the Tonkin Gulf clashes in August 1964: a series of destructive and harassment actions—ground, air and sea raids—conducted under the code name Operation Plan 34A and beginning Feb. 1, 1964; air operations in Laos; and destroyer patrols in the Gulf of Tonkin, under the code name De Soto patrols. (Military planning for the 34A raids was the joint responsibility of the U.S. command in Saigon and the South Vietnamese; the Laos bombing included reconnaissance by U.S. Air Force and Navy jets [with armed escort jets after June 6-7, 1964, when two Navy jets were shot down by enemy ground fire] and strikes by T-28 fighter-bombers carrying the markings of the Laotian Air Force but flown sometimes by pilots of Air America [a private operation run by the CIA] and by Thai pilots; the first destroyer patrol in the Tonkin Gulf was conducted without incident in February and March of 1964, but the presence of the U.S. destroyer Maddox in the Gulf during the second mission resulted in the Tonkin incident.) Of the three phases, the Pentagon analyst emphasized the importance of the 34A raids, saying that the "unequivocal" U.S. responsibility for the raids "carried with it an implicit symbolic and psychological intensification of the U.S. commitment." In addition to the clandestine military operations, the Johnson Administration prepared detailed plans for "increasingly bolder actions" against North Vietnam advocated by Gen. Maxwell D. Taylor, chairman of the Joint Chiefs of Staff. Following a Jan. 23, 1964 NSC meeting at which President Johnson ordered that planning "proceed energetically," Administration officials produced a scenario dated May 23 outlining a 30-day program leading to full-scale, open bombing of North Vietnam. The program included both a plan for air strikes and lists of targets. The scenario was never put into operation as planned, but elements of it were adopted before and after North Vietnamese torpedo boats Aug. 2 and 4 attacked the Maddox. (The existence of the plan was credited for the Administration's ability to retaliate for the Tonkin incident so quickly.) Another part of the scenario was securing the passage of a joint Congressional resolution to back the Administration. In

June of 1964, President Johnson formally asked the CIA if the domino theory was valid. The CIA memo in reply said that: "With the possible exception of Cambodia ... it is likely that no nation in the area would succumb to Communism" if Laos and South Vietnam fell. The CIA memo also said that a continuation of the spread of Communism in the area would be slow and not inexorable.

[24] **Sustained bombing undertaken.** *(Reported in the New York Times June 14.)* The Johnson Administration reached a "general consensus" at a Sept. 7, 1964 strategy meeting that air attacks would probably have to be initiated. Before the meeting, Gen. Taylor, who had succeeded Lodge as ambassador to Saigon, Aug. 18 told Johnson that counterguerrilla measures in the South were not enough and counseled "a carefully orchestrated bombing attack" on North Vietnam. The Joint Chiefs of Staff agreed with Taylor's assessment of the need for bombing. While not rejecting the advice, the Administration decided against immediate bombing or any "provocation strategy"—a decision largely based on President Johnson's upcoming election campaign and on the weakness of the Saigon government. The President's orders resulting from the meeting were for a resumption of the De Soto patrols, reactivation of the 34A coastal raids and arrangements for Laotian ground operations, air strikes and possible U.S. reconnaissance flights. Following a Nov. 1, 1964 Viet Cong attack on U.S. planes and facilities at Bienhoa airfield near Saigon, Johnson set up an interagency working group under William Bundy, assistant secretary of state, to recommend options for Vietnam policy. (In the words of the Pentagon papers, "there appears to have been, in fact, remarkably little latitude for reopening the basic question about U.S. involvement in the Vietnam struggle.") The Bundy group came up with three options, presented to the NSC Nov. 21, 1964: (A) reprisal air strikes and covert military pressures; (B) bombing of the North "at a fairly rapid pace and without interruption" while resisting "pressures for negotiations"; and (C) a gradual escalation of air strikes "against infiltration targets, first in Laos" and then in North Vietnam and then against other targets in North Vietnam, with a possibility of "significant ground deployment to the northern part of South Vietnam." The consensus of the NSC (despite the opposition to bombing expressed by Undersecretary of State George W. Ball) advised a two-part operation: a 30-day program of Option A type attacks followed by the first phase of Option C. In an assessment of the bombing plan, the Pentagon analyst said that the decision was based on "a significant underestimate of the level of the [North Vietnamese] commitment to victory in the South and an overestimate of the effectiveness of U.S. pressures in weakening that resolve." President Johnson approved the plan after it was presented to him Dec. 1 and immediately authorized implementation of the 30-day first phase; but he tied further action to a strengthening of the Saigon government, which was overthrown later in December by dissident army officers. The first U.S. bombing strike came Feb. 7, 1965, following a Viet Cong attack on a U.S. compound at Pleiku. Although executed as a "one-shot, tit-for-tat reprisal," said the analyst, "the drastic U.S. action ... precipitated a rapidly moving sequence of events that transformed the character of the Vietnam war and the U.S. role in it." There was a second U.S. reprisal raid Feb. 11 following a guerrilla attack on U.S. barracks at Quinhon. Johnson gave the order Feb. 13 that March 2 launched a sustained air war against North Vietnam—Operation Rolling Thunder.

[25] **Increasing ground combat involvement.** *(Reported in the New York Times June 15.)* The Pentagon study related that, in the months after the Rolling Thunder bombing campaign was authorized, the Johnson Administration swiftly lost hopes for its success. In the beginning of the campaign, according to the Pentagon analyst, Washington hoped the air assaults "would rapidly convince Hanoi that it should agree to a negotiated settlement to the war in the South." However, "once set in motion, the bombing effort seemed to stiffen rather than soften Hanoi's backbone." The rationale

for the bombing shifted from assaults "dominated by political and psychological considerations" to a "militarily more significant, sustained bombing program" designed to destroy Hanoi's capability to support a war in the South. With the failure of the air war, emphasis began to switch to a ground war. Gen. William C. Westmoreland, American commander in Saigon, March 26 requested (and was backed by the Joint Chiefs of Staff) 17 battalions of U.S. combat troops. President Johnson April 1 decided to use U.S. ground troops for offensive action. He ordered deployment of more troops and "a change in mission" for Marine battalions "to permit their more active use." Johnson's decision met with dissent from two opposite poles. John A. McCone, director of the CIA, argued April 2 that the planned actions were not strong enough and would cause the U.S. to become "mired down in combat in the jungle in a military effort that we cannot win and from which we will have extreme difficulty extracting ourselves." Undersecretary Ball argued in a memo circulated June 28 that neither bombing the North nor fighting guerrillas in the South would effectively advance U.S. interests. Ball suggested, in the words of the Pentagon study, that the U.S. "cut its losses" and withdraw from South Vietnam. He presented the President July 1 with a compromise solution reflecting these beliefs. With a series of Viet Cong successes in "summer offensive" attacks in May and June, President Johnson decided on a troop buildup for offensive action, approving the deployment of 34 battalions July 17 with others to be requested later if needed. (Westmoreland June 7 had requested 44 battalions.) The Joint Chiefs July 30 approved 44 battalions for deployment; and, by the end of the year, 184,314 troops were in South Vietnam. The July 17 decision (kept secret like the April 1 decision) provided the means for change in the role of U.S. combat forces—from the base and enclave security activity of the spring to search-and-destroy operations. "The acceptance of the search-and-destroy strategy," said the Pentagon study, "left the U.S. commitment to Vietnam open-ended. The implications in terms of manpower and money are inescapable." In conclusion, the Pentagon study said, "the major participants in the decision knew the choices and understood the consequences." The deployment "was perceived as a threshold—entrance into an Asian land war. The conflict was seen to be long, with further U.S. deployments to follow." The analyst also perceived a "subtle change of emphasis" in U.S. strategy, from denying the North victory in the South and convincing the enemy he could not win, to defeating the enemy in the South.

[26] 1965-66 escalation. *(Reported in the New York Times July 2.)* The Pentagon study said the massive buildup of U.S. troops in 1965 and 1966 occurred because "no one really foresaw what the troop needs in Vietnam would be" and the enemy's ability to expand forces was "consistently underrated." The study suggested that Westmoreland's battle plan in July 1965 "was derived from what would be available rather than the requirement for manpower being derived from any clearly thought out military plan." According to the study, Westmoreland expected "to have defeated the enemy by the end of 1967" by a three-phase strategy: (Phase I) the commitment of U.S. and allied troops necessary to end the losing trend by the end of 1965; (Phase II) the resumption of the offensive by U.S. and allied troops during the first half of 1966 in high-priority areas necessary to destroy enemy forces, and reinstitution of rural-construction activities; and (Phase III), if the enemy persisted, a period of one to one and a half years following Phase II would be required for the defeat and destruction of remaining enemy forces and base areas. Withdrawal of U.S. forces was to commence after Phase II as South Vietnam became able to establish and maintain internal order and defend its borders. Because Westmoreland "did not take escalatory reactions into account," according to the Pentagon analysis, he would revise upward his estimate of the number of troops needed at each phase of his plan. He requested a total of 175,000 in June 1965, 275,000 in July 1965, 443,000 in December 1965 and 542,000 in June 1966. Neither the requests nor President Johnson's approval of all but the last request were made public. (The refusal of the last request marked the end of automatic approval of troop increases.) The Pentagon study also said that the U.S. air war expansion was based on a "colossal misjudgment" of the effect of bombing on Hanoi's capabilities and will. It said that, in the summer of 1965, the bombing campaign changed from an attempt to break Hanoi's will to a more modest effort to stop infiltration and the flow of supplies to the South. A "major policy dispute" in the spring of 1966, according to the study, was whether the U.S. should bomb North Vietnam's oil storage facilities, a plan endorsed by Presidential Assistant Walt M. Rostow and encouraged by the Joint Chiefs. The CIA advised repeatedly that it was unlikely that bombing oil tanks would "cripple" the enemy, but the attacks were ordered June 22 and begun June 29. By the end of July, it was reported that 70% of North Vietnam's original oil storage capacity had been destroyed, but Hanoi was still able "to meet her ongoing requirements." The strikes were a failure, and Secretary McNamara realized it. They were the last major escalation of the war recommended by him. (The Pentagon papers also indicated that, although military leaders were confident of victory, civilian leaders expressed doubts about the effectiveness of both air and ground efforts—even though they continued to recommend escalation. The Times also indicated that an August 1966 nongovernment scientific panel declared the bombing effort a failure and urged that an electronic barrier be established to stop infiltration and supplies from the North.)

[27] **Turnabout by McNamara.** *(Reported in the New York Times July 3.)* The Pentagon papers reported that Secretary McNamara, his disillusionment with the course of the war deepening, Oct. 14, 1966 recommended to President Johnson a reduction in the bombing of North Vietnam and a cutback in U.S. troop reinforcements. McNamara asked Johnson to "limit the increase in U.S. forces" in 1967 to a total of 470,000 men (100,000 fewer than requested by the military). He asked that a portion of the troops be used for "construction and maintenance of an infiltration barrier" *(see* [26]), recommended a program to "stabilize" the bombing attacks on the North and said "we should consider" a decision to "stop bombing all of North Vietnam" or to shift targets away from Hanoi, Haiphong and areas to the north and concentrate instead "on the infiltration routes." The Joint Chiefs—who had on Oct. 7 urged what the Pentagon analyst called a "full-blown" mobilization of the Army, Navy, Air Force and Marine reserves—reacted swiftly and violently to McNamara's memo. They sent him a memo Oct. 14 saying that they did not concur in his recommendation and that they held the air campaign against the North "to be an integral and indispensable part of overall war effort." President Johnson rejected McNamara's proposal to limit the air war, but did order a territorial limit on the bombing of North Vietnam on March 31, 1968 (17 months after McNamara made his proposal). McNamara's proposal opened a rift in the Administration, with wider debate taking place over troop requests. Gen. Westmoreland March 18, 1967 notified the Joint Chiefs that he needed at least 100,000 men "as soon as possible but not later than 1 July 1968." The request said that, for an "optimum force," he would need 200,000 troops. The Joint Chiefs formally transmitted the request to McNamara April 20, proposing: a mobilization of the reserves; a major troop commitment in the South; an extension of the war into Communist sanctuaries (Laos, Cambodia and possibly North Vietnam); the mining of North Vietnamese ports; and a solid commitment in manpower and resources to a military victory. The recommendation "touched off a searching reappraisal of the course of U.S. strategy in the war." In a May 19, 1967 draft proposal, McNamara, according to the Pentagon analyst, "pointedly rejected" the traditional "high blown formulations of U.S. objectives" and "came forcefully to grips with the old dilemma of ... only limited means to achieve excessive ends" *(see* [20]). McNamara sought to bring U.S. policies into line with two principles: that the U.S. commitment was only to see that the people of South Vietnam were allowed to determine their own future; and that the commitment ceased if

South Vietnam ceased to help itself. He urged that Saigon be persuaded to negotiate for a political settlement—a coalition government—and a cease-fire. The Joint Chiefs responded immediately with three memos renewing their recommendations for 200,000 new troops and air attacks. In a May 31 memo, they said that the "drastic changes" advocated by McNamara "would undermine and no longer provide a complete rationale for our presence in South Vietnam or much of our efforts over the past two years." President Johnson disregarded McNamara's advice and launched a spring air offensive against the North in 1967. However, the President's decisions on troop reinforcements were much closer to McNamara's recommendations than to the demands of the Joint Chiefs.

[28]   **Policy change follows Tet offensive.** *(Reported in the New York Times July 4.)* With the Jan. 31, 1968 attack on the U.S. embassy in Saigon which began the enemy offensive during Tet (the Lunar New Year), President Johnson began to take a new view on American policy in South Vietnam. Before Tet, the Pentagon study indicated, Johnson had tended to discount "negative analyses" of U.S. strategy offered by top civilian advisers in 1967 and had instead embraced "optimistic reports" from military sources. Although Johnson said Feb. 2 that the Tet attack had been "anticipated, prepared for and met," the Pentagon analysis said the offensive took the White House and the Joint Chiefs "by surprise, and its strength, length and intensity prolonged this shock." Secretary McNamara asked for plans to supply emergency reinforcements to Westmoreland; and, on Feb. 12, the Joint Chiefs presented three alternatives—all of which they said would leave the strategic reserve in the U.S. dangerously thin—and recommended that "a decision to deploy reinforcements to Vietnam at this time be deferred." Accord-ing to the analysis, the Joint Chiefs were hoping, "by refusing to scrape the bottom of the barrel any further for Vietnam," to force the President to call up reserves, a step they had long thought essential. Despite the advice, McNamara Feb. 13 approved an emergency deployment of 10,500 troops, a brigade of the 82nd Airborne Division. Johnson went to North Carolina to see the men off Feb. 14. (According to the Pentagon study, Johnson was deeply and significantly moved by the experience.) To determine exactly how many men Westmoreland would need, Johnson sent Joint Chiefs Chairman Gen. Earle G. Wheeler to Saigon in late February. Wheeler's report on the Tet drive was not optimistic. He said that the enemy had gained the initiative with the action and that Westmoreland had said he required 206,756 reinforcements (about half by May 1 and all by the end of 1968). According to the Pentagon analysis, the Administration was now faced with two clear alternatives: to honor the troop request and thereby be forced into Americanization of the war, a call-up of reserve forces and vastly increased expenditures; or to deny the request or cut it, thereby indicating that an upper limit to American involvement in South Vietnam had been reached. Clark Clifford, designated to be sworn in as defense secretary March 1 to replace McNamara, was asked by Johnson Feb. 28 to gather senior advisers for a complete review of U.S. policy. Development of draft memos to the President, to be approved by the Clifford Group, was the work of the International Security Affairs (ISA) office of the Defense Department. An ISA draft memo Feb. 29 said that, even with the requested troop reinforcements, U.S. troops would not be in a position to defeat the enemy and that further escalation would make it difficult to persuade critics "that we are not simply destroying South Vietnam in order to 'save' it and that we genuinely want peace talks." The memo also suggested that growing disaffection with the war, accompanied by growing draft resistance and unrest in the cities over a belief that the U.S. was neglecting domestic problems, could provoke a domestic crisis "of unprecedented proportions." The ISA memo advised that the U.S. "buy the time" needed by the South Vietnamese army rather than wage offensive war. The ISA approach was strongly opposed by military advisers and rejected March 3 by the Clifford Group. The Group's revised memo indicated that it had come to no conclusions on bombing policy and

recommended: deployment of 22,000 more troops, reservation of a decision to deploy the remaining requested troops and approval of a reserve call-up of about 262,000 men. President Johnson March 13 approved a deployment of 30,000 men, later reduced to 13,500. Finally, March 31, the President announced a cutback in the bombing of the North to the 20th Parallel and that he would not seek re-election. According to the Pentagon papers, the President's decision was influenced by increasing public pressure against escalation and the war and by two major considerations: the conviction of his principal civilian advisers that the troop requests by Westmoreland would not make a military victory any more likely; and "a deeply felt conviction of the need to restore unity to the American nation."

See also AGNEW, SPIRO THEODORE; AUSTRALIA [12]

PEOPLE'S COALITION FOR PEACE & JUSTICE—*See* DRAFT & WAR PROTEST [12-17]
PEOPLE'S PARK—*See* STUDENT UNREST [7]
PERON, EVA—*See* ARGENTINA [13, 16]
PERON, JUAN—*See* ARGENTINA [13, 16-17, 20]

PERSIAN GULF STATES—The six Trucial State sheikdoms on the Persian Gulf merged Dec. 2 to form a single nation called the Union of Arab Emirates. Its members were Abu Dhabi, Dubai, Sharja, Ajman, Fujaira and Umm al Quawain. The union was proclaimed at a meeting of the six sheikdom rulers in Dubai. Agreement of the states to merge had been announced July 18. Sheik Zayd ben Sultan of Abu Dhabi was elected president. Sheik Rashid ben Saeed of Dubai was appointed vice president; his crown prince, Sheik Maktoum ben Rashid, was named premier. The union's government was to be located in Abu Dhabi until a new capital was built on the border of Abu Dhabi and Dubai. The independence proclamation said the union was part of the Arab Nation and that it would join the Arab League, as well as the U.N. A new treaty of friendship was signed with Britain later Dec. 2.

See also IRAN; OIL; QATAR; UNITED NATIONS [1]

PERU—Labor developments. The leftist General Confederation of Peruvian Workers (CGTP) announced Jan. 29 that it had been officially recognized by the government. The CGTP, formed in June 1968, was ordered by the government to register as an official labor organization. The government had previously recognized only the moderate-leftist Peruvian Workers Confederation.

About 13,000 miners, according to a report Feb. 8, agreed to end a walkout which had held up mining operations in southern and central Peru since Jan. 26. The strikes, in demand of higher wages, had affected the iron mines of Marcona Mining Co. and the copper mines of Cerro de Pasco Corp., Southern Peru Copper Corp. and several Peruvian-owned firms. Another strike began against Cerro de Pasco Oct. 26, with 16,000 workers striking for higher pay, better working conditions and other benefits. Constitutional guarantees were suspended Nov. 10 in the central Andean region after workers of the mines and plants occupied one of the mines and held two company officials hostage. Five strikers were killed in a clash with police Nov. 11 when police entered the occupied mine to free the two hostages. The strike was ended Nov. 26.

Minister of Mining and Energy Jorge Fernandez announced June 9 the introduction of a new mining law that would grant mine workers 10% of the profits and participation in the management of mining companies. The new law also reaffirmed state ownership of all mineral deposits, soil and subsoil rights and its 200-mile territorial water claim. Fernandez said the law was another step toward a "new Peruvian society." The law did not immediately threaten nationalization of U.S.-owned mines.

The government ended a 15-day teachers' strike Sept. 15 by arresting some union leaders and deporting others on charges of committing subversive acts. Among the six leaders deported was revolutionary leader Hugo Blanco who had been released from prison in 1970.

Government takes control of TV and radio. In the latest of its series of reforms aimed at restructuring Peruvian institutions, the government Nov. 10 placed all television and radio stations under state control. It was the most sweeping formal state intervention in Latin American broadcasting outside Cuba. In a nationwide radio broadcast Nov. 9, Minister of Communications and Transport Brig. Gen. Anibal Meza Cuadra said that Peru's telegraph, Telex and telephone systems also would be placed under broader state control soon. Prior to the government move, the state owned one of Peru's 19 television stations and five of the country's 222 radio stations. Most of the private stations had been owned by five or six families. Under the new General Telecommunications Law, the government acquired "at least 51% of shares in all television stations and 25% of the interest in radio outlets." Of the profits, 25% would be distributed to employees—10% in cash and 15% in bonds of the development corporation Cofide. Employees would share in management of the stations but would not be given ownership rights as in the fishing and manufacturing industries. The new law forbade one person or concern to own more than one television and one radio station in each of Peru's 23 states and required owners of the stations to live at least six months of the year in Peru. All station owners and employees must be Peruvian born, and foreign entertainers were permitted only "at the convenience of the authorities." Initially, the government required all stations to give the Ministry of Education one hour of prime broadcast time each day for cultural and educational programs. The Peruvian content of all programming was ordered raised to at least 60% from the present 30%, and all advertising was to be of Peruvian origin.

Press developments. The government announced that the two dailies Expreso and Extra, which had been seized and turned over to a workers' cooperative in 1970, were to be operated by a special committee appointed by the government. According to a report Feb. 12, the committee's functions were to include determination of the general political stance of the newspapers and appointment and removal of directors. Hernando Aguirre Gamio, acting director of the two papers, resigned his post after he had been censured by the workers' cooperative, it was reported Feb. 12. Reasons for the workers' action were not reported. Efrain Ruiz Caro announced Feb. 23 that he had accepted the committee's appointment to head the papers.

Lima auxiliary bishop held. Msgr. Luis Bambaren, auxiliary Bishop of Lima known as the "slum bishop" for his work in the slum communities surrounding Lima, was arrested May 10 for "disrupting public tranquility," on orders of Interior Minister Armando Artola. The arrests of Bambaren and a U.S. priest, the Rev. Carmelo G. Lamazza of the Maryknoll order, resulted from statements allegedly made by the two concerning a battle the previous week between police and squatters who took over state and private land to form a slum community. The clash ended in one dead and 50 injured. Artola labeled the bishop an "agitator." President Velasco Alvarado declared May 13 that the arrests were a mistake. The bishop was released after 12 hours of detention. According to the president, "the government has no difficulty with the clergy. Our country is Catholic. The members of the government are Catholic." Following protests by leaders of the Roman Catholic Church, Artola resigned a week after the arrests, it was reported May 19.

China relations. Peru and Communist China established diplomatic relations Nov. 2. In a joint communique issued in Peking and Lima, the Peruvian government said it recognized Peking as the sole legal Chinese government and noted that Taiwan was "an inalienable part of the People's Republic of China." The communique announced that China "recognized the sovereignty of Peru over 200 nautical miles of sea, adjacent to its coast." Peru was the third Latin American nation (after Cuba and Chile) to establish diplomatic relations with China.

See also ATOMIC ENERGY [11]; AVIATION [14]; CUBA; HIJACKING [8]; LATIN AMERICA

PESTICIDES—Court orders action on DDT. The U.S. Court of Appeals for the District of Columbia, in a 2-1 ruling Jan. 7, ordered the federal government to issue immediate notices of cancellation of all uses of DDT and to determine whether the pesticide was an "imminent hazard" to public health. The orders were directed to William D. Ruckelshaus, administrator of the Environmental Protection Agency (EPA), which had taken over regulation of pesticides from the Agriculture Department. The court, ruling on a suit brought by four groups—the Environmental Defense Fund, the Sierra Club, the West Michigan Environmental Action Council and the National Audubon Society—said the EPA would have to consider the hazards of DDT to determine whether use of the pesticide should be suspended pending outcome of lengthy cancellation processes. In proceedings on the suit in 1969, Agriculture Secretary Clifford Hardin had canceled some uses of DDT. However, he had refused to cancel all uses and had said he would not suspend the pesticide until the department had decided the cancellation issue.

In another ruling Jan. 7, the court ordered the EPA to reconsider the use of herbicide 2,4,5-T. It said Hardin, in refusing to suspend use of the nonliquid form of the herbicide, had "failed to assign sufficient importance to the risk of harm to human lives." The ruling came in a suit brought by Harrison Wellford, representing the Center for the Study of Responsive Law, and several environmental groups.

In response to the court orders, Ruckelshaus said Jan. 15 he would issue cancellation notices for all uses of DDT. He also said that the EPA would begin a 60-day review Jan. 18 to determine whether DDT and 2,4,5-T should be suspended immediately as environmental hazards. Following the review, Ruckelshaus said March 18 that he had decided against immediate suspension of all uses of DDT and 2,4,5-T. The EPA said "precipitous removal of DDT from interstate commerce would force widespread resort to highly toxic alternatives in pest control on certain crops." In the case of 2,4,5-T, the EPA said the uses that had not been suspended previously "pose no imminent threat to the public and should be permitted to continue" while cancellation proceedings were in process. (Ruckelshaus also said he had issued notices of cancellation for three other pesticides—mirex, aldrin and dieldrin. He declined to suspend the use of the products, but the cancellation notices would set in action a review process to determine their hazards.) In further action on the Environmental Defense Fund suit, the court told the EPA Sept. 22 to make a final determination by Nov. 1 on whether to ban all uses of DDT. The court said the agency had not justified its refusal to impose an outright ban. Ruckelshaus Nov. 1 again refused to impose the total ban.

German DDT ban announced. The West German Agriculture Ministry announced Jan. 12 that the use of DDT as a pesticide would be banned after May 16. The decree came nearly a century after DDT was first discussed as a chemical compound by a German chemist. The Ministry said it had ordered the ban after field studies had been made of harmful after-effects of spraying with DDT. Under the new law, use of the compound after May 16 was punishable with fines up to $2,600. A temporary exemption from the ban was granted to the timber industry so that young trees could be sprayed to protect them from insects. That exemption was to expire in 1974.

See also CHEMICAL & BIOLOGICAL WARFARE; ENVIRONMENT; POLLUTION [11]

PETROLEUM—*See* ALGERIA; CANADA [12, 25]; ENERGY; ENVIRONMENT; FIRES; GREAT BRITAIN [17]; GREECE [19]; INDIANS, AMERICAN; NIGERIA; NORWAY; OIL; POLLUTION [4-6, 11]; VENEZUELA

PHILADELPHIA PLAN—*See* CIVIL RIGHTS [1, 21]

PHILIPPINES—Vice President quits cabinet post. Vice President Fernando Lopez resigned Jan. 15 as secretary of agriculture and national resources, while retaining the vice presidency. Arturo Tanco Jr., undersecretary of agriculture was appointed as acting secretary. Lopez's resignation was linked to a dispute between President Ferdinand E. Marcos and the Lopez family, owners of widespread commercial enterprises. In a Jan. 14 broadcast, Marcos had accused "a pressure group" of fomenting a strike of bus drivers and of providing financial aid to the strikers. He specifically criticized Lopez and his brother Eugenio, a businessman. (Bus drivers had gone on strike over a 6% increase in the price of gasoline. Climaxing the week-long strike, 2,000 students demonstrated Jan. 14 in support of the workers and clashed with police. Four persons were killed and many injured. The drivers agreed Jan. 15 to call off the strike for one week after the oil companies said they would roll back their prices for that period while government auditors checked their books, but the strike was resumed Feb. 1. At least three people were killed in widespread violence throughout Manila. The strike ended Feb. 11.)

Attacks on servicemen. The U.S. embassy Feb. 1 filed a protest with the Philippine government against increasing physical attacks against American servicemen at the Subic Naval Base, 50 miles north of Manila. In attacks against service-men: information supplied by a captured Hukbalahap guerrilla led to the discovery Jan. 8 of a common grave in which the bodies of three U.S. airmen, missing since December 1969, had been buried after the three were slain by Huks; an American airman was killed Feb. 3 outside Clark Air Force Base near Manila, reportedly by three Filippinos attempting to rob him. In other anti-U.S. activities: the Manila headquarters of Esso and Caltex, two American oil companies, were damaged by bombs Jan. 22 set by a group calling itself the People's Revolutionary Front; a bomb exploded on the grounds of the U.S. embassy in Manila Feb. 12.

Christian-Moslem violence. A force of 350 government soldiers were sent to Carmen on Mindinao Island to prevent further trouble after 20 men invaded a Moslem mosque June 17 and killed 61 persons and wounded 18 others with gunfire and hand grenades. Cotabato Province was the scene of a bitter feud between Moslem residents and Christian migrants from other regions, who had allied themselves with primitive tribesmen. By Aug. 10, the death toll in the province was 400 since January, with 178 wounded (see below).

Terrorists disrupt Manila rally. Ten persons were killed and 74 wounded by terrorist grenades at a pre-election rally of the opposition Liberal party in Manila Aug. 21. Among the wounded were all eight senatorial candidates of the party who were to face President Marcos's Nationalist party candidates in November elections. Marcos called the incident the beginning of a subversive Communist campaign to burn Manila and kidnap government leaders. He suspended the election campaign until Nationalists and Liberals decided how to proceed in the face of the violence. In a nationwide broadcast Aug. 23, Marcos announced the indefinite suspension of the right of habeas corpus "for persons currently detained or those who might be detained for the crimes of insurrection or rebellion." Police were permitted to search without warrants and to detain suspects without charges. The Supreme Court ordered the Defense Department Aug. 25 to show cause why suspension of the right of habeas corpus should be continued. The government held agents of the New People's Army (NPA) responsible for the grenade attack. The NPA was a secret antigovernment organization based in central Luzon.

A committee of the Philippines Senate Sept. 6 refuted Marcos's charges that a "clear and present danger of a Communist-inspired insurrection or rebellion" existed. The report, dealing with the situation in central Luzon, north of Manila, where Huk insurgents had operated since World War II, said that the immediate problems in the area were lawlessness, poverty and government corruption. Sen. Jose W. Diokno, a foe of the president, Sept. 4 contended that the government military, or men trained by the military, were responsible for throwing two hand grenades at the rally. Diokno resigned from the Nationalist party in protest. However, Marcos defended the emergency measures Aug. 26, citing an insurgent attack that day on a military command post as evidence that the guerrillas had not given up their plans. Guerrilla forces struck again Sept. 8 at a government army unit in Isabela Province, killing six soldiers. Marcos Sept. 21 restored some of the constitutional freedoms suspended following the rally disruption. He reinstituted the guarantee against indeterminate detention in 39 of 66 provinces, but the right of habeas corpus remained suspended in the Manila area, parts of Luzon and all of Mindinao.

Senate elections. The liberals won at least six of the eight contested seats in the 24-member Senate in elections held Nov. 7. The Nationalist party had held 13 of the uncontested seats prior to the balloting. Elections were also held for more than 15,000 municipal and provincial offices, with the Nationalists ahead in a majority of the races. Casualties on election day included 40 killed and 23 wounded. Since the start of the campaign July 9, 199 persons had been killed and 207 wounded. (In special Senate and municipal elections Nov. 22 in Lanao del Norte Province, held because most of the residents had fled during Christian-Moslem fighting at the time of the regular elections, government soldiers killed 44 Moslems in two incidents. Following an order by Marcos Nov. 26 for an investigation of the shootings, criminal charges were filed against 24 persons, including the mayor of Magsaysay and 21 soldiers. The soldiers, who would normally face court-martial, were ordered held for civilian trial.)

See also HIJACKING [7]; STORMS

PHOSPHATES—*See* POLLUTION [7-8, 11]
PHYSICS—*See* NOBEL PRIZES
PING-PONG—*See* COMMUNIST CHINA-U.S. DETENTE [3-4]; SPORTS

POLAND—Post-riot actions. In an attempt to recover from the December 1970 riots which reportedly had claimed at least 300 lives, the government abandoned two measures believed responsible for the disturbances. The actions came as industrial workers threatened new strikes. The government Jan. 25 delayed for one year the introduction of the controversial wage-incentive system. Under pressure from striking textile workers, the government Feb. 15 announced its intention to revoke March 1 the food price increases also considered responsible for the 1970 disturbances. Premier Pyotr Jaroszewicz said lowering of food prices had been made possible by "substantial credits" from the Soviet Union, but did not specify the amount of the loan.

Personnel changes. *Cabinet.* Interior Minister Kazimierz Switala, widely considered responsible for giving the order to fire on industrial workers in Gdansk during the December riots, asked to resign because of ill health Jan. 23. Switala was replaced by one of his deputies, Franciszek Szlachcic. A two-day session of Parliament ending Oct. 26 approved the replacement of Justice Minister Stanislaw Walczak by Wlodzimierz Berutowicz, of Minister of Culture and Arts Lucien Motyka by Deputy Minister Czwslaw Wisniewski and of Chemical Industry Minister Edward Zawada by Jerzy Olszewski. *Party.* The Central Committee of the Communist party Feb. 7 suspended Wladyslaw Gomulka, former first secretary, for "serious mistakes in recent years," particularly during the December 1970 disturbances. At the same meeting the Central Committee dismissed Zenon Kliszko and Boleslaw Jaszczuk—two of Gomulka's close associates—for "acting irresponsibly and thus contributing to the intensification of the fighting in the Gdansk area." A third member of the committee was also ousted, and resignations from the Politburo were accepted from Ignacy Loga-Sowinski, former head of the Trade Union Council, and Stanley Kociolek, who had appealed to workers in the Gdansk area to return to their jobs. The Central Committee June 24 relieved Mierczyslaw Moczar, a Politburo member considered a rival to CP First Secretary Edward Gierek, of responsibility for internal security of the committee. The official reason was Moczar's election June 22 to the post of chairman of the Supreme Control Chamber, a state agency that audited government financial operations. The same meeting removed Artur Statewicz from the committee's Secretariat.

State Council. Parliament Feb. 13 removed Loga-Sowinski from the Council of State. Gomulka was removed from the State Council May 20. *Parliament.* Gzeslaw Wycech was allowed to resign Feb. 13 as speaker of the Polish Parliament and was replaced by Dyzma Galaj. Kliszko was removed as deputy speaker the same day.

Economic measures taken. The government announced reforms Feb. 24-March 9 designed to bolster the Polish economy. The establishment of a National Bureau of Information, to be administered by the Science and Technology Committee of the Council of Ministers, was reported Feb. 24 after receiving Politburo approval the previous day. The new data bank was expected to absorb a number of computer centers and to improve economic planning. The government Feb. 24 abolished "initial work periods" by which university graduates were required to serve apprenticeships at low wages in positions chosen by the state.

Church gets German lands title. In a move toward the normalization of relations with the Roman Catholic Church, the Polish Parliament June 23 granted the church title to buildings and land in the western and northern parts of the country relinquished by Germany after World War II. The transfer, to be made without payment or taxes, included some 7,000 former church buildings and 2,000 acres of land, much of it church gardens.

Party card exchange begins. The party's Central Control Commission announced June 29 the beginning of a party card exchange, a process by which members relinquished their identity cards to a screening body which would rule on their fitness for continued membership. The announcement predicted the expulsion of "opportunists." According to a July 20 report, Poland's Communist party of nearly two million members was the third largest in the world, following those of China and the Soviet Union.

Party congress held. The Sixth Polish Communist party (Polish United Workers' party) Congress was held in Warsaw Dec. 6-11 to elect party officials and confirm policies initiated as a result of 1970's riots. The meeting was attended by the party leaders of the Soviet Union, Czechoslovakia, Bulgaria, East Germany, Hungary, Rumania and Yugoslavia. Addressing the delegates Dec. 6, First Secretary Gierek said the party's "supreme goal" was the "systematic improvement of living standards." Real earnings during the coming five-year period would increase by 18% over the previous period. Industrial investment was to go up 53%, national income 38%-39%, consumer goods industries investment 98%. A wage policy would be instituted which gave "preference to the growth of productivity and to general economic results" but there would be "a separate program" for low-income groups. The "most important and the most urgent problem" was housing to meet the needs of "some 1,000,000 families," for whom it was planned to build slightly more than that number of new flats. This was 25% more than in the previous five-year plan, Gierek said.

The congress ended Dec. 11 with major but expected changes in the party's hierarchy. Delegates elected a Central Committee expanded from 91 to 115 members, and a Secretariat of 11 (instead of 7) members was chosen. Gierek announced that the Central Committee had elected a Politburo of 11 members, one more than previously, and that three persons prominent in the Gomulka era had been dropped from that body, although they retained seats in the Central Committee. These were Foreign Minister Stefan Jedrychowski, President Jozef Cyrankiewicz and Gen. Moczar. Their places were taken by Mieczyslaw Jagielski, director of economic planning; Henryk Jablonski, minister of education; Gen. Wojciech Jaruselski, defense minister; and Franciszek Szlachcic. All but Szlachcic had been candidate (nonvoting) members of the Politburo.

See also ATOMIC ENERGY [10]; DISARMAMENT; GERMANY, EAST; GERMANY, WEST [1-2]; NOBEL PRIZES; PAKISTAN [42]; SPACE [24]

POLICE—*See* BLACK MILITANTS [5-9, 13-14]; LABOR [7]; SUPREME COURT

POLITICS—Campaign spending reform. A bill to limit the amount presidential and Congressional candidates could spend in election campaigns emerged from a House-Senate conference Dec. 13 and was approved by the Senate Dec. 14. House action was postponed until the next session of Congress. (Separate versions of the bill had been passed by an 88-2 Senate vote Aug. 5 and by a 372-23 House vote Nov. 30.) The bill would limit campaign spending by candidates for federal office to 10¢ per constituent, with not more than 60% of the total to be spent in any one medium (television, radio, newspapers, magazines, billboards or telephones). Television spending would be limited, under the formula, to an $8.4 million total. Broadcasters would be required to sell time to candidates at the lowest rate. Candidates receiving and spending more than $1,000 were required to report contributions and expenditures of more than $100. All funds from fund-raising affairs were required to be reported. Reports were required three times a year and six times in election years. They were to be filed with the Congressional clerks or state officials. The conferees dropped: inclusion of postage for mass mailings in the 60% total; repeal of the equal-time provision for broadcasts; an overall ceiling on campaign spending; and limitations on individual contributions except those from delegates. (The first and third provisions dropped had been included in the House bill; the second and fourth were included in the original Senate bill.)

Republican Party

[2] **Dole named chairman.** The Republican National Committee Jan. 15 approved President Nixon's selection of Sen. Robert J. Dole (Kan.) as the party's national chairman. He succeeded Rep. Rogers C. B. Morton (Md.), previously named by Nixon as secretary of the interior. Dole was considered a conservative, and his selection reportedly had encountered some internal party resistance from liberals. Dole was to retain his Senate seat. The committee Jan. 15 also approved a Nixon suggestion to have two co-chairmen serve with Dole. (The move was seen as an attempt to mollify critics of the Dole appointment.) The co-chairmen were Delaware National Committeeman Thomas B. Evans Jr., an insurance man with a background in working for Negro problems, and Texas National Committeewoman Anne Armstrong. Evans was to work in the areas of administration and organization, Mrs. Armstrong in charge of special programs.

[3] **San Diego named convention site.** The Republican National Committee voted July 23 to hold the party's 1972 presidential convention in San Diego (reportedly President Nixon's personal choice). In being chosen (above Miami Beach, Houston, Chicago, Louisville and San Francisco), San Diego put together a package that included $1.5 million in cash, goods and services from the city, county, state and local business community. Under the plan approved by the committee, the delegates would meet in San Diego Aug. 21, six weeks after the Democrats opened their convention in Miami.

[4] **1972 presidential campaign.** Sen. Robert Taft Jr. (R, Ohio) announced May 27 that he would be a favorite son candidate for president in the Ohio presidential primary as a stand-in for President Nixon. Rep. Paul N. McCloskey Jr. (R, Calif.), a two-term liberal congressman, announced July 9 that he would seek the Republican party's nomination for president, challenging President Nixon in the New Hampshire and California primaries. McCloskey, an opponent of the Indochina war, said he would not wage a one-issue campaign. He mentioned the economy, new domestic priorities and the environment as other key issues in his campaign. The Young Americans for Freedom (YAF), a conservative group, Sept. 5 endorsed, in mock balloting, a ticket of Vice President Spiro T. Agnew for president and New York Conservative Sen. James L. Buckley for vice president. The endorsement came on the second ballot. On the first ballot, California Gov. Ronald Reagan carried 258 votes to 210 for Buckley, 208 for Agnew and 26 for President

Nixon. On the second ballot, Buckley's supporters withdrew his name. Gov. Reagan had made it clear before the convention of the YAF that he did not want its nomination. (President Nixon received 41 votes on the second ballot.) Following the voting, delegates to the YAF convention authorized a $750,000 campaign fund to put "a real conservative" on the ballot in the presidential elections. The votes were seen as a signal to the White House that the young conservatives would not accept a ticket without Agnew and that they were willing to back a challenger to Nixon in the primaries if a conservative candidate emerged. Rep. John M. Ashbrook (R, Ohio) Dec. 29 entered the presidential race as a spokesman for conservative Republicans. Ashbrook, who planned to enter primaries in New Hampshire and Florida, conceded that one purpose of his candidacy was to reverse the "leftward drift" of the Nixon Administration.

Democratic Party

[5] Convention reforms. The Democratic National Committee Feb. 19 approved reform plans for revising the way delegates were selected and the way votes were apportioned for its 1972 national nominating convention. The delegate selection plan, devised by a reform commission, established guidelines that would bar the unit rule, require selection of delegates in the convention year and open the selection process to broader participation by blacks, women and young people. Another guideline would require a favorite son candidate to commit himself to a serious candidacy. Under the plan to apportion votes, the number of votes for each state would be allocated according to a formula counting the state's Democratic vote for president 47% and its Electoral College strength 53%. Under it, the nine most populous states would have a majority of the 3,016 delegate votes. At the 1968 convention, it would have taken at least 13 of the most populous states to combine for a majority. (A U.S. district court in Washington June 16 held the apportionment plan invalid as discriminatory, but that decision was reversed Sept. 30 by the U.S. Court of Appeals for the District of Columbia. Another challenge to the apportionment plan—by Georgia Lt. Gov. Lester G. Maddox—was rejected by a federal appeals court in Washington July 24.) The reform commission, headed by Rep. James G. O'Hara (Mich.) June 11 adopted rules for the 1972 convention banning floor demonstrations, limiting nominating and seconding speeches to 15 minutes and no more than three speakers, giving state delegations their positions on the floor and their place on the role call by lot and limiting favorite son nominations to those obtaining written support of 50 votes, with no more than 20 from any one delegation. The commission completed its task July 30 by approving a rule requiring states to apportion representatives to the convention's standing committees "as equally as possible between men and women" and with "due regard to the race and age of the men and women elected." The panel also approved language to require that each delegate to the convention "expressly agrees that he will not publicly support or campaign for any candidate for presi-dent or vice president other than the nominees of the convention.

[6] Miami chosen as convention site. The Democratic National Committee July 9 formally ratified Miami Beach as the site of the party's 1972 presidential nominating convention. The party's site selection committee had recommended the city June 28. It would be the first Democratic convention in the South since 1928.

[7] Lindsay becomes Democrat. New York Mayor John V. Lindsay Aug. 11 formally switched from the Republican party to the Democratic party "because it offers the best hope for a change in national direction and national leadership in the 1972 election." Lindsay spoke of "a time of realignment" when "progressive Republicans, independents and Democrats must stand together in fighting for common goals" and not struggle "vainly against each other in the net of party alignment."

[8] Presidential contenders agree. Democratic national chairman Lawrence F. O'Brien announced Feb. 10 that major Democratic presidential contenders (Sens. Edmund S. Muskie of Maine, George S. McGovern of South Dakota, Hubert H. Humphrey of Minnesota, Henry M. Jackson of Washington, Edward M. Kennedy of Massachusetts, Harold E. Hughes of Iowa and Fred R. Harris of Oklahoma) had agreed at a meeting the night before to forgo feuding and to concentrate on defeating President Nixon in 1972. O'Brien said he had met with another contender, Sen. Birch Bayh of Indiana, Feb. 2 and Bayh had also "subscribed to the purposes" of the Feb. 9 meeting. O'Brien said the group also agreed to work for party reform, revision of campaign spending legislation, a reduction in the party's $9 million debt, and greater access to free broadcast time. McGovern, Harris, Bayh, Humphrey, Muskie and Rep. Wilbur D. Mills (Ark.) also agreed July 14 to limit each candidate to broadcast spending of 5¢ for each registered voter in each of the 22 primaries scheduled in 1972. If any candidate entered all the primaries, his maximum expense would be $2,819,000.

[9] Presidential contenders. Democrats who announced their candidacy for the presidential nomination in 1972 were: Sen. McGovern (Jan. 18); Sen. Harris (Sept. 24); Rep. Shirley Chisholm (N.Y.), the only black woman in Congress (Sept. 26); Mayor Sam Yorty of Los Angeles (Nov. 16); Sen. Jackson (Nov. 19); Walter E. Fauntroy, the District of Columbia's representative in Congress, as a favorite son candidate in the District's primary (Dec. 7); former Sen. Eugene J. McCarthy (Dec. 17); and Mayor Lindsay (Dec. 28). Those who dropped out of the race were: Sen. Hughes (July 15), who dropped out because he believed he could accomplish more by devoting his full attention as a senator to such issues as narcotics and alcoholism; Sen. Harris (Nov. 10), who dropped out because of lack of funds; and Sen. Bayh (Oct. 12), who removed himself to be with his wife, who was recovering from cancer surgery.

[10] Muskie rules out black on ticket. Sen. Muskie Sept. 8 ruled out a black running mate on the grounds "such a ticket was not electable" and therefore "would not serve the purposes" of either the ticket or the cause of equal rights. Muskie, in Los Angeles, confirmed at a news conference that he had given the view in reply to a question during a private meeting with 35 black leaders in the Watts area Sept. 7. Emphasizing that the exchange had occurred "in the context" of a discussion about how to deal effectively with the problems facing the blacks in America. Muskie said the question of a black vice presidential running mate "was put to me in a way that seemed to call for an honest and direct and frank political judgment." "There are only three answers," he said, "yes, no, or maybe. I chose what I thought was the honest answer." He said his answer was an attempt to convince blacks who might support his candidacy that "what we needed to do was to elect a ticket that would be committed to dealing effectively with questions of racial inequality."

Miscellaneous

[11] Stokes leaving for 'people's lobby.' Cleveland Mayor Carl B. Stokes, elected in 1967 as the first black mayor of a major American city, announced April 16 that he was leaving office after his current term expired to seek development of a "people's lobby" to bring pressure on the two major political parties toward "responsive" presidential candidates in 1972 and toward a reordering of the nation's priorities. Stokes said he would focus his efforts on helping "locked-in minority groups to better understand their role in politics and government." He said his goal would be to gain councilmanic, mayoral and Congressional posts through development of political power at the local level among coalitions of blacks, the poor and liberal whites.

[12] Wallace indicates 1972 race. Gov. George C. Wallace (D, Ala.), a third-party presidential candidate in 1968, indicated Aug. 4 that he would be "a serious candidate in 1972 because I believe that a victory for me is quite possible." Wallace said "the only thing that would keep me out is a meaningful change of direction in the Nixon Administration or the Democratic party." He said he had "no realistic hopes that such miracles will come to pass."

[13] 4th party set. About 200 delegates, representing 28 local parties in 25 states, at the founding convention of the "People's Party" in Dallas Nov. 27 nominated peace activist Dr. Benjamin Spock for president and black educator Julius Hobson for vice president. The delegates considered Spock a stand-in candidate, which some states required before granting ballot slots. They hoped to substitute a politically more prominent candidate if the 1972 Democratic convention failed to name a left-of-center designee. Although the Indochina war remained an issue for the delegates, major attention was also focused on economic concerns.

See also BUSINESS [7]; MINES; NEGROES; NIXON, RICHARD MILHOUS [6]; RACIAL & MINORITY UNREST [3]; TAXES; WELFARE; WOMEN'S RIGHTS

POLLUTION—Ruckelshaus urges action. Environmental Protection Agency (EPA) Administrator William D. Ruckelshaus Jan. 12 called on industry and cities to use available methods to control pollution voluntarily without waiting for development of the "ultimate" technology. He said that antipollution efforts should not be delayed because of the complexities of present laws, with their timetables for compliance and provisions for appeals. He pointed out that, by merely applying present technology to the control of smoke, the 17.5 million tons of smoke and soot particulates emitted annually could be cut by 95% to about 700,000 tons and that basic treatment technology for municipal and industrial wastes had "been available for a generation." He acknowledged that past laws had been too complex and had given too little power to government regulators, but he cited the nation's "willingness to procrastinate, seek excuses and literally break the law or hide behind its complexity."

[2] Citizen action urged. The Citizens' Advisory Council on Environmental Quality, in its annual report to the President May 18, called for public involvement in the fight against pollution. The panel, established in 1969, said many citizens groups had formed in the last two years, and it urged the creation of "ad hoc, single-purpose groups ... to challenge public or private action posing a threat to the environment." The committee asked for a nationwide education program and suggested a clearinghouse of environmental information, claiming that "how-to information for citizens is too often scattered, overlapping, incomplete and sometimes nonexistent." The panel urged federal action to help states create "new towns" near decaying inner cities and to develop recreational facilities and said that more federal funds should be committed to fighting air pollution.

[3] Pollution control costs projected. The President's Council on Environmental Quality, in its second annual report to Congress, said Aug. 6 that the costs of meeting 1975 pollution control standards would be at least $105 billion ($23.7 billion for air pollution control, $38 billion for water and $43.5 billion for solid waste). The council's report said that estimating costs of environmental control was "hazardous," since evidence of pollution costs was "rudimentary" and estimates of control costs depended upon standards not yet set and techniques still being developed. The report said that the investment would save higher costs in health care and damage to the environment and was "well within the capacity of the American economy to absorb." President Nixon was less optimistic in a letter accompanying the report. He warned against seeking "ecological perfection at the cost of bankrupting the very taxpaying enterprises which pay for the social advance the nation seeks." He asked for a realistic approach to environmental problems.

Water Pollution

[4] Oil spills. Two Standard Oil of California tankers, maneuvering in a dense fog, collided near the Golden Gate Bridge in San Francisco Bay Jan. 18, releasing an estimated 840,000 gallons of oil which spread along the California coast for 50 miles. Half of the oil drifted out into the ocean, but a high tide Jan. 19 carried much of it back to the coast. California Standard, responsible for cleaning up the spill, hired 250 workers to spread bales of hay to soak up oil on the shore and to man oil-skimming barges and other machinery to pick up oil-soaked birds. The company Nov. 5 was fined $2,500 for the spill—the maximum fine for a corporate defendant under the 1899 Refuse Act (reactivated by the Nixon Administration). A Standard Oil of New Jersey tanker ran aground in fog Jan. 23 at the mouth of the New Haven (Conn.) harbor and spilled about 385,000 gallons of light, highly refined fuel oil onto Long Island Sound. Ice along the shoreline protected Connecticut beaches from the spill, and the oil was a type that would evaporate. In other oil spill developments: 38 oil companies of the U.S., Japan and Europe signed a voluntary agreement Jan. 14 to provide up to $30 million for cleaning up any spill involving one of the participating companies; the U.S. Navy tanker Manatee, refueling the aircraft carrier Ticonderoga during war games Aug. 20, spilled 230,000 gallons of heavy oil that caused a 65-mile slick along the California coast; a Swedish tanker, unloading at a Standard Oil Co. wharf, spilled 15,000-30,000 gallons of crude oil into San Francisco Bay Sept. 17; four oil companies (the Union Oil Co., Mobil Oil Corp., Gulf Oil Co. and Texaco, Inc.) agreed Nov. 24 to pay $4.5 million damages to 1,560 California property owners whose beaches were affected by the Jan. 29, 1969 offshore oil well blowout in the Santa Barbara Channel.

[5] *Oil drilling permits denied.* Interior Secretary Rogers C. B. Morton announced Sept. 20 that the U.S. had denied permits for two new oil drilling platforms (proposed by Union Oil and the Sun Oil Co.) in the Santa Barbara Channel. In denying the permits, Morton said that the new platforms would be "incompatible" with a 1970 proposal by President Nixon to buy back 35 of the existing 70 leaseholds off the Santa Barbara coast to establish a federal marine sanctuary. (The Interior Department, in an environmental impact statement reported Sept. 2, had proposed resumption of oil drilling off Santa Barbara, suspended following the 1969 spill, saying that "steps have been taken to minimize the possibility of major oil spills resulting from accidents." However, the EPA had said the statement did not adequately assess the risk of spills.)

[6] *Offshore leases halted.* U.S. District Court Judge Charles R. Richey in Washington Dec. 16 issued a preliminary injunction barring the Dec. 21 sale of 78 oil and gas tract leases on the outer continental shelf off Louisiana in the Gulf of Mexico. Richey backed claims of the plaintiffs (the National Resources Defense Council, Inc., the Friends of the Earth and the Sierra Club) that an Interior Department environmental impact statement was inadequate, mainly because it avoided discussion of such possible alternatives to offshore drilling as lifting Texas and Louisiana state production limits, changing natural gas pricing policies or increasing oil import quotas. The leases were to be the start of a program to extend drilling eastward into untapped regions off Mississippi, Alabama and Florida. Eight additional tracts had been withdrawn from sale because of their proximity to wildlife sanctuaries. Richey Dec. 17 ordered the environmental groups to post $100 bond, rejecting government requests of an initial bond of $750,000 and monthly bonds of $2.5 million to cover lost interest on the expected $500 million sale proceeds. A three-judge panel of the U.S. Court of Appeals for the District of Columbia ruled Dec. 20 that sealed bids for the leases could be presented as scheduled the next day, but ordered the bids impounded while the case was being decided.

[7] FTC proposes phosphate warning. The Federal Trade Commission (FTC) announced a proposal Jan. 25 to require a warning on labels of detergents containing phosphates that the additive contributed to water pollution and to require the listing of all ingredients in all detergents. (Environmentalists had argued that phosphates encouraged the growth of aquatic plants, which consumed oxygen needed by other acquatic life and speeded a lake's natural aging by "eutrophication"—a process by which the oxygen in water was depleted.) In other antiphosphate developments: Indiana Gov. Edgar D. Whitcomb April 9 signed the first state law restricting the amount of phosphates (12% or less by 1972 and 3% or less by Jan. 1, 1973) allowed in laundry detergents sold or used in the state; Gov. Kenneth M. Curtis of Maine May 18 signed legislation banning from use or sale in the state (after June 1, 1972) all detergents containing more than 8.7% phosphates by weight; New York and Connecticut, as well as Dade County (Fla.) and Akron (Ohio), also banned high-phosphate detergents.

[8] *Use of phosphates reconsidered.* EPA Administrator Ruckelshaus, Surgeon General Jesse L. Steinfeld, Food and Drug Administration (FDA) Commissioner Dr. Charles C. Edwards Jr. and President's Council on Environmental Quality Chairman Russell Train issued a statement Sept. 15 expressing concern about the leading phosphate substitutes: NTA (nitrilotriacetic acid) and caustic substances such as carbonates and silicates. (Scientific findings had indicated that NTA—no longer used by manufacturers in detergents—could have potential cancer-causing effects and seemed to cause birth defects in laboratory animals. Alkalies, such as caustic soda, could act as eye irritants and cause burns.) The four officials did not deny the environmental dangers of phosphates, but Steinfeld said the alternatives "are highly caustic and clearly constitute a health hazard, which phosphates do not." Steinfeld said: "My advice to the housewife is to use phosphate detergents. They are the safest thing in terms of human health." The joint statement by the four said that, in view of the health hazards of phosphate substitutes, "states and localities are strongly urged to reconsider laws and policies which unduly restrict the use of phosphates in detergents." It said the EPA was surveying bodies of water damaged by phosphates to determine if phosphates could be removed in municipal sewage plants. However, Ruckelshaus said the federal government might have to spend as much as $500 million to upgrade sewage treatment plants to remove phosphates. (Steinfeld Oct. 20 modified his advice to the housewife, admitting that there were noncaustic nonphosphate products on the market and advising consumers to use the phosphates only to avert a possible shift by large detergent makers to the caustic alternatives.)

[9] **Mercury contamination.** The FDA announced Feb. 4 that all stocks of mercury-tainted tuna had been removed from the U.S. market. Dr. Edwards said that the seven-week tuna testing program "showed the problem of mercury in tuna to be less serious than had been feared." He said that about 3.6% of the canned tuna supply had been found contaminated and that about six million pounds of tuna had been removed from stores. The FDA announced at the same time, however, that, at the midway point in its swordfish testing program, about 87% of the samples tested contained more than the .5 parts per million (ppm) declared safe in federal guidelines. The FDA May 6 warned the American public to stop eating swordfish because of mercury contamination. The agency said that more than 90% of the swordfish samples tested during its three-month study contained more than the .5 ppm limit of mercury. The FDA said that, despite industry cooperation and the seizure of 832,000 pounds of contaminated swordfish, it was unable to keep swordfish with excessive mercury levels off the market because the industry was composed of small, scattered operators. The agency had decided on the unprecedented, across-the-board warning because it had been unable to develop a program for certifying the 5%-8% of each swordfish catch likely to meet FDA standards. Dr. Edwards said the warning was particularly important for children, more susceptible to mercury poisoning, and for women of child-bearing age, because of tests indicating that mercury can cause birth defects.

[10]   **Toxic metals measured.** The U.S. Geological Survey March 30 reported that unacceptable levels of cadmium or arsenic had been found in water supplies for 12 urban areas across the nation. (The 720 water samples used in the examination had also been tested for traces of chromium, cobalt, lead, zinc and mercury.) A spokesman said the 1970 tests had been made in rivers and lakes before the water had been treated for drinking, but added that the metals ordinarily were not removed by standard water treatment methods. Concentrations of arsenic above the 50 parts per billion considered safe by the Public Health Service for drinking were found in the water supplies for Wilmington and Charlotte, N.C. Water sources for the following 10 cities were found to have traces of cadmium above the 10 parts per billion considered safe: Birmingham and Huntsville, Ala.; Hot Springs and Little Rock, Ark.; East St. Louis, Ill.; Shreveport, La.; Cape Girardeau and St. Joseph, Mo.; and Pottsville and the Wilkes-Barre, Scranton metropolitan area in Pennsylvania.

[11]   **U.S.-Canada accord on Great Lakes.** The U.S. and Canada agreed June 10 to a joint program designed to eliminate pollution in the Great Lakes by 1975. The accord, accepted in principle and to be translated later into an executive agreement, was based on the recommendations made and published Jan. 14 by the International Joint Commission (IJC) after a six-year study. It was estimated that the cost of the program's objective—to make the polluted waters of the Great Lakes and the St. Lawrence River "clean enough for any fish to live in"—would be $2 billion-$3 billion, with the greatest share to be borne by the U.S. because industrial development on the south shore of the lakes was more advanced. About half the U.S. funds were to come from the federal government, and the rest from state and local governments. The agreement included programs to construct treatment facilities for municipal and industrial wastes and to reduce phosphorus discharges by regulating the use of phosphate detergents. The nations agreed to eliminate mercury and other toxic metal wastes and to control thermal and pesticide pollution as well as radioactive waste. The two governments agreed to institute programs to deal with oil spills and to regulate shipping so as to prevent spills. The accord also included research programs and an expansion of the staff and enforcement policy of the IJC.

[12]   **EPA drops industrial waste standards.**   EPA Administrator Ruckelshaus said July 20 that the EPA would not try to establish national industrial discharge standards, envisioned in a dumping program ordered by President Nixon in December 1970. (Under the program, an estimated 40,000 industries were to apply for permits by July 1 to discharge waste under the 1899 Refuse Act. The deadline had passed with thousands of applications not filed. Permits were to be issued under guidelines established by the EPA.) Ruckelshaus said that regional officials would use their own judgment in issuing permits to discharge wastes in U.S. waterways. The EPA admitted that, without the guidelines, regional officials could impose specific discharge limits on only "a selected minority" of the permits. An EPA July 15 memo had told regional officials to concentrate on "the most seriously polluted waters" and the "major sources of pollution" and that the permits "should also reflect availability of completed modeling studies and other data."

[13]   **PCB controversy.** FDA Commissioner Edwards said Sept. 29 that use of the industrial chemical PCB (polychlorinated biphenyis, produced in the U.S. solely by Monsanto Co.), primarily used as a coolant, was "a potential but not immediate health hazard." His statement was issued while opponents pressed efforts to ban the chemical and incidents of PCB contamination were reported involving turkeys (reported Aug. 6), fish (reported Aug. 4), eggs (reported Aug. 18) and packaged dried foods (reported Sept. 27). Edwards reported that Monsanto would restrict sales to "essential closed-system uses, with no use in food or feed plants." A complete ban, he said, was "not feasible." A conference of Nobel Laureates, according to a report Sept. 22, asked for restrictions on PCB use, warning that concentrations of PCB marine pollution "may reach

levels sufficient to damage ecosystems irreversibly on a worldwide scale before the damage is recognized." In another development, the Senate Environment Subcommittee heard a report Aug. 4 that five Japanese had died and 1,000 had suffered a severe skin disease in 1968 due to PCB concentrations of 200 parts per million in cooking oil. Some of the women afflicted subsequently bore stillborn or defective children.

[14] **Senate OKs water pollution bill.** The Senate Nov. 2 approved a bill to eliminate all water pollution by industries and municipalities by 1985. The bill would concentrate ultimate enforcement power in the EPA, authorize at least $14 billion in matching federal funds for sewage treatment, and provide stiff new penalties for industrial violators. The bill, written largely by Sen. Edmund S. Muskie (D, Me.), would abandon the approach of the 1966 water pollution law, which required states to set overall water quality standards, and base the government's policy on the 1899 Refuse Act. Permits under the act would be issued by state agencies, but the EPA would retain veto powers and could prosecute violators. Under the proposed law, the 1985 goal would be reached in three stages, with current state standards to be enforced by 1976, and all streams and lakes to be adequate for recreation and wildlife propagation by 1981. All industrial plants would be required to incorporate the latest control devices in order to obtain discharge permits. Under the 1899 law, permits had not been required of plants discharging into municipal systems. Penalties would reach a maximum of $50,000 a day (for second violations) and two years in jail. Small businesses would be assisted in conforming to the law by an $800 million loan program. Municipalities would have to have secondary sewage treatment plants under construction by 1974 and meet the same general goals as industry. The EPA would be authorized to contract with localities to build the plants, with up to 70% federal funding. The bill would allow private citizen suits against individual polluters, or against the EPA administrator for failure to enforce the law.

[15] **Ocean dumping bill.** The Senate voted 73-0 Nov. 24 to curb ocean dumping of waste materials. The bill would ban ocean disposal of atomic, chemical and biological weapons and high-level radioactive wastes, and would require EPA permits for all other waste dumping. (A draft agreement to ban dumping of industrial waste in the North Atlantic had been adopted by 12 West European countries Oct. 22.)

Air Pollution

[16] **States sue auto industry.** Eight states filed suit in federal district court March 15 charging the Automobile Manufacturers Association, General Motors Corp., the Ford Motor Co., Chrysler Corp. and American Motors Corp. with conspiring to delay development of antipollution devices. (Twenty other states had filed similar suits in the previous few months and other conspiracy suits had been filed in former years.) The suit sought to force the defendants to speed the development of a pollution-free engine and to install smog-control devices on all new cars and used cars dating back to 1953, when the conspiracy allegedly began. (EPA Administrator Ruckelshaus announced Sept. 24 the development, by the EPA, the Army, Ford Motor Co. and Texaco, Inc., of an experimental automobile engine that met stringent antipollution standards set for 1976 by the 1970 Clean Air Act. The "stratified charge" engine worked by injecting a measured amount of conventional, unleaded fuel directly into the cylinder, bypassing the carburetor. The fuel, enclosed in air, burned more completely than in conventional engines. Ruckelshaus claimed that the engine "means that the truly clean car is not as far away as many people thought"; but Ford immediately disputed the claim, insisting that the engine was only experimental.)

[17] **EPA sets clean air standards.** Ruckelshaus April 30 announced "tough" national standards on the amounts of six major air pollutants permissible by 1975. The standards, issued under provisions of the 1970 Clean Air Act, imposed the following limits on pollutants per cubic meter of air: sulphur oxides, 80 micrograms as an annual mean and a single-day limit of 365 micrograms; particulates (soot and smoke), 75 micrograms as a mean and a limit of 260 micrograms for any single day; carbon monoxide, 10 milligrams in an eight-hour period and 40 milligrams for any one-hour concentration; photochemical oxidants, 160 micrograms in any one-hour concentration; hydrocarbons, 160 micrograms in any three-hour period; and nitrogen oxides, 100 micrograms on any annual average. Under the 1970 Clean Air Act, states had until Jan. 1, 1972 to submit plans for meeting the standards for the six pollutants. The EPA would then either accept the proposals by May 1, 1972 or impose its own standards by July 1, 1972. The states would have until July 1, 1975 to implement the standards. Ruckelshaus said that New York, Chicago, St. Louis, Baltimore, Hartford (Conn.), Buffalo and Philadelphia would have a difficult time meeting the deadline for reducing sulphur oxides and particulates and that Chicago, New York, Los Angeles, Denver, Philadelphia, Washington and Cincinnati would have difficulty meeting the deadline for reducing carbon monoxides. The final version of the air pollution control standards was published Aug. 13.

[18] **'Stringent' exhaust standards set.** Ruckelshaus June 29 announced final regulations for reduction of auto exhaust pollutants as required by the 1970 Clean Air Act. Ruckelshaus said the standards were "stringent" and would "challenge the ingenuity of American industry." He also predicted that the cost of meeting the standards by the 1975 and 1976 deadlines would be "substantial, both to the industry and the consumer." The 1970 act required a 90% reduction in carbon monoxide and hydrocarbon emissions on 1975 models and a 90% reduction in nitrogen oxide emissions on 1976 models. The new EPA rules said this would limit emissions in grams per mile to the following levels: carbon monoxide, 3.4; hydrocarbons, .41; nitrogen oxides, 3 (1973 models), .4 (1976 models). The regulations also set up a new testing procedure to determine emissions, but Ruckelshaus Oct. 18 withdrew proposed regulations requiring producers to provide more accurate measures of emissions for the 1973 and 1974 model years. The regulations would instead take effect in the 1975 model year. The EPA said it doubted industry's ability to acquire the necessary equipment and expertise by 1973.

[19] **Plants shut down in air crisis.** Twenty-three Birmingham, Ala. companies shut down their plants Nov. 18, idling about 25,000 workers, on orders from Federal District Court Judge Sam C. Pointer during an air pollution emergency. The order had been sought by the Justice Department on instructions Nov. 17 from the EPA, and was the first emergency injunction issued under the 1970 Clean Air Act. The federal action came after Jefferson County health officials failed to obtain sufficient cooperation from the city's major industries. A stagnant air mass that covered most of the Eastern seaboard had led to a stagnation alert by the National Weather Service in Birmingham Nov. 15, when air particulate counts reached 771 micrograms per cubic meter, far above the federal pollution alert level of 375. Judge Pointer rescinded the shutdown order Nov. 19 after rain and easterly winds had cleansed the air. Alabama had passed a strict air pollution control bill in 1971, but Gov. George Wallace did not name the enforcement commission until Nov. 15.

[20] **EPA to curb 3 pollutants.** The EPA Dec. 3 proposed new curbs on industrial atmospheric emission of asbestos (which could cause lung damage), mercury (known to cause nervous system damage) and beryllium (which could cause chronic chest disease). Emissions per cubic meter of plant air were limited to 10 grams per day (or a 30-day average of .01 micrograms) for beryllium and a one microgram 30-day average for mercury. No specific emission standard

was set for asbestos, but the rules would require the use of filters to clean gases during mining and manufacture of asbestos products and banned the spraying of buildings with asbestos, unless the spraying were done indoors with air treatment. (The Labor Department, in its first use of emergency powers under the Occupational Safety and Health Act, Dec. 7 ordered a reduction in the maximum asbestos exposure levels for manufacturing and construction workers from 12 to five fibers per milliliter.)

[21] EPA sets industry standards. The EPA Dec. 21 announced final air pollution standards for new or modified plants in five major industries. The rules set limits on emission of particulates, sulphur dioxide, nitrogen oxides and sulphuric acid mist. Plants under the new controls included fossil-fueled steam generators (mostly for electric utilities), large solid waste incinerators, portland cement factories, and sulphuric and nitric acid manufacturers. Existing plants were to be regulated by state programs designed to meet federal air quality standards. New-plant standards were to be set for 18-20 industries in 1972, with a total of 35-40 in the next few years.

See also AUTOMOBILES [11-12]; AVIATION [2]; BUSINESS [8]; CONSERVATION; ENVIRONMENT; FEDERAL BUREAU OF INVESTIGATION [5]; ITALY [19]; JAPAN [11]; LABOR [9]; SWITZERLAND; UNION OF SOVIET SOCIALIST REPUBLICS [7]

POMPIDOU, GEORGES—See CHURCHES [4]; FRANCE [1, 11, 17]; INTERNATIONAL MONETARY DEVELOPMENTS [1, 5, 17-18]

POPE PAUL VI—See CHURCHES [17]; ROMAN CATHOLIC CHURCH [1, 5, 7-9, 11]

POPULAR FRONT FOR THE LIBERATION OF PALESTINE (PFLP)—See MIDDLE EAST [5, 7, 9]; TURKEY [6]

POPULATION—National policy sought. Milton S. Eisenhower, interim president of Johns Hopkins University, and Joseph D. Tydings, former Democratic senator from Maryland, announced in Washington Aug. 10 the formation of the Coalition for a National Population Policy. The coalition, to be chaired by Eisenhower and Tydings, included environmental and family planning organizations and such individual sponsors as United Auto Workers President Leonard Woodcock and Roy E. Wilkins, president of the National Association for the Advancement of Colored People. The organization was formed to support a national policy of zero population growth (ZPG). In addition to backing legislation introduced in Congress to declare a U.S. policy of achieving population stabilization by voluntary means, the coalition planned to press for full funding of the $382 million authorized by the Family Planning Services and Population Research Act, a 1970 bill introduced in the Senate by Tydings. Tydings said Congress had appropriated only $38 million for research and $80.9 million for services.

1971 population figures. The Census Bureau estimated Nov. 2 that the total U.S. population had reached 207,372,000 as of Sept. 1, an increase of 2,159,000 over the corresponding 1970 total. The National Center for Health Statistics announced Oct. 3 that the U.S. fertility rate, or number of births per 1,000 women of child-bearing age, had declined dramatically in 1971, reaching 77.5 by July—the lowest level since the 1930s. In the first seven months of the year, there were about 2.05 million births—down 2% from 1970. The number of births had declined every year between 1961 and 1968 and increased in 1969-70. Demographers suggested that the depressed economy, increasing use of contraceptives, increased urbanization and liberalized abortion laws were factors in the decline.

1970 census reports. The Census Bureau issued a series of reports throughout the year explaining the 1970 decennial census figures. Among the conclusions of the census: despite surveys which indicated that the census had undercounted blacks and other minority group members, an Oct. 20 report showed nonwhite growth during the 1960s at 24% (19.7% for Negroes, 51.4% for American Indians, 94.9% for Filipinos, 83.3% for Chinese, 27.4% for

Japanese and 230% for other minority races including Koreans, Aleuts, Hawaiians, Eskimos, Malayans and Polynesians), compared with an 11.9% increase for whites; the rate of Negro migration from the South to the North had remained nearly the same as the high figures for the 1940s and 1950s, according to a report March 3, with 1.4 million blacks leaving the South to settle primarily in New York (396,000), California (272,000), New Jersey (120,000), Michigan (120,000) and Illinois (120,000); Northern and Western white families were moving to the South in record numbers, according to the same report, with New York losing 638,000 white residents and Illinois, Ohio, Kansas, Iowa and Washington each losing more than 100,000; although the number of illegitimate births to both Negro and white women increased during the 1960s, according to a study released April 19, the rate of Negro illegitimacy declined from 10 times the white rate in 1961 to about seven times the white rate in 1968—a drop in illegitimate Negro children born from 101 for every 1,000 unmarried women in 1961 to 87 for every 1,000 unmarried women in 1968—while white illegitimacy had increased from 10 per 1,000 unmarried women in 1961 to 13 per 1,000 unmarried women in 1968; a report Feb. 13 said the number of Americans living in rural areas declined in the 1960s from 30.1% to 26.5% of the population; nearly 10%, or 20 million, of the American people were over 65 in 1970—an increase of 3.4 million—with a disproportionate number living in the South, especially in Florida, according to a report March 28; the U.S. population center, a statistically determined point around which the American people were equally balanced in number and distance, moved 27 miles west and nine miles South between the 1960 and 1970 censuses, it was reported April 25, continuing a western trend first noted in the second federal census in 1800 and reflecting the population growth of the Southern and Pacific states.

See also ABORTION; BIRTH CONTROL; NEGROES; POVERTY

PORNOGRAPHY—*See* CRIME [3]; OBSCENITY & PORNOGRAPHY

PORTUGAL—Educational reform. Education Minister Veiga Simao, according to report Jan. 8, announced a major educational reform system, including an extension of required schooling from six to eight years, two years of optional kindergarten education and abolition of university entrance examinations. In addition, Simao reported that a chain of polytechnic schools would be established to operate in addition to the three existing universities and that higher education would be made available to all classes of society.

Student unrest. Student disorders, which had disrupted the University of Lisbon during December 1970 and January, resulted in the closing of the Advanced Technical Institute in the city Jan. 18 for an undetermined period of time. A Lisbon court Jan. 27 sentenced two women students and two men to 22 months correctional imprisonment for subversive activities at the Institute and for being members of the outlawed Portuguese Communist party. The four were also deprived of their voting rights for five years. Clashes between students and police erupted at the university Jan. 20. Presidents of student associations the same day demanded the normalization of relations between students and administration, the release of arrested students and an exclusive meeting with Simao. Simao said he would meet jointly with students and university administrators only when classes returned to normal. In other student unrest, about 9,000 students of the University of Coimbra struck Feb. 16-17 to protest the arrest of eight students who had attended an unauthorized meeting protesting a political trial in Lisbon.

Guerrillas raid air base. Bomb explosions in a hangar at the Tancos air base, 100 miles northeast of Lisbon, March 9 destroyed six helicopters and two training planes, according to an official communique. However, the Armed Revolutionary Army (ARA), a clandestine anticolonialist group which claimed responsibility for the sabotage, said at least 14 helicopters and three training planes were destroyed. The ARA said the action was to protest "the shameful colonial war ... waged by the Portuguese fascists and colonialists against the peoples of" Portuguese Africa.

9 convicted for subversion. The Lisbon court of political crimes March 30 convicted the Rev. Joaquim da Rocha Pinto de Andrade, an Angolan priest, and eight others from Portuguese Africa on charges of membership in a Lisbon clandestine organization that supported the African nationalist group, the Popular Movement for the Liberation of Angola (MPLA). One other person was acquitted. The trial had opened Feb. 11. Pinto de Andrade, former chief administrative officer of the Archdiocese of Launda, was sentenced to three years in prison and loss of political rights for 15 years. The prosecution alleged that he was named an "honorary president" of the MPLA in 1962 and had retained membership in the organization since then. The defense pointed out that Pinto de Andrade was in prison in 1962 and denied charges of his membership. His brother, Dr. Mario Pinto de Andrade, was one of the founders of the MPLA. The seven others found guilty of such "subversive activities" as sending letters abroad for the Angolan nationalist movement and collecting funds and medicine for the nationalists received prison sentences ranging from 16 months to four and one-half years. The sentences were considered more severe than expected. Observers felt that the verdicts reflected government concern over the increasing domestic opposition to Portugal's African policies.

Constitutional reforms approved. A special session of the National Assembly, convened June 15 by special decree of Premier Marcello Caetano to vote on constitutional reform proposals, approved a government bill authorizing greater autonomy for Portuguese overseas territories, particularly Angola and Mozambique. Under the bill, the territories were authorized to legislate locally, organize their own administration and raise revenue from a budget drafted and approved by locally elected assemblies. The central government would retain control over defense, guarantee rights for the territories' ethnic groups and preserve the national unity. The assembly also passed a bill July 22 recognizing the juridical identity of religious groups other than the Roman Catholic Church, granting such groups the right to meet without previous authorization and abolishing compulsory religious education in public schools. A bill abolishing formal press censorship—in effect for 40 years—and instituting in its place new rules, which could be replaced by censorship in states of emergency, was approved Aug. 5. Under the law, which required all publications, journalists and foreign news agencies to register with the central information services, editors and reporters who published articles undermining the constitution, institutions, unity and independence were made subject to fines and prison terms. (The government was to publish within six months a decree fixing specific conditions to enact some of the provisions of the press law.)

Arrest of union official protested. Police clashed July 26 in Lisbon with about 1,500 bank clerks who were staging a silent protest march against the arrest of Daniel Cabrita, the secretary of their union. Other clashes occurred July 27 in Lisbon and Aug. 6 in Porto. Cabrita had been arrested June 30 and held without formal charges after sending a letter to the International Labor Organization in Geneva protesting the composition of the Portuguese union delegation, whose members, he said, had been designated by the government without adequate consultation with workers. Cabrita, along with at least 28 other persons accused of belonging to the Portuguese Communist party, was ordered Sept. 29 to stand trial on charges of activities harmful to state security. The security police linked the group to the ARA.

Cabrita's arrest sparked a growing dispute between the government and unions. The Interior Ministry July 26 charged Communist infiltration of the bank clerks' union. It closed the union in Lisbon and Porto July 29 "for an indefinite duration." The union's officials in Lisbon and Porto were suspended from their posts Aug. 9. In an apparent crackdown on the union movement, the government Aug. 4 arrested Antonio dos Santos, secretary of the journalists' union, and his wife, a member of the store clerks' union. No reason for the arrests was disclosed.

U.S.-Portuguese base pact. An agreement under which the U.S. would provide Portugal with up to $436 million in economic credits and aid in exchange for continued air and naval base rights in the Azores until 1974 was announced by the U.S. State Department Dec. 10. The agreement, which authorized U.S. economic aid to Portugal for the first time, became effective that day with the exchange of notes between Secretary of State William P. Rogers and Portuguese Foreign Minister Rui Patricio in Brussels, where the two ministers were attending a NATO ministerial meeting. Under the accord, Washington declared its "willingness" to finance as much as $400 million in Export-Import Bank loans for the purchase of U.S.-produced equipment for Portugal's development program. Each separate loan would be subject to Eximbank's approval. The U.S. also authorized the sale of $30 million worth of surplus farm commodities, the free lease of a U.S. oceanographic ship, $5 million worth of nonmilitary surplus equipment and a $1 million education grant. The last pact authorizing U.S. base rights had expired in 1962, but Portugal had informally permitted the U.S. to continue using the facilities.

Subversion law invoked. The government's announcement that it would invoke Article 109 of the revised constitution to halt subversive acts was reported Nov. 17. The constitution authorized the government to take any measures necessary to curb subversion and provided for National Assembly debate in the event of prolonged incidents. The report said the government had asked the assembly to debate Portugal's "state of subversion." The government acted following bomb explosions in the new North Atlantic Treaty Organization (NATO) headquarters outside Lisbon Oct. 27 and at a NATO military base at Caparica Nov. 8. NATO's main telecommunications center in Lisbon had been bombed in June.

See also AFRICA; AGNEW, SPIRO THEODORE; CHURCHES [3]; EUROPEAN ECONOMIC COMMUNITY [5, 10]; GERMANY, WEST [3]; MOZAMBIQUE; SOUTH AFRICA [13]; ZAMBIA

PORTUGUESE GUINEA—*See* AFRICA; PORTUGAL

POSTAL SERVICE, U.S.—Blount to head new service. Postmaster General Winton Blount said Jan. 13 that he had agreed to stay on as chairman of the postal service's governing board when it became a semi-independent public corporation July 1. Blount would no longer be a member of the President's Cabinet, but would be paid $60,000 a year—the same salary he received as a Cabinet member. The nine members of the governing board (Charles H. Codding Jr., Mayron A. Wright, Crocker Nevin, George E. Johnson, Elmer T. Klassen, Theodore W. Braun, Patrick E. Haggerty, Frederick R. Kappel and Andrew D. Holt), picked as interim governors by President Nixon Jan. 5, named Blount to continue as head of the postal service. Blount and a deputy postmaster general—to be named by Blount—would sit as the 10th and 11th members of the board.

Mail delivery standard set. Blount April 12 announced a new airmail delivery standard—next-day delivery for airmail traveling less than 600 miles, delivery two days after posting for airmail beyond that point. The delivery goal, effective April 22, was to have 95% of the airmail within those limits by July. To be included in the category, the airmail would have to be zip-coded and deposited by 4 p.m. weekdays in specially marked Post Office boxes for delivery in 500 major cities. Blount noted that it was "the first time the postal service has ever stuck its neck out" by pledging a delivery standard.

New postal regions. Blount May 12 announced the reorganization of the postal system into five (from the current 15) major regional offices and the creation of special staffs in Washington, D.C. specializing in mail processing, customer services and support (finance, administration, management information, personnel and international mail). The changes would go into effect when the new postal system became operational July 1. The five regions of the reorganization would be: the Western Region (headquarters in San Francisco), comprising 13 states, including Hawaii and Alaska; the Southern Region (headquarters in Memphis), comprising 11 states from Texas and Oklahoma east to North Carolina; the Central Region (headquarters in Chicago), comprising 13 states from Nebraska east to Ohio; the Eastern Region (headquarters in Philadelphia), comprising 13 states from Virginia north to Maine excluding the New York metropolitan area; and the New York City Region (headquarters in New York City), comprising the New York City metropolitan area, Puerto Rico and the Virgin Islands. The revision would lead to a reduction of management employees, a force currently comprising 6,600 workers.

Court refuses to bar mail hikes. Temporary postal rate increases went into effect May 16 after U.S. District Court Judge William B. Bryant in Washington May 11, the U.S. Court of Appeals in Washington May 14 and Supreme Court Chief Justice Warren E. Burger May 15 rejected efforts by publishers and others to bar them. The rate increases were 20%-33% for second- and third-class mail, to 8¢ an ounce for first-class letters (formerly 6¢), to 11¢ an ounce for airmail letters (formerly 10¢) and 6¢ for postcards (formerly 5¢). The postal service had acted to boost the rates temporarily under the 1970 Postal Reorganization Act, which, it said, authorized such action 100 days after a request had been made for permanent increases. (The service had requested permanent increases Feb. 1, but the new Postal Rates Commission, in the process of taking over the reorganized system, did not begin hearings on the request until May 17.) The publishers brought suit on the ground that the increases were being effected illegally without hearings and due process of law. The courts rejected the publishers' plea, largely out of consideration of the legal tenuousness of ruling on a rate-making provision of the new law which would not be in effect until July 1.

New service inaugurated. The new semi-independent U.S. Postal Service went into effect July 1. A highlight of the ceremony marking the event was a message from President Nixon calling the reorganization "one of the major achievements of my Administration." The new service faced an immediate labor problem: contracts covering seven unions expired along with the old Post Office Department and strike votes were taken by several key units. Negotiations for the initial contract had gone through the 90-day collective bargaining period authorized under the Postal Reform Act and were in a 45-day period for fact-finding. Following that, the legislation provided for compulsory arbitration and an imposed settlement. A strike was prohibited. (The United Federation of Postal Clerks brought suit contending that a "fundamental right" to strike was protected by the Constitution, but a three-judge federal panel April 1 rejected the union's position. The panel said the right to strike was condoned by the 1937 National Labor Relations Act, which withheld that right from public employees.) The new postal service also faced a dispute with black postal workers protesting the "plantation" atmosphere within the system and a court challenge by mass mailers to the May rate increase, as well as a charge of unfair labor practices filed by the unions June 8.

Contract signed. The postal service July 20 signed its first negotiated labor contract with the seven unions. The contract provided for a $1,250 annual wage increase (paid out in installments of $250, beginning July 20), a limited cost-of-living increase and various retroactive payments. (Prior to the 1970 Postal Reform Act, postal wages had been set by Congress.) In addition to the wage boosts, postal workers who had been on the job six months or more would receive a one-time $300 bonus not included in the wage base. Workers with less service would receive proportionally smaller bonuses. The talks were complex, involving 61 demands that covered 2,400 separate and negotiable issues. Collective bargaining deadlines had expired July 18, but the two sides decided to continue bargaining rather than submit the contract to third-party arbitration. Assistant Labor Secretary W. J. Usery Jr. received major credit for bringing the two sides together. Although a majority of issues was left for subsequent negotiation when talks were scheduled to resume Aug. 16, the thorniest problem of job security was resolved. The postal service had sought a freer hand in personnel decisions regarding layoffs and suspensions. In return for the pay increases, management gained increased disciplinary powers and new authority over working arrangements and job scheduling; but workers were protected from layoffs and won a provision ending the substitute system that had allowed the postal service to hire many part-time workers.

Blount resigns, replaced by Klassen. Postmaster General Blount resigned Oct. 29, paving the way for a 1972 campaign for the seat that Sen. John Sparkman (D, Ala.) had held 25 years. (Blount said that he had not yet decided to challenge Sparkman and would return to Alabama to "make up my mind.") The Postal Service's board of governors Dec. 7 named Deputy Postmaster General and postal governor Klassen to succeed Blount. The board also elected postal governor Kappel to replace Blount as chairman of the postal board.

See also OBSCENITY & PORNOGRAPHY

POVERTY—Chicago gang indicted in OEO fraud. Twenty-three members of the Black P Stone Nation, a confederation of black street gangs in Chicago, were indicted April 6 on charges of conspiring to defraud the government of antipoverty funds. The charges were based on a two-year investigation that grew out of 1968 Senate hearings into the $927,341 Office of Economic Opportunity (OEO) program in Chicago. The 23 were charged with drawing salaries for teaching jobs never performed, demanding kickbacks from the $45-a-week salaries paid to job trainees and forging checks and check receipts. Eight of those indicted were already in custody on other charges. Seven other gang members were arrested April 7, and the others were being sought.

U.S. poor rise by 5%. The Census Bureau reported May 7 that the number of poor in the U.S. increased by 5% in 1970 (an increase of 1.2 million persons to 25.5 million), reversing a 10-year trend during which the number of poor decreased by an average of 5% a year. Government analysts attributed the rise to unemployment (averaging 3.5% in 1969 and 4.9% in 1970) and inflation (particularly among families on fixed incomes). In a racial breakdown, the bureau reported that the white poverty population was 17.5 million in 1970 (67% of the total) and black poor people numbered 7.7 million. However, one in three Negroes lived in poverty, compared with one in 10 white persons. Families headed by women—accounting for 14% of the total population—represented 44% of the poverty population. Poverty was about evenly divided between rural and urban areas, but about 90% of the increase in poor families in 1970 came in metropolitan areas.

CRLA accord reached with Reagan. OEO Director Frank C. Carlucci June 29 announced an agreement to restore funds to the controversial California Rural Legal Assistance project (CRLA). California Gov. Ronald Reagan, who had charged the program with improprieties and violations of antipoverty law, agreed to lift his 1970 veto of the project. The agreement, signed July 2, funded CRLA at $2.6 million through 1972. Previously announced restrictions on the activities of CRLA lawyers—such as spare-time representation of certain clients, work on labor union cases or representation of clients before legislative bodies such as town councils—were relaxed in the final agreement, although CRLA attorneys were ordered to attempt negotiation before bringing class action suits against California agencies (a major source of contention between Reagan and the OEO project). The accord also: prohibited use of CRLA facilities by nonproject personnel and picketing and demonstrations by CRLA staff; encouraged better relations between the OEO project and local bar associations; and provided a $2.5 million grant to set up a new project, the California Legal Services Foundation, to experiment with different methods of supplying legal aid to the poor.

Reagan had vetoed a $1.8 million OEO grant to the CRLA on the basis of a report written by California antipoverty director Lewis K. Uhler, a former member of the ultra-conservative John Birch Society. The report charged the CRLA should have concerned itself with civil cases involving individual poor people, but instead had brought class action suits, challenged state and local government policies and entered areas of criminal law. Carlucci had announced Jan. 30 that he would not override the veto "at this time," but would give the CRLA a new $600,000 grant to fund the project through July 31 without conditions. Carlucci said that a commission of lawyers would be named to review Reagan's complaints against the program. (The OEO appointed to the commission Chairman Robert B. Williamson, retired chief justice of the Maine Supreme Court; George R. Currie, retired chief justice of Wisconsin; and Robert B. Lee, a Colorado Supreme Court justice.) He said that the Justice Department and the Civil Service Commission would conduct an inquiry "into possible violations of federal law or federal prohibitions on political activity" and that there would be a review of "fundamental policy questions" raised by Reagan "with a view toward recommending new legislation to Congress." Reagan agreed to the six-month extension as a phase-out period for CRLA. The three-judge commission began hearings in San Francisco April 26; but the Reagan administration formally refused to participate in the hearings, and Reagan called for the resignation of the panel April 27. In calling for the commission's resignation, Reagan said it should "go into the field" and undertake a statewide investigation of CRLA operations rather than conducting an open hearing where the state would have to present testimony to support its charges. The panel, in its report June 30, said that Reagan's charges were "totally irresponsible and without foundation."

New food stamp rules issued. The Agriculture Department July 22 issued new food stamp regulations that would make 1.7 million persons eligible for the first time, but would eliminate or decrease benefits for more than two million other persons currently participating in the program. The rules, which implemented the 1970 Food Stamp Reform Act, also included a new "work requirement" that would make registration for and acceptance of jobs by able-bodied adults a prerequisite for food aid. The regulations set a uniform national eligibility standard, which would allow a family of four with a monthly income of $360 or less to receive some aid. The revised rules particularly benefited "the poorest of the poor"—the estimated 900,000 persons who would receive free food stamps for the first time. (For example, a family of four with a monthly income of less than $30 could now receive free stamps, rather than paying $2 a month for them as formerly.) However, the new rules cut off aid altogether for some 600,000 current participants with incomes above the new national standards. Others would become ineligible because the new rules denied benefits to unrelated groups living in the same household, a provision mandated by Congress to cut off aid to hippie communes. The new rules raised the monthly food stamp allocation for a family of four by $2 to $108, but families with incomes near the maximum eligibility level would have to pay more for their stamps.

Nixon vetoes poverty bill. In a strongly worded message, President Nixon Dec. 9 vetoed a compromise two-year $6 billion bill extending the OEO and setting up a $2 billion child development and day care program. The Senate failed the next day to override the veto by a 51-36 vote—seven short of the necessary two thirds. (The bill, passed in final form by the Senate 63-17 Dec. 2 and the House 210-186 Dec. 7, would have provided free day care to all children in families with incomes up to $4,320, reduced-cost day care for families earning up to $6,960 and full cost care for other children. The programs would have been operated by local government units of at least 5,000 population. The bill would also have authorized meals, education, medical care and social services.) Nixon's primary objection was to the child care provisions of the bill, which he said would "commit the vast moral authority of the national government to the side of communal approaches to child-rearing against the family-centered approach" and would create "a new army of bureaucrats." Other provisions of the bill criticized by Nixon: the provision that the day care programs were to be operated by local government, leaving the states, in Nixon's words, "relegated to an insignificant role"; mandatory fund levels for 15 categorical programs, which Nixon claimed would vitiate the OEO's role as innovator; and the creation of an independent national legal services corporation outside the OEO. (The Administration had favored an independent agency, but Nixon opposed the bill's requirement that 11 of 17 board members, all to be named by the President, be selected from lists drawn by the American Bar Association and other private groups.)

Rulings on rights of poor. The Supreme Court March 2 ruled unanimously that poor people could not be jailed solely because they could not pay fines and ruled over the dissent of Justice Hugo L. Black that people who wanted divorces, but could not afford to pay filing fees and court costs, must have those costs borne by the states. (The first case involved Houston laborer Preston A. Tate, who accumulated $425 in traffic fines and was sentenced to jail to work off the fines; the second case involved five Connecticut welfare mothers who had tried to file divorce suits but could not pay costs of about $60 each.) The court's opinion in the jail-or-fine case, written by Justice William J. Brennan Jr., said states and localities could adopt "alternative" ways of collecting fines, such as installment payments. Justices Black, John M. Harlan and Harry A. Blackmun concurred in the ruling but did not join Brennan's opinion. The majority opinion in the divorce case, written by Justice Harlan, held that the women's right to due process of law had been violated. In concurring opinions, Justices Brennan and William O. Douglas said the court should have based the ruling on the 14th Amendment guarantee of equal protection under the law.

See also AGING; BUDGET; DRAFT & WAR PROTEST [11]; HOUSING; HUNGER; NEGROES; POLITICS [11]; STATE & LOCAL GOVERNMENTS [3-4, 7-9]; WELFARE; WOMEN'S RIGHTS

POWELL, LEWIS F.—*See* SUPREME COURT
POWER—*See* ENERGY; ENVIRONMENT
PRESIDENT'S COMMISSION ON CAMPUS UNREST—*See* STUDENT UNREST [2]
PRESIDENT'S COUNCIL ON ENVIRONMENTAL QUALITY—*See* POLLUTION [3, 8]
PRICE COMMISSION—*See* ECONOMY, U.S. [13-17, 19-20, 23-24]
PRISONERS OF WAR (POWS)—*See* CHURCHES [14]; INDOCHINA WAR [1, 53-57, 59-60, 67-68, 73-75, 79]; SELECTIVE SERVICE SYSTEM [5-6]

PRISONS—First national jail study. Richard E. Velde, associate administrator of the Law Enforcement Assistance Administration (LEAA, a branch of the Justice Department), said Jan. 6 that, in many instances, prisoners, children, habitual offenders and mental incompetents were locked up together in city and county jails "in less than human conditions of overcrowding and filth." Velde's statement was based on a nationwide federal census of such jails, conducted by the U.S. Census Bureau for the LEAA at a cost of $140,000. Before the study, according to Velde, "we didn't even know how many jails there are." The study reported that, as of March 15, 1970, 160,863 persons—including 7,800 juveniles and 83,000 persons who had not been convicted, but were awaiting trial or arraignment—were incarcerated in city and county jails. There were about 4,037 city and county jails in which persons were incarcerated for more than 48 hours. Some 500 of the jails in daily use were built in the 1800s and six in the 1700s. Velde said that the census report would provide the basis for increased assistance from the LEAA for criminal reform programs.

[2] Pilot prison plan for women. The Justice Department announced Aug. 10 creation of a $500,000 model rehabilitation program (jointly sponsored by the government, the United Church of Christ and Delta Sigma Theta, a predominantly Negro national service sorority) for female inmates of federal, state and city prisons. The project involved an 18-month rehabilitation program for 300 female prisoners (100 from various state and local prisons and 200 from the Federal Reformatory for Women at Alderson, W. Va.). Each inmate selected would receive five months of intensive guidance and vocational training. After release, each woman would get one year of rehabilitative assistance from volunteer counselors from the church and the sorority.

[3] Newark jail riots. The Essex County jail in Newark, N.J. was the scene of two short-lived riots in 1971. The first broke out April 27 and was quelled the same day after 200 inmates battled guards, destroyed furniture and set small fires in cell blocks. Two inmates and four guards were injured. The prisoners had complained of overcrowding, lack of recreational facilities and high bail. The second riot, which lasted for two hours Nov. 27, broke out after 90 rebellious inmates ripped open a cell and released a prisoner who was in solitary confinement for allegedly stealing a spoon. No one was injured, but convicts smashed windows and flooded two levels of the jail.

[4] Jackson killed during escape attempt. George Jackson, one of three black convicts (Jackson, John W. Cluchette and Fleeta Drumgo) known as the Soledad Brothers, was shot and killed Aug. 21 as he attempted to escape from the California State Prison at San Quentin. (Jackson and the two others had been incarcerated in a maximum security cellblock awaiting trial on charges of murdering a Soledad Prison guard in January 1970.) According to the original prison report, backed up by a preliminary autopsy report Aug. 23, Jackson was killed by a bullet—which entered his body at the skull and exited from the lower part of his back—fired by a tower guard atop one of the observation towers as Jackson dashed across the prison yard with another convict (who surrendered after Jackson was shot). However, a revised autopsy, completed Sept. 7 and made public Sept. 21, reversed the path of the bullet, saying that the fatal bullet hit Jackson in the lower back and traveled through the body to exit through the skull. San Quentin Warden Louis S. Nelson issued a revised account of Jackson's slaying Sept. 30. According to the account, Jackson was shot by a guard who was prone on the gunwalk at the corner of a cellblock. Nelson said that the guard did not know who he was shooting at, but fired at the convict carrying a gun (Jackson) when he heard someone yell "inmate with a pistol." The guard reportedly was trying to hit Jackson in the legs. About two hours after the break attempt, order was restored by prison guards, state highway troopers and sheriff's deputies. Prison officials said that, after order was restored, guards returned to the cellblock area where the uprising erupted and found in Jackson's cell the bodies of two slain guards, a wounded guard and a dead prisoner. Another guard and another prisoner were found dead in the corridor, where there were also two more wounded guards. All of the dead had had their throats slashed. (Later, guards found the probable weapon—a razor blade fitted into the handle of a toothbrush.)

[5] Stephen M. Bingham, a fugitive attorney sought in connection with the escape attempt, and six other men, all San Quentin convicts, were indicted Aug. 21 on charges of conspiracy to commit escape by violent means, conspiracy to possess a firearm, conspiracy to kidnap correctional officers and five counts of murder. The indictment said that Bingham (reportedly the last person to visit Jackson before his escape attempt) gave Jackson an automatic pistol and clips. Jackson used the gun, the indictment charged, to kill one of the prison guards. The indictment said the other two guards and two prisoners slain "were killed by members of the conspiracy." (The six others indicted were Drumgo, Hugo A. Pinell, John Larry Spain, Willie Tate, David Johnson and Louis N. Talamantes.) Bingham was formally charged with the five counts of murder Aug. 31. Under California law, his alleged complicity made him equally guilty with the perpetrators of a capital crime. (Bingham was last seen the evening of Aug. 21. The Federal Bureau of Investigation joined the nationwide hunt for him Sept. 1 after a U.S. magistrate signed a federal fugitive warrant for his arrest.)

[6]   Attica uprising. Nearly 1,500 state troopers, sheriff's deputies and prison guards staged an air and ground assault Sept. 13 to put down an uprising by 1,200 inmates at the Attica Correctional Facility in Attica, N.Y. The uprising resulted in the death of 42 persons (10 guards and civilian employees held as hostages by rebellious inmates and 32 inmates)—38 of them when the lawmen stormed the prison in upstate New York. (One guard was fatally injured Sept. 9, at the start of the uprising, when convicts threw him from a second-story window in the prison. He died of head injuries Sept. 11. One inmate died of his wounds Sept. 15, another Sept. 23 and a third Sept. 25.) Twenty-eight other hostages were rescued by the invading troopers. The decision to send armed troopers into Attica was made after four days of taut negotiations between the rebels and state correction authorities failed to bring an end to the revolt. New York State Commissioner of Corrections Russell G. Oswald gave the order to have the lawmen move in. He was strongly supported by New York Gov. Nelson Rockefeller, and Rockefeller was supported by President Nixon. Early reports by prison officials said most of the slain hostages died when convicts slashed their throats. Other hostages were said to have been beaten and stabbed to death. (At least two of the dead inmates were also reported to have been slain by other convicts.) However, a medical examiner said Sept. 14, and was verified in his opinion Sept. 19, that official autopsies showed that the nine hostages died of gunshot wounds, with no evidence of slashed throats. Oswald later confirmed that all of the hostages had died of gunshot wounds. According to published reports, none of the convicts had guns during the uprising. These reports led to speculation that the hostages were killed by troopers laying down a hail of bullets as they entered the cellblocks. A pall of tear gas and smoke from fires within the prison hung over the troopers as they stormed Attica, making visibility difficult.

[7] The insurrection began the morning of Sept. 9 when a group of prisoners refused to form into work details. The revolt spread as prisoners, mostly blacks, began breaking windows and burning bedding and other furniture. The rebellious convicts seized 32 guards and civilian employees as hostages and later issued a list of 15 demands that included coverage by state minimum wage laws, an end to censorship of reading materials and no reprisals for the revolt. Oswald met with groups of inmates twice during the day in an effort to secure the release of the hostages. At one negotiating session, the convicts said they wanted specific visitors (including militant civil rights attorney William M. Kunstler and Huey Newton of the Black Panthers) to see the conditions at Attica. Negotiations between Oswald and the rebel leaders continued at an impasse Sept. 10-12—reportedly because of the rebels' demand for complete amnesty and the authorities' unwillingness to grant it. (A U.S. judge Sept. 10 signed an injunction insuring that no administrative reprisals would be taken against the rebels, but the prisoners rejected the injunction as "meaningless.") The convicts added to their list of demands Sept. 10, asking for "speedy and safe transportation out of confinement to a nonimperialistic country" and for a federal takeover of the prison. Attica authorities granted one demand Sept. 10 by permitting outsiders sought by the convicts to enter the prison to witness negotiations and view prison conditions. The observer committee Sept. 12 asked Gov. Rockefeller to intervene, but he declined, saying that "I do not feel that my physical presence on the site can contribute to a peaceful settlement."

[8] Several panels began investigations into the Attica violence. In addition, lawyers from civil rights organizations and legal groups representing almost 1,000 inmates began interviewing prisoners to look into charges they were beaten following the recapture of the prison (The State Department of Correctional Services' chief physician said Sept. 21 that an independent team of doctors' had found there had been no injuries or bruises inflicted on inmates since the revolt was crushed.) Among the groups investigating the uprising: the House Select Committee on Crime, headed by Rep. Claude Pepper (D, Fla.), which interviewed Rockefeller Sept. 17, visited the prison Sept. 18 and began an investigative hearing Nov. 29; a five-man panel set up at Rockefeller's request and co-chaired by Clarence B. Jones, editor and publisher of the Amsterdam News, and Austin H. McCormick, former New York City commissioner of corrections; a special criminal investigation group headed by New York State Deputy Attorney General Robert E. Fischer; a state police unit, headed by New York State Police Capt. Henry F. Williams, who had coordinated the assault on Attica; and a nine-member citizens' committee set up at Rockefeller's request and appointed by a five-judge panel. Rockefeller also asked Attorney General John N. Mitchell Oct. 5 to have the Justice Department investigate charges by Attica inmates that "their rights have been violated." State correctional authorities Sept. 27 had denied convicts' charges that they had been interrogated by state investigators without having been advised of their legal rights. (The Supreme Court Oct. 5 was asked to intervene in the controversy Oct. 5 when lawyers for Attica inmates petitioned Justice Thurgood Marshall to issue a temporary restraining order forbidding questioning of inmates until a lower court decided whether the inmates' rights were being violated. However, the court Oct. 12 refused, by a 6-1 vote, to intervene.)

[9]   New rights panel established. The Justice Department announced Sept. 16 the establishment of the Office of Institutions and Facilities, a new office designed to safeguard the civil rights of the nation's institutional inmates in noncriminal matters. The new office, to be headed by Jesse H. Queen, was to seek to resolve complaints of segregated facilities, discrimination in hiring or other noncriminal matters relative to civil rights violations in hospitals, orphanages or other institutions. Queen said the new unit would stress prison reform.

[10]   Inmates' union formed. A group of convicts, ex-convicts and members of their families Sept. 25 formed the United Prisoners Union (UPU), claiming a membership of 3,000 inmates housed in city, state and federal prisons. The UPU had also drawn up a bill of rights for prison reform as an alternative to what it said would be more bloodshed at prisons. (A bill of rights for Pennsylvania prisoners was issued Oct. 4 by the state to insure inmates of state prisons the right to be treated with dignity as human beings while imprisoned. The bill took the form of the Standard Minimum Rules for the Treatment of Prisoners, adopted by the United Nations in 1955. No nation or U.S. state had enacted the rules into law. They provided that untried prisoners be kept separate from convicted prisoners, untried prisoners would sleep singly in separate rooms, untried prisoners could [within limits] have their food procured at their own expense from outside the prison and corporal punishment would be prohibited.)

[11]   Other prison disturbances. A fight between two rival Chicago street gangs (the Black P Stone Nation and the Disciples) allegedly led to an Oct. 2 riot at an Illinois prison in Pontiac which resulted in the death of two inmates by guards and the injury of seven other inmates and five guards. Officials at Walpole State Prison in Walpole, Mass. locked up all inmates Oct. 5, following nine days of work strikes by prisoners seeking changes in state parole laws and in administrative procedures at the prison. (More than 700 inmates at nearby Norfolk prison colony also staged work stoppages of their own Sept. 28 for prison reform.) Under the lockup orders, all normal activities except visits were halted. Rebellious inmates at the Rahway State Prison in Woodbridge Township, N.J. ended their 24-hour Thanksgiving Day insurrection Nov. 25 by releasing the penitentiary's warden and the last of the five guards they had held hostage. The hostages (all of them injured) were released after New Jersey Gov. William T. Cahill assured the convicts that their demands for reforms at the prison would be considered and after the convicts accepted Cahill's assurances that there would be no physical reprisals, that community representatives would be allowed to accompany inmates to insure that no reprisals were made and that full negotiation would begin on the inmates' demands when the state regained control of the penitentiary. The demands included better medical care, improved inmates' diets, religious freedom and expanded educational opportunities. Cahill appointed a five-man panel Nov. 26 to discuss the grievances with five representatives to be selected by Rahway's inmates. (A force of 150 state policemen had been summoned to the prison, but was not used in quelling the uprising.) Six inmates at the Raiford State Prison in Raiford, Fla. armed themselves with homemade knives Nov. 28 after an attempted escape from the maximum security prison and held four prison guards hostage for three hours before they were recaptured by other guards. No one was hurt in the disturbance.

See also CANADA [11]; CHURCHES [4]; GREECE [2]; KOREA, SOUTH; PUERTO RICO; SECURITY, U.S.

PROPERTY TAXES—See EDUCATION [17]
PSYCHIATRY—See UNION OF SOVIET SOCIALIST REPUBLICS [3]
PUBLIC BROADCASTING SYSTEM (PBS)—See FEDERAL BUREAU OF INVESTIGATION [7]
PUBLIC HOUSING—See HOUSING

PUBLIC LAND—Sale curb urged. The Sierra Club, a conservation group formed in 1892, Feb. 14 urged the "repeal of all existing laws for the disposal of public lands." The club advocated establishment of a national land reserve to maintain and restore public lands and control their commercial use. The group also urged repeal of the 1862 Homestead Act, which allowed private citizens to settle and claim public land, and recommended federal laws to improve forestry practices on public and private lands and the replacement of mining laws with a leasing arrangement providing environmental safeguards. Although the club opposed the commercial bias of the 1970 report of the Public Land Law Commission, it supported the commission's recommendation that states with large federal land tracts be given payments in lieu of taxes rather than, as presently done, share revenue from private use of the land.

Nixon offers beach to California. President Nixon March 31 declared six miles of California beach, currently part of the Camp Pendleton Marine Base, to be excess land in the public domain. The President planned to transfer the land to California as the first in a planned series of such transfers to state and local governments for recreational and other uses. The land would be offered to commercial or industrial bidders if the state and local governments did not acquire it. Nixon's plan to transfer the Pendleton land evoked opposition from members of the House Armed Services Committee, who backed the Marine Corps's contention that the area was needed for training purposes. The committee July 14 wrote into a military construction bill a provision barring transfer of the land without the express approval of Congress.

Wilderness protection sought. The Sierra Club and the Wilderness Society urged President Nixon to act by executive order to save some 60 million acres of wilderness pending studies to determine if the land should be marked for permanent preservation. Spokesmen for the groups Sept. 25 charged that a draft presidential proclamation to save the wilderness acres under consideration by the White House had been blocked by the U.S. Forest Service and lumbering interests. The 1969 Wilderness Act set aside nine million acres of wilderness land and picked 45 million additional acres of federal land to be reviewed for inclusion in wilderness preserves. The organizations said that less than two million acres had emerged from the review process to be included in the wilderness system. President Nixon had asked April 28 for legislation to include another 1.9 million acres, but Congress had taken no action.

Stewart M. Brandborg, executive director of the Wilderness Society, said there was little chance even half of the remaining acres could be reviewed before the deadline under the act ran out in 1974. The proposed presidential order would include about six million additional acres under the land to be reviewed. In a speech Sept. 25, Michael McCloskey, Sierra Club executive director, said the proposed order had the support of the Council on Environmental Quality and the Department of the Interior but that it "faces opposition from the secretary of agriculture, the Forest Service and the forest products industry." He said, if the President failed to act, "then our only option is to try to amend the Wilderness Act itself" to include the proposed acreage in the protected system.

See also BUDGET; ENVIRONMENT; NIXON, RICHARD MILHOUS [1]

PUERTO RICANS—*See* EDUCATION [16]; PUERTO RICO; RACIAL & MINORITY UNREST [2-3, 9]

PUERTO RICO—**Culebra developments.** Secretary of the Navy John H. Chafee signed an agreement Jan. 11, ceding to Puerto Rico most of the Navy's control over the island of Culebra (off the coast of Puerto Rico), which had been used by the Navy for target practice since World War II. Under the agreement, the Navy pledged to: discontinue the firing of Walleye missiles around Culebra; phase out the targets on the island's east coast cays by Jan. 1, 1972; surrender its right to control of the entire shoreline of the island, keeping control only of the shoreline around the property it would retain in the northwest portion of the island; and find an alternate target practice area within "a reasonable time." Puerto Rico pledged to: prevent the construction of buildings in the northwest section where gunnery practice would continue; and try "to obtain the cooperation of everyone in keeping the land and sea safety zones for the remaining target areas clear of people during scheduled training operations." Despite the agreement, the Defense Department April 1 ordered the Navy to refrain from using the island for target practice, although granting the Navy several years to leave. Defense Secretary Melvin Laird said that a final decision on the relocation of Culebra target areas would be reached by the end of 1972 and that studies on alternate target areas would be completed by June 1975. The Defense order, however, said that bombardment with explosive shells on the northwestern part of the island would cease by the end of 1971 and that the Navy would develop "nonexplosive rounds" of ammunition that would emit only smoke upon impact. Laird said he had ordered the Navy to take other steps to ease tensions between it and the islanders: to open to the islanders Flamingo beach, adjacent to the firing range; to construct a road to an alternative beach; to cease the removal of sand from Culebra beaches for Navy use; to take action to prevent unauthorized exploitation of ecological resources; to provide unrestricted air and sea corridors between Culebra and neighboring St. Thomas, Vieques and Puerto Rico; and to use Spanish-speaking Navy officers on the island.

Three killed in student unrest. Police riot squad members Maj. Juan Mercado and Miguel Rosario and Reserve Officers Training Corps cadet Jacinto Gutierrez were shot dead March 11 during a riot at the University of Puerto Rico at Rio Piedras. The rioting broke out following fights between members of student radical groups advocating Puerto Rican independence and cadets of the university's ROTC unit. The battle apparently began when an ROTC cadet appeared on campus in uniform. (The ROTC program had been a source of friction since 1967.) Following the campus violence, which also wounded some 50 others, radical students went through Rio Piedras, attacking stores associated with the U.S. and starting fires. The campus was closed following the riot. Faculty returned to the campus March 16, but there was no word when classes would resume. Police arrested 64 people March 12 in connection with the rioting. Police March 17 arrested Humberto Pagan Hernandez, a third-year student at the university, and charged him with the slaying of Maj. Mercado. Six men and a woman were charged April 10 with rioting and malicious damage in connection with violence in the business district following the campus unrest.

Prison riot ends. Prison authorities announced Aug. 18 that a prison riot at Ponce, the island's second largest city, had been quelled after two nights of violence during which 100 men reportedly took over four wards at the prison. They had refused orders to vacate until police fired tear gas grenades. After the riot, prisoners told newsmen that they were protesting poor food and "cruel treatment by some guards."

Referendum planned. The two major political parties—the New Progressives and the Popular Democrats—announced Aug. 19 an agreement to hold a referendum to decide whether the commonwealth government should ask the U.S. Congress to give Puerto Rican residents the right to vote for President. The decision came after a special commission named by President Nixon and Puerto Rican Gov. Luis A. Ferre issued a report which urged Puerto Rico to seek the presidential franchise under the existing commonwealth arrangement, which subjects residents to most federal laws, but not income taxes. Ferre said he would convene a special session of the legislature to draft a bill that would permit the referendum to be held in December. A constitutional amendment would be necessary to allow Puerto Ricans to vote for President.

See also DRAFT & WAR PROTEST [9]; HIJACKING [1]; RACIAL & MINORITY UNREST [3]; STATE & LOCAL GOVERNMENTS [5]; UNEMPLOYMENT

PULITZER PRIZES—The winners of the 55th annual Pulitzer Prizes in journalism, letters, drama and music were announced in New York May 3 by the president of Columbia University. The winners:

LETTERS: Fiction—none. **Biography**—Lawrence R. Thompson for *Robert Frost: The Years of Triumph, 1915-1938.* **History**—James McGregor Burns for *Roosevelt: The Soldier of Freedom.* **General nonfiction**—John Toland for *The Rising Sun.* **Poetry**—William S. Merwin for *The Carrier of Ladders.* **Music**—Mario Davidowsky for *Synchronisms No. 6 for Piano and Electronic Sound.* **Drama**—Paul Zindel for *The Effect of Gamma Rays on Man-in-the-Moon Marigolds.*

JOURNALISM. International reporting—Jim Hoagland of the Washington Post for reporting on South Africa's apartheid system. **National reporting**—Lucinda Franks and Thomas Powers of United Press International for a 12,000-word study of Diana Oughton, "The Making of a Terrorist." **Local reporting, general**—the staff of the Akron (Ohio) Beacon Journal for its coverage of the shootings at Kent State University. **Local reporting, special**—William H. Jones of the Chicago Tribune for exposing police bribe-taking from local private ambulance companies. **Editorial writing**—Horace J. Davis Jr. of the Gainesville (Fla.) Sun for a series of editorials supporting peaceful desegregation. **Editorial cartoon**—Paul Conrad of the Los Angeles Times. **Distinguished criticism**—Harold C. Schonberg, music critic of the New York Times. **Commentary**—William A. Caldwell of The Record, Hackensack, N.J. for a daily column on local affairs. **Spot news photography**—John P. Filo of the Valley Daily News and the Daily Dispatch of Tarentum and New Kensington, Pa. for coverage of the Kent State shootings including the picture of a girl crying over the body of a student. **Feature photography**—Jack Dykinga of the Chicago Sun-Times for pictures of children in two schools for the retarded. **Meritorious public service**—the Winston-Salem (N.C.) Journal and Sentinel for coverage of environmental problems.

QATAR—The Persian Gulf sheikdom of Qatar declared its independence from Britain Sept. 1 and ended its defense and foreign affairs treaties with the London government. The statement, announced by Sheikh Khalifa Ben Hamad Al Thani, deputy ruler, also expressed Qatar's support for the proposed merger of the Persian Gulf emirates (*see* PERSIAN GULF STATES).

    See also OIL; UNITED NATIONS [1]

RACIAL & MINORITY UNREST—Nixon meets Black Caucus.

President Nixon March 25 conferred with the black members of the House of Representatives (all Democrats) and appointed a White House staff panel to study a list of recommendations made by the group, known as the Congressional Black Caucus. (The caucus had requested the meeting a year before.) The group's far-ranging recommendations expressed the "majority" black viewpoint that representatives of the Nixon Administration, "by word and deed, have at crucial points retreated from the national commitment to make Americans of all races and cultures equal in the eyes of their government." Included in the recommendations: that enforcement of civil rights laws be strengthened; that foreign policy attention to Africa be increased; that American troops be withdrawn from Indochina by the end of 1971 or at least by the end of the current Congress; that a comprehensive manpower program be established to create 600,000 more jobs; that one million youths be employed in the Neighborhood Youth Corps during the summer; that a family of four on welfare be given a guaranteed minimum income of $6,500; and that they be given assurances that the poor would be benefited and represented in the decision-making process of revenue sharing.

[2] Puerto Ricans charge neglect. The Puerto Rican Association for National Affairs threatened Aug. 10 to oppose the nomination of Henry M. Ramirez, a Mexican-American, as chairman of the Cabinet Committee on Opportunities for Spanish Speaking People, after Ramirez dismissed two Puerto Rican staff members the previous day. The association charged that the committee, formed to safeguard the interests of Spanish-Americans in federal programs and to develop new programs, was not sufficiently concerned with Puerto Ricans. A committee spokesman Sept. 6 denied that the staff members had been dismissed for ethnic reasons and claimed that three of the 25 current staff members, as well as several prospective members, were Puerto Rican.

[3] Conference plans political action. The first major conference uniting Mexican-American, Puerto Rican and other Hispanic-American groups voted Oct. 24 to set up a permanent Washington office and summoned a representative convention to determine national political strategy. The conference, attracting about 2,000 participants, including state and local officials, was sponsored by four of the six Spanish-Americans in Congress. (Democratic Sen. Joseph Montoya of New Mexico [a Mexican-American], Democratic Reps. Herman Badillo of New York [a Puerto Rican] and Edward

R. Roybal of California [a Mexican-American] and Republican Rep. Manuel Lujan of New Mexico [a Mexican-American] sponsored the conference. Reps. Henry B. Gonzales and Eligio de la Garza, Democrats of Texas, did not participate.) The conference reached agreement on some issues, but young militants introduced and passed Oct. 24 a measure favoring Puerto Rican independence, despite the wishes of Reps. Badillo and Roybal to leave the matter for the people of Puerto Rico to decide. The militants also precipitated debate on whether to form a separate Spanish-speaking political party, but the debate ended with a resolution to form a study commission.

Major Unrest—State-by-State

[4] Alabama. Tension caused by nearly 14 weeks of organized Negro protests (including, since July, a boycott of white merchants by blacks) in the southwestern Alabama town of Butler was aggravated Sept. 11 as a young black girl, participating in a sit-in demonstration, was run over and fatally injured by a car driven by a white man. Gladden Smith was arrested and charged with murder in connection with the death of the girl, Margaret Ann Knotts. Blacks said that Smith intentionally drove his car over Miss Knotts. Whites insisted that it was an accident.

[5] California. Gustav Montag Jr. was killed and 50 persons injured Jan. 31 when 3,000 Mexican-Americans, rallying in East Los Angeles to protest alleged police brutality during and since an August 1970 riot, battled with Los Angeles County sheriff's deputies. Damage from fires during the battle was estimated at $194,000. Ninety persons were arrested.

[6] Florida. Hundreds of black youths swept through the streets of Jacksonville June 16, looting and hurling firebombs, in the wake of 10 days of racial unrest. The disturbances continued through June 20, with reports of snipers and scattered firebombing. Damage was estimated at about $250,000. Police ordered 274 arrests, most on charges of disorderly conduct. One of the underlying causes of the trouble allegedly was the June 10 fatal shooting of a 15-year-old Negro youth by a policeman. The officer was indicted on a charge of manslaughter.

[7] Georgia. Order was restored to Columbus June 23 after three days of violence. The violence erupted June 19 after a rally was called by black policemen to protest what they described as discrimination by their white superior officers. Following the rally, firebombing and other acts of arson hit stores in Columbus. In all, 48 fires were reported during the unrest. At least six persons were arrested in connection with the disorders.

[8] Louisiana. Firemen summoned to battle two blazes in the black Desire Housing Project (site of numerous racial clashes in 1970) in New Orleans were repulsed Jan. 12 by residents who forced them out of the area with a continuous shower of rocks and bottles. Two buildings, used by the Black Panthers as offices, burned. A New Orleans television station said an anonymous telephone caller claimed the fires had been set in retaliation for the arrest of blacks in the project.

[9] New Jersey—Camden. Racial tensions, fueled by reports that two policemen had beaten a Puerto Rican man, led to a week of sporadic looting and firebombing by Puerto Rican youths in Camden Aug. 16-23. The rioting stemmed from demands by Camden's Puerto Rican community that the two patrolmen be suspended. (They were suspended Aug. 21.) Leaders of the Puerto Rican neighborhoods were also pressing for a greater voice in local government. Four persons were injured during the fighting and more than 200 were arrested on charges of street fighting and curfew violations. **Hoboken.** City authorities and Puerto Rican youth leaders in Hoboken Sept. 6 negotiated a truce ending two days of disturbances marked by window smashing and looting. The informal truce was accepted after city officials agreed to release 35 Puerto Ricans arrested during the disturbances on charges ranging from disorderly conduct to assault with a dangerous weapon. Police said 42 persons had been arrested and eight policemen injured in the disorders. The trouble had begun Sept. 4 when word spread through the city's Puerto Rican community that police were beating two Puerto Rican brothers, accused of assaulting a merchant with a knife in an apparent holdup. A crowd of Puerto Ricans marched on police headquarters. Fighting erupted as police tried to hold back the demonstrators.

[10] North Carolina. Order was restored in Wilmington Feb. 8 after four days of racial violence in which two persons (one black, one white) were shot to death. However, 600 National Guardsmen continued to patrol the streets Feb. 9 to prevent further outbreaks. The unrest was linked to a church which was being used by black students who were boycotting Wilmington's public high school.

[11] South Carolina. An all-white jury in Darlington County Feb. 17 convicted three white men (James D. Marsh, Delmer Kirven and Jeryl Best) of common law rioting in connection with a March 1970 attack on school buses carrying Negro children to newly desegregated public schools in nearby Lamar. (Twenty-two whites had been indicted Feb. 16 on riot charges in the incident.) Kirven was also convicted of assault and battery on a police officer. He and Best were acquitted of charges that they maliciously destroyed property. Kirven was sentenced March 8 to a year in prison (suspended to four months with three years' probation) on the riot charge and to two years (suspended to eight months with three years' probation) on the assault and battery conviction. Best was sentenced to two years in prison (suspended to six months with two years' probation) and fined $1,000. Marsh was sentenced to 18 months (suspended to four months with two years' probation) and fined $100.

[12] Tennesee—*Chattanooga.* A rigid dusk-to-dawn curfew was lifted May 26 after order returned following five nights of racial violence. Two thousand National Guardsmen had moved into the city May 24 after local police were unable to contain arson and sniping in the city's black neighborhoods and on the outskirts of the downtown area. The violence erupted May 21 when a black musician refused to perform at a rock concert in the municipal auditorium. When some of the black youths did not get refunds for their tickets, they began vandalizing the building. Police said that more than 400 persons were arrested during the disorders. One young Negro was killed May 25 by police who said they fired after the youth hurled bricks at them. *Memphis.* An uneasy calm returned to the city Oct. 23 after four nights of violence triggered by the death of a Negro youth (Elton Hayes) in a traffic accident Oct. 14. Hayes died following an alleged high-speed auto chase by police. Police first said he had died of a crushed skull sustained in an accident at the end of the chase, but an autopsy showed that Hayes had suffered two fatal blows to the head. Another black youth with Hayes during the incident said that there was neither a high-speed chase nor an accident. He said that he, Hayes and a third youth were dragged from their vehicle and beaten by police with clubs. As a result of the autopsy finding, 23 members of the Memphis police force were suspended pending an investigation. Nine of the officers were indicted Dec. 9 on charges ranging from first-degree murder to neglect of duty in connection with Hayes's death. Property damage from the rioting following Hayes's Oct. 19 funeral ran into the thousands of dollars, most of it from firebombings.

[13] Texas—*Lubbock.* City officials Sept. 11 lifted a dusk-to-dawn curfew after two nights of racial unrest during which three policemen were wounded. The officials agreed to drop the curfew after Negro leaders complained that intensive police patrolling of Negro neighborhoods was increasing tensions. The disorders broke out Sept. 9 after a 16-year-old black student was shot in the heart by a white classmate in an argument over a pack of cigarettes. *Chicano march.* Up to 2,000 Mexican-Americans marched peacefully through small Texas towns in the Rio Grande Valley March 7 to protest police brutality and to demand economic and political equality for the one million Mexican-Americans in the valley. The march, sponsored by the Mexican-American

Youth Organization (MAYO), began in San Juan with 800 demonstrators and ended in a cemetery in Pharr after a memorial service for five men and boys who had been killed by police during and after civil rights demonstrations in the valley since the summer of 1970.

Military Developments

[14] **Pentagon sets up race program.** Defense Secretary Melvin Laird March 5 announced a pioneering program to improve race relations between blacks and whites serving throughout the armed forces. The keystone of the new directive was an educational program requiring every U.S. soldier to attend classes in race relations upon his entry into the service and to attend six-hour refresher courses each year thereafter. To implement the new program, the Defense Department said it would establish a Defense Race Relations Institute to join the already-formed Defense Race Relations Education Board. The institute would train 1,400 instructors within a year.

[15] **Army policy changes ordered.** The Army March 19 announced major policy changes designed to end housing discrimination against black U.S. servicemen anywhere in the world and insure that all American soldiers—black and white—receive equal treatment under military law. (The new directives came one week after Pentagon officials disclosed that they were meeting with Capt. Curtis R. Smothers, a black military judge who, with six other black servicemen, had petitioned Secretary of the Army Stanley R. Resor in December 1970 to establish a court of inquiry into housing discrimination against black U.S. servicemen in West Germany.) The Army announced eight policy revisions, most of them designed to remedy complaints from black servicemen that European landlords often refused to rent them apartments. According to the revisions, all Army personnel wanting to live off base would have to "process through a housing referral office" that would insure that housing "should be open to all soldiers or it should be open to none." Army commanders were given authority to put off-base housing units off-limits to Army personnel if a landlord discriminated against any soldiers under their command. Under the second set of changes, the Army required that every soldier facing any type of disciplinary action be permitted to consult with a lawyer. Base commanders would be required to post the results of nonjudicial punishment conspicuously on bulletin boards. This, the Army said, would make it more difficult for a commander to impose harsher punishments on black soldiers than on whites for the same offense.

[16] **Racism cited in Air Force.** A 15-man human relations team attached to the Air Force Air Training Command (ATC) July 26 sharply rebuked the manner in which the leadership at many Air Force training bases was dealing with racial problems. The team's report, based on a six-month study of 15 bases, said that there was often a double standard for black and white airmen on such matters as punishment, work details, availability of post exchange products and enforcement of regulations. The study said that "the cause of this is blatant supervisory prejudice in many cases, but for the most part it is the supervisory indifference to human needs." Lt. George B. Simler, who received the report, was reported Sept. 1 to have begun a new "quiet" program to eliminate racial irritations.

[17] **Military racism probed.** Members of the Congressional Black Caucus—co-chaired by Reps. Ronald V. Dellums (D, Calif.) and Shirley Chisholm (D, N.Y.)—held hearings at various military installations in the U.S. Nov. 15 and in Washington Nov. 16-18 to investigate charges of racism in the armed forces. The hearings were dominated by reports that blacks were treated unfairly by the military justice system, that racial tensions had become "explosive" at some bases in the U.S. and abroad and that the Defense Department limited the number of black servicemen stationed in some foreign countries (notably Iceland) at the request of the countries involved. Rep. Dellums said at the conclusion of the hearings that the caucus would seek legislation giving federal

courts jurisdiction over military defendants and would press for more black command officers.

[18] Disorders erupt at Coast base. Black and white servicemen battled one another for four hours May 24 at the Travis Air Force Base near Marysville, Calif. before military police and local lawmen succeeded in quelling the disorders. One fireman died of a heart attack suffered while fighting a blaze that damaged officers' quarters on the base; 10 airmen were injured in fighting; and 97 servicemen were arrested. The trouble erupted when 200 blacks marched on the Travis stockade to protest the detention of three blacks who were being held after an alleged fight with whites May 22. The black airmen found the stockade ringed with military police. As they returned to the barracks area, fighting erupted between some of the protesters and white airmen.

[19] Darmstadt charges dropped. Gen. Michael S. Davison Oct. 22 dropped all charges against 29 black soldiers and rescinded nonjudicial punishment of 17 others resulting from a July 19 racial melee in Darmstadt, West Germany. The charges resulted from a mess hall fight between white and black troops, a subsequent alleged attempt by the accused to prevent an arrest and a demonstration against the arrest. Blacks said the fight had been brought on by a pattern of discrimination and a failure to suppress white racism. They charged lack of fairness in pretrial investigations. Lawyers for the blacks said Oct. 25 that they would file suit to prevent the "illegal and punitive" transfer of the men to other bases.

See also AGRICULTURE [7-9]; BUSINESS [8]; CIVIL RIGHTS [9]; DRAFT & WAR PROTEST [10]; EDUCATION [8-9]; SECURITY, U.S.; STUDENT UNREST [8]; YOUTH

RACISM—*See* CHURCHES [1-6, 8, 15]; RACIAL & MINORITY UNREST
RADIO FREE EUROPE—*See* TELEVISION & RADIO
RADIO LIBERTY—*See* TELEVISION & RADIO
RAHMAN, SHEIK MUJIBUR—*See* PAKISTAN [2-5, 21-22, 26, 29-30]
RAILPAX—*See* RAILROADS

RAILROADS—Amtrak begins. The 182-train Amtrak passenger railroad linking more than 300 cities went into operation May 1 under the National Railroad Passenger Corp., a quasigovernmental corporation authorized by Congress in 1970 to relieve railroads of costly passenger service. (The name Amtrak was chosen by the corporation April 19 in preference to Railpax, its original nickname, which the incorporators thought was too close an association with the deteriorating system it was replacing.) The initiation of the system marked elimination of 178 passenger trains operated up to that time by the individual carriers joining the new system. The reduction of service by almost half its former scope, plus the resultant elimination of jobs, led to lawsuits and Congressional opposition to initiation of Amtrak; but an appeal by railroad unions and passenger groups for a delay was refused April 30 by U.S. District Court Judge Howard F. Corcoran in Washington. His decision—that a delay would unjustifiably frustrate the intent of Congress and subject the public and railroads to harm and that the protection offered to displaced workers (full wages and benefits for up to six years, to be paid by the railroads, not Amtrak) was more than normally provided in such cases—was upheld later the same day by a three-judge panel of the U.S. Court of Appeals. In other Amtrak developments: Amtrak's eight directors (Chief Executive Officer Roger Lewis, John Gilhooley of New York, David W. Kendall of Michigan, Transportation Secretary John Volpe, Frank S. Besson Jr. of Virginia, David E. Bradshaw of Illinois, Catherine May Bedell of Washington and Charles Luna of Ohio) were confirmed by the Senate May 3; Amtrak May 6 announced the restoration of rail service along the "20th Century" route between New York and Chicago by way of Buffalo, N.Y., Erie, Pa., Cleveland and Toledo, Ohio, and South Bend and Gary, Ind., conditional on the assumption by state officials of Ohio, New York and Michigan (to be connected with the line by a shuttle between Toledo and Detroit) of two-thirds of the expected $3 million annual deficit. Amtrak

July 2 issued a revised timetable with the following major additions in service: restoration of the 20th Century route; daily trains between Boston and New York via Worcester and Springfield, Mass.; an experimental tri-weekly train between Minneapolis and Spokane, Wash., with new stops in Minnesota, North Dakota and Montana; through service between Chicago and Norfolk, Va., via Cincinnati and West Virginia; through train service, with no change, from Chicago to Miami and St. Petersburg, Fla., via Indianapolis and Louisville.

Penn Central developments. Among developments surrounding the June 1970 bankruptcy of the Penn Central railroad: Secretary of Commerce Maurice Stans said Feb. 17 that there was no impropriety in connection with his holding of stock in the Great Southwest Corp., a subsidiary of the Penn Central, at a time when the government was negotiating to rescue the railroad from bankruptcy. Stans said that the stocks, acquired as a result of his former partnership in two brokerage firms, were placed in a "blind trust" when he acquired them in 1969; and he did not know if he still owned them. He said he had learned of the stock acquisition "inadvertently" through a letter sent to partners and former partners of the brokerage houses. (Under a blind trust, the beneficiary was not informed of what securities were bought or sold by his portfolio's managers and knew only what he originally put into the trust. Stans was notified of the original acquisition of the Great Southwest shares, but not of any subsequent transactions.) Stans said that he had disqualified himself from all negotiations with the Penn Central and did not attempt to influence the government's decision. In another development, Rep. Wright Patman (D, Tex.), chairman of the House Banking and Currency Committee, March 29 released a report on trading of Penn Central Co. stock prior to its reorganization of the Penn Central Transportation Co. The report called for an investigation by Congress and federal regulatory agencies into the "unloading" by nine institutions (Chase Manhattan Bank of New York, Continental Illinois National Bank & Trust Co. of Chicago, Provident National Bank of Philadelphia, Security Pacific National Bank of Los Angeles, U.S. Trust Co. of New York, Morgan Guaranty Trust Co of New York, Alleghany Corp. of Baltimore and two mutual funds under Alleghany's control—Investors Diversified Services and Investors Mutual, Inc. of Minneapolis) of 1,861,000 Penn Central shares between April 1, 1970 and June 21, 1970. The report alleged that the institutions had taken advantage of privileged insider information concerning the acute situation of the Penn Central without informing the public—thus violating federal securities laws. The report also charged that the Securities and Exchange Commission (SEC), the Interstate Commerce Commission (ICC), the Administration and the press failed in their responsibilities to warn the public about the Penn Central's financial straits. (The ICC, in its first report of a 10-month study by 20 auditors, charged April 19 that the officers and directors of the Penn Central Transportation Co. authorized various accounting measures in 1968-70 to mask from the public the financial plight of the railroad.)

Penn Central divests. The trustees of the Penn Central Transportation Co. reversed a decision not to sell 24 valuable real estate holdings in New York City, announcing June 2 that they were putting the properties up for sale. They had informed the Transportation Department in March that the $21.3 million annual income from the 29 acres of real estate were needed to help defray operating costs of the railroad. Congress had ordered the railroad in January to undertake a major divestiture of its nonrail properties in order to obtain $100 million in federally guaranteed financing. The trustees had announced in March plans to sell $393.6 million in real estate owned by its investment company, Pennsylvania Co. (Pennco). The trustees agreed in principle May 24 to turn over all Pennco's common stock to a group of 53 banks in return for a cancellation of a $300 million loan (extended April 1969) and a pledge for an additional $150 million in equipment financing.

Reading files bankruptcy petition. The Reading Co., corporate parent of the Reading Railroad, Nov. 23 petitioned the U.S. District Court in Philadelphia to reorganize under Section 77 of the Federal Bankruptcy Act. The petition cited its inability to pay about $11.03 million in debts and taxes that would shortly fall due. Reading President Charles E. Bertrand blamed the coal strike (*see* MINES) and sluggish industrial activity as the chief factors behind the petition. (The railroad depended on coal traffic for about 30% of its revenues.) Federal Judge John P. Fullam issued an injunction against enforcement of any judgments, liens or suits that would disturb Reading's assets. The petition said that the railroad had only about $4 million in cash Nov. 19 and anticipated cash receipts through Nov. 30 of about $5.5 million. The Reading was the fifth major railroad to declare bankruptcy within five years.

Labor Developments

Rail engineers pact. The railroads and the Brotherhood of Locomotive Engineers May 13 announced an agreement on wages and work rules for the period of Jan. 1, 1970 through June 30, 1973. The pact would provide a wage increase of about 42% over the 42-month period and would (if other operating employees went along with the changes) permit liberalization of work rules covering: switching operations (extending the yard-crew service area to customers within four miles of a railroad yard and allowing road crews to handle some of their own switching); interdivisional runs (eliminating the requirement that train crews must be changed whenever the train entered a new seniority district—about every 100 miles); and signaling equipment (providing that workers using radios to signal would not receive extra pay over those using older equipment).

Legislation ends strike. A two-day strike by the AFL-CIO Brotherhood of Railroad Signalmen (BRS) that virtually halted rail service on a national scale ended after enactment of emergency legislation May 18 providing more time for negotiations and an interim pay rise of 13.5% for the strikers. Negotiations with the signalmen, in progress for about two years, resulted Nov. 16 in a tentative agreement providing a 46% increase over 42 months. The contract was retroactive to January 1970. (The signalmen had been working without a contract since Jan. 1. The impasse had drawn previous Presidential intervention March 4, when a strike had been threatened but a 60-day cooling-off period had been imposed under the Railway Labor Act. This restriction expired May 15.) The May 17-18 strike effectively closed down rail operations as other rail union members respected the signalmen's picket lines at commuter and intercity rail terminals. (The major exceptions were the Long Island Railroad in New York and the South Shore Line in Chicago.) Some 500,000 rail workers remained away from work. President Nixon May 17 sent Congress a request for emergency legislation requiring a cooling-off period without a strike or lockout until July 1. In the Senate, a substitute proposal May 17 called for a truce period to Oct. 1 and a 17.5% wage rise. In the House, a truce to July 20 and a 13.5% pay hike were considered. The chambers affected a compromise—calling for a cooling-off period until Oct. 1 and a 13.5% pay rise—on the floor of each to avoid a time-consuming joint conference. President Nixon signed the legislation before 11 p.m. May 18, and BRS leader C. J. Chamberlain at 11 p.m. ordered picket lines removed. Restoration of service began immediately. (The signalmen had sought to raise their $3.78 hourly wage by 54% over 36 months, retroactive to Jan. 1.)

UTU strikes end. The selective and spreading railroad strikes by the AFL-CIO United Transportation Union (UTU), which began July 16, ended Aug. 2 after agreement on a 42-month contract with a 42% pay increase and on some changes in key work rules. The pact also provided for a permanent standing labor-management committee to handle economic and rules disputes on a continuing basis. The work rules revisions included: giving the railroads the right to institute interdivisional runs—to be sanctioned by the standing joint committee if home terminals of crew members were thus eliminated;

permitting the carriers to make two-way radios standard equipment for workers and to eliminate extra payment for use of radios; requiring yard crews to provide service to industrial plants built before 1951 if they were within four miles of the yard; and authorizing a requirement, if the lines deemed necessary, for crews taking cars to other rail lines to return with the cars. The pact guaranteed higher compensation if workers were idled because of work rules changes and authorized relocation allowances if necessitated by such changes. A "no reprisal" guarantee was also written into the contract for the workers engaged in the strike action. President Nixon had intervened in the negotiating July 28 by dispatching Assistant Labor Secretary W. J. Usery Jr. to UTU headquarters in Cleveland to meet with union president Charles Luna in an effort to break the negotiating impasse. Nixon July 30 called both sides to the White House to discuss the economic impact of the strike and urge "responsive bargaining" for a quick settlement. (The union had begun its strikes July 16 with actions against the Union Pacific Railroad and the Southern Railway. The strikes were extended July 24 to the Southern Pacific Co. and the Norfolk and Western Railway and July 30 to the Atchison, Topeka and Santa Fe Railway, the Houston Belt & Terminal, the Alton & Southern Railway Companies, the Duluth, Missabe & Iron Range Railway, the Bessemer & Lake Erie, and the Elgin, Joliet and Eastern.)

Strike injunction power backed. The Supreme Court June 1 ruled 5-4 that federal judges could issue injunctions against railroad strikes if they were "the only practical, effective means" of enforcing bargaining obligations under the National Railroad Act. The ruling came in the six-year dispute between brakemen represented by the UTU and the Chicago & Northwestern Railway Co. over crew sizes. Justice Harlan wrote for the majority that a court could use the injunction if it were needed to enforce the railroad act's requirement that negotiators "exert every reasonable effort" to settle disputes without interrupting service.

9-year Florida rail strike ends. A federal district court in Jacksonville Dec. 17 gave preliminary approval to an agreement to end a strike begun Jan. 23, 1963 against the Florida East Coast Railway. The line, with outside help, continued operating except for the first week of the strike. The new agreement called for an out-of-court settlement in which 11 nonoperating unions would be paid $1.5 million in damages and strikers' salaries would be increased 31% Jan. 1, 1972 and 6% more a year later. The old wage paid union employees was $2-$2.50 an hour.

See also LABOR [1]

RAND CORP.—*See* PENTAGON PAPERS [11, 15]
READING RAILROAD—*See* RAILROADS
REAGAN, RONALD—*See* POLITICS [4]; POVERTY

RECORD INDUSTRY—Grammy awards. The musical duo, (Paul) Simon and (Arthur) Garfunkel, received the three most pretigious awards—best record, album and song of the year—at the 1970 Grammy awards announced March 16 by the National Academy of Recording Arts and Sciences. Their bestselling song, "Bridge Over Troubled Water," was also voted best engineered recording (except classical) and the best contemporary song. The other winners:

New artist—the Carpenters; **instrumental arrangement**—Henry Mancini, theme from *Z;* **arrangement accompanying vocalists**—Simon & Garfunkel, "Bridge Over Troubled Water"; **album cover**—Robert Lockhart and Ivan Nagy, B. B. King's "Indianola Mississippi Seeds"; **album notes**—Chris Albertson, Bessie Smith's "The World's Greatest Blues Singer"; **contemporary vocal performance** (female)—Dionne Warwick, "I'll Never Fall In Love Again"; **contemporary vocal performance** (male)—Ray Stevens, "Everything Is Beautiful"; **contemporary vocal performance by a group**—Carpenters, "Close to You"; **contemporary instrumental performance**—Henry Mancini, theme from *Z* and other film music; **rhythm & blues vocal performance** (female)—Aretha Franklin, "Don't Play That

Song"; **rhythm & blues vocal performance** (male)—B. B. King, "The Thrill Is Gone"; **rhythm & blues vocal performance by a duo or group**—The Delfonics, "Didn't I (Blow Your Mind This Time)"; **rhythm & blues song**— Ronald Dunbar and General Johnson, "Patches"; **soul gospel performance**— Edwi: Hawkins Singers, "Every Man Wants To Be Free"; **country vocal performance** (female)—Lynn Anderson, "Rose Garden"; **country vocal performance** (male)—Ray Price, "For The Good Times"; **country performance by a duo or a group**—Johnny Cash and June Carter, "If I Were A Carpenter"; **country instrumental performance**—Chet Atkins and Jerry Reed, "Me and Jerry"; **best country song**—Marty Robbins, "My Woman, My Woman, My Wife"; **sacred performance**—Jake Hess, "Everything Is Beautiful"; **gospel performance**—Oak Ridge Boys, "Talk About the Good Times"; **ethnic or traditional recording**—T-Bone Walker, "Good Feelin'"; **instrumental composition**—Alfred Newman, *Airport* love theme; **score for film or TV special**—John Lennon, Paul McCartney, George Harrison, *Let It Be;* **score from an original cast show album**—Stephen Sondheim, *Company;* **recording for children**—Joan Cooney, *Sesame Street;* **comedy recording**— Flip Wilson, "The Devil Made Me Buy This Dress"; **spoken word recording**— Martin Luther King Jr., "Why I Oppose the War in Vietnam"; **small group jazz performance**—Bill Evans, "Alone"; **large group jazz performance**— Miles Davis, "Bitches Brew"; **album of the year** (classical)—"Berlioz: Les Troyens"; **classical performance** (orchestra)—Pierre Boulez conducting the Cleveland Orchestra, "Stravinsky: Le Sacre Du Printemps"; **chamber music performance**—Eugene Istomin, Isaac Stern, Leonard Rose, "Beethoven: The Complete Piano Trios"; **classical performance instrumental soloist**—David Oistrakh and Mstislav Rostropovich, "Brahms: Double Concerto (Concert in A Minor for Violin and Cello)"; **opera recording**—Colin Davis conducting the Royal Opera House Orchestra and Chorus, "Berlioz: Les Troyens"; **choral performance**—Gregg Smith conducting the Gregg Smith Singers and Columbia Chamber Ensemble, "Ives (New Music of Charles Ives)"; **vocal soloist performance** (classical)—Dietrich Fischer-Dieskau, "Schubert: Lieder"; **engineered recording** (classical)—Pierre Boulez conducting the Cleveland Orchestra, "Stravinsky: Le Sacre Du Printemps."

Songwriters' Hall of Fame. The winners of the first annual election to the Songwriters' Hall of Fame were announced in New York March 9. The 10 winners: Alan Jay Lerner, Dorothy Fields, Duke Ellington, Harold Arlen, Harry Warren, Hoagy Carmichael, Ira Gershwin, Johnny Mercer, James Van Heusen and Rudolf Friml.

RHODESIA—Resettlement completed. The government announced Jan. 14 that it had "completed its task" of resettling Tangwena tribesmen from their ancestral home of Inyanga near the Mozambique border. The tribesmen had resisted government efforts, carried out under the Land Apportionment Act, to move them from the Gaeresi Ranch to Bende, about seven miles away, and to the nearby Holdenby Tribal Trust Land. Rekayi Tangwena, the tribe's unofficial chief, had asked Great Britain to "rescue" his people in a letter Jan. 6. Tangwena appeared in a Salisbury court May 6 on charges of making abusive statements under the Law and Order Maintenance Act. He had reportedly accused the government of using brutality against members of his tribe in an effort to provoke them into retaliatory action during the resettling campaign.

Liberation groups merge. Two black liberation movements—the Zimbabwe (Rhodesia) African People's Union (ZAPU) and the Zimbabwe African National Union (ZANU)—joined to form the Front for the Liberation of Zimbabwe (FROLIZI) Oct. 1. Shelton Siwela, a former guerrilla commander with ZAPU, was elected chairman of the new group's Revolutionary Command Council, which included former Vice President James Chikerema and former National Secretary George Nyandoro (from ZAPU) and former Foreign Affairs Secretary Nathan Shamuyarira (from ZANU).

Chrome import developments. The U.S. House of Representatives Nov. 10 passed a military procurement bill carrying an amendment to permit the importation of Rhodesian chrome in defiance of a United Nations embargo imposed in 1966. The amendment removed the President's authority to ban imports of strategic materials also being imported from a Communist-dominated country. (The U.S. also imported chrome ore from the Soviet Union.) The U.N. General Assembly Nov. 16 protested the passage of the amendment and called on the U.S. to "take the necessary measures" in compliance with past Security Council resolutions and, "bearing in mind its obligations under Article 25 of the Charter of the U.N., to prevent the importation of chrome into the U.S. from Southern Rhodesia." The resolution (passed by a vote of 106-2 with 13 abstentions and 10 absentees) also asked the U.S. to notify the current session of the assembly "of the action taken or envisaged in the implementation of the present resolution." President Nixon Nov. 17 issued a statement saying that he would take no action under the amendment pending the current negotiations between Britain and Rhodesia *(see below)*. The effective date of the amendment was Jan. 1, 1972.

Prospect of black rule accepted. Great Britain Foreign Secretary Sir Alec Douglas-Home and Rhodesian Prime Minister Ian Smith Nov. 24 signed an agreement to end Britain's constitutional debate with Rhodesia's white supremacist government. The pact, approved by the British House of Commons by a 297-269 vote Dec. 1 and by the House of Lords Dec. 3, ended seven years of tension brought on by Rhodesia's seizure of independence in 1965 and paved the way for a lifting of mandatory U.N. economic sanctions. Sir Alec said that the proposals in the document were "fully within the five principles to which the government have constantly adhered in efforts to reach a settlement."

The British principles of unimpeded progress toward majority rule and of immediate improvement in the political status of blacks were to be effected by abolishing a provision in the 1969 constitution which stipulated that blacks became eligible for more seats in the Rhodesian House of Assembly (lower house) when they paid more than 24% of Rhodesia's income taxes. (They currently paid less than 1% of the income taxes.) After the 1970 election, the House had 50 white and 16 black members. Eight of the blacks had been directly elected and eight had been chosen by electoral colleges of government-appointed chiefs. With the amended constitution, the 16 black seats would be retained, but new black voters would be registered on an African Higher Roll, subject to the same qualifications as the European Roll (a high-school education and a yearly income of $1,200 or ownership of property worth $2,400, or no high school education and a yearly income of $1,800 or ownership of property worth $3,600). Two additional black seats would be created and filled by direct election when the number of voters on the Higher Roll reached 6% of those on the European Roll. When the proportion reached 12%, two more seats would be created and filled by indirect election by the tribal colleges. The sequence of alternate direct and indirect elections would continue until parity of black and white seats had been attained. Within one year of the election in which parity was attained, a referendum of all black voters (including those on the African Lower Roll, whose membership standards would be eased) would be held to determine whether the indirectly elected seats should be replaced by directly elected seats—all of them Higher Roll seats unless the legislature provided before the referendum for up to one-quarter of the new seats to be Lower Roll seats. Following the referendum and any subsequent elections, a three-man commission (one black member) would be appointed by the government after consultation with all parties represented in the House to determine if the creation of 10 Common Roll seats would be "acceptable to the people of Rhodesia" or "whether any alternate arrangements would command general support." The Common Roll seats would be filled by a vote of a single constituency composed of all members of the European and Higher Rolls. Each voter would have 10 votes to cast as he chose among the candidates. Afterward, the separate rolls would be retained to fill the existing directly elected seats.

A third principle of guarantees against retroactive amendment of the Rhodesian constitution was fulfilled (from the time of the enactment of the settlement until the filling of Common Roll seats) primarily by a mechanism that required amendments of "specially entrenched" clauses of the constitution to obtain the approval of two-thirds of the House and the Senate voting separately and two-thirds of the black and white members of the House, again voting separately. After the Common Roll seats had been filled, a two-thirds majority of the House would be required for amendment. Among the specially entrenched clauses, as defined by the agreement, were all the provisions detailing aspects of new voting arrangements and an amended Declaration of Rights which forbade new discriminatory laws or the extension of existing discriminatory laws. The Rhodesian government gave an assurance that it would not try to amend the specially entrenched clauses until the first two Higher Roll seats had been filled or three years had elapsed, whichever was sooner.

A fourth British principle of progress toward ending racial discrimination in the colony was reflected in the establishment of a three-member commission (one black member) to examine the question of racial discrimination, particularly the Land Tenure Act, which divided the country's land into equal portions between the blacks and whites. (Rhodesia had a population of about 5,050,000 blacks, 239,000 whites and 25,000 others.) While the Rhodesian government recognized that the commission's findings would "carry special authority," it could ignore the commission's legislative recommendations if it felt that there were "considerations that any government would be obliged to regard as of an overriding character." Until the commission had reported, there were to be no evictions of blacks from white areas. Britain was to provide Rhodesia with $120 million over the following 10 years in economic and educational development aid for black areas, with that sum being matched by the Rhodesian government in addition to its "annual expenditure currently planned." The agreement contained no procedures for verifying that the money actually would be spent on blacks.

The British government's fifth principle—that the agreement be found acceptable to the people of Rhodesia as a whole—was to be implemented by a commission headed by Lord Pearce, chairman of the Press Council, which would travel to Rhodesia and conduct its inquiries there. When the commission had returned a favorable report, economic sanctions would be lifted and the state of emergency in Rhodesia revoked "unless unforeseen circumstances intervene."

Reaction to agreement. An organization opposed to settlement and known as the African National Council was formed in Salisbury Dec. 16 under the leadership of Bishop Abel Muzorewa, head of the United Methodist Church in Rhodesia. The council's first meeting Dec. 18 was attended by approximately 700 blacks. The U.N. also expressed opposition to the settlement. The General Assembly voted 94-8 (22 abstentions) Dec. 21 to condemn the pact as "a flagrant violation of the inalienable rights of the African people of Zimbabwe to self-determination and independence."

See also AFRICA; CHURCHES [2-3]; FOREIGN POLICY; MALAGASY REPUBLIC; ZAMBIA

RICHARDSON, ELLIOTT L.—*See* EDUCATION [7]
ROCKEFELLER, NELSON—*See* PRISONS [6-8]; STUDENT UNREST [5]
ROGERS, WILLIAM P.—*See* CHILE [4]; COMMUNIST CHINA-U.S. DETENTE [7]; DRUG USE & ADDICTION [5, 7]; FEDERAL BUREAU OF INVESTIGATION [6]; FOREIGN AID; FOREIGN POLICY; JAPAN [5]; MIDDLE EAST [36]; NIXON, RICHARD MILHOUS [3]; PORTUGAL
ROLLS-ROYCE LTD.—*See* BUSINESS [3]; GREAT BRITAIN [1, 5]

ROMAN CATHOLIC CHURCH—Dutch bishops accept Simonis. Another episode in a continuing struggle between the Vatican and the generally liberal Roman Catholic hierarchy of the Netherlands was patched up with the acceptance by the Dutch church's bishopric of a conservative as the new bishop of Rotterdam. In a statement issued Jan. 12 after meeting in Haarlem, the bishops expressed concern over the discord within the church that had been caused by the Vatican's appointment of Canon Adrien Simonis. Simonis had reportedly been the only member of the Dutch Pastoral Council to have voted for strict priestly celibacy at the council's January 1970 meeting. Opposition to the appointment had been led by the Rotterdam diocesan pastoral council, an elected body of priests and laymen. Simonis had been the last on a list of eight nominees submitted to the Vatican by the council. At a protest meeting in the first week of January, the council chairman had accused the Vatican of undemocratically using its power to overturn the diocesan recommendations in an attempt to curb the progressive trend of the Dutch church. Executive members of the council resigned their posts, according to a report Feb. 1, to protest the Simonis appointment. A statement by the executive members said they could see no possibility for fruitful cooperation with Simonis. The controversy, however, had apparently been settled at a national level after eight days of consultation between Bernard Cardinal Alfrink, the Dutch primate, and Pope Paul VI were concluded Jan. 26.

[2] Vatican relaxes heresy rules. The Vatican's Congregation for the Doctrine of the Faith published Feb. 4 new procedures to insure objective handling of doctrinal errors regarded as "erroneous or dangerous to the Faith." The 18 new rules included provisions for a "relatore pro auctore," a kind of defense counsel; greater opportunities to defend writings before a final decision; and deeper consultation with the bishop or bishops in an accused theologian's region and with the theologian himself. Under the new procedures, two courses of action would be open: (1) in the case of obvious doctrinal error, the author's bishop would invite him to correct his error, or (2) in the case of possible error, the congregation would assign two experts to study the controversial point, after which the author would be invited to Rome to explain his thinking further if the experts concluded that an error had been committed. The Pope would have ultimate authority in any judgment.

[3] Studies on priests. Two major studies on the Roman Catholic priesthood were made public in 1971—the first a preliminary report on a $500,000 study commissioned by the U.S. National Council of Bishops in 1967 (made public at the council's annual spring meeting April 27-29) and the second a Vatican study on defections from the priesthood (reported Aug. 9). The council's study, authored by the Rev. Carl Armbruster (a Jesuit professor), was the most systematic, in-depth analysis of the priesthood in existence. It drew fire from conservative bishops because of its "subjective" and "existentialist" point of view. The chief point of contention was Armbruster's assertion that no theological basis existed for denying ordination to women and married persons. The sociology part of the report concluded that the most important cause of priests leaving the ministry was loneliness and that conflict with church authorities was the chief problem for those who remained. The sociology section also found—in its survey of 6,000 active priests, 800 priests who had left the ministry and 250 bishops—that support for church teachings against divorce was ebbing but that positions on premarital sex and abortion had not changed significantly. The psychology section of the report found that two-thirds of the priests sampled had "underdeveloped" personalities. The issue of celibacy ran through the report, with a survey showing that an "overwhelming majority" of priests believed that celibacy was an advantage in their work but also showing that 84% of active priests sampled favored optional celibacy. The theological section of the report said that: "The simple fact is that celibacy is a charism [gift] bestowed by the Holy Spirit, and it does not necessarily coincide with the charism of priestly service."

[4] The Vatican study, commissioned by the Sacred Congregation for the Doctrine of the Faith in preparation for the World Synod of Bishops in September (see [9-11]), was a result of a two-year survey of 8,287 priests who received "dispensations from celibacy" from 1939 through March 1969. The report's statistics showed a sharp increase in the number of priests leaving the ministry since 1964. In contrast to a total of 536 priests that left between 1939 and 1963, the total reached 1,906 in 1968 and 1,141 in the first three months of 1969. The report expressed concern over the high total because of a parallel drop in ordinations and an increase of 100 million new Roman Catholics in the last decade. A rapid drop in the average age of those leaving the priesthood meant that priests were leaving at their most active age. Of the 3,047 who left between 1968 and March 1969, 50% were under 36.

[5] **Vatican backs media, curbs secrecy.** The U.S. Catholic Conference published guidelines June 2 established by the Vatican for better use of the communications media and a cutdown on secrecy in church affairs. The 20,000-word document was entitled the Pastoral Instruction for the Application of the Decree of the Second Vatican Ecumenical Council on the Means of Social Communication. It was released after six years of preparation by a commission appointed by Pope Paul. Pointing out that information gaps led to rumor and "dangerous half-truths," the document said "individual Catholics have the right to all the information they need to play their active role in the life of the church." The only restrictions on information should be in "matters that involve the good name of individuals or that touch upon the rights of people whether singly or collectively."

[6] **New Vatican guidelines.** The Vatican June 17 issued new guidelines for religious instruction. The General Catechetical Directory, prepared by the Sacred Congregation for the Clergy, was ordered by the Ecumenical Council Vatican II (1962-65), which asked for a clear statement of the basic church doctrine that should appear in all future Roman Catholic catechisms. The document, reportedly the first of its kind, was designed mainly for bishops as a research stimulus and guide for the preparation of local directories and national catechisms.

[7] **Confirmation rite changed.** Pope Paul decreed Sept. 13 that the traditional laying on of hands, performing the sacrament of confirmation, would be replaced by annointment of the communicant's forehead with sacramental oil in the form of the cross. The reform, in the form of an apostolic constitution, implemented a decision of Vatican II and would become obligatory Jan. 1, 1973. A new word formula used by Eastern (Byzantine) churches since the 4th century in administering the sacrament replaced the 12th century words of the Roman Church; it was interpreted as an ecumenical gesture. The reform also dropped the custom of giving the communicant a slight blow on the cheek.

[8] Mindszenty leaves Hungary. Jozsef Cardinal Mindszenty, 79, ended a 15-year exile in the U.S. embassy in Budapest, Hungary Sept. 28 and traveled to the Vatican where he accepted "the heaviest cross of my life," resigned to living out his life in an exile of "prayer and penitence." The cardinal's departure was announced simultaneously in Rome and Budapest in an official communique which read: "In accordance with an agreement between the Government of the Hungarian People's Republic and the Holy See, Jozsef Cardinal Mindszenty left the territory for good on Tuesday [Sept. 28] and traveled to Rome." The cardinal was warmly received in the Vatican gardens by Pope Paul who, preoccupied with the cardinal's health, had asked Mindszenty "to make the most difficult sacrifice of your life" and end his isolation. The cardinal had repeatedly refused to leave the U.S. embassy sanctuary unless the Hungarian government agreed to his "rehabilitation"— the rescinding of his 1949 conviction and the life sentence he was given for alleged subversive activities against the Communist regime. The cardinal's presence in the American embassy was considered an embarrassment to the U.S. and the Vatican and both were said to be relieved with his departure. It was reported that the Vatican had been negotiating for several years with the Hungarian government on the terms for the cardinal's departure. Details of the agreement were not disclosed, but sources said that in referring to Mindszenty as "Cardinal" in the communique, the Hungarian government acknowledged his position and indirectly rescinded the prison sentence. (Mindszenty arrived in Vienna Oct. 24, presumably to take up residence at a college for Hungarian priests.)

[9] Synod debates celibacy, justice. The third Roman Catholic Synod of Bishops met in Rome Sept. 30-Nov. 6 to deliberate and advise Pope Paul on the problems of the priesthood and justice in a changing world social order. During the five-week synod, the more than 200 delegates (cardinals, bishops, partriarchs of the Eastern-rite churches and heads of male religious orders) deliberated as a papal advisory body under the principle of collegiality adopted by Vatican II. Delegates were both elected from national religious leaderships and appointed by the Pope. (The five-member U.S. delegation included John Cardinal Dearden of Detroit, John Cardinal Krol of Philadelphia, John Cardinal Carberry of St. Louis, Bishop Leo C. Byrne of St. Paul-Minneapolis and Bishop William W. Baum of Springfield, Mo.) The delegates generally reaffirmed papal policies, including traditional priestly celibacy, which appeared for the first time on a synod agenda. However, division on the related subject of ordaining married men produced tumultuous meetings in the synod's last week. The delegates Nov. 2 and Nov. 4 rejected a draft document clause (basically similar both days) which prohibited the admission of married men to the priesthood unless the Pope indicated "that the matter should be subjected to examination." With the permission of Pope Paul, two proposals were submitted to the synod for a final vote Nov. 6. Although the conservatives won in a close tally, 44% supported the liberal stand: 107 delegates voted for the conservative proposal—"Preserving always the right of the Holy Father [to make exceptions], the ordination of married men is not admitted, not even in particular cases"; 87 voted for the liberal proposal—"It belongs only to the Holy Father, in particular cases, on account of pastoral necessities, being attentive to the good of the universal church, to concede a priestly ordination of married men, of a mature age and upright life."

[10] The Synod's discussion of world justice, which opened Oct. 14, failed to pass four-fifths of a final document on world justice Nov. 4, but overwhelmingly supported subsequent revisions and approved the document Nov. 6. Among the recommendations contained in both documents, the synod: endorsed conscientious objection to war; approved in principle formation of a high-level Vatican commission to determine whether women had full rights in the church; criticized the church's identification with the wealthy rather than the poor and urged a modest life style for Catholics in developed areas; urged more ecumenical efforts in working with persons of all faiths in search of justice; and called on rich nations to increase aid to poor nations and give them preferential treatment in world trade.

[11] Delegates to the synod were also told Nov. 3 that the bishops had overwhelmingly rejected a second draft of the Lex Fundamentalis, the church's new charter. The charter had been prepared by the Pontifical Commission for the Revision of the Code of Canon Law in Rome. (The first draft of the constitution—which was to be the first such document in church history—had received strong criticism in the U.S. when it was published in May 1969 because of its conservative and authoritarian tone.) The purpose of the constitution was to be an introductory chapter to a complete revision of church law and a clear statement of fundamental church principles. Of the 1,313 bishops among whom the document had been circulated in the spring, 593 approved the concept of a church constitution, 462 wanted some changes in the basic idea, 251 rejected it outright, 61 said they liked the draft, 798 called for amendments and 422 said it should be scrapped.

[11] **Ukrainians hold 'synod.'** Sixteen bishops of the Eastern-Rite Ukrainian Catholic Church defied the Vatican and voted Oct. 31 to convene their own "synod" to establish an autonomous government for the church. The Vatican, which had united with the Ukrainian Church under the ultimate authority of the Pope 375 years earlier, had denied the Ukrainians the right to hold their synod apart from the Synod of Bishops. Joseph Cardinal Slipyj-Kobernickyj-Dyckowsky, exiled head of the Ukrainian Catholics, formally announced Nov. 1 that the synod was taking place. The synod, which concluded Nov. 5, set up a five-member permanent synod (legislative council) to govern the church, which was illegal in the Soviet Union but had 1.8 million members in the West. The five synod members were: Cardinal Slipyj, Archbishop John Buchko of Rome, Archbishop Ambrose Senyshyn of Philadelphia and Bishop Andrew Sapeliak of Argentina. (In another act of defiance, Oct. 23 Slipyj broke an eight-year silence reportedly imposed on him by the Vatican after his release by Soviet authorities in 1963. In the presence of Pope Paul, Slipyj told the synod that the Vatican had prevented him from speaking out against the "most grave persecution" by the Soviets of 6 million Roman Catholics in the Ukraine.)

See also ARGENTINA [14, 16]; BRAZIL; CAMEROON; CHURCHES [7, 17]; DRAFT & WAR PROTEST [22-23, 29]; EDUCATION [10-11, 18]; GUINEA; ITALY [13]; MALTA; MEXICO; MOTION PICTURES; MOZAMBIQUE; NORTHERN IRELAND; PANAMA; PARAGUAY; PERU; POLAND; SECURITY,U.S.; SOUTH AFRICA [5]; SPAIN [1, 3-4]

ROMNEY, GEORGE—See CIVIL RIGHTS [28]; CONGRESS [11]; HOUSING
RUCKELSHAUS, WILLIAM D.—See PESTICIDES; POLLUTION [1, 8, 12, 16-18]

RUMANIA—1970 economic report. The results of the 1970 economic development plan were reported Jan. 30 by the Central Statistical Board. Measured against the figures for 1969, the following major increases were reported: industrial output 12%, industrial labor productivity 8.8%, national income 7%, real wages 8%, foreign trade 12.7%, building and assembly operations 8.4% and investments 9.3%. The board noted that production quotas had been underfulfilled in the chemical industry, metallurgy and agriculture, the latter in part because of severe flooding in June 1970.

Union congress endorses statutes. At the end of a five-day session in Bucharest, the Sixth Congress of Rumanian Trade Unions March 27 endorsed draft changes in its organizational rules calling for greater autonomy and democracy. Following recommendations made Feb. 10 by Nicolae Ceausescu, Communist party general secretary, the draft statutes envisioned the election of a more representative Executive Bureau and the abolition of "excessive centralism." The new statutes, if enacted, would allow the unions to more "effectively take part in the elaboration, endorsement and implementation of the decisions and measures related to the advancement of society."

Ministries merged. The formation of two new government ministries was announced March 30. The two new ministries: Transport and Telecommunications (to be headed by Florian Danache, who had been named minister of transport Feb. 14), formed from the Ministry of Transport and the Ministry of Posts and Telecommunications; and the Ministry of Mining, Oil and Geology (to be headed by Bujor Almasan, former minister of mines and geology), formed from the Ministry of Oil and the Ministry of Mines and Geology. (Iosif Banc, a vice chairman of the Council of Ministers, had been appointed Jan. 25 to head the newly created Ministry of Agriculture, Food Industry, Forestry and Water Conservation.)

5-year plan approved. The National Assembly Oct. 21 passed a 1971-75 economic development plan which gave priority to heavy industry. The plan called for an overall industrial growth rate of 11%-12.2%, with heavy industry to increase 11.7%-13% and consumer goods to go up 9.5%-11%. Other planned increases: agricultural output 36%-49%, average labor productivity 37%, real income 40%-46%.

Ceausescu tightens controls. On the second day of a Communist party Central Committee plenary session called to discuss ideological controls recommended in August, General Secretary Ceausescu Nov. 4 outlined a program aimed at strengthening "the role played by the party" in Rumanian life. He complained mainly of liberal influences in cultural and artistic matters, blaming the party's Secretariat, over which he presided, for not exerting a firm enough control. He also referred to presumed cases of corruption and called for an end to "the attitudes that are identified in which leadership cadres are ignoring or breaking state laws, probably thinking the laws are not made for them." Henceforth, party organizations throughout the country were to analyze their political "correctness" every six months. Ministries and other central bodies were to give yearly accounts to the Council of Ministers, whose work would be evaluated by the Central Committee. (In a speech endorsed July 6 by the Central Committee, Ceausescu had proposed a series of measures to increase the party's control of ideological and cultural matters by eliminating "bourgeois" influences. The measures included: barring alcoholic drinks from "all entertainment establishments for youth"; and censorship of radio and television programs, artistic performances and literary works if they did not "meet the demands of the political-educational activity of our party." The remarks, which appeared to herald a curtailment of liberal trends, were made following Ceausescu's June 1-9 trip to Communist China.)

See also COMMUNISM, INTERNATIONAL; DISARMAMENT; HIJACKING [11]; SPACE [24]

RURAL DEVELOPMENT—*See* STATE & LOCAL GOVERNMENTS [5]

ST. KITTS-NEVIS-ANGUILLA—Premier Robert Bradshaw was returned to his fifth consecutive term in the confederated state of St. Kitts-Nevis-Anguilla May 10. His ruling Labor party won all seven seats in the House of Assembly for the island of St. Kitts. The opposition party, the People's Action Movement (PAM), gained one seat in Nevis, while another seat went to the Nevis Reformation party. Anguilla, allotted one seat in the Assembly, had declared itself independent of the confederation in 1967 and boycotted the elections. According to Bradshaw, "the mandate is your call for revolutionary change in this country. We can no longer, indeed we will no longer, tolerate obstruction" by the PAM and secessionist Anguilla. The nation's gravest problem, Bradshaw said, was the need for increased economic growth.

See also ANGUILLA; CARIBBEAN; VIRGIN ISLANDS

ST. LUCIA—*See* CARIBBEAN
ST. VINCENT—*See* CARIBBEAN
SALYUT—*See* SPACE [7-9]
SATELLITES—*See* COMMUNIST CHINA-U.S. DETENTE [11]; DEFENSE [8]; DISARMAMENT; SPACE [3, 14-24]
SAUDI ARABIA—*See* AGNEW, SPIRO THEODORE; JORDAN [10]; OIL

SCANDINAVIA—**Nordic ministerial council created.** The premiers of Sweden, Denmark, Norway, Finland and Iceland signed an agreement Feb. 13 establishing a ministerial council to coordinate Scandinavian cooperation. Council decisions on all but procedural matters would have to be reached unanimously. The ministerial council was the only element to survive the Nordic Economic Union (Nordek) plan which was defeated when Finland refused to sign the Nordek treaty in 1970. The five nations had then agreed to revise the Helsinki agreement of 1962 on Nordic cooperation, including creation of the ministerial council. The agreement was signed during the 19th session of the Nordic Council, which met in Copenhagen Feb. 13-19.

SCHOOL PRAYER—*See* EDUCATION [18]
SCHOOLS—*See* EDUCATION

SCIENCE—**Rare atom particle found.** Physicists from the University of California announced Feb. 1 they had discovered a rare particle within the atom. The new particle, called the antiomega-minus baryon, was thought to be the most elusive within the atom. Dr. Gerson Goldhaber of the Lawrence Radiation Laboratory at the university's Berkeley campus said the particle's track in a photograph of a nuclear interaction had led to its discovery. The antiomega-minus baryon was believed to have a lifetime of 15 billionths of a

417

second. Goldhaber said the particle had been found in a search of more than 500,000 photographs. The actual track was discovered by Jane H. Allardt in December 1970.

Medal of Science. The nation's highest award for scientific achievement—the 1970 Medal of Science—was presented by President Nixon May 21 to eight men and a woman in a White House ceremony. The citation for Dr. Barbara McClintock of the Carnegie Institution of Washington was the first to a woman. Other winners: Albert Sabin, developer of the polio vaccine named for him; George E. Mueller, director of the Apollo program from its inception through the landing of men on the moon; Richard D. Brauer, professor of mathematics, Harvard University; Allan R. Sandage, staff member of Hale Observatories, the Carnegie Institution of Washington and the California Institute of Technology; Robert H. Dicke, professor of physics, Princeton University; John C. Slater, professor of physics and chemistry, University of Florida; John A. Wheeler, professor of physics, Princeton; and a posthumous award to Saul Winstein, who died in November 1969 and was a professor of chemistry at the University of California at Los Angeles.

See also ARCHEOLOGY & ANTHROPOLOGY; ASTRONOMY; BIOLOGY; BUDGET; NOBEL PRIZES

SEALE, BOBBY G.—*See* BLACK MILITANTS [11]
SEALS—*See* CONSERVATION
SECURITIES & EXCHANGE COMMISSION (SEC)—*See* BUSINESS [2-3, 10]; GOVERNMENT REORGANIZATION; NIXON, RICHARD MILHOUS [7]; RAILROADS; STOCK MARKET

SECURITY, U.S.—**Berrigan, 5 others indicted.** A federal grand jury in Harrisburg, Pa. Jan. 12 indicted the Rev. Philip F. Berrigan and five others (the Rev. Joseph R. Wenderoth; the Rev. Neil R. McLaughlin; Anthony Scoblick, a former priest; Eqbal Ahmad, a fellow at the Adlai Stevenson Institute of Public Affairs in Chicago; and Sister Elizabeth McAlister of Marymount College) on charges of conspiring to kidnap Henry A. Kissinger, assistant to the President for national security affairs, and of plotting to blow up the heating systems of federal buildings in Washington. The plots were allegedly designed to bring pressure to end the Indochina war. The indictment said that Berrigan and Wenderoth had investigated the Washington tunnel system as part of the plot, which was to include the detonation of dynamite charges "in approximately five locations" on Washington's birthday Feb. 22. The official charges against the six were conspiring to maliciously destroy government property, possessing and transporting explosives across state lines and plotting to kidnap a person across state lines. The alleged plot had been described by Federal Bureau of Investigation (FBI) Director J. Edgar Hoover in Senate testimony in November 1970. The grand jury indictment also named as unindicted co-conspirators: the Rev. Daniel Berrigan, brother of Philip Berrigan; Sisters Beverly Bell and Marjorie A. Schuman; William Davidon, a professor at Haverford (Pa.) College; Thomas Davidson, a former priest; Paul Mayer, a former priest; and Sister Jogues Egan, a member of the Religious Order of the Sacred Heart of Mary in New York. (Sister Jogues was jailed Jan. 26 for refusing to testify before the grand jury, which continued to investigate the conspiracy; but the civil contempt charges against her were dismissed by the 3rd Circuit Court of Appeals May 28. A new hearing was ordered on her claim that the grand jury questions were based on information obtained through illegal wiretapping.)

The six indicted for alleged conspiracy pleaded innocent to the charges at their arraignment Feb. 8. Berrigan had been brought to Harrisburg for the arraignment from Danbury, Conn., where he was serving a 3.5-year sentence in federal prison for destroying draft records at Catonsville, Md. in 1968. The defendants and alleged co-conspirators, with the Berrigans absent, met with newsmen after the arraignment and issued a prepared statement of their innocence. The grand jury April 30 issued a new indictment replacing that issued Jan. 12. The new indictment accused the six alleged conspirators of the same crimes and extended the charges to include John Theodore Glick, currently serving an 18-month sentence in federal prison for a 1970 raid on federal offices in Rochester, N.Y., and Mary Cain Scoblick, a former nun currently married to alleged conspirator Anthony Scoblick. Three persons (Daniel Berrigan, Davidson and Mayer), listed as unindicted co-conspirators in the original indictment, were not named in the new document. The new indictment had attached to it two letters, allegedly exchanged by Philip Berrigan and Sister Elizabeth McAlister. The letter attributed to Sister Elizabeth described a plan to: kidnap "someone like Henry Kissinger"; "issue a set of demands" including a halt to U.S. use of B-52 bombers over North Vietnam, Cambodia and Laos and "release of political prisoners"; hold Kissinger "for about a week," during which he would be tried and the trial filmed for the news media; and then release him. The reply attributed to Berrigan suggested that the plan was too "grandiose" and suggested ways to "weave elements of modesty into it." The alleged reply also warned that the precedent of a kidnaping "opens the door to murder." Attorneys representing the defendants filed a motion May 4 in federal district court in Scranton, Pa. charging the government with violating their clients' rights by releasing the letters. The defense lawyers asked for a contempt of court citation against William S. Lynch, the chief prosecuting attorney, and U.S. Attorney S. John Cottone. (A third letter, from Boyd F. Douglas, a former convict who allegedly supplied the FBI with information, was reported May 16. The letter allegedly expressed Douglas's enthusiasm for the kidnap "plan" and his offer to procure a gun. The report quoted Sister Elizabeth as saying that the letter shocked her by making "it all seem suddenly real and pragmatic.")

All of the eight defendants except McLaughlin (whose trial was postponed because of the death of his father) refused May 25 to enter pleas to the charges against them, which they claimed were designed to stifle opposition to the Indochina war. They attempted to explain their decision not to enter pleas in statements that U.S. District Court Judge R. Dixon Herman accepted as part of the record but refused to allow to be read in court. Herman entered pleas of not guilty for each defendant, as required by law. McLaughlin June 2 also refused to enter a plea, and Herman entered a plea of not guilty for him.

Danbury hunger strike. Five fellow prisoners of the Berrigans began a hunger strike at Danbury Aug. 6 to demand the release of Daniel, an early review of the parole application of Philip and a reform of federal parole procedures and to protest the rebuilding of tiger cage prisons on Con Son Island in South Vietnam (*see* VIETNAM, SOUTH [1]). (The brothers' parole applications had been denied in a routine review July 28.) Paul O'Dwyer, a lawyer representing the Berrigans, said he had been told that the five prisoners had been placed in solitary confinement after distributing leaflets urging prisoners to join the protest. Philip Berrigan and 25 other prisoners were placed in solitary confinement Aug. 9 after joining the protest in support of all "political prisoners." Berrigan and 11 other strikers were transferred Aug. 11 to the federal prison hospital in Springfield, Mo., on grounds of overcrowding in the Danbury infirmary. Seven of the 12, including Berrigan, were returned to Danbury, according to a report Sept. 22. The hunger strike at Danbury ended Sept. 8.

SACB role broadened. President Nixon July 2 issued an executive order broadening the scope of the Subversive Activities Control Board (SACB) by authorizing it to keep a list of subversive groups and to determine, after hearings, whether a group was "totalitarian, fascist, Communist, subversive, or whether it has adopted a policy of unlawfully advocating the commission of acts of force or violence to deny others their rights under the Constitution." The Senate July 19 adopted an appropriations bill amendment prohibiting funding for the expansion, but the amendment was dropped by a House-Senate conference committee. The American Civil Liberties Union (ACLU) Sept. 1 filed suit in federal court in Washington attacking Nixon's July 2 order. The suit asked that the attorney general's list of allegedly subversive groups be banned as unconstitutional and that the SACB be barred from conducting hearings to update the list. The plaintiffs in the suit included antiwar groups and three groups already on the subversives list—the Communist party of the United States, the Industrial Workers of the World (IWW or Wobblies) and the Socialist Workers party.

Detention Act repealed. The House Sept. 14 by a 356-49 vote and the Senate by a voice vote Sept. 16 repealed the Emergency Detention Act (Title 2 of the 1950 Internal Security Act). The act had provided for detention of persons suspected of possible espionage or sabotage in periods of invasion or insurrection. It had never been used and six camps established under it had never been used for detention. There was concern among minority groups, especially Negroes, that the law could be used against them. Japanese-Americans also were wary of the legislation in light of the detention after Pearl Harbor in 1941 of more than 110,000 American citizens of Japanese origin in relocation centers.

See also ESPIONAGE; FEDERAL BUREAU OF INVESTIGATION; PENTAGON PAPERS

SELECTIVE SERVICE SYSTEM—Doctor call-up asked. The Defense Department Feb. 22 asked the Selective Service System to draft 1,531 doctors of medicine, 77 doctors of osteopathy and 536 dentists in 1971 in the first call-up of physicians since 1969. The call-up for dentists was canceled April 12. Selective Service Director Curtis W. Tarr said that the Defense Department would wait until summer to see whether enough dentists would volunteer for military service. If not, the special call would be reissued. Officials of the department said the draft of physicians and osteopaths was necessary because too few medical school graduates were volunteering for military service.

[2] **Board order rescinded.** A spokesman for the Selective Service System said April 13 that it was rescinding an earlier order (disclosed Feb. 17) that would have combined the facilities of a number of smaller draft boards around the country to cut expenses. The order was reversed after the House of Representatives passed an amendment March 31 aimed at halting the economy measure. The order would not have reduced the number of draft boards but merely directed boards to share quarters and clerical personnel.

[3] **Draft lottery for '72 held.** The Selective Service Aug. 5 conducted its third annual draft lottery since Congress authorized the random selection of men into the armed forces in 1969. The new drawing determined the order in which about 2 million young men born in 1952 would be drafted. According to the sequence established, 19-year-olds born Dec. 4 would be the first drafted in 1972 and those born Nov. 1 would be the last chosen.

[4] **'72 draft physicals set.** Despite the expiration of the draft law (*see* [5-6]), the Selective Service System announced Aug. 23 that it would begin to give physical examinations Sept. 1 to the first of 250,000 men who had been assigned lottery numbers 1-50 in the Aug. 5 lottery. Officials also said they would go ahead with plans to examine 20-year-olds holding draft numbers 125-175 for the 1971 draft. A Selective Service spokesman said draft boards were still entitled to provide preinduction physicals early enough for potential draftees to know their physical status and for local draft board officials to have enough time to process the examinations.

[5] **Draft bill passed.** A threatened filibuster by antiwar senators failed to materialize Sept. 21 and the Senate gave final Congressional approval, by a 55-30 vote, to the draft bill which extended military conscription through June 1973. The draft had been suspended since June 30, when the old law expired before Congress had succeeded in passing an extension. The legislation passed (a House-Senate conference version): extended the draft; increased the pay and allowances for servicemen by $2.4 billion a year, effective Oct. 1; gave the President authority to abolish undergraduate deferments for students entering college for the first time after the regular 1970-71 academic year, but retained

the student deferments for men eligible for them during the 1970-71 school year; included a "sense of Congress" declaration calling on President Nixon to withdraw all U.S. troops from Indochina by a "date certain," subject only to the release of all American prisoners of war (*see* INDOCHINA WAR [67]); authorized the Defense Department to experiment with $3,000 combat enlistment bonuses; set a 130,000-man induction ceiling on the number of men that could be called up in fiscal 1972 and provided that no more than 140,000 could be drafted in fiscal 1973 without further Congressional authorization; gave the President authority to conscript men on a national, rather than community, basis; offered draft deferments to men studying for the ministry, but allowed for the drafting of such men if they failed to enter the ministry upon graduation. President Nixon signed the bill Sept. 28, but froze the military pay raise at the same time. The White House said that the raises were "subject to the 90-day wage-price freeze" (*see* ECONOMY, U.S. [8]). The increases were to take effect immediately when the price freeze ended Nov. 13.

[6] *Background.* Hearings on the extension of the draft had begun in February. The House April 1 had approved an extension bill, after delays caused by antiwar representatives' attempts to set a timetable on withdrawal from Indochina. The Senate had passed a draft bill June 24. The two measures were sent to a House-Senate conference after the House June 28 defeated an amendment in the Senate bill calling for withdrawal in nine months if all American prisoners of war were released. The conference in early August changed the Senate amendment to the form which was passed Sept. 21. The conferees had reached agreement on all points except the amendment by June 30.

[7] *Section 20 snarl.* A federal appeals court in Los Angeles Nov. 24 ordered a halt to the induction of draftees from seven Southern California counties into the armed forces pending a review of the new Selective Service Act. (Supreme Court Justice William O. Douglas Dec. 1 intervened in the dispute to also order the government to halt induction in the counties.) The action came in a class-action suit, filed by the Southern California chapter of the American Civil Liberties Union (ACLU), testing Section 20 of the act, which stipulated that no registrants could be inducted prior to 90 days after enactment of the draft legislation unless the President or Senate declared war or a state of national emergency. The ACLU interpreted the section literally to mean that no inductions could take place until Dec. 28. Section 20 was also the focal point of lawsuits brought by draftees in other parts of the country. In Boston, three suits for an injunction delaying induction had been turned down and one was under appeal. In Chicago, U.S. courts had issued 16 temporary restraining orders halting induction procedures pending a review of Section 20.

[8] **Army to release 65,000.** The Army said Oct. 14 that it would release from active duty about 65,000 officers and enlisted men (36,000 draftees, 24,000 volunteers, 4,000 Reserve officers on active duty and 400 senior grade officers) by June 30, 1972 to meet the manpower ceiling of 892,000 ordered by Congress. Army Secretary Robert F. Froehlke said many of those to be released would be men in categories in which the Army was over strength, or men whose tour of duty was about to end. The Nixon Administration had planned to reduce the strength of the Army, at 1,120,000 in 1971, to 942,000 by June 30, 1972; but Congress had ordered a further cut to 892,000 men by the same date. That level would be the lowest Army strength in 11 years.

[9] **Rules revised for system.** In the first major revision of the nation's draft system in four years, the Selective Service Nov. 2 issued new rules and regulations to streamline the system and make it more equitable. The regulations did not change the basic conscription process or make anyone more or less liable to the draft, but did alter procedures for men to follow in dealing with local draft boards. Under the regulations, a new classification, I-H, was set up for men not immediately susceptible to the draft (18-year-olds who, in most cases, would not be called up before their 20th birthday, and men whose

lottery number had not been reached in their year of eligibility); draft boards would no longer keep records other than names and addresses of men classified I-H and such men would not have to communicate with their boards except when they changed addresses. The I-Y classification—men not fit for military service except in a national emergency—was abolished; men with permanent disabilities would be classified 4-F and those with temporary disabilities I-A. Classification 5-A—given to registrants over 26 who had never received deferments and men over 35 who had held deferments—was abolished and draft boards were instructed to destroy 5-A files. The regulations required the Selective Service System, beginning in 1972, to determine after every lottery the highest conceivable number that could be reached by draft calls in that year. Men seeking student deferments had to be full-time students at the end of the 1970-71 school year.

[10]   **Call-ups.** During 1971, draft calls were issued as follows: 17,000 a month for the months of January through April; 10,000 men a month for May and June; 16,000 men a month requested for July and August, but never called up because of the delay in the draft bill (see [5]); none for the month of September, again because of the delay in passage of the draft bill; 10,000 each month for October, November and December (but see [7]).

Conscientious Objectors

[11]   **West Point grad wins discharge.** The American Civil Liberties Union said Feb. 13 that a West Point graduate had won an honorable discharge on the ground that he was a conscientious objector. The ACLU said the favorable action on the discharge application of Cornelius McNeil Cooper Jr. marked the first time a graduate of the academy had been released as a CO.

[12]   **Letter rescinded.** A Selective Service System spokesman confirmed Feb. 17 that Director Tarr had ordered a halt to the sending of a form letter to potential COs warning them that too many objectors could cause the U.S. "to demand each citizen bear his load." The action was taken after the letter came under attack by Rep. Odgen R. Reid (R, N.Y.) and the ACLU. The ACLU said the letter improperly questioned the motives of COs and draft counselors. The Selective Service spokesman indicated that the letter would be altered.

[13]   **Selective exemptions barred.** The Supreme Court ruled March 8 that a young man could not be granted a draft exemption as a CO if he merely opposed the Vietnam war as "unjust" and did not oppose all wars. The court ruled 8-1, with Justice William O. Douglas dissenting, against the appeals of Guy P. Gillette and Louis A. Negre. The court upheld the draft law provision that CO status must be based on opposition to "participation in war in any form." The justices rejected the petitioners' contention that the requirement violated the right of freedom of religion. Justice Thurgood Marshall, writing for the court, said "the exempting provision has focused on individual conscientious belief, not on sectarian affiliation. The relevant individual belief is simply objection to all war, not adherence to any extraneous theological viewpoint." The government had conceded in both cases that the young men were sincere in their objections to the Vietnam war as unjust. But the government argued that its ability to raise manpower for the military would be paralyzed if selective conscientious objection were allowed.

[14]   **Ali conviction overturned.** The Supreme Court reversed the draft conviction and five-year prison sentence of Muhummad Ali, former heavyweight boxing champion, in a unanimous ruling June 28. The court said the Selective Service System had improperly refused to give Ali CO status in 1966 due to advice from the Justice Department that was "simply wrong as a matter of law." Ali, under the name Cassius Clay, had been convicted of refusing induction and sentenced to five years in prison in 1967. He remained free on bail pending appeal. The Justice Department had advised Ali's Louisville, Ky. draft board to reject the fighter's claim to CO status on three grounds—that his antiwar beliefs were not sincere, that they were not based on

religious training and that he did not object to all wars. The board then rejected Ali's claim without giving grounds. The Justice Department later conceded that Ali's beliefs were sincere and religious—grounded in the Black Muslim faith—but it insisted that he did not object to all wars and that the conviction should stand. The court held that whether Ali opposed all wars was immaterial since the draft board had been wrongly advised and gave no indication of what grounds it chose to disallow his claim. The court's vote was 8-0, with Justice Marshall abstaining because he was solicitor general, the government's chief prosecutor, when Ali was indicted.

[15] Religious guideline broadened. Deputy Secretary of Defense David M. Packard signed a directive Aug. 31 broadening the Pentagon's guideline on COs to include "deeply held moral or ethical beliefs" as grounds for discharge as set down in a 1970 Supreme Court decision. Under the widened guideline, servicemen applying for discharge as COs on the basis of their "religious training and belief" need not express belief in a supreme being. The new guideline was incorporated into the Pentagon's directives on COs to better meet the Supreme Court's interpretation of CO status. The court had ruled that a young man who specifically disavowed a religious basis for his antiwar beliefs was nevertheless entitled to CO status if he sincerely objected to all wars. The broadened guideline required the armed services to consider a claim of conscientious objection from a serviceman even though he admitted his beliefs were formed after he had received an induction notice and before he was actually inducted.

[16] Marine officers discharged. Two Marine lieutenants were discharged Sept. 3 as COs. The ACLU, which successfully argued both cases, said Sept. 7 the two were the first officers granted CO discharges by the Marines, although enlisted men had been released as objectors before. Robert C. Randolph, 27, of Lawrenceville, Va. and John P. McDonald, 22 of Farmington, N.Y. said they filed as objectors separately but "leaned to each other for moral support." The Marine Corps had offered both administrative discharges as "leadership failures," but the two refused.

See also BUDGET; DRAFT & WAR PROTEST [11, 22-23]; ECONOMY, U.S. [16]; HIJACKING [2, 15-16]; INDOCHINA WAR [66-67]; WOMEN'S RIGHTS; YOUTH

SELLING OF THE PENTAGON, THE—*See* TELEVISION & RADIO

SENEGAL—Dakar University closed. The government closed Dakar University Feb. 26 for an indefinite period after students refused to take examinations and distributed leaflets hostile to the government. President Leopold Sedar Senghor dissolved the Union of Senegalese Students Feb. 26. The university was reopened March 18 with students required to complete new enrollment procedures and to tender written promises to respect the university's rules. A total of 49 students were not allowed to return.

Cabinet changes. Prime Minister Abdou Diouf made Cabinet changes April 10. Jean Collin became interior minister and was replaced as finance minister by Babacar Ba. Ousmane Seck was named secretary of state for planning; Alioune Diagne became secretary general of the government; Amadou Ly was appointed secretary general of the presidency of the republic; and Diakha Dieng became director of the Cabinet.

New Senegalese bread. The United Nations Development Program (UNDP) March 4 announced creation of a new type of Senegalese bread as a result of a project it had assisted at the Dakar Institute of Food Technology. The bread was expected to save the country $600,000 a year in foreign exchange by replacing 30% of the imported flour with locally grown millet. Senegal planned to promote the new bread by unfreezing the price of heavily subsidized white bread.

See also AFRICA; MIDDLE EAST [37]

SEX DISCRIMINATION—*See* WOMEN'S RIGHTS

SHIPS & SHIPPING—Oklahoma 'seaport' dedicated. President Nixon participated in ceremonies at the Port of Catoosa, Okla. June 5 dedicating a $1.2 billion waterway project making the Verdigris and Arkansas Rivers navigable to the Mississippi River below Memphis, and hence to the sea. The project, including 17 locks and dams connecting a series of lakes and canals for riverboat traffic, was the largest civil works project ever undertaken by the Army Corps of Engineers. It was called the McClellan-Kerr Arkansas River Navigation System after Sen. John L. McClellan (D, Ark.) and the late Sen. Robert S. Kerr (D, Okla.).

Marine disasters. The French cruise ship Antilles went aground and burned Jan. 8 near Mustique, a tiny island in the Caribbean, forcing 650 passengers and crew members to flee in lifeboats. The British luxury liner Queen Elizabeth II picked up most of the survivors. The vessel was declared a total loss.

An American-owned oil tanker, the 83,882-ton Universe Patriot, caught fire and exploded Jan. 21 off the southwestern coast of Sardinia, Italy. Sixteen of the 39 crew members—most of them Japanese—were missing and feared dead. The other 23 were rescued after clinging to two lifeboats and a raft in the Mediterranean overnight. The vessel was owned by the Universal Tank Ship Co. of New York.

The Texaco Oklahoma, a tanker carrying 220,000 barrels of oil from Texas to Boston, split in two March 27 120 miles northeast of Cape Hatteras, N.C. Thirty-three crewmen were listed as missing March 29.

An explosion and fire tore through crew's quarters in the bow of the Norwegian liner Meteor May 22 as the vessel neared the end of an Alaskan cruise, 60 to 80 miles off Van-couver, B.C. Thirty-two crew members were killed. The 67 passengers were removed safely.

A Greek ferryboat carrying at least 1,175 persons—twice the number permitted—caught fire in the Adriatic Sea Aug. 28. The death toll was estimated as high as 54 Aug. 31. The captain of the vessel, the 11,232-ton Heleanna, was charged with multiple homicide and dereliction of duty after he attempted to escape Italy.

The Beethoven II, a ship with about 200 passengers, sank in stormy seas off the central Philippines Nov. 21. As many as 106 people were feared dead.

See also POLLUTION [4, 11]; TERRITORIAL WATERS

SHULTZ, GEORGE P.—*See* CONGRESS [11]; LABOR [10]

SIERRA LEONE—Coup attempt fails. Forces loyal to the government of Prime Minister Siaka P. Stevens succeeded March 23 in thwarting an attempted coup by the commander of the army, Brig. John Bangurah. (Bangurah and three other officers who took part in the attempted coup were executed June 29 after their conviction by a military tribunal.) The unsuccessful coup apparently took the form of a dawn attack on the prime minister's residence and a noon assault on his office. Three government ministers were held hostage and the home of Sir Banja Tejan-Sie, the governor general, was attacked. Bangurah announced on radio March 23 that "the army has been compelled to take control of the situation until further notice," but later the same day Lt. Col. Sam King (the army's third in command) repudiated Bangurah's announcement and stated the support of most of the military for the Stevens government. No details were given about the means by which King had opposed Bangurah. Troops from neighboring Guinea flew into Sierra Leone March 28 at Stevens's request and took up positions around his residence.

Republic declared. The government April 19 proclaimed the country a republic. Stevens was sworn in April 21 as president. The country's republican status had been achieved in several steps by the national parliament, which approved an act April 16 giving itself power to change the constitution without permission from the governor general. (Tejan-Sie had been relieved of his post by the British government pending retirement. He was reportedly replaced in late March by Chief Justice Christopher Okoro-Cole.) Additional legislation, introduced under certificate of emergency procedure, allowed the nation to become a republic with the approval of two-thirds of the members of parliament, provided that the voting should occur in two successive parliaments with a dissolution between the votes. The measure enabled Stevens to use the 1967 Republican Constitution Bill of former Premier Sir Albert Margai. The Republican bill was passed through three readings and committee stage by the parliament April 19 and became law that day. Stevens was sworn in as prime minister and Okoro-Cole was named president. Parliament adopted a constitutional amendment April 21 by which the president of the republic became chief executive, taking over the powers previously exercised by the prime minister. The legislature then unanimously elected Stevens president.

Cabinet changes. President Stevens April 24 swore in Sorie Ibrahim Koroma, minister of agriculture and natural resources, as first vice president and prime minister. The government was reshuffled May 19 to fill the vacancies created by Koroma's appointment and that of L.A.M. Brewa, minister of health, as the new attorney general. A Ministry of Labor, separate from Lands and Mines, was also established. The principal changes: Christian Karama-Taylor (from lands, mines and labor to finance); Semba Forna (from finance to agriculture and natural resources); Cyril Foray (from external affairs to health); Solomon Pratt (to external affairs); and Kawasu Conteh (from provincial resident minister to interior). S.A.T. Koroma became minister of social welfare, F.N. Turay minister of labor and M.O. Cole minister of housing and country planning. Stevens retained the defense portfolio. Stevens Nov. 26 announced the following changes in the Cabinet: Prime Minister Koroma took on the additional portfolio of interior; Conteh became minister of lands and mines; S.W. Gandi-Capio was made responsible for development; A. Khazali became minister of information; and J.C. Hadson-Taylor was put in charge of health.

See also MIDDLE EAST [11]

SIHANOUK, PRINCE NORODOM—*See* CAMBODIA

SINGAPORE—Anti-press moves. The Singapore government launched a campaign against a number of newspapers for allegedly adopting a pro-Communist and antigovernment position and for accepting financial aid from foreign Communist sources. Four executives of the Chinese-language newspaper Nanyang Sing Pao were arrested May 2 on charges of inciting Chinese nationalism and adopting a pro-Communist line. The men were seized under the internal security laws, which permitted indefinite detention without trial.

Prime Minister Lee Kuan Yew charged in a speech May 8 that Chinese Communist agents in Hong Kong had given a Singapore newspaper owner almost $1.35 million to influence his publication. Lee did not name the journal. The prime minister also criticized the Singapore Herald, an English-language newspaper, for being antigovernment and questioned the sources of its finances. Three foreign employees of the Herald were ordered by the government May 17 to leave the country. No specific charges were filed against Robert Reece, an Australian, the newspaper's foreign editor, his wife, Adele Kohl, a Malaysian, the Herald's feature editor, and M.G.G. Pillai, also a Malaysian. The Herald was forced to cease publication May 28 when the government withdrew its printing license.

Another English-language newspaper, The Eastern Sun, ceased publication May 16 following government charges the previous day that its principal owner, Aw Kow, had received $1.2 million in loans from a "Communist intelligence organization in Hong Kong." The editor in chief, Sam Krishniah, and six senior members of his staff resigned after hearing of the government's allegations.

See also AGNEW, SPIRO THEODORE; MALAYSIA

SINO-SOVIET DEVELOPMENTS—After a pause of nearly nine months, Soviet and Communist Chinese propaganda hostilities resumed in March on the eve of the 24th Soviet Communist party Congress. Communist China March 17 accused the Soviet Union of asking liberation movements "to reduce revolutionary violence to the minimum" while itself using "the most savage and brutal means to deal with revolutionary people." The official Soviet press agency Tass denounced China March 21 for its attacks. In the U.S.S.R., the author of a foreign policy work published by the Soviet Academy of Sciences warned China March 17 against playing a "dangerous game" by trying to improve relations with the U.S. (see COMMUNIST CHINA-U.S. DETENTE).

The Soviet Union in August and September carried on an extensive press attack against China which coincided with the signing of a preliminary four-power agreement on Berlin (see GERMAN CONSULTATIONS). Sergei L. Tikhvinsky, a China specialist, Aug. 20 said China was using the threat of Soviet invasion to improve its relations with Western powers and to erect "fortifications along the whole length of the border with the Soviet Union." The government newspaper Isvestia charged Aug. 25 that Peking had rejected "a speedy and full normalization of relations and settlement of all frontier questions on the basis of constructive proposals that meet the national interests of both peoples as suggested by the Soviet Union" at Sino-Soviet border talks. Isvestia speculated that the Chinese were avoiding agreement because "this would tie their hands, prevent them from playing on international differences and from making China into a central power in the world." Several journals, including the Soviet Communist party newspaper Pravda, Sept. 4 urged "political vigilance" against China's foreign policy.

See also BULGARIA; COMMUNIST CHINA-U.S. DETENTE [8, 13]

SIRIK MATAK, SISOWATH—See CAMBODIA
SMOKING—See HEALTH [4-12]

SOCCER—66 die at Glasgow match. Sixty-six persons were killed and 145 injured Jan. 2 when a reinforced steel barrier collapsed under the weight of a surging crowd at the Ibrox soccer stadium in Glasgow, Scotland. The tragedy—worst in the history of British soccer—came after 80,000 spectators rushed toward exits following a hotly contested game between the Glasgow Rangers and the Glasgow Celtics, traditional rivals. A group of Ranger supporters at an exit stairway reportedly attempted to reenter the stadium when they heard their team had scored to tie the game at 1-1. A massive human pileup was created.

Pele leaves Brazil team. Edson Arantes de Nascimento, known to soccer fans as Pele, ended his career with the Brazilian national team July 18 before 130,000 spectators at a match in Rio de Janeiro. Pele would continue to play, however, for Santos, his professional soccer team. Pele played the first half of the game against Yugoslavia and then watched from the sidelines as Brazil erased a 1-0 deficit to gain a 2-2 tie. Pele's first-half appearance with the Brazilian team marked his 110th appearance with the national club.

See also SPORTS

SOCIAL SECURITY—A rider which provided a 10% increase in Social Security benefits was approved by both houses of Congress March 16 as part of legislation raising the ceiling on the national debt. The Social Security rider was attached to the debt ceiling bill in the Senate March 12, after the bill had been passed by the House March 3. Democratic Congressional leaders had attached the rider in order to press for early action on the Social Security increases. Wilbur D. Mills (D, Ark.), chairman of the House Ways and Means Committee, had initiated plans in the current 92nd Congress to combine the increases with provisions on welfare. (The increases had been planned in the 91st Congress, but had expired after they were tied to controversial legislation for welfare changes and trade provisions.) Following unanimous approval by the Senate of the debt ceiling and Social Security provisions, a Senate-House conference committee approved the measure March 15 and it was passed by votes of 358-3 in the House and 76-0 in the Senate.

The increase in Social Security benefits, retroactive to Jan. 1, raised benefits to a minimum of $70.40 a month and a maximum of $213.10 a month (formerly $193.70 a month) for individuals and to a minimum of $105.60 a month and a maximum of $413.71 a month (formerly $376 a month) for couples. A 5% increase was scheduled for the special payments extended to persons 72 and older not qualified for full Social Security benefits. The cost of the increased benefits was estimated at $3.6 billion a year. The payroll tax rate funding the Social Security trust fund, currently at 5.2% was revised to go to 5.85% in 1976 and to 6.05% by 1987. The amount of individual income subject to the payroll tax was to rise from $7,800 to $9,000 effective in 1972.

The House-Senate conferees had eliminated from the bill a Senate-approved provision for new monthly minimums of $100 for individuals and $150 for couples—thus reducing the estimated costs from $5.5 billion to $3.6 billion—and revised the Senate bill to retain the present $1,680 a year in outside earnings permitted persons on Social Security without reduction of benefits.

See also AGING; BUDGET; WELFARE

SOLEDAD BROTHERS—*See* PRISONS [4]
SOLOMON ISLANDS PROTECTORATE—*See* PACIFIC ISLANDS

SOMALIA—Assassin killed. The man who assassinated former President Abdirashid Ali Shermarke in 1969, identified Feb. 10 as Said Yusuf Ismail, was shot by a firing squad March 3 at Las Anod.

Coup foiled. Brig. Gen. Mohamed Ali Samater, secretary of state for defense, declared June 6 that the government had foiled a plot to kill all members of the Supreme Revolutionary Council and "reinstate capitalism" in the country. Samater said the plot, first uncovered May 5, had been headed by Brig. Gen. Salad Gaviere Kedie and Brig. Gen. Mohamed Ainanshe Gulaid.

Cabinet changes. The Supreme Revolutionary Council July 29 announced the following cabinet changes: Brig. Gen. Hussein Kulmiye was named minister of the interior; the Ministry of Justice, Religion and Labor was divided into the Ministry of Justice and Religion, to be headed by Abdulgani Sheik Ahmad, and the Ministry of Labor and Sport, to be headed by Lt. Col. Musa Rabilleh; the Ministry of Industry and Commerce became the Ministry of Industry, headed by Ibrahim Meigag Samatar, and the Ministry of Commerce, headed by Mohamed Warsame.

See also PAKISTAN [42]

SONGMY MASSACRE—*See* WAR CRIMES [1-7]

SOUTH AFRICA—Polaroid to help workers. Apparently in response to picketing of its Boston area headquarters by company employees, the Polaroid Corp. Jan. 13 announced plans to improve conditions of its black employees in South Africa. The plans, described as a one-year "experiment," called on Polaroid's South African distributor and its suppliers to "improve dramatically the salaries and other benefits of their nonwhite employees" and to "train nonwhite employees for important jobs within their companies." Polaroid was to underwrite the educational expenses of 500 black South African students. In other developments in the labor situation of blacks in South Africa: the government announced Feb. 8 that colored workers (those of mixed racial ancestry) would be allowed to work on Johannesburg and Pretoria construction jobs formerly reserved for whites; the Standard Bank of South Africa and Barclays Bank disclosed Aug. 31 their intention of giving black employees the same rate of pay as whites.

[2] **Namibia plebiscite offered.** In a Jan. 27 letter to the International Court of Justice (World Court) at The Hague, South Africa offered to conduct a plebiscite in the territory of Namibia (South-West Africa) to determine whether it should continue to be administered by South Africa or should be taken over by the United Nations. The U.N. Commission on Namibia scored

the move Jan. 29, declaring that the South African government "occupied the territory illegally and therefore did not have the right to formulate such a suggestion." The court March 17 refused "until a later date" to pronounce on the South African request, but ruled June 21 on a request for a pronouncement on Namibia made by the U.N. Security Council in 1970. The court ruled, by a vote of 13-2, that South Africa's administration of the territory was illegal and that South Africa should give up control of the territory immediately. (The court had ruled on the question in 1966, when it held that Liberia and Ethiopia, although members of the defunct League of Nations, had no legal right to question whether South Africa was violating its League mandate by practicing apartheid in Namibia. The 1966 opinion included no ruling on whether apartheid was being practiced.) The June 21 decision said that South Africa was indisputably pursuing in Namibia a policy aimed at achieving "a complete physical separation of races and ethnic groups." The decision also said that the government policy was enforced by "restrictive measures of control" which established "limitations, exclusions or restrictions for the members of the indigenous population groups in certain types of activities, fields of study or of training, labor or employment and also submit them to restrictions or exclusions of residence and movement." The court delivered a supplementary ruling, by a vote of 11-4, that U.N. members were obliged to "abstain from entering into treaty relations with South Africa in all cases in which the government of South Africa purports to act on behalf of, or concerning, Namibia."

3] *Namibia unrest.* Land mine explosions in the Caprivi Strip area of Namibia May 22, Oct. 4 and Oct. 5 killed three persons and wounded 11. The May 22 blast—believed to be the first time that guerrillas had inflicted any fatalities in any territory controlled by South Africa—killed two white policemen and injured seven others, including two black trackers. The Oct. 4 blast injured four policemen, who had been riding in a motor vehicle. The Oct. 5 explosion killed a South African army officer while he was on an inspection trip in the vicinity of the Oct. 4 blast. In an unrelated incident, about 10,000 members of the Ovambo tribe struck businesses in Namibia—including the largest copper mine in the territory—in mid-December. The black workers were striking to protest the government's migratory worker policy under which the Ovambo workers left their homelands in the northern part of Namibia, without their families, on contracts of up to 18 months. The leaders of the tribe had demanded that unless the contract system, due to be overhauled in February 1972, was ended and the workers were allowed to market their skills at higher rates of pay, the Ovambo would expect repatriation to their home areas. A report Dec. 18 said most of the Ovambo population was being repatriated.

[4] Anglican dean arrested. Gonville Aubrey Ffrench-Beytagh, Anglican dean of Johannesburg and a British subject, was taken into official custody without explanation of the causes Jan. 20. He was released on bail Jan. 28 after being charged in a Johannesburg court with crimes of subversion. He was released on condition that he surrender his British passport. The public prosecutor June 30 announced new charges against the dean, who was convicted Nov. 1 and sentenced to five years in prison. An appeal in the case was not expected to be heard before March 1972. Ffrench-Beytagh was convicted of possessing pamphlets from the outlawed African National Congress (ANC) and the South African Communist party; inciting to violence in a speech given at a meeting of the Black Sash, a women's anti-apartheid group; encouraging Louis Kenneth Jordaan, a police agent who posed as the dean's friend, to plan violence against the state; and distributing money for the Defense and Aid Fund, a London-based organization banned in South Africa from giving assistance to the families of political prisoners. He was acquitted on six other counts. At the opening day of his trial in Pretoria Aug. 2, Ffrench-Beytagh denied the charges against him, remarking in subsequent testimony that the ANC pamphlets found by police in his flat had been placed there without his knowledge.

[5] *Other moves against clergy.* Colin Davison, a British-born Anglican clergyman, was expelled from South Africa Feb. 4. Davison had been arrested in 1970 during a protest march against detention of Africans charged with terrorism. Security police, ostensibly investigating into the activities of Ffrench-Beytagh, raided the offices of church and student organizations in different parts of the country in coordinated actions Feb. 25. The raids, conducted in Johannesburg, Cape Town and Port Elizabeth, were carried out against offices of the South African Council of Churches, the Christian Institute, the University Christian Movement and the National Union of South African Students (NUSAS). NUSAS won a court action against the raids March 10 when the Supreme Court declared that the search warrant used in the action had not empowered police to seize goods or documents. The seized NUSAS materials were returned to the organization's office, which was again raided March 11 under a new warrant issued that day. In another move against a clergyman, the Rev. Cosmos Desmond, a British-born Roman Catholic priest, was placed under house arrest June 28 and designated a banned person for five years. No official explanation was given for the move.

[6] **Terrorism Act arrests.** Twenty persons suspected of terrorism were arrested by security police in all parts of the country Feb. 18. No official explanation for the action was given. Those arrested included teachers, lawyers and businessmen—all members of either the Non-European Unity Movement (NEUM) or the African Peoples Democratic Union of South Africa (APDUSA). Both organizations, legally operating in the country, had sought to make the franchise multi-racial. Security police again conducted raids under the act Oct. 24 in Johannesburg, Cape Town, Durban, Port Elizabeth, East London and other cities. The police operation—directed against the homes of 60 clergymen, university teachers, student leaders and newsmen—was an apparent effort to seize illegal political literature. One of the persons taken into custody as a result of the raids died Oct. 27. Police said that he had jumped from a window in Johannesburg's main police station, but the Rand Daily Mail commented Oct. 29 that there had been bars across the station's windows when the station opened in 1967. Two Britons (Quentin Jacobsen and David Smith) and one Australian (Michael Grimley)—all free-lance photographers—were seized Nov. 1 under the Terrorism Act and were reported Nov. 5 to be held in indefinite detention. Police Nov. 18-20 arrested five more persons and detained them under the Terrorism Act.

[7] **Helicopters from Great Britain.** Sir Alec Douglas-Home, British foreign secretary, announced Feb. 22 that the British government planned to sell helicopters to South Africa. (The U.N. had imposed an embargo on arms sales to South Africa, with which the British government had decided in 1964 to comply. The government had announced July 20, 1970, however, that it would consider resuming the sales of arms to South Africa in light of the terms of the 1955 Simonstown Agreement in which Britain ceded the Simonstown naval base to South Africa but retained its use in exchange for certain arms sales to South Africa between 1955 and 1963.) Douglas-Home declared that Britain was "legally obligated" to provide South Africa with seven Wasp helicopters, valued at $2.4 million, under terms of the Simonstown Agreement. The helicopters, of a general purpose variety, were sought for submarine defense work. A British government white paper Feb. 4 had foreshadowed the decision to sell arms. The document, a legal opinion written by Attorney General Sir Peter Rawlinson and Solicitor General Sir Geoffrey Howe, advised that Britain's obligations under the agreement were limited to furnishing Wasp helicopters for antisubmarine frigates and replacing such helicopters already sold.

[8]   **Port Elizabeth riot.** Police opened fire into a crowd of colored persons in Port Elizabeth March 7, wounding 10. (About 20 policemen were hurt by stones.) The disturbance reportedly arose when police tried to arrest a drunk at a meeting called to protest an increase in the bus fare from the colored township to the center of Port Elizabeth. The crowd reportedly tried to prevent the arrest, and a smaller group of about 2,000 surrounded the local police station. Police Minister Stefanus Lourens Muller said March 10 that the crowd had ignored a warning to disperse, and tear gas had proved ineffective due to strong winds. Muller reported that the police had then used batons while the crowd was throwing stones. He said that the police had fired their service revolvers only "after all other measures to restore order had been exhausted and when their lives were in danger."

[9]   **Bantustan developments.** It was reported March 4 that the government had chosen Chief Lucas Mangope to lead Tswanaland toward self-rule. Tswanaland was one of eight bantustans (black homelands) affected by the Bantu Homelands Constitution Bill being considered by the parliament. Under terms of the bill, the government would be able to grant the areas partial self-rule by proclamation. In another action, Paramount Chief Kaiser Matanzima, chief minister of the Transkei government (the most advanced of the bantustans), asked April 13 that the semi-independent Bantu area be allowed to assume more control over its own affairs. Matanzima, known as a supporter of apartheid, asked for "full control of our own affairs" and a larger share of the "white" lands surrounding the Transkei. He warned that race relations would suffer unless the land question was "fairly settled." He said that he would "negotiate with the republican government until they accede to our requests." The South African government indicated refusal of Matanzima's request April 14.

[10]   **New budget introduced.** A 1971-72 budget designed to combat inflation was introduced in the parliament March 31 by Finance Minister Nicolaas D. Diederichs. The document featured a 5% increase in individual income tax as well as increases in the costs of cigarettes and liquor. There was also a 5% "extra savings levy on companies" with the exception of gold and diamond mining firms. Total expenditure for the coming year was expected to reach $5.1 billion with revenue estimated at $5.2 billion.

[11]   **New sports policy?** Prime Minister John Vorster told the South African parliament April 22 that South Africans of all races would be allowed to compete in international sporting events within the country. Vorster said he had no objection to matches between colored or black rugby teams and visiting teams or to an international tennis tournament within the country open to "rated players" of all races. However, the new policy was described as representing no change "on the club, provincial and national levels." The South African leader declared he was opposed to mixed teams representing the country abroad, with the exception of Olympic sports and possibly the Davis Cup tennis series.

[12]   **OAU on dialogue.** The annual three-day summit conference of the Organization of African Unity (OAU) ended June 23 with delegates opposing (by a 28-6 vote with five abstentions) a recommendation for a dialogue with South Africa. The resolution against dialogue had been passed at a ministerial session June 17. It was based on the Lusaka Manifesto of 1969, according to which talks could be initiated with South Africa only if that government met with representatives of its own black majority. The summit conference extended the mandate, established at the 1970 session, of a mission led by Zambian President Kenneth Kaunda which was to visit North America in an attempt to explain OAU opposition to the sale of arms to South Africa. The conference also asked that the U.N. Security Council be called into session to discuss the World Court's decision on Namibia (*see* [2]). (Continuing his opposition to the OAU position, Ivory Coast President Felix Houphouet-

Boigny Oct. 6-9 sent a three-man delegation to South Africa for high-level talks.)

[13] Assembly condemns apartheid. The General Assembly voted 109-2 Nov. 9 to condemn the policy of apartheid in South Africa and to seek a boycott of that country. Only Portugal and South Africa were opposed. The resolution, introduced Nov. 3 by 36 countries, expressed "grave indignation and concern" over "the maltreatment and torture of opponents of apartheid in South Africa and the increased persecution of religious leaders opposed to that policy." It urged governments to "exert all their influence" toward the repeal of "repressive legislation" in South Africa.

    See also AFRICA; AUSTRALIA [10]; AUTOMOBILES [10]; CHURCHES [2-4]; FOREIGN POLICY; TARIFFS & WORLD TRADE [13]; ZAMBIA

SOUTHERN BAPTIST CHURCH—*See* CHURCHES [10-11]
SOUTHERN CHRISTIAN LEADERSHIP CONFERENCE (SCLC)—*See* DRAFT & WAR PROTEST [11]; NEGROES

SOUTHERN YEMEN—China establishes military mission. The U.S. State Department reported March 13 that Communist China had established a military mission in Aden to supplement Peking's economic presence in Southern Yemen. The mission was said to be staffed by several dozen officers. China's $55 million aid program to Southern Yemen centered largely on construction of a paved road from Aden to Mukalla. The highway would enable government security forces to control the valley of Hadhamaut, where armed anti-government tribesmen were operating and receiving assistance from Saudi Arabia.

    Government changes. Salem Ali Rabyee resigned Aug. 1 as chairman of the ruling Presidential Council, but was reappointed to the post by the Provisional Supreme People's Council Aug. 8. A new Presidential Council also was appointed; its members included Ali Masir Mohammed, as premier and defense minister, and Mohammed Salih Awlaqi as foreign affairs minister.

    See also JORDAN [7]

SOUTH PACIFIC FORUM—Government leaders of Australia, New Zealand and five southern Pacific island states, meeting as the South Pacific Forum, announced Aug. 7 the creation of the forum as a permanent regional organization that would hold annual meetings to promote collective diplomacy for the member states. The announcement was made in a communique issued after a three-day meeting in Wellington, New Zealand. The island members were the newly independent islands of Fiji, Western Samoa, Tonga and Nauru, and the self-governing Cook Islands. Among other proposals, the representatives suggested that Fiji, which held membership in the United Nations along with Australia and New Zealand, could represent all the small island states at the U.N. The islands also suggested that the organization set up a joint mission in Japan and proposed changes that would reduce the dominant voting power of Britain, France, the U.S., Australia and New Zealand in the South Pacific Commission, a seven-nation regional development organization. The other two members were Western Samoa and Nauru. In addition, Australia and New Zealand agreed to represent the islands in such areas as international trade and communications.

SOYUZ 10—*See* SPACE [7]
SOYUZ 11—*See* SPACE [8-9]

SPACE—Lunar exploration. *Apollo 14.* Two U.S. astronauts from the spaceship Apollo 14 landed the lunar module (LM) Antares on the moon Feb. 5. Spaceship commander Navy Capt. Alan Bartlett Shepard Jr. (who became the first American to make a space flight by flying the one-man Mercury capsule Freedom 7 May 5, 1961 in sub-orbital flight) and LM pilot Navy Cmdr. Edgar Dean Mitchell (who had never flown in space before) left the LM twice for 4.5-hour working and exploring sessions on the lunar surface during the record 33.5

hours they remained on the moon. (They were the third two-man team to set foot on the earth's natural satellite.) They then returned in the LM's ascent stage to Apollo 14's command-and-service module (CSM), the Kitty Hawk, which had remained in orbit with CSM pilot Air Force Maj. Stuart Allen Roosa aboard. The Apollo 14 astronauts had started their half-million-mile journey Jan. 31 with a launching at Cape Kennedy, Fla. They ended it Feb. 9 with a safe splash-down in the Pacific. The astronauts Jan. 31 developed trouble with a docking (linking) maneuver. The trouble, which caused ground officials to consider canceling the manned landing on the moon, developed after the astronauts had detached the CSM from the third (S4B) stage of their Saturn-5 booster rocket, moved the CSM ahead of the S4B, turned the CSM around and brought it back to the S4B to dock it with the LM, which remained in the open front of the S4B. The astronauts were then to remove the LM from the S4B. However, after the CSM's docking probe had been thrust into the LM's docking collar, the probe's three capture locks failed to attach themselves to the LM's funnel-like drogue. (This "soft" docking was normally followed by a "hard" docking in which 12 docking latches in the CSM's docking ring were attached.) During a period of nearly two hours, the astronauts made five unsuccessful attempts to dock. In each case, the capture locks failed. On their sixth attempt, the astronauts retracted the probe just before contact, by-passed the use of the capture locks and executed the docking procedure by employing only the docking latches. Ground officials debated canceling the landing on the moon because the LM's ascent stage, on returning from the moon, would normally dock with the CSM to facilitate the transfer of the astronauts and their lunar spoils from the LM to the CSM prior to their return to earth. The astronauts spent 4.5 hours early Feb. 1 in dismantling and testing the docking system under directions from ground controllers and found nothing wrong.

[2]　The Apollo 14 mission, conducted by the National Aeronautics and Space Administration (NASA), cost the U.S. an estimated $400 million—or at least $25 million more than any previous Apollo flight. The high (and growing) cost of manned spaceflight had made the Apollo program a subject of controversy and evoked widespread demands that manned spaceflight be replaced with less costly unmanned space projects.

[3]　*Apollo 15.* Two U.S. astronauts (Air Force Col. David Randolph Scott, the flight commander, and Air Force Lt. Col. James Benson Irwin, the "Falcon" LM pilot) drove a 460-pound electric car on the moon July 31-Aug. 2 during three record-breaking days of scientific exploration and experimentation on the lunar surface. The astronauts and their four-wheeled Lunar Rover 1 made the trip to the moon aboard the spaceship Apollo 15 on a $445 million mission described by NASA sources as the most successful from a scientific standpoint of all U.S. manned space flights to date. The 12-day flight started with a perfect liftoff from Cape Kennedy July 26 and ended with a safe splash-down in the Pacific Aug. 7. While the two astronauts explored the moon's surface, CSM pilot Air Force Maj. Alfred Merrill Worden remained in lunar orbit making scientific observations aboard the CSM Endeavor. On July 1, their first day on the moon, the two astronauts made a 5-mile drive in their rover, at speeds of up to 8 mph, to the Hadley Delta area, where they gathered about 51 pounds of lunar material during their 2-hour excursion. They also deployed, about 300 feet from the LM, their Apollo Lunar Surface Experiment Package (ALSEP), a conglomeration of instruments (including a seismometer, a laser reflector, instruments to detect atmosphere and charged particles, a magnetometer and a spectrometer) designed to radio a variety of scientific information back to earth. On Aug. 11, the astronauts' extra-vehicular activity (EVA) lasted a record 7 hours, 13 minutes. They drove their rover 6 miles in a 4-hour excursion and found a rock that geologists at the Manned Spacecraft Center in Houston said might be part of the original lunar crust. By the end of the day, the astronauts had gathered a record total of about 103 pounds of lunar material. The mission's third and final EVA Aug. 2 lasted for four hours,

50 minutes. It increased the total duration of the mission's EVAs on the moon to a record 18 hours, 37 minutes. During the Aug. 2 excursion, the astronauts drove the rover nearly 6.5 miles and brought the vehicle's total mileage on the moon to nearly 17.5 miles. They also took back at least 72 pounds of surface material, raising the total of the mission to more than 226 pounds. Back in the CSM Aug. 2, the astronauts spent the next two days in lunar orbit aboard Endeavor performing additional experiments, taking photos and making scientific observations. (Worden had chief responsibility for this phase of the mission.) On Aug. 4, the TV camera aboard the lunar rover on the moon was activated by radio signal from ground controllers in Houston. The camera transmitted color telecasts for 12 minutes and then stopped, probably due to overheating. The astronauts the same day ejected from the Endeavor a 78.5-pound scientific subsatellite, expected to stay in orbit about a year, which was to radio to earth data on gravitational and magnetic fields and on high energy particles. On Aug. 5, Worden made a 16-minute "space walk" while the CSM was still 196,000 miles from earth—a record distance for such an activity. The purpose was to inspect instruments and to retrieve film cassettes from the instrument bay of the CSM, which was to be jettisoned before re-entry. Worden made three trips between the cabin's hatch and the instrument bay. He had attached to him a 24-foot tether tended by Irwin. All three astronauts wore space suits during the exercise and the cabin was depressurized before the EVA.

[4] *Two Soviet probes.* Soviet space technicians Sept. 2 and 28 launched the unmanned Luna 18 and Luna 19 space vehicles toward the moon atop multi-stage rockets which put them into parking orbit around the earth before sending them into lunar trajectory. Neither launching was announced in advance; nor was the mission's objective made public. Luna 18 reached the vicinity of the moon Sept. 7 and went into an orbit about 60 miles above the lunar surface until Sept. 11, when (after 54 orbits) it crashed into the lunar surface in what was described by Soviet sources as an "unfavorable" landing in a mountainous area near the moon's Sea of Fertility. It was also reported, however, that Luna 18's program of research "has been completely carried out." While in orbit, the probe had reportedly "performed numerous maneuvers" for "testing automatic near-moon navigation methods and securing a landing on the lunar surface." Luna 19 went into lunar orbit Oct. 3 at an altitude of about 84 miles above the moon. The announcement of the probe's launching had hinted that a lunar landing was not planned.

[5] *Soviet car stops.* The U.S.S.R.'s eight-wheeled Lunokhod 1 vehicle's moving parts ceased operation Oct. 4, 10 months and 17 days after it had been landed on the moon by Luna 17 Nov. 17, 1970. The fuel of the car's nuclear heater was exhausted, but the French-made laser reflector mounted on the car would still be used as a fixed astronomical beacon on the moon. Dr. Boris Nepoklonov, scientific chief of the earth-based team that controlled Lunokhod 1's movements on the moon; said in an interview reported Nov. 2 that the vehicle had explored more than 95,000 square yards of the Sea of Rains and had produced data making it "possible to compile an adequate scheme on the terrain covering an area of more than half a million square yards." Nepoklonov said that the car had transmitted to earth "over 500 lunar panoramas," "over 20,000 television pictures, 25 chemical analyses of the ground and hundreds of probes of the physical-mechanical characteristics of the upper layer of the Sea of Rains." He noted that "geologists and selenologists are convinced that the Sea of Rains is one of the oldest formations of the lunar sphere that extends from the equator to the moon's north pole."

[6] **Soviet probe on Venus.** It was reported Jan. 26 that the Soviet interplanetary probe Venera 7 had landed on Venus Dec. 15, 1970 and that weak radio signals from Venera 7 "were received for ... 23 minutes after landing." The announcement noted that this was "the first time that scientific information was relayed directly from the surface of another planet." (Earlier Soviet probes of Venus had been destroyed before reaching the planet's

surface.) The volume of radio signals from the planet was reportedly about 100 times less than during the descent, probably because of a diversion of the axis of the antenna from earth upon landing. The signals were deciphered and analyzed by a "special method" that involved the use of computers. Data received from Venera 7 disclosed that the surface temperature at the landing site was 475 degrees C, allowing a margin of 20 degrees in each direction (847 degrees to 923 degrees Fahrenheit). The surface atmospheric pressure was given as 90 times that on earth, with an allowance of 15 atmospheres on either side. The atmosphere's density was recorded as about 60 times that on earth. The 2,596-pound Venera 7 weighed about 220 pounds more than previous Venera probes because of modifications made to allow the spacecraft to withstand pressures of up to 180 atmospheres and temperatures of up to 986 degrees F. Aerodynamic braking when the probe smashed into Venus's atmosphere reduced its speed in relation to the planet from 7.1 miles a second to 656 feet a second. At an altitude of about 37 miles, when the external pressure was about .7 atmospheres, the parachute opened. (The parachute, which had been redesigned after the previous Venera flights, allowed Venera 7 to drop through the atmosphere much faster than previous Venera probes.)

[7] Soviet orbiting lab launched. Three Soviet cosmonauts (spaceship commander Red Air Force Col. Vladimir A. Statalov, civilian flight engineer Aleksei S. Yeliseyev and civilian test engineer Nikolai N. Rukavishnikov) blasted into orbit in the spaceship Soyuz 10 April 23, docked their spacecraft April 24 with an unmanned "orbital scientific station," the Salyut (Salute, launched April 19). The two linked vehicles flew together in orbit for 5.5 hours and then separated, Soyuz 10, with its three cosmonauts aboard, was brought out of orbit and landed safely in Kazakhstan April 25 while the unmanned Salyut continued to orbit. Both flights were launched from the Baikonur cosmodrome in Kazakhstan. The docking of the two ships was accomplished in two steps, the first (bringing Soyuz 10 to a distance of 195 yards from Salyut) was automatic, the second (further approach and berthing) was manual. The cosmonauts, once docked, carried out "scientific-technical experiments and work on docking and undocking."

[8] *First working crew.* The Salyut received its first working crew June 7. Three cosmonauts (spaceship commander Lt. Col. Georgi Timofeyevich Dobrovolsky, flight engineer Vladislav Nikolayevich Volkov and test engineer Viktor Ivanovich Patsayev) climbed aboard Salyut from their Soyuz 11 spaceship to start a scientific working period of undisclosed duration. (Soyuz 11 had been launched from the Baikonur cosmodrome June 6.) The crew's principal tasks were to check out the space lab, test its navigation instruments and study the earth's geography and atmosphere and the effects of prolonged space flights on men. The three remained on Salyut until June 29, when they "completed the flight program in full" and were "directed to make a landing." The cosmonauts June 24 exceeded the previous space endurance record of 17 days, 16 hours, 58 minutes and 50 seconds which had been set by two Soviet cosmonauts in 1970. During their stay aboard the space laboratory, they consistently reported that they were in excellent health. They exercised vigorously and at length with specially designed equipment to counteract the debilitating effects of weightlessness. In one experiment expected to be of early practical value, the cosmonauts June 15 took spectral photos of Caspian coastal areas for use in farming, land improvement, geodesy and cartography. The data was coordinated with photos obtained simultaneously by Soviet planes.

[9] *Cosmonauts die.* After setting a 24-day endurance record for space flight, the three cosmonauts died early June 30 on their return to earth. Communication with the crew ceased at the end of the operation of the braking engine slowing Soyuz 11's descent through earth's atmosphere. Apparently ground controllers never re-established contact with the crew. A helicopter-borne recovery team landed in the recovery area "simultaneously with" Soyuz 11. Members of the team opened the hatch and found the three cosmonauts lifeless in their seats. Soviet press sources said the dead men appeared to be sleeping peacefully, their faces were calm and there were no signs of a frantic struggle for life. Soviet authorities admitted they were mystified by the deaths and June 30 appointed a special commission to investigate the reasons for the fatal end of the mission. The inquiry commission confirmed July 12 that the deaths had been caused by a "rapid" air pressure drop due to "a loss of the ship's sealing" 20 minutes before landing. Soviet journalist Victor Louis, frequently used by the government to "leak" information to the Western press, had reported July 2 that, "as a result of human error and mechanical failure," "the spacecraft's hatchway opened slightly—enough to suck the cosmonauts' air supply into space." Because of a design fault in the Soyuz 11, Louis said, the cosmonauts had "failed to seal the hatch of their spacecraft properly."

[10] **Soviet probes head for Mars.** The Soviet Union May 19 and 28 launched Mars 2 and Mars 3 (each weighing 10,230 pounds) on six-month journeys designed to take them along 290-million-mile curving paths to the vicinity of the planet Mars. The launchings were announced only after the probes were in successful Martian trajectory. The two probes went into orbit around Mars Nov. 27 and Dec. 2, respectively. Before entering its Martian orbit, Mars 2 sent to the planet's surface (in an apparent crash landing) a capsule containing "a pennant showing the U.S.S.R.'s coat of arms." The capsule was the first manmade object to reach the surface of Mars and the second to land on any planet other than the earth (see [6]). Mars 3 sent down a television-equipped capsule that soft-landed on Mars Dec. 2 and transmitted pictures for 20 seconds before contact was lost. The capsule came down in a hurricane that drove dust particles at speeds of up to 300 mph. The capsule's signals were relayed to the orbiting Mars 3, which stored them and later transmitted them to earth during radio communications sessions held Dec. 2-5. Under a U.S.-Soviet agreement announced in the U.S. Oct. 20, the Russians notified U.S. Jet Propulsion Laboratory (JPL) officials in Pasadena, Calif. of the orbitings and drops. The agreement called for each country to telegraph immediately to the other of all findings "of special interest" made by the Mars probes of the two nations (see [11]).

[11] **U.S. Mars probe.** The U.S. May 30 launched from Cape Kennedy a 2,200-pound probe called Mariner 9. The U.S. flight had a flatter trajectory to Mars than the Soviet probes. The trajectory took the ship on a 247-million-mile trip ending in an orbit around Mars. The Mariner 9 was the second of two virtually identical probes that U.S. space officials had hoped to put into Martian orbit in November. The first of the two, Mariner 8, launched from Cape Kennedy May 8, fell into the Atlantic because of a malfunction in the second stage of the two-stage Atlas-Centaur booster rocket. Mariner 9 became the first manmade object to orbit another planet Nov. 13 when it went into orbit around Mars. The $65 million spacecraft had started taking photos of Mars at a distance of 535,000 miles as it approached the planet Nov. 10. These photos and those taken at the beginning of the orbital phase of the mission revealed the planet to be largely obscured by a tremendous yellow dust storm that had been raging for a month and a half. The probe also photographed Deimos, the smaller of Mars's two moons Nov. 26 and Phobos, the larger moon, Nov. 29-30. In addition to its two cameras—one with a wide-angle lens and the other with a narrow-angle telephoto lens—Mariner 9 carried an infrared radiometer to measure Mars's surface temperature, an infrared spectrometer to provide information on the composition of the planet's surface and to measure surface and atmospheric temperatures, and an ultraviolet spectrometer to study atmospheric composition, structure and pressures. The JPL, which had built Mariner 9 and was directing the mission, reported Nov. 15 that the infrared radiometer had detected an unsuspected 15-square-mile "hot spot" on the Martian surface. The "hot spot" averaged 12 degrees F. above the normal -55 degrees to -60 degrees F. temperature of the surrounding areas. The JPL reported Nov. 19 that an analysis of Mariner 9's orbit and other data had

shown Mars's gravitational field to be very irregular. The analysis had indicated that Mars bulged at the equator. (The planet's flattened poles had been noted previously.)

[12]   **U.S.-Soviet cooperation.** U.S. and Soviet delegations agreed in Moscow Jan. 21 to exchange about three grams of lunar surface material. The U.S. delegation had arrived in Moscow Jan. 16 to discuss U.S.-Soviet space science cooperation following the successful 1970 U.S.-Soviet negotiations on space rescue and on standardizing docking devices. The delegation left Moscow Jan. 21 after agreeing to the formation of international working groups on synchronizing research. In a later development, a joint U.S-Soviet working committee agreed early in December to exchange information on the biological effects of space flight. The agreement was announced Dec. 31. A NASA announcement said that meetings of experts from both nations' space programs, to take place at least once a year, would include "the exchange of pre-, post- and inflight data in sufficient detail to assure a full understanding of the flight experience of each country from a physiological and medical viewpoint."

[13]   **Payment for space object damage.** A United Nations General Assembly committee (having identical membership to the General Assembly) Nov. 11 unanimously approved an international treaty covering payment of compensation for damages caused by objects launched into space. Under the treaty (reportedly drafted in June), a nation was "absolutely liable" to pay any damage, including personal injury, caused on the earth's surface or to aircraft in flight by an object the nation sends into space. Either of the nations concerned in an incident of space object damage could ask for creation of a three-man claims commission which would rule on the merits and amount of the compensation claims. The commission's ruling would be binding only if both parties agreed beforehand.

Satellites

[14]   **U.S. launchings.** A 635-pound scientific satellite, Explorer 43 (also known as the IMP [interplanetary monitoring platform] 8), was sent into orbit March 13 by means of a three-stage Delta rocket launched from Cape Kennedy. The satellite was equipped to collect data on cosmic rays, the solar wind, electric and magnetic fields and radio astronomy. The 1,400-pound OSO (Orbiting Solar Observatory) 7 satellite was sent into a faulty orbit Sept. 29 by means of a two-stage Delta rocket launched from Cape Kennedy. A malfunction in the rocket's second stage brought the satellite into an eccentric rather than circular orbit and caused an initial wobbling in the satellite which delayed the solar orientation needed to recharge the satellite's solar batteries. Radio commands sent from Cape Kennedy and the Goddard Space Flight Center in Greenbelt, Md. corrected the wobbling and sun-orientation faults. The satellite, which also carried a 45-pound satellite to be used in training exercises by Apollo spaceship tracking stations, was equipped to provide data on the sun's corona, solar flares and other solar energy phenomena.

[15]   A scientific satellite designed to collect data on high-energy particles, solar energy, other space phenomena and satellite communications was sent into polar orbit Oct. 17 by means of a Thor-Agena rocket launched from Vandenberg Air Force Base, Calif. The satellite carried a 32-by-6-foot solar power cell that went into space rolled up in a cylinder but was unrolled after the satellite was in orbit. A $10.5 million Tiros improved weather satellite was destroyed Oct. 21, 97 minutes after its launching from Vandenberg. A Delta carrier rocket had brought the 685-pound Tiros into a preliminary polar orbit as scheduled; but, when the rocket was restarted an hour later to carry the satellite into a higher orbit, it was pointed down instead of up. As a result of its disorientation, the satellite plunged back into the atmosphere and was burned over Devon Island, Canada.

[16]   Chinese launch 2nd satellite. Communist China's second earth satellite was sent into orbit March 3 by means of a booster rocket launched from the Shuang-cheng-tze space center in Kansu Province. China March 16 announced that the satellite weighed 486 pounds and orbited the earth every 106 minutes.

[17]   Europa launching fails. An attempt to put an 800-pound West European communications test satellite into synchronous orbit failed Nov. 5 when explosions in the Europa-2 launching rocket's British-built first stage brought the rocket and satellite down into the Atlantic shortly after its launching from the new French space center at Kourou, French Guiana. The 110-ton rocket, developed by the seven-nation European Launcher Development Organization (Eldo), had four stages built, respectively, by Britain, France, West Germany and Italy. The failure was a particular blow to France and West Germany, the Eldo nations most committed to the effort to develop a West European space launching system independent of the U.S. system. (Britain applied Dec. 16 to withdraw from Eldo.)

[18]   France launches two satellites. A 211-pound D-2A scientific satellite, France's seventh satellite, was sent into orbit April 15 by means of a Diamant-B rocket launched from Kourou. The mission of the Tournesol (Sunflower) was to produce data on the distribution of hydrogen in the solar field. A 213-pound D-2A, launched from Kourou Dec. 5 on a mission to study the distribution of hydrogen in the atmosphere, failed to achieve orbit, reportedly because of a malfunction of the Diamant-B's second stage.

[19]   Britain orbits satellite. Great Britain Oct. 28 became the sixth nation to launch its own satellite with its own carrier rocket as a Black Arrow rocket launched from the Woomera space center in South Australia sent into polar orbit a 145-pound satellite dubbed Prospero. Britain's four previous satellites had been launched by the U.S. Further development or use of the Black Arrow had been canceled by British Aerospace Minister Frederick Corfield.

[20]   2 Intelsat-4s launched. The first of a new series of Intelsat-4 commercial communications satellites was sent into preliminary orbit Jan. 25 by means of an Atlas-Centaur rocket assembly launched from Cape Kennedy by NASA on contract to the Communications Satellite Corp. (Comsat), the U.S. member of the 77-(later 81-) member International Telecommunications Satellite Consorium (Intelsat). A radio signal from Andover, Me. Jan. 27 started the 3,094-pound satellite toward its synchronous orbit, in which it would appear to hang motionless over the equator at an altitude of 22,300 miles above the Atlantic. The $13.5 million satellite, launched at a cost of $16 million to Intelsat, was capable of carrying as many as 9,000 simultaneous transatlantic phone conversations. A second Intelsat-4, weighing 3,110 pounds, was launched by NASA under contract to Comsat Dec. 19. The $29.5 million, 17-foot satellite, designed to replace a smaller Intelsat-3 in synchronous orbit 22,300 miles above the Atlantic at the equator, was to relay phone and television communications between the U.S. and Canada in the Western Hemisphere and points in Europe and North Africa.

[21]   Italy launches two satellites. A U.S.-Italian team at the San Marco space platform (which stood on stilts in the Bay of Formosa three miles off the coast of Kenya) launched an Italian-designed-and-built satellite into equatorial orbit April 24 by means of a U.S. four-stage Scout rocket. The 360-pound scientific satellite, designed to collect data on the upper atmosphere, was the third launched from the San Marco site and the fourth in a cooperative program conducted by NASA and the Aerospace Center of Rome University. An Italian team Nov. 15 sent a 114-pound U.S. satellite into orbit by means of a rocket launched from the San Marco site. The satellite's mission was to study the earth's inner magnetosphere.

[22]   Japan launches 2nd, 3rd satellites. Japan's second satellite, a 138.6-pound payload dubbed Tansei (Light Blue) for Tokyo University's school color, was sent into orbit Feb. 16 by means of a four-stage Mu rocket launched by Tokyo University scientists from the Uchinoura space center. Japan's third satellite (and its first operating scientific observation one), a 145-pound payload dubbed Shinsei (New Star),was sent into orbit Sept. 28 by means of a 44-ton Mu rocket fired by a Tokyo University team from Uchinoura. The satellite was designed to develop data on cosmic rays and solar electric waves. Both satellite launchings used the "gravity-turn" technique rather than more reliable guidance and control devices because scientists at the university had refused to develop a system of the latter type for fear it might be adapted to weapons use. It was reported, however, that the scientists, faced with complaints that the gravity-turn system was too unreliable for serious scientific satellite work, had started research on conventional guidance and control.

[23] **Soviet launch series.** The Soviet Union launched 78 satellites in the Cosmos series—Cosmos 390 through Cosmos 454—during the period of Jan. 12-Dec. 16. Eight of the satellites—Cosmos 444-451—were sent up atop a single carrier rocket Oct. 13. It was reported Sept. 6 that four Cosmos satellites—Cosmos 379 sent up Nov. 24, 1970; Cosmos 382 Dec. 2, 1970; Cosmos 398 Feb. 26, 1971; and Cosmos 434 Aug. 12—had apparently been launched to test components for a manned landing on the moon. Cosmos 434 was said to have had a variable-thrust, restartable engine with six times the thrust of the engine of a standard Soyuz manned spacecraft.

[24] Two new Soviet weather satellites in the Meteor series were launched April 17 and Dec. 29. The satellites' mission was to help in weather forecasting and in measuring the heat reflected from the earth. The U.S.S.R. also launched another weather satellite July 16. The 18th and 19th Molniya-1 communications satellites were launched July 28 and Dec. 20. The first satellite in a new Soviet communications satellite series—Molniya-2—was launched Nov. 24. An international space communications organization named Intersputnik was created in Moscow Nov. 15 under an agreement signed by the U.S.S.R. and eight other Communist countries (Bulgaria, Hungary, East Germany, Cuba, Mongolia, Poland, Rumania and Czechoslovakia). The organization was to be open to all states, Communist or otherwise, and was to "coordinate its activities with the International Telecommunications Union as well as with other organizations whose activities are related to the use of communications satellites."

See also BUDGET; COMMUNIST CHINA-U.S. DETENTE [11]; DEFENSE [8]; DISARMAMENT; FOREIGN POLICY

SPAIN—Aftermath of Burgos trial. In what was considered an attempt to stem rightist dissension following the 1970 conclusion of the Burgos trial of Basque nationalists, Generalissimo Francisco Franco Jan. 12 dismissed right-wing Lt. Gen. Fernando Rodrigo Cifuentes, commander of the 9th Military Division headquartered in Granada. The dismissal followed a speech by Roderigo Cifuentes sharply denouncing progressive members of the Roman Catholic church and government members of the Catholic lay group Opus Dei for their liberal stand during the Burgos trial. In another move to ease tensions following the trial, the government Feb. 5 ended the "state of exception"—tantamount to martial law—imposed in the Basque province of Guipuzcoa during the trial. Madrid dropped its special powers of search and banishment, but left in effect the nationwide emergency decree providing for unlimited arrest powers until mid-June. (The government said the measure was necessary because "groups of extreme leftists continue to menace public order" in Seville.) Burgos military courts continued during 1971 to sentence members of ETA, the Basque revolutionary organization. Maria Teresa Arevalo Larrean was sentenced July 27 to 25 years in solitary confinement for a 1970 attack against offices of naval shipyards in Sestao. Miss Arevalo testified she had wanted to seize a mimeograph machine for use in printing propaganda for ETA. Six ETA members July 30 were given prison sentences of up to 21 years for placing a bomb in the television station of Zarauz in August 1968. Ten Basques were given sentences Aug. 1 of from six months to 15 years in prison on charges of treason for their alleged membership in a terrorist group operating in the San Sebastian area since 1966. They were acquitted on charges of rebellion, possession of arms and illegal association.

[2] New labor law approved. A new law reorganizing Spain's labor syndicates was approved by a 451-11 vote of the Cortes (parliament) Feb. 16. The law retained the government-controlled syndicates representing both labor and management in each industry. Within each industry, however, elected worker and employer associations were authorized. The worker associations would present workers' grievances, negotiate contracts, and have the right of appeal to the courts against government interference. Workers would be authorized to hold meetings, but discussion would be restricted by Spain's laws on assembly and speech. The law would not legalize strikes and the government would retain the right to dissolve the associations. In a later development, Generalissimo Franco decreed April 29 that workers would be permitted to hold meetings at their places of work. However, another decree, published May 7, said that unions could not meet spontaneously, but that worker representatives had to ask for permission in writing from union authorities two days in advance.

[3] Concordat deadlock. A foreign ministry communique Feb. 7 called for a new agreement to replace the 1953 Concordat between Spain and the Vatican, which the communique described as "obsolete and outdated." The communique, which expressed hopes for an eventual separation of church and state, came amid press leaks over a deadlock in negotiations for revision of the Concordat. The Vatican's version of the working draft (reportedly rejected in mid-February by a 16-10 vote of Spanish bishops) was published by the press Feb. 2. It would maintain most of the church's temporal privileges, but would revoke the clergy's legal immunity. It would abolish the state's right to choose bishops, but would require the church to inform the government in advance of all nominations of priests and bishops—giving the government effective veto power over candidates. Liberal Spanish bishops and some government officials, who wanted a sharper division between church and state, sharply criticized the Vatican plan. The government version of the draft—leaked to the press Feb. 3—would eliminate state subsidies to the church and abolish some church privileges, including clerical legal immunity, in exchange for exclusive church nomination of bishops.

[4] *Church hierarchy shifted.* Changes in the Roman Catholic Church hierarchy in Spain were announced simultaneously Dec. 4 in Madrid and at the Vatican. The shifts were thought to represent a compromise between liberal and conservative Spanish churchmen, the Vatican and the Spanish government, but some observers felt the shifts bolstered the moderate and progressive factions of the Spanish church. Generalissimo Franco participated in the elections under the Concordat. The shifts: Vicente Cardinal Enrique y Tarancon, the archbishop of Toledo and primate of Spain, was named archbishop of Madrid to succeed the Most Rev. Casimiro Morcillo, who had died in May; Archbishop Marcelo Gonzalez Martin replaced Tarancon as archbishop of Toledo and primate of Spain; the Most Rev. Jose Maria Cirarda Lachionado, apostolic administrator of the Basque stronghold of Bilbao, bishop of Santander and a Basque who had been closely identified with Basque aspirations for home rule, was switched to Cordoba; and the Most Rev. Antonio Anoveros Ataun, bishop of Cadiz and Ceuta, was named bishop of Bilbao. Three other bishops were named to new posts.

[5] Court closes Matesa indictments. Spain's Supreme Court ruled Feb. 24 that there were no grounds for indicting Foreign Minister Gregorio Lopez Bravo and Education Minister Jose Luis Villar Palasi in the Matesa financial scandal involving the mishandling of government export loans. The decision ended court indictments in the case. (Eighteen persons had already been indicted.)

[6] Carlists vow opposition. An estimated 15,000-50,000 Carlists (supporters of the claim to the Spanish throne by exiled Prince Xavier of Bourbon-Parma, who was banished in 1968) defied the government ban on political rallies and declared their official opposition to the Franco regime May 2 after their annual pilgrimage and mass on Monte Jurra, their shrine near the old Carlist capital of Estrella. The Carlists attacked "Franco's sellout to American imperialism" and called for political freedom and amnesty for political prisoners, democratic rights and freedom of the press. The liberal demands were considered surprising in view of the Carlists' traditional conservatism.

[7] Supreme Court decides for press. In a verdict rendered July 2, the Supreme Court annulled a Franco-approved fine against the daily newspaper Madrid. The fine had been levied on Madrid for publishing in 1968 an article critical of a government bill dealing with official secrets. The court, in its first ruling in favor of a newspaper in such a case since the Spanish Civil War, ruled that responsible criticism by the press was beneficial because the press "cannot remain an instrument to be used only as a spokesman for official belief." Despite the court victory, however, Madrid was ordered by the Information Ministry Nov. 25 to cease publication immediately. The ministry charged that the paper's management had illegally failed to report stock transfers since the paper's initial registration, but it was generally assumed that the government closed down the paper because of its independent liberal editorial policy. The government had been pressuring publisher Rafael Calvo Serer, reportedly in self-exile in Paris to avoid government prosecution, to renounce his control of the paper and to replace its moderate editor, Antonio Fontan, with a right-winger. Madrid had been charged with 31 previous violations of the press law since 1966, fined and twice shut down temporarily. Calvo said Nov. 25 that he would appeal the ministry's latest order.

[8] Cortes approves Public Order Law. The Cortes, according to a July 20 report, approved a law under which the government could impose, without trial, fines of up to $14,000 and a maximum sentence of three months in prison on persons disturbing public order. The law, directed at political dissenters, also provided for establishment of special tribunals in case of emergency. A clause requiring a police certificate of good conduct for entrance to universities and other institutions was dropped from the legislation. Enactment of the legislation followed a controversy which developed over the suspension of constitutional guarantees during the Burgos trial (see [1]).

[9] Franco celebrates 35 years in power. Generalissimo Franco told an enthusiastic mass rally, gathered in Madrid to celebrate his 35th anniversary in power Oct. 1, that he would remain as head of the government "as long as God gives me life and clarity of judgment." His remark dispelled rumors that he was planning to hand over power to his designated successor, Prince Juan Carlos de Borbon. (Franco July 6 had decreed that Juan Carlos would substitute for him as head of state and government whenever the general was absent from Spain or ill.) Shortly before the rally, Franco signed a general amnesty for about one-third of the nation's political prisoners. The amnesty freed persons sentenced to six months or less in prison and dropped charges against persons facing penalties of less than six months. Sentences between six months and two years would be reduced by one-half and those from 2-12 years would be cut by one-quarter.

[10] Catalan opposition unites. About 300 Catalan opponents of the Franco regime vowed to work toward the overthrow of the regime at a clandestine meeting held in Barcelona Nov. 7. The meeting, called the Assembly of Catalonia, was attended by a broad opposition front from more than 20 underground political organizations ranging from monarchist to Communist and including businessmen, lawyers, students, artists and workers. The assembly was said to be the biggest opposition meeting since Franco came to power. A four-point program adopted by the assembly called for full amnesty for all political prisoners and exiles, introduction of democratic freedoms, restoration of a special statute granting autonomy to Catalonia, and coordination of all activities of groups opposing the regime. A steering committee was named to draft proposals to implement the program and to prepare for a second session of the assembly. The meeting also pledged to oppose Franco's plans for Juan Carlos to succeed him.

[11] 4-year development plan. Spain's third four-year development plan, covering 1972-75, called for $12 billion in public investment, nearly 60% more than in the previous plan, according to a report Nov. 18. The plan, announced the previous weekend by Planning Minister Laureano Lopez Rodo, also anticipated private investment of $24 billion. An annual economic growth rate of 7%, compared to 6.4% over the past four years, was envisaged. Among the planned programs were the construction of six new universities and 1,120,000 units of government or government-sponsored housing, increases in unemployment compensation and old-age benefits and investments in agricultural development. The plan also provided for incentives to spur consolidation of small industries.

See also AGNEW, SPIRO THEODORE; CUBA; DRUG USE & ADDICTION [9]; EUROPEAN ECONOMIC COMMUNITY [5]; HEALTH [1]

SPANISH-AMERICANS—See RACIAL & MINORITY UNREST [2-3]
SPECIAL DRAWING RIGHTS (SDRS OR PAPER GOLD)—See INTERNATIONAL BANK FOR RECONSTRUCTION AND DEVELOPMENT
SPECK, RICHARD—See CRIME [20]
SPOCK, BENJAMIN—See POLITICS [13]

SPORTS—Table tennis. Table tennis players from Communist China and Japan shared team honors April 5-12 at the 31st World Table Tennis Championships in Nagoya, Japan. For China, the participation of its top men and women players marked the first time since 1965 that it had been represented in the world tournament. China's men's squad, after some difficulty in an early round with Hungary, stopped the Japanese team in the finals, 5-2, to capture the Swaythling Cup, the prize for the men's team title. In the women's division, the Japanese, the reigning world champions, beat Communist China's women's team, 3-1, for the Corbillon Cup for the women's team title. The U.S. men's squad finished 24th in the 54-nation tournament. The U.S. women finished in 21st place. A total of 536 players competed.

Bicycle racing. Eddy Merckx of Belgium became the third man to win three Tour de France bicycle races in a row July 18 as he wheeled into Paris far ahead of his closest challenger. Merckx covered the last lap of the 3,600-kilometer (2,237-mile) race in one hour 10 minutes 32.2 seconds at an average speed of 28.4 miles an hour. The final leg, from Versailles to Paris, was 53.8 kilometers (33.4 miles). Officials gave his overall time, counting bonuses for lap performances, as 96 hours, 45 minutes 14 seconds. The other men to have won three Tours in a row were Jacques Anquetil of France, who won four straight in 1961-64, and Louis Bobet of France in 1953-55.

Volleyball. Cuba earned a berth in the 1972 Olympics volleyball competition in Germany Aug. 22, defeating the U.S. team, 8-15, 15-10, 15-6, 15-8 in Havana. The triumph enabled Cuba to qualify as the North American Zone entrant in the international play in Munich. The Americans and the Cubans reached the finals by defeating the Netherlands Antilles, Mexico and Puerto Rico in the round-robin series.

During their 10-day stay in Havana, the U.S. team, accompanied by a doctor, a trainer and three American journalists, met with Premier Fidel Castro, who attended several of the key matches. Castro told newsmen that Cuba would be interested in a reciprocal volleyball arrangement for a match in the U.S. if the competition involved similar circumstances such as Olympic qualifying tournaments. The volleyballers' stay marked the second time a delegation of American athletes had visited Cuba since Castro took power. In 1969, a team of U.S. fencers were in Havana for the world championships.

U.S. tops field in Pan Am games. A team of U.S. athletes outdistanced teams from 29 other Pan American nations by collecting 218 medals at the sixth Pan American games at Cali, Colombia July 30-Aug. 13. Cuba finished second with 105 medals and Canada was third with 80. The U.S. squad collected 105 gold medals (first-place finishes), 73 silver (second place) and 40 bronze (third place) medals. The Americans were paced by its swimmers and divers who won 26 gold medals.

In team sports, Cuban athletes won the men's and women's volleyball titles. The Cuban men also won the baseball championship. Brazil's men and women captured the basketball titles. Argentina won the soccer championship. The water polo title went to the U.S. The men's basketball championship was marked by elimination of the favored U.S. squad by a complicated scoring system based on point spreads. The U.S. team was scratched Aug. 6 when Brazil beat Cuba, 73-62. Cuba's 62 points enabled it to beat the point spread and eliminate the U.S. Cuba's effort also enabled it to gain the right to face Brazil in the round-robin's final game which Brazil won 63-62.

See also AUSTRALIA |10|; BASEBALL; BASKETBALL; BOXING; FOOTBALL; GOLF; HOCKEY; SOCCER; SOUTH AFRICA |11|; TENNIS; TRACK & FIELD

STANLEY CUP—*See* HOCKEY
STANS, MAURICE—*See* CANADA |26|; CONSERVATION; CONSUMER AFFAIRS |11|; RAILROADS

STATE & LOCAL GOVERNMENTS—Revenue sharing. President Nixon Feb. 4 sent Congress a special message and draft legislation for his proposal on "general revenue sharing" under which states and localities would receive a share of federal revenue with few or no strings attached. Separate messages on the Administration's "special revenue sharing" proposals were sent to Congress later. The President's general revenue sharing plan envisioned a $5 billion fund (increasing, according to Nixon, to perhaps as much as $10 billion by 1980 as the economy grew), automatically financed by taking 1.3% of taxable personal income each year, to be divided among the states on the basis of a state's population and its "tax effort." As for secondary distribution between the states and cities, the message offered an inducement for the states and localities to work out their own "mutually acceptable formula for passing money on to the local level." The inducement was full funding of the state's share of the federal fund. States lacking their own formula would receive only 90% of their share of the federal fund, and this would be distributed under a federal formula with the states getting about half and cities and towns half.

[2] *Crime plan.* President Nixon March 2 asked Congress to approve a $500 million outlay in special revenue sharing funds to help cities and states in their fight against crime. The funds would be distributed to the states on the basis of population. States would not be required to "match" special revenue payments with their own funds or to maintain their present expenditures on law enforcement to qualify for federal funds. Nixon's proposal called for a total federal expenditure of $711 million—$211 million earmarked for programs administered by the Justice Department's Law Enforcement Assistance Administration and $500 to be allocated to the states by the Justice Department. The states would be able to use the funds as they saw fit.

[3] *Manpower training.* The President proposed March 4 that states and cities be permitted to use federal funds to develop public service jobs to train the unemployed. The proposal stipulated that such jobs could not be held longer than two years and should be regarded as a "transitional opportunity" leading to a regular job with a public or private employer. Under the proposal, a number of existing programs would be consolidated into an annual $2 billion program of unearmarked grants to state and local governments representing 100,000 or more persons. Of the proposed $2 billion funding—a one-third increase over existing manpower outlays—85% would be divided among state and local governments by statutory formula according to proportionate

numbers of workers, unemployed persons and low-income adults. The Labor Department would retain 15% for research, development of computerized job banks, experimental manpower programs and local staff training assistance. The proposal also contained a "trigger" feature to automatically release additional funds if the nation's unemployment level ranged 4.5% or higher for three straight months or more. Nixon stressed that his proposal: was optional; allowed state and local governments to devise their own work plans; freed city, county and state governments from matching and maintenance-of-effort restrictions; and dispensed with stringent accountability requirements, except for annual audits and publication of spending plans.

[4] *Urban assistance.* The President's urban assistance program sent to Congress March 5 would merge several major housing and urban development programs into one $2 billion plan to enable local governments to develop their own plans for urban and community development. (In his rural aid message March 10, the President proposed to add $100 million to the urban program to assure continued aid to cities with populations ranging from 20,000 to 50,000.) Of the proposed funding, $1.6 billion would be allocated to urban areas with 50,000 or more persons under a statutory formula taking into account population, degree of substandard housing and proportion of families below the poverty level. The residual $400 million would be distributed at the discretion of the Department of Housing and Urban Development (HUD), chiefly to assure that no recipient received less under the new program than under old programs. Any leftover funds would be distributed to reward communities with outstanding programs and to help those with exceptional problems. The President said his proposal would eliminate numerous federal requirements that would free local communities to write their own rules. Matching of federal funds would also be eliminated under the new program.

[5] *Rural aid.* The President's rural aid message, sent to Congress March 10, would create a new $1.1 billion program for rural development that would replace 11 aid programs but add $179 million in additional funds. The 50 states, Puerto Rico, the Virgin Islands and Guam would receive funds on the basis of such criteria as the state's rural population, rural per capita income relative to the national average and the state's change in rural population. Each state would be required to submit a budget to the Department of Agriculture and HUD outlining the state's plans for urban and rural development, thereby focusing on the interrelationship of the two areas. The plans would not have to have federal approval. (The proposal suffered a setback March 11 when the Senate approved extension of the life of the Appalachian Regional Commission and authorization of funds for seven other regional commissions—including two being formed for the Missouri Basin States and the mid-South. Funds voted by Congress in 1970 to form the latter two commissions were withheld by the Office of Management and Budget because of its plans to phase out such commissions under the revenue sharing program.)

[6] *Transportation.* President Nixon March 18 sent Congress his proposal for combining 23 existing federal transportation grant-in-aid programs into two large revenue sharing funds: a $525 million fund for capital investment in urban mass transit; and a $2.041 billion fund to be allocated to states and cities for "a broad spectrum" of transportation services, such as mass transit, highways and aviation facilities. In line with the Administration's intention to shift priority away from the automobile in urban aid, about $1.5 billion in funds normally earmarked for federal aid to highways could be allocated to other modes of transportation. (This did not include funds for the Interstate Highway System, which was funded from a special trust fund. The Administration would retain the current setup to finish the system, which Nixon estimated was 74% complete.) Allocation of the $2.041 billion fund would be made to the states by a formula involving three ratios: a state's population to the national population; a state's urban population to the national urban population; and a state's geographic area to the total national area. The states would be required to distribute about one-third of their allocation to metropolitan areas of more than 2,500 persons. The remainder could be distributed by the states according to their priorities. Matching requirements would be eliminated.

[7] *School-aid plan.* President Nixon's final revenue sharing message April 6 called for a consolidation of 33 federal programs into five basic grant categories (aid for the disadvantaged, aid for the handicapped, aid to schools in areas with a heavy concentration of federal installations, vocational training and supporting services and supplies) and the addition of $200 million in new funds to the $2.8 billion currently being spent on government programs. It was estimated that 51% of the total allotment in the first-year budget would be apportioned to the disadvantaged. Under the plan, states would be permitted to shift up to 30% of their allocated funds to other education purposes with the exception of funds for the disadvantaged. The states would not be required to submit budget plans to Washington. Allocations would be based on one formula which would distribute funds according to proportionate numbers of low-income pupils, school-age children and children of federal employees in each state. The plan also required states to assist nonpublic school students on an equitable basis in all programs except the "impact aid" program directed at schools educating large numbers of federal employee offspring.

[8] *Mills alternative.* Rep. Wilbur D. Mills (D, Ark.) Nov. 30 introduced revenue sharing legislation as an alternative to the Nixon Administration's plan. The Mills bill would provide $3.5 billion a year to local governments and $1.8 billion a year to state governments for a five-year period, after which Congress would review the plan. Distribution would be made to local governments by a formula based on population and the proportion of low-income families, to states by a formula based on the amount of money raised by the state from income taxes. A state would receive an amount equal to 15% of its collections under its state income tax, up to a ceiling of 6% of the federal income tax collected in that state. For the first two years of the plan, states without an income tax or a low one would receive at least 1% of the federal income tax collected in that state. The state plan featured a "piggy-backing" provision to have the federal government collect the state income taxes that were generally similar in provisions, (not rates) to federal income tax provisions. Spending of the funds by the states and localities under the Mills plan would be restricted to high priority categories, such as public health, safety and transportation and environmental programs.

[9] *Muskie alternative.* Sen. Edmund S. Muskie (D, Me.) early in June had proposed another alternative to the Nixon Administration program. Muskie's proposal would provide an incentive to the states to enact or raise income taxes by adding to their portion from revenue sharing a bonus of 10% of its income tax collections. Other bonuses would be paid states according to need as determined by the percentage of families with poverty-level incomes. It also would extend to individuals or groups the right to sue states or localities using revenue sharing funds in racially discriminatory ways. Muskie's plan was endorsed June 1 by Walter W. Heller, former chairman of the President's Council of Economic Advisers and an originator of the revenue sharing theory.

[10] **State income tax developments.** Rhode Island Feb. 26 levied its first income tax, to be collected at a rate of 20% of the federal income tax. The tax was enacted for the first six months of the year to offset a projected $24.5 million deficit for the current fiscal year. The New Hampshire House of Representatives, by a 219-157 vote May 27, defeated Gov. Walter R. Peterson's proposal for a 3% income tax. New Hampshire remained the only state in the nation without a personal income tax or a general sales tax. A special Connecticut general assembly Aug. 12 repealed a newly enacted (July 8) state graduated income tax and substituted a package raising state sales taxes from 5% to 6.5%—the highest levied by any state. Pennsylvania Aug. 31 enacted a 2.3% flat income tax to replace a graduated income tax (enacted March 4) that had been voided by the state supreme court June 24. The state had already collected and spent some $135 million under the first measure. Collection of the first tax had begun May 1 but had been retroactive to the beginning of 1971.

[11]   Massachusetts lottery voted. The Massachusetts legislature Sept. 27 voted to override a gubernatorial veto and become the fourth state in the Northeast (after New Hampshire, New York and New Jersey) to have an official state lottery. Gov. Francis W. Sargent had vetoed the bill, claiming that a lottery was a poor way of raising money. He said the lottery would be too political because it would be run by a commission under the control of the state treasurer. The lottery was to raise money to aid cities and towns.

[12]   NYC statehood petition rejected. A petition for a November referendum to make New York City a separate state was rejected Sept. 30 by the city clerk because of insufficient valid signatures. Herman Katz turned down the petition in a letter to Rep. Bella Abzug (D, N.Y.), chairman of the 51st state committee that was urging a radical solution to the city's financial difficulties. Katz said at least 20,000 of the 55,398 signatures were invalid, leaving fewer than the necessary 45,000 signatures required for a referendum. He said many were thrown out that were obtained from persons 18-20 years of age because the city charter allowed petition signatures only from persons previously registered to vote.

See also AGING; BUDGET; PUBLIC LAND; RACIAL & MINORITY UNREST [1]; UNEMPLOYMENT

STATE OF THE JUDICIARY—*See* JUDICIARY [7]
STATE OF THE UNION—*See* NIXON, RICHARD MILHOUS [1]
STATE OF THE WORLD—*See* FOREIGN POLICY

STOCK MARKET—NYSE panel breaks tradition. In tradition-shattering moves, the New York Stock Exchange's (NYSE) Committee on Membership Qualifications Jan. 25 endorsed institutional membership on the exchange and recommended negotiated commission rates. The committee ordered the NYSE staff to prepare an action plan on implementation of the two concepts. (The staff recommendations would require the approval of the committee, the board of governors and the exchange's 1,366 members.) The committee coupled the two concepts with the expectation that competitive commissions would be lower than those under the current fixed-rate system and would reduce the pressure by institutions such as mutual funds and investment firms to join the exchange for purposes of cutting brokerage costs by gaining access to lower member rates. The committee action was apparently induced by membership applications by two large mutual funds—Dreyfus Sales Corp. of the Dreyfus Fund (Jan. 13) and Jeffries & Co., a unit of Investors Diversified Services, Inc. (Jan. 20). According to press reports, both Dreyfus and IDS, the nation's largest mutual funds, had threatened the exchange with antitrust suits if their applications were turned down or were not acted upon within a reasonable period. (Jeffries's membership application was rejected Oct. 4.)

NYSE begins negotiated fees. The NYSE, acting in compliance with a Feb. 11 directive from the Securities and Exchange Commission (SEC), April 5 instituted a system of negotiated commission rates on the portions of large stock transactions that exceeded $500,000. The new commission system, opposed by the exchange, introduced price competition for the first time in the exchange's 179-year history and was expected to be adopted by the American Stock Exchange (Amex) and in regional markets. The SEC order grew out of findings by the Justice Department's Antitrust Division that the NYSE's established price-fixed commission system violated antitrust laws unless the SEC declared it to be necessary to the workings of the Securities Exchange Act. In October 1970, the SEC had said that price-fixing on transactions over $100,000 violated the act. The Feb. 11 order thus represented a compromise on the SEC's original ruling. The NYSE board of governors March 31 unanimously approved amendments, to be ratified later by the membership, incorporating the new fee system into the exchange's constitution. The governors acted on the advice of legal counsel to avoid triple-damage antitrust suits by the federal government and private traders. The exchange and member firms attempted resistance to implementation of the new system, but were frustrated by pressure from the SEC to meet the April deadline and by court refusals to postpone implementation.

Martin report on NYSE. William McChesney Martin Jr. Aug. 5 presented to the NYSE governing board a report calling for a full-scale reorganization of the NYSE and creation of a national stock exchange system. The report, on the rules and procedures of the exchange and securities industry, was not binding. It called for: reorganization of the NYSE; continuous review and emphasis on the financial soundness of member firms; additional regulation and improvement of the role of the specialists and the block positioners; prohibition of institutional membership and prohibition of member firm management of mutual funds; prohibition of crediting commissions against any fee charged for investment advice; and greater use of modern communications systems. Martin recommended reorganizing the NYSE governing board to provide greater representation for public and listed corporations and to curb the influence of brokers. He would limit the governing board to policy matters, leaving daily operations to a full-time paid chairman and a non-voting president. He said that the dispute over fixed and negotiated commission rates should be given more study, and he cautioned against an overly rapid expansion of negotiated fees. In other proposals, Martin cited the need for smaller brokerage houses and urged that they be strengthened, and suggested that brokerage firms controlled by foreigners be allowed to become exchange members.

Martin's recommendations requiring government action for creation of a national stock exchange system: development of a national exchange system providing a national auction market for each listed security; consideration of increased requirements for entry into the securities business by broker-dealers; adoption of appropriate segregation requirements with respect to free credit balances [funds left on deposit with brokers when investors sell stock and used by brokers as part of their working capital]; resolution of the differences which result in unequal regulation and the elimination of the "third market," preferably through the development of a national exchange system; additional time to be given to the experiment with negotiated rates before any further change is made; the enactment of legislation granting antitrust exemption to the exchanges coexistent with SEC oversight; a coordinated effort to eliminate the stock certificate; and development of a "consolidated-exchange" tape. Martin recommended creation of a public corporation to operate a central market system formed from the NYSE, Amex and all regional stock exchanges. He said a national exchange system would make possible central reporting of all transactions, prices and volume, and would be a vital aid and spur to investment. To increase the flow of stock orders to the proposed central market, Martin recommended elimination of the "third market" where exchange-listed stocks were traded over-the-counter by securities dealers who were not stock exchange members.

See also BUSINESS [2, 10]

STOKES, CARL B.—*See* ELECTIONS [6]; POLITICS [11]

STORMS—U.S. Tornadoes. At least 90 persons were known dead in an estimated 40-50 tornadoes that tore across northeastern Louisiana, western Mississippi and southern Tennessee Feb. 21. Mississippi was declared a disaster area by President Nixon Feb. 22. Insured property damage in Louisiana and Mississippi was expected to exceed $7.5 million. Eleven persons were killed and more than 100 injured in at least five tornadoes that swept through Kentucky, Illinois and Tennessee April 27-28. The heaviest damage was inflicted in Kentucky, where three tornadoes killed 10 people. President Nixon, acting at the request of Gov. Louie B. Nunn, May 10 declared eight counties in Kentucky a major disaster area. On May 18, the President declared three

Tennessee counties, which had been struck by other tornadoes May 7, major disaster areas.

Wanda kills 25. Tropical storm Wanda lashed across the central Philippines April 26, leaving at least 25 persons dead and more than 100 missing.

Hong Kong gets relief aid. Communist China was reported Aug. 28 to have provided Hong Kong with more than $1.3 million in relief for the devastation caused by a typhoon Aug. 17. The storm had killed more than 90 persons and left 2,500 homeless. The funds were sent by the Chinese Red Cross Society to the Hong Kong branch of the British Red Cross Society.

STRATEGIC ARMS LIMITATION TALKS (SALT)—*See* DISARMAMENT; FOREIGN POLICY

STRIKES—*See* ECONOMY, U.S. [28]; EDUCATION [8-10]; LABOR [1, 6-13]; MINES; POSTAL SERVICE, U.S.; RAILROADS

STUDENTS FOR A DEMOCRATIC SOCIETY (SDS)—*See* DRAFT & WAR PROTEST [4, 6, 9]

STUDENT UNREST—Jury report on Kent held illegal. U.S. District Court Judge William K. Thomas, ruling in Cleveland Jan. 28, upheld 25 grand jury indictments in connection with May 1970 violence at Kent State University which resulted in the death of four students. However, Thomas ruled that the report issued by the jury was illegal and ordered it destroyed within 10 days. The decision came in two suits brought by faculty members and students at Kent State. Thomas refused to throw out the indictments because, he said, "Bad faith in the sense of deliberate willful perversion of law to gain an improper purpose is not directly shown and it will not be inferred." However, he said that former Gov. James A. Rhodes erred in his call for a grand jury report and that the report, if allowed to stand, would "irreparably injure" the defendants' rights to a fair trial. He said the jury "violated the oath of secrecy, . . . took over the duties of a petit [trial] jury and acted as a trying body and determined guilt" and issued a report that was illegal in that it "advises, condemns or commends." Thomas criticized the jury for claiming that its witnesses "have fairly represented every aspect, attitude and point of view concerning the events." He specifically criticized the finding that the events at Kent constituted a riot, arguing that this finding should be left to a regular jury and that "establishing existence of a riot is a basic and essential element of at least 27 of the 43 charged offenses" in the indictments. Thomas' decision to uphold the indictments but destroy the report was upheld by the 6th Circuit U.S. Court of Appeals Oct. 22. The report was officially burned Nov. 15.

[2] *Mitchell drops probe.* Attorney General John N. Mitchell announced Aug. 13 that no federal grand jury would be empaneled to investigate the shooting deaths at Kent. Mitchell said "There is no credible evidence of a conspiracy between National Guardsmen to shoot students on the campus." Mitchell said Justice Department investigations supported the conclusion of the President's Commission on Campus Unrest that the guardsmen's rifle fire against students was "unnecessary, unwarranted and inexcusable." However, he said, no conspiracy had been discovered and a grand jury could not be expected to produce new evidence beyond that already provided by the commission and the Federal Bureau of Investigation (FBI). (The Justice Department's finding contrasted with a private report, released July 20, which was published with funds from the Department of Law, Justice and Community Relations of the United Methodist Church's Board of Christian Social Concerns. That report, based on testimony already on public record, said "a few guardsmen, perhaps no more than eight to ten," from Troop G of the 107th Armored Cavalry had agreed to "punish" the students and opened fire on signal. The report cited a "monumental accumulation of testimony and photographs which support the theory that the shooting was planned and carried out with the intent to kill, maim or injure students." The report, submitted to the Justice Department a month before, was released to the public because the department made no response to its "appeal" for an "immediate and thorough" federal investigation.)

[3] *Kent prosecutions end.* The State of Ohio Dec. 7 dropped for lack of evidence all charges against 20 remaining defendants in the Kent riot trials after two of the first five defendants were cleared, two pleaded guilty and charges against one were dismissed. Ohio Attorney General William Brown said he had concluded some time before that many of the cases could not be prosecuted, and had arranged the trials in the order of the strongest evidence. In the first trial (which began Nov. 22), Jerry Rupe had been convicted Nov. 30 of the misdemeanor of interfering with a fireman, but the jury was unable to reach a verdict on three felony charges. The state then dismissed charges against Peter Bliek, the second defendant. The next two defendants, Larry Shub and Thomas G. Fogelsong, pleaded guilty to first-degree riot charges Dec. 1 and Dec. 6, respectively. Additional charges against Shub were then dropped. Common Pleas Judge Edwin Jones Dec. 7 instructed the jury to find the fifth defendant, Helen Nicholas, not guilty of interfering with a fireman, whereupon Special State Prosecutor John Hayward moved to drop the remaining cases.

[4] Arizona violence. Tucson, Ariz. Mayor James M. Corbett declared a curfew and martial law after a third night of violence Jan. 23 near the campus of the University of Arizona. Six police officers were injured and 41 persons arrested Jan. 23 during an outbreak of firebombing and window breaking. Officials attributed the trouble to "street people" who demanded that a portion of the campus be made a "people's campground" and that the city drop proposed ordinances against hitchhiking, loitering and panhandling. Order was reportedly restored Jan. 24. Campus officials said Jan. 25 that only about 40 of the 148 persons arrested since Jan. 21 were students at the university, which had an enrollment of 25,000 students.

[5] College acquitted in unrest case. Hobart College (Geneva, N.Y.) was acquitted Feb. 8 of criminal coercion charges in connection with campus disorders June 5, 1970. A special grand jury had indicted the college Dec. 18, 1970 for having "recklessly tolerated" threatening actions by students following a drug raid on the campus. New York State Supreme Court Justice Frederick M. Marshall, after a trial that began Feb. 2, directed the jury to acquit the college because he said the prosecution's evidence was insufficient to warrant a conviction. In a later development, a special grand jury appointed by New York Gov. Nelson Rockefeller to investigate the disorder, April 27 recommended "disciplinary action" against Ontario County Sheriff Ray Morrow for his handling of the drug raid that led to the violence. The special grand jury criticized Morrow for using an undercover agent, Thomas (Tommy the Traveler) Tongyai, whose presence during the drug raid touched off the violence. The panel said that Morrow had given Tongyai no training and had "failed to make any investigation into [his] temperament, character, background and suitability . . . beyond conferring with one person."

[6] Santa Cruz building destroyed. A fire which police attributed to arsonists, April 8 destroyed the administration building at the Santa Cruz campus of the University of California, causing $500,000 in damage and destroying irreplaceable student records. (Students at the campus received pass-fail grades and written evaluations rather than letter grades.) In other fires, police said that arson or firebombs caused blazes at the following campuses: the Fletcher School of Law and Diplomacy at Tufts University (Medford, Mass.), where a March 21 fire caused $75,000 damage; the University of Hawaii (Honolulu), where a March 5 blaze caused by gasoline splashed around a campus building followed a fire the week before at a Reserve Officers Training Corps (ROTC) building; and Cornell University (Ithaca, N.Y.), where a March 17 fire damaged a classroom used by the Air Force ROTC unit.

[7] **Berkeley clash marks '69 violence.** Police and sheriff's deputies May 15 confronted 500 demonstrators near the University of California at Berkeley in a clash that resulted in 40 arrests and a number of injuries. The protesters, marking the second anniversary of the "People's Park" battle were responding to editorials in the campus newspaper, the Daily Californian, urging an assembly to "rededicate" the park. (The May 1969 violence, which left one person dead, one blinded and others seriously injured, occurred after the university moved to reclaim a plot of land that students had begun to set up as a park for residents in the area. The plot later was turned into a parking lot.) In the May 15 clash, which apparently involved some people of high-school age, police used tear gas and putty-like bullets designed to control crowds to disperse roving bands that threw rocks and bottles at police. (Following the clash, the Daily Californian's board of publishers ousted three of the paper's editors May 19. The remaining editors announced they would resign to protest the action.)

[8] **University of Florida protests.** A crowd of 2,000 black and white students gathered at the home of University of Florida (Gainesville) President Stephen O'Connell April 15, demanding his resignation and protesting what they called the school's "racist" policies. The incident followed the arrest and suspension of 67 black students the same day during a sit-in outside O'Connell's office. The students called for a program to raise the Negro enrollment at the university by recruiting 500 new students. (There were about 300 black students at the university out of a 22,000 total enrollment.) After the arrests and suspensions were announced, black and white students held a protest rally which police dispersed with riot sticks and tear gas. As the crowd marched to the president's residence, O'Connell gave a television address calling for peace on the campus but rejecting the demands for a recruitment program as "a racial quota" and "racism in reverse."

[9] **Student unrest law voided.** A special three-judge federal panel in Philadelphia ruled 2-1 July 9 that a Pennsylvania statute denying scholarship aid to students involved in campus unrest was unconstitutional. The ruling overturned a 1969 law that required any college in the country with students receiving aid from Pennsylvania to report names of disruptive students to the state, which could deny funds on the basis of a report from a school administrator.

[10] **Bomb suspects indicted for murder.** Four fugitives (Karleton Armstrong, Dwight Armstrong, Leo Frederick Burt and David Sylvan Fine), sought by the FBI for a year, were indicted on murder charges Sept. 1 in connection with the death of Robert Fassnacht, killed when a bomb exploded at the University of Wisconsin in August 1970. Karleton Armstrong was also named on arson counts in connection with three other firebombings in 1969 and 1970.

See also ALGERIA; CHILE [18]; EDUCATION [4, 12]; FRANCE [5]; GREAT BRITAIN [3]; MEXICO; PUERTO RICO; TURKEY [1-2]; URUGUAY [4]; VENEZUELA; YUGOSLAVIA; ZAMBIA

SUBVERSIVE ACTIVITIES CONTROL BOARD (SACB)—See SECURITY, U.S.

SUDAN—Leftist takeover defeated. A group of leftist army officers took control of Africa's largest country July 19, deposing Maj. Gen. Mohammed Gaafar el-Nimeiry. The rebels at first appeared to be in control of the country, but forces loyal to Nimeiry regained power July 22, apparently with the help of Libyan and Egyptian aircraft which carried Sudanese troops from the Suez Canal to al Shagara, about 18 miles from the Sudanese capital of Khartoum. The July 19 coup was led in Khartoum by Maj. Hashem al-Ata, acting in coordination with Maj. Farouk Osman Hamadallah and Lt. Col. Babakr al-Nur Osman (both of whom were in London for medical treatment at the time of the attack). All three had been members of the Free Officers Organization that brought Nimeiry to power in 1969, but had been dismissed from Nimeiry's government in 1970 for Communist sympathies and opposition to the prospective federation of Sudan, Libya and Egypt (*see* MIDDLE EAST [16]). Col. Nur said in London July 20 that Nimeiry was deposed because he had begun to act without the consent of the Revolutionary Command Council and because nationalized industries had been administered in a corrupt manner.

With the help of an armored brigade and the presidential guards, the rebels took less than an hour to secure control of the radio station and other public buildings in Khartoum and Omdurman and to capture Nimeiry. There was no fighting. In Khartoum July 20, the rebel officers formed a new seven-man command council with Nur at its head and Ata as deputy chairman. The council released 49 political prisoners rounded up after the June 29 escape from prison of Communist party Secretary General Abdul Khaliq Magoub. (Although the rebel regime's leftist orientation was evident, its connection with the Communist party was not clear.) The command council also abolished the executive of the Sudanese Socialist Union and other Egyptian-style organizations established by Nimeiry and closed the country's airports.

Counter-coup. The first of the events leading to the counter-coup occurred early July 22 when a BOAC jetliner on the way from London to Khartoum, with Nur, Hamadallah and Maj. Mohammed Magoub Osman (brother of the Communist party leader and a member of the command council) on board, was forced by Libyan authorities to land at Benghazi. Nur and Hamadallah were removed but Magoub Osman was allowed to remain aboard. The plane was in Libyan air space when the pilot received the order to land. He turned the plane back toward the Mediterranean and received permission from Maltese officials to land there, but permission was rescinded when the Maltese discovered the liner was over Libya. Libya July 22 denied that the jetliner had been forced to land in Benghazi, saying it had been "invited" to do so because Khartoum airport was closed and Malta had refused permission for the plane to land there. In Khartoum July 22, troops under the command of Defense Minister Maj. Gen. Khaled Hassan Abbas (out of the country during the coup) attacked the rebel headquarters and the presidential palace where Nimeiry was held prisoner. Nimeiry escaped from the palace during the attack. Heavy fighting was reported in Khartoum before control passed to the loyal troops.

Aftermath of coup. Executions of rebel officers began July 23. Among the executions: Ata by firing squad July 23; Hamadallah by firing squad July 25; Nur by firing squad July 26; and Secretary General Magoub by hanging July 28. (Magoub had denied any foreknowledge of the coup.) In other actions following the coup: Nimeiry July 24 broke diplomatic relations with Iraq, charging it was guilty of "clear interference" in Sudan's internal affairs. (The Iraqi Revolutionary Command Council was reported July 20 to have offered the rebels its full support. Nimeiry July 25 also charged that the Iraqi Baathist party actually participated in the coup plot.) The Sudanese government Aug. 2 ordered the Bulgarian ambassador and the counselor of the Soviet embassy to leave the country. The expulsions (within a week for the Bulgarian ambassador and within 48 hours for the Soviet counselor) were believed ordered because of the envoys' suspected complicity in the coup and the Soviet Union's official opposition to the trial and execution of the plotters. Sudan's ambassador to Moscow and Sofia had been withdrawn Aug. 1.

Communist aides dismissed. Nimeiry Aug. 3 removed from his Cabinet four ministers who had been linked to the Communist party. Foreign Minister Farouk Abou Issa and Labor Minister Maowia Ibrahim had been members of the party before joining Nimeiry's government in 1969. Minister of Communications and Transport Sid Ahmed el-Gak and Irrigation Minister Mustafa Ahmed Ibrahim had been mentioned by the rebel leaders on a list of prospective Cabinet ministers. In another anti-Communist move designed to undermine support for the coup, the government Aug. 7 announced the arrest of 700 more persons it identified as members of the Communist party. (About 1,000 persons had been arrested immediately after the counter-coup.) The August arrests were made in the Blue Nile Province south of Khartoum.

Nimeiry installed as president. Nimeiry was installed as the first elected president of his country Oct. 12 after receiving a 98.6% vote in a two-week national referendum which ended Oct. 1. (The Revolutionary Command Council had promulgated a temporary constitution Aug. 13. The document provided that the country should be a democratic Socialist republic and that its president, named for a term of six years and empowered to appoint and dismiss two or more vice presidents, should also be supreme commander of the armed forces. The President was to be nominated by the Sudanese Socialist Union, the only legal political party, and approved by public referendum. However, according to the document, the first president was to be named by the Revolutionary Command Council, subject to public referendum.) Nimeiry announced a new Cabinet Oct. 13 with Manzur Khaled as foreign minister, Maj. Gen. Hassan again appointed defense minister and Abel al-Eir as minister for southern affairs. Abubakr Awadallah was named first vice president. The Sudanese Socialist Union was proclaimed the only legal political party and Maj. Maamoun Awad Abu Zeid was appointed its secretary general.

Steiner sentenced to 20 years. Rolf Steiner, a West German who went on trial in Khartoum Aug. 2 for allegedly leading a southern Sudanese rebel faction, was sentenced Nov. 9 to 20 years in prison. The first white mercenary ever tried in Africa, Steiner was believed to have fought in Korea, Suez, Indochina, Algeria, Congo (now Zaire) and Biafra. The military tribunal which tried Steiner Sept. 20 recommended the death penalty to Nimeiry, who commuted the sentence to 20 years. Steiner had been accused of entering Sudan illegally, training and leading rebels, preparing them for war and obtaining rebel arms from foreign sources, spreading malicious rumors about Sudan and smuggling medicine and drugs into the country which were distributed without permission. He pleaded guilty to the first charge, but denied the others. The military tribunal found him guilty of all charges except obtaining arms and spreading rumors about the government. Police Commandant Khalifa Karrar, purportedly reading to the tribunal a statement by Steiner, said Aug. 8 that the accused had advised southern rebels to form a unified command, had prepared a plan to defend a hospital against government attack and had taught agricultural skills to the southern Sudanese. Steiner complained Aug. 11 that his statement, forming the basis of Karrar's testimony, had been distorted. Salim Eissa, the defense counsel, drew the admission from Karrar Aug. 12 that Steiner had never taken part in an attack on government troops or committed any act of cruelty and had saved lives on two occasions. In his final submission Sept. 6, Eissa said Steiner should be "sent back home" because he had "meant good for the southern part of our country." Eissa said Steiner was not a mercenary because he had received no pay. It was reported Aug. 17 that Steiner had earlier claimed to have been sent to Sudan by a West German charitable organization called the Society for the Promotion of African Affairs. This effort, according to Steiner, was to develop a route for the shipment of relief supplies. Steiner also reportedly established model farms in rebel territory and trained rebels to defend the farms.

See also COMMUNISM, INTERNATIONAL; MIDDLE EAST [16]

SUEZ CANAL—*See* MIDDLE EAST [1, 3, 17, 27-28, 32-36]; SUDAN; UNITED ARAB REPUBLIC

SUGAR—*See* CUBA

SUPERSONIC TRANSPORT PLANE (SST)—*See* AGNEW, SPIRO THEODORE; AVIATION [1-5]; BUDGET; CONGRESS [1]

SUPREME COURT—**Black resigns.** Associate Justice Hugo L. Black, 85, resigned Sept. 17 after 34 years of service on the Supreme Court. The White House announced that Black had stepped down for "health reasons" and that President Nixon had accepted the resignation "with deep regret." Black had entered the Naval hospital at Bethesda, Md. Aug. 28 for what was described as "treatment of an inflammatory condition of the blood vessels." A hospital spokesman said Sept. 22 that Black was in serious condition but was "remaining stable" after suffering a stroke Sept. 20. (*See* OBITUARIES [Hugo LaFayette Black].) Black's resignation was seen as a loss to the liberal complexion of the (former Chief Justice Earl) Warren court. Black, an ardent New Deal senator from Alabama at the time of his appointment in 1937 by Franklin D. Roosevelt, had been the subject of a bitter fight after his confirmation when it was revealed that he had once belonged to the Ku Klux Klan. However, he joined the majority in landmark decisions broadening racial desegregation in the 1950s and 1960s under the Warren court. His votes on cases concerning First Amendment freedoms of expression and religion were dictated by his absolutist view of the freedoms guaranteed in the Constitution and the Bill of Rights. He held a firm opposition to censorship. He had recently become critical of some liberal criminal law rulings that restricted police rights in wiretapping and searches.

Justice Harlan resigns. Associate Justice John M. Harlan, 72, resigned from the court Sept. 23 because of ill health. Harlan sent his resignation to President Nixon from George Washington University Hospital. His doctor said he was under treatment for "a cancerous process on one of the bones of the lower spine." Harlan had been transferred from Bethesda Naval Hospital, where he had been admitted Aug. 16 with a back ailment. (*See* OBITUARIES [John Marshall Harlan].) Harlan had been appointed by Dwight D. Eisenhower in 1954 after a career as a Wall Street lawyer and a short period of service on the U.S. Court of Appeals. He had been described as the "conservative conscience" of the court and often found himself in the minority on the Warren court. However, many members of the bar considered him the best craftsman among the justices, and men who disagreed with his decisions valued his detailed, scholarly opinions for a considered explication of the conservative argument. He believed in the (Justice Felix) Frankfurter tradition that the Constitution's due process clause should be invoked only as dictated by the judge's conception of the demands of society and judicial precedent. His concept of federalism led him to condone in the states what he forbade as violations of the Bill of Rights by the federal government. He dissented from the Warren court on rulings on such issues as reapportionment with warnings that political and social problems could be solved by legislative rather than judicial action.

Powell, Rehnquist nominated. In a nationally televised broadcast Oct. 21, President Nixon nominated Lewis F. Powell Jr., a Richmond, Va. lawyer, and William H. Rehnquist, an assistant U.S. attorney general, to the Supreme Court vacancies caused by the resignations of Black and Harlan. Nixon said he had selected the two in the belief they shared his judicial philosophy. He described the two as conservatives "but only in a judicial, not in a political sense." Powell was a former president of the American Bar Association (ABA), a past president of the American College of Trial Lawyers and the present president of the American Bar Foundation. Rehnquist headed the Justice Department's Office of Legal Counsel. In selecting the two, the President passed over the names of six persons who were widely regarded as potential nominees and whose qualifications he had asked the ABA to review. (According to published reports, two of the six—Herschel H. Friday, a municipal bond lawyer from Little Rock, Ark., and Judge Mildred L. Lillie of the California Court of Appeals—were Nixon's first choices to fill the court seats. However, the ABA unit voted 11-1 that Judge Lillie was unqualified to sit on the Supreme Court and then split 6-6 on a motion to record the committee as "not opposed" to Friday's nomination. Other names submitted to the ABA judicial fitness committee for evaluation were: Senate Majority Whip Robert C. Byrd [D, W. Va.]; Judge Sylvia Bacon of the District of Columbia Superior Court; Judge Charles Clark of Jackson, Miss., a member of the U.S. Court of Appeals for the 5th Circuit; and Judge Paul H. Roney of St. Petersburg, Fla., also a member of the 5th Circuit U.S. Court of Appeals. Byrd said Oct. 25 that he had asked Nixon not to nominate him. Rep. Richard H. Poff [R, Va.], reportedly Nixon's first choice to replace Black, had withdrawn his name from consideration as a candidate Oct. 2.)

Senate confirms both. With only one dissenting vote, cast by Sen. Fred Harris (D, Okla.) who charged that Powell was "an elitist," the Senate Dec. 6 confirmed the nomination of Powell to Black's seat by an 89-1 vote. Powell was the first Southern conservative to be confirmed to the court since James F. Byrnes of South Carolina in 1941. The Senate Dec. 10 confirmed the nomination of Rehnquist to Harlan's seat, by a 68-26 vote—a wider margin than was generally expected. At least 10 Democrats who usually sided with other liberal senators voted for Rehnquist's confirmation. Both nominees were expected to be sworn in early in January.

Opposition to Rehnquist's nomination was led on the Senate floor by Sen. Birch Bayh (D, Ind.). The opposition, centering about Rehnquist's civil rights stands and his conservative political views, began to coalesce in hearings by the Senate Judiciary Committee Nov. 3-10. In testimony before the committee, Rehnquist Nov. 3 declined to explain the specifics of certain positions he took as a U.S. assistant attorney general because: they were not his personal views but those of a government advocate; his relationship with the attorney general was privileged; and the subjects involved might come up in cases before the Supreme Court. He also sought to defuse some of the criticism expected to come from civil rights groups by recanting his opposition to a public accommodations ordinance adopted in Phoenix in 1964 and by saying he had "come to realize the strong concern of minorities for the recognition" of their civil rights. Clarence Mitchell, director of the National Association for the Advancement of Colored People (NAACP) bureau in Washington, and Joseph L. Rauh Jr., a spokesman for the Americans for Democratic Action (ADA) Nov. 9 charged that Rehnquist was insensitive to the rights of Negroes. The charges evoked an unusual response from committee chairman James O. Eastland (D, Miss.), who issued Nov. 11 a 20-page memorandum as a supplement to the report of the committee hearings in which he accused the two civil rights spokesmen of the "crassest type of character assassination" in their testimony. Organized labor Nov. 10 joined opposition to the nomination, warning that Rehnquist would expand government power at the expense of personal freedom. Rehnquist was also opposed on the basis of his reported membership in Arizonans for Freedom, a precursor of the John Birch Society, and in another ultra-conservative group For America. The reports said Rehnquist had been a member of both groups when he lived in Phoenix. (The reports had surfaced Nov. 17 in files compiled by the late Mrs. Frank Brookes of Phoenix, who had been active in the Methodist Women's Society of Christian Service and its national conference on extremist groups. When Mrs. Brookes died in 1971, her files on right-wing activities in the 1950s and 1960s were sent to an official of a Washington-based organization studying extremism.) Attorney General John N. Mitchell Nov. 17 and Rehnquist Nov. 20 denied that Rehnquist had ever been a member of either group. Sen. Eastland said that an investigation by the Federal Bureau of Investigation had failed to turn up any evidence that Rehnquist had been a member of Arizonans for America. Eastland also produced letters from former members of the defunct group that said Rehnquist was never a member.

On the Senate floor, opponents of the Rehnquist nomination Dec. 6 began a series of long speeches against the nomination. While stopping short of describing their long speeches as the start of a filibuster, the critics said they would talk until their arguments caught the Senate's attention. Rehnquist's supporters declined to take issue with charges leveled by critics and instead charged them with needless obstructionism and delay. Many supporters remained away from the Senate floor during the speeches by critics. The critics reiterated earlier arguments and also cited a new piece of evidence reportedly written by Rehnquist when he was a law clerk to Supreme Court Justice Robert H. Jackson in 1952. The memorandum argued that the court should refuse to overturn the "separate but equal" doctrine in public schools which was then being challenged in a case before the court. Rehnquist said Dec. 8 that the memorandum expressed the views of Justice Jackson and were not his own.

Administration ends prior ABA checks. The Administration Oct. 21 abruptly ended its agreement with the ABA to review the judicial qualifications of Supreme Court nominees before appointing them to the court. (Powell and Rehnquist were not approved by the ABA until Nov. 3. Both received the evaluating committee's highest rating—Powell by a unanimous vote, Rehnquist by a vote of 9-3.) In a letter sent to the ABA, Attorney General Mitchell said the Administration was breaking off the agreement because of "premature disclosures" of the names sent for review. The action came one day after the evaluating committee reported its disapproval of Friday and Judge Lillie. Lawrence E. Walsh, chairman of the committee, said that the disclosure was inevitable in any elaborate checking of candidates by asking the opinions of many people. He said he had earlier warned the Administration that the six names submitted would be leaked and was told that this was an acceptable risk. The White House Oct. 22 strongly denied that the Administration had authorized or in any way condoned disclosure of the names of those on the list. Walsh Nov. 1 issued a report which accused the Justice Department of leaking news of the unfavorable ratings to the press. Implied in the charge was the idea that the leaks were due to the Administration's displeasure at the adverse ratings. The report hinted that the Administration had leaked the information to justify canceling its agreement to submit for prior review the names of potential Supreme Court nominees. Attorney General Mitchell Nov. 1 "categorically" denied the charges.

See also ATOMIC ENERGY [16]; AUTOMOBILES [13-14]; BANKS; CITIZENSHIP, U.S.; CIVIL RIGHTS [1-3, 7, 20-21, 31]; CRIME [15, 19-22]; DRAFT & WAR PROTEST [7-8, 24]; EDUCATION [11, 18]; ELECTIONS [2]; HOUSING; JUDICIARY [1-3, 5, 7, 9, 11]; LABOR [5]; MINES; NEWSPAPERS; OBITUARIES [Hugo La Fayette Black; John Marshall Harlan]; OBSCENITY & PORNOGRAPHY; PENTAGON PAPERS [1, 6-7]; POVERTY; PRISONS [8]; RAILROADS; SELECTIVE SERVICE SYSTEM [7, 13, 15]; VOTING RIGHTS; WELFARE; WOMEN'S RIGHTS

SWAZILAND—The Africa Research Bulletin reported that King Sobhuza II had made the following Cabinet appointments effective July 1: Zonke Amos Khumalo—deputy prime minister, Polycarp Mafeletiven Dlamini—justice, John Mfundza Brighton Sukati—power, works and communications, and Kanyakwexwe Henry Dlamini—minister of state for foreign affairs. ARB reported that Allen Mkhawulo Nxumalo, minister of health, would also be responsible for education.

SWEDEN—Budget presented. The new unicameral Riksdag (parliament) was presented with the 1971-72 state budget at its opening Jan. 12. The document provided for an expenditure of about $10 billion—a 10% increase over the 1970-71 budget. It was designed to encourage industrial investment and exports and to limit private consumption. The only new tax was a 10% levy on newspaper and magazine advertising, expected to raise $5.8 million annually for a plan to aid newspapers with economic difficulties. The budget included increases in government support for basic pensions (13.5%), child support (16.5%) and housing (29.5%). Foreign aid was to increase 25%.

Strike moratorium voted. The Riksdag March 11, by a vote of 279-32, approved an emergency powers bill to ban strikes and lockouts until April 25 to permit intensive negotiations for civil service wage contracts. The government's unprecedented step of interfering in labor negotiations halted Sweden's most serious labor conflict in 25 years, involving the strike of 12,000 and lockout of 35,000 civil servants. The strikes and lockouts had halted railway services and disrupted schools and universities, welfare aid systems, local government and court administration. About 3,000 of Sweden's 5,300 military officers (who belonged to the same union as the railway workers on strike since Feb. 5) had faced a lockout by the government March 10. The world's first lockout of military officers would have been an attempt to deplete the union's strike fund. The strikes began after the government rejected union demands for salary increases ranging from 18% to 23% that would compensate for inflation and high taxes. The government had offered a 7% increase. The white collar and professional strikers reportedly also resented the Social Democratic government's policy of giving high industrial wage differences that narrowed the wage differential between classes. The government March 12 lifted its lockout of 25,000 teachers, which had begun Feb. 19. Passenger trains resumed service March 13.

Industrial wage accord. After seven months of negotiation, the Confederation of Swedish Trade Unions and the Swedish Employers Federation June 22 signed a collective wage accord (proposed by a mediation commission) providing for increases in pay and benefits totaling 28% over three years for 830,000 industrial workers. The agreement called for raising the standard of low-paid workers and for providing shorter working hours, improved sickness benefits and lower pension age. The general agreement would serve as a model for accords to be signed by individual unions before Sept. 30.

Government changes. Premier Olof Palme June 29 announced the appointment of Minister of Industry Krister Wickman as foreign minister to replace Torsten Nilsson, who resigned. Rune Johansson, former minister of the interior, was named minister of industry. The changes were effective July 1.

Constitutional reforms proposed. A Riksdag constitutional committee, dominated by the Social Democrats, recommended Aug. 20 a revised constitution that would maintain the monarch as head of state but strip the next king of most of his power. Under the proposals (effective upon the death of King Gustaf VI Adolph, 88, and the succession of Crown Prince Carl Gustaf), the king would lose his formal right to suggest the name of a new premier during a governmental crisis, would no longer chair the weekly Cabinet meeting and would yield to the government his role as supreme commander of the armed forces. The king would continue ceremonially to open parliament, but would no longer deliver the "throne speech" setting forth government policy. The proposed constitutional reform would also lower the voting age from 20 to 18 and would reduce the age for eligibility to hold a Riksdag seat from 23 to 18. The reform proposals, which would have to be approved by two sessions of the Riksdag and a general election, would not take effect before 1976.

See also ABORTION; EUROPEAN ECONOMIC COMMUNITY [10]; INTERNATIONAL MONETARY DEVELOPMENTS [10, 15]; PAKISTAN [35]; SCANDINAVIA; YUGOSLAVIA

SWITZERLAND—Women win federal vote. Male voters Feb. 7 adopted a constitutional amendment authorizing Swiss women to vote in federal elections and to hold federal office for the first time. With an estimated 57% of the eligible voters voting, 15.5 cantons voted in favor of the amendment, while 6.5 (all German-speaking cantons in the central and eastern parts of Switzerland) voted against it. The amendment had been supported by the nation's major political parties, both houses of the legislature and numerous social organizations, newspapers, businesses and churches. It was estimated that 1.5 million women would be eligible to vote in federal elections, as opposed to the 1.2 million men currently eligible. (By Dec. 12, women had also gained the right to vote in cantonal and local elections in all but four of Switzerland's 22 cantons.)

Jura separatism. Nine members of the Belier movement, a Jura separatist youth organization that sought an autonomous French-speaking canton in the German-speaking Berne canton, were tried in absentia by a court in Lausanne Feb. 22-25 for trespass and breach of peace during demonstrations in 1968. Charges of endangering the constitutional order and unlawful assembly were dropped. Sentences against the nine (in Strasbourg, France during the trial to protest the conduct of their case by the government to the European Commission of Human Rights) ranged from three months' suspended imprisonment and a fine of about $240 for Bernard Varrin, leader of the Beliers in 1968, to smaller fines for other defendants. In later developments: 20 other members of the Belier movement were sentenced June 1 to small fines on the same charges; about 100 members of the movement Sept. 4 used bricks and cement to block the entry to the Berne headquarters of the cantonal authorities; and more than 30,000 people attending a traditional feast day for the Jura region in Delemont Sept. 13 approved, by raised hands, a resolution setting a one-year ultimatum to the government to undertake steps toward creation of an autonomous French-speaking canton in Berne.

Environmental protection voted. A nationwide vote June 6 approved a constitutional amendment that would authorize the government to take necessary measures to combat air and noise pollution. The amendment passed after publication of reports of growing pollution in Swiss lakes. Women participated in the federal vote for the first time since they won suffrage.

Federal elections. Eleven women were elected to the two houses of parliament in federal elections Oct. 30-31. The elections were marked by a sharp upsurge in anti-immigrant sentiment. Two extreme rightist groups advocating immigrant curbs—the National Movement of Republicans and Social Action (formed May 12) and the National Action Against Foreign Penetration—won 11 seats in the 200-member National Council (the lower house), an increase of 10 seats. (Ten of the seats were won in the German-speaking section of Switzerland.) The ruling four-party coalition of Socialists, Radical-Democrats, Christian Democrats and Agrarians won 160 seats, a loss of six since the 1967 elections.

Celio named president. Finance Minister Nello Celio was elected president for 1972 under the annual rotation of the presidency among the seven Cabinet members. Parliament re-elected six of the seven-member coalition Cabinet and elected Kurt Furgler, a Christian Democrat, as justice minister to succeed Ludwig von Moos, who was retiring.

See also DRUG USE & ADDICTION [9]; ESPIONAGE; EUROPEAN ECONOMIC COMMUNITY [10]; INTERNATIONAL MONETARY DEVELOPMENTS [2, 4, 8-10, 13, 15]; JORDAN [12]; PAKISTAN [23]; TARIFFS & WORLD TRADE [2]; TAXES

SYRIA—Lt. Gen. Hafez al-Assad was approved as president of Syria in a nationwide plebiscite held March 12. An official announcement March 13 said 99.2% of the electorate had voted "yes." Assad was sworn in as president for a seven-year term March 14. Assad, who had been premier, had assumed the powers of the presidency Feb. 22 when Ahmed el-Khatib, the nominal head of state, resigned. The formation of a new Syrian cabinet was announced April 3. Its principal members: premier—Maj. Gen. Abd ar-Rahman Khulayfawi; deputy premier & industry minister—Mohammed Talab Hilal; deputy premier & foreign minister—Adib al-Halim Khaddam; finance—Nurallah Nurallah; justice—Adib an-Nahawi; defense—Mutib Shunaywi; and interior—Ali Zaza.

See also FLOODS; JORDAN [3, 6-9]; LIBYA; MIDDLE EAST [1, 4, 11, 15-17, 20]; UNITED ARAB REPUBLIC

TABLE TENNIS—*See* COMMUNIST CHINA-U.S. DETENTE [3-4]; SPORTS
TAFT-HARTLEY ACT—*See* LABOR [1, 10]

TANZANIA—Plotters sentenced. Three men and a woman were sentenced to life imprisonment Feb. 9 on charges of plotting to overthrow and assassinate President Julius K. Nyerere in 1969. Those convicted in Tanzania's first treason trial were: Grey Mtaka, a former editor of The Nationalist, organ of the ruling Tanganyika African National Union (TANU); Bibi Titi Mohamed, former president of a national women's organization; John Chipaka, former secretary of the banned African National Congress, and his brother Elijah Chipaka, a former army captain. Two other accused were acquitted of the major charge but convicted of misprision—having knowledge of the coup and failing to prevent it. They were Michael Kamiliza, former minister of labor, and Col. William Chacha, former Tanzanian military attache in Peking. Both were sentenced to 10 years in prison. Lt. Alfred Mallinga was acquitted of both treason and misprision when the verdicts were handed down Jan. 30.

    See also KENYA; UGANDA

TARIFFS & WORLD TRADE—1970 world trade up. The International Monetary Fund (IMF) reported March 1 that world trade in 1970 had increased in value, but that inflation accounted for an unusually high portion of the increase. Trade in 1970, as measured by world exports, rose by 14.2% to $278 billion, with exports in the fourth quarter reaching a record annual rate of $301.6 billion. The report indicated, however, that "somewhat less than half" of the increase in 1970 was due to higher prices rather than higher volume.

[2] **Kennedy Round cuts.** The fourth of the five annual installments of worldwide tariff cuts took place Jan. 1 in accordance with the Kennedy Round agreements reached in 1967. The office of the General Agreement on Tariffs and Trade (GATT) had reported Dec. 23, 1970 that five nations had already completed, or virtually completed, their scheduled tariff reductions. Argentina was reported to have put its reductions into effect in 1967, Iceland in 1968, Canada and Ireland in 1969 and Switzerland in 1970. In general, their actions were taken to reduce import prices and to help counter inflationary pressures. GATT added that many participants in the Kennedy Round had speeded up their schedule of tariff cuts in actions designed to aid developing nations. (The entry into force of the special agreement on chemicals which had been concluded at the Kennedy Round negotiations was postponed for the third time Jan. 1. The agreement, under which a number of European nations agreed to

457

make additional tariff cuts affecting chemicals and to reduce certain non-tariff barriers in exchange for the U.S. abolition of the American Selling Price [ASP] system of customs valuation on chemicals, was originally scheduled to go into effect Jan. 1, 1969, but had been postponed to Jan. 1, 1970 and then to Jan. 1, 1971. The GATT office reported Dec. 23 that the governments party to the agreement had agreed to extend the entry date until Jan. 1, 1972.)

[3] **Japan curbs textile imports to U.S.** The Japanese Textile Federation announced March 8 that it would voluntarily restrict exports of textiles to the U.S. for a three-year period beginning July 1. The decision drew a critical response from American textile manufacturers and unions. It was rejected by President Nixon March 11. The Japanese textile group hoped that its move would forestall trade-quota legislation pending in the U.S. Congress and would break the impasse in the U.S.-Japanese textile talks, in progress for over two years. The export curbs would apply to cotton and wool textiles and man-made fiber textiles. Yarn and raw materials would be excluded. Exports during the first year of the restrictions would be 5% higher than the previous year, and there would be a 6% boost for each of the two following years. The Japanese federation emphasized that, if other textile-exporting countries (presumably South Korea, Taiwan and Hong Kong) did not enforce similar restrictions, Japan would not do so either. In rejecting the Japanese restrictions, President Nixon said March 11 that his opposition arose because the plan: (1) imposed "only one overall ceiling" on all Japanese textile exports to the U.S., with only a general understanding "to prevent undue distortions" of the present trade pattern, thus permitting specific categories to grow faster than the overall trade; (2) moved back the base date for the plan to March 31, 1972 instead of 1969 as proposed by the U.S.; and (3) "magnifies the potential growth of the sensitive categories by including in the base exports of cotton products" which had already been limited by agreement and had been declining.

[4] Under heavy pressure from the U.S., Japan Oct. 15 initialed a three-year agreement with the U.S. to limit its exports of man-made and woolen textiles to the U.S. (Nixon had warned that the U.S. would impose unilateral quotas if agreement was not reached by Oct. 15.) The agreement would allow an annual growth rate of about 5% for exports of man-made fibers and 1% for woolen goods. In return, the U.S. agreed to remove—retroactive to Oct. 1—its 10% surcharge (*see* ECONOMY, U.S. [8]) on the categories of textiles covered by the agreement. The textile surtax would be removed for all nations. (Japan had signed, according to a GATT report Oct. 13, a three-year extension of an agreement regulating the international cotton textile trade.)

[5] *Hong Kong, Taiwan, Korea accords.* Agreements to curb man-made and woolen textile exports were reached between the U.S. and Hong Kong, Nationalist China and South Korea, the U.S. government announced Oct. 15. The agreements were for five years and were said to permit an annual growth of 7½% in synthetic exports and 1% for woolens. The accords were concluded under the threat of unilateral quotas by the U.S. (Hong Kong had announced a program of voluntary restraints Sept. 15, but the U.S. Sept. 16 rejected the program as unacceptable.)

[6] **Shoes, textile exports to U.S. limited.** A decision to unilaterally restrict export of shoes and textiles to the U.S. was announced July 4 by the Italian Ministry of Foreign Trade. The action was taken after David M. Kennedy, U.S. ambassador at large, warned the Italians in May that the U.S. would restrict imports if they failed to act, according to a report July 12. Under the self-limitation measure, a "statistical visa" would be required for all shoes and textiles leaving Italy for the U.S. It was reported the visas would restrict the volume of exports to a 5% increase over the $280 million worth of textiles and shoes exported in 1970.

[7] Export expansion bill signed. The Export Expansion Finance Act of 1971 was passed by Senate voice vote Aug. 2 and 219-140 House vote Aug. 5. It was signed by President Nixon Aug. 17. The legislation extended the life of the Export-Import Bank to June 30, 1974 and liberalized East-West trade provisions by removing current restrictions against Export-Import Bank credits to nations giving aid to another country in armed conflict with the U.S. A ban against bank-financed trade for countries in armed conflict with the U.S.—i.e. North Vietnam—was retained, as well as a ban against exports to any country of items of war-related material that could be sent to North Vietnam. The ban against financing exports to Communist-bloc countries supplying North Vietnam had been in effect three years. The final House vote represented a reversal of a 207-153 House vote July 8 to retain such a ban.

[8] U.S. surtax. The 10% import surtax imposed by President Nixon Aug. 15 (*see* ECONOMY, U.S. [8]) and lifted Dec. 20 aroused criticism and calls for exemption from Canada, Japan and Latin America, among other nations. Canadian Finance Minister Edgar J. Benson announced Aug. 18 that Canada would seek exemption from the surtax on the grounds that Canada's dollar, which had been floating for 15 months, had not damaged U.S. imports unfairly and that Canada had not undervalued its dollar in relation to the U.S. dollar. A list of 17 demands allegedly formulated by the Nixon Administration as a prerequisite to removal of the surtax for Canada was published Oct. 10. The demands, denied by the U.S. government, included: expansion of the U.S.-Canadian automobile agreement to include cars and "all-terrain" vehicles among duty-free items; increased defense purchases from the U.S. and permission to the U.S. to remove preferential treatment of Canada under defense production sharing arrangements; unilateral reduction of tariffs on manufactured goods; loosening of pressures against foreign companies in Canada; an increase in the number of duty-free items Canadian citizens were allowed to bring back from visits to the U.S.; and revision of a proposed tax reform plan (*see* CANADA [27]) that called for foreign-controlled Canadian companies to pay "substantially higher tax rates" than Canadian-owned concerns. In an attempt to neutralize the impact of the surcharge, the Canadian government Nov. 20 approved a $158 million program for assistance to Canadian firms injured by the surtax.

[9] Japan Aug. 31 requested removal of the surtax, on the ground that its decision to float the yen (*see* INTERNATIONAL MONETARY DEVELOPMENTS [12]) was sufficient reason for the removal. The U.S. and Japan met Sept. 9-10 in an attempt to reach agreement on the trade and monetary demands of each, but no such agreement was reached. The U.S. was pressing for an immediate and substantial revaluation of the yen against the dollar and Japan wanted revocation of the surcharge. Following talks by officials of the two nations Dec. 11-12, Japan announced Dec. 13 that it would remove its import quotas on four agricultural items and cut tariffs on 30 items—including 27 of 28 agricultural and 12 industrial products the U.S. had demanded concessions on in return for lifting its surtax. Japan also pledged to reduce its automobile tariff from 10% to 8% in return for removal of the U.S. surtax from Japanese cars.

[10] An emergency meeting of the Special Commission for Latin American Coordination (CECLA) was convened Sept. 3-5 to adopt a common front to the surtax. The session, attended by representatives of 20 Latin American and Caribbean nations, ended Sept. 5 with the adoption of the Manifesto of Latin America that asked for exemption from the surtax and outlined the position of Latin America in the face of U.S. economy measures. The document pointed out that Latin America should be exempted from the surcharge since "the balance of payments of the Latin nations with the U.S. has traditionally been favorable to that country." The delegates also argued that the surcharge "constitutes a violation of the promises in force that the U.S. has assumed in forums and that are found in such international documents as GATT...." The

Inter-American Economic and Social Council (IA-ECOSOC) met Sept. 13 for eight days of continuous Latin American attacks on the new U.S. economic measures, including the surcharge. During the session, the U.S. attempted to pacify the Latins with a promise to exclude Latin America from a 10% foreign aid cut (*see* FOREIGN AID). The meeting ended Sept. 20 with both sides refusing to retreat from their positions.

[11] *Exemptions granted.* The U.S. Treasury Sept. 1 reversed itself and exempted from the surtax about $1.5 billion to $2 billion worth of merchandise in transit to the U.S. or on the docks by Aug. 16, the effective date of the surcharge. The exemption extended to goods en route to the U.S., tied up in the West Coast dock strike (*see* LABOR [10]), or in bonded warehouses or foreign free trade zones in the U.S. (A bonded warehouse was under bond to the government for payment of duties and taxes on stored goods. A free trade zone was one in which merchandise might be stored and processed free of tariffs.) The Treasury's new order required withdrawal of imported goods from bonded warehouses by Oct. 1 as a condition of the exemption.

[12] *GATT criticism.* The U.S. withstood a barrage of criticism directed at the surtax during an Aug. 24-26 emergency meeting of GATT, called to determine possible violation by the U.S. of GATT's fair trade rules. The meeting established a committee to further study and report on the effects of President Nixon's Aug. 15 protective trade measures. The chief line of arguments revolved around the European Economic Community's (EEC) contention that the U.S. balance of payments deficit was not the result of an unfair trade balance and thus would not be cured by the steps taken, and U.S. insistence that the surtax was needed to assure its economic health. The U.S. delegation said that repeal of the surtax depended on "collective" action by U.S. trade partners to correct the imbalance that led to its imposition. The position was refined Aug. 25 with the statement that the U.S. was seeking a "lasting improvement" in its balance of payments before lifting the surtax. The EEC held that the surtax was "totally incompatible" with GATT rules. The 55-member GATT Council Sept. 16 approved the committee report it had ordered in August. The report: demanded that the U.S. rescind the surtax "within a short time"; said that the surtax, if not removed quickly, would have "far-reaching effects on world trade and trade liberalization"; said that the surtax was an "inappropriate" cure for the "temporary and accidental" U.S. balance of payments problem; declared that the surtax, "to the extent that it raised the incidence of customs bound under Article Two [of the GATT agreement] was not compatible" with GATT rules; and warned that the GATT position was not negotiable and that members affected by the surtax were entitled to take retaliatory measures.

[13] **Sugar bill sent to President.** Congress Oct. 4 sent to the President a three-year extension of the law adjusting sugar quotas for foreign and domestic producers. The bill, a result of a Senate-House conference compromise, had been approved by the Senate Sept. 29 and by the House Oct. 4. The House had originally approved its version of the bill June 10, the Senate its version July 28. The compromise bill contained most of the House bill's features, increasing quota allotments for domestic producers by 300,000 tons and reducing the allotments of several large foreign producers. The bill had roused criticism from Latin American countries, who were affected by the cut in allotments, and from members of the Congressional Black Caucus, who were opposed to giving a 57,747-ton quota to South Africa.

[14] **GATT Assembly.** The EEC and candidate members Britain and Ireland split with the U.S. and other members of GATT on GATT's proposed program for 1972. The rift occurred at a session of the GATT Assembly Nov. 16-26 in Geneva. The differing viewpoints were set forth in a trade policy statement Nov. 26 which recognized that "prolonged debate and confrontation" over trade issues would be "dangerous both economically and politically." The U.S. had asked that the GATT Permanent Council "make appropriate arrangements

for identifying those trade problems capable of prompt resolution and procedures for the settlement of these problems in 1972"; the EEC had opposed any new initiatives until the U.S. revoked its surtax. In other actions Nov. 26, the Assembly accepted a U.S. demand and ordered the GATT secretariat to prepare a study of the impact of preferential trade agreements (e.g., customs unions, free trade associations) on trade flows [see below]. It also granted 16 developing nations dispensation from the most-favored-nation rule in connection with a preferential agreement giving the 16 nations concessions on some 300 imports. The dispensation freed the 16 from having to extend those concessions to other GATT members.

See also ARGENTINA [6, 15]; AVIATION [2]; CANADA [25-26]; COMMUNIST CHINA-U.S. DETENTE [5], CUBA; DENMARK; ECONOMY, U.S. [8-9, 29]; EUROPEAN ECONOMIC COMMUNITY; GREAT BRITAIN [13, 18]; INTERNATIONAL MONETARY DEVELOPMENTS [14, 16-17]; JAPAN [7]; LATIN AMERICA; NIXON, RICHARD MILHOUS [3]; POLLUTION [6]; RHODESIA; ROMAN CATHOLIC CHURCH [10]; TAXES

TARR, CURTIS W.—See SELECTIVE SERVICE SYSTEM [1,12]
TATE, SHARON—See CRIME [7-8]

TAXES, U.S.—Court approves bank data for IRS. The Supreme Court of Switzerland, in a ruling published Jan. 3, authorized federal tax officials to give information to the U.S. Internal Revenue Service (IRS) on dealings with Swiss banks of a U.S. citizen suspected of tax fraud. The tribunal, which had reached the decision Dec. 23, 1970, ruled that under paragraph 16 of the Double Taxation Agreement signed by the U.S. and Switzerland in 1951, Switzerland was obliged to give American officials information available to them under federal law "to prevent offenses involving fraud." In so ruling, the court rejected an appeal by a U.S. citizen, who was not named, against a decision of the Swiss tax authorities to supply information requested by the IRS concerning his dealings with a Swiss bank. The court said the Swiss banking secrecy law of 1934 protected a bank's customer only from routine inquiries about possible tax evasion, but not from inquiries in the more serious matter of tax fraud. The court also held that bank account data could be handed out where the requested information could help forestall or detect a fraud, as well as in cases where fraud had been legally established.

Business tax cuts. President Nixon Jan. 11 set forth new liberalized rules for depreciation write-offs on business equipment, creating a $2.6 billion tax reduction for business in 1971. The rules, designed to act as a long-range stimulus to capital spending by business, would: (1) set up an "asset depreciation range system" to permit a 20% margin period (shortened or extended) over which business could write off the cost of equipment; (2) introduce various technical changes in permissible methods of figuring depreciation, retroactive to Jan. 1; and (3) drop the "reserve ratio test" standard limiting by means of a time schedule the amount of depreciation write-offs. The new regulations would not apply to equipment purchased by electric, gas and telephone companies. The Treasury Department estimated that the business tax cut would result in an $800 million loss in federal revenue for fiscal year 1971 (ending June 30), rising to $4.1 billion in fiscal 1976 and declining to $2.8 billion in fiscal 1980. Two lawyers from the Public Interest Research Group, a Washington law firm founded by consumer advocate Ralph Nader, filed suit in Washington's U.S. District Court Jan. 11 to prohibit the Treasury from implementing the new rules on the grounds that the changes were illegal because the public had not been notified in advance and public hearings had not been held. The two lawyers agreed Jan. 25, however, to withdraw their motion for a preliminary injunction in return for the government's pledge to hold public hearings on the issue.

The Treasury Department June 22 announced a new set of rules in connection with the liberalized write-offs. One of the new features—intended to weaken critics' arguments that the Treasury arbitrarily and illegally set down the guidelines without proper Congressional authority—was the creation of a special office to periodically review the guidelines. The revised plan contained the basic features of the original proposal, but would require more detailed and regular reports on equipment written off, provide easier first-year rules for eligible machinery and equipment and permit deductions for repair and upkeep expenditures based on a "repair allowances" standard. The new plan was adopted retroactively to Jan. 1.

Nader, Common Cause (a citizens' lobby group), the United Auto Workers union, the National Rural Electric Cooperative Association, Rep. Henry S. Reuss (D, Wis.) and real estate developer Ramon L. Posel filed suit July 7 in U.S. District Court in Washington to block the new rules. The suit said the Treasury Department had illegally issued the regulations by administratively enacting the changes without asking Congress to amend the tax laws. (The diversity of the group was intended to improve the plaintiffs' legal standing to bring the suit. According to the doctrine of legal standing, the plaintiff must show that he was significantly affected by the action he is challenging in court.) Reuss, in an apparently unprecedented action, alleged the Treasury action undermined his vote in Congress on the issue and nullified his past opposition as a congressman to subsidies for business taxpayers. Both Nader and Common Cause contended they would be injured because the tax cut of more than $3 billion annually would reduce federal revenues to finance consumer programs. The UAW argued that the new rules would unlawfully subsidize a "particular class of business taxpayers" and discriminate against UAW members. The rural electric co-ops, mostly exempt from federal taxation, said the tax cut would give their competitors, the private power companies, an advantage that would alter the competitive balance between co-ops and private companies. The Jenkintown, Pa. real estate developer said he would be injured competitively by businesses benefitting under the new rules, since real estate and construction were not covered.

Tax bill enacted. A $25.9 billion tax relief bill was passed by both houses of Congress Dec. 9 and signed by President Nixon Dec. 10. Final passage of the House-Senate conference bill came on a 320-74 vote in the House and a 71-6 vote in the Senate. (Differing versions of the bill had been passed by a voice vote in the House Oct. 6 and by a 64-30 vote in the Senate Nov. 22. Faced with a firm position by President Nixon that he would veto the tax bill if it contained either the "budget-busting" amendments added by the Senate or a Senate plan permitting funding of the 1972 presidential campaign with federal revenue, the conference committee abandoned many major Senate amendments, including the campaign-fund plan. (Nixon said the plan would "produce a proliferation of political parties" with the risk that a president could be elected without enough popular mandate to govern properly.) The final conference bill substituted for the plan a compromise plan by which the campaign funding was postponed until 1973, disbursement was delayed until the 1976 presidential campaign and funding was conditioned on another Congressional vote. Also dropped from the bill were provisions calling for: a tax credit of up to $325 a year against the cost of higher education; a tax credit against property taxes paid by the elderly and a double deduction for disabled persons unable to work; an investment credit of 10% (instead of 7%) for some rural and inner-city areas; a diversion of some taxes collected on alcoholic beverages to the highway fund; discretionary presidential authority to impose import quotas and tariff surcharges; and an additional 26 weeks of unemployment compensation for areas where the jobless rate averaged 6% for 13 consecutive weeks.

The final bill: retained a new income tax credit of $12.50 for a single person or $25 for a couple, or deductions of up to $50 or $100, for political contributions; set the personal income tax exemption, currently $650, at $675 for 1971 and $750 for 1972; adopted the House version of the increase in the special minimum standard deduction, from its current level at $1,050 to $1,300 in 1972; limited to a maximum of $400 a month the maximum deductions for the cost of child care and invalid care to families with incomes of $18,000 a year or less (partially available to those with incomes of up to $27,600); accepted the House date of Sept. 22 (Senate date Aug. 15) for retroactive repeal of the excise tax on light trucks; set repeal of the 7% excise tax on autos, effective retroactive to Aug. 15; retained a tax credit for employers of former welfare clients—20% of wages in the first 12 months if the worker stayed another year; adopted a tax incentive for export sales by U.S. firms provided profits were put back into business; and gave the President authority to continue a "Buy American" policy of the investment credit, with the President authorized to bar use of the credit of equipment imported from countries discriminating against U.S. products. The final version of the bill contained a 7% investment credit for business against the cost of equipment, applicable to orders after April 1 or delivered on or before Aug. 15, the credit limited to $50,000 a year if used equipment were purchased. The credit could be claimed in total for the year of purchase or stretched out over the life of the equipment. Other final provisions of the bill included: increasing the regular standard deduction for individual income taxes, currently 13% of income or $1,500, whichever was smaller, to 15% or $2,000, effective in 1972; revising the withholding tax tables to make the amount of tax withheld closer to taxes owed; codifying into law the liberalized equipment depreciation deductions (*see above*); tightening provisions on the confidentiality of tax returns, pertaining to preparation of returns by third parties; and requiring the Administration to make an annual itemized accounting of tax revenue lost from preferential provisions in tax law, such as depletion allowances.

See also BUDGET; BUSINESS [8]; DRAFT & WAR PROTEST [11]; EOCONOMY, U.S. [8-9, 24]; EDUCATION [17]; MILITARY [3]; STATE & LOCAL GOVERNMENTS [1, 8-10]

TAYLOR, MAXWELL D.—*See* PENTAGON PAPERS [23-24]
TEAR GAS—*See* CHEMICAL & BIOLOGICAL WARFARE

TELEVISION & RADIO—Radio Free Europe funding. The House of Representatives, by a 271-12 vote Nov. 19, passed a bill to authorize funds for Radio Free Europe and Radio Liberty for two years and to establish a commission to evaluate international radio broadcasting activities of the two stations. (The stations had been covertly funded by the Central Intelligence Agency [CIA] since the first station was opened in 1950.) The Nixon Administration supported the measure, although it differed from its own proposal for the creation of a nonprofit organization to administer the stations. The House bill was returned to the Senate, which had passed, by voice vote Aug. 2, a bill to provide $35 million to fund the stations for fiscal 1972. The House bill called for a fiscal 1972 funding of $36 million and a fiscal 1973 funding of $38.5 million.

CBS contempt citation killed. The House refused July 13, by a roll-call vote of 226-181, to approve a contempt citation against the Columbia Broadcasting System (CBS) and its president, Dr. Frank Stanton, for their failure to cooperate with an investigation into the CBS television documentary *The Selling of the Pentagon*. Instead, the House sent the proposed citation back to the Commerce Committee, which had recommended it, in effect killing the proposal. The committee had voted July 1, upon the instigation of its chairman, Rep. Harley O. Staggers (D, W. Va.), to seek the citation after Stanton refused to give its investigating subcommittee all the materials used to produce the documentary. Staggers said after the house vote that he would not raise the matter again. The committee had served subpoenas on CBS April 8 and May 26 to provide all televised and untelevised materials used to produce the documentary. (The May 26 subpoena also demanded the appearance of Stanton before the committee.) CBS had refused April 20 to comply with the April 8 subpoena, although it did furnish the subcommittee with the file and transcript of the program as it appeared on television. In appearing before the committee June 24, Stanton again refused to give the committee all the materials used in the program. Stanton said that he had refused to show members of the investigating subcommittee either the raw materials or the editing procedures used on the film on the grounds that the First Amendment guaranteed freedom-of-the-press privileges.

The program, broadcast Feb. 23 and 27, charged that the Pentagon spent nearly $30 million a year to polish its image among Americans by staging elaborate war games, circulating old propaganda-type films and having officers in uniform speak to audiences throughout the U.S. about the menace of Communism. The program was immediately denounced by Rep. F. Edward Hebert (D, La.), chairman of the House Armed Services Committee, and by Vice President Spiro Agnew March 18. CBS rebroadcast the documentary March 23 and followed it with the criticism by Agnew, Hebert and Defense Secretary Melvin Laird and a defense of the film by CBS News President Richard S. Salant.

TV "Emmy" awards. The 23rd annual "Emmy" awards for the 1970-71 television season were presented in Hollywood July 29 by the National Academy of Television Arts and Sciences.

Comedy series—*All in the Family* (CBS). **Variety series (musical category)**—*The Flip Wilson Show* (NBC). **Variety series (talk)**—*The David Frost Show* (Westinghouse Broadcasting System). **Outstanding single program (variety)**—*The Burt Bacharach Special* (CBS). **Actor (comedy series)**—Jack Klugman in *The Odd Couple* (ABC). **Actress (comedy series)**—Jean Stapleton in *All in the Family.* **Actor (drama series)**—Hal Holbrook in "The Senator" segment of *The Bold Ones* (NBC). **Actress (drama series)**—Susan Hampshire in *The First Churchills* (Public Broadcasting System). **Direction (comedy, variety or music)**—Sterling Johnson for *Peggy Fleming at Sun Valley* (NBC). **Writer (special variety, comedy or musical)**—Marty Farrell and Bob Ellison for *The Burt Bacharach Special.* **Director (comedy, variety or music)**—Mark Rowan for *Rowan and Martin's Laugh-In* (NBC). **Supporting actor (comedy series)**—Edward Asner in *The Mary Tyler Moore Show* (CBS). **Supporting actress (comedy series)**—Valerie Harper in *The Mary Tyler Moore Show.* **Supporting actor (drama)**—David Burns in *The Price* on *Hallmark Hall of Fame* (NBC). **Supporting actress (drama)**—Margaret Leighton in *Hamlet* on *The Hallmark Hall of Fame* (NBC). **Dramatic series**—The Senator segment of *The Bold Ones.* **Director (single program in a dramatic series)**—Daryl Duke for "The Day the Lion Died" on "The Senator," **Writing (single program in a dramatic series)**—Joel Oliansky for "To Taste of Death but Once" on "The Senator." **Director (single program in comedy series)**—Jay Sandrich for "Toulouse-Latrec Is One of My Favorite Artists" on *The Mary Tyler Moore Show.* **Writers (single program in a comedy series)**—James L. Brooks and Allan Burns for "Support Your Local Mother" on *The Mary Tyler Moore Show.* Ed Sullivan was awarded the Academy's trustees award "for pioneering in the variety format."

Cable TV agreement. Three broadcasting and cable television organizations (the National Cable Television Association, the Association of Maximum Service Telecasters and the National Association of Broadcasters) Nov. 11 approved an agreement on the future extension of cable television. Under the agreement, cable operators were permitted to import two out-of-town signals without negotiating rights and fees for specific shows. Some compensation, such as a percentage of the cable industry's gross income, was to be negotiated for owners of film copyrights. In the 50 largest markets, cable companies would be permitted to import only programs for which local broadcasters had not purchased exclusive rights. In the next 50 largest markets, exclusive film rights were limited to two years, after which such films would be available to cable companies. The plan, part of which issued from the White House Office of Telecommunications Policy, was designed to slow cable television's growth in the largest markets while extending it from remote rural areas, where it began, into small cities.

See also COMMUNIST CHINA-U.S. DETENTE [4]; FEDERAL BUREAU OF INVESTIGATION [7, 10]; HEALTH [7, 10]; NEWSPAPERS

TENNESSEE VALLEY AUTHORITY (TVA)—See ENVIRONMENT

TENNIS—Laver sweeps Classic. Rod Laver scored a straight-set victory March 19 over Tom Okker to complete his sweep of the 13-match Tennis Champions Classic. Laver overwhelmed Okker, 7-5, 6-2, 6-1, before 8,322 fans at Madison Square Garden in New York. For Laver, the triumph enabled him to complete a sweep of 13 singles matches that promoters had put together for the 2½-month city-to-city Classic. Laver's triumph over Okker earned him $35,000. The 32-year-old Australian earned $160,000 for his 13 victories. Okker earned $15,000 as a losing finalist. Australians Roy Emerson and Ken Rosewall also reached the Classic final matches.

Wimbledon winners. Australia retained its tennis dominance at Wimbledon as John Newcombe and Evonne Goolagong captured the men's and women's All-England championship July 2-3. It was the second consecutive year that two Australians had taken the two top Wimbledon titles. Newcombe, 27, used a battering serve July 3 to stop Stan Smith of Pasadena, Calif., 6-3, 5-7, 2-6, 6-4, 6-4. It was his second straight Wimbledon title and his third in five years. In the women's final, Miss Goolagong, 19, defeated defending champion Mrs. Margaret Court of Australia July 2. With a four-game burst at the start and a string of six in a row to close it up, Miss Goolagong took the match, 6-4, 6-1.

Laver and Emerson defeated Arthur Ashe of Gum Springs, Va. and Dennis Ralston of Bakersfield, Calif. July 2, 4-6, 9-7, 6-8, 6-4, 6-4, to capture the men's doubles title. The women's doubles crown was won by Billie Jean King of Long Beach, Calif. and Rosie Casals of San Francisco July 3. The Americans stopped Miss Goolagong and Mrs. Court 3-6, 6-3, 6-2. Owen Davidson of Australia and Mrs. King won the mixed doubles title July 3 by downing Mrs. Court and Marty Riessen of Evanston, Ill., 3-6, 6-2, 15-13.

U.S. wins Davis Cup. Pfc. Stan Smith, on loan to the U.S. Davis Cup team from the Army, routed Ion Tiriac of Rumania Oct. 10 to give America another Davis Cup triumph in the challenge round competition in Charlotte, N.C. Smith's 8-6, 6-3, 6-0 triumph gave the U.S. Davis Cup squad an insurmountable 3-1 lead over the Rumanians in the five-match series. Rumania's Ilie Nastase won the final match Oct. 11 to trim the U.S. margin to 3-2.

The 1971 competition marked the end of the challenge round system in which the defending Davis Cup nation was pitted against the survivor of a long interzonal tournament. In 1972, the U.S., as the defending titleholder, would also have to compete in the interzonal matches.

Rosewall stops Laver. Laver, who had earned the reputation of never losing a big-money match, finally lost one Nov. 26 as Rosewall defeated him in the first "World Championship of Tennis" in Dallas to earn $50,000, the richest single payoff in tennis history. Rosewall and Laver played almost even in the four-set match but Rosewall prevailed in two tiebreakers to top Laver, 6-4, 1-6, 7-6, 7-6. Laver earned $20,000 to push his 1971 earnings to $292,717. Additionally, his $20,000 loser's purse enabled him to become the first tennis player to pass the million dollar mark in earnings with a nine-year total of $1,006,947.

Federation bans contract pros. The International Lawn Tennis Federation, the ruling body of amateur tennis, announced July 7 that it would impose a ban on contract professionals of the World Championship Tennis (WCT) group from playing in tournaments run by associations affiliated with the federation. Among the tournaments from which the WCT pros would be banned were Wimbledon, the U.S., French and Australian championships. The ban was to go into effect Jan. 1, 1972. The action taken by the federation climaxed a dispute over money demands made by Lamar Hunt, who put together the WCT association.

See also SOUTH AFRICA [11]

TERRITORIAL WATERS—Dispute with Ecuador. During the period of Jan. 11 to Nov. 23, Ecuador seized 50 American tuna fishing boats and released them after the payment of fines and penalties totaling nearly $2 million. The boats were seized during January through March and again in November for fishing without a license in what Ecuador considered to be its territorial waters—200 miles from the Ecuadorian coast. The U.S. recognized only a three-mile territorial limit with a 12-mile fishing limit and thus U.S. boats did not purchase licenses for fishing within the 12-200 mile area. (Licenses cost $350 plus $20 for each ton of a boat's capacity.) All the U.S. boats seized by Ecuador were operating off the coast outside the U.S.-recognized 12 miles. Fines levied by Ecuador were initially paid by the boat owners, but the U.S. government reimbursed the payment and tried to collect the amount from the government which had seized the boats. The State Department admitted, however, that it had "not collected a penny" since boat seizures began in 1966.

In retaliation for the seizure, the State Department announced Jan. 18 that it was suspending all arms sales, credits and guarantees to Ecuador under a Military Sales Act provision which called for a one-year suspension of aid when a nation "seizes or takes into custody or fines an American fishing vessel more than 12 miles from the coast of that country." The State Department also said that U.S. economic assistance scheduled for Ecuador in the remaining months of fiscal 1971—about $25.5 million—would be placed "under review." In response to the arms sales suspension, Ecuador called a special consultative meeting of foreign ministers of the Organization of American States (OAS), charging Jan. 26 that the U.S. had violated Article 19 (prohibiting the use of economic or political coercive measures "to force the sovereign will of another state") of the OAS Charter. The OAS ministers agreed unanimously Jan. 27 to convene the special meeting Jan. 31 over U.S. opposition and abstention from the vote. (The U.S. had suggested that the dispute be sent to the Inter-American Committee on Peaceful Settlements or the International Court of Justice.) The meeting Jan. 31 ended with a vaguely worded resolution, adopted 19-0 with four abstentions, calling on the U.S. and Ecuador to resume early talks on their differences. In a later move, Ecuador Feb. 1 ordered the U.S. to withdraw its military mission from Ecuador. The last of the 27 members of the mission were reported March 3 to have left Ecuador. In an attempt to ease the dispute between the two nations, Assistant Secretary of State for Inter-American Affairs Charles A. Meyer met with Ecuadorian officials Dec. 10-13. Ecuadorian President Jose Maria Velasco Ibarra told Meyer Dec. 12 that Ecuador could not reach any agreement with the U.S. while economic sanctions were in effect against Ecuador. (The U.S. House of Representatives had voted Dec. 8 to cut off all aid to Ecuador because of the seizure of the tuna boats.)

U.S. seizes Cuban fishing boats. Four Cuban fishing vessels were seized off the southern Florida coast Feb. 14 and 25 on charges of fishing within U.S. and Florida territorial waters. The U.S. Coast Guard took into custody Feb. 24 one of the vessels south of the Dry Tortugas Islands after it had been observed fishing within the 12-mile U.S. fishing limit. Three other vessels, which were inside the limit but not observed fishing, were escorted into international waters by the Coast Guard but intercepted by the Florida Marine Patrol Feb. 25. The three were seized and taken to Key West. Florida authorities claimed that an

American fishing boat captain had seen all four boats fishing within the U.S. waters (Florida claimed as its territorial fishing waters the entire area between the mainland and the Florida Keys, which at some points extended well beyond 12 miles.) Florida Feb. 26 dropped its charges against the captains of the three boats it had seized after the federal government said it would prosecute under federal law on the basis of a sworn affadavit by the American boat captain who saw all four fishing. The U.S. District Court in Miami fined the four captains a total of $13,500 March 2 and charged the Cuban government another $12,000 in civil penalties. After the fines had been paid, the four boats, their captains and crews returned to international waters March 3. (The U.S. May 27 arrested four Cuban fishermen for fishing inside U.S. territorial waters. The four were found guilty June 9 by a federal court in Key West and were sentenced to fines of $10,000 each and six months in jail. In apparent retaliation, the Cuban government announced June 10 that it was holding 13 Americans from three vessels [see CUBA]. The four Cuban fishermen were released from federal prison July 6, and the Cuban government released the 13 Americans July 7.)

Brazil enforces new limit. Following up on a decree issued in 1970 which claimed 200 miles of territorial waters, Brazilian President Emilio Garrastazu Medici March 29 signed a decree prohibiting fishing by all foreign vessels within 100 miles of Brazil's coast and requiring a license for fishing within the next 100 miles. Brazil announced June 1 that warships and planes would begin immediate patrol of the 200-mile limit and that the new limits would be "rigorously observed beginning July 30." France and Trinidad & Tobago, according to reports June 1, had begun negotiations on the application for fishing licenses. The U.S., however, insisted that such unilateral claims were not bound by international law and accordingly advised U.S. shrimpers to ignore the 200-mile limit. It was reported that a Brazilian navy gunboat June 16 fired warning shots over one of seven American-owned shrimp boats fishing 40 miles off the Brazilian coast and chased the fleet further off the coast. The State Department said it was investigating the alleged incident, denied by the Brazilian government. A report June 21 said that another incident had occurred between nine American shrimpers and Brazilian planes and warships off the Brazilian northeast coast. The incident, which allegedly took place June 20, did not involve any firing. The shrimpers reportedly were merely ordered to leave the area immediately. (Brazilian diplomatic sources said June 22 that Brazilian warships had received orders to seize foreign fishing boats found within 12 miles of the coast, but that they were only to issue warnings about the new 200-mile limit to boats found within the limit.) The U.S. and Brazil Oct. 25 began negotiations over the 200-mile limit claim. The talks were suspended Oct. 30, but were expected to resume.

U.S. proposes 12-mile limit. The U.S. Aug. 3 changed its position favoring a three-mile territorial water limit and proposed that all nations should have the right to set the limit for territorial seas over which they had jurisdiction at 12 miles from shore. The proposal was made at a meeting of the 86-nation United Nations Committee on the Peaceful Uses of the Seabed, which began deliberations in Geneva July 19 in an attempt to work out treaty articles regulating the exploitation of ocean resources beyond territorial limits. The articles would be submitted to a U.N. conference on the law of the sea scheduled in 1973. The U.S. made its proposal conditional on recognition of the right of transit through straits used for international navigation between one part of the high seas and another, or between the high seas and the territory of a foreign nation. In such cases, all ships and aircraft would enjoy the same freedom of navigation and overflight for transit purposes as they did on the high seas. In another draft treaty—seen as a response to conciliate the coastal developing countries in their desire to reserve fishing rights far off their coasts—the U.S. provided for the establishment of international bodies for regulating fisheries and for measures to insure conservation of the "living resources of the sea." (In a related action, the foreign ministers of 13 Caribbean countries met Nov. 24-26 and adopted a resolution that laid the groundwork for a possible agreement on offshore fishing limits in preparation for the 1973 U.N. conference.)

See also ARGENTINA [11-12]; CUBA; PERU

TERRORISM—See ARGENTINA [11, 13-14]; PARAGUAY

THAILAND—**Premier Thanom seizes power.** A newly formed five-man revolutionary council of military and civilian leaders, headed by Premier Thanom Kittikachorn seized full government powers in a bloodless coup d'etat Nov. 17. Foreign Minister Thanat Khoman and other officials were ousted, but many other key leaders were retained. The council announced Nov. 17 that it had abolished the constitution, dissolved parliament, disbanded the Cabinet and established martial law. It pledged to continue Thailand's anti-Communist and pro-American foreign policy and not to change any existing institutions "beyond necessity." The coup was allegedly aimed at coping with the dangers of Communist insurrection in the northern part of the country, obstruction by parliament members, strikes, terrorism and subversion. There had been a threat, the coup leaders claimed, that the "system of national administration" might be changed to one that would be opposed by King Phumiphol Aduldet and the people.

Power consolidated. Thanom announced the formation Nov. 18 of a 16-man ruling junta headed by him as chairman. The group, called the National Executive Council (NEC), was an enlargement of the revolutionary council. The junta was made up of the leadership of a new Revolutionary party replacing the government-dominated United Thai People's party, which had been abolished at the time of the government overthrow. The principal members of the NEC: Thanom, who dropped his title of premier; Gen. Praphas Charusathien, the army commander and former interior minister, as deputy party leader and director of military affairs; Gen. Kris Sivara, deputy army commander, as secretary of the Revolutionary party; Gen. Prasert Richirawong, former director of the police force, as director of civil affairs; Pote Sarasin, former deputy premier, as Thanom's civilian assistant; Thavil Soonthornsarathoon, former deputy interior minister, as director of civil affairs; and Air Chief Marshals Dawee Chullaspya and Boochoo Chandrbeksa Raiyanond as deputy directors of military affairs. The Revolutionary party Nov. 20 abolished all opposition parties and banned establishment of new ones.

The appointment of a new five-man Cabinet was announced Nov. 26. Thanom assumed the portfolio for foreign affairs. The other Cabinet members also held council positions. They were: Gen. Charusathien—defense, interior and justice; Air Marshal Chullaspya—armed forces chief of staff, agriculture, communications and national development; Sarasin—finance, economy and industry; and Gen. Richirawong—police, education and public health.

See also DRUG USE & ADDICTION [6]; INDOCHINA WAR [29-32]; PENTAGON PAPERS [23]

THANT, U—See DISASTERS; MIDDLE EAST [6, 11, 27, 31-32, 39]; PAKISTAN [33, 40]; UNITED NATIONS [4, 8-12]

THEATER—**Tony awards.** The 25th annual Antoinette Perry (Tony) awards for "distinguished achievement" in the Broadway theater during the 1970-71 season were presented by the League of New York Theaters under the auspices of the American Theater Wing in New York March 28. The winners: **Drama**—*Sleuth.* **Musical**—*Company.* **Dramatic actor**—Brian Bedford, *The School for Wives.* **Dramatic actress**—Maureen Stapleton, *The Gingerbread Lady.* **Musical actor**—Hal Linden, *The Rothschilds.* **Musical actress**—Helen Gallagher, *No, No, Nanette.* **Dramatic supporting actor**—Paul Sand, *Story Theatre.* **Dramatic supporting actress**—Rae Allen, *And Miss Reardon Drinks A Little.* **Musical supporting actor**—Keene Curtis, *The Rothschilds.* **Musical supporting actress**—Patsy Kelly, *No, No, Nanette.* **Dramatic director**—Peter Brook, *A Midsummer Night's Dream.* **Musical director**—Harold Prince, *Company.* **Scenic design**—Boris Aronson, *Company.* **Costume**

design—Raoul Pene du Bois, *No, No, Nanette.* **Lighting design**—H. R. Poindexter, *Story Theatre.* **Choreography**—Donald Saddler, *No, No, Nanette.* **Special awards**—Elliot Norton, Ingram Ash, Playbill magazine, Roger L. Stevens.

N.Y. productions in sharp decline. The number of shows produced on and off Broadway fell steeply during the 1970-71 season, it was reported June 27. Only 45 shows were produced during 1970-71, compared with 69 in the 1969-70 season. Dramas showed the sharpest decline—from 52 to 33. Off-Broadway shows dropped from 125 in 1969-70 to 101 in 1970-71 and dramas again displayed weakness, falling from 102 to 82.

"Fiddler" longest running musical. The story of a Jewish Ukranian dairyman and his five unmarried daughters—Harold Prince's *Fiddler on the Roof*—became the longest running musical on Broadway July 21 when it gave its 2,845th consecutive performance, surpassing *Hello, Dolly! Fiddler,* which opened Sept. 22, 1964 at the Imperial Theater, had played in 32 countries in 16 languages and returned a profit of $6,952,500. Only two other shows, *Life With Father* (3,224 performances) and *Tobacco Road* (3,182) had longer runs.

See also PULITZER PRIZES

THIEU, NGUYEN VAN—*See* DRUG USE & ADDICTION [17]; INDOCHINA WAR [18-19, 56, 63, 76, 79]; VIETNAM, SOUTH
TITO, MARSHAL (JOSIP BROZ)—*See* ITALY [6]

TOGO—According to a report March 27, 27 persons were recently sentenced for their participation in the August 1970 plot against the government of President Etienne Eyadema. Seven were sentenced in absentia, including Noe Kutuklui, the leader of the late President Sylvanus Olympio's banned Togolese Unity party now thought to be held by authorities in Dahomey, who was given 20 years. Alexandre-Jean Osseyi, a police inspector in Lome accused of having been in charge of military aspects of the plot, and four other men were given 10-year sentences. Seven plotters were given five-year sentences and four others were acquitted. The French newspaper Le Monde reported Jan. 13 that Eyadema had released Robert Fiadjoe, one of those under investigation in connection with the plot. Le Monde reported Jan. 7 that three of the accused had died in a prison hospital at Lome of "circulatory collapse."

TONKIN, GULF OF—*See* PENTAGON PAPERS [23]
TORNADOS—*See* STORMS
TORTURE—*See* BRAZIL; NORTHERN IRELAND [1, 10]; PAKISTAN [19]

TRACK & FIELD—**Villanova takes IC4-A titles.** Villanova retained its Intercollegiate Association of Amateur Athletes of America (IC4-A) outdoor track and field championship May 29 in Philadelphia on the strength of a second-place finish in the meet's final event, the mile relay, to move past Maryland, 32-31. It was the Wildcats' 11th outdoor title in the last 15 years. Villanova won the title despite capturing only one first-place finish—by Marty Liquori in the mile with a 4:00.4 clocking. Adelphi finished third with 27 points.

Villanova won another IC4-A indoor title at Princeton, N.J. March 6 by capturing three first-place finishes in track events and a first-place finish in the pole vault to outdistance Pennsylvania and Pittsburgh. Villanova finished with 42 points. Penn and Pitt tied for second with 21. It was Villanova's fifth consecutive IC4-A indoor championship and its 12th in the last 15 years.

Villanova wins NCAA crown. Liquori March 13 led Villanova to the team title in the National Collegiate Athletic Association (NCAA) indoor track and field championship in Detroit. Trailing University of Texas at El Paso by several points. Villanova erased the deficit as Liquori won the mile race in 4:04.7. The Villanova senior had also won the two-mile race March 12 with a 8:37.1 clocking, giving the Wildcats their only two first-place finishes. Villanova finished with 22 points. Texas El Paso was second with 19¼.

U.S., Russia split meet. Track stars from the U.S. and U.S.S.R. split an international dual meet in Berkeley, Calif. July 3, with the American men outscoring their Russian rivals while the Soviet women defeated the American female stars. Trailing by a point entering the final events, the American men rallied to score a 126-110 victory over Russia. The highlight of the U.S. rally was Pat Matzdorf's world-record high jump at 7' 6¼". Matzdorf's effort erased the old mark of 7' 5¾" held by Valery Brumel of the Soviet Union. It was the eighth time in 10 U.S.-U.S.S.R. meets that the American men had topped their Soviet rivals. The Soviet women took five of seven events July 2 and three of six events July 3 on the way to their 76-60 triumph over the American women. It was the ninth time in 10 tries that the Soviet women had defeated the American women's squad.

Liquori tops Ryun by stride. Liquori moved ahead of the pack and held on to defeat Jim Ryun by a stride May 16 in their "Dream Mile" race at the Martin Luther King Games in Philadelphia. Both runners were clocked in 3:54.6 at the tape. The clocking was the fastest mile time in three years. Ryun held the world mark of 3:51.1. The defeat for Ryun was his first since he ended his retirement in 1970.

U.S.-Pan Africa Games. Africa's corps of talented distance runners were the stars of the U.S.-Pan Africa Games in Durham, N.C. July 16-17, but a well-balanced U.S. squad captured team honors by outscoring the Africans, 111-78. A team of U.S. women won the satellite meet, running up a total of 79 points to 53 for a squad of international women opponents. The U.S. victory, however, did not dim the performances of Ethiopia's Mirus Ifter and Kenya's Kipchoge Keino. Ifter won the 10,000-meter run, defeating America's top long-distance runner, Frank Shorter. Keino ran a sensational 3-minute, 37.5-second 1,500-meter race to far outdistance his challengers. His time was equivalent to a 3:54 mile.

Oregon wins cross-country title. Steve Prefontaine led the University of Oregon to the NCAA cross-country championship Nov. 22 in the competition around the six-mile course in Knoxville, Tenn. Prefontaine covered the course in 29 minutes 14 seconds, finishing 40 yards ahead of Garry Bjorklund of Minnesota. (Prefontaine held the NCAA record with his clocking of 28:00.2 set in 1971.) Four of Prefontaine's teammates finished in the top 50 finishers to give Oregon 83 points.

TRANSPORTATION—See BUDGET; CANADA [29]; STATE & LOCAL GOVERMENTS [6, 8]

TRINIDAD & TOBAGO—Election results. Prime Minister Eric Williams' Peoples' National Movement (PNM) won all 36 seats in Parliament in a general election held May 24. The election was fought without major opposition, after A. N. R. Robinson, leader of the major opposition group, the Democratic Labor Party (DLP), withdrew from the race and called for a boycott of the election. It was the PNM's fourth consecutive election victory. The minor parties campaigning against Williams and the PNM were the Democratic Liberation Party, a left-wing faction of the Democratic Labor Party under the leadership of Bhadase Maraj, head of the substantial Hindu community, and the African National Congress. Robinson, who resigned as deputy prime minister during the "Black Power" riots of 1970, had joined the Democratic Labor Party with The Action Committee for Dedicated Citizens (ACDC) in boycotting the election. Williams' party won all 28 contested seats, as well as the remaining eight uncontested seats. Voter abstention totaled approximately 67.1%. The low voter turnout and lack of an opposition precipitated a constitutional crisis. The constitution required selection of an opposition leader in the House, while the document stipulated that there must be at least four members of the opposition in the lower house. This problem was expected to be overcome by a broad interpretation of constitutional provisions.

Emergency declared. Williams declared a state of emergency Oct. 19 as the result of racial trouble. Incidents had occurred between workers and foremen in the yards of two U.S. construction firms employing two thousand men. George Weeks, head of the oil workers union, and two other union leaders were arrested under the emergency regulations.

See also CARIBBEAN; TERRITORIAL WATERS

TRUMAN, HARRY S.—*See* PENTAGON PAPERS [18]

TUNISIA—Congress held, Cabinet formed. A congress of the ruling Destourian Socialist party (PSD) was held at Monastir Oct. 11-14 in the wake of instability caused by the resignations Sept. 4 and 5 of Interior Minister Ahmed Mestiri and Defense Minister Hassib Ben Ammar. The Cabinet, headed by Premier Hedi Nouira, resigned Oct. 26 and a new government was formed three days later.

During the congress Mestiri and his followers won passage of a resolution demanding elections at all political levels and "an end to the practice of designation and choice." Addressing the delegates Oct. 12, Mestiri declared that President Habib Bourguiba should "take the lead in the movement for liberalization [of Tunisian political life] just as he took the lead in the movement for national liberation and the construction of the state." Bourguiba was re-elected president of the party Oct. 14 and announced that he would not seek another term as Tunisian president in 1974. He suggested that Premier Nouira be chosen instead.

Although the congress officially ended Oct. 14, delegates gathered again Oct. 16 to elect the party's 58-member Central Committee. The largest number of votes was polled by Bahi Ladgham, who had been dismissed by Bourguiba as foreign minister in 1970, and second place in the voting went to Mestiri. Premier Nouira placed sixth. Mestiri was suspended from the party Oct. 20 and scheduled to be brought before a disciplinary committee. The government-controlled press later accused him of fostering disunity and of sedition.

Bourguiba appointed Nouira as the party's secretary general Oct. 26 and asked for the Cabinet's resignation. He told the Political Bureau that the congress had seen the "emergence of behavior incompatible with party ethics." The new government, announced Oct. 29, included Nouira as premier and Mohamed Masmoudi as foreign minister. New ministers were Hedi Khefacha (interior), Dhaoui Hannablia (agriculture) and Mohamed Sayah (public works and housing). Bechir Meheddebi had been appointed earlier to replace Hassib Ben Ammar as defense minister.

TUPAMAROS—*See* PARAGUAY; URUGUAY [1, 5, 9-12]

TURKEY—U.S. airmen kidnaped, freed. Four U.S. airmen (Sgt. James J. Sexton and Pvts. Larry J. Heavner, Richard Caraszi and James M. Gholson) were kidnaped by five armed men March 4 as they drove from a radar base outside Ankara to their billets. The kidnapers set a March 6 deadline and demanded $400,000 as a ransom price for not shooting the airmen. The police arrest March 4 of one of the suspects in the kidnap (Mete Ertekin, a student at the Middle East Technical University in Ankara) prompted an additional demand by the kidnapers for his release. In a manifesto delivered to the semi-official Turkish news agency and a radio station March 4, the Turkish People's Liberation Army (TPLA), a new leftist guerrilla group, claimed responsibility for the kidnaping as well as for other terrorist acts. More than 2,000 policemen and militiamen searched for the kidnapers in Ankara. They surrounded the campus of the Middle East Technical University March 5, touching off a riot in which at least one student and one policeman were killed and 20 students injured. (The police used tear gas to dislodge students who barricaded themselves in school buildings with dynamite, guns and fire bombs. About 200 students were arrested.) The four airmen were released by their kidnapers March 8 after the U.S. and Turkish governments had refused to yield to ransom demands. An Ankara military court Oct. 9 imposed death sentences on

18 accused members of the TPLA. The 18 had allegedly admitted their responsibility in the kidnaping and in other violent acts. They were convicted of attempting to overthrow the state through kidnapings, bank robberies and bombings.

[2] **Premier ousted by military.** Premier Suleyman Demirel March 12 announced the resignation of his government in the face of a threatened military coup. The resignation came after Gen. Memduh Tagmac, chief of the general staff, and the commanders of the army, navy and air force submitted a memorandum to President Cevdet Sunay and the leaders of the assembly and senate warning that the armed forces were "determined to seize power" unless a new "strong and respected government" that would rise "above party politics" was promptly formed to halt civil anarchy and enact reforms. The memorandum charged that parliamentary dickering and Demirel's policies had pushed Turkey into "anarchy, fratricide, and social and economic unrest." The ultimatum followed growing impatience by the military with the Demirel government's inability to deal with student riots, leftist agitation, Kurdish separatism and establishment of an underground urban guerrilla organization. Immediately after the memorandum was issued, army leaves were canceled and units in Ankara were placed on partial alert. The threat of a military coup diminished March 16 with the forced retirement of five generals and eight colonels. A sixth general also resigned. It was reported that these officers advocated a military coup without waiting for the politicians to try to form a new government.

[3] **New government formed.** After a week of intensive political and military consultations, President Sunay March 19 designated Nihat Erim, a moderate politician of the opposition Republican People's party, to be the new premier. At Sunay's request, Erim resigned from his political party. (The move appeared to comply with the military demand for a government above party politics.) Erim March 26 announced a 25-member coalition government that included 14 young non-parliamentary technocrats and experts without party affiliation. Five ministers were chosen from the former ruling Justice party and three from the Republican People's party. The Reliance party was also represented in the Cabinet. The Cabinet: Deputy premier in charge of political and administrative affairs—Sadi Kocas; deputy premier in charge of economic affairs—Attila Karaoslmanoglu; ministers of state—Mehmet Ozgunes and Dogan Kitapli; justice—Ismail Arar; national defense—Ferit Melen; interior—Hamdi Omeroglu; foreign affairs—Osman Olcay; finance—Sait Naci Ergin; national education—Sinasi Orel; public works—Cahit Karakas; foreign economic relations—Ozer Derbil; industry and commerce—Ayhan Cilingiroglu; health—Turkan Akyol; customs and monopolies—Haydar Ozalp; agriculture—Orhan Dikmen; communications—Haluk Arik; labor—Attila Sav; power and natural resources—Ihsan Topaloglu; tourism and information—Erol Yilmaz Akcal; construction and housing—Selahattin Baburoglu; rural affairs—Cevdet Aykan; youth and sports—Sezai Ergun; and forestry—Selahattin Inal. The new government April 7 won a vote of confidence (321-46 with 3 abstentions) from the National assembly.

[4] Erim had outlined his government's program to parliament April 2. The plan went far to meet the military's demands for widespread reforms coupled with strong measures to combat political terrorist activity. Assigning top priority to restoration of national security and order, Erim said the government would strengthen laws on associations, freedom of assembly and demonstration marches, strikes and lockouts, and possession of firearms. Erim envisaged a strategy for reforms divided into a short-term (six-month) phase and a long-term phase. The long-term phase appeared to be merely the extension of fundamental reforms. Within the six-month period, the government would set the targets and strategy of the third Five-Year Development Plan. It would also carry out land and agricultural reform, including the limitation of land ownership by an individual family, imposition

of an agricultural tax system, measures to modernize agriculture and improve productivity, and removal of conflicts in agricultural credits and prices policy; financial reforms, including tax administration reform and encouragement of foreign investment in major technological installations; nationalization of strategic minerals such as borax; educational reform; and election reform.

[5] Martial law imposed. The government April 26 proclaimed martial law for one month in 11 of Turkey's 67 provinces. Justice Minister Arar said the Cabinet had acted after consultation with the National Security Council (dominated by the military commanders) because of "a strong, active uprising against the motherland and the republic." The martial law affected Ankara, Istanbul, Izmir, Adana, Eskisehir, Zonguldak, Kocaeli, Sakarya, Hatay, Diyarbakir and Siirt. Military commanders of the 11 provinces announced bans April 27 on unauthorized public meetings and possession of weapons. A curfew was imposed in Ankara. Parliament, meeting in joint session April 28, approved the declaration of martial law with only two dissenting votes. The National Assembly voted two-month extensions of the martial law May 25 (effective May 26), July 23 (effective July 26), Sept. 23 (effective Sept. 26) and Nov. 25 (effective Nov. 26). In the Nov. 25 debate, the government announced that, since the introduction of martial law, police had seized quantities of arms and arrested 785 of the 968 alleged anarchists sought by the government. Of 994 persons subject to trial by military courts, 458 were in preventive detention and 353 had been convicted—18 to capital punishment. In other martial law developments, Parliament May 14 approved without debate, and Sunay May 16 ratified, a law providing for 30-day detention of suspects without charge and the transfer of certain civil offenses to military courts. The National Assembly by a 357-2 vote Sept. 6 and the Senate by a 134-12 vote Sept. 20 approved constitutional amendments designed to restrict basic civil liberties when they conflicted with national security. One of the provisions extended the period that suspects could be held without charge from 24 to 48 hours. The amendments were passed to meet the demands of armed forces commanders that the government curb anarchy.

[6] Kidnaped Israeli diplomat killed. The body of the Israeli consul general in Istanbul, Ephraim Elrom, was found May 23 in an apartment near the Israeli consulate, six days after he had been kidnaped May 17 by four leftist terrorists. He had been shot three times in the head. The TPLA claimed responsibility for the kidnaping. The government said the kidnapers probably belonged to the militant leftist Turkish Revolutionary Youth Federation (Dev-Genc), which had been banned May 12 by court order. Many members of Dev-Genc were thought to belong to the TPLA, which in turn was said to have links with the anti-Israel Popular Front for the Liberation of Palestine. The kidnapers threatened to kill Elrom unless "all revolutionary guerrillas under detention" were released by the evening of May 20. (Elrom was probably killed May 22.) The government immediately rejected the demands and began an intensive search for the kidnaped diplomat and his abductors. The military commander of Istanbul, Gen. Faik Turun May 22 ordered a 15-hour curfew beginning at midnight to permit thorough house searches. By May 24, the government had held for questioning nearly 1,000 persons; many were quickly released. A military court in Istanbul, according to report Dec. 28, sentenced two men and three women to death for their roles in the kidnap-murder of Elrom. They were also convicted of attempting to overthrow the regime and of setting up the outlawed TPLA. The death sentences on the women were commuted to life imprisonment. (One guerrilla sought in the kidnap, Huseyin Cevahir, was killed and another, Mahir Cayan, was seriously wounded June 1 in a police shootout following a 51-hour siege. The two guerrillas had seized Sibel Erkan, the 14-year-old daughter of an army major, May 30 and held her hostage in her home, threatening to kill her unless they were granted safe passage out of Turkey.)

[7] **Ties with Peking set.** Diplomatic relations were established between Turkey and Communist China Aug. 5 after two months of negotiations in Paris. A joint communique issued in Ankara and Peking said Turkey recognized the People's Republic of China as "the sole legal government of China." Ties with Nationalist China were severed. A Foreign Ministry spokesman said Turkey would vote in favor of United Nations membership for Peking (see UNITED NATIONS [7]) but would not vote for the expulsion of Nationalist China. He said that Turkey and Peking would probably not exchange ambassadors until 1972.

[8] **Erim resignation rejected.** President Sunay Oct. 27 refused to accept the resignation of Premier Erim's government on the ground that Erim "enjoyed the full support and confidence of parliament, the Turkish armed forces and Turkish public opinion." The premier agreed to retain his post. The government crisis had begun Oct. 5 with the Justice party's decision to withdraw its members from the Cabinet. The party had charged that Erim's government had lost its nonpartisan nature. Justice party ministers Kitalpi, Ozalp and Akcal resigned. (Erim refused the resignations of the latter two and eliminated Kitalpi's post.) Two Justice party ministers—Karakas and Ergun—refused to resign and were expelled from the party Oct. 14. Erim submitted his resignation early Oct. 27 after failing to reach a compromise with Justice party leader Demirel over their differences, particularly over Justice party opposition to reforms demanded by the military. Erim accused Demirel of inciting the current crisis and revived charges of corruption against Demirel and his family. Gen. Tagmac Oct. 28 called for a solution of the military crisis and warned that the armed forces would "not permit the continuation of the present situation." Yielding to military pressure, the Justice party Nov. 6 revoked its decision to withdraw from the Cabinet and pledged to support Erim's planned reforms.

[9] **Erim resigns again.** Erim resigned Dec. 3 after 14 of his 25 Cabinet members quit over what they charged was the government's inability to implement social reforms demanded by the military. Erim announced the same day that he would head a caretaker government. The ministers, most of whom were appointed from outside parliament, blamed political pressures and the government bureaucracy for obstructing their efforts to implement land and tax reforms and government reorganization. The resignations followed the appointment Dec. 2 of former Finance Minister Mesut Erez, a member of the Justice party, as deputy premier for parliamentary affairs. Erez, a critic of the planned reforms, said he would be involved in economic planning.

[10] **New government formed.** Erim announced a new Cabinet Dec. 11. The 25-member Cabinet was composed of 14 members of parliament (including seven Justice party members and four Republican People's party members) and 11 experts from outside parliament. The new Cabinet was thought to be more moderate, apparently as a concession to parliamentary conservatives who opposed proposed reforms. The Cabinet: ministers of state—Kitapli, Ali Ihsan Gogus, Ilyas Karaoz and Ilhan Oztrak; foreign affairs—Umit Haluk Bayulken; justice—Suat Bilge; defense—Melen; interior—Ferit Kubat; finance—Ergin; education—Arar; public works—Mukadder Oztekin; foreign commerce—Naim Talu; health—Aykan; customs and monopolies—Ozalp; agriculture—Dikmen; communications—Rifki Danisman; labor—Ali Riza Uzuner; industry and technology—Mesut Erez; energy and natural resources—Nezih Devres; tourism and information—Akcal; housing—Serbulent Bingol; youth and sports—Adnan Karakucuk; rural affairs—Necmi Sonmez; and forestry—Inal. The Cabinet was installed in office Dec. 22 after winning a vote of confidence from the National Assembly. The vote was 301-45 with 3 abstentions.

[11] In the government's program, presented to the National Assembly Dec. 16, Erim had again appealed for parliamentary support for reforms. His program, said to be more moderate than his previous one because of

conservative opposition, promised to encourage private investments and promised to work toward a "normally functioning democracy" in Turkey.

See also AGNEW, SPIRO THEODORE; CYPRUS; DRUG USE & ADDICTION [5]; EARTHQUAKES; EUROPEAN ECONOMIC COMMUNITY [5]

TYPHOONS—*See* STORMS

UGANDA—Coup overthrows Obote. President Milton Obote, attending a conference of Commonwealth leaders in Singapore, was deposed Jan. 25 in a coup led by Gen. Idi Amin. Approximately 70 persons were killed in fighting accompanying the takeover, although no indication of major resistance was given. A Kampala radio broadcast Jan. 25 announced the coup and accused Obote of having developed his home region in northern Uganda at the expense of other parts of the country and of having pursued an economic policy for "the rich, big men." Amin declared Jan. 26 that Obote was welcome to return to Uganda as a private citizen and that his Uganda People's Congress would not be disbanded. Obote Jan. 26 announced from neighboring Tanzania that he was still president of Uganda. Following the takeover, the new government Jan. 25 ordered the release of all political prisoners, estimated to number nearly 100, and requested the return of political exiles. (Many of those affected by the order were followers of Sir Edward Mutesa, kabaka [king] of the southern tribe of the Buganda, whom Obote had ousted as president in 1966.) Amin Jan. 28 freed 55 political prisoners, dismissed Obote's Cabinet, ordered that ministries be run by their permanent secretaries and imposed a temporary ban on all political activities. Amin Feb. 1 dismissed all mayors, district councilmen and other local officials until new elections could be held for the offices. Districts were to be run by an administrative secretary responsible to the district commissioner; cities and towns were to be run by town clerks. Amin assumed all legislative and administrative powers Feb. 2 and appointed a 17-man Council of Ministers to assist him in governing the country. The Cabinet included two of Obote's ambassadors and seven former permanent secretaries. The majority of the rest of the group were civilians.

Amin named president. At a press conference Feb. 20, "the soldiers and officers of the Ugandan army" appointed Amin president of the country and promoted him to the rank of full general. Amin then lifted the curfew and state of emergency in Uganda, saying that Obote had used them to settle personal quarrels. An Amin aide, reading a statement of support from the military, declared that the military government "must be in power for at least five years" before elections could be held peacefully and warned that anyone engaging in political activity in the meantime would be "dealt with severely." Amin, however, announced Feb. 22 that the army would not remain in power five years but would "return the country to order everywhere and would then organize free elections." In a related development, the government March 23 decreed a two-year ban on political activity. The ban, including the utterance in

476

public of the name of a political party and the wearing of symbolic uniforms, carried a penalty of 18 months in prison and/or a $1,200 fine.

Reward for Obote, others. The Ugandan government May 13 announced a reward of one million shillings ($139,200) for the return alive of Obote. Rewards of half million shillings each were offered for two of his supporters, Lt. Col. Oyite Ojok and Akena Adoko, head of Obote's disbanded secret police, the General Service Department. The rewards were to be paid "either openly or secretly to anyone, anywhere, in any currency he wishes." According to the announcement, the fugitives were wanted for questioning about a number of matters connected with Obote's regime, particularly "corruption, the operation of the General Service Department, and ... the murder of the late Brig. Gen. Pierino Okova" and his wife in January 1970.

Tanzania border dispute. Amin July 8 threatened to shoot down any aircraft crossing his country's borders with Tanzania, closed by Amin the previous day, and to attack any Tanzanian ships approaching Uganda's shores on Lake Victoria. The warnings were caused by a gradual breakdown of cooperation in the East African Community, whose Uganda-appointed minister of communications, research and social services, Z.H.K. Bigirwenkya, was prevented by Tanzanian police July 5 from taking up his official duties at the community's headquarters in Arusha, Tanzania. Amin July 7 declared persona non grata the community's minister of finance and information, John Malecela, and expelled another Tanzanian, Idi Sumba, director general of the East African Development Bank, whose headquarters were in Kampala. The dispute produced border skirmishes in August, September, October and November, with each side claiming the other had started the fighting. The dispute and the accompanying concern over the future of the East African Community ended Nov. 23 as Amin signed the budgetary appropriations bill of the community and lifted his ban against Malecela and Sumba and Tanzanian President Julius K. Nyerere gave assurances that he would accept Amin's appointments to community posts. Amin had reopened the border with Tanzania Nov. 21 and announced immediate restoration of direct travel and telephone connections between the two countries. Kenya President Jomo Kenyatta was considered primarily responsible for easing tension in the area.

See also AFRICA; KENYA

UKRAINIAN CATHOLIC CHURCH—*See* ROMAN CATHOLIC CHURCH [11]
ULBRICHT, WALTER—*See* GERMANY, EAST
ULSTER—*See* NORTHERN IRELAND

UNEMPLOYMENT—**1971 rates.** Monthly unemployment rates for 1971, on a seasonally adjusted basis were: 6% in January; 5.8% in February; 6% in March; 6.1% in April; 6.2% in May; 5.6% in June; 5.8% in July; 6.1% in August; 6% in September; 5.8% in October; 6% in November; and 6.1% in January.

Job help for unemployed vets. President Nixon announced June 13 a high priority drive for a job placement program for unemployed veterans of the Vietnam war. Expressing concern about the high jobless rate among the veterans—370,000 were jobless, a 10.8% rate compared to an 8.4% rate for non-veterans aged 20-29—Nixon said Labor Secretary James D. Hodgson had his "personal mandate" to head the drive, which would be coordinated with the Jobs for Veterans Committee, a national advisory panel of government, industry and labor leaders, and with the National Alliance of Businessmen. Under the new initiative, veterans would be given priority for on-the-job training financed by the Labor Department; GI benefits would be paid participants in the Manpower Development Training Act and employers would be reimbursed for the extra costs involved; the Transition Program of counseling, training and job placement would be expanded (24,000 were in training); and federal agencies and contractors would be required to list job openings with the U.S. Employment Service.

Public works bill vetoed. President Nixon June 29 vetoed an accelerated public works bill passed in its final form by the Senate June 8 (by a 45-33 vote) and by the House June 15 (by a 275-104 vote). The bill had originally been passed by the Senate March 11 primarily as an extension of aid to Appalachia. The accelerated public works program had been added by the House when it approved the bill April 22. The bill would have provided a four-year, $1.5 billion extension of the Appalachian Regional Commission and a two-year, $2 billion extension of the Public Works and Economic Development Act financing other regional commissions. Nixon's veto was directed at another part of the bill, a $2 billion public works program to provide up to 80% federal grants to areas of high unemployment to build sewers, hospitals, public buildings and other facilities. Nixon described the program (modeled after a Kennedy Administration program, later abandoned) as a "costly and time-consuming method of putting unemployed persons to work." He also said it would stimulate construction jobs, which also had little immediate effect on joblessness, instead of helping "the broad spectrum of the presently unemployed." The Senate July 14 failed to override the President's veto. The 57-36 vote in favor of overriding fell five votes short of the required two-thirds majority.

Emergency job act signed. President Nixon July 12 signed into law the Emergency Employment Act authorizing $2.25 billion to provide public service jobs in the next two years for the unemployed at state and local levels. The bill had been passed by a 75-11 Senate vote June 29 and by a 343-14 House vote July 1. (A bill appropriating $1 billion under the act was approved by the House Aug. 4 and by the Senate Aug. 6 and was signed by the President Aug. 9. About $600 million was allocated to states, effective upon signing of the bill. Specific allocations of $200 million in cities, counties and neighborhoods where the unemployment rate was above 6% were announced Sept. 20.) The bill provided that the government would provide federal funds, whenever the national unemployment rate reached 4.5% of the work force for three consecutive months, for emergency jobs in schools, hospitals, parks, police and fire departments and social service agencies. It included a provision to make funds available to local areas having a 6% jobless rate, even if the national rate fell below 4.5%. Job preference was to be given to veterans who had served in Indochina or Korea within the previous seven years. In signing the bill, Nixon said that it removed his major objections to bills which he had vetoed in December 1970 and June 29 (*see above*). He estimated that the bill would provide 150,000 new jobs, which he said could lead to permanent employment. He added that the job opportunities opened up by the bill would not lead to "entrapment in permanent public subsidy." The jobs provided by the new law would be similar to those envisaged under the two vetoed measures. A key difference, however, was that, under the new law, state and local governments would be required in their applications to give the federal government assurances that the jobs would lead to permanent employment. In addition, the new law would expire in two years. The earlier measures would have been permanent.

Jobless aid extended. Congress Dec. 15 gave final approval to a bill to extend unemployment compensation an additional 13 weeks in states where the jobless rate was 6.5% or more for 13 consecutive weeks. The $274 million estimated cost of the program would be financed from U.S. Treasury funds, which would be replaced if a special unemployment compensation account attained a surplus. The vote in the House Dec. 15 was 194-149. The Senate passed the measure by a voice vote (with only three Senators present). President Nixon signed the bill Dec. 29, but criticized the legislation as "another program of public welfare." Nixon said he had directed the Labor Department to prepare "alternatives to this program, in the event one is needed, which would be properly financed." Nixon objected to the shift from payment of unemployment compensation from employer taxes. He also objected to the legislation's discrimination against "similarly situated workers in other states."

(The bill currently applied to Alaska, California, Connecticut, Maine, Massachusetts, Michigan, New Jersey, Oregon, Puerto Rico, Rhode Island, Vermont and Washington—the areas with more than 6.5% unemployment for 13 consecutive weeks.)

See also AGING; AVIATION [2]; BUDGET; LABOR [3]; LATIN AMERICA; POVERTY; RACIAL & MINORITY UNREST [1]; STATE & LOCAL GOVERNMENTS [3]; TAXES

UNION OF ARAB EMIRATES—*See* PERSIAN GULF STATES ; UNITED NATIONS [1]

UNION OF SOVIET SOCIALIST REPUBLICS (U.S.S.R.)—1970 economic report. The results of the 1970 economic development plan were announced Feb. 3 by the Central Statistical Board. Measured against figures for 1969, the following major increases were reported: national income 8.5%, per capita income 5.2%, industrial productivity 7%, agricultural productivity 8.7%, foreign trade 11%. The figures indicated that the Soviet economy had overcome the effects of a comparatively low 1969 growth rate, although the statistical board observed that the demand for meat and vegetables was not being met. There was evidence that the goals established in the 1966 five-year plan had not been reached. Other figures cited: a 7.4% increase in retail trade turnover, the construction of 2.8 million flats and detached houses, the purchase by the state of 73 million tons of grain from agricultural enterprises and the production of 6.9 million tons of raw cotton.

[2] Consumer prices lowered. A government edict March 1 lowered the prices paid by Soviet citizens on a range of consumer goods. The announcement lowered prices for washing machines, electric razors, ballpoint pens, motorcycles, radio phonographs, raincoats and some household chemicals 16%-38%. The measure was thought to have been taken in order to clear stocks of items no longer in short supply.

[3] Drugging of prisoners charged. In a letter written March 13 and published five days later, two political prisoners (Viktor Feinberg, who had been involved in a protest against the Soviet invasion of Czechoslovakia, and Vladimir Borisov, accused of distributing anti-Soviet leaflets in 1969), both inmates of a Leningrad psychiatric hospital, said that Soviet psychiatric authorities administered mind-altering drugs to political prisoners, threatened them with electric-shock therapy and placed dissidents in the company of mental patients with homicidal tendencies. They added: "Medicine, one of the most humane of professions, is thus being turned into a servile handmaiden of the regime's correction agencies in their hangman functions." The men also charged that prisoners were being held in mental hospitals for as long as 15 years, contrary to a law which limited forced psychiatric treatment to two years. The Soviet practice of confining political prisoners to mental hospitals aroused a variety of other criticism during the year. Vladimir Bukovsky, a Soviet dissident, sent a letter to Western psychiatrists in January asking for help in ending the Soviet practice. The letter purported to contain "exact copies of the diagnoses" of former Maj. Gen. Pyotr G. Grigorenko and asked Western psychiatrists to decide whether the diagnoses "contain enough scientifically based evidence to indicate the mental illness described ... and to indicate the need for isolating these people completely from society." Bukovsky was arrested March 29 on charges of anti-Soviet propaganda and was given a psychiatric examination. Soviet security police were reported Nov. 10 to have informed Bukovsky's mother that an examining panel had found her son normal and that he would be tried soon. In another development, Zhores Medvedev, a Soviet biologist and dissident who was arrested in 1970 and given a forced psychiatric examination, wrote an account of the incident, published in London in mid-September. Medvedev said he had written the book "to call attention to the dangerous tendency of using psychiatry for political purposes, the exploitation of medicine in an alien role as a means of intimidation and punishment—a new and illegal way of isolating people for their views and convictions. (Roy A. Medvedev, brother of the biologist and author of one of the chapters in the book, was reported to have left his job as a historian at Moscow's Academy of Pedagogical Sciences Oct. 12 after police confiscated most of his private papers.) Members of the Soviet Human Rights Committee asked, in a letter published Oct. 23, that the forthcoming World Psychiatric Association Congress, due to open in Mexico City Nov. 28, consider the use of psychiatry for political purposes. The congress Dec. 1 rejected the Soviet appeal, saying that the organization's constitution contained no mechanism for such an action.

[4] Increased power for Soviets. The 55,000 local councils (soviets) exercising local government powers in the U.S.S.R. were to receive more power as a result of a Central Committee decree March 14. Under terms of the decree, the soviets were to receive some of the profits of enterprises situated in their areas, with the amounts to be determined by the national and republican Councils of Ministers. A greater proportion of housing and public amenities were to be transferred from state bodies to local soviet control. Legislation was to be drawn up standardizing the function of the soviets, which differed markedly in urban and in rural areas.

[5] Soviet party congress. The 24th Soviet Communist Party (CP) Congress, attended by nearly 5,000 party members and 101 foreign delegations, was held March 30-April 9 at the Kremlin Palace of Congresses in Moscow. Communist China and Albania did not send delegations to the Congress. The Japanese Communist party, absent from the 1966 congress, sent delegates as the result of a meeting with Soviet party officials in Tokyo (reported March 21). The congress was considered notable more for its affirmation of previous Soviet policies than for its introduction of new ones; it featured renewed emphasis on the prominence of Party General Secretary Leonid Brezhnev. The congress heard a report on domestic and foreign policy by Brezhnev (unanimously adopted April 5) and an economic report by Premier Aleksei N. Kosygin. It elected a Central Committee, which in turn chose a Politburo and a Secretariat. The Central Committee, the party's principal legal organ between congresses, was enlarged from 360 to 390 members. Four men were elevated to full membership in the Politburo, the committee which met weekly to formulate policy, enlarging the Politburo from 11 to 15 members. Brezhnev listed the Politburo members in the following order: Nikolai V. Podgorny, the Soviet president; Premier Kosygin; Mikhail A. Suslov; Andrei P. Kirilenko; Arvid Y. Pelshe; First Deputy Premier Kirill T. Mazurov; First Deputy Premier Dimitri S. Polyansky; Pyotr Y. Shelest; Gennady I. Voronov (*see* [6]); Alexander N. Shelepin; Viktor V. Grishin (newly elevated); Dinmukhamed A. Kunayev (newly elevated); Vladimir V. Shcherbitsky (newly elevated); and Fyodor D. Kulakov. No information was given on the composition of the Secretariat, the body which met daily to implement Politburo decisions. Moscow newspapers April 10 reported the re-election of Brezhnev as general secretary as a separate item ahead of Politburo and Secretariat elections.

[6] Voronov loses premiership. Gennady I. Voronov was removed as premier of the Russian Republic, it was announced July 22. No explanation was given. Voronov, who had held the premiership for nearly nine years, was named chairman of the People's Control Committee, an organization which audited government expenditures. Mikhail E. Solomentsev, a national CP secretary responsible for heavy industry, was appointed July 28 to replace Voronov as premier. A two-day session of the CP Central Committee Nov. 22-23 named Solomentsev as a candidate member of the Politburo, but retained Voronov as a full Politburo member.

[7] Lake Baikal pollution fought. The government and the Communist party Central Committee issued a joint decree Sept. 24 aimed at halting industrial pollution of Lake Baikal in Siberia, the world's largest fresh water lake by volume. (A similar decree issued in February 1969 by the government alone apparently had not been implemented.) The new edict asked government agencies and the Soviet Academy of Sciences to "speed the drafting of plans for organization of the protected zone and for the rules of conservation of the waters of Lake Baikal and the natural resources of the lake's drainage basin." A pulp mill at Baikalsk was given one year to install waste treatment facilities and a mill under construction at Selenginsk was forbidden to open until "appropriate treatment facilities" were ready. Other industries in the area as well as the city of Ulan-Ude were given deadlines for building treatment plants.

[8] 5 year plan approved. The Supreme Soviet ended its winter session Nov. 26 by approving the 1971-75 economic development plan, which had been passed in draft form at the April party congress (*see* [5]), and a $19.9 billion budget for 1972. The budget figure was the same as that for 1971. The new defense budget would represent 10.3% of total expenditures, the third straight annual decline in the defense budget as part of the entire government outlay. The five-year plan emphasized the need to computerize the Soviet economy. It called for an overall industrial growth rate of 42%-46%, with light industry (Group B) expected to increase 44%-48% and heavy industry (Group A) scheduled to grow 41%-45%. Although this was reportedly the first time a five-year plan had given Group B priority, analysts pointed out that the actual amount of money spent on the industrial sector would remain far greater. Labor productivity was slated to rise 36%-40%, accounting for 87%-90% of the planned increase in industrial output and suggesting a scarcity of investment funds. National income was scheduled to increase 37%-40%, with per capita income to go up 30%. Salaries for workers and office employees were to rise 20%-22% and salaries for farmers were expected to increase 30%-35%. An estimated $90 million was to be invested in agriculture in order to "meet more fully the population's growing demand for foodstuffs and industry's for raw materials." Grain production was expected to reach a yearly level of 195 million tons.

Soviet-Jewish Developments

[9] 12th hijacker sentenced. Volf Zalmanson, brother of two Soviet Jews sentenced in December 1970 for an attempted airline hijacking, was given 10 years in prison Jan. 7 for his role in the plot. It was not clear if the sentence was to be carried out in a labor camp or in a regular prison.

[10] *Leningrad Jews sentenced.* Nine Soviet Jews were convicted in a Leningrad court May 20 for their involvement in the attempted hijacking. All nine had been charged with anti-Soviet activity and with "participation in anti-Soviet organization." Five had been accused of stealing state property—a duplicating machine with which they were said to have planned to print anti-Soviet literature. Two—Gilya I. Butman and Mikhail L. Korenblit—were charged with treason. No Western newsmen were admitted to the courtroom during the trial. The sentences handed down May 20 were virtually the same as those requested by the prosecutor. Butman was given a 10-year sentence and Korenblit seven years. The other sentences were: Lassal S. Kaminsky and Lev N. Yagman, five years; Vladimir O. Mogilever, four years; Solomon G. Dreizner, Lev L. Korenblit (Mikhail Korenblit's brother) and Viktor N. Boguslavsky, three years; and Viktor Stilbans, one year. Dreizner, Lev Korenblit and Mogilever had been given lesser sentences because of their "sincere repentance and the fact that they helped uncover the crime at the stage of preliminary investigation." Boguslavsky, convicted of distributing anti-Soviet material, had not been implicated in the hijacking plan.

[11] *4 Riga Jews sentenced.* The Latvian Supreme Court May 27 convicted four Riga Jews of anti-Soviet activity. The four had been charged with producing and circulating an underground newspaper said to have been Zionist and anti-Soviet in content, which had "prepared the ground for" the unsuccessful hijack attempt. The defendants: Arkady A. Shpilberg, sentenced to a three-year term; Mikhail Z. Shepshelovich, sentenced to two years; and Boris M. Maftser and Ruth I. Aleksandrovich, sentenced to one year each. The sentences were the same as those requested by the prosecutor May 26, except in the case of Shpilberg, for whom the prosecutor had asked a four-year confinement.

[12] *Hijackers sentenced in Kishinev.* Nine Soviet Jews were given prison terms by the Moldavian Supreme Court June 30 for their role in the hijack attempt. The nine, most of them engineers or skilled technicians, had been charged with attempting to hijack a plane, stealing and concealing a duplicating machine and the "spreading of materials aimed at subverting the social and state systems of the U.S.S.R." Those sentenced were: David Chernoglaz, five years; Anatoly Goldfeld, four years; Alexander Galperin, two and a half years; Arkady Voloshin, Semyon Levit, Lazar Trakhtenberg, Harry Kizhner and Gilel Shur, two years each; and David Rabinovich, one year.

[13] **Conference asks Jewish freedom.** The World Conference of Jewish Communities on Soviet Jewry, held in Brussels despite the Soviet government's official opposition, concluded a three-day session Feb. 25 with demands for greater freedom for Soviet Jews. A declaration released in the name of the 600 delegates affirmed "solidarity with our Jewish brothers in the Soviet Union" and called on the Soviet government "to recognize the right of Jews who so desire to return to their historic homeland in Israel . . . to enable the Jews in the Soviet Union to exercise fully their right to live in accord with the Jewish cultural and religious heritage. . . . [and] to put an end to the defamation of the Jewish people and of Zionism." The principal event of the conference was the refusal of the meeting's organizers Feb. 24 to grant permission to speak to Rabbi Meir D. Kahane, leader of the U.S.' militant Jewish Defense League (JDL, *see* [15]). Kahane was later detained for questioning by Belgian police and expelled from the country. The Soviet Union repeatedly expressed opposition to the Brussels conference. Rejecting accusations that Soviet Jews were oppressed, Gen. David A. Dragunsky, in Brussels as part of an all-Jewish delegation under the auspices of the Soviet-Belgian Friendship Society, said Feb. 19 that "the granting of emigration visas" to Soviet Jews "will be speeded up" as soon as "peace is restored to the Middle East." Dragunsky remarked: "If we let Jews of military age go to Israel they will swell the ranks of the Israeli army and soldiers and officers. This we do not want to encourage." (Albert I. Ivanov, head of the CP Central Committee section which controlled the Interior Ministry, reportedly said Sept. 20, during an interview with a Soviet Jewish delegation, that Jews with skills needed by the country would not be allowed to emigrate from the Soviet Union. It was reported Nov. 6 that 7,500 Soviet Jews had been allowed to leave the country in 1971.)

[14] **Soviets warn on Jews' harassment.** In a note handed to State Department officials Jan. 4, the Soviet Union charged the U.S. with "conniving at criminal actions" committed by "Zionist extremists" against Soviet representatives in the U.S. The Soviet note said that the U.S. had failed to provide normal working conditions for Soviet officials and it should "not expect that such conditions will be provided for U.S. premises in the Soviet Union." The note referred to anti-Soviet demonstrations by American Jews. U. Alexis Johnson, acting secretary of state, immediately rejected the Soviet note. A State Department spokesman called the anti-Soviet actions "deplorable," but insisted that they were the acts of individuals and that the U.S. government was acting to prevent further actions.

[15] **JDL activities.** Rabbi Kahane—on his way to a New York criminal court to face charges of disorderly conduct, resisting arrest and obstructing governmental administration in connection with JDL activities in 1970—Jan. 19 declared an "indefinite moratorium" on the JDL's campaign, announced Jan. 10, to "follow, question and harass" Soviet diplomats in New York. Kahane declared: "If we don't see any results, we'll go back to our harassment." The harassment had provoked a retaliatory campaign against U.S. diplomats in Moscow, and the situation was worsened by a Jan. 8 bomb explosion outside a Soviet cultural building in Washington and the smashing of a window Jan. 15 at the New York office of the Soviet airline Aeroflot. A bomb exploded April 8 at the New York offices of the Amtorg Trading Corp., the Soviet trading agency. No one was injured in the blast, which damaged the building. The incident drew an official Soviet protest April 24. Six members of the JDL were arrested Sept. 8 in New York City on charges of conspiring to bomb the agency and to plant a bomb in June at the Soviet Union's estate at Glen Cove, N.Y. A seventh member of the JDL, who was in a federal penitentiary serving a sentence on another charge, was also charged in connection with the bombing. (The bomb found June 12 at Glen Cove had been prevented from exploding by a faulty timing device.) Kahane and six other members of the JDL were arrested May 12 after being indicted earlier the same day on charges of conspiracy to violate federal gun and bomb regulations. Kahane July 9 entered a plea of guilty and July 23 was given a five-year suspended sentence, fined $5,000 and placed on probation for five years. Two other JDL members—Chaim Bieber and Stewart Cohen—also received suspended sentences for their role in the conspiracy. Bieber was given a three-year suspended sentence, fined $2,500 and placed on three-year probation. Cohen was given a three-year suspended sentence, fined $500 and placed on three-year probation. In another development, Kahane and Joseph A. Colombo Sr., founder of the Italian-American Civil Rights League and a reputed Mafia chief, announced May 13 that they would join forces to fight what they called harassment by the federal government.

See also ARMAMENTS, INTERNATIONAL; ATOMIC ENERGY [5-7, 19]; AVIATION [5, 14]; CANADA [16, 22, 25]; CARIBBEAN; CEYLON; CHILE [8]; COMMUNIST CHINA-U.S. DETENTE [5, 8]; CUBA; CZECHOSLOVAKIA [6, 8]; DEFENSE [8]; DISARMAMENT; ENERGY; ESPIONAGE; EUROPEAN SECURITY; FOREIGN POLICY; FRANCE [17]; GERMAN CONSULTATIONS; GERMANY, EAST; GERMANY, WEST [1-2]; INDIA; INDOCHINA WAR [71, 72]; JAPAN [4]; KHRUSHCHEV, NIKITA; MEXICO; MIDDLE EAST [1, 3, 20, 23-24, 26, 30]; NIXON, RICHARD MILHOUS [3]; NOBEL PRIZES; NORTH ATLANTIC TREATY ORGANIZATION; OIL; PAKISTAN [40, 42-43]; PENTAGON PAPERS [16, 18-19]; POLAND; RHODESIA; ROMAN CATHOLIC CHURCH [11]; SINO-SOVIET DEVELOPMENTS; SPACE [4-12, 23-24]; SUDAN; TRACK & FIELD; UNITED ARAB REPUBLIC; UNITED NATIONS [8, 10, 12-13]; VIETNAM, NORTH

UNITED ARAB REPUBLIC—Aswan High Dam dedicated. The Aswan High Dam in Egypt was formally dedicated Jan. 15 by U.A.R. President Anwar Sadat and Soviet President Nikolai V. Podgorny. (The dam actually had been in operation for several years, but the last of the 12 turbines had not been installed until July 1970.) The Soviet Union had assisted Egypt in building the project at a cost of more than $1 billion. Construction had begun in 1960. The dam provided Egypt with 10 billion kilowatts of electricity each year, brought 1.3 million acres of new land under cultivation and increased flood control and navigation on the Nile River.

Aly Sabry dismissed. President Sadat dismissed Aly Sabry, one of Egypt's two vice presidents, it was announced May 2. No official explanation was given for the abrupt removal of Sabry, who was regarded as pro-Soviet. Sabry was reported to have been critical of the April 17 agreement to form a federation of Egypt, Syria and Libya (*see* MIDDLE EAST [16]).

Attempted coup smashed. Sadat May 14 disclosed to the nation the smashing of an attempted coup against the Egyptian government. Sadat declared that the alleged plot to oust him had stemmed from the resignations May 13 of six Cabinet members and three top officials of the ruling Arab Socialist Union (ASU). Sadat attributed the coup attempt to opposition to the April 17 federation agreement. He said the plot was discovered when he received tape-recordings May 12 of telephone conversations by members of the ASU Central Committee and a deputy of the National Assembly. The recordings reportedly revealed a plan to forcibly prevent him from addressing the nation following a tumultuous ASU meeting April 25 on the federation.

(The meeting had voted against the federation.) Sadat said he was ordering free elections for a complete reorganization of the ASU and announced the formation of a new Cabinet to replace the six ministers who had resigned. The new Cabinet ministers (the minister who resigned the post in parentheses): war—Gen. Mohammed Ahmed Sadek (Lt. Gen. Mohammed Fawzi); interior—Mahdouh Salem (Sharawy Gomaa); information—Abdel Kader Hatem (Mohammed Fâyek); presidential affairs—Mohammed Ahmed Mohammed (Sami Sharaf); electric power—Ahmed Sultan (Helmy el-Said); and housing—Aly el-Sayed (Saad Zayed). Sadat also appointed Hussein el-Shafel as vice president, replacing Sabry. These other cabinet ministers were dismissed (their replacements in parentheses): Communications Minister Kamal Badir (Abdel Malek Saad); Youth Minister Mohammed Abul Ezz (Mustafa Kamal Tulbah); Scientific Research Minister Ahmed Mustafa Ahmed (Abd al-Wahhab al-Burullusi); Culture Minister Badr el-DinAbu Ghazy (Ismail Ghanim); and Economy Minister Mohammed el-Khawaga (Mohammad Abdullah Marzeban). Sadat May 16 appointed Maj. Gen. Saad Hussein al-Shazli as chief of staff of the armed forces.

Sadat's announcement was followed by the arrest of more than 100 suspected conspirators and a widespread shakeup of the government. Among those jailed were the six ministers who resigned May 13, the three ASU members and Sabry. The National Assembly convened in special session May 14 and voted to expel 18 members suspected of being involved in the aborted coup. Thousands of persons thronged the streets of Cairo May 15 to express their support for Sadat, and the armed forces May 15 pledged their full support for the president. In a further report on the coup, Sadat said May 20: that a Communist-oriented secret faction of the ASU had been responsible for the plot; that the ASU Central Committee had been dissolved; and that the assembly would take over the committee's functions until the ASU was restructured following new elections (held July 1). Sadat also proposed a permanent constitution, replacing the 1967 interim charter. He recommended that the new constitution insure rights for private and cooperative sectors of the largely state-owned economy, a ban against press slander of individuals, trials for all accused and state-paid legal defense for the poor.

Plotters sentenced. A three-man military tribunal in Cairo Dec. 9 sentenced Sabry, Gomaa, Sharaf and Farid Abdel Karim (former secretary of the ASU for the Greater Cairo District of Giza) to death for their connection in the May plot. Sadat immediately commuted their sentences to life in prison. Eighty-seven other persons connected with the plot received sentences ranging from one-year suspended terms to 15 years. Fourteen were acquitted. In a separate trial, a military court gave Lt. Gen. Fawzi a life sentence, later commuted by Sadat to 15 years at hard labor.

Sadat gets 'full powers.' The ASU July 26 gave President Sadat "full powers" to take any steps deemed necessary against Israel to recover all Arab territories lost in the 1967 war. Stressing the need for Egypt to be strong economically as well as militarily in confronting Israel, the ASU congress adopted a 10-year program to double national income and industrial output, rebuild the primitive villages of Egypt and eliminate illiteracy. The party also endorsed Sadat's proposal for reopening the Suez Canal, backed the proposed federation with Libya and Syria and criticized Jordan for its recent drive against the Palestinian commandos.

Sadat consolidates power. President Sadat went further toward restructuring Egypt as he dissolved the legislature Sept. 8 and announced general elections for Oct. 27. Sadat's position was strengthened Sept. 11 when the new constitution he had called for was approved by 99.98% of those voting in a nationwide referedum. The constitution, which went into effect immediately: strengthened guarantees against arbitrary arrest, seizures of property and other police-state abuses; widened the power of the assembly, empowering that body to approve presidential decrees before they became valid and allowing it to override a presidential veto by a two-thirds vote; established councils of specialists, responsible to the president, to provide more efficient and responsive governmental machinery; and established a high constitutional court which could annul legislation it judged to be unconstitutional.

New Cabinet formed. A new Cabinet was formed Sept. 19 as part of Sadat's administrative reforms program. The Ministries of Youth, Labor, Local Administration, National Assembly Affairs and Scientific Research were abolished. Two new ministerial posts were formed—Military Production and Maritime Transport. Sadat ordered the creation of an Academy of Scientific Research and Technology. The new Cabinet: Deputy premier and agriculture—Sayed Marei; deputy premier and information and culture—Hatem; economy and foreign trade, acting minister of supply and internal trade—Marzeban; planning—Sayed Gaballah Sayed; treasury—Abdel Aziz Hegazy; education—Mohammed Hafez Ghanem; religious affairs—Abdel Aziz Kamel; presidential affairs—Mohammed; Cabinet affairs—Ahmed Esmat Abdel Meguid; health and acting minister of social affairs—Ahmed el-Sayed Darwish; Manpower (formerly labor)—Abdel Latif Boltia; civil aviation—Ahmed Nouh; higher education—Mohammed Morsy Ahmed; electric power—Sultan; housing and construction—el Sayed; transport and communications—Soleiman Abdel Hai; irrigation—Mohammed Abdel Rakeeb; petroleum and mineral wealth—Ali Wali; tourism—Ibrahim Naguib; justice—Mohammed Salama; war production—Mohammed Ibrahim Hassan Selim; maritime transport—Vice Adm. Mahmoud Hamdi; and deputy minister of planning—Ismail Sabri Abdullah.

See also HIJACKING [3]; JORDAN [6-7, 10]; LIBYA; MIDDLE EAST [1, 3, 5-6, 11, 15-17, 18-20, 23, 27-29, 31-38]; SUDAN

UNITED AUTOMOBILE WORKERS (UAW)—*See* AUTOMOBILES [1]; LABOR [3, 13]; TAXES
UNITED FARM WORKERS ORGANIZING COMMITTEE (UFWOC)—*See* LABOR [2]
UNITED KINGDOM—*See* GREAT BRITAIN; NORTHERN IRELAND
UNITED MINE WORKERS (UMW)—*See* MINES

UNITED NATIONS (U.N.)—127 members. At the beginning of 1971, the 127 members (joined by Bhutan, Bahrain and Qatar Sept. 21, by Oman Sept. 30 and by the Union of Arab Emirates Dec. 8) of the U.N. were:

Afghanistan	Colombia	Greece	Liberia
Albania	Congo	Guatemala	Libya
Algeria	(Brazzaville)	Guinea	Luxembourg
Argentina	Congo	Guyana	Madagascar
Australia	(Kinshasa)	Haiti	Malawi
Austria	Costa Rica	Honduras	Malaysia
Barbados	Cuba	Hungary	Maldive Is.
Belgium	Cyprus	Iceland	Mali
Bolivia	Czechoslovakia	India	Malta
Botswana	Dahomey	Indonesia	Mauritania
Brazil	Denmark	Iran	Mauritius
Bulgaria	Dominican	Iraq	Mexico
Burma	Republic	Ireland	Mongolia
Burundi	Ecuador	Israel	Morocco
Byelorussia	Equatorial	Italy	Nepal
Cambodia	Guinea	Ivory Coast	Netherlands
Cameroon	El Salvador	Jamaica	New Zealand
Canada	Ethiopia	Japan	Nicaragua
Central African	Fiji	Jordan	Niger
Republic	Finland	Kenya	Nigeria
Ceylon	France	Kuwait	Norway
Chad	Gabon	Laos	Pakistan
Chile	Gambia	Lebanon	Panama
China	Ghana	Lesotho	Paraguay

Peru	Somalia	Togo	U. S.
Philippines	South Africa	Trinidad &	Upper Volta
Poland	Southern Yemen	Tobago	Uruguay
Portugal	Spain	Tunisia	Venezuela
Rumania	Sudan	Turkey	Yemen
Rwanda	Swaziland	Uganda	Yugoslavia
Saudi Arabia	Sweden	Ukraine	Zambia
Senegal	Syria	U. S. S. R.	
Sierra Leone	Tanzania	U. A. R.	
Singapore	Thailand	U. K. (Britain)	

[2]   **Councils.** The membership of the U.N. Security Council, Economic and Social Council and Trusteeship Council as of Jan. 1 (terms expire Dec. 31 of the year indicates): *Security Council*—Permanent members (5): U.S., Britain, France, U.S.S.R. and Nationalist China. Non-permanent members (10): Burundi (1971), Nicaragua (1971), Poland (1971), Sierra Leone (1971), Syria (1971), Argentina (1972), Belgium (1972), Italy (1972), Japan (1972), Somalia (1972). *Economic & Social Council*—Twenty-seven non-permanent members: Indonesia (1971), Jamaica (1971), Norway (1971), Pakistan (1971), U.S.S.R. (1971), Sudan (1971), United Kingdom (1971), Uruguay (1971), Yugoslavia (1971), Brazil (1972), Ceylon (1972), Ghana (1972), Greece (1972), Italy (1972), Kenya (1972), Peru (1972), Tunisia (1972), France (1972), Congo (Kinshasa) (1973), Haiti (1973), Hungary (1973), Lebanon (1973), Madagascar (1973), Malaysia (1973), New Zealand (1973), Niger (1973), U.S. (re-elected) (1973). *Trusteeship Council*—Three permanent members: Nationalist China, France and the U.S.S.R. Trust administering states: Australia, the U.S., Britain. President: Laurence McIntyre of Australia.

[3]   **World Court.** Membership of the International Court of Justice at the Hague (nine-year terms expire Feb. 5 of the year indicated): Sir Gerald Fitzmaurice, Britain (1973); Muhammad Zafrullah Khan, Pakistan (1973); Luis Padilla Nervo, Mexico (1973); Isaac Forster, Senegal (1973); Andre Gros, France (1973); Fouad Ammoun, Lebanon (1976); Cesar Bengzon, Philippines (1976); Sture Petren, Sweden (1976); Manfred Lachs, Poland (1976); Charles D. Onyeama, Nigeria (1976); Federico de Castro, Spain (1979); Hardy C. Dillard, U.S. (1979); Louis Ignacio-Pinto, Dahomey (1979); Eduardo Jimenez de Arechaga, Uruguay (1979) and Platon D. Morozov, U.S.S.R. (1979). President: Muhammad Zafrullah Khan of Pakistan.

[4]   **U.S., Britain withdraw from colonialism committee.** The U.S. and Great Britain withdrew from the 24-member U.N. colonialism committee Jan. 11. Their decisions were announced in separate letters signed by U.S. Ambassador Charles Yost and British Ambassador Sir Colin Crowe, and sent to Secretary General U Thant. Neither Britain nor the U.S. offered explanations for their action, but both had long been critical of the committee's work and had reportedly complained that the unit was dominated by members of the African-Asian and Communist blocs. In the 1970 session of the General Assembly, Britain and the U.S. had voted against a resolution (passed by the committee) which included an assertion that all forms of colonialism constituted crimes against humanity and thus violations of the U.N. Charter.

[5]   **26th Assembly convenes.** The 26th session of the U.N. General Assembly opened in New York Sept. 21 with the election of Adam Malik, Indonesian foreign minister, as its president. (Since this was Asia's year for the presidency, members of the U.N. Asian bloc had agreed on his candidacy two months before.)

[6]   **Korean debate delayed until 1972.** The General Committee, the General Assembly's steering committee, voted Sept. 23 to delete three questions concerning Korea from the Assembly's agenda since North and South Korea were engaging in the first peaceful contacts since the Korean War. The three Korean items were a request for "withdrawal of U.S. and all other foreign forces" from Korea, a proposal for the dissolution of the U.N. Commission for

the Unification and Rehabilitation of Korea (UNCURK), and the report by the commission. The items had been requested for debate by the Soviet Union and other Communist and third-world countries. Britain, however, had proposed that the Assembly table the issues because of the "very important and hopeful development" of talks between the Red Cross societies of the two Koreas (*see* KOREAN NEGOTIATIONS). The committee voted 13-9 with two abstentions for the British proposal. The General Assembly Sept. 25 upheld the committee decision by a vote of 68-28, with 22 abstentions.

[7] **Communist China accepted, Taiwan expelled.** The General Assembly Oct. 25 voted 76-35 (17 abstentions) to approve a motion sponsored by Albania and 20 other nations calling for the seating of the People's Republic of China (Communist China) as the sole representative of China and for the expulsion of Taiwan (Nationalist China). The vote, taken at an unexpected evening session, marked the final defeat for the U.S. in its attempt to keep Nationalist China in the U.N. The vote was greeted with cheers and jubilation from many of the delegates in the Assembly. The Assembly earlier had defeated a U.S. resolution to declare the explusion of Taiwan an important question requiring a two-thirds majority. That vote was 59-55 with 15 abstentions. The assembly had also defeated a move by Saudi Arabia Ambassador Jamil Baroody to delay voting on the key resolutions until Oct. 26. Moments before the vote on the Albanian resolution and after the "important question" issue had been defeated, Liu Chieh, the Chinese Nationalist representative, announced from the podium that his government would no longer take part in the proceedings. He led the Nationalist delegation out of the Assembly.

[8] *Reaction to vote.* In a statement approved by President Nixon, the Administration Oct. 26 welcomed the admission of Communist China as "consistent with the policy of the U.S." but said that, "at the same time, the U.S. deeply regrets the action taken by the U.N. to deprive the Republic of China of representation in that organization." In the U.S. Congress, Sens. James Buckley (Conservative, N.Y.) and Peter Dominick (R, Colo.) said Oct. 27 that they were working on legislation to reduce the U.S. contribution to the U.N.'s specialized agencies. Japanese Premier Eisaku Sato was subjected to bitter attacks from the four opposition parties, labor unions, the press and some members of his own party for backing the U.S. effort to keep Taiwan in the U.N. President Chiang Kai-shek of Nationalist China Oct. 26 denounced the General Assembly for voting the People's Republic into the U.N. Several of Taiwan's newspapers blamed the expulsion on the lack of U.S. sincerity in the final fight. Secretary General Thant expressed sadness at the departure of the Taiwanese, but said the vote "should not be considered in terms of either victory or defeat, but as an essential step towards a more effective and realistic international system." Most Asian governments welcomed the vote; the only two Asian nations to unequivocally criticize it were the two that faced rival Communist regimes—South Korea and South Vietnam. The Soviet Union Oct. 27 applauded the vote as a "triumph of common sense." France Oct. 26 hailed the vote as an act of common sense and realism.

[9] *Background on vote.* U.N. debate on the question of seating of China opened Oct. 18. The U.S. had announced Aug. 2 that it would "support action at the General Assembly this fall calling for seating the People's Republic of China." (At the same time, the U.S. emphasized its continued resistance to any move to expel Nationalist China.) The U.S. move ended 20 years of opposition to Communist China's presence in the U.N. The U.S. Aug. 17 submitted to U Thant for inclusion on the General Assembly agenda a document entitled Representation of China in the U.N. The document included two resolutions: the first declaring the seating of China to be an important question; and the second calling for the admission to membership of the People's Republic and the continuation of Nationalist China's membership. The General Assembly Sept. 24 defeated an Albanian move to reverse a decision by the U.N.'s scheduling committee Sept. 22 to place the U.S. resolution on seating China on the agenda. Albania's own resolution for seating, entered on the agenda in July, was not

challenged. The vote to accept the U.S. resolution was 65-47, with 15 abstentions and three absentees. (The U.S. resolutions were to be considered after the Albanian resolution.)

[10] *China names delegation.* China Nov. 2 announced the appointment of the following delegation to the U.N.: Chiao Kuan-hua, a deputy foreign minister and close associate of Premier Chou En-lai, as head of the nine-man delegation to the General Assembly; Huang Hua, ambassador to Canada, as deputy head of the delegation and permanent representative to the Security Council; Fu Hao, secretary of the Communist party's social department, as representative; Hsiung Hsiang-hui, former charge d'affaires to Britain, as representative; Chen Chu, director of the Foreign Ministry's information department, as representative and assistant to Huang; Tang Ming-chao, member of the CP Central Committee's international department, as deputy representative; An Chih-yuan, a career diplomat, as deputy representative; Wang Hai-jung, deputy director of protocol in the Foreign Ministry and the only woman in the delegation, as deputy representative; and Chang Yung-kuan as deputy representative. The U.S. had announced Nov. 1 that it had waived visa requirements for the Chinese delegates to facilitate their arrival in New York. (The U.S. Nov. 11 also announced its intention of granting Chinese diplomats at the U.N. travel privileges equal to those enjoyed by Soviet officials—unrestricted travel in an area 25 miles in radius from Columbus Circle in New York and travel elsewhere upon 48-hour notice to the U.S. State Department. Both Soviet and Chinese officials were forbidden to visit an area comprising roughly 25% of the U.S. and including strategic installations.) An advance party of six Chinese arrived in New York Nov. 8 to arrange housing and offices for the China delegation. The delegation and 45 other officials arrived in New York Nov. 11 and took their seats in the U.N. Nov. 15. In other China developments in the U.N.: The People's Republic, rather than Taiwan, was recognized Oct. 29 by the U.N. Educational, Scientific and Cultural Organization (UNESCO) as the sole legitimate representative of China to the agency; the U.N. Food and Agriculture Organization, according to report Nov. 5, unanimously voted to invite the People's Republic into the organization; the International Labor Organization (ILO) voted Nov. 16 to seat a delegation from Peking and expel one from Nationalist China; the delegation of the People's Republic took its seat in the Security Council Nov. 23; and the U.N. Dec. 17 withdrew accreditation for two Nationalist Chinese correspondents representing the Central News Agency of China. Secretary General Thant endorsed the order on the ground that the vote ousting Taiwan also applied to employees of the official news agency.

[11] **Raise voted for secretary general.** The General Assembly voted Nov. 29 to raise the salary of the secretary general as of Dec. 1 by $12,500 a year to $62,500, and his pension to $31,250. The vote by a show of hands was 95-0, with eight abstentions. Secretary General Thant would be the first beneficiary of the pension, which was approximately doubled.

[12] **Austrian chosen secretary general.** Kurt Waldheim, Austria's chief delegate to the U.N., was chosen by the Security Council Dec. 21 to succeed Secretary General Thant, who had announced Jan. 18 that he had no wish to remain in the job after his second five-year term expired Dec. 31. The nomination of Waldheim was ratified by a secret ballot in the General Assembly Dec. 22. Waldheim was chosen in the Security Council's third secret session after being vetoed twice by China. (To be elected, a candidate had to have at least nine affirmative votes and no veto against him. Negative votes by any of the five pemanent members of the Security Council—including China—constituted a veto.) In balloting Dec. 21, China's abstention resulted in Waldheim's election with 11 affirmatives, one negative and three abstentions. It was reported Dec. 22 that one of Waldheim's greatest assets was that he was a preferred candidate of the U.S.S.R. and that none of the other big powers strongly opposed him. The U.S. reportedly supported the candidacy of Finnish Ambassador Max Jakobsen, who received nine votes, five against (including the

U.S.S.R.) and one abstention. American officials were reported to believe that Jakobsen would have provided more dynamic leadership of the U.N. at a time when its prestige was at an all-time low. However, Russia, traditionally opposed to a strong secretary general, preferred to see power remain concentrated in the Security Council. There were six candidates in the final balloting: Waldheim; Jakobson; Argentine Ambassador Carlos Ortiz de Rozas, who was vetoed by the U.S.S.R.; Swedish Ambassador Gunnar Jarring; former Foreign Minister Gabriel Valdes of Chile; and Felipe Herrera of Chile, former president of the Inter-American Development Bank.

[13]   **U.N. votes budget for 1972.** On the last day of the 26th session, the General Assembly voted to adopt a $213,124,410 budget for 1972. It was 10.5% higher than the 1971 budget. The Soviet Union voted against the expenditure budget. Britain, France and the U.S. abstained. China did not participate. All had been critical of U.N. spending practices.

See also AFRICA; AUSTRALIA [8]; CHEMICAL & BIOLOGICAL WARFARE; COMMUNIST CHINA-U.S. DETENTE [1]; COPYRIGHTS, INTERNATIONAL; CYPRUS; DISARMAMENT; DISASTERS; FOREIGN AID; FRANCE [17]; JAPAN [12-13]; JORDAN [12]; MICRONESIA; MIDDLE EAST [1, 6, 11, 27-28, 30-31, 33, 35-37, 39]; PAKISTAN [20, 32-34, 42]; PANAMA; PRISONS [10]; RHODESIA; SENEGAL; SOUTH AFRICA [2, 7, 12-13]; SOUTH PACIFIC FORUM; SPACE [13]; TERRITORIAL WATERS; TURKEY

UNITED PRESS INTERNATIONAL (UPI)—*See* CHILE [10]
UNITED PRISONERS UNION (UPU)—*See* PRISONS [10]

UPPER VOLTA — In a decree published Feb. 22, President Sangoule Lamizana established the new cabinet as follows: Gerard Kango Ouedraogo— premier and minister of ex-servicemen's affairs; Capt. Gabriel Some—interior and security; Malick Zorome—justice and keeper of the seals; Joseph Conombo—foreign affairs; Daouda Traore—national defense; Tiemoko Marc Garango—finance and commerce; Diongolo Traore—social affairs; Francois Lompo—public works, transport and town planning; Edouard Yameogo— industry, mines and planning; Capt. Antoine Dakoure—agriculture, animal husbandry, water, forestry resources and tourism; Victor Ouedraogo—labor and civil service; Charles Tamini—national education and culture; Dr. Ali Barraud—health and population; Maj. Bila Jean Zagre—information; Dr. Youl Tigaret—posts and telecommunications; and Capt. Felix Tientaraboum—youth and sports.

URBAN AFFAIRS—*See* NEGROES; STATE & LOCAL GOVERNMENT
URBAN RENEWAL—*See* HOUSING

URUGUAY—Cabinet changes. Interior Minister Antonio Francese, reportedly a hard-liner in the fight against the Tupamaros guerrillas, resigned Jan. 19, apparently at the request of President Jorge Pacheco Areco. Francese was replaced by Gen. Rafael J. Milans, who resigned from the post Jan. 21 and was succeeded by Sen. Santiago de Brum Carbajal. Pacheco was faced with a Cabinet crisis April 2 when three of his ministers resigned. Foreign Minister Jorge Peirano Facio was replaced by Jose Mora Otero; Defense Minister Cesar Borba was succeeded by Frederico Garcia Capurro; and Industry and Commerce Minister Julio Sanguinetti was replaced by Juan Pedro Amestoy. The resignations of Carbajal and Culture Minister Angel Rath were reported June 3. Pacheco temporarily replaced Rath with Capurro. Brig. Gen. Danilo Sena, a staunch anti-Communist, was named to the interior post.

[2]   **Struggle over security measures.** A group of congressmen composed of members of the opposition National party and of the left-wing coalition known as the Frente Amplio (Broad Front, formed Feb. 14) passed a resolution July 14 in the General Legislative Assembly calling for the immediate lifting of security measures taken under the state of seige imposed in June 1969. The resolution was intended to establish civil liberties believed essential for the holding of general elections Nov. 28. The security laws repealed by the congress

permitted press censorship, holding of suspects without charge, banning of demonstrations, public meetings and strikes, and the deportation of any person considered a threat to the government. Other security measures, adopted by the government by decree, were not lifted by the resolution for fear that such action would lead to administrative chaos. (The decrees would have had to be made into law if the full state of emergency were lifted.) President Pacheco reimposed the security laws July 15, touching off a major confrontation with the congress and a 24-hour national strike July 20 by the leftist National Convention of Workers (CNT). The work stoppage was almost entirely effective in paralyzing the country.

[3] **Chamber votes impeachment.** The Chamber of Deputies (lower house) voted July 23 to impeach President Pacheco for his restoration of the repealed security measures. Pacheco had justified his action on the grounds that he had "indisputable" proof "of the designs of certain groups and organizations to destroy the republican-democratic institutions and to attack inherent human rights." The impeachment was initiated by the National party, the Frente Amplio and several dissident members of the President's Colorado party. The groups accused the president of having "violated the constitution" by ignoring the Assembly's repeal of the state of emergency. The Chamber approved the impeachment motion by a 52-2 vote. The impeachment proceedings were brought to a standstill in August. The Senate Aug. 3 decided (by an 18-14 vote) to set up a commission to investigate the Chamber's accusation that the president had violated the constitution. The resolution was opposed by the Frente Amplio, which preferred that the full Senate begin its deliberations immediately. The newly created commission was to give the president 10 days to answer the charges and defend his actions. Pacheco responded Aug. 4 with a brief note in which he reiterated his original reason for reimposing the security measures.

[4] **Rioting follows student's death.** Several hundred students, protesting the death of a fellow student (Heber Nieto) July 24, rioted in front of the University of the Republic July 27, clashing with police who used tear gas to disperse them. Nieto had been one of a group of students stopping vehicles outside the Institute for the Study of Construction and asking for a "toll" to help workers in industrial conflicts and to provide funds for the enlargement of the school's building. The students stoned a bus whose driver refused to comply. Nieto was reportedly killed by police who arrived at the school and began shooting at the students.

[5] **106 Tupamaros escape from prison.** Tupamaro guerrillas Sept. 6 freed 106 Tupamaros and five "common criminals" from the maximum security Punta Carretas prison in an escape through a 40-foot tunnel dug from the house across the street from the prison into a prison cell. (Thirty-eight female Tupamaros had escaped from a maximum security prison in Montevideo July 30.) The stunned government censored news of the escape for seven hours while police and military chiefs met with Pacheco. Uruguyan director of prisons, Col. Pascual Circilo, resigned Sept. 7 and Pacheco named Police Inspector Uruguay Genta to succeed him as prison director. The escape followed several incidents of terrorist activity and police counteraction. The guerrillas had increased their arsenal Aug. 31 by seizing 30 long and short arms from an armory. Soldiers and police were deployed throughout Montevideo Sept. 8 in an unsuccessful attempt to catch the 106 Tupamaros. President Pacheco announced Sept. 9 that, for the first time in the nation's history, the armed forces would be put in full charge of fighting guerrilla subversion. (The police had previously been charged with fighting the Tupamaros.) In a rare radio and television address Sept. 16, the armed forces announced they would fulfill their mission with "the necessary tenacity" to insure final success. It was the first time in 30 years that the military had issued a joint statement. Police Oct. 16 and 19 recaptured seven of the escapees. Two more were arrested Nov. 12.

[6] **Government candidate elected president.** Amid bitter opposition accusations of electoral fraud, the government issued provisional figures Dec. 2

giving its Colorado candidate, Agriculture Minister Juan Maria Bordaberry (hand-picked as an alternate candidate by Pacheco), a narrow 10,843 vote lead over National party candidate Sen. Wilson Ferreira Aldunate in the Nov. 28 presidential elections. Ferreira had won the largest personal vote of 11 presidential candidates, but under the complex Uruguayan electoral system, votes cast for all candidates under the same party accrued to the leading party candidate. Pacheco also ran for a second term, but lost when voters rejected a constitutional amendment, voted on simultaneously with the Nov. 28 election, that would have removed the existing ban on a president succeeding himself. Ferreira, who campaigned on a nationalist program (he would establish diplomatic relations with Cuba and nationalize the banks) and who had been promised a six-month grace period by the Tupamaros, charged the government Dec. 1 with electoral "fraud" and alleged "irregularities" in 38 Montevideo polling districts. About 11,000 votes were at stake. Ferreira also alleged Dec. 2 that 25,000 votes had not been cast for Bordaberry, but for Pacheco. The National party had demanded Dec. 1 that the armed forces supervise an official vote recount begun by the national Electoral Court. Bands of National party supporters, angry that all the votes were not completely counted three days after the polls closed, were organizing protest marches. It was the closest Uruguayan election in 30 years.

[7]   According to report Dec. 2, the Colorado party received 594,800 votes, the National party 583,957 votes, and the Frente Amplio coalition 271,957 votes. More than 70,000 absentee votes remained to be counted, but most observers felt that the odds were with Bordaberry and the Colorados, which had ruled Uruguay for all but eight of the past 106 years. Due to the heavy turnout, the Electoral Court ordered a 4½-hour extension of polling. Voting was obligatory in Uruguay and it was announced for the first time that a fine of about $5 would be levied against those who failed to vote. Non-voters would also face complications in collections of pensions and public paychecks. More than a third of the population depended on the central government for income.

[8]   Uruguayans also voted Nov. 28 to fill elective offices for vice president, municipal officials and congressmen. It was reported Dec. 5 that the National party won 15 of 19 departmental mayoralities. It was also reported that the Colorado party lost Congressional seats to National and Frente Amplio candidates. Figures Dec. 2 reported that the lineup in the Senate would be 13 Colorados, 12 Nationalists, and six Frente Amplio candidates. The House of Deputies would seat 41 Colorados, 40 Nationals and 18 leftists. In the last Congress there were 16 Colorado senators, 11 Nationals and four leftists. The lower house had 48 Colorados, 41 Nationals and 10 leftists.

Kidnapings

[9]   **British envoy captured.** About 20 Tupamaros Jan. 8 kidnaped British Ambassador to Uruguay Geoffrey Jackson as he was being driven to the British embassy in Montevideo. Uruguay immediately began a massive police search for the kidnapers. President Pacheco's government made it clear Jan. 9 that it would not negotiate with the kidnapers for Jackson's release. Pacheco Jan. 11 asked the Assembly for 90-day special police powers to aid in the search for the kidnapers. The 11-member Legislative Commission, serving during the Assembly's annual recess, complied with the request, but reduced the duration of the emergency powers from 90 to 40 days (see [10]). Under the emergency law, habeas corpus was nullified and police were authorized to search homes without warrants and hold suspicious persons indefinitely. A series of calls April 7, requesting Jackson's medical history, said the British ambassador had had a heart attack that day. The Tupamaros released Jackson Sept. 9. Jackson was taken to a hospital for a physical examination. He said he was "feeling fine." The Tupamaros had issued a statement Sept. 8 saying that Jackson would be granted an "amnesty" since there was no further need to hold the ambassador in return for the release of prisoners. The statement referred to the Tupamaros escape Sept. 6 (see [5]).

[10] **Dias Gomide freed.** Brazilian Vice Consul in Montevideo Aloysio Mares Dias Gomide was released outside the city by his Tupamaros kidnapers Feb. 21. His wife, Maria, obtained his freedom after paying a ransom estimated at $250,000-$1 million. (The Tupamaros had originally demanded $1 million ransom.) Dias Gomide, who had been kidnaped July 31, 1970, reported that his kidnapers had treated him "very well" during his captivity, but said he had been kept alone and in one place the entire time. The Tupamaros had issued a communique Feb. 13 stating that negotiations for Dias Gomide's release had been completed and that he would be released after constitutional rights in Uruguay had been restored. (Pacheco had requested that the emergency law suspending constitutional rights be extended, but the Legislative Commission turned down the request Feb. 17 and the decree expired Feb. 20. Pacheco again sought an extension of the decree March 17, but was turned down by the Assembly March 18.)

[11] **Fly freed.** U.S. agronomist Claude L. Fly was released by his Tupamaros kidnapers March 2 after apparently suffering a heart attack while in their custody. Fly had been kidnaped Aug. 7, 1970. Fly, who had a heart condition before the kidnaping, was reported in "delicate condition and resting" March 3. The Tupamaros March 3 issued a statement reporting that Fly had been told Feb. 18 of his release in the near future, but that he had suffered a heart attack Feb. 23. The statement said that Fly's release was part of an amnesty. Fly's wife, Miriam, and son, John, charged March 3 that the Uruguayan government and the U.S. State Department had refused to negotiate with the Tupamaros for Fly's release. (The Tupamaros had reportedly sent a letter to Fly's wife in January, demanding $1 million in ransom for Fly's release. The U.S. State Department Jan. 16 had said that "whether or not the letter is authentic, the U.S. government is not prepared to contribute to a ransom by private individuals.")

[12] **Other kidnapings.** Among other kidnapings in Uruguay: Guido Berro Oribe, Uruguayan attorney general, was kidnaped March 10 and released March 23 after he reportedly admitted, during a "people's tribunal" by the Tupamaros, that Pacheco had pressured the nation's public prosecutors to block the release of detained Tupamaros; Ulyses Pereira Reverbel, director of the state-owned power and telephone company and a confidant of Pacheco, was kidnaped by the Tupamaros March 30; Alfredo Cambon, legal adviser to several Uruguayan companies backed by American funds, was kidnaped June 23 by a left-wing terrorist group called the Organization of the Popular Revolution-33 (OPR-33) and released June 25; Jorge Berembaum, an Argentine-born industrialist, was kidnaped July 12 by the Tupamaros, who demanded $1 million in ransom July 28, and released Nov. 26; Carlos Alberto Laeso, Berembaum's accountant, was kidnaped by the Tupamaros Aug. 18 and released 20 hours later; Luis Fernandez Llado, vice president of a meat-packing company, was kidnaped by the Tupamaros Aug. 18 and released Oct. 10; Michele Ray, a French journalist, was kidnaped by the OPR-33 Nov. 30 and held for 38 hours.

See also ARGENTINA [11]; ATOMIC ENERGY [10]; DOMINICAN REPUBLIC; MIDDLE EAST [39]; PARAGUAY

VATICAN—*See* ROMAN CATHOLIC CHURCH
VENERA 7—*See* SPACE [6]

VENEZUELA—Talks with Colombia. Traditionally friendly relations between Venezuela and Colombia deteriorated during 1971. The two countries Jan. 31 began talks over the alleged illegal immigration of thousands of Colombians into Venezuela, where they had taken jobs of Venezuelans. (It was estimated that 500,000 Colombians were illegally residing in Venezuela.) Despite the talks, relations continued to deteriorate; and Colombia, according to report June 14, sent negotiators into Venezuela to attempt to settle the differences. Press reports from both countries spoke of the danger of war. In addition to the immigration problem, the tense atmosphere was attributed to the question of jurisdiction over the oil-rich Gulf of Venezuela bordering the two countries and the recent move by both countries to increase arms purchases. It was also reported July 17 that Colombia had begun to restrict the flow of contraband cattle, estimated at 300,000 head yearly, from Colombia to Venezuela, causing beef shortages and rising prices in Venezuelan border towns. Several border incidents were reported, and Venezuelan radio and television June 1 falsely reported a Colombian invasion of El Charo Island in the Arauca River. The reports said that troops were being mobilized to confront the Colombians. While fictitious, the reports created a furor on both sides.

Kidnapings. Venezuelan banker Enrique Dao was kidnaped in downtown Caracas Feb. 10 by armed men. He was released about 70 miles west of Caracas March 6, after his relatives had paid a ransom of $150,000-$450,000. Leon Jacobo Taurel, the 13-year-old son of a millionaire department store owner, was kidnaped March 1 on his way to school and released March 4 on the outskirts of Caracas after his father paid a ransom of $900,000. (The boy had been kidnaped in January 1970 under similar circumstances and had been released when his father paid $135,000 ransom.) Millionaire cattleman Rafael Angel Perez was kidnaped March 26 and held near Barinas until March 28 when he was rescued by army helicopters and troops. His kidnapers had demanded $115,000 in ransom. Dominican Ambassador to Venezuela Rafael Bonilla reported Sept. 30 that Mrs. Thelma Frias, consul-general of the Dominican Republic in Venezuela, had been kidnaped by leftist guerrillas in Caracas. The embassy said the kidnapers were members of the Armed Forces of National Liberation and had demanded a $1 million ransom. Venezuelan police Oct. 4 found Mrs. Frias in a Caracas apartment where they said she had been in

493

"voluntary seclusion" for four days. She insisted she had been kidnaped. Mrs. Frias and her adopted son Fausto (Dominican vice counsel in Venezuela) were expelled from Venezuela Oct. 6, and Mrs. Frias was fired from her post the same day.

Oil taxes increased. Venezuela acted March 8 to increase its tax reference base on crude oils by an average 59.5¢ a barrel, effective March 18. In addition, extra charges were imposed for low-gravity crude oil and for the short-haul freight advantage to the U.S. over competitive crude oils from other parts of the world. Venezuela also increased the reference price for heavy industrial fuel oil with high sulphur content by 75¢ a barrel, along with establishing higher prices on low-sulphur fuels. Venezuela again Dec. 21 raised its tax on oil by an average of 32¢ a barrel. Heavy high-sulphur fuel oil was reported to have been raised about 30¢ a barrel, while low-sulphur residual went up an average 75¢ a barrel. In the Dec. 21 decree, there was also a provision that U.S. and other foreign oil companies would have to increase their present production of 3.4 million barrels of oil a day to the 1970 rate of 3.7 million daily or pay increased special taxes. Production drops below 2% of base year 1970 and increases larger that 6% would be penalized by a progressively rising surtax.

Student unrest. Student demonstrations that broke out April 19 continued with increased intensity through May. Two causes of the protests were the issue of Central University in Caracas which had remained closed since October 1970, and the presence of a South Vietnamese delegation at a World Interplanetary Conference that took place in Caracas in mid-April. Since that time, five persons had been killed, 50 injured and 500 persons arrested in violent clashes with police. Minister of Education Hector Hernandez Garabano May 16 ordered all high schools in Caracas and the surrounding state of Miranda closed "indefinitely" after disorders again broke out May 11. The demonstrations had spread to several parts of the country, including La Guaira where one student was killed May 13, San Cristobal, Maracaibo and Merida. Classes were suspended throughout the country May 18. Observers believed that the student disorders were aggravated by political maneuvering between the ruling COPEI party and the opposition Democratic Action (AD). AD blamed the government for the incidents, while COPEI accused AD of instigating the disorders. The government again blamed the political parties for instigating student violence Oct. 26-27 in Caracas and other cities. Classes were suspended to avoid new disturbances after one student was killed and 86 arrested. The students were protesting the closure of the Central University and harsh security force action in student protests.

Hydrocarbons bill. The Chamber of Deputies June 18 and the Senate July 19 passed the Hydrocarbons Reversion Law which would lead to the eventual nationalization of the foreign-owned oil industry and legal national ownership of oil installations and equipment when the 40-year concessions expire in 1983-84. The bill had been criticized by members of the foreign-owned oil industry. Under terms of the legislation, signed by President Rafael Caldera July 30, foreign oil companies would be placed under state direction until the concessions expire. The law gave the government immediate authority to inspect drilling equipment, pipelines and refineries. The state would have the sole right to grant permission for moving equipment from one oil site to another and could determine when and where new wells would be drilled to develop new oil reserves. The law would require oil companies to place between $500 million and $1 billion in a central bank fund to guarantee reversion of the properties to the government and to insure the maintenance of the properties. It also required government authorization for any repatriation of profits and dividends by the oil companies to their parent firms.

Cabinet changes. President Caldera announced July 29 the third Cabinet change since taking office in 1969. Minister of Education Hernandez would become development minister, replacing Haydee Castillo; the deacon of the law faculty of the Central University of Venezuela, Enrique Perez Olivares, was designated minister of education; Brig. Gen. Martin Garcia Villasmil, minister of defense, would be replaced by Vice Admiral Jesus Carbonell Izquierdo.

Gas nationalization. President Caldera Aug. 26 signed into law a modified version of a bill nationalizing the country's natural gas industry. The legislation was originally sponsored by Caldera and the COPEI, but the opposition parties which controlled both houses of Congress introduced certain modifications which led to COPEI's withdrawal of support in the Congress. The legislation established a state monopoly for the extraction of natural gas and stipulated that the government could make use of the product in concessions to international private enterprises without paying compensation. A Senate committee had modified the bill, eliminating the possible participation of private capital in the natural gas export programs. The changes also eliminated the compensation for the gas taken from private firms and limited the type available for exportation. The government had been opposed to the changes, contending that the modifications would limit the government's plans for the investment of $1 billion to export 1.3 billion cubic feet of natural gas daily to the U.S. by 1975.

See also HIJACKING [1]; LATIN AMERICA; OIL

VENUS—*See* SPACE [6]
VETERANS ADMINISTRATION (VA)—*See* DRUG USE & ADDICTION [1, 19]
VIET CONG—*See* COMMUNIST CHINA-U.S. DETENTE [8]; INDOCHINA WAR; PENTAGON PAPERS [21, 24]

VIETNAM, NORTH (PEOPLE'S REPUBLIC OF VIETNAM)—**Elections.** North Vietnamese citizens went to the polls April 11 for the first time since 1964 to elect a new National Assembly. A total of 529 candidates contested 420 seats. The term of the current legislature, elected in 1964, had expired in 1968, but remained in office because of the war. Among the deputies elected in the latest balloting were President Ton Duc Thang, Premier Pham Van Dong, Le Duan, first secretary of the ruling Workers (Communist) party, and Truong Chinh, chairman of the National Assembly. The assembly June 7 re-elected all but one of the nation's top leaders in its first session since the elections. Deputy Premier Pham Hung was dropped from the official list without explanation.

Soviet-North Vietnam accord. The creation of a joint Soviet-North Vietnamese committee to formulate long-term economic, trade, cultural scientific and technological relations between the two nations was announced in a statement broadcast by Hanoi radio Oct. 10, one day after completion of a six-day visit to Hanoi by an official Soviet mission headed by President Nikolai V. Podgorny. The Podgorny delegation also signed new military and economic aid and trade agreements, details of which were not disclosed. The statement reported a Soviet commitment to undertake prospecting and technological studies for a possible hydroelectric project on the Da River in North Vietnam. In addition to a fresh expression of Soviet support for the North Vietnamese war with the U.S., the statement also affirmed Soviet and North Vietnamese support for the political program of the Peking-based National United Front of Cambodia, which called for a U.S. withdrawal and the takeover of power in Cambodia by the Front. (Moscow presently recognized the government of anti-Communist ruler Lon Nol.)

The Podgorny trip closely followed a visit by a Peking economic and military mission to Hanoi and the conclusion of an aid pact between the two nations Sept. 28. Podgorny was the first high-level Soviet official to visit North Vietnam since Soviet Premier Aleksei N. Kosygin attended the funeral of the late President Ho Chi Minh in 1969.

Denmark, Norway set ties. Denmark and Norway announced simultaneously in Copenhagen and Oslo Nov. 25 a decision to establish diplomatic relations with North Vietnam at the ambassadorial level. Their ambassadors to Communist China would also serve as ambassadors to Hanoi. Denmark and Norway were the first members of the North Atlantic Treaty Organization to establish formal relations with North Vietnam.

See also COMMUNIST CHINA-U.S. DETENTE [2, 5]; FLOODS; INDOCHINA WAR; NORWAY; PENTAGON PAPERS [16, 19, 23-27]; TARIFFS & WORLD TRADE [7]

VIETNAM, SOUTH (REPUBLIC OF VIETNAM)—Con Son jail to be rebuilt.

The U.S. mission in Saigon announced Feb. 20 that the U.S. would provide $400,000 to build 288 isolation cells to replace the notorious disciplinary Tiger Cage cells at the South Vietnamese prison on Con Son island, a detention center for political dissidents. The mission said a private American construction firm would build the project. The State Department said Feb. 19 that all prisoners had been removed from Con Son and that the new cells would house only ordinary criminals. In a related development, U.S. journalist Don Luce, who had exposed the tiger cages at Con Son, left South Vietnam May 9 after being ordered to leave. Luce attributed his expulsion to his coverage of the tiger cage story and his continued criticism of the South Vietnamese prison system.

Cabinet shift. Prime Minister Tran Thien Khiem was reported June 11 to have reshuffled his cabinet, transferring one minister, replacing three others and creating a new Ministry of Planning. Finance Minister Nguyen Bich Hue was replaced by his deputy, Ha Xuan Trung. Information Minister Ngo Khac Tinh was shifted to head the Education Ministry, replacing Nguyen Luu Vien, who remained deputy prime minister. Truong Buu Dien was named information minister. Truong Nai Liet replaced Paul Nur as minister of ethnic minorities. Le Tuan Anh was appointed to head the Ministry of Planning.

Presidential Election

Election law. The House of Representatives (lower chamber of the National Assembly) June 3 approved by a 101-21 vote an amendment to the nominating clause of the electoral law. The measure, signed by President Nguyen Van Thieu June 23, required a presidential candidate to have his nomination papers signed by 40 deputies and senators or by 100 members of the elected provincial councils. Thieu, who controlled a majority of the Assembly legislators and of the provincial councils, was the only candidate for the Oct. 3 presidential election who would have little difficulty in meeting the petition requirements. (The House had adopted the measure previously, but it was rejected by the Senate. In order to revive the legislation, the lower chamber had to approve it a second time with a two-thirds majority.)

Candidates enter race. President Thieu July 24 announced his candidacy for re-election. Thieu chose Sen. Tran Van Huong, a former premier, as his vice presidential running mate and Premier Khiem as an alternate running mate. Gen. Duong Van Minh announced his candidacy July 26, but warned that he would withdraw from the contest if he thought it was rigged by the president. Minh selected Dr. Ho Van Minh, deputy speaker of the House as his running mate and Sen. Hong Son as his alternate. Vice President Nguyen Cao Ky submitted his candidacy for the presidency Aug. 4, but his application was rejected by the Supreme Court Aug. 5. The court, which approved Thieu's and Minh's slates the same day, disqualified Ky because 40 of the 102 provincial council signatures submitted by Ky had already signed for Thieu. Ky charged that the signatures were rightfully his because the councilmen had been tricked into endorsing Thieu before passage of the new election law and before they knew Ky would oppose Thieu. Ky said Aug. 12 that the tribunal's decision was illegal and that he still considered himself a candidate. The court Aug. 21 reversed its decision and reinstated Ky as a candidate.

Minh, Ky withdraw. Both Minh (Aug. 20) and Ky (Aug. 23) withdrew from the race charging that Thieu was rigging the election. Both men resisted American pressure to stay in the race. (An aide to Minh disclosed Sept. 3 that U.S. Ambassador Ellsworth Bunker Aug. 19 had offered to finance Minh's campaign. Minh rejected the offer.) With their withdrawal, President Thieu was unopposed, rousing U.S. fears that an uncontested election would have profound political repercussions in South Vietnam and the U.S. Minh's formal withdrawal application, submitted to the Supreme Court, was coupled with several documents which he claimed proved the government was manipulating the election. According to the papers, the Saigon regime was engaging in a countrywide campaign to employ "schemes, ruses and maneuvers directed at political parties" and other groups "in order to persuade wavering people and to manipulate and paralyze opposition blocs." In his statement withdrawing from the race, Ky said "legal irregularities" precluded his remaining a candidate. He accused Thieu of "an indescribable conspiracy to rig the election and use it as a tool for personal gain." Ky proposed that he and Thieu resign to permit the president of the South Vietnamese Senate to form a transition government that would organize new elections. The vice president said he would run in such new elections provided that all province chiefs and other subordinates appointed by Thieu were removed to insure fair balloting. Ky requested the Supreme Court Aug. 26 to remove his name from the slate. The court Sept. 1 announced that Thieu would be the only candidate in the Oct. 3 elections.

Thieu sets majority as goal. President Thieu Sept. 11 officially opened his campaign by declaring that he would resign if he did not receive 50% of the vote in the election. (He had stated Sept. 2 that he regarded the outcome of the election as a test of popular support of his policies and that he would not accept another four-year term "if the results show clearly that the people do not have confidence in me." The White House said Sept. 2 that Thieu's declaration "suggests he is obviously attempting to introduce an element of popular choice to the election." Secretary of State William P. Rogers said Sept. 3 that the U.S. accepted Thieu's decision to run unopposed.) Thieu said that voters wishing to oppose him could cast "an irregular ballot as a ballot expressing nonconfidence." He did not explain what an irregular ballot was, but Saigon sources had reported Sept. 10 that the only proposal Thieu would accept on such ballots was that ballots could be invalidated by mutilating them or throwing them away. The U.S. Sept. 13 publicly called on Thieu to explain how ballots could be cast against him. Thieu confirmed Sept. 20 that a "no confidence" vote could be cast against him by tearing the ballot, marking it in a way that would invalidate it or leaving it blank.

Opposition to Thieu. Opposition to Thieu's unopposed candidacy came from many quarters. A special session of the South Vietnamese Senate Sept. 22 passed a resolution urging Thieu to postpone the elections and organize new ones "in accordance with democratic procedures." The resolution stated that the appearance of only one candidate exacerbated internal unrest, threatened the survival of the country and ignored the wishes of the people. The militant anti-government An Quang Buddhist faction Sept. 16 appealed to its followers and others to boycott the presidential elections. Another Buddhist faction, the Cambodian Buddhist church, denounced Thieu's candidacy Sept. 19 and urged its two million followers to boycott the elections. Demonstrators opposing Thieu's candidacy protested in Saigon Sept. 16 and Sept. 18. There were four separate violent protests Sept. 18—one by 18 anti-Thieu House deputies and three by Buddhist students. It was reported Sept. 23 that the U.S. had warned South Vietnamese generals that any coup carried out against Thieu in the elections would result in a termination of U.S. support for the Saigon government. Vice President Ky Sept. 26 formed the People's Coordinating Committee Against Dictatorship, an opposition group formed to boycott the elections and force the ouster of Thieu. A radical student-based organization, the Committee to Unify All Activities Against the Nguyen Van Thieu Dictatorship, joined the Coordinating Committee Sept. 27. Meanwhile, violent street demonstrations continued in Saigon, prompting Thieu Sept. 29 to order the national police to "shoot down anyone who attempts to burn vehicles in the streets."

Thieu wins 90% of vote. President Thieu was re-elected in the Oct. 3 elections by a 91.5% majority of the 6,311,853 votes cast. The government's election committee announced Oct. 4 that 353,000, or 5.5% had handed in invalid ballots. A total of 87.7% of the eligible voters went to the polls, making it the largest voter turnout in recent South Vietnamese history. (Thieu had also retained a comfortable majority in Aug. 29 elections to the House, although opposition candidates had scored gains.) The South Vietnamese Supreme Court, by an 8-1 vote Oct. 22, ruled that the Thieu election was legally valid. The ruling rejected a suit filed Oct. 6 by Trinh Quoc Khanh, leader of the People's Force Against Dictatorship, urging the justices to declare the balloting unconstitutional and to nullify the results. The South Vietnamese Senate Oct. 19 rejected by a 19-8 vote an opposition motion to investigate charges that the election was rigged. Thieu was inaugurated in Saigon Oct. 31, amid heavy security precautions which included the deployment of about 30,000 government troops and security forces in and around Saigon to cope with a possible Communist effort to disrupt the inauguration. American soldiers, placed on the alert, were permitted to enter South Vietnam's cities and towns only on official business and their trips outside military installations were restricted.

See also COMMUNIST CHINA-U.S. DETENTE |8|; DRUG USE & ADDICTION |14-19|; FLOODS; INDOCHINA WAR; PENTAGON PAPERS |15, 19-20, 22-28|; SECURITY, U.S.; UNITED NATIONS |8|; VENEZUELA; WAR CRIMES

VIETNAM VETERANS AGAINST THE WAR—*See* DRAFT & WAR PROTEST |1, 7-9, 20, 26|; WAR CRIMES |12|

VIRGIN ISLANDS—Governor sworn in. Dr. Melvin H. Evans (R), a black physician, was installed as the first elected governor of the Virgin Islands Jan. 4 with the oath administered by Thurgood Marshall, the first Negro justice on the U.S. Supreme Court. In his inaugural address in Charlotte Amalie, V. I., Evans said "We have come of age."

U.S. ousts aliens. The U.S. Immigration and Naturalization Service began a drive March 2 to oust aliens who had overstayed in the Virgin Islands or entered without a permit. By March 6 more than 1,200 persons had been rounded up, most of them citizens of the British Commonwealth Caribbean islands, and sent home. It was reported March 11 that the expulsions had provoked protests from Donald Halstead, minister of home affairs in Antigua, and Robert Bradshaw, premier of St. Kitts-Nevis-Anguilla, who had flown to St. Thomas to discuss the matter with Gov. Evans. Evans explained that the ousters were a federal issue.

See also STATE & LOCAL GOVERNMENTS |5|

VOICE OF AMERICA—*See* JAPAN |5|
VOLLEYBALL—*See* SPORTS
VOLPE, JOHN A.—*See* AUTOMOBILES |6-7|; RAILROADS
VOLUNTEERS IN SERVICE TO AMERICA (VISTA)—*See* GOVERNMENT REORGANIZATION

VOTING RIGHTS—26th Amendment. The 26th Amendment to the Constitution—lowering the minimum voting age to 18 in all federal, state and local elections—was ratified by the states June 30 when Ohio became the 38th state to approve it. Ohio's action completed the requirement for constitutional amendments of ratification by three-quarters of the states. (The amendment had been given final Congressional approval March 23.) The new amendment was officially certified in a White House ceremony conducted by President Nixon July 5. Ratification by the states was accomplished in the record time of two months, seven days. The old record was six months, six days in 1804 for ratification of the 12th Amendment. Ratification authorized the immediate entry into the electorate of an estimated 11 million 18-to-20-year-olds. (Congress had enacted legislation in 1970 lowering the voting age to 18, but the

Supreme Court held that it could apply only to federal elections. Many states, therefore, faced the costly prospect of maintaining separate registration and voting procedures for federal and local elections. Only Kentucky, Alaska and Georgia permitted 18-year-olds to vote in state and local elections.) The 38 states ratifying the new amendment: Alabama, Alaska, Arizona, Arkansas, California, Colorado, Connecticut, Delaware, Hawaii, Idaho, Illinois, Indiana, Iowa, Kansas, Louisiana, Maine, Maryland, Massachusetts, Minnesota, Michigan, Missouri, Montana, Nebraska, New Hampshire, New Jersey, New York, North Carolina, Ohio, Oregon, Pennsylvania, Rhode Island, South Carolina, Tennessee, Texas, Vermont, Washington, West Virginia and Wisconsin.

In the wake of ratification of the amendment, there arose the question of whether new student voters, attending college away from their permanent residence, should be allowed to register at their college campuses. U.S. Attorney General John N. Mitchell said Sept. 1 that he was opposed to such special "legislative dispensation" because it would discriminate against other voters. However, the supreme courts of California and Michigan ruled Aug. 27 that college students could register and vote at their college communities. A three-judge federal panel in Philadelphia Sept. 27 affirmed an agreement that had been reached by opposing counsel for Pennsylvania and the American Civil Liberties Union (ACLU) allowing students to register to vote on their college campuses if they met other qualifications. The Nevada attorney general ruled Oct. 21 that students could register in their school community if they met county residence requirements and established legal residence away from their parents or guardians. The New Jersey Superior Court ruled June 1 that students could not register on their campuses because they could not show that the school was a permanent home.

Policy on voting laws stiffened. The Justice Department May 25 reported that it would now prevent the enactment of all new voting laws in the South unless the states could show that the new measures were not racially discriminatory. The action, detailed in guidelines reported to Congress May 28, was taken under the Voting Rights Act of 1965, which required that all changes in state and local election laws in seven Southern states had to be cleared by the attorney general or a special U.S. court to make certain that they did not dilute black voting strength. The new guidelines would put the burden of proof that election laws were not discriminatory on the Southern states. Changes which the attorney general could not determine as either discriminatory or nondiscriminatory would not go into effect. Attorney General Mitchell had refused to block new election laws, but reportedly switched his position after coming under pressure from a bipartisan bloc of liberal senators. (Using his authority under the act, Mitchell May 7 rejected a reapportionment plan for Virginia's legislative districts on the ground that the plan discriminated against Negroes. He also overturned a proposal that the city of Richmond annex part of an adjacent suburban county, but approved a third proposal, calling for redrawing Virginia's 10 Congressional districts. However, Mitchell June 10 withdrew his opposition to the Virginia reapportionment plan, which he had opposed because of its creation of multi-member districts, in light of a Supreme Court ruling June 3 approving multi-member districting in Indianapolis. *See below.*)

Reapportionment review denied. The Supreme Court, in an unsigned 6-3 decision June 3, held that reapportionment plans for state legislatures imposed by federal courts could be implemented without approval by the U.S. attorney general or a special federal court. The majority said a federal district court was not within the reach of the 1965 Voting Rights Act. The decision surprised civil rights lawyers, who, supported by the Justice Department, had brought the issue before the court in an appeal from a reapportionment ruling May 14 by a three-judge federal court in Jackson, Miss. The rights advocates contended that impairment of voting rights could come from Southern federal judges as well as from state legislatures or election officials. (The court itself reviewed the reapportionment plan and ordered it revised to provide for single-member legislative districts instead of for at-large elections for Hinds County's 12 state representatives and five senators. The court decision also ordered postponement of the deadline for filing for the August primary in order to allow time to devise the new district subdivision. The district court was given to June 14 to produce the new plan.)

At-large voting upheld. In a separate decision June 3, the court, by a 6-3 decision, upheld at-large elections for state legislators from the metropolitan area of Indianapolis. The ruling reversed a federal court ruling calling for single-member districts to open the system more to minority representation. The majority decision stressed the requirement of "real life" or "in practice" proof of discrimination, as opposed to theory, in finding an apportionment unconstitutional. Deciding otherwise, according to the decision, would "spawn endless litigation" involving contentions not only of racial but also of other discriminations.

See also LIECHTENSTEIN; SWEDEN; SWITZERLAND; WOMEN'S RIGHTS

WALDHEIM, KURT—*See* UNITED NATIONS [12]
WALLACE, GEORGE E.—*See* CIVIL RIGHTS [5]; POLITICS [12]; POLLUTION [19]

WAR CRIMES—Songmy officers cleared. The U.S. Army Jan. 6 dismissed for lack of evidence charges against Lt. Col. David C. Gavin, Lt. Col. William D. Guinn, Maj. Charles C. Calhoun and Maj. Frederick W. Watke. The four had been accused, along with 10 other officers, of suppressing information dealing with the slaying of South Vietnamese civilians at Mylai 4 in the Songmy village complex March 16, 1968. The dismissal action brought to 11 the number of officers cleared. The Army Jan. 29 cleared Maj. Gen. Samuel W. Koster of seven charges of attempting to cover up the alleged massacre at Songmy, but Jan. 30 censured him for alleged negligence for his failure to report and investigate the incident. At the time of the incident, Koster had been commander of the American Division, units of which were involved in the killings. Army Secretary Stanley R. Resor announced May 19 that Koster had been demoted to brigadier general for his failure to conduct an adequate investigation of the slayings. The Army also disciplined Brig. Gen. George H. Young Jr. (Koster's assistant at the time of the massacre) for the same reason by stripping him of his Distinguished Service Medal and by placing a letter of censure in his personal record. (The same two disciplinary measures were invoked against Koster.) It was announced June 11 that Young had been given permission to retire June 30 after 29 years of service.
[2] GIs cleared. A U.S. Army court-martial at Ft. McPherson, Ga. Jan. 14 acquitted Sgt. Charles E. Hutto of murder in the Mylai massacre. Hutto had been charged with intent to murder at least six civilians. The Army Jan. 21-22 dropped charges against the last five enlisted men accused of participating in the massacre. Spec. 4 William F. Doherty was cleared Jan. 21. Dismissal actions were announced Jan. 22 for Sgt. Esequiel Torres, Spec. 4 Robert W. T'Souvas, Pvt. Max Hutson and Pvt. Gerald A. Smith. The dismissals were for insufficient evidence. (In another development, officials in the Justice and Defense Departments said April 8 that they were unable to find legal grounds to try 15 former servicemen allegedly involved in the massacre.)
[3] Calley found guilty. An Army court-martial at Ft. Benning, Ga. March 29 found 1st Lt. William M. Calley Jr. guilty of the premeditated murder of at least 22 South Vietnamese civilians at Mylai. The military jury of six officers March 31 sentenced Calley to life imprisonment at hard labor and ordered his

departure from the Army and the forfeiture of his pay and allowance. However, he was still to retain his officer's status and continue to draw his pay until the case was automatically reviewed by another command. Calley was confined to the Ft. Benning stockade pending appeal. The mandatory sentence was death or life imprisonment. Calley's trial had started Nov. 12, 1970, was adjourned Dec. 17, 1970, resumed Jan. 11, recessed Jan. 18 to permit him to undergo psychiatric tests ordered by the court and started again Feb. 16 following completion of an Army sanity board hearing at Walter Reed Hospital in Washington Feb. 6. The board found Calley "normal in every respect." The Calley jury rendered its verdict after 13 days of deliberation. It convicted him of four specifications of premeditated murder of 22 civilians rather than 102 as charged, because witnesses during the trial had disputed the number of dead at Mylai; some said they had counted fewer than 100 bodies. The first specification charged that Calley killed at least 30 noncombatants at the south end of Mylai. This was reduced by the jury to the murder of "an unknown number, no less than one." The second specification dealt with the slayings of 70 civilians in a ditch outside Mylai. This was reduced to murder of "an unknown number, no less than 20." In the two remaining counts, Calley was found guilty of the premeditated murder of one civilian and of assault with intent to commit the murder of a child. In the case of the child, the original charge was murder, but was not conclusively proven at the trial.

[4] The guilty verdict in the Calley trial evoked tremendous popular opposition. Many persons felt that Calley had been selected as a scapegoat to be punished for the guilt of those who participated in the massacre but had been cleared or not brought to trial. In subsequent developments: President Nixon April 1 ordered the chairman of the Joint Chiefs of Staff to instruct Army authorities to release Calley from the Ft. Benning stockade and return him to his base apartment while his conviction was under review; Nixon announced April 3 that he would personally review the Calley case "before any final sentence is carried out"; the Army refused May 14 to allow Calley to be free from house arrest while his conviction was under review; Lt. Gen. Albert O. Conner, commanding general of the 3rd Army at Ft. McPherson, Aug. 20 reduced Calley's sentence to 20 years, making him eligible for parole in 6-7 years.

[5] **Kotouc cleared.** Capt. Eugene M. Kotouc was acquitted by a military jury at Ft. McPherson April 29 of maiming a Vietcong suspect while interrogating him outside Mylai. The jury of seven career Army officers deliberated a little more than an hour after the 13-day trial. A second charge, alleging that he had assaulted the same prisoner, was dropped April 27 at the direction of the presiding judge, Col. Madison C. Wright 2nd. The Army had charged Kotouc with cutting off part of a finger on the Vietcong suspect's right hand during an interrogation. Kotouc was questioning the prisoner outside of Mylai a few hours after massacre of South Vietnamese men, women and children there. Kotouc testified that he intended only to frighten the suspect when he thrust a knife at him during the interrogation. Kotouc said his hand slipped and the knife cut off part of a finger on the prisoner's right hand. Kotouc confirmed that he had had the suspect's hand bound and spread on a board and that he had made several swiping motions with his knife. He said, however, that he did it to intimidate uncooperative prisoners in an effort to gather information that might save American lives. Before the jurors began to deliberate, Judge Wright said Army regulations in effect at the time of the incident might have led Kotouc to believe it was lawful to threaten a prisoner with violence and physical harm, and his action therefore could be legally justified.

[6] **Medina cleared on Mylai role.** A jury of five officers at Ft. McPherson, Ga. acquitted Capt. Ernest L. Medina Sept. 22 of all charges in connection with the killing of South Vietnamese civilians at Mylai. The jury cleared Medina after deliberating only 60 minutes. The court-martial had begun Aug. 16.

Medina was found not guilty of premeditated murder in the killing of a Vietnamese woman, of involuntary manslaughter in the killing of "not less than 100" Vietnamese civilians and of two counts of assault upon a prisoner by shooting at him twice with a rifle. Medina had originally been charged with the premeditated murder of at least 100 civilians during a search-and-destroy operation by his men through Mylai March 16, 1968. He was also charged with murder in the deaths of a woman and a small boy and with two counts of assault on a prisoner. Col. Kenneth A. Howard, the presiding judge, Sept. 17 threw out the charge that Medina murdered a small boy at Mylai. At the same time, Howard reduced the murder charge that Medina was responsible for the deaths of 100 civilians to involuntary manslaughter. Howard said he had reduced the charge because the government had failed to prove that Medina had any "intent" to kill civilians. (Several times, during his testimony, Medina said he had a poor opinion of Calley, whom he described as an inept officer who had trouble understanding orders. Calley had said his actions at Mylai were under orders from Medina.)

[7] **Henderson acquitted.** The last of the Mylai trials came to an end Dec. 17 as a military jury at Ft. Meade, Md. acquitted Col. Oran K. Henderson of charges that he had covered up the massacre by soldiers in his brigade. Specifically, the jury cleared Henderson of "willful dereliction of duty" in not carrying out a proper investigation of atrocity reports at Mylai, of having failed to report alleged war crimes to his division commander and of lying to a Pentagon investigating committee about Mylai. The verdict was handed down on the 62nd court day of the case, equaling the length of Calley's trial as the longest court-martial in U.S. military history. During the trial, which opened Aug. 23, 106 witnesses took the stand. In addition, the eight jurors studied more than 150 documents including transcripts of Henderson's earlier testimony to a Pentagon inquiry board investigating Mylai. After the verdict, Henderson, the highest ranking officer to face court-martial on Mylai charges, told newsmen he did not plan to remain in the Army.

Other Developments

[8] **Ex-Green Beret admits 1969 slaying.** Robert F. Marasco, a former captain in the U.S. Special Forces who was charged but never tried in the 1969 slaying of a suspected South Vietnamese double agent, said April 2 that he had shot and killed him on orders from the Central Intelligence Agency (CIA). Marasco said he was admitting his complicity in the murder out of a sense of anger over the Calley conviction.

[9] **8 airmen cleared.** The U.S. Army command in Saigon June 4 dropped murder charges against eight airmen in connection with the alleged strafing of Vietnamese civilians from their gunships in September 1970. The Army said the charges had been dropped because of insufficient evidence. The charges against the men had been initiated in November 1970, but the Army did not file charges until May 4. The crewmen were identified as CWO Michael A. Nicholaou, 21; CWO Stephen J. Becker, 23; WO Roland E. Linstad, 21; WO Camille A. Perret, 20; Spec. 5 Dominic Fino, 20; Spec. 5 John N. Enos, 20; Spec. 4 James L. Dunston, 21; and Spec. 4 Charles R. Thompson, 22.

[10] **Herbert cleared.** Army Secretary Robert F. Froehlke Oct. 8 ordered removal of a damaging efficiency report that was added to the file of Lt. Col. Anthony Herbert after he accused two superior officers of covering up alleged atrocities by American soldiers in Vietnam. Froehlke had begun a review of Herbert's case Oct. 3. The removal of the report cleared the way for Herbert, the most decorated enlisted man in the Korean War, to remain in the Army. The report, if it had not been removed, would have forced Herbert to retire from the military by March 1, 1972. The report had charged Herbert with having "no ambition, integrity, loyalty or will for self-improvement" and of having "a terrible appearance." It had been filed by Col. J. Ross Franklin, one of the officers who had been accused by Herbert of covering up stories of

alleged atrocities. The other officer implicated by Herbert was Maj. Gen. John Barnes, his former brigade commander. The Army dropped charges against Franklin July 21 and charges against Barnes Oct. 15. (Herbert had taken and passed a polygraph test on his charges. It was reported Oct. 10 that Army investigators had confirmed seven of 21 allegations made by Herbert of war crimes by U.S. soldiers.) Herbert said Nov. 7 that he would retire from the service in February because of "intolerable" pressures on his family. (While stationed at Ft. McPherson, Herbert was told Oct. 31 that he was under suspicion of being absent without leave. Later he was denied leave to appear on a television talk show. On Nov. 3, the Army ordered him to refrain from speaking to newsmen without specific permission from his commanding officers at Ft. McPherson.)

[11] Donaldson cleared. Brig. Gen. John W. Donaldson was exonerated by the Army Dec. 9 of murder and assault charges accusing him of killing six South Vietnamese citizens in Quangngai Province between November 1968 and January 1969, while he was a brigade commander in South Vietnam. The charges against Donaldson were dropped because "evidence established that no offenses were committed by Gen. Donaldson, then a colonel." Donaldson was the highest-ranking officer accused of war crimes in the Indochina war. He was also the first American general officer to face such charges since Brig. Gen. Jacob H. Smith was charged with war crimes in 1901.

[12] Probe sought. Four Army officers and a Navy officer (Capt. Robert J. Master, Capt. Grier Merwin, Capt. Edward G. Fox, 1st Lt. Louis Font and Lt. (jg.) Peter Dunkelberger), all members of the antiwar Concerned Officers Movement, said Jan. 12 that they were asking that military courts of inquiry be convened to investigate alleged war crimes and atrocities by U.S. troops in Vietnam. The officers said they were requesting the inquiry, under provisions of military law, in letters to the secretaries of the Army and Navy. The five were joined Jan. 20 in their call by Lts. (jg.) John Kent, Edward Shallcross and James Skelly of the Navy and 2nd Lt. Norman Banks of the Air Force. The four said they were joined in their demand for an inquiry by Lt. (jg.) James Schwertman and Lt. Steven Auer of the Navy and 2nd Lt. Ed Kendig of the Marines. In a related development, Reps. John Conyers Jr. (D, Mich.) and John F. Seiberling Jr. (D, Ohio), joined by members of the Vietnam Veterans Against the War, Feb. 5 called for a Congressional investigation of alleged U.S. war crimes in Vietnam.

See also DRAFT & WAR PROTEST [7, 19]

WARSAW PACT—*See* EUROPEAN SECURITY
WATER POLLUTION—*See* POLLUTION[1-15]; UNION OF SOVIET SOCIALIST REPUBLICS [7]
WEATHER—*See* SPACE [15, 24]
WEATHERMEN—*See* DRAFT & WAR PROTEST [4, 6]

WELFARE—Rule on fathers revised. The Nixon Administration Feb. 5 proposed a welfare rule revision, effective in 30 days, governing the amount of work a welfare father could accept while still receiving aid. Currently, a welfare father was considered unemployed and eligible for aid if he worked less than 30 hours a week (35 hours in some states). Under the revision, which would affect about 5% of welfare fathers, a jobless welfare father would be one who worked less than 100 hours a month. More than 100 hours a month would be permitted if the total hours were expected to drop below 100 in future months, as in the case of migrant or farm workers. In the eight states in which Medicaid covered only welfare families, the persons dropped from the rolls would also lose Medicaid benefits.

House passes reform bill. The House of Representatives June 22, by a 288-132 vote, passed an omnibus bill incorporating reform of the welfare system and major changes in Social Security, Medicaid and Medicare programs. A move to delete the welfare reform provision, the Family Assistance Plan (FAP) was defeated June 22 by a 234-187 vote. The FAP approved by the House would guarantee a family of four an annual income of $2,400 and establish uniform national standards for eligibility and benefits. States would be relieved of some current welfare costs and any cost increases over the next five years. The welfare provisions encountered opposition from liberals viewing the income floor as inadequate and conservatives objecting to the concept of an income floor. The House bill was modified by the Ways and Means Committee prior to passage June 22, to require state legislative action to eliminate supplemental welfare payments or food stamp procedure. Liberals had objected that the original bill had no remedy if states accepted the increased federal contributions and reduced their own investment and the amount allotted to poor families. The final provision froze state benefit levels unless positive legislative action were taken by the states.

Income support plan tested. Preliminary results from a federally financed welfare experiment, released May 8, had indicated that a guaranteed minimum income for the working poor would not cause poor people to quit their jobs and live on welfare. Reporting on an experimental program in five Eastern cities, the study said, "There is no evidence indicating a significant decline in weekly family earnings as a result of the income assistance plan." The Office of Economic Opportunity (OEO) project, which began in August 1968, paralleled features of the FAP in that income assistance was extended to about 700 poor families regardless of whether they continued to work or not. The working habits and incomes of the families given assistance were compared with a control group of unaided poor families.

States cut welfare funds. A Health, Education and Welfare Department (HEW) survey, reported July 8, showed that 22 states were reducing welfare benefits or were planning to effect reductions by the end of the year. The survey, submitted to HEW Undersecretary John G. Veneman, said the findings indicated a reversal of a long trend of higher assistance for the poor. The study of family welfare programs said cuts of up to 20% had been ordered in 10 states and reductions by the end of 1971 were possible in 12 additional states. Moves to cut benefits failed in the legislatures of four states. The study listed 1971 aid increases in four states and the District of Columbia and increases were said to be possible in three other states. The 10 states slated for definite reductions were Alabama, Georgia, Kansas, Maine, Nebraska, New Jersey, New Mexico, New York, Rhode Island and South Dakota. The 12 states listed for possible reduction were Arizona, California, Connecticut, Delaware, Idaho, Illinois, Minnesota, New Hampshire, Oregon, Pennsylvania, Texas and Vermont.

10% on relief in big cities. A new HEW study, reported July 16, showed that more than one of 10 residents in the 26 largest U.S. cities received welfare aid. The study, based on February 1971 data, showed a 22.5% increase nationwide in the number of relief clients since the year before. The total number of persons on welfare in the U.S. was reported to be 14.2 million. The study was the first made by HEW that focused on big-city relief rates. The closest comparable study, one based on February 1970 statistics of the 20 largest metropolitan areas, had shown 6.5% on welfare in the metropolitan areas. The report said 10.3% of the residents of the 26 largest cities or the counties that contained them were on relief, compared with 6.9% of the entire U.S. population. Large increases in the big-city relief rolls were shown, with Washington, D.C. leading with a 58% increase over February 1970.

NWRO convention. The National Welfare Rights Organization (NWRO) held its fifth annual convention at Brown University (Providence, R.I.) July 28-Aug. 1, bringing in 1,200 delegates to represent the organization's 125,000 members in 50 states. While continuing to concentrate on welfare reform and the need for an adequate guaranteed annual income for the poor, the organization appeared to be moving toward an effort to organize a broad, populist coalition for political action. In a speech July 29, Dr. George A. Wiley, 39, NWRO executive director, urged the group, already organized across racial lines, to seek a coalition with the working poor, the elderly, women's rights groups, the peace movement, tenants organizations, minority groups and farm, hospital and domestic workers. Workshops July 30 instructed the delegates in political organizing tactics, teaching them how to run for office and influence candidates.

Work rule voted for welfare aid. Congress, by voice votes of both houses, approved legislation Dec. 14 to establish a national work registration requirement for almost all adults receiving welfare aid, many of whom were mothers with dependent children. The legislation, signed by President Nixon Dec. 28, originated in the Senate Dec. 11 as amendments introduced by Sen. Herman Talmadge (D, Ga.) to a minor Social Security bill. They were accepted by a Senate-House conference committee and adopted with little discussion by both houses Dec. 14. The welfare work plan would require, effective July 1, 1972, all those receiving benefits under Aid to Families with Dependent Children to register for work or training unless they were children (under 16), elderly, ill, mothers with children under six years of age, or supporting someone incapacitated. (Under current law, each state determined the registrants and referred "appropriate" welfare recipients for employment.) The federal government would assume 90% of the cost of day care services for children of working mothers, and 100% of the cost of public service jobs for the employable adults in the first year of the new program, 75% in the second year and 50% in the third year.

Court decisions. In a 6-3 ruling Jan. 12, the Supreme Court upheld the right of state and local welfare officials to visit the homes of recipients and to cut off funds from persons who refused to let them enter their homes. (The ruling came in the case of Mrs. Barbara James of New York City, who had refused to allow a city caseworker to enter her home in connection with welfare payments to support her young son. Welfare officials decided to cut off her payments. She brought suit and won a 1969 federal court ruling that the cutoff was illegal.) The court Jan. 18 unanimously upheld a 1967 federal law that was designed to encourage welfare recipients of aid to dependent children to take jobs. The law contained an "income disregard" provision that permitted welfare parents to deduct a portion of their income in determining whether they earned more than the state "need level." (The ruling came in the case of Mrs. Lula Mae Connor of Chicago, who argued that the law was discriminatory because the "income disregard" deduction extended only to persons who were already welfare recipients and not to those who were applying for benefits.) The court June 14 unanimously ruled that states could not deny welfare benefits to needy aliens. In an opinion by Justice Harry Blackmun, the court tied its ruling to a 1969 decision striking down state residency requirements for welfare applicants. (Despite that 1969 ruling, Hawaii June 7, New York June 23 and Connecticut and Illinois July 1 enacted one-year welfare residency requirements. The New York law was declared unconstitutional by a federal court Aug. 9.)

See also AGRICULTURE [8]; BUDGET; NIXON, RICHARD MILHOUS [1]; RACIAL & MINORITY UNREST [1]; TAXES

WEST INDIES—*See* CARIBBEAN
WESTMORELAND, WILLIAM C.—*See* PENTAGON PAPERS [25-28]
WHALING—*See* CONSERVATION
WHITE HOUSE CONFERENCE ON AGING—*See* AGING
WIMBLEDON—*See* TENNIS
WIRETAPS—*See* CRIME [15]; FEDERAL BUREAU OF INVESTIGATION [3-4]; SECURITY, U.S.; SUPREME COURT

WOMEN'S RIGHTS—Sex bias in hiring barred. The Supreme Court Jan. 25 ruled that companies could not deny employment to women with pre-school children unless the same criterion applied to men. In its first sex discrimination ruling on equal hiring provisions of the 1964 Civil Rights Act, the court returned the case for further evidence, contending that "the existence of such conflicting family obligations, if demonstrably more relevant to job performance for a woman than for a man, could arguably be a basis for distinction." The case was an appeal by Mrs. Ida Phillips, who had been denied a job by the Martin Marietta Corp. Lower courts had dismissed her appeal on the ground that she had been denied employment not because of sex alone, but because of her sex plus the factor that she was the parent of young children. In other developments in equal hiring: the Civil Service Commission ruled May 12 that "men only" and "women only" specifications for federal jobs could be continued only if the job required that the employees sleep in common quarters or in certain institutional jobs, such as matron in a women's prison, and not if the job merely required physical strength or the carrying of weapons; Labor Secretary James D. Hodgson Dec. 2 ordered all federal contractors and subcontractors to take "affirmative action" to end "under-utilization of women" in all areas of employment.

Women form political caucus. More than 200 women met in Washington July 10-11 to mobilize the women's rights movement to achieve political power. The National Women's Political Caucus (NWPC) set as its goal the equal representation of women with men at all levels of the nation's political system. The group declared it would support candidates—men and women—who would fight against "sexism, racism, violence and poverty." The NWPC elected a 21-member steering committee to coordinate the group's efforts and planned a full-scale convention in early 1972. The caucus settled on a program, to be carried out by state and local units, to rally support for women candidates, force political parties to accept women in decision-making roles and register new women voters. The NWPC also made public a set of issues adopted as "guidelines" for support of political candidates. The statement said the priority issues were: passage of the proposed equal rights amendment to the Constitution *(see below);* repeal of "all laws that affect a woman's right to decide her own reproductive and sexual life"; amendment of the 1964 Civil Rights Act and extension of the 1963 Equal Pay Act to provide more protection for women; enforcement of existing antidiscrimination legislation and strengthening of the enforcement powers of the Equal Employment Opportunity Commission (EEOC); and elimination of tax inequities involving women and children. The guidelines also called for: programs to end hunger and malnutrition; comprehensive health care; fair and "adequate" housing; preservation of the environment; and an "adequate income for all Americans." The group demanded "comprehensive community-controlled programs" in child care and education and for senior citizens. Other guidelines dealt with working women and "unpaid labor in the home."

NOW convention. More than 750 delegates and 200 observers attended the fifth national conference of the National Organization for Women (NOW) in Los Angeles during the Labor Day weekend. The group, claiming 15,000 members in 180 chapters, officially endorsed the NWPC as an effective instrument for increased political emphasis in the women's movement. Plans were announced to organize local political training programs and resolutions were passed: backing an alliance with poor and minority women; calling for an end to all wars, which were seen as the expression of a masculine mystique; attacking traditional women's volunteer work for helping to keep women in secondary and dependent roles; and supporting freedom in life styles, including lesbianism.

Women mark suffrage day. Women in cities across the country celebrated the 51st anniversary of their right to vote Aug. 26 with marches, rallies, fund-raising events and protests. Although the demonstrations were generally quieter and smaller than those a year ago during the "Women's Strike for Equality," more specific political goals and plans were voiced, as exemplified by the newly formed NWPC. Thousands marched in New York City while a handful of women protested at the stock exchanges. New York Mayor John V. Lindsay proclaimed Women's Rights Day and named the first woman police captain on the city's force. In Washington, NOW and representatives of the National Welfare Rights Organization and the

Teamsters announced plans to lobby for passage of the Equal Rights Amendment to the Constitution. Elsewhere, there were NOW rallies in Winston-Salem, N.C. and Chicago, and money was raised in other cities for women's lobbying activities. An all-day organizing session was held in Boston for the NWPC in the New England Region. A governor's commission in Vermont announced a drive to register more women voters.

House votes equal rights amendment. The House approved and sent to the Senate Oct. 12 by a 354-23 vote a proposed constitutional amendment barring discrimination based on sex. Prior to passage, the House rejected by a 265-87 vote a proposal, opposed by women's rights advocates, to include in the amendment provisions to exempt women from the military draft and to let stand current "protective" work laws. Women's rights advocates contended the latter often were utilized to discriminate against employment or promotion of women.

Idaho sex bias law voided. The Supreme Court Nov. 22, in its first ruling invalidating a state law on the ground of sex discrimination, set aside an Idaho statute that it found to favor men in administration of deceased persons' estates. The vote was 7-0. The court struck down the statute on the ground that it denied women equal protection under the law guaranteed by the 14th Amendment. The decision also marked the first time since the 14th Amendment was enacted in 1868 that the court had held that women had been denied equal legal rights. The court stopped short of ruling that all laws that drew distinctions between men and women should be presumed to be unconstitutional. Women's rights advocates had hoped that the court would take that view. The court held that the Idaho law was "arbitrary" and divided men and women into separate classes "on the basis of criteria wholly unrelated" to the objective of efficiently administering estates. The case had come to the court on an appeal by Sally M. Reed, of Ada County, Ida. She and her former husband, Cecil R. Reed, had filed competing petitions to administer the estate of her deceased son. Reed was selected after the Idaho Supreme Court held that the legislature "evidently concluded that in general men are better able to act as an administrator than women." In overturning that decision, the Supreme Court sent the case back to the Idaho Supreme Court where a decision was to be made between Mr. and Mrs. Reed without regard to sex.

See also CHURCHES [8, 15]; CIVIL RIGHTS [22-24]; DRAFT & WAR PROTEST [9]; ELECTIONS [3]; LIECHTENSTEIN; POLITICS [5]; ROMAN CATHOLIC CHURCH [3, 10]; SWITZERLAND; WELFARE

YAHYA KHAN, AGHA MOHAMMAD—*See* PAKISTAN [2, 4, 15, 20, 24-25, 28-29,31, 39]

YEMEN—Premier Amri resigns, departs. Maj. Gen. Hassan al-Amri was forced to resign as premier of Yemen less than two weeks after forming a new cabinet, Sana radio reported Sept. 4. Amri left Yemen and took up exile in Beirut. He denied reports he had resigned, saying only he was in Lebanon for "rest and medical treatment."

Yemeni and Beirut newspapers reported the following events leading to Amri's ouster: The general placed a telephone call Aug. 25 to the chief of guards at the army's general headquarters, but because of an electronic mixup he reached instead Mohsen al-Harazi, owner of a photography shop in Sana. The misunderstanding led to a sharp argument between the two men and Amri had Harazi brought before him. Harazi was beaten by the guards and Amri. The premier later shot Harazi to death after the guards refused his orders to do so. Abdul Rahman al-Iryani, president of the ruling Republican Council, demanded that Amri either resign from all his posts or stand trial for murder. Amri agreed to step down and was put aboard a plane for Beirut.

Amri's resignation as premier as well as commander in chief and member of the Republican Council was unanimously accepted at an emergency meeting of the legislative Consultative Council Aug. 28. Amri had formed a Cabinet Aug. 23. He had replaced Ahmed Mohammed Noman, who had resigned as premier July 20 because of inability to cope with Yemen's financial deficit. Amri had previously served as premier April 3-July 8, 1969.

See also JORDAN [7]; MIDDLE EAST [7]

YOUNG AMERICANS FOR FREEDOM (YAF)—*See* POLITICS [4]

YOUTH—About 900 youths, aged 14-24, and 500 adults gathered in Estes Park, Colo. April 18 for a four-day White House Conference on Youth. The parley was distinguished from the regular conference on children and youth (held every decade since 1909) in that the problems of youth and children were considered in two separate conferences and the delegates met 1,500 miles from Washington. Critics had charged that the Nixon Administration had isolated the conference in order to avoid confrontations and rigged the selection of delegates to favor those most likely to support Administration views. In answering the charges, conference chairman Stephen Hess said March 26 that an advisory committee of youth had voted to hold the conference outside Washington. He said the delegates were chosen to reflect the demography of the 40 million Americans between the ages of 14 and 24. (College students were slightly overrepresented, comprising 20% of the delegates compared with the 16% of young Americans actually in college; about 40% of the delegates attended high schools and vocational schools; 35% were working young people, and 5% were in the military. The delegates also reflected racial, ethnic and economic balances.)

Concern over the war in Indochina dominated much of the conference. At the closing session April 21, the delegates voted 3-1 to back the majority resolution of the foreign relations study group calling for an immediate halt to U.S. military action in Southeast Asia and withdrawal of American forces and logistical support by the end of the year. They also voted to send telegrams endorsing mass antiwar rallies in Washington and San Francisco April 24.

The preamble to the conference report, to be presented to President Nixon, denounced "slavery and its evil legacy" and said the "annihilation of Indians, genocide, exploitation of labor, and militaristic expansion have been among the most important shortcomings which have undermined the ideals to which the people of this country have aspired." Calling for immediate action on the conference proposals, the preamble concluded, "We are motivated not by hatred, but by disappointment over and love for the unfulfilled potential of this nation." The final draft of the preamble was written by only four persons, but the delegates accorded it a one-minute standing ovation when it was read to the closing session.

The final session also voted 493-127 for a proposal declaring that "any sexual behavior between consenting, responsible individuals must be recognized and tolerated by society as an acceptable life style." The task force on race relations and minorities—which had split into caucuses for American Indians, blacks, European Americans, Asian Americans, Spanish-speaking Americans and "non-ethnic" Americans—came together to urge President Nixon to officially denounce racism as the "cancer of American society." Other recommendations endorsed by the various study groups called for legalization of marijuana and the removal of legal restraints on abortion and personal drug use; an end to the draft by June 30 and amnesty to all draft violators; the resignation of Federal Bureau of Investigation (FBI) Director J. Edgar Hoover and a review board to oversee FBI surveillance; a guaranteed annual income of $6,500 for a family of four; the nationalization of coal mining and an end to strip mining; and the commitment of one-fourth the national budget to education.

YORTY, SAM—*See* POLITICS [9]

YUGOSLAVIA—Constitutional amendments. A committee of the Federal Assembly Feb. 27 published draft constitutional amendments dealing with a proposed collective presidency and giving more power to the republics. The amendments were approved June 18 by the Chamber of Nationalities and became law June 30 with their approval by the Federal Assembly. The measure designed to give the republics more control over their own affairs required the federal government to give up many of its previous functions, but also required each republic to turn over all but 7% to 10% of its foreign exchange holdings to the federal government (*see below*). The new law left federal authorities with control of defense and foreign policy and obliged the government to gain approval from the republics for economic regulations, foreign trade relations and establishment of foreign credit. The collective presidency measure, which required the presidency to secure parliamentary approval for the legislation it initiated and called for the dissolution of both the presidency and the parliament in the event of failure to reconcile differences within nine months, was implemented July 29 with the election of President Josip Broz Tito as chairman of the new presidency. Tito's election took place at a joint session of the Federal Assembly during which the composition of the collective presidency was announced.

The presidency was composed of 22 members—eight presidents of the republican and provincial assemblies (ex-officio members of the federal presidency) and 14 persons chosen by these assemblies. The members, with those serving ex-officio listed first, were: Hamdija Pozderac, Rato Dugonjic and Avgustin Papic (Bosnia-Herzegovina); Nicola Mincev, Kiro Gligorov and Krste Crvenkovski (Macedonia); Sergej Krajger, Marko Bulc and Mitja Ribicic (Slovenia); Dragoslav Markovic, Koca Popovic and Dragi Stamenkovic (Serbia); Jakov Blazevic, Miko Tripalo and Djuro Kladarin (Croatia); Vidoje Zarkovic, Veljko Micunovic and Dobrosav Culafic (Montenegro); Ilija Rajacic and Macas Kelemen (Vovjodina) and Ilijaz Kurtesi and Veli Deva (Kosovo). Ten members of the presidency also belonged to the Presidium of the Communist party and four were members of the party's Executive Bureau. After choosing Tito as their chairman and 23rd member July 29, the members of the presidency elected Krste Crvenkovski as vice chairman for one year.

Premier, Cabinet chosen. The Federal Assembly July 30 elected a premier and 21 other members of the Federal Executive Council (Cabinet), the organ of government directly beneath the collective presidency. Those chosen were: Dsemal Bijedic, the new premier; Muhamed Hadzic, foreign trade secretary, and Ivo Jerkic (Bosnia-Herzegovina); Jakov Sirotkovic, the vice premier, Mirjana Krstinic and Emil Ludviger (Croatia); Vuko Dragesevic, secretary for labor and social policy, Momcilo Cemovic, and Marko Orlandic (Montenegro); Janko Smole, finance secretary, Boris Snuderl and Anton Vratusa (Slovenia); Stejan Andev, Trpe Jakovlevski and Blagoje Popov (Macedonia); Nikola Ljubicic, national defense secretary, Borislav Jovic and Dusan Gligorijevic (Serbia); Boske Dimitrijevic, secretary for the economy, and Imer Pulja (Kosovo); Mirko Tepavac, foreign secretary, and Geza Tikvicki (Vojvodina). Six new members of the council were appointed Dec. 3: Nikola Stojanovic, Luka Banovic, Ivo Kustrak, Mugbil Bejzat, Ivan Franko and Dragan Milojevic.

Envoy assassinated in Sweden. Vladimir Rolovic, Yugoslavia's ambassador to Sweden, died April 15 in a Stockholm hospital as a result of bullet wounds inflicted April 7 by two Croatian terrorists, later identified as Andjelko Brajkowic and Miro Barzico. The two entered the embassy on the pretext of obtaining passports and shot Rolovic a number of times. Mira Stemphihar, a secretary, was wounded trying to protect the ambassador. The two Croats and a third man suspected of aiding them were charged with murder April 16 in a Stockholm court. Brajkowic and Barzico, who told the court they would "never be sorry" for the ambassador because he had "murdered thousands of Croats between 1941 and 1945," were sentenced July 14 to life imprisonment. Also sentenced to two-year terms for complicity were Marinko Lemo and Stanislav Milicevic. Ante Stojanov, the group's leader, was given four years. (The assassination had prompted President Tito to hold a meeting of the League of Communists' Presidium April 28-30 to discuss disputes between members of Yugoslavia's national groups. The meeting reportedly ended with "complete unity" of views on how to overcome "the present situation.")

Student strike ends. Nearly 30,000 students at Zagreb University in Croatia, the country's wealthiest republic, ended an 11-day strike Dec. 3 after President Tito Dec. 1 asked that measures be taken against them. The students had opposed the provision in the constitutional amendments requiring the republics to turn over foreign exchange earnings (*see above*). Tito said that the students did "not even know what is at stake when the foreign currency system is involved." He declared that they did not have the support of the working class and that they were aided by persons outside the country. (It was reported that, while workers' councils in the factories had condemned the strike, individual employees had signed resolutions endorsing it.) The end of the strike was decided at a rally on the Zagreb campus attended by 7,000 students.

Croat leaders resign. Leading Croat party officials, responding to charges made by Tito in his Dec. 1 address that they had failed to effectively resist the nationalist movement in the republic, resigned at a meeting of the Croatian party's Central Committee Dec. 12. Those who resigned were: Mrs. Savka Dabcevic-Kucar, the committee's president; Pero Pirker, secretary of its Executive Bureau; Marko Koprtla, member of the Executive Bureau; Gen. Janko Bobetko, member of the Central Committee; and Miko Tripalo, a member of both the Yugoslav Communist party Executive Bureau and the Yugoslav presidency. The committee Dec. 13 announced replacements for those removed from the Croat CP and said it intended to effect "the liquidation of all nationalist and chauvinist hotbeds in our society." The dismissal of Croatian leaders was followed by four nights of rioting and demonstrations in Zagreb Dec. 13-16 as 3,000-5,000 students chanted Croatian slogans. Police used nightsticks to restore order. Some 170 students were arrested Dec. 13 and 14. (Thirteen student leaders had been arrested Dec. 12 because they allegedly had "by their acts and speeches incited violent and anti-constitutional change in the social and state order and the overthrow of the representative bodies and their political executive organs.")

Croatian premier resigns. Dragutin Haramija Dec. 22 resigned as Croatian prime minister. Haramija, who declared he no longer had the trust of responsible persons in the government, was joined in his decision to step down by his deputy prime minister, Vjekoslav Prpic, and by two vice presidents of the Croatian National Assembly, Makso Bace and Milivoj Rukavina. Haramija was replaced Dec. 28 by Ivo Perisin, a deputy of the Croatian Assembly and governor of the National Bank of Yugoslavia.

Amendment system altered. Yugoslav Premier Bijedic said Dec. 27 that tentative changes had been worked out in the system by which each of the country's six republics was obliged to turn foreign exchange earnings over to the central government. Under the new system, export firms would be allowed to retain as much as 20% of their hard currency earnings. Firms engaged in the tourist industry could keep up to 40%.

See also AVIATION [14]; DRUG USE & ADDICTION [9]; ITALY [6]

ZAIRE—*See* CONGO, DEMOCRATIC REPUBLIC OF THE; MIDDLE EAST [37]; SUDAN

ZAMBIA—Cabinet changes. Changes of personnel at Cabinet level were announced in three separate actions during January and in one action June 3. President Kenneth Kaunda was reported Jan. 1 to have reinstated the previous day all but one (Henry Shambanse, minister for the Northwestern Province, who was tried and fined March 11) of the Cabinet ministers and other public officials suspended in November 1970 on charges of tampering with government funds. The announcement came after the government's director of public prosecution reported no evidence of misconduct against those suspended. Kaunda created two new ministries Jan. 7—the Ministry of Mines and Mining Development, with Humphrey Mulemba as minister, and the Ministry of Legal Affairs, with Fitzpatrick Chuula, the attorney general, as minister. Mulemba was replaced as minister of commerce and industry by Justin Chimba. Chimba was suspended by Kaunda Jan. 29 pending results of a commission of inquiry established Jan. 26 to investigate charges of tribal bias within the government. Chimba, a Bemba from the Northern Province, Jan. 25 had accused the government of discrimination against his tribe in the selection for government positions of importance and had accused Reuben Kamanga, a non-Bemba and former Zambian vice president, of raping his secretary. The judicial commission June 1 denied the charges and exonerated Kamanga. Kaunda June 3 dismissed Chimba, Dingiswayo Banda (minister of power, transport and works) and Nephas Tembo (minister of state for provincial and local government and culture). The judicial commission's report had criticized the manner in which the latter two ministers and five senior officials had disposed of loan funds intended for public use. Banda was replaced by Fwanyanga Mulikita, minister of labor and social services; Mulikita's former post was taken by Wilson Chakulya.

Fear Portuguese blockade. President Kaunda March 22 asked diplomats of more than 30 nations for help in fighting what he said was a Portuguese blockade of Zambian imports levied in reprisal for the capture of five Portuguese nationals in January by members of the Mozambique Revolutionary Council (COREMO). Kuanda said the blockade was resulting in a pileup of Zambian goods at Nacala and Beira in Mozambique and at Lobito Bay in Angola. He denied any connection with the capture of the Portuguese and said he would have tried to secure the release of the men if Portugal had

513

made the request through normal diplomatic channels. Kaunda spoke of the danger of a Portuguese invasion and accused authorities in Mozambique of holding three Zambians. Portugal denied that there was a blockade of Zambian goods in Beira.

UNIP gets constitution. At the conclusion of a four-day general conference in Mulungushi May 10, the governing United National Independence party (UNIP) elected Central Committee members and adopted a new constitution designed, according to Kaunda, to broaden "the scope of leadership" so that Central Committee members would be selected on a national rather than tribal basis. Kaunda said that membership in the committee would not automatically lead to a Cabinet appointment and said he favored "as much distinction as possible" between party and government officers. The Zambian leader was elected secretary general of UNIP May 10 and his entire Central Committee was returned unopposed. Those named to the committee were Mainza Chona, Simon Kapwepwe, Reuben Kamanga, Elijah Mudenda, Sikota Wina, Solomon Kalulu, Humphrey Mulumba, Wesley Nyirenda, Alexander Chikwanda, Wilson Chakulya, Grey Zulu, Aaron Milner, Clement Mwanashiku, Alex Shapi, Jethro Mutti, Stephen Sikonde, Josephat Litana, Mary Fulano and Dorothy Kapanza.

Troops close university. Government troops July 15 closed the University of Zambia after student militants took control of the campus July 14 to protect 10 of their leaders who had written a letter opposing Kaunda's "inconsistency toward issues in Southern Africa." (The July 12 letter had protested Kaunda's order banning demonstrations on arms sales to South Africa following a July 7 march on the French embassy. The order had asked that Kaunda be allowed to handle the matter in his own way. The student letter charged Kaunda with communicating with South Africa and said it was expecting too much of them and of the nation to ask that the matter be left to Kaunda.) A large group of demonstrators led by Fines Bulawayo, a minister of state, marched on the campus July 14, reportedly with the intention of punishing the authors of the letter. When the demonstrators were met by students who barred the university's gates, they abandoned their plans but presented a petition to the university's vice chancellor calling on him to shut down the campus and dismiss the student leaders. A government spokesman said July 15 that the authors of the letter would not be admitted when the campus reopened Aug. 30, but that other students could fill out normal readmission forms.

Socialist opposition formed. Dissident members of the UNIP, including major figures among the Bemba, formed a Socialist opposition party, the United Progressive party (UPP), Aug. 22 and vowed to seek general elections. The move was announced by Simon Kapwepwe, a former vice president considered the leading Bemba politician, who had resigned Aug. 3 as minister of local government and culture. (Former minister Chimba was also a member of the UPP.) Kapwepwe charged corruption in the government and said that Zambia's leaders were "the victims of the flattery of the imperialists, South Africa and the West." The UPP's constitution, submitted Aug. 24 to the Lusaka district secretary's headquarters along with an application for registration as a society, said the party would "pursue a Socialist policy" and would work "to stamp out all forms of capitalism, tribalism and sectionalism." About 75 members of the UPP were arrested Sept. 20 on orders of President Kaunda, who charged the men with gun-running and with sending Zambians abroad for guerrilla training. (Kapwepwe was not detained.) The arrests, believed to have been made mostly in the Northern, Central and Copperbelt Provinces, followed Aug. 27 allegations by Kaunda that Kapwepwe's establishment of the UPP had been "part and parcel of an international intrigue against the Zambian revolution." He alleged the move was aided by South Africa, Rhodesia and Portugal. Kapwepwe denied the charge Aug. 31 and also denied Sept. 22 that members of his party had engaged in gun-running or in sending Zambians abroad to study guerrilla warfare. He also announced

Sept. 22 that 10 University of Zambia students had offered to fill some of the UPP positions vacated by the detained leaders. It was not determined whether the students were those not allowed to return to the university.

Rhodesian blacks deported. It was reported Dec. 14 that 129 members of the Rhodesian black liberation movement had been deported to Rhodesia (reportedly in August) because they were working for that country's secret services. Other sources reported that the deportations had occurred partly because of rivalry among different liberation groups and partly because some of the guerrillas had supported plans for forming the UPP.

ZERO POPULATION GROWTH (ZPG)—*See* POPULATION
ZIMBABWE—*See* RHODESIA